Christian Writers' Market Guide | 2005

THE REFERENCE TOOL FOR THE CHRISTIAN WRITER

SALLY E. STUART

SHAW BOOKS

an imprint of WATERBROOK PRESS

Christian Writers' Market Guide 2005
A SHAW BOOK
Published by WaterBrook Press
2375 Telstar Dr., Suite 160
Colorado Springs, CO 80920
A division of Random House, Inc.

ISSN 1080-3955

ISBN 0-87788-200-2

Printed in the United States of America
2005

10 9 8 7 6 5 4 3 2 1

CONTENTS

III. PERIODICALS

For information on how to receive the market guide automatically every year and freeze the price at $24.99, plus postage, for future editions, or for information on getting the guide at a discounted group rate or getting books on consignment for your next seminar or conference, contact me at the address or numbers above.

HOW TO USE THIS BOOK

The purpose of this market guide is to make your marketing job easier and more targeted. However, it will serve you well only if you put some time and effort into studying its contents and using it as a springboard for discovering and becoming an expert on those publishers best suited to your writing topics and style.

   Below you will find information on its general setup and instructions for its use. In order to help you become more of an expert on marketing, I am including an explanation of each entry in the alphabetical listings for both the book section and the periodical section. Be sure to study these before trying to use this book.

   1.   Spend some time initially getting acquainted with the contents and setup of this resource book. You cannot make the best use of it until you know exactly what it has to offer.

   2.   Study the contents pages, where you will find listings of all the periodical and book topics. When selecting a topic, be sure to check related topics as well. Some cross-referencing will often be helpful. For example, if you have a novel that deals with doctor-assisted suicide, you might find the list for adult novels and the list for controversial issues and see which publishers are on both lists. Those would be good potential markets. In the topical sections you will find a letter "R" following publishers who accept reprints (pieces that have been printed in other publications but for which you retain the rights). You will find a dollar sign ($) in front of the paying markets. That will help you pick those out quickly when getting paid is your necessary goal for a particular piece.

   3.   The primary/alphabetical listings for book and periodical publishers contain those publishers who answered the questionnaire and those who did not. The listings preceded by an asterisk (*) are those publishers who didn't respond and whose information I was unable to update from other sources. Those with a number symbol (#) were updated from their printed guidelines or other current sources. Since the information in those two groups was not verified by the publisher, you are encouraged to send for sample copies or catalogs and writer's guidelines before submitting to them or get that information by e-mail or on their Websites. A plus sign (+) indicates a new listing.

   4.   In each **book publisher listing** you will find the following information (as available) in this format:

   a)   Name of publisher

   b)   Address, phone and fax numbers, e-mail address, Website

   c)   Denomination or affiliation

   d)   Name of editor—This may include the senior editor's name, followed by the name of another editor to whom submissions should be sent. In a few cases, several editors are named with the type of books each is responsible for. Address to appropriate editor.

   e)   Sometimes a statement of purpose

   f)   Sometimes a list of imprint names

   g)   Number of inspirational/religious titles published per year

   h)   Number of submissions received annually

   i)   Percentage of books from first-time authors

   j)   In the past, it has indicated only those publishers who do not accept manuscripts through agents. If it said nothing about agents, you could assume they did accept manuscripts through agents. Some listings will indicate whether they accept, prefer, require, or don't accept manuscripts through agents.

   k)   The percentage of books from freelance authors they subsidy publish (if any). This does not refer to percentage paid by author. If percentage of subsidy is over 50%, the publisher will be listed in a separate section under Subsidy Publishers.

l) Whether they reprint out-of-print books from other publishers

m) Preferred manuscript length in words or pages; if pages, it refers to double-spaced manuscript pages.

n) Average amount of royalty, if provided. If royalty is a percentage of wholesale or net, it is based on price paid by bookstores or distributors. If it is on retail price, it is based on cover price of the book.

o) Average amount paid for advances. Whether a publisher pays an advance or not is noted in the listing; if they did not answer the question, there is no mention of it.

p) Whether they make any outright purchases and amount paid. In this kind of sale, an author is paid a flat fee and receives no royalties.

q) Average first printing (number of books usually printed for a first-time author)

r) Average length of time between acceptance of a manuscript and publication of the work

s) Whether they consider simultaneous submissions. This means you can send a query or complete manuscript simultaneously to more than one publisher, as long as you advise everyone involved that you are doing so.

t) Length of time it should take them to respond to a query/proposal or to a complete manuscript (when two lengths of time are given, the first generally refers to a query and the latter to a complete manuscript). Give them a one-month grace period beyond that and then send a polite follow-up letter if you haven't heard from them.

u) Whether a publisher "accepts," "prefers," or "requires" the submission of an *accepted* manuscript on disk (do not send your unsolicited manuscripts/submissions on disk). Most publishers now do accept or require that books be sent on a computer disk (usually along with a hard copy) or by e-mail, but since each publisher's needs are different, that information will be supplied to you by the individual publisher when the time comes. This section also indicates, if they accept submissions by e-mail, whether they want it sent as an attachment or copied into the message.

v) If they have a preference, it will indicate what Bible version they prefer.

w) It will also indicate if they do print-on-demand publishing.

x) Availability and cost for writer's guidelines and book catalogs—If the listing says "guidelines," it means they are available for a #10 (business size) SASE with a first-class stamp. The cost of the catalog (if any), the size of envelope, and amount of postage are given, if specified (affix stamps to envelope; don't send loose). Tip: If postage required is more than $1.42, I suggest you put $1.42 in postage on the envelope and clearly mark it "Media Mail." (That is enough for up to 1 pound.) (Please note that if the postage rates increase this year, this amount may change. Check with your local post office.) If the listing says "free catalog," it means you need only request it; they do not ask for payment or SASE. Note: If sending for both guidelines and catalog, it is not necessary to send two envelopes; guidelines will be sent with catalog. If guidelines are available by e-mail or Website, that will be indicated.

y) Nonfiction Section—Preference for query letter, book proposal, or complete manuscript, and if they accept phone, fax, or e-queries (if it does not say they accept them, assume they do not; this reference applies to fiction as well as nonfiction). If they want a query letter, send just a letter describing your project. If they want a query letter/proposal, you can add a chapter-by-chapter synopsis and the number of sample chapters indicated. If not specified, send one to three chapters. This is often followed by a quote from them about their needs or what they don't want to see.

z) Fiction Section—Same information as nonfiction section

aa) Special Needs—If they have specific topics needs, especially those that are not included in the subject listings, they are indicated here.

bb) Ethnic Books—Usually specifies which ethnic groups they target or any particular needs

cc) Also Does—Indicates which publishers also publish booklets, pamphlets, tracts, or e-books dd) Photos—Indicates if they accept freelance photos for book covers. If interested, contact them for details or photography guidelines.

ee) Tips—Specific tips provided by the editor/publisher.

Note: At the end of some listings you will find an indication that the publisher receives mailings of book proposals from The Writer's Edge (see Editorial Services/Illinois for an explanation of that service) and/or First Edition (see index).

5. In each **periodical listing** you will find the following information (as available) in this format:

a) Name of periodical

b) Address, phone, fax, e-mail address, Website

c) Denomination or affiliation

d) Name of editor and editor to submit to (if different)

e) Theme of publication—This will help you understand their particular slant.

f) Format of publication, frequency of publication, number of pages and size of circulation—Tells whether magazine, newsletter, journal, tabloid, newspaper, or take-home paper. Frequency of publication indicates quantity of material needed. Number of pages usually indicates how much material they can use. Circulation indicates the amount of exposure your material will receive and often indicates how well they might pay or the probability that they will stay in business.

g) Subscription rate—Amount given is for a one-year subscription in the country of origin. I suggest you subscribe to at least one of your primary markets every year to become better acquainted with its specific focus.

h) Date established—Included only if 2003 or later

i) Openness to freelance; percentage freelance written. Again this year this information has been expanded to indicate the percentage of unsolicited freelance and the percentage of assigned. Since not all publishers have responded to this question, some will still give the two percentages combined or indicate only the unsolicited number. If they buy only a small percentage, it often means they are open but receive little that is appropriate. The percentage of freelance written indicates how great your chances are of selling to them. When you have a choice, choose those with the higher percentage, but only if you have done your homework and know they are an appropriate market for your material.

j) Preference for query or complete manuscript also tells if they want a cover letter with complete manuscripts and whether they will accept phone, fax, or e-mail queries. (If it does not mention cover letters or phone, fax, or e-mail queries, assume they do not accept them.)

k) Payment schedule, payment on acceptance (they pay when the piece is accepted) or publication (they pay when it is published), and rights purchased. (See glossary for definitions of different rights.)

l) If a publication does not pay, or pays in copies or subscription, that is indicated in bold, capital letters.

m) If a publication is not copyrighted, that is indicated. That means you should ask for your copyright notice to appear on your piece when they publish it, so your rights will be protected.

n) Preferred word lengths and average number of manuscripts purchased per year (in parentheses)

o) Response time—The time they usually take to respond to your query or manuscript submission (add at least two weeks for delays for mailing).

p) Seasonal material (also refers to holiday)—Holiday or seasonal material should reach them at least the specified length of time in advance.

q) Acceptance of simultaneous submissions and reprints—If they accept simultaneous submissions, it means they will look at submissions (usually timely topic or holiday material) sent simultaneously to several publishers. Best to send to nonoverlapping markets (such as denominational), and be sure to always indicate that it is a simultaneous submission. Reprints are pieces you have sold previously, but to which you hold the rights (which means you sold only first or one-time rights to the original publisher and the rights reverted to you as soon as they were published).

r)   If they accept, prefer, or require submissions on disk or by e-mail. Many now prefer an e-mail submission, rather than on disk. Most will want a query or hard copy first. If it does not say they prefer or require disks, you should wait and see if they ask for them. If they accept an e-mail submission, it will indicate whether they want it as an attached file or copied into the message. If it says they accept e-mail submissions, but doesn't indicate a preference, it usually means they will take it either way.

s)   Average amount of kill fee, if they pay one (see glossary for definition)

t)   Whether or not they use sidebars (see glossary for definition), and whether they use them regularly or sometimes

u)   Their preferred Bible version is indicated. The most popular version is the NIV (New International Version). If no version is indicated, they usually have no preference. See glossary for Bible Versions list.

v)   For the second time, this year it will indicate if they accept submissions from children or teens. These young writers will find a list of the publishers open to submissions from them in the topical listings under "Young Writer Markets."

w)   Availability and cost for writer's guidelines, theme list, and sample copies—If the listing says "Guidelines," it means they are available for a #10 SASE (business size) with a first-class stamp. Many more now have guidelines available by e-mail or Website, and the listing will indicate that. The cost for a sample copy, the size of envelope, and number of stamps required are given, if specified (affix stamps to envelope; don't send loose). Tip: If postage required is more than $1.42, I suggest you put $1.42 in postage on the envelope and clearly mark it "Media Mail." (That is enough for up to one pound.) If the listing says "free sample copy," it means you need only to request them; they do not ask for payment or SASE. Note: If sending for both guidelines and sample copy, it is not necessary to send two envelopes; guidelines will be sent with sample copy. If a listing doesn't mention guidelines or sample copy, they probably don't have them.

x)   "Not in topical listings" means the publisher has not supplied a list of topics they are interested in. Send for their guidelines or study sample copies to determine topics used.

y)   Poetry—Name of poetry editor (if different). Average number of poems bought each year. Types of poetry; number of lines. Payment rate. Maximum number of poems you may submit at one time.

z)   Fillers—Name of fillers editor (if different). Types of fillers accepted; word length. Payment rate.

aa)   Columns/Departments—Name of column editor. Names of columns in the periodical (information in parentheses gives focus of column); word length requirements. Payment rate. Be sure to see sample before sending ms or query. Most columns require a query.

bb)   Special Issues or Needs—Indicates topics of special issues they have planned for the year or unique topics not included in regular subject listings

cc)   Ethnic—Any involvement they have in the ethnic market

dd)   Contest—Information on contests they sponsor or how to obtain that information. See Contest section at back of book for full list of contests. They are listed by genre—poetry, fiction, nonfiction, etc.

ee)   Tips—Tips from the editor on how to break into this market or how to be successful as an author.

ff)   At the end of some listings you will find a notation as to where that particular periodical placed in the Top 50+ Christian Periodical list in 2004, and/or their place in previous years. This list is compiled annually to indicate the most writer-friendly publications. To receive a complete listing, plus a prepared analysis sheet and writer's guidelines for the top 50 of those markets, send $25 (includes postage) to: Sally Stuart, 1647 S.W. Pheasant Dr., Aloha, OR 97006, or order from this Website: www.stuartmarket.com.

Some listings also include EPA winners. These awards are made annually by the Evangelical Press Association (a trade organization for Christian periodicals). We have also indicated the top 10 best-selling magazines in Christian retail stores.

6.   It is important that you adhere closely to the guidelines set out in these listings. If a publisher asks for a query only, do not send a complete manuscript. Following these guidelines will mark you as a professional.

7.   If your manuscript is completed, select the proper topical listing and target audience, and make up a list of possible publishers. Check first to see which ones will accept a complete manuscript (if you want to send it to those that require a query, you will have to write a query letter or book proposal to send first). Please do not assume that your manuscript will be appropriate for all those on the list. Read the primary listing for each, and if you are not familiar with a publisher, read their writer's guidelines and study one or more sample copies or book catalog. (The primary listings tell how to get these.) Be sure the slant of your manuscript fits the slant of the publisher.

8.   If you have an idea for an article, short story, or book but you have not written it yet, a reading of the appropriate topical listing will help you decide on a possible slant or approach. Select some publishers to whom you might send a query about your idea. If your idea is for an article, do not overlook the possibility of writing on the same topic for a number of different periodicals listed under that topic, either with the same target audience or another from the list that indicates an interest. For example, you could write on money management for a general adult magazine, a teen magazine, a women's publication, or a magazine for pastors. Each would require a different slant, but you would get a lot more mileage from that idea.

9.   If you do not have an idea, simply start reading through the topical listings or the primary listings. They are sure to trigger any number of book or magazine article ideas you could go to work on.

10.   If you run into words or terms you are not familiar with, check the glossary at the back of the book for definitions.

11.   If you need someone to look at your material to evaluate it or to give it a thorough editing, look up the section on Editorial Services and find someone to send it to for such help. That often will make the difference between success or failure in publishing.

12.   If you are a published author with other books to your credit, you may be interested in finding an agent. Unpublished authors generally don't need or won't be able to interest an agent. However, some agents will consider unpublished authors (their listing will indicate that), but you must have a completed manuscript before you approach an agent (see agent list). Christian agents are at a premium, so realize it will be hard to find an agent unless you have had some success in book writing. The agent list also includes secular agents who handle religious/inspirational material.

13.   Check the Group list to find a group to join in your area. Go to the Conference list to find a conference you might attend this year. Attending a conference every year or two is almost essential to your success as a writer, especially when you get into book writing.

14.   **ALWAYS SEND AN SASE WITH EVERY QUERY OR MANUSCRIPT**, unless your cover letter indicates that you do not want it returned. If that is the case, send a #10 SASE for their acceptance or rejection, and indicate that's what you are doing in your cover letter.

15.   **DO NOT RELY SOLELY ON THE INFORMATION PROVIDED IN THIS MARKET GUIDE.** It is just that—a guide—and is not intended to be complete by itself. It is important to your

success as a freelance writer that you learn how to use writer's guidelines and study book catalogs or sample copies before submitting to any publisher. Be a professional!

ADDITIONAL RESOURCES TO HELP WITH YOUR WRITING AND MARKETING

Note: Here are additional resources to help with your every writing need. They are divided into interest areas to help you make the best selections. See instructions for ordering at the end of the list.

GENERAL HELPS

1. **Sally Stuart's Guide to Getting Published**—At last, the author of the *Christian Writers' Market Guide* has compiled all the information you need to understand and function in the world of Christian publishing. Takes you through all the steps needed to be successful as a freelance writer. Serves as both a text and a reference book. One of the most important and useful resources you'll ever find for your writing library. $17, postpaid.

2. **New! The Little Style Guide to Great Christian Writing and Publishing**—At last an up-to-date style guide that deals with style concerns unique to Christian writing and editing. $16 postpaid.

3. **Just Write! An Essential Guide for Launching Your Writing Career**—Information on how to do research, common grammatical pitfalls, writing for children, interviewing, and short stories—plus much more. $15 postpaid.

4. **The Complete Guide to Christian Writing and Speaking**—A how-to handbook for beginning and advanced writers and speakers written by the 19 members of the editorial staff of *The Christian Communicator.* $18 postpaid.

5. **The Complete Guide to Writing for Publication**—Written by top experts in the field. Contains chapters on various genres of fiction, marketing tips, and writing for children, plus everything you wanted to know about writing for publication. $18 postpaid.

6. **How to Write What You Love—and Make a Living at It**—Discusses how to find a distinctive style, make time to write, negotiate contracts, contact agents, secure copyrights, and make multiple sales. $16 postpaid.

7. **Small, Easy Ways to Break into Print**—Becoming a columnist, writing and selling micro fiction, holiday articles, using an almanac, and publication release forms. $5 postpaid.

8. **New! The Real American Dream: Creating Independence & Running a One-Person Business**—Let this workbook coach you, step by step, through creating a one-person business and freedom and control of your life as a professional writer. $26 postpaid.

FICTION RESOURCES

9. **Getting into Character: Seven Secrets a Novelist Can Learn from Actors**—A valuable resource for the novelist wanting to create multidimensional characters. $19 postpaid.

10. **How to Write and Sell a Christian Novel**—Leads you step by step through the process of writing a novel. $15 postpaid.

11. **The Professional Way to Write Dialogue**—$5 postpaid.

12. **The Professional Way to Create Characters**—$5 postpaid.

INTERNET RESOURCES

13. **WriterSpeaker.Com**—A friendly guide to Internet research and marketing. Plus how to set up and promote your own Website. $18 postpaid.

14. **2005 Internet Directory of Christian Publishers**—A handy listing of nearly 900 Christian publishers who have Websites or e-mail addresses. This resource now comes spiral bound for easier reference. $10 postpaid.

LEGAL CONCERNS

15. **Permissions Packet**—A compilation of over 16 pages of information directly from publishers on how and when to ask permission to quote from other people's material or from Bible paraphrases. Information not available elsewhere in printed form. $6 postpaid.

16. **Copyright Law: What You Don't Know Can Cost You**—Answers all the questions about rights and copyright law that affect you as a writer. Simple Q&A format followed by the actual wording of the law. Includes reproducible copyright forms and instructions. $18 postpaid.

17. **Updated! Totally Honest Tax Tips for Writers**—Answers all those tax questions specifically applicable to the Christian writer. $10 postpaid.

MARKETING RESOURCES

18. **2005 Christian Writers' Market Guide on Computer Disk**—in ASCII Text on 3.5" HD disk or CD, for quick marketing reference. This is currently in text form as it appears in the book, not in a database. (May be available in a database this year. E-mail for information.) $30 postpaid.

19. **2005 Top 50+ Christian Periodical Publishers Packet**—Includes a list of the Top 50+ "writer-friendly" periodicals, preprepared analysis sheets, and publisher's guidelines for each of the top 50, plus a master form for analyzing your own favorite markets. Saves more than $40 in postage and 25-30 hours of work. $25, postpaid. New packet every year.

20. **A Market Plan for More Sales**—A step-by-step plan to help you be successful in marketing. Includes 5 reproducible forms. $5 postpaid.

21. **Keeping Track of Your Periodical Manuscripts**—These pages can be duplicated to keep track of every step involved in sending out your periodical manuscripts to publishers. $5 postpaid.

22. **Keeping Track of Your Book Manuscripts**—A similar booklet summarizing the steps in tracking a book manuscript from idea to publication. $5 postpaid.

23. **How to Submit a Book Proposal to a Publisher**—Contains all you need to know to present a professional-looking book proposal to a publishing house (includes a sample book proposal). $5 postpaid.

24. **How to Submit an Article or Story to a Publisher**—Shows how to write a query, prepare a professional-looking manuscript, and more. $5 postpaid.

25. **Marketing Manuscripts**—Locating the markets, analyzing magazines, page set-up, book proposals, query letters, and literary agents. $5 postpaid.

NONFICTION RESOURCES

26. **Effective Magazine Writing**—Gives a clear understanding of each step of the magazine writing process. From the former editor of *Decision* magazine. $14 postpaid.

27. **Write on Target: A Five-Phase Program for Nonfiction Writers**, by Dennis Hensley and Holly Miller—The craft of writing, the nuts and bolts, finding your niche, selling your manuscript, and mapping your future success as a writer. $16 postpaid.

28. **How to Write That Sure-Sell Magazine Article**—Contains a 3-step writing plan for articles, a list of article types, 12 evaluation questions, a sample manuscript page, and more. $5 postpaid.

29. **How to Write Personal Experience Articles**—Includes how to write a query letter/sample, components of the personal experience article, interviewing tips, and more. $5 postpaid.

30. **New! How to Write and Sell Interviews and Personality Profiles**—Effective listening skills, open-ended questions, sample interview, photo release form, and basics of interviewing. $5 postpaid.

31. **The Art of Researching the Professional Way**—$5 postpaid.

32. **Interviewing the Professional Way**—$5 postpaid.

SELF PROMOTION

33. **You Can Market Your Book: All the Tools You Need to Sell Your Published Book**—All the best resources and ideas for promoting and selling your book—from someone who has done it successfully. $18 postpaid.

34. **A Savvy Approach to Book Sales: Marketing Advice to Get the Buzz Going**—by Elaine Wright Colvin. A wealth of information on how to promote your self-published book, as well as many ideas for the author wanting to boost the sales of a book from a royalty publisher. $16 postpaid.

SPECIALTY AREAS

35. **Screenwriting: A Manual for Christian Writers**—Written by the director of *Act One: Writing for Hollywood.* $18 postpaid.

36. **The Christian Poet**—Everything you need to know to write salable poetry. $13 postpaid.

37. **Updated! You Can Do It: A Guide to Christian Self-Publishing**—Takes you step-by-step through the process of self-publishing, including the preparation, cost, and promotion of the book. $13 postpaid.

38. **Preparing for a Writing Conference**—A spiral-bound pamphlet that helps you prepare effectively for your first—or next—writer's conference. $7 postpaid

39. **How to Write a Picture Book**—An inside look at how to write, format, and lay out a children's picture book, with tips for those all-important finishing touches. $5 postpaid.

40. **How to Write Daily Devotionals That Inspire**—Includes the basic format and patterns for daily devotionals, marketing tips, 12 evaluation questions, and polishing. $5 postpaid.

41. **Agents: What You Need to Know**—Includes why an agent would want you for a client, do you need an agent, and signing with an agent. $5 postpaid.

42. **Writing and Selling Comedy and Humor**—Includes forms of comedy, markets for humor, how to be funny, and how to stimulate humorous thinking. $5 postpaid.

43. **Ghostwriting, Co-Authoring and Collaborations**—Ghostwriting basics, expense sheets, payment guidelines, multiauthor contracts, breaking in, working with book editors, and using a pen name. $5 postpaid.

44. **Writing Junior Books the Professional Way** (writing for ages 8-12)—$5 postpaid.

45. **Writing for Young Adults the Professional Way**—$5 postpaid.

46. **How to Develop a Professional Writers' Group**—$5 postpaid.

SPIRITUAL/PERSONAL HELPS

47. **How to Keep a Spiritual Journal**—Learning to set up and maintain a regular spiritual journal can be one of the best tools for a successful Christian writer. $17 postpaid.

48. **100 Plus Motivational Moments for Writers and Speakers**—A devotional book specifically for writers and speakers written by successful writers and speakers. $13 postpaid.

49. **Write His Answer: A Bible Study for Christian Writers**—A Bible-study guide that deals specifically with the struggles of the Christian writer. $15 postpaid.

50. **Managing Stress as a Freelance Writer**—Stress response, self-assessment exercise, coping, handling anger and stress from editors. $5 postpaid.

51. **Time Management for Writers**—How to make time for writing, life map, time-management contract, etc. $5 postpaid.

Note: Any of the above $5 booklets may be purchased at 2 for $9, 4 for $17, 6 for $25, 8 for $33, 10 for $40, or 12 for $47.

To order any of the above resources, send a list of what you want with your check or money order to: Sally E. Stuart, 1647 S.W. Pheasant Dr., Aloha OR 97006, (503)642-9844. Fax (503)848-3658; stuartcwmg@aol.com. Or order by credit card through PayPal on Website: www.stuartmarket.com.

RESOURCES FOR WRITERS

Below you will find a variety of resources that will help you as you carry out your training or work as a freelance writer. In addition to the resources here, also check out the separate listings for groups, conferences, editorial services, and contests. You are encouraged to spend some time checking out these resources, as they represent a wealth of knowledge and contacts that will help you be more successful in this business of writing and publishing. Note that we have added three new sections this year: Denominations, Full-time Freelancing, and Speaking, as well as 280 new resources throughout.

Many thanks to Donna Fleisher, of I'll Read It! Editorial Services (Oregon), who stepped in to update this section. Her dedication to the task has resulted in our largest resource section to date. If you have additions or corrections to the listing, feel free to contact us.

(*) New category this year
(+) New listing this year

CONNECTING WITH OTHER WRITERS

AUTHOR'S DEN. Website: www.authorsden.com. Where authors and readers come together. Discover and meet thousands of authors and readers from around the world.

CHRISTIAN WRITERS' GROUP (CWG). Website: http://christianwritersgroup.org. A discussion group and organization for published or aspiring, born-again writers. Purposes: To share ideas, tips, conference/seminar information, encouragement, support, and prayer requests. Editors/publishers also welcome. Offers scholarships for writers' conferences. To join, send a blank e-mail to: CWG-subscribe@yahoogroups.com or sign up on Website. Director and list owner: Lisa Wiener. Membership (300+) open.

DISCUSSION FORUMS. Freelance Writing: Website for Today's Working Writers. Website: www.freelancewriting.com. Numerous forums to meet and network with other writers.

+FCW's FREE LIST SERVE. (Fellowship of Christian Writers), http://groups.yahoo.com/groups.com, or send an email to FCW-subscribe@yahoo.com. List is moderated. Must apply online at Yahoo groups and fill out questionnaire. 600+ members. Has weekly topics, daily interaction, markets, encouragement, tips, definitions, prayer, contests, and more. Online critique groups for fiction, nonfiction, children's, and poetry for list members which must be joined after you join the main list. Members may also be paired with an accountability partner, if you wish. 600+ members.

INTERNATIONAL@WRITERS CLUB. Website: http://members.tripod.com/awriters/iwc.htm. Provides writers worldwide with a host of services and opportunities including a base for networking, job opportunities, and invaluable writing resources.

KINGDOM WRITERS. Leaders: Marilyn Phemister (marilyp@larned.com) and Sue Hoover (Szanne@sprynet.com). An e-mail critique group and fellowship for Christian writers. You may submit work for critique and critique the works of others in return. To subscribe, send a blank e-mail message to: KingdomWriters-subscribe@egroups.com. Website: www.angelfire.com/ks/kingwrit/index.html. Membership (124 and growing) open.

+SMALL PUBLISHERS, ARTISTS, AND WRITERS NETWORK (SPAWN). Website: www.spawn.org. Local networking chapters and newsletter. To start a new chapter, e-mail Patricia@spawn.org.

WORDS OF WORSHIP. Online critique group for Christian fiction writers. Subscribe at their Website: http://groups.yahoo.com/group/wordsofworship or send an e-mail to: wordsofworship-subscribe@ yahoogroups.com.

WORDSMITH SHOPPE. Website: http://wordsmithshoppe.com. This is a Christian writers group that offers a free weekly e-mail newsletter, Wordsmith Shoppe News, with over 500 subscribers. The newsletter contains information of general interest to writers including conference listings, contests, and other writing opportunities. A twice-weekly chat meets Tuesdays at 10:00 p.m. ET and Thursdays at 2:00 p.m. ET. To view past issues of the newsletter go to http://wssnewsonline.com/file_archives.htm.

+WRITING.COM. Website: www.writing.com. The online community for readers and writers of all ages and interests. Over 50,000 active members.

THE WRITERS VIEW. Website: http://groups.yahoo.com/group/TheWritersView. Over 450 members. A great network of authors, editors, agents, freelance writers, journalists, publicists, and publishers. Offers focused panel discussions with 13 CBA professionals for intermediate, advanced, and professional writers.

YAHOO CHRISTIAN WRITERS CLUB. Website: http://clubs.yahoo.com/clubs/christianwritersclub. A place for Christians who write. Over 300 members.

DENOMINATIONS*

+CHRISTIANITY, CULTS & RELIGIONS. Rose Publishing, 4455 Torrance Blvd. #259, Torrance CA 90503. (310)370-7152. Toll-free (800)532-4278. E-mail: RosePublishing@aol.com. Website: www.rose-publishing.com. A wall chart or pamphlet charting 18 world religions and cults at a glance.

+COMPARISON CHART OF CHRISTIAN BELIEFS. Website: www.saintaquinas.com/christian_comparison.html.

+DENOMINATIONAL DIFFERENCES FOR SPEAKERS, by Marita Littauer. A ten-page booklet explaining the major differences between denominations. To order, call (600)433-6633 or e-mail erin@classervices.com. $5.

DENOMINATIONAL THEOLOGY. Website: http://apu.edu/~bstone/theology/trad.html. Check out the theology of various denominations.

+HANDBOOK OF DENOMINATIONS IN THE U.S., by Frank Spencer Mead and Samuel S. Hill, Abingdon Press (2001), ISBN 068706831, $20.

+THE UNAUTHORIZED GUIDE TO CHOOSING A CHURCH, by Carmen Renee Berry, Brazos Press (2003), ISBN 1587430363, $19. A conversational guide that discusses the nuances between denominations.

+WORLD RELIGIONS. Website: http://religion.rutgers.edu/vri/index.html. The Religion Department at Rutgers University offers this site with information about world religions.

ELEMENTS OF STYLE

THE ASSOCIATED PRESS STYLEBOOK AND BRIEFING ON MEDIA LAW. Edited by Norm Goldstein. Basic Books (2004), ISBN 0465004881, $17.95.

+THE CHICAGO MANUAL OF STYLE. Website: www.press.uchicago.edu/Misc/Chicago/cmosfaq/cmosfaq.html. The definitive guide (15th edition) online.

A CHRISTIAN WRITER'S MANUAL OF STYLE, by Hudson & Townsend. Zondervan (2004), ISBN 0310487714, $19.99. Good for unique spellings, capitalization, etc., of religious terms.

CITATION SITE. Citation Styles Online. Website: www.bedfordstmartins.com/online/citex.html. Shows you all the correct versions of citation style.

+CLEAR ENGLISH. Website: www.clearenglish.net/grammar.htm. Online references and resources to help with grammar and usage.

COLUMBIA GUIDE TO ONLINE STYLE, by Janice R. Walker and Todd Taylor, Columbia University

Press, New York (1998). $35.00 hardback, $17.50 paperback. Available at local bookstores. Website: www.columbia.edu/cu/cup/cgos/idx_basic.html.

ELEMENTS OF STYLE. William Strunk Jr.'s classic online. Websites: www.oualline.com/style; www.diku.dk/hjemmesider/studerende/myth/EOS; www.crockford.com/wrrrld/style.html; www.bartleby.com/141.

+ONLINE ENGLISH COURSES. Website: http://owl.english.purdue.edu/sitemap.html. Purdue University's Owl English Online courses.

+STYLE AND PROOFREADING HELPS. Websites: www.proofread.com; www.theslot.com; www.webgrammar.com; www.editavenue.com/writingtip.asp?cid=1600; www.mla.org, for more scholarly works; www.rbs0.com, for more technical writers; http://uwadmnweb.uwyo.edu/Pubrel/publications/StyleManual.htm.

FIND: BOOKS

ABEBOOKS.COM. Website: www.abebooks.com. If you tell them what book you want, they can tell you which stores carry it. You then work directly with the appropriate store to order the book.

+ALIBRIS BOOKS. Website: www.alibris.com. Over 40 million new, used, out-of-print, and hard-to-find books.

ALLBOOKS4LESS.COM. Website: www.AllBooks4Less.com. Inexpensive prices on books.

+BIBLIOFIND. Website: www.bibliofind.com. Searches over 10 million used and rare books, periodicals, and ephemera offered for sale by thousands of booksellers worldwide.

BOOKSINPRINT.COM. "The world's most inclusive, most accurate, most up-to-date, uniquely unbiased—and most trusted—database of book, audiobook, and video titles." For subscription information, visit: www.bowker.com or www.booksinprint.com or call toll-free (888)269-5372.

BOOK WIRE. Website: www.bookwire.com. The most comprehensive online portal into the book industry.

CHRISTIAN BOOK DISTRIBUTORS (CBD). Website: www.christianbook.com. Check out what's selling in the marketplace. Books can be found by publisher, author, or subject.

FETCHBOOK. Website: www.fetchbook.info. A quick way to compare prices of new and used books.

HALF.COM. An inexpensive source for both Christian and secular books. Also a place to sell books you no longer need. Not an auction; sellers list books they have and their asking price, and you pick the ones you want. Details on the Website: www.Half.com.

INTERNATIONAL BOOKS IN PRINT. Send details of your new book to: IBIP, Bowker, Windsor Court, East Grinstead House, East Grinstead, West Sussex RH19 1XA, United Kingdom. E-mail: IBIP@Bowker.co.uk.

+KREGEL BOOKS. Website: www.gospelcom.net/kregel. Offers new, used, and hard-to-find Christian books, publications, and resources.

OUT OF PRINT BOOKS. Website: http://marylaine.com/bookbyte/getbooks.html. Excellent guide on how to find out of print books by Marylaine Block.

THE WRITE RESOURCE. Websites: www.writerswrite.com; www.readersread.com. Contains hundreds of categorized links to best book-related sites on the Web.

FIND: INFORMATION

ASK-AN-EXPERT PAGE. Website: www.K12Science.org/askanexpert.html. Also see: www.askanexpert.com or www.askjeeves.com. The Yearbook of Experts, Authorities, and Spokespersons is another Website that lists hundreds of links to experts in dozens of categories. Website: www.yearbook.com.

BIOGRAPHICAL INFORMATION. Website: www.biography.com. Short biographies on over 25,000 personalities.

COUNTRIES. These sites give information on various countries of the world: CIA's World Factbook. Website: www.cia.gov/cia/publications/factbook; Library of Congress' Portals to the World. Website: www.loc.gov/rr/international/portals.html; Country Reports. Website: www .countryreports.org.

FEDERAL CITIZEN INFORMATION CENTER. Website: www.helenginger.com/links_govt_ crime_pg.htm. Brochures on just about any subject. News, links, topics, resources, fun stuff, and more.

HOLIDAYS/FESTIVALS. To find information on holidays and festivals worldwide, visit: www .holidayfestival.com.

HOW STUFF WORKS. Website: www.howstuffworks.com. Explains machines and processes with text, pictures, and animations.

INFORMATION PLEASE. Website: www.InfoPlease.com. This 50-year-old print resource is now available on the Internet.

MAG PORTAL. Website: www.MagPortal.com. This site lets you search for articles online simultaneously, without having to visit each magazine's Website individually.

WRITERS' KNOWLEDGE SWAP. Website: http://groups.yahoo.com/group/writerswap. An information-exchange mailing list for writers doing research. Membership 250+.

FIND: QUOTES

BARTLETT'S FAMILIAR QUOTATIONS. Website: www.bartleby.com. Just enter the word or words and it gives you the quotations.

JOURNALISM QUOTES. Website: www.schindler.org/quote.shtml.

THE QUOTABLE WRITER, by William A. Gordon. McGraw Hill. ISBN 0071355766, $14.95. Quotes by writers on writing. Available at your local bookstore. To read excerpts from this book, go to: http://members.aol.com/williamagordon/writers_quotations.html.

WEBSITES FOR QUOTATIONS. Website: www.itools.com. Go to "Research Tools" section, then click on "Quotations." Search by topic, author, etc., including Bible quotations. Also: www.quotationspage.com; www.quoteland.com; www.aphids.com/quotes/index.shtml; www.brainyquote.com; www.startingpage.com/html/quotations.html; www.cybernation .com/victory/quotations/directory.html; www.geocities.com/Athens/7186; http://members .aol.com/Jainster/Quotes/quotes.html; www.quotablequotes.net; www.motivational quotes.com; www.thinkexist.com/English; www.madwed.com. Click on the quotations section. The quotations are numbered, authors are in alphabetical order under each topic, and a short bio of each author is included where possible.

+WORD CRAFTERS. Bob Kelly, 10225 E. Stoney Vista Dr., Sun Lakes AZ 85248. (480)895-7617. Fax (480)895-7618. E-mail: quotes@robsoncom.net. Website: www.wordcrafters.info. Free Quotation Search Service and newsletters.

FIND: STATISTICS

BARNA RESEARCH GROUP. Website: www.barna.org/FlexPage.aspx?Page=Home. Click on "Ministry Resources" for information about the intersection of faith and culture in the US. Some subjects include: church health, discipleship, stewardship, youth, evangelism, leaders, and trends.

+BUREAU OF JUSTICE STATISTICS. Website: www.ojp.usdoj.gov/bjs.

INDUSTRY STATISTICS. To find out statistics about the book industry (i.e. how many books sold last year), check out: www.publishers.org/industry/index.cfm.

INTERNET STATISTICS. Website: www.nua.ie/surveys. "The world's leading resource for Internet trends and statistics."

THE PEW FORUM ON RELIGION & PUBLIC LIFE. Research and discussion of issues about the intersection of religion and public affairs. Website: www.pewforum.org.

STATISTICS SOURCE. Website: www.nilesonline.com/data.

UNIVERSITY OF MICHIGAN'S DOCUMENT CENTER STATISTICAL RESOURCES ON THE WEB. Website: www.lib.umich.edu/govdocs/stats.html.

FREELANCE JOBS

CREATIVE FREELANCERS. Website: www.freelancers.com. Connecting freelancers and clients for over twenty years.

FREELANCE WRITING: Website for Today's Working Writer. Job Bank at: www.freelance writing.com/fjb.html.

JOB SITES. Websites: www.writerfind.com/freelance_jobs; www.writejobs.com/jobs; www.writers digest.com; http://telecommuting.about.com/smallbusiness/telecommuting/msub29.htm; www.gospelcom.net/epa/jobs.html; www.prostogo.com; http://allfreelance.com; www .freelanceworkexchange.com; www.nytimes.com/pages/jobs/index.html; www.mediabistro .com; www.writetools.com/jobs.html.

JOURNALISM JOBS & SIMILAR SITES. Website: www.journalismjobs.com; www.news jobs.net; www.sunoasis.com/intern.html; www.writejobs.com; www.newslink.org/joblink.html; www.iwantmedia.com/jobs/index.html.

WORLDWIDE FREELANCE. Website: www.worldwidefreelance.com. Extensive lists of travel writing markets, Christian markets, technology markets, and more. E-mail to subscribe: wwfw-subscribe@topica.com.

WRITING EMPLOYMENT CENTER. Website: www.poewar.com/jobs.htm.

FULL-TIME FREELANCING*

+ABOUT FREELANCING. Website: www.freelancewrite.about.com. Provides the essentials for freelance writers.

+CLARITY IN COMMUNICATIONS. Website: www.claricomm.com/freelance.shtml. Susanne M. Alexander, pres. Coaching for freelance writers.

+THE E-MYTH REVISITED, by Michael E. Gerber. ISBN: 0887307280. This book looks at and dispels myths involved with starting and maintaining your own business. Available at www.amazon.com.

+FREELANCE BIDDING SERVICES. Websites: www.elance.com. Writers, editors, and other professionals in a broad range of fields bid for projects posted by companies looking for freelance workers; www.guru.com. An online marketplace for freelance talent.

+FREELANCE WRITERS. Website: www.freelancewriters.com. Global, searchable directory of freelance writers. Add your information for a $39 fee per year. Also offers legal information, a community bulletin board, and e-mail service.

+FREELANCE WRITING ORG. INT'L. Website: www.fwointl.com. Site offers more than 2,200 links to writing resources in over 40 categories.

+FUNDS FOR WRITERS. Website: www.fundsforwriters.com. Helping writers earn a living doing what they love.

+HEALTH INSURANCE CONCERNS. Websites: www.christianet.com/blessed; www.biblical healthcare.com. These sites are not insurance sites, rather they are biblically based Medi-Share alternatives.

For examples, see the Website e-zine *Common Scents Stardusterzine* at: www.crosstel
.net/~stardust. Contact: Ron Ferguson, PO Box 173, Gore OK 74435. Phone/Fax (918)464-
2873. E-mail: stardust@crosstel.net.

LANGUAGE/VOCABULARY

ACRONYM AND ABBREVIATION LIST. Website: www.AcronymFinder.com. Allows you to
search for over 169,000 acronyms, abbreviations, and definitions about all subjects,
including information technology, business, telecommunications, military, government,
and much more.

+APHORISMS. Website: www.aphorismsgalore.com.

AUSTRALIAN SLANG DICTIONARY. Website: www.koalanet.com.au/australian-slang.html.

CLICHÉ FINDER. Website: www.westegg.com/cliche. Also see: www.plainenglish.co.uk for the
Plain English Campaign against clichés.

COMMON ERRORS IN ENGLISH. Website: www.wsu.edu/~brians/errors/errors.html.

+DE-MYSTIFYING BUZZWORDS. Website: www.buzzwhack.com. Sign up for the buzzword of
the day.

DIALECT SURVEY. Website: http://hcs.harvard.edu/~golder/dialect/index.html. You can take
the survey and also see a map of the survey results. Over a hundred questions.

THE DIALECTIZER. Website: www.rinkworks.com/dialect. Converts English to Redneck, Jive,
Cockney, Elmer Fudd, Swedish Chef, or Pig Latin.

DICTIONARY.COM. Website: www.dictionary.com. Type in the word you are looking for, and if
there is no match, it makes suggestions that are hyperlinked so you can check the meaning to make sure it is the word you are actually seeking.

ENGLISH LESSONS. Website: www.englishpage.com. Free online English lessons.

+ENGLISH WORDS AND PHRASES. Website: www.worldwidewords.org. What words mean,
where they came from, how they have evolved, and the ways people misuse them.

+FUN WITH WORDS. Website: www.fun-with-words.com. "The Wordplay Website."

GOOGLE LANGUAGE TOOLS. Website: www.google.com/language_tools?hl=en. Allows you to
search by specific languages or countries and translates texts.

GRAMMAR. Websites: www.grammarcheck.com. Free weekly e-mail newsletter that helps
improve your grammar, punctuation, and writing skills; http://webster.commnet.edu/
grammar. Offers an exhaustive index of grammar and composition references; www
.edufind.com/english/grammar; www.grammarlady.com; www.ruthvilmi.net/hut/help/
grammar_help.

+IDIOMS. Website: www.idiomsite.com. Learn the origin of phrases that have found their way
into our everyday language.

LANGUAGE CONSTRUCTION KIT. Website: www.zompist.com/kit.html. Create your own language.

LEXICAL SITE. Website: www.lexfn.com. Goes beyond giving synonyms; it also links words so
that synonyms, antonyms, or words related by any of 16 different criteria may be found.

LINGUISTICS. Website: www.sfwa.org/members/elgin/Linguistics/RWL05.html. A lesson, *Real
World Linguistics 101* by Suzette Haden Elgin.

OXYMORON: CONTRADICTORY WORDS. Website: www.oxymoronlist.com. Here's a self-
proclaimed "Largest List of Oxymorons Ever Collected Online!"

THE PHRASE FINDER. Website: http://phrases.shu.ac.uk/meanings/index.html. Get the mean-
ings and origins of phrases, sayings, clichés, and quotes.

PRONUNCIATION GUIDE. The Voice of America Pronunciation Guide. Website: http://
ibb7.ibb.gov/pronunciations.

SLANG. Website: www.slangsite.com. Here's a site where you can find the latest hip lingo.

+TEEN LINGO. Website: www.thesourcefym.com/teenlingo.

TRANSLATIONS. Websites: http://babelfish.altavista.com/translate.dyn. Babelfish Translations. Type anything in English and it will translate it into either Spanish, French, Portuguese, Italian, German—or the other way around; http://translate.google.com/translate_t. Instantly translates from English to German, Spanish, French, Italian, and Portuguese, and from each of these into the others. Will even translate Website addresses; http://translation2 .paralink.com. English, French, German, Russian, and Spanish.

THE VOCABULA REVIEW. Website: www.vocabula.com. An online journal about the state of the English language, with tips on grammar, articles, and more.

A WORD A DAY. Website: www.wordsmith.org/awad/index.html. This is the Website for the mailing list by the same name. At the Website you can sign up to get a new word and its definition sent each day. The Merriam-Webster Website also offers a word-a-day at: www .m-w.com. To subscribe to Hebrew word-a-day, go to: http://HebrewResources.com. Another site is www.mywordaday.com. It features a word a day with definitions, photos, etc. Check out the "Additional Services" page for more links to interesting sites. Also see: www.nationalreview.com/word/word.asp; http://dictionary.reference.com/wordoftheday.

+WORD COUNTER. Website: www.wordcounter.com. Rank the most frequently used words in any body of text.

WORD POLICE. Website: www.theatlantic.com/unbound/wordpolice/six.

WORDS. Websites: www.wordspy.com; www.verbatimmag.com. Two sources of popular new words or new uses.

+WORTHLESS WORD OF THE DAY. Website: http://home.mn.rr.com/wwftd.

LEGAL CONCERNS

ASJA CONTRACTS WATCH. Offers free e-newsletter from the American Society of Journalists and Authors that keeps writers up to date on latest contract developments. See Website to subscribe: www.asja.org.

BOOKS FOR LEGAL CONCERNS. *The Copyright Permission and Libel Handbook: A Step-by-Step Guide for Writers, Editors, and Publishers* by Lloyd J. Jassin and Steve C. Schecter. *The Practical Guide to Libel Law* by Neil J. Rosini. *The Writer's Legal Companion* by Brad Bunnin and Peter Beren. Covers contracts, agents, copyright, taxes, libel, permissions, and more. Books available through local retailer.

+COPYRIGHT AND COPY WRONGS. Website: www.education-world.com/a_curr/ curr280a.shtml. Multipart article for teachers and writers.

COPYRIGHT AND PUBLISHING LAW ATTORNEY. Randolph Law Offices LLP, Sallie G. Randolph, 520 Franklin St., Buffalo NY 14202. (716)885-1847. E-mail: Sallie@author law.com. Website: www.authorlaw.com. Offers full legal services to writers at affordable rates.

+COPYRIGHT INFORMATION. Websites: www.templetons.com/brad/copymyths.htm. Brad Templeton's article gives important information on copyrights; www.writing-world .com/rights/topten.shtml. Answers the top ten questions about copyright permissions.

+COPYRIGHT LAW. Website: www.booksatoz.com/copyrigh/whatis.htm. Explains exactly what the copyright law is, how long it lasts, and other basics.

COPYRIGHT LAW—LIBRARY OF CONGRESS COPYRIGHT OFFICE, 101 Independence Ave. SE, Washington DC 20559-6000. (202)707-3000. Website: www.copyright.gov. Available in Spanish: www.copyright.gov/espanol. You may call or write for forms, or get them from the Website. To view the most current copyright rates, go to: www.copyright.gov/docs/ fees.html. Also check out these copyright information sites: www.benedict.com and www.whatiscopyright.org. For difficult questions, call (202)707-5959.

COPYRIGHT PIRACY. Website: www.sharpwriter.com/content/piracy.htm. Offers one writer's experience with pirates.

FAIR BUSINESS PRACTICES BRANCH, COMPETITION BUREAU, INDUSTRY CANADA. Website: http://competition.ic.gc.ca. Contact about illegal or unethical behavior by an agent or publisher in Canada. You also might notify or contact The Canadian Author's Assn. at: Box 419, Campbellford ON K0L 1L0, Canada. (705)653-0323. Toll-free (866)216-6222. Fax (705)653-0593. E-mail: admin@canauthors.org. Website: www.canauthors.org.

THE FEDERAL TRADE COMMISSION, BUREAU OF CONSUMER PROTECTION, Consumer Response Center (CRC). (202)382-4357. Website: www.ftc.gov. Contact about illegal or unethical behavior by an agent or publisher in the U.S.; access, complete, and transmit to the CRC the FTC's Public Complaint Form at the Website.

FREEDOM OF INFORMATION ACT BY THE SOCIETY OF PROFESSIONAL JOURNALISTS. Website: http://spj.org/foia.asp.

INTELLECTUAL PROPERTY LAW. Website: www.intelproplaw.com. Look up copyrights or connect to legal reference sites.

+INTERNATIONAL TRADEMARK ASSN. Website: www.inta.org. Offers free information about trademarks and a Trademark Hotline for free and immediate answers on spelling and proper usage.

LEGAL SITE FOR WRITERS. Daniel N. Steven, Publishing Attorney and Consultant. Website: www.publishlawyer.com. The legal resource for publishing professionals.

NOLO: Law for All. Website: www.nolo.com/encyclopedia/tc_ency.html. Includes comprehensive legal explanations about trademarks and copyrights.

+PATENT CAFÉ. Website: www.patentcafe.com. "Intellectual Property Management."

PERMISSIONS CONTACTS. Websites: www.publist.com. Lists over 150,000 publications with basic information, including who to contact for permissions; www.ucpress.edu/press/authors/perms.html.

PLAGIARISM. For articles dealing with plagiarism, go to: www.writersweekly.com/search.html and enter the search word Plagiarism.

+THE PUBLISHING LAW CENTER, Lloyd L. Rich, Property Rights Attorney, 1163 Vine St., Denver CO 80206. (303)388-5215. E-mail: info@publaw.com. Website: www.publaw.com. Offers a free newsletter.

SMALL BUSINESSES. Website: www.businesslaw.gov. Launched by the Small Business Administration to provide indexes in one central location and links to credible sources of information such as licenses, permits, e-commerce, and exporting. The site also includes information specific to each state and territory.

+TRADE BOOK PUBLISHING AGREEMENT CHECKLIST. Website: www.copylaw.com/forms/pubchk.html. Gives a good overview of items commonly found in a book publishing agreement.

+U.S. PATENT AND TRADEMARK OFFICE. Website: www.uspto.gov. Trademark process information in easy terms.

U.S. POSTAL INSPECTION SERVICE/FRAUD, CHILD EXPLOITATION AND FORFEITURE DIVISON. Website: www.usps.com. Click on "Postal Inspectors" then "Mail Fraud" or contact Inspection Service Operations Support Group, Attn: Mail Fraud, Ste. 1250, 222 S. Riverside Plaza, Chicago IL 60606-6100 about incidents of potential mail fraud.

VOLUNTEER LAWYERS FOR THE ARTS, 1 East 53rd St., 6th Fl., New York NY 10022. (212)319-2787, ext. 1. Fax (212)752-6575. E-mail: askvla@vlany.org. Website: www.vlany.org.

WARNINGS. A Website to check out when you are having trouble getting payment or wondering about the legitimacy of a publisher is: www.writersweekly.com/search.html and enter the search words Whispers and Warnings. Also see: www.nwu.org/alerts/alrthome.htm.

WRITER'S POCKET TAX GUIDE. Website: www.foolscap-quill.com. An annual tax guide book.

Note: If you are the victim of fraud or have questions/concerns about an agent or publisher, contact the Better Business Bureau in their town, as well as their local attorney general or their state attorney general's office of consumer protection. You can also contact the Better Business Bureau online to see if a certain company has any complaints on file at: www.bbb.org.

MARKET SOURCES

ANTHOLOGIES ONLINE. Website: www.anthologiesonline.com. A listing of anthologies looking for contributors. Writers should subscribe and send in brief bio and best writing sample (up to 1,200 words total) to apply to become a feature writer.

BOOK MARKETING/PROMOTION CHECKLIST: 22 Ways to Promote and Sell Books, by John B. McHugh. Free. Website: www.johnbmchugh.com. Click on Free McHugh Publications.

CANADIAN MAGAZINE PUBLISHERS ASSN., 425 Adelaide St., Ste. 700, Toronto ON M5V 3C1 Canada. (416)504-0274. Fax (416)504-0437. E-mail: cmpainfo@cmpa.ca. Website: www.cmpa.ca.

CANADIAN MARKETS. *Canadian Markets* (and other publications) at Website: www.pwac.ca/resources/publications.htm; Directory of members at www.writers.ca, which is a free searchable database; *Roughing It in the Market: A Survival Toolkit for the Savvy Writer,* 54 Wolseley St., Ste. 203., Toronto ON M5T 1A5; www.booklocker.com/books/1188.html for the e-book *A Writer's Guide to Canadian Markets and On-line Resources* by Diana M. VandeHoef.

CHRISTIAN WRITERS' MARKET GUIDE WEBSITE. Website: www.stuartmarket.com. Sally Stuart's Website with information on the latest guide, links to the Websites or e-mail of all the Christian publishers or publications that have them, and a listing of conferences for the year. Lots more in the works.

FIRST EDITION MANUSCRIPT SERVICE. Website: www.ecpa.org. Click on 1st Edition. This is an online submission service provided by the 82 ECPA publishing houses. Fee is $79.

GILA QUEEN'S GUIDE TO MARKETS. Kathy Ptacek, ed., PO Box 97, Newton NJ 07860-0097. (973)579-1537. Website: http://GilaQueen.us. An e-mail newsletter for writers and artists.

IDEAMARKETERS.COM. Contact: Marnie L. Pehrson, dir., 514 Old Hickory Ln., Ringgold GA 30736. (706)866-2295. E-mail: webmaster@ideamarketers.com. Website: www.ideamarketers.com. A media-matching service that unites writers and publishers. Writers post their articles for free, and they are stored in a searchable database. Publishers, Web masters, and e-zine editors can then come and find content. There is a link at the top of each article they can click on to ask author's permission to use article.

LINKS TO FOREIGN MAGAZINES & NEWSPAPERS. Websites: http://dir.yahoo.com/News_and_Media/By_Region/countries; www.cmpa.ca (Canadian); www.vicnet.net.au/~ozlit (Australian); www.newsdirectory.com.

+LITERARY JOURNALS. Website: www.jefferybahr.com/Publications/default.htm. Links to literary journals, journal response times, statistics, ranking, and more.

LITERARY MARKETPLACE. Website: www.literarymarketplace.com. General market guide put out by Information Today, Inc., 143 Old Marlton Pike, Medford NJ 08055. Toll-free (800)300-9868. E-mail: custserv@infotoday.com. Cost $299. Online version is $399.

+ONLINE MARKETS FOR WRITERS. Website: www.marketsforwriters.com. This book is the guide for online markets.

PATHWAYS CHRISTIAN WRITERS RESOURCES. Website: www.angelfire.com/ca4/Pathways. From Australia, this site lists 112 Christian publishers, some in Australia and England, plus links to other writers' sites and how-to help.

PUBLISHER'S CATALOGS. Website: www.lights.com/publisher. Includes over 7,700 publishers. Search by publisher's name or city; takes you to the publisher's Website.

PUBLISHERS MARKETING ASSOCIATION ONLINE. Website: http://pma-online.org. Lists basic contact information on hundreds of publishers.

PUBLISHERS OF CHRISTIAN MATERIALS. Website: www.idisciple.net/christianpublishers .shtml. Lists Websites of Christian publishers.

PUBLIST. Website: www.publist.com. List over 150,000 publications with basic contact information.

ROSEDOG.COM. Website: www.rosedog.com. Connects writers, agents and publishers at no cost to any of them.

SHELOVESGOD.COM. Contact: Marnie L. Pehrson, dir., 514 Old Hickory Ln., Ringgold GA 30736. (706)866-3395. E-mail: webmaster@SheLovesGod.com. Website: www.SheLoves God.com. A community for Christian women. Read and/or submit faith-promoting articles, stories, testimonies & poems. Writers post their submissions for free and they are stored in a searchable database. Churches, editors, women's groups, and others can then come and find content. There is a link at the top of each item that they can click on to ask author's permission to reprint.

WEB-ZINE ARTICLE DISTRIBUTION SITES. Websites: www.ideamarketers.com and www .EzineArticles.com. Free content for your e-zine or Website.

WOODEN HORSE PUBLISHERS. Market database for nonfiction writers at: www.wooden horsepub.com. Also contains an extensive glossary for writers.

WRITER'S DIGEST WEBSITE. Website: www.writersdigest.com. Lots of writer's helps, including copies of writer's guidelines you can print right off the site. Website for guidelines: www.writersdigest.com/guidelines.asp.

WRITER'S EDGE. Website: www.WritersEdgeService.com. Their list includes 75 participating publishers.

WRITER'S GUIDELINES DATABASE. Website: www.freelancewriting.com/guidelines/pages/ index.html. Lists over 580 writer's guidelines to paying markets.

+WRITERS MARKET. Website: www.writersmarket.com. A searchable database of over 5,600 writing markets. Listings are updated daily. Site also includes Submission Tracker, Expert Advice articles, Market Watch, Agent Q&A, and much more.

WRITER'S RELIEF, INC., 245 Teaneck Rd., #3, Ridgefield Park NJ 07660. (201)641-3003. Fax (201)641-1253. E-mail: Ronnie@wrelief.com. Website: www.wrelief.com. An author's submission service, handling your manuscript submissions for an hourly rate of $45-60 plus postage and copying (after initial free reading), or a flat fee after completing review. Prepares manuscripts, proofreads, writes query and cover letters, tracks submissions, keeps records, etc.

YAHOO'S LIST OF CHRISTIAN PUBLICATIONS ON THE WEB. Go to Yahoo's search engine (www.yahoo.com). Click on Society and Culture: Religion: Faith and Practices: Christianity.

PROMOTION

ARTICLES AND BOOKS OF INTEREST. *The Art of Creating an Unfair Advantage: 200+ Ideas to Market Yourself and Your Books* edited by Ted Decorte. To read article, go to www.geocities.com/MadisonAvenue/Boardroom/4278/aaideas.html; *35 Ways to Make Your Next Book Signing an Event* by Larry James. Website: www.writerswrite.com/ journal/jan00/james.htm; other book-signing articles: www.writing-world.com/promotion/ james.shtml; www.writing-world.com/promotion/booksignings.shtml; Book: *You CAN Market Your Book!* by Carmen Leal (ACW 2003). Website: www.writerspeaker.com/ YCMYB/YouCan.asp; Book: *Sell Yourself Without Selling Your Soul* by Susan Harrow (HarperCollins 2002). Website: www.prsecrets.com.

AUTHORLINK. Website: www.authorlink.com. Includes a place to advertise and sell self-published books.

BANNERS/POSTERS. Websites: www.poster.com; www.brittenmedia.com. Visual Display Solutions also offers merchandising and display products. Call toll-free (800)688-5104 for information.

BOOK MARKETING UPDATE. Edited by John Kremer. A 12-page newsletter for book writers to help gain national publicity and more book sales. Cost is $297/year (24 issues/year). Contact: Open Horizons, PO Box 205, Fairfield IA 52556. Toll-free (800)796-6130. (641)472-6130. Fax (641)472-1560. E-mail: info@bookmarket.com. Website: www.bookmarket.com.

BOOKWIRE. Website: www.bookwire.com. This is an author tour database for Internet browsers. Lets general public and industry professionals know about authors touring in their area.

BROCHURES/BUSINESS CARDS. Contact: Bill Spilman, Innovative Media Solutions, 529 N. Cherry St., Galesburg IL 61401. (309)342-3211. Fax (309)342-3212. E-mail: bill@innovativemediasolutions.com.

+CHRISTIAN-BASED TALK SHOW. Kevin Wayne Johnson hosts a one-hour Internet-based Christian talk show carried by VoiceAmerica. Websites: www.writingforthelord.com; www.voiceamerica.com. For more information: (410)340-8633; E-mail: Kevin@writingforthelord.com.

CHRISTIAN E-AUTHORS. Website: http://christianeauthor.com. Purpose of site is to promote the electronic works of inspirational authors from around the world. Site offers a books page showcasing a variety of e-books in different genres. Author links take you directly to member Websites for more information on each author. A links page offers a glimpse into the world of e-books and e-publishing. A Yahoo list group, banner, logos, and link exchanges are also available.

+FRUGAL MARKETING. Website: www.frugalmarketing.com. Shel Horowitz offers tips and information and his book, *Grassroots Marketing: Getting Noticed in a Noisy World.*

GUERRILLA MARKETING FOR WRITERS, by Jay Conrad Levinson, Rick Frishman, and Michael Larson. Ideas on how to promote your book on the Internet, including using your own Website to increase sales. Available at local bookstores, Writer's Digest book club, or find information at: www.writersdigest.com/store/booksearch.asp.

GUIDE TO FREELANCERS. Website: www.epassoc.org. Click on Freelance Guide or call (763)535-4793. A joint project of the Evangelical Press Association, Associated Church Press, and Christian Newspaper Association. This annual guide is distributed free of charge to hundreds of Christian periodical editors, and is designed to help them find freelance writers, photographers, and artists. Indexed by specialty and location. Listings available to professional freelancers for a small fee.

HOW TO GET PUBLISHED by Michael LaRocca. A free e-book that will help you improve your writing, find a publisher, and promote it after the sale. Website: http://freereads.topcities.com/fictionwritingtips.html.

INTERNET FOR CHRISTIANS NEWSLETTER. Weekly newsletter from gospelcom.net that highlights and reviews Websites of interest to Christians. Website: www.gospelcom.net/ifc/newsletter.shtml. Submit your news, press releases, humorous anecdotes, and Web addresses by e-mail to ifc@internetforchristians.org.

INTERVIEWS. Website: www.willwrite4food.com. Will do author interviews; Website: http://citv.com/broadcast/interviews. The Christian Internet Radio & Television Network.

+IT'S A NEW DAY, Box 2010, Winnipeg MB R3C 3R3, Canada. (204)949-3333. Fax (204)949-3334. E-mail: staff@newday.com. Website: www.newday.org. Trinity Television's one-hour show offers interview opportunities to authors.

+MAILING LISTS. ParaLists, Dan Poynter, PO Box 4232-189, Santa Barbara CA 93140-4232. (805)968-7277. Toll-free (800)727-2782. Fax (805)968-1379. Website: www.parapub .com. ParaLists offers many categories of book promotion mailing lists that may be rented.

+MANAGING CLIPS. Website: www.claricomm.com/fw_clips.shtml.

MARKETING HELP. Website: http://cba.know-where.com/cba. Search for Christian bookstores in your area, or any area you might want to target. Website: www.stretcher.com/stories/ 01/010409j.cfm. Tips on marketing yourself without money.

MARKETING TIP OF THE WEEK NEWSLETTER. Website: http://bookmarket.com. Plus other helps for promoting your book.

MEDIA KIT. "How to Prepare a Media Kit." Website: www.publicityhound.com/mediakitspeak.

MEDIA LISTS. Publicity Tools is a source for unlimited-use media lists, including Book Industry, Christian, Library, Radio, Newspapers, and National Media Lists. Call toll-free (888)330-4919.

+MINI-CD BUSINESS CARDS. Website: www.cardiscs.com.

NRB DIRECTORY OF RELIGIOUS MEDIA. Produced by National Religious Broadcasters and available for purchase online, it contains nearly 4,700 entries consisting of radio & TV stations/programs/program producers and key personnel e-mail addresses, print and music, agencies, and services. The printed version will be discontinued after the 2002 release, but the electronic versions (CD and download) will continue to be produced and updated. NRB Store Website: www.nrb.org. Contact: Valerie Fraedrich, 9510 Technology Dr., Manassas VA 20110. (703)330-7000, ext. 516. E-mail: vfraedrich@nrb.org.

+ONLINE PRESS RELEASE DISTRIBUTION SERVICE. Website: www.prweb.com. Also offers press release tips and templates.

+PREMIUM POST CARDS. The U.S. Post Office will print and mail customized postcards. Website: www.usps.com/netpost/premiumpostcard.htm.

+PRESS KITS. Website: www.murdermustadvertise.com/FAQ/PressKit.html. Advice on what a press kit should contain and how to make yours stand out.

PRESS RELEASES. Websites: www.prsa.org. Offers information about chapters and other resources; www.prweek.com. A weekly magazine, offering news of interest to PR writers; www.Imediafax.com. A "Trash Proof News Release Tutorial" can be downloaded for free; www.stetson.edu/~rhansen/prhowto.html; www.press-release-writing.com/10_essential _tips.htm; www.thewritemarket.com/articles/pond.htm; www.thewritemarket.com/ articles/moore.htm; www.thewritemarket.com/articles/ventura5.htm; www.thewritemarket .com/articles/lock.htm; Book: *Handbook of Strategic Public Relations and Integrated Communications,* edited by Clarke L. Caywood (McGraw-Hill).

+PRINTING. Websites: www.megacolor.com; www.qualityprintingcheap.com; www.cfre.com.

+PUBLICITY HOUND. Joan Stewart, 3434 County KK, Port Washington WI 53074. (263)284-7451. Fax (262)284-1737. E-mail: jstewart@publicityhound.com. Website: www.publicity hound.com. Excellent site for everything publicity.

RADIO-TV INTERVIEW REPORT, Bradley Communications, PO Box 1206, Lansdowne PA 19050-8206. (610)259-0707. Fax (610)284-3704. E-mail: contactus@rtir.com. Website: www.rtir.com. Authors pay to have their profile included in this publication that goes to over 4,000 radio and TV producers who are looking for talk-show guests.

A SAVVY APPROACH TO BOOK SALES: Marketing Advice to Get the Buzz Going, by Elaine Wright Colvin. $13 postpaid from Christian Writers Marketplace, 1647 S.W. Pheasant Dr., Aloha OR 97006.

STICKERS. Websites: http://ebookisle.com/general/accessories.htm (60 for $2.00); www.maysmall .com/order.htm (10 for $3.00); www.spannet.org/stickers.htm (200 for $10); www.abflink.com/abflink/dept.asp?dept%5Fid=121; www.bookweb.org/graphics/pdfs/ orderform.pdf (1,000 for $6).

+TALK RADIO STATIONS. Websites: http://newslink.org/rneradi.html; www.radio-locator .com. Search for stations on either site.

PROMOTION: BOOK REVIEWERS

+BOOK CROSSING. Website: www.bookcrossing.com. Book Crossing encourages people to "release books into the wild," to leave books in public places for anyone to pick up and read for free. Register your book online, then "release" it. When someone picks up your book and reads it, he/she is then encouraged to go to the site and leave feedback about it. Over a million books are registered.

+BOOKS AND AUTHORS. Website: www.booksandauthors.net. Seeking book reviews and reviewers. E-mail: editor@booksandauthors.net.

CHRISTIAN BOOK PREVIEWS.COM. Website: www.christianbookpreviews.com. Features book excerpts, reviews, author bios, and interviews. Also offers a price comparison tool for buyers who want to find the best prices online before purchasing.

CO-OP REVIEWERS DATABASE. A free co-op review site listing reviews by genre (including: Christian, Spiritual, Religion, and Inspirational). Website: www.bookzonepro.com/reviewers.

+EXTREME CHRISTIANITY. Website: www.eczine.com/features/reviews. Brian Groce, publisher. See submission guidelines on site or e-mail: info@eczine.com.

GLORY GIRLS, 33290 W. 14 Mile Rd. #482, W. Bloomfield MI 48322. Website: www.glory girlsread.net. Reading groups for African American Christian women who love God and like to read. If you would like the group to consider your book, send 3 copies of each work, press kit, and contact information to the address above.

THE MIDWEST BOOK REVIEW, 278 Orchard Dr., Oregon WI 53575. (608)835-7937. E-mail: mbr@execpc.com. Website: www.midwestbookreview.com. James Cox, ed-in-chief. Send copy of your book to be reviewed for library resource newsletters, etc.

WEBSITES FOR BOOK REVIEWS. Websites: www.barnesandnoble.com; www.christian books.com; www.amazon.com; www.churchfolk.com. Click on Book Club section; www.byauthor.com. Will link to authors' Websites. Includes a newsletter; www.christianity today.com/books; www.bookreviewcafe.com; www.cbaonline.org. Click on CBA Market-place; www.romantictimes.com; www.libraryjournal.com; www.christianity.net; www .thewordonromance.com; www.theromancereadersconnection.com; http://come.to/ bookreviews. The Author's Choice Book Review site. Reviews several books every month, mainly from CBA, and in all categories. Maintained by Carolyn R. Scheidies; A Christian book-review network with close to 1,200 members on the Internet. Most are highly moti-vated writers and buyers of books. E-mail: BookClub3000@YahooGroups.com.

PROMOTION: PUBLICISTS

PATRICIA AVERY; AVERY PR. E-mail: averypr@gbronline.com. Specializes in cultural/issue/ family values—oriented titles, high-profile projects, as well as offering marketing recom-mendations to authors.

B & B MEDIA GROUP. Client Development: Tina Jacobson. Toll-free (800)927-0517. E-mail: tjacobson@tbbmedia.com. Website: www.tbbmedia.com. We are a full service publicity and public relations media communications firm that works with publishers, speakers, writers, and organizations.

BOOKMAN MARKETING. Website: www.bookmanmarketing.com. Toll-free (800)342-6068. E-mail: information@bookmanmarketing.com.

CLASS PROMOTIONAL SERVICES, LLC., 3830 Sienna St., Oceanside CA 92056. (760)630-2677. Fax (760)630-9355. Contact: Kim Garrison. E-mail: Interviews@classervices.com.

Website: www.classervices.com. Click on Promotional Services. Specializing in radio and TV interview campaigns for Christian authors, speakers, and ministries. CLASS Promotional Services is a division of Christian Leaders, Authors & Speakers Services, which provides resources, training, and promotion for Christian authors and speakers.

CREATIVE RESOURCES. Contact: Don Otis, PO Box 1665, Sandpoint ID 83864. (208)263-8055. Fax (208)263-9055. E-mail: CMResource@aol.com. A Christian consulting and publicity firm that schedules 2,000 broadcast interviews annually and arranges numerous reviews, articles, and interviews in major publications. Provides services for direct mail, communications, and media relations to parachurch groups, publishers, broadcast ministries, and others. Publishes *Media Connections,* which links individuals, organizations, and media.

DECHANT HUGHES ASSOCIATES INC. Public Relations/Media Tours. Contacts: Kelly Hughes, president; 1440 N. Kingsbury, Chicago IL 60622. (312)280-8126. Fax (312)280-8362. E-mail: dha@dechanthughes.com. Website: www.dechanthughes.com.

+DOBSON MEDIA GROUP. Melanie Dobson, 7970 Telegraph Dr., Colorado Springs CO 80920. (719)282-3822. E-mail: melanie@dobsonmedia.com. Website: http://dobsonmedia.com.

GUEST FINDER. Website: www.guestfinder.com. A place to get noticed for possible interviews, plus tips on being a better guest. E-mail: info@guestfinder.com. Also see: www.newsbuzz.com for their GreatGuests Newsletter.

GUTHRIE COMMUNICATIONS. Contact: Nancy Guthrie, 904 Little Bridge Pl., Nashville TN 37221. (615)376-4430. E-mail: nancyguthrie@comcast.net.

+INTEGRATED BOOK MARKETING. Sharon H. Castlen, PO Box 321, Kings Park NY 11754. (631)979-5990. E-mail: ibmarket@optonline.net. Integrates publicity with distribution to generate the greatest sales.

JAKASA PRODUCTIONS. Contact: Jacqueline Cromartie, 108 Fairview Pkwy., Lafayette LA 70508. (328)981-6179.

+ANNIE JENNINGS; PUBLICIST. Offers TV, radio, and print publicity opportunities, teleseminars, and extensive book promotion. (908)281-6201. Fax (908)281-5221. E-mail: annie@anniejenningspr.com. Website: anniejenningspr.com.

MCCLURE/MUNTSINGER PUBLIC RELATIONS. Contact: Jana Muntsinger, PO Box 804, Franklin TN 37065. (804)754-2118. E-mail: jana@mmpublicrelations.com. Website: www.mmpublicrelations.com.

MEDIA RELATIONS. A public-relations/marketing/media firm. Contact: Susan J. Coker, Media Relations, 826 Thatcher Way, Franklin TN 37064. (615)599-4685. Fax (615)599-4689.

MINISTRY MARKETING SOLUTIONS. Pamela Perry, Publicist. (248)426-2300. E-mail: info@ministrymarketingsolutions.com. Website: www.ministrymarketingsolutions.com. A consulting firm that provides a blend of capabilities in marketing, public relations, ghost writing, publishing, special event planning, fund raising, and providing Christian resource links.

+MRB CONSULTING. Michele R. Buc, 2820 Hazelwood Dr., Ste. C-7, Nashville TN 37212. E-mail: MicheleRBuc@aol.com. Specializes in unique campaigns directed to target markets.

PHENIX & PHENIX, 2525 W. Anderson Lane, Ste. 540, Austin TX 78757. (512)478-2028. Fax (512)478-2117. Website: www.bookpros.com. A literary publicity firm specializing in finding readers for your books through extensive media contacts.

PR-LINK PUBLIC RELATIONS. Website: www.pr-link.com. (513)233-9090. E-mail: info@pr-link.com.

+PROMOTE YOURSELF PUBLIC RELATIONS AND SEMINARS. Raleigh Pinskey, PO Box 701, Carefree AZ 85377. Toll-free (800)249-7322. E-mail: raleigh@promoteyourself.com. Website: www.promoteyourself.com. Offers free monthly newsletter, articles, and tips.

+PUBLICITY HOUSE. Tim Shook, PO Box 38704, Colorado Springs CO 80937. (719)579-6472. Website: www.publicityhouse.com.

BEVERLY RYKERD PUBLIC RELATIONS. Beverly Rykerd, PO Box 88180, Colorado Springs CO 80908. (719)495-3920. E-mail: brykerd@ix.netcom.com.

WYNN-WYNN MEDIA. Jeane Wynn, 410 N. Chickasaw Ave., Claremore OK 74017. (918)283-1834. E-mail: wynn@onenet.net.

REFERENCE TOOLS

+ALMANACS. Website: www.infoplease.com/almanacs.html. Search dozens of almanacs at once. Topics include history, government, biography, sports, arts, entertainment, business, finance, consumer resources, health, science, and weather.

+AMERICAN DIALECT SOCIETY. Website: www.americandialect.org. Offers e-mail discussion list, Words of the Year, and reference links.

BARTLEBY'S REFERENCE LIBRARIES. Website: www.bartleby.com. *American Heritage Dictionary:* www.bartleby.com/61. Over 90,000 entries, 900 full-page color illustrations, and 70,000 audio word pronunciations. *The Columbia Encyclopedia:* www.bartleby.com/65. Over 150,000 entries. *Strunk's Elements of Style:* www.bartleby.com/141; *The Encyclopedia of World History:* www.bartleby.com/67; *Roget's II: The New Thesaurus:* www.bartleby.com/62; Quotations: www.bartleby.com/quotations; *Gray's Anatomy:* www.bartleby.com/107.

+COMPUTER-USER HIGH-TECH DICTIONARY. Website: www.computeruser.com/resources/dictionary. Includes emoticons, file types, chat stuff, domains, HTML tags, and much more.

+DEPT. OF DEFENSE DICTIONARY OF MILITARY TERMS. Website: www.dtic.mil/doctrine/jel/doddict.

DICTIONARY.COM. Website: www.dictionary.com. Type in the word you are looking for, and if there is no match, it makes suggestions that are hyperlinked so you can check the meaning to make sure it is the word you are actually seeking.

ENCYCLOPEDIA BRITANNICA. Website: www.britannica.com.

FREE INTERNET ENCYCLOPEDIA. Website: www.cam-info.net/enc.html

+THE JARGON DICTIONARY. Website: http://info.astrian.net/jargon.

+LAW DICTIONARY. Website: www.duhaime.org/diction.htm. Also offers references to many other law topics. Be sure to check out the Law Fun page for jokes and great dumb stuff.

MERRIAM-WEBSTER ONLINE DICTIONARY/THESAURUS. Website: http://m-w.com.

ONELOOK DICTIONARIES. Website: www.onelook.com. Definitions from over 900 dictionaries.

OXFORD ENGLISH DICTIONARY. Website: www.oed.com.

REFERENCE BOOKS ONLINE. Website: www.xrefer.com. Allows you to search for words or phrases in 60 online encyclopedias, dictionaries, quotation books, biographical sources, and gazetteers published by HarperCollins, Oxford University Press, Penguin UK, and other major houses.

RESEARCH & RESOURCES FOR WRITERS. Website: www.fontayne.com/ink. Links to lots of great sites, such as Bartlett's Familiar Quotations, other quotation resources, grammar/style notes, a rhyming dictionary, speech writing resources, etc.

+RHYMING DICTIONARY. Website: www.rhymezone.com.

+ROGET'S DESCRIPTIVE WORD FINDER: A Dictionary/Thesaurus of Adjectives and Adverbs, by Barbara Ann Kipfer (Writer's Digest Books, 2003). $24.99. ISBN: 1582971706.

ROGET'S ONLINE THESAURUS. Website: www.thesaurus.com.

SUPER SEARCHER, AUTHOR, SCRIBE: Successful Writers Share Their Internet Research Secrets by Loraine Page. Website: www.supersearchers.com. A book that features in-depth interviews with 15 writers who regularly use the Internet as a research tool.

Website links to nearly 300 Internet resources recommended in the book. Available at your local bookstore for $24.95 (ISBN: 0-910965-58-7) or call (800)300-9868.

VISUAL THESAURUS. Website: www.visualthesaurus.com. A visual representation of the English language. Be sure to take the Guided Tour.

A WEB OF ON-LINE DICTIONARIES. Website: www.yourdictionary.com. Linked to more than 1800 dictionaries in over 250 different languages.

+WEBOPEDIA. Website: www.webopedia.com. Online dictionary/encyclopedia.

WORD WEB. Website: www.wordweb.info. Free dictionary you can download.

WORLD BOOK ONLINE. Website: www.worldbook.com.

+WORLD FACTBOOK. Website: www.odci.gov/cia/publications/factbook. Published by the U.S. Central Intelligence Agency, the *World Factbook* offers data on every country in the world, including maps, background, geography, people, government, economy, and military.

RESEARCH: BIBLE

ARCHAEOLOGY. Website: www.bib-arch.org. Lists links related to archaeology and Bible scholarship.

BIBLE ANSWER MACHINE. Website: http://BibleAnswerMachine.ww7.com.

BIBLE GATEWAY. Website: http://bible.gospelcom.net. Searches different Bible versions in over 30 languages.

+BIBLEPROBE. Website: www.bibleprobe.com. A nondenominational reference site for Christians and Jews.

BIBLE PROPHECY. Website: www.armageddonbooks.com. Links to over 285 Bible prophecy sites on the Web.

+THE BIBLE STUDIES FOUNDATION. Website: www.bible.org. Home of the Net Bible.

BIBLE STUDY TOOLS. Websites: www.biblestudytools.com; www.biblestudytools.net; www.e-sword.net. A free Bible Study software with many free add-ons.

BIBLE TIMES & CUSTOMS. Website: www.middletownbiblechurch.org/biblecus/biblec.htm. Includes topics such as: Customs and Manners, Bible Measurements, Eating and Dressing, Transportation and Communication, Farming, Animals, Occupations, and Holidays.

CHRISTIAN INFORMATION MINISTRIES/RESEARCH SERVICE. Cecil R. Price, ThM, Senior Researcher, PO Box 141055, Dallas TX 75214. (214)827-0057. E-mail: crprice@email.com. Provides fee-based custom research and information retrieval for authors, churches, individuals, publishers, ministries, speakers; primary topics related to the Bible, theology, and Christian living. Basic research fee $35/hr. (2 hr. min.) plus expenses such as photocopying and shipping.

+CHURCHLINK. Website: www.churchlink.com.au. Christian Resource Networking.

CONCORDANCE. *Where to Find It in the Bible: The Ultimate A-Z Resource* by Ken Anderson (Thomas Nelson Publishers). A topical concordance listing contemporary topics and issues. Available at local bookstores.

CROSS DAILY. Website: www.crossdaily.com. Click on "Bible Search."

ONEPLACE.COM. Website: www.oneplace.com. Provides Bible study tools, such as words in Greek and Hebrew, and Strong's Concordance.

ONLINE BIBLE. Website: www.onlinebible.net.

+STUDY LIGHT. Website: www.studylight.org. Study resources, forums, and weekly columns, plus an outstanding collection of historical Bible maps.

UNBOUND BIBLE. Website: http://unbound.biola.edu. A collection of searchable Bibles, consisting of ten English versions, Greek and Hebrew versions, four ancient versions, and 42 other languages.

VINE'S EXPOSITORY DICTIONARY OF NEW TESTAMENT WORDS. Website: www.menfak
.no/bibel/vines.html.
VIRTUAL CHRISTIANITY: Bibles. Website: www.internetdynamics.com/pub/vc/bibles.html. A
comprehensive list of online Bibles in English and other languages.

RESEARCH: LIBRARIES

THE DIGITAL LIBRARY. Website: www.hti.umich.edu/cgi/b/bib/bib-idx?c-dlfcoll. Indexes hundreds of collections from libraries and museums with raw material of social history:
diaries, manuscripts, pictures, sheet music, campaign buttons, oral histories, films,
recordings, etc.
+E-LIBRARY. Website: www.highbeam.com. Search magazines, books, newspapers, maps, TV
and radio transcripts.
THE LIBRARY OF CONGRESS. Website: www.loc.gov.
LIBRARYSPOT. Website: www.libraryspot.com. A free gateway to more than 5,000 libraries
worldwide.
PROJECT BARTLEBY. Website: www.bartleby.com. The most comprehensive public reference
library ever published on the Web.
REFDESK. Website: www.refdesk.com. Well-organized and useful information.
RESEARCH LIBRARY. Website: www.researchlibrary.net.

RESEARCH: NEWS

+ABYZ NEWS LINKS. Website: www.abyznewslinks.com. Links to more than 16,000 U.S. and
international newspapers and other media.
ARCHIVED NEWSPAPERS. To find something in an archived newspaper, check out Newspaper
Links at: www.newspaperlinks.com; U.S. News Archives on the Web at: www.ibiblio.org/
slanews/internet/archivesindex.html; http://newslibrary.com.
ASSIST NEWS SERVICE. Founded by journalist and author Dan Wooding. Website: www.assist
news.net. Provides a wide variety of national and international stories that go to 2,400
media around the world.
BBC NEWSLINE. Website: www.bbc.co.uk/newsline. Desktop news center delivering updates
automatically throughout the day.
+CHRISTIAN NEWSPAPERS. Website: www.christiannewsassoc.com.
CHRISTIAN SCIENCE MONITOR NEWS SITE. Website: www.csmonitor.com.
+DAILY ROTATION. Website: www.dailyrotation.com. Collects and displays links to the latest
tech news stories from over 250 different sites.
DEMOSSNEWSPOND.COM. Website: www.DeMossNewsPond.com. Offers primary news about
some of the major faith-based organizations, leaders, and enterprises in the world.
Designed specifically for the media (reporters, editors, producers), the site is filled with
timely and reliable story leads and interactive resources.
DESKTOP NEWS. Website: http://desktopnews.com. Delivers news to your desktop on a com-
pact toolbar.
EP NEWS SERVICE. c/o Bryan Malley, Minnesota Christian Chronicle, 7317 Cahill Rd., Ste.
201, Minneapolis MN 55439. (952)562-1234. E-mail: editor@mcchronicle.com.
+FIND ARTICLES. Website: www.findarticles.com. From LookSmart.
+JOURNALISM NET (UK). Website: www.journalismnet.com/uk/index.htm. Portal of online
tools and worldwide news.
NEWSPAPER DIRECTORY. Website: www.newsd.com.

+NEWSPAPERS.COM. Website: www.newspapers.com. Exceptional tool for referencing the world's newspapers.

THE NEWSROOM HOMEPAGE. Website: http://assignmenteditor.com. Connect to virtually any newspaper in the world, check news wires, access maps, and people finders, etc.

NEWS STORY RESEARCH. Website: www.newstream.com. Offers keyword searches on news stories. Search for specific news items at: www.newstrawler.com.

NEWS STORY SOURCES. Websites: www.ap.org; http://dailynews.yahoo.com; www.slate .com/code/todayspapers/todayspapers.asp; www.newshub.com; http://totalnews.com; www.newsindex.com; http://fullcoverage.yahoo.com; www.all-links.com/newscentral; http://news.google.com; www.newseum.org/todaysfrontpages. Lets you view the current front pages of 163 newspapers from 25 different countries; http://newslink.org. You can pull up all media (newspaper, TV, radio) by city.

USA WEEKEND. Website: www.usaweekend.com. Click on "Local Newspapers." Links to over 590 newspapers, listed by state.

RESOURCES: CHILDREN'S WRITING

BLUE PHANTOM CRITIQUE GROUP FOR CHILDREN'S WRITERS. Website: www.blue phantomwriters.com. Free critique group and newsletter.

+BOOKS OF INTEREST. *How to Write A Children's Book and Get It Published* by Barbara Seuling. Wiley & Sons (1991). ISBN: 0684193434; *How to Write and Sell Children's Picture Books* by Jean E. Karl. Writers Digest Books (1994); *Children's Writer Guide to 2005* by Susan Tierney. Order at www.writersbookstore.com or call the Institute of Children's Literature at (800)443-6078. ICL also offers several other books for children's writers.

THE CHILDREN'S BOOK COUNCIL, 12 W. 37th St., 2nd Fl., New York NY 10018-7480. (212)966-1990. Fax (212)966-2073. E-mail: info@cbcbooks.org. Website: www.cbcbooks .org. Go to the Publishing FAQs page for marketing information and beginner instruction for writers and illustrators of children's books, plus lots of good links.

CHILDREN'S BOOK PUBLISHERS. Website: www.scils.rutgers.edu/%7Ekvander/Children Lit/publish.html. Lists links to various children's book publishers.

THE CHILDREN'S LITERATURE WEB GUIDE. Website: www.acs.ucalgary.ca/~dkbrown. Internet resources related to books for children and young adults.

+CHILDREN'S WRITER NEWSLETTER. Website: www.childrenswriter.com. A 12-page monthly newsletter in two sections reporting on the marketplace for children's writing, and current news, trends, and tips in the publishing industry. Susan Tierney, Editor.

CHILDREN'S WRITING SUPERSITE. Children's Book Insider LLC, 901 Columbia Rd., Fort Collins CO 80525. (970)495-0056. Toll-free (800)807-1916. E-mail: mail@write 4kids.com. Website: www.write4kids.com. To subscribe to the free e-zine *Children's Book Insider,* and for more free offers, go to the Website. Also includes market news, tutorials, FAQ, files to download, surveys, and links to other resources for children's writers.

CONTESTS. Check the Contests section in this guide for "Writing for Children/Young Adult Contests."

GLORY PRESS/PROF. DICK BOHRER, MS, MA (teacher, 39 years; editor, 11 years including editor of two newspapers and managing editor of *Moody Monthly;* author of 16 books), PO Box 624, West Linn OR 97068. (503)638-7711. E-mail: dickbohrer@juno.com. Offers 3 writing courses: "4+20 Ways to Write Stories for Christian Kids," "4+20 Ways, Christian, to Write Features Like a Pro," and "4+20 Ways, Christian, to Write What You Think." Charges $35 for each manual plus $1 per double-spaced typed page plus SASE for editing and critiquing assignments of poems, stories, and books. Asks for written testimony regarding applicant's salvation testimony of how he/she came to faith in Christ. References: gude@juno.com; k&kyoung@stic.net; asrduff@aol.com.

INSTITUTE OF CHILDREN'S LITERATURE, 93 Long Ridge Rd., West Redding CT 06896. (203)792-8600. Toll-free (800)243-9645. Fax (203)792-8406. E-mail: information services@InstituteChildrensLit.com. Website: www.InstituteChildrensLit.com. Writing programs and aptitude tests, plus a chat room and other resources for writers.

INTERVIEWS. Websites: www.robinfriedman.com; www.olswanger.com. Both of these author sites have wonderful interviews with editors and agents.

+PICTURE-BOOK.COM. Website: www.picture-book.com. "The online resource for children's illustrators, publishers, and book lovers."

THE SOCIETY OF CHILDREN'S BOOK WRITERS AND ILLUSTRATORS, 8271 Beverly Blvd., Los Angeles CA 90048. (323)782-1010. Fax (323)782-1892. E-mail: membership@ scbwi.org. Website: www.scbwi.org. Founded in 1971, this is the professional organization for children's book writers and illustrators. Over 16,000 members. Site includes a newsletter, critique groups, workshops, market resources, and other general information.

TRENDS IN CHILDREN'S PUBLISHING. Website: www.underdown.org/trends.htm.

VERLA KAY'S WEBSITE FOR CHILDREN'S WRITERS. Website: www.verlakay.com.

+WRITING FOR CHILDREN WORKSHOP. Website: www.bethanyroberts.com/ForWriters .htm. Offers writer quotes, tips, FAQs, resources, book recommendations, and a directory of children's authors and illustrators.

RESOURCES: ETHNIC WRITERS

AFRICAN-AMERICAN GUIDE TO WRITING AND PUBLISHING NONFICTION by Jewell Parker Rhodes (Broadway Books). ISBN: 0767905784.

ASIAN AMERICAN JOURNALISTS ASSN. (AAJA), 1182 Market St., Ste. 320, San Francisco CA 94102. (415)346-2051. Fax (415)346-6343. E-mail: National@aaja.org. Website: www.aaja.org. A nonprofit organization whose mission is to encourage Asian Pacific Americans to enter ranks of journalism, to work for fair and accurate coverage of Asian Pacific Americans, and to increase the number of Asian Pacific American journalists and news managers in the industry. 2,000 members.

BLACK WRITERS UNITED. The offshoot of Black Writers Alliance, Black Writers United exists to promote fellowship and the sharing of resources and information among writers. Join at: http://groups.yahoo.com/group/bwunited.

+CENTER FOR RESEARCH LIBRARIES. Website: wwwcrl.uchicago.edu. Offers 2,000 titles of periodicals and newspapers published by various ethnic groups in North America.

COPYRIGHT INFORMATION IN SPANISH. Website: www.copyright.gov/espanol.

+EDITOR & PUBLISHER. Website: www.editorandpublisher.com. The trade magazine for the newspaper industry publishes an annual yearbook. Its ethnic-press section lists newspapers by group, with contact information. Order yearbook on Website.

+MANY VOICES, ONE CITY: The Independent Press Assn.'s Guide to the Ethnic Press of New York City. Contact: Abby Scher, IPA, New York, at (212)279-1442 or e-mail: ipany@indypress.org. Website: www.indypress.org.

MAYNARD INSTITUTE, 409—13th St., 9th Fl., Oakland CA 94612. (510)891-9202. Fax (510)891-9565. E-mail: mije@maynardije.org. Website: www.maynardije.org. Provides advanced training and services nationally to help news media reflect the nation's diversity in content, staffing, and business operations.

+MULTICULTURAL MARKETING RESOURCES. Website: www.multicultural.com. Lists annual seminars and conferences of interest to marketing professionals targeting all ethnic backgrounds.

NATIONAL ASSN. OF BLACK JOURNALISTS (NABJ), University of Maryland, 8701A Adelphi Rd., Adelphi MD 20783-1716. (301)445-7100. Fax (301)445-7101. E-mail: nabj@nabj .org. Website: www.nabj.org. Goal is to strengthen ties among African American journalists and promote and communicate the importance of diversity in newsrooms. 3,300 members.

NATIONAL ASSN. OF HISPANIC JOURNALISTS (NAHJ), 1000 National Press Building, Washington DC 20045-2100. Toll-free (888)346-6245. (202)662-7145. Fax (202)662-7144. E-mail: nahj@nahj.org. Website: www.nahj.org. Dedicated to the recognition and professional advancement of Hispanics in the news industry. Approx. 1,500 members.

NATIVE AMERICAN JOURNALISTS ASSN. (NAJA), 555 N. Dakota St., Vermillion SD 57069. (605)677-5282. Fax (866)694-4264. E-mail: info@naja.com. Website: www.naja.com. To encourage, inspire, enhance, and empower Native American communicators. Includes news articles, archives, and links.

ORGANIZATION OF BLACK SCREENWRITERS, 1968 W. Adams Blvd., Los Angeles CA 90018. (323)735-2050. Fax (323)735-2051. E-mail: obswriter@sbcglobal.net. Website: www .obswriter.com. Helps African American writers get their work presented to Hollywood.

UNITY: Journalists of Color, 1601 N. Kent St., Ste. 1003, Arlington VA 22209. (703)469-2100. Fax (703)469-2108. E-mail: info@unityjournalists.org. Website: www.unityjournalists .org. Four national minority journalism associations (AAJA, NABJ, NAHJ, NAJA) seeking to promote diversity within the nation's media.

RESOURCES: FICTION WRITING

AMERICAN CHRISTIAN ROMANCE WRITERS (ACRW), PO Box 101066, Palm Bay FL 32910-1066. Rachel Hauck, pres. E-mail: info@acrw.net. Website: www.acrw.net. "To encourage writers of Christian romance and women's fiction, develop their skills, educate them in the market, and be a fellowship for writers of like interests." E-mail loop, online courses, and newsletter. Sponsors an annual conference and writing contest.

+AMERICAN CRIME WRITERS LEAGUE, 18645 SW Farmington Rd. #255, Aloha OR 97007. Website: www.acwl.org. Dues $35/year.

AT-HOME WRITING WORKSHOPS. Director: Marlene Bagnull, LittD, Write His Answer Ministries, 316 Blanchard Rd., Drexel Hill PA 19026. E-mail: mbagnull@aol.com. Website: www.writehisanswer.com. Fiction, 10 units, $255. Units may also be purchased individually for $30.

+BOOKS OF INTEREST. *Self-Editing for Fiction Writers: How to Edit Yourself into Print* by Renni Browne and Dave King, HarperResource (2004). $13.95. ISBN: 0060545690; *The First Five Pages: A Writer's Guide to Staying Out of the Rejection Pile* by Noah Lukeman, Fireside (2000). ISBN: 068485743X; *Behind the Stories* by Diane Eble, Bethany House (2002). ISBN: 0764224638. Book is based on interviews with Christian novelists. Provides readers with the "behind the story" of many of CBA's best-selling fiction writers; *Sometimes the Magic Works: Lessons from a Writing Life* by Terry Brooks, Del Rey (2004). ISBN: 0345465512.

CHAPTER A WEEK. A group for those who love Christian fiction and want to sample a chapter a week from some of the finest writing in the genre. Those who sign up will receive a free chapter excerpt each week along with information about how to order the book. To subscribe, go to: http://groups.yahoo.com/group/ChapteraWeek. Note: They are not soliciting material at this time.

CHARACTER BIOGRAPHY. Use these Websites to help develop a character biography or personality profile for your fiction characters: www.queendom.com/tests/personality/ index.html; www.davideck.com; www.2h.com/Tests/personality.phtml; www.susettewilliams .com/Workshops/CharacterSheet.htm.

CHARACTER NAME SOURCES. Websites: www.babynames.com; www.census.gov/genealogy/ names; www.ssa.gov. Their lists of registered Americans go back decades and also give the top ten (or so) names for the year you inquire about; www.ivillage.com/namefinder; www.babycenter.com/babyname/index.html; www.babynamenetwork.com; www.faithful family.net/babynames/index/php; www.behindthename.com; www.geocities.com/edgarbook/ names/welcome.html; medieval names: www.panix.com/~mittle/names/english.shtml; www.parenthoodweb.com/parent_cfmfiles/babynames.cfm; www.kleimo.com/random/ name.cfm. Randomly generates names from the U.S. Census.

CHARACTER NAME SOURCES OF DIFFERENT NATIONALITIES. Websites: African names: www.namesite.com/namesite/mainpage.html; Afrocentric names: www.swagga.com/ name.htm; Arabic names, masculine: www.ummah.org.uk/family/masc.html; Arabic names, feminine: www.ummah.org.uk/family/fem.html; Chinese names: www.mandarin tools.com/chinesename.html.

CONTESTS. Check the Contest section in this guide for "Fiction Contests."

CRIME MYSTERY WRITING/FORENSIC SITES. Websites: http://flash.lakeheadu.ca/ ~pals/forensics; www.visualexpert.com; www.tritechusa.com; www.crime-scene-investigator .net; www.pimall.com/nais/home.html. This is the site for the National Assn. of Investigative Specialists; http://dir.yahoo.com/Society_and_Culture/Crime. Yahoo's Crime Directory; www.officer.com. Offers links to agencies, criminal justice, investigations, special ops, most-wanted worldwide and other law enforcement sites; http://foia.fbi.gov. This Freedom of Information Act site offers an electronic reading room with categories such as espionage, famous persons, gangster era, historical interests, unusual phenomena, and violent crimes.

+ECLECTIC FICTION. Website: www.eclectics.com. Site offers a newsletter, links, articles, and a helpful character trait tracking chart.

FAITH, HOPE & LOVE is the inspirational chapter of Romance Writers of America. Dues for the chapter are $24/yr., but you must also be a member of RWA to join (dues $75/yr.). Chapter offers these services: online list service for members, a Website, 20-pg. bimonthly newsletter, annual contest, connects critique partners by mail or e-mail, and latest romance market information. To join, contact RWA National Office, 16000 Stuebner Airline Rd., Ste. 140, Spring TX 77379. (832)717-5200. Fax (832)717-5201. Website: www .rwanational.com. Or go to FHL Website: www.faithhopelove-rwa.org. E-mail: info@ rwanational.com. Over 150 members in FHL, over 8500 in RWA.

+FEDERAL CITIZEN INFORMATION CENTER. Website: www.pueblo.gsa.gov. Need information about your character's livelihood? The Center offers free and low-cost booklets about nearly everything.

FICTION & SCI-FI/FANTASY E-GROUPS. Website: http://groups.yahoo.com. Type into box: Christian_fic2 (for genre fiction), or ChristSF (for science fiction and Christianity). A Christian fantasy site is: www.christianfantasy.com. A Christian sci-fi site is www.christian-fandom .org.

+FICTIONETTE/SHORT STORIES. Website: www.fictionette.com. With a free membership comes the ability to submit and critique short fiction works.

+FICTION FACTOR. Website: www.fictionfactor.com. Free monthly newsletter, plus tips and articles on writing better fiction, promoting and marketing your work, and more.

FICTION FIX NEWSLETTER: The Nuts and Bolts of Crafting Better Fiction. Website: www.coffeehouseforwriters.com/news.html.

FICTION HOW-TO ESSAYS. Website: www.storyispromise.com. Essays on the craft of writing by Bill Johnson.

+FICTION LINKS. Website: http://story.exis.net/masterlink. 1001 links to articles about writing fiction.

FICTION WRITER'S CONNECTION. Website: www.fictionwriters.com. Provides help with novel writing and information on finding agents/editors and getting published. Website includes newsletters (online and hard copy), critiquing, editor/agent information, free tip sheets and consultations, and scam warnings. Toll-free (800)248-2758. E-mail: Bcamenson@ aol.com.

FICTION WRITING CLASSES (F2K). Website: http://fiction.4-writers.com/creative-writing-classes.shtml.

FREE CHRISTIAN FICTION. Website: www.edelayne.com. Fiction writer Elizabeth Delayne's site offers free fiction as well as links to other Christian fiction sites.

+THE HISTORICAL NOVEL SOCIETY. Website: www.historicalnovelsociety.org. Founded in 1997, this group aims to promote all aspects of historical fiction. Offers an annual conference, discussion list, book reviews, and more. E-mail: histnovel@aol.com.

+LEGAL INFORMATION INSTITUTE. Website: www4.law.cornell.edu/uscode. Is your character in trouble with the law? Learn about court processes and other legalities.

MYSTERYNET NETWORK, 3616 Far West Blvd. #117-298, Austin TX 78731. (512)342-8377. E-mail: comment@MysteryNet.com. Website: www.mysterynet.com.

MYSTERY WRITERS OF AMERICA, 17 E. 47th St., 6th Fl., New York NY 10017. (212)888-8171. Fax (212)888-8107. E-mail: mwa@mysterywriters.org. Website: www.mystery writers.org.

MYSTERY WRITERS SITES OF INTEREST. Websites: www.cluelass.com; www.crime.org; http://crime.about.com; www.MurderMustAdvertise.com. Offers an e-mail discussion list for authors wanting to promote new mystery books; www.deadlypleasures.com.

NOVEL ADVICE. Website: www.noveladvice.com. Online courses, chat sessions, and writing links.

NOVEL PRO. Website: http://novelcode.com. Software that helps organize ideas, work on pieces of the story without getting lost, brainstorm creation of characters and scenes, etc. Cost is $29.95.

ONLINE NEWSLETTER. Website: www.fictionaddiction.net. E-mail: newsletter@fiction addiction.net.

+ROBIN'S NEST. Website: www.robinsnest.com. Offers links, articles, online courses, and workshops for all genres fiction writers.

ROMANCE WRITERS. Websites: www.eHarlequin.com; www.rchzine.com.

ROMANCE WRITERS OF AMERICA, 16000 Stuebner Airline Rd. Ste. 140, Spring TX 77379. (832)717-5200. Fax (832)717-5201. E-mail: info@rwanational.org. Website: www .rwanational.org.

SCIENCE FICTION AND FANTASY WRITERS OF AMERICA, Jane Jewell, exec. dir., PO Box 877, Chestertown MD 21620. (207)861-8078. E-mail: execdir@sfwa.org. Website: www.sfwa.org.

SCIENCE FICTION LANGUAGE. Website: www.langmaker.com.

SCIENCE FICTION SITE. Ralan Conley's SpecFic & Humor Webstravaganza. Website: www .ralan.com.

SHORT MYSTERY FICTION SOCIETY. Website: www.thewindjammer.com/smfs.

+SISTERS IN CRIME, PO Box 442124, Lawrence KS 66044-8933. (785)842-1325. Website: www.sistersincrime.org.

SPECULATIVE (sci-fi & fantasy) FICTION LINKS. Spicy Green Iguana, Inc. Website: www.spicygreeniguana.com.

STORYCRAFT STORY DEVELOPMENT SOFTWARE. Website: www.writerspage.com. Guides writers through the entire process of writing novels, screenplays, teleplays, plays, and short stories.

SYNOPSES. "Conquering the Dreaded Synopsis" by Lisa Gardner. Website: www.rosecity romancewriters.com.

+TIME TICKER. Website: www.timeticker.com. Keep track of characters in other time zones.

TOP 100 FICTIONAL CHARACTERS. Website: www.fictional100.com. Features the most influential characters in world literature and legend. Compiled by Lucy Pollard-Gott. Also check: www.npr.org/programs/totn/features/2002/mar/020319.characters.html for *Book* magazine's list of the top 100 fictional characters since 1900.

+TRADEMARK SEARCHES. If you are concerned that you may have chosen a name for a fictitious business or brand in your story that exists in real life, go to: www.uspto .gov/web/menu/tmebc/index.html and click Search. In Canada, go to: http://strategis.ic .gc.ca/sc_mrksv/cipo/tm/tm_main-e.html.

VICTORIAN SETTING. Websites: www.victorianweb.org. Provides history and cultural information for fiction set in the Victorian age; www.thelondonhouse.co.uk; www.victorian london.org.

WEBSITES OF CHRISTIAN FICTION AUTHORS. Connect to over 30 sites at: www.deehenderson .com.

WESTERN WRITERS OF AMERICA. Website: www.westernwriters.org. For membership information, contact: Larry K. Brown, 209 E. Iowa, Cheyenne WY 82009. E-mail: member ship@westernwriters.org. Current membership over 600 published writers.

WRITER'S BLOCKS 3.0. Website: www.writersblocks.com. Organize story elements for your fiction.

WRITER'S DIGEST SCHOOL, 4700 E. Galbraith Rd., Cincinnati OH 45236. Toll-free (800)759-0963. Fax (513)531-0798. E-mail: wds@fwpubs.com. Website: www.writers digest.com/wds. Novel Writing Workshop, Writing & Selling Short Stories, and others. This is a secular course, but you may request a Christian instructor.

+XIANWORLDVIEW.COM. Website: www.xianworldview.com. From a Christian world view, this site provides book reviews, articles, interviews, forums, and other Science Fiction and Fantasy resources.

RESOURCES: POETRY WRITING

ACADEMY OF AMERICAN POETS, 588 Broadway, Ste. 604, New York NY 10012-3210. (212)274-0343. Fax (212)274-9427. Website: www.poets.org. Site offers 500 poet biographies, 1,500 poems, 100 RealAudio poet clips, poetry exhibits, essays, and a National Poetry Map.

ALBANY POETRY WORKSHOP. Website: www.sonic.net/poetry/albany.

CONTESTS. Check the Contest section in this guide for "Poetry Contests."

+CREATIVE-POEMS.COM. Website: www.creative-poems.com. "Join the world's friendliest free poetry site. Add poems to be rated and commented on. Then rate and comment on other's poetry as well." Over 4000 members.

CROSSHOME.COM. A site where Christian poetry is featured. To have your work considered, go to: www.crosshome.com/poetry.shtml.

+DIRECTORY OF POETRY PUBLISHERS. Website: http://acqweb.library.vanderbilt .edu/acqweb/pubr/poem.htm.

+FELLOWSHIP OF CHRISTIAN POETS, John and Marilyn Marinelli, cofounders. PO Box 93345, Lakeland FL 33804. Offers books, a newsletter, contests, critiques, and members are guaranteed publication of 52 poems per year, one per week, in the Library of Poetic Expression. Dues: $35/year.

HAIKU. Websites devoted to haiku: www.gardendigest.com/poetry/index.htm; www.execpc .com/~ohaus/haiku.html; www.everypoet.com/absurdities/index.htm. The following

organizations also provide additional resources for haiku writers: BRITISH HAIKU SOCI-
ETY, David Cobb, pres., Sinodun, Shalford, Braintree, Essex CM7 5HN, England. Website:
www.britishhaikusociety.org; HAIKU OZ, Janice Bostok, contact officer. E-mail: haikuoz@
yahoo.com. Website: www.haikuoz.org; HAIKU SOCIETY OF AMERICA, Membership Secre-
tary, 333 E. 47th St. New York NY 10017, Website: www.hsa-haiku.org; WORLD HAIKU
CLUB, Susumu Takiguchi, chairman, Leys Farm, Roucham, Bicestor, Oxfordshire OX25 4
RA, England. Website: www.worldhaikuclub.org. Also check out *The Haiku Box* by Lonnie
Hull DuPont, Tuttle Publishing (2001). ISBN: 1582900302.

+ONLINE POETRY CLASSROOM. Website: www.onlinepoetryclassroom.org. Online classes
geared toward high school poetry teachers, but helpful for all poets.

POETIC VOICES. Website: www.poeticvoices.com. A ton of information for poets, including
market listings, contests, conferences, articles, columns, and more.

+POETRY AND WRITERS PORTAL. Website: www.voicesnet.com/poetrylinks.htm. Offers an
international contest, forums, an e-zine, audio, self-publishing options, and more.

THE POETRY LIST. Website: www.thepoetrylist.com. A free up-to-date listing of domestic, foreign, and online literary journals that regularly publish poetry.

POETRY SOCIETY OF AMERICA, 15 Gramercy Park, New York NY 10003. (212)254-9628.
Website: www.poetrysociety.org.

POETS & WRITERS. Website: www.pw.org. Publishing advice, conference list, grants and
awards, literary links, news from the writing world, and resources.

RHYMING DICTIONARY. Website: www.rhymer.com.

THE SCROLL. Website: www.Christian-poetry.com/thescroll.html. E-mail: thescroll@
Christian-poetry.com. Online Christian magazine designed to share Christian poetry, creative writing, and articles.

UNIVERSITY OF BUFFALO POETRY LINKS. Website: http://wings.buffalo.edu/epc/connects/
poetrywebs.html.

+WRITING POETRY by Shelly Tucker, GoodYear Books. A very "reader-friendly" book with
clear examples of imagery, figures of speech, and guidelines for free and rhymed verse.
Find a copy at www.alibris.com.

RESOURCES: SCREENWRITING/SCRIPTWRITING

ACADEMY OF MOTION PICTURE ARTS AND SCIENCES, 8949 Wilshire Blvd., Beverly Hills
CA 90211-1972. (310)247-3000. Fax (310)859-9351 or (310)859-9619. E-mail: ampas@
oscars.org. Website: www.oscars.org. Script library, Academy Players Directory, and listings for industry events.

+ACADEMY WRITERS CLINIC, 2118 Wilshire Blvd., Ste. 160A, Santa Monica CA 90403. E-mail:
info@academywriters.com. Website: www.academywriters.com. For screenwriters who
wish to improve their art, sell their material, and be discovered.

ACT ONE: Writing for Hollywood. Contact: Barbara R. Nicolosi, 1763 N. Gower St., Hollywood CA 90028. (323)462-1348. Fax (323)462-2550. E-mail: Actone@fpch.org. Website:
www.ActOneprogram.com. Speakers include: Randall Wallace (*Braveheart*) and Angelo
Pizzo (*Rudy*). Limited to 30 students. This is a month-long intensive training session for
screenwriters. See Website for dates and for information about weekend seminars.

AMERICAN SCREENWRITERS ASSOCIATION, 269 S. Beverly Dr., Ste. 2600, Beverly Hills CA
90212-3807. Toll-free phone/fax (866)265-9091. E-mail: asa@asascreenwriters.com.
Website: www.asascreenwriters.com. Nonprofit group that encourages the public's participation in and knowledge of screenwriting as a literary art form.

ANGELIC ENTERTAINMENT, 555 W. Beech St., Ste. 225, San Diego CA 92101-2957.
(619)238-8234. E-mail: mark@angelicentertainment.com. Website: www.AngelicEnter

tainment.com. An entertainment group in search of properties in manuscript and/or screenplay form. Their mission is to produce "content-responsible" entertainment. Go to the Website to view their credits and experience.

ART WITHIN. Contact: Bryan Coley, artistic director, 1940 Minnewil Ln., Marietta GA 30068, (770)565-8804. E-mail: artwithin@artwithin.org. Website: www.artwithin.org. A professional theater company whose emphasis is new works that uniquely blend hope and truth from a Christian perspective and that are relevant to a contemporary (secular) audience.

+BOOKS OF INTEREST. *The Writers Journey: Mythic Structure for Writers* by Christopher Vogler (Michael Weise Productions). ISBN: 0941188701; *Screen Play: The Foundations of Screenwriting* by Syd Field (MJF Books); *The Writer's Guide to Writing Your Screenplay* and *The Writer's Guide to Selling Your Screenplay* by Cynthia Whitcomb (Kalmbach Publishing). Find both books at www.thewriterbooks.com.

CHRISTIAN DRAMA NORTHWEST. An e-mail group for those interested in drama. Website: http://groups.yahoo.com/groups/CDNW.

CHRISTIANS IN HOLLYWOOD. Contact: Victorya Rogers Communications, PO Box 30202, Edmond OK 73003. (405)341-7621. Fax (405)348-3343. E-mail: victorya@victorya.com. Websites: www.victorya.com and www.thrillinglife.com. A publication for Christians interested in breaking into Hollywood.

CHRISTIANS IN THEATER ARTS, PO Box 26471, Greenville SC 29616. (864)679-1898. E-mail: information@cita.org. Website: www.cita.org. Holds an annual conference.

COLLABORATOR SOFTWARE/SERVICES FOR SCREEN WRITERS AND NOVELISTS. Website: www.collaborator.com.

THE COMPLETE BOOK OF SCRIPTWRITING by J. Michael Straczynski, Writer's Digest Books, $19.99. Order at: www.writersdigest.com or through local bookstore. ISBN: 1582971587.

CREATIVE SCREENWRITING, 6404 Hollywood Blvd., Ste. 415, Los Angeles CA 90028. Toll-free (800)727-6978. (323)957-1405. Fax (323)957-1406. E-mail: info@creativescreen writing.com. Website: www.creativescreenwriting.com. A magazine for professional screenwriters. Website also offers a discussion group.

+DONE DEAL. Website: www.scriptsales.com. A wealth of resources for screenwriters.

THE DRAMA IMPROVEMENT CONFERENCE. Greater Portland Area, October. Contact: Judy Straalsund, PO Box 19844, Portland OR 97280-0844. (503)245-6919. E-mail: ttc.pdx@att.net. Website: www.tapestrytheatre.org. Geared to all Christian dramatists, and features workshops, performances, networking, forums, and a book table. Playwrights are encouraged to attend.

DRAMASHARE CHRISTIAN DRAMA THEATRE RESOURCES, 82 St. Lawrence Crescent, Saskatoon SK S7K 1G5 Canada. Toll-free (877)363-7262. Fax (306)653-0653. E-mail: contactus@ dramashare.org. Website: www.dramashare.org. Supports those involved in Christian drama ministry worldwide, with how-to manuals, scripts, seminars, and newsletters.

DRAMATIC EXCHANGE. Website: http://dramex.org. A script exchange site where playwrights can post unpublished scripts and readers/producers can look for plays.

THE DRAMATISTS GUILD OF AMERICA, 1501 Broadway, Ste. 701, New York NY 10036. (212)398-9366. Fax (212)944-0420. E-mail: Igor@Dramaguild.com. Website: www .dramaguild.com. Professional association of playwrights, composers, and lyricists with over 6,000 members.

DRAMA WORKSHOP. Website: http://Chdramaworkshop.homestead.com/Home.html. "Nuts & Bolts of Dramatic Writing." Includes: dramatic structures, script formats, screenwriting, reading list, and exercises.

ESSAYS. An index of essays on the craft of dramatic writing can be found at www.storyis promise.com.

FADE IN ONLINE. Website: www.fadeinonline.com. Annual screenplay and fiction competition.

GETTING YOUR ACTS TOGETHER by Frank V. Priore. A complete step-by-step guide on how to write and sell a full-length play for the school market. ISBN: 0963749846. This and other books available at: www.writersbookcase.com.

GRIZZLY ADAMS PRODUCTIONS, PO Box 1987, Loveland CO 80539. (970)663-3820. Fax (970)663-6487. E-mail: grizzlyadamstv@aol.com. Website: www.grizzlyadams.tv. Producers of network television "Encounters with the Unexplained" (PAX-TV Network) and home videos, including Christian films. Producer for a variety of networks. Occasionally on the lookout for beginning screenwriters.

HOLLYWOOD CREATIVE DIRECTORY, IFILM Publishing, 1024 N. Orange Dr., Hollywood CA 90038. (323)308-3606. Toll-free (800)815-0503. Fax (323)308-3493. Website: www.hcdonline.com. Comes out 3 times a year. Lists production companies and staff (the ones who option or buy screenplays for production). Commonly referred to as the "Phonebook to Hollywood." They also publish the Hollywood Representation Directory—managers, agents, attorneys, publicity.

HOLLYWOOD JESUS. Website: www.hollywoodjesus.com. Movie reviews and pop culture from a spiritual point of view.

+HOLLYWOOD LIT SALES. Website: www.hollywoodlitsales.com. A place to submit screenplays and to learn how to write them.

HOLLYWOOD SCRIPTWRITING. Website: www.HowToWriteScripts.com. Teaches how to go from idea, to screenplay, to sale. Also includes free newsletter and links.

ILLINOIS/CHICAGO SCREENWRITING COMPETITION. Website: www.illinoisbiz.biz/film/index.html. This is a biennial event sponsored by the Chicago and Illinois Film Offices to support and promote local screenwriters. It is offered exclusively to Illinois resident writers who have completed a feature-length script. Winners receive a cash prize and their scripts are sent to a select group of production companies and Hollywood producers and studios. Call (312)814-8711 for general information. Contact: Debbie Beck (Chicago Film office) at (312)744-9275 or Todd Lizak (Illinois Film office) at (312)814-2100.

INKTIP.COM. Website: www.InkTip.com. The fastest and easiest way to give your screenplays more exposure.

INTER-MISSION. Website: www.inter-mission.net. A community of Christians involved in the arts.

INTERNATIONAL SCREENPLAY COMPETITION. Website: http://writersdigest.com/contests/internat_screenplay.asp. Sponsored by the American Screenwriters Association and Writer's Digest.

+MAVERICK BLUEPRINT SCREENWRITING COMPETITION. ScriptShark Contests, 520 Broadway St., Ste. 230, Santa Monica CA 90401. (310)393-9999. Fax (310)393-7799. E-mail: scriptshark@filmtracker.com. Website: www.maverickblueprint.com. Maverick Films will read the top 100 scripts with guaranteed representation for the top three winners.

MOVIEBYTES.COM. Website: www.moviebytes.com. Screenwriting contests and markets online.

ONLINE SCREENWRITING AND WRITING COURSES. Website: www.absolutewrite.com/classes. John Jarvis and Christina Hamlett teach beginning screenwriters and novelists how to go from idea to completed manuscript in online classes.

ORGANIZATION OF BLACK SCREENWRITERS, 1968 W. Adams Blvd., Los Angeles CA 90018. (323)735-2050. Fax (323)735-2051. E-mail: obswriter@sbcglobal.net. Website: www.obswriter.com. Helps African American writers get their work presented to Hollywood.

THE PLAYWRIGHTS GUILD OF CANADA. (formerly The Playwrights Union of Canada.) (416)703-0201. Fax (416)703-0059. E-mail: info@playwrightsguild.ca. Website: www.puc.ca. A national association of professional playwrights. Approx. 440 members.

PLAYWRITING SEMINARS. Website: www.vcu.edu/artweb/playwriting. "An opinionated Web companion on the Art & Craft of Playwriting."

SCREENPLAY FESTIVAL. Website: www.screenplayfestival.com. Annual festival to submit your screenplay.

+SCREENPLAY MASTERY. Website: www.screenplaymastery.com. Michael Hauge offers coaching and consultation services dedicated to the art, craft, and business of screenwriting. His site offers articles, services, newsletters, and events for entertainment professionals. Call toll-free (800)477-1947.

SCREENWRITERS MAGAZINE. Website: www.screenwritersutopia.com.

SCR(i)PT MAGAZINE. Website: www.scriptmag.com. The magazine for the craft and business of screenwriting. Subscribe online and also check out screenwriting advice and contests.

+SCRIPT SHARK, 520 Broadway St., Ste. 230, Santa Monica CA 90401. (310)393-9999. Fax (310)393-7799. E-mail: scriptshark@filmtracker.com. Website: www.scriptshark.com. Helps screenwriters connect to studios, agents, managers, and production companies. Newsletter provides Film Tracker Insider Report, Reader Portfolios, and specials. Also provides professional analysis of your script.

SCRIPT VIKING. Website:www.scriptviking.com. Evaluates, develops, and sells scripts.

+SCRIPTS WANTED. Bob Jones University Press publishes four new plays per year. They are willing to purchase full-length plays with original, well-rounded characters, innovative, believable plots and an underlying world-view that is compatible with the Christian philosophy as revealed in the Holy Bible. For more information, e-mail: plarson@bju.edu. They accept e-mail submissions and hard copy submissions sent to: Drama Scripts, Secondary Authors Department, Bob Jones University Press, Greenville SC 29614.

SCRIPTWRITERS NETWORK. Website: http://scriptwritersnetwork.com. Also see: www .screenwriters.com; www.screenwriter.com.

SCRIPTWRITING CONFERENCES. Website: www.writersdigest.com/conferences. Type in "Scriptwriting" in the Search box.

SCRIPTWRITING RECOMMENDED BOOKS. *Making a Good Script Great* by Linda Seger; *Writing Screenplays That Sell* by Michael Hauge; *Story* by Robert McKee; *The Writer's Journey* by Chris Vogler; *Writing Treatments That Sell* by Ken Atchity.

SELLING TO HOLLYWOOD. Website: www.sellingtohollywood.com. American Screenwriters Assn. International Screenwriters Conference.

+SOFTWARE FOR SCREEN/SCRIPT WRITERS. Add-ons: ScreenStyle at www.screen style.com; Script Werx at www.originalvision.com; Script Wizard at www.warrenassoc.com; ScriptWright 2000 at www.kois.com/ink; HollyWord at www.hollyword.com. Programs: Final Draft at www.finaldraft.com; Movie Magic Screenwriter 2000 at www.screenplay.com; Scriptware at www.scriptware.com; Page 2 stage at www.page2stage.com. Download and try the free demos before buying. More software at www.writersstore.com/products.php?cPath=22.

SPIRITUAL THEATER INTERNATIONAL. Website: www.spiritualtheater.com. Looking for new play submissions. Send plays to: Spiritual Theater Intl., PO Box 538, Littleton CO 80160. Attn: New Play Submissions. When submitting, include a copy of the release form found on Website. For more information contact: carl@spiritualtheater.com.

STORIE ARTS, INC., 407 S. Vail Ave., Arlington Heights IL 60005. (847)843-2047. E-mail: info@storie.com. Website: www.storie.com. A Christian film/video company looking for original scripts to be produced as film shorts, half-hour shows for broadcast/video, or feature-length films. Producing for various markets including youth, comedy, and drama.

STUDIO NOTES. Website: www.studionotes.com. E-mail: info@studionotes.com. A place where writers can receive a level of professional feedback and access denied those outside the Hollywood system.

WRITE BROTHERS, INC. (formerly Screenplay Systems, Inc.), 138 N. Brand Blvd., Ste. 201, Glendale CA 91203. Toll-free (800)847-8679. Fax (818)843-8364. Websites: www.screen play.com; www.write-bros.com. Software for writing screenplays and stories.

WRITER'S FILM PROJECT (WFP). Website: www.chesterfield-co.com. Offers fiction, theater, and film writers the opportunity to begin a career in screenwriting. Up to 5 writers will be chosen to participate. Selected writers form a yearlong screenwriting workshop, using their storytelling skills to begin a career in film. Send application and submissions to: The Chesterfield Film Company—Writer's Film Project, 1158—26th St., PMB 544, Santa Monica CA 90403. (213)683-3977. E-mail: info@chesterfield-co.com.

THE WRITERS STORE. Website: www.writersstore.com. Essentials for writers and filmmakers.

+ZOETROPE. Website: www.zoetrope.com. "The Virtual Studio is a submission destination and collaboration tool for filmmakers—a community where artists can submit and workshop original work and where producers can make movies using build-in production tools." Membership is free.

RESOURCES: SONGWRITING

Note: Also see "Music Markets" in Periodical section.

+ADORATION PUBLISHING, CO. Website: www.adorationpublishing.com. E-mail: larry@ adorationpublishing.com. Publishes choral and instrumental music for Christian worship.

THE ART OF WRITING LOVE SONGS by Pamela Phillips Oland, Allworth Press, ISBN 158115271, $19.95. Order this book and many others at www.allworth.com.

+CHORDANT MUSIC GROUP. EMI Music/Chordant Music Group Distribution. Website: www.chordant.com. Click on Products, then Labels for Chordant labels.

THE CHRISTIAN MEDIA DIRECTORY. Christian Media, PO Box 448, Jacksonville OR 97530. (541)899-8888. E-mail: James@christianmedianetwork.com. Website: www.christian medianetwork.com. Easy-to-use guide to the Christian music, film, and video business. 21st Century Edition on CD-ROM. Also has *The Christian Artist Survival Guide: How to Produce, Manufacture, Distribute & Promote an Independent Christian Record* and the *Christian Retail Directory,* listing distribution outlets and wholesalers.

CHRISTIAN MUSIC DIRECTORIES/CHRISTIAN MUSIC FINDER. Resource Publications, Inc., 160 E. Virginia St., #290, San Jose CA 95112-5876. Toll-free (888)273-7782. Fax (408)287-8748. E-mail: info@rpinet.com. Website: www.rpinet.com/products/cmf.html. A comprehensive information source for Christian music. Christian Music Finder is available on CD-ROM.

CHRISTIAN MUSIC ONLINE. Website: www.cmo.com.

CHRISTIAN SONGWRITING ORGANIZATION. Website: www.christiansongwriting.org. A group for songwriters to share ideas/experiences and to critique each other's work.

THE DRAMATISTS GUILD OF AMERICA, 1501 Broadway, Ste. 701, New York NY 10036. (212)398-9366. Fax (212)944-0420. E-mail: Igor@dramaguild.com. Website: www.drama guild.com. Professional association of playwrights, composers, and lyricists.

FINDING A COLLABORATOR. Helpful article at: www.writersdigest.com/articles/excerpts/ 99songmarket_find_collaborator.asp.

+GOSPEL MUSIC ASSN., 1205 Division St., Nashville TN 37203. (615)242-0303. Fax (615)254-9755. Website: www.gospelmusic.org. For submission opportunities, click "Got Talent?"

+INDIEHEAVEN. Website: www.indeheaven.com. Information and resources for independent Christian artists, radio stations, venues. Offers the *50 Point Tune-up* song evaluation.

THE INSIDE TRACK TO GETTING STARTED IN CHRISTIAN MUSIC. Reed Arvin, editor. Harvest House Publishers. ISBN: 0736902678. How to become a solo or ensemble performer in Christian music, and to live a life that may include wealth and fame while remaining true to Christ's calling. Also focuses on basic poetic techniques for lyric writers.

THE NASHVILLE SONGWRITERS ASSOCIATION INTERNATIONAL, 1701 West End Ave., 3rd Fl., Nashville TN 37203. (615)256-3354. Toll-free (800)321-6008. Fax (615)256-0034. E-mail: nsai@NashvilleSongwriters.com. Website: www.nashvillesongwriters.com. Over 100 workshops around the country.

THE NATIONAL ACADEMY OF RECORDING ARTS AND SCIENCES, 3402 Pico Blvd., Santa Monica CA 90405. (310)392-3777. Fax (310)399-3090. E-mail: info@grammyfoundation .com. Website: www.grammy.com/academy. Presents the Grammy Awards. Also engages in professional educational activities, such as seminars; provides scholarships; offers associate memberships.

PERFORMING RIGHTS SOCIETIES. These three groups collect royalties due their members from radio, TV, and concert performances. The three societies are ASCAP (American Society of Composers, Authors and Publishers), 1 Lincoln Plaza, New York NY 10023. (212)621-6000. E-mail: info@ascap.com. Website: www.ascap.com. BMI (Broadcast Music Inc.), 320 W. 57th St., New York NY 10019-3790. (212)586-2000. Website: http://bmi.com. SESAC (not an acronym), 55 Music Square East, Nashville TN 37203. (615)320-0055. Fax (615)329-9627. Website: www.sesac.com.

+PROVIDENT MUSIC GROUP, 741 Cool Springs Blvd. E., Franklin TN 37067. Website: www.providentmusic.com. Site provides links to retailers, Provident labels, artists, concerts, jobs, FAQs, features, and more.

RESOURCES & CONTESTS. Website: www.musesmuse.com.

RHYMING DICTIONARY. Website: www.rhymer.com.

THE SONGWRITERS GUILD, 1222—16th Ave. S., Ste. 25, Nashville TN 37212. (615)329-1782. Fax (615)329-2623. E-mail: nash@songwritersguild.com. Website: www.song writers.org. Protects the rights of songwriters.

THE SONGWRITER'S MARKET GUIDE. Website: www.writersdigest.com. Search for The Songwriter's Market.

+SONGWRITING COMPETITION. International Songwriting Competition, Zero Governors Ave., #6, Medford MA 02155. (781)306-0441. Website: www.songwritingcompetition.com.

SONGWRITING LINKS. Website: www.lyricist.com.

YOU CAN WRITE SONG LYRICS by Terry Cox. ISBN: 0898799899. $14.99. Order at www.writers digest.com.

RESOURCES: YOUNG WRITERS

CONFERENCES. Check "Christian Writers' Conferences and Workshops" section in this guide for those that provide a separate track or sessions for young writers.

CONTESTS. A Mystery writing contest for kids is offered at: http://kids.mysterynet.com.

CREATIVE WRITING FOR TEENS. Website: http://teenwriting.about.com/teens/teenwriting. Devoted to helping young authors develop their writing skills and creativity. Covers over 30 subjects. Lots of links listed too.

+JO: JOURNALISM ONLINE, 6118 Bend of River, Dunn NC 28334. Phone/fax (910)980-1126. E-mail: publisher@teenlight.org. Website: www.writershelper.org/workshop. Annette Dammer, administrator. Offers a free online workshop to Christian teens and homeschooling families.

+JUST4TEENS. Website: www.lovepoetscafe.net/teens. Site where teens can post stories and poems.

LISSA EXPLAINS IT ALL. Website: www.lissaexplains.com. An excellent site for learning HTML (the language in which Web pages are written), especially for kids, but equally helpful for any HTML novice.

PERIODICAL MARKETS. Check "Periodical Topics" in this guide for "Young Writer Markets."

SECULAR PERIODICAL MARKETS. Creative Kids: www.prufrock.com/prufrockjournals magazines.cfm; *Potluck Children's Literary Magazine*: http://members.aol.com/_ht_a/ potluckmagazine/index.html; *Merlyn's Pen:* www.merlynspen.com; *Skipping Stones:* www.efn.org/~skipping/submissions.htm; *Stone Soup:* www.stonesoup.com; *Teen Ink Magazine:* http://teenink.com; *WordDance.com*: www.worddance.com/tips.html; *The Writers' Slate:* www.writingconference.com/writer's.htm; *Young Voices Magazine:* www.young voicesmagazine.com. Also, check out: www.jhu.edu/~gifted/ts/writing_resources.htm and www.merlynspen.com/publish.html for a list of links to publications that publish student writings.

STORYBOOK WEAVER DELUXE. A computer CD for children ages 8-12 that encourages writing by offering story ideas, background pictures, objects, and other options. For more information, go to www.riverdeep.net/support/product_support/s/strybkwv11569.jhtml.

UPPER ROOM MINISTRIES. Website: www.MethodX.org. At this site young adults can reflect on their faith through music, personal journal space, reviews, and more.

+THE WRITE STUFF. Website: www.geocities.com/writestuffclub. A club for young adult writers ages 13 to 23.

WRITING WITH WRITERS. Website: http://teacher.scholastic.com/writewit/index.htm. Students work with authors, editors, and illustrators in exclusive workshops designed to guide them in developing their writing skills.

YAHOOLIGANS. Website: www.yahooligans.com. Search engine for kids. Geared toward elementary age children or adults seeking information in a simple format.

YOUNG AUTHOR EDITION OF WRITING SMARTER NOT HARDER by Colleen Reese. A how-to book for elementary-school-age children. Great for children's writing classes or homeschoolers. To order a copy, send $7.95, plus $1.50 shipping to: Kaleidoscope Press, 2507—94th Ave. E., Edgewood WA 98371, or call (253)848-1116. *Writing Smarter Not Harder* (for jr. high through adults) is also available for $13.95 plus $1.50 shipping.

YOUNG WRITERS CLUBHOUSE. Real Kids, Real Adventures, PO Box 461572, Garland TX 75046-1572. Website: www.realkids.com. From author Deborah Morris: tips on how to get started writing, a writing contest, an e-mail list, and a critique group for kids.

YOUNG WRITERS SERIES. *Young Writers Contest Manual, Young Writers Market Manual* and *Young Writers Manuscript Manual* by Penny Lent. For kindergarten to college-age students interested in selling nonfiction, poetry, photos, and art. To order, send $7.95, plus $1.50 shipping, for each book to: Kaleidoscope Press, 2507—94th Ave. E., Edgewood WA 98371, or call (253)848-1116.

SEARCH ENGINES

ALTAVISTA. Website: www.altavista.com.

+A9. Website: http://a9.com. Amazon.com's search engine. "In addition to Web search results, we present book results from Amazon.com that include 'Search Inside the Book.' "

ASKME. Website: www.askme.com. Under writing, look for 17 subtopics, including fiction writing, copyright law, and publishing.

BRITANNICA. Website: www.britannica.com. The *Encyclopedia Britannica*'s Website. Includes the Britannica Internet Guide, all of the articles in the *Encyclopedia Britannica,* and much more.

+CHRISTIAN SEARCH ENGINES. Websites: www.christianlink.com; www.crosssearch.com; www .crosswalk.com; www.everythingchristian.org; www.his-net.com; www.ibelieve.com; www.injesus.com; www.praize.com; www.religiousresources.org; www.chritech.com; www .worthylinks.com.

+CNET. Website: http://cnet.com. A conglomeration of dozens of tech sites and tools.

COPERNIC. Website: www.copernic.com. A meta-search engine.

DIRECT SEARCH. Website: www.freepint.com/gary/direct.htm. A growing compilation of links to the search interfaces of resources not easily searchable from general search tools.

DITTO. Website: www.ditto.com. A family-friendly image search engine; will not link to any offensive images.

DOGPILE. Website: www.dogpile.com. Uses over a dozen search engines to find your search topic.

EXPERT CLICK. Website: www.expertclick.com. Search for experts by topic, geography, or organization.

FREEALITY INTERNET SEARCH ENGINES. Website: www.freeality.com. Links to search engines.

GOOGLE. Website: www.google.com. Sorts hits based on how "popular" they are—in other words, by how many other sites point to that particular hit.

+GOOGLE PRINT. Website: http://print.google.com/print/faq.html.

GOOGLE WEBQUOTES. Website: http://labs.google.com/cgi-bin/webquotes. Annotates the results of your Google search with comments from other Websites. This offers a convenient way to get a third party's opinion about each of the returns for your search, providing you with more information about that site's credibility and reputation.

HOTBOT. Website: www.hotbot.com.

INFO. Website: www.info.com. Displays results from 12 search engines.

KARNAK. Website: www.karnak.com. Specifically designed for structured and productive research. You can construct a personal library of past research topics for easy referral.

LISTFISH. Website: www.listfish.com. Specifically designed to help you find e-mail publications, and is updated regularly. Topics include science, computers, sports, fashion, government, culture, and even a category for Internet users who are under 21.

LOOKSMART. Website: www.looksmart.com. Find resources for improving your writing and getting published.

LYCOS. Website: www.lycos.com.

METOR SEARCH ENGINE. Website: www.metor.com. A more comprehensive search engine with both general and specific collections of sites.

MSN. Website: www.msn.com.

QUICKBROWSE. Website: www.quickbrowse.com. Service that combines your favorite sites into a single page for faster viewing.

SEARCH ENGINE WATCH. Website: www.searchenginewatch.com. Good site to learn information about search engines. Click on "Web Searching Tips" to learn how to search the Web.

711.NET. Website: www.711.net. A Christian-oriented search engine that includes categories such as apologetics, Bible, faith, church, and theology.

TURBO10 METASEARCH ENGINE. Website: http://turbo10.com. Topics are generated for each search and are listed in a pull down menu at the top of the search results to help refine it to the most specific search.

VIVISIMO. Website: http://vivisimo.com/. New clustering search engine.

YAHOO! Website: www.yahoo.com; http://search.yahoo.com.

SERVICES FOR WRITERS

Note: Check out these services before hiring any of them. Their listing here in no way indicates an endorsement.

AGENT RESEARCH & EVALUATION, INC., 25 Barrow St., New York, NY 10014. (212)924-9942. Fax (212)924-1864. E-mail: info@agentresearch.com. Website: www.agentresearch

.com. Tracks public record of literary agents and agents for the sale of dramatic and other subsidiary rights involving books and manuscripts. Database contains over 2,000 agents and more than 20,000 of their clients. Offers two consulting services—The Fingerprint and Dead Reckoning—and a new agent list and publishes a newsletter, *Talking Agents.*

ALL ABOUT QUOTES. Website: www.allaboutquotes.com/Daily.asp. Do you use quotations in your writing and speaking? Subscribe to the free daily e-mail quote service.

BUSINESS CARDS. Website: www.VistaPrint.com. They offer 250 free business cards.

CANADIAN SUBSIDY DIRECTORY. A guide containing more than 2,800 direct and indirect financial subsidies, grants, and loans offered by government departments and agencies, foundations, associations, and organizations. Cost is $49.95. Order from one of the following distributors: Canadian Business Resource Center: (250)381-4822 or Fureteur Bookstore: (450)465-5597 or fax (450)465-8144.

CHRISTIAN INFORMATION MINISTRIES/RESEARCH SERVICE. Cecil R. Price, ThM, Senior Researcher, PO Box 141055, Dallas TX 75214. (214)827-0057. E-mail: crprice@ email.com. Provides fee-based custom research and information retrieval for authors, churches, individuals, publishers, ministries, speakers; primary topics related to the Bible, theology, and Christian living. Basic research fee $35/hr. (2 hr. min.) plus expenses such as photocopying and shipping.

+CHRISTIAN MARKETING GROUP. Contact: Karen Whiting, 10936 SW 156th Pl. Miami FL 33196. (954)463-0982. Website: www.karenhwhiting.com.

CLASS PERSONAL MENTOR. Florence Littauer, who leads CLASS (Christian Leaders and Speakers Seminars) is offering to be a personal mentor to a limited number of CLASS graduates. This will be done in small classes in her home in Palm Springs, CA. For more information, contact: CLASS, 3830 Sienna St., Oceanside CA 92056. (760)630-2677. Fax (760)630-9355.

CORRESPONDENCE COURSE FOR MANUSCRIPT EDITING. The University of Wisconsin offers a correspondence course in manuscript editing for those wanting to do editing on a professional level or for writers wanting to improve their personal editing skills. Contact: University of Wisconsin Research Park, 505 S. Rosa Rd., Madison WI 53719-1257. Toll-free (877)895-3276. (608)262-2011. Fax (608)262-4096. E-mail: info@learn.uwsa.edu. Ask about Manuscript Editing C350-A52. Website: http://learn.wisconsin.edu/il.

EDITORIAL SERVICES. Lynda Lotman offers various services to writers and editors. Find the specific service you need in one of the Websites she coordinates: www.EnglishEdit.com; www .ManuscriptEditing.com; www.QueryLetters.com; www.SciFiEditor.com; www.Statistics Tutors.com; www.DissertationWriting.com; www.DissertationAdvisors.com; www.Book-Editing .com; www.WritingNetwork.com.

E-MAIL LISTS. Sources for free mailing list companies. Websites: www.christianemailservice .com; www.topica.com; http://groups.yahoo.com; http://groups.google.com.

FAX SERVICES WHEN YOU DON'T HAVE A FAX. You can now receive faxes through an existing e-mail address. Check out these sites: www.efax.com and www.faxaway.com. Both offer free trial.

FIRST EDITION MANUSCRIPT SERVICE. Now your book can be submitted to over 70 Christian publishers in one simple step by logging on to www.1stedition.org. First edition is an online manuscript service of the Evangelical Christian Publishers Assn. Fee is $79.

FREE E-MAIL SERVICES. Website: www.juno.com. Provides a free service to those who want the ability to correspond with others by e-mail, but don't need additional access to the Internet. Sign up online or call toll-free (800)879-5866 to order a Juno CD for $9.95. For another option to set up a free e-mail address, check out www.mail.com. For a guide to free Internet Providers, go to www.fepg.net.

LOGOS RESEARCH SYSTEMS, 1313 Commercial St., Bellingham WA 98225-4372. (360)527-1700. Toll-free (800)875-6467. Fax (360)527-1700. E-mail: customerservice@logos.com. Website: www.logos.com. Publishes the all-new Logos Bible Software Series X-Scholar's Library, Pastor's Library, and the Bible Study Library. Over 3,000 titles from more than 100 publishers are now compatible with the system.

MANUSCRIPT BOXES. To obtain rugged boxes for mailing manuscripts, contact: Papyrus Place, 2210 Goldsmith Ln., Louisville KY 40218. (502)451-9748. Fax (502)451-5487. Website: www.papyrusplace.com. E-mail: info@papyrusplace.com.

MANUSCRIPT TRACKING PROGRAM. Website: www.sandbaggers.8m.com. Free download.

MARKETING LISTS. Toll-free (888)330-4919. E-mail: sendlistinfo@netscape.net. If they don't have the list you need, they will compile a custom list according to your specifications. Lists include: Libraries, Bookstores, Media, and more.

POSTAGE CHART. Writer's Postage Chart. Website: www.mirror.org/terry.hickman/Postage.htm. Gregory Koster and Terry Hickman's postage rates for mailing manuscripts to and from most English-speaking countries.

P. L. SCHLACHTER CONSULTING INC, PO Box 22443, Denver, CO 80222. (303)588-2351. E-mail: software@livebytheword.com. For more info: www.livebytheword.com. Will work with you directly to develop custom software designed to meet your needs, regardless of your industry. Developed database for the *Christian Writers' Market Guide.*

SCORE (Service Corps of Retired Executives). Website: www.score.org. Offers free advice to small businesses by e-mail.

STAMPS.COM. Website: www.stamps.com. Free software for printing postage on your computer.

TELEPHONE HANDSET RECORDING CONTROL. To record phone calls for interviewing purposes. Available at Radio Shack. Website: www.radioshack.com. Enter Product #43-1237. $15-20.

TRANSLATORS. Slavic Christian Publishing (SCP). Group specializes in English-Russian translation of Christian materials. Contact: Bogdan Michka, exec. dir., SCP Group, PO Box 13111, Salem OR 97309. (503)589-9906. Fax (503)589-9908. E-mail: scpg@cityofgod.org. Website: www.cityofgod.org/scpgroup/scp.htm. Other translators: Julia Borovik. E-mail: boroviki@mail.ru. Charges $4/page or $3.50/page for more than 100 pages. She provides services over the Internet as she is a Ukrainian resident; Lean Terentyeva. E-mail: terentyeva@ukr.net. A professional Christian translator, with 8 years of experience. Russian/English; Francisco Chavarria. E-mail: inspanish@juno.com. Translator and registered court interpreter. Spanish/English.

ULINE. Website: www.uline.com. Sells a variety of mailing supplies. Order by phone, online, or catalog.

WRITERS' EDGE. Website: www.WritersEdgeService.com. Submission and critique service. Their list includes 75 participating publishers.

SPEAKING*

+AMERICAN SPEAKERS BUREAU, 10151 University Blvd. #197, Orlando FL 32817. (407)826-4248. Fax (407)629-7752. E-mail: info@speakersbureau.com. Website: www.speakersbureau.com.

CLASS PERSONAL MENTOR. Florence Littauer, who leads CLASS (Christian Leaders and Speakers Seminars) is offering to be a personal mentor to a limited number of CLASS graduates. This will be done in small classes in her home in Palm Springs, CA. For more information, contact: CLASS, 3830 Sienna St., Oceanside CA 92056. (760)630-2677. Fax (760)630-9355.

CLASS PROMOTIONAL SERVICES, LLC., 3830 Sienna St., Oceanside CA 92056. (760)630-2677. Fax (760)630-9355. Contact: Kim Garrison. E-mail: Interviews@classervices.com. Website: www.classervices.com. Click on Promotional Services. Specializing in radio and

TV interview campaigns for Christian authors, speakers, and ministries. CLASS Promotional Services is a division of Christian Leaders, Authors & Speakers Services, which provides resources, training, and promotion for Christian authors and speakers.

+DAYBOOK NEWS. Website: www.daybooknews.com. Information and updates on press releases, conferences, speaking engagements, conventions, and book release dates.

NATIONAL SPEAKERS ASSN., 1500 S. Priest Dr., Tempe AZ 85281. (480)968-2552. Fax (480)968-0911. Website: www.nsaspeaker.org. Convention and training for professional speakers. Puts out *Professional Speaker Magazine.*

+ONE-SHEET PRINTING. Website: www.cfre.com. Click on Personal Brochures.

ONLINE SPEAKERS BUREAU. Website: www.espeakersbureau.com. Allows speakers to register their background information online so meeting planners have greater access to available talent and can contact speakers directly. For more information, contact pjdoland@espeakersbureau.com.

+SEMINAR FINDER. Website: www.seminarfinder.com. Locate professional seminars, continuing education classes and Web-based training programs on a variety of topics.

+SERMON AND SPEECH ILLUSTRATIONS. Website: www.bible.org/illus/illustoc.htm. Over 10,000 illustrations in their database.

SPEAKERS. Website: www.christianspeakerservice.com. Lists Christian speakers and artists available for church, corporate, and civic events.

+SPEAKER SPOTLIGHT, 7247 W. Colt #300, Boise ID 83709. (208)362-6611. Website: www.speakerspotlight.com. Add your link to their directory.

+SPEAKING.COM. Website: www.speaking.com. Speakers platform. (415)920-9027. E-mail: speakers@speaking.com.

+SPEECH COACHING. Websites: http://fripp.com/forspeaker.html; www.professional speaker.com/catalog.htm.

+TOASTMASTERS. Website: www.toastmasters.org. Worldwide speaking organization offering tips for professionals and nonprofessionals alike.

VOICE COACHING. Roy Hanschke, voice coach. Toll-free (800)795-7429. Website: www.voicepersonality.com. Ron Hanschke does voice coaching via audiotape. He listens to your tape, critiques it, and records instructions to you, which are cut into your tape where the correction is needed.

+WOMEN'S MINISTRY. Website: www.womensministry.net. Ideas, resources, and information exchange among Christian women and worldwide ministry organizations.

WRITERSPEAKER.COM. Website: www.writerspeaker.com. Offers all kinds of help for the writer or speaker, including a free newsletter. Editor Carmen Leal is seeking subscribers (it's free) and also submissions of articles. Although there is no payment, she will include a generous bio at the end of your piece with e-mail and Website contact information.

WEB PAGE DEVELOPMENT/RESOURCES

CHRISTIAN WEB DESIGN AND HOSTING. Website: www.webtechdg.com. WebTech Design Group: a full service Christian company offering site design, hosting, domain registration, and more.

CREATE-IT 101: Basic HTML. Website: www.geocities.com/Karenw/index.html. Great tutorial on making Web pages.

DOMAIN NAMES. To see if the domain name you want to use is already in use, go to: www.net worksolutions.com/cgi-bin/whois/whois. To register your domain name, go to: www.net worksolutions.com; http://my.register.com; or www.namezero.com. For domain name system management and a list of accredited registrars, go to: www.icann.org/registrars/ accredited-list.html. Other sites for domain names include: www.names4ever.com; www .godaddy.com; www.homewithgod.com; www.westhost.com.

FREE COUNTERS. Websites: www.sitemeter.com. Other fee-based counters are at www.super stats.com and www.thecounter.com.

FREE GREETING CARDS. Website: http://associates.123greetings.com.

FREE ONLINE CUSTOMER SERVICE. Website: http://humanclick.com.

FREE POLLS. Website: www.freepolls.com.

FREE WEB-BASED E-MAIL SERVICE. Website: www.zzn.com.

FREE WEB TOOLS. Website: www.bravenet.com. Some tools include guest books, message forums, counters, polls, site searches, audio clips, and more.

HELPFUL WEBSITES. Websites: www.BigNoseBird.com; www.hotwired.com/webmonkey. Free Websites that offer downloads of the language and free CGI scripts.

HOMESTEAD WEB SERVER. Website: www.homestead.com.

HOW TO PROMOTE YOUR WEBSITE. Website: www.wilsonweb.com.

LISSA EXPLAINS IT ALL. Website: www.lissaexplains.com. An excellent site for learning HTML (the language in which Web pages are written), especially for kids, but equally helpful for any HTML novice.

MAINTAINING YOUR WEBSITE. Website: www.workz.com.

MEDIA BUILDER. Website: www.mediabuilder.com. Offers free fonts and Web graphics to use on your Web page.

OURCHURCH.COM. Website: www.OurChurch.com. Free Christian Web server; easy to use.

SCRIPT ARCHIVE. Website: www.scriptarchive.com. Interactive Website gadgets. Site includes working CGI scripts that you can install on your server. Some programming skills required, as well as permission from your ISP or Web-hosting service to install and run your own CGI programs.

+SEARCH ENGINE OPTIMIZATION & SUBMISSION. Website: www.webtechdg.com. Click on "Free Resource Page." Before you submit your site to search engines, let then evaluate your site for search engine readiness free. After they let you know what is needed to make your site rank higher in major search engines, you can submit your site to over 200 search engines from their site for free.

WEB HOSTS. Websites: www.wyenet.com; www.arkwebs.com; www.halfpricehosting.com; www .catalog.com; www.freepagehosting.com; www.westhost.com; www.ilovejesus.com; www.true path.com; http://smallbusiness.yahoo.com/webhosting. For a list of the "100 Best Web Site & Domain Hosting Services," go to: http://100best-web-site-and-domain-hosting-services.com.

WEB PAGE DESIGN. Websites: www.section508.gov/; www.webaim.org/standards/508/check list; www.fresnostate.edu/webaccess/; www.webposition.com.

WEBSITE OPTIMIZATION. Website: http://websiteoptimization.com/speed/toc. Website Optimization (WSO) is a series of techniques that minimize Web page file sizes and maximize page display speeds.

WEBSITE WORKSTATION. Website: www.davesite.com/webstation. All kinds of advice on Website design, etc.

WEB-ZINE ARTICLE DISTRIBUTION SITES. Websites: www.ideamarketers.com; www .EzineArticles.com. Free articles to put on your Web page.

WRITERSPEAKER WEB DESIGN AND DEVELOPMENT. Gary Scott, PO Box 9426, Naples FL 34101-9426. E-mail: Gary@writerspeaker.com. Website: www.writerspeaker.com. A Christian company whose focus is helping writers and speakers set up effective Websites.

WEBSITES OF INTEREST TO WRITERS: GENERAL

ABSOLUTE WRITE. Website: www.absolutewrite.com. Good links, market info, and Q&As.

ACW PRESS: RESOURCES FOR THE CHRISTIAN WRITER. Website: www.acwpress.com/ links.htm. Links to lots of great resources.

ALL WRITING SERVICES, (formerly AuthorShowcase). Website: www.allwritingservices.com. Offers a variety of services for writers.

AMERICAN CHRISTIAN WRITERS. Website: www.ACWriters.com.

AMERICAN JOURNALISM REVIEW'S NEWS LINK. Website: www.newslink.org. Links more than 60 Websites including The Freedom Forum, Pulitzer Prizes, American Society of Magazine Editors, American Society of Newspaper Editors, Newsletter Publishers Assn., and the Committee to Protect Journalists.

+BIOGRAPHIES. Website: www.amillionlives.com. A large guide to posthumous biographies.

+BOOK BLOG. Website: www.bookblog.net.

+BOOKZONE. Website: www.bookzonepro.com. Current information for writers and publishers, plus a newsletter, service directory, events calendar, and reviewers' database.

+BURRYMAN WRITERS CENTER. Website: www.burryman.com. Lists freelance jobs, resources for fiction and nonfiction writers, working professionals and beginners.

CHRISTIAN E-AUTHORS. Website: www.christianeauthor.com. Offers support to Christian authors with a specific call to write for the Internet. Welcomes e-book/e-zine authors, poets, playwrights, publishers, online ministries, and those interested in learning more about writing for the Internet. Discussion list, Website, workshops.

CHRISTIAN MINISTRY LINKS. Website: www.CrossSearch.com. Links to over 40 Christian ministries.

CHRISTIAN PARADISE. Website: www.christianparadise.com. A great site for just about everything Christian, from music and entertainment to articles by some great writers.

+CHRISTIAN RETAILING. Website: www.christianretailing.com. Monitors the heartbeat of the Christian retail industry. Offers free newsletter.

CHRISTIANWRITERS.COM. Website: http://christianwriters.com. A free online writers' resource community. Their mission is to provide a supportive, family atmosphere where writers may easily access the tools and resources to create, market, and publish their work.

COFFEEHOUSE FOR WRITERS. Website: www.coffeehouseforwriters.com. Online writing workshops, critique groups, discussion lists, contests, and newsletter.

+COOL STUFF FOR WRITERS. Website: www.CoolStuff4Writers.com. Find mugs and shirts and other cool stuff, or buy a gift certificate for that writer you love.

COURSE MATERIALS. Website: http://ocw.mit.edu. MIT's OpenCourseWare site. Course materials from MIT classes, at no charge.

+CRITIQUE AND DISCUSSION FORUMS. Website: www.writersbbs.com.

CROSSHOME. Website: www.crosshome.com. Your Christian home on the Internet.

DEDICATED AUTHOR. Website: http://groups.yahoo.com/group/eDedicatedAuthor. Free online newsletter for professional Christian writers. Includes tips for conference directors, notes for speakers, writing exercises, self-editing tips, and writing opportunities. Also open to submissions of material in above-mentioned areas. Editor, Sheila Seifert. Over 450 members.

ECONOMY INFORMATION. Website: www.dismal.com. Economic data you can use in your writing.

ERIC MAISEL'S CREATIVITY NEWSLETTER. Website: www.ericmaisel.com. To subscribe to this online newsletter, go to creativitynewsletter-subscribe@egroups.com.

THE EUROPEAN CHRISTIAN WRITERS' RESOURCES WEBSITE. Websites: www.abidemi .sanusi.name; www.christianwriter.co.uk. Ms. Abidemi Sanusi, ed. E-mail: info@abidemi .sansusi.name.

EXPERTS. Website: www.experts.com. A diverse source of experts, academic and otherwise. A directory that lists expertise of more than 1,000 University of Southern California scientists, scholars, administrators, and physicians as a service to editors, reporters, and producers can be found at: http://uscnews3.usc.edu/experts/index.html. Also, check out: www .profnet.com.

E-ZINES. Websites: www.zinebook.com; www.e-zinez.com.

FAITH WRITERS. Website: www.faithwriters.com. Offers free services and information for writers, readers, and publishers.

+FAITHFUL READER. Website: www.faithfulreader.com. Helps a writer keep track of current market trends by providing book reviews, author interviews, excerpts, a devotional, and more.

+FEDERAL CITIZEN INFORMATION CENTER. Website: www.pueblo.gsa.gov. Information about anything and everything one could need. Free and low-cost booklets.

FEDWORLD INFORMATION NETWORK. Website: www.fedworld.gov. Source of federal reports for your research.

+FOG INDEX FOR READABILITY. Website: www.helpforschools.com/ELLKBase/practitioners tips/Fog_Index_Readability.shtml.

FREELANCE HELP. Website: www.freelancehelp.com. Help for writers, illustrators, graphic designers, photographers, and Web designers.

FREELANCE SUCCESS. Website: www.freelancesuccess.com.

FREELANCE WRITING: Website for Today's Working Writer. Website: www.freelance writing.com. Links to all kinds of resources, including a Job Bank and current contests.

+THE GENDER GENIE. Website: www.bookblog.net/gender/genie.html. Find out if your writing voice is male or female.

GUIDE TO LITERARY AGENTS. Website: http://literaryagents.org.

IBELIEVE.COM. Website: www.ibelieve.com. One of the most active Christian Websites.

I LOVE TO WRITE. John Riddle, Christian writer and conference speaker. Blue Moon Communications, 6 Basset Pl., Bear DE 19701. E-mail: Ilovetowrite@ilovetowrite.com. Website: www.ilovetowrite.com. Includes many resources for writers, including the e-book *How I Made $66,270 in 9 Months Writing for Websites.* Order it and receive the free e-book *Getting a Book Contract in 30 Days or Less.*

+INDEPENDENT CHRISTIAN MEDIA NETWORK. Website: www.christianindy.com. A site for writers, photographers, recording artists, painters, and any independent Christian artist to showcase his/her talents to the world. Also designs and hosts Websites.

INTERNET FOR CHRISTIANS. A book by Quentin J. Schultze, Gospel Films, Inc., $7.99. Available at your local Christian bookstore. Author also offers a free newsletter, *Internet for Christians.* To subscribe, send a blank e-mail to: ifc-subscribe@lists.gospelcom.net. Website: www.gospelcom.net/ifc (includes hyperlinks to all listed sites).

INTERNET-RESOURCES.COM. Website: www.internet-resources.com/writers. A wealth of valuable resource links.

IUNIVERSE.COM/AUTHOR TOOLKIT. Website: www.iuniverse.com/authortoolkit/default.asp.

KAZOODLES. Website: http://groups.yahoo.com/group/kazoodles. Bimonthly newsletter featuring e-zines, lists, books, and sites on writers and writing.

+LITERARY RESOURCES. Website: http://newark.rutgers.edu/~jlynch/Lit. Links to sites dealing with English and American literature.

MAGAZINE ARTICLE. Website: www.pcmag.com/article2/0,4149,1043161,00.asp. Article from PC Magazine about print-on-demand (POD). PC Magazine has rated six POD firms and lists the results.

+MAGAZINES FOR WRITERS. *The Writer.* Website: www.writermag.com. *Writer's Digest.* Website: www.writersdigest.com.

MAGAZINE SUBSCRIPTIONS. Website: www.magazinevalues.com. A great source for really cheap magazines, including 24 religious magazines.

+MOM WRITERS. Website: www.momwriters.com. Support, encouragement, and tips for mothers who write. Discussion group at http://groups.yahoo.com/group/momwriters.

+MR. MAGAZINE. Website: www.mrmagazine.com. Provides the latest information on consumer magazines, including the 30 Most Notable Launches of the previous year.

+MY HIDDEN TALENT. Website: www.myhiddentalent.com. A place to read other writers' work and get your work reviewed.

+MY WRITER BUDDY. Website: www.writerbuddy.com. "A community and reference center for writers of all ages, writing interests, and experience. Provides mutual support, assistance, and friendship."

+ON THIS DAY IN HISTORY. Website: www.dmarie.com/timecap. Details about any period in history.

101 WRITING ANSWERS. Website: www.101writinganswers.com. A directory of writing and related sources. Lists associations, forums, and groups, writing by genre, markets, and showcasing, and much more. Has a link to publishing and media resources.

PAGE ONE LITERARY NEWSLETTER. Website: www.pageonelit.com.

+PAGE WISE. Website: www.essortment.com/in/hobbies.writing. Site contains a large assortment of helpful articles to answer any question about writing.

PHONE BOOK SEARCH USA. Websites: www.switchboard.com; www.infobel.com/teldir.

+PICTURES OF PUBLISHING. Website: www.geocities.com/visualsofpublish. A very informative slide show of 50 photos related to the New York publishing community.

POSTAGE RATES WORLDWIDE. Website: www.geocities.com/wallstreet/exchange/1161/index.htm. International postage rates. Writers living in foreign countries seeking US postage, order online at: www.usps.gov.

PRAYER WALKING. Websites: www.dailyprayerwalking.com; www.janetmchenry.com. Janet Holm McHenry, speaker and author of *Looking Up: Encouragement to Pursue a Life of Prayer; Prayerwalk;* and *Daily Prayerwalk.*

PUBLIC OPINION POLLS. Website: www.pollingreport.com. Add substance to your articles with the latest opinion poll results.

RADIO STATIONS. Website: www.radio-locator.com/cgi-bin/home. The MIT List of Radio Stations on the Internet, or "radio-locator." Over 10,000 radio stations from all around the world.

REJECTIONS. "Read 'Em and Weep" at www.rejectioncollection.com. A place to post your rejections and vent your frustrations. Contact: PO Box 443, Shrub Oak NY 10588-0443.

+RIGHT WRITING. Website: www.right-writing.com. W. Terry Whalin, best-selling author and longtime editor, wants to help anyone with his/her written communication, from novels to thank-you letters. Offers the e-zine *Right Writing News.*

+SELF-PUBLISHING. Website: www.parapublishing.com. And check out Dan Poynter's book *The Self-Publishing Manual.* Also check out www.instantpublisher.com.

SHARP WRITER. Website: www.sharpwriter.com. A site with quick references and lots of useful writer's links.

SPEAKERS. Website: www.christianspeakerservice.com. Lists Christian speakers and artists available for church, corporate, and civic events.

TIME WARNER CHRISTIAN BOOKS NEWSLETTER. Free monthly newsletter. Sign up at their Website: www.twbookmark.com. Click on "e-Newsletter" then on "Christian" from the list provided. The site lists Christian books and allows you to read the first chapter of the book for free.

TIME ZONE CONVERTER. Website: www.timezoneconverter.com.

+TOASTED CHEESE. Website: www.toasted-cheese.com. Excellent site providing forums, chats, news, musings, book reviews, and the Toasted Cheese Literary Journal.

TOURBUS. Website: www.TOURBUS.com. An informative e-newsletter about what's happening on the Internet, including information on current Internet viruses and hoaxes.

WILLWRITE4FOOD.COM. Website: www.willwrite4food.com. Geared toward creating community between writers. Forums, updates on the markets, a list of writers conferences, articles on writing, and more.

+WRITE DIRECTIONS. Website: www.writedirections.com. Articles, resources, bookstore, and consulting by Beth Mende Conny. E-mail: beth@writedirections.com.

+WRITE FROM HOME. Website: www.writefromhome.com. "Helping writers manage kids and clips under one roof."

WRITE TO INSPIRE.COM. Website: www.writetoinspire.com. A site for inspirational and Christian writers. Seeking articles from Christian writers that will help other writers hone their skills or pursue their call.

+WRITERS' BREAK. Website: www.writersbreak.com. Articles, interview, and links.

WRITER'S FREE REFERENCE. Website: www.writers-free-reference.com. Contains maps, encyclopedias, copyright information, zip codes, telephone directories, currency conversions, distance calculations, and more.

+WRITER'S HAVEN. Contact: Beverly Caruso, PO Box 1388, Lake Elsinore CA 92530. (909)245-4082. E-mail: Rancho@across2u.com. Website: www.across2u.com/haven .html. A haven where Christian writers who need time and solitude to write will not be interrupted. Room and board included. Write for available dates, and for information about upcoming writer's seminars.

THE WRITER'S MIND. Website: www.thewritersmind.com. Site lists agents and publishers by genre.

A WRITER'S PRAYER. Website: www.booksandauthors.net/Fromtheauthor/LBlock.html. A prayer that offers some food for thought to which all writers can relate.

+WRITERS' WORDS GLOSSARY. Website: www.everywriter.com/newwriters.htm.

WRITERSPEAKER.COM. Website: www.writerspeaker.com. Offers all kinds of help for the writer or speaker, including a free newsletter. Editor Carmen Leal is seeking subscribers (it's free) and also submissions of articles. Although there is no payment, she will include a generous bio at the end of your piece with e-mail and Website contact information.

+WRITING CORNER. Website: www.writingcorner.com. Links to agents, markets, newsletters, writing schools, recommended books, and grammar tips.

+WRITING GROUPS. Website: www.6ftferrets.com. Tips for starting and maintaining a group.

WRITING RESOURCES. For lists of publishers, writing links, resources, and research sites, go to Websites: www.susettewilliams.com; www.seliterary.homestead.com/links.html.

YOU CAN WRITE. Website: www.youcanwrite.com/. Good site for nonfiction writers but with a boatload of good information for others, too.

WEBSITES OF INTEREST TO WRITERS: SPECIALTY TOPICS

+ASSOCIATED PRESS PHOTO ARCHIVE. Website: http://photoarchive.ap.org.

+ASSN. OF PERSONAL HISTORIANS. Website: www.personalhistorians.org. Information for memoir writing.

CHRISTIAN HISTORY. Websites: www.christianhistory.net; www.gospelcom.net/chi/index.html.

CLOTHING OF PAST ERAS. Website: http://members.aol.com/nebula5/tcpinfo2.html#history. Covers everything from ancient Greece to the Middle Ages to the 1950s.

COMIX35 CHRISTIAN COMICS TRAINING. Nathan Butler, PO Box 27470, Albuquerque NM 87125-7470. (505)232-3500. Fax (775)307-8202. E-mail: comix35@comix35.org. Website: www.comix35.org. Various international locations. Often has editors in attendance; no agents. Another contact person for writers interested in scripting a comic or other aspects of comic ministry is Len Cowan. E-mail: Len@comix35.org.

DOMESTIC ABUSE. Website: www.womeninneed.org. An outreach recovery program for domestic and intimate partner abuse.

EDUCATORS. Websites: www.teacherfocus.com; www.enduref.org. More than 2000 unique lesson plans submitted by teachers; www.merlot.com. MERLOT, the Multimedia Educational

Resource for Learning and Online Teaching, is a free, peer-reviewed collection of over 8,000 different online learning tools and simulations developed mostly by college professors around the world.

ENGLISH ROYALTY. Website: www.royal.gov.uk.

GLASS BLOWING. Website: www.lamberts.de/elambhom.htm. Check here for answers to your questions about mouth-blown glass and lots of other kinds of glass (i.e. restoration, flashed, crackled, cathedral) and glass around the world.

HISTORY CHANNEL. Website: www.historychannel.com. Historical research by topic, time, event, etc. Also check out: www.historynet.com.

HOMESCHOOLING. Websites: www.homeschoolheadquarters.com; www.hsrc.com; www.cross walk.com/family/home_school. For writers in homeschool market.

INDEPENDENT CHRISTIAN MEDIA NETWORK. Website: www.christianindy.com. A Website for writers, photographers, recording artists, painters, and any independent Christian artists.

+INTERNET IMAGES. Make sure your book's cover is on the Internet. Search at: http://images.google.com. Type in your book's ISBN number without hyphens.

JOIN HANDS. If writing for pastors, Christian education leaders, or music directors, you may find some helpful resources at www.woodlakebooks.com or www.logosproductions.com.

MEDLINE PLUS. Website: www.nlm.nih.gov/medlineplus/. Dedicated to medical professionals and experts of all kinds. From a medical encyclopedia to all kinds of drug information.

MEMOIRS. Website: www.turningmemories.com. A resource for memoirs. Has articles that are extremely helpful in getting started.

MOVIES. Internet Movie Database. Website: www.imdb.com. Free, searchable database of over 260,000 film and television productions made since 1892; www.metacritic.com. Movie Reviews. A place where movie fans easily find the most important reviews for each new movie.

NEWSPAPERS AND MAGAZINES. Website: www.prLeads.com. Learn about articles before they are written. Dan Janal will supply you with target leads on the subjects you select. Then you contact the editor or freelancer to help him or her with the article. E-mail: Dan@prLeads.com.

PARENT SOUP. Website: www.parentsoup.com. For writers of parenting articles.

PASTORAL WRITING RESOURCES. Website: www.pastors.com. Roger Palms, former pastor and editor of *Decision* magazine for 22 years, also has a Website: www.pastorswrite.com. It offers help for pastors, evangelists, missionaries, church workers, and writers.

THE PEOPLE'S COMIC BOOK NEWSLETTER. Website: www.jazmaonline.com. Submit scripts, story lines and fan art. Home of the Jazma League of Justice. Offers free galleries. Submit your drawings and writings to: Paul Dale Roberts, Publisher, People's Comic Book Newsletter, 5606 Moonlight Way, Elk Grove CA 95758-6837. E-mail: Silhouet98@cs.com.

PROPHETIC NEWS SITES. Website: www.prophezine.com. News about Israel from a Zionist perspective. Discussion group at: http://groups.yahoo.com/group/zincisrael.

REGENCY ERA. Website: www.regencylibrary.com.

REVIEW COPY HELPER. Website: www.twowriters.net/reviewcopies.html. A site for book reviewers to get publisher contact information.

+TRAVEL WRITING TIPS. Website: www.travelwritingtips.com.

TRAVELWRITERS.COM. Website: www.travelwriters.com. E-source for travel writers. Contact info on over 800 travel publications. Free market news and press trip announcements.

UPPER ROOM MINISTRIES. Website: www.MethodX.org. Young adults can reflect on their faith through music, personal journal space, reviews, and more. Good resource for those whose target audience is teens/young adults.

+U.S. MILITARY INFORMATION. Websites: www.usmilitary.com; www.defenselink.mil; www.dtic.mil/doctrine/jel/doddict. Army Websites: www.army.mil; www.goarmy.com;

www.army.mil/usar; www.qmfound.com/army_heraldry.htm. Navy Websites: www.navy.mil; www.navyjobs.com; www.navyseals.com. Air force Websites: www.af.mil; www.airforce .com. Marine Websites: www.usmc.mil; www.marines.com; www.marinecorps.com; www.usmc.mil/marinelink/ind.nsf/ranks. Coast Guard Websites: www.uscg.mil; www.gocoastguard.com; www.cgaux.org. Special Ops Website: www.specialoperations.com.

VICTORIAN ERA. Websites: www.victorianlondon.org; www.victorianweb.org; www.thelondon house.co.uk.

WOMEN'S WRITING RESOURCES. Website: www.womensministry.net.

WORD COUNT. *Word Counts: What Is a Wo*rd? by Chuck Rothman. Website: www.sfwa.org/ writing/wordcount.htm.

+WORLD WAR II INFO. Websites: www.ibiblio.org/pha; www.worldwar2history.info.

WRITERS' SOFTWARE

DRAMATICA PRO. Website: http://storymind.com.

M3PRO. Manuscript and Marketing Manager Professional. Website: www.pbtechnologies.net. Contact: Randy Brown. E-mail: rbrown@pbtechnologies.net. Allows writers to track manuscripts, submissions, markets and contacts, goals, payments, and expenses. Also gives users a wide variety of customizable reports.

NOVEL PRO 2.0. Website: http://novelcode.com. Software that helps organize ideas, work on pieces of the story without getting lost, brainstorm creation of characters and scenes, etc. Cost is $29.95.

+OUTLOOK EXPRESS ADD-INS. Website: www.SperrySoftware.com.

QUICKPLOT. Website: www.characterpro.com/quickplot.html. Freeware program to help organize your thoughts in the planning stages.

S.A.M.M. Website: www.sandbaggers.8m.com/samm.htm. A manuscript tracking freeware program.

+SCREEN/SCRIPT WRITING SOFTWARE. See Resources Section: Screenwriting/Scriptwriting.

+STORYBASE. Website: www.storybase.net. Toll-free (800)833-7568.

STORYCRAFT STORY DEVELOPMENT SOFTWARE. Website: www.storycraft.org. Guides writers through the entire process of writing novels, screenplays, teleplays, plays, and short stories.

STORYVIEW 2.0. Website: www.storyview.com. A writing tool that lets you create the elements of your story and arrange them on a timeline. You add the building blocks of your story in any order and immediately see any gaps.

STORYWEAVER. Website: http://storymind.com.

WORD MENU. Website: www.wordmenu.com. Word Menu (by Write Brothers, Inc.) organizes words by the way we actually use them: by subject matter. Cost: $34.95.

WRITE PRO. Website: www.writepro.com. Also, FictionMaster, by Sol Stein and WritePro.

WRITE-BRAIN. Website: www.write-brain.com. Software to help you plot and write your stories.

WRITER'S BLOCKS 3.0. Website: www.writersblocks.com. Organize story elements for your fiction.

+WRITER'S SUPERCENTER. Website: www.writerssupercenter.com. Offers a wide variety of software to help writers of all genres and forms.

WRITING MANAGEMENT SOFTWARE. Website: www.asmoday.com/WA.htm. Can download on trial basis. Costs $49.95.

WRITING INSTRUCTION: CDs/CASSETTE TAPES

THE CHRISTIAN COMMUNICATOR MANUSCRIPT CRITIQUE SERVICE CASSETTE HANDS-ON COURSE. For information contact: Susan Titus Osborn, 3133 Puente St., Fullerton CA 92835-1952. (714)990-1532. Toll-free (877)428-7992. E-mail:

Susanosb@aol.com. Website: www.christiancommunicator.com. Offers basic writing course available by cassette. Includes 6 lessons on 12 cassettes, handouts, and critiqued assignments. Cost for entire course: $180, by the lesson: $35. Completion of entire course entitles you to one unit of Continuing Education Credit (CEU) from Pacific Christian College of Hope International University for an additional $30.

CHRISTIAN WRITERS LEARNING CENTER. Website: www.ACWriters.com. Over 1,500 cassette tapes to choose from. Cost is $5-6 each, depending on quantity. Request the complete catalog by contacting American Christian Writers, PO Box 110390, Nashville TN 37222. (800)21-WRITE. Call for free catalog.

CREATIVE CHRISTIAN MINISTRIES, PO Box 12624, Roanoke VA 24027. (540)342-7511. Fax (540)342-7929. E-mail: ccmbbr@juno.com. Website: www.CreativeChristianMinistries .com. Tapes on a variety of topics for Christian writers (recorded at past writers' conferences by top writer/speakers).

+JOYFUL MINISTRY RESOURCE CD. More than 75 e-books have been burned onto one CD for a virtual library of ministry resources. For information, write: India Christian Partnership, 12 Edsall St., Hamburg NJ 07419. E-mail: joyfulministry@37.com.

NO FEAR STRATEGIES FOR PUBLISHING YOUR FIRST ARTICLES AND BOOK. David Sandford's 45-minute audio seminar. For a copy of the seminar, send a check for $15 to: David Sanford, 6406 NE Pacific St., Portland OR 97213.

WRITE HIS ANSWER MINISTRIES. Director: Marlene Bagnull, LittD, 316 Blanchard Rd., Drexel Hill PA 19026. E-mail: mbagnull@aol.com. Website: www.writehisanswer.com. Tapes on 20+ topics, $5 ea. Topics include: Taking the Pain Out of Marketing; Writing Manuscripts That Sell and Touch Lives; Turning Personal Experience into Print; and Self-Publishing. Tapes of Marlene's 8.5-hour Christian Writers Seminar (emphasis on writing for periodicals) are $28.95 and 6-hour Book Writers Seminars are $23.95 and include handouts.

WRITE-TO-PUBLISH CONFERENCE. Director: Lin Johnson, 9731 N. Fox Glen Dr. #6F, Niles IL 60714-4222. E-mail: lin@writetopublish.com. Website: www.writetopublish.com. Bring speakers from the Write-to-Publish Conference into your home and car via these cassettes. Tapes from past conferences on all aspects of writing and publishing, as well as editors' panels telling what they are looking for now. $5 each, $4 for 21 or more. Lists are available on the Website, or send SASE to above address.

WRITING INSTRUCTION: CORRESPONDENCE COURSES

AMERICAN SCHOOL OF CHRISTIAN WRITING. Website: www.ACWriters.com. This division of American Christian Writers offers a 3-year, 36-lesson correspondence course that covers the entire field of Christian writing. Students may purchase full course or selected portions. Several payment plans available. For school brochure contact: American Christian Writers, PO Box 110390, Nashville TN 37222. (800)21-WRITE.

ASSOCIATED WRITING PROGRAMS, George Mason University, MS 1E3, Fairfax VA 22030. (703)993-4301. Fax (703)993-4302. E-mail: awp@awpwriter.org. Website: www.awp writer.org.

AT-HOME WRITING WORKSHOPS. Director: Marlene Bagnull, LittD, Write His Answer Ministries, 316 Blanchard Rd., Drexel Hill PA 19026. E-mail: mbagnull@aol.com. Website: www.writehisanswer.com. Offers 3 courses of study with 5-10 study units in each. (1) Putting Your Best Foot Forward (lays foundation for your writing ministry), 5 units, $145; (2) Nonfiction (articles, tracts, curriculum, devotionals, how-tos, etc., plus planning a nonfiction book and book proposal), 10 units, $272; (3) Fiction, 10 units, $255. Units may also be purchased individually for $30-34.

CHRISTIAN WRITERS INSTITUTE CORRESPONDENCE COURSES. Website: www.AC Writers.com. This 55-year-old institution, founded by veteran publisher Robert Walker, is a division of American Christian Writers. Offers six, 1-year courses with an assigned instructor/mentor. Writing assignments are given with a goal of having a publishable manuscript by the end of each course. Two payment plans available. Contact: Christian Writers Institute, PO Box 110390, Nashville TN 37222. (800)21-WRITE.

CORRESPONDENCE COURSE FOR MANUSCRIPT EDITING. Website: http://learn.wisconsin .edu/il. The University of Wisconsin offers a correspondence course in manuscript editing for those wanting to do editing on a professional level or for writers wanting to improve their personal editing skills. Reasonable cost. Contact: University of Wisconsin Research Park, 505 S. Rosa Rd., Madison WI 53719-1257. Toll-free (877)895-3276. (608)262-2011. Fax (608)262-4096. E-mail: info@learn.uwsa.edu. Ask about Manuscript Editing C350-A52.

GLORY PRESS/PROF. DICK BOHRER, MS, MA (teacher, 39 years; editor, 11 years including editor of two newspapers and managing editor of *Moody Monthly;* author of 16 books), PO Box 624, West Linn OR 97068. (503)638-7711. E-mail: dickbohrer@juno.com. Offers 3 writing courses called "4+20 Ways to Write Stories for Christian Kids," "4+20 Ways, Christian, to Write Features Like a Pro," and "4+20 Ways, Christian, to Write What You Think." Charges $35 for each manual plus $1 per double-spaced typed page plus SASE for editing and critiquing assignments of poems, stories, and books. Asks for written testimony regarding applicant's salvation testimony of how he/she came to faith in Christ. References: gude@juno.com; k&kyoung@stic.net; asrduff@aol.com.

THE INSTITUTE OF CHILDREN'S LITERATURE, 93 Long Ridge Rd., West Redding CT 06896. Toll-free (800)243-9645. (203)792-8600. Fax (203)792-8406. E-mail: information services@InstituteChildrensLit.com. Website: www.InstituteChildrensLit.com. Several writing programs and a writing aptitude test; also a chat room and other resources for writers.

JERRY B. JENKINS CHRISTIAN WRITERS GUILD, PO Box 88196, Black Forest CO 80908. Toll-free (866)495-5177. Fax (719)495-5181. E-mail: contactus@christianwriters guild.com. Website: www.christianwritersguild.com. Contact: Rick Anderson. This organization, formerly owned and directed by Norman Rohrer, is now owned by Jerry B. Jenkins, author of the Left Behind series. Offering annual guild memberships, correspondence courses, associated benefits (advocacy, health insurance, etc.), workshops, and conferences. Call for a Free Starter Kit.

LONG RIDGE WRITERS GROUP, 95 Long Ridge Rd., West Redding CT 06896. Toll-free (800)624-1476. Fax (203)792-8406. E-mail: studentservices@longridgewriters group.com. Website: www.longridgewritersgroup.com. Secular correspondence course, but you may request a Christian instructor.

RIGHTEOUS WRITING. Dr. Kenneth Gentry, PO Box 1874, Fountain Inn SC 29644. E-mail: kennethgentry@cs.com. Website: www.kennethgentry.com. Intensive writing course covering research, library strategy, note taking, cultivating a topic, outlining, polishing, avoiding pitfalls, approaching editors, copyrighting, marketing, and more.

WRITER'S DIGEST SCHOOL, 4700 E. Galbraith Rd., Cincinnati OH 45236. Toll-free (800)759-0963. Fax (513)531-0798. E-mail: wds@fwpubs.com. Website: www.writersdigest .com/wds. Novel Writing Workshop, Writing & Selling Short Stories, Writing & Selling Nonfiction Articles, and others. This is a secular correspondence course, but you may request a Christian instructor.

THE WRITING ACADEMY SEMINAR. Inez Schneider, New Member Coordinator, 4010 Singleton Rd., Rockford IL 61114. (815)877-9675. E-mail: pattyk@wams.org. Website: www .wams.org. Sponsors year-round Christian correspondence writing program and annual seminar in various locations.

WRITING SERVICES INSTITUTE (WSI), Marsha L. Drake, #109—4351 Rumble St., Burnaby

B.C. V5J 2A2, Canada. Phone/fax (604)321-3555. E-mail: writeone@shaw.ca. Offers several correspondence and online courses: Write for Fun and Profit; Write for Success; Write Fiction from Plot to Print; Write with Power; Write for You: Magazine Article Writing; Write Yes!; Write Now: Young Author's Tutorial; Write Right—With Computers; and Write On! Write or e-mail for details and information on correspondence courses. Also writes company histories, biographies, résumés, and offers online tutorials. Charges negotiable fees for consultation, editing, and critique. See: www.vsb-adult-ed.com for more information on courses and author biography.

WRITING INSTRUCTION: E-MAIL/INTERNET COURSES

ABSOLUTE WRITE UNIVERSITY. Website: www.absoluteclasses.com. Online courses in photojournalism, romance writing, writing children's picture books, creativity, spiritual writing, and more.

BARNES & NOBLE ONLINE WRITING COURSES. Website: www.bn.com. Click on "B&N University."

THE CHRISTIAN COMMUNICATOR MANUSCRIPT CRITIQUE SERVICE E-MAIL HANDS-ON COURSE. For information contact: Susan Titus Osborn, 3133 Puente St., Fullerton CA 92835-1952. (714)990-1532. Toll-free (877)428-7992. E-mail: Susanosb@aol.com. Website: www.christiancommunicator.com. Offers basic writing course available by e-mail. Includes 6 lessons online, handouts, and critiqued assignments. Cost for entire course: $150, by the lesson: $30. Completion of entire course entitles you to one unit of Continuing Education Credit (CEU) from Pacific Christian College of Hope International University for an additional $30.

COFFEEHOUSE FOR WRITERS. Website: http://members.tripod.com/coffeehouse4writers. Offers a variety of 4-week writing workshops for $80.

E-MAIL NEWSLETTERS FOR WRITERS. Websites: www.publishersweekly.com; www.parapub .com; www.writetoinspire.com; www.writing-world.com.

EPISTLEWORKS CREATIONS, JoAnn Reno Wray, 812 W. Glenwood St., Broken Arrow OK 74011-6419. (918)451-4017. Website: http://epistleworks.com. E-mail: epistle1@epistle works.com. Call/write/e-mail (prefer). E-mail writing classes on: Writing and Marketing Devotions, Slash & Burn: Self-Editing for writers, Laughing All the Way: Bank on Your Sense of Humor, and Interview Techniques. Each class is 6 lessons with a writing exercise per lesson, which is critiqued. Final lesson helps writer craft submission to markets. $50 for each class, or buy on CD in PDF format for $15 with no feedback. Booklets available on: *Most Everything You Wanted to Know About Newsletters,* $10.00 + S&H, and *On Critique— What It Is and Isn't.* PDF on disk with forms for critique groups to use—$7.50. *Your Bungee Cord of Tips for Humor Writers*—with tips from and by professional humor writers, $10.00 + S & H. Experienced artist, writer, and editor since 1974. Can create logos, business cards, brochures, letterhead, and T-shirt designs. Chalk Talk Ministry. Does Pastel Portraits. Experienced speaker on writing topics; taught at national, local, and regional conferences and groups. Sells illustrated bookmarks and framed poems. Hundreds of links on her site to guidelines, research sites, resources for writers, news services, greeting card markets, and more.

HOW TO LAND HIGH-PAYING ASSIGNMENTS. Website: www.dougschmidt.com. Encourages writers to "seek the assignment, NOT the sale." Shows aspiring writers how to get an editor's attention without spending hours, days, and weeks on a manuscript.

LIFE WRITE. Website: http://LifeWrite.com. Free 9-lesson writing course.

NOVELCRAFT ONLINE CLASSES. Website: www.noveladvice.com. Courses for writers, $50-100.

ONLINELEARNING.NET/UCLA EXTENSION. Website: www.onlinelearning.net. Offers an extensive selection of writing courses. Call toll-free (800)784-8436 for a free copy of the UCLA Extension Writers' Program Quarterly or e-mail the program at learnonline@educate.com.

ONLINE WORKSHOPS BY MARY EMMA ALLEN, 55 Binks Hill Rd., Plymouth NH 03264. Fax (603)536-4851. E-mail: me.allen@juno.com. Website: http://homepage.fcgnetworks.net/jetent/mea. Topics include: Column Writing 101, Introduction to Self-Publishing, Writing for Children, Writing Your Family History, Writing for Regional Markets, Writing for the Weekly Newspaper, Travel Writing Workshops, Marketing Your Manuscripts, Poetry Writing Workshop, Writing & Publishing on the Internet, and others. She also develops writing workshops for children.

ONLINE WRITING COURSES. Website: www.ed2go.com/courses.html. Click on "Writing Courses" for a list of 15 online writing classes.

PARADIGM ONLINE WRITING ASSISTANT. Website: www.powa.org. An interactive, menu-driven, online writer's guide. Useful for all writers, from inexperienced to advanced.

SHADES OF ROMANCE ONLINE CONFERENCE. Website: www.sormag.com/conference.html. A free annual conference, usually seven days.

VIRTUAL UNIVERSITY. Website: http://vu.org/calendar.html. Offers online courses for writers.

+WRITERS' HELPER, 6118 Bend of River, Dunn NC 28334. Phone/fax (910)980-1126. E-mail: publisher@teenlight.org. Website: www.writershelper.org/workshop.htm. Annette Dammer, administrator. Dedicated to Christian writers and their dreams. Interactive, easy-to-use, online workshops taught by Christian published authors. Many free resources, workshops, e-zine, and support group. Home of the free, award-winning "Write From the Bible" workshop.

WRITERS ONLINE WORKSHOPS, 4700 E. Galbraith Rd., Cincinnati OH 45236. (513)531-0798. Toll-free (800)759-0963. E-mail: wdwowadmin@fwpubs.com. Website: www.Writers OnlineWorkshops.com. Beginning to advanced workshops in fiction, nonfiction, proposal writing, and more. This is a secular Internet-based course, but you may request a Christian instructor. Sponsored by Writer's Digest.

WRITERS ON THE NET. Website: www.writers.com. Online classes and a Writing Tips section.

WRITERS WEEKLY UNIVERSITY. Website: http://writersweekly.com/wwu/courses. Offers online courses for writers. Topics include: plot, characters, life stories, grant writing, marketing, and novels.

WRITING BASICS. Website: www.write4christ.com. E-books that integrate faith and writing.

WRITING CLASSES. Website: www.writingclasses.com.

THE WRITING SCHOOL HOME PAGE. Website: www.mythbreakers.com/writingschool.

WRITING INSTRUCTION: MISCELLANEOUS HELPS

BOOKS ON WRITING. *Art and Soul: 156 Ways to Free Your Creative Spirit* by Pam Grout (2000), Kansas City: Andrews McNeel. *On Writing: A Memoir of the Craft* by Stephen King (2000), Scribner. *Forest for the Trees: An Editor's Advice to Writers* by Betsy Lerner (2000), Riverhead Books.

CARTOONING. Website: www.cartoon.org/home.htm. Website for the International Museum of Cartoon Art. Includes information on how to become a cartoonist. Click on "Advice."

CHAPBOOKS FOR WRITERS. Elizabeth Rosian has a series of concise chapbooks for writers: *Getting Published: 101 Steps to Writing Freelance Articles; A Journey in Journalism: 101 Steps to Writing a Memorable Journal; Writing Meaningful Letters: 101 Steps to Writing Letters that Make a Difference; Greetings for All Occasions: 101 Steps to Writ-*

ing Thoughtful Greeting Cards; Welcome to the Web: 101 Steps to Writing for the World Wide Web. $3.50 each or $15 for a set of five. E-mail: blrosian@charter.net.

+COMIC BOOKS. Website: www.jazmaonline.com. Offers information for aspiring comic book writers with interviews, reviews, message board, and classifieds.

E-BOOK PUBLISHING. *How to Get Your E-Book Published: An Insider's Guide to the World of Electronic Publishing* by Richard Curtis and William Thomas Quick. ISBN: 1582970955.

THE ECLECTIC WRITER. How-to articles for writers. Website: www.eclectics.com/writing/writing.html.

EDITING. Website: www.queryletters.com. Provides in-depth editing of fiction and nonfiction manuscripts. See also the Editorial Services section in the back of this Market Guide.

EEI PRESS. Linda Jorgensen, Mgr., EEI Press, 66 Canal Center Plaza, Ste. 200, Alexandria VA 22314-5507. (703)683-0683. Fax (703)683-4915. E-mail: info@eeicommunications.com. Website: www.eeicommunications.com. Publishes reference books and self-instructional manuals for professional editors, proofreaders, and educators. Also publishes a subscription newsletter, *The Editorial Eye.*

+FAT FREE WRITING. Website: http://home.comcast.net/~garbl/writing/concise.htm. An annotated directory of Websites that give advice on cutting the fat from your writing.

+FIFTEEN WRITING EXERCISES. Website: www.poewar.com/articles/15_exercises.htm.

FREELANCE WRITING. Website: www.suite101.com/topics/page.cfm/1639. Practical helps for freelancers, such as how to write a query letter.

+GETTING ORGANIZED. Websites: www.onlineorganizing.com; www.succeedinginbusiness .com/catalog. Offers many e-books, including *Winning the Fight Between You and Your Desk* by Jeffrey Mayer.

+GLOSSARY OF PUBLISHING TERMS. Website: www.picture-book.com/news.asp?listingid=44.

THE GRAMMAR LADY. Website: www.grammarlady.com.

GUIDE TO GRAMMAR AND WRITING. Website: www.ccc.commnet.edu/grammar.

MANUSCRIPT FORMAT. For a sample and instructions on format for an article or a book, go to: www.shunn.net/format.html, or www.sfwa.org/writing/format_betancourt.htm.

+NONFICTION BOOK PROPOSAL. Website: http://co.essortment.com/bookproposal_rjwi .htm.

PERSONAL WRITING COACH. Dr. Mary Ann L. Diorio, Certified Writing Coach, Certified Behavioural Consultant, Certified Biblical Counselor. (856)327-1231. Fax (856)327-0291. E-mail: MaryAnn@lifecoachingforwriters.com. Website: www.lifecoachingforwriters.com. Expert help for those stuck in a rut or confused about what direction to take. Guarantees results and positive changes in your writing career.

+PRINT ON DEMAND. Website: www.booksandtales.com/pod. *An Incomplete Guide to Print on Demand Publishers* by Clea Saal compares different POD publishers and their services.

PROFESSIONAL WRITING DEGREE. Website: www.tayloru.edu. Taylor University Fort Wayne has initiated the country's first "Professional Writing" major at an accredited Christian university. The four-year bachelor of arts program includes freelance writing, fiction, business and technical writing, journalism, scriptwriting, public relations, editorial and opinion writing, TV and radio news broadcasting, speech writing, and academic research writing. Write to Office of Admissions, TUFW, 1025 W. Rudisill Blvd., Fort Wayne IN 46807. (260)744-8647. Fax (260)744-8660. E-mail: dnhensley@tayloru.edu.

Q&A COLUMN. The University of Chicago Press (publisher of the *Chicago Manual of Style,* 15th edition) has a Q&A column written by their Manuscript Editing Department on their Website: www.press.uchicago.edu/Misc/Chicago/cmosfaq.html.

QUERY LETTERS. Websites: www.elainenichols.com. Click on Articles for "The Editor Friendly Query"; http://personal.rockbridge.net/gavaler/TheArtoftheQuery.html. The Art of the Query; www.writing-world.com/basics/query.shtml. How to Write a Successful Query Letter; www.writing-world.com/basics/email.shtml. Preparing E-mail Queries; www.powernet.net/~scrnplay/Queryletterbk.html. Query letter sample; www.eclectics.com/articles/query.html; www.poewar.com/articles/query_letter.htm; www.jkelman.com/misc/query letter.html; www.geocities.com/charlottedillon2000/query.html.

RENSSELEAR WRITING CENTER ONLINE HANDOUTS. Website: www.rpi.edu/web/writing center/handouts.html. Includes 12 one-page handouts on Basic Prose Styles, and 18 handouts on Basic Punctuation and Mechanics.

SALLY STUART'S GUIDE TO GETTING PUBLISHED. This book tells you everything you need to know about how to write for publication and get published. $17 postpaid from Christian Writers Marketplace, 1647 S.W. Pheasant Dr., Aloha OR 97006. Website: www.stuart market.com.

SPIRITUAL JOURNAL. Ron Klug has revised his book *How to Keep a Spiritual Journal: A Guide to Journal Keeping for Inner Growth and Personal Discovery* (Augsburg Books, 2002). For the writer, a journal is a safe place to practice writing, to capture ideas and material, and to explore the writing process. This substantial revision of a widely read book on journaling from a Christian perspective offers dozens of writing exercises, a new chapter on writing for healing, and ideas on how to harvest the journal. Included is a guide for forming a journaling group and an extensive bibliography of books, tapes, and Websites. You may order the guide ($17 postpaid) from Christian Writers Marketplace, 1647 S.W. Pheasant Dr., Aloha OR 97006. Website: www.stuartmarket.com.

SUBMISSIONS. Website: www.yudkin.com/flfaq.htm. Article about freelance writing and submission procedures.

TEACHING RESOURCES. *You Can Improve Your Students' Writing Skills Immediately* by David Melton; *Writing Toward Home* by Georgia Heard; and *Where I'm From* by George Ella Lyon.

TESTIMONIES. Website: www.gospelcom.net/guide/resources/angie/php. Article showing how to make a testimony target non-Christian readers. Also in English, click on Leia em Ingles.

WRITER'S APPRENTICE. Website: www.writersapprentice.com. Tina Miller, publisher. Free print magazine for new and intermediate writers.

WRITER'S ULTIMATE RESOURCE GUIDE. Website: www.writersdigest.com. This book contains 84 conferences, 25 writing books that belong on your shelf, specific contact information and Website links, and much more.

WRITERS WEEKLY. Website: www.writersweekly.com/index-starterkit.htm. Free Internet newsletter for writers. Subscribe and receive the free e-book *How to Be a Freelance Writer* (with 103 paying markets).

WRITING ARTICLES. Website: www.writing.org. Durant Imboden's articles for writers.

WRITING UPDATE FROM WRITER'S DIGEST. This is a periodic, free e-mail newsletter from the editors at Writer's Digest that includes up-to-date writing-related news and tips. Subscribe at their Website: www.writersdigest.com.

WRITING WORKSHOPS FOR CHILDREN AND ADULTS. Offered by Mary Emma Allen, author, journalist, columnist. Offered at conferences, schools, colleges, senior centers, church groups, etc. Topics include: Column Writing 101, Introduction to Self-Publishing, Writing for Children, Writing Your Family History, Writing for Regional Markets, Marketing Your Manuscripts, Poetry Writing Workshop, Writing & Publishing on the Internet, Writing for Christian Publications, and others. She also develops writing workshops for children. Contact: Mary Emma Allen, 55 Binks Hill Rd., Plymouth NH 03264. Fax

(603)536-4851. Website: http://homepage.fcgnetworks.net/jetent/mea. E-mail: me
.allen@juno.com.

WRITING WORLD. Website: www.writing-world.com. Good site for writers including a step-by-
step guide to launching a writing career and other important tips.

YOU CAN BE A COLUMNIST, by Charlotte Digregorio (1993), Baker & Taylor. $13.95. Avail-
able at www.alibris.com.

TOPICAL/SUBJECT LISTINGS OF BOOK PUBLISHERS

One of the most difficult aspects of marketing is trying to determine which publishers might be interested in the book you want to write. This topical listing was designed to help you do just that.

First, look up your topic of interest in the following lists. If you don't find the specific topic, check the list of topics in the table of contents, find any related topics, and pursue those. Once you have discovered which publishers are interested in a particular topic, the next step is to secure writer's guidelines and book catalogs from those publishers. Just because a particular publisher is listed under your topic, don't assume that it would automatically be interested in your book. It is your job to determine whether your approach to the subject will fit within the unique scope of that publisher's catalog. It is also helpful to visit a Christian bookstore to actually see some of the books produced by each publisher you are interested in pursuing.

Note, too, that the primary listings for each publisher indicate what the publisher prefers to see in the initial contact—a query, book proposal, or complete manuscript.

R—Indicates which publishers reprint out-of-print books from other publishers.

An asterisk (*) following a topic indicates it is a new topic this year.

An (s) before a listing indicates it is a publisher listed in the Subsidy Publishers' section and does at least 50% subsidy publishing or print-on-demand. Please note that some of these publishers do some royalty publishing as well (check their listings), so if you aren't interested in a subsidy deal, you can contact them indicating you are interested only in a royalty contract.

APOLOGETICS

ACU Press
Alba House—R
Allegiance Books—R
Ambassador-Emerald—R
(s)-American Binding—R
AMG Publishers—R
Baker Books
Bethany House
(s)-Black Forest—R
(s)-Brentwood—R
Bridge-Logos
Broadman & Holman
Canadian Inst. for Law—R
Canon Press—R
Canticle Books—R
(s)-Catholic Answers—R
Charisma House—R
Christian Focus—R
Christian Publications—R
Christian Writers Ebook—R
College Press—R
Conciliar Press—R
Continuum Intl.—R
(s)-Creation House—R
Crossway Books
Discovery House—R
Eerdmans Publishing—R

(s)-Emmaus Road Pub.—R
(s)-Essence—R
Fair Havens—R
(s)-Fairway Press—R
Good News Publishers
Greenwood Publishing
(s)-Guardian Books—R
HarperSanFrancisco
Harvest House
Hensley Publishing—R
Hiddenspring Books
Inkling Books—R
InterVarsity Press—R
Kregel—R
Lighthouse Trails Publishing—R
Lightwave Publishing
Lutterworth Press
Magnus Press—R
Master Books
(s)-Master Design—R
Messianic Jewish—R
Millennium III—R
Monarch Books—R
Moody Publishers
Multnomah
New Leaf Press—R
Oregon Catholic Press—R
Our Sunday Visitor—R
P & R Publishing—R

Pacific Press
Pauline Books—R
Pickwick Publications—R
(s)-Promise Publishing
(s)-Providence House—R
Quintessential Books—R
Read 'N Run—R
Regnery—R
Rose Publishing
Sheed & Ward—R
St. Anthony Messenger
Still Waters Revival—R
Tate Publishing
Trinity Foundation—R
Tyndale House—R
Tyndale House/SaltRiver
Univ. Press of America—R
Victor Books
W Publishing Group
Whitaker House—R
World Publishing—R
Zondervan

ARCHAEOLOGY

Algora Publishing—R
(s)-American Binding—R
Baker Books
Baker Tritten
Basic Books—R

Baylor Univ. Press—R
(s)-Black Forest—R
(s)-Brentwood—R
Christian Writers Ebook—R
Christopher Publishing
Conciliar Press—R
Continuum Intl.—R
(s)-Creation House—R
Dover Publications—R
Eerdmans Publishing—R
(s)-Elderberry Press
(s)-Essence—R
Facts on File
Fair Havens—R
(s)-Fairway Press—R
FaithWalk Publishing
Four Courts Press—R
(s)-Guardian Books—R
HarperSanFrancisco
Hendrickson—R
Hiddenspring Books
Hill Street Press—R
InterVarsity Press—R
Johns Hopkins—R
Kregel—R
(s)-Longwood—R
Lutterworth Press
(s)-Master Design—R
Monarch Books—R
Mt. Olive College Press
New Seeds Books—R
New York Univ. Press
Oxford University
Pacific Press
(s)-Promise Publishing
(s)-Providence House—R
PublishAmerica
Read 'N Run—R
Rose Publishing
Tate Publishing
Third World Press—R
Trinity Press Intl.—R
Univ. Press of America—R
World Publishing—R
Yale Univ. Press—R

AUTOBIOGRAPHY

Ambassador-Emerald—R
(s)-American Binding—R
Baker Books
Baylor Univ. Press—R
Bethany House
BJU/Journey Forth—R
Blue Dolphin
(s)-Book Publishers Network
(s)-Brentwood—R
Carey Library, Wm.—R

Charisma House—R
Christian Focus—R
Christian Writers Ebook—R
Christopher Publishing
Continuum Intl.—R
Created in Christ
(s)-Creation House—R
Cross Cultural—R
(s)-Elderberry Press
(s)-Essence—R
Fair Havens—R
(s)-Fairway Press—R
Friends United Press—R
Genesis Communications
Genesis Press
Georgetown Univ. Press
Greenwood Publishing
(s)-Guardian Books—R
Guernica Editions—R
(s)-Hannibal Books—R
HarperSanFrancisco
Hill Street Press—R
His eBooks
Lighthouse Trails Publishing—R
(s)-Lightning Star Press—R
Liguori
Living Books for All
(s)-Longwood—R
Lutterworth Press
(s)-McDougal Publishing—R
Monarch Books—R
New Seeds Books—R
Pacific Press
(s)-Promise Publishing
(s)-Providence House—R
PublishAmerica
Read 'N Run—R
Regnery—R
(s)-Robbie Dean Press—R
Rose Publishing
Selah Publishing—R
(s)-So. Baptist Press—R
Still Waters Revival—R
Tate Publishing
(s)-TEACH Services—R
Univ. Press of America—R
(s)-VESTA—R
VMI Publishers
Whitaker House—R
(s)-Word for Word
Zondervan

BIBLE/BIBLICAL STUDIES

Abingdon Press
ACU Press
Ambassador-Emerald—R
(s)-American Binding—R

AMG Publishers—R
Baker Books
Baker Tritten
Baptist Pub. House
Baylor Univ. Press—R
Bethany House
(s)-Brentwood—R
Bridge Resources
Broadman & Holman
Canon Press—R
Canticle Books—R
Carey Library, Wm.—R
(s)-Catholic Answers—R
Cerdic-Publications
Chalice Press
Charisma House—R
Christian Ed. Pub.
Christian Writers Ebook—R
Christopher Publishing
College Press—R
Conciliar Press—R
Contemporary Drama Service
Continuum Intl.—R
Created in Christ
(s)-Creation House—R
Cross Cultural—R
CSS Publishing
(s)-DCTS Publishing—R
Editores Betania-Caribe
Editorial Portavoz—R
Educational Ministries
(s)-Emmaus Road Pub.—R
(s)-Essence—R
Fair Havens—R
(s)-Fairway Press—R
FaithWalk Publishing
Fortress Press
Forward Movement
Genesis Communications
Geneva Press
Good Book—R
Greenwood Publishing
Group Publishing
(s)-Guardian Books—R
Harcourt Religion
HarperSanFrancisco
Harrison House
Harvest House
Hendrickson—R
Hensley Publishing—R
Hiddenspring Books
Holy Cross—R
Inkling Books—R
InterVarsity Press—R
Judson Press
Libros Liguori
Lightwave Publishing

Living Books for All
Logion Press
(s)-Longwood—R
Lutterworth Press
Magnus Press—R
(s)-Master Design—R
(s)-McDougal Publishing—R
MegaGrace Books
Mercer Univ. Press—R
Messianic Jewish—R
Monarch Books—R
New Hope—R
New Leaf Press—R
Openbook—R
Oregon Catholic Press—R
Our Sunday Visitor—R
P & R Publishing—R
Pacific Press
Paradise Research—R
Pathway Press
Paulist Press
Pickwick Publications—R
Pilgrim Press—R
(s)-Poetry of Today
(s)-Promise Publishing
(s)-Providence House—R
PublishAmerica
Read 'N Run—R
(s)-Robbie Dean Press—R
Rose Publishing
Shaw Books—R
Sheed & Ward—R
Shining Star
Smyth & Helwys
(s)-So. Baptist Press—R
St. Anthony Messenger
Tate Publishing
Trinity Press Intl.—R
UMI Publishing—R
United Church Pub.
Univ. Press of America—R
(s)-VESTA—R
VMI Publishers
Walk Worthy—R
Westminster John Knox
Woodland Gospel
(s)-Word for Word
World Publishing—R
Yale Univ. Press—R
Youth Specialties
Zondervan

BIBLE COMMENTARY

Ambassador-Emerald—R
(s)-American Binding—R
Baker Books

Baptist Pub. House
Baylor Univ. Press—R
(s)-Black Forest—R
Bridge-Logos
Canon Press—R
Carey Library, Wm.—R
(s)-Catholic Answers—R
Chariot Books
Christian Focus—R
Christian Writers Ebook—R
Christopher Publishing
College Press—R
Conciliar Press—R
Continuum Intl.—R
(s)-Creation House—R
Crossway Books
Discovery House—R
Doubleday
Editores Betania-Caribe
Editorial Portavoz—R
Eerdmans Publishing—R
(s)-Elderberry Press
(s)-Emmaus Road Pub.—R
(s)-Fairway Press—R
Forward Movement
Four Courts Press—R
Greenwood Publishing
(s)-Guardian Books—R
Harrison House
Hendrickson—R
Hiddenspring Books
Holy Cross—R
Inkling Books—R
InterVarsity Press—R
Kregel—R
Libros Liguori
Living Books for All
Lutterworth Press
(s)-Master Design—R
Messianic Jewish—R
Monarch Books—R
New Canaan
New Leaf Press—R
Openbook—R
Oregon Catholic Press—R
Our Sunday Visitor—R
Oxford University
P & R Publishing—R
Pauline Books—R
Paulist Press
Pickwick Publications—R
(s)-Promise Publishing
(s)-Providence House—R
PublishAmerica
Read 'N Run—R
Rose Publishing

Sheed & Ward—R
St. Anthony Messenger
Twenty-Third Publications
Tyndale House—R
UMI Publishing—R
Victor Books
Westminster John Knox
(s)-WinePress—R
(s)-Word for Word
World Publishing—R
Zondervan

BIOGRAPHY

Algora Publishing—R
Ambassador-Emerald—R
(s)-American Binding—R
Baker Books
Baker Tritten
Ballantine Books
Barbour Publishing
Basic Books—R
Baylor Univ. Press—R
Bethany House
BJU/Journey Forth—R
(s)-Black Forest—R
Blue Dolphin
(s)-Book Publishers Network
Branden Publishing
(s)-Brentwood—R
Bridge-Logos
Canon Press—R
Canticle Books—R
Carey Library, Wm.—R
(s)-Catholic Answers—R
Charisma House—R
Charisma Kids
Christian Focus—R
Christian Writers Ebook—R
Christopher Publishing
Conciliar Press—R
Continuum Intl.—R
Created in Christ
(s)-Creation House—R
Cross Cultural—R
Crossroad Publishing—R
Cumberland House
Dimension Books—R
Eerdmans Publishing—R
Eerdmans/Young Readers
(s)-Elderberry Press
(s)-Essence—R
Facts on File
Fair Havens—R
(s)-Fairway Press—R
FaithWalk Publishing
Genesis Press

Georgetown Univ. Press
Greenwood Publishing
(s)-Guardian Books—R
(s)-Hannibal Books—R
HarperSanFrancisco
Hill Street Press—R
His eBooks
ICS Publications—R
Inkling Books—R
Jossey-Bass
Kaleidoscope Press—R
Lighthouse Trails Publishing—R
Liguori
Living Books for All
(s)-Longwood—R
Lutterworth Press
Magnus Press—R
(s)-Master Design—R
(s)-McDougal Publishing—R
Mercer Univ. Press—R
Monarch Books—R
Mt. Olive College Press
New Hope—R
New Seeds Books—R
Northfield
Our Sunday Visitor—R
P & R Publishing—R
Pacific Press
Paulist Press
PREP Publishing—R
(s)-Promise Publishing
(s)-Providence House—R
PublishAmerica
Quintessential Books—R
Read 'N Run—R
Regnery—R
(s)-Robbie Dean Press—R
Scarecrow Press—R
Scepter Publishers—R
Selah Publishing—R
Sheed & Ward—R
Shoreline—R
(s)-So. Baptist Press—R
Still Waters Revival—R
Summit Pub. Group—R
Tate Publishing
(s)-TEACH Services—R
United Church Pub.
Univ. of AR Press—R
Univ. Press of America—R
(s)-VESTA—R
VMI Publishers
W Publishing Group
Whitaker House—R
Woodland Gospel
(s)-Word for Word

Yale Univ. Press—R

BOOKLETS

(s)-American Binding—R
Baptist Pub. House
Canon Press—R
(s)-Catholic Answers—R
Charisma House—R
Christian Writers Ebook—R
Concordia
Created in Christ
(s)-Creation House—R
(s)-Essence—R
Fair Havens—R
FamilyLife Publishing
(s)-Fruit-Bearer Pub.
Genesis Communications
Good Book—R
(s)-Guardian Books—R
(s)-Insight Publishing
InterVarsity Press—R
Intl. Awakening—R
Jubilant Press—R
Libros Liguori
(s)-Lightning Star Press—R
Lightwave Publishing
Liguori
Living Books for All
(s)-Longwood—R
(s)-Master Design—R
MegaGrace Books
(s)-One World—R
Our Sunday Visitor—R
P & R Publishing—R
Pacific Press
Paradise Research—R
Paulist Press
(s)-Providence House—R
Read 'N Run—R
(s)-Robbie Dean Press—R
Rose Publishing
St. Anthony Messenger
Tate Publishing
Trinity Foundation—R
Twenty-Third Publications
(s)-WinePress—R
(s)-Xulon Press—R

CANADIAN/FOREIGN

Canadian Inst. for Law—R
Cerdic-Publications
Christian Focus—R
Continuum Intl.—R
(s)-Essence—R
(s)-Guardian Books—R
Guernica Editions—R

Hidden Brook Press
His eBooks
Hunt Publishing, John
(s)-Inheritance Publications—R
Kindred Productions
Lightwave Publishing
Living Books for All
Lutterworth Press
Monarch Books—R
Northstone—R
Openbook—R
Shoreline—R
Skysong Press
Still Waters Revival—R
Tate Publishing
United Church Pub.
Univ./Ottawa Press
Verbinum
(s)-VESTA—R
Wood Lake Books—R
(s)-Word Alive
Writers Exchange

CELEBRITY PROFILES

Baker Books
(s)-Black Forest—R
Blue Dolphin
Bridge-Logos
Christian Writers Ebook—R
Continuum Intl.—R
(s)-Creation House—R
(s)-Essence—R
(s)-Fairway Press—R
FaithWalk Publishing
Genesis Press
Good News Publishers
Greenwood Publishing
(s)-Guardian Books—R
HarperSanFrancisco
Hay House
Hill Street Press—R
Judson Press
Liguori
(s)-Promise Publishing
(s)-Providence House—R
Read 'N Run—R
Selah Publishing—R
Shaw Books—R
Tate Publishing
TowleHouse—R
VMI Publishers
Whitaker House—R
Woodland Gospel

CHILDREN'S BOARD BOOKS

(s)-Ambassador House

Big Idea, Inc.
Candy Cane Press
Canon Press—R
Eerdmans/Young Readers
Fair Havens—R
Kregel—R
Kregel Kidzone—R
Tate Publishing
ZonderKidz

CHILDREN'S EASY READERS

Ambassador Books
(s)-Ambassador House
Baker Books
Big Idea, Inc.
Branden Publishing
Canon Press—R
Chariot Books
Charisma Kids
Conciliar Press—R
(s)-Creation House—R
Creative Teaching
Eerdmans/Young Readers
(s)-Emmaus Road Pub.—R
(s)-Essence—R
Fair Havens—R
(s)-Fairway Press—R
Faith Kids Books
Genesis Communications
Green Pastures Press—R
(s)-Guardian Books—R
Honor Kidz
Hunt Publishing, John
Inkling Books—R
Legacy Press—R
(s)-Lightning Star Press—R
Lightwave Publishing
Liguori
Lutterworth Press
McRuffy Press
OnStage Publishing
Pacific Press
Pauline Books—R
Read 'N Run—R
(s)-Robbie Dean Press—R
Standard Publishing
Tate Publishing
Tyndale House—R
VMI Publishers
ZonderKidz

CHILDREN'S PICTURE BOOKS

Ambassador Books
(s)-Ambassador House
Baker Books

Big Idea, Inc.
(s)-Black Forest—R
(s)-Book Publishers Network
Boyds Mills Press—R
Candy Cane Press
Canon Press—R
Chariot Books
Charisma Kids
Christian Focus—R
Conciliar Press—R
Concordia
Devoted to You
Editorial Portavoz—R
Eerdmans/Young Readers
(s)-Elderberry Press
(s)-Essence—R
(s)-Fairway Press—R
Faith Communications
Faith Kids Books
Genesis Communications
(s)-Guardian Books—R
Hunt Publishing, John
Illumination Arts
Kaleidoscope Press—R
Kregel—R
Kregel Kidzone—R
Lamplighter—R
(s)-Lightning Star Press—R
Lightwave Publishing
Liguori
Lutterworth Press
OnStage Publishing
Pauline Books—R
Pelican Publishing—R
(s)-Poetry of Today
Read 'N Run—R
Selah Publishing—R
Tate Publishing
Third World Press—R
Tyndale House—R
Warner Press
ZonderKidz

CHRIST*

(s)-American Binding—R
AMG Publishers—R
Baker Tritten
(s)-Black Forest—R
Canticle Books—R
(s)-Catholic Answers—R
Chariot Books
Charisma House—R
Charisma Kids
Christian Writers Ebook—R
Christopher Publishing
(s)-Creation House—R
(s)-Emmaus Road Pub.—R

Forward Movement
Hiddenspring Books
InterVarsity Press—R
Kregel—R
(s)-Longwood—R
Magnus Press—R
(s)-Master Design—R
Multnomah
Pilgrim Press—R
(s)-Poetry of Today
(s)-Providence House—R
PublishAmerica
Resource Publications
Rose Publishing
St. Anthony Messenger
Tate Publishing
VMI Publishers
Wesleyan Publishing
Whitaker House—R

CHRISTIAN BUSINESS*

(s)-American Binding—R
(s)-Black Forest—R
Chariot Books
Charisma House—R
Christian Writers Ebook—R
(s)-Creation House—R
(s)-Emmaus Road Pub.—R
Genesis Communications
(s)-Hannibal Books—R
InterVarsity Press—R
(s)-Longwood—R
Millennium III—R
Multnomah
(s)-Poetry of Today
(s)-Providence House—R
Quintessential Books—R
Rose Publishing
St. Anthony Messenger
Tate Publishing
VMI Publishers
Westminster John Knox
Whitaker House—R

CHRISTIAN EDUCATION

ACU Press
Ambassador-Emerald—R
(s)-American Binding—R
Andros Book Publishing
Baker Books
Baker Tritten
Baptist Pub. House
Baylor Univ. Press—R
Big Idea, Inc.
(s)-Black Forest—R
(s)-Brentwood—R
Bridge Resources

Bridge-Logos
Broadman & Holman
Canon Press—R
Chalice Press
Chariot Books
Christian Ed. Pub.
Christian Writers Ebook—R
Christopher Publishing
College Press—R
Contemporary Drama Service
Created in Christ
(s)-Creation House—R
Cross Cultural—R
CSS Publishing
(s)-DCTS Publishing—R
Doubleday
Educational Ministries
(s)-Emmaus Road Pub.—R
(s)-Essence—R
ETC Publications
Fair Havens—R
(s)-Fairway Press—R
Faith Alive Resources
Forward Movement
Gospel Publishing House
Group Publishing
(s)-Guardian Books—R
Harcourt Religion
Hendrickson—R
Hensley Publishing—R
Hiddenspring Books
Hill Street Press—R
Holy Cross—R
Hunt Publishing, John
Kregel—R
Legacy Press—R
Lightwave Publishing
Liturgical Press
Lutterworth Press
Master Books
(s)-Master Design—R
Meriwether—R
Millennium III—R
Monarch Books—R
New Canaan
New Hope—R
New Leaf Press—R
Nexgen
Openbook—R
Oregon Catholic Press—R
Our Sunday Visitor—R
P & R Publishing—R
Pacific Press
Pathway Press
Paulist Press
Pflaum Publishing Group
Pilgrim Press—R

(s)-Poetry of Today
(s)-Providence House—R
PublishAmerica
Quintessential Books—R
Rainbow Publishers—R
Reference Service
Religious Education
Resource Publications
(s)-Robbie Dean Press—R
Rose Publishing
Scarecrow Press—R
Smyth & Helwys
(s)-So. Baptist Press—R
St. Anthony Messenger
Standard Publishing
Still Waters Revival—R
Tate Publishing
Trinity Foundation—R
UMI Publishing—R
United Church Pub.
Univ. Press of America—R
Wood Lake Books—R
Wordsmiths

CHRISTIAN HOME-SCHOOLING

Ambassador-Emerald—R
Andros Book Publishing
Baker Books
Big Idea, Inc.
(s)-Brentwood—R
Bridge-Logos
Broadman & Holman
Canon Press—R
Christian Publications—R
Christian Writers Ebook—R
Created in Christ
(s)-Creation House—R
Crossway Books
(s)-Emmaus Road Pub.—R
(s)-Essence—R
ETC Publications
Fair Havens—R
(s)-Fairway Press—R
(s)-Guardian Books—R
(s)-Hannibal Books—R
Harcourt Religion
Harvest House
Hensley Publishing—R
Hill Street Press—R
Hunt Publishing, John
Inkling Books—R
Jubilant Press—R
Kaleidoscope Press—R
Legacy Press—R
(s)-Longwood—R
(s)-Master Design—R

Multnomah
New Leaf Press—R
Oregon Catholic Press—R
Our Sunday Visitor—R
P & R Publishing—R
Pacific Press
(s)-Providence House—R
Rainbow Publishers—R
Resource Publications
(s)-Robbie Dean Press—R
Rose Publishing
Scarecrow Press—R
Standard Publishing
Still Waters Revival—R
Tate Publishing
Virginia Pines Press

CHRISTIAN LIVING

Abingdon Press
(s)-Ambassador House
Ambassador-Emerald—R
(s)-American Binding—R
AMG Publishers—R
Baker Books
Baker Tritten
Baptist Pub. House
Barbour Publishing
Baylor Univ. Press—R
Beacon Hill Press
Bethany House
(s)-Black Forest—R
(s)-Brentwood—R
Bridge-Logos
Broadman & Holman
Canon Press—R
Canticle Books—R
Chalice Press
Chariot Books
Charisma House—R
Christian Focus—R
Christian Publications—R
Christian Writers Ebook—R
Christopher Publishing
Cladach Publishing—R
Continuum Intl.—R
Created in Christ
(s)-Creation House—R
Cross Cultural—R
Crossway Books
CSS Publishing
(s)-DCTS Publishing—R
Dimensions for Living
Discovery House—R
Editorial Portavoz—R
Eerdmans Publishing—R
Elijah Press
(s)-Emmaus Road Pub.—R

(s)-Essence—R
Fair Havens—R
(s)-Fairway Press—R
FaithWalk Publishing
Focus on the Family—R
Forward Movement
Friends United Press—R
(s)-Fruit-Bearer Pub.
Genesis Communications
Good News Publishers
Green Key Books
Green Pastures Press—R
Greenwood Publishing
(s)-Guardian Books—R
HarperSanFrancisco
Harrison House
Harvest House
Haworth Press—R
Hendrickson—R
Hensley Publishing—R
Hiddenspring Books
Hill Street Press—R
Holy Cross—R
Howard Publishing
Hunt Publishing, John
(s)-Impact Christian—R
InterVarsity Press—R
Jireh Publishing
Jossey-Bass
Judson Press
Kindred Productions
Kregel—R
Lamplighter—R
Langmarc
Life Cycle Books—R
Lighthouse Trails Publishing—R
Liturgical Press
Living Books for All
(s)-Longwood—R
Lutterworth Press
Magnus Press—R
(s)-Master Design—R
(s)-McDougal Publishing—R
MegaGrace Books
Monarch Books—R
Moody Publishers
Morehouse
Multnomah
Nelson Books
New Leaf Press—R
Openbook—R
Oregon Catholic Press—R
Our Sunday Visitor—R
P & R Publishing—R
Paraclete Press—R
Paradise Research—R
Pathway Press

Pilgrim Press—R
(s)-Poetry of Today
PREP Publishing—R
(s)-Providence House—R
PublishAmerica
Quintessential Books—R
Read 'N Run—R
RiverOak—R
Rose Publishing
Selah Publishing—R
Shaw Books—R
Shining Star
Small Helm Press—R
Smyth & Helwys
St. Anthony Messenger
Standard Publishing
Still Waters Revival—R
Tate Publishing
Tau-Publishing—R
(s)-TEACH Services—R
Tyndale House—R
Tyndale House/SaltRiver
UMI Publishing—R
United Church Pub.
Univ. Press of America—R
VMI Publishers
W Publishing Group
Wesleyan Publishing
Westminster John Knox
Whitaker House—R
(s)-Winer Foundation—R
Woodland Gospel
(s)-Word for Word
World Publishing—R
Zondervan

CHRISTIAN SCHOOL BOOKS

Andros Book Publishing
Baker Books
Baker Tritten
Baylor Univ. Press—R
Big Idea, Inc.
Broadman & Holman
Christian Liberty Press
Christian Writers Ebook—R
Created in Christ
(s)-Creation House—R
ETC Publications
(s)-Fairway Press—R
Forward Movement
(s)-Guardian Books—R
Hunt Publishing, John
Inkling Books—R
Kaleidoscope Press—R
Lutterworth Press
(s)-Master Design—R

New Canaan
Our Sunday Visitor—R
Pacific Press
(s)-Poetry of Today
(s)-Providence House—R
Rainbow Publishers—R
(s)-Robbie Dean Press—R
Rose Publishing
(s)-So. Baptist Press—R
Tate Publishing
Trinity Foundation—R
Wood Lake Books—R
Wordsmiths

CHURCH HISTORY

Abingdon Press
Algora Publishing—R
Ambassador-Emerald—R
(s)-American Binding—R
American Cath. Press—R
Baker Books
Baker Tritten
Baptist Pub. House
Baylor Univ. Press—R
(s)-Black Forest—R
Broadman & Holman
Canon Press—R
Canticle Books—R
Carey Library, Wm.—R
(s)-Catholic Answers—R
Christian Focus—R
Christian Publications—R
Christian Writers Ebook—R
Christopher Publishing
Cistercian—R
College Press—R
Concordia
Continuum Intl.—R
Created in Christ
(s)-Creation House—R
Cross Cultural—R
Crossroad Publishing—R
Crossway Books
Discovery House—R
Doubleday
Editorial Portavoz—R
Eerdmans Publishing—R
Elijah Press
(s)-Emmaus Road Pub.—R
Fair Havens
(s)-Fairway Press—R
FaithWalk Publishing
Fortress Press
Forward Movement
Four Courts Press—R
Geneva Press
Green Pastures Press—R

Greenwood Publishing
HarperSanFrancisco
Hendrickson—R
Hiddenspring Books
Holy Cross—R
InterVarsity Press—R
Intl. Awakening—R
Johns Hopkins—R
Kregel—R
Libros Liguori
(s)-Longwood—R
Loyola Press
Lutterworth Press
(s)-Master Design—R
Millennium III—R
Monarch Books—R
New Canaan
Our Sunday Visitor—R
Oxford University
P & R Publishing—R
Pacific Press
Paulist Press
Pickwick Publications—R
(s)-Promise Publishing
(s)-Providence House—R
PublishAmerica
Quintessential Books—R
Resource Publications
Rose Publishing
Scepter Publishers—R
Selah Publishing—R
Sheed & Ward—R
Shoreline—R
Smyth & Helwys
Summit Pub. Group—R
Tate Publishing
Trinity Foundation—R
Twenty-Third Publications
Univ. of AR Press—R
Univ. Press of America—R
Univ./Ottawa Press
Victor Books
Westminster John Knox
Whitaker House—R
Wood Lake Books—R
World Publishing—R

CHURCH LIFE

Abingdon Press
ACU Press
Ambassador-Emerald—R
(s)-American Binding—R
AMG Publishers—R
Baker Books
Baptist Pub. House
Baylor Univ. Press—R
Bethany House

(s)-Black Forest—R
(s)-Brentwood—R
Bridge-Logos
Broadman & Holman
Canon Press—R
Chalice Press
Charisma House—R
Charisma Kids
Christian Focus—R
Christian Writers Ebook—R
Christopher Publishing
Continuum Intl.—R
(s)-Creation House—R
Cross Cultural—R
Crossway Books
CSS Publishing
(s)-DCTS Publishing—R
Destiny Image—R
Doubleday
Educational Ministries
Eerdmans Publishing—R
(s)-Emmaus Road Pub.—R
(s)-Essence—R
Fair Havens—R
(s)-Fairway Press—R
FaithWalk Publishing
Forward Movement
Friends United Press—R
Gospel Publishing House
Greenwood Publishing
Group Publishing
(s)-Guardian Books—R
HarperSanFrancisco
Harrison House
Hendrickson—R
Hill Street Press—R
Holy Cross—R
Hunt Publishing, John
(s)-Impact Christian—R
InterVarsity Press—R
Judson Press
Kregel—R
Libros Liguori
Lighthouse Trails Publishing—R
Living Books for All
Lutterworth Press
(s)-Master Design—R
Monarch Books—R
Multnomah
Nexgen
Openbook—R
OSL Publications—R
Our Sunday Visitor—R
P & R Publishing—R
Pacific Press
Pathway Press
Paulist Press

Pilgrim Press—R
(s)-Promise Publishing
(s)-Providence House—R
PublishAmerica
Read 'N Run—R
RiverOak—R
Selah Publishing—R
Smyth & Helwys
Tate Publishing
Twenty-Third Publications
United Church Pub.
VMI Publishers
W Publishing Group
Wesleyan Publishing
Westminster John Knox
Whitaker House—R
(s)-Winer Foundation—R
Wood Lake Books—R
Woodland Gospel
Youth Specialties
Zondervan

CHURCH RENEWAL

Abingdon Press
Ambassador-Emerald—R
(s)-American Binding—R
Baker Books
Baylor Univ. Press—R
Bethany House
(s)-Black Forest—R
(s)-Brentwood—R
Bridge-Logos
Broadman & Holman
Canon Press—R
Canticle Books—R
Carey Library, Wm.—R
Charisma House—R
Charisma Kids
Christian Focus—R
Christian Writers Ebook—R
Continuum Intl.—R
Created in Christ
(s)-Creation House—R
Cross Cultural—R
Crossroad Publishing—R
CSS Publishing
Destiny Image—R
Dimension Books—R
Doubleday
Eerdmans Publishing—R
(s)-Emmaus Road Pub.—R
(s)-Essence—R
Fair Havens—R
(s)-Fairway Press—R
FaithWalk Publishing
Forward Movement
Geneva Press

Greenwood Publishing
Group Publishing
(s)-Guardian Books—R
Hendrickson—R
Hill Street Press—R
Holy Cross—R
Hunt Publishing, John
(s)-Impact Christian—R
InterVarsity Press—R
Intl. Awakening—R
Jossey-Bass
Judson Press
Kregel—R
Libros Liguori
(s)-Longwood—R
Lutterworth Press
Magnus Press—R
(s)-Master Design—R
(s)-McDougal Publishing—R
MegaGrace Books
Monarch Books—R
Openbook—R
Oregon Catholic Press—R
OSL Publications—R
P & R Publishing—R
Pacific Press
Paulist Press
Pilgrim Press—R
(s)-Promise Publishing
(s)-Providence House—R
PublishAmerica
Read 'N Run—R
Resource Publications
Selah Publishing—R
(s)-Sermon Select Press
Smyth & Helwys
(s)-So. Baptist Press—R
Tate Publishing
Twenty-Third Publications
United Church Pub.
VMI Publishers
Westminster John Knox
Whitaker House—R

CHURCH TRADITIONS

(s)-American Binding—R
Baker Books
Baylor Univ. Press—R
(s)-Black Forest—R
Bridge-Logos
Broadman & Holman
Carey Library, Wm.—R
(s)-Catholic Answers—R
Charisma House—R
Christian Writers Ebook—R
Christopher Publishing
Conciliar Press—R

Continuum Intl.—R
Created in Christ
(s)-Creation House—R
Cross Cultural—R
Crossroad Publishing—R
CSS Publishing
Doubleday
Eerdmans Publishing—R
(s)-Emmaus Road Pub.—R
(s)-Essence—R
(s)-Fairway Press—R
FaithWalk Publishing
Forward Movement
Greenwood Publishing
(s)-Guardian Books—R
HarperSanFrancisco
Hendrickson—R
Hiddenspring Books
Hill Street Press—R
Holy Cross—R
Hunt Publishing, John
Inkling Books—R
InterVarsity Press—R
Libros Liguori
Liguori
Lutterworth Press
(s)-Master Design—R
Openbook—R
Oregon Catholic Press—R
OSL Publications—R
Our Sunday Visitor—R
Pacific Press
Pauline Books—R
Paulist Press
(s)-Promise Publishing
(s)-Providence House—R
PublishAmerica
Read 'N Run—R
Tate Publishing
Twenty-Third Publications
United Church Pub.
VMI Publishers
Whitaker House—R
Wood Lake Books—R

COMPILATIONS

(s)-American Binding—R
Baylor Univ. Press—R
(s)-Brentwood—R
Christian Writers Ebook—R
Continuum Intl.—R
(s)-Creation House—R
(s)-Fairway Press—R
Gilgal
Group Publishing
HarperSanFrancisco
Lighthouse Trails Publishing—R

(s)-Longwood—R
Lutterworth Press
Obadiah Press
Our Sunday Visitor—R
(s)-Promise Publishing
(s)-Providence House—R
PublishAmerica
RiverOak—R
Tate Publishing
Univ. Press of America—R
VMI Publishers
Whitaker House—R
Woodland Gospel
(s)-Word for Word

CONTROVERSIAL ISSUES

Algora Publishing—R
Ambassador-Emerald—R
(s)-American Binding—R
AMG Publishers—R
Baker Books
(s)-Black Forest—R
Blue Dolphin
(s)-Brentwood—R
Bridge-Logos
Broadman & Holman
Canadian Inst. for Law—R
Canon Press—R
Canticle Books—R
(s)-Catholic Answers—R
Chalice Press
Charisma House—R
Christian Focus—R
Christian Writers Ebook—R
Conciliar Press—R
Continuum Intl.—R
(s)-Creation House—R
Cross Cultural—R
Destiny Image—R
(s)-Essence—R
(s)-Fairway Press—R
FaithWalk Publishing
Focus on the Family—R
Genesis Press
Greenwood Publishing
(s)-Guardian Books—R
(s)-Hannibal Books—R
HarperSanFrancisco
Haworth Press—R
Hay House
Hendrickson—R
Hill Street Press—R
Hunt Publishing, John
Iceagle Press—R
Inkling Books—R
InterVarsity Press—R
Jireh Publishing

Jossey-Bass
Kregel—R
Life Journey Books—R
Lighthouse Trails Publishing—R
Lutterworth Press
Magnus Press—R
(s)-Master Design—R
Millennium III—R
Monarch Books—R
Multnomah
New Leaf Press—R
New Seeds Books—R
Openbook—R
Pilgrim Press—R
(s)-Poetry of Today
(s)-Promise Publishing
(s)-Providence House—R
Quintessential Books—R
Read 'N Run—R
Regnery—R
Rising Star Press
RiverOak—R
(s)-Robbie Dean Press—R
Selah Publishing—R
Still Waters Revival—R
Tate Publishing
United Church Pub.
Virginia Pines Press
VMI Publishers
Whitaker House—R

COOKBOOKS

(s)-American Binding—R
AMG Publishers—R
Ballantine Books
(s)-Black Forest—R
(s)-Book Publishers Network
(s)-Brentwood—R
Christian Writers Ebook—R
Christopher Publishing
Countryman, J.
Crane Hill—R
(s)-Creation House—R
Cumberland House
Dover Publications—R
(s)-Elderberry Press
(s)-Fairway Press—R
Genesis Communications
(s)-Guardian Books—R
(s)-Hannibal Books—R
Hill Street Press—R
Jubilant Press—R
Liguori
(s)-Longwood—R
Pacific Press
Pelican Publishing—R
(s)-Providence House—R

PublishAmerica
Read 'N Run—R
Siloam Press
(s)-So. Baptist Press—R
Summit Pub. Group—R
Tate Publishing
(s)-TEACH Services—R

COUNSELING AIDS

Ambassador-Emerald—R
(s)-American Binding—R
Baker Books
Bethany House
(s)-Black Forest—R
(s)-Brentwood—R
Bridge-Logos
Broadman & Holman
Charisma House—R
Christian Writers Ebook—R
Christopher Publishing
Continuum Intl.—R
Created in Christ
(s)-Creation House—R
CSS Publishing
Dimension Books—R
Editorial Portavoz—R
(s)-Elderberry Press
(s)-Essence—R
Fair Havens—R
(s)-Fairway Press—R
FaithWalk Publishing
Genesis Communications
(s)-Guardian Books—R
Harcourt Religion
Harrison House
Haworth Press—R
Hill Street Press—R
InterVarsity Press—R
Judson Press
Kaleidoscope Press—R
Kregel—R
Life Cycle Books—R
Life Journey Books—R
(s)-Longwood—R
Lutterworth Press
(s)-McDougal Publishing—R
MegaGrace Books
Monarch Books—R
Openbook—R
Pilgrim Press—R
(s)-Promise Publishing
(s)-Providence House—R
Read 'N Run—R
RiverOak—R
(s)-Robbie Dean Press—R
(s)-Sermon Select Press
Silas Publishing—R

(s)-So. Baptist Press—R
Tate Publishing
United Church Pub.
VMI Publishers
Youth Specialties

CREATION SCIENCE

Allegiance Books—R
Ambassador-Emerald—R
(s)-American Binding—R
AMG Publishers—R
(s)-Black Forest—R
Canon Press—R
Christian Focus—R
Christian Writers Ebook—R
(s)-Creation House—R
Editorial Portavoz—R
(s)-Elderberry Press
(s)-Essence—R
Fair Havens—R
(s)-Fairway Press—R
Green Pastures Press—R
(s)-Guardian Books—R
Hendrickson—R
Hill Street Press—R
Inkling Books—R
Kaleidoscope Press—R
Lightwave Publishing
(s)-Longwood—R
(s)-Master Design—R
Millennium III—R
New Leaf Press—R
Pacific Press
(s)-Promise Publishing
(s)-Providence House—R
Rose Publishing
Tate Publishing
Whitaker House—R

CULTS/OCCULT

Ambassador-Emerald—R
AMG Publishers—R
Baker Books
Baker Tritten
Bethany House
(s)-Black Forest—R
Bridge-Logos
Broadman & Holman
(s)-Catholic Answers—R
Christian Focus—R
Christian Writers Ebook—R
Conciliar Press—R
Continuum Intl.—R
Created in Christ
(s)-Creation House—R
CSS Publishing
Editorial Portavoz—R

(s)-Essence—R
(s)-Fairway Press—R
Greenwood Publishing
(s)-Guardian Books—R
Harrison House
Harvest House
Hill Street Press—R
Iceagle Press—R
(s)-Impact Christian—R
InterVarsity Press—R
Lighthouse Trails Publishing—R
Lutterworth Press
Open Court—R
P & R Publishing—R
(s)-Promise Publishing
(s)-Providence House—R
Read 'N Run—R
RiverOak—R
Rose Publishing
Scarecrow Press—R
Selah Publishing—R
Tate Publishing
Whitaker House—R

CURRENT/SOCIAL ISSUES

Algora Publishing—R
Allegiance Books—R
Ambassador Books
Ambassador-Emerald—R
(s)-American Binding—R
AMG Publishers—R
Baker Books
Baker Tritten
Beacon Hill Press
Bethany House
(s)-Black Forest—R
Blue Dolphin
(s)-Brentwood—R
Bridge-Logos
Broadman & Holman
Canadian Inst. for Law—R
(s)-Catholic Answers—R
Chalice Press
Charisma House—R
Christian Focus—R
Christian Publications—R
Christian Writers Ebook—R
Christopher Publishing
Continuum Intl.—R
Created in Christ
(s)-Creation House—R
Cross Cultural—R
Crossway Books
(s)-DCTS Publishing—R
Destiny Image—R
Discovery House—R
Editorial Portavoz—R

Eerdmans Publishing—R
(s)-Elderberry Press
(s)-Essence—R
(s)-Fairway Press—R
FaithWalk Publishing
Georgetown Univ. Press
Greenwood Publishing
(s)-Guardian Books—R
HarperSanFrancisco
Harrison House
Haworth Press—R
Hendrickson—R
Hill Street Press—R
Inkling Books—R
InterVarsity Press—R
Jossey-Bass
Judson Press
Kregel—R
Lamplighter—R
Life Cycle Books—R
Life Journey Books—R
Lighthouse Trails Publishing—R
Liguori
(s)-Longwood—R
Loyola Press
Lutterworth Press
Millennium III—R
Monarch Books—R
Multnomah
New Hope—R
New Leaf Press—R
Openbook—R
Oxford University
Pilgrim Press—R
(s)-Poetry of Today
(s)-Promise Publishing
(s)-Providence House—R
PublishAmerica
Quintessential Books—R
Read 'N Run—R
Regnery—R
Rising Star Press
RiverOak—R
Scarecrow Press—R
Selah Publishing—R
Sheed & Ward—R
Small Helm Press—R
Smyth & Helwys
St. Anthony Messenger
Still Waters Revival—R
Tate Publishing
United Church Pub.
Univ./Ottawa Press
(s)-VESTA—R
VMI Publishers
W Publishing Group
Whitaker House—R

Wood Lake Books—R

CURRICULUM

Andros Book Publishing
Baker Tritten
Baptist Pub. House
Big Idea, Inc.
Canon Press—R
Chariot Books
Christian Ed. Pub.
Christian Focus—R
Christian Liberty Press
Created in Christ
(s)-Creation House—R
Easum, Bandy & Assoc.
(s)-Elderberry Press
(s)-Fairway Press—R
Gospel Publishing House
Group Publishing
Harcourt Religion
Hill Street Press—R
InterVarsity Press—R
Master Books
(s)-Master Design—R
Monarch Books—R
Openbook—R
(s)-Providence House—R
Rainbow Publishers—R
Rose Publishing
Scarecrow Press—R
Smyth & Helwys
Standard Publishing
Tate Publishing
UMI Publishing—R
Univ. Press of America—R
W Publishing Group
Youth Specialties

DATING/SEX

AMG Publishers—R
Ballantine Books
Canon Press—R
(s)-Catholic Answers—R
Chariot Books
Charisma House—R
Christian Writers Ebook—R
Created in Christ
(s)-Creation House—R
Discovery House—R
(s)-Emmaus Road Pub.—R
FaithWalk Publishing
Focus on the Family—R
Frederick Fell—R
Genesis Communications
Genesis Press
Greenwood Publishing
HarperSanFrancisco

Harrison House
Harvest House
Iceagle Press—R
InterVarsity Press—R
Jubilant Press—R
Kregel—R
Life Journey Books—R
(s)-Longwood—R
(s)-Master Design—R
Multnomah
(s)-Providence House—R
PublishAmerica
Quintessential Books—R
Rose Publishing
Silas Publishing—R
Tate Publishing
VMI Publishers
Walk Worthy—R
Whitaker House—R
Youth Specialties

DEATH/DYING

ACTA Publications
Algora Publishing—R
Ambassador Books
(s)-American Binding—R
AMG Publishers—R
Baker Books
Barbour Publishing
(s)-Black Forest—R
Blue Dolphin
(s)-Book Publishers Network
Bridge-Logos
Chariot Books
Charisma House—R
Christian Focus—R
Christian Writers Ebook—R
Christopher Publishing
Continuum Intl.—R
Created in Christ
(s)-Creation House—R
CSS Publishing
Discovery House—R
Editorial Portavoz—R
Eerdmans Publishing—R
(s)-Emmaus Road Pub.—R
(s)-Essence—R
Fair Havens—R
(s)-Fairway Press—R
FaithWalk Publishing
Focus on the Family—R
Forward Movement
Genesis Communications
Gilgal
Greenwood Publishing
(s)-Guardian Books—R
HarperSanFrancisco

Harrison House
Harvest House
Haworth Press—R
Hendrickson—R
Hiddenspring Books
Hill Street Press—R
Hunt Publishing, John
InterVarsity Press—R
Life Cycle Books—R
Life Journey Books—R
Liguori
Liturgy Training
(s)-Longwood—R
Lutterworth Press
(s)-Master Design—R
Monarch Books—R
Morehouse
New Seeds Books—R
Openbook—R
OSL Publications—R
Pacific Press
Paulist Press
Pilgrim Press—R
PREP Publishing—R
(s)-Promise Publishing
(s)-Providence House—R
PublishAmerica
Read 'N Run—R
RiverOak—R
Rose Publishing
Sheed & Ward—R
Siloam Press
Smyth & Helwys
St. Anthony Messenger
Tate Publishing
Twenty-Third Publications
VMI Publishers
Whitaker House—R

DEVOTIONAL BOOKS

Abingdon Press
ACTA Publications
ACU Press
Ambassador Books
(s)-Ambassador House
Ambassador-Emerald—R
(s)-American Binding—R
AMG Publishers—R
Baker Books
Baker Tritten
Baptist Pub. House
Barbour Publishing
(s)-Black Forest—R
(s)-Brentwood—R
Bridge-Logos
Broadman & Holman
Canticle Books—R

Chariot Books
Charisma House—R
Christian Focus—R
Christian Publications—R
Christian Writers Ebook—R
Christopher Publishing
Concordia
Contemporary Drama Service
Continuum Intl.—R
Countryman, J.
Created in Christ
(s)-Creation House—R
Cross Cultural—R
CSS Publishing
Devoted to You
Dimensions for Living
Discovery House—R
Doubleday
Easum, Bandy & Assoc.
Editorial Portavoz—R
(s)-Essence—R
Fair Havens—R
(s)-Fairway Press—R
FaithWalk Publishing
FamilyLife Publishing
Focus on the Family—R
Forward Movement
Friends United Press—R
(s)-Fruit-Bearer Pub.
Genesis Communications
Gilgal
Glory Bound Books
Good Book—R
Green Key Books
Green Pastures Press—R
Greenwood Publishing
Group Publishing
(s)-Guardian Books—R
(s)-Hannibal Books—R
HarperSanFrancisco
Harrison House
Harvest House
Hendrickson—R
Hensley Publishing—R
Hiddenspring Books
Honor Books
Honor Kidz
Hunt Publishing, John
(s)-Impact Christian—R
Inkling Books—R
Inspirio Gifts
InterVarsity Press—R
Jireh Publishing
Judson Press
Kregel—R
Lamplighter—R
Legacy Press—R

Libros Liguori
(s)-Lightning Star Press—R
Lightwave Publishing
Liguori
Living Books for All
Lutterworth Press
Magnus Press—R
(s)-Master Design—R
(s)-McDougal Publishing—R
MegaGrace Books
Monarch Books—R
Multnomah
New Seeds Books—R
Openbook—R
Opine Publishing—R
Our Sunday Visitor—R
P & R Publishing—R
Paraclete Press—R
Pauline Books—R
Paulist Press
Pilgrim Press—R
(s)-Poetry of Today
(s)-Promise Publishing
(s)-Providence House—R
PublishAmerica
Read 'N Run—R
RiverOak—R
Selah Publishing—R
Smyth & Helwys
St. Anthony Messenger
Standard Publishing
Tate Publishing
(s)-TEACH Services—R
Tyndale House—R
United Church Pub.
VMI Publishers
W Publishing Group
Whitaker House—R
(s)-Winer Foundation—R
(s)-Word for Word
World Publishing—R
Youth Specialties
Zondervan

DISCIPLESHIP

ACU Press
Ambassador-Emerald—R
(s)-American Binding—R
AMG Publishers—R
Baker Books
Baker Tritten
Baptist Pub. House
Barbour Publishing
Baylor Univ. Press—R
Beacon Hill Press
Bethany House
(s)-Black Forest—R

(s)-Brentwood—R
Bridge-Logos
Broadman & Holman
Canticle Books—R
Carey Library, Wm.—R
Chalice Press
Chariot Books
Charisma House—R
Charisma Kids
Christian Focus—R
Christian Writers Ebook—R
College Press—R
Continuum Intl.—R
Created in Christ
(s)-Creation House—R
Cross Cultural—R
Crossway Books
CSS Publishing
(s)-DCTS Publishing—R
Discovery House—R
Doubleday
Editorial Portavoz—R
Educational Ministries
(s)-Essence—R
Fair Havens—R
(s)-Fairway Press—R
FaithWalk Publishing
Genesis Communications
Good News Publishers
Gospel Publishing House
Group Publishing
(s)-Guardian Books—R
HarperSanFrancisco
Harrison House
Hensley Publishing—R
Hiddenspring Books
Hill Street Press—R
Hunt Publishing, John
Inkling Books—R
InterVarsity Press—R
Jossey-Bass
Judson Press
Kregel—R
Lamplighter—R
Lightwave Publishing
Liguori
Living Books for All
(s)-Longwood—R
Magnus Press—R
(s)-Master Design—R
(s)-McDougal Publishing—R
MegaGrace Books
Monarch Books—R
Moody Publishers
Multnomah
New Hope—R
Nexgen

Openbook—R
OSL Publications—R
P & R Publishing—R
Pacific Press
Pathway Press
Paulist Press
Pilgrim Press—R
(s)-Promise Publishing
(s)-Providence House—R
Read 'N Run—R
RiverOak—R
Rose Publishing
Shaw Books—R
Smyth & Helwys
(s)-So. Baptist Press—R
Standard Publishing
Tate Publishing
VMI Publishers
W Publishing Group
Wesleyan Publishing
Whitaker House—R
(s)-Winer Foundation—R
Youth Specialties

DIVORCE

Ambassador Books
(s)-American Binding—R
AMG Publishers—R
Baker Books
Bethany House
(s)-Black Forest—R
(s)-Brentwood—R
Bridge-Logos
Chariot Books
Charisma House—R
Christian Focus—R
Christian Writers Ebook—R
Continuum Intl.—R
Created in Christ
(s)-Creation House—R
Editorial Portavoz—R
(s)-Essence—R
Fair Havens—R
(s)-Fairway Press—R
Faith One
FaithWalk Publishing
Greenwood Publishing
(s)-Guardian Books—R
Harvest House
Haworth Press—R
Hill Street Press—R
InterVarsity Press—R
Jubilant Press—R
Life Journey Books—R
Liguori
Monarch Books—R
Pacific Press

(s)-Promise Publishing
(s)-Providence House—R
PublishAmerica
Read 'N Run—R
Regnery—R
RiverOak—R
(s)-Robbie Dean Press—R
Silas Publishing—R
(s)-So. Baptist Press—R
Tate Publishing
VMI Publishers
Whitaker House—R

DOCTRINAL

ACU Press
Ambassador-Emerald—R
(s)-American Binding—R
AMG Publishers—R
Baker Books
Baptist Pub. House
Baylor Univ. Press—R
Beacon Hill Press
Bethany House
(s)-Black Forest—R
(s)-Brentwood—R
Bridge-Logos
Broadman & Holman
Canon Press—R
Canticle Books—R
(s)-Catholic Answers—R
Charisma House—R
Christian Focus—R
Christian Publications—R
Christian Writers Ebook—R
College Press—R
Continuum Intl.—R
Created in Christ
(s)-Creation House—R
Cross Cultural—R
CSS Publishing
(s)-DCTS Publishing—R
Discovery House—R
Doubleday
Editorial Portavoz—R
(s)-Emmaus Road Pub.—R
(s)-Essence—R
Fair Havens—R
(s)-Fairway Press—R
Friends United Press—R
(s)-Guardian Books—R
HarperSanFrancisco
Harrison House
Hendrickson—R
Hill Street Press—R
Holy Cross—R
(s)-Impact Christian—R
InterVarsity Press—R

Intl. Awakening—R
Kregel—R
Libros Liguori
Lighthouse Trails Publishing—R
Liturgical Press
Living Books for All
Lutterworth Press
Magnus Press—R
(s)-Master Design—R
MegaGrace Books
Millennium III—R
Monarch Books—R
Openbook—R
Oregon Catholic Press—R
Our Sunday Visitor—R
P & R Publishing—R
Pacific Press
Pauline Books—R
Pickwick Publications—R
(s)-Promise Publishing
(s)-Providence House—R
Read 'N Run—R
RiverOak—R
Rose Publishing
Scepter Publishers—R
Shaw Books—R
(s)-So. Baptist Press—R
Still Waters Revival—R
Tate Publishing
Trinity Foundation—R
UMI Publishing—R
Whitaker House—R
World Publishing—R

DRAMA

A.D. Players Theater
(s)-American Binding—R
Baker's Plays—R
Baker Tritten
Big Idea, Inc.
(s)-Black Forest—R
(s)-Brentwood—R
Contemporary Drama Service
Created in Christ
(s)-Creation House—R
CSS Publishing
Easum, Bandy & Assoc.
(s)-Elderberry Press
Eldridge Pub.
Fair Havens—R
(s)-Fairway Press—R
Genesis Press
Group Publishing
(s)-Guardian Books—R
Iceagle Press—R
InterVarsity Press—R
Lillenas

Meriwether—R
Monarch Books—R
New Hope—R
OnStage Publishing
Openbook—R
Players Press—R
(s)-Poetry of Today
Read 'N Run—R
(s)-So. Baptist Press—R
Spiritual Theater
Tate Publishing
United Church Pub.
(s)-Word for Word
Youth Specialties

E-BOOKS

Algora Publishing—R
Booklocker Jr.
Booklocker.com
Broadman & Holman
Canon Press—R
Christian Writers Ebook—R
College Press—R
Created in Christ
Cross Cultural—R
Descant Publishing
Easum, Bandy & Assoc.
His eBooks
Jireh Publishing
Jossey-Bass
Jubilant Press—R
(s)-Lightning Star Press—R
Liguori
(s)-Master Design—R
MountainView
(s)-One World—R
Paradise Research—R
(s)-Poetry of Today
Read 'N Run—R
(s)-Robbie Dean Press—R
Selah Publishing—R
Smyth & Helwys
Tyndale House—R
Whitaker House—R
Writers Exchange
(s)-Xulon Press—R

ECONOMICS

Algora Publishing—R
Allegiance Books—R
(s)-American Binding—R
Baker Books
Basic Books—R
(s)-Brentwood—R
Canadian Inst. for Law—R
Christian Writers Ebook—R
Christopher Publishing

(s)-Creation House—R
Cross Cultural—R
Dimension Books—R
(s)-Essence—R
Fair Havens—R
(s)-Fairway Press—R
FaithWalk Publishing
(s)-Guardian Books—R
Haworth Press—R
Hill Street Press—R
InterVarsity Press—R
Lutterworth Press
Monarch Books—R
New York Univ. Press
Northfield
Oregon Catholic Press—R
(s)-Promise Publishing
(s)-Providence House—R
Read 'N Run—R
Regnery—R
RiverOak—R
Sheed & Ward—R
Summit Pub. Group—R
Tate Publishing
Trinity Foundation—R
Univ. Press of America—R
VMI Publishers
Whitaker House—R
(s)-Word for Word

ENVIRONMENTAL ISSUES

Algora Publishing—R
Allegiance Books—R
(s)-American Binding—R
Baker Books
Basic Books—R
Baylor Univ. Press—R
(s)-Black Forest—R
Blue Dolphin
Chalice Press
Christian Writers Ebook—R
Christopher Publishing
CSS Publishing
Eerdmans/Young Readers
(s)-Elderberry Press
(s)-Essence—R
Facts on File
Fair Havens—R
(s)-Fairway Press—R
FaithWalk Publishing
Georgetown Univ. Press
(s)-Guardian Books—R
HarperSanFrancisco
Haworth Press—R
Hill Street Press—R

InterVarsity Press—R
Jeremy P. Tarcher
Johns Hopkins—R
Judson Press
Liturgy Training
Lutterworth Press
Monarch Books—R
Openbook—R
Oxford University
Paragon House
(s)-Promise Publishing
Read 'N Run—R
RiverOak—R
Sheed & Ward—R
(s)-So. Baptist Press—R
St. Anthony Messenger
Tate Publishing
United Church Pub.
Univ. Press of America—R
VMI Publishers

ESCHATOLOGY

Ambassador-Emerald—R
Baker Books
Baptist Pub. House
(s)-Black Forest—R
Bridge-Logos
Broadman & Holman
Canon Press—R
Charisma House—R
Christian Focus—R
Christian Writers Ebook—R
College Press—R
Continuum Intl.—R
(s)-Creation House—R
(s)-DCTS Publishing—R
Editores Betania-Caribe
Fair Havens—R
(s)-Fairway Press—R
Four Courts Press—R
(s)-Guardian Books—R
HarperSanFrancisco
Hiddenspring Books
Hill Street Press—R
Kregel—R
Lighthouse Trails Publishing—R
Liguori
(s)-Longwood—R
Lutterworth Press
(s)-Master Design—R
Millennium III—R
Monarch Books—R
Multnomah
Openbook—R
Oregon Catholic Press—R
OSL Publications—R

P & R Publishing—R
Pacific Press
Paulist Press
Pickwick Publications—R
(s)-Promise Publishing
(s)-Providence House—R
Selah Publishing—R
Tate Publishing
Victor Books
Whitaker House—R
(s)-WinePress—R

ETHICS

ACU Press
Alba House—R
Algora Publishing—R
(s)-American Binding—R
Andros Book Publishing
Baker Books
Baylor Univ. Press—R
Bethany House
(s)-Black Forest—R
(s)-Book Publishers Network
(s)-Brentwood—R
Broadman & Holman
(s)-Catholic Answers—R
Chalice Press
Charisma House—R
Christian Focus—R
Christian Writers Ebook—R
Christopher Publishing
Conciliar Press—R
Continuum Intl.—R
(s)-Creation House—R
Cross Cultural—R
CSS Publishing
Discovery House—R
Doubleday
Dover Publications—R
Eerdmans Publishing—R
Eerdmans/Young Readers
(s)-Elderberry Press
(s)-Essence—R
Fair Havens—R
(s)-Fairway Press—R
FaithWalk Publishing
Fortress Press
Geneva Press
Georgetown Univ. Press
Greenwood Publishing
(s)-Guardian Books—R
HarperSanFrancisco
Haworth Press—R
Hiddenspring Books
Hill Street Press—R
Holy Cross—R

Inkling Books—R
InterVarsity Press—R
Jossey-Bass
Judson Press
Libros Liguori
Life Cycle Books—R
Liguori
(s)-Longwood—R
Lutterworth Press
Monarch Books—R
New Seeds Books—R
Open Court—R
Openbook—R
Opine Publishing—R
Oregon Catholic Press—R
Oxford University
P & R Publishing—R
Pacific Press
Paulist Press
Pickwick Publications—R
Pilgrim Press—R
(s)-Poetry of Today
(s)-Promise Publishing
(s)-Providence House—R
Quintessential Books—R
Read 'N Run—R
Regnery—R
Rising Star Press
RiverOak—R
Sheed & Ward—R
Smyth & Helwys
Spence Publishing
St. Augustine's Press—R
Still Waters Revival—R
Tate Publishing
Trinity Foundation—R
Trinity Press Intl.—R
Twenty-Third Publications
United Church Pub.
Univ. Press of America—R
Univ./Ottawa Press
Victor Books
VMI Publishers
Walk Worthy—R
Westminster John Knox
Wood Lake Books—R
Yale Univ. Press—R

ETHNIC/CULTURAL

ACU Press
(s)-Alfred Ali Literary—R
(s)-American Binding—R
Baker Books
Baker Tritten
Basic Books—R
Baylor Univ. Press—R

(s)-Black Forest—R
Broadman & Holman
Carey Library, Wm.—R
Chalice Press
Christian Writers Ebook—R
Christopher Publishing
College Press—R
Concordia
Continuum Intl.—R
(s)-Creation House—R
Cross Cultural—R
Doubleday
Editores Betania-Caribe
Facts on File
(s)-Fairway Press—R
FaithWalk Publishing
Fortress Press
Friends United Press—R
Genesis Press
Georgetown Univ. Press
(s)-Guardian Books—R
Guernica Editions—R
Haworth Press—R
Hensley Publishing—R
Hiddenspring Books
Hill Street Press—R
Holy Cross—R
Howard Publishing
InterVarsity Press—R
Judson Press
Kaleidoscope Press—R
Libros Liguori
Liguori
Living Books for All
Lutterworth Press
Moody Publishers
New York Univ. Press
Oregon Catholic Press—R
Pacific Press
Pilgrim Press—R
(s)-Poetry of Today
(s)-Promise Publishing
(s)-Providence House—R
PublishAmerica
Read 'N Run—R
(s)-Robbie Dean Press—R
Rose Publishing
Shaw Books—R
Standard Publishing
Tate Publishing
Third World Press—R
UMI Publishing—R
United Church Pub.
Univ. of AR Press—R
Univ. Press of America—R
(s)-VESTA—R

VMI Publishers
Walk Worthy—R

EVANGELISM/ WITNESSING

Abagail Press
ACU Press
Ambassador-Emerald—R
(s)-American Binding—R
Baker Books
Baker Tritten
Baptist Pub. House
Barbour Publishing
Baylor Univ. Press—R
Bethany House
(s)-Black Forest—R
(s)-Brentwood—R
Bridge-Logos
Broadman & Holman
Carey Library, Wm.—R
Chariot Books
Charisma House—R
Christian Focus—R
Christian Writers Ebook—R
Christopher Publishing
Church Growth Inst.
Continuum Intl.—R
Created in Christ
(s)-Creation House—R
Crossway Books
CSS Publishing
(s)-DCTS Publishing—R
Discovery House—R
Editorial Portavoz—R
(s)-Essence—R
Fair Havens—R
(s)-Fairway Press—R
Faith Alive Resources
Faith One
FaithWalk Publishing
Forward Movement
Friends United Press—R
Genesis Communications
Gospel Publishing House
Group Publishing
(s)-Guardian Books—R
(s)-Hannibal Books—R
Harrison House
Harvest House
Hiddenspring Books
Hunt Publishing, John
(s)-Impact Christian—R
InterVarsity Press—R
Judson Press
Kregel—R
Lamplighter—R

(s)-Lightning Star Press—R
Living Books for All
(s)-Longwood—R
Lutterworth Press
(s)-Master Design—R
(s)-McDougal Publishing—R
MegaGrace Books
Millennium III—R
Monarch Books—R
Moody Publishers
Multnomah
New Hope—R
New Leaf Press—R
Nexgen
Openbook—R
P & R Publishing—R
Pacific Press
Pilgrim Press—R
(s)-Poetry of Today
(s)-Promise Publishing
(s)-Providence House—R
Read 'N Run—R
RiverOak—R
Rose Publishing
Selah Publishing—R
(s)-So. Baptist Press—R
Still Waters Revival—R
Tate Publishing
Tyndale House—R
VMI Publishers
W Publishing Group
Wesleyan Publishing
Whitaker House—R
Woodland Gospel

EXEGESIS

Baker Books
Baptist Pub. House
Baylor Univ. Press—R
(s)-Black Forest—R
Bridge-Logos
Canon Press—R
(s)-Catholic Answers—R
Christian Focus—R
Christian Writers Ebook—R
Cistercian—R
College Press—R
Continuum Intl.—R
(s)-Creation House—R
Discovery House—R
Eerdmans Publishing—R
(s)-Essence—R
Fair Havens—R
(s)-Fairway Press—R
Geneva Press
Greenwood Publishing
(s)-Guardian Books—R

Hendrickson—R
Hiddenspring Books
InterVarsity Press—R
Johns Hopkins—R
Lutterworth Press
(s)-Master Design—R
(s)-McDougal Publishing—R
Monarch Books—R
Openbook—R
Oregon Catholic Press—R
Oxford University
P & R Publishing—R
Paulist Press
Pickwick Publications—R
(s)-Promise Publishing
(s)-Providence House—R
Read 'N Run—R
Tate Publishing
Twenty-Third Publications
VMI Publishers
Westminster John Knox
Whitaker House—R

EXPOSÉS

(s)-American Binding—R
Baker Books
(s)-Black Forest—R
(s)-Brentwood—R
Christian Writers Ebook—R
(s)-Fairway Press—R
Greenwood Publishing
(s)-Guardian Books—R
Iceagle Press—R
Lighthouse Trails Publishing—R
Lutterworth Press
Open Court—R
(s)-Promise Publishing
Read 'N Run—R
(s)-So. Baptist Press—R

FAITH

Abingdon Press
ACTA Publications
Ambassador Books
(s)-Ambassador House
Ambassador-Emerald—R
(s)-American Binding—R
AMG Publishers—R
Baker Books
Baker Tritten
Baptist Pub. House
Baylor Univ. Press—R
(s)-Black Forest—R
Bridge-Logos
Canticle Books—R
Charisma House—R
Christian Focus—R

Christian Writers Ebook—R
Christopher Publishing
Continuum Intl.—R
Created in Christ
(s)-Creation House—R
Cross Cultural—R
Crossway Books
(s)-DCTS Publishing—R
Destiny Image—R
Discovery House—R
Doubleday
Editores Betania-Caribe
Educational Ministries
Eerdmans Publishing—R
Eerdmans/Young Readers
(s)-Elderberry Press
(s)-Emmaus Road Pub.—R
(s)-Essence—R
Fair Havens—R
(s)-Fairway Press—R
Faith Communications
Faith One
FaithWalk Publishing
(s)-Fruit-Bearer Pub.
Genesis Communications
Genesis Press
Good News Publishers
Gospel Publishing House
Greenwood Publishing
Group Publishing
(s)-Guardian Books—R
HarperSanFrancisco
Harrison House
Harvest House
Hendrickson—R
Hensley Publishing—R
Hiddenspring Books
Hill Street Press—R
InterVarsity Press—R
Jireh Publishing
Jossey-Bass
Legacy Publishers
Loyola Press
Lutterworth Press
Magnus Press—R
(s)-Master Design—R
(s)-McDougal Publishing—R
MegaGrace Books
Monarch Books—R
Multnomah
(s)-Omega House—R
Openbook—R
Opine Publishing—R
Oregon Catholic Press—R
Our Sunday Visitor—R
P & R Publishing—R
Pacific Press

Paraclete Press—R
Paradise Research—R
Paulist Press
Pickwick Publications—R
Pilgrim Press—R
(s)-Poetry of Today
PREP Publishing—R
(s)-Promise Publishing
(s)-Providence House—R
PublishAmerica
Quintessential Books—R
Read 'N Run—R
Rising Star Press
RiverOak—R
Rose Publishing
Scepter Publishers—R
Selah Publishing—R
Shaw Books—R
St. Anthony Messenger
Tate Publishing
(s)-TEACH Services—R
Twenty-Third Publications
Tyndale House—R
UMI Publishing—R
Virginia Pines Press
VMI Publishers
W Publishing Group
Wesleyan Publishing
Whitaker House—R
(s)-WinePress—R
(s)-Word for Word
Youth Specialties

FAMILY LIFE

ACTA Publications
ACU Press
Ambassador Books
(s)-Ambassador House
Ambassador-Emerald—R
(s)-American Binding—R
AMG Publishers—R
Andros Book Publishing
Baker Books
Baker Tritten
Baptist Pub. House
Barbour Publishing
Beacon Hill Press
Bethany House
Big Idea, Inc.
(s)-Black Forest—R
Blue Dolphin
(s)-Book Publishers Network
(s)-Brentwood—R
Bridge-Logos
Broadman & Holman
Canon Press—R
Chalice Press

Chariot Books
Charisma House—R
Christian Family
Christian Focus—R
Christian Publications—R
Christian Writers Ebook—R
Christopher Publishing
Cladach Publishing—R
College Press—R
Concordia
Continuum Intl.—R
Created in Christ
(s)-Creation House—R
Crossway Books
CSS Publishing
(s)-DCTS Publishing—R
Destiny Image—R
Devoted to You
Dimensions for Living
Discovery House—R
Editorial Portavoz—R
Eerdmans/Young Readers
(s)-Elderberry Press
(s)-Emmaus Road Pub.—R
(s)-Essence—R
Fair Havens—R
(s)-Fairway Press—R
Faith Communications
FaithWalk Publishing
Focus on the Family—R
(s)-Fruit-Bearer Pub.
Genesis Communications
Glory Bound Books
Green Key Books
Green Pastures Press—R
Greenwood Publishing
(s)-Guardian Books—R
Harrison House
Harvest House
Haworth Press—R
Hensley Publishing—R
Hiddenspring Books
Hill Street Press—R
Ideals Books
InterVarsity Press—R
Jireh Publishing
Judson Press
Lamplighter—R
Life Cycle Books—R
Life Journey Books—R
Lightwave Publishing
Liguori
Living Books for All
(s)-Longwood—R
Loyola Press
Lutterworth Press
(s)-Master Design—R

(s)-McDougal Publishing—R
Monarch Books—R
Morehouse
Multnomah
New Hope—R
New Leaf Press—R
Openbook—R
Our Sunday Visitor—R
P & R Publishing—R
Pacific Press
Pauline Books—R
Peter Pauper Press
Pilgrim Press—R
(s)-Poetry of Today
PREP Publishing—R
(s)-Promise Publishing
(s)-Providence House—R
PublishAmerica
(s)-Quiet Waters
Quintessential Books—R
Read 'N Run—R
(s)-Recovery Communications
RiverOak—R
Rose Publishing
Selah Publishing—R
Shaw Books—R
Silas Publishing—R
(s)-So. Baptist Press—R
Sower's Press
Spence Publishing
St. Anthony Messenger
Still Waters Revival—R
Tate Publishing
Twenty-Third Publications
Tyndale House—R
VMI Publishers
W Publishing Group
Whitaker House—R
Wood Lake Books—R
Woodland Gospel
(s)-Word for Word

FICTION: ADULT/ RELIGIOUS

Ambassador Books
(s)-Ambassador House
Ambassador-Emerald—R
(s)-American Binding—R
Baker Books
Baker's Plays—R
Barbour Publishing
Bethany House
(s)-Black Forest—R
Blue Dolphin
(s)-Book Publishers Network
Bridge Resources
Broadman & Holman

Canon Press—R
Cerdic-Publications
Charisma House—R
Christian Writers Ebook—R
Christopher Publishing
Cladach Publishing—R
(s)-Creation House—R
Cross Cultural—R
Crossroad Publishing—R
Crossway Books
(s)-DCTS Publishing—R
Descant Publishing
Destiny Image—R
Eerdmans Publishing—R
(s)-Elderberry Press
Elijah Press
(s)-Essence—R
Fair Havens—R
(s)-Fairway Press—R
FaithWalk Publishing
Focus on the Family—R
Frederick Fell—R
Genesis Communications
Genesis Press
Green Pastures Press—R
(s)-Guardian Books—R
Guernica Editions—R
HarperSanFrancisco
Harvest House
Hay House
HeartQuest
Heartsong Presents
His eBooks
Howard Publishing
(s)-Insight Publishing—R
Jireh Publishing
Kregel—R
Lighthouse Trails Publishing—R
(s)-Lightning Star Press—R
(s)-Longwood—R
Love Inspired
(s)-McDougal Publishing—R
Messianic Jewish—R
Millennium III—R
Moms In Print
Moody Publishers
MountainView
Mt. Olive College Press
Multnomah
Northfield
(s)-Omega House—R
Opine Publishing—R
Pacific Press
(s)-Pleasant Word—R
(s)-Poetry of Today
(s)-Providence House—R

PublishAmerica
Quintessential Books—R
Read 'N Run—R
RiverOak—R
Scepter Publishers—R
Selah Publishing—R
(s)-Self Publish Press—R
Shamarah
Shaw Books—R
Silas Publishing—R
Steeple Hill
(s)-Strong Tower
Vintage Romance
Virginia Pines Press
VMI Publishers
Walk Worthy—R
Westbow Press
Whitaker House—R
(s)-WinePress—R
Wood Lake Books—R
(s)-Word for Word
(s)-Xulon Press—R
Zondervan

FICTION: ADVENTURE

Ambassador Books
(s)-Ambassador House
Ambassador-Emerald—R
(s)-American Binding—R
Baker Books
Baker's Plays—R
Baker Tritten
Bethany House
BJU/Journey Forth—R
(s)-Black Forest—R
(s)-Book Publishers Network
(s)-Brentwood—R
Broadman & Holman
Canon Press—R
Chariot Books
Christian Ed. Pub.
Christian Focus—R
Christian Writers Ebook—R
Christopher Publishing
(s)-Creation House—R
Crossway Books
(s)-Elderberry Press
(s)-Essence—R
Fair Havens—R
(s)-Fairway Press—R
FaithWalk Publishing
Focus on the Family—R
Forward Movement
Genesis Communications
Glory Bound Books

Group Publishing
(s)-Guardian Books—R
Harvest House
Howard Publishing
(s)-Insight Publishing—R
Kaleidoscope Press—R
Kregel—R
Lighthouse Trails Publishing—R
(s)-Lightning Star Press—R
(s)-Longwood—R
MountainView
Multnomah
OnStage Publishing
Opine Publishing—R
PREP Publishing—R
(s)-Providence House—R
PublishAmerica
Read 'N Run—R
Selah Publishing—R
(s)-Self Publish Press—R
Shamarah
(s)-So. Baptist Press—R
Tweener Press
Virginia Pines Press
VMI Publishers
Whitaker House—R
(s)-WinePress—R
ZonderKidz
Zondervan

FICTION: ALLEGORY

(s)-Ambassador House
(s)-American Binding—R
Baker Books
Baker Tritten
(s)-Black Forest—R
Canon Press—R
Charisma House—R
Christian Focus—R
Christian Writers Ebook—R
(s)-Creation House—R
CSS Publishing
(s)-Elderberry Press
(s)-Essence—R
(s)-Fairway Press—R
Genesis Communications
Group Publishing
(s)-Guardian Books—R
Howard Publishing
(s)-Insight Publishing—R
Multnomah
Opine Publishing—R
(s)-Providence House—R
Read 'N Run—R
Selah Publishing—R
VMI Publishers

Whitaker House—R
(s)-WinePress—R

FICTION: BIBLICAL

(s)-Ambassador House
(s)-American Binding—R
Baker Books
Baker's Plays—R
Baker Tritten
(s)-Black Forest—R
(s)-Brentwood—R
Canon Press—R
Charisma House—R
Charisma Kids
Christian Focus—R
Christian Writers Ebook—R
Christopher Publishing
Cladach Publishing—R
College Press—R
(s)-Creation House—R
Creative Teaching
(s)-DCTS Publishing—R
Destiny Image—R
Eerdmans Publishing—R
(s)-Elderberry Press
Fair Havens—R
(s)-Fairway Press—R
Forward Movement
Genesis Communications
Group Publishing
(s)-Guardian Books—R
Howard Publishing
(s)-Insight Publishing—R
(s)-Longwood—R
Messianic Jewish—R
Moody Publishers
Mt. Olive College Press
Multnomah
(s)-Omega House—R
Opine Publishing—R
Pacific Press
(s)-Poetry of Today
PREP Publishing—R
(s)-Providence House—R
PublishAmerica
Quintessential Books—R
Ragged Edge—R
Read 'N Run—R
(s)-Self Publish Press—R
(s)-So. Baptist Press—R
Steeple Hill
(s)-Strong Tower
VMI Publishers
Walk Worthy—R
Whitaker House—R
(s)-WinePress—R

(s)-Word for Word
ZonderKidz

FICTION: CHICK LIT*

Christian Writers Ebook—R
(s)-Elderberry Press
Howard Publishing
(s)-Insight Publishing—R
Kregel—R
Love Inspired
Multnomah
Opine Publishing—R
PublishAmerica
RiverOak—R
Steeple Hill
Westbow Press
(s)-WinePress—R

FICTION: CONTEMPORARY

Ambassador Books
(s)-Ambassador House
(s)-American Binding—R
Baker Books
Baker Tritten
Bethany House
(s)-Black Forest—R
(s)-Brentwood—R
Broadman & Holman
Canon Press—R
Chariot Books
Charisma Kids
Christian Ed. Pub.
Christian Focus—R
Christian Writers Ebook—R
Cladach Publishing—R
(s)-Creation House—R
Creative Teaching
Crossway Books
Descant Publishing
Destiny Image—R
(s)-Elderberry Press
(s)-Essence—R
(s)-Fairway Press—R
FaithWalk Publishing
Focus on the Family—R
Glory Bound Books
(s)-Guardian Books—R
HarperSanFrancisco
Harvest House
HeartQuest
Heartsong Presents
Hill Street Press—R
Howard Publishing
Iceagle Press—R
(s)-Insight Publishing—R
Jireh Publishing

Kindred Productions
Kregel—R
Lighthouse Trails Publishing—R
(s)-Longwood—R
Love Inspired
(s)-McDougal Publishing—R
MegaGrace Books
Meriwether—R
Moody Publishers
MountainView
Mt. Olive College Press
Multnomah
Northfield
(s)-One World—R
OnStage Publishing
Opine Publishing—R
(s)-Providence House—R
PublishAmerica
Putnam's Sons, G. P
Quintessential Books—R
Read 'N Run—R
RiverOak—R
(s)-Self Publish Press—R
(s)-So. Baptist Press—R
Steeple Hill
Third World Press—R
Tweener Press
VMI Publishers
Walk Worthy—R
Westbow Press
Whitaker House—R
(s)-WinePress—R
Zondervan

FICTION: ETHNIC

(s)-American Binding—R
Baker Books
Baker Tritten
(s)-Black Forest—R
Blue Dolphin
Boyds Mills Press—R
Canon Press—R
Christian Focus—R
Christian Writers Ebook—R
(s)-Creation House—R
(s)-DCTS Publishing—R
Destiny Image—R
(s)-Elderberry Press
(s)-Essence—R
(s)-Fairway Press—R
Focus on the Family—R
Genesis Communications
(s)-Guardian Books—R
Guernica Editions—R
(s)-Insight Publishing—R
Kaleidoscope Press—R

Living Books for All
Messianic Jewish—R
(s)-One World—R
Opine Publishing—R
(s)-Poetry of Today
PublishAmerica
Putnam's Sons, G. P
Third World Press—R
Walk Worthy—R
(s)-WinePress—R

FICTION: FANTASY

(s)-American Binding—R
AMG Publishers—R
Baker Tritten
Big Idea, Inc.
BJU/Journey Forth—R
(s)-Black Forest—R
(s)-Book Publishers Network
Canon Press—R
Chariot Books
Charisma House—R
Christian Writers Ebook—R
(s)-Creation House—R
Descant Publishing
Destiny Image—R
Dover Publications—R
(s)-Elderberry Press
(s)-Fairway Press—R
Forward Movement
Genesis Communications
(s)-Guardian Books—R
(s)-Insight Publishing—R
Multnomah
OnStage Publishing
PublishAmerica
Putnam's Sons, G. P
Read 'N Run—R
Shamarah
VMI Publishers
Whitaker House—R
(s)-WinePress—R
ZonderKidz

FICTION: FRONTIER

Ambassador-Emerald—R
(s)-American Binding—R
Baker Books
Baker Tritten
Bethany House
BJU/Journey Forth—R
(s)-Black Forest—R
(s)-Brentwood—R
Canon Press—R
Christian Writers Ebook—R
Christopher Publishing
(s)-Elderberry Press

(s)-Fairway Press—R
Glory Bound Books
(s)-Guardian Books—R
Howard Publishing
(s)-Insight Publishing—R
Kaleidoscope Press—R
(s)-Longwood—R
MountainView
Opine Publishing—R
(s)-Poetry of Today
PublishAmerica
Read 'N Run—R
RiverOak—R
(s)-Self Publish Press—R
(s)-So. Baptist Press—R
VMI Publishers
Whitaker House—R
(s)-WinePress—R
ZonderKidz

FICTION: FRONTIER/ROMANCE

Ambassador-Emerald—R
(s)-American Binding—R
Baker Books
Barbour Publishing
Bethany House
(s)-Black Forest—R
(s)-Brentwood—R
Christian Writers Ebook—R
(s)-Elderberry Press
(s)-Fairway Press—R
(s)-Guardian Books—R
Heartsong Presents
Howard Publishing
(s)-Insight Publishing—R
(s)-Lightning Star Press—R
(s)-Longwood—R
Love Inspired
MountainView
Multnomah
Opine Publishing—R
(s)-Poetry of Today
PREP Publishing—R
PublishAmerica
Read 'N Run—R
RiverOak—R
(s)-Self Publish Press—R
(s)-So. Baptist Press—R
Vintage Romance
VMI Publishers
Whitaker House—R
(s)-WinePress—R

FICTION: HISTORICAL

Ambassador Books
Ambassador-Emerald—R

(s)-American Binding—R
Baker Books
Baker's Plays—R
Baker Tritten
Bethany House
BJU/Journey Forth—R
(s)-Black Forest—R
Boyds Mills Press—R
(s)-Brentwood—R
Broadman & Holman
Canon Press—R
Chariot Books
Charisma House—R
Charisma Kids
Christian Focus—R
Christian Writers Ebook—R
Christopher Publishing
(s)-Creation House—R
Crossroad Publishing—R
Crossway Books
Eerdmans Publishing—R
Eerdmans/Young Readers
(s)-Elderberry Press
(s)-Essence—R
Fair Havens—R
(s)-Fairway Press—R
Faith Kids Books
Green Pastures Press—R
(s)-Guardian Books—R
Howard Publishing
Iceagle Press—R
(s)-Inheritance Publications—R
(s)-Insight Publishing—R
(s)-Longwood—R
Love Inspired
Millennium III—R
Moody Publishers
MountainView
Northfield
OnStage Publishing
Opine Publishing—R
P & R Publishing—R
(s)-Providence House—R
PublishAmerica
Putnam's Sons, G. P
Quintessential Books—R
Ragged Edge—R
Read 'N Run—R
RiverOak—R
(s)-Self Publish Press—R
Shamarah
(s)-So. Baptist Press—R
Third World Press—R
VMI Publishers
Whitaker House—R
(s)-WinePress—R
ZonderKidz

Zondervan

FICTION: HISTORICAL/ ROMANCE

Ambassador-Emerald—R
(s)-American Binding—R
Baker Books
Barbour Publishing
Bethany House
(s)-Black Forest—R
(s)-Book Publishers Network
(s)-Brentwood—R
Broadman & Holman
Christian Writers Ebook—R
(s)-Elderberry Press
(s)-Fairway Press—R
(s)-Guardian Books—R
HeartQuest
Heartsong Presents
Howard Publishing
(s)-Insight Publishing—R
(s)-Longwood—R
Love Inspired
MountainView
Multnomah
Opine Publishing—R
(s)-Poetry of Today
PublishAmerica
Putnam's Sons, G. P
Read 'N Run—R
RiverOak—R
(s)-Self Publish Press—R
(s)-So. Baptist Press—R
Steeple Hill
Vintage Romance
VMI Publishers
Whitaker House—R
(s)-WinePress—R

FICTION: HUMOR

Ambassador Books
(s)-Ambassador House
Ambassador-Emerald—R
(s)-American Binding—R
Baker Books
Baker's Plays—R
Baker Tritten
Big Idea, Inc.
BJU/Journey Forth—R
(s)-Black Forest—R
Canon Press—R
Christian Writers Ebook—R
Christopher Publishing
(s)-Elderberry Press
(s)-Essence—R
(s)-Fairway Press—R
Focus on the Family—R

Genesis Communications
Glory Bound Books
(s)-Guardian Books—R
Howard Publishing
(s)-Insight Publishing—R
Kaleidoscope Press—R
(s)-Longwood—R
Love Inspired
Meriwether—R
OnStage Publishing
Opine Publishing—R
(s)-Poetry of Today
PublishAmerica
Putnam's Sons, G. P
Read 'N Run—R
RiverOak—R
Selah Publishing—R
Shamarah
Vintage Romance
VMI Publishers
(s)-WinePress—R
ZonderKidz

FICTION: JUVENILE (Ages 8-12)

Ambassador Books
(s)-Ambassador House
Ambassador-Emerald—R
(s)-American Binding—R
Baker Books
Baker's Plays—R
Baker Tritten
Bethany House
Big Idea, Inc.
BJU/Journey Forth—R
(s)-Black Forest—R
Boyds Mills Press—R
Branden Publishing
Canon Press—R
Chariot Books
Christian Focus—R
(s)-Creation House—R
(s)-DCTS Publishing—R
Dover Publications—R
Eerdmans/Young Readers
(s)-Elderberry Press
(s)-Essence—R
Fair Havens—R
(s)-Fairway Press—R
Faith Kids Books
Forward Movement
Genesis Communications
Glory Bound Books
Green Pastures Press—R
Group Publishing
(s)-Guardian Books—R
His eBooks

(s)-Insight Publishing—R
Kaleidoscope Press—R
Kindred Productions
Kregel—R
Lamplighter—R
Legacy Press—R
(s)-Lightning Star Press—R
Lightwave Publishing
Liguori
(s)-Longwood—R
Moody Publishers
Multnomah
Northfield
OnStage Publishing
Opine Publishing—R
P & R Publishing—R
Pacific Press
Pelican Publishing—R
(s)-Pleasant Word—R
PublishAmerica
Putnam's Sons, G. P
Read 'N Run—R
(s)-Robbie Dean Press—R
Selah Publishing—R
(s)-Self Publish Press—R
Third World Press—R
Tweener Press
VMI Publishers
Walk Worthy—R
(s)-WinePress—R
ZonderKidz

FICTION: LITERARY

Ambassador Books
(s)-Ambassador House
Ambassador-Emerald—R
(s)-American Binding—R
Baker Books
BJU/Journey Forth—R
(s)-Black Forest—R
Broadman & Holman
Canon Press—R
Christian Writers Ebook—R
Christopher Publishing
Cladach Publishing—R
Crane Hill—R
Crossway Books
Dover Publications—R
Eerdmans Publishing—R
Eerdmans/Young Readers
(s)-Elderberry Press
(s)-Fairway Press—R
FaithWalk Publishing
Focus on the Family—R
Genesis Press
(s)-Guardian Books—R
Guernica Editions—R

Hill Street Press—R
Howard Publishing
(s)-Insight Publishing—R
Love Inspired
Millennium III—R
Moody Publishers
Mt. Olive College Press
Multnomah
Northfield
OnStage Publishing
Opine Publishing—R
(s)-Poetry of Today
PREP Publishing—R
PublishAmerica
Putnam's Sons, G. P
Quintessential Books—R
Read 'N Run—R
RiverOak—R
(s)-Self Publish Press—R
Shamarah
Skysong Press
Steeple Hill
Third World Press—R
Virginia Pines Press
VMI Publishers
Walk Worthy—R
(s)-WinePress—R

FICTION: MYSTERY/ROMANCE

(s)-Ambassador House
(s)-American Binding—R
Baker Books
Bethany House
(s)-Black Forest—R
(s)-Book Publishers Network
(s)-Brentwood—R
Chariot Books
Christian Writers Ebook—R
Destiny Image—R
(s)-Elderberry Press
(s)-Fairway Press—R
Genesis Press
(s)-Guardian Books—R
Harvest House
Heartsong Presents
Howard Publishing
(s)-Insight Publishing—R
Kregel—R
(s)-Lightning Star Press—R
(s)-Longwood—R
Love Inspired
MountainView
Multnomah
OnStage Publishing
Opine Publishing—R

PREP Publishing—R
PublishAmerica
Read 'N Run—R
RiverOak—R
Selah Publishing—R
(s)-Self Publish Press—R
(s)-So. Baptist Press—R
Steeple Hill
Vintage Romance
VMI Publishers
Whitaker House—R
(s)-WinePress—R
Zondervan

FICTION: MYSTERY/ SUSPENSE

(s)-Ambassador House
Ambassador-Emerald—R
(s)-American Binding—R
Baker Books
Bethany House
(s)-Black Forest—R
Christian Ed. Pub.
Christian Focus—R
Christian Writers Ebook—R
Cumberland House
Descant Publishing
(s)-Elderberry Press
(s)-Essence—R
Fair Havens—R
(s)-Fairway Press—R
Focus on the Family—R
Glory Bound Books
(s)-Guardian Books—R
HeartQuest
Howard Publishing
(s)-Insight Publishing—R
Kregel—R
(s)-Longwood—R
Love Inspired
Moody Publishers
MountainView
Mt. Olive College Press
Multnomah
OnStage Publishing
Opine Publishing—R
PublishAmerica
Putnam's Sons, G. P
Read 'N Run—R
Selah Publishing—R
(s)-Self Publish Press—R
VMI Publishers
(s)-WinePress—R
ZonderKidz
Zondervan

FICTION: NOVELLAS

(s)-American Binding—R
Baker Books
Canon Press—R
Chariot Books
Christian Writers Ebook—R
(s)-Elderberry Press
(s)-Fairway Press—R
(s)-Guardian Books—R
Howard Publishing
(s)-Insight Publishing—R
MegaGrace Books
MountainView
Opine Publishing—R
PublishAmerica
Read 'N Run—R
Vintage Romance
(s)-Word for Word

FICTION: PLAYS

A.D. Players Theater
(s)-American Binding—R
Baker's Plays—R
(s)-Brentwood—R
Bridge Resources
Canon Press—R
Dover Publications—R
Eldridge Pub.
(s)-Essence—R
(s)-Fairway Press—R
Group Publishing
(s)-Guardian Books—R
Lillenas
Meriwether—R
Mt. Olive College Press
Players Press—R
Read 'N Run—R
Resource Publications
(s)-So. Baptist Press—R
Third World Press—R

FICTION: ROMANCE

Ambassador Books
(s)-Ambassador House
(s)-American Binding—R
Baker Books
Barbour Publishing
Bethany House
(s)-Black Forest—R
Christian Writers Ebook—R
(s)-Elderberry Press
(s)-Fairway Press—R
Genesis Press
(s)-Guardian Books—R
(s)-Hannibal Books—R

Harvest House
HeartQuest
Heartsong Presents
Howard Publishing
Iceagle Press—R
(s)-Insight Publishing—R
(s)-Lightning Star Press—R
(s)-Longwood—R
Love Inspired
MountainView
Multnomah
OnStage Publishing
Opine Publishing—R
(s)-Poetry of Today
PREP Publishing—R
PublishAmerica
Read 'N Run—R
RiverOak—R
Selah Publishing—R
Steeple Hill
Vintage Romance
VMI Publishers
Whitaker House—R
(s)-WinePress—R

FICTION: SCIENCE FICTION

(s)-American Binding—R
(s)-Black Forest—R
Canon Press—R
Charisma House—R
Christian Writers Ebook—R
Descant Publishing
Destiny Image—R
Dover Publications—R
(s)-Elderberry Press
Fair Havens—R
(s)-Fairway Press—R
Forward Movement
Genesis Communications
Genesis Press
Group Publishing
(s)-Guardian Books—R
Howard Publishing
(s)-Insight Publishing—R
(s)-Lightning Star Press—R
Multnomah
OnStage Publishing
(s)-Poetry of Today
PublishAmerica
Putnam's Sons, G. P
Read 'N Run—R
RiverOak—R
Skysong Press
VMI Publishers
Whitaker House—R

(s)-WinePress—R
ZonderKidz

FICTION: SHORT STORY COLLECTION

(s)-American Binding—R
Baker Books
Baker Tritten
(s)-Black Forest—R
Canon Press—R
Christian Writers Ebook—R
(s)-DCTS Publishing—R
Eerdmans Publishing—R
(s)-Elderberry Press
(s)-Essence—R
(s)-Fairway Press—R
Glory Bound Books
Green Pastures Press—R
Group Publishing
(s)-Guardian Books—R
(s)-Insight Publishing—R
Kaleidoscope Press—R
(s)-Lightning Star Press—R
(s)-Longwood—R
MountainView
Mt. Olive College Press
Opine Publishing—R
PublishAmerica
Read 'N Run—R
RiverOak—R
Third World Press—R
VMI Publishers
Walk Worthy—R
Whitaker House—R

FICTION: SPECULATIVE

(s)-American Binding—R
Baker Books
Canon Press—R
Charisma House—R
Christian Writers Ebook—R
(s)-Elderberry Press
Howard Publishing
Iceagle Press—R
(s)-Insight Publishing—R
Multnomah
PublishAmerica
RiverOak—R
VMI Publishers
Whitaker House—R
(s)-WinePress—R

FICTION: TEEN/YOUNG ADULT

Ambassador Books
(s)-Ambassador House

(s)-American Binding—R
AMG Publishers—R
Baker Books
Baker Tritten
Bethany House
Big Idea, Inc.
BJU/Journey Forth—R
(s)-Book Publishers Network
Boyds Mills Press—R
Canon Press—R
Christian Focus—R
Christian Writers Ebook—R
(s)-Creation House—R
Eerdmans/Young Readers
(s)-Elderberry Press
(s)-Essence—R
Fair Havens—R
(s)-Fairway Press—R
Faith Communications
Focus on the Family—R
Forward Movement
Genesis Communications
Glory Bound Books
Green Pastures Press—R
Group Publishing
(s)-Guardian Books—R
(s)-Insight Publishing—R
Kregel—R
(s)-Lightning Star Press—R
(s)-Longwood—R
Moody Publishers
MountainView
Multnomah
New Canaan
Northfield
Opine Publishing—R
P & R Publishing—R
(s)-Pleasant Word—R
PublishAmerica
Putnam's Sons, G. P
Ragged Edge—R
Read 'N Run—R
Selah Publishing—R
Third World Press—R
Virginia Pines Press
Walk Worthy—R
(s)-WinePress—R
Youth Specialties
Zondervan

FICTION: WESTERNS

(s)-American Binding—R
Baker Books
Baker Tritten
BJU/Journey Forth—R
(s)-Black Forest—R

Canon Press—R
Christian Writers Ebook—R
(s)-Elderberry Press
(s)-Fairway Press—R
Glory Bound Books
Howard Publishing
(s)-Insight Publishing—R
(s)-Longwood—R
Opine Publishing—R
(s)-Poetry of Today
PublishAmerica
RiverOak—R
VMI Publishers
Whitaker House—R
(s)-WinePress—R

FORGIVENESS

(s)-American Binding—R
Baker Tritten
(s)-Black Forest—R
Charisma House—R
Christian Writers Ebook—R
Christopher Publishing
Continuum Intl.—R
Created in Christ
(s)-Creation House—R
Crossway Books
(s)-DCTS Publishing—R
Doubleday
Editorial Portavoz—R
Eerdmans Publishing—R
Eerdmans/Young Readers
(s)-Elderberry Press
(s)-Emmaus Road Pub.—R
Fair Havens—R
FaithWalk Publishing
Genesis Communications
Good News Publishers
Gospel Publishing House
Greenwood Publishing
Harrison House
Hiddenspring Books
Howard Publishing
InterVarsity Press—R
Jossey-Bass
Life Journey Books—R
(s)-Master Design—R
MegaGrace Books
Morehouse
Multnomah
Opine Publishing—R
Our Sunday Visitor—R
Pacific Press
Pilgrim Press—R
(s)-Providence House—R
PublishAmerica
Silas Publishing—R

St. Anthony Messenger
Tate Publishing
Twenty-Third Publications
VMI Publishers
Whitaker House—R

GAMES/CRAFTS

Ambassador-Emerald—R
Baker Books
Barbour Publishing
Big Idea, Inc.
Christian Focus—R
Contemporary Drama Service
(s)-Creation House—R
Creative Teaching
Devoted to You
(s)-Essence—R
(s)-Fairway Press—R
Frederick Fell—R
(s)-Guardian Books—R
Harcourt Religion
Harvest House
Hunt Publishing, John
Jubilant Press—R
Judson Press
Kaleidoscope Press—R
Legacy Press—R
Lightwave Publishing
Lutterworth Press
Meriwether—R
Monarch Books—R
Players Press—R
Rainbow Publishers—R
Rose Publishing
Shining Star
Standard Publishing
Tate Publishing
Wood Lake Books—R
(s)-Word for Word

GIFT BOOKS

ACTA Publications
Ambassador Books
Ambassador-Emerald—R
(s)-American Binding—R
Baker Books
Ballantine Books
Barbour Publishing
Big Idea, Inc.
(s)-Black Forest—R
Blue Mountain Arts
(s)-Book Publishers Network
Bridge-Logos
Broadman & Holman
Chariot Books
Christian Focus—R
Christian Writers Ebook—R

Concordia
Contemporary Drama Service
Countryman, J.
(s)-Creation House—R
Cumberland House
(s)-DCTS Publishing—R
Devoted to You
Dimensions for Living
Editorial Portavoz—R
Eerdmans Publishing—R
(s)-Elderberry Press
(s)-Essence—R
(s)-Fairway Press—R
Faith Communications
FamilyLife Publishing
Focus on the Family—R
Genesis Communications
Green Pastures Press—R
(s)-Guardian Books—R
HarperSanFrancisco
Harvest House
Hensley Publishing—R
Hill Street Press—R
Howard Publishing
Hunt Publishing, John
Judson Press
Kaleidoscope Press—R
Liguori
(s)-Longwood—R
Lutterworth Press
Mt. Olive College Press
Multnomah
New Leaf Press—R
Opine Publishing—R
Our Sunday Visitor—R
Paulist Press
Peter Pauper Press
(s)-Poetry of Today
(s)-Promise Publishing
(s)-Providence House—R
(s)-Robbie Dean Press—R
Shaw Books—R
Tate Publishing
VMI Publishers
Whitaker House—R
(s)-WinePress—R
Woodland Gospel

GROUP STUDY BOOKS

(s)-American Binding—R
AMG Publishers—R
Baker Books
Baker Tritten
Baptist Pub. House
(s)-Brentwood—R
Bridge Resources
Carey Library, Wm.—R

Charisma House—R
Christian Focus—R
Christian Writers Ebook—R
Christopher Publishing
Continuum Intl.—R
Created in Christ
(s)-Creation House—R
CSS Publishing
Easum, Bandy & Assoc.
Educational Ministries
(s)-Emmaus Road Pub.—R
(s)-Essence—R
Fair Havens—R
(s)-Fairway Press—R
Focus on the Family—R
Genesis Communications
Gospel Publishing House
(s)-Guardian Books—R
Harvest House
Hensley Publishing—R
Hill Street Press—R
InterVarsity Press—R
Judson Press
Liguori
(s)-Longwood—R
Lutterworth Press
(s)-Master Design—R
Monarch Books—R
New Hope—R
Nexgen
Oregon Catholic Press—R
P & R Publishing—R
Pacific Press
Pilgrim Press—R
(s)-Promise Publishing
(s)-Providence House—R
Rose Publishing
Smyth & Helwys
(s)-So. Baptist Press—R
Tate Publishing
UMI Publishing—R
VMI Publishers
(s)-Word for Word

HEALING

Abagail Press
(s)-American Binding—R
Baker Books
Bethany House
(s)-Black Forest—R
Blue Dolphin
(s)-Book Publishers Network
(s)-Brentwood—R
Bridge-Logos
Canticle Books—R
Chariot Books
Charisma House—R

Christian Focus—R
Christian Writers Ebook—R
Christopher Publishing
Continuum Intl.—R
Created in Christ
(s)-Creation House—R
CSS Publishing
Destiny Image—R
(s)-Essence—R
(s)-Fairway Press—R
Faith One
FaithWalk Publishing
Gilgal
Greenwood Publishing
(s)-Guardian Books—R
HarperSanFrancisco
Harrison House
Haworth Press—R
Hay House
Hensley Publishing—R
Hiddenspring Books
Hill Street Press—R
Hunt Publishing, John
Iceagle Press—R
(s)-Impact Christian—R
InterVarsity Press—R
Jireh Publishing
Jossey-Bass
Life Journey Books—R
(s)-Lightning Star Press—R
Liguori
Living Books for All
Loyola Press
Lutterworth Press
Magnus Press—R
(s)-McDougal Publishing—R
Monarch Books—R
Northstone—R
(s)-Omega House—R
Oregon Catholic Press—R
OSL Publications—R
Pacific Press
Paradise Research—R
Paulist Press
Pilgrim Press—R
PREP Publishing—R
(s)-Promise Publishing
(s)-Providence House—R
PublishAmerica
Read 'N Run—R
(s)-Recovery Communications
RiverOak—R
Selah Publishing—R
Silas Publishing—R
Siloam Press
(s)-So. Baptist Press—R
Tate Publishing

United Church Pub.
VMI Publishers
Whitaker House—R
Wood Lake Books—R

HEALTH

(s)-American Binding—R
Baker Books
Ballantine Books
Basic Books—R
Bethany House
(s)-Black Forest—R
Blue Dolphin
(s)-Book Publishers Network
(s)-Brentwood—R
Bridge-Logos
Charisma House—R
Christian Writers Ebook—R
Christopher Publishing
Cladach Publishing—R
Continuum Intl.—R
Crane Hill—R
Created in Christ
(s)-Creation House—R
(s)-Elderberry Press
(s)-Essence—R
Facts on File
Fair Havens—R
(s)-Fairway Press—R
Faith One
Frederick Fell—R
Genesis Communications
Greenwood Publishing
(s)-Guardian Books—R
HarperSanFrancisco
Harrison House
Harvest House
Haworth Press—R
Hay House
Hill Street Press—R
Hunt Publishing, John
Jeremy P. Tarcher
Kaleidoscope Press—R
Legacy Publishers
Life Cycle Books—R
Lighthouse Trails Publishing—R
Liguori
(s)-Longwood—R
Loyola Press
Lutterworth Press
Monarch Books—R
Pacific Press
(s)-Promise Publishing
(s)-Providence House—R
Read 'N Run—R
(s)-Recovery Communications
Regnery—R

RiverOak—R
Shaw Books—R
Silas Publishing—R
Siloam Press
(s)-So. Baptist Press—R
Square One—R
Summit Pub. Group—R
Tate Publishing
(s)-TEACH Services—R
Third World Press—R
(s)-VESTA—R
VMI Publishers
Whitaker House—R
Wood Lake Books—R

HISTORICAL

Algora Publishing—R
Allegiance Books—R
Ambassador-Emerald—R
(s)-American Binding—R
Baker Books
Basic Books—R
Bethany House
(s)-Black Forest—R
(s)-Book Publishers Network
(s)-Brentwood—R
Canon Press—R
Carey Library, Wm.—R
(s)-Catholic Answers—R
Cerdic-Publications
Christian Focus—R
Christian Writers Ebook—R
Christopher Publishing
Cistercian—R
Conciliar Press—R
Continuum Intl.—R
(s)-Creation House—R
Cross Cultural—R
Cumberland House
Custom Communications
Dimension Books—R
Eerdmans Publishing—R
Eerdmans/Young Readers
(s)-Elderberry Press
(s)-Essence—R
ETC Publications
Facts on File
Fair Havens—R
(s)-Fairway Press—R
FaithWalk Publishing
Four Courts Press—R
Friends United Press—R
Greenwood Publishing
(s)-Guardian Books—R
HarperSanFrancisco
Hill Street Press—R

Holy Cross—R
Hunt Publishing, John
(s)-Impact Christian—R
Inkling Books—R
InterVarsity Press—R
Johns Hopkins—R
Judson Press
Liguori
(s)-Longwood—R
Lutterworth Press
Magnus Press—R
(s)-Master Design—R
Mercer Univ. Press—R
Monarch Books—R
Mt. Olive College Press
New York Univ. Press
Northstone—R
OnStage Publishing
Oregon Catholic Press—R
Oxford University
(s)-Promise Publishing
(s)-Providence House—R
PublishAmerica
Quintessential Books—R
Read 'N Run—R
Regnery—R
RiverOak—R
Rose Publishing
Scepter Publishers—R
(s)-So. Baptist Press—R
St. Augustine's Press—R
Still Waters Revival—R
Tate Publishing
Third World Press—R
Trinity Foundation—R
United Church Pub.
Univ. of AR Press—R
Univ. Press of America—R
Univ./Ottawa Press
(s)-VESTA—R
Virginia Pines Press
Whitaker House—R
(s)-Winer Foundation—R
Wood Lake Books—R
(s)-Word for Word

HOLIDAY/SEASONAL

Ambassador Books
(s)-American Binding—R
Baker Tritten
Chariot Books
Charisma House—R
Christian Writers Ebook—R
Christopher Publishing
Continuum Intl.—R
(s)-Creation House—R

Cumberland House
Doubleday
Educational Ministries
Eerdmans/Young Readers
Focus on the Family—R
Genesis Communications
Glory Bound Books
Gospel Publishing House
Greenwood Publishing
Harvest House
InterVarsity Press—R
(s)-Longwood—R
(s)-Master Design—R
Meriwether—R
Our Sunday Visitor—R
P & R Publishing—R
(s)-Providence House—R
Tate Publishing
VMI Publishers
Whitaker House—R

HOLY SPIRIT

(s)-American Binding—R
Baker Tritten
Baylor Univ. Press—R
(s)-Black Forest—R
Canticle Books—R
Charisma House—R
Christian Writers Ebook—R
Christopher Publishing
Continuum Intl.—R
Created in Christ
(s)-Creation House—R
Destiny Image—R
(s)-Emmaus Road Pub.—R
(s)-Fruit-Bearer Pub.
Gospel Publishing House
Greenwood Publishing
(s)-Hannibal Books—R
Harrison House
Iceagle Press—R
InterVarsity Press—R
Kregel—R
Magnus Press—R
(s)-Master Design—R
Multnomah
Our Sunday Visitor—R
P & R Publishing—R
Pacific Press
Pathway Press
Pilgrim Press—R
(s)-Poetry of Today
(s)-Providence House—R
PublishAmerica
Rose Publishing
Tate Publishing

VMI Publishers
Wesleyan Publishing
Westminster John Knox
Whitaker House—R
(s)-Word for Word

HOMESCHOOLING RESOURCES

Andros Book Publishing
Baker Books
Big Idea, Inc.
(s)-Book Publishers Network
(s)-Brentwood—R
Broadman & Holman
Canon Press—R
Christian Focus—R
Christian Publications—R
Christian Writers Ebook—R
Created in Christ
(s)-Creation House—R
(s)-Emmaus Road Pub.—R
Fair Havens—R
(s)-Fairway Press—R
(s)-Hannibal Books—R
Heart of Wisdom
Jubilant Press—R
(s)-Master Design—R
McRuffy Press
New Canaan
Our Sunday Visitor—R
P & R Publishing—R
(s)-Providence House—R
Rainbow Publishers—R
Rose Publishing
Scarecrow Press—R
Shaw Books—R
Tate Publishing
Virginia Pines Press
(s)-Word for Word
Wordsmiths

HOMILETICS

Abingdon Press
Alba House—R
Baker Books
(s)-Black Forest—R
Bridge-Logos
Broadman & Holman
Chalice Press
Christian Focus—R
Christian Writers Ebook—R
Cistercian—R
Continuum Intl.—R
(s)-Creation House—R
CSS Publishing
(s)-DCTS Publishing—R

Eerdmans Publishing—R
Fair Havens—R
(s)-Fairway Press—R
Group Publishing
(s)-Guardian Books—R
Hendrickson—R
Hiddenspring Books
InterVarsity Press—R
Judson Press
Kregel—R
Logion Press
Lutterworth Press
(s)-Master Design—R
Monarch Books—R
Oregon Catholic Press—R
OSL Publications—R
Paulist Press
(s)-Promise Publishing
(s)-Providence House—R
Resource Publications
Twenty-Third Publications
Victor Books
VMI Publishers
Westminster John Knox
Whitaker House—R
Wood Lake Books—R

HOW-TO

(s)-American Binding—R
Baker Books
Ballantine Books
Bethany House
(s)-Black Forest—R
Blue Dolphin
(s)-Book Publishers Network
(s)-Brentwood—R
Bridge-Logos
Broadman & Holman
Christian Focus—R
Christian Writers Ebook—R
Christopher Publishing
Church Growth Inst.
(s)-Creation House—R
Descant Publishing
Destiny Image—R
Discovery House—R
Educational Ministries
(s)-Elderberry Press
(s)-Essence—R
Fair Havens—R
(s)-Fairway Press—R
FaithWalk Publishing
Frederick Fell—R
Genesis Communications
Gilgal
Greenwood Publishing

(s)-Guardian Books—R
(s)-Hannibal Books—R
Harcourt Religion
Hill Street Press—R
Hunt Publishing, John
Inkling Books—R
InterVarsity Press—R
Jeremy P. Tarcher
Judson Press
Kaleidoscope Press—R
(s)-Lightning Star Press—R
Lillenas
(s)-Longwood—R
Lutterworth Press
MegaGrace Books
Meriwether—R
Monarch Books—R
Mt. Olive College Press
Oregon Catholic Press—R
Pacific Press
Perigee Books
Players Press—R
(s)-Poetry of Today
(s)-Promise Publishing
(s)-Providence House—R
Read 'N Run—R
(s)-Recovery Communications
RiverOak—R
(s)-So. Baptist Press—R
Standard Publishing
Still Waters Revival—R
Tate Publishing
VMI Publishers
Walk Worthy—R
Wilshire Book—R
(s)-Winer Foundation—R
(s)-Word for Word

HUMOR

(s)-American Binding—R
AMG Publishers—R
Baker Books
Ballantine Books
(s)-Black Forest—R
Blue Dolphin
(s)-Brentwood—R
Bridge-Logos
Broadman & Holman
Canon Press—R
Chariot Books
Christian Writers Ebook—R
Countryman, J.
Crane Hill—R
(s)-Creation House—R
CSS Publishing
Dimension Books—R

(s)-Elderberry Press
(s)-Essence—R
(s)-Fairway Press—R
Friends United Press—R
Genesis Communications
Glory Bound Books
(s)-Guardian Books—R
(s)-Hannibal Books—R
Harvest House
Hill Street Press—R
Hunt Publishing, John
Ideals Books
InterVarsity Press—R
Judson Press
Kaleidoscope Press—R
Liguori
(s)-Longwood—R
Loyola Press
Lutterworth Press
Meriwether—R
Monarch Books—R
OnStage Publishing
Pacific Press
PREP Publishing—R
(s)-Promise Publishing
(s)-Providence House—R
PublishAmerica
Read 'N Run—R
Regnery—R
RiverOak—R
Selah Publishing—R
(s)-So. Baptist Press—R
Tate Publishing
VMI Publishers
Walk Worthy—R
(s)-Word for Word

INSPIRATIONAL

ACU Press
(s)-Alfred Ali Literary—R
Ambassador Books
(s)-Ambassador House
Ambassador-Emerald—R
(s)-American Binding—R
AMG Publishers—R
Baker Books
Baker Tritten
Baptist Pub. House
Barbour Publishing
Baylor Univ. Press—R
Beacon Hill Press
Bethany House
(s)-Black Forest—R
Blue Dolphin
(s)-Book Publishers Network
(s)-Brentwood—R

Bridge-Logos
Broadman & Holman
Canticle Books—R
Catholic Book Publishing
Charisma House—R
Charisma Kids
Christian Focus—R
Christian Publications—R
Christian Writers Ebook—R
Christopher Publishing
Cladach Publishing—R
Continuum Intl.—R
Countryman, J.
Crane Hill—R
Created in Christ
(s)-Creation House—R
Cross Cultural—R
Crossway Books
CSS Publishing
(s)-DCTS Publishing—R
Destiny Image—R
Dimensions for Living
Discovery House—R
Doubleday
Eerdmans/Young Readers
(s)-Elderberry Press
(s)-Essence—R
Fair Havens—R
(s)-Fairway Press—R
Faith Communications
FaithWalk Publishing
Focus on the Family—R
Frederick Fell—R
Friends United Press—R
Genesis Communications
Genesis Press
Gilgal
Glory Bound Books
Good Book—R
Green Key Books
(s)-Guardian Books—R
Harrison House
Harvest House
Hay House
Hensley Publishing—R
Hiddenspring Books
Hill Street Press—R
Honor Books
Honor Kidz
Hunt Publishing, John
ICS Publications—R
Ideals Books
(s)-Impact Christian—R
InterVarsity Press—R
Jossey-Bass
Judson Press

Kaleidoscope Press—R
Kindred Productions
Kregel—R
Lamplighter—R
Langmarc
Lighthouse Trails Publishing—R
(s)-Lightning Star Press—R
Liguori
Living Books for All
(s)-Longwood—R
Lutterworth Press
Magnus Press—R
(s)-Master Design—R
(s)-McDougal Publishing—R
MegaGrace Books
Messianic Jewish—R
Monarch Books—R
Multnomah
New Leaf Press—R
Opine Publishing—R
Our Sunday Visitor—R
P & R Publishing—R
Pacific Press
Paulist Press
Perigee Books
Peter Pauper Press
Pilgrim Press—R
(s)-Poetry of Today
PREP Publishing—R
(s)-Promise Publishing
(s)-Providence House—R
PublishAmerica
Read 'N Run—R
RiverOak—R
Rose Publishing
Selah Publishing—R
Shaw Books—R
Smyth & Helwys
(s)-So. Baptist Press—R
St. Anthony Messenger
Tate Publishing
Tau-Publishing—R
(s)-TEACH Services—R
TowleHouse—R
Tyndale House—R
United Church Pub.
VMI Publishers
W Publishing Group
Wesleyan Publishing
Whitaker House—R
(s)-Winer Foundation—R
Wood Lake Books—R
Woodland Gospel
(s)-Word for Word
Zondervan

LEADERSHIP

ACU Press
(s)-American Binding—R
Baker Books
Baptist Pub. House
Baylor Univ. Press—R
Beacon Hill Press
(s)-Black Forest—R
(s)-Book Publishers Network
Bridge Resources
Bridge-Logos
Broadman & Holman
Chalice Press
Chariot Books
Charisma House—R
Christian Focus—R
Christian Publications—R
Christian Writers Ebook—R
Christopher Publishing
Church Growth Inst.
College Press—R
Continuum Intl.—R
Created in Christ
(s)-Creation House—R
Crossway Books
CSS Publishing
(s)-DCTS Publishing—R
Destiny Image—R
Discovery House—R
Editorial Portavoz—R
(s)-Elderberry Press
(s)-Essence—R
Fair Havens—R
(s)-Fairway Press—R
FaithWalk Publishing
Focus on the Family—R
Frederick Fell—R
Genesis Communications
Gospel Publishing House
Greenwood Publishing
Group Publishing
(s)-Guardian Books—R
Harrison House
Harvest House
Hiddenspring Books
Hill Street Press—R
InterVarsity Press—R
Judson Press
Lamplighter—R
Liguori
Living Books for All
(s)-Longwood—R
Lutterworth Press
(s)-Master Design—R
(s)-McDougal Publishing—R

MegaGrace Books
Monarch Books—R
Multnomah
Neibauer Press—R
Openbook—R
Oregon Catholic Press—R
Paulist Press
Pilgrim Press—R
(s)-Promise Publishing
(s)-Providence House—R
PublishAmerica
Quintessential Books—R
Read 'N Run—R
Selah Publishing—R
Standard Publishing
Tate Publishing
Tyndale House/SaltRiver
UMI Publishing—R
Univ. Press of America—R
VMI Publishers
Wesleyan Publishing
Whitaker House—R
(s)-Winer Foundation—R
Wood Lake Books—R

LITURGICAL STUDIES

American Cath. Press—R
Baker Books
Baylor Univ. Press—R
Blue Dolphin
(s)-Brentwood—R
Canon Press—R
(s)-Catholic Answers—R
Catholic Book Publishing
Cerdic-Publications
Chalice Press
Christian Writers Ebook—R
Christopher Publishing
Cistercian—R
Conciliar Press—R
Continuum Intl.—R
(s)-Creation House—R
Cross Cultural—R
CSS Publishing
Eerdmans Publishing—R
(s)-Emmaus Road Pub.—R
(s)-Fairway Press—R
Forward Movement
Greenwood Publishing
(s)-Guardian Books—R
Hendrickson—R
Hiddenspring Books
Holy Cross—R
Johns Hopkins—R
Judson Press
Liturgy Training

Lutterworth Press
Morehouse
New Seeds Books—R
Openbook—R
Oregon Catholic Press—R
OSL Publications—R
Oxford University
Paulist Press
Pilgrim Press—R
(s)-Promise Publishing
(s)-Providence House—R
PublishAmerica
Read 'N Run—R
(s)-So. Baptist Press—R
Trinity Press Intl.—R
Twenty-Third Publications
United Church Pub.
Univ. Press of America—R

MARRIAGE

Ambassador Books
(s)-Ambassador House
AMG Publishers—R
Baker Books
Baptist Pub. House
Barbour Publishing
Beacon Hill Press
Bethany House
(s)-Black Forest—R
(s)-Brentwood—R
Bridge-Logos
Broadman & Holman
Canon Press—R
(s)-Catholic Answers—R
Cerdic-Publications
Chalice Press
Chariot Books
Charisma House—R
Christian Focus—R
Christian Publications—R
Christian Writers Ebook—R
Christopher Publishing
College Press—R
Continuum Intl.—R
Created in Christ
(s)-Creation House—R
Crossway Books
CSS Publishing
Destiny Image—R
Dimensions for Living
Discovery House—R
Doubleday
Editorial Portavoz—R
Eerdmans Publishing—R
(s)-Elderberry Press
(s)-Emmaus Road Pub.—R

(s)-Essence—R
Fair Havens—R
(s)-Fairway Press—R
FaithWalk Publishing
FamilyLife Publishing
Focus on the Family—R
Genesis Communications
Greenwood Publishing
Group Publishing
(s)-Guardian Books—R
(s)-Hannibal Books—R
Harrison House
Harvest House
Haworth Press—R
Hendrickson—R
Hensley Publishing—R
Hiddenspring Books
Hill Street Press—R
InterVarsity Press—R
Jubilant Press—R
Judson Press
Legacy Publishers
Life Journey Books—R
Liguori
Living Books for All
(s)-Longwood—R
Loyola Press
Lutterworth Press
(s)-Master Design—R
(s)-McDougal Publishing—R
Millennium III—R
Moms In Print
Monarch Books—R
Multnomah
Northfield
Openbook—R
Oregon Catholic Press—R
P & R Publishing—R
Pacific Press
Paulist Press
Pilgrim Press—R
(s)-Promise Publishing
(s)-Providence House—R
PublishAmerica
(s)-Quiet Waters
Quintessential Books—R
Ragged Edge—R
Read 'N Run—R
RiverOak—R
(s)-Robbie Dean Press—R
Rose Publishing
Scepter Publishers—R
Selah Publishing—R
Shaw Books—R
Silas Publishing—R
(s)-So. Baptist Press—R
Sower's Press

Spence Publishing
St. Anthony Messenger
Standard Publishing
Still Waters Revival—R
Tate Publishing
(s)-TEACH Services—R
Twenty-Third Publications
Tyndale House—R
VMI Publishers
W Publishing Group
Whitaker House—R
(s)-Word for Word

MEMOIRS

(s)-American Binding—R
Baker Books
Ballantine Books
Basic Books—R
(s)-Book Publishers Network
Christian Focus—R
Christian Writers Ebook—R
Christopher Publishing
Continuum Intl.—R
(s)-Creation House—R
Crossroad Publishing—R
Cumberland House
Descant Publishing
(s)-Elderberry Press
Fair Havens—R
(s)-Fairway Press—R
FaithWalk Publishing
(s)-Fruit-Bearer Pub.
Glory Bound Books
Greenwood Publishing
(s)-Hannibal Books—R
HarperSanFrancisco
Hill Street Press—R
Ideals Books
Jossey-Bass
Lighthouse Trails Publishing—R
Lutterworth Press
Pacific Press
(s)-Promise Publishing
(s)-Providence House—R
PublishAmerica
Shoreline—R
Tate Publishing
TowleHouse—R
Tyndale House/SaltRiver
Univ. Press of America—R
VMI Publishers
Whitaker House—R

MEN'S BOOKS

Ambassador Books
Ambassador-Emerald—R
AMG Publishers—R

Baker Books
Baptist Pub. House
Beacon Hill Press
Bethany House
(s)-Black Forest—R
Blue Dolphin
Bridge-Logos
Broadman & Holman
Canon Press—R
Chalice Press
Christian Writers Ebook—R
Christopher Publishing
College Press—R
Continuum Intl.—R
Created in Christ
(s)-Creation House—R
Crossway Books
CSS Publishing
Dimensions for Living
Discovery House—R
Editorial Portavoz—R
(s)-Elderberry Press
(s)-Emmaus Road Pub.—R
(s)-Essence—R
Fair Havens—R
(s)-Fairway Press—R
Faith Communications
FaithWalk Publishing
Focus on the Family—R
Genesis Communications
(s)-Guardian Books—R
Harvest House
Hensley Publishing—R
Hiddenspring Books
Hill Street Press—R
Inkling Books—R
InterVarsity Press—R
Judson Press
Life Journey Books—R
Liguori
(s)-Longwood—R
Loyola Press
Lutterworth Press
Magnus Press—R
(s)-McDougal Publishing—R
Monarch Books—R
Multnomah
Openbook—R
Oregon Catholic Press—R
Pacific Press
Pilgrim Press—R
(s)-Poetry of Today
(s)-Promise Publishing
(s)-Providence House—R
Read 'N Run—R
RiverOak—R
Selah Publishing—R

St. Anthony Messenger
Tate Publishing
VMI Publishers
W Publishing Group
Whitaker House—R
(s)-Word for Word

MIRACLES

Ambassador-Emerald—R
(s)-American Binding—R
Baker Books
(s)-Black Forest—R
(s)-Brentwood—R
Bridge-Logos
Charisma House—R
Christian Writers Ebook—R
Christopher Publishing
Continuum Intl.—R
(s)-Creation House—R
Cross Cultural—R
CSS Publishing
(s)-Elderberry Press
(s)-Essence—R
(s)-Fairway Press—R
Friends United Press—R
Genesis Communications
Greenwood Publishing
Harrison House
Harvest House
Hiddenspring Books
Iceagle Press—R
(s)-Impact Christian—R
Living Books for All
Loyola Press
Lutterworth Press
(s)-McDougal Publishing—R
Monarch Books—R
Pacific Press
(s)-Promise Publishing
(s)-Providence House—R
Read 'N Run—R
Selah Publishing—R
(s)-So. Baptist Press—R
Tate Publishing
VMI Publishers
Whitaker House—R

MISSIONARY

ACU Press
Ambassador-Emerald—R
(s)-American Binding—R
Baker Books
Baptist Pub. House
Baylor Univ. Press—R
(s)-Black Forest—R
(s)-Brentwood—R
Carey Library, Wm.—R

Charisma House—R
Christian Focus—R
Christian Writers Ebook—R
Christopher Publishing
Continuum Intl.—R
Created in Christ
(s)-Creation House—R
Cross Cultural—R
CSS Publishing
Discovery House—R
(s)-Essence—R
Fair Havens—R
(s)-Fairway Press—R
FaithWalk Publishing
Friends United Press—R
Genesis Communications
Glory Bound Books
Greenwood Publishing
(s)-Guardian Books—R
(s)-Hannibal Books—R
Harrison House
InterVarsity Press—R
Judson Press
Lamplighter—R
Lighthouse Trails Publishing—R
Living Books for All
Logion Press
(s)-Longwood—R
Lutterworth Press
(s)-Master Design—R
(s)-McDougal Publishing—R
Messianic Jewish—R
Monarch Books—R
New Hope—R
Pacific Press
(s)-Promise Publishing
(s)-Providence House—R
PublishAmerica
(s)-Quiet Waters
Read 'N Run—R
Rose Publishing
(s)-So. Baptist Press—R
Tate Publishing
VMI Publishers

MONEY MANAGEMENT

(s)-American Binding—R
Baker Books
Barbour Publishing
Basic Books—R
Bethany House
Blue Dolphin
(s)-Book Publishers Network
(s)-Brentwood—R
Bridge-Logos
Chariot Books
Christian Writers Ebook—R

Christopher Publishing
Created in Christ
(s)-Creation House—R
Editorial Portavoz—R
(s)-Elderberry Press
(s)-Essence—R
Fair Havens—R
(s)-Fairway Press—R
FaithWalk Publishing
Focus on the Family—R
Genesis Communications
Greenwood Publishing
(s)-Guardian Books—R
Harrison House
Harvest House
Hensley Publishing—R
Jubilant Press—R
Legacy Publishers
Life Journey Books—R
Lutterworth Press
Moms In Print
Moody Publishers
Multnomah
Northfield
Pacific Press
(s)-Promise Publishing
(s)-Providence House—R
Read 'N Run—R
Regnery—R
RiverOak—R
Silas Publishing—R
(s)-So. Baptist Press—R
Summit Pub. Group—R
Tate Publishing
VMI Publishers
Walk Worthy—R
Wesleyan Publishing
Whitaker House—R
(s)-Winer Foundation—R
(s)-Word for Word

MUSIC-RELATED BOOKS

ACU Press
Ambassador-Emerald—R
American Cath. Press—R
Baker Books
Christian Writers Ebook—R
Christopher Publishing
Contemporary Drama Service
Countryman, J.
Dimension Books—R
(s)-Essence—R
(s)-Fairway Press—R
FaithWalk Publishing
(s)-Guardian Books—R
Hill Street Press—R
Judson Press

Liturgy Training
Lutterworth Press
MegaGrace Books
Oregon Catholic Press—R
OSL Publications—R
(s)-Promise Publishing
Read 'N Run—R
Scarecrow Press—R
Standard Publishing
Tate Publishing
United Church Pub.
VMI Publishers
Whitaker House—R

NOVELTY BOOKS FOR KIDS

Baker Books
Baker Tritten
Big Idea, Inc.
(s)-Creation House—R
Creative Teaching
(s)-Fairway Press—R
Kregel Kidzone—R
Legacy Press—R
Lutterworth Press
Our Sunday Visitor—R
(s)-Poetry of Today
(s)-Promise Publishing
Standard Publishing
Tate Publishing
(s)-Word for Word

PAMPHLETS

Baptist Pub. House
Christian Writers Ebook—R
Concordia
(s)-Essence—R
Forward Movement
(s)-Fruit-Bearer Pub.
Good Book—R
Good News Publishers
(s)-Guardian Books—R
Intl. Awakening—R
Libros Liguori
Liguori
Living Books for All
(s)-Longwood—R
Neibauer Press—R
Our Sunday Visitor—R
Paradise Research—R
Paulist Press
Read 'N Run—R
Rose Publishing
St. Anthony Messenger
Trinity Foundation—R

PARENTING

ACU Press

(s)-Ambassador House
(s)-American Binding—R
AMG Publishers—R
Andros Book Publishing
Baker Books
Baker Tritten
Ballantine Books
Baptist Pub. House
Barbour Publishing
Basic Books—R
Beacon Hill Press
Bethany House
(s)-Black Forest—R
(s)-Book Publishers Network
(s)-Brentwood—R
Bridge-Logos
Broadman & Holman
Chalice Press
Chariot Books
Charisma House—R
Christian Family
Christian Focus—R
Christian Publications—R
Christian Writers Ebook—R
Christopher Publishing
College Press—R
Conciliar Press—R
Concordia
Continuum Intl.—R
Created in Christ
(s)-Creation House—R
Crossway Books
CSS Publishing
Devoted to You
Dimensions for Living
Discovery House—R
Editorial Portavoz—R
(s)-Essence—R
Fair Havens—R
(s)-Fairway Press—R
FamilyLife Publishing
Focus on the Family—R
(s)-Fruit-Bearer Pub.
Genesis Communications
Greenwood Publishing
Group Publishing
(s)-Guardian Books—R
Harrison House
Harvest House
Hensley Publishing—R
Hiddenspring Books
Hill Street Press—R
InterVarsity Press—R
Jeremy P. Tarcher
Jubilant Press—R
Judson Press
Kaleidoscope Press—R

Kregel—R
Life Journey Books—R
Lightwave Publishing
Liguori
Living Books for All
(s)-Longwood—R
(s)-Master Design—R
(s)-McDougal Publishing—R
Moms In Print
Monarch Books—R
Morehouse
Multnomah
Northfield
Openbook—R
P & R Publishing—R
Pacific Press
Paulist Press
(s)-Promise Publishing
(s)-Providence House—R
PublishAmerica
Quintessential Books—R
Read 'N Run—R
RiverOak—R
(s)-Robbie Dean Press—R
Rose Publishing
Scepter Publishers—R
Selah Publishing—R
Shaw Books—R
Silas Publishing—R
Square One—R
Standard Publishing
Still Waters Revival—R
Tate Publishing
Twenty-Third Publications
Tyndale House—R
VMI Publishers
W Publishing Group
Walk Worthy—R
Whitaker House—R
Wood Lake Books—R
(s)-Word for Word

PASTORS' HELPS

Abingdon Press
Ambassador-Emerald—R
(s)-American Binding—R
AMG Publishers—R
Baker Books
Baptist Pub. House
Beacon Hill Press
Bethany House
(s)-Brentwood—R
Broadman & Holman
Christian Focus—R
Christian Publications—R
Christian Writers Ebook—R
Christopher Publishing

Church Growth Inst.
Continuum Intl.—R
Created in Christ
(s)-Creation House—R
Cross Cultural—R
CSS Publishing
(s)-DCTS Publishing—R
Editorial Portavoz—R
(s)-Essence—R
Fair Havens—R
(s)-Fairway Press—R
Fortress Press
Forward Movement
Gospel Publishing House
Greenwood Publishing
Group Publishing
(s)-Guardian Books—R
Harcourt Religion
Harrison House
Haworth Press—R
Hendrickson—R
InterVarsity Press—R
Judson Press
Kregel—R
Living Books for All
(s)-Master Design—R
Monarch Books—R
Multnomah
Neibauer Press—R
Openbook—R
Oregon Catholic Press—R
P & R Publishing—R
Pathway Press
Pilgrim Press—R
(s)-Promise Publishing
(s)-Providence House—R
Read 'N Run—R
(s)-Sermon Select Press
(s)-So. Baptist Press—R
Standard Publishing
Tate Publishing
Twenty-Third Publications
Victor Books
VMI Publishers
(s)-Winer Foundation—R
(s)-Word for Word

PERSONAL EXPERIENCE

Abagail Press
Ambassador-Emerald—R
(s)-American Binding—R
Baker Books
(s)-Black Forest—R
(s)-Brentwood—R
Canon Press—R
Charisma House—R

Chicken Soup Books
Christian Focus—R
Christian Writers Ebook—R
Christopher Publishing
Continuum Intl.—R
Created in Christ
(s)-Creation House—R
(s)-DCTS Publishing—R
Destiny Image—R
(s)-Essence—R
Fair Havens—R
(s)-Fairway Press—R
FaithWalk Publishing
Friends United Press—R
(s)-Fruit-Bearer Pub.
Gilgal
Green Pastures Press—R
Greenwood Publishing
(s)-Guardian Books—R
Hensley Publishing—R
Iceagle Press—R
Lamplighter—R
Lighthouse Trails Publishing—R
Living Books for All
(s)-Longwood—R
Lutterworth Press
Magnus Press—R
(s)-Master Design—R
(s)-McDougal Publishing—R
Monarch Books—R
Pacific Press
(s)-Promise Publishing
(s)-Providence House—R
PublishAmerica
Read 'N Run—R
RiverOak—R
Shaw Books—R
Shoreline—R
(s)-So. Baptist Press—R
Tate Publishing
Twenty-Third Publications
(s)-VESTA—R
VMI Publishers
W Publishing Group
Whitaker House—R
(s)-Winer Foundation—R
(s)-Word for Word

PERSONAL GROWTH

Abagail Press
(s)-Alfred Ali Literary—R
Ambassador Books
(s)-Ambassador House
Ambassador-Emerald—R
(s)-American Binding—R
AMG Publishers—R
Baker Books

Barbour Publishing
Bethany House
(s)-Black Forest—R
(s)-Book Publishers Network
Broadman & Holman
Canon Press—R
Charisma House—R
Charisma Kids
Christian Focus—R
Christian Writers Ebook—R
Christopher Publishing
Continuum Intl.—R
Created in Christ
(s)-Creation House—R
CSS Publishing
(s)-DCTS Publishing—R
Destiny Image—R
Discovery House—R
(s)-Essence—R
Fair Havens—R
(s)-Fairway Press—R
FaithWalk Publishing
Frederick Fell—R
(s)-Fruit-Bearer Pub.
Genesis Communications
Green Pastures Press—R
Greenwood Publishing
(s)-Guardian Books—R
Hay House
Hensley Publishing—R
Hiddenspring Books
Hill Street Press—R
Howard Publishing
Iceagle Press—R
InterVarsity Press—R
Jossey-Bass
Judson Press
Langmarc
Life Journey Books—R
Liguori
Living Books for All
Lutterworth Press
Magnus Press—R
(s)-Master Design—R
(s)-McDougal Publishing—R
MegaGrace Books
Monarch Books—R
Openbook—R
OSL Publications—R
Pacific Press
Pathway Press
Paulist Press
Pilgrim Press—R
(s)-Promise Publishing
(s)-Providence House—R
PublishAmerica
Quintessential Books—R

Read 'N Run—R
Rising Star Press
RiverOak—R
Shaw Books—R
Silas Publishing—R
Tate Publishing
(s)-TEACH Services—R
Twenty-Third Publications
Tyndale House—R
United Church Pub.
VMI Publishers
W Publishing Group
Wesleyan Publishing
Whitaker House—R
(s)-Winer Foundation—R
(s)-Word for Word

PERSONAL RENEWAL

Abagail Press
(s)-Alfred Ali Literary—R
Ambassador-Emerald—R
AMG Publishers—R
Baker Books
Bethany House
(s)-Black Forest—R
Blue Dolphin
Broadman & Holman
Canon Press—R
Charisma House—R
Charisma Kids
Christian Focus—R
Christian Writers Ebook—R
Christopher Publishing
Continuum Intl.—R
Created in Christ
(s)-Creation House—R
CSS Publishing
(s)-DCTS Publishing—R
Destiny Image—R
Discovery House—R
Doubleday
(s)-Essence—R
Fair Havens—R
(s)-Fairway Press—R
FaithWalk Publishing
Focus on the Family—R
Forward Movement
Friends United Press—R
(s)-Fruit-Bearer Pub.
Genesis Communications
Green Pastures Press—R
Greenwood Publishing
(s)-Guardian Books—R
(s)-Hannibal Books—R
HarperSanFrancisco
Haworth Press—R
Hensley Publishing—R

Hill Street Press—R
(s)-Impact Christian—R
InterVarsity Press—R
Intl. Awakening—R
Jossey-Bass
Judson Press
Life Journey Books—R
Liguori
Living Books for All
(s)-Longwood—R
Lutterworth Press
(s)-Master Design—R
(s)-McDougal Publishing—R
MegaGrace Books
Monarch Books—R
(s)-Omega House—R
Openbook—R
OSL Publications—R
P & R Publishing—R
Pacific Press
Pilgrim Press—R
(s)-Promise Publishing
(s)-Providence House—R
PublishAmerica
Read 'N Run—R
RiverOak—R
Shaw Books—R
Silas Publishing—R
Tate Publishing
Tyndale House—R
United Church Pub.
VMI Publishers
Wesleyan Publishing
Whitaker House—R
(s)-Winer Foundation—R
(s)-Word for Word

PHILOSOPHY

ACU Press
Alba House—R
Algora Publishing—R
Baker Books
Basic Books—R
Baylor Univ. Press—R
(s)-Black Forest—R
(s)-Brentwood—R
Cambridge Univ. Press
Cerdic-Publications
Christian Writers Ebook—R
Christopher Publishing
Continuum Intl.—R
Cross Cultural—R
CSS Publishing
Dover Publications—R
Eerdmans Publishing—R
(s)-Elderberry Press
(s)-Essence—R

(s)-Fairway Press—R
FaithWalk Publishing
Friends United Press—R
Greenwood Publishing
(s)-Guardian Books—R
Hiddenspring Books
Hill Street Press—R
Inkling Books—R
InterVarsity Press—R
Jeremy P. Tarcher
Larson Publications
Lutterworth Press
Mercer Univ. Press—R
Monarch Books—R
Open Court—R
Oxford University
Paragon House
Paulist Press
(s)-Promise Publishing
(s)-Providence House—R
PublishAmerica
Quintessential Books—R
Read 'N Run—R
Regnery—R
Scarecrow Press—R
St. Augustine's Press—R
Still Waters Revival—R
Tate Publishing
Third World Press—R
Trinity Foundation—R
Univ. Press of America—R
(s)-VESTA—R
VMI Publishers
Whitaker House—R
(s)-Winer Foundation—R
(s)-Word for Word
Yale Univ. Press—R

PHOTOGRAPHS (FOR COVERS)

Abingdon Press
(s)-Alfred Ali Literary
(s)-Black Forest
(s)-Brentwood
Bridge-Logos
Canadian Inst. for Law
Canon Press
Carey Library, Wm.
(s)-Catholic Answers
Christian Focus
Church Growth Inst.
Cistercian
Conciliar Press
Continuum Intl.
Created in Christ
(s)-Creation House
Cross Cultural

Devoted to You
(s)-Essence
ETC Publications
(s)-Express Publishers
Fair Havens
FaithWalk Publishing
Glory Bound Books
(s)-Guardian Books
Guernica Editions
Harcourt Religion
Intl. Awakening
Jireh Publishing
Jubilant Press
(s)-Lightning Star Press
Living Books for All
(s)-Longwood
Millennium III
MountainView
Neibauer Press
New Canaan
New Hope
Oregon Catholic Press
Our Sunday Visitor
Paulist Press
Players Press
(s)-Poetry of Today
(s)-Providence House
Quintessential Books
Read 'N Run
Rising Star Press
(s)-Robbie Dean Press
Selah Publishing
Sheed & Ward
St. Anthony Messenger
Tau-Publishing
(s)-TEACH Services
Touch Publications
TowleHouse
Trinity Foundation
Twenty-Third Publications
United Methodist Publishing
Univ. of AR Press
Virginia Pines Press
Wilshire Book
(s)-WinePress

POETRY

(s)-American Binding—R
(s)-Black Forest—R
(s)-Book Publishers Network
Boyds Mills Press—R
(s)-Brentwood—R
Canon Press—R
Christian Writers Ebook—R
Christopher Publishing
Cladach Publishing—R
Continuum Intl.—R

Created in Christ
Eerdmans/Young Readers
(s)-Elderberry Press
(s)-Essence—R
(s)-Fairway Press—R
(s)-Fruit-Bearer Pub.
Glory Bound Books
(s)-Guardian Books—R
Guernica Editions—R
Hidden Brook Press
Image Books—R
Lamplighter—R
(s)-Lightning Star Press—R
Lutterworth Press
Moms In Print
(s)-Poems by Me—R
(s)-Poetry of Today
(s)-Poets Cove Press
(s)-Promise Publishing
PublishAmerica
Read 'N Run—R
(s)-Robbie Dean Press—R
Selah Publishing—R
(s)-So. Baptist Press—R
Tate Publishing
(s)-VESTA—R
Vintage Romance
(s)-Word for Word

POLITICAL

Algora Publishing—R
Allegiance Books—R
Baker Books
Basic Books—R
Baylor Univ. Press—R
(s)-Black Forest—R
(s)-Brentwood—R
Canadian Inst. for Law—R
Christian Writers Ebook—R
Christopher Publishing
Continuum Intl.—R
(s)-Creation House—R
Cross Cultural—R
(s)-Elderberry Press
(s)-Essence—R
(s)-Fairway Press—R
Georgetown Univ. Press
Greenwood Publishing
(s)-Guardian Books—R
Hill Street Press—R
Inkling Books—R
Judson Press
Lutterworth Press
Mercer Univ. Press—R
Millennium III—R
Monarch Books—R
New York Univ. Press

Open Court—R
(s)-Promise Publishing
(s)-Providence House—R
PublishAmerica
Quintessential Books—R
Read 'N Run—R
Regnery—R
Scarecrow Press—R
Spence Publishing
Still Waters Revival—R
Tate Publishing
Third World Press—R
United Church Pub.
Univ. Press of America—R
VMI Publishers

PRAYER

Abingdon Press
ACU Press
Ambassador-Emerald—R
(s)-American Binding—R
American Cath. Press—R
AMG Publishers—R
Baker Books
Baker Tritten
Barbour Publishing
Baylor Univ. Press—R
Beacon Hill Press
Bethany House(s)-Black Forest—R
(s)-Brentwood—R
Bridge-Logos
Broadman & Holman
Catholic Book Publishing
Chariot Books
Charisma House—R
Charisma Kids
Christian Focus—R
Christian Publications—R
Christian Writers Ebook—R
Christopher Publishing
College Press—R
Continuum Intl.—R
Created in Christ
(s)-Creation House—R
Cross Cultural—R
CSS Publishing
(s)-DCTS Publishing—R
Destiny Image—R
Diamond Eyes—R
Discovery House—R
Doubleday
Eerdmans Publishing—R
Eerdmans/Young Readers
(s)-Elderberry Press
(s)-Emmaus Road Pub.—R
(s)-Essence—R
Fair Havens—R

(s)-Fairway Press—R
Faith One
FaithWalk Publishing
FamilyLife Publishing
Focus on the Family—R
Forward Movement
Friends United Press—R
(s)-Fruit-Bearer Pub.
Genesis Communications
Good News Publishers
Gospel Publishing House
Green Pastures Press—R
Greenwood Publishing
(s)-Guardian Books—R
Harcourt Religion
HarperSanFrancisco
Harrison House
Harvest House
Hensley Publishing—R
Hiddenspring Books
Hill Street Press—R
Holy Cross—R
Iceagle Press—R
ICS Publications—R
(s)-Impact Christian—R
InterVarsity Press—R
Intl. Awakening—R
Jireh Publishing
Judson Press
Kregel—R
Libros Liguori
(s)-Lightning Star Press—R
Lightwave Publishing
Liguori
Liturgy Training
Living Books for All
(s)-Longwood—R
Lutterworth Press
(s)-Master Design—R
(s)-McDougal Publishing—R
Monarch Books—R
Moody Publishers
Morehouse
Multnomah
New Hope—R
New Leaf Press—R
New Seeds Books—R
Openbook—R
OSL Publications—R
Our Sunday Visitor—R
P & R Publishing—R
Pacific Press
Paraclete Press—R
Pauline Books—R
Paulist Press
Pilgrim Press—R

(s)-Promise Publishing
(s)-Providence House—R
Read 'N Run—R
RiverOak—R
Rose Publishing
Scepter Publishers—R
Selah Publishing—R
Shaw Books—R
Smyth & Helwys
(s)-So. Baptist Press—R
Standard Publishing
Still Waters Revival—R
Tate Publishing
(s)-TEACH Services—R
Twenty-Third Publications
Tyndale House—R
United Church Pub.
VMI Publishers
W Publishing Group
Walk Worthy—R
Wesleyan Publishing
Westminster John Knox
Whitaker House—R
(s)-Winer Foundation—R
Wood Lake Books—R
Woodland Gospel
(s)-Word for Word
Zondervan

PRINT-ON-DEMAND

(s)-American Binding—R
(s)-Black Forest—R
Blue Dolphin
Booklocker Jr.
Booklocker.com
(s)-Brentwood—R
Christian Writers Ebook—R
Continuum Intl.—R
Created in Christ
Crossroad Publishing—R
(s)-Elderberry Press
(s)-Express Publishers
Genesis Communications
Georgetown Univ. Press
Inkling Books—R
(s)-Insight Publishing—R
(s)-Lightning Star Press—R
(s)-One World—R
(s)-Pleasant Word
(s)-Poems by Me—R
(s)-Poetry of Today
PublishAmerica
(s)-Robbie Dean Press—R
(s)-Self Publish Press—R
(s)-Strong Tower
Univ. Press of America—R

VMI Publishers
(s)-Word Alive
(s)-Xulon Press—R

PROPHECY

Ambassador-Emerald—R
(s)-American Binding—R
Baker Books
Baylor Univ. Press—R
(s)-Black Forest—R
Blue Dolphin
(s)-Brentwood—R
Bridge-Logos
Broadman & Holman
Charisma House—R
Charisma Kids
Christian Focus—R
Christian Writers Ebook—R
Christopher Publishing
Continuum Intl.—R
Created in Christ
(s)-Creation House—R
CSS Publishing
(s)-Elderberry Press
(s)-Essence—R
Fair Havens—R
(s)-Fairway Press—R
FaithWalk Publishing
(s)-Fruit-Bearer Pub.
Greenwood Publishing
(s)-Guardian Books—R
Harrison House
Harvest House
Iceagle Press—R
Kregel—R
Living Books for All
(s)-Longwood—R
Lutterworth Press
(s)-Master Design—R
(s)-McDougal Publishing—R
Millennium III—R
Monarch Books—R
Multnomah
P & R Publishing—R
Pacific Press
(s)-Promise Publishing
(s)-Providence House—R
Read 'N Run—R
RiverOak—R
Selah Publishing—R
Small Helm Press—R
(s)-So. Baptist Press—R
Still Waters Revival—R
Tate Publishing
Victor Books
VMI Publishers

W Publishing Group
Whitaker House—R
(s)-Word for Word

PSYCHOLOGY

Basic Books—R
Baylor Univ. Press—R
Bethany House
(s)-Black Forest—R
Blue Dolphin
(s)-Brentwood—R
Christian Focus—R
Christian Writers Ebook—R
Christopher Publishing
Continuum Intl.—R
Created in Christ
(s)-Creation House—R
Dimension Books—R
(s)-Elderberry Press
(s)-Essence—R
Fair Havens—R
(s)-Fairway Press—R
FaithWalk Publishing
Genesis Communications
Greenwood Publishing
(s)-Guardian Books—R
Haworth Press—R
Hiddenspring Books
Hill Street Press—R
InterVarsity Press—R
Jeremy P. Tarcher
Jossey-Bass
Judson Press
Larson Publications
Life Journey Books—R
Liguori
Lutterworth Press
Monarch Books—R
New Seeds Books—R
New York Univ. Press
Open Court—R
P & R Publishing—R
Paragon House
(s)-Promise Publishing
(s)-Providence House—R
PublishAmerica
Quintessential Books—R
Read 'N Run—R
(s)-Recovery Communications
Religious Education
Silas Publishing—R
(s)-So. Baptist Press—R
Tate Publishing
Third World Press—R
Tyndale House—R
Univ. Press of America—R

VMI Publishers
Wilshire Book—R
(s)-Winer Foundation—R
Yale Univ. Press—R

RACISM

(s)-Alfred Ali Literary—R
American Cath. Press—R
Baker Books
(s)-Black Forest—R
Christian Writers Ebook—R
Christopher Publishing
Continuum Intl.—R
(s)-Creation House—R
Cross Cultural—R
(s)-DCTS Publishing—R
Destiny Image—R
Eerdmans/Young Readers
(s)-Fairway Press—R
FaithWalk Publishing
Greenwood Publishing
Hendrickson—R
Hiddenspring Books
Hill Street Press—R
InterVarsity Press—R
Jossey-Bass
Lutterworth Press
Monarch Books—R
Oxford University
Paulist Press
Pilgrim Press—R
(s)-Promise Publishing
(s)-Providence House—R
Summit Pub. Group—R
Univ. Press of America—R
VMI Publishers
(s)-Word for Word

RECOVERY BOOKS

Ambassador Books
(s)-Ambassador House
Baker Books
(s)-Black Forest—R
Broadman & Holman
Charisma House—R
Christian Writers Ebook—R
Christopher Publishing
Continuum Intl.—R
(s)-Creation House—R
CSS Publishing
(s)-Essence—R
Fair Havens—R
(s)-Fairway Press—R
Faith Communications
FaithWalk Publishing
Genesis Communications

Gilgal
Good Book—R
Greenwood Publishing
(s)-Guardian Books—R
(s)-Hannibal Books—R
HarperSanFrancisco
Harvest House
Haworth Press—R
Hill Street Press—R
Iceagle Press—R
Judson Press
Life Journey Books—R
Liguori
(s)-McDougal Publishing—R
Monarch Books—R
Our Sunday Visitor—R
Paradise Research—R
(s)-Promise Publishing
(s)-Providence House—R
Read 'N Run—R
(s)-Recovery Communications
RiverOak—R
Silas Publishing—R
Siloam Press
Tate Publishing
Tyndale House—R
VMI Publishers
Whitaker House—R
Wilshire Book—R

REFERENCE BOOKS

Ambassador-Emerald—R
AMG Publishers—R
Baker Books
Baylor Univ. Press—R
Bethany House
(s)-Black Forest—R
Branden Publishing
(s)-Brentwood—R
Bridge-Logos
Chariot Books
Christian Focus—R
Christian Writers Ebook—R
Christopher Publishing
Continuum Intl.—R
(s)-Creation House—R
CSS Publishing
Dover Publications—R
Editorial Portavoz—R
Eerdmans Publishing—R
(s)-Elderberry Press
Facts on File
(s)-Fairway Press—R
FaithWalk Publishing
(s)-Guardian Books—R
HarperSanFrancisco

Hendrickson—R
Hill Street Press—R
Hunt Publishing, John
(s)-Impact Christian—R
InterVarsity Press—R
Intl. Awakening—R
Johns Hopkins—R
Judson Press
Kaleidoscope Press—R
Kregel—R
Lightwave Publishing
Liguori
Living Books for All
Lutterworth Press
(s)-Master Design—R
MegaGrace Books
Messianic Jewish—R
Millennium III—R
Monarch Books—R
New Leaf Press—R
Oregon Catholic Press—R
Oxford University
(s)-Promise Publishing
(s)-Providence House—R
Read 'N Run—R
Religious Education
Rose Publishing
Scarecrow Press—R
Sheed & Ward—R
(s)-So. Baptist Press—R
Square One—R
Still Waters Revival—R
Tate Publishing
Third World Press—R
Tyndale House—R
Univ. Press of America—R
(s)-VESTA—R
Victor Books
Whitaker House—R
(s)-Word for Word
World Publishing—R

RELIGION

Abingdon Press
ACTA Publications
ACU Press
(s)-Alfred Ali Literary—R
Ambassador-Emerald—R
(s)-American Binding—R
Baker Books
Baker Tritten
Ballantine Books
Basic Books—R
Baylor Univ. Press—R
Bethany House
(s)-Black Forest—R

Blue Dolphin
(s)-Brentwood—R
Broadman & Holman
Cambridge Univ. Press
Canticle Books—R
(s)-Catholic Answers—R
Cerdic-Publications
Charisma House—R
Christian Writers Ebook—R
Christopher Publishing
Continuum Intl.—R
Created in Christ
(s)-Creation House—R
Cross Cultural—R
Crossway Books
CSS Publishing
Descant Publishing
Dimension Books—R
Doubleday
Educational Ministries
Eerdmans Publishing—R
Eerdmans/Young Readers
(s)-Elderberry Press
(s)-Emmaus Road Pub.—R
(s)-Essence—R
Facts on File
(s)-Fairway Press—R
FaithWalk Publishing
FamilyLife Publishing
Fortress Press
Friends United Press—R
Georgetown Univ. Press
Greenwood Publishing
(s)-Guardian Books—R
HarperSanFrancisco
Harvest House
Hiddenspring Books
Hill Street Press—R
Holy Cross—R
Hunt Publishing, John
(s)-Impact Christian—R
InterVarsity Press—R
Jeremy P. Tarcher
Johns Hopkins—R
Judson Press
Kregel—R
Larson Publications
Libros Liguori
Liguori
Liturgy Training
Lutterworth Press
Magnus Press—R
(s)-Master Design—R
(s)-McDougal Publishing—R
Mercer Univ. Press—R
Messianic Jewish—R

Millennium III—R
Monarch Books—R
Mt. Olive College Press
New Hope—R
New Seeds Books—R
New York Univ. Press
Northstone—R
Open Court—R
Oregon Catholic Press—R
OSL Publications—R
Our Sunday Visitor—R
Oxford University
P & R Publishing—R
Pacific Press
Paraclete Press—R
Paragon House
Paulist Press
Pilgrim Press—R
(s)-Poetry of Today
PREP Publishing—R
(s)-Promise Publishing
(s)-Providence House—R
PublishAmerica
Ragged Edge—R
Read 'N Run—R
Regnery—R
Religious Education
Rising Star Press
RiverOak—R
Rose Publishing
Shaw Books—R
Sheed & Ward—R
Smyth & Helwys
(s)-So. Baptist Press—R
Spence Publishing
Square One—R
Still Waters Revival—R
Tate Publishing
Tau-Publishing—R
Third World Press—R
Trinity Press Intl.—R
Twenty-Third Publications
United Church Pub.
Univ. of AR Press—R
Univ. Press of America—R
(s)-VESTA—R
VMI Publishers
W Publishing Group
Westminster John Knox
Whitaker House—R
Wood Lake Books—R
(s)-Word for Word
Yale Univ. Press—R

RELIGIOUS TOLERANCE

(s)-American Binding—R

American Cath. Press—R
Baker Books
Baylor Univ. Press—R
(s)-Black Forest—R
Canticle Books—R
Charisma House—R
Christian Writers Ebook—R
Christopher Publishing
Continuum Intl.—R
Created in Christ
Cross Cultural—R
Doubleday
Eerdmans/Young Readers
(s)-Elderberry Press
(s)-Fairway Press—R
FaithWalk Publishing
Greenwood Publishing
Hill Street Press—R
InterVarsity Press—R
Johns Hopkins—R
Lutterworth Press
New Canaan
Paragon House
Paulist Press
(s)-Poetry of Today
(s)-Promise Publishing
(s)-Providence House—R
PublishAmerica
Rising Star Press
Tate Publishing
VMI Publishers
Westminster John Knox
(s)-Word for Word

RETIREMENT

(s)-American Binding—R
Baker Books
Barbour Publishing
Bethany House
(s)-Book Publishers Network
Broadman & Holman
Chalice Press
Christian Publications—R
Christian Writers Ebook—R
Christopher Publishing
College Press—R
Continuum Intl.—R
(s)-Creation House—R
Discovery House—R
(s)-Elderberry Press
(s)-Essence—R
Fair Havens—R
(s)-Fairway Press—R
Greenwood Publishing
(s)-Guardian Books—R
Hill Street Press—R

Judson Press
Life Journey Books—R
Liguori
(s)-Longwood—R
Lutterworth Press
(s)-Promise Publishing
(s)-Providence House—R
Read 'N Run—R
Regnery—R
(s)-So. Baptist Press—R
Square One—R
Tate Publishing
United Church Pub.

SCHOLARLY

Baker Books
Baylor Univ. Press—R
(s)-Black Forest—R
Canon Press—R
Chariot Books
Christian Focus—R
Christian Writers Ebook—R
Christopher Publishing
Cistercian—R
Continuum Intl.—R
(s)-Creation House—R
Cross Cultural—R
Crossway Books
Eerdmans Publishing—R
(s)-Elderberry Press
(s)-Essence—R
Fair Havens—R
(s)-Fairway Press—R
Fortress Press
Four Courts Press—R
Georgetown Univ. Press
Gospel Publishing House
Greenwood Publishing
(s)-Guardian Books—R
Haworth Press—R
Hendrickson—R
Hill Street Press—R
(s)-Impact Christian—R
Inkling Books—R
InterVarsity Press—R
Intl. Awakening—R
Kregel—R
Lutterworth Press
(s)-Master Design—R
Mercer Univ. Press—R
Millennium III—R
Monarch Books—R
Mt. Olive College Press
New Leaf Press—R
New Seeds Books—R
New York Univ. Press

Oregon Catholic Press—R
OSL Publications—R
Our Sunday Visitor—R
P & R Publishing—R
Paragon House
Pickwick Publications—R
Pilgrim Press—R
(s)-Promise Publishing
(s)-Providence House—R
(s)-Quiet Waters
Read 'N Run—R
Religious Education
Scarecrow Press—R
Shaw Books—R
Smyth & Helwys
Trinity Foundation—R
Trinity Press Intl.—R
Univ. of AR Press—R
Univ. Press of America—R
Univ./Ottawa Press
(s)-VESTA—R
Victor Books
VMI Publishers
Westminster John Knox
Whitaker House—R
Youth Specialties

SCIENCE

Allegiance Books—R
(s)-American Binding—R
Baker Books
(s)-Black Forest—R
Boyds Mills Press—R
Broadman & Holman
Christian Focus—R
Christian Writers Ebook—R
Christopher Publishing
Continuum Intl.—R
(s)-Creation House—R
Cross Cultural—R
(s)-Elderberry Press
Facts on File
Fair Havens—R
(s)-Fairway Press—R
Glory Bound Books
Greenwood Publishing
(s)-Guardian Books—R
Harvest House
Hill Street Press—R
Inkling Books—R
InterVarsity Press—R
Kaleidoscope Press—R
Lutterworth Press
Master Books
(s)-Master Design—R
Millennium III—R

Monarch Books—R
New Leaf Press—R
OnStage Publishing
Open Court—R
Oxford University
(s)-Promise Publishing
(s)-Providence House—R
Read 'N Run—R
Regnery—R
Summit Pub. Group—R
Whitaker House—R

SELF-HELP

(s)-Alfred Ali Literary—R
Ambassador Books
(s)-American Binding—R
Baker Books
Ballantine Books
(s)-Black Forest—R
Blue Dolphin
(s)-Book Publishers Network
Bridge-Logos
Broadman & Holman
Charisma House—R
Christian Writers Ebook—R
Christopher Publishing
Continuum Intl.—R
(s)-Creation House—R
(s)-DCTS Publishing—R
Descant Publishing
Destiny Image—R
Dimensions for Living
(s)-Essence—R
Fair Havens—R
(s)-Fairway Press—R
FaithWalk Publishing
Focus on the Family—R
Frederick Fell—R
(s)-Fruit-Bearer Pub.
Genesis Communications
Genesis Press
Glory Bound Books
Good Book—R
(s)-Guardian Books—R
Harvest House
Hay House
Hiddenspring Books
Hill Street Press—R
InterVarsity Press—R
Jeremy P. Tarcher
Judson Press
Langmarc
Life Journey Books—R
(s)-Lightning Star Press—R
Liguori
(s)-Longwood—R

Lutterworth Press
MegaGrace Books
Monarch Books—R
Mt. Olive College Press
New Seeds Books—R
Northstone—R
Openbook—R
P & R Publishing—R
Paradise Research—R
Paulist Press
Perigee Books
Peter Pauper Press
Pilgrim Press—R
(s)-Poetry of Today
(s)-Promise Publishing
(s)-Providence House—R
Ragged Edge—R
Read 'N Run—R
RiverOak—R
(s)-Robbie Dean Press—R
Selah Publishing—R
Silas Publishing—R
Square One—R
Summit Pub. Group—R
Tate Publishing
(s)-TEACH Services—R
Third World Press—R
United Church Pub.
VMI Publishers
Walk Worthy—R
Whitaker House—R
Wilshire Book—R
(s)-Winer Foundation—R
(s)-Word for Word

SENIOR ADULT CONCERNS

(s)-American Binding—R
AMG Publishers—R
Baker Books
Bethany House
(s)-Black Forest—R
Chalice Press
Chariot Books
Charisma House—R
Christian Publications—R
Christian Writers Ebook—R
Christopher Publishing
Continuum Intl.—R
Created in Christ
(s)-Creation House—R
Discovery House—R
Educational Ministries
(s)-Essence—R
Fair Havens—R
(s)-Fairway Press—R
Genesis Communications

Gospel Publishing House
(s)-Guardian Books—R
Haworth Press—R
Hensley Publishing—R
Hill Street Press—R
Judson Press
Life Journey Books—R
Liguori
(s)-Longwood—R
Monarch Books—R
Oregon Catholic Press—R
(s)-Poetry of Today
(s)-Promise Publishing
(s)-Providence House—R
Read 'N Run—R
Rose Publishing
Shaw Books—R
(s)-So. Baptist Press—R
St. Anthony Messenger
Tate Publishing
United Church Pub.
VMI Publishers

SERMONS

Alba House—R
Ambassador-Emerald—R
(s)-American Binding—R
Baker Books
(s)-Brentwood—R
Christian Focus—R
Christian Writers Ebook—R
Christopher Publishing
Church Growth Inst.
Cistercian—R
Continuum Intl.—R
Created in Christ
(s)-Creation House—R
CSS Publishing
(s)-DCTS Publishing—R
Editorial Portavoz—R
Educational Ministries
(s)-Elderberry Press
Fair Havens—R
(s)-Fairway Press—R
Group Publishing
(s)-Guardian Books—R
Hiddenspring Books
Judson Press
Liturgical Press
(s)-Master Design—R
(s)-McDougal Publishing—R
Monarch Books—R
Oregon Catholic Press—R
Pacific Press
Paulist Press
(s)-Promise Publishing

(s)-Providence House—R
Read 'N Run—R
(s)-Sermon Select Press
(s)-So. Baptist Press—R
Still Waters Revival—R
Tate Publishing
United Church Pub.
VMI Publishers

SINGLES ISSUES

(s)-Ambassador House
AMG Publishers—R
Baker Books
Barbour Publishing
Bethany House
(s)-Brentwood—R
Bridge-Logos
Broadman & Holman
Chariot Books
Charisma House—R
Christian Writers Ebook—R
Continuum Intl.—R
(s)-Creation House—R
Destiny Image—R
Discovery House—R
(s)-Elderberry Press
(s)-Essence—R
Fair Havens—R
(s)-Fairway Press—R
FaithWalk Publishing
Genesis Communications
Greenwood Publishing
(s)-Guardian Books—R
Harrison House
Hensley Publishing—R
Hill Street Press—R
Jubilant Press—R
Judson Press
Kregel—R
Life Journey Books—R
Liguori
(s)-McDougal Publishing—R
Monarch Books—R
Multnomah
Oregon Catholic Press—R
P & R Publishing—R
Pacific Press
Perigee Books
(s)-Poetry of Today
(s)-Promise Publishing
(s)-Providence House—R
Quintessential Books—R
Read 'N Run—R
(s)-Robbie Dean Press—R
Rose Publishing
Tate Publishing

VMI Publishers
Walk Worthy—R
Whitaker House—R
(s)-Word for Word

SOCIAL JUSTICE ISSUES

Allegiance Books—R
Baker Books
Baylor Univ. Press—R
Bethany House
(s)-Black Forest—R
(s)-Brentwood—R
Broadman & Holman
Canadian Inst. for Law—R
Chalice Press
Christian Focus—R
Christian Writers Ebook—R
Christopher Publishing
Continuum Intl.—R
(s)-Creation House—R
Cross Cultural—R
Crossroad Publishing—R
CSS Publishing
(s)-DCTS Publishing—R
Destiny Image—R
Doubleday
Eerdmans Publishing—R
Eerdmans/Young Readers
(s)-Essence—R
(s)-Fairway Press—R
Georgetown Univ. Press
Greenwood Publishing
(s)-Guardian Books—R
Haworth Press—R
Hiddenspring Books
Hill Street Press—R
Inkling Books—R
InterVarsity Press—R
Jossey-Bass
Judson Press
Libros Liguori
Life Cycle Books—R
Liturgy Training
Lutterworth Press
Monarch Books—R
Openbook—R
Oregon Catholic Press—R
Our Sunday Visitor—R
Paulist Press
Pilgrim Press—R
(s)-Poetry of Today
(s)-Promise Publishing
(s)-Providence House—R
Quintessential Books—R
Read 'N Run—R
Regnery—R

Shaw Books—R
Sheed & Ward—R
St. Anthony Messenger
Still Waters Revival—R
Tate Publishing
United Church Pub.
Univ./Ottawa Press
VMI Publishers
Whitaker House—R
Youth Specialties

SOCIOLOGY

Algora Publishing—R
Allegiance Books—R
(s)-American Binding—R
Baker Books
Basic Books—R
Baylor Univ. Press—R
Bethany House
(s)-Black Forest—R
(s)-Brentwood—R
Carey Library, Wm.—R
Cerdic-Publications
Christian Writers Ebook—R
Christopher Publishing
Continuum Intl.—R
(s)-Elderberry Press
(s)-Essence—R
(s)-Fairway Press—R
FaithWalk Publishing
Greenwood Publishing
(s)-Guardian Books—R
Haworth Press—R
Hiddenspring Books
Hill Street Press—R
InterVarsity Press—R
Judson Press
Lutterworth Press
(s)-McDougal Publishing—R
Monarch Books—R
New York Univ. Press
Oxford University
(s)-Promise Publishing
(s)-Providence House—R
Quintessential Books—R
Read 'N Run—R
RiverOak—R
Still Waters Revival—R
Tate Publishing
Third World Press—R
Univ. Press of America—R
VMI Publishers

SPIRITUAL GIFTS

ACTA Publications
(s)-American Binding—R

Baker Books
(s)-Black Forest—R
Bridge-Logos
Broadman & Holman
Canticle Books—R
Charisma House—R
Christian Focus—R
Christian Writers Ebook—R
Christopher Publishing
Continuum Intl.—R
Created in Christ
(s)-Creation House—R
Crossroad Publishing—R
Destiny Image—R
Editores Betania-Caribe
(s)-Essence—R
Fair Havens—R
(s)-Fairway Press—R
Faith One
FaithWalk Publishing
Gospel Publishing House
Greenwood Publishing
Group Publishing
(s)-Guardian Books—R
Harrison House
Hensley Publishing—R
Hiddenspring Books
Hill Street Press—R
Iceagle Press—R
InterVarsity Press—R
Living Books for All
Lutterworth Press
Magnus Press—R
(s)-Master Design—R
Monarch Books—R
Multnomah
(s)-Omega House—R
Oregon Catholic Press—R
Our Sunday Visitor—R
P & R Publishing—R
Pacific Press
(s)-Poetry of Today
(s)-Promise Publishing
(s)-Providence House—R
Read 'N Run—R
RiverOak—R
(s)-Robbie Dean Press—R
Selah Publishing—R
Silas Publishing—R
Tate Publishing
Tau-Publishing—R
VMI Publishers
W Publishing Group
Wesleyan Publishing
Whitaker House—R
(s)-WinePress—R

(s)-Word for Word

SPIRITUALITY

Abingdon Press
ACTA Publications
ACU Press
Alba House—R
(s)-Alfred Ali Literary—R
Ambassador Books
(s)-Ambassador House
(s)-American Binding—R
AMG Publishers—R
Baker Books
Ballantine Books
Basic Books—R
Baylor Univ. Press—R
Bethany House
(s)-Black Forest—R
Blue Dolphin
(s)-Book Publishers Network
(s)-Brentwood—R
Broadman & Holman
Canticle Books—R
Chalice Press
Charisma House—R
Christian Focus—R
Christian Writers Ebook—R
Christopher Publishing
Cistercian—R
Continuum Intl.—R
Created in Christ
(s)-Creation House—R
Cross Cultural—R
Crossway Books
CSS Publishing
Descant Publishing
Destiny Image—R
Dimension Books—R
Doubleday
Educational Ministries
Eerdmans Publishing—R
Eerdmans/Young Readers
Elijah Press
(s)-Emmaus Road Pub.—R
(s)-Essence—R
Fair Havens—R
(s)-Fairway Press—R
Faith Communications
FaithWalk Publishing
FamilyLife Publishing
Forward Movement
Four Courts Press—R
Friends United Press—R
Genesis Communications
Good News Publishers
Greenwood Publishing

(s)-Guardian Books—R
(s)-Hannibal Books—R
HarperSanFrancisco
Hay House
Hendrickson—R
Hiddenspring Books
Hill Street Press—R
Holy Cross—R
Howard Publishing
(s)-Impact Christian—R
InterVarsity Press—R
Johns Hopkins—R
Jossey-Bass
Judson Press
Kregel—R
Larson Publications
Libros Liguori
Liguori
Living Books for All
Loyola Press
Lutterworth Press
Magnus Press—R
(s)-Master Design—R
Monarch Books—R
Morehouse
Multnomah
New Seeds Books—R
Northstone—R
Openbook—R
Oregon Catholic Press—R
OSL Publications—R
Our Sunday Visitor—R
Oxford University
P & R Publishing—R
Pacific Press
Paraclete Press—R
Paragon House
Pauline Books—R
Paulist Press
Perigee Books
Peter Pauper Press
Pilgrim Press—R
PREP Publishing—R
(s)-Promise Publishing
(s)-Providence House—R
PublishAmerica
Quintessential Books—R
Ragged Edge—R
Read 'N Run—R
Regnery—R
Resource Publications
Rising Star Press
RiverOak—R
Selah Publishing—R
Shaw Books—R
Sheed & Ward—R

Smyth & Helwys
(s)-So. Baptist Press—R
St. Anthony Messenger
Tate Publishing
Tau-Publishing—R
Twenty-Third Publications
Tyndale House—R
United Church Pub.
Victor Books
VMI Publishers
W Publishing Group
Wesleyan Publishing
Whitaker House—R
(s)-Winer Foundation—R
Wood Lake Books—R
(s)-Word for Word

SPIRITUAL LIFE*

(s)-American Binding—R
AMG Publishers—R
Baker Tritten
Baptist Pub. House
(s)-Black Forest—R
Canticle Books—R
Charisma House—R
Christian Publications—R
Christian Writers Ebook—R
Christopher Publishing
Created in Christ
Doubleday
(s)-Emmaus Road Pub.—R
FaithWalk Publishing
Forward Movement
Genesis Communications
Gospel Publishing House
Harrison House
Hiddenspring Books
InterVarsity Press—R
Jossey-Bass
Kregel—R
Legacy Publishers
(s)-Longwood—R
MegaGrace Books
Multnomah
Nelson Books
New Seeds Books—R
Paradise Research—R
Pathway Press
Pilgrim Press—R
(s)-Poetry of Today
(s)-Providence House—R
PublishAmerica
Resource Publications
Rose Publishing
Tate Publishing
(s)-TEACH Services—R

Tyndale House/SaltRiver
Victor Books
VMI Publishers
Wesleyan Publishing
Whitaker House—R
(s)-Word for Word

SPIRITUAL WARFARE

(s)-American Binding—R
Baker Books
Baylor Univ. Press—R
(s)-Black Forest—R
Bridge-Logos
Broadman & Holman
Carey Library, Wm.—R
Charisma House—R
Christian Focus—R
Christian Writers Ebook—R
Continuum Intl.—R
Created in Christ
(s)-Creation House—R
CSS Publishing
Destiny Image—R
Editores Betania-Caribe
Editorial Portavoz—R
(s)-Essence—R
(s)-Fairway Press—R
FaithWalk Publishing
Genesis Communications
Greenwood Publishing
(s)-Guardian Books—R
Harrison House
Harvest House
Hiddenspring Books
Iceagle Press—R
(s)-Impact Christian—R
Jireh Publishing
Lamplighter—R
Legacy Publishers
(s)-Lightning Star Press—R
Living Books for All
(s)-Longwood—R
Lutterworth Press
(s)-Master Design—R
(s)-McDougal Publishing—R
Monarch Books—R
Multnomah
(s)-Omega House—R
Paradise Research—R
(s)-Poetry of Today
(s)-Promise Publishing
(s)-Providence House—R
Read 'N Run—R
Selah Publishing—R
Tate Publishing
Virginia Pines Press

W Publishing Group
Whitaker House—R
(s)-Winer Foundation—R

SPORTS/RECREATION

Ambassador Books
(s)-Ambassador House
(s)-American Binding—R
Baker Books
Ballantine Books
Bridge-Logos
Canon Press—R
Christian Focus—R
Christian Writers Ebook—R
Christopher Publishing
Continuum Intl.—R
Cumberland House
(s)-Essence—R
Facts on File
(s)-Fairway Press—R
Genesis Communications
Good News Publishers
Greenwood Publishing
(s)-Guardian Books—R
Hill Street Press—R
Lutterworth Press
New York Univ. Press
(s)-Promise Publishing
(s)-Providence House—R
Read 'N Run—R
Tate Publishing
TowleHouse—R
VMI Publishers

STEWARDSHIP

Ambassador-Emerald—R
(s)-American Binding—R
Baker Books
Baptist Pub. House
(s)-Black Forest—R
Chalice Press
Charisma House—R
Christian Focus—R
Christian Writers Ebook—R
College Press—R
Continuum Intl.—R
Created in Christ
(s)-Creation House—R
CSS Publishing
Discovery House—R
Educational Ministries
(s)-Emmaus Road Pub.—R
(s)-Essence—R
Fair Havens—R
(s)-Fairway Press—R
FaithWalk Publishing

Forward Movement
Genesis Communications
Geneva Press
(s)-Guardian Books—R
Harrison House
Hensley Publishing—R
Hill Street Press—R
Judson Press
Lightwave Publishing
Liguori
Lutterworth Press
(s)-Master Design—R
(s)-McDougal Publishing—R
Multnomah
Neibauer Press—R
Openbook—R
Oregon Catholic Press—R
Pacific Press
Pilgrim Press—R
(s)-Promise Publishing
(s)-Providence House—R
Read 'N Run—R
RiverOak—R
Shaw Books—R
Tate Publishing
United Church Pub.
VMI Publishers
Wesleyan Publishing
Westminster John Knox
Whitaker House—R
(s)-Winer Foundation—R

THEOLOGY

ACU Press
Alba House—R
Ambassador-Emerald—R
(s)-American Binding—R
American Cath. Press—R
AMG Publishers—R
Baker Books
Baptist Pub. House
Baylor Univ. Press—R
Bethany House
(s)-Black Forest—R
Blue Dolphin
(s)-Brentwood—R
Bridge Resources
Bridge-Logos
Broadman & Holman
Canon Press—R
Canticle Books—R
(s)-Catholic Answers—R
Cerdic-Publications
Chalice Press
Chariot Books
Christian Focus—R

Christian Writers Ebook—R
Christopher Publishing
Cistercian—R
College Press—R
Conciliar Press—R
Continuum Intl.—R
Created in Christ
(s)-Creation House—R
Cross Cultural—R
Crossroad Publishing—R
Crossway Books
CSS Publishing
Dimension Books—R
Discovery House—R
Doubleday
Eerdmans Publishing—R
(s)-Emmaus Road Pub.—R
(s)-Essence—R
Fair Havens—R
(s)-Fairway Press—R
FaithWalk Publishing
Fortress Press
Friends United Press—R
Geneva Press
Georgetown Univ. Press
(s)-Guardian Books—R
HarperSanFrancisco
Harvest House
Hendrickson—R
Hiddenspring Books
Hill Street Press—R
Holy Cross—R
(s)-Impact Christian—R
Inkling Books—R
InterVarsity Press—R
Intl. Awakening—R
Judson Press
Kregel—R
Lighthouse Trails Publishing—R
Liguori
Liturgical Press
Liturgy Training
Lutterworth Press
Magnus Press—R
(s)-Master Design—R
Mercer Univ. Press—R
Millennium III—R
Monarch Books—R
Multnomah
New Seeds Books—R
Open Court—R
Openbook—R
Oregon Catholic Press—R
OSL Publications—R
Our Sunday Visitor—R
Oxford University

P & R Publishing—R
Pacific Press
Paulist Press
Pickwick Publications—R
Pilgrim Press—R
(s)-Poetry of Today
(s)-Promise Publishing
(s)-Providence House—R
PublishAmerica
Quintessential Books—R
Read 'N Run—R
Religious Education
RiverOak—R
Shaw Books—R
Sheed & Ward—R
Smyth & Helwys
(s)-So. Baptist Press—R
St. Augustine's Press—R
Still Waters Revival—R
Tate Publishing
Trinity Foundation—R
Trinity Press Intl.—R
Twenty-Third Publications
Tyndale House—R
UMI Publishing—R
Univ. Press of America—R
Victor Books
VMI Publishers
Westminster John Knox
Whitaker House—R

TIME MANAGEMENT

(s)-American Binding—R
Baker Books
Barbour Publishing
(s)-Black Forest—R
Broadman & Holman
Chariot Books
Christian Writers Ebook—R
Christopher Publishing
Continuum Intl.—R
(s)-Creation House—R
(s)-DCTS Publishing—R
(s)-Elderberry Press
(s)-Essence—R
Fair Havens—R
(s)-Fairway Press—R
Genesis Communications
(s)-Guardian Books—R
Harvest House
Hensley Publishing—R
Hill Street Press—R
Life Journey Books—R
Lutterworth Press
Moms In Print
Monarch Books—R

(s)-Promise Publishing
(s)-Providence House—R
Read 'N Run—R
RiverOak—R
Summit Pub. Group—R
Tate Publishing
VMI Publishers
Walk Worthy—R
Whitaker House—R
(s)-Winer Foundation—R

TRACTS

Baptist Pub. House
Christian Writers Ebook—R
(s)-Essence—R
(s)-Fruit-Bearer Pub.
Good News Publishers
Gospel Tract Society
(s)-Guardian Books—R
Intl. Awakening—R
Lamplighter—R
Libros Liguori
Liguori
(s)-Longwood—R
Neibauer Press—R
(s)-One World—R
Read 'N Run—R
Rose Publishing
Tract League
Trinity Foundation—R

TRAVEL

(s)-American Binding—R
Baker Books
Ballantine Books
(s)-Black Forest—R
(s)-Brentwood—R
Bridge-Logos
Christian Writers Ebook—R
Christopher Publishing
Crane Hill—R
Cumberland House
(s)-Elderberry Press
(s)-Essence—R
(s)-Fairway Press—R
FaithWalk Publishing
Greenwood Publishing
(s)-Guardian Books—R
Hill Street Press—R
Ideals Books
Image Books—R
Liguori
Lutterworth Press
(s)-Promise Publishing
(s)-Providence House—R
Read 'N Run—R

Tate Publishing
United Church Pub.
Whitaker House—R

WOMEN'S ISSUES

Ambassador Books
(s)-Ambassador House
Ambassador-Emerald—R
AMG Publishers—R
Baker Books
Ballantine Books
Baptist Pub. House
Barbour Publishing
Basic Books—R
Beacon Hill Press
Bethany House
(s)-Black Forest—R
Blue Dolphin
(s)-Book Publishers Network
Bridge-Logos
Broadman & Holman
Cerdic-Publications
Chalice Press
Chariot Books
Charisma House—R
Christian Focus—R
Christian Writers Ebook—R
Christopher Publishing
College Press—R
Continuum Intl.—R
Created in Christ
(s)-Creation House—R
Crossway Books
Destiny Image—R
Discovery House—R
(s)-Essence—R
Fair Havens—R
(s)-Fairway Press—R
Faith Communications
FaithWalk Publishing
FamilyLife Publishing
Fortress Press
Genesis Communications
Genesis Press
Gospel Publishing House
Greenwood Publishing
(s)-Guardian Books—R
Guernica Editions—R
Harrison House
Harvest House
Haworth Press—R
Hensley Publishing—R
Hill Street Press—R
Howard Publishing
Inkling Books—R
InterVarsity Press—R

Jeremy P. Tarcher
Johns Hopkins—R
Jossey-Bass
Jubilant Press—R
Judson Press
Kregel—R
Legacy Publishers
Life Cycle Books—R
Life Journey Books—R
Lighthouse Trails Publishing—R
(s)-Lightning Star Press—R
Liguori
(s)-Longwood—R
Loyola Press
Lutterworth Press
(s)-Master Design—R
(s)-McDougal Publishing—R
Monarch Books—R
Moody Publishers
Multnomah
New Hope—R
New Leaf Press—R
New York Univ. Press
Openbook—R
Oregon Catholic Press—R
P & R Publishing—R
Perigee Books
Pilgrim Press—R
(s)-Poetry of Today
(s)-Promise Publishing
(s)-Providence House—R
PublishAmerica
Read 'N Run—R
RiverOak—R
(s)-Robbie Dean Press—R
Scarecrow Press—R
Selah Publishing—R
Sheed & Ward—R
(s)-So. Baptist Press—R
Still Waters Revival—R
Summit Pub. Group—R
Tate Publishing
Third World Press—R
Twenty-Third Publications
Univ. of AR Press—R
VMI Publishers
W Publishing Group
Whitaker House—R
(s)-Word for Word

WORLD ISSUES

Algora Publishing—R
Allegiance Books—R
Baker Books
Bethany House
(s)-Black Forest—R

Blue Dolphin
Bridge-Logos
Carey Library, Wm.—R
Chalice Press
Charisma House—R
Christian Focus—R
Christian Writers Ebook—R
Christopher Publishing
Continuum Intl.—R
(s)-Creation House—R
Cross Cultural—R
(s)-Essence—R
Fair Havens—R
(s)-Fairway Press—R
FaithWalk Publishing
Georgetown Univ. Press
Greenwood Publishing
(s)-Guardian Books—R
Guernica Editions—R
Harrison House
Hill Street Press—R
InterVarsity Press—R
(s)-Longwood—R
Lutterworth Press
Monarch Books—R
New Leaf Press—R
New Seeds Books—R
Pilgrim Press—R
(s)-Promise Publishing
(s)-Providence House—R
Quintessential Books—R
Read 'N Run—R
Regnery—R
RiverOak—R
Rose Publishing
Selah Publishing—R
Shaw Books—R
Still Waters Revival—R
Tate Publishing
Tyndale House—R
United Church Pub.
(s)-VESTA—R
VMI Publishers
Whitaker House—R

WORSHIP

Abingdon Press
Ambassador-Emerald—R
(s)-American Binding—R
Baptist Pub. House
Baylor Univ. Press—R
(s)-Black Forest—R
Broadman & Holman
Canon Press—R
Chariot Books
Charisma House—R
Charisma Kids

Christian Writers Ebook—R
Christopher Publishing
College Press—R
Continuum Intl.—R
Created in Christ
(s)-Creation House—R
Destiny Image—R
Doubleday
Educational Ministries
(s)-Emmaus Road Pub.—R
Faith Alive Resources
FaithWalk Publishing
Forward Movement
Greenwood Publishing
Harrison House
Hiddenspring Books
Hill Street Press—R
Iceagle Press—R
InterVarsity Press—R
Kregel—R
Life Journey Books—R
(s)-Master Design—R
Multnomah
Nexgen
P & R Publishing—R
Pacific Press
Paulist Press
Pickwick Publications—R
Pilgrim Press—R
(s)-Poetry of Today
(s)-Providence House—R
PublishAmerica
Resource Publications
Rose Publishing
Selah Publishing—R
Tate Publishing
Victor Books
VMI Publishers
W Publishing Group
Wesleyan Publishing
Westminster John Knox
Whitaker House—R

WORSHIP RESOURCES

Abingdon Press
American Cath. Press—R
Baker Books
Baylor Univ. Press—R
Bethany House
Catholic Book Publishing
Chalice Press
Charisma House—R
Christian Writers Ebook—R
Continuum Intl.—R
Created in Christ
(s)-Creation House—R
CSS Publishing

(s)-DCTS Publishing—R
(s)-Elderberry Press
(s)-Emmaus Road Pub.—R
(s)-Essence—R
Fair Havens—R
(s)-Fairway Press—R
Faith Alive Resources
FaithWalk Publishing
FamilyLife Publishing
Forward Movement
Geneva Press
Greenwood Publishing
Group Publishing
(s)-Guardian Books—R
Hiddenspring Books
Hill Street Press—R
InterVarsity Press—R
Judson Press
Liturgical Press
Liturgy Training
(s)-Master Design—R
Openbook—R
Oregon Catholic Press—R
OSL Publications—R
Our Sunday Visitor—R
Paulist Press
Pilgrim Press—R
(s)-Poetry of Today
(s)-Promise Publishing
(s)-Providence House—R
Read 'N Run—R
Resource Publications
Smyth & Helwys
Standard Publishing
Tate Publishing
Twenty-Third Publications
United Church Pub.
VMI Publishers
Wesleyan Publishing
Westminster John Knox
Wood Lake Books—R

WRITING HOW-TO

(s)-American Binding—R
(s)-Black Forest—R
Bridge-Logos
Christian Writers Ebook—R
Diamond Eyes—R
(s)-Essence—R
(s)-Fairway Press—R
FaithWalk Publishing
Genesis Communications
Green Pastures Press—R
(s)-Guardian Books—R
Jubilant Press—R
Lillenas
(s)-Poetry of Today

(s)-Promise Publishing
(s)-Providence House—R
PublishAmerica
Selah Publishing—R
Shaw Books—R
Square One—R
VMI Publishers
Write Now—R

YOUTH BOOKS
(Nonfiction)

Note: Listing denotes books for 8- to 12-year-olds, junior highs, or senior highs. If all three, it will say "all." If no age group is listed, they did not specify.

Ambassador Books (All)
(s)-Ambassador House
Ambassador-Emerald—R
(s)-American Binding—R
  (Jr./Sr. High)
AMG Publishers—R (Jr. High)
Baker Books
Baker Tritten (All)
Barbour Publishing
Bethany House
Big Idea, Inc. (8-12/Jr. High)
BJU/Journey Forth—R
(s)-Black Forest—R (All)
Boyds Mills Press—R
Broadman & Holman
Canon Press—R
Charisma Kids (8-12/Jr. High)
Christian Ed. Pub.
Christian Focus—R
Christian Writers Ebook—R (All)
Concordia

Contemporary Drama Service
(s)-Creation House—R (All)
CSS Publishing
Educational Ministries
Eerdmans/Young Readers
(s)-Emmaus Road Pub.—R (All)
(s)-Essence—R
Facts on File
Fair Havens—R
(s)-Fairway Press—R
FamilyLife Publishing
Friends United Press—R
Genesis Communications
Genesis Press
Glory Bound Books (All)
Green Pastures Press—R (8-12)
(s)-Guardian Books—R
Harcourt Religion (Sr. High)
Harrison House (All)
Health Communications
Hensley Publishing—R
Honor Kidz (8-12)
Judson Press
Kaleidoscope Press—R
Kregel—R (All)
Lamplighter—R
Legacy Press—R
Lightwave Publishing
Lutterworth Press
McRuffy Press (8-12)
Moody Publishers
New Canaan
New Hope—R
OnStage Publishing
Oregon Catholic Press—R
P & R Publishing—R (Jr. High)
Pacific Press
Pauline Books—R

Pelican Publishing—R (8-12)
Pflaum Publishing Group (All)
Read 'N Run—R
Shining Star
(s)-So. Baptist Press—R
Still Waters Revival—R
Tate Publishing (All)
VMI Publishers (All)
Wood Lake Books—R
World Publishing—R
Youth Specialties (Jr./Sr. High)

YOUTH PROGRAMS

(s)-American Binding—R
Baker Books
Christian Writers Ebook—R
Church Growth Inst.
Concordia
Contemporary Drama Service
(s)-Creation House—R
CSS Publishing
Educational Ministries
(s)-Fairway Press—R
Gospel Publishing House
Group Publishing
(s)-Guardian Books—R
Harcourt Religion
Hensley Publishing—R
Judson Press
Langmarc
Liguori
Lutterworth Press
Openbook—R
Pflaum Publishing Group
Pilgrim Press—R
Read 'N Run—R
Standard Publishing
Tate Publishing

ALPHABETICAL LISTINGS OF BOOK PUBLISHERS

(*) An asterisk before a listing indicates unconfirmed or no information update.
(#) A number symbol before a listing indicates it was updated from their guidelines or other current sources.
(+) A plus sign before a listing indicates it is a new listing this year and was not included last year.

If you do not find the publisher you are looking for, check the General Index. See the introduction to that index for the codes used to identify the current status of each unlisted publisher. If you do not understand all the terms or abbreviations used in these listings, read the "How to Use This Book" section.

+ABAGAIL PRESS, PO Box 1477, Cordova TN 38088-1477. (902)752-0322. Nondenominational. Alexandra F. Clair, ed.; John A. Bailey, acq. ed. Every believer has a testimony and story, and we want to give voice to some of those stories. No reprints. Prefers 50,000-80,000 wds., or 225-300 pgs. Royalty 8-12% of net; advance $1. Print-on-demand publisher (no charge to author). Publication within 6 mos. Considers simultaneous submissions. Responds in 3-6 wks. Guidelines on Website; no catalog.
   Nonfiction: Proposal/first 2 chapters; prefers mail query.
   Tips: "Looking for personal stories about or by those who overcome challenges in Christian faith. True stories of salvation, healing, and deliverance. We want well-written material, conversational, honest." Offers advice and help with promotion.

ABINGDON PRESS, 201—8th Ave. S., PO Box 801, Nashville TN 37202. (615)749-6301. Fax (615)749-6512. E-mail: (first initial and last name) @umpublishing.org. Website: www.abingdonpress.com. United Methodist Publishing House. Editors: Harriett Jane Olson, ed. dir.; Ron Kidd, gen. interest bks.; Robert Ratcliff, professional and academic bks.; Paul Franklyn, reference bks.; Joseph A. Crowe, gen. interest bks.; Peg Augustine, children's bks.; Crys Zinkiewicz, youth bks. Books and church supplies directed primarily to a mainline religious market. Imprint: Dimensions for Living (see separate listing). Publishes 120 titles/yr. Receives 3,000 submissions annually. Less than 5% of books from first-time authors. Accepts mss through agents. No reprints. Prefers 144 pgs. Royalty 5-10% on retail; advance. Average first printing 3,500-4,000. Publication within 18 mos. Prefers no simultaneous submissions. Requires requested ms on disk. Responds in 8-12 wks. Prefers NRSV or a variety of which NRSV is one. Guidelines (also by e-mail); free catalog.
   Nonfiction: Proposal/2 chapters; no phone/fax/e-query.
   Ethnic Books: African American, Hispanic, Native American, Korean.
   Photos: Accepts freelance photos for book covers.
   Tips: "We develop and produce materials to help more people in more places come to know and love God through Jesus Christ and to choose to serve God and neighbor."

ACTA PUBLICATIONS, 4848 N. Clark St., Chicago IL 60640-4711. (773)271-1030. Fax (773)271-7399. E-mail: actapublications@aol.com. Website: www.actapublications.com. Catholic. Gregory F. Augustine Pierce, pres. & co-publisher. Resources for the "end user" of the Christian faith. Publishes 10 titles/yr. Receives 65 submissions annually. 50% of books from first-time authors. Prefers 150-200 pgs. Royalty 10-12% of net; no advance. Average first printing 3,000. Publication within 1 yr. Responds in 2 mos. Prefers NRSV. Guidelines; catalog for 9x12 SAE/2 stamps.
   Nonfiction: Query or proposal/1 chapter; no phone/fax/e-query.

Tips: "Most open to books that are useful to a large number of average Christians. Read our catalog and one of our books first."

ACU PRESS, 1648 Campus Ct., Abilene TX 79601, or ACU Station Box 29138, Abilene TX 79699. (325)674-2720. Fax (325)674-6471. E-mail: LEMMONST@acu.edu. Website: www .acu.edu/acupress, or www.hillcrestpublishing.com. Church of Christ/Abilene Christian University. Thom Lemmons, ed.; Charme Robarts, asst. ed. Guidance in the religious life for members and leaders of the denomination. Publishes 10 titles/yr. Receives 100 submissions annually. 10% of books from first-time authors. Royalty 10%. Average first printing 5,000. Publication within 3 mos. Considers simultaneous submissions. Responds in 1 mo. Catalog.

Nonfiction: Proposal/3 chapters.

+A.D. PLAYERS THEATER, 2710 W. Alabama, Houston TX 77-98. (713)526-2721. E-mail: lee@adplayers.org. Website: www.adplayers.org. Lee Walker, literary mngr. Produces full-length plays and musicals with Judeo-Christian world-view; interested only in scripts suitable for production. Payment negotiable. Guidelines available by e-mail or Website.

Fiction: Play scripts only; phone/fax/e-query OK. "Send synopsis and/or brief scene or demo tape/CD. Include scripts and cast list."

Tips: "Our only consideration is whether the scripts are suitable for production in our theater—we don't publish them."

ALBA HOUSE, 2187 Victory Blvd., Staten Island NY 10314-6603. (718)761-0047. Fax (718)761-0057. E-mail: Edmund_Lane@juno.com. Website: albahouse.org. Catholic/Society of St. Paul. Edmund C. Lane SSP, ed-in-chief; Frank Sadowski, SSP, ed.; Father Victor Viberti, SSP, acq. ed. Imprint: St. Pauls. Publishes 24 titles/yr. Receives 450 submissions annually. 20% of books from first-time authors. No mss through agents. Reprints books. Prefers 124 pgs. Royalty 7-10% on retail; no advance. Average first printing 3,500. Publication within 9 mos. Prefers requested ms on disk. Responds in 1-2 mos. Free guidelines/catalog.

Nonfiction: Query.

Special Needs: Spirituality in the Roman Catholic tradition; lives of the saints.

ALGORA PUBLISHING, 222 Riverside Dr., 16th Fl., New York NY 10025-6809. (212)678-0232. Fax (212)663-9805. E-mail: editors@algora.com. Website: www.algora.com. Martin DeMers, acq. ed. Focus is on politics and international affairs, also history of religion. Publishes 25 titles/yr. Receives 700 submissions annually. 20% of books from first-time authors. Accepts mss through agents. Reprints books. Prefers 90,000 wds. Royalty 7.5-12% of net; advance to $1,000. Publication within 10 mos. Considers simultaneous submissions. Responds in 1-2 mos. Guidelines & catalog online.

Nonfiction: Prefers e-mail query; or send proposal/3 chapters, or complete ms.

Tips: "We publish well-researched, well-documented academic-type books for the educated, general reader. We help first-time writers get their project ready for publication."

ALLEGIANCE BOOKS, 10640 Main St., #204, Fairfax VA 22030. (703)934-4411. Fax (703)934-0174. E-mail: tfreiling@allegiancepress.com. Website: www.allegiancepress.com. Xulon Press. Tom Freiling, pub. Gives readers the truth about today's most relevant cultural and public policy issues from a Christian world-view. Publishes 12 titles/yr. 20% of books from first-time authors. Prefers mss through agents. Reprints books. Prefers 200-400 pgs. Royalty 15-20% of net. Average first printing 10,000. Publication within 9-18 mos. Considers simultaneous submissions. Prefers requested mss by e-mail. Guidelines on Website; no catalog.

Nonfiction: Proposal/2 chapters; e-query OK.

Tips: Most open to history, political, or current events.

AMBASSADOR BOOKS, INC., 91 Prescott St., Worcester MA 01605-1702. (508)756-2893. Fax (508)757-7055. E-mail: info@ambassadorbooks.com. Website: www.ambassador books.com. Catholic. Kathryn Conlan, acq. ed. Books of intellectual and spiritual excellence.

Publishes 7 titles/yr. Receives 2,000 submissions annually. 50% of books from first-time authors. Accepts mss through agents. No reprints. Royalty 8-12% of retail; no advance. Publication within 1 yr. Considers simultaneous submissions. Responds in 3-4 mos. Prefers NAB. Guidelines (also by e-mail/Website); free catalog (or on Website).

Nonfiction: Query; no phone/fax/e-query.

Fiction: Query. Juvenile, young adult, and adult; picture books.

Photos: Accepts freelance photoss for book covers.

Tips: "Most open to books that will have a positive impact on readers' lives. Must be well written and fit with our mission."

#AMBASSADOR-EMERALD, INTL., 427 Wade Hampton Blvd., Greenville SC 29609. (864)235-2434. Fax (864)235-2491. E-mail: authors@emeraldhouse.com, or info@emerald house.com. Website: www.emeraldhouse.com. European office: Ambassador Productions, Providence House, Ardenlee, Belfast BT6 8QJ, N. Ireland. Phone 028 90450010. Fax 028 90739659. E-mail: info@ambassador-productions.com. Emerald House Group, Inc. Tomm Knutson, ed. Dedicated to spreading the gospel of Christ and empowering Christians through the written word. Publishes 55 titles/yr. Receives 400 submissions annually. 15% of books from first-time authors. Accepts mss through agents. **SUBSIDY PUBLISHES 1%.** Reprints books. Prefers 150-200 pgs. Royalty 5-15% of net; advance $1,000. Average first printing 5,000. Publication within 1 yr. Considers simultaneous submissions. Prefers requested ms on disk or by e-mail. Responds in 3 mos. Prefers KJV. Guidelines (also by e-mail); free catalog.

Nonfiction: Query only; fax/e-query OK.

Fiction: Query only; fax/e-query OK. All ages.

Tips: "We're most open to nonfiction writing for women."

AMERICAN CATHOLIC PRESS, 16565 State St., South Holland IL 60473-2025. (708)331-5485. Fax (708)331-5484. E-mail: acp@acpress.org. Website: www.acpress.org, or www .leafletmissal.com. Catholic worship resources. Father Michael Gilligan, ed. dir. Publishes 4 titles/yr. Receives 10 submissions annually. Reprints books. Pays $25-100 for outright purchases only. Average first printing 3,000. Publication within 1 yr. Considers simultaneous submissions. Responds in 2 mos. Prefers NAS. No guidelines; catalog for SASE.

Nonfiction: Query first; no phone/fax/e-query.

Tips: "We publish only materials on the Roman Catholic liturgy. Especially interested in new music for church services."

AMG PUBLISHERS, 6815 Shallowford Rd. (37421), PO Box 22000, Chattanooga TN 37422. Toll-free (800)266-4977. (423)894-6060. Fax (800)265-6690 or (423)894-9511. E-mail: danp@amginternational.org. Website: www.amgpublishers.com. AMG International. Dan Penwell, dir. of product development/acquisitions: Dr. Warren Baker, sr. ed.; Richard Steele, assoc. ed. To provide biblically oriented books for reference, learning, and personal growth. Publishes 30 titles/yr. Receives 1,500 submissions annually. 20% of books from first-time authors. Accepts mss through agents. Reprints books. Prefers 50,000 wds. or 175 pgs. Royalty 10-16% of net; advance $1,500 and up. Average first printing 3,000. Publication within 1 yr. Accepts simultaneous submissions. Prefers accepted ms by mail. Responds in 1-4 mos. Prefers KJV, NASB, NIV, NKJV, NLT. Guidelines (also by e-mail/Website); catalog for 9x12 SAE/5 stamps.

Nonfiction: Query letter first; e-query OK. "Looking for well-written nonfiction. We have a broad interest in biblically oriented books."

Fiction: Teen fantasy.

Special Needs: Women's issues and men's issues.

Also Does: Bible software, Bible audio cassettes, CD-ROMs.

Tips: "Most open to a book that is well thought out, clearly written, and finely edited. A professional proposal, following our specific guidelines, has the best chance of acceptance."

Note: This publisher serviced by The Writer's Edge.

ANDROS BOOKS PUBLISHING, PO Box 12080, Prescott AZ 86304. (928)778-4491. Fax (928)778-4620. E-mail: androsbks@aol.com. Website: www.hometown.aol.com/androsbks. Small publisher. Susanne Bain, pub. Specializes in homeschooling and parental involvement in education. Prefers 200 pgs. Considers simultaneous submissions. Responds within 6 wks. No e-mail submissions (mail only). Guidelines (also by e-mail); no catalog.

Nonfiction: Query only first; no phone/fax query, e-query OK.

Tips: "We are currently seeking uplifting works about homeschool and positive parental involvement in children's education or continuing education. We prefer how to do it or how we did it from homeschooling parents only. We want personal experience."

AUGSBURG BOOKS, 100 S. 5th St., Ste. 700 (55402), Box 1209, Minneapolis MN 55440-1209. (612)330-3300. Fax (612)330-3215. Website: www.augsburgfortress.org. No freelance submissions.

Note: This publisher is serviced by The Writer's Edge.

BAKER BOOKS, Box 6287, Grand Rapids MI 49516-6287. (616)676-9185. Fax (616)676-9573. Website: www.bakerbooks.com, or www.thenarrowroad.net. Baker Publishing Group. No freelance submissions. Submit only through an agent, Writer's Edge, or ECPA First Edition.

BAKER'S PLAYS, PO Box 699222, Quincy MA 02269-9222. (617)745-0805. Fax (617)745-9891. Website: www.bakersplays.com. Deidre Shaw, ed. Publishes 2-8 titles/yr. Receives 800 submissions annually. 60% of plays from first-time authors. Accepts mss through agents. Reprints books. Book royalty 10%; performance royalty 50%; no advance. Average first printing 1,000. Publication within 8-10 mos. Considers simultaneous submissions. Accepts requested ms on disk. Responds in 6-8 mos. Free guidelines (also on Website); no catalog.

Plays: Complete ms. "Most open to plays that involve biblical stories or skits on modern Christian life."

Contest: High School Play Writing Contest. Deadline: January 30. No entry fee. Prizes: $500 (with publication), $250, $100. Plays about the high-school experience or appropriate for high school productions. Requires a signature from a sponsoring drama or English teacher. May not be held every year.

Tips: "We currently publish full-length plays, one-act plays for young audiences, theater texts and musicals, plays written by high schoolers, with a separate division which publishes plays for religious institutions. The ideal time to submit work is from September to April." If your play has been produced, send copies of press clippings.

+BAKER TRITTEN PRESS, PO Box 277, Winona Lake IN 46590. (574)269-6100. Fax (574)269-6130. E-mail: info@btconcepts.com. Website: www.btconcepts.com. Marvin G. Baker, ed-in-chief. Imprints: Tweener Press; Innovative Christian Publications. Books for 8- to 12-year-olds. Publishes 4-5 religious titles/yr. New publisher. 50% of books from first-time authors. Accepts mss through agents. No reprints. Prefers 20,000-40,000 wds. Royalty 7-10% on retail; no advance. Average first printing 2,500. Publication within 1 yr. No simultaneous submissions. Responds in 1 mo. Accepts mss on disk or by e-mail. Prefers NIV. No guidelines; catalog available soon.

Nonfiction: Proposal/3 chapters; no phone query; fax/e-query OK.

Fiction: Proposal/3 chapters; no phone query; fax/e-query OK.

BALLANTINE BOOKS, 1540 Broadway, New York NY 10036. (212)782-9000. Website: www.randomhouse.com/BB. A Division of Random House. Dan Smetanka, religion ed. General publisher that does a few religious books. Mss from agents only. Royalty 8-15%; variable advances. Guidelines on Website; no catalog.

BANTAM BOOKS—See Doubleday.

BAPTIST PUBLISHING HOUSE, 4613 Loop 245, Texarkana AR 71854. (870)772-0054. Fax

(870)772-5451. E-mail: jerome@bph.org. Website: www.bph.org. Baptist Missionary Assn. of America. Jerome Cooper, production dir.; Charles Reddin, adult ed.; Jerry Sawrie, youth ed.; and Amelia Beasley, children's ed. Focuses on Bible study, discipleship, and training material; providing resources for evangelical congregations and personal spiritual development. Imprint: Mirror Press. Publishes 1-2 titles/yr. Receives 10-20 submissions annually. 10% of books from first-time authors. No mss through agents. No reprints. Prefers 150-300 pgs. Outright purchase (all books assigned as work-for-hire); no advance. Average first printing 2,000. Publication within 3 mos. No simultaneous submissions. Prefers requested ms on disk. Responds in 3 mos. Prefers KJV. No guidelines; free catalog.

> **Nonfiction**: Query letter only; e-query OK.
>
> **Also Does**: Booklets, pamphlets, tracts.

BARBOUR PUBLISHING, INC., 1810 Barbour Dr., PO Box 719, Uhrichsville OH 44683. (740)922-6045. Fax (740)922-5948. E-mail: info@barbourbooks.com. Website: www.barbourbooks.com. Paul Muckley, editorial director. (pmuckley@barbourbooks.com); Rebecca Germany (rgermany@barbourbooks.com), sr. ed. for romance and women's fiction (novels & novellas); Shannon Hill (shill@barbourbooks.com), ed-at-large for suspense, historical, military, sci-fi, and youth-focused and other nonfiction titles; Kelly Williams (kwilliams@barbourbooks.com), mng. ed. Distributes Christian books at value prices. Imprints: Barbour Books (fiction and nonfiction) and Heartsong Presents (romance-see separate listing). Publishes 200 titles/yr. (80 fiction titles). Receives 2,000 submissions annually. 20% of books from first-time authors. Few mss through agents. Prefers 50,000 wds. (novels & nonfiction). Royalty 8-12% of net; outright purchases $500-5,000; advance $500-7,500. Average first printing 15,000-20,000. Publication within 2 yrs. Considers simultaneous submissions. Responds in 3-6 mos. Prefers NIV, KJV. Guidelines (also by e-mail/Website); catalog $2.

> **Nonfiction**: Proposal/3 chapters; no phone/fax/e-query.
>
> **Fiction**: Proposal/2 chapters to Rebecca Germany, fiction ed. Novellas 20,000 wds. "We are interested in a mystery/romance series." See separate listing for Heartsong Presents.
>
> **Special Needs**: Card Books that can be sold with an envelope.
>
> **Tips**: "We seek solid, evangelical books with the greatest mass appeal. A good title on practical Christian living will go much farther with Barbour than will a commentary on Jude. Do your homework before sending us a manuscript; send material that will work well within our publishing philosophy."
>
> ****Note**: This publisher serviced by The Writer's Edge.

BARCLAY PRESS, 110 S. Elliott Rd., Newberg OR 97132-2144. (503)538-9775. Fax (503)538-7033. E-mail: info@barclaypress.com. Website: www.barclaypress.com. Friends/Quaker. Dan McCracken, gen. mngr. No unsolicited manuscripts.

> ****Note**: This publisher serviced by The Writer's Edge.

BASIC BOOKS, 387 Park Ave. South, 12th Fl., New York NY 10016-8810. (212)340-8100. Fax (212)340-8115. Website: www.basicbooks.com. Elizabeth Maguire, VP, assoc. ed. Perseus Books Group. Secular publisher that does books on religion and spirituality. Publishes 100 titles/yr. Receives 800 submissions annually. 5% of books from first-time authors. Accepts mss through agents. Reprints books. Royalty 10-15% on retail; advance to $10,000. Publication within 1 yr. Considers simultaneous submissions. Responds in 3-6 mos. No submissions on disk or by e-mail. Prefers NIV. Guidelines on Website; free catalog.

> **Nonfiction**: Query by mail, or send proposal/3 chapters. No complete mss. "We do not do poetry, romance, children's books, or conventional thrillers."

BAYLOR UNIVERSITY PRESS, One Bear Pl., #97363, Waco TX 76798-7308. (254)710-3164. Fax (254)710-3440. E-mail: Carey_Newman@baylor.edu. Website: www.baylorpress.com. Baptist. Carey C. Newman, dir. Imprint: Markham Press Fund. Academic press producing scholarly books on religion and social sciences; church-state studies. Publishes 4 titles/yr. Receives 120 submissions annually. 10% of books from first-time authors. Accepts mss through agents. Reprints books. Prefers 250 pgs. Royalty 10% of net; no advance. Average first printing 1,000. Publication within 1 yr. Responds in 2 mos. No guidelines; free catalog.

Nonfiction: Query/outline; no phone query, e-query OK. Looking for academic books.

BEACON HILL PRESS OF KANSAS CITY, PO Box 419527, Kansas City MO 64141. (816)931-1900. Fax (816)753-4071. E-mail: bjp@bhillkc.com. Website: www.bhillkc.com. Nazarene Publishing House/Church of the Nazarene. Bonnie Perry, pub. dir.; Richard Buckner, ministry line ed.; Judi Perry, trade ed. A Christ-centered publisher that provides authentically Christian resources that are faithful to God's Word and relevant to life. Imprint: Beacon Hill Books. Publishes 40 titles/yr. Accepts mss through agents. Prefers 30,000-60,000 wds. or 250 pgs. Royalty 12-14% of net; advance; some outright purchases. Average first printing 5,000. Publication within 2 yrs. Considers simultaneous submissions. Responds in 3 mos. or longer. Free guidelines/catalog.

Nonfiction: Proposal/2 chapters; no phone/fax query. "Looking for practical Christian living, felt needs, Christian care, spiritual growth, and ministry resources."

Tips: "Nearly all our titles come through acquisitions, and the number of freelance submissions has declined dramatically. If you wish to submit, follow guidelines above. You are always welcome to submit after sending for guidelines."

**Note: This publisher serviced by The Writer's Edge.

BETHANY HOUSE PUBLISHERS, 11400 Hampshire Ave. S., Bloomington MN 55438. (952)829-2500. Fax (952)996-1304 or (952)829-2768. Website: www.bethany house.com. Baker Publishing Group. Submit to nonfiction, fiction or juvenile ed. To publish books communicating biblical truth that will inspire and challenge people in both spiritual and practical areas of life. Publishes 90-100 titles/yr. 2% of books from first-time authors. Accepts mss through agents. No reprints. Negotiable royalty, on net, and advance. Publication within 1 yr. Considers simultaneous submissions. Responds in 4-6 wks. Guidelines for fiction/nonfiction/juvenile on Website; no catalog.

Nonfiction: One-page fax query only; all unsolicited submissions returned unopened. "Seeking well-planned and developed books in the following categories: personal growth, deeper-life spirituality, contemporary issues, women's issues, reference, applied theology, and inspirational."

Fiction: One-page fax query only; all unsolicited submissions returned unopened. "We publish adult fiction in several genres, teen/young adult fiction, and children's fiction series (6-12 yrs.)."

Tips: "We do not accept unsolicited queries or proposals via telephone, regular mail, or e-mail, but will consider one-page queries sent by facsimile (fax) and directed to Adult Nonfiction, Adult Fiction, or Young Adult/Children."

**Note: This publisher serviced by The Writer's Edge.

+BIG IDEA, INC., 230 Franklin Rd., Franklin TN 37064. (615)224-2200. E-mail: cindy.kenney@ bigidea.com. Website: www.bigidea.com. Classic Media. Cindy Kenney, sr. mng. ed. To creatively impact the lives of children, ages 2 through 12, with stories that teach biblical values. Publishes 15-20 titles/yr. Receives 1,000 submissions annually. 25% of books from first-time authors. Accepts mss through agents. No reprints. Prefers 1,500-2,000 wds. Negotiable outright purchase (no royalties); no advance. Average first printing 10,000-20,000. Publication within 18 mos. Considers simultaneous submissions. Responds in 4-6 mos. Prefers NIRV or NIV. No catalog (see online).

Nonfiction: Query first; complete ms for picture or board books; no phone/fax query; e-query OK.

Fiction: Query first; complete ms for picture books; no phone/fax query; e-query OK.

Special Needs: Looking for picture books and tween books.

Tips: "Come up with stories/materials that are highly innovative, clever, witty, and teach a biblical value."

BJU PRESS/JOURNEY FORTH, 1700 Wade Hampton Blvd., Greenville SC 29614. (864)370-1800, ext. 4350. Fax (864)298-0268, ext. 4324. E-mail: jb@bju.edu. Website: www.bjup.com. Bob Jones University Press. Nancy Lohr, youth ed. Our goal is to publish excellent, trustworthy books for children. Publishes 10 titles/yr. Receives 500 submissions annually. 30% of books from first-time authors. Accepts mss through agents. Reprints books. Royalty on net; outright purchases (for first-time authors). Average first printing 5,000. Publication within 12-18 mos. Considers simultaneous submissions. Responds in 8-12 wks. Requires KJV. Guidelines (also by e-mail/Website); catalog for 9x12 SAE/3 stamps.

Nonfiction: Proposal/3 chapters or complete ms; no phone/fax/e-query.

Fiction: Proposal/5 chapters or complete ms. For children & teens. "We prefer overtly Christian or Christian world-view."

Tips: "While there are many devotional/Bible-study books for children on the market, we continue to focus our efforts on well-crafted fiction and biographies. We are not currently looking to publish children's devotionals or study books. Not currently accepting picture books."

**Note: This publisher serviced by The Writer's Edge.

BLUE DOLPHIN PUBLISHING, INC., PO Box 8, Nevada City CA 95959. (530)265-6925. Fax (530)265-0787. E-mail: Bdolphin@netshel.net. Website: www.bluedolphinpublishing.com. Paul M. Clemens, pub. Imprint: Pelican Pond (fiction). Books that help people grow in their social and spiritual awareness. Publishes 20-24 titles/yr. (includes 10-12 print-on-demand). Receives 4,800 submissions annually. 90% of books from first-time authors. Prefers about 60,000 wds. or 200-300 pgs. Royalty 10-15% of net; no advance. Average first printing 300, then on demand. Publication within 10 mos. Considers simultaneous submissions. Requires requested ms on disk. Responds in 3-6 mos. Guidelines (also on Website); catalog for 6x9 SAE/2 stamps.

Nonfiction: Query or proposal/1 chapter; no phone/e-query. "Looking for books that will increase people's spiritual and social awareness. We will consider all topics."

Fiction: Query/2-pg. synopsis. Pelican Pond Imprint. Will consider all genres for all ages, except children's board books or picture books.

Tips: "We look for topics that would appeal to the general market, are interesting, different, and will aid in the growth and development of humanity. See Website before submitting."

Note: This publisher also publishes books on a range of topics, including cross-cultural spirituality. They also offer a co-publishing arrangement, not necessarily a royalty deal.

#BOOKLOCKER.COM, INC., PO Box 2399, Bangor ME 04402-2399. Fax (207)262-5544. Website: www.booklocker.com. E-books or print-on-demand. Royalty varies according to product/price. Prices and terms on Website; also contract. No questionnaire returned.

#BOOKLOCKER JR, PO Box 2399, Bangor ME 04402-2399. Fax (207)262-5544. Website: www.booklocker.com/getpublished/published.html. E-books or print-on-demand. Seeking submissions from young authors, under 18 years. Royalty varies according to product/price. Prices and terms on Website; also contract. Not included in topical listings. No questionnaire returned.

*BORDEN BOOKS, 6532 E. 71st St., Ste. 105, Tulsa OK 74133. Dave Borden, ed. Not included in topical listings. No questionnaire returned.

BOYDS MILLS PRESS, 815 Church St., Honesdale PA 18431-1895. (570)253-1164. Fax (570)253-0179. E-mail: admin@boydsmillspress.com. Website: www.boydsmills press.com. Highlights for Children. Larry Rosler, ed. dir. Publishes a wide range of literary children's titles, for preschool through young adult; very few religious. Publishes 50 titles/yr. Receives 10,000 submissions annually. 40% of books from first-time authors. Reprints books. Royalty 4-12% on retail; advances vary. Considers simultaneous submissions. Responds in 1 mo. Guidelines and catalog on Website.

Nonfiction: Query/proposal package, outline, 1 sample chapter; no fax or e-query.

Fiction: Outline/synopsis/3 chapters for novels; complete ms for picture books. "We are always interested in multicultural settings."

Tips: "Looking for picture books for pre-readers that contain simple, focused, and fun concepts for children ages 3-5, and concept books. We are primarily a general trade book publisher. For us, if stories include religious themes, the stories should still have a wide enough appeal for a general audience."

#BRANDEN PUBLISHING CO., PO Box 812094, Wellesley MA 02482. Fax (781)790-1056. Adolph Caso, ed. Books by or about women, children, military, Italian American or African American themes; religious fiction. Reprints books. Royalty 5-10% of net; advance $1,000 max. Incomplete topical listings. No questionnaire returned.

Nonfiction: Paragraph query only with author's vita & SASE; no fax query.

Fiction: Paragraph query only with author's vita & SASE. Ethnic, religious fiction.

BRAZOS PRESS, PO Box 6287, Grand Rapids MI 49516-6287. Division of Baker Publishing Group. No freelance. Submit through Writer's Edge or ECPA First Edition.

BRIDGE-LOGOS, PO Box 141630, Gainesville FL 32614-1640. (352)472-7900. Fax (352)472-7908. E-mail: editorial@bridgelogos.com. Website: www.bridgelogos.com. Beverly G. Browning, mng. ed. Purpose is to clearly define God's changeless Word to a changing world. Imprints: Logos, Bridge, Selah, and Synergy. Publishes 25 titles/yr. Receives 510 submissions annually. 40% of books from first-time authors. **SUBSIDY PUBLISHES 12%.** Prefers 180 pgs. Royalty 6-25% of net; some advances, $1,000-10,000. Average first printing 5,000. Publication within 6 mos. Considers simultaneous submissions. Responds in 15 wks. No disk. Guidelines (also by e-mail/Website); no catalog.

Nonfiction: Query only. "Most open to evangelism, spiritual growth, self-help, and education."

Special Needs: Reference, biography, current issues, controversial issues, church renewal, women's issues, and Bible commentary.

Photos: Accepts freelance photos for book covers.

Tips: "Have a great message, a well-written manuscript, and a specific plan and willingness to market your book. Looking for previously published authors with an active ministry who are experts on their subject."

BRIDGE RESOURCES/WITHERSPOON PRESS, 100 Witherspoon St., Louisville KY 40202-1396. Toll-free (888)728-7228. (502)569-5202. E-mail: ssorem@ctr.pcusa.org. Website: www.pcusa.org/cmd/cmp. Congregational Ministries Publishing/Presbyterian Church (U.S.A.) Sandra M. Sorem, pub. Prefers NRSV. Publishes nonfiction works that help congregations fulfill their ministries and individuals more thoroughly understand the Presbyterian Church (U.S.A.); Bible studies, resources for children, youth and adults; bringing those with special needs into fuller participation; lay leadership. Reformed theology only. Guidelines on Website. Incomplete topical listings.

Nonfiction: Proposal/sample chapters. "Treatment/sample chapters required for consideration."

BROADMAN & HOLMAN, 127—9th Ave. N., Nashville TN 37234-0115. (615)251-2438. Fax (615)251-3752. E-mail: courtney.brooks@lifeway.com. Website: www.broadmanholman.com. Book and Bible division of Lifeway Christian Resources. Leonard Goss, ed. dir.; David Shepherd, Sr. VP-publisher. Publishes books in the conservative, evangelical tradition by and for the larger Christian world. Publishes 100 titles/yr. Receives 3,000 submissions annually. 10% of books from first-time authors. Prefers 60,000-80,000 wds. Variable royalty on net;

advance. Average first printing 5,000. Publication within 12-18 mos. Considers simultaneous submissions. Responds in 3 mos. Requires requested ms on disk. Prefers HCSB, NIV, NASB. Guidelines; no catalog.

Nonfiction: Proposal only first; no phone/fax query.

Fiction: Prefers adult contemporary. Full synopsis/2 chapters.

Ethnic: Spanish translations.

Also Does: Rocket e-books.

Tips: "Follow guidelines when submitting. Be informed about the market in general and specifically related to the book you want to write." Expanding into fiction, gift books, and children's books.

**Note: This publisher serviced by The Writer's Edge.

CAMBRIDGE UNIVERSITY PRESS, 40 W. 20th St., New York NY 10011-4211. Toll-free (800)872-7423. (212)924-3900. Fax (212)691-3239. E-mail: information@cup.org. Specific e-mails on Website. Website: www.cup.org. University of Cambridge. Andrew Beck, religion ed. (abeck@cup.org).

Nonfiction: Proposal; no complete mss.

CANADIAN INSTITUTE FOR LAW, THEOLOGY & PUBLIC POLICY, INC., 7203—90th Ave., Edmonton AB T6B 0P5 Canada. (780)465-4581. Fax (780)465-4581. E-mail: ciltpp@cs.com. Website: www.ciltpp.com. Will Moore, pres. Integrating Christianity with the study of law and political science. Publishes 2-4 titles/yr. Receives 4-5 submissions annually. 1% of books from first-time authors. Accepts mss through agents. Reprints books. Royalty 7% of retail; no advance. Average first printing 1,000. Publication within 12-24 mos. No simultaneous submissions. Responds in 6-12 mos. Prefers NIV. Free guidelines (also by e-mail)/catalog.

Nonfiction: Proposal/1 chapter. "Looking for books integrating Christianity with law and political science."

Photos: Accepts freelance photos for book covers.

CANDY CANE PRESS, 535 Metroplex Dr., Ste. 250, Nashville TN 37211. Toll-free (800)586-2572. (615)333-0478. Fax (888)815-2759. Website: www.idealspublications.com. Ideals Publications/Guideposts. Patricia Pingry, ed.; submit to Peggy Schaefer, mng. ed. Board books for 3- to 5-year-olds (holiday oriented, religious, or Americana). Publishes 5-10 titles/yr. Maximum 1,000 wds. Royalty; variable advance. Responds in 2 mos. Send for guidelines/catalog.

Fiction: Complete mss for board books.

Tips: "We are looking in particular for subjects pertaining to holidays (Christmas, Valentine, Easter, etc.), either secular or religious."

CANON PRESS, PO Box 8729, Moscow ID 83843. (208)882-1456. Fax (208)882-1568. E-mail: canonads@moscow.com. Website: www.canonpress.org. Christ Church (Reformed; Presbyterian). J.C. Evans, ed. Aims to expand "medieval Protestantism" in terms of truth, beauty, and goodness. Publishes 10-15 titles/yr. Receives 150 submissions annually. 10% of books from first-time authors. Accepts mss through agents. Reprints books. Prefers 100-300 pgs. Royalty on retail; no advance. Average first printing 3,000. Publication within 1 yr. Considers simultaneous submissions. Prefers accepted ms by e-mail. Responds in 1 mo. Prefers NKJV. Guidelines (also by e-mail/Website); free catalog.

Nonfiction: Query first; no phone/fax query; e-query OK.

Fiction: Query first. "We want literary fiction, but not genre."

Also Does: Booklets, e-books (soon).

Tips: "Most open to books from a Trinitarian world-view. Avoid the typical, modern, sentimental evangelical thinking, as well as intellectualistic Presbyterianism. We delight in beauty and humor, creation, and the reformed tradition. Please consult guidelines on Website before submitting."

CANTICLE BOOKS, PO Box 2666, Carlsbad CA 92018. (760)806-3743. Fax (760)806-3689. E-mail: magnuspres@aol.com. Website: www.magnuspress.com. Imprint of Magnus Press. Warren Angel, ed. dir. To publish biblical studies by Catholic authors which are written for the average person and which minister life to Christ's Church. Publishes 2 titles/yr. Receives 60 submissions annually. 50% of books from first-time authors. Accepts submissions through agents. Reprints books. Prefers 125-375 pgs. Royalty 6-12% on retail; no advance. Average first printing 5,000. Publication within 1 yr. Considers simultaneous submissions. Accepts requested ms on disk. Responds in 1 mo. Guidelines (also by e-mail); free catalog.

    Nonfiction: Query or proposal/2-3 chapters; fax query OK. "Looking for spirituality, thematic biblical studies, unique inspirational/devotional books."

    Tips: "Our writers need solid knowledge of the Bible and a mature spirituality that reflects a profound relationship with Jesus Christ. Most open to well-researched, popularly written biblical studies geared to Catholics, or personal experience books which share/emphasize a person's relationship with Christ."

CASCADIA PUBLISHING HOUSE, 126 Klingerman Rd., Telford PA 18969. (215)723-9125. E-mail: editor@cascadiapublishinghouse.com. Website: www.cascadiapublishinghouse.com. Mennonite. Michael A. King, ed. Imprint: DreamSeeker Books. Open to freelance; uses little unsolicited. Some books are subsidized by interested institutions. Not included in topical listings. No questionnaire returned.

    Nonfiction: Query only/vita; e-query OK.

CATHOLIC BOOK PUBLISHING CO., 77 West End Rd., Totowa NJ 07512. (973)890-2400. Fax (973)890-2410. E-mail: info@catholicbookpublishing.com. Website: http://catholicbook publishing.com. Catholic. Anthony Buono, mng. ed. Inspirational books for Catholic Christians. Acquired Resurrection Press and World Catholic Press. Publishes 15-20 titles/yr. Receives 75 submissions annually. 30% of books from first-time authors. No mss through agents. Variable royalty or outright purchases; no advance. Average first printing 3,000. Publication within 12-15 mos. No simultaneous submissions. Responds in 2-3 mos. Catalog for 9x12 SAE/5 stamps.

    Nonfiction: Query letter only; no phone/fax query.

    Tips: "We publish mainly liturgical books, Bibles, Missals, and prayer books. Most of the books are composed in-house or by direct commission with particular guidelines. We strongly prefer query letters in place of full manuscripts."

*CERDIC-PUBLICATIONS, PJR-RIC, 11, Rue Jean Sturm, 67520 Nordheim, France. Phone (03)88.87.71.07. Fax (03)88.87.71.25. Marie Zimmerman, dir. Publishes 3-5 titles/yr. 50+% of books from first-time authors. Prefers 230 pgs. The first print run in the field of law in religion does not make money; no payment. Average first printing 2,200. Publication within 3 mos.(varies). Considers simultaneous submissions. Responds in 4 wks. No guidelines; free catalog.

    Nonfiction: Complete ms; phone/fax query OK. "Looking for books on law and religion. All topics checked in topical listings must relate to the law."

    Tips: "We publish original studies in law of religion (any) with preference for young, beginning authors; in French only."

CHALICE PRESS, Box 179, St. Louis MO 63166-0179. (314)231-8500. Fax (314)231-8524. E-mail: chalice@cbp21.com. Website: www.chalicepress.com. Christian Church (Disciples of Christ). Dr. Jane McAvoy, ed. dir.; Dr. Trent Butler, sr. ed. Books for a thinking, caring church; in Bible, theology, ethics, homiletics, pastoral care, Christian education, Christian living, and spiritual growth. Publishes 50 titles/yr. Receives 500 submissions annually. 15% of books from first-time authors. No mss through agents. Prefers 144-160 pgs. for general books, 160-300 pgs. for academic books. Royalty 14-18% of net. Average first printing 2,500-3,000. Publication within 1 yr. Accepts simultaneous submissions. Requires requested proposal and ms by e-mail. Responds in 1-3 mos. Guidelines on Website; catalog for 9x12 SAE/2 stamps.

Nonfiction: Proposal/1 chapter; e-proposal preferred. "Looking for books in evangelism, leadership, and spiritual growth."

CHARIOT BOOKS—See Cook Communications Ministries.

CHARIOT VICTOR PUBLISHING—See Cook Communications Ministries.

CHARISMA HOUSE, 600 Rinehart Rd., Lake Mary FL 32746. (407)333-0600. Fax (407)333-7100. E-mail: charismahouse@strang.com. Website: www.charismahouse.com. Strang Communications. Submit to Acquisitions Asst. To inspire and equip people to live a Spirit-led life and walk in the divine purpose for which they were called. Imprints: Creation House Press (co-publishing), Siloam (health), CharismaKids. Publishes 40 titles/yr. Receives 600+ submissions annually. 15% of books from first-time authors. Accepts mss through agents. Reprints books. Prefers 50,000+ wds. Royalty 4-18%; outright purchases of $1,500-5,000; advance. Average first printing 7,500. Publication within 18 mos. Considers simultaneous submissions. Accepts requested ms on disk or by e-mail. Responds in 6-8 mos. Guidelines by e-mail/Website; free catalog.

Nonfiction: Proposal/1-2 chapters; no phone/fax query; e-query OK.

Fiction: Query first. For adults. Also open to supernatural thrillers or spiritual-warfare novels. "Looking for speculative fiction and sophisticated historical fiction in eras and events when Christ and Christianity were part of the culture (medieval, biblical, crusades, Awakenings, etc.)."

CHARISMAKIDS, 600 Rinehart Rd., Lake Mary FL 32746. (407)333-0600. Fax (407)333-7100. E-mail: matuszak@strang.com. Website: www.charismakids.com. Strang Communications. Pat Matuszak, ed. Books to help children experience God's presence, find His purpose for their lives, and receive the power of the Holy Spirit. Publishes 12 titles/yr. Receives 100s of submissions annually. 10% of books from first-time authors. Prefers mss through agents. No reprints. Prefers 2,400 wds. or 32 pgs. Royalty on net; advance. Average first printing 10,000. Publication within 1 yr. Considers simultaneous submissions. Responds in 6 mos. Guidelines & catalog on Website.

Nonfiction: Proposal/1 chapter; fax/e-query OK.

Fiction: Proposal/1 chapter. Charismatic children's books; for children 4-8 years.

Ethnic Books: Black, Charismatic.

Tips: "Most open to books with a Charismatic world-view for children."

CHICKEN SOUP BOOKS—See listing in Periodical section.

CHOSEN BOOKS, Division of Baker Publishing Group, 3985 Bradwater St., Fairfax VA 22031-3702. (703)764-8250. Fax (703)764-3995. E-mail: JECampbell@aol.com. Website: www.bakerbooks.com. Charismatic. Jane Campbell, ed. dir. No freelance. Submit through Writer's Edge or ECPA First Edition.

CHRISTIAN ED. PUBLISHERS, Box 26639, San Diego CA 92196. (858)578-4700. Fax (858)578-2431 (for queries only). E-mail: Editor@cepub.com or Jackelson@cepub.com. Website: www.ChristianEdWarehouse.com. Janet Ackelson, asst. ed. An evangelical publisher of Bible Club materials for ages two through high school, church special-event programs, and Bible-teaching craft kits. Publishes 80 titles/yr. Receives 150 submissions annually. 10% of books from first-time authors. No mss through agents. Outright purchases for .03/wd.; no advance. Publication within 1 yr. No simultaneous submissions. Accepts requested ms on disk or by e-mail. Responds in 3-5 mos. Prefers NIV, KJV. Guidelines (also by e-mail); catalog for 9x12 SAE/4 stamps.

Nonfiction: Query only; phone/fax/e-query OK. Bible studies, curriculum, and take-home papers.

Fiction: Query only. Juvenile fiction for take-home papers. "Each story is about 900 wds. Write for an application; assignments only."

Special Needs: Open to freelance illustrators. Send files in Adobe Illustrator.

Tips: "All writing done on assignment. Request our guidelines, then complete a writer application before submitting. Need Bible-teaching ideas for preschool through sixth grade. Also publishes Bible stories for preschool and primary take-home papers, 200 words."

+CHRISTIAN FAMILY PUBLICATIONS, 58 S. Bay Ave., Islip NY 11751. E-mail: Gfedele@ cmp.com. Website: www.christianfamilybooks.com. Gene Fedele, ed. Incomplete topical listings. No questionnaire returned.

CHRISTIAN FOCUS PUBLICATIONS, LTD., Geanies House, Fearn, Tain, Ross-shire IV20 1TW Scotland UK. Phone +44 (0) 1862 871011. Fax +44 (0) 1862 871699. E-mail: info@christianfocus.com. Website: www.christianfocus.com. Willie Mackenzie, adult editorial mngr.; Catherine McKenzie, children's ed. Focuses on having strong biblical content. Imprints: Mentor, Christian Heritage, Christian Focus, Christian Focus 4 Kids. Publishes 90 titles/yr. Receives 300+ submissions annually. 10% of books from first-time authors. Accepts mss through agents. Reprints books. Royalty on net or outright purchase. Publication within 24 mos. Considers simultaneous submissions. Accepts requested ms on disk. Responds typically in 4 mos. Guidelines on Website; free catalog.

Nonfiction: Proposal/2 chapters; fax/e-query OK.

Fiction: Complete ms. For children and teens only. See guidelines for descriptions of children's fiction lines.

Photos: Accepts freelance photos for book covers.

Tips: "We are 'reformed,' though we don't insist all our authors would consider themselves reformed." A prize-winning British publisher with good worldwide coverage.

CHRISTIAN LIBERTY PRESS, 502 W. Euclid Ave., Arlington Heights IL 60064. (847)259-4444. Fax (847)259-2941. Website: www.christianlibertypress.com. Publishing arm of Christian Liberty Academy. Curriculum. Incomplete topical listings. No questionnaire returned.

CHRISTIAN PUBLICATIONS, 3825 Hartzdale Dr., Camp Hill PA 17011. (717)761-7044. Fax (717)761-7273. E-mail: editorial@christianpublications.com. Website: www.christian publications.com. Christian and Missionary Alliance. Gretchen Nesbit, asst. ed. Publishes books which emphasize the deeper Christian life. Publishes 20 titles/yr. Receives 250 submissions annually. 30% of books from first-time authors. Reprints books. Prefers 50,000 wds. or 150-300 pgs. Royalty 5-10% of retail; variable advance. Average first printing 3,000-5,000. Publication within 15 mos. Considers simultaneous submissions on full proposals. Requires requested ms on disk. Responds in 6-8 wks. Guidelines (also by e-mail/Website); no catalog.

Nonfiction: Query or proposal/2 chapters; fax query OK. "Looking for books on spiritual growth and women's concerns (Bible-based)."

Tips: "Most open to Christian living with depth, homeschooling resources, and church/Christian history. The books we publish are selected for their potential to promote real spiritual growth in the lives of our readers."

**Note: This publisher serviced by The Writer's Edge.

CHRISTIAN WRITER'S EBOOK NET, PO Box 446, Ft. Duchesne UT 84026. (435)772-3429. E-mail: editor@writersebook.com. Website: www.writersebook.com. Nondenominational/ Evangelical Christian. Linda Kay Stewart Whitsitt, ed-in-chief; Terry Gordon Whitsitt, asst. ed. Gives first-time authors the opportunity to bring their God-given writing talent to the Christian market. Publishes 30 titles/yr. Receives 200 submissions annually. 95% of books from first-time authors. Accepts mss through agents. **SUBSIDY PUBLISHES 25%.** Reprints books. Prefers 60+ pgs. Royalty 35-50%; no advance. E-Books only. Publication within 6 mos. Considers simultaneous submissions. Electronic queries and submissions only; mss need to be in electronic form (MS Word, WordPerfect, ASCII, etc.) to be published; send by e-mail (preferred). Responds in 1-2 mos. Guidelines on Website.

   Nonfiction: E-query only. Any topic.

   Fiction: E-query only. Any genre.

   Also Does: Booklets, pamphlets, tracts.

   Tips: "Make sure your work is polished and ready for print. The books we publish are sold in our online store. If you are not sure what an e-book is, check out our Website's FAQ page."

THE CHRISTOPHER PUBLISHING HOUSE, 24 Rockland St., Hanover MA 02339. (781)826-7474. Fax (781)826-5556. E-mail: cph@atigroupinc.com. Website: www.atigroupinc.com. Member of the ATI Group. Nancy A. Kopp, mng. ed. Produces fine quality books for the public's reading enjoyment. Publishes 6-8 titles/yr. Receives 200+ submissions annually. 90% of books from first-time authors. **SUBSIDY PUBLISHES 8-10%.** Prefers 100+ pgs. Royalty 5-30% of net; no advance. Average first printing 2,000. Publication within 12-14 mos. Considers simultaneous submissions. Responds in 6-8 wks. No e-mail submissions. Guidelines (also by e-mail/Website); catalog for #10 SAE/2 stamps.

   Nonfiction: Complete ms. Most topics; no juvenile material.

   Fiction: Complete ms. Adult only. About 100 pgs.

CHURCH & SYNAGOGUE LIBRARY ASSN. INC., PO Box 19357, Portland OR 97280-0357. (503)244-6919. Fax (503)977-3734. E-mail: csla@worldaccessnet.com. Website: www.worldaccessnet.com/~csla. Karen Bota, ed. An interfaith group set up to help librarians set up and organize/reorganize their religious libraries. Publishes 6 titles/yr. No mss through agents. No royalty. Average first printing 750. Catalog.

CHURCH GROWTH INSTITUTE, PO Box 7, Elkton MD 21922-0007. E-mail: cgimail@churchgrowth.org. Website: www.churchgrowth.org. Ephesians Four Ministries. Cindy G. Spear, resource development dir. Providing practical tools for leadership, evangelism, and church growth. Publishes 4 titles/yr. Receives 40 submissions annually. 7% of books from first-time authors. No mss through agents. Prefers 64-160 pgs. Royalty 6% on retail or outright purchase; no advance. Average first printing 100. Publication within 1 yr. Considers simultaneous submissions. Responds in 3 mos. Requires requested ms on disk. Guidelines; catalog for 9x12 SAE/3 stamps, or on Website.

   Nonfiction: Proposal/1 chapter; no phone/fax; e-query OK. "We prefer our writers to be experienced in what they write about, to be experts in the field."

   Special Needs: Topics that help churches grow spiritually and numerically; leadership training; attendance and stewardship programs; new or unique ministries (how-to). Self-discovery and evaluation tools, such as our Spiritual Gifts Inventory and Spiritual Growth Survey.

   Photos: Accepts freelance photos for book covers.

   Tips: "Most open to a practical manual or audio album (CDs/audiotapes and workbooks) for the pastor or other church leaders—something unique with a special niche. Must be practical and different from anything else on the same subject—or must be a topic/slant few others have published. Also very interested in evaluation tools as mentioned above. Please no devotionals, life testimonies, commentaries, or studies on books of the Bible."

CISTERCIAN PUBLICATIONS, INC., WMU Station, 1903 W. Michigan Ave., Kalamazoo MI 49008-5415. (269)387-8920. Fax (269)387-8390. E-mail: cistpub@wmich.edu. Website: www.spencerabbey.org/cistpub. Catholic/Order of Cistercians of the Strict Observance.

Dr. E. Rozanne Elder, ed. dir. Works of monastic tradition and studies that foster renewal, spirituality, and ongoing formation of monastics. Publishes 8-14 titles/yr. Receives 30 submissions annually. 50% of books from first-time authors. No mss through agents. Reprints books. Prefers 204-286 pgs. Royalty on net; no advance. Average first printing 1,500. Publication within 2-10 yrs. Requires requested ms on disk. No guidelines; free style sheet/catalog.

Nonfiction: Query only; no phone query; fax query OK. History, spirituality, and theology.

Photos: Accepts freelance photos for book covers.

Tips: "We publish only on the Christian Monastic Tradition. Most open to a translation of a monastic text, or study of a monastic movement, author, or subject."

CLADACH PUBLISHING, Santa Rosa CA. Mailing address: PO Box 336144, Greeley CO 80633. E-mail: staff@cladach.com. Website: www.cladach.com. Independent Christian publisher. Catherine Lawton, pub./ed. Seeks to influence those inside and outside the body of Christ by giving a voice to little-known but talented writers with a clear, articulate, and Christ-honoring vision. Publishes 2-3 titles/yr. Receives 100 submissions annually. 90% of books from first-time authors. Accepts mss through agents. Reprints books. Prefers 128-300 pgs. Royalty 7-10% on net. Average first printing 1,000. Publication within 1 yr. Considers simultaneous submissions. Requires accepted submissions on disk. Responds in 3-6 mos. Guidelines on Website; catalog for #10 SAE/1 stamp.

Nonfiction: Query letter or proposal/1-3 chapters; e-query OK.

Fiction: Query letter or proposal/1-3 chapters. For adults. "Prefers stories depicting inner struggles and real-life issues. Would like to see Christian world-view, literary fiction."

Tips: "Write from your heart and experience, true to the Word of God. Most open to books that inspire or meet a need and that the author can help market."

COLLEGE PRESS PUBLISHING CO., INC., 223 W. Third St. (64801), Box 1132, Joplin MO 64802. Toll-free (800)289-3300. (417)623-6280. Fax (417)623-8250. Website: www .collegepress.com. Christian Church/Church of Christ. Dru Ashwell, exec. ed. Christian materials that will help fulfill the Great Commission and promote unity on the basis of biblical truth and intent. Imprint: Forerunner Books. Publishes 15-20 titles/yr. Receives 300-400 submissions annually. 1-5% of books from first-time authors. Reprints books. Prefers 250-300 pgs. (paperback) or 300-600 pgs.(hardback). Royalty 5-15% of net; no advance. Average first printing 3,000. Publication within 9-12 mos. Considers simultaneous submissions. Requires requested ms on disk; no e-mail submissions. Responds in 2-3 mos. Prefers NIV, NASB, NAS. Guidelines (also by e-mail/Website); catalog for 9x12 SAE/5 stamps.

Nonfiction: Query only, then proposal/2-3 chapters; no phone/fax query. "Looking for Bible study, reference, divorced leaders, blended families, and leadership."

Ethnic Books: Reprints their own books in Spanish.

Also Does: E-books.

Tips: "We are interested in biblical studies and resources that come from an 'Arminian' view and/or 'amillennial' slant."

CONARI PRESS, PO Box 612, York Beach ME 03910-0612. Toll-free (800)423-7087. Fax (877)337-3309. E-mail: orders@redwheelweiser.com. Website: www.conari.com or www.redwheelweiser.com. Now an imprint of Red Wheel/Weiser, LLC. Ms. Pat Bryce, ed. Books on spirituality, personal growth, parenting, and social issues. Publishes 30 titles/yr. Incomplete topical listings. No questionnaire returned.

CONCILIAR PRESS, PO Box 76, Ben Lomand CA 95005. Toll-free (800)967-7377. (831)336-5118. Fax (831)336-8882. E-mail: marketing@conciliarpress.com. Website: www.conciliar press.com. Antiochian Orthodox Christian Archdiocese of N.A., Father Thomas Zell, ed. Publishes 5-10 titles/yr. Receives 50 submissions annually. 20% of books from first-time authors. Accepts mss through agents. **SUBSIDY PUBLISHES 10%**. Reprints books. Royalty;

no advance. Average first printing 5,000. Prefers e-mail submission. Prefers NKJV. Guidelines (also by e-mail); catalog for 9x12 SAE/5 stamps.

Nonfiction: Query only; phone/fax/e-query OK.

Photos: Accepts freelance photos for book covers.

CONCORDIA ACADEMIC PRESS, 3558 S. Jefferson Ave., St. Louis MO 63118-3968. (314)268-1000. Fax (314)268-1329. E-mail: mark.sell@cph.org. Website: www.concordiaacademicpress.org. Lutheran Church/Missouri Synod. Imprint of Concordia Publishing House. Mark E. Sell, ed. Scholarly and professional books in biblical studies, 16th-century studies, historical theology, and theology and culture. Publication within 2 yrs. Responds in 8-12 wks. Guidelines on Website.

Tips: "Freelance submissions are welcome. Prospective authors should consult the guidelines at the Website for an author prospectus and submissions guidelines."

CONCORDIA PUBLISHING HOUSE, 3558 S. Jefferson Ave., St. Louis MO 63118-3968. (314)268-1000. Fax (314)268-1329. Website: www.cph.org. Lutheran Church/Missouri Synod. Peggy Kuethe: children's resources, children's and family devotions, teaching resources, adult nonfiction and devotionals; Mark Sell: academic books; Fred Baue: pastoral and congregational resources; Hector Hoppe: multiethnic resources; Brandy Overton: guidelines for adults, children's resources. Publishes 30 titles/yr. Receives 3,000 submissions annually. 10% of books from first-time authors. Royalty 2-12% on retail; some outright purchases; some advances $500-1,500. Average first printing 6,000-8,000. Publication within 2 yrs. Considers simultaneous submissions. Responds in 6 mos. Prefers accepted submissions on disk. Prefers NIV. Guidelines (also by e-mail/Website); catalog for 9x12 SAE/4 stamps.

Nonfiction: Proposal/2 chapters; no phone/fax query. No poetry, personal experience, or biography.

Ethnic Books: Hispanic; Asian American.

Also Does: Pamphlets, booklets.

Tips: "Publishes Christ-centered resources for The Lutheran Church-Missouri Synod. Most open to family, devotional, and teaching resources. Any proposal should be Christ centered, Bible based, and life directed. It must be creative in its presentation of solid scriptural truths."

**Note: This publisher serviced by The Writer's Edge.

CONTEMPORARY DRAMA SERVICE—See Meriwether Publishing, Ltd.

CONTINUUM INTERNATIONAL PUBLISHING, Tower Bldg., 11 York Rd., London SE1 7NX England. Phone 0207 922 0880. Fax 0207 922 0881. E-mail: info@continuumbooks.com. Website: www.continuumbooks.com. R. J. Baird-Smith, pub. dir.; Philip J. Law, publishing dir. of T and T Clark Intl. Imprints: Morehouse; T and T Clark/Sheffield Academic Press; Burns & Oates. Publishes 250-300 titles/yr. Receives 1,000 submissions annually. 5% of books from first-time authors. Accepts mss through agents. Does print-on-demand. Reprints books. Royalty to 15%; advance. Publication within 9 mos. Considers simultaneous submissions. Guidelines by e-mail; free catalog.

Nonfiction: Proposal/1 chapter; phone/fax/e-query OK.

Photos: Accepts freelance photos for book covers.

Contest: Trinity Prize.

Note: This publisher is tied to Continuum, Morehouse Publishing, Living the Good News, and Trinity Press International.

COOK COMMUNICATIONS MINISTRIES, 4050 Lee Vance View, Colorado Springs CO 80918. (719)536-0100. Fax (719)536-3269. E-mail: athenk@cookministries.org. Website: www.cookministries.com. Dan Benson, ed. dir.; Lora Riley, mng. ed.; submit to Editorial Assistant. Discipleship is foundational; everything we publish needs to move the reader one step closer to maturity in Christ. Brands: NexGen (for teachers or program leaders who want Bible-based discipleship resources); Victor (Bible and study resources for serious Bible students); Life Journey (guides for Christian families seeking biblical answers to life problems); Honor Books (devotional books that inspire and motivate, packaged as gift books); RiverOak (historical, contemporary fiction); Faith Kidz (equipping kids—birth to age 12—for life; see separate listing). Publishes 125 titles/yr. 10% of books from first-time authors. Prefers mss through agents. Average first printing 5,000. Publication within 1-2 yrs. Considers simultaneous submissions. Responds in 3-6 mos. Prefers requested ms on disk. Prefers NIV. Guidelines (also by e-mail/Website).

Nonfiction: Proposal/2 chapters. All book proposals must be sent via Website: www.cook ministries.com/proposals.

Fiction: Proposal/3 chapters or complete ms. All book proposals must be sent via Website: www.cookministries.com/proposals.

Tips: "Most open to a book that combines expertise with experience—both are important here."

**Note: This publisher serviced by The Writer's Edge.

J. COUNTRYMAN, PO Box 141000, Nashville TN 37214-1000. (615)902-3134. Fax (615)902-3200. Website: www.jcountryman.com. Thomas Nelson Inc. Troy Johnson, pub./exec. VP; Terri Gibbs, VP, acq. and product development. Gift-book imprint presenting strong, Bible-based messages in beautifully designed books. No longer accepting unsolicited manuscripts or proposals.

**Note: This publisher serviced by The Writer's Edge.

CRANE HILL PUBLISHERS, 3608 Clairmont Ave., Birmingham AL 35222. (205)714-3007, ext. 28. Fax (205)714-3008. E-mail: cranemail@cranehill.com. Website: www.cranehill.com. Lee Howard, ed. Publishes a few religious titles. Receives 500 submissions annually. 50% of books from first-time authors. Accepts mss through agents. Reprints books. Length varies. Royalty; no advance. Publication within 1-2 yrs. Considers simultaneous submissions. Responds in 2-6 mos. No guidelines; free catalog.

Nonfiction: Query only; no phone query.

Fiction: Query only. Literary fiction only.

CREATED IN CHRIST, PUBLISHING DIVISION, 3725 Golfe Links Dr., Snellville GA 30039. Toll-free (877)886-6260. Fax (530)618-5767. E-mail: cicpublishing@ureach.com. Website: www.cicpublishing.org. International Gospel Fellowship. Lloyd Ocampo, dir. Develops and publishes written materials based on biblical teachings that tear down walls of denomination and religion. 100% of books from first-time authors. No mss through agents. 100% print-on-demand. No reprints. Prefers 700 pgs. Pay 10-45% royalty on net; no advance. Publication within 3 mos. Considers simultaneous submissions. Accepts manuscripts on disk or by e-mail. Guidelines by e-mail or Website.

Nonfiction: Complete ms.; no phone query, fax/e-query OK.

Photos: Accepts freelance photos for book covers.

Tips: "Most open to church manuals, or spiritual teachings that foster relationship development with God."

+CREATIVE TEACHING PRESS, 15342 Graham St., Huntington Beach CA 92649. (714)895-5047. Fax (714)895-5087. E-mail: carolea.williams@creativeteaching.com. Website: www .creativeteaching.com. Rebecca Cleland, ed. Currently publishes Christian decoratives, but branching out into teacher's resource books and children's readers. Publishes 50 titles/yr. Outright purchases (amount to be decided). Publication within 9-12 mos. Considers simultaneous submissions. Accepts disk or e-mail submissions. Guidelines on Website; free catalog.

Nonfiction: Proposal; e-query OK.

Fiction: For children. Proposal; e-query OK.

Special Needs: Sunday school activity books.

Tips: "Most open to teacher resource books for use by a Christian school teacher or Sunday school teacher; grades prekindergarten through 3rd grade." Submission form on Website.

CROSS CULTURAL PUBLICATIONS, INC., PO Box 506, Notre Dame IN 46556. Toll-free (800)561-6526 (219)273-6526. Fax (219)273-5973. E-mail: crosscult@aol.com. Website: www.crossculturalpub.com. Catholic. Cyriac K. Pullapilly, gen. ed. Promotes intercultural and interfaith understanding. Imprint: CrossRoads Books. Publishes 20 titles/yr. Receives 5,000-7,000 submissions annually. 10% of books from first-time authors. Accepts mss through agents. Reprints books. Prefers 250 pgs. Royalty 10% on net; no advance. Publication within 6 mos. Considers simultaneous submissions. Requires requested ms on disk. Responds in 3-4 mos. No guidelines; free catalog.

   Nonfiction: Prefers query letter/sample chapters; will accept a proposal; e-query OK.

   Fiction: Prefers query letter/sample chapters; will accept a proposal; e-query OK. For adults only.

   Ethnic Books: Seeks to serve the cross-cultural, intercultural, and multicultural aspects of religious traditions.

   Also Does: Will soon be doing e-books.

   Photos: Accepts freelance photos for book covers.

   Tips: "Most open to solidly researched, well-written books on serious issues: intercultural, interfaith topics. Do a thorough job of writing/editing, etc. Have something constructive, noble, and worthwhile to say."

THE CROSSROAD PUBLISHING CO., 481—8th Ave., Ste. 1550, New York NY 10001-1820. (212)868-1801. Fax (212)868-2171. E-mail: ask@crossroadpublishing.com. Website: www.crossroadpublishing.com. Dr. John Jones, exec. mngr. Books on religion, spirituality, and personal growth that speak to the diversity of backgrounds and beliefs; books that inform, enlighten, and heal. Imprints: see below. Publishes 50 titles/yr. Receives 1,200 submissions annually. 50% of books from first-time authors. Prefers mss through agents. **SUBSIDY PUBLISHES 5%**. Does print-on-demand. Reprints books. Prefers 50,000-60,000 wds. or 160-176 pgs. Royalty 8-10-12% of net; small advance (more for established authors). Average first printing 5,000. Publication within 1 yr. Considers simultaneous submissions. Responds in 3-4 mos. Accepts requested ms on disk. Guidelines by e-mail.

   Nonfiction: Proposal/2 chapters; fax/e-query OK. Books that explore and celebrate the Christian life.

   Fiction: Proposal/2 chapters; fax/e-query OK. For adults. Prefers historical fiction that focuses on important figures or periods in the history of Christianity. Must have a spiritual purpose or message.

   Crossroad Carlisle: Roy Carlisle, sr. ed.; PO Box 13212, Oakland CA 94661-0212; (510)482-1444; fax (508)355-8181; e-mail: rok47@aol.com. Celebrating the wise and literate expression of Christian faith within the Protestant, Evangelical, and Orthodox traditions in books of nonfiction and fiction.

   Crossroad 8th Avenue: Nonfiction and fiction on the world's religious, cultural, and healing traditions of further dialog, understanding, and respect among all peoples of good faith.

   Crossroad Faith & Formation: Supporting the faith families of tomorrow with educational and formative materials for parishes, small Christian communities, and lay and religious congregations.

   Herder & Herder: 200 years of international publishing in the service of theology and church. Monographs, reference works, theological, and philosophical discourse.

CROSS TRAINING PUBLISHING, PO Box 1541, Grand Island NE 68802. Toll-free (800)430-8588. Fax (308)384-9974. E-mail: gordon@crosstrainingpublishing.com. Website: www.crosstrainingpublishing.com. Gordon Thiessen, pub. Sports books for children and adults.

CROSSWAY BOOKS, 1300 Crescent St., Wheaton IL 60187. (630)682-4300. Fax (630)682-4785. E-mail: editorial@gnpcb.org. Website: www.crosswaybooks.org. A division of Good News Publishers. Marvin Padgett, VP editorial; submit to Jill Carter, editorial administrator. Publishes books that combine the Truth of God's Word with a passion to live it out, with unique and compelling Christian content. Publishes 80 titles/yr. Receives 2,500 submissions annually. 1% of books from first-time authors. Accepts mss through agents. No reprints. Prefers 25,000 wds. & up. Royalty 10-21% of net; advance varies. Average first printing 5,000-10,000. Publication within 18 mos. Considers simultaneous submissions. Requires requested ms on disk (compatible with Microsoft Word). Responds in 6-8 wks. Prefers ESV. Guidelines (also on Website); free catalog.

Nonfiction: Query only, then proposal/2 chapters; fax query OK; no e-query or submissions by e-mail.

Fiction: Proposal/2 chapters (no complete mss); no e-query or submissions by e-mail. Adult.

Also Does: Tracts. See Good News Publishers.

Tips: No unsolicited submissions—which will not be returned.

**Note: This publisher serviced by The Writer's Edge and First Edition.

CSS PUBLISHING CO., PO Box 4503, 517 S. Main St., Lima OH 45802-4503. (419)227-1818. Fax (419)228-9184. E-mail: trhoads@csspub.com. Website: www.csspub.com. Terry Rhoads, ed.; Stan Purdum, acq. ed. Serves the needs of pastors, worship leaders, and parish program-planners in the broad Christian mainline of the American church. Publishes 60 titles/yr. Receives 1,200-1,500 submissions annually. 50% of books from first-time authors. **SUBSIDY PUBLISHES 40%** through Fairway Press. Prefers 100-125 pgs. Royalty 3-7% or outright purchases for $25-400. Average first printing 1,000. Publication within 6-10 mos. Considers simultaneous submissions. Requires requested mss by mail. Responds in 3 wks. to 3 mos.; final decision within 6 mos. Accepts requested ms on disk. Prefers NRSV. Free guidelines (also on Website)/catalog.

Nonfiction: Query or proposal/3 chapters; fax/e-query OK (no attachments); complete ms for short works. "Looking for pastoral resources for ministry. Our material is practical in nature."

Fiction: Complete ms. Easy-to-perform dramas and pageants for all age groups. "Our drama interest primarily includes Advent, Christmas, Epiphany, Lent, and Easter. We do not publish long plays."

Tips: "Suggest what you can do to help promote the book."

#CUMBERLAND HOUSE PUBLISHING, 431 Harding Industrial Dr., Nashville TN 37211. (615)832-1171. Fax (615)832-0633. E-mail: info@cumberlandhouse.com. Website: www.cumberlandhouse.com. Tilly Katz, ed. dir. Historical nonfiction, cooking, mystery, and Christian titles. Publishes 60 titles/yr. Receives 1,300 submissions annually. 50% of books from first-time authors. Accepts mss through agents. Royalty. No simultaneous submissions. Prefers accepted ms on disk; no e-mail submissions. Responds in 3-6 mos. Guidelines on Website. Incomplete topical listings. No questionnaire returned.

Nonfiction: Query/outline; fax query OK; no e-query. See guidelines for how to submit cookbooks.

Fiction: Query only. Southern mystery/suspense.

Tips: "Most open to history or biography. In your cover letter, briefly describe the book and the market for the book. In a statement or two indicate who you are and why you have written or plan to write the book you are proposing."

CUSTOM COMMUNICATIONS SERVICES, INC./SHEPHERD PRESS/CUSTOM BOOK, 77 Main St., Tappan NY 10983. (845)365-0414. Fax (845)365-0864. E-mail: customusa@aol.com. Website: www.customstudios.com. Norman Shaifer, pres. Publishes 50-75 titles/yr. 50% of books from first-time authors. No mss through agents. Royalty on net; some outright purchases for specific assignments. Publication within 6 mos. Responds in 1 mo. Guidelines.

Nonfiction: Query/proposal/chapters. "Histories of individual congregations, denominations, or districts."

Tips: "Find stories of larger congregations (750 or more households) who have played a role in the historic growth and development of the community or region."

DAVID C. COOK PUBLISHING CO.—See Cook Communications Ministries.

*DESCANT PUBLISHING, PO Box 12973, Mill Creek WA 98082. (206)235-3357. Fax (646)365-7513. E-mail: bret@descantpub.com. Website: www.descantpub.com. Bret Sable, nonfiction ed.; Alex Royal, fiction ed. Secular publisher that does books on religion and spirituality, and religious fiction. Publishes 10-12 titles/yr. Does some e-books. Receives 1,200 submissions annually. 50% of books from first-time authors. Accepts mss through agents. Royalty 6-15%. Publication within 18 mos. Considers simultaneous submissions. Responds in 3 mos. Guidelines for SASE.

Nonfiction: For adults and children. Query by mail.

Fiction: Adult. Query by mail.

DESTINY IMAGE PUBLISHERS, PO Box 310, Shippensburg PA 17257. (717)532-3040. Fax (717)532-9291. E-mail: dlm@destinyimage.com. Website: www.destinyimage.com. Don Milam, ed. mngr. Publishes biblically sound prophetic words to strengthen the church as a whole. Imprints: Destiny Image, Revival Press, Treasure House, Fresh Bread. Publishes 36 titles/yr. Receives 1,500 submissions annually. 10% of books from first-time authors. Accepts mss through agents. **SUBSIDY PUBLISHES 1-2%.** Reprints books. Prefers 128-190 pgs. Royalty 10-15% on net; no advance. Average first printing 10,000. Publication within 9 mos. Considers simultaneous submissions. No disk or e-mail submissions. Responds in 1-3 wks. Guidelines on Website; free catalog.

Nonfiction: Query or proposal/chapters; no e-query. Charges a $25 fee for unsolicited manuscripts (enclose).

Fiction: Proposal. Adult. Biblical.

Tips: "Most open to books on the deeper life, Charismatic interest." See Website for Manuscript Submission Questionnaire.

DEVOTED TO YOU BOOKS, 515 County Rd. 18, Wrenshall MN 55797-9103. Toll-free (800)704-7250. E-mail: info@devotedtoyoubooks.com. Website: www.devotedtoyoubooks.com. Non-denominational. Tracy Ryks, pub. Seeks to teach children that God is present in their lives today; children's picture books for ages 1-8. Publishes 2 titles/yr. No reprints. Royalty; no advance. Publication within 18 mos. Considers simultaneous submissions. Responds in 2-4 mos. Prefers NIV. Guidelines on Website; free catalog.

Nonfiction: Complete ms or mock-up dummy book; e-submission OK. Now open to picture stories.

Fiction: Complete ms (dummy of book); e-submission OK. Contemporary children's picture books. "Books that portray God working in children's lives, prayer, or those that teach children how to develop a personal relationship with Jesus."

Special Needs: "We are looking for contemporary Christian picture books that show God in children's lives. Also parenting books—could be in devotional form—that inspire parents. Not how-to tips on parenting; we prefer books that make parents better parents by reminding them of their blessings, something heartwarming and inspirational."

Photos: Accepts freelance photos for book covers.

Contest: Sponsors a contest.

Tips: "Most open to contemporary books for today, children's picture books, and inspirational parenting. Creative, innovative books that meet the needs of a changing society without compromising or changing our core Christian beliefs."

DIAMOND EYES PUBLISHING, 2309 Mountain Spruce St., Ocoee FL 347651. Toll-free (888)769-9931. Fax (208)977-1164. E-mail: Wordsarelife@yahoo.com. Website: www.depublishing.com. Submit to Acquisitions Department. Imprints: Trident Books, Lauren's Box, House of Truth. Books that view life from God's perspective. Publishes 2-3 titles/yr. Receives 120 submissions annually. 80% of books from first-time authors. Accepts mss through agents. Accepts reprints. Prefers under 75,000 words or 250 pgs. Royalty 10% on retail; no advance. Average first printing 2,000-3,000. Publication within 9-10 mos. Considers simultaneous submissions. Responds in 4-6 wks. Prefers KJV. Guidelines on Website; no catalog.

Nonfiction: Query only by e-mail preferred (can send by mail). No phone/fax query. "Need prophecy pertaining to writing a book; prayer pertaining to writing a book; and writers' helps."

Photos: Accepts freelance photos for book covers.

Tips: "Looking for writers' helps, journals for writers, success stories for compilation book. We also accept drama and screenplay instruction."

DIMENSION BOOKS, INC., PO Box 9, Starrucca PA 18462. (570)727-2486. Fax (570)727-2813. Catholic; general nonfiction. Thomas P. Coffey, ed. Publishes 18 titles/yr. Receives 97 submissions annually. 2% of books from first-time authors. Reprints books. Royalty 10-15% on retail; advance. Average first printing 6,000-20,000. Publication within 9 mos. Considers simultaneous submissions. Responds in 2-5 wks. Catalog for #10 SAE/1 stamp.

Nonfiction: Query first. Christian spirituality, music, biography, and psychology.

DIMENSIONS FOR LIVING, 201—8th Ave. S., Nashville TN 37203. Fax (615)749-6512. Website: www.abingdonpress.com. United Methodist Publishing House. Joseph A. Crowe, ed.; submit to Shirley Briese (sbriese@umpublishing.org). Books for the general Christian reader. Publishes 120 titles/yr. Receives 2,000 submissions annually. Less than 1% of books from first-time authors. No reprints. Prefers 144 pgs. Royalty 7.5% on retail; some outright purchases; no advance. Average first printing 3,000. Publication within 2 yrs. Requires requested ms on disk. Responds in 6-8 wks. Guidelines; free catalog.

Nonfiction: Proposal/2 chapters; no phone query. Open to inspiration/devotion, self-help, home/family, special occasion gift books."

DISCOVERY HOUSE PUBLISHERS, PO Box 3566, Grand Rapids MI 49501. Toll-free (800)653-8333. (616)942-9218. Fax (616)957-5741. E-mail: dhp@dhp.org, or dph@rbc.net. Website: www.dhp.org. RBC Ministries. Carol Holquist, pub.; submit to ms. review ed. Publishes books that foster Christian growth and godliness. Publishes 12-18 titles/yr. Accepts mss through agents. Reprints books. Royalty 10-14% on net; no advance. Publication within 12-18 mos. Considers simultaneous submissions. Requires accepted mss on disk or by e-mail. Responds in 4-6 wks. Guidelines (also by e-mail/Website); free catalog.

Nonfiction: Query letter only; e-query OK.

Also Does: Bible study software.

**Note: This publisher serviced by The Writer's Edge.

DOUBLEDAY RELIGIOUS PUBLISHING, 1745 Broadway, New York NY 10019. (212)782-9762. Fax (212)782-8338. E-mail: mrapkin@randomhouse.com, or tmurphy@randomhouse.com. Website: www.randomhouse.com. Random House, Inc. Michelle Rapkin, VP, Dir. of Religious Publishing; submit to Trace Murphy, ed-in chief. Imprints: Image, Galilee, Doubleday Hardcover, Three Leaves, Anchor Bible Commentaries. Publishes 45-50 titles/yr. Receives 1,500 submissions annually. 10% of books from first-time authors. Requires mss through agents. Royalty 7.5-15% on retail; advance. Average first printing varies. Publication within 8 mos. Considers simultaneous submissions. Responds in 4 mos. No disk. No guidelines; catalog for 9x12 SAE/3 stamps.

Nonfiction: Agented submissions only. Proposal/3 chapters; no phone query.

Ethnic Books: African American; Hispanic.

Tips: "Most open to a book that has a big and well-defined audience. Have a clear proposal, lucid thesis, and specified audience."

DOVER PUBLICATIONS, INC., 31 E. 2nd St., Mineola NY 11501-3852. (516)294-7000. Fax (516)873-1401 or (516)742-6953. E-mail: rights@doverpublications.com. Website: www.doverpublications.com. Paul Negri, ed-in-chief. Publishes some religious titles, reprints only. Makes outright purchases. Query. Free catalog online.

Nonfiction: Query. Religion topics.

EASUM, BANDY & ASSOCIATES, INC., PO Box 780, Port Aransas TX 78373-0780. (361)749-5364. Fax (361)749-5800. E-mail: easum@easumbandy.com, or bandy@easumbandy.com. Website: www.easumbandy.com. Bill Easum, pub. Submit to Sandra Pearson (attached file to: Sandra@easumbandy.com). E-book publisher. Company keeps 20% of proceeds from sales of book. Guidelines on Website (click on "Publishing").

Nonfiction: Produces books in Adobe format to be downloaded. Author sets price.

Special Needs: Does workbooks, study guides, PowerPoint presentations, and curriculum.

Also Does: Audio, video.

EDITORES BETANIA-CARIBE, PO Box 141000, Nashville TN 37214. Toll-free (800)322-7423. (615)902-2372/2375. Fax (615)883-9376. E-mail: info@editorialcaribe.com, or ecaribe@bellsouth.net. Website: www.caribebetania.com. Subsidiary of Thomas Nelson. Tod Shuttleworth, VP/Publisher; Juan Rojas, ed. Targets the needs and wants of the Hispanic community. Imprints: Betania and Caribe. Publishes 45 titles/yr. Receives 50 submissions annually. 90% of books from first-time authors. No mss through agents. Prefers 192 pgs. Royalty on net; advance $500. Average first printing 4,000. Publication within 15 mos. Accepts e-mail submissions. No guidelines; free catalog.

Nonfiction: Query letter only; no phone/fax/e-query. "We currently have a backlog of 18 months."

Ethnic Books: Hispanic imprint.

Also Does: Computer games.

Tips: "Most open to Christian books based on the Bible."

EDITORIAL PORTAVOZ, PO Box 2607, Grand Rapids MI 49501-2607. Toll-free (800)733-2607. (616)451-4775. Fax (616)451-9330. E-mail: editor@portavoz.com. Website: www.portavoz.com. Spanish Division of Kregel Publishing. Andres Schwartz, ed. dir. To provide trusted, biblically based resources that challenge and encourage Spanish-speaking individuals in their Christian lives and service. Publishes 40+ titles/yr. 2-5% of books from first-time authors. Accepts mss through agents. Does print-on-demand. No reprints. Negotiable royalty on net; negotiable advance. Purchases artwork outright. Average first printing 5,000. Publication within 13 mos. Considers simultaneous submissions. Responds in 2-4 mos. Guidelines on Website.

Nonfiction: Send proposal by e-mail or CD-ROM, with 2-3 chapters. "Looking for original Spanish reference works."

EDITORIAL UNILIT, 1360 N.W. 88th Ave., Miami FL 33172-3093. Toll-free (800)767-7726. (305)592-6136. Fax (305)592-0087. Website: www.editorialunilit.com. Spanish House. Submit to The Editor. To glorify God by providing the church and Spanish-speaking people with the tools to communicate clearly the gospel of Jesus Christ and help them grow in their relationship with Him and His church.

**Note: This publisher selected as Publisher of the Year (1999) by the Spanish Evangelical Publishers Assn.

EDUCATIONAL MINISTRIES, 165 Plaza Dr., Prescott AZ 86303. (928)771-8601. Fax (928)771-8621. E-mail: edmin2@aol.com. Website: www.educationalministries.com. Linda

Davidson, ed. Our liberal theology sets us apart—our books do not give pat answers. Periodicals: *Church Educator* and *Church Worship*. Publishes 2-3 titles/yr. Receives 30 submissions annually. 15% of books from first-time authors. No mss through agents. No reprints. Outright purchases; no advance. Average first printing 500. Publication within 6 mos. Considers simultaneous submissions. Prefers accepted ms on disk. Responds in 2-3 mos. Guidelines; catalog for 9x12 SAE/3 stamps.

> **Nonfiction**: Complete ms; phone query OK.

EERDMANS BOOKS FOR YOUNG READERS, 255 Jefferson SE, Grand Rapids MI 49503. Toll-free (800)253-7521. (616)459-4591. Fax (616)459-6540. E-mail: jzylstra@ eerdmans.com; or youngreaders@eerdmans.com. Website: www.eerdmans.com/young readers. Wm. B. Eerdmans Publishing. Judy Zylstra, ed-in-chief. Books that nurture children's faith in God and help children and young people understand and explore life in God's world. Publishes 12-15 titles/yr. Receives 3,000 submissions annually. 5% of books from first-time authors. Age-appropriate length. Royalty 5-7% of retail; advance to previously published authors. Average first printing 10,000 (picture books) and 5,000-6,000 (chapter books/novels). Publication within 1-3 yrs. Considers simultaneous submissions. Responds in 2 mos. Guidelines (also by e-mail/Website); catalog for 9x12 SAE/4 stamps.

> **Nonfiction**: Proposal/3-4 chapters for book length; complete ms for picture books; no phone/fax/e-query. For children and teens.

> **Fiction**: Proposal/3 chapters for book length; complete ms for picture books. For children and teens.

> **Tips**: "Please do not send illustrations with picture book manuscripts unless you are a professional illustrator. When submitting artwork, send color copies, not originals."

> ****Note**: This publisher serviced by The Writer's Edge.

ELDRIDGE CHRISTIAN PLAYS & MUSICALS, PO Box 14367, Tallahassee FL 32317. Toll-free (800)95-CHURCH. Fax (800)453-5179. E-mail: info@95church.com. Website: www .95church.com. Independent Christian drama publisher. Susan Shore, religious ed. To provide superior religious drama to enhance preaching and teaching, whatever your Christian denomination. Publishes 12 plays and 1-2 musicals/yr. Receives 350-400 plays annually. 75% of plays from first-time authors. One-act to full-length plays. Outright purchases of $100-1,000 on publication; no advance. Publication within 1 yr. Considers simultaneous submissions. Responds in 1-3 mos. Requires requested ms on disk or by e-mail. Free guidelines (also by e-mail or Website)/catalog.

> **Plays**: Complete ms; e-query OK. For children, teens, and adults.

> **Special Needs**: Always looking for high quality Christmas and Easter plays but open to other holiday and "anytime" Christian plays too. Can be biblical or current day, for performance by all ages, children through adult.

> **Tips**: "Have play produced at your church and others prior to submission, to get out the bugs. At least try a stage reading."

ELIJAH PRESS, Meadow House Communications, Inc., PO Box 317628, Cincinnati OH 45231-7628. (513)521-7362. Fax (513)521-7364. E-mail: info@elijahpress.com. Website: www.elijahpress.com. Publishes quality religious/spiritual fiction and nonfiction books and tapes on and related to Christian living, church history, and spiritual reflection. S. R. Davis, ed. Publishes 3-5 titles/yr. Prefers 50,000-100,000 wds. Responds in 1 mo. Incomplete topical listings.

> **Nonfiction**: One-page query; must have completed ms; no phone/e-query.

> **Fiction**: Accepts fiction.

EMMAUS ROAD PUBLISHING, 827 N. Fourth St., Steubenville OH 43952. Toll-free (800)398-5470. (740)281-2404. Fax (740)283-4011. E-mail: shughes@emmausroad.org. Website: www.emmausroad.org. Catholics United for Faith. Regis Flaherty, ed. Publishes 8-10 titles/yr. Receives 40-50 submissions annually. 25% of books from first-time authors. Reprints books. Royalty on net; advance $500. Publication within 1 yr. Considers simultaneous submissions. Guidelines on Website; free catalog.

Nonfiction: Complete ms.

ETC PUBLICATIONS, 700 E. Vereda del Sur, Palm Springs CA 92262. (760)325-5352. Fax (760)325-8841. E-mail: etcbooks@earthlink.net. LeeOna S. Hostrop, sr. ed. Publishes textbooks for the Christian and secular markets at all levels of education. Publishes 3 textbook/yr. Receives 50 submissions annually. 90% of books from first-time authors. Accepts mss through agents. No reprints. Prefers 128-256 pgs. Royalty 5-15% of net; no advance. Average first printing 1,500-2,500. Publication within 6 mos. No simultaneous submissions. Responds in 10 days. No guidelines (use *Chicago Manual of Style*); catalog for #10 SAE/1 stamp.

Nonfiction: Query only; e-query OK. "We are interested only in Christian-oriented state history textbooks to be used in Christian schools and by homeschoolers."

Photos: Accepts freelance photos for book covers.

Tips: "Open only to state histories that are required at a specific grade level and are Christian oriented, with illustrations."

FACTS ON FILE, INC., 132 W. 31st St., 17th Floor, New York NY 10011. Toll-free (800)322-8755. (212)967-8800. Fax (212)967-3903. E-mail: llikoff@factsonfile.com, or editorial@factsonfile.com. Website: http://factsonfile.com. Laurie Likoff, ed. dir. School and library reference and trade books (for middle- to high-school students) tied to curriculum and areas of cross-cultural studies, including religion. Imprints: Facts on File, Checkmark Books. Publishes 3-5 religious titles/yr. Receives 10-20 submissions annually. 2% of books from first-time authors. No books through agents. No reprints. Prefers 224-480 pgs. Royalty 10-15% on retail; outright purchases of $2,000-10,000; advance $10,000. Some work-for-hire. Average first printing 5,000. Publication within 9-12 mos. Considers simultaneous submissions. Responds in 2 mos. Requires requested ms on disk. Guidelines (also by e-mail/Website)/free catalog.

Nonfiction: Query only; fax/e-query OK.

Tips: "Most open to reference books tied to curriculum subjects or disciplines."

FAIR HAVENS PUBLICATIONS, PO Box 1238, Gainesville TX 76241-1238. Toll-free (800)771-4861. (940)668-6044. Fax (940)668-6984. E-mail: fairhavens@fairhavenspub.com. Website: www.fairhavenspub.com. John C. Newton, gen. ed.; J. Ray Smith, chief ed.; D. Joan Smith, children's ed. Produces quality books, teaching and evangelistic literature, audiotapes and videotapes, CD-ROMs, dramas, and artworks that inspire faith and courage. Publishes 5 titles/yr. Receives 200 submissions annually. 25% of books from first-time authors. Accepts mss through agents. **SUBSIDY PUBLISHES 10%.** Reprints books. Prefers 250-300 pgs. Royalty 10-18% on net; no advance for first-time authors; negotiable for published authors. Average first printing 4,000 (runs 3,000-12,000). Publication within 8 mos. Considers simultaneous submissions. Requires requested ms on disk. Responds in 6 wks. Prefers NIV. Guidelines on Website; no catalog.

Nonfiction: Proposal/3 chapters; no phone/fax/e-query.

Fiction: Proposal/2 chapters; for all ages.

Special Needs: Biography, Bible prophecy, personal experience, animal stories, inspirational, how-to, trend analysis, self-help, and ministry aids.

Also Does: Booklets, audio & videotapes, CD-ROMs, dramas, artwork.

Photos: Accepts freelance photos for book covers.

Tips: "We prefer books that follow traditional standards of grammar and style."

+FAITH ALIVE CHRISTIAN RESOURCES, 2850 Kalamazoo Ave. SE, Grand Rapids MI 49560. Toll-free (800)333-8300. (616)224-0819. E-mail: editors@faithaliveresources.org. Website:

www.faithaliveresources.org. CRC Publications/Christian Reformed Church. Incomplete topical listings. No questionnaire returned.

FAITH COMMUNICATIONS, 3201 S.W. 15th St., Deerfield Beach FL 33442. (954)360-0909. Fax (954)360-0034. E-mail: susant@hcibooks.com. Website: www.hcibooks.com. Christian imprint of Health Communications, Inc. Submit to Editorial Committee. No phone/e-queries. Guidelines on Website. Incomplete topical listings. No questionnaire returned.

FAITH KIDZ BOOKS, 4050 Lee Vance View, Colorado Springs CO 80918. (719)536-3271. Fax (719)536-3265. Website: www.cookministries.com. Cook Communications. Heather Gemmen, sr. ed. Publishes inspirational books for children, ages 1-12, with a strong spiritual emphasis. Publishes 40-50 titles/yr. Receives 1,000-1,500 submissions annually. Accepts mss through agents. Variable royalty on retail, or outright purchase $2,000-10,000; advance $5,000. Publication within 18 mos. Considers simultaneous submissions. Responds in 6 mos. Guidelines on Website; free catalog.

    Nonfiction: Proposal via their Website: www.cookministries.com/proposals. For picture books send complete manuscript.

    Fiction: Prefers proposals from previously published authors or agents.

FAITH ONE PUBLISHING, PO Box 90000, Los Angeles CA 90009. (323)758-3777. Fax (323)758-7991. E-mail: donorsvcs@faithdome.org. Website: www.faithdome.org. Ever Increasing Faith Ministries. Stanley O. Williford, ed. Primary focus is to publish works by the pastors and ministers of the Crenshaw Christian Center. Publishes 5-8 titles/yr. Receives 10-25 submissions annually. 15% of books from first-time authors. No mss through agents. No guidelines or catalog.

    Nonfiction: Query only.

    Tips: "We have not yet begun to pay for manuscripts."

FAITHWALK PUBLISHING, 333 Jackson St., Grand Haven MI 49417. (616)846-9360. Fax (616)846-0072. E-mail: submissions@faithwalkpub.com. Website: www.faithwalkpub .com Dirk Wierenga, ed. Called to publish books which appeal to seekers and believers who might otherwise never purchase a religious book. Publishes 8 titles/yr. Receives 300 submissions annually. 25% of books from first-time authors. Accepts mss through agents. No reprints. Prefers 160-356 pages. Royalty 7-10% of retail; advance. Average first printing 5,000. Publication within 9-12 mos. Considers simultaneous submissions (if stipulated). Accepts requested ms by e-mail. Responds in 2-3 mos. Prefers NIV, NRSV. Guidelines (also by e-mail); catalog.

    Nonfiction: Proposal/1-2 chapters; e-query OK. No children's or gift books.

    Fiction: Proposal/1-2 chapters; e-query OK. Adult; adventure, contemporary, and literary.

    Photos: Accepts freelance photos for book covers.

FAMILYLIFE PUBLISHING, PO Box 7111, Little Rock AR 72212. Toll-free (800)404-5052. E-mail from Website. Website: www.familylife.com. Campus Crusade for Christ. Mike Hefner, materials mngr. FamilyLife Publishing exists to create. Publishes 3-12 titles/yr. Receives 50 submissions annually. 1% of books from first-time authors. Prefers mss through agents. Royalty 2-18% of net; rarely pays advance. Average first printing 25,000. Publication within 24 mos. Considers simultaneous submissions. Responds in 3 mos. on queries; 6 mos. on proposals/manuscripts. Prefers NASB, ESV, NIV. Guidelines (also by e-mail/Website); catalog on Website or for 9x12 SAE/4 stamps. Note: This company is seeking a new editor, so it is being very selective about accepting freelance material.

    Nonfiction: Query first; fax/e-query OK.

    Also Does: Booklets; multipiece activity packs.

    Tips: "Most open to multipiece, interactive products. Before you submit to us, be sure to read our writer's guidelines and The Family Manifesto (both on Website). If you don't know who we are or what we do, please send your material elsewhere. Most of what we publish is generated from inside our organization. Your opportunity to be published here is very slim."

+FIRST FRUITS OF ZION, PO Box 620099, Littleton CO 80162-0099. Fax (303)933-0997. Website: www.FFOZ.org. Hope Egan, ed. A nonprofit ministry devoted to strengthening the love and appreciation of the Body of Messiah for the land, people, and Scripture of Israel. Publishes 2-6 titles/yr. No mss through agents. Royalty; no advance. Publication within 6 mos. Considers simultaneous submissions. Responds in 1 mo. Prefers NASB. Catalog for 9x12 SAE/4 stamps. Not included in topical listings.

    Nonfiction: Query first; no phone/fax/e-query.

    Special Needs: Books on Hebrew roots.

    Tips: "Be very familiar with our material before submitting to us."

FOCUS ON THE FAMILY BOOK PUBLISHING AND RESOURCE DEVELOPMENT, 8605 Explorer Dr., Colorado Springs CO 80920-1051. (719)531-3400. Fax (719)268-4841. E-mail: kussjc@fotf.org. Website: www.family.org. Mark Maddox, sr. ed. (maddoxmh@aol.com); submit to Julie Kuss, acq. mngr. Dedicated to the preservation of marriage and the family. Publishes 15-20 titles/yr. Receives 750 submissions annually. Reprints books. Prefers 40,000 wds. or 200 pgs. Royalty 10-22% of net; some outright purchases; advance varies. Average first printing 15,000. Publication within 20 mos. Considers simultaneous submissions. Requires requested ms on disk. Responds in 8-10 wks. Prefers NIV. Guidelines by e-mail; free resources catalog.

    Nonfiction: Query Letter only; e-query OK. Most open to a fresh look at a parenting or marital issue.

    Fiction: Proposal/2-3 chapters; hard copy only. Adult fiction set from 1900 to present day. No prairie/Old West stories, or science fiction. Stories must incorporate traditional family values. Submit to Lissa Halls Johnson at above address.

    Tips: "What we do is act as an author, creating our own resources and books that best fit our ministry needs. We either write the books in-house, or find freelance writers willing to partner with us on a work-for-hire basis. We also work with an author's original material if it matches our ministry goals." Be sure to read guidelines before submitting anything to this publisher.

    **Note: This publisher serviced by The Writer's Edge.

FORTRESS PRESS, Box 1209, Minneapolis MN 55440-1209. (612)330-3300. Fax (612)330-3215. Website: www.fortresspress.com. J. Michael West, ed-in-chief; submit to Dr. K. C. Hanson, acq. ed. Publishes religious academic books. Publishes 60 titles/yr. Receives 500-700 submissions annually. 10% of books from first-time authors. Accepts mss through agents. Royalty on retail. Publication within 1-2 yrs. Considers simultaneous submissions. Responds in 3 mos. Guidelines on Website; free catalog (call 1-800-328-4648).

    Nonfiction: Proposal/1 chapter. "Please study guidelines before submitting."

    Ethnic Books: African American studies.

FORWARD MOVEMENT, 412 Sycamore St., Cincinnati OH 45202. Toll-free (800)543-1813. (513)721-6659. Fax (513)721-0729. E-mail: esgleason@forwarddaybyday.com. Website: www.forwardmovement.org. Episcopal. Edward S. Gleason, ed. dir. To help rejuvenate the life of the church. Publishes 12 titles/yr. Receives 1,000 submissions annually. 50% of books from first-time authors. No mss through agents. Rarely reprints books. Prefers 150 pgs. One-time honorarium; no advance. Average first printing 5,000. Publication within 9 mos. Considers simultaneous submissions. Prefers requested ms on disk. Responds in 1-2 mos. Prefers NRSV. Guidelines; free catalog.

    Nonfiction: Query for book, complete ms if short; no phone/fax/e-query.

    Fiction: Query. For teens. Biblical. Send for guidelines.

    Ethnic Books: Hispanic pamphlets.

Also Does: Booklets, 4-32 pgs.; pamphlets 4-8 pgs.; tracts.

Tips: "We sell primarily to a mainline Protestant audience. Most open to books that deal with the central doctrines of the Christian faith."

FOUR COURTS PRESS, 7 Malpas St., Dublin 8, Ireland. International phone +3531 4534668. Fax +3531 4534672. Marlin Fanning, ed. Imprint: Open Air. Publishes 5 titles/yr. Receives 40 submissions annually. 10% of books from first-time authors. Accepts mss through agents. Reprints books. Prefers 70,000 wds. Royalty 10% of net; sometimes no royalty is paid; no advance. Average first printing 500-700. Publication within 6-10 mos. Considers simultaneous submissions. Responds in 2-10 wks. Prefers RSV. Guidelines being revised; free catalog.

Nonfiction: Query only; unsolicited mss will not be returned. Phone/fax/e-query OK. "We're looking for scholarly/academic books."

FREDERICK FELL PUBLISHERS, INC., 2131 Hollywood Blvd., Ste. 305, Hollywood FL 33020-6750. (954)925-0555. Fax (954)925-5244. E-mail: dlessne@fellpub.com, or info@fellpub.com. Website: www.fellpub.com. Barbara Newman, sr. ed. General publisher that publishes 2-4 religious titles/yr. Receives 100 submissions annually. 95% of books from first-time authors. Reprints books. Prefers 60,000 wds. or 200-300 pgs. Royalty 6-15% on retail; advance of $500-10,000. Average first printing 7,500. Publication within 1 yr. Considers simultaneous submissions. Responds in 4-6 wks. Requires submissions by e-mail. Guidelines on Website.

Nonfiction: Complete ms; no phone/fax/e-query. Looking for self-help and how-to books. Include a clear marketing and promotional strategy.

Fiction: Complete ms; no phone/fax/e-query. For adults; adventure and historical. "Looking for great story lines, with potential movie prospects."

Tips: "Spirituality, optimism, and a positive attitude have international appeal. Steer clear of doom and gloom; less sadness and more gladness benefits all." Also publishes New Age books.

FRIENDS UNITED PRESS, 101 Quaker Hill Dr., Richmond IN 47374. (765)962-7573. Fax (765)966-1293. E-mail: friendspress@fum.org. Website: www.fum.org. Friends United Meeting (Quaker). Barbara Bennett Mays, ed. To gather persons into a fellowship where Jesus Christ is known as Lord and Teacher. Publishes 2 titles/yr. Receives 180 submissions annually. 50% of books from first-time authors. No mss through agents. **SUBSIDY PUBLISHES 5%**. Reprints books. Prefers 200 pgs. Royalty 7% of net; no advance. Average first printing 1,000-1,500. Publication within 1 yr. Considers simultaneous submissions. Responds in 3 mos. Prefers requested ms on disk or by e-mail. Guidelines (also on Website); free catalog.

Nonfiction: Proposal/2 chapters; fax/e-query OK.

Ethnic Books: Howard Thurman Books (African American).

Tips: "Most open to Quaker authors. Looking for Quaker-related spirituality, or current faith issues/practice addressed from a Quaker experience or practice."

#GENESIS COMMUNICATIONS/EVERGREEN PRESS, 9350 Dauphin Island Parkway, Theodore AL 36582. Toll-free (800)367-8203. Fax (877)768-0857. E-mail: kathy@evergreen777.com. Website: www.evergreenpressbooks.com. Nondenominational. Kathy Banashak, sr. ed. Publishes books that empower people for breakthrough living by being practical, biblical, and engaging. Imprints: Evergreen Press, Gazelle Press. Publishes 30 titles/yr. Receives 250 submissions annually. 40% of books from first-time authors. Accepts mss through agents. **SUBSIDY PUBLISHES 35%**. Does print-on-demand. No reprints. Prefers 96-160 pgs. Royalty on net; no advance. Average first printing 4,000. Publication within 6 mos. Considers simultaneous submissions. Requires requested ms on disk or by e-mail. Responds in 4-6 wks. Guidelines (also by e-mail); free catalog.

Nonfiction: Complete ms; phone/fax/e-query OK.

Fiction: For all ages. Complete ms; phone/fax/e-query OK.

Special Needs: Business, finance, personal growth, women's issues, family/parenting, relationships, prayer, humor, and angels.

Also Does: Booklets.

Tips: "Most open to books with a specific market (targeted, not general) that the author is qualified to write for and that is relevant to today's believers and seekers. Author must also be open to editorial direction."

GENESIS PRESS, INC., PO Box 101, Columbus MS 39703-0101. (662)329-9927. Fax (662)329-9399. E-mail: editor@genesis-press.com. Website: www.genesis-press.com. Niani Colom, acq. ed. Wants to approach romance with a classy, realistic, and fun, yet inspirational, Christian outlook. Imprints: Indigo Christian Romance; Indigo Glitz, and Indigo Vibe (all fiction); and Mount Blue (Christian living). Publishes 2 titles/yr. Receives 300+ submissions annually. 75% of books from first-time authors. **SOME SUBSIDY**. No reprints. Prefers 75,000-100,000 wds. Royalty 6-8% of net; advance $750. Average first printing 15,000. Publication within 6 mos. Considers simultaneous submissions. Responds in 3 mos. Guidelines by e-mail/Website; free catalog.

Nonfiction: Proposal/3 chapters; no phone/fax/e-query.

Fiction: Proposal/3 chapters; no phone/fax/e-query. Christian/inspirational romance. Prefers African American or cross-cultural fiction. Also does teen fiction for 12- to 18-year-olds, and fiction for 21- to 30-year-olds (under Indigo Vibe Imprint).

Ethnic Books: African American and multicultural.

GENEVA PRESS, 100 Witherspoon St., Louisville KY 40202-1396. Toll-free (800)227-2872. (502)569-5613. Fax (502)569-5113. E-mail: ldowell@presbypub.com. Website: www.genevapress.com, or www.ppcpub.com. Presbyterian Church (USA). Submit to Lori Dowell, ed. asst. Imprint of Presbyterian Publishing Corp. Publishes in three categories: (1) heritage, history, doctrine, policy, and institutions of the denomination; (2) theological, social, and ethical issues confronting the church; and (3) congregational mission (books for Christian educators, pastors, lay leaders, and laity); for a Presbyterian-specific audience. Publishes 10 titles/yr. Receives 1,500 submissions annually. 10% of books from first-time authors. Accepts mss through agents. No reprints. Average length 120-250 pgs. Royalty on retail; no advance for first-time authors. Average first printing 2,000. Publication within 10 mos. Considers simultaneous submissions. Accepts e-mail submissions; prefers hard copy by mail. Responds within 8 wks. Prefers NRSV. Guidelines by e-mail/Website; free catalog.

Nonfiction: Proposal/1 chapter; fax/e-query OK.

GEORGETOWN UNIVERSITY PRESS, 3240 Prospect St. NW, Washington DC 20007. (202)687-5889. Fax (202)687-6340. E-mail: reb7@georgetown.edu, or gupress@george town.edu. Website: www.press.georgetown.edu. Georgetown University. Richard Brown, dir. Scholarly books in religion, theology, ethics, and other fields, with an emphasis on cross-disciplinary and cross-cultural studies. Publishes 10 titles/yr. Receives 100 submissions annually. 10% of books from first-time authors. Accepts mss through agents. No reprints. Prefers 80,000 wds. Royalty 8-12% on net; negotiable advance. Average first printing 2,000-3,000. Publication within 9-10 mos. Considers simultaneous submissions. Requires requested ms on disk. Responds in 6-8 wks. Prefers NRSV. Does print-on-demand. Guidelines on Website; free catalog.

Nonfiction: Proposal/1 chapter; fax/e-query OK. "Should be thoroughly researched and original."

Special Needs: Work relations, theology, ethics—with scholarly bent.

Ethnic Books: Hispanic.

Also Does: CD-ROMs.

Photos: Accepts freelance photos for book covers.

GILGAL PUBLICATIONS, Box 3399, Sunriver OR 97707. Phone/fax (541)593-8418. E-mail: judyo@gilgal.com. Website: www.gilgal.com. Judy Osgood, exec. ed. Focuses on collections of meditations on specific themes. Publishes 1 title/yr. Receives 100+ submissions annually. 25-30% of submissions from first-time authors. No mss through agents. Pays $25/meditation on acceptance, plus 2 copies of the book. Average first printing 3,000. Publication time varies. Responds in 1-2 mos. No disk. Guidelines on Website.

> **Nonfiction**: Complete ms (after reading guidelines); fax query OK. "Our books are all anthologies on coping with stress and resolving grief. Not interested in other book mss. Currently interested in meditations on bereavement of various kinds."
>
> **Tips**: "For the foreseeable future, we will only be continuing our Gilgal Meditation Series and will not be buying book manuscripts."

GLORY BOUND BOOKS, PO Box 278, Cass City MI 48726. Phone/fax (989)635-7520. E-mail: info@gloryboundenterprises.com. Website: www.thegloryboundbookcompany.com. Leah Berry, pub. Sharing with children and families around the world that there is a home in heaven that can never be taken from them and that the family of God waits to welcome them in. Publishes 10+ titles/yr. (growing). New publisher. 100% of books from first-time authors. No mss through agents. No reprints. Prefers 5,000 wds. Royalty 25% of net; no advance. Average first printing 500. Publication within 12-24 mos. Considers simultaneous submissions. Responds in 3 mos. Prefers KJV (but not limited to). Guidelines on Website; catalog $1/#10 SAE/2 stamps.

> **Nonfiction**: Complete ms; no phone/fax/e-query. "We are specifically looking for family-type or ministry memoirs, missionary adventure books, and science for children. Submissions in all categories are welcome."
>
> **Fiction**: Complete ms by mail only; no phone/fax/e-query. "Humorous family fiction. Life is funny—give us a giggle and make us smile! I Peter 1:18."
>
> **Special Needs**: "We specialize in fables and poetry books." Looking for humorous books and mystery novels.
>
> **Ethnic Books**: Actively seeking foreign language submissions with English translation.
>
> **Photos**: Accepts freelance photos for book covers.
>
> **Contest**: Sponsors a contest; see contest listings.
>
> **Tips**: "We cherish the humor of family life and the nostalgic moments that weave us together. Our books are rich in feeling and descriptive detail, literally transporting the reader to another time and place. Take us on a journey through the eyes of a child or let us peek through the window of a family's home. Allow us to become a part of the experience where children and families have allowed Jesus to become their friend." Charges a $10 handling fee, payable by check in US funds to Glory Bound Books.

GOOD BOOK PUBLISHING COMPANY, PO Box 837, Kihei HI 96753-0837. Phone/fax (808)874-4876. E-mail: dickb@dickb.com. Website: www.dickb.com/index.shtml.Christian/ Protestant/Bible Fellowship. Ken Burns, pres. Researches and publishes books on the biblical/Christian roots of Alcoholics Anonymous. Publishes 1 title/yr. Receives 8 submissions annually. 80% of books from first-time authors. No mss through agents. Reprints books. Prefers 250 pgs. Royalty 10%; no advance. Average first printing 3,000. Publication within 2 mos. Considers simultaneous submissions. Responds in 1 wk. No disk. Prefers KJV. No guidelines; free catalog.

> **Nonfiction**: Proposal; no phone/fax/e-query. Books on the spiritual history and success of A. A.; 12-step spiritual roots.
>
> **Also Does**: Pamphlets, booklets.

GOOD NEWS PUBLISHERS, 1300 Crescent St., Wheaton IL 60187. (630)682-4300, ext. 308. Fax (630)682-4785. E-mail: gdennis@goodnews-crossway.org. Website: www.goodnews publishers.org. Geoffrey L. Dennis, dir. Tracts only; publishing the gospel message in an attractive and relevant format. Publishes 30 tracts/yr. Receives 500 submissions annually. 2% of tracts from first-time authors. Prefers 650-800 wds. Pays about $150 or a quantity of tracts. Average first printing 250,000. Publication within 16 mos. Considers simultaneous submissions. Responds in 6 wks. Prefers ESV. Guidelines; free tract catalog.

   Tracts: Complete ms.

   Also Does: Pamphlets.

+**GOSPEL PUBLISHING HOUSE**, 1445 N. Boonville Ave, Springfield MO 65802. (417)831-8000. E-mail: newproducts@gph.org. Website: www.gospelpublishing.com. Assemblies of God. Julie Horner, ed. The majority of titles specifically address Pentecostal audiences in a variety of ministries in the local church. Publishes 10-15 titles/yr. Receives 250 submissions annually. 25% of books from first-time authors. Accepts mss through agents. No reprints. Royalty 5-10% on retail; no advance. Average first printing 5,000. Publication within 1 yr. Considers simultaneous submissions. Responds in 4 mos. Requires accepted mss on disk or by e-mail. Guidelines on Website; free catalog.

   Nonfiction: Proposal/1 chapter; no phone query, e-query OK. "Looking for Holy Spirit; Pentecostal focus for pastors, local church lay leaders, and individuals; children's ministry programs and resources."

   Ethnic Books: Hispanic.

   Tips: "Most open to a new program or resource for children's ministry or evangelistic outreach."

GOSPEL TRACT SOCIETY, INC., PO Box 1118, Independence MO 64051. (816)461-6086. Fax (816)461-4305. Gospel Tract Society, Inc. David Buttram, ed. All tracts must be camera-ready (artwork, typeset, etc.). "We always need good, Bible-based articles that will fit a tract format. We also use poems in tract form."

+**GREEN KEY BOOKS**, 2514 Aloha Pl., Holiday FL 34691. Toll-free (888)900-0197. (727)934-0927. Fax (888)278-3300. E-mail: acquisitions@greenkeybooks.com. Website: www.greenkeybooks.com. Christian publisher. Submit to Attn: Acquisitions. Responds in 6-8 wks. Guidelines on Website. Incomplete topical listings. No questionnaire returned.

   Nonfiction: Query first; fax/e-query OK. Query can include a synopsis or brief project outline.

+**GREEN PASTURES PRESS**, HC 67 Box 91-A, Mifflin PA 17058. (717)436-9115. Mennonite. Don L. Martin, ed. High-quality, inspirational, character-building literature for children & young people. Publishes 1-4 titles/yr. Reprints books. Prefers 100-200 pgs. Royalty on net. Prefers KJV. No guidelines; free catalog.

   Nonfiction: Query first; phone query OK. "Looking for children's devotionals."

   Fiction: For all ages. Query first; phone query OK. "Looking for short-story collections and inspirational children's fiction. We prefer historical fiction; we are very conservative and avoid romance, violence, women preachers, and evangelism of children who are too young to understand."

   Tips: "We are most open to well-researched historical Christian fiction for middle grades to teens; short stories with moral and inspirational value; and children's or family devotionals."

GREENWOOD PUBLISHING GROUP/PRAEGER PUBLISHERS, 88 Post Road West, Westport CT 06881. (203)226-3571. Fax (203)226-6009. E-mail: sstaszak@greenwood.com. Website: www.Greenwood.com. Reed Elsevier Co. Suzanne Staszak-Silva, sr. ed. Imprints: Greenwood and Praeger. Publishes 5-30 titles/yr. Receives 40-60 submissions annually. No reprints. Prefers up to 100,000 wds. Royalty on net; some advances. Average first printing 1,500. Publication within 8-10 mos. Considers simultaneous submissions. Requires accepted ms on disk. Responds in 1-3 mos. Guidelines (by e-mail or Website); free catalog.

   Nonfiction: Book proposal/1-2 chapters or all chapters available; e-query OK.

Special Needs: Religious studies (general interest); criminology (general interest); literary studies.

Ethnic Books: Black studies (general interest); Islamic studies; Jewish studies.

Tips: "Most open to general interest books."

GROUP PUBLISHING, INC., 1515 Cascade Ave., Loveland CO 80539-0481. Toll-free (800)447-1070. (970)669-3836. Fax (970)679-4373. E-mail: kloesche@grouppublishing.com. Website: www.grouppublishing.com. Nondenominational. Dave Thornton, dir. of prod. dev.; Mikal Keefer, children's and youth ed.; Matt Lockhart, adult & pastoral ed.; Kerri Loesche, book/curriculum ed. Imprints: Group Books. To encourage Christian growth in children, youth, and adults with resources that are R.E.A.L. (relational, experiential, applicable, learner based). Publishes 40 titles/yr. Receives 1,000+ submissions annually. 5% of books from first-time authors. Prefers mss through agents. Some subsidy. No reprints. Prefers 128-250 pgs. Outright purchases of $25-3,000 or royalty of 6-10% of net; advance $1,500. Average first printing 5,000. Publication within 12-18 mos. Considers simultaneous submissions. Responds in 3 mos. Requires requested ms on disk. Prefers NIV. Guidelines on Website; no catalog.

Nonfiction: Query or proposal/2 chapters; no phone/fax/e-query. "Looking for practical ministry tools for pastors, youth workers, C. E. directors, and teachers with an emphasis on active learning. Read *Why Nobody Learns Much of Anything at Church: And How to Fix It* and *The Dirt on Learning* and *The 1 Thing* by Thom & Joani Schultz."

Tips: "Most open to a practical resource that will help church leaders change lives."

****Note**: This publisher serviced by The Writer's Edge.

GUERNICA EDITIONS, PO Box 117, Sta. P, Toronto ON M5S 2S6 Canada. (416)658-9888. Fax (416)657-8885. E-mail: guernicaeditions@cs.com. Website: www.guernicaeditions.com. Antonio D'Alfonso, ed. Interested in the next generation of writers. Publishes 1 religious title/yr. Receives 100 submissions annually. 5% of books from first-time authors. No mss through agents. Reprints books. Prefers 100 pgs. Royalty 8-10% of retail; some outright purchases of $200-5,000; $200-2,000 advance. Average first printing 1,500. Publication within 10 mos. Responds in 1-6 mos. Requires requested ms on disk; no e-mail. No guidelines (read one of our books to see what we like); catalog online.

Nonfiction: Query first; no phone/fax/e-query. "Looking for books on world issues."

Fiction: Query first. "Looking for short and profound literary works."

Ethnic Books: Concentration on other cultures. "We are involved in translations and ethnic issues."

Photos: Accepts freelance photos for book covers.

Tips: "Know what we publish. We're interested in books that bridge time and space; works that fit our editorial literary policies."

HARCOURT RELIGION PUBLISHERS, 6277 Sea Harbor Dr., Orlando FL 32887. Toll-free (800)922-7696. (407)345-3800. Fax (407)345-3798 (to Sebrina Kersanac for submissions). Website: www.harcourtreligion.com. Catholic. Craig O'Neil, sr. ed. Catholic educational market; high school curriculum. Publishes 50-100 titles/yr. Receives 100-300 submissions annually. Variable royalty or outright purchase; rarely pays advance. Average first printing 1,000-3,000. Publication within 1 yr. Considers simultaneous submissions. Responds in 6 mos. Free catalog.

Nonfiction: Complete ms. "Looking primarily for school and parish textbooks."

Photos: Accepts freelance photos for book covers. Submit to Lynn Molony, production mngr.

HARPERSANFRANCISCO, 353 Sacramento St., #500, San Francisco CA 94111-3653. (415)477-4400. Fax (415)477-4444. E-mail: hcsanfrancisco@harpercollins.com. Website:

www.harpercollins.com. Religious division of HarperCollins. Stephen W. Hanselman, pub.; Michael G. Maudlin, ed. dir. Strives to be the preeminent publisher of the most important books across the full spectrum of religion and spiritual literature, adding to the wealth of the world's wisdom by respecting all traditions and favoring none; emphasis on quality Christian spirituality and literary fiction. Publishes 75 titles/yr. Receives 10,000 submissions annually. 5% of books from first-time authors. Prefers mss through agents. No reprints. Prefers 160-256 ms pgs. Royalty 7.5-15% on retail; advance $20,000-100,000. Average first printing 10,000. Publication within 12 mos. Considers simultaneous submissions. Responds in 3 mos. Requires requested ms on disk. No guidelines/catalog.

Nonfiction: Proposal/1 chapter; fax query OK.

Fiction: Complete ms; contemporary adult fiction.

Tips: "Agented proposals only."

HARRISON HOUSE PUBLISHERS, Box 35035, Tulsa OK 74153. Toll-free (800)888-4126. (918)523-5400. E-mail: customerservice@harrisonhouse.com. Website: www.harrison house.com. Evangelical/charismatic. Julie Lechlider, mng. ed. To challenge Christians to live victoriously, grow spiritually, and know God intimately. Publishes 20 titles/yr. 5% of books from first-time authors. No mss through agents. No reprints. Royalty on net or retail; no advance. Average first printing 5,000. Publication within 12-24 mos. Responds in 6 mos. No guidelines or catalog. Not currently accepting proposals or manuscripts.

Nonfiction: Query first; then proposal/table of contents/1 chapter; no phone/fax query; e-query OK.

HARVEST HOUSE PUBLISHERS, 990 Owen Loop North, Eugene OR 97402. (541)343-0123. E-mail: admin@harvesthousepublishers.com. Evangelical. Books and products that affirm biblical values and help people grow spiritually strong. Publishes 190 titles/yr. No longer accepting unsolicited submissions, proposals, queries, etc.

Nonfiction: Self-help; Christian living.

Fiction: Interesting women's fiction.

**Note: This publisher serviced by The Writer's Edge and First Edition.

THE HAWORTH PASTORAL PRESS, an imprint of The Haworth Press, 10 Alice St., Binghamton NY 13904-1580. Toll-free (800)429-6784. (607)722-5857. Fax (607)771-0012. E-mail: getinfo@haworthpress.com. Website: www.haworthpress.com. Bill Palmer, mng. ed. Publishes 10 titles/yr. Receives 100 submissions annually. 60% of books from first-time authors. Reprints books. Prefers up to 250 pgs. Royalty 7-15% of net; advance $500-1,000. Average first printing 1,500. Publication within 1 yr. Requires requested ms on disk. Responds in 2 mos. Guidelines; free catalog.

Nonfiction: Proposal/3 chapters; no phone/fax query. "Looking for books on psychology/social work, etc., with a pastoral perspective."

HAY HOUSE, INC., PO Box 5100, Carlsbad CA 92018-5100. (760)431-7695. Fax (760)431-6948. E-mail: slittrell@hayhouse.com. Website: www.hayhouse.com. Jill Kramer, ed. dir.; Shannon Littrell, submissions ed. (slittrell@hayhouse.com). Books to help heal the planet. Publishes 1 religious title/yr. Receives 200 religious submissions annually. 5% of books from first-time authors. Agented submissions only. Prefers 70,000 wds. or 250 pgs. Royalty. Average first printing 5,000. Publication within 12-15 mos. Considers simultaneous submissions. Responds in 1-2 mos. Guidelines (also by e-mail); free catalog for SASE.

Nonfiction: Proposal/3 chapters; hard copy only. "Looking for self-help/spiritual with a unique ecumenical angle."

Also Does: Some gift books.

Tips: "We are looking for books with a unique slant, ecumenical, but not overly religious. We want an open-minded approach." Includes a broad range of religious titles, including New Age.

HEALTH COMMUNICATIONS, INC., 3201 S.W. 15th St., Deerfield Beach FL 33442. (954)360-0909 (no phone calls). Fax (954)360-0034. E-mail: editorial@hcibooks.com. Website: www.hci-online.com, or www.hcibooks.com. Submit to Editorial Committee or Children's Editor. Nonfiction that emphasizes self-improvement, personal motivation, psychological health, and overall wellness; recovery/addiction, self-help/psychology, health/wellness, soul/spirituality, inspiration, women's issues, relationships, and family. Imprints: HCI Teens and Simcha Press. Publishes 40 titles/yr. 20% of books from first-time authors. Accepts mss through agents. Prefers 250 pgs. Royalty 15% of net. Publication within 9 mos. Considers simultaneous submissions. Responds in 1-3 mos. Must get and follow guidelines for submission. Guidelines (also on Website); catalog for 9x12 SASE. Not in topical listings.

> **Nonfiction**: Query/outline and 2 chapters; no phone/fax/e-query. Needs books for Christian teens.

HEART OF WISDOM PUBLISHERS, 146 Chriswood Ln., Stafford VA 22556-6601. (540)752-2593. E-mail: info@heartofwisdom.com. Website: www.heartofwisdom.com. Publishes a variety of academic materials to help Christian families bring up children with a heart's desire for and knowledge of the Lord. Robin Sampson, ed. Query only. Guidelines at: http://homeschoolunitstudies.com/guidelines.htm.

> **Special Needs**: Currently accepting queries for high-quality history, science, and life skills unit studies for grades 4-12. Not accepting any other titles.
>
> **Tips**: "We market to home educators and Christian schools."

HEARTQUEST/TYNDALE HOUSE PUBLISHERS, PO Box 80, Wheaton IL 60189-0080. (630)668-8300. Fax (630)784-5011. E-mail: through Website. Website: www.tyndale.com; or www.heartquest.com. Anne Goldsmith, acq. ed. Romance imprint. To encourage and challenge readers in their faith journey and Christian walk. Accepts mss through agents or by request only. Prefers 75,000-90,000 wds. (contemporary), and 100,000+ wds. (historical). Responds in 3 mos. Royalty on net; advance. Guidelines (also by e-mail).

> **Fiction**: One-to-two-page query/synopsis/3 chapters; no phone/fax query. "Must incorporate three plot lines—action, emotion, and faith (see guidelines for details). None set in Civil War period."
>
> **Also Does**: E-books.
>
> **Tips**: "We are actively acquiring contemporary and historical romances for our HeartQuest romance line. Also looking for suspense novels and women's fiction. We look for strong writing, gripping stories, and powerful Christian content. We publish historical romances (set in 1600-1945), contemporary romances, and 3-book series."

HEARTSONG PRESENTS, Imprint of Barbour Publishing, Inc., PO Box 721, 1810 Barbour Dr., Uhrichsville, OH 44683. (740)922-7280. Fax (740)922-5948. E-mail: fictionsubmit@barbourbooks.com, or info@heartsongpresents.com. Website: www.heartsongpresents.com. Jim & Tracie Peterson, mng. eds. Produces affordable, wholesome entertainment through a book club that also helps to enhance and spread the gospel. Publishes 52 titles/yr. Receives 800+ submissions annually. 10% of books from first-time authors. Prefers 45,000-50,000 wds. Royalty 8% of net; advance $2,200. Average first printing 15,000-20,000. Publication within 1 yr. Considers simultaneous submissions. Responds in 9-12 wks. Requires electronic submission; no proposals via regular mail. Prefers KJV for historicals; NIV for contemporary. Guidelines (also by e-mail/Website); no catalog.

> **Fiction**: Proposal/3-4 chapters; electronic submissions only (fictionsubmit@barbourbooks.com). Adult. "We publish 2 contemporary and 2 historical romances every 4 weeks. We cover all topics and settings. Specific guidelines available."
>
> **Tips**: "Romance only, with a strong conservative-Christian theme. Read our books and study our style before submitting."

HENDRICKSON PUBLISHERS, 140 Summit St., PO Box 3473, Peabody MA 01961. (978)532-6546. Fax (978)531-8146. E-mail: editorial@hendrickson.com. Website: www.hendrickson.com. Dawn Harrell, assoc. ed. To provide biblically oriented books for reference, learning, and personal growth. Publishes 25-35 titles/yr. Receives 500-600 submissions annually. 25% of books from first-time authors. Accepts mss through agents. Reprints books. Prefers 200-500 pgs. Royalty 10-14% of net; some advances. Average first printing 3,000. Publication within 12-18 mos. Considers simultaneous submissions. Responds in 1-3 mos. Prefers accepted ms by e-mail. Follow *Chicago Manual of Style*. Prefers NIV. Guidelines (also on Website); catalog for 9x12 SAE/$1.42 postage (mark "Media Mail").

> **Nonfiction**: Proposal/1-2 chapters; fax/e-query OK. "Looking for popular reference material." Also publishes academic books through their Academic Book Division.

> **Special Needs**: Books that help the reader's confrontation and interaction with Scripture, leading to a positive change in thought and action; books that give a hunger to studying, understanding, and applying Scripture; books that encourage and facilitate personal growth in such areas as personal devotions and a skillful use of the Bible.

> **Tips**: "Most open to books about current 'hot' topics in churches; books that help readers understand and explore Scripture and early church history; and books that encourage Bible study and application of theology in practical life."

> ****Note**: This publisher serviced by The Writer's Edge.

HENSLEY PUBLISHING, 6116 E. 32nd St., Tulsa OK 74135. (918)664-8520. Fax (918)664-8562. E-mail: editorial@hensleypublishing.com. Website: www.hensleypublishing.com. Terri Kalfas, dir. of publishing. To edify and challenge the readers to a higher level of spiritual maturity in their Christian walk; Bible study only. Publishes 5-10 titles/yr. Receives 800 submissions annually. 50% of books from first-time authors. Accepts mss through agents. Reprints books. Prefers up to 250 pgs. Royalty on net; some outright purchases; no advance. Average first printing 5,000. Publication within 12-18 mos. Considers simultaneous submissions. Requires requested ms on disk, in MAC format or e-mail submissions. Responds in 2 mos. Guidelines (also on Website); catalog for 9x12 SAE/2 stamps.

> **Nonfiction**: Query first, then proposal/first 3 chapters; no phone/fax query. "Looking for Bible studies of varying length for use by small or large groups or individuals."

> **Tips**: "Most open to topical Bible studies with personal application."

> ****Note**: This publisher serviced by The Writer's Edge.

HIDDEN BROOK PRESS, 412-701 King St. W., Toronto ON M5V 2W7 Canada. (416)504-3966. Fax (801)751-1837. E-mail: writers@hiddenbrookpress.com. Website: www.hiddenbrookpress.com. Richard M. Grove, ed. Poetry books.

HIDDENSPRING BOOKS, 997 Macarthur Blvd., Mahwah NJ 07430. (201)825-7300. Fax (201)825-8345. E-mail: Info@hiddenspringbooks.com. Website: www.hiddenspringbooks.com, or www.paulistpress.com. Paulist Press. Paul McMahon, mng. ed. A mainstream Catholic publishing house that specializes in parish and theology resources. Publishes 95 titles/yr. Receives 700 submissions annually. 30-40% of books from first-time authors. Accepts mss through agents. 10% subsidy. No reprints. Prefers 160 pgs. Royalty 8% on net; advance $1,000. Average first printing 5,000. Publication within 18 mos. Considers simultaneous submissions. Accepts ms on disk. Responds in 2 mos. Prefers NIV. Guidelines on Website; free catalog.

> **Nonfiction**: Proposal/1 chapter, or complete ms.; phone query OK.

> **Tips**: "Most open to books on classic spirituality and prayer."

#HILLCREST PUBLISHING, 1648 Campus Ct., Abilene TX 79601. Toll-free (877)816-4455. (325)674-6950. Fax (325)674-6471. E-mail: Lemmonst@acuprs.acu.edu, or contact@hillcrestpublishing.com. Website: www.hillcrestpublishing.com. To provide books, software, and other media of the highest quality and value, that will honor the God who is revealed in the Holy Bible, encourage the spiritual quest and personal devotion, and promote service to others. Not included in topical listings. No questionnaire returned.

HILL STREET PRESS, 191 E. Broad St., Ste. 209, Athens GA 30601-2848. (706)613-7200. Fax (706)613-7204. E-mail: editorial@hillstreetpress.com. Website: www.hillstreetpress.com. Patrick Allen (allen@hillstreetpress.com) & Judy Long (long@hillstreetpress.com), eds. Liberal, ecumenical, progressive. Imprint: Hill Street Classics. Publishes 1-2 titles/yr. Receives 75-100 submissions annually. 40% of books from first-time authors. Prefers mss through agents. Reprints books. Prefers 50,000-85,000 wds. Royalty; sometimes gives advance. First printing varies. Publication within 12-15 mos. Considers simultaneous submissions. Responds in 6-8 mos. Guidelines on Website; catalog online only.

> **Nonfiction**: Proposal/3 chapters/query letter/résumé; no phone/fax/e-query. "All electronic submissions are returned unread."
>
> **Fiction**: Proposal/3 chapters/query letter/résumé; no phone/fax/e-query. Contemporary and literary. Not encouraging fiction submissions at this time, except by previously published authors.
>
> **Ethnic Books**: Jewish, Black.
>
> **Tips**: "Most open to a book that is short, ecumenical, and liberal."

HIS eBOOKS, UK PO Box 15, Southwold, Suffolk, United Kingdom 1P18 6JX. Phone +44 1502 725069. Fax +44 1502 725482. E-mail: editor@hisbooks.co.uk. Website: www.his books.co.uk. Vic Ramsey, ed. Evangelical Christian e-book publisher. Incomplete topical listings.

> **Nonfiction**: Contact by e-mail with a brief synopsis of the manuscript (4 pgs. maximum)
>
> **Fiction**: Contact by e-mail with a brief synopsis of the manuscript (4 pgs. maximum).

HOLY CROSS ORTHODOX PRESS, 50 Goddard Ave., Brookline MA 02445. (617)731-3500. Fax (617)850-1460. E-mail: tcontos@hcoc.edu. Greek Orthodox. Tanya Contos, editorial mngr. Academic and general works of interest to Orthodox Christians in church history, worship, spirituality, and life. No freelance for at least the next two years.

HONOR BOOKS, Devotional books that inspire and motivate, packaged as gift books. Submit to The Editor. See Cook Communications Ministries for details.

HONOR KIDZ, 4050 Lee Vance View, Colorado Springs CO 80918. Toll-free (800)708-5550. (719)536-0100. E-mail through Website. Website: www.cookministries.com/books/honor. Inspirational/devotional books for children. Children's imprint of Honor Books. No freelance submissions. Accepting submissions only through The Writer's Edge or First Edition.

HOURGLASS BOOKS, PO Box 132, Antioch IL 60002-0132. E-mail: editor@hour glassbooks.com. Website: www.hourglassbooks.com/submissions.html. Gina Frangello & Molly McQuade, eds. Publishes anthologies of short stories assembled around a common theme. Accepts reprints and simultaneous submissions. Shared royalties for contributors to the anthologies.

> **Fiction**: Submit by e-mail (copied into message). Literary fiction only. Currently working on "Leaving Home," a collection of stories about the experience of departure and change. No word limits, or fixed closing dates.

HOWARD PUBLISHING CO., INC., 3117 N. 7th St., West Monroe LA 71291. (318)396-3122. Fax (318)397-1882. E-mail: dennyb@howardpublishing.com. Website: www.howard publishing.com. John Howard, pres.; Denny Boultinghouse, exec. ed.; submit to Manuscript Review Committee. Christian publisher. Imprint: Howard Fiction. Publishes 46 titles/yr. Receives 600 submissions annually. 10% of books from first-time authors. Prefers 200-250 pgs. Negotiable royalty & advance. Average first printing 10,000. Publication within 16 mos. Considers simultaneous submissions. Accepted ms by e-mail. Responds in 6-8 mos. No disk. Prefers NIV. Free guidelines (also on Website); no catalog.

> **Nonfiction**: Query letter only; e-query OK.

Fiction: Query letter only; e-query OK (Twhalin@howardpublishing.com). Adult.

Tips: "Our authors must first be Christ-centered in their lives and writing, then qualified to write on the subject of choice. Public name recognition is a plus. Authors who are also public speakers usually have a ready-made audience."

**Note: This publisher serviced by The Writer's Edge.

+ICEAGLE PRESS, PO Box 681, Ocoee FL 34761. E-mail: submit@iceaglepress.com. Website: www.iceaglepress.com. Jessica Adriel, ed. Estab. 2004. Publishes 4 titles/yr. Receives 400+ submissions annually. 65% of books from first-time authors. Accepts mss through agents. Reprints books. Prefers under 65,000 wds., or 225 pgs. Royalty 10% on net; few outright purchases. Publication within 6-12 mos. Considers simultaneous submissions. Responds in 2-6 wks. Guidelines on Website; catalog on Website or for SASE.

Nonfiction: Query first, e-query OK. No phone/fax query.

Fiction: Query first, e-query OK. No phone/fax query. "Looking for modern-day romance, spiritual thrillers, or medieval/Renaissance novels; primarily for young adults."

Special Needs: "Exposés on occult involvement and how you got out. Why you wish you never joined, and what you think you can do to reach others about to be drawn in. Read our latest book, *Inverted Angel,* if you want to see the type of material we are looking for."

Tips: "Prepare yourself, read other books like yours, and study marketing. A book is only as good as its promoter."

ICS PUBLICATIONS, 2131 Lincoln Rd. NE, Washington DC 20002-1199. Toll-free (800)832-8389. (202)832-8489. Fax (202)832-8967. E-mail: editorial@icspublications.org. Website: www.icspublications.org. Catholic/Institute of Carmelite Studies. John Sullivan, ed. pro tem. For those interested in the Carmelite tradition with focus on prayer and spirituality. Publishes 6 titles/yr. Receives 30 submissions annually. 10% of books from first-time authors. Reprints books. Prefers 200 pgs. Royalty 2-6% on retail; some outright purchases; advance $500. Average first printing 3,000-7,000. Publication within 2 yrs. Considers simultaneous submissions. Accepts requested ms on disk. Responds in 2 mos. No guidelines; catalog for 7x10 SAE/2 stamps.

Nonfiction: Query or outline/1 chapter; phone/fax/e-query OK.

Tips: "Most open to translation of Carmelite classics; popular introductions to Carmelite themes which show a solid grasp of the tradition."

IDEALS CHILDREN'S BOOKS, 535 Metroplex Dr., Ste. 250, Nashville TN 37211. Toll-free (800)586-2572 (615)333-0478. Website: www.idealspublications.com. Ideal Publications/Guideposts. Patricia Pingry, pub. Hard- and soft-cover books for 3- to 10-year-olds. Publishes 5-10 titles/yr. Maximum 1,000 wds. Royalty; variable advance. Responds in 8-12 wks. Send for guidelines/catalog.

Fiction: Complete mss for picture books; sample chapters for children's chapter books; no fax/e-mail. No original artwork.

Tips: "We are looking in particular for subjects pertaining to holidays (Christmas, Valentine, Easter, etc.), either secular or religious." Address submissions to: Submissions, Ideals Children's Books (at above address).

IDEALS PUBLICATIONS, 535 Metroplex Dr., Ste. 250, Nashville TN 37211. Toll-free (800)932-2145. (615)333-0478. Website: www.idealspublications.com. *Guideposts.* Patricia Pingry, pub.; submit to Peggy Schaefer, mng. ed. Imprint: Candy Cane Press. Publishes 8-10 adult and 25-30 children's titles/yr. Variable advance. Publication within 18 mos. Considers simultaneous submissions. Responds in 2 mos. Guidelines.

Nonfiction: Accepting manuscripts. Subjects include memoirs, humorous family stories, inspiration, reflections on nature, patriotism, or travel.

ILLUMINATION ARTS PUBLISHING CO., INC., PO Box 1865, Bellevue WA 98009. (425-644-7185. Fax (425)644-9274. E-mail: LiteInfo@Illumin.com. Website: www.Illumin.com.

Ruth Thompson, ed. dir. Publishes high quality, enlightening children's picture books with enduring, inspirational, and spiritual values (inspirational, not religious). Prefers 500-1,500 wds. Royalty. Responds in 1 mo. Guidelines on Website.

Nonfiction: Complete ms/cover letter.

Fiction: Complete ms/cover letter.

Special Needs: Picture books only.

Tips: "Include a description of what makes your book special or different from others currently on the market."

INKLING BOOKS, 6528 Phinney Ave. N., Seattle WA 98103. (206)365-1624. Fax (206)838-1542. E-mail: editor@inklingbooks.com. Website: www.InklingBooks.com. Michael W. Perry, pub. Publishes 6 titles/yr. No mss through agents. Reprints books. Prefers 150-400 pgs. No advance. Print-on-demand. Publication within 2 mos. No guidelines or catalog. Not currently accepting submissions.

INTERNATIONAL AWAKENING PRESS, 139 N. Washington, PO Box 232, Wheaton IL 60189. Phone/fax (630)653-8616. E-mail: internationalawakening@juno.com. Website: www .intl-awaken.com. Intl. Awakening Ministries, Inc. Richard Owen Roberts, pres. Scholarly books on religious awakenings or revivals. Publishes 4 titles/yr. Receives 12 submissions annually. Reprints books. Royalty negotiated; no advance. Average first printing 3,000. Publication within 6 mos. Responds in 3 mos. Prefers requested ms on disk. Any translation; no paraphrases. No guidelines; free catalog.

Nonfiction: Query only; no phone/fax/e-query. "Looking for scholarly theology, especially Bible commentaries, church history, and revival-related material."

Also Does: Booklets, pamphlets, tracts.

Photos: Accepts freelance photos for book covers.

INTERVARSITY PRESS, Box 1400, Downers Grove IL 60515-1426. Receptionist: (630)734-4000. Fax (630)734-4200. E-mail: submissions@ivpress.com. Website: www.ivpress.com. InterVarsity Christian Fellowship. Andrew T. LePeau, ed. dir.; submit to Elaina Whittenhall, ms reviewer. IVP books are characterized by a thoughtful, biblical approach to the Christian life that transforms the hearts, souls, and minds of readers in the university, church, and the world, on topics ranging from spiritual disciplines to apologetics, to current issues, to theology. Imprint: LifeGuide Bible Studies. Publishes 90 titles/yr. Receives 2,500 submissions annually. 15% of books from first-time authors. Accepts mss through agents. Reprints books. Prefers 50,000 wds. or 200 pgs. Negotiable royalty on retail or outright purchase; negotiable advance. Average first printing 5,000. Publication within 18 mos. Considers simultaneous submissions. Responds in 1-12 wks. Prefers NIV, NRSV. Accepts e-mail submissions on acceptance. Guidelines (also by e-mail/Website); catalog for 9x12 SAE/$1.42 postage (mark "Media Mail").

Nonfiction: Query only first, with detailed letter according to our submissions guidelines, then proposal with 2 chapters; e-query OK.

Ethnic Books: Especially looking for ethnic writers (Black, Hispanic, Asian) this year.

Also Does: Booklets, 5,000 wds.; e-books.

Tips: "We look for a thoughtful, fresh approach. We shy away from simple answers. Writers who are nuanced, subtle, discerning, and perceptive will get farther at IVP. Writers who know and read IVP books regularly will have the best sense of what kind of books work for us. We are especially interested in apologetics, spiritual disciplines, Christianity and society issues, and theology and doctrine."

**Note: This publisher serviced by The Writer's Edge.

JEREMY P. TARCHER, 375 Hudson St., New York NY 10014. (212)366-2000. Fax (212)366-2670. Website: www.penguinputnam.com. Penguin Putnam, Inc. Mitch Horowitz, Wendy Hubbert, Sara Carder, eds. Publishes ideas and works about human consciousness that are large enough to include matters of spirit and religion. Publishes 40-50 titles/yr. Receives 1,500 submissions annually. 10% of books from first-time authors. Accepts mss through agents. Royalty 5-8% of retail; advance. Considers simultaneous submissions. Free catalog.

Nonfiction: Query. Religion.

JIREH PUBLISHING CO., PO Box 4263, San Leandro CA 94579-0263. (510)276-3322. E-mail: jaholman@yahoo.com. Website: www.jirehpublishing.com. Janice Holman, ed. To spread the gospel and teach the Word of God throughout the world. Publishes 4-6 titles/yr. Receives 100 submissions annually. 95% of books from first-time authors. Accepts mss through agents. No reprints. Prefers 96+ pgs. Royalty 10-12% on net; no advance. Average first printing 500-1,000. Publication within 18 mos. Accepts simultaneous submissions. Responds in 4-6 wks. Guidelines (also on Website); catalog on Website.

  Nonfiction: Proposal/3 chapters; fax/e-query OK. "Looking for manuscript which helps teach believers how to walk by faith and receive all the blessings that God has for them." Likes to see first and last chapter.

  Fiction: Proposal/3 chapters. Adult only. Contemporary, mystery/romance, and mystery/suspense.

  Also Does: E-books.

  Photos: Accepts freelance photos for book covers.

  Tips: "We are looking for authors who would like to work with us to create e-books (initially fiction titles)." Responds only to accepted manuscripts.

JOHN HUNT PUBLISHING, LTD., 46A West St., Alresford, Hampshire, United Kingdom S024 9AU. Phone 44 01962 736880. Fax 44 01962 736881. E-mail: office@johnhunt-publishing .com, or sandra@johnhunt-publishing.com. Website: www.johnhunt-publishing.com. John Hunt, pub.; Anne O'Rorke, ed. Imprints: Hunt & Thorpe; John Hunt Publishing Ltd.; O Books; Arthur James Ltd. Color Christian books for the international market, particularly for children. Publishes 40 titles/yr. Receives 300 submissions annually. 2% of books from first-time authors. Royalty 2-10% of net; outright purchases of $100-1,000; advance $250. Average first printing 10,000. Publication within 18 mos. No simultaneous submissions. Responds in 1 wk. No disk. No guidelines; free catalog.

  Nonfiction: Proposal/1 chapter by mail only; no phone query.

JOHNS HOPKINS UNIVERSITY PRESS, 2715 N. Charles St., Baltimore MD 21218-4363. (410)516-6900. Fax (410)516-6968. Website: www.press.jhu.edu. Nondenominational. Henry Tom, exec. ed. Publishes 4-6 religious titles/yr. Receives 50-75 submissions annually. 10-25% of books from first-time authors. Accepts mss through agents. Reprints books. Prefers 100,000 wds. Publication within 10-12 mos. Considers simultaneous submissions only on proposals. Guidelines/catalog on Website.

  Nonfiction: Query only; no phone/fax/e-query.

JOSSEY-BASS, A John Wiley & Sons Imprint, 989 Market St., 5th Floor, San Francisco CA 94103-1741. (415)782-3145. Fax (415)433-0499. E-mail: Sfullert@jbp.com. Website: www.jossey-bass.com. John Wiley & Sons, Inc. Sheryl Fullerton, exec. ed.; Julianna Gustafson, ed. Because of a nondenominational focus on practice and renewal of faith and secular corporate ownership, they are able to reach the broadest range of markets and readership. Imprint: Religion in Practice. Publishes 40 titles/yr. Receives hundreds of submissions annually. Up to 25% of books from first-time authors. Accepts mss through agents. No reprints. Prefers 60,000 wds. or 250 pgs. Royalty negotiable on net; advance. Average first printing 10,000. Publication within 1 yr. Considers simultaneous submissions. Responds in 1 mo. Prefers NRSV, NIV. Guidelines (also by e-mail); free catalog.

  Nonfiction: Proposal/2 chapters; e-query OK. "Looking for fresh, vital resources to deepen faith and Christian identity."

  Also Does: E-books.

Tips: "Our mission is transforming lives through the renewal and practice of faith and through a spirituality that engages with the world. We therefore look for writers who are able to write about faith in ways that speak to that mission, especially books on Christian spirituality and Christian living for a general readership. Writers should have fresh ideas clearly positioned among existing books in the market and should have a platform (and/or track record) from which to promote and market themselves, as well as clearly relevant credentials."

+JUBILANT PRESS: An Electronic Publisher, PO Box 6421, Longmont CO 80501. E-mail: jubilantpress@aol.com. Website: www.JubilantPress.com. Supports Right to the Heart Ministries. Linda Shepherd, pub. Publishes downloadable e-books with instant information to change your life. Publishes 20 titles/yr. Acquires by invitation only. 0% of books from first-time authors. Accepts mss through agents. Reprints books. Prefers 20-100 pgs. Pays for the right to publish, plus a percentage of author's online sales (author must have an active Web page); variable advance. Publication within 6 mos. Prefers NIV. Guidelines on Website.

Nonfiction: Brief e-mail query only; no phone/fax query.

Special Needs: Cookbooks (Crockpot, low carb, and others), wedding helps, funeral helps, birthday party helps, kid games, weight-loss helps.

Photos: Accepts freelance photos for book covers.

Tips: "Submissions accepted by invitation only. Best to send a brief e-mail with description of your idea. Please see our Web page to best understand our publishing program. Most open to a how-to, informational book with a 'need-to-know' marketability."

JUDSON PRESS, Box 851, Valley Forge PA 19482-0851. (610)768-2128. Fax (610)768-2441. Website: www.judsonpress.com. American Baptist Churches USA. Randy Frame, acq. ed.; Laura Alden, pub. Publishes 15 titles/yr. Receives 200 submissions annually. 15% of books from first-time authors. Accepts mss through agents. No reprints. Prefers 140-180 pgs., or 30,000-40,000 wds. Royalty 10-15% on net; some work-for-hire agreements; advance $500. Average first printing 4,500. Publication within 8 mos. Considers simultaneous submissions. Responds in 3 mos. Free guidelines (also on Website; click on Free Downloads)/catalog.

Nonfiction: Proposal/2 chapters.

Ethnic Books: African American.

Tips: "Authors should avoid books based primarily on their own experiences and personal reflections. Writing style must be engaging, and the writer should be well qualified to address the topic. We want books that are unusually well written."

**Note: This publisher serviced by The Writer's Edge.

JUST FOLKS PUBLISHING CO., PO Box 2012, Columbus IN 47202. (812)372-1663. E-mail: eb@hsonline.net. Website: www.prayerofhannah.com. Kenn Gividen, ed. Query; phone/fax query OK. New publisher. Not included in topical listings.

KINDRED PRODUCTIONS, 169 Riverton Ave., Winnipeg MB R2L 2E5 Canada. (204)669-6575. Fax (204)654-1865. E-mail: kindred@mbconf.ca. Website: www.kindredproductions.com. Mennonite Brethren. Marilyn Hudson, mngr. To resource the churches within the denomination (Anabaptist perspective) for Christlike living and ministry. Publishes 2-3 titles/yr. Receives 30 submissions annually. 90% of books from first-time authors. No mss through agents. **SUBSIDY PUBLISHES 5%**. No reprints. Prefers 60,000 wds. or 213 pgs. Royalty 10-15% on net; no advance. Average first printing 1,000-2,000. Publication within 9-12 mos. Considers simultaneous submissions. Responds within 4-5 mos. Requires requested ms on disk or by e-mail. Prefers NIV. Free guidelines (also by e-mail)/catalog.

Nonfiction: Proposal/2-3 chapters; no phone query, fax/e-query OK. "Looking for books that help people meet God in a nonthreatening way. Only accepting unsolicited manuscripts for inspirational reading books. A crossover potential preferred, but not mandatory."

Tips: "Most open to inspirational books that help people in everyday life encounter a relevant God. No deep theology. Material with a human interest element is best."

KREGEL KIDZONE, PO Box 2607, Grand Rapids MI 49501-2607. (616)451-4775. Fax (616)451-9330. E-mail: acquisitions@kregel.com. Website: www.kregelpublications.com. Submit to Acquisitions Editor. Publishes books and collateral materials that target both the spiritual and educational development of children. Royalty; some outright purchases. Publication within 16 mos. Considers simultaneous submissions. Responds in 2-3 mos. Guidelines (also by e-mail/Website); catalog for 9x12 SAE/3 stamps.

Fiction: Query, or complete ms (if 32 pages or less): no phone/fax/e-query. "Do not send original material, as we recycle all materials once they have been reviewed."

Tips: "Don't bind materials, other than with a paperclip or spring clip."

KREGEL PUBLICATIONS, PO Box 2607, Grand Rapids MI 49501-2607. (616)451-4775. Fax (616)451-9330. Website: www.kregelpublications.com. Evangelical/Conservative. Dennis R. Hillman, pub.; Jim Weaver, academic & professional books ed.; submit to Acquisitions Editor. To provide tools for ministry and Christian growth from a conservative, evangelical perspective. Imprints: Kregel Kidzone, Kregel Academic and Professional, and Kregel Classics. Publishes 90 titles/yr. Receives 800+ submissions annually. 20% of books from first-time authors. Reprints books. Royalty 12-16% of net; some outright purchases. Average first printing 5,000. Publication within 16 mos. Considers simultaneous submissions. Responds in 2-3 mos. Guidelines (also by e-mail/Website); catalog for 9x12 SAE/3 stamps.

Nonfiction: Query only; no phone/fax/e-query.

Fiction: For all ages. Query only; no phone/fax/e-query. "Looking for high-quality contemporary fiction with strong Christian themes and characters."

Tips: "We are expanding our line of children's products. Engaging stories and great art are a must. Also we are adding more fiction, but again, we are very selective. Strong story lines with an evident spiritual emphasis are required."

**Note: This publisher serviced by The Writer's Edge.

**Named a 2002 Publishers Weekly "Small Publisher Standout."

LAMPLIGHTER PUBLISHERS, Box 2315, Brandon FL 33509-2315. (813)685-7387. Fax (813)655-3066. E-mail: lamplighterpub@cs.com. Nondenominational. R. A. Ellinger, ed. To enlighten, educate, and entertain. No mss through agents. Makes outright purchase on acceptance. Average first printing 500-1,000. Publication within 1 yr. Considers simultaneous submissions. Accepts e-queries. Responds in 6-8 wks. Prefers KJV. Guidelines by e-mail; no catalog.

Nonfiction: Query first; e-query OK.

Fiction: For children, including picture books. Query first. "Fiction is confined to children's publications and should follow guidelines."

Special Needs: "We are looking for writers who specialize in short, moral subjects for children's tracts, no more than 500 words per tract. Topics need to be Bible based with strong moral applications. Send SASE for a sample."

Tips: "Writers should incorporate biblically sound principles with Bible reference (KJV) only. We want a clear, concise reading with no sympathy for sin or immorality. We expect submissions to be readable and double spaced on good quality paper; easy to read and understand."

LANGMARC PUBLISHING, PO Box 90488, Austin TX 78709-0488. (512)394-0989. Fax (512)394-0829. E-mail: langmarc@booksails.com. Website: www.langmarc.com. Lutheran. Lois Qualben, pub. Focuses on spiritual growth of readers. Publishes 4 titles/yr. Receives 200 submissions annually. 50% of books from first-time authors. No mss through agents. No reprints. Prefers 150-300 pgs. Royalty 10-13% on net; no advance. Average first printing varies. Publication usually within 1 yr. Considers simultaneous submissions. Responds in

2-4 mos. Requires requested ms on disk. Prefers NIV. Guidelines (also by e-mail/Website); catalog for #10 SAE/1 stamp.

Nonfiction: Proposal/3 chapters; no phone query. "Most open to inspirational books."

LARSON PUBLICATIONS/PBPF, 4936 NYS Rte. 414, Burdett NY 14818-9729. (607)546-9342. Fax (607)546-9344. E-mail: larson@lightlink.com. Website: www.larsonpublications.org. Paul Cash, dir. Books cover philosophy, psychology, religion, and spirituality. Publishes 4-5 titles/yr. Receives 1,000 submissions annually. 5% of books from first-time authors. Variable royalty; rarely gives an advance. Publication within 1 yr. Considers simultaneous submissions. Responds in 4 mos. Prefers NIV. Catalog on Website.

Nonfiction: Query by mail/outline.

LEGACY PRESS, PO Box 261129, San Diego CA 92196. (858)668-3260. Fax (858)668-3328. E-mail: rainbowed@earthlink.net. Website: www.rainbowpublishers.com. Rainbow Publishers. Christy Scannell, ed. dir. Publishes nondenominational nonfiction for children in the evangelical Christian market. Publishes 15 titles/yr. Receives 250 submissions annually. 50% of books from first-time authors. Reprints books. Prefers 150 pgs. & up. Royalty 8% & up on net; advance $500+. Average first printing 5,000. Publication within 2 yrs. Considers simultaneous submissions. Prefers requested ms on disk. Responds in 3 mos. Prefers NIV. Guidelines (also on Website); catalog for 9x12 SAE/2 stamps.

Nonfiction: Proposal/3-5 chapters; no e-queries. "Looking for nonfiction for girls and boys ages 2-12."

Fiction: Proposal/2-5 chapters. Juvenile only. Must include an additional component beyond fiction (e.g., devotional, Bible activities, etc.)

Special Needs: Nonfiction for ages 10-12, particularly Christian twists on current favorites, such as cooking, jewelry making, games, etc.

Tips: "All books must offer solid Bible teaching in a fun, meaningful way that appeals to kids. Research popular nonfiction for kids in the general market, then figure out how to present those fun ideas in ways that teach the Bible. As a smaller publisher, we seek to publish unique niche books that stand out in the market."

+LEGACY PUBLISHERS INTERNATIONAL, 1301 S. Clinton St., Denver CO 80247. (303)283-7480. Fax (303)283-7536. Website: www.legacyinternationalpublishers.com. Catalog. Incomplete topical listings. No questionnaire returned.

LIBROS LIGUORI, 1 Liguori Dr., Liguori MO 63057-9999. (636)464-2500. Fax (636)464-8449. E-mail: imartinez@liguori.org or mkessler@liguori.org. Website: www.liguori.org. Spanish division of Liguori Publications. Israel Martinez (636)223-1367 and Mathew Kessler (636)223-1471, eds. To spread the gospel in the Hispanic community by means of low-cost publications. Publishes 5 titles/yr. Receives 6-8 submissions annually. 5% of books from first-time authors. Prefers up to 30,000 wds. Royalty 8-10% of net or outright purchases of $450 (book and booklet authors get royalties; pamphlet authors get $400 on acceptance); advance. Average first printing 3,500-5,000. Publication within 18 mos. No simultaneous submissions. Requires accepted mss on electronic file. Responds in 4-8 wks. Free guidelines/catalog.

Nonfiction: Proposal/2 chapters; fax/e-query OK. "Looking for issues families face today—substance abuse, unwanted pregnancies, etc.; family relations; religion's role in immigrants' experiences, pastoral Catholic faith."

Ethnic Books: Focuses on Spanish-language products.

Also Does: Pamphlets, booklets, tracts, PC software, clip art.

Tips: "Contact us before writing. It's much easier to work together from the beginning of a project. We need books on the Hispanic experience in the U.S. Keep it concise, avoid academic/theological jargon, and stick to the tenets of the Catholic faith. Avoid abstract arguments."

+LIFE CHANGING MEDIA, 10777 W. Sample Rd., Unit 302, Coral Springs FL 33065-3768. (954-554-1921. E-mail: Paul@lifechangingmedia.net. Website: www.lifechangingmedia .net. Life Changing Publications. Paul Gundotra, pres.; submit to Sindhu Roy (submissions@lifechangingmedia.net). Considers simultaneous submissions (if informed). Guidelines on Website. Not included in topical listings. No questionnaire returned.

> **Nonfiction**: Query first; e-query OK. "Please include a description of the book project, brief bio including publishing history. Let us know if you have the ability for public speaking."

LIFE CYCLE BOOKS, LPO Box 1008, Niagara Falls NY 14304-1008. Toll-free (800)214-5849. (970)493-2257. Fax (970)493-2257. E-mail: paulb@lifecyclebooks.com. Website: www.life cyclebooks.com. Paul Broughton, gen. mngr.; submit to The Editor. Specializes in pro-life material. Publishes 1-3 titles/yr. Receives 50 submissions annually. 50% of books from first-time authors. Reprints books. Royalty 8% of net; outright purchase of brochure material, $250+; advance $100-300. **SUBSIDY PUBLISHES 10%**. Publication within 10 mos. Responds in 6 wks. Free catalog.

> **Nonfiction**: Query or complete ms. "Our emphasis is on pro-life and pro-family titles."
> **Tips**: "We are most involved in publishing leaflets of about 1,500 words, and we welcome submissions of manuscripts of this length."

+LIFE JOURNEY BOOKS, 4050 Lee Vance View, Colorado Springs CO 80918. (719)536-0100. Fax (719)536-3269. Website: www.cookministries.com. Mary McNeil, acq. ed. Guides for Christian families seeking biblical answers to life problems. Prefers mss through agents. Reprints books. Royalty 8-14% on net; advance $5,000. Average first printing 5,000. Publication within 9-12 mos. Considers simultaneous submissions. Responds in 3-9 mos. Prefers NIV. Guidelines on Website; no catalog.

> **Nonfiction**: Proposal via their Website.
> **Special Needs**: Family life and senior adult concerns.
> ****Note**: This publisher serviced by The Writer's Edge.

LIFESONG PUBLISHERS, PO Box 183, Somis CA 93066. (805)655-5644. E-mail: mailbox@lifesongpublishers.com. Website: www.lifesongpublishers.com. Laurie Donahue, pub. Provides Christian families with tools that will aid in spiritual and relational development of family members. Publishes 4 titles/yr. No mss through agents. No reprints. **SOME SUBSIDY**. Royalty 5-10% of net; small advance. Publication within 6 mos. Considers simultaneous submissions. Responds in 2-4 wks. No guidelines; Catalog for 9x12 SAE/2 stamps. Not included in topical listings.

> **Nonfiction**: Proposal/3 chapters; e-query OK. "Looking for an author with an existing ministry."

LIFT EVERY VOICE, 820 N. LaSalle Blvd., Chicago IL 60610. (312)329-2101. Fax (312)329-2144. E-mail: acquisitions@moody.edu. Website: www.moodypublishers.org. African American imprint of Moody Publishers. Moody Bible Institute and Institute for Black Family Development. Submit to Acquisitions Coordinator. To advance the cause of Christ through publishing African American Christians who educate, edify, and disciple Christians. Not included in topical listings.

+LIGHTHOUSE TRAILS PUBLISHING, PO Box 958, Silverton OR 97381. (503)873-9092. Fax (503)873-7380. E-mail: editor@lighthousetrails.com. Website: www.lighthousetrails.com. David Dombrowski, acq. ed. Books that align with the Word of God, rather than with what is popular or trendy. Publishes 1-2 titles/yr. Receives 25-50 submissions annually. 50% of books from first-time authors. Accepts mss through agents. Reprints books. Prefers 144-300 pgs. Royalty 12-17% of net, or 20% of retail; no advance. Average first printing 2,500. Publication within 6-9 mos. Considers simultaneous submissions. Requires accepted ms on disk. Responds in 2-4 wks. Prefers NKJV, NIV, KJV. Guidelines and catalog on Website.

> **Nonfiction**: Proposal/2-3 chapters; no phone/fax query; e-query OK.

Fiction: Proposal/2-3 chapters.

Special Needs: Clearly written exposés on false doctrines that have infiltrated the church or true stories of those who have courageously protected children.

Tips: "Any book we consider will not only challenge the educated, professional reader, but also be able to reach young adults who may have less experience and comprehension. Our books will include human interest and personal experience scenarios as a means of getting the point across. Read a couple of our books to better understand the style of writing we are looking for."

LIGHTWAVE PUBLISHING, INC., 26275—98th Ave, Maple Ridge BC V2W 1K3 Canada. (604)462-7890. Fax (604)462-8208. E-mail: mikal@lightwavepublishing.com. Website: www.lightwavepublishing.com. Interdenominational. Mikal Marrs, admin. To help children understand the basics of the Christian faith and to help parents pass these values on to their children. Publishes 15 titles/yr. Receives 95 submissions annually. No mss through agents. Work-for-hire only (pays an hourly or per-project rate, amount depends on project size; wages up front, on delivery of manuscript). Publication within 4-8 mos. No simultaneous submissions. Responds in 2 mos. (if requested). Guidelines; catalog on Website.

Nonfiction: Query only to inquire about work-for-hire and send résumé; e-query only. Please do not submit unsolicited material.

Fiction: Query only.

Special Needs: Writers with solid biblical foundation and understanding who will work-for-hire. They buy all rights to the work.

Also Does: Some booklets.

Tips: "We come up with a book idea, then hire a writer/researcher, with expertise in that particular field, to write it."

**Note: This publisher serviced by The Writer's Edge.

LIGUORI PUBLICATIONS, 1 Liguori Dr., Liguori MO 63057-9999. Toll-free (800)325-9521. (636)464-2500. Fax (636)464-8449. E-mail: jbauer@liguori.org. Website: www.liguori.org. Catholic/Redemptorists. Judy Bauer, mng. ed. Spreading the gospel of Jesus Christ, primarily through the print and electronic media. Imprints: Faithware, Libros Liguori, Liguori Books, and Liguori/Triumph. Publishes 30 titles/yr. Prefers 100-300 pgs. for books; 40-100 pgs. for booklets; pamphlets 16-18 pgs. Variable royalty; outright purchase of pamphlets for $400; advance varies. Average first printing 3,500-5,000 on books & booklets, 10,000 on pamphlets. Publication within 2 yrs. No simultaneous submissions. Accepts requested ms on disk. Responds in 9-13 wks. Prefers NRSV. Guidelines (also by e-mail/Website); catalog for 9x12 SASE.

Nonfiction: Proposal/1 chapter (complete ms for pamphlets); phone/fax/e-query OK. "Looking for spirituality, classics, saints, prayer, travel, parenting, and family life."

Fiction: Complete ms. "Generally we don't do fiction, but will consider children's picture books, allegory or biblical books for children, with strong Catholic appeal."

Ethnic Books: Publishes books in Spanish. See separate listing for Libros Liguori.

Also Does: Booklets, pamphlets, tracts, computer games, screen savers; e-books (electronic publishing division does 4 books/yr.).

Tips: "Manuscripts accepted by us must have strong, middle-of-the-road, practical spirituality."

LILLENAS PUBLISHING CO., Program Builder Series and Other Drama Resources, Box 419527, Kansas City MO 64141-6527. (816)931-1900. Fax (816)412-8390. E-mail: drama@lillenas.com. Website: www.lillenasdrama.com. Kimberly R. Messer, product line mngr. Imprint: Lillenas Drama Resources. Publishes 10-12 titles/yr. Accepts mss through agents. Royalty 10% for drama resources; outright purchase of program builder material; no advance. No simultaneous submissions. Responds in 4 mos. Guidelines (also by e-mail/Website); catalog.

Drama Resources: Query or complete ms; phone/fax/e-query OK. Accepts readings, one-act and full-length plays, program and service features, monologues, and sketch collections.

Special Needs: Sketch collections and plays; full-length and one-act plays for adults. Seasonal; children's or youth 5-minute sketches.

Tips: "Most open to biblically based sketches and plays that have small- to medium-sized casts and are easy to stage; short sketches—4 to 8 minutes."

LION PUBLISHING, 4050 Lee Vance View, Colorado Springs CO 80918-7102. (719)536-3271. Cook Communications. Accepts no freelance submissions.

THE LITURGICAL PRESS, PO Box 7500, St. John's Abbey, Collegeville MN 56321-7500. Toll-free (800)858-5450. (320)363-2213. Fax (800)445-5899 or (320)363-3299. E-mail: mtwomey@osb.org. Website: www.litpress.org. St. John's Abbey (a Benedictine group). Imprints: Liturgical Press Books, Michael Glazier Books, and Pueblo Books. Mark Twomey, mng. ed. Academic manuscripts to Linda Maloney (lmmaloney@csbsju.edu). Publishes 70 titles/yr. Prefers 100-300 pgs. Royalty 10% of net; some outright purchases; no advance. No simultaneous submissions. Responds in 3 mos. Guidelines (also on Website); free catalog.

Nonfiction: Query/proposal. Adult only.

Tips: "We publish liturgical, scriptural, and pastoral resources."

LITURGY TRAINING PUBLICATIONS, Archdiocese of Chicago, 1800 N. Hermitage Ave., Chicago IL 60622-1101. Toll-free (800)933-1800. (773)486-8970, ext. 264. Fax (773)486-7094. E-mail: editors@ltp.org. Website: www.LTP.org. Catholic/Archdiocese of Chicago. Margaret Brennan, ed. (mbrennan@ltp.org); Paul Zalonski (pzalonski@ltp.org). Resources for liturgy in Christian life. Publishes 25 titles/yr. Receives 150 submissions annually. 50% of books from first-time authors. Variable royalty. Average first printing 2,000-5,000. Publication within 1 yr. Considers simultaneous submissions. Responds in 2-10 wks. Requires requested ms on disk. Catalog.

Nonfiction: Proposal/1 chapter; phone/fax/e-query OK.

LIVING BOOKS FOR ALL, PO Box 98425 (TST), Kowloon, Hong Kong. Phone 852 2723 1525. Fax 852 2366 6519. E-mail: clchk@hkstar.com. Website: www.hkstar.com/~clchk. CLC Ministries International, Hong Kong. Mrs. Mare Allison, ed. Prefers books of interest to Asians or Western readers interested in Asia. Imprint: Bellman House (Chinese); Living Books for All (LBA) English. Publishes 1-5 titles/yr. Receives 20 submissions annually. Considers Chinese translations of English books and English translations of Chinese books. Prefers up to 200 pgs. Royalty 5% on retail or payment in copies of book; no advance. Average first printing 3,000. Publication within 1 yr. Considers simultaneous submissions. Prefers requested ms on disk or by e-mail in Rich Text Format (.RTF). Responds in 1-3 mos. Guidelines (by e-mail or Website, www.hkstar.com/~clchk/lbaguide.html.); free Chinese book catalog.

Nonfiction: Query; proposal with 3 chapters (up to 30 pages), or complete ms; e-query preferred.

Fiction: "Fiction for adults in an Asian context."

Ethnic Books: For Asian market.

Also Does: Pamphlets, booklets.

Photos: Would consider freelance photos for book covers.

Tips: "Write in direct, personal, inclusive style; then simplify. No dissertations. We are looking for Chinese manuscripts." Prefers American spelling to English spelling. Accepts manuscripts in English or Chinese.

LIVING THE GOOD NEWS, 600 Grant St., Ste. 400, Denver CO 80203. Fax (303)832-4971. Division of the Morehouse Group. Not currently accepting submissions.

LOGION PRESS, 1445 N. Boonville Ave., Springfield MO 65802. (417)862-2781, ext. 3315.

Fax (417)866-1146. E-mail: dkingsriter@ag.org. Website: www.ag.org. Assemblies of God. Submit to Director of Christian Higher Education. Academic line of Gospel Publishing House; primarily college textbooks. Publishes on occasional basis. No mss through agents. Prefers up to 185,000 wds. Royalty on retail; some advances. Average first printing 3,500. Publication within 1 yr. No simultaneous submissions. Responds in 3 mos. Requires requested ms on disk. Free guidelines/catalog.

Nonfiction: Proposal/1-2 chapters.

Tips: "Books must not contradict our statement of Fundamental Truths that all our ministers must sign annually. Most open to religion/biblical textbooks."

#LONGLEAF PUBLISHING, 320 Thornwood Dr., Atlanta GA 30328. E-mail: manuscripts@ longleafpublishing.com. Dedicated to bringing awareness and action to preserve our natural world and understand our need to live in harmony with the environment. Publishes fiction, nonfiction, poetry, and children's literature. Not included in topical listings. No questionnaire returned.

+LOS ANGELES DESIGNERS' THEATRE, PO Box 1883, Studio City CA (1614. (323)650-9600. E-mail: ladesigners@juno.com. Full-length comedy, drama, musicals, adaptations; can incorporate religious, social, or political themes. 6-8 plays/season. Receives 1,200 submissions annually. 100% freelance. Royalty. Responds in 4-5 mos.

Plays: Query first; e-query OK.

LOVE INSPIRED, 233 Broadway, Ste. 1001, New York NY 10279-0001. (212)553-4200. Fax (212)277-8969. E-mail: JoanMarlow_Golan@harlequin.ca. Website: www.Steeple Hill.com. Harlequin Enterprises. Tara Gavin, ed. dir.; submit to any of the following: Joan Marlow Golan, sr. ed.; Krista Stroever, ed.; Diane Dietz, asst. ed. Mass-market Christian romance novels. Imprints: Steeple Hill (single-title trade paperback women's fiction), see separate listing. Publishes 60-65 titles/yr. Receives 500-1,000 submissions annually. 15% of books from first-time authors. Prefers mss through agents. No reprints. Prefers 70,000-75,000 wds. or 300-320 pgs. Royalty on net; advance. Publication within 12-24 mos. Requires accepts ms on disk/hard copy. Responds in 3 mos. Prefers KJV. Guidelines by e-mail/Website: no catalog.

Fiction: Query letter or 3 chapters and up to 5-page synopsis; no phone/fax/e-query.

Special Needs: These contemporary "sweet" romances feature Christian characters facing the many challenges of life and love in today's world. Drama, humor, and even a touch of mystery or suspense can take place in the series. Any subplots should come directly from the main story. Secondary characters (children, family, friends, neighbors, fellow church members, etc.) can also help contribute to a substantial and gratifying story. An element of faith should be well integrated into the plot. And the conflict between the main characters should be an emotional one.

Tips: "We want character-driven fiction, with appealing author voice that inspires, from historicals and contemporary, across a broad spectrum of subgenres: relationship novels, family sagas, Christian chick lit, suspense, mysteries, thrillers, 'weepies,' and romance."

LOYAL PUBLISHING, PO Box 1414, Bend OR 97709-1414. (541)549-8890. Fax (541)549-8879. E-mail: editorial@loyalpublishing.com. Website: www.loyalpublishing.com. Submit to Book Editor. To draw the heart of mankind to God, to remain faithful to His precepts, and to walk in His ways. Not included in topical listings. No questionnaire returned.

Nonfiction: Accepts mss by e-mail in a zipped file (see Website for full instructions). Books, children's books, and educational materials.

**Note: Multnomah Publishers has purchased certain publishing rights from this publisher.

LOYOLA PRESS, 3441 N. Ashland Ave., Chicago IL 60657. Toll-free (800)621-1008. (773)281-1818. Fax (773)281-0152. E-mail: durepos@loyolapress.com. Website: www.loyola press.org. Catholic. Joseph Durepos, acq. ed. Serving faith formation in the Jesuit tradition.

Publishes 40 titles/yr. Open to first-time authors. Accepts mss through agents. Prefers 40,000-80,000 wds. or 200-400 pgs. Variable royalty on net; advances $5,000-25,000. Average first printing 7,500-15,000. Considers simultaneous submissions. Responds in 8-10 wks. Prefers NRSV (Catholic Edition). Guidelines on Website.

Nonfiction: Proposal/sample chapters; no phone query; e-query OK.

Tips: "Looking for family, faith, and social/spiritual issues."

**Note: This publisher serviced by The Writer's Edge.

THE LUTTERWORTH PRESS/JAMES CLARKE & CO. LTD., PO Box 60, Cambridge CB1 2NT England. Phone +44 1223 350865. Fax +44 1223 366951. E-mail: publishing@lutterworth.com. Website: www.lutterworth.com. Adrian Brink, ed. Imprints: The Lutterworth Press (general); James Clarke & Co. (academic/reference). Publishes 10 titles/yr. Receives 100 submissions annually. 90% of books from first-time authors. **SUBSIDY PUBLISHES 2%.** Royalty on retail; some advances. Publication within 18 mos. No simultaneous submissions. Responds in 3 mos. Requires requested ms on disk. No guidelines; free catalog.

Nonfiction: Proposal/2 chapters. Most open to nonfiction.

+MACALESTER PARK PUBLISHING, 24558—546th Ave., Austin MN 55912. (507)396-0135. Toll-free fax (800)407-9078. Sue Franklin, owner.

#MADISON BOOKS/COOPER SQUARE PRESS, 200 Park Ave. S., Ste. 1109, New York NY 10003-1503. (212)529-3888, ext. 313. Fax (212)529-4223. E-mail: rplotkin@rowman.com. Website: www.coopersquarepress.com. Rowman and Littlefield Publishing Group. Ross Plotkin, ed. asst. Religion topics. Publishes 40 titles/yr. Receives 1,200 submissions annually. 15% of books from first-time authors. Accepts mss through agents. Reprints books. Royalty 10-15% of net. Publication within 1 yr. Considers simultaneous submissions. Responds in 2-3 mos. Guidelines: catalog for 9x12 SAE/4 stamps. Incomplete topical listings. No questionnaire returned.

Nonfiction: Query with outline, sample chapters, and SASE; no e-query.

MAGNUS PRESS, PO Box 2666, Carlsbad CA 92018. (760)806-3743. Fax (760)806-3689. E-mail: magnuspres@aol.com. Website: www.magnuspress.com. Warren Angel, ed. dir. To publish biblical studies that are written for the average person and that minister life to Christ's Church. Imprint: Canticle Books. Publishes 6 titles/yr. Receives 60 submissions annually. 50% of books from first-time authors. Accepts submissions through agents. Reprints books. Prefers 125-375 pgs. Graduated royalty on retail; no advance. Average first printing 5,000. Publication within 1 yr. Considers simultaneous submissions. Accepts requested ms on disk. Responds in 1 mo. Guidelines (also by e-mail); free catalog.

Nonfiction: Query or proposal/2-3 chapters; fax query OK. "Looking for spirituality, thematic biblical studies, unique inspirational/devotional books, e.g. *Sports Stories and the Bible.*"

Tips: "Our writers need solid knowledge of the Bible and a mature spirituality that reflects a profound relationship with Jesus Christ. Most open to a popularly written biblical study that addresses a real concern/issue in the church at large today."

**Note: This publisher serviced by The Writer's Edge.

MASTER BOOKS, PO Box 726, Green Forest AR 72638. (870)438-5288. Fax (870)438-5120. E-mail: nlp@newleafpress.net. Website: www.masterbooks.net. Imprint of New Leaf Press. Jim Fletcher, ed.; Roger Howerton, acq. ed. Publishes 12-15 titles/yr. Receives 1,200 submissions annually. 10% of books from first-time authors. Prefers 140-240 pgs. Royalty 10% of net; no advance. Average first printing 5,000. Considers simultaneous submissions. Responds in 90 days or longer. Free catalog.

Nonfiction: Query. "Looking for biblical creationism, biblical science, creation/evolution debate material." No fiction, poetry, or personal stories.

Special Needs: Children's books and homeschool science books.

MCDOUGAL PUBLISHING, PO Box 3595, Hagerstown MD 21742. (301)797-6637. Fax (301)733-2767. E-mail: publishing@mcdougal.org. Website: www.mcdougalpublishing.com. Pentecostal/Charismatic, nondenominational. Diane McDougal, pres.; Jeanette Biesecker, mng. ed. Publishes books for the Body of Christ. Imprints: McDougal Publishing, Fairmont Books, Parable Publishing, and Serenity Books. Publishes 15-20 titles/yr. Receives 150 submissions annually. 70% of books from first-time authors. Accepts mss through agents. **SUBSIDY PUBLISHES 20%**. Reprints books. Prefers 80-192 pgs. Royalty 10-15% of net; no advance. Average first printing 3,000-5,000. Publication within 6 mos. Considers simultaneous submissions. Responds in 2 mos. Guidelines (also on Website); free catalog.

    Nonfiction: Proposal/1-2 chapters (preferred); phone/fax/e-query OK. "Looking for titles on all topics relevant to the Christian life."

    Fiction: Complete ms. "Now considering adult fiction for authors with an established market; no romance."

    Tips: "Know who your audience is, and write to that audience. Also, keep focused on one central theme."

+MCRUFFY PRESS, PO Box 212, Raymore MO 64083. (888)967-1200. Fax (888)967-1300. E-mail: brian@mcruffy.com. Website: www.mcruffy.com. Brian Davis, ed. Christian publisher of children's trade books, children's audio, and homeschool materials. Open to freelance. Incomplete topical listings. No questionnaire returned.

+MEGAGRACE BOOKS, PO Box 80180, Las Vegas NV 89180-0180. Phone/fax (702)243-4895. E-mail: ds@scherf.com, or grace@megagrace.com. Websites: www.megagrace.com, or www.scherf.com/scherfbooks.htm. Dietmar Scherf, ed. Books that positively discuss and teach the pure grace message of the Bible. Imprint: Scherf Books. Publishes 2 titles/yr. Receives 500 submissions annually. 90% of books from first-time authors. No mss through agents. No reprints. Prefers 40,000-50,000 wds. (nonfiction), or 90,000-120,000 wds. (fiction). Royalty 5-10% of retail or outright purchase; no advance. Average first printing 2,000-5,000. Publication within 18 mos. Considers simultaneous submissions. No mss by disk or e-mail. Responds in 4-6 wks. Prefers KJV, NASB, or Amplified. Guidelines and catalog on Website.

    Nonfiction: Query first/SASE; no phone/fax/e-query. "Looking for Christian living and spiritual life books."

    Fiction: Query first/SASE; no phone/fax/e-query. Adult. "All books must be solidly grounded in the pure grace message as revealed in the Bible, and as explained on our Website."

    Also Does: Audio CDs on the pure grace of God.

    Photos: Accepts freelance photos for book covers.

    Tips: "We like books that gently help folks discover the pure grace of God."

#MERCER UNIVERSITY PRESS, 1400 Coleman Ave., Macon GA 31207-0003. (478)301-2880. Fax (478)301-2264. E-mail: jolley_ma@mercer.edu. Website: www.mupress.org. Baptist. Marc Jolley, mng. ed. Publishes 15 titles/yr. Receives 200 submissions annually. 75% of books from first-time authors. Accepts mss through agents. Some reprints. Royalty on net; no advance. Average first printing 800-1,200. Publication within 15 mos. Prefers requested ms on disk; no e-mail submissions.

    Nonfiction: Proposal/2 chapters; fax/e-query OK. "We are looking for books on history, philosophy, theology, and religion, including history of religion, philosophy of religion, Bible studies, and ethics." No religious fiction, only Southern literary.

MERIWETHER PUBLISHING LTD./CONTEMPORARY DRAMA SERVICE, 885 Elkton Dr., Colorado Springs CO 80918. (719)594-4422. Fax (719)594-9916. E-mail: MerPCDS@ aol.com. Website: www.meriwetherpublishing.com. Arthur L. Zapel, ed.; submit to Rhonda

Wray, Christian ed. Publishes 2-3 titles/yr.; 30 plays/yr. Primarily a publisher of plays for Christian and secular; must be acceptable for use in a wide variety of Christian denominations. Imprint: Contemporary Drama Service. Publishes 3 bks./25 plays/yr. Receives 800 submissions annually (mostly plays). 50% of books from first-time authors. Accepts mss through agents. Reprints books. Prefers 200 pgs. Royalty 10% of net or retail, or fee arrangement; no advance. Average first printing of books 2,500, plays 500. Publication within 1 yr. Considers simultaneous submissions. Requires accepted mss on disk; no e-mail submissions. Responds in 3-5 wks. Guidelines (also on Website); catalog $2.

Nonfiction: Query only for books; fax/e-query OK. "Looking for creative worship books, i.e., drama, using the arts in worship, how-to books with ideas for Christian education." Submit books to Meriwether.

Fiction: Plays only, for all ages. Always looking for Christmas and Easter plays (1 hour maximum). Send complete manuscript. Submit plays to Contemporary Drama.

Special Needs: Collections of church dramas. Drama, theater, how-to in relation to theater, drama ministry, and Christian education; collection of skits, scripts, or sketches.

Tips: "Our books are on drama or any creative, artistic area that can be a part of worship. Writers should familiarize themselves with our catalog before submitting to ensure that their manuscript fits with the list we've already published." Contemporary Drama Service wants easy-to-stage comedies, skits, one-act plays, large-cast musicals, and full-length comedies for schools (junior high through college), and churches (including chancel dramas for Christmas and Easter).

MESSIANIC JEWISH PUBLISHERS, 6204 Park Heights Ave., Baltimore MD 21215. (410)358-6471, ext. 206. Fax (410)764-1376. E-mail: editor@messianicjewish.net. Website: www.MessianicJewish.net. Lederer/Messianic Jewish Communications. Janet Chaiet, mng. ed. Books that build up the Messianic Jewish community, witness to unbelieving Jewish people, or help Christians understand their Jewish roots. Imprints: Lederer Books, Remnant Press (subsidy only). Publishes 10-12 titles/yr. Receives 100+ submissions annually. 50% of books from first-time authors. No mss through agents. Reprints books. Prefers 50,000-88,000 wds. Royalty 7-15% of net. Average first printing 5,000. Publication within 12-24 mos. No simultaneous submissions. Responds in 3-6 mos. Requires requested ms on disk. Prefers Complete Jewish Bible. Guidelines (also by e-mail); free catalog.

Nonfiction: Write or call for submission guidelines first. Messianic Judaism, Jewish evangelism, or Jewish roots of Christian faith. "Must have Messianic Jewish theme and demonstrate familiarity with Jewish culture and thought."

Fiction: Write or call for submission guidelines first. For adults. Jewish only.

Ethnic Books: Jewish; Messianic Jewish.

Tips: "Must request guidelines before submitting book proposal; all submissions must meet our requirements. Looking for Messianic Jewish commentaries. Books must address one of the following: Jewish evangelism, Jewish roots of Christianity, or Messianic Judaism."

MILLENNIUM III PUBLISHERS, 174 N. Moore Rd., Simpsonville SC 29680. (864)967-7344. E-mail: willramsey@millenniatech.info. Website: www.paradigmbooks.info. Willard Ramsey, sr. ed. Restoring our culture to a Christian world-view. Publishes 4-5 titles/yr. Receives 40-50 submissions annually. 50% of books from first-time authors. Accepts mss through agents. Reprints books. Prefers 250-300 pgs. Royalty 10-15% on net; some advances. Publication within 10-12 mos. Considers simultaneous submissions. Responds in 6 wks. Prefers NKJV. Guidelines; free catalog.

Nonfiction: Query; proposal/2 chapters; phone/e-query OK.

Fiction: Proposal/2 chapters; phone/e-query OK. "Looking for historical novels of the 'Great Awakening' period—how were the churches and their message different then?"

Photos: Accepts freelance photos for book covers.

Tips: "Most open to nonfiction books applying Christian solutions to contemporary cultural problems."

+MOMS IN PRINT: The Exclusive Publisher for Moms, PO Box 241, Round Hill VA 20141. (540)338-2596. Fax (703)750-0229. E-mail: editors@momsinprint.com, or submissions@momsinprint.com. Website: www.momsinprint.com. General publisher. Terry Doherty, sr. ed. Publishes select works by a wide variety of Mom authors, producing top quality books readers will cherish. Royalty. Responds in 2 mos. Guidelines on Website. Incomplete topic listings. No questionnaire returned.

Nonfiction: Proposal/3 chapters to submissions@momsinprint.com.

Fiction: Proposal/3 chapters to submissions@momsinprint.com.

Also Does: Poetry.

Tips: "We believe that every Mom should have the opportunity to share her creative writing skills, while expressing personal thoughts, dreams, emotions, and helpful information in print for the benefit of readers worldwide."

MONARCH BOOKS, Mayfield House, 256 Banbury Rd., Oxford OX2 7DH, United Kingdom. Phone +44 (0) 1865 302750. Fax +44 (0) 1865 302757. E-mail: monarch@lion hudson.com. Website: www.lionhudson.com. Lion Hudson PLC. Tony Collins, editorial dir. Publishes primarily for the evangelical Christian market, providing tools and resources for Christian leaders; publishes and distributes in U.S. and Canada through an arrangement with Kregel Books. Publishes 35 titles/yr. Receives 800-1,000 submissions annually. 20% of books from first-time authors. Accepts mss through agents. Prefers 50,000 wds. or 192 pgs. Royalty 10-15% on net; advance. Average first printing 5,000. Publication within 9 mos. Considers simultaneous submissions. Requires requested ms on disk or by e-mail. Responds in 6 wks. Prefers NIV. Guidelines by e-mail; free catalog.

Nonfiction: Proposal with 2 chapters; phone/fax/e-query OK. Looking for books of substance.

Tips: "Looking for books that are original, well presented, and have a clear purpose and market. Think about who you are writing for. What will a reader get as a benefit from reading your book?"

MOODY PUBLISHERS, 820 N. LaSalle Blvd., Chicago IL 60610. Fax (312)329-2144. E-mail: Acquisitions@moody.edu. Website: www.moodypublishers.org. Imprint: Northfield Publishing, and Lift Every Voice (African American). Moody Bible Institute. Submit to Acquisitions Coordinator. To provide books that evangelize, edify the believer, and educate concerning the Christian life. Publishes 65-70 titles/yr. Receives 3,500 submissions annually. 1% of books from first-time authors. Accepts mss through agents. Royalty on net; advance $500-50,000. Average first printing 10,000. Publication within 1 yr. No simultaneous submissions. Requires requested ms on disk. Responds in 2-3 mos. Prefers NAS, NLT, NIV. Guidelines (also by e-mail); catalog for 9x12 SASE/$1.42 postage (mark "Media Mail").

Nonfiction: Proposal/3 chapters; no phone/fax/e-query. "For nonfiction, we review only those proposals that come from professional literary agents." Closed to all other unsolicited mss.

Fiction: Proposal/3-5 chapters; for all ages. "We are seeking compelling fiction that will provide readers with an enjoyable and enriching reading experience and will motivate them toward biblical thinking and Christlike living. Our fiction must reinforce the overall mission of Moody Publishers by edifying, evangelizing, and/or educating readers through well-crafted stories." No picture book or romance genre fiction.

Ethnic Books: African American.

Tips: "Get to know Moody, and tell us why your book is a good fit for us. Most open to books where the writer is a recognized expert and already has a platform to promote the book."

**Note: This publisher serviced by The Writer's Edge.

MOREHOUSE PUBLISHING CO., 4775 Linglestown Rd., Harrisburg PA 17112. (717)541-8130. Fax (717)541-8136. E-mail: morehouse@morehouse.com. Website: www.morehousepublishing.com. Episcopalian. Debra Farrington, ed. dir.; submit to Nancy Fitzgerald, sr. ed. Publishes 25 titles/yr. Accepts mss through agents. No reprints. Royalty 10% of net; advance $1,000-2,000. Average first printing 3,000. Publication within 18 mos. Considers simultaneous submissions. Responds in 4-8 wks. Guidelines (also on Website); for free catalog call (800)877-0012.

   Nonfiction: Proposal/1 chapter; no phone/fax/e-query.

   Special Needs: Spirituality, Episcopal oriented.

   Tips: "We primarily accept books in our stated categories that are written by Episcopalians and written from an Anglican perspective."

MOUNT OLIVE COLLEGE PRESS, 634 Henderson St., Mount Olive NC 28365. (919)658-2502. Dr. Pepper Worthington, ed. Publishes 5 titles/yr. Receives 1,000 submissions annually. 70% of books from first-time authors. Prefers 220 pgs. Negotiated royalty. Average first printing 500. Publication within 1-3 yrs. No simultaneous submissions. Responds in 6-12 mos. No disk. Free guidelines/catalog.

   Nonfiction: Proposal/3 chapters; no phone query. Religion. For poetry submit 6 sample poems.

   Fiction: Proposal/3 chapters. Religious; literary.

MOUNTAINVIEW PUBLISHING COMPANY, 1284 Overlook Dr., Sierra Vista AZ 85635-5512. E-mail: leeemory@earthlink.net. Website: www.trebleheartbooks.com. Division of Treble Heart Books. Lee Emory, ed./pub. Online Christian publisher. Receives 300 submissions annually. 13% of books from first-time authors. Prefers 50,000-100,000 wds. Royalty 35% of retail; no advance. Books are published electronically, available on disk or downloaded into buyer's computer; also available in trade-sized print. Publication usually within 12 mos. No simultaneous submissions (a 90-day exclusive is required on all submissions). Responds in 3-4 mos. Guidelines on Website.

   Nonfiction: Submissions to: submissions@trebleheartbooks.com. Seeking excellent nonfiction, inspirational books.

   Fiction: E-mail submissions only. Historical romances, 80,000-100,000 wds.; contemporary romances, 65,000-80,000 wds.; novellas 20,000-30,000 wds. preferred (considers 35,000-40,000). "Seeking high-quality manuscripts; not necessarily romances. Looking for good mainstream and traditional inspirationals in most categories."

   Photos: Accepts some high quality freelance photos for book covers.

   Tips: "All inspirational fiction should contain a faith element. Challenge the reader to think, to look at things through different eyes. Avoid head-hopping and clichés; avoid heavy-handed preaching. No sci-fi or fantasy or dark angel stories. Send consecutive chapters, not random."

MULTNOMAH PUBLISHERS, Box 1720, 204 W. Adams St., Sisters OR 97759. (541)549-1144. Fax (541)549-0432. E-mail: editorial@multnomahbooks.com. Websites: www.multnomahbooks.com; www.letstalkfiction.com. Imprint information listed below. Publishes 75 titles/yr. Multnomah is currently not accepting unsolicited manuscripts, proposals, or queries; no proposals for biographies, poetry, or children's books. Queries will be accepted through literary agents and at writers' conferences at which a Multnomah representative is present.

   Multnomah Books: Christian living and popular theology books.

   Multnomah Fiction: Well-crafted fiction that uses truth to change lives.

   Multnomah Gifts: Substantive topics with beautiful, lyrical writing.

   Also Does: E-books.

   **Note: This publisher serviced by The Writer's Edge (especially for fiction).

NAVPRESS, Box 35001, Colorado Springs CO 80935. (719)548-9222. Website: www.navpress .org or www.gospelcom.net/navs/NP. "We are no longer accepting any unsolicited submissions, proposals, queries, etc."

**Note: This publisher serviced by The Writer's Edge.

NAZARENE PUBLISHING HOUSE—See Beacon Hill Press of Kansas City.

NEIBAUER PRESS, 20 Industrial Dr., Warminster PA 18974. (215)322-6200. Fax (215)322-2495. E-mail: Nathan@neibauer.com. Website: www.ChurchGrowthCenter.com. Nathan Neibauer, ed. For Evangelical/Protestant clergy and church leaders. Publishes 8 titles/yr. Receives 100 submissions annually. 5% of books from first-time authors. No mss through agents. Reprints books. Prefers 200 pgs. Royalty on net; some outright purchases; no advance. Average first printing 1,500. Publication within 6 mos. Considers simultaneous submissions. Responds in 4 wks. Prefers e-mail submissions. Prefers NIV. No guidelines/catalog.

Nonfiction: Query or proposal/2 chapters; fax query OK.

Also Does: Pamphlets, tracts.

Photos: Accepts freelance photos for book covers.

Tips: "Publishes only religious books on stewardship and church enrollment, stewardship and tithing, and church enrollment tracts."

NELSON BOOKS, (formerly Thomas Nelson Publishers) PO Box 141000, Nashville TN 37214. (615)889-9000. Fax (615)902-2747. Website: www.thomasnelson.com. A division of Thomas Nelson, Inc. Jonathan Merkh, pub.; Brian Hampton, assoc. pub. Imprints: Oliver Nelson and Nelson Business. Publishes 42 titles/yr. Less than 5% of books from first-time authors. Prefers mss through agents. No reprints. Accepts no unsolicited mss. Prefers 65,000-95,000 wds. Royalty. No guidelines.

Nonfiction: Query letter only first; no unsolicited mss. "Looking for nonfiction dealing with the relationship and/or application of biblical principles to everyday life, 65,000-95,000 words."

**Note: This publisher serviced by First Edition and The Writer's Edge.

#NEW CANAAN PUBLISHING CO., INC., PO Box 752, New Canaan CT 06840. Phone/fax (203)966-3408. E-mail: info@newcanaanpublishing.com. Website: www.newcanaan publishing.com. Kathy Mittelstadt, ed. Children's books with strong educational and moral content, for grades 1-9; also aggressively building its Christian titles list. Publishes 4 titles/yr. Receives 1,000 submissions annually. 50% of books from first-time authors. Accepts mss through agents. Prefers 20,000-50,000 wds. or 120-250 pgs. Royalty 8-10% of net; occasional advance. Average first printing 500-5,000. Publication within 1 yr. Accepts simultaneous submissions. Responds in 3-4 mos. Requires requested ms on disk; no e-mail submissions. Guidelines and catalog on Website, or for #10 SASE.

Nonfiction: Query letter; proposal/2-3 chapters or complete ms; no e-query. Does not return submissions.

Fiction: Query letter; proposal/2-3 chapters or complete ms; no e-query. For children and teens, 6-14 yrs. "We want children's books with strong educational and moral content; 10,000-20,000 wds." Now accepts picture books.

Special Needs: Middle-school-level educational books.

Photos: Accepts freelance photos for book covers.

Tips: "Looking for teen/youth fiction and religious instructional materials for teens/youth."

NEW HOPE, Box 12065, Birmingham AL 35202-2065. (205)991-8100. Fax (205)991-4015. E-mail: new_hope@wmu.org. Website: www.newhopepubl.com. Imprint of Woman's Missionary Union; Auxiliary to Southern Baptist Convention. Becky Yates, pub. dir.; Rebecca England, ed. Publishes Christian nonfiction for women and families, and books with a missions or ministry focus. Publishes 24-32 titles/yr. Receives 350 submissions annually. 25%

of books from first-time authors. Accepts mss through agents. Reprints books occasionally. Prefers 150-250 pgs. Royalty or outright purchase. Average first printing 5,000-10,000. Publication within 2 yrs. Considers simultaneous submissions. Responds in 3 mos. Requires requested ms on disk or by e-mail. Guidelines (also on Website); catalog for 9x12 SAE/3 stamps.

Nonfiction: Complete ms or proposal/3 chapters; no phone/fax/e-query. "All that we publish must have a missions/ministry emphasis."

Photos: Accepts freelance photos for book covers.

**Note: This publisher serviced by The Writer's Edge.

NEW LEAF PRESS, PO Box 726, Green Forest AR 72638-0726. (870)438-5288. Fax (870)438-5120. E-mail: nlp@newleafpress.net. Website: www.newleafpress.net. Jim Fletcher, ed.; Roger Howerton, acq. ed. Endeavors to bring the lost to Christ and understanding to the Body of Christ. Imprint: Master Books and Balfour Books. Publishes 25-30 titles/yr. Receives 1,200 submissions annually. 15% of books from first-time authors. Accepts mss through agents. Reprints books. Prefers 100-400 pgs. Variable royalty on net; rarely gives advance. Average first printing 5,000. Publication within 12 mos. Considers simultaneous submissions. Requires accepted ms on disk. Responds in 3 mos. Prefers KJV. Guidelines (also by e-mail); catalog for 9x12 SAE/5 stamps.

Nonfiction: Proposal/2 chapters; no phone/fax query. "Looking for gift books, Christian living, creation-science, and scholarly works." No fiction, poetry, or personal stories.

Tips: "Send us a gift book or something very unique that's different from anything out there."

+NEW SEEDS BOOKS, 300 Massachusetts Ave., Boston MA 02115. (617)424-0030. Fax (617)236-1563. E-mail: doneal@shambhala.com. Website: www.shambhala.com. Shambhala Publications, Inc. David O'Neal, mng. ed. A new imprint devoted to publishing works of the Christian contemplative traditions, cross-traditionally; also new and readable translations of classic texts. Accepts mss through agents. Reprints books. Length open. Royalty; advance. Average first printing 10,000-30,000. Publication within 1 yr. Considers simultaneous submissions. Responds in 6 wks. Prefers accepted ms on disk or by e-mail. Guidelines; free catalog.

Nonfiction: Query, proposal/2 chapters, or complete ms; e-query OK.

NEW YORK UNIVERSITY PRESS, 838 Broadway, 3rd Floor, New York NY 10003-4812. (212)998-2575. Fax (212)995-3833. E-mail: information@nyupress.org. Website: www.nyupress.nyu.edu. Jennifer Hammer, religion ed. Embraces ideological diversity. Publishes 100 titles/yr. Receives 800-1,000 submissions annually. 30% of books from first-time authors. Few mss through agents. Royalty on net. Publication within 10-12 mos. Considers simultaneous submissions. Initial response usually within 1 mo. (peer reviewed). Guidelines on Website.

Nonfiction: Query or proposal/1 chapter.

Tips: "As a university press, we primarily publish works with a scholarly foundation written by PhDs affiliated with a university department."

+NEXGEN. For teachers or program leaders who want Bible-based discipleship resources. Janet Lee, sr. product mgr. See Cook Communications Ministries for details.

NORTHFIELD PUBLISHING CO., 820 N. LaSalle Blvd., Chicago IL 60610. (312)329-8047. Fax (312)329-2019. E-mail: acquisitions@moody.edu. Website: www.moodypublishers.org. Imprint of Moody Publishers. Chris Johnson, acq. coord. Books for non-Christians or those exploring the faith. Publishes 3-5 titles/yr. 1% of books from first-time authors. Royalty on net; advance $500-50,000. Publication within 1 yr. No simultaneous submissions. Responds in 2-3 mos. Guidelines (also by e-mail/Website); catalog for 9x12 SAE/2 stamps. Incomplete topical listings.

Nonfiction: Proposal/2-3 chapters. "We decline all unsolicited proposals."

Fiction: For all ages.

NORTHSTONE PUBLISHING, 9025 Jim Bailey Rd., Kelowna BC V4V 1R2 Canada. (250)766-2778. Fax (250)766-2736. E-mail: acquisitions@woodlake.com. Website: www.wood lakebooks.com. Imprint of Wood Lake Books, Inc. Michael Schwartzentruber, ed. To provide high quality products promoting positive social and spiritual values. Publishes 6 titles/yr. Receives 900 submissions annually. 30% of books from first-time authors. Prefers 192-256 pgs. Royalty 7.5-10% of retail; some advances $1,000. Average first printing 4,000. Publication within 18 months. Considers simultaneous submissions. Prefers requested ms on disk, or by e-mail. Guidelines (also by e-mail/Website); catalog $2.

Nonfiction: Proposal/2 chapters; phone/fax/e-query OK.

Tips: "Most open to truth-seeking, life-affirming books that promote positive social and spiritual values. Although we publish from a Christian perspective, we seek to attract a general audience. Our target audience is interested in spirituality and values, but may not even attend church (nor do we assume that they should)."

+NORTHWESTERN PUBLISHING HOUSE, 1250 N. 113th St., Milwaukee WI 53226-3284. Toll-free (800)662-6022. Fax (414)475-7684. E-mail: braunj@nph.wels.net. Website: www.nph.net. Lutheran. Rev. John A. Braun, VP of publishing services. Open to freelance. Responds in 2-3 mos. Guidelines on Website (www.nph.net/cgi-bin/site.pl?aboutUs Manuscript). Not included in topical listings. No questionnaire returned.

Nonfiction: Complete ms./cover letter; or query letter/outline.

OBADIAH PRESS, 607 N. Cleveland St., Merrill WI 54452. Phone/fax (715)536-3167. E-mail: tina@obadiahpress.com. Website: www.obadiahpress.com. Nondenominational/Christian. Tina L. Miller, ed-in-chief. Publishes 2-5 titles/yr. 90% of books from first-time authors. Royalty 12% of net. Prefers e-query or complete ms. By mail. Not currently accepting submissions except for their anthologies. Guidelines on Website.

Tips: "We publish only a few books each year and work very closely with our authors. Check the Website before submitting as we are not currently accepting proposals or submissions except stories for our anthologies."

ONE WORLD/BALLANTINE BOOKS, 1540 Broadway, New York NY 10036. (212)782-8378. Fax (212)782-8442. E-mail: adiggs@randomhouse.com. Website: www.randomhouse.com. Anita Diggs, sr. ed. Imprint of Ballantine Books. Novels that are written by and focus on African Americans, but from an American perspective. Publishes 24 titles/yr. Receives 850 submissions annually. 50% of books from first-time authors. Submissions from agents only. No reprints. Prefers 80,000 wds. Royalty 7.5-15% on retail; advance $40,000-200,000. Average first printing 10,000. Publication within 18 mos. Considers simultaneous submissions. Responds in 2 mos. No disk or e-mail. No guidelines/catalog. Not accepting submissions at this time. Note: No unsolicited submissions, proposals, manuscripts, or queries at this time.

Fiction: Proposal/3 chapters; no phone/fax/e-query. "Contemporary/ethnic novels only; for African American women."

Ethnic Books: All are ethnic books.

Tips: "You must understand African American culture and avoid time-worn stereotypes."

ONSTAGE PUBLISHING, 214 E. Moulton NE, Decatur AL 35601. Toll-free (888)420-8879. (256)308-2300. Fax (256)308-9712. Website: www.onstagebooks.com. Dianne Hamilton, sr. ed. (dianne@onstagebooks.com). Children's book publisher. Open to freelance. 80% of books from first-time authors. No mss through agents. No reprints. Prefers 3,000-9,000 wds. for ages 6-8; 10,000-40,000 wds. for ages 9-12; and 40,000-60,000 wds. for ages 12 and up. Royalty on retail; advance. Average first printing varies. Considers simultaneous submissions (if advised). Responds in 2-4 mos. Guidelines by e-mail; catalog for 3 stamps.

Nonfiction: Not currently looking for nonfiction, so query first.

Fiction: Proposal/3 chapters or complete ms; no phone/fax/e-query. "We publish books for children or teens."

Tips: "Study our catalog, and get a sense of the kind of books we publish, so you'll know whether your projects is right for us."

OPENBOOK PUBLISHERS, GPO Box 1368, Adelaide, Australia 5001. Phone 08 8124 0003. Fax 08 8223 4552. E-mail: johnp@openbook.com.au. Website: www.openbook.com.au. Lutheran Church of Australia. John Pfitzner, ed. Australian resources for Christians of all denominations. Publishes 20 titles/yr. Receives 100+ submissions annually. 60% of books from first-time authors. Reprints books. Prefers 160 pgs. Royalty 10-15% of net; no advance. Average first printing 1,000-2,000. Publication within 6 mos. Considers simultaneous submissions. Prefers accepted ms by e-mail. Responds in 6 wks. No guidelines/catalog.

Nonfiction: Complete ms; phone/fax/e-query OK.

Tips: "Most open to resources for use in congregations and homes. Authors need to present or apply the Christian faith in new and fresh ways. Material needs to meet a felt need among readers and needs to be life related."

#OPEN COURT PUBLISHING CO., 332 S. Michigan Ave., Ste. 1100, Chicago IL 60604-9968. Toll-free (800)815-2280. Fax (815)224-2256. E-mail: opencourt@caruspub.com. Website: www.opencourtbooks.com. Carus Publishing Co. David Ramsay Steele, ed. dir. Liberal publisher with a focus on comparative religion. Publishes 4 religious titles/yr. Receives 1,200 submissions annually. 20% of books from first-time authors. Accepts mss through agents. Reprints books. Prefers 250-300 pgs. Royalty 5-12% of net; advance $1,000. Average first printing 500 (cloth), 1,500 (paperback). Publication within 1-3 yrs. No simultaneous submissions. Responds in 6 mos. Free catalog.

Nonfiction: Proposal/2 chapters/résumé/vita; no e-query.

Tips: "We're looking for works of high intellectual quality for a scholarly or general readership on comparative religion, philosophy of religion, and religious issues."

OPINE PUBLISHING, 5113 W. Running Brook Rd., Columbia MD 21044. (443)745-1004. Fax (410)730-0917. E-mail: info@opinebooks.com. Website: www.opinebooks.com, or www.opinepublishing.com. Jean Purcell, pub. Christian books on faith, marriage, and single life, plus award-winning family humor and fiction for all ages. Imprint: Touchstone. 80% of books from first-time authors. Accepts mss through agents. Reprints books. Royalty 9.5-12.5% and up, on net; no advance. Publication within 12-18 mos. Considers simultaneous submissions (if notified). Accepts submissions by e-mail (attached file). Responds in 6-8 wks. Prefers NIV or NASB. Guidelines on Website; no catalog.

Nonfiction: Query/3 chapters/250-word bio. No phone/fax query, e-query OK.

Fiction: Query by e-mail. "Only through an experienced book agent."

Also Does: Opine Publishing has a new "Writers Mission" that is focused on guiding new authors' professional development; it is primarily for writers who have or are working on their first or second book manuscript. This mission is built into the Opine contract offer.

Photos: Accepts freelance photos for book covers.

Tips: "We like expressive, approachable, friendly, intelligent, and well-founded writing aimed at bringing refreshing hope and love from Christian writers. We want our readers to enjoy and be inspired by our books."

OREGON CATHOLIC PRESS, PO Box 18030, Portland OR 97218-0030. Toll-free (800)548-8749. (503)281-1191. Fax (800)462-7329. E-mail: Liturgy@ocp.org. Website: www.ocp.org. John Limb, pub.; Kathleen Orozco, music ed.; Geri Eathan, Website editor/general questions (geri@ocp.org); submit to "Attn: Manuscript Proposal." To enhance the worship in the Catholic Church in the United States. Imprint: Pastoral Press. Publishes 10 titles/yr. Receives 72 submissions annually. 5% of books from first-time authors. No mss through agents. Reprints books. Royalty 5-12% of net; no advance. Average first printing 500. Publication within 6 mos. Considers simultaneous submissions. Prefers requested ms on disk; no e-mail submissions. Responds in 3-6 mos. Free catalog.

Nonfiction: Proposal/1 chapter; no phone/fax/e-query. "Looking for pastoral and liturgical books."

Ethnic Books: Hispanic/Spanish language.

Photos: Accepts freelance photos for book covers.

Tips: "Most open to Catholic liturgical works."

ORIGINAL WORD PUBLISHERS, PO Box 799, Roswell GA 30077. Toll-free (800)235-9673. (770)552-8879. E-mail: drgoodwin@mindspring.com. Website: www.originalword.com. Dr. Charles Goodwin, ed. A transdenominational, nonprofit teaching ministry devoted to biblical studies.

OSL PUBLICATIONS, PO Box 22279, Akron OH 44302-0079. (330)535-8656. Fax (330)535-8656. E-mail: books@Saint-Luke.org. Website: www.Saint-Luke.org. Order of St. Luke. Timothy J. Crouch, O.S.L., dir. of pub. Publishes 3 titles/yr. Receives 10 submissions annually. 40% of books from first-time authors. No mss through agents. Reprints books. Prefers to 200 pgs. Royalty 5-10%; no advance. Average first printing 1,000. Publication within 9 mos. Considers simultaneous submissions. Free guidelines/catalog.

Nonfiction: Query only.

Tips: "Our primary focus is centered around publishing materials that aid in discovering a sacramental spirituality and provide practical liturgical resources."

OUR SUNDAY VISITOR, INC., 200 Noll Plaza, Huntington IN 46750-4303. Toll-free (800)348-2440. (260)356-8400. Fax (260)356-8472. E-mail: booksed@osv.com. Website: www .osv.com. Catholic. Greg Erlandson, pub./pres.; Jacquelyn Lindsey, ed. dev. mngr.; submit to Acquisitions Editors: Jacquelyn Lindsey, Michael Dubruiel, and Beth McNamara (religious ed.). To assist Catholics to be more aware and secure in their faith and capable of relating their faith to others. Publishes 60 titles/yr. Receives 1,000 submissions annually. 10% of books from first-time authors. Prefers not to work through agents. Reprints books. Royalty 10-12% of net; advance varies. Average first printing 5,000. Publication within 1 yr. Considers simultaneous submissions. Responds in 3 mos. Requires requested ms on disk. Free guidelines (also by e-mail); catalog for 9x12 SASE.

Nonfiction: Proposal/2 chapters; e-query OK. "Most open to devotional books (not first person), church history, heritage and saints, the parish, prayer, and family."

Also Does: Pamphlets, booklets.

Photos: Occasionally accepts freelance photos for book covers.

Tips: "All books published must relate to the Catholic Church; unique books aimed at our audience. Give as much background information as possible on author qualification, why the topic was chosen, and unique aspects of the project. Follow our guidelines. We are expanding our religious education product line and programs."

OXFORD UNIVERSITY PRESS, 198 Madison Ave., New York NY 10016-4314. (212)726-6000. Fax (212)726-6440. E-mail: cynthia.read@oup.com. Website: www.oup.com. Academic press. Cynthia Read, exec. ed. Service to academic community. Publishes 60+ titles/yr. Receives hundreds of submissions annually. 20% of books from first-time authors. Accepts mss through agents. No reprints. Prefers 250 pgs. Royalty & advance negotiable. Average first printing 900. Publication within 1 yr. Considers simultaneous submissions. Responds in 3 mos. Requires disk. Prefers NRSV. Free catalog.

Nonfiction: Proposal/2 chapters. "Most open to academic books."

Tips: "Author should be affiliated with an institution of higher learning, or have established a track record in publishing (books or journalism). We do not publish inspirational or devotional literature or poetry or fiction."

PACIFIC PRESS PUBLISHING ASSN., Box 5353, Nampa ID 83653-5353. (208)465-2570. Fax (208)465-2531. E-mail: booksubmissions@pacificpress.com. Website: www.pacific press.com. Seventh-day Adventist. David Jarnes, book ed.; submit to Tim Lale, acq. ed. Books of interest and importance to Seventh-day Adventists and other Christians of all ages. Publishes 30 titles/yr. Receives 500 submissions annually. 5% of books from first-time authors. Accepts mss through agents. Prefers 40,000-70,000 wds. or 128-256 pgs. Royalty 12-15% of net; advance $1,500. Average first printing 5,000. Publication within 12-24 mos. Considers simultaneous submissions. Responds in 3 mos. Requires requested ms on disk, or by e-mail. Guidelines at www.pacificpress.com/writers/books.htm; free catalog.

> **Nonfiction**: Query only; e-query OK.
>
> **Fiction**: Query only; almost none accepted; adult/biblical. Children's books: "Must be on a uniquely Seventh-day Adventist topic. No talking animals."
>
> **Ethnic Books**: Occasionally publishes for ethnic market.
>
> **Also Does**: Booklets.
>
> **Tips**: "Most open to spirituality, inspirational, Christian living, or gift books. Our Website has the most up-to-date information, including samples of recent publications. Do not send full manuscript unless we request it after reviewing your proposal."

P & R PUBLISHING CO., PO Box 817, Phillipsburg NJ 08865. (908)454-0505. Fax (908)454-0859. E-mail: susan@prpbooks.com. Website: www.prpbooks.com. Allan Fisher, publications dir.; Barbara Lerch and Melissa Craig, acq. eds. Devoted to stating, defending, and furthering the gospel in the modern world. Publishes 40 titles/yr. Receives 250 submissions annually. 5% of books from first-time authors. Accepts mss through agents. Reprints books. Prefers 140-240 pgs. Royalty 10-14% of net; no advance. Average first printing 4,000. Publication within 8-10 mos. Considers simultaneous submissions. Responds in 1-3 mos. Free guidelines (also by e-mail/Website)/catalog.

> **Nonfiction**: Proposal/1-3 chapters; fax/e-query OK.
>
> **Also Does**: Booklets.
>
> **Tips**: "Clear, engaging, and insightful applications of reformed theology to life. Offer us fully developed proposals and polished sample chapters. All books must be consistent with the Westminster Confession of Faith."
>
> ****Note**: This publisher serviced by The Writer's Edge.

PARACLETE PRESS, PO Box 1568, Orleans MA 02653. (508)255-4685. Fax (508)255-5705. E-mail: mail@paracletepress.com. Website: www.paracletepress.com. Ecumenical. Lillian Miao, sr. ed. Publishes 20 titles/yr. Receives 160 submissions annually. Few books from first-time authors. Reprints few books. Prefers 170-300 pgs. Royalty 10-12% of retail or net; advance. Average first printing 3,000-5,000. Publication within 12-18 mos. Considers simultaneous submissions. Responds in 6-8 wks. Requires hard copy. Prefers NIV, KJV, NKJV, RSV, NRSV. Guidelines (also by e-mail); catalog for 9x12 SAE/3 stamps.

> **Nonfiction**: Proposal/2 chapters; no phone/fax/e-query. "Looking for books on deeper spirituality that appeal to all denominations."
>
> **Contests**: Paraclete Fiction Award. See details in Contest Section.
>
> **Tips**: Vision statement: "In all times, in different branches of the Christian family, there are people who have written, sung, or spoken things that encouraged us to give our lives to God and to listen to His voice. We gather and share these treasures."
>
> ****Note**: This publisher serviced by The Writer's Edge.

PARADISE RESEARCH PUBLICATIONS, INC., PO Box 837, Kihei HI 96753-0837. Phone/fax (808)874-4876. E-mail: dickb@dickb.com. Website: www.dickb.com/index.shtml. Ken Burns, VP. Imprint: Tincture of Time Press. Publishes 5 titles/yr. Receives 8 submissions annually. 80% of books from first-time authors. No mss through agents. Reprints books. Prefers 250 pgs. Royalty 10% of retail; no advance. Average first printing 5,000. Publication within 2 mos. Considers simultaneous submission. Responds in 1 wk. No disk. Prefers KJV. No guidelines; free catalog.

Nonfiction: Query only; no phone/fax/e-query. Books on the biblical/Christian history of early Alcoholics Anonymous.

Also Does: Pamphlets, booklets, e-books.

Tips: "Most open to healing of alcoholism/addiction by power of God."

PARAGON HOUSE, 2285 University Ave. W., Ste. 200, St. Paul MN 55114-1635. (651)644-3087. Fax (651)644-0997. E-mail: paragon@paragonhouse.com. Website: www.paragon house.com. Rosemary Yokoi, acq. ed. Serious nonfiction and texts with an emphasis on religion and philosophy. Imprints: New Era Books, Athena, Omega. Publishes 12-15 titles/yr. Receives 5,000 submissions annually. 20% of books from first-time authors. Accepts mss through agents. No reprints. Prefers 250 pgs. Royalty 7-15% (usually 10%) of net; advance $1,000. Average first printing 2,000-3,000. Publication within 10-18 mos. Considers few simultaneous submissions. Prefers requested ms as hard copy; accepts disk. Responds in 3 mos. Guidelines (by e-mail/Website); catalog available online.

Nonfiction: Query; proposal/2-3 chapters, or complete ms; no phone/fax/e-query. "Looking for scholarly overviews of religious teachers and movements; textbooks in philosophy; new information, theories, ecumenical subjects; and reference books."

PATHWAY PRESS, 1080 Montgomery Ave., Cleveland TN 37311. (423)478-7592. Fax (423)478-7616. E-mail: bill_george@pathwaypress.org. Website: www.pathwaypress.org. Church of God (Cleveland TN). Bill George, ed. Publishes 14-16 titles/yr. . Receives 120 submissions annually. 25% of books from first-time authors. Prefers 120-300 pgs. Royalty 10% of wholesale; no advance. Average first printing 2,500-5,000. Publication within 12-18 mos. Guidelines on Website (www.pathwaypress.org/Evangel).

Nonfiction: Proposal/1-3 chapters; no phone/fax/e-query. "Manuscripts returned only when accompanied by an SASE."

Tips: "Pathway markets to evangelical readers and publishes from a Pentecostal/Charismatic perspective. Acquisitions committee meets quarterly."

PAULINE BOOKS & MEDIA, 50 Saint Pauls Ave., Boston MA 02130-3491. (617)522-8911. Fax (617)541-9805. E-mail: editorial@pauline.org. Website: www.pauline.org. Catholic. Sr. Madonna Ratliff, acq. ed.; Sr. Patricia Edward Jablonski, children's ed. To help clarify Catholic belief and practice for the average reader. Publishes 25-35 titles/yr. Receives 1,300 submissions annually. 25% of books from first-time authors. No ms through agents. Royalty 8-12% of net; advance $300-500. Average first printing 3,000. Publication within 2 yrs. Responds in 3 mos. Requires requested ms on disk. Prefers NRSV. Guidelines (also by e-mail/Website); free catalog.

Nonfiction: Proposal/2-3 chapters, fax/e-query OK. "Looking for books on Catholic faith and moral values, spiritual growth and development, and Christian formation for families."

Tips: "Open to religion teacher's resources and adult catechetics. No biographical or autobiographical material."

PAULIST PRESS, 997 Macarthur Blvd., Mahwah NJ 07430. (201)825-7300. Fax (201)825-8345. E-mail: info@paulistpress.com. Website: www.paulistpress.com. Catholic. Paul McMahon, mng. ed. Catholic publisher that publishes books for a broad spiritual market with a particular focus on ecumenism, reconciliation, and dialog with people in search of faith. Imprints: Newman Press; HiddenSpring. Publishes 90 titles/yr. Receives 1,000 submissions annually. 5% of books from first-time authors. Accepts mss through agents. Prefers 100-400 pgs. Royalty 10% of net; advance $1,000. Average first printing 3,500. Publication within 10 mos. Considers simultaneous submissions. Requires requested ms on disk. Responds in 2 mos. Prefers NRSV. Guidelines on Website; free catalog.

Nonfiction: Proposal/3 chapters or complete ms; phone query OK. "Looking for theology

(Catholic and ecumenical Christian), popular spirituality, liturgy, and religious education texts." Children's books for 2-5, 5-8, 8-12, 9-14 years, as per guidelines; complete ms.
Ethnic Books: A few Hispanic.
Also Does: Booklets, pamphlets.
Photos: Accepts freelance photos for book covers.
Tips: "Most open to good spirituality books that have solid input and a clear sense of tradition behind them. Demonstrate grounded convictions. Stay well read. Pay attention to contemporary social needs."

PELICAN PUBLISHING CO., INC., PO Box 3110, Gretna LA 70054-3110. (504)368-1175. Fax (504)368-1195. E-mail: editorial@pelicanpub.com. Website: www.pelicanpub.com. Nina Kooij, ed. To publish books of quality and permanence that enrich the lives of those who read them. Imprint: Firebird Press. Publishes 5 titles/yr. Receives 250 submissions annually. No books from first-time authors. Accepts mss through agents. Reprints books. Prefers 200+ pgs. Royalty; some advances. Publication within 9-18 mos. No simultaneous submissions. Responds in 1 mo. Requires requested ms on disk. Prefers KJV. Guidelines (also on Website); catalog for 9x12 SAE/$1.42 postage (mark "Media Mail").
Nonfiction: Proposal/2 chapters; no phone/fax/e-query. Children's picture books to 1,100 wds.; middle readers about Louisiana (ages 8 & up) at least 25,000 wds.; cookbooks at least 200 recipes.
Fiction: Complete ms. For ages 5-8 only.
Tips: "On inspirational titles we need a high-profile author who already has an established speaking circuit so books can be sold at these appearances."

PERIGEE BOOKS, 375 Hudson St., New York NY 10014. (212)366-2000. Fax (212)366-2365. Website: www.penguin.com. Penguin Group (USA), Inc. John Duff, pub.; Sheila Curry Oakes, exec. ed.; Michelle Howry, ed. (spirituality). Publishes 3-5 spirituality titles out of 55-60 titles/yr. Receives 300 submissions annually. 30% of books from first-time authors. Strongly prefers mss through agents (but accepts freelance). Prefers 60,000-80,000 wds. Royalty 6-15%; advance $5,000-150,000. Average first printing varies. Publication within 18 mos. Considers simultaneous submissions. Responds in 2-6 mos. No guidelines or catalog.
Nonfiction: Query only; no phone/e-query; fax query OK. Looking for spiritual, prescriptive, self-help, and women's issues; no memoirs or personal histories.

PETER PAUPER PRESS, 202 Mamaroneck Ave., Ste. 400, White Plains NY 10601-5376. Toll-free (800)833-2311. (914)681-0144. Fax (914)681-0389. E-mail: pauperp@aol.com, or epoyet@peterpauper.com. Website: www.peterpauper.com. Elizabeth Poyet, ed. dir.; Nick Beilenson, ed. (nbeilenson@peterpauper.com). Does small-format illustrated gift books. Imprint: Inspire Books (evangelical imprint). Publishes 2 religious titles/yr. Receives 30 submissions annually. 0% of books from first-time authors. Accepts mss through agents. No reprints. Prefers 800-2,000 wds. Outright purchase only, $250-1,000. Average first printing 10,000. Publication within 1 yr. Considers simultaneous submissions. Requires requested ms on disk. Responds in 1 mo. Guidelines (request by e-mail that a copy be faxed); no catalog.
Nonfiction: Query by mail or e-mail. General inspirational themes.
Tips: "We want original aphorisms, 67-75 to a book. Title should be focused on a holiday or special occasion, family such as mother, sister, graduation, new baby, wedding, etc."

+PFLAUM PUBLISHING GROUP, 2621 Dryden Rd., Ste. 300, Dayton OH 45439. (937)293-1415. Fax (937)293-1310. E-mail: kcannizzo@pflaum.com, or jeanlarkin@pflaum.com. Website: www.pflaum.com. Peter Li Education Group/Catholic. Karen Cannizzo, ed. dir., or Jean Larkin, ed. dir. Religious education resources for Catholic young people (preschool through high school), plus resources for catechists and teachers who work with Catholic young people. Publishes 10-20 titles/yr. Receives 25 submissions annually. 10% of books from first-time authors. Prefers mss through agents. No reprints. Royalty on net or outright purchase; advance depends on author arrangement. Average first printing 2,000. Publication within 9 mos. No simultaneous submissions. Requires accepted ms on disk or by e-mail. Responds as soon as possible. Prefers NRSV. Guidelines (also by e-mail); free catalog.

Nonfiction: Proposal/chapters; e-query OK. "We like user-friendly resources."

PICKWICK PUBLICATIONS, 215 Incline Way, San Jose CA 95139-1526. (408)224-6777. Fax (408)224-6686. E-mail: dyh1@aol.com. Website: www.pickwickpublications.com. Dikran Y. Hadidian, ed. Publishes 2-4 titles/yr. Receives several dozen submissions annually. 60% of books from first-time authors. No mss through agents. Reprints books. Royalty on net; no advance. Publication within 12 mos. No simultaneous submissions. No e-mail submissions. Responds in 3 mos. Guidelines (also by e-mail/Website); catalog for 9x12 SAE/5 stamps.

Nonfiction: Proposal; phone/fax/e-query OK.

THE PILGRIM PRESS, 700 Prospect Ave. E., Cleveland OH 44115-1100. (216)736-3755. Fax (216)736-2207. E-mail: stavetet@ucc.org. Website: www.thepilgrimpress.com. United Church of Christ. Timothy G. Staveteig, pub.; Kim Sadler, ed. dir. Church and educational resources. Publishes 54 titles/yr. Receives 500 submissions annually. 30% of books from first-time authors. Prefers mss through agents. Reprints books. Royalty 10% of net; or work-for-hire, one-time fee; negotiable advance. Average first printing 2,000. Publication within 18 mos. No simultaneous submissions. Responds in 13 wks. Accepts submissions on disk or by e-mail. Guidelines (also by e-mail); free catalog.

Nonfiction: Proposal/2 chapters; e-query via Website.

Special Needs: Children's sermons, worship resources, youth materials, and religious materials for ethnic groups.

Ethnic Books: African American, Native American, Asian American, Pacific Islanders, and Hispanic.

Photos: Accepts freelance photos for book covers.

Tips: "Most open to well-written manuscripts that address mainline Protestant-Christian needs and that use inclusive language and follow the *Chicago Manual of Style.*"

*PISTIS PRESS, 2408 Arbuton Ave., Baltimore MD 21230. (410)409-9721. Fax (410)644-1957. Scott Stubblefield, ed. Not included in topical listings. No questionnaire returned.

PLAYERS PRESS, INC., PO Box 1132, Studio City CA 91614-0132. (818)789-4980. Robert W. Gordon, ed. To create is to live life's purpose. Publishes only dramatic works. Publishes 1-5 religious titles/yr. Receives 50-100 submissions annually. 15-20% of books from first-time authors. Accepts mss through agents. Reprints books. Variable length. Variable royalty and advance. Average first printing 1,000-10,000. Publication within 12 mos. No simultaneous submissions. No submissions by disk or e-mail. Responds in 3 wks. on query; 3-12 mos. on ms. Guidelines; catalog for 9x12 SAE/5 stamps.

Nonfiction/Plays: Query only; no phone/fax/e-query. "Theatrical musicals; theater/film/television how-tos; plays and theater crafts."

Special Needs: Theatre education.

Photos: Accepts freelance photos for book covers.

Tips: "Most open to plays and books on theater, film, and television; also how-to."

PREP PUBLISHING, 1110 1/2 Hay St., Fayetteville NC 28305. (910)483-6611. Fax (910)483-2439. Website: www.prep-pub.com. PREP, Inc. Anne McKinney, mng. ed. (mckinney@prep-pub.com); submit to Frances Sweeney (sweeney@prep-pub.com). Books to enrich people's lives and help them find joy in human experience. Publishes 10 titles/yr. Receives 1,500+ submissions annually. 85% of books from first-time authors. Reprints books. Prefers 250 pgs. Royalty 6-10% of retail; advance. Average first printing 3,000-5,000.

Publication within 18 mos. Considers simultaneous submissions. Responds in 1 mo. Guidelines (also on Website) & catalog for #10 SAE/2 stamps.

Nonfiction: Query only; no phone query.

Fiction: Query only (cover letter and up to 3-page synopsis). If you send a complete manuscript (send to Janet Abernathy), include a check for $150 for a paid critique. All ages. "We are attempting to grow our Judeo-Christian fiction imprint."

Tips: "Rewrite, rewrite, rewrite with your reader clearly in focus."

PUBLISHAMERICA, PO Box 151, Frederick MD 21705. (240)529-1031. Fax (301)631-9073. E-mail: authors@PublishAmerica.com. Website: www.PublishAmerica.com. Miranda Prather, editorial dir. A secular print-on-demand publisher that also publishes a number of Christian titles. Imprints; PublishBritannica and PublishIslandica. Publishes 550 titles/yr. Receives 800 submissions annually. 80% of books from first-time authors. Accepts mss through agents. No reprints. Prefers 50,000-60,000 wds., or 225 pgs. Royalty 8-12.5% of net; no advance. Publication within 6 mos. Considers simultaneous submissions. Accepts e-mail submissions. Responds in 2-4 wks. Guidelines (also by e-mail/Website); catalog online.

Nonfiction: Query first; then complete ms; fax/e-query OK.

Fiction: Query first; then complete ms; fax/e-query OK. "We are open to review all forms of fiction, excluding picture books and screenplays."

Tips: "We encourage new talent to query us. We are particularly interested in works by or about people who overcome a serious challenge in life."

*G. P. PUTNAM'S SONS, a division of Penguin/Books for Young Readers, 345 Hudson St., 14th Floor, New York NY 10014. (212)366-2000. Fax (212)366-2666. Website: www.penguin putnam.com. Submit to Children's Manuscript Editor. Imprint: G. P. Putnam's Sons. Publishes 45 titles/yr. Accepts mss through agents. Variable royalty on retail; variable advance. Considers simultaneous submissions. No disk or e-mail submissions. Responds in 6 mos. Guidelines free.

Nonfiction: Query only. "We publish some religious/inspirational books and books for ages 2-18."

Fiction: For children or teens. Complete ms for picture books; proposal/3 chapters for novels. Primarily picture books or middle-grade novels.

QUINTESSENTIAL BOOKS, PO Box 8755, Kansas City MO 64114-0755. (816)214-4289. Fax (816)561-4109. E-mail: mjanson@quintessentialbooks.com. Website: www.quintessential books.com. Maryl Janson, dir. of acq. Books that will challenge people to think deeply and live passionately in accordance with sound principles. Publishes 3-4 titles/yr. Receives 75-100 submissions annually. 10% of books from first-time authors. Reprints books. Prefers 60,000-70,000 wds. or 224 pgs. Royalty on net; advance. Average first printing varies. Publication within 18 mos. Considers simultaneous submissions. Responds in 3-4 mos. Accepts requested ms on disk. Prefers NIV. Guidelines (also by e-mail).

Nonfiction: Query only; no phone/fax query. "Looking for family/parenting, personal responsibility, and leadership."

Fiction: Query only. For teens & adults.

Photos: Accepts freelance photos for book covers.

Tips: "Most open to something that is crisp, fresh, provocative, cutting-edge/iconoclastic, but kind/generous at the same time."

RAGGED EDGE PRESS, 63 W. Burd St., PO Box 152, Shippenburg PA 17257. (717)532-2237. Fax (717)532-6110. E-mail: marketing@whitemane.com, or editorial@whitemane.com. Website: www.whitemane.com. White Mane Publishing Co., Inc. Harold E. Collier, acq. ed. Christian, social science, and self-help books to make a difference in people's lives. Publishes 10-15 titles/yr. Receives 50-75 submissions annually. 50% of books from first-time authors. **SUBSIDY PUBLISHES 20%.** Reprints books. Prefers 200 pgs. Variable royalty on net; no advance. Average first printing 3,000. Publication within 1 yr. Considers simultaneous submissions. Responds in 30-90 days. Free guidelines (also by e-mail)/catalog.

Nonfiction: Query only; fax query OK.

Fiction: Query only. Adult fiction.

Tips: "Most open to a Protestant book in the middle of the spectrum."

RAINBOW PUBLISHERS, Box 261129, San Diego CA 92196. (858)668-3260. Fax (858)668-3328. E-mail: rainbowed@earthlink.net. Website: www.rainbowpublishers.com. Christy Scannell, ed. dir. Publishes Bible-teaching, reproducible books for children's teachers. Publishes 20 titles/yr. Receives 250 submissions annually. 50% of books from first-time authors. Reprints books. Prefers 96 pgs. Outright purchases $640 & up. Average first printing 2,500. Publication within 2 yrs. Considers simultaneous submissions. Responds in 3 mos. No disk or e-mail submissions. Prefers NIV. Guidelines (also on Website); catalog for 9x12 SAE/2 stamps.

Nonfiction: Proposal/2-5 chapters; no phone/e-query. "Looking for fun and easy ways to teach Bible concepts to kids, ages 2-12."

Special Needs: Creative puzzles and unique games.

Tips: "Request a catalog or visit your Christian bookstore to see what we have already published. We have over 100 titles and do not like to repeat topics, so a proposal needs to be unique for us but not necessarily unique in the market. Most open to writing that appeals to teachers who work with kids and Bible activities that have been tried and tested on today's kids. No preachy, old-fashioned methods."

READ 'N RUN BOOKS, PO Box 294, Rhododendron OR 97049. Crumb Elbow Publishing. Michael P. Jones, pub. Books of lasting interest. Publishes 2 titles/yr. Receives 150 submissions annually. 90% of books from first-time authors. Reprints books. Royalty 30-50% of net; no advance; **SOME COOPERATIVE PUBLISHING**. Average first printing 500-1,000. Publication within 1 yr. Considers simultaneous submissions. Responds in 2-5 wks. No disk. Guidelines; catalog $3.

Nonfiction: Complete ms; no phone/fax query. "Looking for books on cults/occult, history, and prophecy."

Fiction: Complete ms. Any type; any age. Looking for historical fiction of the Northwest, Oregon, or the West.

Ethnic Books: Open to ethnic books.

Also Does: Booklets, pamphlets, tracts, e-books, postcards, note cards, posters.

Photos: Accepts freelance photos for book covers.

Contest: Poetry contest. Send SASE for information.

Tips: "Nature and history are two areas we are seriously looking at but are also interested in poetry and short-story collections." Send copies only; no originals.

+REFERENCE SERVICE PRESS, 5000 Windplay Dr., Ste. 4, El Dorado Hills CA 95762. (916)939-9620. Fax (916)939-9626. E-mail: findaid@aol.com. Website: www.rspfunding .com. Stuart Hauser, ed. Books related to financial aid and Christian higher education. Publishes 1 title/yr. Receives 3-5 submissions annually. Most books from first-time authors. No reprints. Royalty 10% on net; usually no advance. Publication within 5 mos. May consider simultaneous submissions. No guidelines; free catalog for 2 stamps.

Nonfiction: Proposal/several chapters.

Special Needs: Financial aid directories for Christian college students.

REGAL BOOKS, 2300 Knoll Dr., Ventura CA 93003. Does not accept unsolicited manuscripts.

**Note: This publisher serviced by The Writer's Edge.

REGNERY PUBLISHING, One Massachusetts Ave. N.W., Washington DC 20001. Toll-free (888)219-4747. (202)216-0600. Fax (202)216-0612. E-mail: submissions@regnery.com, or editorial@regnery.com. Website: www.regnery.com. Eagle Publishing. Harry Crocker, exec. ed.; submit to Submissions Editor. Trade publisher that does scholarly Catholic books and evangelical Protestant books. Imprint: Gateway Editions. Publishes 2-4 religious titles/yr. Receives 30-50 submissions annually. Few books from first-time authors. Requires mss through agents. Reprints books. Prefers 250-500 pgs. Royalty 8-15% on retail; advances to $50,000. Average first printing 5,000. Publication within 1 yr. Considers simultaneous submissions. Responds in 3 mos. Free catalog.

  Nonfiction: Accepts manuscripts through agents only. Proposal/1-3 chapters or query; no fax/e-query. Looking for history, popular biography, and popular history.

  Tips: "Religious books should relate to politics, history, current affairs, biography, and public policy. Most open to a book that deals with a topical issue from a conservative point of view—something that points out a need for spiritual renewal or a how-to book on finding spiritual renewal."

RELIGIOUS EDUCATION PRESS, 5316 Meadow Brook Rd., Birmingham AL 34242. (205)991-1000. Fax (205)991-9669. E-mail: releduc@ix.netcom.com. Website: www.bham.net/releduc. Unaffiliated. James Michael Lee, ed. Mission is specifically directed toward helping fulfill, in an interfaith and ecumenical way, the Great Commission. Publishes 5-6 titles/yr. Receives 500 submissions annually. 40% of books from first-time authors. Prefers 200-500 pgs. Royalty 5% of net; advance. Average first printing 2,000. Publication within 9 mos. Responds in 1 mo. Requires requested ms on disk. Guidelines; free catalog.

  Tips: "We are not accepting manuscripts for the foreseeable future."

RESOURCE PUBLICATIONS, INC., 160 E. Virginia St., Ste. 290, San Jose CA 95112-5876. (408)286-8505. Fax (408)287-8748. E-mail: info@rpinet.com. Website: www.rpinet.com. William Burns, pub. Publishes 10 titles/yr. Receives 450 submissions annually. 30% of books from first-time authors. Prefers 50,000 wds. Royalty 8% of net; rare advance. Average first printing 3,000. Publication within 1 yr. Responds in 10 wks. Prefers requested ms on disk. Guidelines on Website; catalog for 9x12 SAE/$1.42 postage (mark "Media Mail").

  Nonfiction: Proposal/1 chapter; phone/fax/e-query OK.

  Fiction: Query. Adult/teen/children. Only read-aloud stories for storytellers; fables and parables. "Must be useful in ministerial, counseling, or educational settings."

  Also Does: Computer programs; aids to ministry or education.

  Tips: "Know our market. We cater to ministers in Catholic and mainstream Protestant settings. We are not an evangelical house or general interest publisher."

REVELL BOOKS, Box 6287, Grand Rapids MI 49516. (616)676-9185. Fax (616)676-2315. E-mail: lhdupont@bakerbooks.com. Website: www.bakerbooks.com. Baker Publishing Group. No freelance. Submit through Writer's Edge or ECPA First Edition.

REVIEW AND HERALD PUBLISHING ASSN., 55 W. Oak Ridge Dr., Hagerstown MD 21740-7390. (301)393-3000. Fax (301)393-4055. E-mail: editorial@rhpa.org. Website: www.rhpa.org. Seventh-day Adventist. Richard Coffen, VP/editorial; Jeannette Johnson, acq. ed. No freelance.

RISING STAR PRESS, PO Box 66378, Scotts Valley CA 95067-6378. (831)461-0604. Fax (831)461-0445. E-mail: editor@risingstarpress.com, or RSPEditor@earthlink.net. Website: www.RisingStarPress.com. Donna Jacobsen, acq. ed. Overall focus is on intellect/values/spiritual agreement in life and work. Publishes 2 titles/yr. Receives 200 submissions annually. 90% of books from first-time authors. No mss through agents. Length open. Royalty 15% of net; average advance $750. Average first printing 2,000. Publication within 10 mos. Considers simultaneous submissions. Responds in 6-8 wks. Prefers accepted mss by e-mail; disk OK. Guidelines on Website; no catalog.

Nonfiction: Query only; e-query OK.

Photos: Accepts freelance photos for book covers.

Tips: "Books are selected based on the combination of fit with the company mission, consistency between the author's words and life, and marketability. Looking for books on 'open' and 'accepting' religion as a topic."

RIVEROAK PUBLISHING, Historical and contemporary fiction. Jeff Dunn, acq. ed. See Cook Communications Ministries for details.

ROSE PUBLISHING, 4455 Torrance Blvd., #259, Torrance CA 90503. Toll-free (800)532-4278. (310)370-7152. Fax (310)370-7492. E-mail: rosepublishing@aol.com (make subject "Carol"). Website: www.rose-publishing.com. Nondenominational. Carol Witte, mng. ed. Publishes primarily Bible studies; Sunday school wall charts and visual aids. Publishes 5-10 titles/yr. 5% of projects from first-time authors. No mss through agents. Royalty or outright purchases. Publication within 18 mos. Considers simultaneous submissions. Responds in 2-3 mos. Catalog for 9x12 SAE/4 stamps.

Nonfiction: Not books, mainly booklets, wall charts, or PowerPoints.

Special Needs: Query with sketch of proposed chart (nonreturnable); fax query OK; e-query OK if less than 100 wds. (copied into message). No e-mail attachments. Basic wall charts that every Sunday school classroom needs; reference wall charts that make difficult Bible topics or theological topics easier; wall charts for children and youth; wall charts on Old Testament and New Testament topics; study guides and worksheets (grades 4-8) on Creation and evolution, life of Jesus, the Exodus, sharing your faith with skeptics, salvation, and armor of God; and wall chart on feasts of Israel, apologetics, Great Commission, modern heroes, Bible study methods, "reasons to believe," past, and comfort in time of trouble.

Tips: "Now accepting more freelance submissions. Material for children, youth, Bible study charts and study guides, pamphlets, maps, time lines, and Power Points." No fiction.

SCARECROW PRESS, 4501 Forbes Blvd., Ste. 200, Lanham MD 20706. (301)459-3366. Fax (301)429-5747. E-mail: mray@scarecrowpress.com. Website: www.scarecrowpress.com. Rowman & Littlefield Publishing Group. Submit to Melissa Ray, religion ed. Provides reference and professional materials for librarians. Publishes 150-200 titles/yr. Receives 600-700 submissions annually. 20% of books from first-time authors. Accepts mss through agents. Reprints books. Prefers 250-300 pgs. Royalty 5-15% of net; no advance. Average first printing 500. Publication within 9 mos. No simultaneous submissions. Responds in 2-4 mos. Requires requested ms on disk. Guidelines on Website; free catalog.

Nonfiction: Proposal/2-3 chapters; e-query OK. "Looking for reference, religion, and scholarly books." New: educational administration.

Tips: "Most open to reference, music, and scholarly books. Should be well researched and address issues from a scholarly point of view. We consider submissions only from college-educated writers."

SCEPTER PUBLISHERS, INC., PO Box 211, New York NY 10018. (212)354-0670. Fax (212)354-0736. E-mail: scepter@scepterpublishers.org. Website: www.scepterpublishers.org. Catholic. Bernard Browne, ed. Books on how to struggle to live faith and virtue in one's daily life. Publishes 20 titles/yr. 0-2% of books from first-time authors. Accepts mss through agents. Reprints books. Prefers 200-250 pgs. Royalty on net; advance $2,000-10,000. Average first printing 2,000. Publication within 24 mos. No simultaneous submissions. Responds after 12 mos. No guidelines; free catalog.

Nonfiction: Query only first; no phone/fax/e-query.

Fiction: Query only first; no phone/fax/e-query.

Tips: "Looking for short, practical books addressing reader needs."

SCRIPTURE PRESS—See Cook Communications Ministries.

SELAH PUBLISHING GROUP, LLC., 12705 Rullman Dr., Dillsboro IN 47018. Toll-free (877)616-6451. Fax (866)777-8909. E-mail: garlen@selahbooks.com. Website: www .selahbooks.com. Garlen Jackson, pub. A publisher that does not water down the author's message. Publishes 45 titles/yr. Receives 20 submissions annually. 75% of books from first-time authors. Prefers mss through agents. Reprints books. Prefers 40,000 wds. or 144 pgs. Royalty 12-18% of net; no advance. Average first printing 2,500. Publication within 6 mos. No simultaneous submissions. Prefers requested ms on disk. Responds in 2 mos. Prefers ASV. Guidelines by e-mail; free catalog.

> **Nonfiction**: Complete ms; no phone/fax/e-query.
>
> **Fiction**: Complete ms; no phone/fax/e-query. For all ages.
>
> **Also Does**: E-books.
>
> **Photos**: Accepts freelance photos for book covers.
>
> **Tips**: "Most open to time-sensitive, current events, and controversial books. Writers should spend more time selling who they are in regards to character and integrity."

SHAMARAH PUBLICATIONS, INC., PO Box 250692, Franklin MI 48025-1576. E-mail: shamarah@twmi.rr.com. Website under construction. Ross Heron, pub. Publishes novels that convey messages and ideas by supernatural influences that cause the reader to develop behaviors that demonstrate spiritual awareness and maturity. Publishes 2 titles/yr. (projected). Receives 25-200 submissions annually. No mss through agents. No reprints. Prefers 100,000+ wds. Negotiable royalty on retail and negotiable advance. Average first printing 2,000 (hardcover). Publication within 18 mos. Considers simultaneous submissions. Responds in 3 mos. Guidelines (also by e-mail); no catalog.

> **Fiction**: Adult. "Christian-based, inspirational fiction with literary value, timeless and multidimensional content. Story must appeal to readers' sensitivities and elicit their introspection."
>
> **Tips**: "Requesting guidelines prior to proposal submission is a must."

SHAW BOOKS, 2375 Telstar Dr., Ste. 160, Colorado Springs CO 80920. (719)590-4999. Fax (719)590-8977. Website: www.shawbooks.com. Imprint of WaterBrook Press/Random House. Elisa Stanford, ed. Publishes books on health and wellness, family and education, creative nonfiction, and books "blending faith, life, and the arts." Imprints: Writers' Palette and Fisherman Bible Study guides. Publishes 20-25 titles/yr. 10-20% of books from first-time authors. Royalty on net. Queries accepted (attn: Editorial) but not unsolicited mss. Guidelines on Website.

> **Nonfiction**: Query only; no phone/fax/e-query.
>
> **Tips**: "We are looking for unique manuscripts on the above topics that add a fresh voice to the subject."
>
> ****Note**: This publisher serviced by The Writer's Edge.

SHEED & WARD, 1332 N. Halsted St., Ste. 302, Chicago IL 60622-2694. (312)664-5844. Fax (312)664-5846. E-mail: jeremy.langford@rowman.com. Website: www.sheedandward .com. Rowman & Littlefield Publishers, Inc. Jeremy Langford, ed. dir. Publishes books of contemporary impact and enduring merit in Catholic-Christian thought and action. Publishes 30 titles/yr. Receives 300-500 submissions annually. 1% of books from first-time authors. Does print-on-demand. Reprints books. Prefers 35,000-65,000 wds. Royalty 8-12.5% of net; flexible advance. Average first printing 3,000. Publication within 9 mos. No simultaneous submissions. Responds in 1 mo. Requires requested ms on disk. Prefers NAB, NRSV (Catholic editions). Guidelines (also on Website); free catalog.

> **Nonfiction**: Proposal/2 chapters; phone/fax/e-query OK. "Looking for parish ministry (health care, spirituality, leadership, general trade books for mass audiences, sacraments, small group, or priestless parish facilitating books)."
>
> **Photos**: Accepts freelance photos for book covers.

Tips: "Looking for general trade titles and academic titles (oriented toward the classroom) in areas of spirituality, parish ministry, leadership, sacraments, prayer, faith formation, Church history, and scripture."

SHINING STAR PUBLICATIONS, 3195 Wilson Dr. N.W., Grand Rapids MI 49544. Toll-free (800)609-1735. Division of McGraw Hill Children's Publishing. Not currently accepting freelance submissions.

+SHORELINE, 23 Ste-Anne, Ste-Anne-de-Bellevue QC H9X 1L1 Canada. Phone/fax (514)457-5733. E-mail: shoreline@sympatico.ca. Website: www.shorelinepress.ca. Judith Isherwood, ed. Supports first-time authors of books that show creativity, originality, and care in nonfiction or creative nonfiction. Publishes 1 religious title/yr. 99% of books from first-time authors. Doesn't prefer mss through agents. Occasionally reprints books. Prefers under 200 pgs. Royalty 10% on retail; no advance. In some cases pays 10 copies of the book, plus 40% discount on additional purchases (no royalties). Average first printing 500. Publication within 1 yr. Catalog for #10 SAE/1 stamp.

    Nonfiction: Query/1-2 chapters; e-query OK.

    Tips: "Most open to a true-life experience, memoir or biography; a history of the church or of a church."

SILAS PUBLISHING, (formerly Silas Interactive Multimedia) 1154 Westchester Dr., Lilburn GA 30047. E-mail: info@silasinteractive.com. Website: www.silasinteractive.com. Independent Christian publisher. Scott Philip Stewart, ed. Publishes Christian care books and software to help 21st century Christians and seekers and those who minister to them. Publishes 10 titles/yr. Receives 60 submissions annually. 80% of books from first-time authors. Accepts mss through agents. Reprints books. Royalty 10-12% of net; some outright purchases; some advances. Publication within 6 mos. Considers simultaneous submissions, if notified. Accepts requested manuscript on disk or by e-mail. Responds in 1 wk. Guidelines by e-mail/Website.

    Nonfiction: Proposal/2-3 chapters; prefers e-mail query.

    Fiction: Novella-length, "self-help" fiction (see Website for details).

    Special Needs: Self-help, personal growth, counseling aids, resources for peer and professional Christian caregivers and counselors.

    Also Does: Interactive multimedia; book/CD sets

    Tips: "Most open to grace-full self-help/personal growth books written from a unique angle designed to help hurting believers and seekers and those who minister to them."

+SILOAM PRESS, 600 Rinehart Rd., Lake Mary FL 32746. (407)333-0600. Website: www .strang.com. Strang Communications. Jeff Gerke, sr. ed. Health and fitness books from a Christian perspective. Publishes 12-15 titles/yr. Prefers mss through agents. Prefers 35,000-60,000 wds. Royalty; advance. Considers simultaneous submissions. Responds in 4-6 mos. Guidelines on Website.

    Nonfiction: Query first; no phone/fax query; e-query OK.

    Special Needs: Fitness, health issues, nutrition, medical issues, relationships, sex and intimacy, alternative medicine (no New Age), integrative medicine, conventional medicine, and emotional health.

    Tips: "Wellness is a major concern in America, and Christians want timely answers grounded in Scripture and informed by the latest science. The ideal Siloam author is professionally qualified to write on his or her topic, writes well and with passion, has an established audience or marketing platform, writes from an evangelical world-view, and writes on a health or fitness topic about which a wide Christian audience will be interested."

SKYSONG PRESS, 35 Peter St. S., Orillia ON L3V 5A8 Canada. E-mail: skysong@bconnex.net. Website: www.bconnex.net/~skysong. Steve Stanton, ed. Imprints: Dreams & Visions, Sky Song. Publishes 2+ titles/yr. Guidelines on Website.

    Fiction: Publishers of Christian literary fiction under the imprints Dreams & Visions, Sky

Songs, and Skysong Science Fiction. "New authors should not submit novel manuscripts. Send us something for Dreams & Visions (see periodical section) first."

SMALL HELM PRESS, 622 Baker St., Petaluma CA 94952-2525. (707)763-5757. E-mail: smallhelm@comcast.com. Website: http://smallhelm.home.attbi.com. Alice Pearl Evans, pub. Interprets direction in contemporary life. Publishes 1 title/yr. Receives few submissions. Reprints books. Prefers 96-224 printed pgs. Outright purchase, negotiable. Average first printing 1,000-2,000. Publication within 9 mos. Considers simultaneous submissions. Responds in 2-4 wks. Prefers NIV. Guidelines (also on Website); catalog for 9x12 SAE/3 stamps. Note: This company is moving and is in a time of transition so is not accepting submissions at this time.

SMYTH & HELWYS PUBLISHING, INC., 6316 Peake Rd., Macon GA 31210-3960. Toll-free (800)747-3016. (478)757-0564. Fax (478)757-1305. E-mail: mcelroy@helwys.com. Website: www.helwys.com. Dr. Keith Gammons, book ed. (keith@helwys.com); Mark McElroy, sr. ed. Quality resources for the church, the academy, and individual Christians who are nurtured by faith and informed by scholarship. Publishes 25-30 titles/yr. Receives 600 submissions annually. 40% of books from first-time authors. Prefers 144 pgs. Royalty 7%. Considers simultaneous submissions. Responds in 3 mos. Free guidelines (also by e-mail/Website); free catalog.

Nonfiction: Query only; fax/e-query OK. "Manuscripts requested for topics appropriate for mainline church and seminary/university textbook market."

Also Does: E-books. Copies of print books and original books. Go to: www.next sunday.com.

Tips: "Most open to books with a strong secondary or special market. Niche titles and short-run options available for specialty subjects."

*SOWER'S PRESS, PO Box 666306, Marietta GA 30066. Phone/fax (770)977-3784. Jamey Wood, ed. Books to further establish the ministries of speakers and teachers. Publishes 2-3 titles/yr. Responds in 1 mo.

Nonfiction: Proposal/chapters. Marriage and family books.

SPENCE PUBLISHING COMPANY, 111 Cole St., Dallas TX 75207-7101. Toll-free (888)773-6782. (214)939-1700. Fax (214)939-1800. E-mail: muncy@spencepublishing.com. Website: www.spencepublishing.com. Thomas Spence, pub.; Mitchell Muncy, ed-in-chief. Commentary on social and cultural issues related to education, ethics, religion, public life, politics, law, marriage, family, and the arts. Publishes 8-10 titles/yr. Royalty 12% of net; modest advance. Considers simultaneous submissions. Responds in 1-2 mos. Guidelines; free catalog on Website. Incomplete topical listings.

Nonfiction: Query or proposal/1 chapter (no complete manuscripts). Religion.

SPIRITUAL THEATER INTERNATIONAL, PO Box 538, Littleton CO 80160. E-mail: Carl@ spiritualtheater.com. Website: www.spiritualtheater.com. Carl Anderson, pres. Submit to: New Plays Submissions. Seeks plays for purchase or production. Buys all rts. Guidelines & submission form on Website.

Special Needs: Each year they feature their best works at a Spiritual Theater Festival, where a panel of judges selects one new play for full production. To be considered for the Festival, submit plays by February 1.

SQUARE ONE PUBLISHERS, 115 Herricks Rd., New Hyde Park NY 11040-5341. (516)535-2010. Fax (516)535-2014. E-mail: sq1info@aol.com. Website: www.squareonepublishers .com. Rudy Shur, ed. Strives to satisfy readers' hunger for knowledge by providing reliable information on meaningful topics, including religion. Publishes 6 religious titles/yr. Receives 100 submissions annually. 35% of books from first-time authors. Prefers mss through agents. Reprints books. Prefers 80,000 wds. Royalty 10-15% of net; advance $2,500 & up. Average first printing 6,000-8,000. Publication within 12-18 mos. Considers simultaneous submissions. Accepts requested ms on disk. Responds in 4 wks. Guidelines on Website; free catalog.

Nonfiction: Query with overview, table of contents, author information, potential audience, and SASE; no phone/fax/e-query.

Tips: "Inspirational books and books on spirituality that do not overly focus on one particular denomination would have the greatest appeal to our firm."

ST. ANTHONY MESSENGER PRESS and **FRANCISCAN COMMUNICATIONS**, 28 W. Liberty St., Cincinnati OH 45202. Toll-free (800)488-0488. (513)241-5615, ext. 123. Fax (513)241-0399. E-mail: StAnthony@AmericanCatholic.org. Website: www.AmericanCatholic.org. Catholic. Lisa Biedenbach, ed. dir. (lisab@AmericanCatholic.org); Katie Carroll, book ed; Mary Hackett, book ed. Seeks to publish affordable resources for living a Catholic-Christian lifestyle. Imprints: Servant Books, Franciscan Communications, Fischer Productions, and Ikonographics (videos). Publishes 30-40 titles/yr. Receives 350 submissions annually. 5% of books from first-time authors. Accepts mss through agent. Reprints books (seldom). Prefers 25,000-50,000 wds. or 100-300 pgs. Royalty 10-14% on net; advance $1,000. Average first printing 5,000. Publication within 18 mos. No simultaneous submissions. Requires accepted ms on disk; e-mail OK. Responds in 4-6 wks. Prefers NRSV. Guidelines (also by e-mail/Website); free catalog.

Nonfiction: Query only/500-wd. summary; fax/e-query OK. "Looking for family-based catechetical programs; living the Catholic-Christian life at home and in workplace; and Franciscan topics."

Special Needs: Catholic identity; spirituality; resources for new and inactive Catholics.

Ethnic Books: Hispanic, occasionally.

Also Does: Pamphlets, booklets.

Tips: "Most open to books with sound Catholic doctrine that include personal experiences or anecdotes applicable to today's culture. Our books are decidedly Catholic."

****Note**: 2001 First Place Best Website—Catholic Press Assn. of the U.S. and Canada.

ST. AUGUSTINE'S PRESS, PO Box 2285, South Bend IN 46680. (574)291-3500. Fax (574)291-3700. E-mail: bruce@staugustine.net. Website: www.staugustine.net. A conservative, nondenominational (although mostly Catholic) scholarly publisher of academic titles, mainly in academic philosophy, theology, and cultural history. Bruce Fingerhut, pres. Publishes 20-40 titles/yr. Receives 100+ submissions annually. 5% of books from first-time authors. Accepts mss through agents. Reprints books. Royalty 6-15% of net; advance $1,000. Average first printing 1,000. Publication within 1 yr. Considers simultaneous submissions. Responds in 3 mos. No guidelines; free catalog.

Nonfiction: Query or proposal/chapters. "Most of our titles are philosophy."

Tips: "Most open to books on subjects or by authors similar to what/who we already publish."

STANDARD PUBLISHING, 8121 Hamilton Ave., Cincinnati OH 45231. (513)931-4050. Fax (513)931-0950. E-mail: customerservice@standardpub.com. Website: www.standardpub.com. Standex Intl. Corp. Ruth Frederick, children's ministry resources; Paul Learned, adult/teen ministry resources; Bruce Stoker, acq. ed. An evangelical Christian publisher of curriculum, classroom resources, teen resources, children's books, and drama. Following are the consumer departments for this company (see guidelines for details): Children's & Tween books (ages birth-12)—publishes 30 titles/yr.; 25% freelance. Teen/Young Adult Books (ages 13-22)—contact Dale Reeves (dreeves@standardpub.com), teen/young ad. book editor. Christian Living/Inspirational/Theology—new trade line of titles for adults exists to present biblical truth in a broadly accessible way to help adults develop deeper, stronger relationships with God and with other people. Royalty & work-for-hire; advance. Average first printing 10,000 (depends on product). Publication within 18 mos. Considers simultaneous submissions.

Responds in 3 mos. Prefers NIV, ICB. Guidelines (also by e-mail/Website); catalog $2. Website for submissions information: www.standardpub.com/writers_guidelines.html.

Nonfiction: Query to Christian Education Team, Children's Editor, Teen Editor; no phone/fax query. E-mail them for permission to send query by e-mail. "Well-presented, clearly stated cover letters are very useful."

Also Does: Toys and games; about 10/yr. Jen Holder, acq. ed. See guidelines for details.

**Note: This publisher serviced by The Writer's Edge.

STEEPLE HILL, 233 Broadway, Ste. 1001, New York NY 10279-0001. (212)553-4200. Fax (212)277-8969. E-mail: JoanMarlow_Golan@harlequin.ca. Website: www.Steeple Hill.com. Harlequin Enterprises. Submit to any of the following: Joan Marlow Golan, exec. ed.; Krista Stroever, ed.; Diane Dietz, asst. ed. Single title, trade paperback Christian women's fiction that will help women guide themselves and their families toward purpose-ful, task-driven lives. Lines: Love Inspired (mass-market category romances), see separate listing; Romantic Suspense line (no name yet); Steeple Hill Café (women's fiction). Publishes 100-108 titles/yr. Receives 500-1,000 submissions annually. 15% of books from first-time authors. Prefers mss through agents. No reprints. Prefers 80,000-125,000 wds. or 350-500 pgs. Royalty on retail; competitive advance. Publication within 12-24 mos. Considers simulta-neous submissions for trade books, not for mass market. Requires accepted ms on disk/hard copy. Responds in 3 mos. Prefers KJV. Guidelines (also by e-mail/Website): no catalog.

Fiction: Query letter or 3 chapters and up to 5-page synopsis; no phone/fax/e-query.

Tips: "We want quality inspirational novels that focus on the more complex and thought-fully developed stories, with many characters, subplots, and so on. They are mostly character-driven, depicting sympathetic protagonists as they learn important lessons about the power of faith. Subgenres include relationship novels, contemporary and historical romances, family dramas, Christian chick lit, romantic suspense, mysteries, and thrillers. Most interested in romantic suspense, chick lit, and mom lit."

STILL WATERS REVIVAL BOOKS, 4710—37A Ave., Edmonton AB T6L 3T5 Canada. (708)450-3730. Fax (708)468-1096. E-mail: swrb@swrb.com. Website: www.swrb.com. Covenanter Church. Reg Barrow, pres. Publishes 100 titles/yr. Receives few submissions. Very few books from first-time authors. Reprints books. Prefers 128-160 pgs. Negotiated royalty or outright purchase. Considers simultaneous submissions. Catalog for 9x12 SAE/2 stamps.

Nonfiction: Proposal/2 chapters.

Tips: "Only open to books defending the Covenanted Reformation, nothing else."

THE SUMMIT PUBLISHING GROUP, 3649 Conflans Rd., #103, Irving TX 75061. (972)399-8856. Fax (972)313-9060. E-mail: jbertolet@tapestrypressinc.com. Website: www.tapes trypressinc.com. Tapestry Press, Inc. Jill Bertolet, pub. Secular publisher of contemporary nonfiction books, including some religious; custom publishing or partnership between author and publisher. Publishes 10-15 titles/yr. Receives 1,000 submissions annually. 50% of books from first-time authors. Accepts mss through agents. Reprints books. Royalty on net; small advance. Publication within 6-12 mos. Considers simultaneous submissions. Responds in 3-6 mos. Guidelines on Website; no catalog.

Nonfiction: Query only; fax/e-query OK. Looking for gardening, cooking, and business.

Tips: "Books need national distribution appeal. Author's media experience, contacts, and exposure are a strong plus."

#TAN BOOKS AND PUBLISHERS, INC., 2020 Harrison Ave., PO Box 424, Rockford IL 61105. Toll-free (800)437-5876, ext. 205. (815)226-7777. Fax (815)226-7770. E-mail: editor@ tanbooks.com. Website: www.TanBooks.com. Catholic. Thomas A. Nelson, ed. Not included in topical listings. No questionnaire returned.

TAPESTRY PRESS, INC., 3649 Conflans Rd., #103, Irving TX 75061. (972)399-8856. Fax (972)313-9060. E-mail: jbertolet@tapestrypressinc.com, or info@tapestrypressinc.com.

Website: www.tapestrypressinc.com. Jill Bertolet, pub. Secular publisher of contemporary nonfiction books, including some religious; custom publishing or partnership between author and publisher. Publishes 10-15 titles/yr. Receives 1,000 submissions annually. 50% of books from first-time authors. Accepts mss through agents. Reprints books. Royalty on net. Publication within 6-12 mos. Considers simultaneous submissions. Responds in 3-6 mos. Guidelines on Website; no catalog.

Nonfiction: Query only; fax/e-query OK. Looking for gardening, cooking, and business.

Tips: "Books need national distribution appeal. Author's media experience, contacts, and exposure are a strong plus."

+TATE PUBLISHING & ENTERPRISES, LLC., 1716 W. State Hwy. 152, Mustang OK 73064-1505. (405)376-4900. Fax (405)376-4401. E-mail: info@tatepublishing.com. Website: www.tatepublishing.com. David Dolphin, sr. ed.; submit to Dr. Richard Tate. Publishes 120 titles/yr. Receives 3,600 submissions annually. 95% of books from first-time authors. Prefers mss through agents. No reprints. Has a division for self-publishers. Any length. Royalty 15-40% on retail; variable advance. First printing varies. Publication within 1 week. Considers simultaneous submissions. Requires e-mail submissions. Responds in 2 days. Any Bible version. Guidelines by e-mail/Website; free catalog.

Nonfiction: Proposal with synopsis & 1 chapter; phone/fax/e-query OK. "Looking for books that sell."

Fiction: Proposal with synopsis & 1 chapter; phone/fax/e-query OK.

Ethnic Books: Hispanic

Photos: Rarely accepts freelance photos for book covers.

Contest: Not this year, but forthcoming.

Tips: "We invest resources in every work we accept, and only accept first-time authors."

TAU-PUBLISHING, 1422 E. Edgemont Ave., Phoenix AZ 85006. (602)264-4828. Fax (602)248-9656. E-mail: phoenixartist@msn.com. Website: www.tau-publishing.org. Catholic. Jeffrey Campbell, pub. Imprints: Aleph-First. Publishes 3-4 titles/yr. Receives 25 submissions annually. 50% of books from first-time authors. Prefers mss through agents. **SOME SUBSIDY.** Reprints books. Prefers 25,000-50,000 wds. or 100-200 pgs. Royalty on net; no advance. Average first printing 3,000. Publication within 8 mos. Considers simultaneous submissions. Responds in 4-6 mos. Guidelines on Website; no catalog.

Nonfiction: Query; fax/e-query OK. "Looking for Catholic inspirational material; reflections and meditations."

Photos: Accepts freelance photos for book covers.

THIRD WORLD PRESS, PO Box 19730, Chicago IL 60619. (773)651-0700. Fax (773)651-7286. E-mail: GwenMTWP@aol.com. Website: www.ThirdWorldPressInc.com. Gwendolyn Mitchell, ed. African American publisher. Publishes 20 titles/yr. Receives 200-300 submissions annually. 20% of books from first-time authors. Few mss through agents. Reprints books. Royalty on retail; advance varies. Publication within 18 mos. Considers simultaneous submissions. Responds in 6 mos. Guidelines; free catalog. Note: this company is open to submissions in July only.

Nonfiction: Query by mail, or proposal/5 chapters.

Fiction: Query by mail, or proposal/5 chapters. African American.

Ethnic Books: African American.

Tips: "Submit complete manuscript for poetry; must be African American centered."

TOMMY NELSON, a division of Thomas Nelson, Inc., 402 BNA Dr., Bldg. 100, Ste. 600, Nashville TN 37217. (615)889-9000. Dan Lynch, Sr. VP & pub.; Amy Parker, ed. of children's books (2-14 yrs.). Children's books and products. Submissions only through agents, by referral from one of their authors, through a manuscript service, or by meeting an editor at a conference.

**Note: This publisher serviced by First Edition and The Writer's Edge.

+**TORCH LEGACY PUBLICATIONS**, 2780 Valley Ridge Dr., Atlanta GA 30032; PO Box 165046, Irving TX 75016. (214)235-9334 or (404)284-9619. E-mail: danielwhyteiii@yahoo.com. Website: www.torchlegacy.com. Torch Ministries, Intl. Daniel Whyte III, pres. Dedicated to publishing Bible-based books of all genres by and for African Americans and others.

TOUCH PUBLICATIONS, 10055 Regal Row Ste. 180, Houston TX 77040-3254. Toll-free (800)735-5865. (281)497-7901, or (713)896-7478. Fax (281)497-0904, or (713)896-1874. E-mail: sboren@touchusa.org. Website: www.touchusa.org. Touch Outreach Ministries. Scott Boren, dir. of publishing. To empower pastors, group leaders, and members to transform their lives, churches, and the world through basic Christian communities called cells. Publishes 8 titles/yr. Receives 25 submissions annually. 40% of books from first-time authors. Reprints books. Prefers 75-200 pgs. Royalty 10-15% of net; no advance. Average first printing 2,000. Guidelines (also by e-mail). Not in topical listings.

    Nonfiction: Query only. "Must relate to cell church life."

    Photos: Accepts freelance photos for book covers.

    Tips: "Our market is extremely focused. We publish books, resources, and discipleship tools for churches, using a cell group strategy."

TOWLEHOUSE PUBLISHING, 394 W. Main St., Ste. B-9, Hendersonville TN 37075. (615)822-6405. Fax (615)822-5535. E-mail: vermonte@aol.com. Website: www.towlehouse.com. Mike Towle, pres. A sports-oriented publisher—mostly golf, baseball, football, and basketball—interested in books with a Christian angle. Publishes 8-10 titles/yr. Receives 250 submissions annually. 50% of books from first-time authors. Accepts mss through agents. Reprints books. Prefers 25,000-30,000 wds. Royalty 8% of net; negotiable advance. Average first printing 5,000. Publication within 6 mos. Considers simultaneous submissions. Responds in 3-4 mos. Prefers requested ms on disk. No guidelines; catalog for #10 SAE/2 stamps.

    Nonfiction: Proposal/2 chapters; fax/e-query OK. "Looking for sports books, especially golf."

    Photos: Accepts freelance photos for book covers.

THE TRACT LEAGUE, 2627 Elmridge Dr., Grand Rapids MI 49544-1390. (616)453-7695. Fax (616)453-2460. E-mail: info@tractleague.com. Website: www.tractleague.com. Publishes very few tracts from outside writers, but willing to look at ideas. Submit to General Manager.

THE TRINITY FOUNDATION, PO Box 68, Unicoi TN 37692. (423)743-0199. Fax (423)743-2005. E-mail: jrob1517@aol.com. Website: www.trinityfoundation.org. John W. Robbins, pres. To promote the logical system of truth found in the Bible. Publishes 6 titles/yr. Receives 3 submissions annually. No books from first-time authors. No mss through agents. Reprints books. Prefers 200 pgs. Outright purchase; free books; no advance. Average first printing 2,000. Publication within 9 mos. No simultaneous submissions. Requires requested ms on disk. Responds in 2 mos. No guidelines; catalog for 3 stamps.

    Nonfiction: Query letter only. Open to Calvinist/Clarkian books, Christian philosophy, economics, and politics.

    Also Does: Pamphlets, booklets, tracts.

    Photos: Accepts freelance photos for book covers.

    Tips: "Most open to doctrinal books; nonfiction, biblical, and well-reasoned books, theologically sound, clearly written, and well organized."

TRINITY PRESS INTERNATIONAL, PO Box 1321, Harrisburg PA 17105. (717)671-8130. Fax (717)671-8136. E-mail: hcarriga@morehousegroup.com. Website: www.trinitypressintl .com. The Morehouse Group. Henry L. Carrigan Jr., ed. dir. A nondenominational, academic religious publisher. Publishes 40 titles/yr. Receives 150-200 submissions annually. 3% of books from first-time authors. Reprints books. Royalty 10% of net; advance $500 & up.

Average first printing 2,000. Publication within 9 mos. Considers simultaneous submissions. Responds in 3-6 mos. Prefers RSV, NRSV. Guidelines (also by e-mail); free catalog.

Nonfiction: Proposal/1 chapter, or complete ms; fax/e-query OK. "Religious material only in the area of Bible studies, theology, ethics, etc." No dissertations or essays.

Special Needs: Religion and film; American religious history; and religion and science.

Tips: "Most open to a book that is academic, to be used in undergraduate biblical studies, theology, or religious studies programs."

TROITSA BOOKS, 400 Oser Ave., Hauppauge NY 11788-3619. (631)231-7269. Fax (631)231-8175. E-mail: Novaeditorial@earthlink.net. Website: www.novapublishers.com. Imprint of Nova Science Publishers, Inc. Frank Columbus, ed. Publishes 5-20 titles/yr. Receives 50-100 submissions annually. No mss through agents. Various lengths. Royalty; no advance. Publication within 6-18 mos. Considers simultaneous submissions. Accepts requested ms on disk or by e-mail (prefers e-mail for all submissions and correspondence). Responds in 1 mo. Free guidelines/catalog.

Nonfiction: Proposal/2 chapters by e-mail.

Fiction: Proposal/2 chapters by e-mail. For adults.

Photos: Accepts freelance photos for book covers.

+TWEENER PRESS, 555 Gidley Dr., Ste. D, Grand Haven MI 49417. (616)846-8550. Fax (616)846-8575. Website: www.gospelstoryteller.com. Focuses on tweeners (8- to 12-year-olds) and those who love them. Incomplete topical listings. No questionnaire returned.

Fiction: "Fiction that captures the imagination and interest of this forgotten age group will demonstrate healthy relationships that present strong Christian values without sermonizing."

TWENTY-THIRD PUBLICATIONS, PO Box 180, Mystic CT 06355. Toll-free (800)321-0411. (860)536-2611, ext. 141. Fax (860)536-5674. E-mail: ttpubsedit@aol.com. Website: www.twentythirdpublications.com. Catholic/Bayard. Gwen Costello, pub.; Mary Carol Kendzia, ed. dir. Publishes 45 titles/yr. Receives 50 submissions annually. 45% of books from first-time authors. Accepts mss through agents. No reprints. Royalty on net; advance $1,000. Average first printing 3,000. Publication within 1 yr. Considers simultaneous submissions (say so). Requires requested ms on disk or by e-mail. Responds in 1 mo. Prefers NRSV (Catholic Edition). Guidelines (also by e-mail); free catalog.

Nonfiction: Proposal/2 chapters; phone/e-query OK.

Also Does: Booklets, CD-ROMs.

Photos: Accepts freelance photos for book covers.

Tips: "Most open to pastoral, catechetical, or spirituality books."

TYNDALE HOUSE PUBLISHERS, 351 Executive Dr., Carol Stream IL 60188. Toll-free (800)323-9400. (630)668-8300. E-mail: manuscripts@tyndale.com. Fax (800)684-0247. Website: www.tyndale.com. Submit to Manuscript Review Committee; Anne Goldsmith, acq. ed. Imprints: HeartQuest (see separate listing). Publishes 200 titles/yr. 2% of books from first-time authors. Reprints books. Royalty; outright purchase of some children's books; advance negotiable. Average first printing 5,000-10,000. Publication within 18 mos. Responds in 3 mos. Prefers NLT. No unsolicited mss. Guidelines (also by e-mail); catalog on Website.

Nonfiction: Query from agents or published authors only; no phone/fax query. Also producing e-books.

Fiction: "We accept queries only from agents, Tyndale authors, authors known to us from other publishers, or other people in the publishing industry. Novellas, 25,000-30,000 words; novels 75,000-100,000 words. All must have an evangelical Christian message."

Also Does: E-books.

****Note**: This publisher serviced by The Writer's Edge.

+TYNDALE HOUSE/SALTRIVER BOOKS, 351 Executive Dr., Carol Stream IL 60188. (630)668-8300. Website: www.tyndale.com. Janis Long Harris, sr. acq. ed. A new nonfiction crossover imprint with a goal of "publishing thought-provoking books that draw readers further along in their journey of Christian faith—or to Christian faith."

Tips: "SaltRiver Books will seek to provide accessibly intelligent conversation starters in such areas as spiritual formation, spiritual memoir, leadership, apologetics, and life with God in the real world."

**Note: This publisher serviced by The Writer's Edge.

UMI PUBLISHING, 1551 Regency Court, Calumet IL 60409. Toll-free (800)860-8642. (708)868-7100. Fax (708)868-6759. E-mail: khall@urbanministries.com. Website: www .urbanministries.com. Urban Ministries, Inc. Carl Jeffrey Wright, pub.; Kathryn Hall, mng. ed. Called of God to create, produce, and distribute quality Christian education products; to provide quality Christian educational services that will empower God's people, especially in the Black community; to evangelize, disciple, and equip people for serving Christ, his Kingdom, and his church. Publishes 2-4 titles/yr. Receives 25-40 submissions annually. 85% of books from first-time authors. Accepts mss through agents. Reprints books. Prefers 256 pgs. Royalty to 40%; no advance. Average first printing 2,500-5,000. Publication within 2 yrs. Acknowledges receipt within 4 wks.; accepts or rejects in 6-12 mos. Prefers accepted ms on disk. Prefers KJV or NIV. Guidelines by e-mail; free catalog.

Nonfiction: Query/proposal/complete ms; no phone/fax/e-query.

Special Needs: Christian living, theology, Christian education, and Christian doctrine.

Ethnic Books: Black.

Tips: "Follow guidelines for submissions (strictly); send query letter first."

**Note: This publisher serviced by The Writer's Edge.

UNITED CHURCH PRESS, 700 Prospect Ave. E., Cleveland OH 44115-1100. (216)736-3715. Fax (216)736-3703. E-mail: sadlerk@ucc.org, or stavetet@ucc.org. Website: www.pilgrim press.com. No freelance; see listing for Pilgrim Press.

UNITED CHURCH PUBLISHING HOUSE, 3250 Bloor St. W., Ste. 300, Toronto ON M8X 2Y4 Canada. (416)231-7680. Fax (416)231-3103. E-mail: bookpub@united-church.ca. Website: www.united-church.ca/ucph. The United Church of Canada. Rebekah Chevalier, sr. ed. Publishes spiritual and socially important books that raise awareness of timely issues. Publishing new books on a limited basis. Not currently accepting manuscripts.

UNITED METHODIST PUBLISHING HOUSE—See Abingdon Press or Dimensions for Living.

UNIVERSITY OF ARKANSAS PRESS, 201 Ozark Dr., Fayetteville AR 72701. (479)575-3246. Fax (479)575-6044. E-mail: uapress@uark.edu. Website: www.uapress.com. Lawrence Malley, ed. Academic publisher. Accepts mss through agents. Reprints books. Prefers 300 pgs. Royalty; no advance. Average first printing 1,000-2,000. Publication within 1 yr. Reluctantly considers simultaneous submissions. Requires accepted ms on disk. No guidelines; free catalog.

Nonfiction: Query. "All our books are scholarly." Looking for regional books.

Photos: Accepts freelance photos for book covers.

UNIVERSITY OF OTTAWA PRESS, 542 King Edward Ave., Ottawa ON K1N 6N5 Canada. (613)562-5246. Fax (613)562-5247. E-mail: press@uottawa.ca. Website: www.uottawa press.ca. Ruth Bradley-St-Cyr, ed-in-chief. Promotes scholarly, academic publications; no inspirational. Publishes 20-25 titles/yr. Receives 75 submissions annually. 10-20% of books from first-time authors. No mss through agents. No reprints. Prefers 300-400 pgs. Royalty 8% of net; no advance. Average first printing 1,000. Publication within 6 mos. Accepts simultaneous submissions. Responds in 2 wks. Requires requested ms on disk. Free guidelines (also by e-mail)/catalog.

Nonfiction: Query only first; e-query OK. Scholarly/academic books only. Social scientific study of religion. No devotionals or memoirs.

Special Needs: Postdoctoral and senior academic research in social sciences and humanities. Scholarly work with supporting footnotes/references/bibliography. Primary research, usually by individual or team of individuals with PhD in Religious Studies, Ethics, Theology, History, or Philosophy (peer review required).

Tips: "Do not send SASE with U.S. stamps. UOP is the oldest French-language university in North America and the only officially bilingual (French/English) university press in Canada."

UNIVERSITY PRESS OF AMERICA, 4501 Forbes Blvd., Ste. 200, Lanham MD 20706. (301)459-3366. Fax (301)429-5749. E-mail: submitupa@univpress.com. Website: www.univpress.com. Rowman & Littlefield Publishing Group/academic. Judith Rothman, VP & dir.; acq. eds.: Nicole Caddigan, David Chao, and Joseph Parry. Publishes scholarly works in the social sciences and humanities; established by academics for academics. Imprint: Hamilton Books (biographies & memoirs). Publishes 50 religious titles/yr. Receives 700 submissions annually. 75% of books from first-time authors. Accepts mss through agents. **SOME SUBSIDY.** Does print-on-demand. Reprints books. Prefers 90-300 pgs. Royalty up to 12% of net; no advance. Average first printing 200-300. Publication within 4-6 mos. Considers simultaneous submissions. Accepts e-mail submissions. Responds in 2 wks. Accepts requested ms on disk or by e-mail. Guidelines (also by e-mail/Website); free catalog.

Nonfiction: Proposal/3 chapters or complete ms; phone/fax/e-query OK. "Looking for scholarly manuscripts."

Ethnic Books: African studies; Black studies.

Tips: "Most open to timely, thoroughly researched, and well-documented books. Moderately controversial topics. We publish academic and scholarly books only. Authors are typically affiliated with a college, university, or seminary."

*VERBINUM, ul. Ostrobramska 98, 04-118 Warszawa, Poland. Phone (+48 22)610 78 70. Fax (+48 22)610 77 75. E-mail: verbinum@wa.onet.pl. Catholic. Fr. George Skrabania SVD, dir. Concentrates mainly on Bible apostolate, science of religion and mission, cultural anthropology, ecumenism, and children's books. Not in topical listings. Did not return questionnaire.

VICTOR BOOKS, Theology books. Craig Bubeck, acq. ed. See Cook Communications Ministries for details.

+VINTAGE ROMANCE PUBLISHING, LLC. E-mail: submissions@vrpublishing.com. Website: http://vrpublishing.com. Old-fashioned romance set in the 1900s through the 1960s. Open to first-time authors. Prefers 35,000-75,000 wds. or novellas up to 25,000 wds. No simultaneous submissions; asks for a one-month exclusive. Responds in 1 mo. Guidelines on Website.

Fiction: Query first via e-query; no attachments.

Special Needs: Romantic poetry for publication in a biannual anthology; up to 40 lines. Submit a minimum of 3 poems to: poetry@vrpublishing.com, with "Poetry" typed in subject window.

VIRGINIA PINES PRESS, 7092 Jewell-North, Kinsman OH 44428. (330)876-3504. Fax (209)882-5803. E-mail: virginiapines@nlc.net. Website: http://virginiapines.com. Helen C. Caplan, pub. Publishes fiction with a Christian viewpoint and creative nonfiction that helps document 21st century America. Publishes 3-5 titles/yr. Receives 40-50 submissions annually. 90% of books from first-time authors. Accepts mss through agents. No reprints. Prefers 80,000-100,000 wds. Royalty 6-8% on net; some outright purchases; no advance. Average first printing 1,000. Publication within 8 mos. Considers simultaneous submissions. Prefers requested ms on disk. Responds in 1-10 mos. Prefers NKJV. Guidelines on Website; free catalog.

Nonfiction: Query, proposal, or complete ms; phone/fax/e-query OK. "We are always on the lookout for third-person, full-length, creative nonfiction works to which we give top priority."

Fiction: Query, proposal, or complete ms; phone/fax/e-query OK. "Looking for excellent, full-length spiritual warfare works that teach by example of the characters within the story how to identify spiritual warfare in daily life and how to become victorious over these types of attacks on family, finances, business, and peace of mind."

Photos: Accepts freelance photos for book covers.

Contest: Sponsors several cover design contests each year. See Website for details of current contest.

+VMI PUBLISHERS, 26306 Metolius Meadows Dr., Camp Sherman OR 97730. (541)595-2403. Fax (541)595-5822. E-mail: bill@vmipublishers.com. Website: www.vmipublishers.com. Virtue Ministries, Inc. Bill and Nancie Carmichael, pubs. Partnering with new authors. Publishes 8-12 titles/yr. Receives dozens of submissions annually. 95% of books from first-time authors. Accepts mss through agents. No reprints. Print-on-demand. Prefers 65,000+ wds., or 192-400 pgs. Royalty 12-18% of net; no advance. Average first printing varies. Publication within 6-12 mos. Considers simultaneous submissions. Requires accepted mss on disk or by e-mail. Responds in 2 mos. Guidelines on Website.

Nonfiction: Query first by e-mail only.

Fiction: Query first by e-mail only. For all ages. "Anything Christian or inspirational that is well written, especially from new authors."

Also Does: "We coach new writers in our writers' breakaways (www.writersbreak away.com)."

Tips: "Most open to well-written books. Our niche is new authors with something significant to say and who have the ability to partner with us."

W PUBLISHING GROUP, PO Box 141000, Nashville TN 37214. (615)889-9000. Fax (615)902-2112. Website: www.Wpublishinggroup.com. Thomas Nelson, Inc. David Moberg, pub.; Greg Daniel, exec. ed. Publishes 75 titles/yr. Less than 3% of books from first-time authors. Prefers mss through agents. No reprints. Does not accept unsolicited manuscripts. Prefers 65,000-95,000 wds. Royalty. No guidelines.

Nonfiction: Query letter only first; no unsolicited ms. "Nonfiction dealing with the relationship and/or application of biblical principles to everyday life; 65,000-95,000 words."

**Note: This publisher serviced by The Writer's Edge.

WALK WORTHY PRESS, 33290 W. 14 Mile Rd., #482, West Bloomfield MI 48322. (248)737-1747. Fax (248)737-1766. E-mail: editor@walkworthypress.net. Website: www.walkworthy press.net. Denise Stinson, pub. Primarily fiction for the African American Christian. Publishes 10 titles/yr. Receives 200 submissions annually. 95% of books from first-time authors. Accepts mss through agents. Reprints books. Prefers 75,000-100,000 wds., or 300 pgs. Royalty 10-15% on retail; variable advance. Average first printing varies. Publication within 9 mos. Considers simultaneous submissions (if informed). No disk or e-mail submissions. Responds in 6-8 wks. Prefers KJV, NKJV, NIV, Amplified. Guidelines on Website; free catalog.

Nonfiction: Proposal/2 chapters; no phone/fax/e-query. "We do primarily fiction. Our nonfiction is generally from authors who have a high profile."

Fiction: Complete ms; no phone/fax/e-query. Seasoned fiction author may send proposal/3 chapters. For all ages. Contemporary, ethnic, fantasy, juvenile, literary, short-story collection. Big commercial fiction.

Ethnic Books: African American.

Tips: "Present a good package. Read our books first. Do a story synopsis, not book-jacket copy. We like manuscripts that explore little-explored areas of life in Christian books."

WARNER PRESS, PO Box 2499, 1200 E. 5th St., Anderson IN 46018. (765)644-7721. Fax (765)640-8005. E-mail: krhodes@warnerpress.org. Website: www.warnerpress.com, or www.chog.org. Church of God/Anderson IN. Eric King, pres.; Karen Rhodes, sr. ed. This publisher publishes only greeting cards, bulletins, coloring books or activity books (predominately Bible stories), puzzle books, a limited number of children's story books, and some longer inspirational poetry (to 20 lines). No unsolicited manuscripts for children's story books. See listing in greeting card section. Guidelines on Website.

WATERBROOK PRESS, Random House Inc., 2375 Telstar Dr., Ste. 160, Colorado Springs CO 80920. (719)590-4999. Fax (719)590-8977. Website: www.waterbrookpress.com. Dudley Delffs, fiction ed. Imprint: Shaw Books. Accepts no freelance.
   **Note: This publisher serviced by The Writer's Edge.

WESLEYAN PUBLISHING HOUSE, PO Box 50434, Indianapolis IN 46250-0434. (317)774-3853. Fax (317)774-3860. E-mail: wph@wesleyan.org. Website: www.wesleyan.org/wph. The Wesleyan Church. Lawrence Wilson, ed. dir. Aims to ignite a passion for God in all of life. Publishes 15 titles/yr. Receives 150 submissions annually. 10-20% of books from first-time authors. Accepts mss through agents. No reprints. Prefers 25,000-40,000 wds. Royalty; no advance. Average first printing 3,000. Publication within 10-12 mos. Considers simultaneous submissions. Accepts requested ms by e-mail. Responds in 2 mos. Prefers NIV. Guidelines on Website; free catalog.
   Nonfiction: Proposal/2 chapters; no phone/fax/e-query.
   Tips: "Most open to books that help the reader take the next step in spiritual maturing or deal with an issue or problem in life. We are not looking for Bible studies, memoirs, or devotionals."

+WESTBOW PRESS, PO Box 141000, Nashville TN 37215. (615)889-9000. Website: www.WestBowPress.com. Thomas Nelson, Inc. Allen Arnold, pub.; Jenny Baumgartner and Ami McConnell, acq. eds. Fiction from a Christian world-view. Publishes 25 titles/yr. Prefers mss through agents; does not accept unsolicited manuscripts. Prefers 100,000 wds. Royalty. No guidelines; free catalog.
   Fiction: Proposal with at least 3 chapters.

WESTMINSTER JOHN KNOX PRESS, 100 Witherspoon St., Louisville KY 40202-1396. (502)569-5613. Fax (502)569-5113. E-mail: ldowell@presbypub.com. Website: www.wjkbooks.com. Presbyterian Publishing Co./Presbyterian Church (USA). Submit to Lori Dowell. Addresses the needs of the Christian community by fostering religious and cultural dialog by contributing to the intellectual, moral, and spiritual nurture of the church and broader human family. Publishes 50 titles/yr. Receives 1,000-2,000 submissions annually. Less than 10% of books from first-time authors. Accepts mss through agents. Prefers 140-300 pgs. Royalty on retail or net; advance up to $500. Average first printing 2,000. Publication within 12-24 mos. Considers simultaneous submissions. Responds in 6-8 wks. Prefers NRSV. Guidelines (also by e-mail); free catalog.
   Nonfiction: Proposal/1 chapter according to guidelines; fax/e-query OK. Looking mostly for Bible studies, ethics, spirituality, and theology.
   Tips: "Most open to religious/theological scholarship."

+WHITAKER HOUSE, 30 Hunt Valley Circle, New Kensington PA 15068. (724)334-7000. Fax (724)334-1200. E-mail: publisher@whitakerhouse.com. Website: www.whitakerhouse.com. Whitaker Corp. John David Kudrick, sr. ed. "As we proclaim the gospel through the written word, we are willing to look at authors with good ideas but a lack of writing ability." Publishes 40-50 titles/yr. Receives 1,000 submissions annually. 33% of books from first-time authors. Accepts mss through agents. **SUBSIDY PUBLISHES 25%**. No print-on-demand. Reprints books. Prefers 50,000 wds. Royalty 10-22% on retail; some variable advances. Average first printing 10,000. Publication within 1 yr. Considers simultaneous submissions. Prefers accepted ms by e-mail. Responds in 6 mos. Prefers NIV. Guidelines by e-mail/Website; catalog on Website.

Nonfiction: Query only first; phone/fax/e-query OK. "Looking for timely, well-crafted manuscripts that show an author's knowledge of current issues and the Christian book market."

Fiction: Query only first.

Ethnic Books: Hispanic translations of current English titles.

Tips: "Most open to a high-quality, well-thought-out, compelling piece of work. Do the research and work required by our guidelines. Include a large amount of real-life illustrations."

+WHITE STONE BOOKS, PO Box 2835, Lakeland FL 33806. (866)253-8622. Fax (800)830-5688. E-mail: info@whitestonebooks.com. Website: www.whitestonebooks.com. Christian books. Not included in topical listings. No questionnaire returned.

WILLIAM CAREY LIBRARY, PO Box 40129, Pasadena CA 91104. (626)720-8210. Fax (626)794-0477. E-mail: publishing@WCLBook.com, or info@WCLBooks.com. Website: www.wclbooks.com. Greg Parsons, mngr. Purpose is to publish the best in Evangelical Christian Mission literature. Imprint: Mandate Press. Publishes 10-15 titles/yr. Reprints books. Variable lengths. Royalty 10% on net; no advance. Publication time varies. Prefers KJV. Free catalog.

Nonfiction: Query only; e-query OK. "As a specialized publisher, we do only books and studies of church growth, missions, world issues, and ethnic/cultural issues."

Special Needs: Anthropology and cross-cultural.

Photos: Accepts freelance photos for book covers.

Tips: "We mostly look for books on missions and evangelization, also unreached people groups—books missionaries and mission-minded people would find useful and encouraging."

WILLIAM MORROW, 10 E. 53rd St., New York NY 10022. (212)207-7000. Fax (212)207-7145. Website: www.harpercollins.com. Imprint of HarperCollins Publishers. General trade imprint; religious titles published by HarperSanFrancisco. Agented submissions only.

WILSHIRE BOOK COMPANY, 12015 Sherman Rd., North Hollywood CA 91605-3781. (818)765-8579. Fax (818)765-2922. E-mail: mpowers@mpowers.com. Website: www.mpowers.com. A secular publisher of motivational books. Melvin Powers, pres.; Marcia Grad, ed. Books that help you become who you choose to be tomorrow. Publishes 6 titles/yr. 90% of books from first-time authors. Reprints books. Prefers 30,000 wds. or 128-160 pgs. Royalty 5% on retail; variable advance. Average first printing 5,000. Publication within 6 mos. Considers simultaneous submissions. No disk or e-mail submissions. Responds in 2 mos. Guidelines (also by e-mail/Website)/catalog for SAE/2 stamps.

Nonfiction: Complete ms; phone/e-query OK. Fables for adults that teach principles of psychological/spiritual growth.

Photos: Accepts freelance photos for book covers.

Tips: "We are looking for adult allegories such as *Illusions*, by Richard Bach, *The Little Prince*, by Antoine de Saint Exupery, and *The Greatest Salesman in the World*, by Og Mandino. Analyze each one to discover what elements make it a winner. Duplicate those elements in your own style, using a creative, new approach and fresh material. We need 30,000-60,000 words."

WM. B. EERDMANS PUBLISHING CO., 255 Jefferson Ave. S.E., Grand Rapids MI 49503. Toll-free (800)253-7521. (616)459-4591. Fax (616)459-6540. E-mail: info@eerdmans.com. Website: www.eerdmans.com. Protestant/Academic/Theological. Jon Pott, ed-in-chief. Imprint: Eerdmans Books for Young Readers. Publishes 120-130 titles/yr. Receives 3,000-4,000 submissions annually. 10% of books from first-time authors. Accepts mss through agents. Reprints books. Royalty; occasional advance. Average first printing 4,000. Publication within 1 yr. Considers simultaneous submissions. Responds in 6 wks. to query; longer for mss. Guidelines on Website; free catalog.

Nonfiction: Proposal/2-3 chapters; no fax/e-query. "Looking for religious approaches to contemporary issues; spiritual growth; scholarly works."

Fiction: Proposal/chapter; no fax/e-query. "We are looking for adult novels with high literary merit."

Tips: "Most open to material with general appeal, but well-researched, cutting-edge material that bridges the gap between evangelical and mainline worlds."

**Note: This publisher serviced by The Writer's Edge.

WOOD LAKE BOOKS, INC., 9025 Jim Bailey Rd., Kelowna BC V4V 1R2 Canada. (250)766-2778. Fax (250)766-2736. E-mail: acquisitions@woodlake.com. Website: www.woodlake books.com. Ecumenical/mainline; Wood Lake Books, Inc. Michael Schwartzentruber, series ed. Publishes quality resources that respond to the needs of the ecumenical church and promote spiritual growth and commitment to God. Imprint: Northstone Publishing. Publishes 3 titles/yr. Receives 300 submissions annually. 25% of books from first-time authors. Reprints books. Prefers 200-250 pgs. Royalty on net; compiler's fee (for compilations) $1,000-3,000; some advances $1,000. Average first printing 3,000-4,000. Publication within 18-24 mos. Considers simultaneous submissions. Prefers requested ms on disk. Responds in 6-12 wks. Guidelines; catalog $2.

Nonfiction: Query or proposal/2 chapters; fax/e-query OK. "Books with inclusive language and mainline, Protestant interest."

Tips: "Most open to books with inclusive language, mainline/liberal theology, truth seeking, life affirming, and those that deal positively with life and faith. We publish books, curriculum, and resources for the mainline church. All queries and submissions should reflect this in their theological approach."

+WOODLAND GOSPEL PUBLISHING HOUSE, 118 Woodland Dr. Ste. 1101, Chapmanville WV 25508. (304)752-7500. Fax (304)369-0800. E-mail: kdavis@woodlandpress.com. Website: www.woodlandgospel.com. Woodland Press LLC. Cheryl Davis, ed; submit to Mike Collins. Publishes 7 titles/yr. Receives 150 submissions annually. 90% of books from first-time authors. Accepts mss through agents. No reprints. Prefers 60,000 wds. or 230 pgs. Royalty on net; no advance. Average first printing 2,000. Publication within 1 yr. No simultaneous submissions. Responds in 2 mos. No mss by disk or e-mail. No guidelines or catalog.

Nonfiction: Proposal/3 chapters; no phone/fax/e-query.

WORDSMITHS, 1355 Ferry Rd., Grants Pass OR 97526. (541)476-3080. Fax (541)474-9756. E-mail: frode@jsgrammar.com. Website: www.jsgrammar.com. Frode Jensen, ed. To supply quality materials for homeschools and Christian schools. Receives 8-10 submissions annually. No mss through agents. No reprints. Prefers 100-300 pgs. Royalty on net; no advance. Average first printing 2,000-5,000. Publication time varies. Will e-mail info on request.

Nonfiction: Proposal/outline; no phone/fax query; e-query OK. "We're most open to educational materials, textbook and workbook formats, having to do with language."

Tips: "I am open to books that are educational in nature, primarily text books. Most of my existing market is for junior high and high school, but books for lower grades would be acceptable."

WORLD PUBLISHING (formerly World Bible Publishing). Website: www.World Publishing.com. Terry W. Draughon, VP/pub. Publishes 5-10 bks./yr.; 15-20 Bibles. Receives 200-300 submissions annually. 1% of books from first-time authors. Accepts mss through agents. Reprints books. Prefers 200-375 pgs. Royalty 5-12% of net; advance $1,000. Average first printing 5,000-10,000. Publication within 18 mos. Considers simultaneous submissions.

Responds in 3 mos. Prefers requested ms on disk. No guidelines; catalog for $3/9x12 SAE/5 stamps.

Nonfiction: Proposal/1-2 chapters; no phone/fax/e-query. "Looking for well-written devotional/inspirational books with a unique approach."

Tips: "In addition to Bibles, we now do reference books, children's books, Christian living books, and audio Bibles."

****Note**: This publisher serviced by The Writer's Edge.

WRITE NOW PUBLICATIONS, 5501 N. 7th Ave., PMB 502, Phoenix AZ 85013. (602)336-8910. Fax (602)532-7123. E-mail: stevelaube@acwpress.com. Website: www.writenow publications.com. Steven R. Laube, exec. ed. To train and develop quality Christian writers; books on writing and speaking for writers and speakers. Royalty division of ACW Press. Publishes 1-2 titles/yr. Receives 6 submissions annually. 0% from first-time authors. Accepts mss through agents. Reprints books. Royalty 10% of net. Average first printing 3,000. Publication within 12 mos. Considers simultaneous submissions. Requires requested ms on disk. No guidelines/catalog.

Nonfiction: Writing how-to only. Query letter only; e-query OK.

WRITERS EXCHANGE E-PUBLISHING, PO Box 372, Atherton QLD 4883, Australia. E-mail: writers@writers-exchange.com. Website: www.writers-exchange.com/epublishing. E-book publisher. Sandy Cummins, sr. ed. All contracts and agreements are available on the Website. Publishes books in different categories, including one for Christian books. Guidelines on Website. Not included in topical listings.

Nonfiction: Proposal.

Fiction: Proposal.

Tips: "Looking for children's fiction that reveals deeper Christian truths or theology, not just fluff."

YALE UNIVERSITY PRESS, 302 Temple St. (06511), PO Box 209040, New Haven CT 06520. (203)432-0960. Fax (203)432-0948. E-mail: larisa.heimert@yale.edu. Website: www.yale .edu/yup. Lara Heimert, ed./religion. Publishes 10 religious titles/yr. Receives 200 submissions annually. 15% of books from first-time authors. Accepts mss through agents. Reprints books. Prefers up to 100,000 wds. or 400 pgs. Royalty from 0% to standard trade royalties; advance $0-100,000. Average first printing varies by field. Publication within 1 yr. Considers simultaneous submissions. Requires requested ms on disk.; no e-mail submissions. Responds in 1-2 mos. Free guidelines (also on Website, www.yalebooks.com)/catalog for #10 SASE.

Nonfiction: Query; fax query OK. "Excellent and salable scholarly books."

Contest: Yales Series of Younger Poets competition. Open to poets under 40 who have not had a book of poetry published. Submit manuscripts of 48-64 pages in February only. Entry fee $15. Send SASE for guidelines (also on Website).

YOUTH SPECIALTIES, 300 S. Pierce St., El Cajon CA 92020. (619)440-2333. Fax (619)440-0582. E-mail: nicole@YouthSpecialties.com, or ys@youthspecialties.com. Website: www.youthspecialties.com. Nondenominational. Roni Meek, mng. ed.; Dave Urbanski, sr. developmental ed.; submit to Nicole Davis, product asst. Christian resources for youth workers to use in their youth groups. Publishes 40 titles/yr. Receives 60 submissions annually. 25% of books from first-time authors. Prefers mss through agents. Some subsidy. Reprints books. Royalty depends on the author; advance. Average first printing 2,000-3,000. Publication within 8 mos. Considers simultaneous submissions. Responds in 1.5 mos. Accepts requested manuscripts by e-mail. Guidelines on Website; free catalog

Nonfiction: Proposal/3 chapters.

Fiction: Proposal/3 chapters. For teens/YA.

ZERUBBABEL PRESS, PO Box 1710, Blowing Rock NC 28605. (828)295-7982. Fax (828)295-7900. E-mail: zpressnc@aol.com. Zerubbabel, Inc. Nondenominational. Sanda Cooper, ed-in-chief. Reprints out-of-print Christian books; does not solicit mss. Publishes 1 title/yr. 100% of books from first-time authors. No mss through agents. Reprints books only. No guidelines/catalog.

Tips: "Our mission is to further the great high calling of the Lord Jesus to carry His Gospel to the whole world, and one way we accomplish this is through literature."

ZONDERKIDZ, 5300 Patterson SE, Grand Rapids MI 49530-0002. (616)698-3400. Fax (616)698-3326. E-mail: zpub@zondervan.com. Website: www.zonderkidz.com. Zonder-van/HarperCollins. Bruce Nuffer, children's pub. Children's book lines of Zondervan; ages 12 and under. No longer accepting unsolicited manuscripts or proposals by air or surface mail. Submit your proposal electronically to First Edition, or fax to Book Proposal Review Editor, (616)698-3454. No e-mail submissions.

Special Needs: This imprint covers five areas: devotionals, picture books, Bibles/Bible sto-rybooks, special format books, and partnerships with groups such as Mothers of Preschoolers, Young Women of Faith, Focus on the Family, etc.

ZONDERVAN, General Trade Books; Academic and Professional Books, 5300 Patterson SE, Grand Rapids MI 49530-0002. Toll-free (800)226-1122. (616)698-6900. Fax (616)698-3439. E-mail: zprod@zondervan.com. Website: www.zondervan.com. HarperCollins Pub-lishers. Submit hard copy (no e-mails) to Manuscript Proposal Review Editor only. Seeks to meet the needs of people with resources that glorify Jesus Christ and promote biblical principles. Publishes 120 trade titles/yr. Receives about 3,000 submissions annually. 20% of books from first-time authors. Prefers 50,000 wds. Royalty 14% of net (12% on mass-market paperbacks); variable advance. Publication within 1-2 yrs. Considers simultaneous submissions. Responds in 3 mos. Prefers NIV. Prefers requested ms on disk. Further sub-missions information at www.zondervan.com/desk/subguide.asp. Catalogs can be seen at http://catalogs.google.com/catalogs?q=zondervan&btnG=Google+Search.

Nonfiction: Proposal/2 chapters; no phone/e-query. "When faxing, proposal should include the book title; a table of contents (2 or 3 sentence description of each chapter); a brief description of the proposed book, including its unique contribution and why you feel it should be published; your intended reader; and your vita, including your qualifications to write the book. The proposal should be no more than 5 pages. If we're interested, we will respond within 6 weeks. You may fax your proposal to the Manuscript Proposal Review Editor, (616)698-3454."

Fiction: Proposal/2 chapters. Publishes 4 each, contemporary and historical, per year.

Children's Lines: ZonderKidz (see separate listing).

Ethnic Books: Vida Publishers division: Spanish and Portuguese.

Tips: "Absolutely stellar prose that meets demonstrated needs of our market always receives a fair and sympathetic hearing. Great writing, great content always catch our attention."

SUBSIDY PUBLISHERS

WHAT YOU NEED TO KNOW ABOUT SUBSIDY PUBLISHERS

In this section you will find any publishers who do 50% or more subsidy publishing. For our purposes, I am defining a subsidy publisher as any publisher that requires the author to pay for any part of the publishing costs. They may call themselves by a variety of names, such as a book packager, a cooperative publisher, a self-publisher, or simply someone who helps authors get their books published. Note that some of these also do at least some royalty publishing, so they could be approached as any other royalty publisher. You just need to realize that they are likely to offer you a subsidy deal, so indicate in your cover letter that you are only interested in a royalty arrangement, if that is the case.

As technology makes book publishing more accessible, and with the refinement of desktop publishing, more subsidy publishers have sprung up, and there has been an increase in confusion over who or what type of subsidy publishing is legitimate, and what publishers fall in with what we call "vanity publishers." As many of the legitimate publishers (and even some questionable ones) try to distance themselves from the reputation of the vanity publisher, they have come up with a variety of names to try to form definite lines of distinction. Unfortunately, it has only served to confuse the authors who might use their services. It is my hope in offering this separate listing that I can help you understand what this side of publishing entails, what to look for in a subsidy publisher, as well as what to look out for. To my knowledge the following publishers are legitimate subsidy publishers and are not vanity publishers, but I cannot guarantee that. It is important that as a writer you understand that any time you are asked to send money for any part of the production of your book, you are entering into a nontraditional relationship with a publisher. In this constantly changing field it becomes a matter of buyer beware.

Realize, too, that some of these publishers will publish any book, as long as the author can afford to pay for it. Others are as selective about what they publish as a royalty publisher would be, or they publish only certain types of books. Fortunately I'm seeing more publishers who are being selective; consequently, the professional quality of subsidy books is improving overall. Many will do only nonfiction—no novels or children's books. These distinctions will be important as you seek the right publisher for your project.

Because there is so much confusion about subsidy publishing, with many authors going into agreements with these publishers having little or no knowledge of what to expect or even what is typical in this situation, many have come away unhappy or disillusioned. For that reason I frequently get complaints from authors who feel they have been cheated or taken advantage of. (Of course, I sometimes get similar complaints about the royalty publishers listed in this book.) Each complaint brings with it an expectation that I should drop that publisher from this book. Although I am sensitive to their complaints, I also have come to the realization that I am not in a position to pass judgment on which publishers should be dropped. It has been my experience in publishing that for every complaint I get on a publisher, I can usually find several other authors who will sing the praises of the same publisher. For that reason, I feel I can serve the needs of authors better by giving them some insight into what to expect from a subsidy publisher and what kinds of terms should send up a red flag.

Because I am not an expert in this field and because of space limitations, I will keep this brief. Let me clarify first that unless you know your book has a limited audience or you have your own method of distribution (such as being a speaker who can sell your own books when you speak), I recommend that you try all the appropriate royalty publishers first. If you are unsuccessful with the royalty publishers but feel strongly about seeing your book published and have the financial resources to do so (or have your own distribution), one of the following publishers may be able to help you.

You can go to a local printer and take your book through all the necessary steps yourself, but a legitimate subsidy publisher has the contacts, know-how, and resources to make the task easier and often less expensive. It is always good to get more than one bid to determine whether the terms you are being offered are fair and competitive with other such publishers. Note that this listing is beginning to also include printers who offer the necessary services to help you complete the printing process yourself, so you will want to check out those as well.

There is not currently any kind of watchdog organization for subsidy publishers, and since I do not have direct knowledge about all of the publishers listed below, I would recommend that no matter who makes you a first offer, you get a second one from ACW Press, Essence Publishing (in Canada), Longwood Communications, WinePress, or Xulon Press (for print-on-demand and small print runs). These are ones I can personally recommend.

As with any contract, have someone review it before signing anything. I do such reviews, as do a number of others listed in the Editorial Services section of this book. Be sure that any terms agreed upon are IN WRITING. Verbal agreements won't be binding. A legitimate subsidy publisher will be happy to provide you with a list of former clients as references (if they aren't, watch out). Don't just ask for that list; follow through and contact more than one of those references. Get a catalog of their books or a list of books they have published, and try to find them or ask them to send you a review copy of one or two books they have published. Use those to check the quality of their work, the bindings, etc. See if their books are available through Amazon.com or similar online services. Get answers to all your questions before you commit yourself to anything.

Keep in mind that the more copies of a book that are printed, the lower the cost per copy, but never let a publisher talk you into publishing more (or fewer) copies than you think is reasonable. Also, find out up front, and have included in the contract, whether and how much promotion the publisher is going to do. Some will do as much as a royalty publisher; others do none at all. If they are not doing promotion, and you don't have any means of distribution yourself, it may not be a good idea to pursue subsidy publication. You don't want to end up with a garage full of books you can't sell. Following this section I am including the names and addresses of Christian book distributors. I don't know which ones will consider distributing a subsidy-published book, so you will want to contact them to find out before you sign a contract. For more help on self-publishing, go to: www.bookmarket.com/index.html.

LISTING OF SUBSIDY PUBLISHERS

Below is a listing of any publishers that do 50% or more subsidy publishing (author pays some or all of the production costs). Before entering into dealings with any of these publishers, be sure to read the preceding section on what you need to know.

(*) An asterisk before a listing indicates no or unconfirmed information update.

(#) A number symbol before a listing indicates it was updated from their guidelines or other current sources.

(+) A plus sign before a listing indicates it is a new listing this year or was not included last year.

ACW PRESS, 1200 Hwy. 231 South, #273, Ozark AL 36360. (877)868-9673. Fax (334)774-3375. E-mail: juliewood@acwpress.com. Website: www.acwpress.com. Steven R. Laube, owner; Julie Wood, gen. mngr.; Chuck Dean, sales dir. A self-publishing book packager. Imprint: Write Now Publications. Publishes 40 titles/yr. Reprints books. **SUBSIDY PUBLISHES**

95%. Average first printing 2,500. Publication within 4-5 mos. Prefers accepted ms by e-mail. Responds in 1 wk. Guideline booklet (also on Website). Not in topical listings; will consider any nonfiction or fiction topic.

Tips: "We offer a high quality publishing alternative to help Christian authors get their material into print. High standards, high quality. If authors have a built-in audience, they have the best chance to make self-publishing a success." Has complete marketing program available to authors.

ALFRED ALI LITERARY WORKS, INC., 21750 Winchester St., Southfield MI 48076. (248)356-5111. Fax (248)356-1367. E-mail: AALiterary@aol.com. Website: www .AlfredAli.com. San Serif, ed. Spreading the word on how the Word of God can change and improve lives. Publishes 1 title/yr. Receives 5 submissions annually. 80% of books from first-time authors. Accepts mss through agents. Reprints books. **SUBSIDY PUBLISHES 70%.** Prefers 210 pgs. Royalty 25% of retail; no advance. Average first printing 1,000-5,000. Publication within 9 mos. Accepts e-mail submissions. No guidelines; catalog $3.

Nonfiction: Query only; fax query OK.

Ethnic Books: Publishes for the African American market.

Photos: Accepts freelance photos for book covers.

Tips: "Most open to books that are based on inspiration that leads to self-awareness."

#AMBASSADOR HOUSE, 8005 Cattle Dr., Austin TX 78749-3288. Fax (512)291-5768. E-mail: ambpress@sprynet.com. Website: www.ambhouse.com. Nondenominational. Sandra Myers, pub. Publishes 1-2 titles/yr. Receives 10+ submissions annually. 90% of books from first-time authors. No mss through agents. **SUBSIDY PUBLISHES 95%.** Royalty 35-95%; no advance. Average first printing 1,000. Publication within 2 mos. Considers simultaneous submissions. No disk or e-mail submissions. Responds in 1 mo. Guidelines (also by e-mail); free catalog.

Nonfiction: Query or proposal/3 chapters; phone/fax/e-query OK. "Especially want political, prophecy, end times."

Fiction: Query or proposal/3 chapters. "Purposeful advancement of situational, historical, prophetic, political, and end-times education."

Tips: "Our goal is to help individuals with important messages self-publish their books and get the marketing, public relations, and distribution they need. We will strive to ensure that bookstores, and ultimately bookstore customers, know that these crucial books exist."

AMERICAN BINDING & PUBLISHING CO., PO Box 2259, Rockport TX 78381. Toll-free (800)863-3708. E-mail: magpub@pyramid3.net. Website: www.americanbindingpublishing .com. Rose Magner, pub. Publishes 60/yr. Receives 200 submissions annually. 95% of books from first-time authors. No mss through agents. Reprints books. **SUBSIDY PUBLISHES 100%.** Prefers 200 pgs. Royalty 15% on retail; no advance. Print-on-demand. Publication within 2 wks. Considers simultaneous submissions. Requires requested ms on disk (Microsoft Word format). Responds in 2 wks. Any Bible version. Guidelines (also by e-mail); free catalog. Not included in topical listings.

Nonfiction: Complete ms; phone/e-query OK. Will consider any topic.

Fiction: Complete ms; phone/e-query OK. For all ages; all genres.

Ethnic Books: Hispanic.

Photos: Accepts freelance photos for book covers.

Tips: "We are print-on-demand; authors are responsible for their own marketing. We will consider any topic—nonfiction or fiction."

+AMPELOS PRESS, 316 Blanchard Road, Drexel Hill, PA 19026. Phone/fax (610)626-6833. E-mail: mbagnull@aol.com. Website: www.writehisanswer.com. Marlene Bagnull, LittD, pub./ed. Services (depending on what is needed) include critiquing, editing, proofreading, typesetting, and cover design. Publishes 1-3 titles/yr. SUBSIDY PUBLISHES 100%. Query only. Not included in topical listings (see Tips).

Tips: "Our vision statement reads: 'Strongly, unashamedly, uncompromisingly Christ-centered. Exalting the name of Jesus Christ. Seeking to teach His ways through holding up the Word of God as the Standard.' (Ampelos is the Greek word for 'vine' in John 15:5.)"

BLACK FOREST PRESS, PO Box 6342, Chula Vista CA 91909-6342. Toll-free (800)451-9404. Fax (619)482-8704. E-mail: bfp1@blackforestpress.com. Website: www.blackforest press.com. Mary Inbody, sr. ed.; Sue Van Gundy, acq. ed. A self-publishing company; also does print-on-demand (POD); beginning e-books. Imprints: Kinder Books (children's adventure books); Dichter Books (Ethnic & Poetry); Abenteuer Books; Sonnenschein Books; Segen Books (religious). Publishes 100 titles/yr. (including POD). Receives 2,000 submissions annually. 75% of books from first-time authors. Accepts mss through agents. **SUBSIDY PUBLISHES 60%** (helps people get published). Reprints books. Prefers 75-350 pgs. Royalty 100% to authors; 68% to authors for Website purchases; promotional contracts vary; no advance. Average first printing 2,000-3,000. Publication within 4.5 months. Considers simultaneous submissions. Requires requested ms on disk. Responds in 2-3 wks. Prefers NLT or modern Bible versions. Free 90-page catalog (also on Website).

Nonfiction: Query/phone number; phone/fax/e-query OK. "Looking for true testimonials and books on angels; also contemporary Christian issues."

Fiction: Query. For all ages. "Looking for historical novels and Civil War books; 150-350 pages."

Ethnic Books: Publishes for Black and Hispanic markets.

Photos: Accepts freelance photos for book covers.

Tips: "Looking for books on vital Christian issues; books with literary merit and significant lessons for life."

+BOOK PUBLISHERS NETWORK, PO Box 2256, Bothell WA 98041. (425)483-3040. Fax (425)483-3098. E-mail: sherynhara@earthlink.net. Publishes 5-8 titles/yr. Receives 20 submissions annually. 100% of books from first-time authors. Accepts mss through agents. **100% SUBSIDY**. Reprints books. No preference on length. No royalty/advance. Publication within 3 mos. Considers simultaneous submissions. Responds in 1 mo. Guidelines (also by e-mail); no catalog.

Nonfiction: Proposal or complete ms.; phone/fax/e-query OK.

Fiction: Proposal or complete ms.; phone/fax/e-query OK.

Photos: Accepts freelance photos for book covers.

BRENTWOOD CHRISTIAN PRESS, 4000 Beallwood Ave., Columbus GA 31904. Toll-free (800)334-8861. (706)576-5787. Fax (706)317-5808. E-mail: Brentwood@aol.com. Website: www.BrentwoodBooks.com. Mainline. U.D. Roberts, exec. ed. Publishes 267 titles/yr. Receives 2,000 submissions annually. Reprints books. **SUBSIDY PUBLISHES 95%**. Offers InstaBooks and Just in Time publishing (print-on-demand). Average first printing 500. Publication within 1 mo. Considers simultaneous submissions. Responds in 2 days. Guidelines.

Nonfiction: Complete ms. "Collection of sermons on family topics; poetry; relation of Bible to current day."

Fiction: Complete ms. "Stories that show how faith helps overcome small, day-to-day problems."

Photos: Accepts freelance photos for book covers.

Tips: "Keep it short; support facts with reference." This publisher specializes in small print runs of 300-1,000. Can best serve the writer who has a completed manuscript.

+BROWN BOOKS PUBLISHING GROUP, 16200 N. Dallas Pkwy., Dallas TX 75248. (972)381-0009. Fax (972)248-4336. E-mail: debra@brownbooks.com. Website: www.brownbooks .com. Milli A. Brown, pub. Publishes books in the areas of self-help, religion/inspirational, relationships, business, mind/body/spirit, and women's issues. **SUBSIDY PUBLISHES 100%**.

+CATHOLIC ANSWERS, 2020 Gillespie Way, El Cajon CA 92020. (619)387-7200. Fax (619)387-0042. Trask Tapperson, dir. of publications. Publishes 10-20 titles/yr. Accepts mss through agents. **SUBSIDY PUBLISHER**. Does print-on-demand. Reprints books. Prefers 30,000 wds. Royalty on retail; advance $500. Average first printing 5,000. Publication within 6 mos. No simultaneous submissions. Prefers RSV. No guidelines; free catalog.
   Nonfiction: Query first; no phone/fax/e-query.
   Photos: Accepts freelance photos for book covers.
   Tips: "Most open to Catholic apologetics and evangelization."

CREATION HOUSE PRESS, 600 Rinehart Rd., Lake Mary FL 32746-4872. (407)333-0600. Fax (407)333-7100. E-mail: allen.quain@strang.com. Strang Communications Co. Allen Quain, mngr. To inspire and equip people to live a Spirit-led life and to walk in the divine purpose for which they were created. Imprints: Charisma House, Siloam Press, CharismaKids. Publishes 50-100 titles/yr. Receives 500 submissions annually. 80% of books from first-time authors. Accepts mss through agents. **CO-PUBLISHES 100%**. No print-on-demand. Reprints books. Prefers 25,000+ wds. or 100-200 pgs. Royalty 12-18% of net; no advance. Average first printing 5,500. Publication within 5 mos. Considers simultaneous submissions. Responds in 6-12 wks. Open to submissions on disk or by e-mail. Guidelines (also by e-mail/Website); free catalog.
   Nonfiction: Proposal or complete ms.; phone/fax/e-query OK. "Open to any books that are well-written and glorify Jesus Christ."
   Fiction: Proposal or complete ms.; phone/fax/e-query OK. For all ages. "Fiction must have a biblical world-view and point the reader to Christ."
   Photos: Accepts freelance photos for book covers.
   Tips: "We use the term 'co-publishing' to describe a hybrid between conventional royalty publishing and self or subsidy publishing, utilizing the best of both worlds. We produce a high quality book for our own inventory, market it, distribute it, and pay the author a royalty on every copy sold. In return, the author agrees to buy, at a deep discount, a portion of the first print run."

DCTS PUBLISHING, PO Box 40216, Santa Barbara CA 93140. Toll-free (800)965-8150. Fax (805)653-6522. E-mail: dennis@dctspub.com. Website: www.dctspub.com. Dennis Hamilton, ed. Books are designed to enrich the mind, encourage the heart, and empower the spirit. Publishes 5 titles/yr. Receives 25 submissions annually. 35% of books from first-time authors. No mss through agents. **SUBSIDY PUBLISHES 70%**. Reprints books. Prefers 100-300 pgs. Royalty 17% of retail; no advance. Average first printing 3,500. Publication within 6-8 mos. No simultaneous submissions. Prefers KJV. Guidelines; catalog for #10 SAE/1 stamp.
   Nonfiction: Query or proposal/2-3 chapters; e-query OK.
   Fiction: Query or proposal/2-3 chapters; e-query OK. Adult, biblical, ethnic, juvenile, or short story collections.

ELDERBERRY PRESS, 1393 Old Homestead Rd., 2nd Floor, Oakland OR 97462. Phone/fax (541)459-6043. E-mail: editor@elderberrypress.com. Website: www.elderberrypress .com. David W. St. John, exec. ed. Publishes 15 titles/yr. Receives 150-250 submissions annually. 90% of books from first-time authors. No mss through agents. **SUBSIDY PUBLISHES 50%**. Does print-on-demand. Royalty 10-25%; no advance. Publication within 3 mos. Considers simultaneous submissions. Accepts disk or e-mail submissions. Responds in 1 mo. Guidelines on Website; free catalog. Will consider any nonfiction or fiction topic. Not included in topical listings.
   Nonfiction: Complete ms; phone/fax/e-query OK. "We consider all topics."
   Fiction: Complete ms; phone/fax/e-query OK. All genres for all ages.

#END TIME WAVE PUBLICATIONS, PO Box 1314, Newark NJ 07101. Website: www.endtime

wave.com. Perry Malory, pub. **SUBSIDY PUBLISHER**. Prices and guidelines on Website. Not included in topical listings. No questionnaire returned.

ESSENCE PUBLISHING CO., INC., 20 Hanna Ct., Belleville ON K8P 5J2 Canada. (613)962-2360. Toll-free (800)238-6376. Fax (613)962-3055. E-mail: publishing@essence group.com. Website: www.essencegroup.com. Essence Communications Group. Cathy Jol, submissions ed.; Rikki-Anne McNaught, publishing mgr.; Renee VanderWindt and Stephanie VanderMuelen, eds. Provides affordable, short-run book publishing to the Christian community. Imprints: Guardian Books (see separate listing), Epic Press (secular). Publishes 100-150+ titles/yr. Receives 250+ submissions annually. 75% of books from first-time authors. **SUBSIDY PUBLISHES 90%**. Reprints books. Any length. Average first printing 500-1,000. Publication within 3-5 mos. Considers simultaneous submissions. Responds in 3-4 wks. Prefers requested ms on disk. Guidelines (also by e-mail/Website); catalog online (www.essencebookstore.com).

Nonfiction: Complete ms; phone/fax/e-query OK. Accepts all topics.

Fiction: Complete ms. All genres for all ages. Also picture books.

Also Does: Pamphlets, booklets, tracts.

Contest: The Essence Treasury Writing Competition.

Photos: Accepts freelance photos for book covers.

EXPRESS PUBLISHERS, 4000 Beallwood Ave., Columbus GA 31904. Toll-free (800)334-8861. (706)576-5787. Fax (706)317-5808. E-mail: Brentwood@aol.com. Website: www.Express Publishers.com. Mainline. U. D. Roberts, exec. ed. Division of Brentwood Christian Press. Publishes 30 titles/yr. Reprints books. **SUBSIDY PUBLISHES 95%**. Offers an improved print-on-demand process that will produce a book in a week. Average first printing 500. Publication within 1 wk. Considers simultaneous submissions. Responds in 2 days. Guidelines.

Nonfiction & Fiction: Complete ms.

Photos: Accepts freelance photos for book covers.

Tips: "We can deliver a 'Book Complete in One Week,' which has a limited market but fills a vital void when a ministry or group wants distribution of detailed news on a current topic in print immediately, at low cost. This could supplement the Internet or stand alone as a printed book."

FAIRWAY PRESS, subsidy division for CSS Publishing Company, 517 S. Main St., Box 4503, Lima OH 45802-4503. (419)227-1818. Fax (419)228-9184. Website: www.csspub.com. Teresa Rhoads, ed.; submit to Stan Purdum. Imprint: Express Press. Publishes 100 titles/yr. Receives 200-300 submissions annually. 80% of books from first-time authors. Reprints books. **SUBSIDY PUBLISHES 100%**. Royalty to 50%; no advance. Average first printing 500-1,000. Publication within 6-9 mos. Considers simultaneous submissions. Responds in up to 1 mo. Prefers requested ms on disk; no e-mail submissions. Prefers NRSV. Free guidelines (also on Website)/catalog for 9x12 SAE.

Nonfiction: Complete ms; phone/fax/e-query OK. All types. "Looking for manuscripts with a Christian theme, and seasonal material."

Fiction: Complete ms. For adults, teens, or children; all types. No longer producing anything in full color or with four-color illustrations.

FRUIT-BEARER PUBLISHING, PO Box 777, Georgetown DE 19947. (302)856-6649. Fax (302)856-7742. E-mail: candy.abbott@verizon.net. Website: www.fruitbearer.com. Branch of Candy's Creations. Candy Abbott, pres. Offers editing services and advice for self-publishers. Publishes 5-10 titles/yr. Receives 10-20 submissions annually. 90% of books from first-time authors. **SUBSIDY PUBLISHES 100%.** No reprints. Average first printing 30-5,000. Publication within 1-6 mos. Responds in 3 mos. Brochure for #10 SAE/1 stamp.

Nonfiction: Proposal/2 chapters; phone/fax/e-query OK.

Also Does: Pamphlets, booklets, tracts.

Photos: Accepts freelance photos for book covers.

Tips: "Accepting limited submissions."

GESHER—See Winer Foundation.

GUARDIAN BOOKS, 20 Hanna Ct., Belleville ON K8P 5J2 Canada. Toll-free (800)238-6376. (613)962-3294. Fax (613)962-3055. E-mail: publishing@essencegroup.com. Website: www.essencegroup.com. Essence Communications Group. Renee VanderWindt, submissions ed.; Lori Mackay, ed.; Rikki-Anne McNaught, mngr.; Gus Henne, marketing. Provides affordable, short-run book publishing to the Christian community. Imprints: Guardian Books, Epic Press (secular). Publishes 40-50 titles/yr. Receives 250+ submissions annually. 75% of books from first-time authors. **SUBSIDY PUBLISHES 90%.** Reprints books. Any length. Average first printing 500-1,000. Publication within 3-5 mos. Considers simultaneous submissions. Responds in 3-4 wks. Prefers requested ms on disk. Guidelines (also by e-mail/Website); free catalog.

Nonfiction: Complete ms; phone/fax/e-query OK. Accepts all topics.

Fiction: Complete ms. All genres for all ages. Also picture books.

Also Does: Pamphlets, booklets, tracts.

Photos: Accepts freelance photos for book covers.

+HANNIBAL BOOKS, PO Box 461592, Garland TX 75046-1592. (972)487-5710. Fax (972)487-7960. E-mail: hannibalbooks@earthlink.net. Website: www.hannibalbooks.com. KLMK Communications, Inc. Louis Moore, pub. Evangelical Christian publisher specializing in missions, marriage and family, and critical issues. Publishes 8-10 titles/yr. Receives 50 submissions annually. 80% of books from first-time authors. Accepts mss through agents. **SUBSIDY PUBLISHES 100%;** no POD. Reprints books. Prefers 50,000-60,000 wds. Royalty on net or outright purchase; no advance. Average first printing 2,000-3,000. Publication within 3 mos. Considers simultaneous submissions. Responds in 3 mos. Prefers NIV. Guidelines by e-mail; free catalog.

Nonfiction: Book Proposal/1-3 chapters; no phone/fax/e-query. "Looking for missionary, marriage restoration, homeschooling, and devotionals."

Fiction: Book Proposal/1-3 chapters; no phone/fax/e-query. "We like missionary romance novels."

Tips: "We are looking for go-get-'em new authors with a passion to be published."

IMPACT CHRISTIAN BOOKS, INC., 332 Leffingwell Ave., Ste. 101, Kirkwood MO 63122. (314)822-3309. Fax (314)822-3325. E-mail: info@impactchristianbooks.com. Website: www.impactchristianbooks.com. William D. Banks, pres. Books of healing, miraculous deliverance, and spiritual warfare; drawing individuals into a deeper walk with God. Publishes 20+ titles/yr. Receives 20-50 submissions annually. 50-70% of books from first-time authors. No mss through agents. **SUBSIDY PUBLISHES 50-70%.** Reprints books. Average first printing 5,000. Publication within 2 mos. Considers simultaneous submissions. Responds by prior arrangement in 30 days. Requires requested ms on disk. Guidelines; catalog for 9x12 SAE/5 stamps. Not in topical listings.

Nonfiction: Query only; phone/fax query OK. Outstanding personal testimonies and Christ-centered books.

INHERITANCE PUBLICATIONS, Box 154, Neerlandia AB T0G 1R0 Canada. U.S. address: Box 366, Pella IA 50219. Toll-free (800)563-3594. (780)674-3949. Fax (775)890-9118. E-mail: inhpub@telusplanet.net. Website: www.telusplanet.net/public/inhpub/webip/ip.htm. Roelof Janssen, ed. E-mail: inhpubl@telusplanet.net Website: www.telusplanet.net/public/inhpubl/webip/ip.htm. Reprints books. **SUBSIDY PUBLISHER.** Accepting historical novels only.

Tips: "A book must be very good for us to publish it. We do mostly old books."

INSIGHT PUBLISHING GROUP, 8801 S. Yale, Ste. 410, Tulsa OK 74137. (918)493-1718. Fax

(918)493-2219. E-mail: info@freshword.com. Website: www.freshword.com. Christian Publisher. John Mason, ed. Owned by a best-selling author who established the company to serve authors. Publishes 50 titles/yr. Receives 50 submissions annually. 50% of books from first-time authors. Accepts mss through agents. Does print-on-demand. Reprints books. Prefers 160 pgs. Royalty 15-17% on net; no advance. Average first printing 5,000. Publication within 6 mos. Considers simultaneous submissions. Requires disk or e-mail submission. Responds in 2 mos. Guidelines by e-mail/Website; no catalog. Will consider most fiction and nonfiction topics. Incomplete topical listings.

Nonfiction: Complete ms; phone/fax/e-query OK.

Fiction: Complete ms; phone/fax/e-query OK. Nondenominational Christian. For all ages.

Also Does: Booklets.

Tips: "We help people self-publish. To those authors we can offer a variety of services including distribution and small print runs. Most open to books that are unique, authentic, and relevant."

KENOSIS PUBLISHING, LLC., 20532 El Toro Rd., Ste. 209, Mission Viejo CA 92692. (949)951-8969. E-mail: questions@kenosispublishing.com. Website: www.kenosispublishing.com. Bob Butkins, ed. **100% SUBSIDY.** Not in topical listings. No questionnaire returned.

+LIGHTNING STAR PRESS, PO Box 730393, San Jose CA 95173. (408)270-0572. Fax (425)645-0423. E-mail: jessie@lightningstarpress.com. Website: www.lightningstar press.com. Submit to The Editor. Publishes 2-4 titles/yr. Receives 50 submissions annually. 99% of books from first-time authors. Accepts mss through agents. **99% SUBSIDY.** Does print-on-demand. Reprints books. Prefers 32+ pgs. No royalty or advance. Average first printing 100+. Publication within 6 mos. Considers simultaneous submissions. Responds in 1-2 wks. Accepts e-mail submissions. Guidelines on Website; no catalog.

Nonfiction: Complete ms or proposal/2 chapters; phone/fax/e-query OK

Fiction: Complete ms or proposal/3 chapters; phone/fax/e-query OK

Photos: Accepts freelance photos for book covers.

LONGWOOD COMMUNICATIONS, 3037 Clubview Dr., Orlando FL 32822. (407)737-0406. Fax (407)737-7378. E-mail: longcomm@bellsouth.net. Murray Fisher, VP. A service for authors who cannot get their books accepted by a traditional house. Publishes 8 titles/yr. Receives 70-80 submissions annually. 95% of books from first-time authors. No mss through agents. **30% SUBSIDY.** Reprints books. Any length. Outright purchases. Average first printing 5,000. Publication within 10-14 wks. Considers simultaneous submissions. Prefers accepted ms on disk. Responds in 2 wks. Any Bible version. No guidelines or catalog.

Nonfiction: Complete ms; phone/fax/e-query OK. Almost any topic as long as it's Christian and builds up the Body of Christ. Looking for books to strengthen individuals and the church.

Fiction: Complete ms. For all ages.

Also Does: Booklets, pamphlets, tracts.

Photos: Accepts freelance photos for book covers.

Tips: "Looking for well-written, basic Christian books: building up the church, Christian growth, and stories about real people."

+MARKETINGNEWAUTHORS.COM, 2910 E. Eisenhower Parkway, Ann Arbor MI 48108. (734)975-0028. Fax (734)973-9475. E-mail: Fairyha@aol.com. Website: www.Marketing NewAuthors.com. Imprint of Robbie Dean Press. To primarily serve authors who wish to self-publish. Dr. Fairy C. Hayes-Scott, owner. 100% of books from first-time authors. Accepts mss through agents. **SUBSIDY PUBLISHES 100%.** Reprints books. Length flexible. Publication within 6 mos. Considers simultaneous submissions. Responds in 2-6 wks. Guidelines by e-mail/Website. Offers 7 different marketing plans; see Website.

THE MASTER DESIGN, PO Box 17865, Memphis TN 38187-0865. Phone/fax (901)309-9655.

E-mail: info@masterdesign.org. Website: www.masterdesign.org. S. Faithe Finley, submissions ed. Prefers to publish books that advance Christ's Kingdom. Imprint: Macbeth Publishers (educational/homeschool materials). Publishes 10-15 titles/yr. Receives 40-50 submissions annually. 85% of books from first-time authors. No mss through agents. **90% SUBSIDY.** No print-on-demand. Reprints books. Prefers 50-300 pgs. Author pays all costs. Average first printing 3,000. Publication within 5 mos. Considers simultaneous submissions. Responds in 2-3 wks. Prefers NASB, KJV. Requires requested ms on disk or by e-mail (preferred). Guidelines & catalog on Website.

> **Nonfiction**: Proposal/3 chapters; fax query OK; prefers e-query.
>
> **Ethnic/Foreign Books**: Accepts foreign-language books and books for overseas.
>
> **Also Does**: E-books.
>
> **Tips**: "Most open to Bible-focused books, studies, commentaries, or books aimed at the homeschool market." Also sells books directly from Website.

OMEGA HOUSE PUBLISHING, PO Box 68, Three Rivers MI 49093. (269)273-7070. Nondenominational. Zendra Manley, ed. To distribute and increase knowledge in the body of Christ (Hosea 4:6). Publishes 5 titles/yr. Receives 60 submissions annually. 95% of books from first-time authors. No mss through agents. **90% SUBSIDY.** Reprints books. Prefers 80-500 pgs. Royalty 8-10% of net; no advance. Average first printing 2,000-5,000. Publication within 6 mos. Considers simultaneous submissions. Responds in 2 wks. No disk. Guidelines; no catalog.

> **Nonfiction**: Query; no phone query.
>
> **Special Needs**: Renewal, inspirational, healing.
>
> **Tips**: "Manuscripts are turned down that do not bring glory to God and that are less than marketable. Most open to scripturally referenced manuscripts that are anointed to transform lives; no personal experiences."

ONE WORLD PRESS, PO Box 2501, Prescott AZ 86302. (928)445-2081. Fax (928)717-1779. E-mail: oneworldpress@mail.com. Joe Zuccarello, operation mngr. Publishes many titles/yr. Receives 25-50 submissions annually. 50% of books from first-time authors. Accepts mss through agents. **SUBSIDY PUBLISHES 100%.** Reprints books. Does print-on-demand. Average first printing up to author. Publication within 2 mos. Considers simultaneous submissions. Responds in 2-4 wks. No guidelines or catalog. Incomplete topical listings (open to most topics/genres).

> **Nonfiction & Fiction:** Complete manuscript. All ages. "We publish about anything within decency and reason."
>
> **Also Does**: Booklets, e-books, pamphlets, tracts.

PLEASANT WORD, 1730 Railroad St., PO Box 428, Enumclaw WA 98022. Toll-free (800)326-4674. (360)802-9758. Fax (360)802-9992. E-mail: info@pleasantword.com. Website: www.pleasantword.com. WinePress Publishing. David Dean, pub.; Athena Dean, acq. ed. **100% SUBSIDY.** Print-on-demand division. Publishes 300+ titles/yr. Receives 500+ submissions annually. 80% of books from first-time authors. Accepts mss through agents. Reprints books. Any length, 48 to 740 pgs. Color picture books in soft cover only, 28-120 pgs. Royalty; no advance. Publication within 45-90 days. Considers simultaneous submissions. Responds online. Guidelines & catalog on Website.

> **Nonfiction**: Complete ms submitted online through Website; e-queries OK. "We accept all topics except books that promote the prosperity doctrine, 'Toronto Blessing,' or women in leadership over men."
>
> **Fiction**: Complete ms submitted online through Website; e-queries OK. Fiction for all ages.
>
> **Tips**: "Most subsidy/POD publishers will publish anything if you are willing to pay for it. We turn down unscriptural manuscripts and others that have no chance of recouping the original investment."

POEMS BY ME, 4000 Beallwood Ave., Columbus GA 31904. Toll-free (800)334-2828. E-mail: Brentwood@aol.com. Website: www.PoemsByMe.com. Brentwood Christian Press. Joyce Warren, ed. Poetry that is spiritual, personal, emotional. Receives 80 submissions annually. 75% of books from first-time authors. Accepts mss through agents. **100% SUBSIDY**. Print-on-demand. Reprints books. Need at least 40 poems for a book. Same-week response.

#POETRY OF TODAY PUBLISHING, 2075 Stanford Village Dr., Antioch TN 37013-4450. (615)337-2725. Fax (347)823-9608. E-mail: editor@poetryoftoday.com. Website: www.poetryoftoday.com. Christian Business. Patrice M. Brooks, pub. Publishes 10-12 titles/yr. Receives 25-40 submissions annually. 95% of books from first-time authors. Accepts mss through agents. **SUBSIDY PUBLISHES 75%**. Print-on-demand. No reprints. Prefers 80 pgs. min. Royalty 60% on retail; no advance. Average first printing open. Publication within 3 mos. Considers simultaneous submissions. Requires disk. Responds in 1-2 mos. Prefers KJV. Guidelines by e-mail/Website; no catalog at this time.

   Nonfiction: Complete ms; phone/fax/e-query OK.

   Fiction: Complete ms; phone/fax/e-query OK. For all ages; biblical and literary. "Looking for spiritual poetry and novels."

   Also Does: E-books.

   Photos: Accepts freelance photos for book covers.

   Contest: Sponsors a monthly poetry contest.

   Tips: "We're looking for Christian poetry that is well written, new, inspiring, and educational. We specialize in first-time authors."

POET'S COVE PRESS, 4000 Beallwood Ave., Columbus GA 31904. Toll-free (800)334-8861. (706)576-5787. E-mail: Brentwood@aol.com. Website: www.BrentwoodBooks.com. Subsidiary of Brentwood Publishers Group. U.D. Roberts, exec. dir. Publishes 75 titles/yr. **SUBSIDY OR CUSTOM PUBLISHES 100%**. Specializes in self-publishing books of religious or inspirational poetry, in small press runs of under 500 copies. Publication in 45 days. Same-day response.

   Tips: "Type one poem per page; include short bio and photo with first submission."

PROMISE PUBLISHING, PO Box 10759, Santa Ana CA 92711-0759. (714)997-8450. Fax (714)997-5545. E-mail: marybelle@ix.netcom.com. Listed on Barnes & Noble Website. M. B. Steele, VP. Publishes 6 titles/yr. 50% of books from first-time authors. **100% COOPERATIVE PUBLISHING** in support of ministry organizations. Royalty 10% of net (negotiable); no advance. Average first printing 5,000. Publication within 6 mos. Considers simultaneous submissions. Preacceptance talks determine acceptance.

   Nonfiction: Query or proposal/3 chapters; phone/fax/e-query OK. "We are interested in missionary books or Bible studies."

   Special Needs: "We are interested in a topic if it is not contradictory to the Bible."

   Tips: "Most open to established ministries that will use the books for their constituency."

PROVIDENCE HOUSE PUBLISHERS, 238 Seaboard Ln., Franklin TN 37067. Toll-free (800)321-5692. (615)771-2020. Fax (615)771-2002. E-mail: mvanhook@providence house.com. Website: www.providence-publishing.com. Providence Publishing Corp. Nancy Wise, mng. ed.; Michael S. VanHook, acq. ed. A private publisher that supplies a complete list of services including editorial, design, production, marketing, and inventory management. Imprint: Hillsboro Press. Publishes 12 titles/yr. Receives 50 submissions annually. 90% of books from first-time authors. Accepts mss through agents. **SUBSIDY PUBLISHES 100%**. No print-on-demand. Reprints books. Average first printing 2,000-3,000. Publication within 9 mos. Considers simultaneous submissions. Responds in 1-4 wks. Requires accepted ms on disk. Prefers NIV, NKJV. Guidelines (also by e-mail/Website); no catalog.

   Nonfiction: Complete ms; phone/fax/e-query OK. "Looking for historical and biographical books this year."

Fiction: Complete ms; phone/fax/e-query OK. "We seldom do fiction."

Also Does: Booklets.

Photos: Accepts freelance photos for book covers.

Tips: "Most open to books that are orthodox/evangelical Christian and that the author has a willingness to personally market."

QUIET WATERS PUBLICATIONS, PO Box 34, Bolivar MO 65613-0034. (417)326-5001. Fax (617)249-0256. E-mail: QWP@usa.net. Website: www.QuietWatersPub.com. Stephen Trobisch, ed. Books on marriage, family, and missions. Open to freelance submissions.

RECOVERY COMMUNICATIONS, INC., PO Box 19910, Baltimore MD 21211. (410)243-8352. Fax (410)243-8558. E-mail: tdrews3879@aol.com. Website: www.GettingThem Sober.com. Toby R. Drews, ed. Publishes 4-6 titles/yr. No mss through agents. **SUBSIDY PUBLISHER.** Prefers 110 pgs. Co-op projects; no royalty or advance. Average first printing 5,000. Publication within 9 mos. Excellent nationwide distribution and marketing in bookstores. Send for their free information packet.

    Nonfiction: Query only.

    Tips: "Although technically we are a subsidy publisher, we are more of a hybrid publisher in that we give the author enough free books to sell in the back of the room to totally recoup all the money they have paid; plus we share 50/50 on net sales at bookstores. Over half of our authors have gotten their money back and made a great profit. We are also aggressive in our pursuit of catalog sales and foreign rights sales (we recently sold to a German publisher). We also individually coach all our authors, at no cost to them, to help them successfully obtain speaking engagements."

ROBBIE DEAN PRESS, 2910 E. Eisenhower Parkway, Ann Arbor MI 48108. (734)973-9511. Fax (734)973-9475. E-mail: Fairyha@aol.com. Website: www.RobbieDeanPress.com. Interested in works that are multiculturally appealing and that approach a topic in a unique manner. Dr. Fairy C. Hayes-Scott, owner. Publishes 1 title/yr. Receives 20 submissions annually. 100% of books from first-time authors. Accepts mss through agents. **SUBSIDY PUBLISHES 75%.** Does print-on-demand. Reprints books. Length flexible. Royalty 10-20%; no advance. Average first printing 250. Publication within 6 mos. Considers simultaneous submissions. Responds in 2-6 wks. Guidelines by e-mail; free catalog.

    Nonfiction: Query first. "We're open to new ideas."

    Fiction: "We seldom do fiction." For children only.

    Ethnic Books: Multicultural.

    Also Does: Booklets; e-books; computer games.

    Photos: Accepts freelance photos for book covers.

    Tips: "Most open to self-help, reference, senior adult topics, and parenting."

SELF PUBLISH PRESS, 4000 Beallwood Ave., Columbus GA 31904. Toll-free (800)334-8861. (706)576-5787. Fax (706)317-5808. E-mail: Brentwood@aol.com. Website: www .PublishMyBook.com. Brentwood Publishing Group. U.D. Roberts, exec. ed.; submit to Marie Warren, ed. All books must be family suitable. Receives 100 submissions annually. 98% of books from first-time authors. Accepts mss through agents. **SUBSIDY PUBLISHES 98%.** Does print-on-demand. Offers InstaBooks and Just in Time publishing (print-on-demand). Reprints books. Prefers 64-300 pgs. Publication within 1 mo. Considers simultaneous submissions. Responds in 3 days. Guidelines on Website; no catalog.

    Nonfiction: Complete ms/diskette; no phone/fax/e-query. All religious—for family or youth.

    Fiction: Complete ms/diskette; no phone/fax/e-query. For all ages.

SERMON SELECT PRESS, 4000 Beallwood Ave., Columbus GA 31904. Toll-free (800)334-8861. (706)576-5787. Fax (706)317-5808. E-mail: Brentwood@aol.com. Website: www.BrentwoodBooks.com. Subsidiary of Brentwood Publishers Group. U. D. Roberts, exec. dir. **SUBSIDY OR CUSTOM PUBLISHES 100%**. Focus is on sermon notes, outlines, illustrations, plus news that pastors would find interesting. Publishes 100 copies. Cost of about $3-4/book. Publication in 45 days. Same-day response.

SOUTHERN BAPTIST PRESS, 4000 Beallwood, Columbus GA 31904. Toll-free (800)334-8861. (706)576-5787. E-mail: Brentwood@aol.com. Website: www.SouthernBaptist Press.com. U.D. Roberts, exec. ed. Publishes 25 books/yr. Receives 600 submissions annually. Reprints books. **SUBSIDY OR CUSTOM PUBLISHES 95%**. Average first printing 500. Publication within 2 mos. Considers simultaneous submissions. Responds in 1 week. Guidelines.

> **Nonfiction**: Complete ms. "Collections of sermons on family topics; poetry; relation of Bible to current day."
> **Fiction**: Complete ms. "Stories that show how faith helps overcome small, day-to-day problems."
> **Tips**: "Keep it short; support facts with reference."

#STEP-BY-STEP PUBLICATIONS, PO Box 369, Cloverdale IN 46120. Toll-free (800)709-8097. E-mail: sbs@sbspub.com. Submit to The Editor. Publishes 1-2 titles/yr. **SUBSIDY PUBLISHES 100%**. Guidelines and price list on Website. Not included in topical listings (accepts almost any topic). No questionnaire returned.

STRONG TOWER PUBLISHING, PO Box 973, Milesburg PA 16853. E-mail: strongtower pubs@aol.com. Website: www.strongtowerpublishing.com. Heidi L. Nigro, pub. Looks for books that challenge the reader to think more deeply about their faith and scriptural truths; must be biblically responsible, doctrinally defensible, and consistent with their statement of faith. Publishes 1-2 titles/yr. 50% of books from first-time authors. No mss through agents. No reprints. **PRINT-ON-DEMAND 100%**. Royalty on retail; no advance. Average first printing 200. Publication within 3-4 mos. No guidelines or catalog. Information and prices on Website.

> **Nonfiction**: Query.
> **Fiction**: Query. Adult biblical.
> **Tips**: "We recommend that all first-time authors have their manuscript professionally edited. We will consider putting first-time authors into print, but by invitation only. That invitation comes only after the manuscript has been thoroughly evaluated and we have discussed the pros and cons of our unique on-demand publishing model with the author."

SYNERGY PUBLISHERS, PO Box 141630, Gainesville FL 32614-1640. (352)472-7900. E-mail: submissions@bridgelogos.com. Website: www.bridgelogos.com. **CO-OP PUBLISHING** imprint of Bridge-Logos. Pays for cost of production and royalties, but author is required to buy a certain number of books up front. Not included in topical listings. No questionnaire returned.

TEACH SERVICES, INC., 254 Donovan Rd., Brushton NY 12916. (518)358-2125. Fax (518)358-3028. E-mail: publishing@TEACHservices.com. Website: www.teachservices .com. Timothy Hullquist, pres.; submit to Wayne Reid, acq. ed. To publish uplifting books for the lowest price. Publishes 40-50 titles/yr. Receives 100 submissions annually. 35% of books from first-time authors. No mss through agents. **SUBSIDY PUBLISHES 75%** (author has to pay for first printing, then publisher keeps it in print). Reprints books. Prefers 45,000 wds. or 96 pgs. Royalty 10% of retail; no advance. Average first printing 2,000. Publication within 6 mos. Requires requested ms on disk. Responds in 2 wks. Prefers KJV. Guidelines (also by e-mail/Website)/catalog for #10 SAE/2 stamps.

> **Nonfiction**: Query only; no phone/fax query. "Looking for books on nutrition."
> **Special Needs**: Personal testimonies.
> **Photos**: Accepts freelance photos for book covers.

VESTA PUBLICATIONS, LTD., Box 32, Cornwall ON K6H 5R9 Canada. (613)932-2135. Fax

(613)932-7735. E-mail: sgill@ican.net, or stefgill@hotmail.com. Websites: www.author den.com/stephengill, or http://home.ican.net/~sgill. General trade publisher that does a few religious titles; focus is on world peace. Stephen Gill, ed. Publishes 4 titles/yr. Receives 20-60 submissions annually. 95% of books from first-time authors. No mss through agents. **SUBSIDY PUBLISHES 90%** (author pays about 50% of cost). Reprints books. Any length. Royalty 15% of net; no advance. Average first printing 1,500. Publication within 3 mos. No simultaneous submissions. Responds in 4-7 wks. Requires requested ms on disk. Catalog for SAE/IRCs.

> **Nonfiction**: Proposal/1 chapter; phone query OK.

> **Tips**: "Most open to scholarly/religious books."

WINEPRESS PUBLISHING, PO Box 428, 1730 Railroad St., Enumclaw WA 98022. Toll-free (800)326-4674. (360)802-9758. Fax (360)802-9992. E-mail: info@winepresspub.com or athena@winepresspub.com. Website: www.winepresspub.com. David Dean, pub.; Athena Dean, acq. ed. Books that challenge readers to think about their Christianity and the need for holy lives. Publishes 50+ titles/yr. Receives 500+ submissions annually. 70% of books from first-time authors. Accepts mss through agents. **BOOK PACKAGERS 95%**. Reprints books. Lengths range from 48-1,300 pgs. Author pays production costs, keeps all income from sales. Average first printing 3,000 (2,500 min.). Publication in 4-5 mos. Considers simultaneous submissions. Responds in 48-72 hrs. Accepts requested ms on disk. Prefers NIV. Free guidelines (also on Website)/catalog. Not included in topical listings because they consider any topic or genre.

> **Nonfiction**: Complete ms; phone/fax/e-query OK. Publishes any topic as long as it's biblical or glorifies God.

> **Fiction**: Complete ms. All ages and all genres.

> **Also Does**: Booklets, gift books, Bibles, full-color children's books. Offers a print-on-demand program with competitive prices for less than 2,500 copies.

> **Photos**: Accepts freelance photos for book covers.

> **Tips**: "As the leader in quality self-publishing, we offer professional book packaging for Christian writers. We not only offer a full line of editorial, design, layout, and printing services, but cutting-edge marketing, publicity, promotion, order fulfillment, warehousing, and distribution as well. Our in-house team of professionals is committed to serving our authors with excellent customer service and honest advice. We don't purchase rights to books and choose not to partner with messages that don't glorify God. All manuscripts that do not have a reasonably good chance of selling at least 1,000 copies are encouraged to take advantage of our print-on-demand services (see Pleasant Word listing)."

WINER FOUNDATION, PO Box 33373, Philadelphia PA 19142-3373. (215)365-3350. Fax (215)365-3325. E-mail: info@winerfoundation.org. Website: www.winerfoundation.org. Robert Winer, pres. Helping people walk in all that God intends for them. Publishes 4 titles/yr. **SUBSIDY PUBLISHES 90%.** Reprints books. Prefers 150-250 pgs. Royalty 3-10% of retail; advance $250-500. Average first printing 3,000-5,000. Publication within 6-8 mos. Considers simultaneous submissions. Requires requested ms on disk (Word, WordPerfect, or .RTF format). Responds in 1-2 mos. Prefers NKJV. Guidelines (also by e-mail); no catalog.

> **Nonfiction**: Proposal with 2-3 chapters; e-query OK. "Books on deeper spirituality to help people mature in the Lord."

> **Special Needs**: Messianic Jewish in addition to general Christianity.

> **Tips**: "Most open to books that fulfill our mission statement."

WORD ALIVE PRESS, 131 Cordite Rd., Winnipeg MB R3W 1S1 Canada. (866)967-3782, ext. 203. Fax (800)352-9272. E-mail: Cschmidt@wordalive.ca. C. Schmidt, ed. At least 12,000 wds. or 100 pgs. **100% PRINT-ON-DEMAND**.

WORD FOR WORD PUBLISHING CO., 14 MetroTech Center, Brooklyn NY 11201-3824. (718)222-9673. E-mail: info@WordForWord.us. Website: www.WordForWord.us. Michelle A. Edwards, ed. Specializes in religious publications. Imprints: Key-A-Teese Productions and A & E Publications. Publishes 15-20 titles/yr. Receives 200+ submissions annually. 90% of books from first-time authors. **SUBSIDY PUBLISHES 90%.** All profits belong to author; flexible payment plan. No minimum length. Average first printing 1,000. Publication within 3 mos. Responds in 1-2 wks. Prefers KJV; accepts any version. Will consider most Christian topics.

> **Nonfiction & Fiction:** Query only first; e-query OK. "Looking for books that enlighten, empower, and glorify God."

> **Tips**: "'Write the vision and make it plain, that he may run that readeth it' (Hab. 2:2). Then, actively promote your books. We go as you pay." Will transcribe from tapes.

WRITE HAND PUBLISHING, 105 Willow Dr., Andalusia AL 36420. (334)222-9212. E-mail: webmail@writehand.com. Website: www.writehand.com. George Payne, ed. Reprints books. Publication within 2 mos. Not a subsidy publisher; helps Christians self-publish their books. Prefers you call for information. No catalog.

> **Nonfiction**: Phone query only. Open to anything Christian.

> **Photos**: Accepts freelance photos for book covers.

XLIBRIS, 436 Walnut St., 11th Floor, the Independence Bldg., Philadelphia PA 19106. Toll-Free (888)795-4274, ext. 278. E-mail: info@xlibris.com. Website: www.xlibris.com. Random House. Mercedes Bournias, publishing consultant. Can produce novels to 700 pages and picture books to 24 pages. Not included in topical listings. No questionnaire returned.

XULON PRESS, INC., 10640 Main St., Ste. 204, Fairfax VA 22030. Toll-free (866)381-2665. Fax (407)339-9898. E-mail: kkochenburger@xulonpress.com. Website: www.xulon press.com. Tom Freiling, pres./CEO.; Karen Kochenburger, ed. Uses digital and print-on-demand technologies to help Christian authors get published. Publishes 1,000 titles/yr. Receives 2,500 submissions annually. 80% of books from first-time authors. **SUBSIDY PUBLISHES 80%.** Reprints books. Any length. Royalty 20-25% of net; no advance. Print-on-demand. Publication within 2 mos. Considers simultaneous submissions. Responds in 1 mo. Not in topical listings; will consider all appropriate Christian topics. Guidelines on Website; free catalog.

> **Nonfiction**: Phone/fax/e-query OK.

> **Fiction**: Phone/fax/e-query OK.

> **Also Does**: Booklets, e-books.

> **Photos**: Accepts freelance photos for book covers.

> **Tips**: "We offer publishing, distribution, and marketing services. Our books are available in bookstores and on the Internet. Our bimonthly catalog is mailed to 4,000 bookstores and media channels, and we publicize our books at trade shows, including at the annual CBA convention."

> ****Note**: This publisher (royalty division) serviced by The Writer's Edge.

LISTING OF CHRISTIAN BOOK/MUSIC/GIFT DISTRIBUTORS

*ALLIANCE—MUSIC, 4250 Coral Ridge Dr., Coral Springs FL 33065-7615. Toll-free (800)267-3794. Fax (954)255-4825. Music.

AMAZON ADVANTAGE PROGRAM, Go to Amazon.com, scroll down to "Make Money" section in left-hand column, and click on "Advantage." Site to contact if you want Amazon to distribute your book.

ANCHOR DISTRIBUTORS, 30 Hunt Valley Cir., New Kensington PA 15068. Toll-free (800)444-4484. (724)334-7000. Fax (800)765-1960 or (724)334-1200. E-mail: customerservice@

anchordistributors.com. Website: www.anchordistributors.com. Donna Bonarati, intl. sales mngr. (800)444-4484, ext. 246.

APPALACHIAN DISTRIBUTORS, PO Box 1573, 522 Princeton Rd., Johnson City TN 37601. Toll-free (800)289-2772. Fax (800)759-2779. Website: www.appalink.com. A full-service distributor with two locations. Includes the homeschool market.

B. BROUGHTON CO., LTD., 2105 Danforth Ave., Toronto ON M4C 1K1 Canada. (416)690-4777. Fax (416)690-5357. E-mail: sales@bbroughton.com. Website: www.bbroughton.com. Canadian distributor.

CBA MAILING LISTS OF CHRISTIAN BOOKSTORES, PO Box 62000, Colorado Springs CO 80962-2000. Fax (719)272-3510. Available for rental. Four different lists available, including nonmember stores, 7,500 addresses ($149); member stores, 1,800 addresses ($649); chain-store headquarters (51) plus largest independent stores 1,000 addresses ($449); or a combined list of all stores, 9,300 addresses ($699). Prices subject to change. Call toll-free (800)252-1950 for full details.

CHRISTIAN BOOK DISTRIBUTORS, PO Box 7000, Peabody MA 01961-7000. Toll-free (800)247-4784. (978)977-5080. Fax (978-977-5010). Website: www.christianbooks.com.

CHRISTIAN DISTRIBUTION SERVICE, 1933 Whitfield Park Look, Sarasota FL 34243. Toll-free (800)905-4306, ext. 250. Fax (800)777-2525. E-mail: info@bookworld.com. Website: www.christiandistribution.com. General CBA products.

+THE CHRISTIAN MARKETPLACE, (formerly Y.O.U.R. Stores, Inc.) 13695 Goldmark Dr. #3322, Dallas TX 75240-4215. Toll-free (888)282-2016. (214)575-7557. E-mail: support@ thechristianmarketplace.com. Website: www.yourstores.com. Bea Kassees, pres. Distributes gift products.

CONEXUS MULTIFAITH MEDIA, PO Box 39218, Solon OH 44139. Toll-free (877)784-7779. (440)349-0495. E-mail: info@conexuspress.com. Website: www.conexuspress.com. Distributes interreligious/interfaith and comparative religion resources, including books, music, videos, CD-ROMs, gift items, etc. James T. Cloud, owner.

+CONSORTIUM BOOK SALES & DISTRIBUTION, INC., 1045 Westgate Dr., Ste. 90, St. Paul MN 55114. Toll-free (800)283-3572. Website: www.cbsd.com.

COOK COMMUNICATIONS CANADA, 55 Woodslee Ave., Box 98, Paris ON N3L 3E5 Canada. Toll-free (800)263-2664. Fax (800)461-8575. E-mail: custserv@cook.ca. Website: www .cook.ca. Can distribute only in Canada.

DICKSONS, PO Box 368, Seymour IN 47274. (812)522-1308. Fax (812)522-1319. E-mail: marketing@dicksonsgifts.com. Website: www.dicksonsgifts.com. Distributes gift products only. Website includes a list of additional distributors.

EFULFILLMENT SERVICE, INC., 6893 Sullivan Rd., Grawn MI 49637. (231)276-5057, ext. 100. Fax (231)276-5074. E-mail: alc@efulfillmentservice.com, or info@efulfillment service.com. Website: www.efulfillmentservice.com. John Lindberg, pres. Services include storage and order fulfillment.

FAITHWORKS, 9247 Hunterboro Dr., Brentwood TN 37027. Toll-free(877)323-4550. (615)221-6442. Fax (612)221-6442. E-mail: lcarpenter@faithworksonline.com. Website: www.faithworksonline.com. Christian products, including books, music, videos, audiotapes, and software.

FOUNDATION DISTRIBUTING INC., 9 Cobbledick St., PO Box 98, Orono ON L0B 1M0 Canada. (905)983-1188. Fax (905)983-1190. E-mail: info@fdi.ca. Website: www.fdi.ca. Canadian distributor.

+GENESIS MARKETING, Toll-free (800)627-2651.

+GL SERVICES, 1957 Eastman Ave., Ventura CA 93003. Toll-free (800)628-2878. A division of Gospel Light.

+GODSPEED COMPUTING'S DIGITAL DISTRIBUTION SYSTEM, #210, 3553—31st St. N.W., Calgary AB T2L 2K7 Canada. Toll-free (866)463-7733. (403)274-6510. Fax (403)282-1238. E-mail: sales@godspeedcomputing.com, or info@godspeedcomputing .com. Website: http://godspeedcomputing.com. E-book distributor.

INGRAM BOOK GROUP/DISTRIBUTION, One Ingram Blvd., LaVergne TN 37086-1986. Toll-free (800)937-8000. (615)793-5000. Website: www.ingrambookgroup.com. The best way to have your book/product distributed by this company is to go through one of their trading partners. For a list of distributing partners and more information, visit their Website.

KEY MARKETING GROUP, PO Box 162, Jenks OK 74037. Toll-free (866)862-2278. (918)369-9293. Fax (413)723-4384. E-mail: info@keymarketingroup.net. Website: www .keymarketinggroup.net. Bryan Norris, owner.

LIGHTNING SOURCE, INC., 1246 Heil Quaker Blvd., LaVergne TN 37086. (615)213-5815. Fax (615)213-4426. E-mail: inquiry@lightningsource.com. Website: www.lightning source.com.

MALACO CHRISTIAN DISTRIBUTION, 3023 W. Northside Dr., Jackson MS 39213. (877)462-3623, Fax (877)270-4508. E-mail: tgoodwin@malaco.com. Website: www.malaco.com. Tony Goodwin, mng. dir. of sales. Music distributor.

MCBETH CORPORATION, Fulfillment and Distribution Headquarters, PO Box 400, Chambersburg PA 17201. Toll-free (800)876-5112. (717)263-5600. Fax (800)876-5110 or (717)263-5600. E-mail: mcbethcorp@earthlink.net. Distributes Christian gift products.

R. G. MITCHELL FAMILY BOOKS, INC., 565 Gordon Baker Rd., Willowdale ON M2H 2W2, Canada. (416)499-4615. Fax (416)499-6340. E-mail: info@rgm.ca. Website: www.rgm.ca. David Freeland, pres.

#MUSIC/CD/TAPE DISTRIBUTOR, PO Box 1298, Decatur AL 35602-1298. Contact: Brian Baer.

NEW DAY CHRISTIAN DISTRIBUTORS, 126 Shivel Dr., Hendersonville TN 37075. Toll-free (800)251-3633. (615)822-3633. Fax (800)361-2533. E-mail: info@newdaychristian .com. Music (primarily), books, Bibles, gift items.

NEW LIFE PUBLICATIONS, 375 Hwy. 74 South, Ste. A, Peachtree City GA 30269. Toll-free (800)235-7255, or (800)827-2788. Fax (800)514-7072, or (770)631-9916. Website: www.nlpdirect.com.

*NOAH'S ARK DISTRIBUTION, 28545 Felix Valdez Ave., Ste. B4, Temecula CA 92590-1859. Toll-free (800)562-8093. (760)723-3101. Fax (760)723-1443. E-mail: Noahtwo@ juno.com. Contact: Scott Vanyo, manager.

*NOBLE MARKETING GROUP, 19216 S.E. 46th Pl., Issaquah WA 98027. (615)221-0992. Fax (615)221-0962. Book distributor.

PALM DIGITAL MEDIA. Website: www.palmdigitalmedia.com. Partnering with Lightning Source, Inc. to distribute e-books.

THE PARABLE GROUP, 3563 Empleo St., San Luis Obispo CA 93401. Toll-free (800)366-6031, ext. 525. Fax (800)543-2136. E-mail: info@parable.com. Website: www.parable.com. A marketing program for Christian bookstores.

PUBLISHERS GROUP WEST, National Headquarters: 1700 Fourth St., Berkeley CA 94710. (510)528-1444. Fax (510)528-3444. E-mail: info@pgw.com. Website: www.pgw.com. Send all inquiries to National Headquarters. Distribution Center: 1170 Trademark Dr., Reno NV 89511. (775)850-2500. Fax (775)850-2501.

PUBLISHERS MARKETING ASSN., 627 Aviation Way, Manhattan Beach CA 90266-7107. (310)372-2732. Fax (310)374-3342. E-mail: info@pma-online.org. Website: www .pma-online.org. Trade association of independent publishers. Provides cooperative marketing programs for books, e-books, and audiobooks. Jan Nathan, exec. dir.

QUALITY BOOKS, 1003 W. Pines Rd., Oregon IL 61061. (815)732-4450. Fax (815)732-4499.

E-mail: carolyn.olson@quality-books.com. Website: www.quality-books.com. Contact: Carolyn Olson. Distributes small press books, videos, audios, DVDs, and CD-ROMs to secular libraries. Asks for 1 copy of the book, plus 30 covers.

SPRING ARBOR DISTRIBUTORS, PO Box 3006, One Ingram Blvd., Mailstop 671, La Vergne TN 37086. Toll-free (800)395-4340. Fax (615)213-5192 or (800)876-0186. E-mail: custserv@springarbor.com. Website: www.springarbor.com. Contact: Karen K. Bishop, Director National Sales. Books, music, Bibles; no gift items or church supplies.

WHITAKER HOUSE PUBLISHERS, 30 Hunt Valley Cir., New Kensington PA 15068. Toll-free (877)793-9800. (724)334-7000. Fax (800)765-1960 or (724)334-1200. E-mail: sales@whitakerhouse.com. Donna Bonarati, intl. sales mngr. (800)444-4484, ext. 246.

+WINDFLOWER DISTRIBUTORS, 67 Flett Ave., Winnipeg MB R2K 3N3 Canada. (204)668-7475. Fax (204)661-8530. E-mail: mennonitebooks@brandtfamily.com. Website: www.mennonitebooks.com. Brandt Family Enterprises. Gilbert Brandt, pres. Book distributor.

WORD ALIVE, INC., 131 Cordite Rd., Winnipeg MB R3W 1S1 Canada. Toll-free (800)665-1468. Fax (800)352-9272. E-mail: orderdesk@wordalive.ca. Website: www.wordalive.ca.

MARKET ANALYSIS

ALL PUBLISHERS IN ORDER OF MOST BOOKS PUBLISHED PER YEAR

PublishAmerica 550 (POD)
Continuum Intl. 250-300
Barbour Publishing 200
Tyndale House 200
Harvest House 190
United Methodist 175
Scarecrow Press 150-200
Cook Communications 125
Eerdmans 120-130
Abingdon Press 120
Baptist Publishing House 120
Zondervan 120
Basic Books 100
Broadman & Holman 100
Hazelden Publishing 100
New York Univ. Press 100
Bethany House 90-100
Christian Focus 90
InterVarsity Press 90
Paulist Press 90
Crossway 85
Christian Ed. Publishers 80
Standard Publishing 75-100
HarperSanFrancisco 75
Multnomah 75
W Publishing Group 75
Liturgical Press 70
Moody Publishers 65-70
Tommy Nelson 65
Love Inspired 60-65
Steeple Hill 60-65
Honor Books 60+
Oxford University 60+
CSS Publishing 60
Fortress Press 60
Kregel 60
Our Sunday Visitor 60
Ambassador-Emerald 55
Pilgrim Press 54
Heartsong Presents 52
Harcourt Religion 50-100
Custom Commun. 50-75
Boyds Mills Press 50
Chalice Press 50
Crossroad Publishing 50
Liguori Publications 50
G. P. Putnam's Sons 50
University Press 50
Westminster/John Knox 50

ZonderKidz 50
Capall Bann 46
Howard Publishing 46
Doubleday Religion 45-50
Editores Betania-Caribe 45
RiverOak 45
Selah Publishing 45
Twenty-Third Publications 45
Nelson Books 42
Faith Kids Books 40-50
Peter Pauper Press 40-50
Jeremy P. Tarcher 40-50
Shaw Books 40-45
Editorial Portavoz 40+
Beacon Hill Press 40
Charisma House 40
Group Publishing 40
Health Communications 40
John Hunt Publishing 40
Jossey-Bass 40
Legacy Press 40
Loyola Press 40
P & R Publishing 40
Youth Specialties 40
Eldridge 35 (plays)
Monarch Books 35
Trinity Press Intl. 35
AMG Publishers 30-40
Hendrickson 30-40
St. Anthony Mess. Press 30-40
Christian Writers E-Book 30
Concordia 30
Genesis Communications 30
Good News Publishers 30 (tracts)
Thomas More 30
Pacific Press 30
Sheed & Ward 30
Pauline Books 25-35
New Leaf Press 25-30
Smyth & Helwys 25-30
Algora Publishing 25
Bridge-Logos 25
Libros Liguori 25
Liturgy Training 25
Meriwether 25 (plays)
Morehouse Publishing 25
WestBow Press 25
New Hope 24-32
Alba House 24

One World 24
St. Augustine's Press 20-40
Univ. of Ottawa Press 20-25
Blue Dolphin 20-24
CharismaKids 20
Christian Publications 20
Cross Cultural 20
Jubilant Press 20
Openbook Publishers 20
Paraclete Press 20
Rainbow Pub./Rainbow Books 20
Resource Publications 20
Scepter Publishers 20
Shining Star 20
Third World Press 20
Dimension Books 18
Big Idea 15-20
Catholic Book Publishing 15-20
College Press 15-20
Focus on the Family 15-20
McDougal Publishing 15-20
Judson Press 15
Lightwave Publishing 15
Mercer Univ. Press—R 15
Rainbow Pub./Legacy Press 15
Still Waters 15
Wesleyan Publishing House 15
Pathway Press 14-16
Discovery House 12-18
Master Books 12-15
Paragon House 12-15
Siloam Press 12-15
Allegiance Press 12
Forward Movement 12
Lamplighter Publishers 12
Promise Press/Suspense 12
Pflaum Publishing 10-20
Canon Press 10-15
Carey Library, Wm. 10-15
Gospel Publishing House 10-15
Ragged Edge 10-15
Summit Pub. Group 10-15
Tapestry Press 10-15
Descant Publishing 10-12
Eerdmans/Young Readers 10-12
Hiddenspring Books 10-12
Lillenas 10-12
Messianic Jewish Publishers 10-12
Starburst Publishers 10-12

Glory Bound Books 10+
ACTA Publications 10
ACU Press 10
BJU Press/Journey Forth 10
Georgetown University Press 10
Haworth Press 10
Lutterworth Press 10
Oregon Catholic Press 10
PREP Publishing 10
Silas Publishing 10
Walk Worthy Press 10
Yale Univ. Press 10
Cistercian Publications 8-14
Emmaus Road 8-10
Holy Cross Orthodox 8-10
Millennium III 8-10
Spence Publishing 8-10
TowleHouse Publishing 8-10
FaithWalk Publishing 8
Neibauer Press 8
Touch Publications 8
Ambassador Books 7
Woodland Gospel 7
Christopher Pub. Hs. 6-8
Americana Publishing 6
Church & Synagogue Libraries 6
ICS Publications 6
Inkling Books 6
Magnus Press 6
Northstone Publishing 6
Square One Publishers 6
Trinity Foundation 6
Wilshire Book Co. 6
Greenwood Publishing 5-30
Troitsa Books 5-20
Conciliar Press 5-10
Hensley Publishing 5-10
Rose Publishing 5-10
World Publishing 5-10
Faith One Publishing 5-8
Perigee Books 5-8
Religious Education Press 5-6
Fair Havens Publications 5
Four Courts Press 5
Mt. Olive College Press 5
Paradise Research 5
Pelican Publishing 5
Friends United Press 4-6
Jireh Publishing 4-6
Baker Tritten 4-5

Larson Publications 4-5
Pickwick Publications 4-5
American Catholic Press 4
Baylor Univ. Press 4
Church Growth Institute 4
Iceagle Press 4
Intl. Awakening Press 4
Langmarc Publishing 4
LifeSong Publishers 4
New Canaan 4
Open Court 4
FamilyLife Publishing 3-12
Cerdic-Publications 3-5
Facts on File 3-5
Northfield Publishing 3-5
Virginia Pines Press 3-5
Quintessential Books 3-4
Tau-Publishing 3-4
ETC Publications 3
Meriwether 3
OSL Publications 3
Wood Lake Books 3
Baker's Plays 2-8
First Fruits of Zion 2-6
Obadiah Press 2-5
Canadian Institute for Law 2-4
Frederick Fell 2-4
Regnery Publishing 2-4
UMI Press 2-4
Cladach Publishing 2-3
Daybreak Books/Rodale 2-3
Diamond Eyes 2-3
Educational Ministries 2-3
Kindred Productions 2-3
Sower's Press 2-3
Canticle Books 2
Devoted to You 2
Genesis Press 2
Read 'N Run Books 2
Rising Star Press 2
Shamarah Publications 2
Barclay Press 1-5
Living Books for All 1-5
Green Pastures Press 1-4
Life Cycle Books 1-3
Hill Street Press 1-2
Players Press 1-2
Write Now 1-2
Gilgal Publications 1
Goetz 1

Good Book 1
Guernica Editions 1
Hay House 1
Noveledit 1
Shoreline 1
Small Helm Press 1

SUBSIDY PUBLISHERS

Xulon Press 1,000
Pleasant Word 300+
Brentwood 267
Essence Publishing 100-150+
Black Forest Press 100
Fairway Press 100
Poet's Cove Press 75
American Binding 60
Creation House Press 50-100
WinePress 50+
Insight Publishing Group 50
Guardian Books 40-50
TEACH Services 40-50
ACW Press 40
Express Publishers 30
Southern Baptist Press 25
Impact Christian Books 20+
Word for Word 15-20
Elderberry Press 15
Providence House 12
Catholic Answers 10-20
Master Design 10-15
Poetry of Today 10-12
Hannibal Books 8-10
Longwood Communications 8
Promise Publishing 6
Fruit-Bearer Publishing 5-10
Book Publishers 5-8
DCTS Publishing 5
Omega House 5
Recovery Communications 4-6
VESTA Publications 4
Winer Foundation 4
Lightning Star Press 2-4
Ampelos Press 1-3
Ambassador House 1-2
Step-By-Step 1-2
Strong Tower Publishing 1-2
Alfred Ali Literary 1
Robbie Dean Press 1

BOOK PUBLISHERS WITH THE MOST BOOKS ON THE BESTSELLER LIST FOR THE LAST YEAR

Note: This tally is based on actual sales in Christian bookstores reported July 2003 to June 2004 (most recent information available). This year's listings reflect the more specific Bestseller topics adopted midyear in 2003, with 21 specific categories. These lists will be even more helpful in determining who is the most successful with different genres. Numbers behind the names indicate the number of titles each publisher had on that bestseller list during the year. The combined list indicates the total number a particular publisher had on all the lists added together. It is interesting to note that in the past the number of publishers on the combined list has varied from a few publishers the first few years (starting at about 26 in 1993), to a much broader number for a couple of years (all time high of 60 in 1996), and then started to drop again in 1998. By last year it was about 58, and this year it dropped to 54. It is interesting to note that there are very dominant leaders in each category. With a combined total of 97 titles this year (89 last year), Barbour has once again shown themselves able not only to produce best-selling books, but to do it in a broad range of categories. This year Zondervan moved ahead of Multnomah into second place, but both of those companies had considerably fewer books on the lists—Zondervan dropping from 71 to 64, and Multnomah from 72 to 50. A close analysis of who is on this list and in what categories will tell you a lot about what publishers to go to with certain projects.

GENERAL INTEREST
1. Barbour 15
2. Hendrickson 3
3. Howard 3
4. Bethany House 1
5. Chosen Books 1
6. Frontier Research 1
7. InterVarsity 1
8. Kregel 1
9. Multnomah 1
10. Oracle House 1
11. Regal 1
12. Tyndale House 1
13. White Stone 1
14. W Publishing 1

BIBLICAL STUDIES
1. Nelson 14
2. Zondervan 8
3. Barbour 4
4. Lifeway 3
5. NavPress 3
6. Regal 2
7. Bantam Books 1
8. Broadman & Holman 1
9. Focus on the Family 1
10. Harvest House 1
11. Moody Publishers 1
12. Multnomah 1
13. New Hope 1
14. Oracle House 1
15. Tyndale House 1

16. WaterBrook 1
17. W Publishing 1

CHARISMATIC BOOKS
1. Warner Faith 4
2. Whitaker House 4
3. Harrison House 1
4. Nelson Books 1
5. Spirit-Filled Books 1

CHRISTIAN LIVING
1. W Publishing 14
2. Nelson Books 12
3. Multnomah 9
4. Zondervan 7
5. Barbour 4
6. Warner Faith 4
7. WaterBrook 3
8. Charisma 2
9. Integrity 2
10. Broadman & Holman 1
11. Chosen 1
12. Crossway 1
13. Howard 1
14. Legacy Press 1
15. Moody Publishers 1
16. Regal 1
17. Tyndale House 1

CHURCH & MINISTRY
1. Zondervan 9
2. Standard 4
3. Broadman & Holman 3

4. Baker 1
5. Liturgy Training 1
6. Nelson Books 1
7. Regal 1

INSPIRATIONAL
1. Barbour 5
2. Multnomah 3
3. Tyndale House 3
4. W Publishing 3
5. Cook 2
6. Broadman & Holman 1
7. Charisma 1
8. Nelson Books 1
9. Warner Faith 1
10. Zondervan 1

MARRIAGE
1. Harvest House 4
2. Multnomah 2
3. Family Life 1
4. Legacy 1
5. Moody 1
6. Revell 1

PARENTING
1. Broadman & Holman 2
2. Howard 2
3. Moody 2
4. Harvest House 1
5. Multnomah 1
6. Nelson Books 1
7. Tyndale House 1

8. WaterBrook 1
9. W Publishing 1
10. Zondervan 1

PRAYER
1. Multnomah 6
2. Harrison House 3
3. Whitaker House 3
4. Zondervan 3
5. Broadman & Holman 2
6. Harvest House 2
7. Nelson Books 2
8. Barbour 1
9. J. Countryman 1
10. InterVarsity 1
11. Regal 1

RELATIONSHIPS
1. Multnomah 6
2. Barbour 1
3. Harrison House 1
4. Harvest House 1
5. Nelson Books 1
6. Revell 1
7. Tyndale House 1
8. Zondervan 1

SPIRITUAL GROWTH
1. Broadman & Holman 5
2. Zondervan 5
3. Multnomah 2
4. Nelson Books 2
5. Barbour 1
6. Charisma 1
7. Impact 1
8. NavPress 1
9. WarnerFaith 1

THEOLOGY
1. Nelson Books 3
2. Whitaker House 3
3. Tyndale House 2
4. Multnomah 1
5. Regal 1
6. Victor 1
7. Warner Faith 1
8. Zondervan 1

WOMEN'S INTEREST
1. Harvest House 7
2. Multnomah 4
3. Howard 2
4. Nelson Books 2
5. WaterBrook 2
6. Bethany House 1
7. Destiny Image 1
8. Integrity 1
9. Moody 1
10. Zondervan 1

FICTION: GENERAL
1. Tyndale 19
2. Zondervan 11
3. Barbour 8
4. W Publishing 5
5. Bethany House 4
6. Multnomah 4
7. Viking 3
8. Warner Faith 3
9. WestBow Press 3
10. Broadman & Holman 2
11. Bantam Books 1
12. Crossway 1
13. Harvest House 1
14. NavPress 1
15. WaterBrook 1

FICTION: HISTORICAL
1. Bethany House 18
2. Tyndale House 8
3. Barbour 6
4. Harvest House 4
5. Multnomah 2
6. Revell 2
7. WaterBrook 2

FICTION: ROMANCE
1. Barbour 16
2. Multnomah 7
3. Harvest House 5
4. Tyndale 2

CHILDREN'S BIBLE STORY BOOKS
1. Cook 6
2. Standard 4
3. Dalmation Press 3
4. ZonderKidz 2
5. Baker 1
6. Barbour 1
7. Broadman & Holman 1
8. Concordia 1
9. Integrity 1
10. Moody Publishing 1
11. Tommy Nelson 1
12. Tyndale Kids 1

CHILDREN'S BOOKS
1. ZonderKidz 20
2. Tommy Nelson 11
3. Standard 6
4. Tyndale Kids 6
5. Crossway 5
6. Barbour 3
7. Broadman & Holman 2
8. Cook 2
9. Legacy Press 2
10. Moody 2
11. Concordia 1

12. Howard 1

YOUNG ADULT BOOKS
1. Tyndale Kids 14
2. Barbour/Discovery 2
3. NavPress 2
4. Nelson Books 2
5. WaterBrook 2
6. Baker 1
7. Broadman & Holman 1
8. Harvest House 1
9. Honor Books 1
10. Moody 1
11. Tommy Nelson 1
12. Revell 1
13. Zondervan 1

DEVOTIONALS
1. Zondervan 7
2. Barbour 5
3. Broadman & Holman 3
4. J. Countryman 3
5. Nelson Books 2
6. Kregel 2
7. W Publishing 2
8. Harvest House 1
9. Honor Books 1
10. Ideals Publications 1
11. Integrity 1
12. Multnomah 1
13. Warner Faith 1

GIFT BOOKS
1. Barbour 25
2. J. Countryman 17
3. Zondervan 8
4. Multnomah 5
5. Broadman & Holman 3
6. Tyndale House 2
7. W Publishing 2
8. Christian Publications 1
9. Honor Books 1
10. Howard 1
11. Regal 1

COMBINED BESTSELLER LISTS (combination of previous 21 lists)
1. Barbour 97
2. Zondervan 64
3. Multnomah 50
4. Nelson Books 49
5. Tyndale House 32
6. Broadman & Holman 30
7. W Publishing 29
8. Harvest House 28
9. Bethany House 24
10. ZonderKidz 22
11. J. Countryman 21

12. Tyndale Kids 21
13. Warner Faith 15
14. Standard 14
15. Tommy Nelson 13
16. WaterBrook 12
17. Howard 10
18. Moody 10
19. Regal 10
20. Whitaker House 10
21. Crossway 7
22. FaithKidz/Chariot 7
23. NavPress 7
24. Harrison House 5
25. Integrity 5
26. Revell 5

27. Charisma House 4
28. Cook 4
29. Legacy 4
30. Baker 3
31. Dalmation Press 3
32. Hendrickson 3
33. Lifeway 3
34. Viking 3
35. Bantam 2
36. Chosen Books 2
37. Concordia 2
38. Honor Books 2
39. InterVarsity 2
40. Oracle House 2
41. Christian Publications 1

42. Destiny Image 1
43. Family Life 1
44. Focus on the Family 1
45. Frontier Research 1
46. Honor Books 1
47. Ideals Publications 1
48. Impact Christian 1
49. Kregel 1
50. Liturgy Training 1
51. New Hope 1
52. Spirit-Filled Books 1
53. Victor Books 1
54. WestBow 1

TOP 50 BOOK PUBLISHERS.

This is a new list this year based on which publishers had the most books on the list of the Top 50 books each month. It varies from the combined list above in that it tracks the top 50 sellers regardless of genre. It is interesting to note that there are only 26 publishers with books on this list during the year.

1. Zondervan 26
2. Barbour 25
3. Nelson Books 19
4. Multnomah 18
5. Tyndale House 15
6. W Publishing 15
7. Broadman & Holman 10
8. Harvest House 9
9. J. Countryman 8

10. Bethany House 3
11. Charisma 3
12. Lifeway 3
13. Moody 3
14. Warner Faith 3
15. WaterBrook 3
16. Crossway 2
17. Integrity 2
18. Revell 2

19. Bantam 1
20. Cook 1
21. Dalmation Press 1
22. Honor Books 1
23. Howard 1
24. Regal 1
25. Standard 1
26. Viking 1

BOOK TOPICS MOST POPULAR WITH PUBLISHERS

Note: The numbers following the topics indicate how many publishers said they were interested in seeing a book on that topic. To find the list of publishers interested in each topic, go to the Topical Listings for books (see Table of Contents).

1. Christian Living 130
2. Inspirational 128
3. Spirituality 126
4. Prayer 124
5. Religion 121
6. Family Life 119
7. Devotional Books 116
8. Bible/Biblical Studies 111
9. Theology 109
10. Marriage 106
11. Faith 104
12. Women's Issues 101
13. Biography 99
14. Parenting 98
15. Fiction: Adult/Religious 92
16. Discipleship 91

17. Christian Education 91
18. Current/Social Issues 89
19. Ethics 89
20. Church History 87
21. Church Life 87
22. Historical 85
23. Evangelism/Witnessing 84
24. Personal Growth 82
25. Apologetics 78
26. Leadership 78
27. Self-help 78
28. Church Renewal 77
29. Doctrinal 76
30. Personal Renewal 75
31. Death/Dying 73
32. Healing 73

33. Controversial Issues 73
34. Bible Commentary 70
35. Fiction: Contemporary 69
36. Youth Books (nonfiction) 69
37. Scholarly 67
38. Reference Books 66
39. Men's Books 66
40. How-to 65
41. Health 65
42. Ethnic/Cultural 64
43. Photographs (for Covers) 63
44. Gift Books 63
45. Fiction: Juvenile (ages 8-12) 62
46. Autobiography 61
47. Social Justice Issues 61
48. Fiction: Historical 60

49. Pastors' Helps 60
50. Spiritual Gifts 59
51. Fiction: Adventure 59
52. Personal Experience 56
53. Philosophy 56
54. Psychology 56
55. Church Traditions 56
56. Humor 54
57. Worship Resources 54
58. Prophecy 54
59. Missionary 53
60. Counseling Aids 53
61. Fiction: Biblical 53
62. Worship 53
63. Stewardship 52
64. Fiction: Literary 51
65. Group Study Books 51
66. Money Management 51
67. Spiritual Warfare 51
68. Singles Issues 50
69. Fiction: Teen/Young Adult 49
70. Archaeology 49
71. World Issues 49
72. Liturgical Studies 48
73. Christian Homeschooling 47
74. Recovery Books 46
75. Divorce 45
76. Eschatology 45
77. Children's Picture Books 45
78. Booklets 44
79. Spiritual Life 44
80. Forgiveness 44

81. Environmental Issues 44
82. Exegesis 43
83. Senior Adult Concerns 43
84. Political 43
85. Sermons 40
86. Sociology 40
87. Fiction: Mystery/Suspense 40
88. Homiletics 40
89. Science 39
90. Cults/Occult 39
91. Children's Easy Readers 39
92. Fiction: Mystery/Romance 39
93. Dating/Sex 38
94. Economics 38
95. Holy Spirit 38
96. Miracles 38
97. Memoirs 38
98. Fiction: Romance 38
99. Fiction: Humor 38
100. Poetry 37
101. Drama 36
102. Time Management 34
103. Religious Tolerance 34
104. Fiction: Historical/Romance 34
105. Retirement 33
106. Curriculum 33
107. Games/Crafts 32
108. Cookbooks 32
109. Homeschooling Resources 32
110. Fiction: Frontier/Romance 32
111. E-books 31
112. Christ 31

113. Fiction: Science Fiction 31
114. Fiction: Frontier 31
115. Creation Science 31
116. Racism 31
117. Christian School Books 31
118. Fiction: Ethnic 30
119. Print-on-demand 29
120. Celebrity Profiles 29
121. Fiction: Fantasy 29
122. Canadian/Foreign 29
123. Holiday/Seasonal 28
124. Sports/Recreation 28
125. Fiction: Short Story Collection 28
126. Music-related Books 28
127. Travel 27
128. Fiction: Allegory 26
129. Youth Programs 25
130. Compilations 25
131. Writing How-to 23
132. Christian Business 22
133. Pamphlets 22
134. Fiction: Plays 21
135. Fiction: Westerns 19
136. Tracts 18
137. Fiction: Novellas 17
138. Fiction: Speculative 15
139. Exposés 15
140. Novelty Books For Kids 14
141. Fiction: Chick Lit 12
142. Children's Board Books 10

COMMENTS

If you are a fiction writer, you are more likely to sell adult fiction (92 possible publishers—7 more than last year) than you are juvenile fiction (62 publishers—3 more than last year), or teen fiction (49 publishers—2 more than last year). These figures indicate that the fiction market is still improving for all three age ranges.

The most popular fiction genres with publishers are (1) Contemporary, 69 markets, (2) historical, 60 markets, (3) Adventure, 59 markets, (4) Biblical, 53 markets, (5) literary, 51 markets, (6) mystery/suspense, 40 markets, and (7) mystery/romance, 33 markets. This year, contemporary moved ahead of historical, and mystery/romance moved up as well. All the numbers above show an increase in actual markets for each genre, for the fifth year in a row.

This year the book market for poetry went up slightly from 34 to 37. That compares to only 16 in 1994, a 53% increase in the last eleven years. With the market just holding its own, most poets will still want to consider self-publishing (look for subsidy publishers listed in another section of this book), or sell to periodicals. Go to the periodical topical listings in this book to find 197 markets for poetry (ten less than last year).

Compared to last year, the same 14 topics are at the top, but each in a different location, with Christian Living at the top.

SUMMARY OF INFORMATION ON CHRISTIAN BOOK PUBLISHERS FOUND IN THE ALPHABETICAL LISTINGS

Note: The following numbers are based on the maximum total estimate for each company. For example, if a company gave a range of 5-10, the averages were based on the higher number, 10. This information will be valuable in determining if the contract offered by your publisher is in line with other publishers in some of these areas. For further help, check the section on editorial services to find those who offer contract evaluations, which are most valuable.

TOTAL MANUSCRIPTS RECEIVED

Two hundred fifty-six publishers indicated they received a combined total of about 231,006 manuscripts during the year. That is an average of 902 manuscripts per publisher, per year, a decrease of about 3% compared to last year. The drop is likely tied to the fact that more publishers are not accepting freelance submissions. It is easy to see why many publishers are refusing to review unsolicited manuscripts. This year some publishers who do accept freelance indicated an increase in the number of manuscripts received. The actual number of manuscripts received ranges from 1 to 10,000 per publisher.

NUMBER OF BOOKS PUBLISHED

Three hundred and twelve publishers reported that they will publish a combined total of 11,735 titles during the coming year. That is an average of almost 38 books per publisher (about 3 more per publisher than last year). The actual number per publisher ranges from 1 to 1,000. If each publisher actually publishes his maximum estimate of books for the year, about 5% of the manuscripts submitted will be published (up about 1% from last year).

AVERAGE FIRST PRINT RUN

Based on 219 book publishers who indicated their average first print run, the average first printing of a book for a new author is just under 4,600 books. That's about the same as last year. Actual print runs ranged from 200 to 20,000 copies. These numbers indicate that publishers are generally publishing about the same number of titles but fewer copies of those titles.

ROYALTIES

Of the 292 publishers who indicated that they paid royalties, 67 (23%) pay on the retail price, 155 (53%) pay on the wholesale price or net, and the remaining 70 did not indicate which. Not all gave specific percentages for their royalties, but of those who did, the average royalty based on the retail price of the book was 8.2% to 13.4% (compared to 8% to 11.8% last year). Actual royalties on retail varied from 2% to 50%. The average royalty based on net varied from 9.5% to 14.3% (compared to 9.4% to 13.9% last year). The average royalties in both categories are up this year. Actual royalties on net varied from 2% to 50%. The recommended royalty based on net is 18%, but only 14% of the Christian publishers counted here are paying 18% or higher.

ADVANCES

Two hundred and sixty-one publishers responded to the question about whether they paid advances. Of those, 140 paid advances, and 121 did not, which means those who do still outnumber those who don't. Of those who pay advances, only 21% (54 publishers) gave a specific amount. The average advance for those 54 ranged from $2,674 to $15,597—a considerable increase compared to last year when the averages were $1,793 to $11,218. These percentages have increased the last two years. Many publishers are reluctant to give actual figures and tend toward the conservative when reporting them, so it's difficult to track this accurately. The actual range is from $250 to $50,000, so ask for the amount that you need or deserve based on past publishing history. (Although one publisher indicated they pay up to a $1 million advance, we didn't include them in order to keep these averages realistic.) Most publishers pay more for established authors or potentially best-selling books. It is not unusual for a first-time author to get no advance or a small one. Once you have one or more books published, feel free to ask for an advance, and raise the amount for each book. Don't be afraid to ask for an advance, even on a first book, if you need the money to support you while you finish the manuscript. Although some publishers say they don't give an advance or are reluctant to name an amount, the truth is, many of those publishers do give advances when warranted.

REPORTING TIME

Waiting for a response from an editor is often the hardest part of the writing business. Of the 288 editors who indicated how long you should have to wait for a response from them, the average time was just over 12 weeks (1 week less than last year). However, since the times they actually gave ranged from 1 to 52 weeks, be sure to check the listing for the publisher you are interested in. Give them a 2- to 4-week grace period; then feel free to write a polite letter asking about the current status of your manuscript. Give them another month to respond, and if you don't hear anything, you can call as a last resort or ask for your manuscript to be returned.

E-MAIL AND WEBSITES

Since such a large percentage of the publishers now have e-mail and Websites, we are no longer tracking these numbers or percentages.

PREFERRED BIBLE VERSION

Book publishers list their preferred Bible versions as NIV, KJV, NRSV, and NKJV, in that order. Each publisher's preference is indicated in the regular listings.

TOPICAL LISTINGS OF PERIODICALS

As soon as you have an article or story idea, look up that topic in the following topical listings (see table of contents for a full list of topics). Study the appropriate periodicals in the primary/alphabetical listings (as well as their writers' guidelines and sample copies) and select those that are most likely targets for the piece you are writing.

Note that most ideas can be written for more than one periodical if you slant them to the needs of different audiences, for example, current events for teens, or pastors, or women. Have a target periodical and audience in mind before you start writing. Each topic is divided by age group/audience, so you can pick appropriate markets for your particular slant.

If the magazine prefers or requires a query letter, be sure to write that letter first and then follow any guidelines or suggestions they make if they give you a go-ahead.

R—Takes reprints
(*)—Indicates new topic this year
($)—Indicates a paying market

APOLOGETICS

ADULT/GENERAL
Alliance Life
$-Catholic Insight
$-Celebrate Life—R
Channels—R
Christian Online
$-Christian Research
Church Herald & Holiness—R
Discerning Poet—R
$-Discipleship Journal—R
Evangelical Advocate—R
$-Faith & Family
Grand Valley Observer—R
$-Horizons (adult)—R
$-Light & Life
$-Lookout—R
$-Montgomery's Journey
$-National Catholic
$-North American Voice—R
$-Our Sunday Visitor
$-Plain Truth—R
$-Presbyterian Record—R
Priscilla Papers—R
Sword and Trumpet—R
Sword of the Lord—R
$-Testimony—R
$-Today's Christian—R
Victory News—R

PASTORS/LEADERS
$-Christian Century—R
Theological Digest—R
$-This Rock

BIBLE STUDIES

ADULT/GENERAL
AGAIN—R
$-alive now!—R
Alliance Life
$-Arlington Catholic
Bread of Life—R
Breakthrough Intercessor—R
$-Catholic Peace Voice—R
$-CGA World—R
Christian Bible Studies.com
Christian Computing—R
Christian Motorsports
Christian Online
Christian Ranchman
$-Christianity Today—R
Church Herald & Holiness—R
Connecting Point—R
Creation Care—R
$-Culture Wars—R
$-Direction
$-Foursquare World Advance—R
$-Gem—R
$-Generation X—R
Grand Valley Observer—R
Heartlight—R
Highway News—R
HopeKeepers—R
$-Indian Life—R
$-Interchange
$-Light & Life
Literary TNT—R
$-Lookout—R
$-Lutheran—R

$-Lutheran Journal—R
Mature Times—R
$-Mature Years—R
Methodist History
$-New Freeman—R
$-New Wineskins—R
$-North American Voice—R
$-Our Sunday Visitor
$-Plain Truth—R
$-Positive Thinking—R
PrayerWorks—R
$-Precepts for Living
Priscilla Papers—R
Quaker Life—R
Singles Scoop—R
$-Sojourners
$-Spiritual Life
Spiritual Voice—R
$-St. Anthony Messenger
Star of Zion
Sword and Trumpet—R
Sword of the Lord—R
$-Testimony—R
thegoodsteward.com—R
Trumpeter—R
$-U.S. Catholic
Victory News—R
$-War Cry—R
$-Way of St. Francis—R

CHILDREN
$-Celebrate
$-Juniorway
$-Primary Street

CHRISTIAN EDUCATION/LIBRARY
$-Children's Ministry
Church & Synagogue Lib.—R
$-Church Educator—R
$-Group
$-Preschool Playhouse
$-Religion Teacher's Journal

MISSIONS
Railroad Evangelist—R
Women of the Harvest

PASTORS/LEADERS
$-African American Pulpit
Angelos—R
$-Building Church Leaders.com
$-Catholic Servant
$-Emmanuel
$-Evangelicals Today—R
$-Let's Worship
$-Ministries Today
$-Pastoral Life—R
Pulpit Helps—R
Quarterly Review
Sewanee Theological Review
Sharing the Practice—R
Strategic Adult Ministries—R
Theological Digest—R
$-Word & World

TEEN/YOUNG ADULT
$-Conqueror—R
$-J.A.M.: Jesus and Me
$-Passageway.org—R
Setmag.com—R
$-Student Leadership—R
Teen Light—R
TeensForJC.com—R
Transcendmag.com—R
$-With—R
$-Young Christian—R
$-Young Salvationist—R
YouthWalk

WOMEN
ChurchWoman
$-Horizons (women)—R
Right to the Heart—R
True Woman
$-Women by Grace—R

BOOK EXCERPTS

ADULT/GENERAL
AGAIN—R
$-alive now!—R
$-Animal Trails—R
Books & Culture

$-Bridal Guides—R
$-Catholic Digest—R
$-Catholic New Times—R
Channels—R
$-Charisma
$-Chicken Soup—R
Christian Motorsports
Christian Observer
$-Christian Renewal—R
$-Culture Wars—R
$-Door—R
Evangelical Advocate—R
$-Generation X—R
$-Home Times—R
HopeKeepers—R
$-Indian Life—R
Jewel Among Jewels
Literary TNT—R
Mature Times—R
Metro Voice—R
New Heart—R
$-New Man—R
$-New Wineskins—R
$-Nostalgia Magazine—R
Parents & Teens—R
$-Portland Magazine
$-Power for Living—R
Priscilla Papers—R
$-Prism—R
Regent Business—R
Sacred Journey—R
$-SCP Journal—R
Singles Scoop—R
Spiritual Voice—R
$-Spring Hill Review—R
Steps
$-Testimony—R
thegoodsteward.com—R
$-Today's Christian—R
Tributes—R
Trumpeter—R
$-U.S. Catholic
$-United Church Observer—R
$-Upscale Magazine
Victory News—R
Walk This Way—R

CHILDREN
$-Guide—R

MISSIONS
Intl. Jour./Frontier—R

PASTORS/LEADERS
$-Christian Century—R
$-Emmanuel
$-Ministries Today

$-Ministry & Liturgy—R
Pastors.com—R
Pulpit Helps—R
Sharing the Practice—R
$-Worldwide Challenge
$-Youthworker

TEEN/YOUNG ADULT
$-Boundless Webzine—R
$-Passageway.org—R
Setmag.com—R
Teen Light—R
TeensForJC.com—R
Transcendmag.com—R

WOMEN
$-Godly Business Woman
Hearts at Home—R
$-Link & Visitor—R
$-MOMsense—R
$-SpiritLed Woman

WRITERS
BOOK Magazine
$-Money the Write Way—R

BOOK REVIEWS

ADULT/GENERAL
African Voices—R
AGAIN—R
$-America
$-Anglican Journal
$-Arlington Catholic
Barefoot Path—R
Books & Culture
$-Cathedral Age
$-Catholic Insight
$-Catholic Peace Voice—R
$-CBA Marketplace
Channels—R
$-Charisma
Christian Computing—R
Christian Journal—R
Christian Media—R
Christian Motorsports
Christian Observer
$-Christian Parents Section
Christian Radio Weekly
$-Christian Renewal—R
$-Christian Research
$-Christian Retailing
$-Christian Social Action—R
$-Christianity Today—R
$-Christianweek
$-Commonweal
$-Cornerstone Christian—R
Creation Care—R

$-Cresset
Crosshome.com
$-Culture Wars—R
Discerning Poet—R
Divine Ascent
$-Dovetail—R
$-Eureka Street
Evangelical Advocate—R
$-Faith & Family
$-Faith Today
$-First Things
Fuse Magazine
$-Generation X—R
Good News Journal
Hannah to Hannah—R
$-Home Times—R
HopeKeepers—R
$-Impact—R
$-Indian Life—R
$-Inland NW Christian
$-Interchange
$-Interim—R
Jewel Among Jewels
$-Joy & Praise
$-Layman
Literary TNT—R
Maranatha News—R
Mars Hill Review
Mature Times—R
Methodist History
MovieGuide
Mutuality—R
$-New Wineskins—R
$-North American Voice—R
$-Parabola—R
Parents & Teens—R
Penwood Review
Perspectives
$-Plain Truth—R
$-Prairie Messenger—R
$-Presbyterian Record—R
$-Presbyterians Today—R
Priscilla Papers—R
$-Prism—R
Quaker Life—R
Radix—R
Reformed Quarterly
Regent Business—R
$-Relevant
Rhubarb
Rose & Thorn
Sacred Journey—R
$-Science & Spirit
$-SCP Journal—R
$-Silver Wings—R
Singles Scoop—R

$-Social Justice—R
$-Sojourners
$-Spiritual Life
Spiritual Voice—R
$-Spring Hill Review—R
Star of Zion
Steps
Studio—R
$-Testimony—R
thegoodsteward.com—R
Time of Singing—R
Tributes—R
Trumpeter—R
$-Upscale Magazine
Valparaiso Poetry—R
Victory News—R
$-Voice of the Lord
Walk This Way—R
$-Way of St. Francis—R
$-Weavings—R
Winsome Wit—R
$-Wireless Age—R

CHILDREN
Barefoot for Kids—R
$-SHINE brightly—R

CHRISTIAN EDUCATION/LIBRARY
$-Caravan
Catholic Library World
Christian Early Education—R
Christian Librarian—R
Christian Library Journal—R
Church & Synagogue Lib.—R
$-Church Libraries—R
Jour./Christianity/Foreign Languages
Jour./Ed. & Christian Belief—R
$-Journal/Adventist Educ.—R
Journal/Christian Education
$-Momentum
$-Teachers of Vision—R

MISSIONS
East-West Church
$-Evangelical Missions—R
Missiology
OpRev Equipper—R
Women of the Harvest

MUSIC
$-CCM Magazine
Hymn

PASTORS/LEADERS
$-African American Pulpit
$-Catechumenate
$-Christian Century—R

Christian Education Journal (CA)—R
Cross Currents
$-Diocesan Dialogue—R
$-Emmanuel
$-Enrichment—R
$-Evangelical Baptist—R
$-Evangelicals Today—R
$-Five Stones—R
$-Horizons (pastor)—R
Journal/Pastoral Care—R
$-Leadership—R
$-Let's Worship
Lutheran Forum—R
$-Lutheran Partners—R
$-Ministries Today
Ministry in Motion—R
$-Pastoral Life—R
Pulpit Helps—R
$-Sermon Notes—R
Sharing the Practice—R
Strategic Adult Ministries—R
$-This Rock
$-WCA News—R
$-Word & World
$-Worship Leader

TEEN/YOUNG ADULT
$-Boundless Webzine—R
$-Devo'Zine—R
$-J.A.M.: Jesus and Me
Setmag.com—R
Teen Light—R
TeensForJC.com—R
Transcendmag.com—R

WOMEN
Anna's Journal—R
Christian Woman's Page—R
ChurchWoman
Footprints
$-Godly Business Woman
Hearts at Home—R
$-Horizons (women)—R
$-inSpirit—R
Praise
Right to the Heart—R
True Woman

WRITERS
$-Advanced Chris. Writer—R
$-Areopagus (UK)
Author-Me.com
$-Christian Communicator—R
$-Cross & Quill—R
$-Fellowscript—R
$-Money the Write Way—R
$-Spirit-Led Writer—R

$-Tickled by Thunder
Upper Case
$-WIN-Informer
Writer's Lifeline
Writers Gazette
$-Writers' Journal

CANADIAN/FOREIGN MARKETS

ADULT/GENERAL
Anglican
$-Abilities
$-Anglican Journal
$-Annals of St. Anne
$-Atlantic Catholic
$-Aujourd'hui Credo—R
$-B.C. Catholic—R
BC Christian News
Bread of Life—R
$-Canada Lutheran—R
Canadian Lutheran
Canadian Mennonite
Catalyst
$-Catholic Insight
$-Catholic New Times—R
Catholic Register
Channels—R
$-Christian Courier (CAN)—R
$-Christian Herald—R
$-Christian Renewal—R
$-Christianweek
$-Common Ground—R
Creation
Crossway/Newsline—R
Crux
$-Dreams & Visions—R
$-Eureka Street
$-Faith & Friends—R
$-Faith Today
Fellowship Magazine
Friend
$-Impact—R
$-Indian Life—R
Insight (for blind)
Insound
Interactive E-Poetry
$-Interim—R
Intouch
Island Catholic News
$-Living Light News—R
Mature Times—R
$-Mennonite Brethren—R
$-Mennonite Historian—R
$-Messenger of St. Anthony
$-Messenger of the Sacred Heart
Mosaic (Canadian Baptist)

Mosaic (Free Methodist)
$-New Freeman—R
$-Peeks & Valleys—R
Plowman—R
$-Prairie Messenger—R
$-Presbyterian Record—R
Rhubarb
$-Shantyman—R
Singles Scoop—R
Studio—R
$-Testimony—R
Time for Rhyme—R
TJ
$-United Church Observer—R
Walk This Way—R
War Cry (Canada)—R

CHRISTIAN EDUCATION/LIBRARY
$-Caravan
$-Christian Educators Journal—R
Jour. of Christian Education

DAILY DEVOTIONALS
$-Rejoice!
$-Words of Life

MISSIONS
Catholic Missions In Canada
Glad Tidings

PASTORS/LEADERS
$-Evangelical Baptist—R
$-Evangelicals Today—R
$-Horizons (pastor)—R
Ministry Matters
Technologies for Worship—R
Theological Digest—R

WOMEN
Christian Women Today—R
$-Esprit—R
Footprints
Life Tools for Women
$-Link & Visitor—R
Making Waves
Tapestry (Canada)
Women Today—R

WRITERS
$-Areopagus (UK)
Author Network E-zine
$-Brady Magazine—R
$-Canadian Writer's Journal—R
$-Exchange—R
$-Fellowscript—R
$-Tickled by Thunder
Writer's Lifeline
Writers Gazette

Writers Manual

CELEBRITY PIECES

ADULT/GENERAL
American Tract Society—R
$-Angels on Earth
$-Arlington Catholic
Breakthrough Intercessor—R
$-Catholic Digest—R
$-Celebrate Life—R
$-Charisma
Christian Journal—R
Christian Motorsports
Christian Online
Christian Radio Weekly
Christian Ranchman
$-Christian Social Action—R
$-Cornerstone Christian—R
$-Door—R
$-Episcopal Life—R
$-Faith & Family
$-Generation X—R
$-God Allows U-Turns—R
Good News Journal
$-Grit
$-Guideposts—R
Heartlight—R
$-Home Times—R
HopeKeepers—R
$-Indian Life—R
$-Inside Journal—R
Jewel Among Jewels
$-Light & Life
$-Live—R
$-Living Light News—R
Maranatha News—R
Metro Voice—R
$-Minnesota Christian—R
$-Montgomery's Journey
Mutuality—R
$-New Man—R
$-New Wineskins—R
$-Nostalgia Magazine—R
$-Positive Thinking—R
$-Power for Living—R
$-Priority!
$-Prism—R
Sacred Journey—R
Spiritual Voice—R
$-Spring Hill Review—R
$-St. Anthony Messenger
$-Testimony—R
thegoodsteward.com—R
$-Today's Christian—R
$-Today's Pentecostal Evangel
Trumpeter—R

$-Vibrant Life—R
Victory News—R
$-War Cry—R
$-Wireless Age—R

CHILDREN
$-American Girl
$-Cadet Quest—R
$-Children's Magic Window
$-Guide—R
$-Guideposts for Kids
$-High Adventure—R
$-SHINE brightly—R
Skipping Stones
$-Winner—R

CHRISTIAN EDUCATION/LIBRARY
$-Children's Ministry

MISSIONS
$-Worldwide Challenge

MUSIC
Christian Music Weekly—R
Tradition

PASTORS/LEADERS
$-Catholic Servant
$-Interpreter
Ministry in Motion—R
$-Pastoral Life—R

TEEN/YOUNG ADULT
$-Boundless Webzine—R
$-Brio—R
$-Brio & Beyond
$-Essential Connection
$-J.A.M.: Jesus and Me
$-Passageway.org—R
Setmag.com—R
$-Sharing the VICTORY—R
Teen Light—R
TeensForJC.com—R
Transcendmag.com—R
$-Young Salvationist—R

WOMEN
$-Godly Business Woman
$-Journey
$-MOMsense—R

WRITERS
Cochran's Corner—R
Upper Case

CHRISTIAN BUSINESS

ADULT/GENERAL
Alliance Life
$-Angels on Earth

Breakthrough Intercessor—R
$-CBA Marketplace
$-Christian Courier (CAN)—R
Christian Journal—R
$-Christian Leader—R
Christian Motorsports
Christian News NW—R
Christian Online
Christian Ranchman
$-Christian Retailing
$-Christianweek
Church Herald & Holiness—R
$-Columbia
$-Cornerstone Christian—R
Disciple's Journal—R
Discovery—R
$-Faith Today
$-Gem—R
$-Generation X—R
$-God Allows U-Turns—R
Good News Journal
$-Gospel Today—R
$-Guideposts—R
Heartlight—R
Highway News—R
$-Indian Life—R
$-Light & Life
Literary TNT—R
$-Living—R
$-Lookout—R
Maranatha News—R
Marketplace
$-MESSAGE
Metro Voice—R
$-Minnesota Christian—R
$-Montgomery's Journey
$-New Freeman—R
$-New Man—R
$-NRB Magazine—R
$-Our Sunday Visitor
$-Power for Living—R
$-Presbyterian Record—R
$-Prism—R
Quaker Life—R
Regent Business—R
$-Resource—R
$-Science & Spirit
$-Social Justice—R
$-St. Anthony Messenger
$-Testimony—R
thegoodsteward.com—R
$-Today's Christian—R
$-Together—R
Trumpeter—R
Victory News—R
$-War Cry—R

$-Wireless Age—R

CHRISTIAN EDUCATION/LIBRARY
$-Resource—R
$-Youth & CE Leadership

MISSIONS
$-Evangelical Missions—R
Missiology
$-Worldwide Challenge

PASTORS/LEADERS
$-African American Pulpit
$-Catholic Servant
$-Christian Camp—R
$-Christian Century—R
$-Evangelicals Today—R
$-Interpreter
$-Ministries Today
$-Pastoral Life—R
Pastors.com—R
Sharing the Practice—R
Technologies for Worship—R
$-Today's Parish—R
$-WCA News—R
$-Your Church—R

TEEN/YOUNG ADULT
$-J.A.M.: Jesus and Me

WOMEN
Christian Women Today—R
$-Godly Business Woman
Right to the Heart—R

WRITERS
$-Money the Write Way—R

CHRISTIAN EDUCATION

ADULT/GENERAL
African Voices—R
$-America
$-Anglican Journal
$-Arlington Catholic
$-B.C. Catholic—R
Breakthrough Intercessor—R
$-Canada Lutheran—R
$-Catholic New Times—R
$-Catholic Parent
$-Catholic Peace Voice—R
$-Celebrate Life—R
Channels—R
Christian C. L. RECORD—R
$-Christian Courier (CAN)—R
$-Christian Examiner
$-Christian Home & School
Christian Journal—R
$-Christian Leader—R

Christian Motorsports
Christian News NW—R
Christian Observer
Christian Online
Christian Ranchman
$-Christian Renewal—R
$-Christian Retailing
$-Christianweek
Church Herald & Holiness—R
$-Columbia
$-Company—R
$-Cornerstone Christian—R
$-Covenant Companion—R
$-Culture Wars—R
$-Direction
$-Eclectic Homeschool
Evangelical Advocate—R
$-Faith Today
$-Foursquare World Advance—R
$-Gem—R
$-Generation X—R
$-God Allows U-Turns—R
Good News Journal
$-Gospel Today—R
Grand Valley Observer—R
Heartlight—R
$-Home Times—R
$-Homeschooling Today—R
$-Indian Life—R
$-Inland NW Christian
$-Interchange
Jewel Among Jewels
$-Layman
$-Light & Life
Literary TNT—R
$-Living Church
$-Lookout—R
$-Lutheran Digest—R
Mature Times—R
$-Messenger of the Sacred Heart
Methodist History
Metro Voice—R
$-Montgomery's Journey
$-National Catholic
$-New Freeman—R
$-New Wineskins—R
$-Our Sunday Visitor
Perspectives
$-Precepts for Living
Presbyterian Outlook
$-Presbyterian Record—R
$-Priority!
$-Prism—R
Quaker Life—R
$-SCP Journal—R

Singles Scoop—R
$-Social Justice—R
$-St. Anthony Messenger
Star of Zion
Sword and Trumpet—R
Sword of the Lord—R
$-Testimony—R
thegoodsteward.com—R
$-Together—R
Trumpeter—R
$-U.S. Catholic
Victory News—R
$-War Cry—R
$-Way of St. Francis—R
$-Wesleyan Life—R

CHILDREN
$-Adventures
$-Celebrate
$-Focus/Clubhouse
$-Juniorway
$-My Friend
$-Primary Street

CHRISTIAN EDUCATION/LIBRARY
$-Caravan
$-Catechist
$-Children's Ministry
Christian Early Education—R
$-Christian Educators Journal—R
Christian Librarian—R
Christian School Education
$-Church Educator—R
$-Evangelizing Today's Child—R
$-Group
$-Ideas Unlimited—R
Jour. of Christian Education
Jour./Christianity/Foreign Languages
Jour./Ed. & Christian Belief—R
$-Journal/Adventist Educ.—R
Journal/Christian Education
$-Kids' Ministry Ideas—R
$-Leader in C. E. Ministries
$-Momentum
$-Preschool Playhouse
$-Religion Teacher's Journal
$-Resource—R
$-Teachers Interaction
$-Teachers of Vision—R
$-Today's Catholic Teacher—R
$-Youth & CE Leadership

MISSIONS
$-Evangelical Missions—R
Missiology

PASTORS/LEADERS
$-African American Pulpit
$-Barefoot—R
$-Building Church Leaders.com
$-Catholic Servant
$-Christian Century—R
Christian Education Journal (CA)—R
Cross Currents
$-Enrichment—R
$-Eucharistic Ministries—R
$-Evangelical Baptist—R
$-Evangelicals Today—R
$-Five Stones—R
$-Interpreter
$-Lutheran Partners—R
$-Ministries Today
$-Ministry & Liturgy—R
Ministry in Motion—R
$-Pastoral Life—R
Pastors.com—R
Quarterly Review
$-RevWriter Resource
Sharing the Practice—R
Technologies for Worship—R
$-Today's Parish—R
$-Word & World
$-Youthworker

TEEN/YOUNG ADULT
$-J.A.M.: Jesus and Me
Setmag.com—R
Teen Light—R
TeensForJC.com—R
Transcendmag.com—R
$-Young Adult Today—R

WOMEN
$-Godly Business Woman
$-inSpirit—R
Just Between Us—R
Right to the Heart—R

CHRISTIAN LIVING

ADULT/GENERAL
AGAIN—R
$-alive now!—R
$-Alive!—R
Alliance Life
$-America
American Tract Society—R
$-Angels on Earth
$-Annals of St. Anne
$-Arlington Catholic
$-B.C. Catholic—R
$-Beacon
$-Bible Advocate—R
Bread of Life—R

Breakthrough Intercessor—R
$-Bridal Guides—R
$-Canada Lutheran—R
$-Catholic Digest—R
$-Catholic Forester—R
$-Catholic New York
$-Catholic Parent
$-Celebrate Life—R
$-CGA World—R
Channels—R
$-Charisma
Chattels of the Heart—R
$-Chicken Soup—R
Christian Bible Studies.com
$-Christian Courier (CAN)—R
Christian Courier (WI)—R
$-Christian Examiner
Christian Journal—R
$-Christian Leader—R
Christian Motorsports
Christian Observer
Christian Online
$-Christian Parenting—R
Christian Radio Weekly
Christian Ranchman
$-Christian Social Action—R
$-Christianity Today—R
$-Christianweek
Church Herald & Holiness—R
$-Church of God EVANGEL
$-Columbia
$-Commonweal
Connecting Point—R
$-Cornerstone Christian—R
$-Covenant Companion—R
Crossway/Newsline—R
$-Culture Wars—R
$-Decision
Desert Call—R
$-Direction
$-Discipleship Journal—R
Divine Ascent
$-Eclectic Homeschool
$-Evangel—R
Evangelical Advocate—R
$-Faith & Family
$-Faith & Friends—R
$-Faith Today
$-Family Digest—R
$-Fellowship Focus—R
$-Focus on the Family
$-Foursquare World Advance—R
$-Gem—R
$-Generation X—R
$-God Allows U-Turns—R

$-Good News—R
Good News Journal
$-Gospel Today—R
Gospel Tract—R
Grand Valley Observer—R
$-Guideposts—R
Hannah to Hannah—R
Heartlight—R
Highway News—R
$-Home Times—R
$-Homeschooling Today—R
HopeKeepers—R
$-Horizons (adult)—R
$-Indian Life—R
$-Inland NW Christian
$-Interchange
Jewel Among Jewels
Keys to Living—R
$-Layman
Leaves—R
$-Light & Life
$-Liguorian
Literary TNT—R
$-Live—R
$-Living—R
$-Living Church
$-Lookout—R
$-Lutheran—R
$-Lutheran Digest—R
$-Lutheran Journal—R
Maranatha News—R
$-Marian Helper—R
$-Marriage Partnership—R
Mature Times—R
$-Mature Years—R
$-Men of Integrity—R
$-Mennonite Brethren—R
$-MESSAGE
MESSAGE/Open Bible—R
$-Messenger of the Sacred Heart
Methodist History
Metro Voice—R
$-Minnesota Christian—R
$-Montgomery's Journey
Mutuality—R
$-New Freeman—R
New Heart—R
$-New Man—R
$-New Wineskins—R
$-North American Voice—R
$-Nostalgia Magazine—R
$-Oblates
$-Our Sunday Visitor
Parents & Teens—R
$-Physician—R

$-Plain Truth—R
Plowman—R
$-Positive Thinking—R
$-Power for Living—R
PrayerWorks—R
$-Presbyterian Record—R
$-Presbyterians Today—R
$-Psychology for Living—R
$-Purpose—R
Quaker Life—R
Regent Business—R
$-Relate—R
$-Science & Spirit
$-SCP Journal—R
$-Seek—R
$-Senior Living
$-Signs of the Times—R
$-Silver Wings—R
Singles Scoop—R
$-Social Justice—R
Southwest Kansas
$-Spiritual Life
$-St. Anthony Messenger
$-Standard—R
Storyteller—R
Sword and Trumpet—R
Sword of the Lord—R
$-Testimony—R
thegoodsteward.com—R
$-Today's Christian—R
$-Today's Pentecostal Evangel
$-Together—R
Trumpeter—R
$-U.S. Catholic
$-United Church Observer—R
$-Vibrant Life—R
Victory News—R
$-Vision—R
$-War Cry—R
$-Way of St. Francis—R
$-Wesleyan Life—R
$-Young Christian—R

CHILDREN
$-Adventures
Barefoot for Kids—R
$-BREAD/God's Children—R
$-Club Connection
$-Courage—R
$-Focus/Clubhouse
$-Focus/Clubhouse Jr.
$-High Adventure—R
$-Juniorway
$-My Friend
$-Partners—R
$-Passport—R

$-Pockets—R
$-Primary Street
$-SHINE brightly—R

CHRISTIAN EDUCATION/LIBRARY
Church & Synagogue Lib.—R
$-Church Educator—R
$-Group
$-Resource—R
$-Teachers Interaction
$-Teachers of Vision—R
$-Youth & CE Leadership

MISSIONS
$-Evangelical Missions—R
Missiology
$-One
Women of the Harvest
$-Worldwide Challenge

PASTORS/LEADERS
$-African American Pulpit
Angelos—R
$-Building Church Leaders.com
$-Catholic Servant
Cell Group—R
$-Christian Century—R
$-Emmanuel
$-Eucharistic Ministries—R
$-Evangelical Baptist—R
$-Evangelicals Today—R
$-Interpreter
$-Ministries Today
Ministry in Motion—R
Net Results
$-Pastoral Life—R
Pastors.com—R
$-Proclaim—R
Pulpit Helps—R
Quarterly Review
$-Rev.
$-Review for Religious
$-RevWriter Resource
Sharing the Practice—R
$-Spiritual Spinach—R
Steps
Technologies for Worship—R
$-Today's Christian Preacher—R
$-Word & World

TEEN/YOUNG ADULT
$-Boundless Webzine—R
$-Brio & Beyond
$-Conqueror—R
$-Devo'Zine—R
$-Essential Connection
$-J.A.M.: Jesus and Me

$-Passageway.org—R
$-Real Faith in Life—R
Setmag.com—R
$-Sharing the VICTORY—R
$-Student Leadership—R
Teen Light—R
TeensForJC.com—R
Transcendmag.com—R
$-With—R
$-Young and Alive—R
$-Young Christian—R
$-Young Salvationist—R

WOMEN
$-At the Center—R
Christian Woman's Page—R
$-Esprit—R
$-Godly Business Woman
Hearts at Home—R
$-Horizons (women)—R
$-inSpirit—R
$-Journey
Just Between Us—R
$-Link & Visitor—R
Lutheran Woman's Quar.
$-MOMsense—R
P31 Woman—R
Right to the Heart—R
$-Today's Christian Woman—R
True Woman
$-Woman's Touch—R
$-Women Alive!—R
$-Women by Grace—R
Women of the Cross—R
Women Today—R

CHURCH GROWTH

ADULT/GENERAL
AGAIN—R
Alliance Life
$-America
Breakthrough Intercessor—R
$-Bridal Guides—R
$-Catholic Peace Voice—R
Channels—R
$-Charisma
Christian Bible Studies.com
$-Christian Examiner
Christian Journal—R
$-Christian Leader—R
Christian Motorsports
Christian News NW—R
Christian Online
$-Christianweek
Church Herald & Holiness—R
$-Covenant Companion—R

$-Culture Wars—R
$-Direction
$-Discipleship Journal—R
Evangelical Advocate—R
$-Faith Today
$-Fellowship Focus—R
$-Gem—R
$-Generation X—R
$-Good News—R
Grand Valley Observer—R
$-Indian Life—R
$-Inside Journal—R
$-Interchange
Jewel Among Jewels
$-Layman
$-Light & Life
$-Liguorian
$-Living Church
$-Lookout—R
$-Messenger of the Sacred Heart
$-Minnesota Christian—R
$-National Catholic
$-New Freeman—R
$-New Wineskins—R
$-North American Voice—R
$-On Mission
$-Our Sunday Visitor
Presbyterian Outlook
$-Presbyterians Today—R
Quaker Life—R
$-Signs of the Times—R
$-St. Anthony Messenger
Star of Zion
Sword and Trumpet—R
Sword of the Lord—R
$-Testimony—R
thegoodsteward.com—R
Trumpeter—R
Victory News—R

CHRISTIAN EDUCATION/LIBRARY
$-Caravan
$-Children's Ministry
Church & Synagogue Lib.—R

MISSIONS
$-Evangelical Missions—R
Missiology
$-PIME World—R
$-Wesleyan Life—R
$-Worldwide Challenge
$-Youth & CE Leadership

PASTORS/LEADERS
$-African American Pulpit
$-Building Church Leaders.com

$-Catholic Servant
$-Christian Century—R
$-Church Growth Network—R
$-Clergy Journal—R
$-Creator—R
$-Enrichment—R
$-Eucharistic Ministries—R
$-Evangelical Baptist—R
$-Evangelicals Today—R
$-Five Stones—R
$-Horizons (pastor)—R
Interpretation
$-Interpreter
Jour./Amer. Soc./Chur. Growth—R
$-Let's Worship
$-Ministries Today
$-Ministry
$-Ministry & Liturgy—R
Ministry in Motion—R
Net Results
$-Pastoral Life—R
Pastors.com—R
$-Priest
Pulpit Helps—R
$-Rev.
$-RevWriter Resource
$-Sermon Notes—R
Sharing the Practice—R
Technologies for Worship—R
$-WCA News—R
$-Worship Leader
$-Your Church—R

TEEN/YOUNG ADULT
$-Passageway.org—R
Setmag.com—R
TeensForJC.com—R
Transcendmag.com—R
$-Young Christian—R

WOMEN
$-inSpirit—R
Just Between Us—R
Right to the Heart—R

CHURCH HISTORY

ADULT/GENERAL
African Voices—R
$-America
$-Arkansas Catholic—R
$-Bridal Guides—R
$-Catholic Digest—R
$-Catholic Insight
$-Catholic Peace Voice—R
$-Catholic Sentinel
Channels—R

$-Christian History & Biography—R
Christian Online
$-Christian Renewal—R
$-Christianity Today—R
Church Herald & Holiness—R
$-Columbia
$-Company—R
$-Covenant Companion—R
$-Cresset
$-Direction
Divine Ascent
Evangel, The
$-Family Digest—R
Friends Journal—R
$-Generation X—R
Grand Valley Observer—R
$-Horizons (adult)—R
$-Indian Life—R
Journal of Church & State
$-Light & Life
$-Liguorian
$-Lutheran Journal—R
Maranatha News—R
$-Mennonite Historian—R
$-Messiah Magazine
Methodist History
$-National Catholic
$-New Wineskins—R
$-North American Voice—R
$-Nostalgia Magazine—R
$-Our Sunday Visitor
PrayerWorks—R
Priscilla Papers—R
$-Purpose—R
Re:generation Quarterly
$-Science & Spirit
$-Social Justice—R
$-St. Anthony Messenger
Star of Zion
Sword and Trumpet—R
$-Testimony—R
thegoodsteward.com—R
Trumpeter—R
Victory News—R
$-Way of St. Francis—R
$-Young Christian—R

CHILDREN
$-BREAD/God's Children—R
$-Courage—R
$-Primary Pal (IL)

CHRISTIAN EDUCATION/LIBRARY
Catholic Library World
$-Teachers Interaction

MISSIONS
$-Evangelical Missions—R
Missiology
Railroad Evangelist—R

PASTORS/LEADERS
$-African American Pulpit
Angelos—R
$-Christian Century—R
Cross Currents
$-Eucharistic Ministries—R
Interpretation
$-Interpreter
$-Ministries Today
$-Pastoral Life—R
$-Priest
$-Review for Religious
$-Theology Today
$-This Rock

TEEN/YOUNG ADULT
$-Breakaway
$-Essential Connection
$-Living My Faith
$-Passageway.org—R
$-Real Faith in Life—R
Setmag.com—R
TeensForJC.com—R
Transcendmag.com—R
$-Young Christian—R

WOMEN
$-History's Women—R
$-Horizons (women)—R
$-Link & Visitor—R
$-SpiritLed Woman

WRITERS
Cochran's Corner—R

CHURCH LIFE

ADULT/GENERAL
AGAIN—R
Alliance Life
$-America
Breakthrough Intercessor—R
$-Bridal Guides—R
$-Catholic Digest—R
$-Catholic Insight
$-Catholic Sentinel
Channels—R
Christian Journal—R
$-Christian Leader—R
Christian Motorsports
Christian Online
$-Christian Standard—R
$-Christianweek
Church Herald & Holiness—R

$-Columbia
$-Company—R
$-Cornerstone Christian—R
$-Covenant Companion—R
$-Decision
$-Direction
Evangelical Advocate—R
$-Faith & Family
$-Faith Today
$-Family Digest—R
$-Fellowship Focus—R
$-Gem—R
$-Generation X—R
$-God Allows U-Turns—R
$-Good News—R
Grand Valley Observer—R
Hannah to Hannah—R
$-Horizons (adult)—R
$-Impact—R
$-Interchange
Leaves—R
$-Light & Life
$-Liguorian
$-Living Church
$-Lookout—R
$-Lutheran Digest—R
$-Lutheran Journal—R
Maranatha News—R
$-Men of Integrity—R
$-Mennonite Historian—R
MESSAGE/Open Bible—R
$-Minnesota Christian—R
$-Montgomery's Journey
Mutuality—R
$-National Catholic
$-New Freeman—R
$-New Wineskins—R
$-North American Voice—R
$-Nostalgia Magazine—R
$-Our Sunday Visitor
$-Prairie Messenger—R
PrayerWorks—R
$-Precepts for Living
$-Presbyterian Record—R
$-Presbyterians Today—R
Priscilla Papers—R
$-Purpose—R
Quaker Life—R
$-Relate—R
$-Silver Wings—R
$-St. Anthony Messenger
Star of Zion
$-Testimony—R
thegoodsteward.com—R
$-Today's Christian—R
$-Today's Pentecostal Evangel

Trumpeter—R
Victory News—R
$-Vision—R
$-Way of St. Francis—R
$-Wesleyan Life—R

CHILDREN
$-Juniorway
$-Primary Street

CHRISTIAN EDUCATION/LIBRARY
$-Caravan
$-Children's Ministry
$-Church Educator—R
$-Group
$-Momentum
$-Resource—R
$-Youth & CE Leadership

MISSIONS
$-Evangelical Missions—R

PASTORS/LEADERS
$-African American Pulpit
$-Barefoot—R
$-Building Church Leaders.com
$-Catholic Servant
Cell Group—R
$-Christian Century—R
$-Clergy Journal—R
$-Emmanuel
$-Enrichment—R
$-Eucharistic Ministries—R
$-Evangelical Baptist—R
$-Evangelicals Today—R
$-Five Stones—R
$-Horizons (pastor)—R
Interpretation
$-Interpreter
$-Leadership—R
$-Lutheran Partners—R
$-Ministries Today
$-Ministry
$-Ministry & Liturgy—R
Ministry in Motion—R
Net Results
$-Pastoral Life—R
Pastors.com—R
$-Priest
Pulpit Helps—R
Quarterly Review
$-Rev.
$-Review for Religious
$-RevWriter Resource
Sharing the Practice—R
Steps
Technologies for Worship—R

Theological Digest—R
$-WCA News—R
$-Worship Leader

TEEN/YOUNG ADULT
$-J.A.M.: Jesus and Me
$-Passageway.org—R
Teen Light—R
$-Young Christian—R

WOMEN
Handmaiden—R
$-Horizons (women)—R
$-inSpirit—R
Right to the Heart—R
$-SpiritLed Woman

CHURCH MANAGEMENT

ADULT/GENERAL
$-America
Breakthrough Intercessor—R
$-Bridal Guides—R
Channels—R
Christian Computing—R
$-Christian Leader—R
Christian News NW—R
Christian Online
$-Christian Standard—R
$-Christianweek
$-Cornerstone Christian—R
$-Culture Wars—R
$-Direction
Disciple's Journal—R
Evangelical Advocate—R
$-Faith Today
$-Fellowship Focus—R
$-Gem—R
$-Generation X—R
$-God Allows U-Turns—R
$-Good News, Etc—R
$-Gospel Today—R
$-Layman
$-Living Church
$-Lookout—R
$-Lutheran Digest—R
Metro Voice—R
$-New Freeman—R
$-Our Sunday Visitor
$-Presbyterians Today—R
Priscilla Papers—R
Quaker Life—R
Regent Business—R
$-St. Anthony Messenger
Star of Zion
$-Testimony—R
thegoodsteward.com—R
Trumpeter—R

$-U.S. Catholic
Victory News—R
$-Wesleyan Life—R
$-Young Christian—R

CHRISTIAN EDUCATION/LIBRARY
$-Children's Ministry
$-Church Educator—R
$-Resource—R
$-Youth & CE Leadership

MISSIONS
$-Evangelical Missions—R

PASTORS/LEADERS
$-African American Pulpit
$-Building Church Leaders.com
$-Catholic Servant
$-Christian Century—R
Christian Management—R
$-Church Growth Network—R
$-Clergy Journal—R
$-Enrichment—R
$-Evangelical Baptist—R
$-Evangelicals Today—R
$-Five Stones—R
Interpretation
$-Interpreter
Jour./Amer. Soc./Chur. Growth—R
$-Leadership—R
$-Ministries Today
$-Ministry
Ministry in Motion—R
Net Results
OpRev Equipper—R
$-Pastoral Life—R
Pastors.com—R
$-Priest
Pulpit Helps—R
Quarterly Review
$-Rev.
$-RevWriter Resource
Sharing the Practice—R
Technologies for Worship—R
$-Word & World
$-Worship Leader
$-Your Church—R
$-Youthworker

WOMEN
Just Between Us—R
Right to the Heart—R

CHURCH OUTREACH

ADULT/GENERAL
AGAIN—R
$-Alive!—R

$-America
$-Beacon
$-Bible Advocate—R
Breakthrough Intercessor—R
$-Bridal Guides—R
$-Cathedral Age
$-Catholic Forester—R
$-Catholic Sentinel
Channels—R
$-Charisma
$-Christian Leader—R
Christian Motorsports
Christian News NW—R
Christian Online
$-Christian Research
$-Christian Social Action—R
$-Christian Standard—R
$-Christianweek
Church Herald & Holiness—R
$-Church of God EVANGEL
$-Columbia
$-Company—R
$-Cornerstone Christian—R
$-Covenant Companion—R
$-Culture Wars—R
$-Decision
$-Direction
$-Episcopal Life—R
$-Evangel—R
Evangelical Advocate—R
$-Faith & Friends—R
$-Faith Today
$-Fellowship Focus—R
$-Gem—R
$-God Allows U-Turns—R
$-Good News—R
HopeKeepers—R
$-Layman
$-Light & Life
$-Liguorian
Literary TNT—R
$-Living Church
$-Lookout—R
$-Lutheran—R
$-Lutheran Digest—R
Maranatha News—R
Mature Times—R
MESSAGE/Open Bible—R
Metro Voice—R
$-Minnesota Christian—R
$-National Catholic
$-New Freeman—R
$-New Wineskins—R
$-On Mission
$-Our Sunday Visitor

$-Precepts for Living
Presbyterian Outlook
$-Presbyterians Today—R
Priscilla Papers—R
$-Prism—R
Quaker Life—R
$-Relate—R
$-Science & Spirit
$-SCP Journal—R
Singles Scoop—R
$-Social Justice—R
$-St. Anthony Messenger
$-St. Joseph's Messenger—R
Sword of the Lord—R
$-Testimony—R
thegoodsteward.com—R
$-Today's Christian—R
Trumpeter—R
$-U.S. Catholic
Victory News—R
$-Vision—R
$-Way of St. Francis—R
$-Wesleyan Life—R
$-Young Christian—R

CHILDREN
$-Juniorway
$-Kids' Ministry Ideas—R
$-Primary Street
$-SHINE brightly—R

CHRISTIAN EDUCATION/LIBRARY
$-Caravan
$-Children's Ministry
$-Church Educator—R
$-Group
$-Journal/Adventist Educ.—R
$-Resource—R
$-Youth & CE Leadership

MISSIONS
$-Evangelical Missions—R
Missiology
$-One
$-PIME World—R
Railroad Evangelist—R
Wesleyan World—R
$-Worldwide Challenge

PASTORS/LEADERS
$-African American Pulpit
$-Barefoot—R
$-Building Church Leaders.com
$-Catholic Servant
Cell Group—R
$-Christian Century—R
$-Church Growth Network—R

$-Clergy Journal—R
Cornerstone Youth—R
$-Emmanuel
$-Enrichment—R
$-Eucharistic Ministries—R
$-Evangelical Baptist—R
$-Evangelicals Today—R
$-Five Stones—R
Interpretation
$-Interpreter
Jour./Amer. Soc./Chur. Growth—R
$-Leadership—R
$-Let's Worship
$-Lutheran Partners—R
$-Ministries Today
$-Ministry
$-Ministry & Liturgy—R
Ministry in Motion—R
Net Results
$-Pastoral Life—R
Pastors.com—R
$-Priest
Pulpit Helps—R
Quarterly Review
$-Rev.
$-RevWriter Resource
Sharing the Practice—R
Steps
Technologies for Worship—R
$-Today's Parish—R
$-WCA News—R
$-Word & World
$-Worship Leader

TEEN/YOUNG ADULT
$-Conqueror—R
$-J.A.M.: Jesus and Me
Teen Light—R
$-With—R
$-Young Christian—R

WOMEN
$-inSpirit—R
$-Journey
Just Between Us—R
$-Passageway.org—R
Right to the Heart—R
Setmag.com—R
$-SpiritLed Woman
TeensForJC.com—R
Transcendmag.com—R
Women Today—R

CHURCH TRADITIONS

ADULT/GENERAL
AGAIN—R

$-America
$-Arkansas Catholic—R
Breakthrough Intercessor—R
$-Bridal Guides—R
$-Canada Lutheran—R
$-Catholic Digest—R
$-Catholic Forester—R
$-Celebrate Life—R
Channels—R
$-Christian Examiner
$-Christian History & Biography—R
$-Christian Leader—R
Christian Online
$-Christian Research
$-Columbia
$-Cresset
Desert Call—R
$-Direction
$-Faith & Family
$-Faith Today
$-Family Digest—R
$-Gem—R
$-Generation X—R
$-Gospel Today—R
$-Impact—R
$-Indian Life—R
$-Light & Life
$-Liguorian
$-Living Church
$-Lutheran Journal—R
Maranatha News—R
$-Mennonite Historian—R
$-National Catholic
$-New Freeman—R
$-New Wineskins—R
$-North American Voice—R
$-Nostalgia Magazine—R
$-Our Sunday Visitor
Perspectives
PrayerWorks—R
$-Presbyterian Record—R
Priscilla Papers—R
$-Science & Spirit
$-Seeds
$-St. Anthony Messenger
Star of Zion
$-Testimony—R
thegoodsteward.com—R
$-Together—R
Trumpeter—R
Victory News—R
$-Way of St. Francis—R
$-Young Christian—R

CHILDREN
$-Celebrate

$-My Friend

CHRISTIAN EDUCATION/LIBRARY
$-Caravan
$-Catechist
$-Children's Ministry
$-Religion Teacher's Journal
$-Teachers Interaction
$-Youth & CE Leadership

MISSIONS
Missiology

MUSIC
Tradition

PASTORS/LEADERS
$-African American Pulpit
$-Building Church Leaders.com
$-Eucharistic Ministries—R
$-Evangelicals Today—R
$-Interpreter
$-Ministries Today
$-Pastoral Life—R
Pastors.com—R
$-Priest
Quarterly Review
$-Review for Religious
Sharing the Practice—R
Theological Digest—R

TEEN/YOUNG ADULT
$-Passageway.org—R
Setmag.com—R
Teen Light—R
TeensForJC.com—R
Transcendmag.com—R
$-Young Christian—R

WOMEN
Handmaiden—R
$-Horizons (women)—R

WRITERS
Cochran's Corner—R

CONTROVERSIAL ISSUES

ADULT/GENERAL
AGAIN—R
$-America
American Tract Society—R
$-Bible Advocate—R
$-Catholic Peace Voice—R
$-Celebrate Life—R
Channels—R
$-Charisma
Christian Bible Studies.com
$-Christian Courier (CAN)—R

$-Christian Examiner
$-Christian Home & School
Christian Media—R
Christian Motorsports
Christian Online
Christian Radio Weekly
$-Christian Renewal—R
$-Christian Response—R
$-Christian Social Action—R
$-Christian Standard—R
$-Christianity Today—R
$-Christianweek
$-Commonweal
$-Cornerstone Christian—R
$-Cresset
Crossway/Newsline—R
$-Culture Wars—R
Discovery—R
$-Door—R
$-Dovetail—R
Evangelical Advocate—R
$-Faith Today
$-First Things
$-Generation X—R
$-God Allows U-Turns—R
$-Good News—R
$-Gospel Today—R
Grand Valley Observer—R
$-Home Times—R
$-Homeschooling Today—R
$-Interim—R
$-Layman
$-Light & Life
Literary TNT—R
$-Living Church
$-Lookout—R
$-Lutheran—R
Mature Times—R
$-MESSAGE
Metro Voice—R
$-Minnesota Christian—R
MovieGuide
Mutuality—R
$-National Catholic
$-New Man—R
$-New Wineskins—R
$-North American Voice—R
$-Now What?—R
$-Our Sunday Visitor
Perspectives
$-Plain Truth—R
$-Prairie Messenger—R
$-Presbyterian Record—R
Priscilla Papers—R
$-Prism—R
$-Psychology for Living—R

Rhubarb
Sacred Journey—R
$-Science & Spirit
$-SCP Journal—R
Singles Scoop—R
$-Social Justice—R
Spiritual Voice—R
$-Spirituality & Health
$-Spring Hill Review—R
$-St. Anthony Messenger
$-Testimony—R
thegoodsteward.com—R
$-Today's Christian—R
Trumpeter—R
$-U.S. Catholic
Victory News—R
$-War Cry—R
$-Way of St. Francis—R
Winsome Wit—R
$-World & I—R
Xavier Review
$-Young Christian—R

CHILDREN
$-Passport—R
Skipping Stones

CHRISTIAN EDUCATION/LIBRARY
$-Children's Ministry
$-Church Educator—R
$-Teachers Interaction
$-Teachers of Vision—R
$-Today's Catholic Teacher—R

MISSIONS
East-West Church
$-Evangelical Missions—R
Intl. Jour./Frontier—R
Missiology
$-Worldwide Challenge

MUSIC
Hymn

PASTORS/LEADERS
$-African American Pulpit
$-Building Church Leaders.com
$-Christian Camp—R
$-Christian Century—R
$-Clergy Journal—R
Cross Currents
$-Emmanuel
$-Eucharistic Ministries—R
$-Interpreter
$-Let's Worship
$-Ministry & Liturgy—R
$-Pastoral Life—R

$-Priest
Pulpit Helps—R
Strategic Adult Ministries—R
Theological Digest—R
$-This Rock
$-Word & World
$-Worship Leader
$-Youthworker

TEEN/YOUNG ADULT
$-Boundless Webzine—R
$-Brio—R
$-Brio & Beyond
$-Insight—R
$-J.A.M.: Jesus and Me
$-Passageway.org—R
Setmag.com—R
$-Student Leadership—R
Teen Light—R
TeensForJC.com—R
Transcendmag.com—R
$-With—R
$-Young Salvationist—R

WOMEN
$-Esprit—R
$-Godly Business Woman
$-inSpirit—R
$-SpiritLed Woman
Women Today—R

WRITERS
$-Areopagus (UK)
Cochran's Corner—R

CRAFTS

ADULT/GENERAL
$-Cappers
$-CGA World—R
Christian Online
$-Eclectic Homeschool
$-Faith & Family
$-Generation X—R
$-Grit
$-Living—R
$-Mature Living
$-World & I—R
$-Young Christian—R

CHILDREN
$-Adventures
Barefoot for Kids—R
$-BREAD/God's Children—R
$-Cadet Quest—R
$-Celebrate
$-Children's Magic Window
$-Courage—R
$-Focus/Clubhouse

$-Focus/Clubhouse Jr.
$-Guideposts for Kids
$-My Friend
$-On the Line—R
$-Pockets—R
$-PrayKids!—R
$-SHINE brightly—R
$-Story Friends—R

CHRISTIAN EDUCATION/LIBRARY
$-Catechist
$-Children's Ministry
$-Evangelizing Today's Child—R
$-Religion Teacher's Journal
$-Teachers Interaction

TEEN/YOUNG ADULT
$-Brio—R
$-Brio & Beyond
$-Guideposts Sweet 16—R
$-J.A.M.: Jesus and Me
Setmag.com—R
Teen Light—R
TeensForJC.com—R
Transcendmag.com—R

WOMEN
Keeping Hearts & Home
$-MOMsense—R
P31 Woman—R
$-Women by Grace—R

CREATION SCIENCE

ADULT/GENERAL
$-Catholic New Times—R
$-Christian Courier (CAN)—R
$-Christian Examiner
Christian Observer
$-Christian Renewal—R
$-Christian Research
Creation
$-Creative Nonfiction
Discovery—R
Evangelical Advocate—R
$-Faith Today
Grand Valley Observer—R
$-Homeschooling Today—R
Literary TNT—R
$-Live—R
$-Living—R
$-Lookout—R
Maranatha News—R
$-Minnesota Christian—R
MovieGuide
$-New Freeman—R
$-Social Justice—R

$-St. Anthony Messenger
$-Standard—R
Sword and Trumpet—R
Sword of the Lord—R
$-Testimony—R
thegoodsteward.com—R
$-Today's Pentecostal Evangel
Trumpeter—R
Victory News—R
$-War Cry—R
$-Young Christian—R

CHILDREN
Barefoot for Kids—R
$-BREAD/God's Children—R
$-Courage—R
$-Nature Friend
$-Primary Pal (IL)

CHRISTIAN EDUCATION/LIBRARY
$-Journal/Adventist Educ.—R

PASTORS/LEADERS
$-Building Church Leaders.com
Cross Currents
$-Pastoral Life—R
Pulpit Helps—R

TEEN/YOUNG ADULT
$-Boundless Webzine—R
$-J.A.M.: Jesus and Me
$-Passageway.org—R
$-Real Faith in Life—R

WOMEN
$-Godly Business Woman

CULTS/OCCULT

ADULT/GENERAL
Alliance Life
$-America
American Tract Society—R
$-Charisma
$-Christian Examiner
$-Christian Renewal—R
$-Christian Research
$-Christianity Today—R
$-Culture Wars—R
Discovery—R
$-Faith Today
$-God Allows U-Turns—R
$-Lookout—R
Metro Voice—R
$-Minnesota Christian—R
New Heart—R
$-Now What?—R
$-On Mission

$-SCP Journal—R
$-Shantyman—R
$-Social Justice—R
$-Testimony—R
thegoodsteward.com—R
Trumpeter—R
Victory News—R
$-Voice of the Lord

MISSIONS
Intl. Jour./Frontier—R
Missiology

PASTORS/LEADERS
$-Building Church Leaders.com
$-Interpreter
Journal/Pastoral Care—R
$-This Rock
$-Word & World

TEEN/YOUNG ADULT
$-Passageway.org—R
$-Real Faith in Life—R
Setmag.com—R
$-Teenage Christian—R
TeensForJC.com—R
Transcendmag.com—R

WOMEN
$-SpiritLed Woman

CURRENT/SOCIAL ISSUES

ADULT/GENERAL
$-Alive!—R
Alliance Life
$-America
American Tract Society—R
$-Anglican Journal
$-Apocalypse Chronicles—R
$-Arlington Catholic
$-B.C. Catholic—R
$-BGC World—R
$-Bible Advocate—R
$-Catholic Insight
$-Catholic New York
$-Catholic Peace Voice—R
Channels—R
$-Charisma
Christian Bible Studies.com
$-Christian Courier (CAN)—R
Christian Courier (WI)—R
$-Christian Examiner
$-Christian Home & School
$-Christian Leader—R
Christian Motorsports
Christian News NW—R
Christian Observer

Christian Online
$-Christian Parenting—R
Christian Ranchman
$-Christian Renewal—R
$-Christian Research
$-Christian Social Action—R
$-Christian Standard—R
$-Christianity Today—R
$-Christianweek
$-Church of God EVANGEL
$-Columbia
$-Commonweal
$-Cornerstone Christian—R
$-Cresset
$-Culture Wars—R
$-Direction
Discovery—R
$-Door—R
$-Dovetail—R
$-Eureka Street
Evangelical Advocate—R
$-Faith & Family
$-Faith Today
$-First Things
$-Foursquare World Advance—R
Friends Journal—R
$-Gem—R
$-Generation X—R
$-God Allows U-Turns—R
$-Good News—R
Good News Journal
Grand Valley Observer—R
Hannah to Hannah—R
Heartlight—R
Highway News—R
$-Home Times—R
$-Homeschooling Today—R
$-Indian Life—R
Indiana Christian News
$-Inland NW Christian
$-Interchange
$-Interim—R
Island Catholic News
Journal of Church & State
$-Layman
$-Liberty—R
$-Light & Life
$-Liguorian
Literary TNT—R
$-Living—R
$-Lookout—R
$-Lutheran—R
$-Marian Helper—R
Mature Times—R
$-Men of Integrity—R

Men of the Cross—R
$-Mennonite Brethren—R
$-MESSAGE
MESSAGE/Open Bible—R
Metro Voice—R
$-Minnesota Christian—R
$-Montgomery's Journey
Mutuality—R
$-National Catholic
$-New Freeman—R
New Heart—R
$-New Man—R
$-New Wineskins—R
$-North American Voice—R
$-Now What?—R
$-Our Sunday Visitor
Perspectives
$-Plain Truth—R
Plowman—R
$-Prairie Messenger—R
$-Presbyterian Record—R
Priscilla Papers—R
$-Prism—R
$-Psychology for Living—R
$-Purpose—R
Quaker Life—R
Re:generation Quarterly
$-Relevant
Sacred Journey—R
$-SCP Journal—R
$-Seeds
$-Senior Living
$-Shantyman—R
$-Silver Wings—R
Singles Scoop—R
$-Social Justice—R
$-Sojourners
$-Special Living—R
Spiritual Voice—R
$-Spirituality & Health
$-Spring Hill Review—R
$-St. Anthony Messenger
$-St. Joseph's Messenger—R
$-Testimony—R
thegoodsteward.com—R
$-Today's Christian—R
$-Together—R
Trumpeter—R
Victory News—R
$-War Cry—R
$-Way of St. Francis—R
West Wind Review
Winsome Wit—R
$-World & I—R
$-Young Christian—R

CHILDREN
$-Club Connection
$-Guideposts for Kids
$-Passport—R
Skipping Stones

CHRISTIAN EDUCATION/LIBRARY
$-Caravan
$-Catechist
$-Children's Ministry
$-Church Educator—R
$-Evangelizing Today's Child—R
$-Momentum

MISSIONS
Missiology
$-New World Outlook
$-PIME World—R
Women of the Harvest
$-Worldwide Challenge

MUSIC
$-CCM Magazine

PASTORS/LEADERS
$-African American Pulpit
$-Building Church Leaders.com
$-Catholic Servant
$-Christian Camp—R
$-Christian Century—R
$-Clergy Journal—R
$-Eucharistic Ministries—R
$-Evangelicals Today—R
$-Horizons (pastor)—R
$-Interpreter
Journal/Pastoral Care—R
$-Pastoral Life—R
$-Priest
Pulpit Helps—R
Quarterly Review
$-Rev.
$-RevWriter Resource
Sharing the Practice—R
Steps
Strategic Adult Ministries—R
Theological Digest—R
$-Theology Today
$-This Rock
$-WCA News—R
$-Word & World
Youth Culture
$-Youthworker

TEEN/YOUNG ADULT
$-Boundless Webzine—R
$-Brio—R
$-Brio & Beyond

$-Conqueror—R
$-Devo'Zine—R
$-J.A.M.: Jesus and Me
$-Passageway.org—R
Setmag.com—R
Teen Light—R
$-Teenage Christian—R
TeensForJC.com—R
Transcendmag.com—R
$-With—R
$-Young Adult Today—R
$-Young Salvationist—R

WOMEN
Christian Woman's Page—R
$-Esprit—R
$-Godly Business Woman
Handmaiden—R
Hearts at Home—R
$-Horizons (women)—R
$-inSpirit—R
$-Journey
$-Link & Visitor—R
Making Waves
$-SpiritLed Woman
Women Today—R

WRITERS
$-Areopagus (UK)
Beginnings
$-Writer

DEATH/DYING

ADULT/GENERAL
AGAIN—R
$-Alive!—R
American Tract Society—R
$-Arlington Catholic
$-Bible Advocate—R
Breakthrough Intercessor—R
$-Celebrate Life—R
Channels—R
$-Chicken Soup—R
Christian Bible Studies.com
$-Christian Leader—R
Christian Online
$-Christian Parenting—R
Christian Ranchman
$-Christian Social Action—R
$-Christianity Today—R
$-Cornerstone Christian—R
$-Creative Nonfiction
$-Cresset
$-Cup of Comfort—R
$-Dovetail—R
$-Evangel—R
Evangelical Advocate—R

$-Faith & Family
$-Faith Today
$-Gem—R
$-Generation X—R
$-God Allows U-Turns—R
$-Guideposts—R
Heartlight—R
Highway News—R
$-Homeschooling Today—R
HopeKeepers—R
$-Horizons (adult)—R
$-Interim—R
$-Liguorian
Mature Times—R
$-Men of Integrity—R
$-MESSAGE
$-Messenger of the Sacred Heart
$-Minnesota Christian—R
$-National Catholic
$-New Freeman—R
New Heart—R
$-New Wineskins—R
$-North American Voice—R
$-Now What?—R
$-Our Sunday Visitor
Perspectives
$-Physician—R
$-Plain Truth—R
$-Positive Thinking—R
$-Prairie Messenger—R
Presbyterian Outlook
$-Presbyterians Today—R
$-Prism—R
$-Psychology for Living—R
Quaker Life—R
$-Relate—R
Sacred Journey—R
$-Shantyman—R
$-Signs of the Times—R
$-Silver Wings—R
Singles Scoop—R
$-Social Justice—R
$-Spring Hill Review—R
$-St. Anthony Messenger
$-Testimony—R
thegoodsteward.com—R
$-Today's Christian—R
Tributes—R
Trumpeter—R
Victory News—R
$-War Cry—R
$-Way of St. Francis—R
$-Wesleyan Life—R

CHILDREN
$-Guideposts for Kids

Skipping Stones

CHRISTIAN
EDUCATION/LIBRARY
$-Church Educator—R

PASTORS/LEADERS
$-African American Pulpit
$-Building Church Leaders.com
$-Catholic Servant
$-Christian Camp—R
$-Christian Century—R
$-Clergy Journal—R
$-Eucharistic Ministries—R
$-Evangelical Baptist—R
$-Interpreter
Journal/Pastoral Care—R
$-Pastoral Life—R
$-Priest
Pulpit Helps—R
$-Rev.
Sharing the Practice—R
$-Today's Christian Preacher—R

TEEN/YOUNG ADULT
$-Brio—R
$-Brio & Beyond
$-Passageway.org—R
Setmag.com—R
Teen Light—R
TeensForJC.com—R
Transcendmag.com—R
$-With—R
$-Young Salvationist—R

WOMEN
$-Esprit—R
$-Godly Business Woman
$-Horizons (women)—R
$-inSpirit—R
Reflections
$-SpiritLed Woman
Women Today—R

WRITERS
Beginnings
Cochran's Corner—R

DEVOTIONALS/
MEDITATIONS

ADULT/GENERAL
$-alive now!—R
$-Animal Trails—R
$-Annals of St. Anne
$-Arlington Catholic
Barefoot Path—R
Bread of Life—R
Breakthrough Intercessor—R

$-Bridal Guides—R
$-Catholic Peace Voice—R
CBN.com—R
$-CGA World—R
$-Charisma
Chattels of the Heart—R
$-Chicken Soup—R
Christian Journal—R
Christian Motorsports
Christian Online
Christian Ranchman
$-Christianity Today—R
Church Herald & Holiness—R
$-Cornerstone Christian—R
$-Covenant Companion—R
Creation Care—R
Crosshome.com
Divine Ascent
$-Evangel—R
Evangelical Advocate—R
$-Faith & Family
$-Faith & Friends—R
$-Family Digest—R
$-Foursquare World Advance—R
$-Gem—R
$-Good News—R
Good News Journal
Gospel Tract—R
Hannah to Hannah—R
Heartlight—R
Highway News—R
HopeKeepers—R
$-Ideals—R
Indiana Christian News
$-Interchange
Jewel Among Jewels
Keys to Living—R
Leaves—R
LifeTimes Catholic
$-Liguorian
Literary TNT—R
$-Living Church
$-Lookout—R
Maranatha News—R
$-Mature Living
Mature Times—R
$-Mennonite Brethren—R
$-Messenger of the Sacred Heart
Metro Voice—R
Mutuality—R
$-National Catholic
$-New Freeman—R
New Heart—R
$-New Wineskins—R
$-North American Voice—R
$-Positive Thinking—R

PrayerWorks—R
$-Presbyterian Record—R
$-Prism—R
Quaker Life—R
$-Queen of All Hearts
Radix—R
$-Seeds
$-Signs of the Times—R
$-Silver Wings—R
Singles Scoop—R
Spiritual Voice—R
$-Sports Spectrum
$-St. Anthony Messenger
$-Standard—R
Star of Zion
Sword of the Lord—R
$-Testimony—R
thegoodsteward.com—R
$-Today's Christian—R
$-Today's Pentecostal Evangel
Trumpeter—R
$-U.S. Catholic
Victory News—R
$-Vision—R
$-War Cry—R
$-Way of St. Francis—R
$-Weavings—R
$-Young Christian—R

CHILDREN
$-Club Connection
$-Keys for Kids—R
$-Pockets—R
$-Primary Pal (IL)
Skipping Stones

CHRISTIAN EDUCATION/LIBRARY
$-Caravan
$-Children's Ministry
Church & Synagogue Lib.—R
$-Church Educator—R
$-Group

DAILY DEVOTIONALS
Anchor Devotional
Closer Walk
Daily Dev. for Deaf
$-Daily Meditation
Daily Walk
$-Devotions
Family Walk
Forward Day by Day
Fruit of the Vine
Home Altar
Indeed
Penned from the Heart

$-Quiet Hour
Quiet Walk
$-Rejoice!
$-Secret Place
Soul Journey
$-These Days
$-Upper Room
$-Word in Season
$-Words of Life

MISSIONS
Women of the Harvest

PASTORS/LEADERS
$-Barefoot—R
$-Catholic Servant
$-Church Worship
$-Emmanuel
$-Evangelical Baptist—R
$-Evangelicals Today—R
Journal/Pastoral Care—R
$-Priest
Pulpit Helps—R
$-RevWriter Resource
Sharing the Practice—R

TEEN/YOUNG ADULT
$-Breakaway
$-Brio—R
$-Brio & Beyond
$-Conqueror—R
$-Devo'Zine—R
$-Passageway.org—R
$-Real Faith in Life—R
Setmag.com—R
Teen Light—R
TeensForJC.com—R
Transcendmag.com—R
$-With—R
$-Young Adult Today—R
$-Young and Alive—R
$-Young Christian—R
$-Young Salvationist—R

WOMEN
Christian Woman's Page—R
ChurchWoman
$-Godly Business Woman
$-Horizons (women)—R
$-Journey
Keeping Hearts & Home
$-Melody of the Heart
$-Woman's Touch—R
$-Women Alive!—R
$-Women by Grace—R

WRITERS
Beginnings

$-Cross & Quill—R
$-Spirit-Led Writer—R
Upper Case
$-WIN-Informer

DISCIPLESHIP

ADULT/GENERAL
$-alive now!—R
Alliance Life
$-Arlington Catholic
$-BGC World—R
$-Bible Advocate—R
Bread of Life—R
Breakthrough Intercessor—R
$-Canada Lutheran—R
$-Catholic New Times—R
$-Charisma
Chattels of the Heart—R
Christian Bible Studies.com
Christian Journal—R
$-Christian Leader—R
Christian Motorsports
Christian Online
Christian Ranchman
$-Christian Standard—R
$-Christianity Today—R
$-Christianweek
Church Herald & Holiness—R
$-Cornerstone Christian—R
Creation Care—R
$-Decision
$-Direction
$-Discipleship Journal—R
$-Evangel—R
Evangelical Advocate—R
$-Faith & Family
$-Faith & Friends—R
$-Faith Today
$-Fellowship Focus—R
$-Gem—R
$-Good News—R
Grand Valley Observer—R
Heartlight—R
Highway News—R
$-Homeschooling Today—R
$-Indian Life—R
$-Inland NW Christian
Jewel Among Jewels
$-Layman
$-Light & Life
$-Liguorian
Literary TNT—R
$-Lookout—R
$-Men of Integrity—R
Men of the Cross—R

MESSAGE/Open Bible—R
Metro Voice—R
$-Minnesota Christian—R
$-Montgomery's Journey
Mosaic (Canadian Baptist)
$-National Catholic
$-New Freeman—R
$-New Wineskins—R
$-North American Voice—R
$-NRB Magazine—R
Perspectives
PrayerWorks—R
$-Precepts for Living
$-Prism—R
$-Purpose—R
Quaker Life—R
Regent Business—R
$-Signs of the Times—R
$-St. Anthony Messenger
$-St. Joseph's Messenger—R
$-Standard—R
$-Stewardship—R
Sword of the Lord—R
$-Testimony—R
thegoodsteward.com—R
$-Today's Christian—R
Trumpeter—R
$-U.S. Catholic
Victory News—R
Walk This Way—R
$-War Cry—R
$-Way of St. Francis—R
$-Wesleyan Life—R
$-Young Christian—R

CHILDREN
$-BREAD/God's Children—R
$-Club Connection
$-Evangelizing Today's Child—R
$-Juniorway
$-Passport—R
$-Primary Street

CHRISTIAN EDUCATION/LIBRARY
$-Church Educator—R
$-Evangelizing Today's Child—R
$-Group
$-Resource—R

MISSIONS
Missiology
$-PIME World—R
Wesleyan World—R
$-Worldwide Challenge

PASTORS/LEADERS
$-African American Pulpit

Angelos—R
$-Barefoot—R
$-Building Church Leaders.com
$-Catholic Servant
Cell Group—R
$-Christian Camp—R
Christian Education Journal (CA)—R
$-Church Growth Network—R
$-Clergy Journal—R
$-Emmanuel
$-Eucharistic Ministries—R
$-Evangelical Baptist—R
$-Evangelicals Today—R
$-Interpreter
Jour./Amer. Soc./Chur. Growth—R
$-Leadership—R
$-Lutheran Partners—R
$-Ministry
$-Ministry & Liturgy—R
Ministry in Motion—R
Net Results
$-Pastoral Life—R
$-Priest
$-Proclaim—R
Quarterly Review
$-Rev.
$-Review for Religious
$-RevWriter Resource
Sharing the Practice—R
Steps
Theological Digest—R
$-Word & World
$-Youthworker

TEEN/YOUNG ADULT
$-Boundless Webzine—R
$-Brio—R
$-Brio & Beyond
$-Conqueror—R
$-Devo'Zine—R
$-Passageway.org—R
$-Real Faith in Life—R
Setmag.com—R
$-SHINE brightly—R
$-Student Leadership—R
Teen Light—R
$-Teenage Christian—R
TeensForJC.com—R
Transcendmag.com—R
$-With—R
$-Young Salvationist—R

WOMEN
Christian Woman's Page—R
Christian Women Today—R
$-Esprit—R
$-Godly Business Woman

$-inSpirit—R
$-Journey
Just Between Us—R
$-Link & Visitor—R
P31 Woman—R
Right to the Heart—R
$-SpiritLed Woman
$-Today's Christian Woman—R
$-Woman's Touch—R
$-Women Alive!—R
$-Women by Grace—R
Women of the Cross—R

DIVORCE

ADULT/GENERAL
Alliance Life
$-America
American Tract Society—R
$-Angels on Earth
$-Arlington Catholic
$-Bible Advocate—R
Breakthrough Intercessor—R
$-Bridal Guides—R
$-Catholic Digest—R
$-Charisma
Christian Bible Studies.com
$-Christian Examiner
$-Christian Home & School
Christian Motorsports
Christian Online
$-Christian Parenting—R
Christian Ranchman
$-Christian Social Action—R
$-Creative Nonfiction
$-Culture Wars—R
$-Cup of Comfort—R
$-Dovetail—R
$-Faith Today
$-Focus on the Family
$-Gem—R
$-Generation X—R
$-God Allows U-Turns—R
$-Guideposts—R
Highway News—R
$-Home Times—R
$-Homeschooling Today—R
$-Indian Life—R
$-Interim—R
$-Liguorian
$-Living—R
$-Living Church
$-MESSAGE
Metro Voice—R
$-Minnesota Christian—R
$-National Catholic

$-New Freeman—R
New Heart—R
$-New Wineskins—R
$-Now What?—R
Parents & Teens—R
$-Physician—R
$-Positive Thinking—R
Priscilla Papers—R
$-Prism—R
$-Psychology for Living—R
$-Shantyman—R
$-Signs of the Times—R
$-Smart Families—R
$-Social Justice—R
Spiritual Voice—R
$-Spring Hill Review—R
$-St. Anthony Messenger
$-Testimony—R
thegoodsteward.com—R
$-Today's Christian—R
Trumpeter—R
$-U.S. Catholic
Victory News—R
$-War Cry—R
$-World & I—R
$-Young Christian—R

CHILDREN
$-Guideposts for Kids
$-Winner—R

CHRISTIAN EDUCATION/LIBRARY
$-Catechist
$-Children's Ministry

MISSIONS
$-Worldwide Challenge

PASTORS/LEADERS
$-Building Church Leaders.com
$-Interpreter
Journal/Pastoral Care—R
$-Ministry
$-Pastoral Life—R
$-Priest
Pulpit Helps—R
$-Rev.
Sharing the Practice—R
Strategic Adult Ministries—R
$-Word & World

TEEN/YOUNG ADULT
$-Brio—R
$-Brio & Beyond
$-Listen—R
$-Passageway.org—R
Teen Light—R

$-Teenage Christian—R

WOMEN
$-Esprit—R
$-Godly Business Woman
$-MOMsense—R
Reflections
$-SpiritLed Woman
$-Women by Grace—R
Women Today—R

WRITERS
Beginnings
Cochran's Corner—R

DOCTRINAL

ADULT/GENERAL
AGAIN—R
$-America
$-Anglican Journal
$-B.C. Catholic—R
$-Bible Advocate—R
Breakthrough Intercessor—R
Channels—R
$-Charisma
Christian Media—R
Christian Motorsports
Christian Online
$-Christian Research
$-Christianity Today—R
Church Herald & Holiness—R
$-Cresset
$-Culture Wars—R
$-Faith & Family
$-Faith Today
$-First Things
$-Generation X—R
Grand Valley Observer—R
$-Homeschooling Today—R
$-Horizons (adult)—R
$-Impact—R
$-Layman
$-Light & Life
$-Liguorian
$-Lookout—R
Mature Times—R
$-Men of Integrity—R
$-MESSAGE
MESSAGE/Open Bible—R
Metro Voice—R
$-National Catholic
$-New Freeman—R
$-New Wineskins—R
$-North American Voice—R
$-Our Sunday Visitor
Priscilla Papers—R
$-Queen of All Hearts

$-SCP Journal—R
Singles Scoop—R
$-Social Justice—R
$-St. Anthony Messenger
Sword and Trumpet—R
Sword of the Lord—R
$-Testimony—R
thegoodsteward.com—R
$-This Rock
Trumpeter—R
$-U.S. Catholic
Victory News—R
$-Young Christian—R

CHRISTIAN EDUCATION/LIBRARY
$-Catechist

MISSIONS
Intl Jour./Frontier—R
Missiology
$-Worldwide Challenge

PASTORS/LEADERS
$-Building Church Leaders.com
$-Catholic Servant
$-Christian Century—R
$-Emmanuel
$-Eucharistic Ministries—R
$-Evangelical Baptist—R
$-Ministry
$-Pastoral Life—R
Pulpit Helps—R
Quarterly Review
Sewanee Theological Review
Theological Digest—R
$-Theology Today
$-This Rock
$-Word & World
$-Worship Leader

TEEN/YOUNG ADULT
$-Essential Connection
$-Passageway.org—R
$-Real Faith in Life—R
$-Student Leadership—R
$-Teenage Christian—R

WOMEN
$-SpiritLed Woman

ECONOMICS

ADULT/GENERAL
$-America
$-Bridal Guides—R
$-Catholic Peace Voice—R
$-CBA Marketplace
Christian C. L. RECORD—R

Christian Media—R
Christian Motorsports
Christian Online
Christian Ranchman
$-Christian Renewal—R
$-Christian Retailing
$-Christian Social Action—R
$-Covenant Companion—R
$-Cresset
$-Culture Wars—R
$-Faith & Family
$-Faith Today
$-First Things
$-Generation X—R
Good News Journal
Highway News—R
$-Home Times—R
$-Homeschooling Today—R
$-Layman
$-Light & Life
$-Liguorian
Metro Voice—R
MovieGuide
$-National Catholic
$-New Freeman—R
$-NRB Magazine—R
$-Positive Thinking—R
$-Presbyterian Record—R
$-Prism—R
Regent Business—R
$-Relevant
$-SCP Journal—R
$-Social Justice—R
Spiritual Voice—R
$-Spring Hill Review—R
$-St. Anthony Messenger
$-Testimony—R
thegoodsteward.com—R
Trumpeter—R
$-U.S. Catholic
Victory News—R
$-World & I—R

PASTORS/LEADERS
$-Building Church Leaders.com
$-Christian Century—R
$-Interpreter
$-Pastoral Life—R
$-Priest
$-Rev.
$-Today's Parish—R
$-Word & World

TEEN/YOUNG ADULT
Setmag.com—R
Teen Light—R
TeensForJC.com—R

Transcendmag.com—R

WOMEN
$-Godly Business Woman

ENCOURAGEMENT

ADULT/GENERAL
Alliance Life
$-Animal Trails—R
Barefoot Path—R
$-Bible Advocate—R
$-Brave Hearts
$-Bridal Guides—R
$-Catholic Digest—R
Channels—R
Chattels of the Heart—R
Christian Journal—R
Christian Online
Christian Ranchman
$-Cup of Comfort—R
$-Eclectic Homeschool
$-Evangel—R
Evangelical Advocate—R
$-Faith & Family
$-Faith & Friends—R
$-Faith Today
$-Family Digest—R
$-Generation X—R
$-God Allows U-Turns—R
Grand Valley Observer—R
Hannah to Hannah—R
Highway News—R
$-Homeschooling Today—R
Keys to Living—R
$-Light & Life
$-Liguorian
Literary TNT—R
$-Living—R
$-Lookout—R
$-Lutheran Digest—R
$-Mature Living
$-Men of Integrity—R
New Heart—R
$-New Wineskins—R
$-North American Voice—R
$-Over the Back Fence—R
PrayerWorks—R
$-Purpose—R
Quaker Life—R
Regent Business—R
Sacred Journey—R
$-Seek—R
$-Senior Living
$-Silver Wings—R
$-Testimony—R
$-Today's Christian—R

$-Together—R
Tributes—R
Victory News—R
$-Wesleyan Life—R
$-Young Christian—R

CHILDREN
Barefoot for Kids—R
$-BREAD/God's Children—R
$-Cadet Quest—R

CHRISTIAN EDUCATION/LIBRARY
$-Children's Ministry
Christian Early Education—R

PASTORS/LEADERS
$-Building Church Leaders.com
$-Evangelical Baptist—R
Ministry in Motion—R

TEEN/YOUNG ADULT
$-Brio—R
$-Brio & Beyond
Teen Light—R
$-Young Christian—R

WOMEN
Christian Woman's Page—R
$-Esprit—R
$-inSpirit—R
$-MOMsense—R
P31 Woman—R
$-SpiritLed Woman
$-Today's Christian Woman—R
$-Woman's Touch—R
$-Women by Grace—R

ENVIRONMENTAL ISSUES

ADULT/GENERAL
$-Anglican Journal
$-Catholic Forester—R
$-Catholic Peace Voice—R
Christian Bible Studies.com
$-Christian Courier (CAN)—R
Christian Motorsports
Christian Online
$-Christian Social Action—R
$-Common Ground—R
$-Commonweal
$-Covenant Companion—R
Creation Care—R
$-Cresset
Desert Call—R
$-Faith Today
$-Generation X—R
Hard Row to Hoe
$-Home Times—R

$-Indian Life—R
$-Layman
$-Light & Life
$-Liguorian
$-Living Church
$-Lookout—R
$-Lutheran—R
Mature Times—R
Metro Voice—R
$-Minnesota Christian—R
$-National Catholic
$-New Freeman—R
$-New Wineskins—R
$-North American Voice—R
Pegasus Review—R
Perspectives
Plowman—R
$-Prairie Messenger—R
Presbyterian Outlook
$-Prism—R
$-Purpose—R
Quaker Life—R
Sacred Journey—R
$-Science & Spirit
$-SCP Journal—R
$-Seeds
Singles Scoop—R
Spiritual Voice—R
$-Spring Hill Review—R
$-St. Anthony Messenger
$-St. Joseph's Messenger—R
$-Testimony—R
thegoodsteward.com—R
Trumpeter—R
Victory News—R
$-War Cry—R
$-Way of St. Francis—R
$-World & I—R
$-Young Christian—R

CHILDREN
$-Guideposts for Kids
$-My Friend
$-On the Line—R
$-Pockets—R
$-SHINE brightly—R
Skipping Stones

PASTORS/LEADERS
$-Building Church Leaders.com
$-Christian Camp—R
$-Christian Century—R
$-Eucharistic Ministries—R
$-Interpreter
Journal/Christian Education
$-Lutheran Partners—R
$-Pastoral Life—R

$-Rev.
$-Word & World

TEEN/YOUNG ADULT
$-Devo'Zine—R
$-Passageway.org—R
Setmag.com—R
$-Student Leadership—R
Teen Light—R
TeensForJC.com—R
Transcendmag.com—R
$-With—R

WOMEN
$-Esprit—R
$-Godly Business Woman
$-inSpirit—R
Reflections

ESSAYS

ADULT/GENERAL
African Voices—R
$-Ancient Paths—R
$-Annals of St. Anne
$-Arlington Catholic
Barefoot Path—R
Books & Culture
Breakthrough Intercessor—R
$-Catholic Answer
$-Catholic Digest—R
$-Catholic Parent
$-Catholic Peace Voice—R
Chattels of the Heart—R
$-Chicken Soup—R
$-Christian Courier (CAN)—R
Christian Motorsports
Christian Online
$-Christian Parents Section
$-Christian Renewal—R
$-Commonweal
$-Company—R
$-Cornerstone Christian—R
Creation Care—R
$-Creative Nonfiction
$-Cresset
$-Culture Wars—R
$-Cup of Comfort—R
$-Direction
$-Door—R
$-Dovetail—R
$-Eureka Street
$-Faith Today
$-First Things
$-Flutters of the Heart
$-Gem—R
$-Generation X—R
Hannah to Hannah—R

Highway News—R
$-Home Times—R
$-Image/WA
$-Impact—R
$-Interim—R
$-Liguorian
Literary TNT—R
$-Living—R
Mars Hill Review
Metro Voice—R
Mutuality—R
$-National Catholic
$-New Wineskins—R
$-Over the Back Fence—R
$-Parabola—R
Pegasus Review—R
Penwood Review
Perspectives
$-Plain Truth—R
$-Portland Magazine
$-Presbyterian Record—R
$-Prism—R
Re:generation Quarterly
Rose & Thorn
Sacred Journey—R
$-SCP Journal—R
$-Senior Living
$-Spiritual Life
$-Spring Hill Review—R
SR: A Journal—R
$-St. Anthony Messenger
Storyteller—R
$-Testimony—R
thegoodsteward.com—R
$-Tidewater Parent—R
Tributes—R
Trumpeter—R
Valparaiso Poetry—R
Victory News—R
$-War Cry—R
$-Way of St. Francis—R
$-World & I—R
Xavier Review

CHILDREN
$-Nature Friend
Skipping Stones

CHRISTIAN EDUCATION/LIBRARY
Catholic Library World

MISSIONS
Missiology
$-PFI World Report—R
$-PIME World—R
Railroad Evangelist—R

MUSIC
$-Creator—R

PASTORS/LEADERS
$-African American Pulpit
$-Catholic Servant
$-Christian Century—R
Cross Currents
$-Emmanuel
Journal/Pastoral Care—R
$-Pastoral Life—R
Sharing the Practice—R
Steps
Theological Digest—R
$-Word & World
$-Youthworker

TEEN/YOUNG ADULT
$-Boundless Webzine—R
$-Passageway.org—R
Setmag.com—R
Teen Light—R
TeensForJC.com—R
Transcendmag.com—R
$-Young and Alive—R

WOMEN
Anna's Journal—R
$-Godly Business Woman
$-MOMsense—R

WRITERS
Author-Me.com
BOOK Magazine
$-Byline
Cochran's Corner—R
$-Money the Write Way—R
Once Upon a Time—R
$-Spirit-Led Writer—R
$-Writer's Apprentice
$-Writer's Digest—R

ETHICS

ADULT/GENERAL
AGAIN—R
$-Angels on Earth
Breakthrough Intercessor—R
$-Canada Lutheran—R
Catalyst
$-Catholic Digest—R
$-Catholic Insight
$-Catholic Parent
$-Catholic Peace Voice—R
Channels—R
Christian Bible Studies.com
$-Christian Courier (CAN)—R
$-Christian Examiner
Christian Journal—R

Christian Media—R
Christian Motorsports
Christian Observer
Christian Online
$-Christian Renewal—R
$-Christian Research
$-Christianity Today—R
$-Commonweal
$-Cresset
$-Culture Wars—R
$-Dovetail—R
$-Faith & Family
$-Faith Today
$-First Things
$-Generation X—R
Good News Journal
Grand Valley Observer—R
Highway News—R
$-Home Times—R
$-Homeschooling Today—R
$-Horizons (adult)—R
$-Indian Life—R
$-Interim—R
Island Catholic News
Journal of Church & State
$-Layman
$-Light & Life
$-Liguorian
$-Living—R
$-Living Church
$-Lookout—R
Maranatha News—R
$-Men of Integrity—R
$-Mennonite Brethren—R
Metro Voice—R
$-National Catholic
$-New Freeman—R
New Heart—R
$-New Wineskins—R
$-NRB Magazine—R
$-Our Sunday Visitor
Pegasus Review—R
Perspectives
$-Physician—R
$-Positive Thinking—R
$-Prairie Messenger—R
Presbyterian Outlook
$-Presbyterian Record—R
Priscilla Papers—R
$-Prism—R
Quaker Life—R
Regent Business—R
$-Relevant
Sacred Journey—R
$-Science & Spirit

$-Seeds
$-Silver Wings—R
$-Social Justice—R
$-Sojourners
$-Spring Hill Review—R
$-St. Anthony Messenger
$-Testimony—R
thegoodsteward.com—R
Trumpeter—R
Victory News—R
$-War Cry—R
$-Wesleyan Life—R
$-World & I—R
$-Young Christian—R

CHILDREN
$-BREAD/God's Children—R
Skipping Stones

CHRISTIAN EDUCATION/LIBRARY
$-Caravan
Christian Librarian—R
Journal/Christian Education
$-Teachers Interaction

MISSIONS
$-Worldwide Challenge

PASTORS/LEADERS
$-African American Pulpit
$-Building Church Leaders.com
$-Christian Century—R
$-Clergy Journal—R
Cross Currents
$-Evangelical Baptist—R
$-Interpreter
Journal/Pastoral Care—R
$-Leadership—R
$-Pastoral Life—R
$-Priest
Quarterly Review
$-Rev.
Sewanee Theological Review
Sharing the Practice—R
Theological Digest—R
$-Theology Today
$-This Rock
$-Word & World
$-Youthworker

TEEN/YOUNG ADULT
$-Devo'Zine—R
$-Passageway.org—R
$-Real Faith in Life—R
Setmag.com—R
Teen Light—R
$-Teenage Christian—R

TeensForJC.com—R
Transcendmag.com—R
$-With—R
$-Young Salvationist—R

WOMEN
$-Godly Business Woman
Handmaiden—R
$-inSpirit—R

WRITERS
Beginnings

ETHNIC/CULTURAL PIECES

ADULT/GENERAL
African Voices—R
AGAIN—R
$-Arlington Catholic
$-Beacon
Breakthrough Intercessor—R
$-Bridal Guides—R
$-Catholic Digest—R
$-Catholic Peace Voice—R
$-CBA Marketplace
$-Celebrate Life—R
Channels—R
Christian Bible Studies.com
$-Christian Courier (CAN)—R
Christian Motorsports
Christian News NW—R
Christian Online
$-Christian Parenting—R
$-Christianity Today—R
$-Christianweek
$-Columbia
Creation Care—R
$-Direction
$-Dovetail—R
$-Episcopal Life—R
Evangelical Advocate—R
$-Faith & Family
$-Faith Today
$-Foursquare World Advance—R
$-Gem—R
$-Generation X—R
$-God Allows U-Turns—R
$-Good News—R
$-Gospel Today—R
Grand Valley Observer—R
Hannah to Hannah—R
Highway News—R
$-Home Times—R
$-Homeschooling Today—R
$-Impact—R
$-Indian Life—R
Journal of Church & State
$-Light & Life

$-Liguorian
$-Lookout—R
Maranatha News—R
Mature Times—R
$-Men of Integrity—R
$-Mennonite Historian—R
$-MESSAGE
MESSAGE/Open Bible—R
$-Minnesota Christian—R
Mutuality—R
$-National Catholic
$-New Freeman—R
$-New Wineskins—R
$-North American Voice—R
$-On Mission
$-Plain Truth—R
$-Prairie Messenger—R
$-Presbyterian Record—R
Priscilla Papers—R
$-Prism—R
$-Purpose—R
Quaker Life—R
Sacred Journey—R
$-Science & Spirit
$-Seeds
Singles Scoop—R
Spiritual Voice—R
$-Spirituality & Health
$-Spring Hill Review—R
$-St. Anthony Messenger
Star of Zion
$-Testimony—R
thegoodsteward.com—R
$-Today's Christian—R
$-Today's Pentecostal Evangel
Trumpeter—R
$-Upscale Magazine
Victory News—R
$-War Cry—R
West Wind Review
$-World & I—R
Xavier Review
$-Young Christian—R

CHILDREN
$-Faces
$-Focus/Clubhouse
$-Guideposts for Kids
$-On the Line—R
Skipping Stones
$-Story Friends—R

CHRISTIAN EDUCATION/LIBRARY
$-Children's Ministry
$-Evangelizing Today's Child—R

MISSIONS
$-Evangelical Missions—R
Missiology
$-One
OpRev Equipper—R
Women of the Harvest
$-World Pulse—R

PASTORS/LEADERS
$-African American Pulpit
$-Building Church Leaders.com
$-Christian Century—R
$-Eucharistic Ministries—R
$-Five Stones—R
$-Interpreter
Journal/Pastoral Care—R
$-Lutheran Partners—R
Net Results
$-Pastoral Life—R
$-Priest
$-Rev.
Sharing the Practice—R
$-Worship Leader

TEEN/YOUNG ADULT
$-Boundless Webzine—R
$-Conqueror—R
$-Devo'Zine—R
$-Essential Connection
$-Passageway.org—R
$-Real Faith in Life—R
Setmag.com—R
$-Student Leadership—R
Teen Light—R
TeensForJC.com—R
Transcendmag.com—R
$-With—R
$-Young Christian—R
$-Young Salvationist—R

WOMEN
$-Esprit—R
$-Godly Business Woman
$-Horizons (women)—R
$-inSpirit—R
$-Link & Visitor—R
$-MOMsense—R
Reflections
$-SpiritLed Woman

EVANGELISM/WITNESSING

ADULT/GENERAL
$-Alive!—R
Alliance Life
American Tract Society—R
$-Anglican Journal
$-Annals of St. Anne

$-Beacon
$-BGC World—R
$-Bible Advocate—R
Bread of Life—R
Breakthrough Intercessor—R
$-Canada Lutheran—R
Channels—R
$-Charisma
Chattels of the Heart—R
Christian Bible Studies.com
Christian Courier (WI)—R
$-Christian Leader—R
Christian Motorsports
Christian Online
$-Christian Parenting—R
Christian Ranchman
$-Christian Research
Church Herald & Holiness—R
$-Cornerstone Christian—R
Creation Care—R
Crossway/Newsline—R
$-Decision
$-Discipleship Journal—R
$-Episcopal Life—R
$-Evangel—R
Evangelical Advocate—R
$-Faith & Family
$-Faith Today
$-Focus on the Family
$-Gem—R
$-God Allows U-Turns—R
$-Good News—R
Gospel Tract—R
Grand Valley Observer—R
Hannah to Hannah—R
Highway News—R
$-Horizons (adult)—R
$-Indian Life—R
$-Inland NW Christian
$-Layman
Leaves—R
$-Light & Life
Literary TNT—R
$-Live—R
$-Living Church
$-Lookout—R
$-Lutheran—R
$-Lutheran Journal—R
Maranatha News—R
Mature Times—R
$-Men of Integrity—R
$-Mennonite Brethren—R
MESSAGE/Open Bible—R
Metro Voice—R
$-Minnesota Christian—R
$-Montgomery's Journey

$-New Freeman—R
New Heart—R
$-New Wineskins—R
$-North American Voice—R
$-Oblates
$-On Mission
$-Plain Truth—R
$-Power for Living—R
PrayerWorks—R
$-Priority!
$-Prism—R
$-Purpose—R
Quaker Life—R
Regent Business—R
$-SCP Journal—R
$-Seek—R
$-Shantyman—R
Sharing—R
$-Signs of the Times—R
Singles Scoop—R
Spiritual Voice—R
$-St. Anthony Messenger
$-Standard—R
Sword of the Lord—R
$-Testimony—R
thegoodsteward.com—R
$-This Rock
$-Today's Christian—R
$-Today's Pentecostal Evangel
Trumpeter—R
$-Up
Victory News—R
$-Voice of the Lord
$-War Cry—R
$-Way of St. Francis—R
$-Wesleyan Life—R
$-Young Christian—R

CHILDREN
$-BREAD/God's Children—R
$-Club Connection
$-Courage—R
$-Focus/Clubhouse
$-Focus/Clubhouse Jr.
$-Kids' Ministry Ideas—R
$-Primary Pal (IL)
$-SHINE brightly—R

CHRISTIAN EDUCATION/LIBRARY
$-Children's Ministry
$-Church Educator—R
$-Evangelizing Today's Child—R
$-Group
$-Religion Teacher's Journal
$-Resource—R
$-Youth & CE Leadership

MISSIONS
$-Evangelical Missions—R
Intl. Jour./Frontier—R
$-Leaders for Today
Missiology
OpRev Equipper—R
Wesleyan World—R
$-Worldwide Challenge

MUSIC
Christian Music Weekly—R
Quest—R

PASTORS/LEADERS
$-African American Pulpit
Angelos—R
$-Building Church Leaders.com
Cell Group—R
$-Christian Century—R
Christian Education Journal (CA)—R
$-Church Growth Network—R
$-Clergy Journal—R
$-Emmanuel
$-Eucharistic Ministries—R
$-Evangelical Baptist—R
$-Evangelicals Today—R
$-Five Stones—R
$-Horizons (pastor)—R
$-Interpreter
Jour./Amer. Soc./Chur. Growth—R
$-Let's Worship
$-Lutheran Partners—R
$-Ministries Today
Ministry in Motion—R
$-Pastoral Life—R
Pastors.com—R
$-Preaching
$-Priest
Pulpit Helps—R
Quarterly Review
$-Rev.
$-Review for Religious
$-RevWriter Resource
$-Sermon Notes—R
Sharing the Practice—R
$-This Rock
$-WCA News—R
$-Youthworker

TEEN/YOUNG ADULT
$-Breakaway
$-Brio & Beyond
$-Conqueror—R
$-Devo'Zine—R
$-Essential Connection
$-Passageway.org—R
$-Real Faith in Life—R

Setmag.com—R
$-Student Leadership—R
$-Teenage Christian—R
TeensForJC.com—R
Transcendmag.com—R
$-With—R
$-Young Christian—R
$-Young Salvationist—R

WOMEN
$-At the Center—R
Footprints
$-Godly Business Woman
$-Horizons (women)—R
$-inSpirit—R
$-Journey
Just Between Us—R
$-Link & Visitor—R
P31 Woman—R
Right to the Heart—R
$-SpiritLed Woman
$-Woman's Touch—R
$-Women Alive!—R

EXEGESIS

ADULT/GENERAL
$-alive now!—R
$-Bible Advocate—R
$-Catholic Insight
Channels—R
Christian Ranchman
$-Christianity Today—R
Creation
Evangelical Advocate—R
Grand Valley Observer—R
$-Light & Life
$-Living Church
$-Lookout—R
$-National Catholic
$-New Freeman—R
$-Plain Truth—R
PrayerWorks—R
$-Presbyterian Record—R
Priscilla Papers—R
Regent Business—R
$-St. Anthony Messenger
Sword and Trumpet—R
$-Testimony—R
Victory News—R

MISSIONS
Missiology

PASTORS/LEADERS
$-African American Pulpit
Angelos—R
$-Building Church Leaders.com

$-Emmanuel
$-Enrichment—R
$-Passageway.org—R
$-Pastoral Life—R
Pulpit Helps—R
Sharing the Practice—R
Theological Digest—R
$-Theology Today
Trumpeter—R
$-Young Adult Today

FAITH

ADULT/GENERAL
African Voices—R
$-Animal Trails—R
$-Arkansas Catholic—R
Barefoot Path—R
$-Believer's Bay
$-BGC World—R
$-Bible Advocate—R
$-Brave Hearts
Bread of Life—R
$-Bridal Guides—R
$-Catholic Digest—R
$-Catholic Insight
$-Catholic Peace Voice—R
Channels—R
Christian Bible Studies.com
$-Christian Courier (CAN)—R
Christian Journal—R
$-Christian Leader—R
$-Christian Networks Journal
Christian Online
Christian Ranchman
$-Christian Research
$-Christianity Today—R
$-Christianweek
$-Columbia
$-Cornerstone Christian—R
$-Covenant Companion—R
$-Cresset
$-Cup of Comfort—R
$-Decision
$-Direction
Disciple's Journal—R
$-Discipleship Journal—R
$-Dovetail—R
$-Evangel—R
Evangelical Advocate—R
$-Faith & Family
$-Faith & Friends—R
$-Faith Today
$-Family Digest—R
$-Gem—R
$-Generation X—R

$-God Allows U-Turns—R
Good News Journal
Gospel Tract—R
Grand Valley Observer—R
Hannah to Hannah—R
Highway News—R
$-Home Times—R
HopeKeepers—R
Jewel Among Jewels
LifeTimes Catholic
$-Light & Life
$-Liguorian
Literary TNT—R
$-Live—R
$-Living—R
$-Lutheran Journal—R
Maranatha News—R
$-Marriage Partnership—R
Mature Times—R
$-Men of Integrity—R
$-Minnesota Christian—R
$-Montgomery's Journey
$-National Catholic
$-New Freeman—R
New Heart—R
$-New Wineskins—R
$-North American Voice—R
$-Now What?—R
$-Our Sunday Visitor
Parents & Teens—R
Pegasus Review—R
Perspectives
$-Plain Truth—R
$-Positive Thinking—R
$-Prairie Messenger—R
PrayerWorks—R
$-Precepts for Living
$-Presbyterian Record—R
$-Priority!
Priscilla Papers—R
$-Psychology for Living—R
Quaker Life—R
Reformed Quarterly
Re:generation Quarterly
$-Relate—R
Sacred Journey—R
$-Seek—R
$-Signs of the Times—R
Singles Scoop—R
Southwest Kansas
Spiritual Voice—R
$-St. Anthony Messenger
$-St. Joseph's Messenger—R
Sword and Trumpet—R
Sword of the Lord—R
$-Testimony—R

thegoodsteward.com—R
$-Today's Christian—R
$-Together—R
Trumpeter—R
$-U.S. Catholic
$-United Church Observer—R
$-Up
Victory News—R
$-Way of St. Francis—R
$-Weavings—R
$-Wesleyan Life—R
$-World & I—R
$-Young Christian—R

CHILDREN
Barefoot for Kids—R
$-BREAD/God's Children—R
$-Courage—R
$-Focus/Clubhouse
$-Focus/Clubhouse Jr.
$-Juniorway
$-Our Little Friend—R
$-Partners—R
$-Passport—R
$-Primary Street
$-Primary Treasure—R
$-SHINE brightly—R

CHRISTIAN EDUCATION/LIBRARY
$-Catechist
Catholic Library World
$-Children's Ministry
Christian Librarian—R
$-Group
$-Momentum
$-Teachers of Vision—R
$-Youth & CE Leadership

MISSIONS
Missiology
$-One
$-PIME World—R

MUSIC
Christian Music Weekly—R

PASTORS/LEADERS
$-African American Pulpit
$-Building Church Leaders.com
Christian Education Journal (CA)—R
$-Clergy Journal—R
$-Emmanuel
$-Eucharistic Ministries—R
$-Evangelical Baptist—R
$-Evangelicals Today—R
$-Interpreter
Ministry in Motion—R

$-Pastoral Life—R
$-Proclaim—R
Quarterly Review
$-Rev.
$-Review for Religious
Sharing the Practice—R
Theological Digest—R
$-Worship Leader

TEEN/YOUNG ADULT
$-Boundless Webzine—R
$-Breakaway
$-Brio—R
$-Brio & Beyond
$-Conqueror—R
$-Devo'Zine—R
$-J.A.M.: Jesus and Me
$-Passageway.org—R
Setmag.com—R
$-Student Leadership—R
TeensForJC.com—R
Transcendmag.com—R
$-With—R
$-Young Adult Today—R
$-Young and Alive—R
$-Young Christian—R
$-Young Salvationist—R

WOMEN
Christian Woman's Page—R
ChurchWoman
$-Esprit—R
$-Godly Business Woman
$-Horizons (women)—R
$-inSpirit—R
$-Journey
Just Between Us—R
Life Tools for Women
P31 Woman—R
Reflections
$-SpiritLed Woman
$-Today's Christian Woman—R
$-Woman's Touch—R
$-Women Alive!—R
$-Women by Grace—R

WRITERS
$-Areopagus (UK)
Beginnings

FAMILY LIFE

ADULT/GENERAL
African Voices—R
AGAIN—R
$-Alive!—R
Alliance Life
$-America

$-Angels on Earth
$-Annals of St. Anne
$-Arkansas Catholic—R
$-Arlington Catholic
At Home with Our Faith
$-B.C. Catholic—R
Barefoot Path—R
$-Beacon
$-Believer's Bay
$-BGC World—R
$-Bible Advocate—R
$-Brave Hearts
Bread of Life—R
Breakthrough Intercessor—R
$-Bridal Guides—R
$-Canada Lutheran—R
$-Cappers
$-Catholic Digest—R
$-Catholic Forester—R
$-Catholic New Times—R
$-Catholic Parent
CBN.com—R
$-CGA World—R
Channels—R
$-Charisma
$-Chicken Soup—R
Christian Bible Studies.com
Christian C. L. RECORD—R
$-Christian Courier (CAN)—R
Christian Courier (WI)—R
$-Christian Home & School
Christian Journal—R
$-Christian Leader—R
Christian Motorsports
Christian Online
$-Christian Parenting—R
Christian Ranchman
$-Christian Renewal—R
$-Christianweek
$-Columbia
Connecting Point—R
$-Cornerstone Christian—R
$-Covenant Companion—R
$-Culture Wars—R
$-Cup of Comfort—R
$-Decision
Disciple's Journal—R
$-Dovetail—R
$-Eclectic Homeschool
Evangelical Advocate—R
$-Faith & Family
$-Faith & Friends—R
$-Faith Today
$-Family Digest—R
$-Fellowship Focus—R
$-Focus on the Family

$-Foursquare World Advance—R
$-Gem—R
$-God Allows U-Turns—R
Gold Country Families—R
Good News Journal
$-Grit
$-Guideposts—R
Hannah to Hannah—R
Heartlight—R
Highway News—R
$-Home Times—R
$-Homeschooling Today—R
HopeKeepers—R
$-Horizons (adult)—R
$-Ideals—R
$-Indian Life—R
Indiana Christian News
$-Inland NW Christian
$-Interim—R
Jewel Among Jewels
$-Joy & Praise
Keys to Living—R
$-Kiwanis
$-Layman
LifeTimes Catholic
$-Light & Life
$-Liguorian
Literary TNT—R
$-Live—R
$-Living—R
$-Living Church
$-Living Light News—R
$-Lookout—R
$-Lutheran—R
$-Lutheran Digest—R
Maranatha News—R
$-Marriage Partnership—R
Mature Times—R
$-Mature Years—R
$-Men of Integrity—R
$-MESSAGE
$-Messenger
Metro Voice—R
$-Minnesota Christian—R
$-Montgomery's Journey
Mutuality—R
$-New Freeman—R
$-New Man—R
$-New Wineskins—R
$-North American Voice—R
$-Nostalgia Magazine—R
$-Oblates
$-Our Sunday Visitor
$-Over the Back Fence—R
Parents & Teens—R
Pegasus Review—R

$-Physician—R
$-Plain Truth—R
$-Positive Thinking—R
$-Power for Living—R
$-Prairie Messenger—R
PrayerWorks—R
$-Presbyterian Record—R
Priscilla Papers—R
$-Psychology for Living—R
$-Purpose—R
Quaker Life—R
$-Relate—R
Sacred Journey—R
$-Science & Spirit
$-Seek—R
$-Signs of the Times—R
$-Smart Families—R
$-Social Justice—R
Southwest Kansas
$-Special Living—R
Spiritual Voice—R
$-Spring Hill Review—R
$-St. Anthony Messenger
$-Standard—R
Steps
Storyteller—R
Sword and Trumpet—R
$-Testimony—R
thegoodsteward.com—R
$-Tidewater Parent—R
$-Today's Christian—R
$-Together—R
Trumpeter—R
$-U.S. Catholic
$-United Church Observer—R
$-Vibrant Life—R
Victory News—R
$-Vision—R
$-War Cry—R
$-Way of St. Francis—R
$-Wesleyan Life—R
West Wind Review
Winsome Wit—R
$-World & I—R
$-Young Christian—R

CHILDREN
$-Adventures
Barefoot for Kids—R
$-BREAD/God's Children—R
$-Celebrate
$-Club Connection
$-Focus/Clubhouse
$-Focus/Clubhouse Jr.
$-Guideposts for Kids
$-My Friend

$-Partners—R
$-Pockets—R
$-SHINE brightly—R
Skipping Stones
$-Winner—R
Young Gentleman's Monthly

CHRISTIAN EDUCATION/LIBRARY
$-Caravan
$-Children's Ministry
$-Church Educator—R
$-Momentum

MISSIONS
$-One
Women of the Harvest
$-Worldwide Challenge

PASTORS/LEADERS
$-African American Pulpit
$-Barefoot—R
$-Building Church Leaders.com
$-Catholic Servant
$-Christian Camp—R
$-Evangelical Baptist—R
$-Evangelicals Today—R
Journal/Pastoral Care—R
$-Pastoral Life—R
$-Priest
Pulpit Helps—R
$-Rev.
Sharing the Practice—R
$-Spiritual Spinach—R
Steps
$-Today's Christian Preacher—R
$-Today's Parish—R
$-Word & World
Youth Culture
$-Youthworker

TEEN/YOUNG ADULT
$-Brio—R
$-Brio & Beyond
$-Conqueror—R
$-Listen—R
$-Passageway.org—R
$-Real Faith in Life—R
Setmag.com—R
Teen Light—R
TeensForJC.com—R
Transcendmag.com—R
$-With—R
$-Young Adult Today—R
$-Young and Alive—R
$-Young Christian—R

WOMEN
Christian Woman's Page—R

Crowned with Silver
$-Esprit—R
$-Extreme Joy
$-Godly Business Woman
Handmaiden—R
Hearts at Home—R
$-Horizons (women)—R
$-inSpirit—R
$-Journey
Just Between Us—R
Keeping Hearts & Home
Life Tools for Women
$-Link & Visitor—R
Lutheran Woman's Quar.
$-MOMsense—R
P31 Woman—R
Reflections
Shalom Bayit
$-Simple Joy
$-SpiritLed Woman
$-Today's Christian Woman—R
$-Welcome Home
$-Woman's Touch—R
$-Women Alive!—R
$-Women by Grace—R
Women Today—R

FILLERS: ANECDOTES

ADULT/GENERAL
$-Alive!—R
$-Angels on Earth
$-Animal Trails—R
Barefoot Path—R
$-Bridal Guides—R
$-Catholic Digest—R
Channels—R
$-Chicken Soup—R
Christian Courier (WI)—R
Christian Journal—R
Christian Motorsports
$-Christian Parenting—R
Christian Ranchman
$-Christian Response—R
Church Herald & Holiness—R
$-Decision
Desert Call—R
Disciple's Journal—R
$-DisciplesWorld
$-Faith & Family
$-Family Digest—R
$-Foursquare World Advance—R
$-Gem—R
$-Generation X—R
$-God Allows U-Turns—R
Good News Journal
Grand Valley Observer—R

$-Grit
Heartlight—R
Highway News—R
$-Home Times—R
$-Impact—R
Jewel Among Jewels
$-Live—R
$-Living—R
$-Lutheran Digest—R
$-Lutheran Journal—R
Maranatha News—R
$-Mature Living
Mature Times—R
Metro Voice—R
MovieGuide
New Heart—R
$-North American Voice—R
$-Nostalgia Magazine—R
$-Presbyterian Record—R
$-Presbyterians Today—R
$-Purpose—R
Singles Scoop—R
Spiritual Voice—R
$-St. Anthony Messenger
Star of Zion
Steps
Tributes—R
Victory News—R
$-War Cry—R
$-Way of St. Francis—R
$-Young Christian—R

CHILDREN
$-Children's Magic Window
$-Club Connection
$-Guideposts for Kids
$-High Adventure—R
Skipping Stones

CHRISTIAN EDUCATION/LIBRARY
Christian Librarian—R
$-Religion Teacher's Journal

MISSIONS
Railroad Evangelist—R
Women of the Harvest

MUSIC
$-Church Pianist
$-Creator—R

PASTORS/LEADERS
$-Eucharistic Ministries—R
Ministry in Motion—R
$-Pastoral Life—R
Sharing the Practice—R
Steps

TEEN/YOUNG ADULT
Teen Light—R
$-Young Christian—R
$-Young Salvationist—R

WOMEN
Anna's Journal—R
Hearts at Home—R
Just Between Us—R
Right to the Heart—R
$-Today's Christian Woman—R
$-Woman's Touch—R
$-Women by Grace—R

WRITERS
$-Areopagus (UK)
$-Byline
Cochran's Corner—R
$-Cross & Quill—R
$-Fellowscript—R
$-Money the Write Way—R
Once Upon a Time—R
Romancing the Christian Heart—R
$-Tickled by Thunder
Write Touch
$-Writers' Journal

FILLERS: CARTOONS

ADULT/GENERAL
African Voices—R
$-alive now!—R
$-Alive!—R
Alliance Life
American Tract Society—R
$-Angels on Earth
$-Animal Trails—R
$-Bridal Guides—R
$-Catholic Digest—R
$-Catholic Forester—R
$-CBA Marketplace
Channels—R
$-Chicken Soup—R
Christian Computing—R
Christian Journal—R
Christian Motorsports
Christian Ranchman
Church Herald & Holiness—R
$-Commonweal
Connecting Point—R
$-Cornerstone Christian—R
$-Culture Wars—R
Disciple's Journal—R
$-DisciplesWorld
Discovery—R
$-Door—R
$-Eureka Street
$-Evangel—R

$-Faith & Family
$-Faith & Friends—R
$-Family Digest—R
$-Foursquare World Advance—R
$-Gem—R
Good News Journal
$-Gospel Today—R
$-Grit
Heartlight—R
Highway News—R
$-Impact—R
$-Inside Journal—R
$-Interchange
$-Joy & Praise
$-Liguorian
$-Lutheran—R
$-Lutheran Digest—R
Maranatha News—R
$-Mature Living
Mature Times—R
$-Mature Years—R
MESSAGE/Open Bible—R
Metro Voice—R
MovieGuide
New Heart—R
$-North American Voice—R
Pegasus Review—R
$-Physician—R
Plowman—R
$-Power for Living—R
$-Presbyterian Record—R
$-Presbyterians Today—R
$-Purpose—R
Singles Scoop—R
$-Sojourners
$-Special Living—R
Spiritual Voice—R
$-Spring Hill Review—R
$-St. Anthony Messenger
Star of Zion
Steps
Storyteller—R
thegoodsteward.com—R
Trumpeter—R
$-United Church Observer—R
Victory News—R
$-Way of St. Francis—R
$-Wireless Age—R
$-Young Christian—R

CHILDREN
$-Adventures
$-American Girl
Barefoot for Kids—R
$-Children's Magic Window
$-Club Connection

$-High Adventure—R
$-On the Line—R
$-Passport—R
$-SHINE brightly—R
Skipping Stones
$-Story Friends—R

CHRISTIAN EDUCATION/LIBRARY
$-Children's Ministry
Christian Librarian—R
$-Group
$-Journal/Adventist Educ.—R
$-Teachers of Vision—R
$-Today's Catholic Teacher—R
$-Youth & CE Leadership

MISSIONS
Mission Frontiers
Railroad Evangelist—R

MUSIC
Christian Music Weekly—R
$-Church Pianist
$-Creator—R
$-Senior Musician—R
Tradition

PASTORS/LEADERS
$-Catholic Servant
$-Christian Century—R
Christian Management—R
$-Clergy Journal—R
$-Diocesan Dialogue—R
$-Eucharistic Ministries—R
$-Horizons (pastor)—R
$-Leadership—R
$-Lutheran Partners—R
$-Preaching
$-Priest
Pulpit Helps—R
$-Rev.
$-Sabbath School Leadership—R
$-Sermon Notes—R
Sharing the Practice—R
$-Small Group Dynamics—R
Steps
$-WCA News—R
$-Your Church—R

TEEN/YOUNG ADULT
$-Listen—R
Setmag.com—R
Teen Light—R
TeensForJC.com—R
Transcendmag.com—R
$-With—R
$-Young Christian—R
$-Young Salvationist—R

WOMEN
Hearts at Home—R
Just Between Us—R
$-Today's Christian Woman—R
$-Women Alive!—R

WRITERS
$-Byline
Cochran's Corner—R
$-Cross & Quill—R
Heaven—R
Once Upon a Time—R
Upper Case
$-Writers' Journal

FILLERS: FACTS

ADULT/GENERAL
$-Alive!—R
Alliance Life
$-Angels on Earth
$-Animal Trails—R
$-Bible Advocate—R
Bread of Life—R
$-Bridal Guides—R
$-Catholic Digest—R
$-CBA Marketplace
$-Chicken Soup—R
Christian Courier (WI)—R
Christian Motorsports
Christian Ranchman
$-Christian Response—R
$-Cornerstone Christian—R
Desert Call—R
Disciple's Journal—R
$-Gem—R
$-Generation X—R
$-God Allows U-Turns—R
Good News Journal
Grand Valley Observer—R
Highway News—R
$-Interchange
Jewel Among Jewels
$-Joy & Praise
Keys to Living—R
$-Lutheran Digest—R
$-Lutheran Journal—R
$-Mature Living
Mature Times—R
MESSAGE/Open Bible—R
MovieGuide
$-North American Voice—R
$-Nostalgia Magazine—R
$-Presbyterian Record—R
Singles Scoop—R
Spiritual Voice—R
$-St. Anthony Messenger

Sword and Trumpet—R
Sword of the Lord—R
$-Vibrant Life—R
Victory News—R
$-Way of St. Francis—R
$-Young Christian—R

CHILDREN
$-Adventures
Barefoot for Kids—R
$-Children's Magic Window
$-Club Connection
$-Guideposts for Kids
$-High Adventure—R
$-On the Line—R

CHRISTIAN EDUCATION/LIBRARY
$-Religion Teacher's Journal
$-Teachers of Vision—R
$-Today's Catholic Teacher—R

PASTORS/LEADERS
$-Interpreter
$-Pastoral Life—R
Pulpit Helps—R
Strategic Adult Ministries—R

TEEN/YOUNG ADULT
$-Real Faith in Life—R
Setmag.com—R
Teen Light—R
TeensForJC.com—R
Transcendmag.com—R
$-Young Christian—R
$-Young Salvationist—R

WOMEN
Anna's Journal—R
Hearts at Home—R

WRITERS
$-Areopagus (UK)
$-Money the Write Way—R
Write Touch
$-Writers' Journal

FILLERS: GAMES

ADULT/GENERAL
$-Alive!—R
$-Angels on Earth
$-CGA World—R
Christian Motorsports
$-Christian Parents Section
Christian Ranchman
Connecting Point—R
$-Cornerstone Christian—R
Disciple's Journal—R
$-Faith & Friends—R

$-Gem—R
Good News Journal
Heartlight—R
$-Lutheran Journal—R
$-Mature Living
Mature Times—R
MovieGuide
$-Nostalgia Magazine—R
Singles Scoop—R
Spiritual Voice—R
$-Spring Hill Review—R
Star of Zion
Victory News—R
$-Young Christian—R

CHILDREN
$-Adventures
$-American Girl
Barefoot for Kids—R
$-Children's Magic Window
$-Club Connection
$-Courage—R
$-Guide—R
$-Guideposts for Kids
$-High Adventure—R
$-On the Line—R
$-Pockets—R
$-Primary Pal (IL)
$-SHINE brightly—R

CHRISTIAN EDUCATION/LIBRARY
$-Group
$-Religion Teacher's Journal

PASTORS/LEADERS
$-Rev.

TEEN/YOUNG ADULT
$-Conqueror—R
$-Listen—R
Setmag.com—R
Teen Light—R
TeensForJC.com—R
Transcendmag.com—R
$-Young Salvationist—R

WOMEN
Keeping Hearts & Home

WRITERS
$-Areopagus (UK)
Cochran's Corner—R

FILLERS: IDEAS

ADULT/GENERAL
$-Angels on Earth
$-Animal Trails—R
Barefoot Path—R

$-Bridal Guides—R
$-Catholic Parent
$-CBA Marketplace
$-CGA World—R
$-Christian Home & School
Christian Motorsports
$-Christian Parenting—R
Christian Ranchman
$-Cornerstone Christian—R
Disciple's Journal—R
$-Gem—R
$-Generation X—R
$-God Allows U-Turns—R
Good News Journal
Heartlight—R
Highway News—R
Jewel Among Jewels
Metro Voice—R
MovieGuide
$-North American Voice—R
$-Presbyterian Record—R
$-Seek—R
Spiritual Voice—R
$-St. Joseph's Messenger—R
Victory News—R
$-Young Christian—R

CHILDREN
Barefoot for Kids—R
$-Children's Magic Window
$-Club Connection
$-Guideposts for Kids
$-High Adventure—R
$-Pockets—R

CHRISTIAN EDUCATION/LIBRARY
$-Children's Ministry
$-Group
$-Religion Teacher's Journal
$-Teachers Interaction
$-Youth & CE Leadership

MUSIC
$-Creator—R
$-Senior Musician—R

PASTORS/LEADERS
$-Church Worship
$-Enrichment—R
$-Interpreter
$-Lutheran Partners—R
$-Pastoral Life—R
$-Pray!—R
$-Rev.
$-RevWriter Resource
$-Small Group Dynamics—R

$-Spiritual Spinach—R
Strategic Adult Ministries—R
$-WCA News—R

TEEN/YOUNG ADULT
$-Campus Life—R
$-Real Faith in Life—R
$-Young Christian—R

WOMEN
Hearts at Home—R
P31 Woman—R
Right to the Heart—R
$-Woman's Touch—R

WRITERS
$-Areopagus (UK)
Dedicated Author
Just Between Us—R
$-Money the Write Way—R
Once Upon a Time—R
$-Tickled by Thunder
Write Touch
$-Writers' Journal

FILLERS: JOKES

ADULT/GENERAL
$-Angels on Earth
$-Catholic Digest—R
Christian Journal—R
Christian Motorsports
Christian Ranchman
$-Cornerstone Christian—R
Disciple's Journal—R
$-Faith & Friends—R
$-Gem—R
$-Generation X—R
Good News Journal
$-Grit
Heartlight—R
$-Home Times—R
$-Impact—R
$-Interchange
$-Joke Writers
Keys to Living—R
$-Liguorian
$-Lutheran—R
$-Lutheran Digest—R
Maranatha News—R
$-Mature Years—R
MovieGuide
New Heart—R
$-Seek—R
Spiritual Voice—R
$-St. Anthony Messenger
Star of Zion
thegoodsteward.com—R

Victory News—R
$-Young Christian—R

CHILDREN
Barefoot for Kids—R
$-Children's Magic Window
$-Club Connection
$-Guideposts for Kids
$-High Adventure—R
$-On the Line—R
$-Pockets—R

MUSIC
$-Creator—R

PASTORS/LEADERS
$-Joke Writers
Sharing the Practice—R
$-Spiritual Spinach—R

TEEN/YOUNG ADULT
Setmag.com—R
Teen Light—R
TeensForJC.com—R
Transcendmag.com—R

WOMEN
$-Women Alive!—R
$-Women by Grace—R

WRITERS
$-Areopagus (UK)
$-Writers' Journal

FILLERS: KID QUOTES

ADULT/GENERAL
$-Animal Trails—R
Barefoot Path—R
$-Bridal Guides—R
$-Chicken Soup—R
Christian Journal—R
$-Cornerstone Christian—R
$-DisciplesWorld
$-Fellowship Focus—R
Highway News—R
Keys to Living—R
$-North American Voice—R
Spiritual Voice—R
$-Upscale Magazine
Victory News—R
$-Young Christian—R

CHILDREN
Barefoot for Kids—R
$-Children's Magic Window

CHRISTIAN EDUCATION/LIBRARY
$-Children's Ministry

PASTORS/LEADERS
$-Eucharistic Ministries—R

WOMEN
Footprints

FILLERS: NEWSBREAKS

ADULT/GENERAL
$-Angels on Earth
$-Anglican Journal
$-Arkansas Catholic—R
$-B.C. Catholic—R
$-Canada Lutheran—R
$-Catholic New Times—R
$-Catholic Telegraph
$-CBA Marketplace
$-Celebrate Life—R
Christian Courier (WI)—R
Christian Journal—R
Christian Motorsports
Christian Ranchman
$-Christian Renewal—R
$-Cornerstone Christian—R
Disciple's Journal—R
Friends Journal—R
$-Gem—R
$-God Allows U-Turns—R
Good News Journal
Heartlight—R
Highway News—R
$-Home Times—R
$-Indian Life—R
Maranatha News—R
Metro Voice—R
MovieGuide
$-NRB Magazine—R
Re:generation Quarterly
Spiritual Voice—R
Sword of the Lord—R
Victory News—R

CHILDREN
$-Club Connection

CHRISTIAN
EDUCATION/LIBRARY
Christian Librarian—R

MISSIONS
OpRev Equipper—R

PASTORS/LEADERS
$-Spiritual Spinach—R
Strategic Adult Ministries—R
Sword and Trumpet—R

TEEN/YOUNG ADULT
$-Real Faith in Life—R

WOMEN
Anna's Journal—R

WRITERS
$-Areopagus (UK)
$-Writers' Journal

FILLERS: PARTY IDEAS

ADULT/GENERAL
$-Animal Trails—R
$-Bridal Guides—R
Christian Ranchman
$-Cornerstone Christian—R
Disciple's Journal—R
Good News Journal
Highway News—R
MovieGuide
Spiritual Voice—R
Victory News—R
$-Young Christian—R

CHILDREN
$-Adventures
Barefoot for Kids—R
$-Club Connection
$-Guideposts for Kids
$-On the Line—R

CHRISTIAN
EDUCATION/LIBRARY
$-Pastoral Life—R

MUSIC
$-Creator—R
$-Senior Musician—R

TEEN/YOUNG ADULT
$-Conqueror—R
Setmag.com—R
Teen Light—R
TeensForJC.com—R
Transcendmag.com—R
$-Young Christian—R

WOMEN
Hearts at Home—R
Keeping Hearts & Home
P31 Woman—R
Right to the Heart—R

WRITERS
$-Areopagus (UK)

FILLERS: PRAYERS

ADULT/GENERAL
$-Angels on Earth
$-Animal Trails—R
Barefoot Path—R
$-Brave Hearts

$-Bridal Guides—R
$-CGA World—R
Channels—R
Christian Journal—R
Christian Motorsports
Christian Online
Christian Ranchman
Church Herald & Holiness—R
$-Cornerstone Christian—R
Desert Call—R
Disciple's Journal—R
$-Family Digest—R
$-Gem—R
$-God Allows U-Turns—R
Good News Journal
Gospel Tract—R
Heartlight—R
Highway News—R
Jewel Among Jewels
$-Joy & Praise
Keys to Living—R
LifeTimes Catholic
Literary TNT—R
$-Mature Years—R
MovieGuide
$-North American Voice—R
Plowman—R
$-Presbyterian Record—R
Spiritual Voice—R
Star of Zion
Tributes—R
Victory News—R
$-Way of St. Francis—R
$-Young Christian—R

CHILDREN
Barefoot for Kids—R
$-Pockets—R
$-Primary Pal (IL)
$-SHINE brightly—R

CHRISTIAN
EDUCATION/LIBRARY
$-Religion Teacher's Journal
$-Teachers Interaction

PASTORS/LEADERS
$-Clergy Journal—R
$-Pastoral Life—R

TEEN/YOUNG ADULT
Setmag.com—R
Teen Light—R
TeensForJC.com—R
Transcendmag.com—R
$-Young Christian—R
$-Young Salvationist—R

WOMEN
Anna's Journal—R
Just Between Us—R
Keeping Hearts & Home
Right to the Heart—R

WRITERS
$-Areopagus (UK)
Cochran's Corner—R
$-Cross & Quill—R
$-WIN-Informer
$-Writers' Journal

FILLERS: PROSE

ADULT/GENERAL
$-Angels on Earth
$-Animal Trails—R
$-Bible Advocate—R
Bread of Life—R
$-Bridal Guides—R
Christian Motorsports
Christian Ranchman
$-Decision
Desert Call—R
Disciple's Journal—R
Discovery—R
$-Faith & Family
$-Gem—R
$-Generation X—R
$-God Allows U-Turns—R
Good News Journal
$-Grit
Heartlight—R
Highway News—R
$-Indian Life—R
$-Live—R
MovieGuide
Pegasus Review—R
Plowman—R
$-Presbyterian Record—R
$-Presbyterians Today—R
Re:generation Quarterly
Spiritual Voice—R
Sword and Trumpet—R
Sword of the Lord—R
$-Today's Pentecostal Evangel
Victory News—R
$-Way of St. Francis—R
$-Wireless Age—R
$-Young Christian—R

CHILDREN
$-Guideposts for Kids
$-Partners—R

PASTORS/LEADERS
$-Pastoral Life—R

$-Spiritual Spinach—R

TEEN/YOUNG ADULT
$-Brio—R
$-Conqueror—R
$-Real Faith in Life—R
Setmag.com—R
Teen Light—R
TeensForJC.com—R
Transcendmag.com—R
$-Young Christian—R

WOMEN
Anna's Journal—R
$-Melody of the Heart
$-Today's Christian Woman—R

WRITERS
$-Areopagus (UK)
Romancing the Christian Heart—R
Upper Case
Write Touch
$-Writer
$-Writers' Journal

FILLERS: QUIZZES

ADULT/GENERAL
$-Alive!—R
$-Angels on Earth
$-Animal Trails—R
$-Bridal Guides—R
Christian Motorsports
Christian Online
Christian Ranchman
Church Herald & Holiness—R
Disciple's Journal—R
$-Door—R
$-Faith & Friends—R
$-Gem—R
Good News Journal
$-Home Times—R
$-Impact—R
Literary TNT—R
$-Lutheran Journal—R
Mature Times—R
MovieGuide
$-North American Voice—R
$-Nostalgia Magazine—R
Singles Scoop—R
Spiritual Voice—R
thegoodsteward.com—R
$-Vibrant Life—R
Victory News—R
$-Young Christian—R

CHILDREN
Barefoot for Kids—R
$-Cadet Quest—R

$-Club Connection
$-Focus/Clubhouse
$-Guide—R
$-Guideposts for Kids
$-Nature Friend
$-On the Line—R
$-Partners—R
$-SHINE brightly—R
Skipping Stones
$-Story Mates—R

MUSIC
$-Senior Musician—R

TEEN/YOUNG ADULT
$-Conqueror—R
$-Guideposts Sweet 16—R
$-Real Faith in Life—R
Setmag.com—R
Teen Light—R
TeensForJC.com—R
Transcendmag.com—R
$-Young Christian—R
$-Young Salvationist—R

WOMEN
Anna's Journal—R
Footprints
$-Melody of the Heart

WRITERS
$-Areopagus (UK)
Once Upon a Time—R
$-WIN-Informer
$-Writers' Journal

FILLERS: QUOTES

ADULT/GENERAL
Alliance Life
$-Angels on Earth
$-Animal Trails—R
Barefoot Path—R
$-Bible Advocate—R
Bread of Life—R
$-Bridal Guides—R
$-Catholic Digest—R
$-Chicken Soup—R
Christian Journal—R
Christian Motorsports
Christian Ranchman
$-Christian Response—R
$-Culture Wars—R
Desert Call—R
Disciple's Journal—R
$-DisciplesWorld
$-Faith & Friends—R
$-Gem—R
$-Generation X—R

$-God Allows U-Turns—R
Good News Journal
$-Grit
Heartlight—R
$-Home Times—R
Jewel Among Jewels
Keys to Living—R
$-Lutheran Journal—R
MESSAGE/Open Bible—R
Metro Voice—R
MovieGuide
$-North American Voice—R
Pegasus Review—R
$-Seek—R
Spiritual Voice—R
$-Spring Hill Review—R
$-St. Anthony Messenger
Storyteller—R
Victory News—R
$-Young Christian—R

CHILDREN
$-Adventures
Barefoot for Kids—R
$-Partners—R
Skipping Stones

MISSIONS
Railroad Evangelist—R

PASTORS/LEADERS
$-Pastoral Life—R
Pulpit Helps—R
Strategic Adult Ministries—R

TEEN/YOUNG ADULT
Teen Light—R
$-Young Christian—R

WOMEN
Anna's Journal—R
Footprints
Just Between Us—R
Right to the Heart—R

WRITERS
$-Areopagus (UK)
$-Money the Write Way—R
Romancing the Christian Heart—R
$-WIN-Informer
$-Writers' Journal

FILLERS: SHORT HUMOR

ADULT/GENERAL
$-Alive!—R
$-Angels on Earth
$-Animal Trails—R
Barefoot Path—R
$-Bridal Guides—R

$-Chicken Soup—R
Christian Journal—R
Christian Motorsports
Christian Online
Christian Ranchman
Church Herald & Holiness—R
$-Cornerstone Christian—R
Disciple's Journal—R
$-DisciplesWorld
$-Door—R
Friends Journal—R
$-Gem—R
$-Generation X—R
$-God Allows U-Turns—R
Good News Journal
Gospel Tract—R
$-Grit
Heartlight—R
Highway News—R
$-Home Times—R
$-Impact—R
Keys to Living—R
Literary TNT—R
$-Living—R
$-Lutheran—R
$-Lutheran Digest—R
Maranatha News—R
$-Mature Living
Mature Times—R
MESSAGE/Open Bible—R
Metro Voice—R
MovieGuide
New Heart—R
$-North American Voice—R
Plowman—R
$-Presbyterian Record—R
$-Presbyterians Today—R
$-Purpose—R
Rose & Thorn
$-Seek—R
Singles Scoop—R
Spiritual Voice—R
Steps
Victory News—R
Winsome Wit—R
$-Young Christian—R

CHILDREN
Barefoot for Kids—R
$-Children's Magic Window
$-Club Connection
$-Guideposts for Kids
$-SHINE brightly—R

CHRISTIAN EDUCATION/LIBRARY
Christian Librarian—R

MISSIONS
Women of the Harvest

MUSIC
$-Creator—R
$-Senior Musician—R

PASTORS/LEADERS
$-Catholic Servant
$-Enrichment—R
$-Eucharistic Ministries—R
$-Interpreter
$-Leadership—R
$-Pastoral Life—R
$-Sermon Notes—R
Sharing the Practice—R
$-Spiritual Spinach—R
Steps

TEEN/YOUNG ADULT
$-Real Faith in Life—R
Setmag.com—R
Teen Light—R
TeensForJC.com—R
Transcendmag.com—R
$-Young Christian—R
$-Young Salvationist—R

WOMEN
Hearts at Home—R
Just Between Us—R
Keeping Hearts & Home
$-Melody of the Heart
$-Women Alive!—R
$-Women by Grace—R

WRITERS
$-Areopagus (UK)
$-Byline
$-Christian Communicator—R
$-Fellowscript—R
Once Upon a Time—R
$-Tickled by Thunder
Write Touch
$-Writers' Journal

FILLERS: TIPS

ADULT/GENERAL
Alliance Life
$-Animal Trails—R
Barefoot Path—R
$-Bridal Guides—R
Highway News—R
Jewel Among Jewels
$-Special Living—R
Storyteller—R
Victory News—R

CHILDREN
$-Adventures
Barefoot for Kids—R
$-Cadet Quest—R
$-Children's Magic Window

PASTORS/LEADERS
Ministry in Motion—R

TEEN/YOUNG ADULT
Setmag.com—R
Teen Light—R
TeensForJC.com—R
Transcendmag.com—R
$-Young Christian—R

WRITERS
$-Brady Magazine—R
$-Fellowscript—R
$-Money the Write Way—R
Once Upon a Time—R
Romancing the Christian Heart—R
$-Writers' Journal

FILLERS: WORD PUZZLES

ADULT/GENERAL
$-Alive!—R
$-Animal Trails—R
$-Bridal Guides—R
$-CGA World—R
Christian Journal—R
Christian Ranchman
Connecting Point—R
$-Cornerstone Christian—R
Disciple's Journal—R
$-Evangel—R
$-Faith & Friends—R
Friends Journal—R
$-Gem—R
Good News Journal
$-Gospel Today—R
Heartlight—R
$-Horizons (adult)—R
$-Impact—R
$-Joy & Praise
Maranatha News—R
$-Mature Living
$-Mature Years—R
MovieGuide
$-North American Voice—R
$-Power for Living—R
Spiritual Voice—R
$-Spring Hill Review—R
$-Standard—R
Star of Zion
Victory News—R

$-Young Christian—R

CHILDREN
$-Adventures
$-American Girl
$-Cadet Quest—R
$-Children's Magic Window
$-Club Connection
$-Courage—R
$-Focus/Clubhouse
$-Guide—R
$-Guideposts for Kids
$-Nature Friend
$-On the Line—R
$-Our Little Friend—R
$-Partners—R
$-Passport—R
$-Pockets—R
$-Primary Pal (IL)
$-SHINE brightly—R
Skipping Stones
$-Story Friends—R
$-Story Mates—R

CHRISTIAN EDUCATION/LIBRARY
$-Religion Teacher's Journal
$-Youth & CE Leadership

PASTORS/LEADERS
Pulpit Helps—R

TEEN/YOUNG ADULT
$-Conqueror—R
$-Real Faith in Life—R
Setmag.com—R
Teen Light—R
TeensForJC.com—R
Transcendmag.com—R
$-Young Christian—R
$-Young Salvationist—R

WOMEN
Footprints
$-Melody of the Heart

WRITERS
Heaven—R
$-Writers' Journal

FOOD/RECIPES

ADULT/GENERAL
$-Bridal Guides—R
$-Cappers
$-Catholic Parent
$-CGA World—R
Christian C. L. RECORD—R
Christian Online
$-Cornerstone Christian—R

$-Dovetail—R
$-Faith & Family
$-Faith & Friends—R
$-Grit
$-Home Times—R
$-Ideals—R
$-Impact—R
Keys to Living—R
$-Lutheran Digest—R
$-Lutheran Journal—R
$-Mature Living
$-MESSAGE
$-Montgomery's Journey
$-Nostalgia Magazine—R
Parents & Teens—R
Spiritual Voice—R
$-St. Anthony Messenger
Victory News—R
$-World & I—R
$-Young Christian—R

CHILDREN
$-American Girl
Barefoot for Kids—R
$-Cadet Quest—R
$-Celebrate
$-Club Connection
$-Focus/Clubhouse
$-Focus/Clubhouse Jr.
$-Guideposts for Kids
$-On the Line—R
$-Pockets—R
$-SHINE brightly—R
Skipping Stones

MISSIONS
Women of the Harvest

TEEN/YOUNG ADULT
$-Brio—R
Setmag.com—R
Teen Light—R
TeensForJC.com—R
Transcendmag.com—R
$-Young Christian—R

WOMEN
Christian Women Today—R
$-Extreme Joy
$-Godly Business Woman
Hearts at Home—R
Keeping Hearts & Home
$-Melody of the Heart
$-MOMsense—R
Praise
$-Simple Joy
True Woman
$-Welcome Home

$-Woman's Touch—R
$-Women by Grace—R
Women Today—R

HEALING

ADULT/GENERAL
Alliance Life
$-Angels on Earth
$-Animal Trails—R
$-Brave Hearts
Breakthrough Intercessor—R
$-Bridal Guides—R
$-Canada Lutheran—R
$-Catholic New Times—R
$-Celebrate Life—R
$-CGA World—R
Channels—R
$-Charisma
Christian Motorsports
Christian Online
Christian Ranchman
Connecting Point—R
$-Cornerstone Christian—R
$-Cup of Comfort—R
Evangelical Advocate—R
$-Faith Today
$-Foursquare World Advance—R
$-Gem—R
$-Good News—R
$-Guideposts—R
HopeKeepers—R
$-Light & Life
$-Liguorian
$-Live—R
Maranatha News—R
Metro Voice—R
$-National Catholic
New Heart—R
$-North American Voice—R
$-Now What?—R
$-Positive Thinking—R
Prayer Closet
Quaker Life—R
Sacred Journey—R
$-SCP Journal—R
Sharing—R
$-Sound Body—R
$-Spiritual Life
Spiritual Voice—R
$-St. Anthony Messenger
Steps
$-Testimony—R
thegoodsteward.com—R
$-Today's Christian—R
Tributes—R

Trumpeter—R
$-United Church Observer—R
Victory News—R
$-Vision—R
$-World & I—R
$-Young Christian—R

CHILDREN
$-BREAD/God's Children—R

PASTORS/LEADERS
$-African American Pulpit
$-Christian Century—R
$-Emmanuel
$-Interpreter
Journal/Pastoral Care—R
$-Ministry
$-Priest
Sharing the Practice—R
Steps
$-Word & World

TEEN/YOUNG ADULT
$-Young Christian—R

WOMEN
ChurchWoman
$-Esprit—R
$-Godly Business Woman
$-inSpirit—R
$-SpiritLed Woman
$-Woman's Touch—R

WRITERS
$-Areopagus (UK)

HEALTH

ADULT/GENERAL
$-Alive!—R
$-Angels on Earth
$-Anglican Journal
$-B.C. Catholic—R
Breakthrough Intercessor—R
$-Canada Lutheran—R
$-Catholic Forester—R
$-Catholic New Times—R
CBN.com—R
$-Celebrate Life—R
$-CGA World—R
Channels—R
$-Charisma
Christian Bible Studies.com
$-Christian Courier (CAN)—R
Christian Courier (WI)—R
Christian Journal—R
Christian Motorsports
Christian Online

$-Christian Social Action—R
$-Christianweek
$-Common Ground—R
$-Cornerstone Christian—R
Creation Care—R
Disciple's Journal—R
Discovery—R
$-Faith Today
$-Gospel Today—R
$-Grit
$-Guideposts—R
Hannah to Hannah—R
Highway News—R
$-Home Times—R
HopeKeepers—R
$-Inland NW Christian
$-Inside Journal—R
$-Joy & Praise
$-Kiwanis
Life Tools for Women
$-Lifeglow—R
$-Light & Life
$-Living—R
$-Lutheran Digest—R
$-Marriage Partnership—R
$-Mature Years—R
$-MESSAGE
Metro Voice—R
$-Montgomery's Journey
New Heart—R
$-New Man—R
$-Physician—R
$-Positive Thinking—R
Quaker Life—R
$-Relevant
Sacred Journey—R
$-SCP Journal—R
$-Senior Living
$-Sound Body—R
$-Special Living—R
Spiritual Voice—R
$-Spring Hill Review—R
$-St. Anthony Messenger
$-Studio Classroom
$-Testimony—R
thegoodsteward.com—R
$-Today's Christian—R
Tributes—R
Trumpeter—R
$-Upscale Magazine
$-Vibrant Life—R
Victory News—R
$-War Cry—R
$-World & I—R
$-Young Christian—R

CHILDREN
$-American Girl
Barefoot for Kids—R
$-BREAD/God's Children—R
$-Club Connection
$-Guideposts for Kids
$-On the Line—R
$-SHINE brightly—R
$-Winner—R

CHRISTIAN EDUCATION/LIBRARY
$-Children's Ministry
$-Teachers of Vision—R

PASTORS/LEADERS
$-African American Pulpit
$-Building Church Leaders.com
$-Christian Camp—R
$-Christian Century—R
$-Interpreter
Journal/Pastoral Care—R
$-Lutheran Partners—R
$-Rev.
$-Word & World

TEEN/YOUNG ADULT
$-Brio—R
$-Brio & Beyond
$-Devo'Zine—R
$-Listen—R
Setmag.com—R
TeensForJC.com—R
Transcendmag.com—R
$-Young and Alive—R

WOMEN
$-At the Center—R
Christian Women Today—R
ChurchWoman
$-Esprit—R
$-Godly Business Woman
Hearts at Home—R
$-inSpirit—R
Keeping Hearts & Home
Lutheran Woman's Quar.
$-MOMsense—R
$-SpiritLed Woman
$-Today's Christian Woman—R
$-Welcome Home
Women Today—R

HISTORICAL

ADULT/GENERAL
AGAIN—R
$-America
$-Angels on Earth

$-Animal Trails—R
$-Arlington Catholic
$-Bridal Guides—R
$-Cappers
$-Cathedral Age
$-Catholic Answer
$-Catholic New Times—R
$-Catholic Peace Voice—R
$-Celebrate Life—R
Channels—R
Christian C. L. RECORD—R
$-Christian Courier (CAN)—R
$-Christian History & Biography—R
Christian Motorsports
Christian Observer
Christian Online
$-Christian Renewal—R
$-Christianity Today—R
$-Company—R
$-Cresset
Dallas/Ft. Worth Heritage
$-Dovetail—R
$-Eclectic Homeschool
Evangelical Advocate—R
$-Faith Today
$-Generation X—R
Grand Valley Observer—R
$-Grit
$-Home Times—R
$-Indian Life—R
Journal of Church & State
$-Layman
$-Lifeglow—R
$-Light & Life
$-Mature Living
$-Mennonite Historian—R
$-Messiah Magazine
Methodist History
$-National Catholic
$-New Freeman—R
$-New Wineskins—R
$-North American Voice—R
$-Nostalgia Magazine—R
$-Our Sunday Visitor
$-Over the Back Fence—R
$-Power for Living—R
PrayerWorks—R
Presbyterian Outlook
Priscilla Papers—R
$-SCP Journal—R
Sharing—R
$-Social Justice—R
$-Spring Hill Review—R
$-St. Anthony Messenger
Star of Zion

Storyteller—R
$-Testimony—R
thegoodsteward.com—R
$-Tidewater Parent—R
Trumpeter—R
$-Upscale Magazine
Victory News—R
$-Way of St. Francis—R
$-Wireless Age—R
$-World & I—R
$-Young Christian—R

CHILDREN
$-BREAD/God's Children—R
$-Children's Magic Window
$-Guideposts for Kids
$-High Adventure—R
$-My Friend
$-On the Line—R
Skipping Stones
Young Gentleman's Monthly

CHRISTIAN EDUCATION/LIBRARY
$-Teachers of Vision—R

MISSIONS
East-West Church
Missiology
Women of the Harvest
$-Worldwide Challenge

MUSIC
$-Church Pianist
$-Creator—R

PASTORS/LEADERS
$-African American Pulpit
$-Ministry
$-Pastoral Life—R
Sewanee Theological Review
Sharing the Practice—R
Theological Digest—R
$-Today's Parish—R
$-Word & World

TEEN/YOUNG ADULT
$-Breakaway
$-Listen—R
$-Passageway.org—R
$-Real Faith in Life—R
Setmag.com—R
$-Student Leadership—R
TeensForJC.com—R
Transcendmag.com—R
$-Young Adult Today—R
$-Young and Alive—R
$-Young Christian—R

WOMEN
$-History's Women—R
Just Between Us—R
Shalom Bayit
$-SpiritLed Woman

WRITERS
$-Areopagus (UK)
Cochran's Corner—R
$-Tickled by Thunder

HOLIDAY/SEASONAL

ADULT/GENERAL
$-alive now!—R
$-Alive!—R
American Tract Society—R
$-Angels on Earth
$-Animal Trails—R
$-Annals of St. Anne
$-Arlington Catholic
Barefoot Path—R
$-BGC World—R
Breakthrough Intercessor—R
$-Bridal Guides—R
$-Canada Lutheran—R
$-Cathedral Age
$-Catholic Digest—R
$-Catholic Forester—R
$-Catholic New York
$-Catholic Parent
$-CGA World—R
Channels—R
$-Charisma
$-Chicken Soup—R
Christian C. L. RECORD—R
$-Christian Courier (CAN)—R
Christian Courier (WI)—R
$-Christian Home & School
Christian Motorsports
Christian Online
$-Christian Parenting—R
$-Christian Renewal—R
$-Christian Retailing
$-Christianweek
Connecting Point—R
$-Cornerstone Christian—R
$-Covenant Companion—R
Desert Call—R
Discovery—R
$-Dovetail—R
$-Eclectic Homeschool
$-Evangel—R
Evangelical Advocate—R
$-Faith Today
$-Family Digest—R
$-Fellowship Focus—R

$-Foursquare World Advance—R
$-Gem—R
$-Generation X—R
Good News Journal
Gospel Tract—R
$-Guideposts—R
Hannah to Hannah—R
Heartlight—R
Highway News—R
$-Home Times—R
$-Horizons (adult)—R
$-Ideals—R
$-Indian Life—R
$-Inside Journal—R
Jewel Among Jewels
$-Lifeglow—R
$-Light & Life
$-Live—R
$-Living—R
$-Living Church
$-Lookout—R
$-Lutheran Digest—R
$-Mature Living
Mature Times—R
$-Mature Years—R
$-Men of Integrity—R
$-MESSAGE
MESSAGE/Open Bible—R
$-Messenger
$-Minnesota Christian—R
$-Montgomery's Journey
$-National Catholic
$-North American Voice—R
$-Oblates
$-Our Sunday Visitor
$-Over the Back Fence—R
Parents & Teens—R
Pegasus Review—R
$-Plain Truth—R
$-Positive Thinking—R
$-Power for Living—R
$-Prairie Messenger—R
PrayerWorks—R
$-Priority!
$-Psychology for Living—R
$-Purpose—R
Quaker Life—R
$-Relate—R
Sacred Journey—R
$-Seek—R
Sharing—R
Singles Scoop—R
$-Smart Families—R
$-Special Living—R
Spiritual Voice—R

$-Spring Hill Review—R
$-St. Anthony Messenger
$-St. Joseph's Messenger—R
$-Standard—R
Star of Zion
Storyteller—R
$-Testimony—R
thegoodsteward.com—R
$-Today's Christian—R
$-Together—R
Tributes—R
Trumpeter—R
$-U.S. Catholic
$-United Church Observer—R
$-Vibrant Life—R
Victory News—R
$-War Cry—R
$-Wesleyan Life—R
$-World & I—R
$-Young Christian—R

CHILDREN
Barefoot for Kids—R
$-Celebrate
$-Club Connection
$-Courage—R
$-Focus/Clubhouse
$-Focus/Clubhouse Jr.
$-Guideposts for Kids
$-Juniorway
$-My Friend
$-Nature Friend
$-On the Line—R
$-Partners—R
$-Pockets—R
$-Primary Pal (IL)
$-Primary Street
$-SHINE brightly—R
Skipping Stones
$-Winner—R

CHRISTIAN EDUCATION/LIBRARY
$-Catechist
$-Children's Ministry
$-Church Educator—R
$-Evangelizing Today's Child—R
$-Leader in C. E. Ministries
$-Resource—R
$-Teachers of Vision—R
$-Today's Catholic Teacher—R

MISSIONS
Railroad Evangelist—R
Women of the Harvest
$-Worldwide Challenge

MUSIC
$-Church Pianist
$-Creator—R
Quest—R

PASTORS/LEADERS
$-African American Pulpit
$-Catholic Servant
$-Christian Century—R
$-Enrichment—R
$-Five Stones—R
$-Interpreter
$-Ministry & Liturgy—R
Ministry in Motion—R
$-Pastoral Life—R
Pulpit Helps—R
$-Rev.

TEEN/YOUNG ADULT
$-Brio—R
$-Brio & Beyond
$-Conqueror—R
$-Essential Connection
$-Listen—R
$-Real Faith in Life—R
Setmag.com—R
Teen Light—R
$-Teenage Christian—R
TeensForJC.com—R
Transcendmag.com—R
$-Young and Alive—R
$-Young Christian—R
$-Young Salvationist—R

WOMEN
Anna's Journal—R
Christian Woman's Page—R
Christian Women Today—R
$-Esprit—R
Handmaiden—R
Hearts at Home—R
$-History's Women—R
$-Horizons (women)—R
$-inSpirit—R
Lutheran Woman's Quar.
$-MOMsense—R
P31 Woman—R
$-Today's Christian Woman—R
$-Woman's Touch—R
$-Women by Grace—R
Women Today—R

WRITERS
$-Areopagus (UK)

HOMESCHOOLING

ADULT/GENERAL
$-Anglican Journal

$-Arlington Catholic
Barefoot Path—R
Breakthrough Intercessor—R
$-CBA Marketplace
Channels—R
$-Charisma
Christian C. L. RECORD—R
Christian Computing—R
$-Christian Examiner
Christian Motorsports
Christian Observer
Christian Online
$-Christian Parenting—R
$-Cornerstone Christian—R
Creation Care—R
Disciple's Journal—R
Discovery—R
$-Dovetail—R
$-Eclectic Homeschool
$-Faith & Family
$-Faith Today
Good News Journal
$-Home Times—R
$-Homeschooling Today—R
$-Interim—R
$-Light & Life
Metro Voice—R
$-Minnesota Christian—R
Parents & Teens—R
$-Psychology for Living—R
$-Smart Families—R
$-Social Justice—R
$-St. Anthony Messenger
$-Testimony—R
thegoodsteward.com—R
Trumpeter—R
Victory News—R
$-Wesleyan Life—R
$-World & I—R

CHILDREN
$-BREAD/God's Children—R
$-Focus/Clubhouse
$-Guideposts for Kids
Skipping Stones

CHRISTIAN EDUCATION/LIBRARY
$-Children's Ministry
Jour./Ed. & Christian Belief—R

MISSIONS
Women of the Harvest

PASTORS/LEADERS
$-Pastoral Life—R

TEEN/YOUNG ADULT
$-Passageway.org—R
Teen Light—R

WOMEN
Christian Woman's Page—R
Crowned with Silver
Hearts at Home—R
Shalom Bayit

HOMILETICS

ADULT/GENERAL
Channels—R
Church Herald & Holiness—R
Grand Valley Observer—R
$-Lookout—R
Maranatha News—R
$-New Wineskins—R
Priscilla Papers—R
$-St. Anthony Messenger
$-Stewardship—R
$-Testimony—R
Trumpeter—R
$-U.S. Catholic
Victory News—R
$-Way of St. Francis—R

PASTORS/LEADERS
$-African American Pulpit
Angelos—R
$-Barefoot—R
$-Clergy Journal—R
$-Emmanuel
$-Evangelical Baptist—R
Interpretation
$-Leadership—R
$-Lutheran Partners—R
$-Pastoral Life—R
$-Preaching
Preaching On-Line—R
$-Priest
$-Proclaim—R
Quarterly Review
Sewanee Theological Review
Sharing the Practice—R
$-Spiritual Spinach—R

WOMEN
$-SpiritLed Woman

HOW-TO

ADULT/GENERAL
$-Bridal Guides—R
$-CBA Marketplace
$-Celebrate Life—R
$-CGA World—R
Channels—R

$-Charisma
Christian Bible Studies.com
$-Christian Home & School
Christian Journal—R
Christian Motorsports
Christian Observer
Christian Online
$-Christian Parenting—R
$-Christian Retailing
$-Church of God EVANGEL
Connecting Point—R
$-Cornerstone Christian—R
Creation Care—R
Discovery—R
$-Dovetail—R
$-Eclectic Homeschool
$-Faith & Family
$-Faith Today
$-Family Digest—R
$-Generation X—R
Good News Journal
$-Home Times—R
$-Inland NW Christian
Jewel Among Jewels
$-Joy & Praise
$-Light & Life
$-Living Church
$-Lutheran Digest—R
$-Marriage Partnership—R
$-Mennonite Historian—R
$-MESSAGE
$-Montgomery's Journey
Mutuality—R
$-On Mission
$-Physician—R
$-Positive Thinking—R
PrayerWorks—R
Regent Business—R
$-Smart Families—R
$-St. Anthony Messenger
Storyteller—R
$-Testimony—R
thegoodsteward.com—R
$-Tidewater Parent—R
$-Today's Christian—R
Tributes—R
Trumpeter—R
$-Vibrant Life—R
Victory News—R
$-World & I—R

CHILDREN
$-High Adventure—R
$-Kids' Ministry Ideas—R
$-PrayKids!—R

CHRISTIAN EDUCATION/LIBRARY
Catholic Library World
$-Children's Ministry
Christian Librarian—R
Christian Library Journal—R
Church & Synagogue Lib.—R
$-Church Educator—R
$-Church Libraries—R
$-Group
$-Ideas Unlimited—R
$-Kids' Ministry Ideas—R
$-Leader in C. E. Ministries
$-Religion Teacher's Journal
$-Resource—R
$-Teachers Interaction
$-Teachers of Vision—R
$-Today's Catholic Teacher—R
$-Youth & CE Leadership

MISSIONS
$-PFI World Report—R

MUSIC
Tradition

PASTORS/LEADERS
$-Building Church Leaders.com
$-Evangelical Baptist—R
$-Evangelicals Today—R
$-Interpreter
$-Ministry & Liturgy—R
Ministry in Motion—R
Net Results
$-Newsletter Newsletter
$-Rev.
$-RevWriter Resource
$-Sabbath School Leadership—R
$-Small Group Dynamics—R
$-WCA News—R
$-Worship Leader
$-Your Church—R
$-Youthworker

TEEN/YOUNG ADULT
$-Boundless Webzine—R
$-Brio—R
$-Brio & Beyond
$-Listen—R
$-Real Faith in Life—R
Setmag.com—R
Teen Light—R
TeensForJC.com—R
Transcendmag.com—R
$-Young and Alive—R

WOMEN
Christian Women Today—R

$-Esprit—R
Just Between Us—R
$-Melody of the Heart
$-MOMsense—R
Reflections
Right to the Heart—R
$-Today's Christian Woman—R
Women Today—R

WRITERS
Author-Me.com
$-Byline
$-Christian Communicator—R
$-Cross & Quill—R
$-Exchange—R
$-Money the Write Way—R
NW Christian Author—R
Once Upon a Time—R
$-Spirit-Led Writer—R
$-Writer's Digest—R

HOW-TO ACTIVITIES (JUV.)

ADULT/GENERAL
$-Animal Trails—R
Channels—R
Christian Online
$-Christian Parenting—R
$-Christian Parents Section
$-Cornerstone Christian—R
Creation Care—R
$-Dovetail—R
$-Eclectic Homeschool
$-Faith & Family
$-Generation X—R
Good News Journal
$-Homeschooling Today—R
$-Indian Life—R
Keys to Living—R
$-Light & Life
$-Living—R
$-Lutheran Digest—R
$-Smart Families—R
Spiritual Voice—R
$-St. Anthony Messenger
$-World & I—R
$-Young Christian—R

CHILDREN
$-American Girl
Barefoot for Kids—R
$-BREAD/God's Children—R
$-Cadet Quest—R
$-Celebrate
$-Children's Magic Window
$-Club Connection

$-Courage—R
$-Faces
$-Focus/Clubhouse
$-Focus/Clubhouse Jr.
$-Guide—R
$-Guideposts for Kids
$-High Adventure—R
$-Kids' Ministry Ideas—R
$-My Friend
$-Nature Friend
$-On the Line—R
$-Partners—R
$-Pockets—R
$-Preschool Playhouse
$-Primary Pal (IL)
$-SHINE brightly—R
Skipping Stones
$-Story Friends—R
$-Winner—R

CHRISTIAN EDUCATION/LIBRARY
$-Catechist
$-Children's Ministry
$-Church Educator—R
$-Evangelizing Today's Child—R
$-Group
$-Kids' Ministry Ideas—R
$-Preschool Playhouse
$-Religion Teacher's Journal
$-Teachers Interaction
$-Teachers of Vision—R

PASTORS/LEADERS
$-Building Church Leaders.com
$-Evangelical Baptist—R
$-Interpreter
$-Rev.

TEEN/YOUNG ADULT
$-Breakaway
Teen Light—R
$-Young Christian—R
$-Young Salvationist—R

WOMEN
$-Godly Business Woman
Just Between Us—R
Reflections

HUMOR

ADULT/GENERAL
$-Alive!—R
Alliance Life
American Tract Society—R
$-Angels on Earth
$-Animal Trails—R
Barefoot Path—R

Bread of Life—R
$-Bridal Guides—R
$-Cadet Quest—R
$-Catholic Digest—R
$-Catholic Forester—R
$-Catholic Parent
$-Catholic Peace Voice—R
$-CGA World—R
Channels—R
$-Charisma
Chattels of the Heart—R
$-Chicken Soup—R
Christian C. L. RECORD—R
Christian Computing—R
$-Christian Courier (CAN)—R
$-Christian Home & School
Christian Journal—R
Christian Motorsports
Christian Online
$-Christian Parenting—R
$-Christian Parents Section
Christian Radio Weekly
$-Christianity Today—R
$-Church of God EVANGEL
Connecting Point—R
$-Cornerstone Christian—R
$-Cup of Comfort—R
Disciple's Journal—R
$-DisciplesWorld
$-Door—R
$-Dovetail—R
$-Evangel—R
Evangelical Advocate—R
$-Faith & Family
$-Faith Today
$-Gem—R
$-Generation X—R
$-God Allows U-Turns—R
Good News Journal
Gospel Tract—R
Hannah to Hannah—R
Highway News—R
$-Home Times—R
$-Homeschooling Today—R
$-Indian Life—R
$-Inland NW Christian
$-Lifeglow—R
$-Light & Life
Literary TNT—R
$-Living—R
$-Living Church
$-Living Light News—R
$-Lutheran—R
$-Lutheran Digest—R
Maranatha News—R

$-Marriage Partnership—R
$-Mature Living
Mature Times—R
$-Minnesota Christian—R
$-National Catholic
$-New Freeman—R
New Heart—R
$-New Wineskins—R
$-Nostalgia Magazine—R
$-Over the Back Fence—R
$-ParentLife
Pegasus Review—R
Plowman—R
$-Positive Thinking—R
PrayerWorks—R
$-Presbyterian Record—R
$-Psychology for Living—R
Quaker Life—R
Re:generation Quarterly
$-Relate—R
Rhubarb
Rose & Thorn
Sacred Journey—R
$-Seek—R
$-Senior Living
$-Signs of the Times—R
$-Silver Wings—R
Singles Scoop—R
$-Smart Families—R
Spiritual Voice—R
$-St. Anthony Messenger
Storyteller—R
$-Testimony—R
thegoodsteward.com—R
$-Tidewater Parent—R
$-Today's Christian—R
$-Together—R
Trumpeter—R
Victory News—R
$-Vision—R
$-War Cry—R
$-Weavings—R
Winsome Wit—R
$-World & I—R
Xavier Review
$-Young Christian—R

CHILDREN
Barefoot for Kids—R
$-Cadet Quest—R
$-Children's Magic Window
$-Club Connection
$-Guide—R
$-High Adventure—R
$-My Friend
$-On the Line—R

$-SHINE brightly—R
$-Story Friends—R
$-Winner—R

CHRISTIAN EDUCATION/LIBRARY
$-Group
$-Youth & CE Leadership

MISSIONS
Women of the Harvest
$-Worldwide Challenge

MUSIC
$-Church Pianist
$-Creator—R
Quest—R

PASTORS/LEADERS
$-Catholic Servant
$-Enrichment—R
$-Eucharistic Ministries—R
$-Evangelical Baptist—R
$-Evangelicals Today—R
$-Five Stones—R
$-Joke Writers
$-Leadership—R
$-Ministries Today
$-Ministry & Liturgy—R
$-Pastoral Life—R
Pulpit Helps—R
$-Rev.
$-Sermon Notes—R
Sharing the Practice—R
$-Small Group Dynamics—R
$-Spiritual Spinach—R
$-Today's Parish—R
$-WCA News—R

TEEN/YOUNG ADULT
$-Boundless Webzine—R
$-Breakaway
$-Brio—R
$-Essential Connection
$-Guideposts Sweet 16—R
$-Listen—R
$-Passageway.org—R
$-Real Faith in Life—R
Setmag.com—R
Teen Light—R
TeensForJC.com—R
Transcendmag.com—R
$-With—R
$-Young and Alive—R
$-Young Christian—R
$-Young Salvationist—R

WOMEN
$-Esprit—R

Hearts at Home—R
$-inSpirit—R
$-Journey
Just Between Us—R
Keeping Hearts & Home
Lutheran Woman's Quar.
$-Melody of the Heart
$-MOMsense—R
Reflections
$-SpiritLed Woman
$-Today's Christian Woman—R
$-Women by Grace—R
Women Today—R

WRITERS
$-Areopagus (UK)
Beginnings
$-Byline
$-Christian Communicator—R
$-Exchange—R
$-Fellowscript—R
Once Upon a Time—R
$-WIN-Informer

INNER LIFE

ADULT/GENERAL
Barefoot Path—R
$-BGC World—R
$-Bible Advocate—R
$-Bridal Guides—R
$-Catholic Digest—R
Channels—R
Christian Bible Studies.com
Christian Journal—R
$-Cup of Comfort—R
$-Discipleship Journal—R
Divine Ascent
$-Faith & Family
$-Faith Today
$-Generation X—R
Hannah to Hannah—R
Highway News—R
LifeTimes Catholic
$-Light & Life
Literary TNT—R
$-Living—R
$-Lookout—R
Mature Times—R
$-Mature Years—R
$-Men of Integrity—R
Men of the Cross—R
$-National Catholic
$-New Wineskins—R
$-North American Voice—R
$-Now What?—R
$-Positive Thinking—R

$-Presbyterians Today—R
Quaker Life—R
Reformed Quarterly
Regent Business—R
$-Relate—R
Sacred Journey—R
$-Silver Wings—R
Singles Scoop—R
Spiritual Voice—R
$-Testimony—R
$-Together—R
Victory News—R
$-World & I—R

CHILDREN
$-BREAD/God's Children—R

CHRISTIAN EDUCATION/LIBRARY
$-Teachers of Vision—R

PASTORS/LEADERS
$-Building Church Leaders.com
$-Evangelical Baptist—R
Journal/Pastoral Care—R

TEEN/YOUNG ADULT
$-Brio & Beyond
Setmag.com—R
TeensForJC.com—R
Transcendmag.com—R
$-Young Christian—R

WOMEN
Christian Woman's Page—R
$-Esprit—R
$-inSpirit—R
Praise
Right to the Heart—R
$-Today's Christian Woman—R
$-Woman's Touch—R
Women of the Cross—R

INSPIRATIONAL

ADULT/GENERAL
African Voices—R
$-alive now!—R
Alliance Life
$-Angels on Earth
$-Annals of St. Anne
$-Arlington Catholic
Barefoot Path—R
$-Brave Hearts
Bread of Life—R
Breakthrough Intercessor—R
$-Bridal Guides—R
$-Canada Lutheran—R
$-Cappers

$-Catholic Answer
$-Catholic Forester—R
$-Catholic New Times—R
$-Catholic Parent
$-Catholic Peace Voice—R
$-Celebrate Life—R
$-CGA World—R
Channels—R
$-Charisma
Chattels of the Heart—R
$-Chicken Soup—R
Christian Bible Studies.com
Christian Journal—R
Christian Motorsports
Christian Online
$-Christian Parents Section
Christian Radio Weekly
Christian Ranchman
Church Herald & Holiness—R
$-Church of God EVANGEL
Connecting Point—R
$-Cornerstone Christian—R
$-Covenant Companion—R
$-Cup of Comfort—R
$-Decision
$-Direction
Divine Ascent
$-Evangel—R
Evangelical Advocate—R
$-Faith & Family
$-Faith Today
$-Family Digest—R
$-Flutters of the Heart
$-Focus on the Family
$-Foursquare World Advance—R
$-Gem—R
$-God Allows U-Turns—R
$-Good News—R
Good News Journal
$-Gospel Today—R
Gospel Tract—R
Grand Valley Observer—R
$-Grit
$-Guideposts—R
Hannah to Hannah—R
Heartlight—R
Heartwarmers
Highway News—R
$-Home Times—R
HopeKeepers—R
$-Ideals—R
$-Indian Life—R
$-Inland NW Christian
Insight (for blind)
$-Joy & Praise
Keys to Living—R

Leaves—R
$-Lifeglow—R
$-Light & Life
$-Liguorian
Literary TNT—R
$-Live—R
$-Living—R
$-Living Church
$-Lookout—R
$-Lutheran—R
$-Lutheran Digest—R
Maranatha News—R
$-Marian Helper—R
$-Mature Living
Mature Times—R
$-Mennonite Brethren—R
$-MESSAGE
MESSAGE/Open Bible—R
$-Messenger of the Sacred Heart
$-Minnesota Christian—R
$-Montgomery's Journey
Mutuality—R
$-National Catholic
$-New Freeman—R
New Heart—R
$-North American Voice—R
$-Oblates
$-Over the Back Fence—R
Parents & Teens—R
Pegasus Review—R
$-Plain Truth—R
Plowman—R
$-Positive Thinking—R
$-Power for Living—R
$-Prairie Messenger—R
PrayerWorks—R
$-Precepts for Living
$-Presbyterian Record—R
$-Psychology for Living—R
$-Purpose—R
Quaker Life—R
$-Queen of All Hearts
$-Relate—R
Sacred Journey—R
$-Seeds
$-Seek—R
$-Shantyman—R
$-Silver Wings—R
Singles Scoop—R
Southwest Kansas
Spiritual Voice—R
$-St. Anthony Messenger
$-St. Joseph's Messenger—R
$-Standard—R
Star of Zion
$-Stewardship—R

Storyteller—R
Sword and Trumpet—R
Sword of the Lord—R
$-Testimony—R
thegoodsteward.com—R
$-Today's Christian—R
$-Together—R
Trumpeter—R
$-United Church Observer—R
$-Upscale Magazine
Victory News—R
$-Vision—R
$-War Cry—R
$-Way of St. Francis—R
$-Wesleyan Life—R
$-World & I—R
$-Worldwide Challenge
$-Young Christian—R

CHILDREN
Barefoot for Kids—R
$-BREAD/God's Children—R
$-Cadet Quest—R
$-Club Connection
$-Guide—R
$-High Adventure—R
$-Juniorway
$-Partners—R
$-Primary Street
$-SHINE brightly—R

CHRISTIAN EDUCATION/LIBRARY
$-Children's Ministry
Church & Synagogue Lib.—R
$-Journal/Adventist Educ.—R
$-Teachers of Vision—R

MISSIONS
Women of the Harvest

MUSIC
$-Creator—R
Quest—R
$-Resource—R
$-Senior Musician—R
Tradition

PASTORS/LEADERS
$-African American Pulpit
$-Building Church Leaders.com
$-Catholic Servant
Cell Group—R
$-Emmanuel
$-Evangelical Baptist—R
$-Evangelicals Today—R
Journal/Pastoral Care—R
$-Leadership—R

$-Let's Worship
$-Ministry
$-Pastoral Life—R
Pulpit Helps—R
$-Rev.
Sharing the Practice—R
Technologies for Worship—R

TEEN/YOUNG ADULT
$-Breakaway
$-Brio—R
$-Conqueror—R
$-Guideposts Sweet 16—R
$-J.A.M.: Jesus and Me
$-Passageway.org—R
Setmag.com—R
Teen Light—R
$-Teenage Christian—R
TeensForJC.com—R
Transcendmag.com—R
$-With—R
$-Young Christian—R

WOMEN
Christian Woman's Page—R
Christian Women Today—R
$-Esprit—R
$-Godly Business Woman
Handmaiden—R
Hearts at Home—R
$-Horizons (women)—R
$-inSpirit—R
$-Journey
Just Between Us—R
Lutheran Woman's Quar.
P31 Woman—R
Reflections
Right to the Heart—R
$-SpiritLed Woman
$-Today's Christian Woman—R
$-Woman's Touch—R
$-Women Alive!—R
Women of the Cross—R

WRITERS
$-Areopagus (UK)
$-Byline
Once Upon a Time—R
$-Writer's Digest—R

INTERVIEWS/PROFILES

ADULT/GENERAL
AGAIN—R
$-Alive!—R
American Tract Society—R
$-Anglican Journal
$-Arlington Catholic

$-BGC World—R
Books & Culture
Breakthrough Intercessor—R
$-Catholic New York
$-Catholic Parent
$-Catholic Peace Voice—R
CBN.com—R
$-Celebrate Life—R
Channels—R
$-Charisma
Christian C. L. RECORD—R
Christian Courier (WI)—R
Christian Journal—R
Christian Motorsports
Christian News NW—R
Christian Observer
Christian Online
$-Christian Parents Section
Christian Ranchman
$-Christianity Today—R
$-Christianweek
$-Columbia
$-Cornerstone Christian—R
Creation Care—R
$-Culture Wars—R
Desert Call—R
$-Direction
Divine Ascent
$-Door—R
$-Dovetail—R
$-Eclectic Homeschool
$-Episcopal Life—R
$-Faith Today
$-Gem—R
$-Generation X—R
$-God Allows U-Turns—R
$-Good News—R
$-Gospel Today—R
$-Grit
$-Guideposts—R
Heartlight—R
$-Home Times—R
$-Indian Life—R
$-Inside Journal—R
$-Interim—R
$-Joy & Praise
$-Layman
$-Lifeglow—R
$-Light & Life
$-Liguorian
$-Living Church
$-Lookout—R
$-Lutheran—R
Maranatha News—R
Mars Hill Review

$-Mennonite Historian—R
$-MESSAGE
$-Messenger
Metro Voice—R
$-Minnesota Christian—R
$-Montgomery's Journey
Mutuality—R
$-National Catholic
New Heart—R
$-New Man—R
$-North American Voice—R
$-Nostalgia Magazine—R
$-Over the Back Fence—R
$-Physician—R
$-Portland Magazine
$-Positive Thinking—R
$-Power for Living—R
PrayerWorks—R
$-Precepts for Living
Presbyterian Outlook
$-Presbyterian Record—R
$-Priority!
$-Prism—R
Quaker Life—R
Regent Business—R
$-Relate—R
$-Relevant
Rose & Thorn
Sacred Journey—R
$-Science & Spirit
$-SCP Journal—R
$-Senior Living
Spiritual Voice—R
$-Spring Hill Review—R
$-St. Anthony Messenger
$-Stewardship—R
$-Testimony—R
thegoodsteward.com—R
$-Tidewater Parent—R
$-Today's Christian—R
Tributes—R
Trumpeter—R
$-United Church Observer—R
$-Upscale Magazine
Valparaiso Poetry—R
Victory News—R
$-War Cry—R
$-Way of St. Francis—R
$-Weavings—R
$-Wireless Age—R
$-World & I—R

CHILDREN
$-Faces
$-Juniorway
$-My Friend

$-Pockets—R
$-Primary Street
$-SHINE brightly—R
Skipping Stones

CHRISTIAN EDUCATION/LIBRARY
$-Children's Ministry
Christian Early Education—R
Christian Librarian—R
Christian Library Journal—R
$-Church Libraries—R

MISSIONS
East-West Church
$-Evangelical Missions—R
$-Leaders for Today
$-One
OpRev Equipper—R
$-PFI World Report—R
$-World Pulse—R
$-Worldwide Challenge

MUSIC
Quest—R

PASTORS/LEADERS
$-African American Pulpit
Angelos—R
$-Building Church Leaders.com
$-Catholic Servant
Cell Group—R
$-Christian Camp—R
$-Christian Century—R
$-Evangelicals Today—R
$-Leadership—R
$-Ministries Today
$-Ministry & Liturgy—R
Ministry in Motion—R
$-Pastoral Life—R
$-Rev.
$-RevWriter Resource
$-Sermon Notes—R
$-This Rock
$-Youthworker

TEEN/YOUNG ADULT
$-Boundless Webzine—R
$-Brio & Beyond
$-Essential Connection
$-Guideposts Sweet 16—R
$-Insight—R
$-J.A.M.: Jesus and Me
$-Listen—R
$-Passageway.org—R
Setmag.com—R
$-Sharing the VICTORY—R
Teen Light—R

$-Teenage Christian—R
TeensForJC.com—R
Transcendmag.com—R
$-Young and Alive—R
$-Young Salvationist—R
YouthWalk

WOMEN
Hearts at Home—R
$-Horizons (women)—R
$-Journey
$-MOMsense—R
$-Today's Christian Woman—R

WRITERS
$-Advanced Chris. Writer—R
$-Areopagus (UK)
BOOK Magazine
$-Christian Communicator—R
$-Cross & Quill—R
$-Exchange—R
$-Fellowscript—R
$-Money the Write Way—R
NW Christian Author—R
Once Upon a Time—R
Upper Case
Writer's Lifeline
Writers Manual
Writes of Passage

LEADERSHIP

ADULT/GENERAL
African Voices—R
Alliance Life
$-Angels on Earth
Breakthrough Intercessor—R
$-CGA World—R
Channels—R
$-Christian Courier (CAN)—R
$-Christian Leader—R
Christian Motorsports
Christian Ranchman
$-Christian Retailing
$-Christian Standard—R
$-Christianweek
$-Church of God EVANGEL
$-Cornerstone Christian—R
$-Culture Wars—R
$-Decision
Disciple's Journal—R
$-Faith Today
$-Fellowship Focus—R
$-Foursquare World Advance—R
$-Gem—R
$-Generation X—R
$-Good News—R
Grand Valley Observer—R

Heartlight—R
$-Inland NW Christian
$-Layman
$-Light & Life
Literary TNT—R
$-Living Church
$-Lookout—R
Mutuality—R
$-National Catholic
$-New Freeman—R
$-New Wineskins—R
$-NRB Magazine—R
Presbyterian Outlook
$-Presbyterian Record—R
Priscilla Papers—R
$-Prism—R
Quaker Life—R
Re:generation Quarterly
Regent Business—R
Sacred Journey—R
Spiritual Voice—R
$-St. Anthony Messenger
$-Stewardship—R
$-Testimony—R
thegoodsteward.com—R
Trumpeter—R
$-United Church Observer—R
Victory News—R
Walk This Way—R
$-Way of St. Francis—R
$-Wesleyan Life—R
$-Wireless Age—R
$-World & I—R
$-Young Christian—R

CHILDREN
$-Club Connection

CHRISTIAN EDUCATION/LIBRARY
Catholic Library World
$-Children's Ministry
Christian Early Education—R
$-Church Educator—R
$-Group
$-Ideas Unlimited—R
Journal/Christian Education
$-Leader in C. E. Ministries
$-Momentum
$-Resource—R
$-Teachers Interaction
$-Today's Catholic Teacher—R
$-Youth & CE Leadership

MISSIONS
$-Leaders for Today
$-Worldwide Challenge

PASTORS/LEADERS
$-African American Pulpit
Angelos—R
$-Barefoot—R
$-Building Church Leaders.com
$-Catholic Servant
Cell Group—R
$-Christian Camp—R
$-Christian Century—R
Christian Education Journal (CA)—R
Christian Management—R
$-Church Growth Network—R
$-Church Worship
$-Clergy Journal—R
$-Emmanuel
$-Enrichment—R
$-Eucharistic Ministries—R
$-Evangelical Baptist—R
$-Evangelicals Today—R
$-Five Stones—R
$-Horizons (pastor)—R
Jour./Amer. Soc./Chur. Growth—R
$-Leadership—R
$-Lutheran Partners—R
$-Ministries Today
$-Ministry
Ministry in Motion—R
Net Results
$-Pastoral Life—R
Pastors.com—R
Pulpit Helps—R
Quarterly Review
$-Rev.
$-RevWriter Resource
$-Sabbath School Leadership—R
$-Sermon Notes—R
Sharing the Practice—R
Steps
Theological Digest—R
$-WCA News—R
$-Word & World
$-Worship Leader
$-Your Church—R
$-Youthworker

TEEN/YOUNG ADULT
$-Brio—R
Setmag.com—R
$-Student Leadership—R
Teen Light—R
$-Teenage Christian—R
TeensForJC.com—R
Transcendmag.com—R

WOMEN
$-Esprit—R
$-Godly Business Woman

$-Horizons (women)—R
$-inSpirit—R
Just Between Us—R
Right to the Heart—R
$-SpiritLed Woman
Women Today—R

LITURGICAL

ADULT/GENERAL
AGAIN—R
$-alive now!—R
$-Arlington Catholic
Breakthrough Intercessor—R
$-Catholic Parent
$-CGA World—R
Channels—R
Christian Motorsports
$-Commonweal
$-Cresset
$-Culture Wars—R
Divine Ascent
$-Dovetail—R
$-Episcopal Life—R
$-Liguorian
$-Living Church
$-Lutheran Journal—R
$-Messenger
$-Messenger of the Sacred Heart
$-National Catholic
$-New Wineskins—R
$-North American Voice—R
$-Our Sunday Visitor
$-Prairie Messenger—R
$-Silver Wings—R
$-St. Anthony Messenger
$-Testimony—R
$-Way of St. Francis—R

CHRISTIAN EDUCATION/LIBRARY
$-Church Educator—R

MUSIC
$-Church Pianist
Hymn

PASTORS/LEADERS
$-African American Pulpit
$-Catechumenate
$-Catholic Servant
$-Christian Century—R
$-Church Worship
$-Clergy Journal—R
Cross Currents
$-Diocesan Dialogue—R
$-Emmanuel
$-Eucharistic Ministries—R

$-Interpreter
$-Leadership—R
$-Lutheran Partners—R
$-Ministries Today
$-Ministry & Liturgy—R
$-Parish Liturgy—R
$-Pastoral Life—R
Pastors.com—R
$-Priest
Quarterly Review
$-Reformed Worship
$-RevWriter Resource
Sewanee Theological Review
Sharing the Practice—R
$-Spiritual Spinach—R
$-Today's Parish—R
$-Word & World

WOMEN
$-Horizons (women)—R

MARRIAGE

ADULT/GENERAL
$-Alive!—R
Alliance Life
$-America
$-Angels on Earth
$-Arlington Catholic
$-BGC World—R
Bread of Life—R
Breakthrough Intercessor—R
$-Bridal Guides—R
$-Canada Lutheran—R
$-Catholic Digest—R
$-Catholic Forester—R
$-Catholic Parent
$-Celebrate Life—R
Channels—R
$-Charisma
Christian Bible Studies.com
Christian C. L. RECORD—R
$-Christian Courier (CAN)—R
$-Christian Examiner
$-Christian Home & School
Christian Journal—R
$-Christian Leader—R
Christian Motorsports
Christian Online
$-Christian Parenting—R
Christian Ranchman
$-Christian Social Action—R
$-Christianweek
$-Columbia
$-Cornerstone Christian—R
$-Culture Wars—R
$-Cup of Comfort—R

$-Decision
Disciple's Journal—R
$-Discipleship Journal—R
$-Dovetail—R
$-Evangel—R
Evangelical Advocate—R
$-Faith & Family
$-Faith Today
$-Family Digest—R
$-Fellowship Focus—R
$-Focus on the Family
$-Foursquare World Advance—R
$-Gem—R
$-Generation X—R
$-God Allows U-Turns—R
Good News Journal
Grand Valley Observer—R
$-Guideposts—R
Hannah to Hannah—R
Heartlight—R
Highway News—R
$-Home Times—R
$-Homeschooling Today—R
$-Indian Life—R
$-Inside Journal—R
$-Interim—R
$-Joy & Praise
$-Layman
$-Light & Life
$-Liguorian
$-Living—R
$-Living Church
$-Living Light News—R
$-Lookout—R
$-Lutheran—R
$-Lutheran Digest—R
$-Marriage Partnership—R
Mature Times—R
$-Men of Integrity—R
$-Mennonite Brethren—R
$-MESSAGE
Metro Voice—R
$-Montgomery's Journey
Mutuality—R
$-New Freeman—R
$-New Man—R
$-New Wineskins—R
$-North American Voice—R
$-Nostalgia Magazine—R
$-Our Sunday Visitor
Pegasus Review—R
$-Physician—R
$-Plain Truth—R
$-Positive Thinking—R
$-Prairie Messenger—R
$-Presbyterian Record—R

Priscilla Papers—R
$-Prism—R
$-Psychology for Living—R
$-Purpose—R
Quaker Life—R
$-Shantyman—R
$-Signs of the Times—R
Singles Scoop—R
$-Smart Families—R
$-Social Justice—R
Spiritual Voice—R
$-Spring Hill Review—R
$-St. Anthony Messenger
$-Standard—R
$-Testimony—R
thegoodsteward.com—R
$-Today's Christian—R
$-Together—R
Trumpeter—R
$-U.S. Catholic
$-Vibrant Life—R
Victory News—R
$-War Cry—R
$-Wesleyan Life—R
$-World & I—R
$-Young Christian—R

MISSIONS
$-Worldwide Challenge

PASTORS/LEADERS
$-African American Pulpit
Angelos—R
$-Building Church Leaders.com
$-Catholic Servant
Cell Group—R
$-Christian Century—R
$-Evangelical Baptist—R
$-Evangelicals Today—R
$-Interpreter
Journal/Pastoral Care—R
$-Lutheran Partners—R
$-Ministries Today
$-Pastoral Life—R
$-Priest
$-Rev.
Sharing the Practice—R
$-Spiritual Spinach—R
$-Today's Parish—R
$-Word & World

TEEN/YOUNG ADULT
$-Boundless Webzine—R
$-Brio—R
Setmag.com—R
Teen Light—R
TeensForJC.com—R

Transcendmag.com—R
$-Young Adult Today—R
$-Young and Alive—R

WOMEN
Anna's Journal—R
Christian Woman's Page—R
Crowned with Silver
$-Esprit—R
$-Extreme Joy
$-Godly Business Woman
Hearts at Home—R
$-inSpirit—R
$-Journey
Just Between Us—R
Lutheran Woman's Quar.
$-MOMsense—R
P31 Woman—R
Reflections
Shalom Bayit
$-Simple Joy
$-SpiritLed Woman
$-Today's Christian Woman—R
True Woman
$-Welcome Home
$-Woman's Touch—R
$-Women Alive!—R
$-Women by Grace—R
Women of the Cross—R
Women Today—R

MEN'S ISSUES

ADULT/GENERAL
Alliance Life
$-Annals of St. Anne
$-Arlington Catholic
$-Beacon
$-BGC World—R
Bread of Life—R
Breakthrough Intercessor—R
$-Catholic Forester—R
$-Catholic New Times—R
$-Catholic Parent
Channels—R
$-Charisma
$-Chicken Soup—R
Christian Bible Studies.com
$-Christian Examiner
Christian Journal—R
$-Christian Leader—R
Christian Motorsports
Christian Online
$-Christian Parenting—R
Christian Ranchman
$-Christian Social Action—R
$-Christianweek

$-SpiritLed Woman
$-Woman's Touch—R

MISSIONS

ADULT/GENERAL
AGAIN—R
$-Alive!—R
Alliance Life
$-Anglican Journal
$-B.C. Catholic—R
Breakthrough Intercessor—R
Channels—R
$-Charisma
Christian Bible Studies.com
$-Christian Leader—R
Christian Motorsports
Christian Online
$-Christianity Today—R
$-Christianweek
Church Herald & Holiness—R
Connecting Point—R
$-Culture Wars—R
$-Discipleship Journal—R
$-Episcopal Life—R
Evangelical Advocate—R
$-Faith Today
$-Gem—R
$-Good News—R
Gospel Tract—R
$-Horizons (adult)—R
$-Layman
$-Light & Life
$-Liguorian
Literary TNT—R
$-Live—R
$-Living Church
$-Lookout—R
$-Lutheran—R
$-Lutheran Journal—R
Maranatha News—R
Mature Times—R
$-Men of Integrity—R
$-Montgomery's Journey
$-National Catholic
$-New Freeman—R
New Heart—R
$-New Wineskins—R
$-North American Voice—R
$-On Mission
$-Our Sunday Visitor
$-Power for Living—R
PrayerWorks—R
Presbyterian Outlook
Priscilla Papers—R
$-Prism—R
Quaker Life—R

$-Seeds
$-Silver Wings—R
Singles Scoop—R
Spiritual Voice—R
$-St. Anthony Messenger
$-Standard—R
Sword and Trumpet—R
Sword of the Lord—R
$-Testimony—R
thegoodsteward.com—R
$-Today's Christian—R
Trumpeter—R
$-U.S. Catholic
Victory News—R
$-Voice of the Lord
Walk This Way—R
$-Way of St. Francis—R
$-Wireless Age—R

CHILDREN
$-BREAD/God's Children—R
$-Focus/Clubhouse

CHRISTIAN EDUCATION/LIBRARY
$-Children's Ministry
$-Church Educator—R
$-Courage—R
$-Group
$-Youth & CE Leadership

MISSIONS
$-American Baptists in Mission
Catholic Missions In Canada
East-West Church
$-Evangelical Missions—R
Glad Tidings
I.E.
Intl. Jour./Frontier—R
$-Leaders for Today
Missiology
Mission Frontiers
$-New World Outlook
$-One
OpRev Equipper—R
$-PFI World Report—R
$-PIME World—R
Railroad Evangelist—R
Wesleyan World—R
Women of the Harvest
$-World Pulse—R
$-Worldwide Challenge

MUSIC
Quest—R

PASTORS/LEADERS
$-African American Pulpit

$-Building Church Leaders.com
$-Clergy Journal—R
$-Emmanuel
$-Enrichment—R
$-Evangelical Baptist—R
$-Evangelicals Today—R
$-Lutheran Partners—R
$-Ministries Today
Ministry in Motion—R
$-Pastoral Life—R
Pastors.com—R
Pulpit Helps—R
$-Rev.
Sharing the Practice—R
$-Word & World
$-Youthworker

TEEN/YOUNG ADULT
$-Brio—R
$-Brio & Beyond
$-Conqueror—R
$-Devo'Zine—R
$-Passageway.org—R
$-Real Faith in Life—R
$-Student Leadership—R
Teen Light—R
$-With—R
$-Young Salvationist—R

WOMEN
$-Godly Business Woman
$-Horizons (women)—R
$-inSpirit—R
Just Between Us—R
$-Link & Visitor—R
$-SpiritLed Woman

MONEY MANAGEMENT

ADULT/GENERAL
$-Anglican Journal
$-Bridal Guides—R
$-Catholic Forester—R
$-Catholic Parent
$-CBA Marketplace
CBN.com—R
$-CGA World—R
Channels—R
Christian Bible Studies.com
Christian C. L. RECORD—R
Christian Journal—R
Christian Motorsports
Christian Online
$-Christian Parenting—R
Christian Ranchman
$-Christianweek
$-Church of God EVANGEL
Connecting Point—R

$-Cornerstone Christian—R
Disciple's Journal—R
$-Faith & Family
$-Faith Today
$-Gem—R
$-Generation X—R
Gospel Tract—R
Heartlight—R
Highway News—R
$-Home Times—R
$-Homeschooling Today—R
$-Inland NW Christian
$-Layman
$-Lifeglow—R
$-Light & Life
$-Living—R
$-Lookout—R
$-Men of Integrity—R
$-MESSAGE
$-Montgomery's Journey
$-North American Voice—R
$-NRB Magazine—R
Parents & Teens—R
$-Physician—R
Quaker Life—R
$-Relevant
$-Signs of the Times—R
$-Smart Families—R
Spiritual Voice—R
$-St. Anthony Messenger
$-Testimony—R
thegoodsteward.com—R
$-Today's Christian—R
$-Together—R
Trumpeter—R
Victory News—R
$-War Cry—R
$-Wesleyan Life—R
$-World & I—R
$-Young Christian—R

CHILDREN
$-BREAD/God's Children—R

CHRISTIAN EDUCATION/LIBRARY
$-Church Educator—R
$-Momentum

PASTORS/LEADERS
$-Building Church Leaders.com
Cell Group—R
$-Enrichment—R
$-Evangelical Baptist—R
$-Evangelicals Today—R
$-Interpreter
$-Ministries Today

Ministry in Motion—R
$-Pastoral Life—R
Pastors.com—R
$-Rev.
Sharing the Practice—R
$-Today's Christian Preacher—R
$-Today's Parish—R
$-Your Church—R
$-Youthworker

TEEN/YOUNG ADULT
$-Boundless Webzine—R
$-Brio & Beyond
$-Conqueror—R
$-Real Faith in Life—R
Teen Light—R
$-Young and Alive—R
$-Young Christian—R

WOMEN
Christian Women Today—R
$-Godly Business Woman
$-Horizons (women)—R
$-inSpirit—R
Just Between Us—R
Life Tools for Women
$-Today's Christian Woman—R
True Woman
$-Woman's Touch—R
Women Today—R

MOVIE REVIEWS*

ADULT/GENERAL
CBN.com—R
Mars Hill Review
MovieGuide
$-Nostalgia Magazine—R
Perspectives
Reformed Quarterly
Spiritual Voice—R
$-Spring Hill Review—R

WOMEN
Praise

MUSIC REVIEWS

ADULT/GENERAL
$-Arlington Catholic
$-Catholic Peace Voice—R
$-CBA Marketplace
CBN.com—R
Channels—R
$-Charisma
Christian Journal—R
Christian Media—R
$-Christian Parenting—R
Christian Radio Weekly

$-Christian Renewal—R
$-Christian Retailing
$-Christianweek
$-Commonweal
$-Cornerstone Christian—R
$-Cresset
Crosshome.com
$-Faith & Family
$-Faith Today
Fuse Magazine
Heartlight—R
$-Home Times—R
$-Indian Life—R
$-Interim—R
$-Joy & Praise
Literary TNT—R
Mars Hill Review
MovieGuide
$-New Man—R
Parents & Teens—R
$-Presbyterians Today—R
$-Prism—R
Quaker Life—R
Reformed Quarterly
$-Relevant
Rose & Thorn
$-Sojourners
Spiritual Voice—R
$-Spring Hill Review—R
$-Testimony—R
Trumpeter—R
Victory News—R
Winsome Wit—R
$-Wireless Age—R
$-World & I—R

CHILDREN
$-Cadet Quest—R
$-Club Connection

CHRISTIAN EDUCATION/LIBRARY
$-Church Libraries—R

MISSIONS
Women of the Harvest

MUSIC
$-CCM Magazine
Christian Music Weekly—R
$-Creator—R
Hymn
Quest—R
Tradition

PASTORS/LEADERS
$-Christian Century—R
$-Interpreter

$-Ministries Today
$-Pastoral Life—R
$-Reformed Worship
Technologies for Worship—R
$-Worship Leader

TEEN/YOUNG ADULT
$-Boundless Webzine—R
$-Brio & Beyond
$-Devo'Zine—R
Setmag.com—R
Teen Light—R
$-Teenage Christian—R
TeensForJC.com—R
Transcendmag.com—R
$-With—R
$-Young Salvationist—R

WOMEN
$-Godly Business Woman
Praise

NATURE

ADULT/GENERAL
$-Alive!—R
Angel Face
$-Animal Trails—R
Barefoot Path—R
$-Brave Hearts
$-Cappers
$-Catholic New Times—R
Chattels of the Heart—R
$-Christian Courier (CAN)—R
$-Christian Renewal—R
$-Covenant Companion—R
Creation
Creation Care—R
$-Cresset
$-Cup of Comfort—R
$-Eclectic Homeschool
$-Gem—R
$-Grit
$-Ideals—R
Keys to Living—R
$-Lifeglow—R
$-Light & Life
$-Lutheran Digest—R
Maranatha News—R
$-Nostalgia Magazine—R
$-Over the Back Fence—R
Pegasus Review—R
Plowman—R
PrayerWorks—R
Sacred Journey—R
$-Science & Spirit
Spiritual Voice—R

$-Spring Hill Review—R
$-St. Anthony Messenger
Storyteller—R
$-Testimony—R
thegoodsteward.com—R
TJ
Trumpeter—R
Victory News—R
$-Vision—R
$-World & I—R
$-Young Christian—R

CHILDREN
Barefoot for Kids—R
$-BREAD/God's Children—R
$-Cadet Quest—R
$-Club Connection
$-Focus/Clubhouse
$-Focus/Clubhouse Jr.
$-Guide—R
$-My Friend
$-Nature Friend
$-Partners—R
$-Passport—R
Skipping Stones
$-Story Friends—R

PASTORS/LEADERS
$-Pastoral Life—R
$-Rev.
$-Word & World

TEEN/YOUNG ADULT
$-Devo'Zine—R
Teen Light—R
$-Teenage Christian—R
$-Young and Alive—R

WOMEN
$-Extreme Joy
$-inSpirit—R
Reflections

NEWS FEATURES

ADULT/GENERAL
$-Arkansas Catholic—R
$-Atlantic Catholic
BC Christian News
$-BGC World—R
$-Cappers
$-Catholic Insight
$-Catholic Peace Voice—R
CBN.com—R
$-Christian Examiner
Christian Journal—R
Christian News NW—R
Christian Radio Weekly
$-Christian Renewal—R

$-Christian Research
$-Christian Retailing
$-Christianweek
Compass Direct
$-Disaster News Network
$-Dovetail—R
Evangel, The
Evangelical Advocate—R
$-Faith Today
$-Fellowship Focus—R
$-Generation X—R
$-Grit
$-Impact—R
$-Indian Life—R
Indiana Christian News
Island Catholic News
$-Liberty—R
$-Light & Life
$-MESSAGE
Metro Voice—R
$-National Catholic
$-Our Sunday Visitor
$-Plain Truth—R
$-Portland Magazine
PrayerWorks—R
$-Science & Spirit
Spiritual Voice—R
$-Spring Hill Review—R
$-St. Anthony Messenger
Sword and Trumpet—R
$-Testimony—R
thegoodsteward.com—R
$-Today's Christian—R
Trumpeter—R
$-Upscale Magazine
Victory News—R
$-War Cry—R
War Cry (Canada)—R
$-Wireless Age—R
$-World & I—R

CHILDREN
$-Pockets—R
Skipping Stones

PASTORS/LEADERS
$-Building Church Leaders.com
$-Interpreter
Pastors.com—R
Pulpit Helps—R

TEEN/YOUNG ADULT
Teen Light—R

WOMEN
$-Today's Christian Woman—R

WRITERS

$-Fellowscript—R
$-Money the Write Way—R

NEWSPAPERS/
TABLOIDS

$-Anglican Journal
$-Arkansas Catholic—R
$-Arlington Catholic
$-Atlantic Catholic
$-B.C. Catholic—R
B.C. Christian News
$-Catholic New Times—R
$-Catholic New York
Catholic Register
$-Catholic Sentinel
$-Catholic Telegraph
$-Christian Courier (CAN)—R
Christian Courier (WI)—R
$-Christian Examiner
$-Christian Herald—R
Christian Journal—R
Christian Media—R
Christian News NW—R
Christian Observer
Christian Ranchman
$-Christian Renewal—R
$-Christianweek
$-Common Ground—R
$-Cornerstone Christian—R
Dallas/Ft. Worth Heritage
Disciple's Journal—R
Discovery—R
$-Episcopal Life—R
Faro de Luz
$-Good News, Etc.—R
Good News Journal
$-Grit
$-Home Times—R
Indiana Christian News
$-Indian Life—R
$-Inland NW Christian
$-Inside Journal—R
Insight (for the blind)
$-Interchange
$-Interim—R
Island Catholic News
$-Layman
$-Living—R
$-Living Light News—R
Maranatha News—R
$-Messenger
Messianic Times
Metro Voice—R
Mid-South Christian

$-Minnesota Christian—R
$-National Catholic
Network
$-New Freeman—R
New Frontier
$-Our Sunday Visitor
$-Prairie Messenger—R
PrayerWorks—R
Pulpit Helps—R
$-Senior Living
$-Shantyman—R
Southwest Kansas
Spiritual Voice—R
Star of Zion
Sword of the Lord—R
$-Tidewater Parent—R
$-Together—R

NOSTALGIA*

ADULT/GENERAL
$-Animal Trails—R
$-Bridal Guides—R
Chattels of the Heart—R
$-Cup of Comfort—R
Discerning Poet—R
$-Grit
$-Lutheran Digest—R
$-Mature Living
$-Nostalgia Magazine—R
$-Over the Back Fence—R
PrayerWorks—R
Storyteller—R
$-Testimony—R
$-Tidewater Parent—R
Victory News—R

WOMEN
Crowned with Silver

ONLINE PUBLICATIONS

ADULT/GENERAL
$-America
$-Anglican Journal
$-Apocalypse Chronicles—R
Barefoot Path—R
$-Believer's Bay
Books & Culture
$-Cathedral Age
$-Catholic Digest—R
CBN.com—R
$-Charisma
Christian Computing—R
$-Christian Examiner
$-Christian Home & School
Christian Media—R
Christian Online

$-Christian Parents Section
Christian Single Online
$-Christian Standard—R
$-Christianity Today—R
$-Columbia
$-Company—R
Compass Direct
$-Connection—R
Crosshome.com
$-Decision Online
$-Disaster News Network
Disciple's Journal—R
Discovery—R
$-Drama Ministry—R
$-Eclectic Homeschool Online
$-First Things
$-Flutters of the Heart
Fuse
$-Gateway S-F—R
Gold Country Families—R
Heartlight—R
Heartwarmers
$-Impact—R
Inspire
Interactive E-Poetry
$-Interim—R
Jewel Among Jewels
LifeTimes Catholic
Literary TNT—R
$-Lookout—R
$-Lutheran—R
$-Lutheran Digest—R
$-Marian Helper—R
Men of the Cross—R
$-Messenger of St. Anthony
$-Messianic Sci-Fi
$-Minnesota Christian—R
$-National Catholic
$-New Wineskins—R
$-Now What?—R
$-NRB Magazine—R
$-On Mission
Parents & Teens—R
$-Passageway.org—R
PrayerWorks—R
Regent Business—R
$-Relate—R
$-RelevantMagazine.com
Rose & Thorn
Sacred Journey—R
Salt of the Earth
$-Signs of the Times—R
SingleAgain.com
$-Smart Families—R
$-Sojourners

$-Sound Body—R
SR: A Journal—R
$-St. Anthony Messenger
$-Studio Classroom
$-Testimony—R
thegoodsteward.com—R
TJ
$-Today's Christian—R
$-Today's Pentecostal Evangel
Tributes—R
Trumpeter—R
$-Upscale
$-U.S. Catholic
Valparaiso Poetry
Walk This Way—R
$-War Cry—R
Winsome Wit—R
$-World & I—R

CHILDREN
$-American Girl
Barefoot for Kids—R
$-Focus/Clubhouse
Focus/Clubhouse Jr.
$-Guideposts for Kids
$-Keys for Kids—R
$-My Friend

CHRISTIAN EDUCATION/LIBRARY
Christian Library Journal—R
$-Ideas Unlimited—R

DAILY DEVOTIONALS
Forward Day by Day

MISSIONS
Mission Frontiers
OpRev Equipper—R
$-World Pulse—R

MUSIC
$-CCM Magazine

PASTORS/LEADERS
$-Barefoot—R
$-Christian Camp—R
Interpretation
$-Leadership—R
Ministry in Motion—R
Net Results
$-Newsletter Newsletter
Pastors.com—R
Plugged In
Preaching On-Line—R
$-PreachingToday.com
Pulpit Helps—R
$-Rev.
$-RevWriter Resource

$-Sermon Notes—R
$-Small Group Dynamics—R
Strategic Adult Ministries—R
Technologies for Worship—R
$-WCA News—R
Youth Culture
$-Youthworker

TEEN/YOUNG ADULT
$-Boundless Webzine—R
Journalism Online
$-Passageway.org—R
Setmag.com—R
$-Student Leadership—R
Teen Light—R
TeensForJC.com—R
Transcendmag.com—R
$-Young Salvationist—R

WOMEN
Anna's Journal—R
$-At the Center—R
Christian Woman's Page—R
Christian Women Today—R
$-Extreme Joy
$-History's Women—R
Life Tools for Women
$-Melody of the Heart
Right to the Heart—R
$-Simple Joy
True Woman
$-Women by Grace—R
Women of the Cross—R
Women Today—R
Women's Ministry

WRITERS
Author Network E-zine
Author-Me.com
ChristianWriters.com
Dedicated Author
$-Money the Write Way—R
Romancing/Christian Heart—R
$-Spirit-Led Writer—R
Teachers & Writers
WriteToInspire.com
$-Writing Parent—R

OPINION PIECES

ADULT/GENERAL
$-Annals of St. Anne
$-Arkansas Catholic—R
$-Arlington Catholic
$-B.C. Catholic—R
$-Bible Advocate—R
$-Bridal Guides—R
$-Catholic New Times—R

$-Catholic New York
$-Catholic Peace Voice—R
$-Charisma
$-Christian Courier (CAN)—R
$-Christian Examiner
Christian Motorsports
Christian News NW—R
$-Christian Renewal—R
$-Christian Research
$-Christianity Today—R
$-Christianweek
$-Commonweal
$-Cresset
$-Culture Wars—R
$-DisciplesWorld
$-Door—R
$-Episcopal Life—R
$-Faith Today
$-First Things
$-Generation X—R
Good News Journal
Grand Valley Observer—R
Highway News—R
$-Home Times—R
$-Indian Life—R
$-Inland NW Christian
$-Interim—R
$-Light & Life
Literary TNT—R
$-Living Church
$-Lookout—R
$-Lutheran—R
$-Mennonite Brethren—R
$-Messenger
Metro Voice—R
$-Minnesota Christian—R
$-National Catholic
$-New Freeman—R
$-NRB Magazine—R
$-Our Sunday Visitor
$-Plain Truth—R
$-Portland Magazine
$-Prairie Messenger—R
PrayerWorks—R
Presbyterian Outlook
$-Presbyterian Record—R
Re:generation Quarterly
Regent Business—R
$-Seeds
$-Social Justice—R
Spiritual Voice—R
$-St. Anthony Messenger
$-Testimony—R
thegoodsteward.com—R
Trumpeter—R

$-U.S. Catholic
$-United Church Observer—R
Victory News—R
$-Way of St. Francis—R
Winsome Wit—R
$-World & I—R
$-Young Christian—R

CHRISTIAN EDUCATION/LIBRARY
Catholic Library World

MISSIONS
Glad Tidings
OpRev Equipper—R

PASTORS/LEADERS
$-Evangelical Baptist—R
Journal/Pastoral Care—R
$-Pastoral Life—R
Pulpit Helps—R
$-Rev.
Steps
$-This Rock
$-Word & World
$-Worship Leader

TEEN/YOUNG ADULT
$-Boundless Webzine—R
$-Listen—R
Setmag.com—R
Teen Light—R
TeensForJC.com—R
Transcendmag.com—R
$-Young Christian—R

WOMEN
Anna's Journal—R
Reflections

WRITERS
$-Advanced Chris. Writer—R
$-Areopagus (UK)
$-Christian Communicator—R
$-Exchange—R
$-Fellowscript—R
$-Money the Write Way—R

PARENTING

ADULT/GENERAL
American Tract Society—R
$-Angels on Earth
$-Annals of St. Anne
$-Arlington Catholic
At Home with Our Faith
Breakthrough Intercessor—R
$-Bridal Guides—R
$-Canada Lutheran—R
$-Catholic Digest—R

$-Catholic Forester—R
$-Catholic New Times—R
$-Catholic Parent
$-Celebrate Life—R
$-Charisma
$-Chicken Soup—R
Christian Bible Studies.com
$-Christian Courier (CAN)—R
$-Christian Home & School
Christian Journal—R
Christian Motorsports
Christian Observer
$-Christian Parenting—R
$-Christian Parents Section
Christian Ranchman
$-Christian Renewal—R
$-Christian Social Action—R
$-Columbia
$-Cornerstone Christian—R
Creation Care—R
$-Culture Wars—R
$-Cup of Comfort—R
Disciple's Journal—R
$-Dovetail—R
$-Eclectic Homeschool
Evangelical Advocate—R
$-Faith & Family
$-Faith Today
$-Family Digest—R
$-Fellowship Focus—R
$-Focus on the Family
$-Foursquare World Advance—R
$-Gem—R
$-Generation X—R
Gold Country Families—R
Good News Journal
Heartlight—R
Highway News—R
$-Home Times—R
$-Homeschooling Today—R
HopeKeepers—R
$-Indian Life—R
$-Inside Journal—R
$-Interim—R
Jewel Among Jewels
$-Light & Life
$-Liguorian
Literary TNT—R
$-Living—R
$-Living Light News—R
$-Lookout—R
$-Lutheran—R
$-Lutheran Digest—R
$-Lutheran Journal—R
Maranatha News—R

$-Marriage Partnership—R
$-Men of Integrity—R
$-Mennonite Brethren—R
$-MESSAGE
Metro Voice—R
$-Montgomery's Journey
MovieGuide
Mutuality—R
$-New Freeman—R
$-New Man—R
$-New Wineskins—R
$-North American Voice—R
$-Our Sunday Visitor
$-ParentLife
Parents & Teens—R
Pegasus Review—R
$-Plain Truth—R
$-Positive Thinking—R
$-Power for Living—R
$-Prairie Messenger—R
PrayerWorks—R
$-Psychology for Living—R
$-Purpose—R
Quaker Life—R
$-Relate—R
$-Signs of the Times—R
Singles Scoop—R
$-Smart Families—R
$-Social Justice—R
Southwest Kansas
$-Special Living—R
Spiritual Voice—R
$-St. Anthony Messenger
$-St. Joseph's Messenger—R
$-Standard—R
Steps
Storyteller—R
$-Testimony—R
thegoodsteward.com—R
$-Tidewater Parent—R
$-Today's Christian—R
$-Together—R
Trumpeter—R
$-Vibrant Life—R
Victory News—R
$-Vision—R
$-War Cry—R
$-Way of St. Francis—R
$-Wesleyan Life—R
$-World & I—R

CHRISTIAN EDUCATION/LIBRARY
$-Adventures
$-Children's Ministry

MISSIONS
$-Worldwide Challenge

PASTORS/LEADERS
$-African American Pulpit
$-Building Church Leaders.com
$-Catholic Servant
$-Evangelical Baptist—R
$-Evangelicals Today—R
$-Interpreter
$-Pastoral Life—R
Pulpit Helps—R
$-Rev.
Sharing the Practice—R
$-Spiritual Spinach—R
Strategic Adult Ministries—R
Youth Culture
$-Youthworker

WOMEN
$-At the Center—R
Christian Woman's Page—R
Crowned with Silver
$-Esprit—R
$-Extreme Joy
$-Godly Business Woman
Handmaiden—R
Hearts at Home—R
$-inSpirit—R
Just Between Us—R
Keeping Hearts & Home
$-Link & Visitor—R
Lutheran Woman's Quar.
$-MOMsense—R
P31 Woman—R
Reflections
Shalom Bayit
$-Simple Joy
$-SpiritLed Woman
$-Today's Christian Woman—R
True Woman
$-Welcome Home
$-Woman's Touch—R
$-Women Alive!—R
$-Women by Grace—R

PEACE ISSUES*

ADULT/GENERAL
$-Bridal Guides—R
Christian Bible Studies.com
$-Generation X—R
$-Living—R
$-National Catholic
$-Prairie Messenger—R
Quaker Life—R
Rhubarb
Sacred Journey—R

$-Silver Wings—R
$-Testimony—R
$-Together—R
Victory News—R

CHILDREN
$-Pockets—R

PASTORS/LEADERS
$-Building Church Leaders.com

TEEN/YOUNG ADULT
Teen Light—R

WOMEN
$-Horizons (women)—R
$-inSpirit—R

PERSONAL EXPERIENCE

ADULT/GENERAL
AGAIN—R
$-alive now!—R
Alliance Life
$-Angels on Earth
$-Annals of St. Anne
$-B.C. Catholic—R
$-Bible Advocate—R
$-Brave Hearts
Bread of Life—R
Breakthrough Intercessor—R
$-Bridal Guides—R
$-Catholic Digest—R
$-Catholic Forester—R
$-Catholic New Times—R
$-Catholic New York
$-Catholic Peace Voice—R
$-Celebrate Life—R
$-CGA World—R
Channels—R
Chattels of the Heart—R
$-Chicken Soup—R
Christian Bible Studies.com
$-Christian Courier (CAN)—R
$-Christian Home & School
Christian Journal—R
Christian Motorsports
Christian Observer
Christian Online
Christian Ranchman
$-Christianity Today—R
$-Commonweal
$-Cornerstone Christian—R
Crossway/Newsline—R
Crossway/Newsline—R
$-Cup of Comfort—R
$-Decision
$-Door—R
$-Dovetail—R

$-Eclectic Homeschool
$-Evangel—R
$-Faith Today
$-Family Digest—R
$-Gem—R
$-Generation X—R
$-God Allows U-Turns—R
Good News Journal
Grand Valley Observer—R
$-Grit
$-Guideposts—R
Hannah to Hannah—R
Highway News—R
$-Home Times—R
HopeKeepers—R
$-Horizons (adult)—R
$-Ideals—R
$-Indian Life—R
$-Inland NW Christian
$-Inside Journal—R
$-Interim—R
Jewel Among Jewels
Keys to Living—R
Leaves—R
$-Light & Life
$-Liguorian
Literary TNT—R
$-Live—R
$-Living—R
$-Living Church
$-Lookout—R
$-Lutheran—R
$-Lutheran Digest—R
$-Lutheran Journal—R
Maranatha News—R
$-Marian Helper—R
$-Marriage Partnership—R
$-Mennonite Brethren—R
$-MESSAGE
MovieGuide
Mutuality—R
$-New Freeman—R
New Heart—R
$-New Wineskins—R
$-North American Voice—R
$-Nostalgia Magazine—R
$-Now What?—R
$-Oblates
$-Over the Back Fence—R
Parents & Teens—R
$-Portland Magazine
$-Positive Thinking—R
PrayerWorks—R
$-Presbyterian Record—R
$-Psychology for Living—R

Quaker Life—R
$-Queen of All Hearts
$-Relate—R
Sacred Journey—R
$-SCP Journal—R
$-Seeds
$-Seek—R
$-Senior Living
$-Shantyman—R
Sharing—R
$-Signs of the Times—R
$-Silver Wings—R
$-Spiritual Life
Spiritual Voice—R
$-Spring Hill Review—R
$-St. Anthony Messenger
$-Standard—R
Steps
Storyteller—R
$-Testimony—R
thegoodsteward.com—R
$-Tidewater Parent—R
$-Today's Christian—R
$-Together—R
Trumpeter—R
$-Up
$-Upscale Magazine
Victory News—R
$-Vision—R
$-War Cry—R
$-Way of St. Francis—R
$-Wesleyan Life—R
$-World & I—R
$-Young Christian—R

CHILDREN
Barefoot for Kids—R
$-Cadet Quest—R
$-Club Connection
$-Faces
$-Guide—R
$-Partners—R
$-SHINE brightly—R
Skipping Stones

CHRISTIAN EDUCATION/LIBRARY
$-Children's Ministry
$-Group
$-Journal/Adventist Educ.—R
$-Teachers of Vision—R

MISSIONS
$-PIME World—R
Railroad Evangelist—R
Women of the Harvest
$-Worldwide Challenge

MUSIC
Tradition

PASTORS/LEADERS
$-African American Pulpit
$-Building Church Leaders.com
$-Catholic Servant
Cell Group—R
$-Evangelical Baptist—R
$-Evangelicals Today—R
$-Interpreter
Journal/Pastoral Care—R
$-Pastoral Life—R
$-Rev.
$-Sabbath School Leadership—R
Sharing the Practice—R
$-Spiritual Spinach—R
Steps
Strategic Adult Ministries—R
Theological Digest—R
$-Today's Parish—R
$-Worship Leader
$-Youthworker

TEEN/YOUNG ADULT
$-Boundless Webzine—R
$-Breakaway
$-Brio—R
$-Brio & Beyond
$-Campus Life—R
$-Listen—R
$-Passageway.org—R
$-Real Faith in Life—R
Setmag.com—R
$-Sharing the VICTORY—R
Teen Light—R
TeensForJC.com—R
Transcendmag.com—R
$-Young Christian—R

WOMEN
Anna's Journal—R
Christian Woman's Page—R
$-Esprit—R
$-Extreme Joy
$-Godly Business Woman
Handmaiden—R
Hearts at Home—R
$-Horizons (women)—R
$-inSpirit—R
Just Between Us—R
$-Melody of the Heart
$-MOMsense—R
Reflections
$-SpiritLed Woman
$-Today's Christian Woman—R
$-Welcome Home
$-Woman's Touch—R

$-Women Alive!—R
Women of the Cross—R

WRITERS
$-Areopagus (UK)
$-Brady Magazine—R
$-Byline
$-Exchange—R
$-Money the Write Way—R
Once Upon a Time—R

PERSONAL GROWTH

ADULT/GENERAL
$-alive now!—R
Alliance Life
$-Annals of St. Anne
$-BGC World—R
$-Bible Advocate—R
Bread of Life—R
Breakthrough Intercessor—R
$-Bridal Guides—R
$-Catholic Digest—R
$-Catholic Forester—R
$-Catholic New Times—R
$-Catholic Peace Voice—R
Channels—R
Chattels of the Heart—R
Christian Bible Studies.com
$-Christian Courier (CAN)—R
Christian Journal—R
Christian Online
Christian Ranchman
$-Church of God EVANGEL
$-Common Ground—R
$-Cup of Comfort—R
$-Decision
Divine Ascent
$-Dovetail—R
$-Evangel—R
Evangelical Advocate—R
$-Faith & Family
$-Faith & Friends—R
$-Faith Today
$-Family Digest—R
$-Gem—R
$-Generation X—R
$-God Allows U-Turns—R
Good News Journal
Grand Valley Observer—R
Hannah to Hannah—R
Highway News—R
$-Home Times—R
HopeKeepers—R
$-Indian Life—R
Jewel Among Jewels
$-Joy & Praise
Keys to Living—R

Leaves—R
$-Light & Life
$-Liguorian
Literary TNT—R
$-Living—R
$-Living Church
$-Lookout—R
Maranatha News—R
$-Marriage Partnership—R
$-Mature Living
Mature Times—R
$-Mature Years—R
Men of the Cross—R
Mutuality—R
New Heart—R
$-New Wineskins—R
$-North American Voice—R
$-Now What?—R
Parents & Teens—R
$-Positive Thinking—R
PrayerWorks—R
$-Psychology for Living—R
Quaker Life—R
Regent Business—R
Sacred Journey—R
$-Seek—R
Singles Scoop—R
Spiritual Voice—R
$-St. Anthony Messenger
$-Standard—R
Steps
$-Stewardship—R
Storyteller—R
$-Testimony—R
thegoodsteward.com—R
$-Today's Christian—R
$-Together—R
Tributes—R
Trumpeter—R
$-Up
Victory News—R
$-Vision—R
Walk This Way—R
$-War Cry—R
$-Way of St. Francis—R
$-World & I—R
$-Young Christian—R

CHILDREN
$-BREAD/God's Children—R
$-Cadet Quest—R
$-Guide—R
Skipping Stones

CHRISTIAN EDUCATION/LIBRARY
$-Children's Ministry

$-Group
$-Resource—R
$-Teachers Interaction
$-Youth & CE Leadership

MISSIONS
Women of the Harvest

PASTORS/LEADERS
$-African American Pulpit
$-Barefoot—R
$-Building Church Leaders.com
Christian Management—R
$-Emmanuel
$-Eucharistic Ministries—R
$-Evangelical Baptist—R
$-Evangelicals Today—R
$-Interpreter
Journal/Pastoral Care—R
Ministry in Motion—R
$-Pastoral Life—R
$-Rev.
Sharing the Practice—R
Steps
Theological Digest—R

TEEN/YOUNG ADULT
$-Brio—R
$-Brio & Beyond
$-Passageway.org—R
Setmag.com—R
$-Sharing the VICTORY—R
Teen Light—R
TeensForJC.com—R
Transcendmag.com—R
$-With—R
$-Young Adult Today—R
$-Young Christian—R
$-Young Salvationist—R

WOMEN
Anna's Journal—R
Christian Woman's Page—R
$-Esprit—R
$-Godly Business Woman
Hearts at Home—R
$-inSpirit—R
$-Journey
Just Between Us—R
$-MOMsense—R
P31 Woman—R
Reflections
Right to the Heart—R
$-SpiritLed Woman
$-Today's Christian Woman—R
$-Woman's Touch—R
$-Women by Grace—R

WRITERS
$-Areopagus (UK)

PHOTO ESSAYS

ADULT/GENERAL
$-Animal Trails—R
$-Bridal Guides—R
$-Cornerstone Christian—R
$-Faith & Family
$-Home Times—R
$-Indian Life—R
Maranatha News—R
$-Nostalgia Magazine—R
$-Presbyterian Record—R
Quaker Life—R
Sacred Journey—R
$-Senior Living
$-Spring Hill Review—R
$-St. Anthony Messenger
$-Today's Christian—R
$-U.S. Catholic
$-Way of St. Francis—R
$-World & I—R
$-Young Christian—R

CHILDREN
$-Children's Magic Window
$-Faces
Skipping Stones

MISSIONS
$-One

PASTORS/LEADERS
$-Interpreter

TEEN/YOUNG ADULT
$-Passageway.org—R
Setmag.com—R
Teen Light—R
TeensForJC.com—R
Transcendmag.com—R
$-Young Christian—R

WOMEN
$-Horizons (women)—R
Reflections

PHOTOGRAPHS

Note: "Reprint" indicators (R) have been deleted from this section and "B" for black & white glossy prints or "C" for color transparencies inserted. An asterisk (*) before a listing indicates they buy photos with articles only.

ADULT/GENERAL
African Voices—B
alive now!—B/C

Alive!—B
American Tract Society
Ancient Paths—B
Anglican Journal—B/C
*Animal Trails—B/C
*Annals of St. Anne—B/C
*Arkansas Catholic—C
Arlington Catholic—B
Barefoot Path—B/C
Beacon
BGC World—C
Bible Advocate—C
Brave Hearts
*Bridal Guides—B/C
Canada Lutheran—B
*Cathedral Age—B
*Catholic Digest—B/C
Catholic Forester—B/C
Catholic New Times
Catholic New York—B
Catholic Parent
Catholic Peace Voice—B/C
Catholic Sentinel—B/C
Catholic Telegraph—B
CBA Marketplace—C
*Celebrate Life—C
Channels
Charisma—C
*Christian Courier (CAN)—B
Christian Drama—B/C
*Christian Examiner—C
*Christian History & Biography—B/C
Christian Home & School—C
Christian Journal—B/C
Christian Leader—B/C
*Christian Motorsports—B
*Christian Online
Christian Parenting—B/C
Christian Radio Weekly
Christian Retailing—C
Christian Social Action—B
*Christian Standard—B/C
*Christianity Today—C
Church of God EVANGEL—C
*Commonweal—B/C
*Company
Connecting Point—B
Cornerstone Christian
Covenant Companion—B/C
Cresset
Culture Wars—B/C
*DisciplesWorld
Dovetail—B
Episcopal Life—B
Eureka Street
*Evangel—B

Evangelical Advocate—B/C
Faith & Family—C
*Faith & Friends—C
*Faith Today—C
Fellowship Focus—B
Focus on the Family—B/C
Foursquare World Advance
Good News Journal
Gospel Today
Gospel Tract—C
*Grand Valley Observer—C
*Grit—B/C
*Guideposts—B/C
Highway News—B
*Home Times—B/C
Homeschooling Today—B/C
*Horizons (adult)
Impact—B/C
Indian Life—B/C
Inland NW Christian—B
*Inside Journal—B
Interchange—B
*Interim—B/C
*Layman—B
Leaves—B/C
Liberty—B/C
*Lifeglow—B/C
Light & Life—B/C
*Liguorian—C
Literary TNT—C
Live—B/C
Living—B/C
Living Church—B/C
*Living Light News—B/C
Lookout—B/C
Lutheran—B
*Lutheran Journal—C
*Maranatha News—B
Marian Helper—B/C
*Mature Living
*Mature Years—C
Mennonite Brethren—B
MESSAGE—B/C
Messenger—B
*Minnesota Christian
Montgomery's Journey
Mutuality—B/C
*New Heart—C
New Wineskins—B/C
North American Voice—B
Nostalgia Magazine—B/C
*On Mission—C
Our Sunday Visitor—B/C
Over the Back Fence—C
Parabola—B
Power for Living—B

Presbyterian Outlook—B/C
Presbyterian Record—B/C
Presbyterians Today—B/C
*Priority!
Prism—B/C
*Psychology for Living—C
*Purpose—B
Quaker Life—B/C
Rhubarb—B
Sacred Journey—B/C
SCP Journal—B/C
*Seek—C
Signs of the Times—C
Sojourners—C
*Special Living—B/C
Spiritual Life—B
Spiritual Voice
Sports Spectrum—C
Spring Hill Review—B
*St. Anthony Messenger—B/C
Standard—B
*Star of Zion
*Storyteller—B
*Testimony—B/C
*Today's Christian—B/C
Today's Pentecostal Evangel—B/C
Together—B/C
Trumpeter
*United Church Observer—B/C
*Up
Upscale Magazine
*Vibrant Life—C
Vision—B/C
*Voice of the Lord
*Walk This Way—C
War Cry—B/C
War Cry (Canada)
Way of St. Francis—B
Wesleyan Life—C
West Wind Review—B
White Wing Messenger—C
*World & I—B/C
*Young Christian—B/C

CHILDREN
American Girl—C
Barefoot for Kids—B/C
Celebrate—C
*Children's Magic Window—C
*Courage
Faces
*Focus/Clubhouse—C
*Focus/Clubhouse Jr.—C
Guideposts for Kids—C
*My Friend—C
Nature Friend—B/C
On the Line—B/C

*Pockets—B/C
PrayKids!—C
Primary Pal (IL)
SHINE brightly—C
*Skipping Stones—B/C
Story Friends—B
*Winner—C

CHRISTIAN EDUCATION/LIBRARY
*Christian Early Education—C
Christian Librarian—B
Church Educator—B
*Church Libraries—B/C
Evangelizing Today's Child—B/C
Journal/Adventist Educ.—B
Leader in C. E. Ministries—B
Religion Teacher's Journal—C
*Teachers Interaction—B
*Teachers of Vision—C
*Today's Catholic Teacher—C

DAILY DEVOTIONALS
Secret Place—B/C
Upper Room
Words of Life—B/C

MISSIONS
Evangelical Missions
Intl. Jour./Frontier
*New World Outlook—C
*One—C
OpRev Equipper—B/C
PFI World Report
*PIME World—B/C
*Wesleyan World
*World Pulse

MUSIC
Christian Music Weekly—B
*Creator—B/C
*Tradition

PASTORS/LEADERS
*Angelos—B
Catholic Servant
*Christian Camp—C
Christian Century—B/C
Christian Management—C
Clergy Journal—B
Environment & Art—B/C
Eucharistic Ministries—B/C
Evangelical Baptist—B/C
*Interpreter—C
Leadership—B
Lutheran Forum—B
*Lutheran Partners—B
Mennonite Brethren—B
Ministry—B

Pray!
Rev.—C
*Setmag.com
*This Rock—B/C
Today's Parish—B/C
WCA News—C
*Worship Leader—C
Your Church—C

TEEN/YOUNG ADULT
Boundless Webzine
Breakaway—C
Brio—C
Campus Life—C
Conqueror—B/C
Essential Connection—B/C
Listen—B/C
Passageway.org—B/C
*Real Faith in Life—B
*Sharing the VICTORY—C
Student Leadership—B/C
Teen Light—C
*TeensForJC.com
*Transcendmag.com
With—B
Young Adult Today—B
*Young and Alive—B
*Young Christian—B/C

WOMEN
Anna's Journal—B
At the Center—C
*Esprit—B
Hearts at Home—B/C
*Journey
*Link & Visitor—B
MOMsense—B/C
Right to the Heart
Women Alive!—B

WRITERS
*Beginnings—B
*Byline
Cochran's Corner—B
*Once Upon a Time
Tickled by Thunder
*Writer's Digest—B

POETRY

ADULT/GENERAL
African Voices—R
$-alive now!—R
$-Ancient Paths—R
Angel Face
Barefoot Path—R
$-Believer's Bay
$-Bible Advocate—R
$-Brave Hearts

Bread of Life—R
Breakthrough Intercessor—R
$-Bridal Guides—R
$-Catholic Peace Voice—R
Channels—R
$-Christian Courier (CAN)—R
Christian Journal—R
Christian Motorsports
Christian Online
Christian Publisher.com
Christian Ranchman
$-Christian Social Action—R
$-Commonweal
Connecting Point—R
$-Cornerstone Christian—R
$-Covenant Companion—R
$-Cresset
Crosshome.com
$-Culture Wars—R
$-Decision
Desert Call—R
Discerning Poet—R
$-DisciplesWorld
$-Door—R
$-Dovetail—R
$-Eureka Street
$-Evangel—R
$-First Things
Friends Journal—R
Fuse Magazine
$-Gem—R
Good News Journal
$-Grit
Hannah to Hannah—R
Hard Row to Hoe
Highway News—R
$-Home Times—R
$-Ideals—R
$-Image/WA
$-Impact—R
$-Indian Life—R
Interactive E-Poetry
Jewel Among Jewels
Keys to Living—R
Leaves—R
$-Liberty—R
LifeTimes Catholic
$-Light & Life
$-Liguorian
Literary TNT—R
$-Live—R
$-Lutheran Digest—R
$-Lutheran Journal—R
Mars Hill Review
$-Mature Living
Mature Times—R

$-Mature Years—R
$-Mennonite Brethren—R
$-Miraculous Medal
New Heart—R
$-New Wineskins—R
$-North American Voice—R
$-Over the Back Fence—R
$-Peeks & Valleys—R
Pegasus Review—R
Penned from the Heart
Penwood Review
Perspectives
Plowman—R
$-Prairie Messenger—R
$-Presbyterian Record—R
Priscilla Papers—R
$-Purpose—R
Quaker Life—R
$-Queen of All Hearts
Radix—R
Re:generation Quarterly
Rhubarb
Rose & Thorn
Sacred Journey—R
Sharing—R
$-Silver Wings—R
Singles Scoop—R
$-Sojourners
Spiritual Voice—R
$-Spring Hill Review—R
$-St. Anthony Messenger
$-St. Joseph's Messenger—R
$-Standard—R
Star of Zion
Storyteller—R
Studio—R
Sword and Trumpet—R
$-Testimony—R
Time for Rhyme—R
Time of Singing—R
Tributes—R
$-U.S. Catholic
Valparaiso Poetry—R
Victory News—R
$-Vision—R
$-War Cry—R
$-Weavings—R
West Wind Review
Winsome Wit—R
$-World & I—R
Xavier Review
$-Young Christian—R

CHILDREN
$-Adventures
$-Celebrate

$-Children's Magic Window
$-Focus/Clubhouse Jr.
$-Guideposts for Kids
$-On the Line—R
$-Partners—R
$-Pockets—R
$-SHINE brightly—R
Skipping Stones
$-Story Friends—R
$-Story Mates—R

CHRISTIAN EDUCATION/LIBRARY
$-Church Educator—R
$-Teachers of Vision—R
$-Today's Catholic Teacher—R

DAILY DEVOTIONALS
$-Secret Place
$-These Days

MISSIONS
Railroad Evangelist—R
Women of the Harvest

MUSIC
$-Church Pianist
Quest—R
$-Senior Musician—R

PASTORS/LEADERS
$-Catechumenate
$-Christian Century—R
Cross Currents
$-Emmanuel
Journal/Pastoral Care—R
$-Lutheran Partners—R
Pulpit Helps—R
$-Review for Religious
Sharing the Practice—R
$-Spiritual Spinach—R
$-Theology Today

TEEN/YOUNG ADULT
$-Campus Life—R
$-Devo'Zine—R
$-Essential Connection
$-Insight—R
Setmag.com—R
$-Student Leadership—R
Teen Light—R
$-Teenage Christian—R
TeensForJC.com—R
Transcendmag.com—R
$-Young Christian—R
$-Young Salvationist—R

WOMEN
Anna's Journal—R

$-Esprit—R
Footprints
Handmaiden—R
Hearts at Home—R
$-Link & Visitor—R
$-Melody of the Heart
Praise
Reflections
$-Welcome Home

WRITERS
$-Areopagus (UK)
Author Network E-zine
Author-Me.com
Beginnings
$-Byline
$-Christian Communicator—R
Cochran's Corner—R
$-Cross & Quill—R
Heaven—R
Omnific—R
Once Upon a Time—R
Romancing the Christian Heart—R
$-Tickled by Thunder
Upper Case
$-WIN-Informer
Write Touch
$-Writer's Digest—R
$-Writers' Journal

POLITICAL

ADULT/GENERAL
African Voices—R
$-Anglican Journal
$-Arlington Catholic
Catalyst
$-Catholic Insight
$-Catholic New Times—R
$-Catholic Peace Voice—R
Christian C. L. RECORD—R
$-Christian Courier (CAN)—R
Christian Courier (WI)—R
$-Christian Examiner
Christian Media—R
Christian Motorsports
$-Christian Renewal—R
$-Christian Social Action—R
$-Christianity Today—R
$-Commonweal
$-Cornerstone Christian—R
Creation Care—R
$-Cresset
$-DisciplesWorld
$-Faith Today
$-First Things
$-Generation X—R

$-Home Times—R
$-Inland NW Christian
$-Interim—R
Journal of Church & State
$-Light & Life
Metro Voice—R
$-Minnesota Christian—R
$-National Catholic
$-New Wineskins—R
$-Our Sunday Visitor
Presbyterian Outlook
$-Prism—R
Re:generation Quarterly
$-SCP Journal—R
$-Social Justice—R
$-Sojourners
$-Spring Hill Review—R
$-St. Anthony Messenger
$-Testimony—R
thegoodsteward.com—R
Trumpeter—R
$-U.S. Catholic
Victory News—R
$-World & I—R

MISSIONS
OpRev Equipper—R

PASTORS/LEADERS
$-Christian Century—R
$-Interpreter
$-Spiritual Spinach—R
Theological Digest—R
$-Word & World

TEEN/YOUNG ADULT
$-Inteen—R
$-With—R

WOMEN
$-Horizons (women)—R

PRAYER

ADULT/GENERAL
African Voices—R
AGAIN—R
$-alive now!—R
$-Angels on Earth
$-Annals of St. Anne
Barefoot Path—R
$-Believer's Bay
$-BGC World—R
$-Bible Advocate—R
Bread of Life—R
Breakthrough Intercessor—R
$-Bridal Guides—R
$-Canada Lutheran—R
$-Catholic Digest—R

$-Catholic New Times—R
$-Catholic Peace Voice—R
$-Celebrate Life—R
$-CGA World—R
$-Charisma
Chattels of the Heart—R
Christian Bible Studies.com
Christian Journal—R
$-Christian Leader—R
Christian Motorsports
Christian Online
Christian Ranchman
$-Christian Research
$-Christianity Today—R
$-Christianweek
$-Columbia
Connecting Point—R
$-Cornerstone Christian—R
$-Covenant Companion—R
Creation Care—R
$-Culture Wars—R
$-Decision
Desert Call—R
$-Direction
$-Discipleship Journal—R
Divine Ascent
$-Dovetail—R
$-Episcopal Life—R
$-Evangel—R
Evangelical Advocate—R
$-Faith & Family
$-Faith Today
$-Family Digest—R
$-Foursquare World Advance—R
$-Gem—R
$-God Allows U-Turns—R
$-Good News—R
Good News Journal
Gospel Tract—R
Heartlight—R
Highway News—R
$-Home Times—R
$-Horizons (adult)—R
$-Inland NW Christian
Leaves—R
$-Lifeglow—R
$-Light & Life
$-Liguorian
Literary TNT—R
$-Live—R
$-Living Church
$-Lookout—R
$-Lutheran—R
$-Lutheran Digest—R
$-Lutheran Journal—R
Maranatha News—R

$-Marian Helper—R
$-Marriage Partnership—R
$-Mature Living
Mature Times—R
$-Mature Years—R
$-Men of Integrity—R
$-Mennonite Brethren—R
$-MESSAGE
Metro Voice—R
$-Minnesota Christian—R
$-Montgomery's Journey
$-National Catholic
$-New Freeman—R
$-New Wineskins—R
$-North American Voice—R
$-Now What?—R
Pegasus Review—R
Perspectives
$-Plain Truth—R
Plowman—R
$-Positive Thinking—R
Prayer Closet
PrayerWorks—R
$-Precepts for Living
Presbyterian Outlook
$-Presbyterian Record—R
$-Presbyterians Today—R
$-Priority!
Quaker Life—R
$-Queen of All Hearts
Sacred Journey—R
$-Seeds
$-Signs of the Times—R
$-Silver Wings—R
Singles Scoop—R
$-Social Justice—R
$-Spiritual Life
Spiritual Voice—R
$-St. Anthony Messenger
Sword of the Lord—R
$-Testimony—R
thegoodsteward.com—R
$-Today's Christian—R
Trumpeter—R
$-U.S. Catholic
Victory News—R
$-Vision—R
$-War Cry—R
$-Way of St. Francis—R
$-Wesleyan Life—R
$-Young Christian—R

CHILDREN
Barefoot for Kids—R
$-BREAD/God's Children—R
$-Club Connection

$-High Adventure—R
$-Juniorway
$-Passport—R
$-PrayKids!—R
$-Primary Street
$-SHINE brightly—R

CHRISTIAN EDUCATION/LIBRARY
$-Catechist
Catholic Library World
$-Children's Ministry
$-Church Educator—R
$-Evangelizing Today's Child—R
$-Religion Teacher's Journal
$-Resource—R
$-Teachers of Vision—R
$-Youth & CE Leadership

MISSIONS
Intl. Jour./Frontier—R
$-PFI World Report—R
Railroad Evangelist—R
Wesleyan World—R
$-Worldwide Challenge

MUSIC
$-Creator—R
Quest—R

PASTORS/LEADERS
$-African American Pulpit
Angelos—R
$-Barefoot—R
$-Building Church Leaders.com
$-Catholic Servant
Christian Education Journal (CA)—R
$-Church Worship
$-Diocesan Dialogue—R
$-Emmanuel
$-Enrichment—R
$-Eucharistic Ministries—R
$-Evangelical Baptist—R
$-Evangelicals Today—R
$-Interpreter
Journal/Pastoral Care—R
$-Leadership—R
$-Ministries Today
$-Ministry
$-Ministry & Liturgy—R
$-Pastoral Life—R
Pastors.com—R
$-Pray!—R
$-Priest
$-Proclaim—R
Pulpit Helps—R
$-Reformed Worship
$-Rev.

$-RevWriter Resource
Sewanee Theological Review
Sharing the Practice—R
$-Spiritual Spinach—R
Theological Digest—R
$-Theology Today
$-Today's Christian Preacher—R
$-Today's Parish—R
$-Word & World
$-Worship Leader

TEEN/YOUNG ADULT
$-Breakaway
$-Conqueror—R
$-Inteen—R
$-J.A.M.: Jesus and Me
$-Passageway.org—R
$-Real Faith in Life—R
Setmag.com—R
$-Student Leadership—R
Teen Light—R
$-Teenage Christian—R
TeensForJC.com—R
Transcendmag.com—R
$-Vision—R
$-With—R
$-Young and Alive—R
$-Young Christian—R
$-Young Salvationist—R

WOMEN
Christian Woman's Page—R
$-Esprit—R
Footprints
$-Horizons (women)—R
$-inSpirit—R
$-Journey
Just Between Us—R
Lutheran Woman's Quar.
P31 Woman—R
Reflections
$-SpiritLed Woman
$-Today's Christian Woman—R
$-Woman's Touch—R
$-Women Alive!—R
Women of the Cross—R

WRITERS
$-Areopagus (UK)

PROPHECY

ADULT/GENERAL
$-Apocalypse Chronicles—R
$-Believer's Bay
Breakthrough Intercessor—R
$-Charisma
$-Christian Leader—R

Christian Media—R
Christian Motorsports
Christian Online
$-Christian Research
Evangelical Advocate—R
$-Foursquare World Advance—R
Gospel Tract—R
Maranatha News—R
$-MESSAGE
Metro Voice—R
Midnight Call
$-New Freeman—R
$-North American Voice—R
PrayerWorks—R
$-SCP Journal—R
Spiritual Voice—R
$-St. Anthony Messenger
Sword of the Lord—R
$-Testimony—R
thegoodsteward.com—R
Trumpeter—R
Victory News—R
$-Voice of the Lord
$-Young Christian—R

CHILDREN
$-BREAD/God's Children—R

MUSIC
Tradition

PASTORS/LEADERS
$-African American Pulpit
$-Building Church Leaders.com
$-Interpreter
$-Ministries Today
$-Pastoral Life—R
Pastors.com—R
Pulpit Helps—R
Sharing the Practice—R
$-Word & World

TEEN/YOUNG ADULT
$-Inteen—R
$-Real Faith in Life—R
Setmag.com—R
TeensForJC.com—R
Transcendmag.com—R

WOMEN
$-SpiritLed Woman

PSYCHOLOGY

ADULT/GENERAL
$-Bridal Guides—R
$-Catholic New Times—R
$-Catholic Peace Voice—R
$-Christian Courier (CAN)—R

Christian Motorsports
Christian Online
$-Creative Nonfiction
$-Dovetail—R
Evangelical Advocate—R
$-Gem—R
$-Generation X—R
$-Light & Life
$-Psychology for Living—R
Quaker Life—R
$-Relevant
$-Science & Spirit
$-SCP Journal—R
$-Social Justice—R
$-Spiritual Life
Spiritual Voice—R
$-Spirituality & Health
$-Spring Hill Review—R
$-St. Anthony Messenger
$-Testimony—R
thegoodsteward.com—R
Trumpeter—R
$-Vibrant Life—R
Victory News—R
$-World & I—R

CHRISTIAN EDUCATION/LIBRARY
$-Church Educator—R

PASTORS/LEADERS
$-African American Pulpit
$-Building Church Leaders.com
Cell Group—R
Journal/Pastoral Care—R
$-Ministries Today
$-Pastoral Life—R
Sharing the Practice—R
Steps
$-Word & World

PUPPET PLAYS
$-Children's Ministry
$-Christian Creative Arts
$-Club Connection
$-Evangelizing Today's Child—R
Lillenas
Maranatha News—R
Sharing the Practice—R
$-SHINE brightly—R
Teen Light—R

RACISM

ADULT/GENERAL
$-Catholic Peace Voice—R
Christian Bible Studies.com
Christian C. L. RECORD—R

$-Christian Social Action—R
$-Christianity Today—R
$-Creative Nonfiction
$-Cresset
$-Dovetail—R
$-Faith Today
$-Generation X—R
$-Indian Life—R
$-Interchange
$-Light & Life
$-Liguorian
$-Living—R
$-Lookout—R
$-Men of Integrity—R
$-MESSAGE
$-Minnesota Christian—R
Mutuality—R
$-New Wineskins—R
$-North American Voice—R
$-Our Sunday Visitor
$-Plain Truth—R
Priscilla Papers—R
Quaker Life—R
$-Spirituality & Health
$-St. Anthony Messenger
$-Testimony—R
thegoodsteward.com—R
$-Today's Christian—R
$-Together—R
Trumpeter—R
$-U.S. Catholic
$-Upscale Magazine
Victory News—R
$-World & I—R

CHILDREN
$-Our Little Friend—R
$-Primary Treasure—R
Skipping Stones

MISSIONS
Missiology

PASTORS/LEADERS
$-African American Pulpit
$-Building Church Leaders.com
$-Christian Century—R
Cross Currents
$-Emmanuel
$-Eucharistic Ministries—R
$-Interpreter
$-Lutheran Partners—R
$-Pastoral Life—R

TEEN/YOUNG ADULT
$-Campus Life—R
$-Passageway.org—R
Setmag.com—R

$-Student Leadership—R
Teen Light—R
TeensForJC.com—R
Transcendmag.com—R

WOMEN
ChurchWoman
$-Esprit—R
$-Horizons (women)—R
$-inSpirit—R
Making Waves
$-SpiritLed Woman

WRITERS
Teachers & Writers

RELATIONSHIPS

ADULT/GENERAL
Alliance Life
$-Angels on Earth
$-Annals of St. Anne
$-BGC World—R
$-Bible Advocate—R
Bread of Life—R
Breakthrough Intercessor—R
$-Bridal Guides—R
$-Canada Lutheran—R
$-Catholic Digest—R
$-Catholic Forester—R
$-Celebrate Life—R
Channels—R
$-Charisma
$-Chicken Soup—R
Christian Bible Studies.com
Christian Journal—R
$-Christian Leader—R
Christian Motorsports
Christian Online
Christian Ranchman
$-Christianweek
$-Cornerstone Christian—R
$-Creative Nonfiction
$-Cup of Comfort—R
Desert Call—R
$-Discipleship Journal—R
$-Dovetail—R
Evangelical Advocate—R
$-Faith Today
$-Foursquare World Advance—R
$-Gem—R
$-Generation X—R
$-God Allows U-Turns—R
Good News Journal
$-Gospel Today—R
Grand Valley Observer—R
$-Guideposts—R
Hannah to Hannah—R

Heartlight—R
Heartwarmers
Highway News—R
$-Home Times—R
$-Homeschooling Today—R
HopeKeepers—R
$-Horizons (adult)—R
$-Indian Life—R
$-Inside Journal—R
$-Interchange
Jewel Among Jewels
Keys to Living—R
$-Lifeglow—R
$-Light & Life
$-Liguorian
Literary TNT—R
$-Live—R
$-Living—R
$-Lookout—R
$-Lutheran Digest—R
$-Marriage Partnership—R
Mature Times—R
$-Mature Years—R
$-Men of Integrity—R
Men of the Cross—R
$-Mennonite Historian—R
$-MESSAGE
Metro Voice—R
$-Montgomery's Journey
Mutuality—R
New Heart—R
$-New Man—R
$-New Wineskins—R
$-Our Sunday Visitor
Parents & Teens—R
Pegasus Review—R
$-Plain Truth—R
$-Positive Thinking—R
$-Prairie Messenger—R
PrayerWorks—R
Priscilla Papers—R
$-Purpose—R
Quaker Life—R
$-Relate—R
$-Relevant
Sacred Journey—R
$-Science & Spirit
$-Seeds
$-Signs of the Times—R
$-Silver Wings—R
Singles Scoop—R
$-Smart Families—R
$-Special Living—R
Spiritual Voice—R
$-Spring Hill Review—R
$-St. Anthony Messenger

$-Standard—R
Storyteller—R
$-Testimony—R
thegoodsteward.com—R
$-Today's Christian—R
$-Together—R
Trumpeter—R
$-U.S. Catholic
$-Upscale Magazine
$-Vibrant Life—R
Victory News—R
$-Vision—R
Walk This Way—R
$-War Cry—R
$-Wesleyan Life—R
$-World & I—R
$-Young Christian—R

CHILDREN
Barefoot for Kids—R
$-BREAD/God's Children—R
$-Cadet Quest—R
$-Club Connection
$-High Adventure—R
$-My Friend
$-Passport—R
$-SHINE brightly—R
$-Winner—R

CHRISTIAN EDUCATION/LIBRARY
$-Resource—R
$-Teachers of Vision—R
$-Youth & CE Leadership

MISSIONS
$-Worldwide Challenge

PASTORS/LEADERS
$-African American Pulpit
$-Building Church Leaders.com
Cell Group—R
$-Evangelical Baptist—R
$-Evangelicals Today—R
$-Interpreter
Journal/Pastoral Care—R
$-Ministries Today
$-Ministry
$-Pastoral Life—R
$-Rev.
Sharing the Practice—R
Steps
Strategic Adult Ministries—R
Theological Digest—R
$-Word & World
$-Youthworker

TEEN/YOUNG ADULT
$-Boundless Webzine—R

$-Brio—R
$-Brio & Beyond
$-Conqueror—R
$-Guideposts Sweet 16—R
$-Listen—R
$-Passageway.org—R
$-Real Faith in Life—R
Setmag.com—R
$-Student Leadership—R
Teen Light—R
$-Teenage Christian—R
TeensForJC.com—R
Transcendmag.com—R
$-With—R
$-Young and Alive—R
$-Young Christian—R

WOMEN
$-At the Center—R
$-Esprit—R
$-Extreme Joy
Hearts at Home—R
$-Horizons (women)—R
$-inSpirit—R
$-Journey
Just Between Us—R
Life Tools for Women
$-Link & Visitor—R
Lutheran Woman's Quar.
$-MOMsense—R
P31 Woman—R
Reflections
$-Simple Joy
$-SpiritLed Woman
$-Today's Christian Woman—R
$-Welcome Home
$-Woman's Touch—R
$-Women by Grace—R
Women of the Cross—R
Women Today—R

RELIGIOUS FREEDOM

ADULT/GENERAL
$-America
$-Arlington Catholic
Breakthrough Intercessor—R
$-Catholic New Times—R
$-Catholic Peace Voice—R
Channels—R
$-Charisma
Christian Bible Studies.com
Christian C. L. RECORD—R
Christian Courier (WI)—R
$-Christian Examiner
$-Christian Leader—R
Christian Motorsports
Christian News NW—R

SALVATION TESTIMONIES

ADULT/GENERAL
Alliance Life
American Tract Society—R
$-Believer's Bay
$-BGC World—R
$-Bible Advocate—R
Breakthrough Intercessor—R
Channels—R
Chattels of the Heart—R
Christian Bible Studies.com
Christian Journal—R
Christian Motorsports
Christian Online
Christian Ranchman
Church Herald & Holiness—R
$-Church of God EVANGEL
Connecting Point—R
Crossway/Newsline—R
$-Decision
Evangelical Advocate—R
$-Faith Today
$-Gem—R
Gospel Tract—R
Grand Valley Observer—R
$-Guideposts—R
Highway News—R
$-Home Times—R
$-Indian Life—R
$-Inside Journal—R
Leaves—R
$-Lifeglow—R
$-Light & Life
Literary TNT—R
$-Lookout—R
Maranatha News—R
Mature Times—R
$-Men of Integrity—R
$-Mennonite Brethren—R
$-New Freeman—R
New Heart—R
$-North American Voice—R
$-Now What?—R
Parents & Teens—R
$-Power for Living—R
$-SCP Journal—R
$-Seek—R
$-Shantyman—R
$-Signs of the Times—R
$-Silver Wings—R
Singles Scoop—R
Spiritual Voice—R
$-St. Anthony Messenger
Sword of the Lord—R
$-Testimony—R

thegoodsteward.com—R
$-Today's Christian—R
$-Together—R
Trumpeter—R
$-Up
Victory News—R
$-War Cry—R
$-Wesleyan Life—R
$-Young Christian—R

CHILDREN
$-BREAD/God's Children—R
$-Club Connection

CHRISTIAN EDUCATION/LIBRARY
$-Evangelizing Today's Child—R

MISSIONS
Railroad Evangelist—R
$-Worldwide Challenge

PASTORS/LEADERS
$-African American Pulpit
$-Building Church Leaders.com
Cell Group—R
$-Evangelicals Today—R
$-Interpreter
$-Ministry
$-Pastoral Life—R
Pulpit Helps—R
$-Small Group Dynamics—R

TEEN/YOUNG ADULT
$-Breakaway
$-Inteen—R
$-Passageway.org—R
Setmag.com—R
TeensForJC.com—R
Transcendmag.com—R
$-With—R

WOMEN
$-Esprit—R
Footprints
$-Godly Business Woman
$-History's Women—R
Praise
$-SpiritLed Woman
Women Today—R

WRITERS
$-Areopagus (UK)

SCIENCE

ADULT/GENERAL
$-Catholic New Times—R
Christian C. L. RECORD—R
$-Christian Courier (CAN)—R

Christian Motorsports
$-Christian Social Action—R
$-Creative Nonfiction
$-Cresset
$-Eclectic Homeschool
$-Faith Today
$-Home Times—R
$-Light & Life
$-Lutheran Digest—R
Metro Voice—R
$-Minnesota Christian—R
$-National Catholic
$-New Freeman—R
$-Science & Spirit
$-SCP Journal—R
$-Spirituality & Health
$-Spring Hill Review—R
$-St. Anthony Messenger
$-Testimony—R
thegoodsteward.com—R
TJ
Trumpeter—R
$-World & I—R
$-Young Christian—R

CHILDREN
$-Children's Magic Window
$-Guideposts for Kids
$-My Friend
$-Nature Friend

PASTORS/LEADERS
$-Building Church Leaders.com
$-Lutheran Partners—R
$-Word & World

TEEN/YOUNG ADULT
$-Inteen—R
$-Passageway.org—R
Setmag.com—R
TeensForJC.com—R
Transcendmag.com—R
$-Young Christian—R

WOMEN
$-Esprit—R

SELF-HELP

ADULT/GENERAL
$-Bridal Guides—R
$-Catholic Digest—R
$-CGA World—R
Christian Journal—R
Christian Motorsports
Disciple's Journal—R
$-Dovetail—R
$-Family Digest—R
Hannah to Hannah—R

$-Lifeglow—R
$-Light & Life
$-Living—R
$-Marriage Partnership—R
$-MESSAGE
$-North American Voice—R
$-Smart Families—R
$-Social Justice—R
$-Special Living—R
Spiritual Voice—R
$-St. Anthony Messenger
$-Standard—R
Steps
$-Testimony—R
thegoodsteward.com—R
Trumpeter—R
$-Vibrant Life—R
Victory News—R
$-Vision—R
$-World & I—R

CHILDREN
$-Winner—R

MISSIONS
Women of the Harvest

PASTORS/LEADERS
$-Building Church Leaders.com
Cell Group—R
$-Evangelicals Today—R
Journal/Pastoral Care—R
$-Rev.
Steps

TEEN/YOUNG ADULT
$-Conqueror—R
$-Guideposts Sweet 16—R
Setmag.com—R
Teen Light—R
$-Teenage Christian—R
TeensForJC.com—R
Transcendmag.com—R
$-Young and Alive—R
$-Young Christian—R

WOMEN
$-MOMsense—R
Reflections
$-Today's Christian Woman—R

WRITERS
$-Money the Write Way—R

SENIOR ADULT ISSUES

ADULT/GENERAL
$-Alive!—R
$-Angels on Earth
$-Anglican Journal

$-Annals of St. Anne
$-B.C. Catholic—R
Breakthrough Intercessor—R
$-Canada Lutheran—R
$-Catholic Forester—R
$-Catholic New Times—R
$-CGA World—R
Christian Bible Studies.com
$-Christian Home & School
Christian Journal—R
Christian Motorsports
$-Christianweek
Church Herald & Holiness—R
Discovery—R
$-Dovetail—R
Evangelical Advocate—R
$-Family Digest—R
$-Gem—R
$-Home Times—R
$-Homeschooling Today—R
$-Indian Life—R
$-Lifeglow—R
$-Light & Life
$-Liguorian
$-Live—R
$-Lookout—R
$-Lutheran—R
Maranatha News—R
$-Mature Living
$-Mature Years—R
Metro Voice—R
$-New Freeman—R
$-North American Voice—R
$-Power for Living—R
PrayerWorks—R
$-Resource—R
$-Senior Living
$-Smart Families—R
$-Spring Hill Review—R
$-St. Anthony Messenger
Star of Zion
$-Testimony—R
thegoodsteward.com—R
$-Today's Christian—R
Trumpeter—R
Victory News—R
$-Vision—R
$-War Cry—R
$-Wesleyan Life—R

CHRISTIAN EDUCATION/LIBRARY
$-Church Educator—R
$-Youth & CE Leadership

MISSIONS
$-Worldwide Challenge

MUSIC
$-Senior Musician—R

PASTORS/LEADERS
$-Building Church Leaders.com
$-Diocesan Dialogue—R
$-Eucharistic Ministries—R
$-Evangelical Baptist—R
$-Evangelicals Today—R
$-Interpreter
$-Pastoral Life—R
$-Rev.
Sharing the Practice—R
$-Word & World

WOMEN
$-Esprit—R
Reflections
$-Today's Christian Woman—R

SERMONS

ADULT/GENERAL
$-Arlington Catholic
Breakthrough Intercessor—R
$-Cathedral Age
Christian Motorsports
Christian Ranchman
Church Herald & Holiness—R
Creation Care—R
$-Lutheran Journal—R
Maranatha News—R
Pegasus Review—R
$-Seeds
$-St. Anthony Messenger
Star of Zion
$-Stewardship—R
Sword of the Lord—R
$-Testimony—R
Trumpeter—R
$-Way of St. Francis—R
$-Weavings—R

PASTORS/LEADERS
$-African American Pulpit
$-Church Worship
$-Clergy Journal—R
$-Enrichment—R
$-Evangelicals Today—R
$-In Season
$-Preaching
Preaching On-Line—R
$-Priest
$-Proclaim—R
Pulpit Helps—R
$-Rev.
$-Sermon Notes—R
Sharing the Practice—R

$-Spiritual Spinach—R
$-Sunday Sermons—R
Theological Digest—R
$-Today's Parish—R

SHORT STORY: ADULT/RELIGIOUS

African Voices—R
$-alive now!—R
$-Alive!—R
$-Ancient Paths—R
$-Angelica
$-Animal Trails—R
Anna's Journal—R
$-Annals of St. Anne
$-Areopagus (UK)
Author Network E-zine
Beginnings
$-Believer's Bay
$-Bridal Guides—R
$-Catholic Forester—R
$-CGA World—R
$-Christian Century—R
$-Christian Courier (CAN)—R
$-Christian Educators Journal—R
$-Christian Home & School
Christian Journal—R
Christian Online
Christian Radio Weekly
Christian Ranchman
$-Christian Renewal—R
Christian Woman's Page—R
Church & Synagogue Lib.—R
Cochran's Corner—R
Connecting Point—R
$-Cornerstone Christian—R
$-Covenant Companion—R
Dragons, Knights & Angels
$-Dreams & Visions—R
$-Esprit—R
$-Eureka Street
$-Evangel—R
$-Faith & Family
$-Fellowship Focus—R
$-Five Stones—R
Footprints
Fuse Magazine
$-Gem—R
$-Gems of Truth—R
Good News Journal
$-Grit
Hard Row to Hoe
Heartlight—R
Heaven—R
Highway News—R

$-Home Times—R
$-Horizons (adult)—R
$-Horizons (women)—R
$-Ideals—R
$-Image/WA
$-Impact—R
$-Indian Life—R
Inspire
$-inSpirit—R
$-Liguorian
$-Live—R
$-Living—R
$-Living Light News—R
$-Lutheran Journal—R
Lutheran Woman's Quar.
$-Mature Living
Mature Times—R
$-Mature Years—R
$-Melody of the Heart
$-Mennonite Brethren—R
$-Messenger of the Sacred Heart
$-Miraculous Medal
$-My Legacy—R
$-National Catholic
$-New Wineskins—R
$-North American Voice—R
$-Peeks & Valleys—R
Pegasus Review—R
Perspectives
Plowman—R
PrayerWorks—R
$-Presbyterian Record—R
$-Purpose—R
$-Queen of All Hearts
Railroad Evangelist—R
Seeds of Hope
$-Seek—R
$-Shades of Romance—R
Singles Scoop—R
Spiritual Voice—R
$-Spring Hill Review—R
$-St. Anthony Messenger
$-St. Joseph's Messenger—R
St. Linus Review
$-Standard—R
Storyteller—R
Studio—R
$-Studio Classroom
$-Testimony—R
Upper Case
$-U.S. Catholic
Victory News—R
$-Vision—R
$-Voice of the Lord
$-War Cry—R
$-Wesleyan Life—R

West Wind Review
Winsome Wit—R
$-Women Alive!—R
$-Women by Grace—R
Write Touch

SHORT STORY: ADVENTURE

ADULT
$-Alive!—R
$-Animal Trails—R
$-Annals of St. Anne
Beginnings
$-Byline
$-Christian Century—R
Christian Journal—R
Christian Radio Weekly
Cochran's Corner—R
$-Cornerstone Christian—R
$-Dreams & Visions—R
Fuse Magazine
$-Gem—R
Heartlight—R
Inspire
$-Live—R
$-Miraculous Medal
$-My Legacy—R
$-Peeks & Valleys—R
PrayerWorks—R
Rose & Thorn
Spiritual Voice—R
St. Linus Review
$-Standard—R
Storyteller—R
$-Tickled by Thunder
Victory News—R
$-Vision—R
$-Voice of the Lord
$-Weavings—R

CHILDREN
$-American Girl
Barefoot for Kids—R
$-BREAD/God's Children—R
$-Cadet Quest—R
$-Celebrate
$-Children's Magic Window
Cochran's Corner—R
Connecting Point—R
$-Courage—R
$-Focus/Clubhouse
$-Focus/Clubhouse Jr.
$-High Adventure—R
$-My Friend
$-Primary Pal (IL)
Skipping Stones
$-Story Friends—R

TEEN/YOUNG ADULT

$-Brio & Beyond
Cochran's Corner—R
$-Inteen—R
Setmag.com—R
Teen Light—R
$-Teenage Christian—R
TeensForJC.com—R
Transcendmag.com—R
$-Young Adult Today—R
$-Young Christian—R
$-Young Salvationist—R

SHORT STORY: ALLEGORY

ADULT

$-Animal Trails—R
$-Byline
$-Christian Century—R
Christian Journal—R
Cochran's Corner—R
$-Covenant Companion—R
$-Dreams & Visions—R
Fuse Magazine
$-Gem—R
Heartlight—R
$-Indian Life—R
Inspire
$-Mennonite Brethren—R
$-My Legacy—R
$-New Wineskins—R
$-North American Voice—R
$-Plain Truth—R
PrayerWorks—R
$-Prism—R
Railroad Evangelist—R
Spiritual Voice—R
St. Linus Review
Studio—R
Victory News—R
$-Vision—R
Walk This Way—R

CHILDREN

Cochran's Corner—R
$-Nature Friend
$-SHINE brightly—R
Skipping Stones

TEEN/YOUNG ADULT

$-Breakaway
Cochran's Corner—R
$-Conqueror—R
$-Student Leadership—R
Teen Light—R
$-With—R

$-Young Salvationist—R

SHORT STORY: BIBLICAL

ADULT

$-Animal Trails—R
$-Annals of St. Anne
Bread of Life—R
$-CGA World—R
Christian Journal—R
Christian Online
Christian Ranchman
Church & Synagogue Lib.—R
$-Church Worship
Cochran's Corner—R
Connecting Point—R
$-Cornerstone Christian—R
$-Dreams & Visions—R
$-Esprit—R
$-Evangel—R
$-Gem—R
Heartlight—R
$-Horizons (women)—R
$-Lutheran Journal—R
Lutheran Woman's Quar.
$-Mennonite Brethren—R
$-Miraculous Medal
$-My Legacy—R
$-National Catholic
$-New Wineskins—R
Perspectives
PrayerWorks—R
$-Presbyterian Record—R
$-Purpose—R
Railroad Evangelist—R
$-Seek—R
Spiritual Voice—R
St. Linus Review
Sword of the Lord—R
$-U.S. Catholic
Victory News—R
$-War Cry—R
$-Wesleyan Life—R

CHILDREN

Barefoot for Kids—R
$-BREAD/God's Children—R
Cochran's Corner—R
$-Evangelizing Today's Child—R
$-Focus/Clubhouse
$-Focus/Clubhouse Jr.
$-MESSAGE
$-Nature Friend
$-North American Voice—R
$-Pockets—R
$-PrayKids!—R

TEEN/YOUNG ADULT

$-Breakaway
Cochran's Corner—R
$-Conqueror—R
$-Inteen—R
Setmag.com—R
$-Student Leadership—R
Teen Light—R
$-Teenage Christian—R
TeensForJC.com—R
Transcendmag.com—R
$-Young Adult Today—R
$-Young Christian—R

SHORT STORY: CONTEMPORARY

ADULT

African Voices—R
$-Ancient Paths—R
$-Angelica
$-Animal Trails—R
$-Annals of St. Anne
Author-Me.com
Beginnings
$-Bridal Guides—R
$-Byline
$-Canada Lutheran—R
$-Christian Century—R
$-Christian Courier (CAN)—R
Christian Radio Weekly
$-Christian Renewal—R
Cochran's Corner—R
Connecting Point—R
$-Cornerstone Christian—R
$-Covenant Companion—R
$-Dreams & Visions—R
$-Esprit—R
$-Evangel—R
Fuse Magazine
$-Gem—R
Hard Row to Hoe
Heartlight—R
Highway News—R
$-Home Times—R
$-Ideals—R
$-Indian Life—R
Inspire
$-Liguorian
$-Living Light News—R
Mature Times—R
$-Miraculous Medal
$-My Legacy—R
$-National Catholic
$-New Wineskins—R
$-Peeks & Valleys—R

Perspectives
Railroad Evangelist—R
$-Seek—R
Singles Scoop—R
Spiritual Voice—R
$-Spring Hill Review—R
$-St. Anthony Messenger
$-St. Joseph's Messenger—R
St. Linus Review
$-Standard—R
Storyteller—R
Studio—R
$-Tickled by Thunder
$-U.S. Catholic
Victory News—R
$-War Cry—R
West Wind Review

CHILDREN
$-American Girl
Barefoot for Kids—R
$-BREAD/God's Children—R
$-Cadet Quest—R
$-Canada Lutheran—R
$-Celebrate
Cochran's Corner—R
$-Courage—R
$-Evangelizing Today's Child—R
$-Focus/Clubhouse
$-Focus/Clubhouse Jr.
$-Guideposts for Kids
$-My Friend
$-On the Line—R
$-Partners—R
$-Pockets—R
$-Primary Pal (IL)
$-SHINE brightly—R
Skipping Stones
$-Story Friends—R

TEEN/YOUNG ADULT
$-BREAD/God's Children—R
$-Breakaway
$-Brio & Beyond
$-Campus Life—R
Cochran's Corner—R
$-Essential Connection
$-Listen—R
$-Real Faith in Life—R
Setmag.com—R
Teen Light—R
$-Teenage Christian—R
TeensForJC.com—R
Transcendmag.com—R
$-Young Christian—R

SHORT STORY: ETHNIC

ADULT
African Voices—R
$-Animal Trails—R
$-Bridal Guides—R
$-Byline
$-CGA World—R
Cochran's Corner—R
$-Dreams & Visions—R
$-Gem—R
Hard Row to Hoe
$-Indian Life—R
$-Live—R
$-Peeks & Valleys—R
$-Purpose—R
Spiritual Voice—R
$-Spring Hill Review—R
St. Linus Review
Studio—R
Victory News—R

CHILDREN
$-BREAD/God's Children—R
Cochran's Corner—R
$-Focus/Clubhouse
$-Focus/Clubhouse Jr.
$-My Friend
Skipping Stones

TEEN/YOUNG ADULT
$-BREAD/God's Children—R
Cochran's Corner—R
Setmag.com—R
Teen Light—R
TeensForJC.com—R
Transcendmag.com—R
$-Young Christian—R
$-Young Salvationist—R

SHORT STORY: FANTASY

ADULT
$-Angelica
Author-Me.com
Beginnings
$-Byline
Cochran's Corner—R
Connecting Point—R
Dragons, Knights & Angels
$-Dreams & Visions—R
$-Esprit—R
Fuse Magazine
$-Gem—R
$-Impact—R
Inspire
$-My Legacy—R
$-Peeks & Valleys—R

$-Presbyterian Record—R
Rose & Thorn
Spiritual Voice—R
$-Spring Hill Review—R
St. Linus Review
Storyteller—R
$-Tickled by Thunder
Victory News—R

CHILDREN
Barefoot for Kids—R
$-Children's Magic Window
Cochran's Corner—R
$-Guideposts for Kids
$-SHINE brightly—R

TEEN/YOUNG ADULT
Cochran's Corner—R
$-Inteen—R
Setmag.com—R
Teen Light—R
TeensForJC.com—R
Transcendmag.com—R
$-With—R
$-Young Adult Today—R
$-Young Salvationist—R

SHORT STORY: FRONTIER

ADULT
$-Animal Trails—R
Beginnings
$-Byline
$-Cappers
Cochran's Corner—R
Connecting Point—R
Fuse Magazine
$-Gem—R
$-Indian Life—R
Inspire
$-Miraculous Medal
$-My Legacy—R
$-Peeks & Valleys—R
Spiritual Voice—R
$-Spring Hill Review—R
St. Linus Review
Storyteller—R
$-Tickled by Thunder
Victory News—R
$-Voice of the Lord

CHILDREN
Cochran's Corner—R
$-Guideposts for Kids
$-High Adventure—R
$-SHINE brightly—R

TEEN/YOUNG ADULT
Cochran's Corner—R

Teen Light—R
$-Young Christian—R

SHORT STORY: FRONTIER/ROMANCE

$-Bridal Guides—R
$-Byline
Cochran's Corner—R
Connecting Point—R
$-Dreams & Visions—R
$-Gem—R
$-Grit
Inspire
$-Miraculous Medal
$-My Legacy—R
Romancing the Christian Heart—R
St. Linus Review
Spiritual Voice—R
Storyteller—R
Teen Light—R
Victory News—R
$-Young Christian—R

SHORT STORY: HISTORICAL

ADULT
$-Alive!—R
$-Ancient Paths—R
$-Animal Trails—R
$-Bridal Guides—R
$-Byline
$-Cappers
$-Christian Renewal—R
Cochran's Corner—R
Connecting Point—R
$-Cornerstone Christian—R
$-Esprit—R
Fuse Magazine
$-Gem—R
$-Grit
Heartlight—R
$-Home Times—R
$-Ideals—R
$-Indian Life—R
Inspire
$-Live—R
Lutheran Woman's Quar.
$-Mature Living
Mature Times—R
$-Miraculous Medal
$-My Legacy—R
$-National Catholic
$-North American Voice—R
$-Peeks & Valleys—R
Perspectives

$-Presbyterian Record—R
Railroad Evangelist—R
Rose & Thorn
$-Seek—R
Singles Scoop—R
Spiritual Voice—R
$-Spring Hill Review—R
St. Linus Review
Storyteller—R
Studio—R
Victory News—R
$-Voice of the Lord

CHILDREN
Barefoot for Kids—R
Cochran's Corner—R
$-Courage—R
$-Focus/Clubhouse
Friend
$-Guideposts for Kids
$-High Adventure—R
$-Nature Friend
$-SHINE brightly—R
Skipping Stones

TEEN/YOUNG ADULT
$-BREAD/God's Children—R
Cochran's Corner—R
$-Inteen—R
Teen Light—R
$-Young Adult Today—R
$-Young Christian—R

SHORT STORY: HISTORICAL/ROMANCE

African Voices—R
$-Areopagus (UK)
$-Bridal Guides—R
$-Byline
Cochran's Corner—R
Connecting Point—R
$-Dreams & Visions—R
$-Gem—R
$-Grit
Inspire
$-Miraculous Medal
$-My Legacy—R
Romancing the Christian Heart—R
Spiritual Voice—R
$-St. Anthony Messenger
St. Linus Review
Storyteller—R
Teen Light—R
Victory News—R
$-Voice of the Lord
$-Young Christian—R

SHORT STORY: HUMOROUS

ADULT
$-Alive!—R
$-Ancient Paths—R
$-Animal Trails—R
Author-Me.com
Beginnings
$-Byline
$-Canada Lutheran—R
$-Catholic Forester—R
$-CGA World—R
$-Christian Courier (CAN)—R
Christian Journal—R
Christian Radio Weekly
Christian Woman's Page—R
Church & Synagogue Lib.—R
Cochran's Corner—R
Connecting Point—R
$-Cornerstone Christian—R
$-Covenant Companion—R
$-Dreams & Visions—R
$-Esprit—R
$-Five Stones—R
Fuse Magazine
$-Gem—R
Gospel Tract—R
Heartlight—R
$-Home Times—R
Inspire
$-Live—R
$-Living Light News—R
$-Mature Living
Mature Times—R
$-Mature Years—R
$-Miraculous Medal
$-My Legacy—R
$-National Catholic
$-Over the Back Fence—R
$-Peeks & Valleys—R
Plowman—R
PrayerWorks—R
$-Presbyterian Record—R
$-Seek—R
Singles Scoop—R
Spiritual Voice—R
$-Spring Hill Review—R
$-St. Joseph's Messenger—R
St. Linus Review
Storyteller—R
$-Tickled by Thunder
$-U.S. Catholic
Victory News—R
West Wind Review
Winsome Wit—R

CHILDREN
Barefoot for Kids—R
$-Cadet Quest—R
$-Children's Magic Window
Cochran's Corner—R
$-Courage—R
$-Focus/Clubhouse
$-Focus/Clubhouse Jr.
$-Guideposts for Kids
$-My Friend
$-SHINE brightly—R
Skipping Stones
$-Story Friends—R

TEEN/YOUNG ADULT
$-Breakaway
$-Brio—R
$-Campus Life—R
Cochran's Corner—R
$-Essential Connection
$-Inteen—R
$-Listen—R
Setmag.com—R
$-Student Leadership—R
Teen Light—R
$-Teenage Christian—R
TeensForJC.com—R
Transcendmag.com—R
$-With—R
$-Young Adult Today—R
$-Young Christian—R
$-Young Salvationist—R
YouthWalk

SHORT STORY: JUVENILE
$-Adventures
$-American Girl
$-Animal Trails—R
$-Areopagus (UK)
Barefoot for Kids—R
$-Beginner's Friend—R
$-BREAD/God's Children—R
$-Bridal Guides—R
$-Cadet Quest—R
$-Catholic Forester—R
$-Celebrate
$-Children's Magic Window
$-Christian Home & School
$-Christian Parents Section
$-Christian Renewal—R
Church & Synagogue Lib.—R
$-Church Educator—R
Cochran's Corner—R
$-Courage—R
$-Discoveries—R
$-Evangelizing Today's Child—R

$-Faith & Family
$-Focus/Clubhouse
$-Focus/Clubhouse Jr.
$-Guideposts for Kids
$-High Adventure—R
$-Home Times—R
$-Indian Life—R
$-Junior Companion—R
$-Living—R
$-MESSAGE
$-My Friend
$-My Legacy—R
$-Nature Friend
$-On the Line—R
$-Partners—R
$-Pockets—R
$-Presbyterian Record—R
$-Primary Pal (IL)
$-Primary Pal (KS)—R
Setmag.com—R
$-SHINE brightly—R
Skipping Stones
Spiritual Voice—R
$-Story Friends—R
Storyteller—R
Sword of the Lord—R
TeensForJC.com—R
$-Today's Catholic Teacher—R
Transcendmag.com—R
$-United Church Observer—R
$-Voice of the Lord
$-War Cry—R
$-Winner—R
Write Touch
$-Young Christian—R
Young Gentleman's Monthly
$-Young Salvationist—R

SHORT STORY: LITERARY

ADULT
African Voices—R
$-Ancient Paths—R
Author-Me.com
Beginnings
BOOK Magazine
$-Byline
$-Christian Century—R
$-Christian Courier (CAN)—R
Cochran's Corner—R
$-Covenant Companion—R
$-Dreams & Visions—R
$-Esprit—R
$-First Things
$-Gem—R
Hard Row to Hoe
$-Image/WA

Inspire
$-Mennonite Brethren—R
$-Miraculous Medal
$-My Legacy—R
$-National Catholic
$-New Wineskins—R
Perspectives
Rose & Thorn
$-Seek—R
Spiritual Voice—R
$-Spring Hill Review—R
$-St. Anthony Messenger
St. Linus Review
$-Standard—R
Storyteller—R
Studio—R
$-Tickled by Thunder
Victory News—R
$-War Cry—R
West Wind Review
Xavier Review

CHILDREN
Cochran's Corner—R
$-My Friend
Reflections
Skipping Stones
$-Story Friends—R

TEEN/YOUNG ADULT
Cochran's Corner—R
Reflections
Teen Light—R
$-Young Salvationist—R

SHORT STORY: MYSTERY/ROMANCE
Beginnings
$-Bridal Guides—R
$-Byline
Cochran's Corner—R
Connecting Point—R
$-Dreams & Visions—R
$-Gem—R
$-Grit
Inspire
$-Miraculous Medal
Reflections
Romancing the Christian Heart—R
Setmag.com—R
$-Shades of Romance—R
Spiritual Voice—R
$-Standard—R
St. Linus Review
Storyteller—R
Teen Light—R
TeensForJC.com—R

Transcendmag.com—R
Victory News—R
$-Young Christian—R

SHORT STORY: MYSTERY/SUSPENSE

ADULT

$-Animal Trails—R
Author-Me.com
Beginnings
$-Bridal Guides—R
$-Byline
$-Cappers
Christian Radio Weekly
Cochran's Corner—R
Connecting Point—R
$-Dreams & Visions—R
Fuse Magazine
$-Gem—R
$-Grit
Heartlight—R
$-Indian Life—R
Inspire
$-Miraculous Medal
$-My Legacy—R
$-Peeks & Valleys—R
Spiritual Voice—R
$-Spring Hill Review—R
St. Linus Review
Storyteller—R
$-Tickled by Thunder
Victory News—R
$-Voice of the Lord

CHILDREN

$-American Girl
Barefoot for Kids—R
$-Cadet Quest—R
$-Children's Magic Window
Cochran's Corner—R
$-Courage—R
$-Focus/Clubhouse
$-Guideposts for Kids
$-My Friend
$-On the Line—R
$-SHINE brightly—R

TEEN/YOUNG ADULT

$-Brio & Beyond
Cochran's Corner—R
$-Inteen—R
Setmag.com—R
Teen Light—R
TeensForJC.com—R
Transcendmag.com—R
$-Young Adult Today—R
$-Young Christian—R

$-Young Salvationist—R

SHORT STORY: PARABLES

ADULT

$-alive now!—R
$-America
$-Animal Trails—R
$-Annals of St. Anne
$-Bridal Guides—R
$-Christian Courier (CAN)—R
Christian Journal—R
Christian Woman's Page—R
$-Church Worship
Cochran's Corner—R
$-Cornerstone Christian—R
$-Covenant Companion—R
$-Dreams & Visions—R
$-Esprit—R
$-Five Stones—R
$-Gem—R
Heartlight—R
Highway News—R
$-Impact—R
$-Indian Life—R
$-Lutheran—R
$-Lutheran Journal—R
Mature Times—R
$-Mennonite Brethren—R
$-MESSAGE
$-New Wineskins—R
$-North American Voice—R
Perspectives
$-Plain Truth—R
PrayerWorks—R
$-Presbyterian Record—R
Railroad Evangelist—R
$-Seek—R
Singles Scoop—R
Spiritual Voice—R
St. Linus Review
$-Testimony—R
Victory News—R

CHILDREN

Barefoot for Kids—R
$-Church Educator—R
Cochran's Corner—R
$-Faces
$-Guideposts for Kids
$-High Adventure—R
$-MESSAGE
$-My Friend
$-SHINE brightly—R
Skipping Stones

TEEN/YOUNG ADULT

$-Breakaway
$-Church Educator—R
Cochran's Corner—R
$-Inteen—R
Setmag.com—R
$-Student Leadership—R
Teen Light—R
TeensForJC.com—R
$-Testimony—R
Transcendmag.com—R
$-With—R
$-Young Adult Today—R
$-Young Christian—R

SHORT STORY: PLAYS

$-Areopagus (UK)
Beginnings
$-Christian Creative Arts
Christian Drama
$-Church Worship
$-Courage—R
$-Drama Ministry—R
$-Esprit—R
$-Faces
$-Guideposts for Kids
$-J.A.M.: Jesus and Me
$-New Wineskins—R
Setmag.com—R
$-SHINE brightly—R
$-Spring Hill Review—R
Teen Light—R
TeensForJC.com—R
Transcendmag.com—R
$-Voice of the Lord

SHORT STORY: ROMANCE

ADULT

$-Alive!—R
$-Animal Trails—R
Author-Me.com
Beginnings
$-Bridal Guides—R
$-Byline
$-Cappers
Cochran's Corner—R
Connecting Point—R
$-Cornerstone Christian—R
$-Dreams & Visions—R
$-Gem—R
$-Grit
Inspire
$-Miraculous Medal
$-Peeks & Valleys—R

Romancing the Christian Heart—R
Rose & Thorn
$-Shades of Romance—R
Spiritual Voice—R
$-St. Joseph's Messenger—R
St. Linus Review
Storyteller—R
Victory News—R

TEEN/YOUNG ADULT
$-Brio—R
Cochran's Corner—R
Reflections
Setmag.com—R
Teen Light—R
TeensForJC.com—R
Transcendmag.com—R
$-With—R
$-Young Christian—R
$-Young Salvationist—R

SHORT STORY: SCIENCE FICTION

ADULT
African Voices—R
$-Angelica
Author-Me.com
Beginnings
$-Byline
Cochran's Corner—R
Connecting Point—R
Dragons, Knights & Angels
$-Dreams & Visions—R
Fuse Magazine
$-Gateway S-F—R
$-Gem—R
Inspire
$-Messianic Sci-Fi
$-Peeks & Valleys—R
Rose & Thorn
Spiritual Voice—R
$-Spring Hill Review—R
St. Linus Review
Storyteller—R
$-Tickled by Thunder
Victory News—R

CHILDREN
$-Children's Magic Window
Cochran's Corner—R

TEEN/YOUNG ADULT
$-Breakaway
Cochran's Corner—R
$-Inteen—R
$-J.A.M.: Jesus and Me
Teen Light—R

$-With—R
$-Young Adult Today—R
$-Young Salvationist—R

SHORT STORY: SKITS

ADULT
$-Church Worship
$-Cornerstone Christian—R
$-Drama Ministry—R
$-Esprit—R
$-Five Stones—R
Mature Times—R
$-New Wineskins—R
Singles Scoop—R

CHILDREN
Barefoot for Kids—R
$-Faces
$-SHINE brightly—R

TEEN/YOUNG ADULT
$-J.A.M.: Jesus and Me
Setmag.com—R
$-Student Leadership—R
Teen Light—R
TeensForJC.com—R
Transcendmag.com—R

SHORT STORY: SPECULATIVE

ADULT
$-Angelica
$-Dreams & Visions—R
Fuse Magazine
Inspire
$-National Catholic
$-Spring Hill Review—R
St. Linus Review
Storyteller—R
$-Tickled by Thunder
Victory News—R

TEEN/YOUNG ADULT
Setmag.com—R
Teen Light—R
TeensForJC.com—R
Transcendmag.com—R

SHORT STORY: TEEN/YOUNG ADULT

$-Animal Trails—R
$-BREAD/God's Children—R
$-Breakaway
$-Bridal Guides—R
$-Brio—R
$-Brio & Beyond
$-Cadet Quest—R

$-Campus Life—R
$-Canada Lutheran—R
$-Catholic Forester—R
$-Christian Parents Section
Church & Synagogue Lib.—R
$-Church Educator—R
Cochran's Corner—R
$-Conqueror—R
Dragons, Knights & Angels
$-Essential Connection
$-Evangel—R
$-Fellowship Focus—R
$-High Adventure—R
$-Home Times—R
$-Indian Life—R
$-Inteen—R
$-J.A.M.: Jesus and Me
$-Liguorian
$-Listen—R
$-Partners—R
$-Presbyterian Record—R
$-Real Faith in Life—R
Reflections
Setmag.com—R
$-SHINE brightly—R
Skipping Stones
Spiritual Voice—R
$-St. Anthony Messenger
Storyteller—R
$-Student Leadership—R
Sword of the Lord—R
Teen Light—R
$-Teenage Christian—R
TeensForJC.com—R
$-Testimony—R
Transcendmag.com—R
$-Voice of the Lord
$-War Cry—R
West Wind Review
$-With—R
Write Touch
$-Young Adult Today
$-Young Christian—R
$-Young Salvationist—R
$-Youth Compass (KS)—R
YouthWalk

SHORT STORY: WESTERNS*

ADULT
Author-Me.com
$-Dreams & Visions—R
Fuse Magazine

SINGLES ISSUES

ADULT/GENERAL
African Voices—R

Alliance Life
$-Annals of St. Anne
$-BGC World—R
$-Bible Advocate—R
Breakthrough Intercessor—R
$-Bridal Guides—R
Channels—R
$-Christian Examiner
Christian Journal—R
Christian Motorsports
Christian Online
$-Christian Parenting—R
Christian Ranchman
$-Christian Single
$-Christian Social Action—R
$-Christianweek
$-Cornerstone Christian—R
Crossway/Newsline—R
$-Discipleship Journal—R
$-Dovetail—R
$-Evangel—R
Evangelical Advocate—R
$-Faith Today
$-Foursquare World Advance—R
$-Gem—R
$-Generation X—R
Good News Journal
Heartlight—R
$-Home Times—R
$-Homeschooling Today—R
$-Indian Life—R
$-Joy & Praise
$-Layman
$-Light & Life
$-Liguorian
$-Living—R
$-Lookout—R
$-Lutheran—R
Mature Times—R
$-Men of Integrity—R
$-MESSAGE
Metro Voice—R
$-Montgomery's Journey
Mutuality—R
$-New Man—R
$-Our Sunday Visitor
$-Pastoral Life—R
$-Power for Living—R
$-Presbyterian Record—R
Priscilla Papers—R
$-Psychology for Living—R
Quaker Life—R
Singles Scoop—R
$-Smart Families—R
$-St. Anthony Messenger
$-Testimony—R

thegoodsteward.com—R
$-Today's Christian—R
$-Together—R
Trumpeter—R
$-U.S. Catholic
$-Vibrant Life—R
Victory News—R
$-War Cry—R
$-World & I—R

CHRISTIAN EDUCATION/LIBRARY
$-Youth & CE Leadership

MISSIONS
Women of the Harvest
$-Worldwide Challenge

MUSIC
Quest—R

PASTORS/LEADERS
$-Christian Century—R
$-Eucharistic Ministries—R
$-Evangelical Baptist—R
$-Interpreter
$-Ministries Today
$-Pastoral Life—R
$-Rev.
Sharing the Practice—R
Strategic Adult Ministries—R
$-Word & World

TEEN/YOUNG ADULT
$-Boundless Webzine—R
$-Inteen—R
$-Passageway.org—R
Setmag.com—R
Teen Light—R
TeensForJC.com—R
Transcendmag.com—R

WOMEN
Anna's Journal—R
$-At the Center—R
Christian Woman's Page—R
Christian Women Today—R
$-Godly Business Woman
$-inSpirit—R
$-MOMsense—R
Reflections
Shalom Bayit
$-SpiritLed Woman
$-Today's Christian Woman—R
True Woman
$-Woman's Touch—R
$-Women by Grace—R
Women Today—R

SOCIAL JUSTICE

ADULT/GENERAL
$-Arlington Catholic
Catalyst
$-Catholic New Times—R
$-Catholic Peace Voice—R
Channels—R
$-Charisma
Christian Bible Studies.com
$-Christian Courier (CAN)—R
$-Christian Leader—R
Christian Motorsports
Christian Online
$-Christian Social Action—R
$-Christianity Today—R
$-Christianweek
$-Columbia
$-Commonweal
$-Company—R
$-Covenant Companion—R
$-Cresset
$-Culture Wars—R
Desert Call—R
$-Dovetail—R
$-Faith & Family
$-Faith Today
$-Foursquare World Advance—R
$-Gem—R
$-Generation X—R
$-Home Times—R
$-Indian Life—R
$-Inland NW Christian
Island Catholic News
$-Layman
$-Light & Life
$-Liguorian
$-Living—R
$-Lookout—R
$-Men of Integrity—R
$-Mennonite Brethren—R
$-Minnesota Christian—R
Mutuality—R
$-National Catholic
$-New Wineskins—R
$-North American Voice—R
$-Our Sunday Visitor
$-Prairie Messenger—R
$-Presbyterian Record—R
$-Priority!
Priscilla Papers—R
$-Prism—R
$-Purpose—R
Quaker Life—R
Salt of The Earth
$-Science & Spirit

$-Silver Wings—R
$-Social Justice—R
$-Sojourners
$-Spiritual Life
$-Spring Hill Review—R
$-St. Anthony Messenger
$-St. Joseph's Messenger—R
$-Testimony—R
thegoodsteward.com—R
$-Today's Christian—R
$-Together—R
Trumpeter—R
$-U.S. Catholic
$-United Church Observer—R
Victory News—R
$-Way of St. Francis—R
$-World & I—R
$-Young Christian—R

CHILDREN
$-Pockets—R
Skipping Stones

CHRISTIAN EDUCATION/LIBRARY
Catholic Library World
$-Church Educator—R
$-Journal/Adventist Educ.—R
$-Momentum
$-Religion Teacher's Journal

MISSIONS
Missiology
$-One

PASTORS/LEADERS
$-African American Pulpit
$-Building Church Leaders.com
$-Christian Century—R
$-Clergy Journal—R
$-Emmanuel
$-Interpreter
$-Ministries Today
$-Pastoral Life—R
Quarterly Review
$-Rev.
Sharing the Practice—R
$-Theology Today

TEEN/YOUNG ADULT
$-Boundless Webzine—R
$-Devo'Zine—R
$-Passageway.org—R
Setmag.com—R
$-Teenage Christian—R
TeensForJC.com—R
Transcendmag.com—R
$-Young Salvationist—R

WOMEN
$-Esprit—R
$-Horizons (women)—R
$-inSpirit—R
Making Waves

SOCIOLOGY

ADULT/GENERAL
$-Anglican Journal
$-Catholic New Times—R
$-Catholic Peace Voice—R
$-Christian Courier (CAN)—R
Christian Online
$-Christian Social Action—R
$-Commonweal
$-Culture Wars—R
$-Dovetail—R
Evangelical Advocate—R
$-Faith Today
$-Gem—R
$-Generation X—R
Journal of Church & State
$-Light & Life
$-Montgomery's Journey
$-National Catholic
Priscilla Papers—R
$-Science & Spirit
$-SCP Journal—R
$-Social Justice—R
Spiritual Voice—R
$-Spring Hill Review—R
$-St. Anthony Messenger
$-Testimony—R
thegoodsteward.com—R
Trumpeter—R
Victory News—R
$-World & I—R

CHRISTIAN EDUCATION/LIBRARY
$-Church Educator—R

PASTORS/LEADERS
$-African American Pulpit
$-Building Church Leaders.com
$-Eucharistic Ministries—R
$-Interpreter
$-Pastoral Life—R
$-Rev.
Theological Digest—R
$-Word & World
Youth Culture

TEEN/YOUNG ADULT
$-Inteen—R
Setmag.com—R
TeensForJC.com—R

Transcendmag.com—R

WOMEN
$-inSpirit—R

SPIRITUAL GIFTS

ADULT/GENERAL
African Voices—R
Alliance Life
$-Arkansas Catholic—R
$-Bible Advocate—R
Bread of Life—R
$-Bridal Guides—R
Channels—R
Christian Bible Studies.com
$-Christian Leader—R
Christian Online
Christian Ranchman
$-Christianity Today—R
$-Cornerstone Christian—R
$-Covenant Companion—R
$-Cup of Comfort—R
$-Discipleship Journal—R
$-Dovetail—R
Evangelical Advocate—R
$-Faith & Family
$-Faith & Friends—R
$-Faith Today
$-Light & Life
$-Liguorian
Literary TNT—R
$-Lookout—R
Maranatha News—R
Mature Times—R
$-Mature Years—R
$-Men of Integrity—R
Mutuality—R
$-New Freeman—R
$-New Wineskins—R
$-North American Voice—R
$-Positive Thinking—R
$-Presbyterian Record—R
Priscilla Papers—R
Quaker Life—R
Regent Business—R
Sacred Journey—R
$-Silver Wings—R
Singles Scoop—R
Spiritual Voice—R
$-St. Anthony Messenger
$-Stewardship—R
Sword and Trumpet—R
$-Testimony—R
thegoodsteward.com—R
$-Today's Christian—R
$-Together—R

Trumpeter—R
Victory News—R
$-Voice of the Lord
$-Way of St. Francis—R
$-Young Christian—R

CHILDREN
$-BREAD/God's Children—R
$-Our Little Friend—R
$-Primary Treasure—R
$-SHINE brightly—R

PASTORS/LEADERS
$-African American Pulpit
$-Building Church Leaders.com
$-Evangelicals Today—R
$-Interpreter
Ministry in Motion—R
$-Pastoral Life—R
$-Review for Religious
$-RevWriter Resource
Sharing the Practice—R
$-Worship Leader

TEEN/YOUNG ADULT
$-Passageway.org—R
Setmag.com—R
Teen Light—R
TeensForJC.com—R
Transcendmag.com—R
$-With—R
$-Young Christian—R

WOMEN
$-Esprit—R
$-Godly Business Woman
$-Horizons (women)—R
$-inSpirit—R
$-Journey
Just Between Us—R
P31 Woman—R
Right to the Heart—R
$-SpiritLed Woman
$-Women by Grace—R

SPIRITUAL LIFE

ADULT/GENERAL
Barefoot Path—R
$-BGC World—R
$-Bible Advocate—R
$-Bridal Guides—R
$-Catholic Digest—R
$-Catholic Peace Voice—R
CBN.com—R
Channels—R
Chattels of the Heart—R
Christian Bible Studies.com
$-Christian Examiner

Christian Journal—R
Christian Online
$-Christian Research
$-Christianweek
$-Cup of Comfort—R
$-Discipleship Journal—R
Divine Ascent
$-Eclectic Homeschool
$-Faith & Family
$-Faith & Friends—R
$-Faith Today
$-Family Digest—R
$-God Allows U-Turns—R
Highway News—R
$-Homeschooling Today—R
$-Horizons (adult)—R
$-Light & Life
Literary TNT—R
$-Lookout—R
$-Lutheran Journal—R
$-Men of Integrity—R
Men of the Cross—R
$-Montgomery's Journey
$-National Catholic
New Heart—R
$-New Wineskins—R
$-North American Voice—R
PrayerWorks—R
$-Presbyterians Today—R
Priscilla Papers—R
Quaker Life—R
Reformed Quarterly
Re:generation Quarterly
Regent Business—R
$-Relevant
Sacred Journey—R
$-Science & Spirit
$-Seek—R
$-Signs of the Times—R
$-Silver Wings—R
$-St. Anthony Messenger
$-Stewardship—R
Sword and Trumpet—R
$-Testimony—R
$-Today's Christian—R
$-Together—R
$-U.S. Catholic
$-Up
Victory News—R
$-Young Christian—R

CHILDREN
Barefoot for Kids—R
$-BREAD/God's Children—R
$-Focus/Clubhouse

CHRISTIAN EDUCATION/LIBRARY
$-Children's Ministry
$-Youth & CE Leadership

MISSIONS
Missiology

PASTORS/LEADERS
$-Building Church Leaders.com
Christian Education Journal (CA)—R
$-Clergy Journal—R
$-Evangelical Baptist—R
Journal/Pastoral Care—R
Ministry in Motion—R
$-RevWriter Resource
$-This Rock
$-WCA News—R

TEEN/YOUNG ADULT
$-Breakaway
$-Young Christian—R

WOMEN
Christian Woman's Page—R
$-Horizons (women)—R
$-inSpirit—R
P31 Woman—R
Right to the Heart—R
Women of the Cross—R

SPIRITUAL RENEWAL*

ADULT/GENERAL
Alliance Life
Barefoot Path—R
$-Bridal Guides—R
Chattels of the Heart—R
Christian Bible Studies.com
Christian Journal—R
Christian Online
Church Herald & Holiness—R
$-Cup of Comfort—R
$-Evangel—R
Evangelical Advocate—R
Literary TNT—R
$-Mature Living
$-Men of Integrity—R
Men of the Cross—R
$-New Wineskins—R
PrayerWorks—R
Quaker Life—R
Re:generation Quarterly
$-Relevant
Sacred Journey—R
Spirituality For Today
Sword and Trumpet—R
$-Testimony—R
$-Today's Christian—R

Victory News—R

MISSIONS
Missiology

PASTORS/LEADERS
$-Building Church Leaders.com
$-Lutheran Partners—R
Ministry in Motion—R

TEEN/YOUNG ADULT
Teen Light—R

WOMEN
$-Horizons (women)—R
$-inSpirit—R
$-Woman's Touch—R

SPIRITUAL WARFARE

ADULT/GENERAL
AGAIN—R
Alliance Life
$-Angels on Earth
$-Believer's Bay
$-BGC World—R
$-Bible Advocate—R
Breakthrough Intercessor—R
$-Celebrate Life—R
$-CGA World—R
Channels—R
$-Charisma
Christian Bible Studies.com
$-Christian Leader—R
Christian Motorsports
Christian Online
Christian Ranchman
$-Christian Research
$-Christianity Today—R
$-Cornerstone Christian—R
Evangelical Advocate—R
$-Faith & Friends—R
$-Faith Today
$-Gem—R
$-Good News—R
Gospel Tract—R
Heartlight—R
Leaves—R
$-Light & Life
Literary TNT—R
Maranatha News—R
$-Men of Integrity—R
$-MESSAGE
$-New Freeman—R
New Heart—R
$-New Wineskins—R
$-North American Voice—R
Prayer Closet
PrayerWorks—R

Quaker Life—R
Spiritual Voice—R
$-St. Anthony Messenger
Sword and Trumpet—R
Sword of the Lord—R
$-Testimony—R
thegoodsteward.com—R
$-Today's Pentecostal Evangel
Trumpeter—R
Victory News—R
$-Voice of the Lord

CHILDREN
$-BREAD/God's Children—R
$-High Adventure—R

MISSIONS
Missiology
Railroad Evangelist—R

PASTORS/LEADERS
$-Building Church Leaders.com
Cell Group—R
$-Church Growth Network—R
$-Evangelicals Today—R
Journal/Pastoral Care—R
$-Let's Worship
$-Ministries Today
$-Pastoral Life—R
Pastors.com—R
$-Rev.
Sharing the Practice—R

TEEN/YOUNG ADULT
$-Brio—R
$-Passageway.org—R
Setmag.com—R
Teen Light—R
TeensForJC.com—R
Transcendmag.com—R

WOMEN
$-Godly Business Woman
Handmaiden—R
$-inSpirit—R
Just Between Us—R
Praise
$-Women Alive!—R
$-Women by Grace—R

SPIRITUALITY

ADULT/GENERAL
African Voices—R
AGAIN—R
$-alive now!—R
Alliance Life
American Tract Society—R
$-Angels on Earth

$-Annals of St. Anne
$-Arkansas Catholic—R
$-Arlington Catholic
Barefoot Path—R
$-Bible Advocate—R
Bread of Life—R
Breakthrough Intercessor—R
$-Bridal Guides—R
$-Cathedral Age
$-Catholic Digest—R
$-Catholic New Times—R
$-Catholic Parent
$-Catholic Peace Voice—R
$-CGA World—R
Channels—R
$-Charisma
Chattels of the Heart—R
Christian Bible Studies.com
$-Christian Courier (CAN)—R
$-Christian Home & School
Christian Journal—R
$-Christian Leader—R
Christian Motorsports
Christian Online
$-Christianity Today—R
$-Christianweek
$-Columbia
$-Common Ground—R
$-Commonweal
$-Cornerstone Christian—R
$-Covenant Companion—R
Crossway/Newsline—R
$-Culture Wars—R
$-Cup of Comfort—R
Desert Call—R
Divine Ascent
$-Door—R
$-Dovetail—R
$-Episcopal Life—R
$-Faith & Family
$-Faith & Friends—R
$-Faith Today
$-Gem—R
$-Generation X—R
$-God Allows U-Turns—R
$-Good News—R
Good News Journal
$-Grit
$-Guideposts—R
Heartlight—R
$-Horizons (adult)—R
$-Inland NW Christian
Island Catholic News
Leaves—R
$-Lifeglow—R
LifeTimes Catholic

$-Light & Life
$-Liguorian
Literary TNT—R
$-Living—R
$-Living Church
$-Lookout—R
$-Lutheran—R
Mature Times—R
$-Mature Years—R
$-Men of Integrity—R
$-Mennonite Brethren—R
$-Messenger of the Sacred Heart
$-National Catholic
$-New Freeman—R
New Heart—R
$-New Wineskins—R
$-North American Voice—R
$-Oblates
$-Parabola—R
Parents & Teens—R
Pegasus Review—R
Perspectives
$-Portland Magazine
$-Positive Thinking—R
$-Prairie Messenger—R
Presbyterian Outlook
$-Presbyterian Record—R
$-Presbyterians Today—R
Priscilla Papers—R
$-Prism—R
Quaker Life—R
$-Queen of All Hearts
Sacred Journey—R
$-SCP Journal—R
$-Seek—R
Singles Scoop—R
$-Social Justice—R
$-Spiritual Life
Spiritual Voice—R
$-St. Anthony Messenger
$-St. Joseph's Messenger—R
$-Standard—R
Star of Zion
$-Stewardship—R
Sword and Trumpet—R
$-Testimony—R
thegoodsteward.com—R
$-Today's Christian—R
$-Together—R
Trumpeter—R
$-U.S. Catholic
$-Up
Victory News—R
$-War Cry—R
$-Way of St. Francis—R
$-Weavings—R

$-World & I—R
$-Young Christian—R

CHILDREN
$-BREAD/God's Children—R
$-Passport—R
Skipping Stones

CHRISTIAN EDUCATION/LIBRARY
$-Church Educator—R
Jour./Ed. & Christian Belief—R
Journal/Christian Education
$-Religion Teacher's Journal

MISSIONS
$-Evangelical Missions—R
Missiology
$-Worldwide Challenge

MUSIC
Quest—R

PASTORS/LEADERS
$-African American Pulpit
$-Barefoot—R
$-Building Church Leaders.com
$-Christian Century—R
Christian Education Journal (CA)—R
$-Church Worship
$-Clergy Journal—R
$-Diocesan Dialogue—R
$-Emmanuel
$-Eucharistic Ministries—R
$-Evangelical Baptist—R
$-Evangelicals Today—R
$-Interpreter
Journal/Pastoral Care—R
$-Lutheran Partners—R
$-Ministries Today
$-Ministry
Ministry in Motion—R
$-Pastoral Life—R
Pastors.com—R
$-Proclaim—R
Quarterly Review
$-Reformed Worship
$-Rev.
$-Review for Religious
$-RevWriter Resource
Sharing the Practice—R
$-Spiritual Spinach—R
Theological Digest—R
$-Theology Today
$-Today's Parish—R
$-Word & World
$-Worship Leader
$-Youthworker

TEEN/YOUNG ADULT
$-Inteen—R
$-Passageway.org—R
Setmag.com—R
$-Teenage Christian—R
TeensForJC.com—R
Transcendmag.com—R
$-With—R
$-Young Adult Today—R
$-Young and Alive—R
$-Young Christian—R
$-Young Salvationist—R

WOMEN
Christian Woman's Page—R
ChurchWoman
$-Esprit—R
$-Godly Business Woman
Handmaiden—R
Hearts at Home—R
$-Horizons (women)—R
$-inSpirit—R
Just Between Us—R
Lutheran Woman's Quar.
$-SpiritLed Woman
$-Today's Christian Woman—R

WRITERS
$-Areopagus (UK)

SPORTS/RECREATION

ADULT/GENERAL
$-Angels on Earth
$-Arlington Catholic
$-Bridal Guides—R
Christian Courier (WI)—R
Christian Motorsports
Christian Radio Weekly
Christian Ranchman
$-Christian Renewal—R
Connecting Point—R
$-Cornerstone Christian—R
$-Faith Today
$-Gem—R
$-Gospel Today—R
$-Guideposts—R
$-Home Times—R
$-Lifeglow—R
$-Light & Life
$-Living Light News—R
Metro Voice—R
$-Minnesota Christian—R
$-New Freeman—R
$-New Man—R
$-Smart Families—R
Spiritual Voice—R
$-Sports Spectrum

$-St. Anthony Messenger
Storyteller—R
$-Testimony—R
thegoodsteward.com—R
$-Today's Christian—R
Victory News—R
$-World & I—R
$-Young Christian—R

CHILDREN
Barefoot for Kids—R
$-BREAD/God's Children—R
$-Cadet Quest—R
$-Club Connection
$-Focus/Clubhouse
$-Guideposts for Kids
$-High Adventure—R
Skipping Stones

CHRISTIAN EDUCATION/LIBRARY
$-Children's Ministry

MISSIONS
$-Worldwide Challenge

MUSIC
Quest—R

PASTORS/LEADERS
Cornerstone Youth—R
$-Interpreter
$-Rev.
$-Spiritual Spinach—R

TEEN/YOUNG ADULT
$-Boundless Webzine—R
$-Breakaway
$-Brio—R
$-Brio & Beyond
$-Inteen—R
$-Listen—R
$-Passageway.org—R
$-Real Faith in Life—R
Setmag.com—R
$-Sharing the VICTORY—R
TeensForJC.com—R
Transcendmag.com—R
$-Young Christian—R

WOMEN
$-Esprit—R
Reflections

STEWARDSHIP

ADULT/GENERAL
Alliance Life
$-Angels on Earth
$-BGC World—R

Breakthrough Intercessor—R
$-Celebrate Life—R
Channels—R
Christian Bible Studies.com
$-Christian Courier (CAN)—R
$-Christian Leader—R
Christian Motorsports
Christian Online
$-Christian Social Action—R
$-Christianweek
Church Herald & Holiness—R
$-Cornerstone Christian—R
$-Covenant Companion—R
Creation Care—R
$-Cresset
$-Discipleship Journal—R
Evangelical Advocate—R
$-Faith Today
$-Family Digest—R
$-Fellowship Focus—R
$-Gem—R
Grand Valley Observer—R
$-Layman
$-Lifeglow—R
$-Light & Life
$-Liguorian
$-Live—R
$-Living Church
$-Lutheran Digest—R
$-Lutheran Journal—R
Mature Times—R
$-Men of Integrity—R
$-MESSAGE
$-North American Voice—R
$-NRB Magazine—R
$-Our Sunday Visitor
$-Positive Thinking—R
$-Power for Living—R
Presbyterian Outlook
$-Presbyterian Record—R
$-Prism—R
$-Purpose—R
Quaker Life—R
Regent Business—R
$-Seeds
Singles Scoop—R
$-St. Anthony Messenger
$-Stewardship—R
$-Testimony—R
thegoodsteward.com—R
$-Today's Christian—R
Trumpeter—R
$-U.S. Catholic
$-United Church Observer—R
Victory News—R
$-Wireless Age—R

CHILDREN
$-BREAD/God's Children—R
Skipping Stones

CHRISTIAN EDUCATION/LIBRARY
$-Church Educator—R
$-Momentum

MISSIONS
Wesleyan World—R

PASTORS/LEADERS
$-African American Pulpit
$-Building Church Leaders.com
Cell Group—R
$-Christian Camp—R
Christian Management—R
$-Clergy Journal—R
$-Evangelical Baptist—R
$-Evangelicals Today—R
$-Five Stones—R
$-Interpreter
$-Let's Worship
$-Ministries Today
$-Ministry
Net Results
$-Pastoral Life—R
$-Priest
Quarterly Review
$-Rev.
$-RevWriter Resource
Sharing the Practice—R
Theological Digest—R
$-Your Church—R

TEEN/YOUNG ADULT
$-Passageway.org—R
Setmag.com—R
Teen Light—R
TeensForJC.com—R
Transcendmag.com—R
$-With—R
$-Young Salvationist—R

WOMEN
$-Esprit—R
$-Godly Business Woman
$-Horizons (women)—R
$-inSpirit—R
Just Between Us—R
P31 Woman—R
$-Today's Christian Woman—R

TAKE-HOME PAPERS

ADULT/GENERAL
$-Evangel—R

$-Gem—R
$-Gems of Truth—R
$-Horizons—R
$-Live—R
$-Lookout—R
$-Power for Living—R
$-Purpose—R
$-Seek—R
$-Standard—R
$-Vision—R

CHILDREN
$-Adventures
$-Beginner's Friend—R
$-Celebrate
$-Courage—R
$-Discoveries—R
$-Junior Companion—R
$-Juniorway
$-Our Little Friend—R
$-Partners—R
$-Passport—R
$-PrayKids!—R
$-Preschool Playhouse
$-Primary Pal (IL)
$-Primary Pal (KS)—R
$-Primary Treasure—R
$-Promise
$-Seeds
$-Story Mates—R

TEEN/YOUNG ADULT
$-Insight—R
$-Youth Compass (KS)—R

THEOLOGICAL

ADULT/GENERAL
AGAIN—R
$-alive now!—R
$-America
$-Anglican Journal
$-Annals of St. Anne
$-Arkansas Catholic—R
$-Arlington Catholic
$-B.C. Catholic—R
Breakthrough Intercessor—R
$-Catholic New Times—R
$-Catholic Peace Voice—R
Channels—R
$-Charisma
$-Christian Courier (CAN)—R
$-Christian Leader—R
Christian Motorsports
Christian Online
$-Christian Renewal—R
$-Christian Research
$-Christian Standard—R

$-Christianity Today—R
Church Herald & Holiness—R
$-Commonweal
Creation Care—R
$-Cresset
$-Culture Wars—R
$-DisciplesWorld
Divine Ascent
$-Dovetail—R
$-Episcopal Life—R
$-Eureka Street
Evangelical Advocate—R
$-Faith Today
$-First Things
$-Good News—R
Grand Valley Observer—R
$-Horizons (adult)—R
Journal of Church & State
$-Layman
$-Light & Life
$-Liguorian
$-Living Church
$-Lookout—R
$-Lutheran—R
$-Lutheran Journal—R
Maranatha News—R
Mature Times—R
$-Men of Integrity—R
$-Messenger of the Sacred Heart
$-Minnesota Christian—R
$-National Catholic
$-New Freeman—R
$-New Wineskins—R
$-North American Voice—R
$-Our Sunday Visitor
$-Plain Truth—R
$-Prairie Messenger—R
Presbyterian Outlook
Priscilla Papers—R
$-Queen of All Hearts
Reformed Quarterly
Re:generation Quarterly
$-Science & Spirit
$-SCP Journal—R
Singles Scoop—R
$-Social Justice—R
$-Spiritual Life
SR: A Journal—R
$-St. Anthony Messenger
Star of Zion
$-Testimony—R
thegoodsteward.com—R
Trumpeter—R
$-U.S. Catholic
$-United Church Observer—R
Victory News—R

$-Way of St. Francis—R

CHRISTIAN EDUCATION/LIBRARY
$-Church Educator—R
$-Teachers Interaction

MISSIONS
East-West Church
Missiology
$-Worldwide Challenge

PASTORS/LEADERS
$-African American Pulpit
$-Building Church Leaders.com
$-Catechumenate
$-Christian Century—R
Christian Education Journal (CA)—R
$-Church Growth Network—R
$-Church Worship
Cross Currents
$-Diocesan Dialogue—R
$-Emmanuel
$-Eucharistic Ministries—R
$-Evangelical Baptist—R
$-Evangelicals Today—R
$-Horizons (pastor)—R
Jour./Amer. Soc./Chur. Growth—R
Journal/Pastoral Care—R
Lutheran Forum—R
$-Lutheran Partners—R
$-Ministries Today
$-Ministry
$-Ministry & Liturgy—R
$-Pastoral Life—R
Pastors.com—R
$-Priest
$-Proclaim—R
Quarterly Review
$-Review for Religious
Sewanee Theological Review
Sharing the Practice—R
$-Spiritual Spinach—R
$-Theology Today
$-This Rock
$-Today's Parish—R
$-Word & World
$-Worship Leader
$-Youthworker

TEEN/YOUNG ADULT
$-Inteen—R
$-Passageway.org—R
Setmag.com—R
TeensForJC.com—R
Transcendmag.com—R

WOMEN
$-Godly Business Woman
$-Horizons (women)—R
Making Waves

THINK PIECES

ADULT/GENERAL
$-alive now!—R
$-Alive!—R
$-Annals of St. Anne
Barefoot Path—R
$-Catholic Forester—R
$-Catholic New Times—R
$-Catholic Peace Voice—R
$-CGA World—R
Chattels of the Heart—R
Christian C. L. RECORD—R
$-Christian Courier (CAN)—R
Christian Journal—R
$-Christian Leader—R
Christian Online
$-Christian Social Action—R
$-Christian Standard—R
$-Christianity Today—R
$-Commonweal
$-Cornerstone Christian—R
Creation Care—R
$-Cresset
Desert Call—R
$-Door—R
$-Dovetail—R
$-Episcopal Life—R
$-Faith Today
$-First Things
$-Gem—R
$-Generation X—R
Good News Journal
Grand Valley Observer—R
Heartlight—R
$-Home Times—R
$-Layman
$-Lifeglow—R
$-Light & Life
Literary TNT—R
$-Lutheran—R
$-Lutheran Digest—R
$-MESSAGE
Metro Voice—R
$-New Wineskins—R
Pegasus Review—R
Penwood Review
$-Positive Thinking—R
PrayerWorks—R
Presbyterian Outlook
Rhubarb

$-Science & Spirit
Spiritual Voice—R
$-Spring Hill Review—R
$-St. Anthony Messenger
$-Stewardship—R
$-Testimony—R
thegoodsteward.com—R
$-Today's Christian—R
Trumpeter—R
Victory News—R
$-Way of St. Francis—R
Winsome Wit—R
$-World & I—R

CHILDREN
$-Courage—R

CHRISTIAN EDUCATION/LIBRARY
$-Children's Ministry

MUSIC
Quest—R

PASTORS/LEADERS
$-Building Church Leaders.com
$-Catholic Servant
$-Evangelicals Today—R
$-Interpreter
Journal/Pastoral Care—R
$-Ministries Today
Pastors.com—R
$-Rev.
Sharing the Practice—R
Strategic Adult Ministries—R
$-This Rock
$-Word & World

TEEN/YOUNG ADULT
$-Boundless Webzine—R
$-Breakaway
$-Conqueror—R
$-Passageway.org—R
$-Real Faith in Life—R
Setmag.com—R
TeensForJC.com—R
Transcendmag.com—R
$-Vision—R

WOMEN
Anna's Journal—R
$-Godly Business Woman
$-inSpirit—R
Reflections

WRITERS
$-Areopagus (UK)
$-Money the Write Way—R

TIME MANAGEMENT

ADULT/GENERAL
Alliance Life
Breakthrough Intercessor—R
$-Bridal Guides—R
$-Catholic Forester—R
$-CBA Marketplace
Christian Bible Studies.com
Christian Journal—R
Christian Online
$-Christian Parenting—R
$-Cornerstone Christian—R
Disciple's Journal—R
Evangelical Advocate—R
$-Gem—R
$-Generation X—R
Good News Journal
$-Home Times—R
$-Homeschooling Today—R
$-Lifeglow—R
$-Light & Life
$-Living—R
$-Living Light News—R
$-Lookout—R
$-Men of Integrity—R
$-NRB Magazine—R
Parents & Teens—R
$-Positive Thinking—R
Quaker Life—R
Regent Business—R
Spiritual Voice—R
$-St. Anthony Messenger
$-Stewardship—R
$-Testimony—R
thegoodsteward.com—R
$-Today's Christian—R
$-Together—R
Trumpeter—R
Victory News—R
$-Wireless Age—R
$-World & I—R
$-Young Christian—R

CHILDREN
$-Guideposts for Kids

CHRISTIAN EDUCATION/LIBRARY
$-Children's Ministry
Christian Librarian—R
$-Resource—R
$-Youth & CE Leadership

PASTORS/LEADERS
$-Barefoot—R
$-Building Church Leaders.com

Christian Management—R
$-Enrichment—R
$-Evangelicals Today—R
$-Interpreter
$-Pastoral Life—R
Pastors.com—R
$-Priest
$-Rev.
$-RevWriter Resource
Sharing the Practice—R
$-Today's Christian Preacher—R
$-WCA News—R

TEEN/YOUNG ADULT
Setmag.com—R
$-Student Leadership—R
Teen Light—R
TeensForJC.com—R
Transcendmag.com—R
$-Young and Alive—R
$-Young Christian—R

WOMEN
$-Extreme Joy
$-Godly Business Woman
Hearts at Home—R
$-inSpirit—R
$-Journey
Just Between Us—R
Life Tools for Women
$-MOMsense—R
P31 Woman—R
Reflections
Right to the Heart—R
$-Simple Joy
$-Today's Christian Woman—R
Women Today—R

WRITERS
$-Advanced Chris. Writer—R
$-Christian Communicator—R
$-Fellowscript—R
$-Money the Write Way—R
$-Writer
$-Writer's Apprentice
$-Writers' Journal
Writes of Passage

TRAVEL

ADULT/GENERAL
$-Alive!—R
$-Angels on Earth
$-Arlington Catholic
$-Bridal Guides—R
$-Cappers
$-Charisma
$-Christian Parenting—R

$-Common Ground—R
$-Cornerstone Christian—R
$-Cresset
$-DisciplesWorld
$-Family Digest—R
$-Gem—R
$-Generation X—R
Good News Journal
$-Grit
Highway News—R
$-Interchange
$-Joy & Praise
$-Lifeglow—R
$-Mature Living
$-Mature Years—R
MovieGuide
$-Over the Back Fence—R
Sacred Journey—R
$-Senior Living
$-Special Living—R
Spiritual Voice—R
$-Spring Hill Review—R
Storyteller—R
$-Studio Classroom
$-Testimony—R
$-Tidewater Parent—R
$-Today's Christian—R
$-Upscale Magazine
Victory News—R
$-World & I—R
$-Young Christian—R

CHILDREN
Barefoot for Kids—R
$-High Adventure—R
Skipping Stones

MISSIONS
$-One
OpRev Equipper—R
$-PIME World—R

MUSIC
Tradition

PASTORS/LEADERS
$-Rev.
$-Spiritual Spinach—R

TEEN/YOUNG ADULT
Setmag.com—R
Teen Light—R
$-Teenage Christian—R
TeensForJC.com—R
Transcendmag.com—R
$-Young and Alive—R
$-Young Christian—R

WOMEN
$-Godly Business Woman
Reflections

WRITERS
$-Money the Write Way—R

TRUE STORIES

ADULT/GENERAL
$-Alive!—R
$-Ancient Paths—R
$-Angels on Earth
$-Animal Trails—R
Barefoot Path—R
$-Bible Advocate—R
Breakthrough Intercessor—R
$-Bridal Guides—R
$-Catholic Digest—R
$-Catholic New Times—R
Channels—R
Christian Journal—R
Christian Motorsports
Christian Observer
Christian Online
Christian Ranchman
$-Christianweek
Church Herald & Holiness—R
$-Cornerstone Christian—R
Creation Care—R
$-Creative Nonfiction
Crossway/Newsline—R
$-Culture Wars—R
$-Cup of Comfort—R
$-Dovetail—R
$-Faith & Family
$-Foursquare World Advance—R
$-Gem—R
$-Generation X—R
$-God Allows U-Turns—R
Good News Journal
Grand Valley Observer—R
$-Grit
$-Guideposts—R
Hannah to Hannah—R
Heartlight—R
Highway News—R
$-Home Times—R
HopeKeepers—R
$-Horizons (adult)—R
$-Indian Life—R
$-Lifeglow—R
$-Light & Life
$-Live—R
$-Lutheran—R
$-Lutheran Digest—R
Maranatha News—R

Men of the Cross—R
$-Mennonite Historian—R
MESSAGE/Open Bible—R
Metro Voice—R
New Heart—R
$-New Wineskins—R
$-Nostalgia Magazine—R
$-Over the Back Fence—R
Parents & Teens—R
$-Physician—R
$-Plain Truth—R
$-Power for Living—R
PrayerWorks—R
$-Priority!
$-Relate—R
Sacred Journey—R
$-Science & Spirit
$-SCP Journal—R
$-Seeds
$-Seek—R
$-Signs of the Times—R
Spiritual Voice—R
$-Spring Hill Review—R
$-St. Anthony Messenger
$-St. Joseph's Messenger—R
Storyteller—R
$-Testimony—R
thegoodsteward.com—R
$-Today's Christian—R
$-Today's Pentecostal Evangel
Trumpeter—R
$-Up
Victory News—R
$-Vision—R
$-War Cry—R
War Cry (Canada)—R
$-Young Christian—R

CHILDREN
Barefoot for Kids—R
$-BREAD/God's Children—R
$-Cadet Quest—R
$-Celebrate
$-Club Connection
$-Courage—R
$-Focus/Clubhouse
$-Guide—R
$-High Adventure—R
$-Nature Friend
$-Our Little Friend—R
$-Partners—R
$-Pockets—R
$-Primary Treasure—R
$-SHINE brightly—R
Skipping Stones
$-Story Friends—R

$-Winner—R

CHRISTIAN EDUCATION/LIBRARY
$-Group

MISSIONS
$-Leaders for Today
$-Worldwide Challenge

MUSIC
Quest—R

PASTORS/LEADERS
Cell Group—R
$-Evangelicals Today—R
$-Interpreter
$-Pastoral Life—R
Sharing the Practice—R
$-Spiritual Spinach—R

TEEN/YOUNG ADULT
$-Boundless Webzine—R
$-Breakaway
$-Brio—R
$-Brio & Beyond
$-Conqueror—R
$-Essential Connection
$-Guideposts Sweet 16—R
$-Insight—R
$-Listen—R
$-Passageway.org—R
$-Real Faith in Life—R
Setmag.com—R
Teen Light—R
TeensForJC.com—R
Transcendmag.com—R
$-With—R
$-Young and Alive—R
$-Young Christian—R
$-Young Salvationist—R

WOMEN
$-Godly Business Woman
Hearts at Home—R
$-History's Women—R
$-inSpirit—R
Just Between Us—R
Reflections
$-Women by Grace—R
Women of the Cross—R

WRITERS
$-Areopagus (UK)

VIDEO REVIEWS

ADULT/GENERAL
$-Arlington Catholic
Barefoot Path—R

$-Catholic Peace Voice—R
$-CBA Marketplace
Channels—R
Christian Journal—R
Christian Radio Weekly
$-Christian Renewal—R
$-Cornerstone Christian—R
Desert Call—R
$-Dovetail—R
$-Eureka Street
$-Faith & Family
$-Indian Life—R
$-Interim—R
Maranatha News—R
MovieGuide
$-New Man—R
Parents & Teens—R
$-Presbyterians Today—R
Quaker Life—R
Reformed Quarterly
$-Relevant
Rose & Thorn
Spiritual Voice—R
$-Spring Hill Review—R
$-Testimony—R
Trumpeter—R
Victory News—R
Winsome Wit—R
$-Wireless Age—R

CHILDREN
$-Club Connection

CHRISTIAN EDUCATION/LIBRARY
Catholic Library World
Christian Library Journal—R
$-Church Libraries—R
East-West Church
Jour./Christianity/Foreign Languages

PASTORS/LEADERS
$-Christian Century—R
$-Evangelicals Today—R
$-Interpreter
$-Lutheran Partners—R
$-Ministries Today
$-Pastoral Life—R
Sharing the Practice—R
$-Worship Leader

TEEN/YOUNG ADULT
$-Devo'Zine—R
Setmag.com—R
TeensForJC.com—R
Transcendmag.com—R

WRITERS
$-Fellowscript—R

WEBSITE REVIEWS

ADULT/GENERAL
Barefoot Path—R
$-Catholic Peace Voice—R
$-Christian Parents Section
$-Christianity Today—R
$-Dovetail—R
$-Generation X—R
$-Indian Life—R
Jewel Among Jewels
$-MESSAGE
$-New Wineskins—R
$-Relevant
Rose & Thorn
Spiritual Voice—R
Storyteller—R
$-Upscale Magazine
Victory News—R
$-Wireless Age—R
$-World & I—R

CHRISTIAN EDUCATION/LIBRARY
Christian Librarian—R
Christian Library Journal—R
$-Teachers Interaction

MISSIONS
East-West Church
OpRev Equipper—R

PASTORS/LEADERS
Ministry in Motion—R
$-Pastoral Life—R

TEEN/YOUNG ADULT
$-Campus Life—R
Setmag.com—R
TeensForJC.com—R
Transcendmag.com—R

WOMEN
$-Today's Christian Woman—R

WRITERS
$-Money the Write Way—R
$-Writers' Journal

WOMEN'S ISSUES

ADULT/GENERAL
$-alive now!—R
$-Anglican Journal
$-Annals of St. Anne
$-Arlington Catholic
$-Beacon
$-BGC World—R

Breakthrough Intercessor—R
$-Catholic Forester—R
$-Catholic New Times—R
$-Catholic Parent
$-Catholic Peace Voice—R
$-CBA Marketplace
$-Celebrate Life—R
$-CGA World—R
$-Charisma
Chattels of the Heart—R
$-Chicken Soup—R
Christian Bible Studies.com
Christian C. L. RECORD—R
$-Christian Courier (CAN)—R
$-Christian Examiner
Christian Journal—R
$-Christian Leader—R
Christian News NW—R
Christian Online
$-Christian Parenting—R
Christian Ranchman
$-Christian Social Action—R
$-Christianweek
$-Columbia
$-Cornerstone Christian—R
Crossway/Newsline—R
$-Cup of Comfort—R
Disciple's Journal—R
$-Dovetail—R
$-Eclectic Homeschool
$-Episcopal Life—R
Evangelical Advocate—R
$-Faith & Family
$-Faith Today
$-Foursquare World Advance—R
$-Gem—R
$-God Allows U-Turns—R
Good News Journal
$-Gospel Today—R
Hannah to Hannah—R
Heartlight—R
Heartwarmers
$-Home Times—R
$-Homeschooling Today—R
HopeKeepers—R
$-Indian Life—R
$-Interim—R
$-Joy & Praise
$-Layman
$-Light & Life
$-Liguorian
$-Live—R
$-Lookout—R
$-Lutheran—R
Maranatha News—R

$-Marriage Partnership—R
$-Mennonite Brethren—R
$-MESSAGE
Metro Voice—R
$-Montgomery's Journey
Mutuality—R
$-National Catholic
$-New Freeman—R
$-New Wineskins—R
$-North American Voice—R
$-Our Sunday Visitor
$-ParentLife
$-Prairie Messenger—R
Presbyterian Outlook
Priscilla Papers—R
$-Psychology for Living—R
Quaker Life—R
$-Smart Families—R
Spiritual Voice—R
$-St. Anthony Messenger
$-St. Joseph's Messenger—R
Steps
Storyteller—R
$-Testimony—R
thegoodsteward.com—R
$-Today's Christian—R
$-Today's Pentecostal Evangel
$-Together—R
Trumpeter—R
$-U.S. Catholic
$-United Church Observer—R
$-Vibrant Life—R
Victory News—R
$-Vision—R
$-War Cry—R
West Wind Review
$-World & I—R

CHRISTIAN EDUCATION/LIBRARY
Christian Early Education—R
$-Resource—R
$-Teachers of Vision—R

MISSIONS
East-West Church
Missiology
Women of the Harvest
$-Worldwide Challenge

PASTORS/LEADERS
$-African American Pulpit
$-Building Church Leaders.com
Cell Group—R
$-Enrichment—R
$-Eucharistic Ministries—R
$-Evangelicals Today—R

$-Interpreter
Journal/Pastoral Care—R
$-Lutheran Partners—R
$-Ministries Today
$-Ministry
$-Pastoral Life—R
$-Rev.
Sharing the Practice—R
$-Word & World
$-Youthworker

TEEN/YOUNG ADULT
$-Boundless Webzine—R
Setmag.com—R
Teen Light—R
TeensForJC.com—R
Transcendmag.com—R
$-Vision—R

WOMEN
Anna's Journal—R
$-At the Center—R
Christian Woman's Page—R
Christian Women Today—R
Crowned with Silver
$-Esprit—R
$-Extreme Joy
Footprints
$-Godly Business Woman
Handmaiden—R
Hearts at Home—R
$-Horizons (women)—R
$-inSpirit—R
$-Journey
Just Between Us—R
Keeping Hearts & Home
Life Tools for Women
$-Link & Visitor—R
Lutheran Woman's Quar.
Making Waves
$-Melody of the Heart
$-MOMsense—R
P31 Woman—R
Praise
Reflections
Right to the Heart—R
Shalom Bayit
Share
$-Simple Joy
$-SpiritLed Woman
Tapestry (Canada)
Tapestry (GA)
$-Today's Christian Woman—R
True Woman
$-Welcome Home
$-Woman's Touch—R
$-Women Alive!—R

$-Women by Grace—R
Women of the Cross—R
Women Today—R
$-Women's Faith & Spirit
Women's Ministry

WRITERS
Beginnings

WORKPLACE ISSUES
ADULT/GENERAL
Alliance Life
$-BGC World—R
Channels—R
Christian Bible Studies.com
$-Christian Examiner
Christian Journal—R
Christian News NW—R
Christian Online
$-Christian Retailing
$-Christianweek
$-Evangel—R
Evangelical Advocate—R
$-Faith & Friends—R
$-Faith Today
$-Generation X—R
$-Gospel Today—R
Highway News—R
$-Light & Life
$-Living—R
Maranatha News—R
Marketplace
$-Men of Integrity—R
Men of the Cross—R
$-Montgomery's Journey
New Heart—R
$-Our Sunday Visitor
$-Positive Thinking—R
$-Prairie Messenger—R
Quaker Life—R
Re:generation Quarterly
Regent Business—R
$-Relate—R
$-Relevant
$-Testimony—R
$-Today's Christian—R
$-Together—R
$-U.S. Catholic
Victory News—R
$-Wireless Age—R
$-World & I—R

CHRISTIAN EDUCATION/LIBRARY
Catholic Library World
$-Children's Ministry
Christian Early Education—R

Christian Librarian—R
$-Teachers of Vision—R
$-Today's Catholic Teacher—R

PASTORS/LEADERS
$-Building Church Leaders.com

TEEN/YOUNG ADULT
Teen Light—R

WOMEN
$-inSpirit—R
$-Journey
Life Tools for Women
Making Waves
$-MOMsense—R
$-Today's Christian Woman—R
Women of the Cross—R
Women Today—R

WORLD ISSUES
ADULT/GENERAL
AGAIN—R
$-Alive!—R
$-America
American Tract Society—R
$-Annals of St. Anne
$-Arlington Catholic
Breakthrough Intercessor—R
$-Catholic Peace Voice—R
$-CGA World—R
$-Charisma
Christian Bible Studies.com
$-Christian Examiner
Christian Journal—R
$-Christian Leader—R
Christian Motorsports
Christian Observer
Christian Online
$-Christian Renewal—R
$-Christian Social Action—R
$-Christianweek
$-Commonweal
$-Cornerstone Christian—R
Creation Care—R
$-Culture Wars—R
$-Dovetail—R
$-Evangel—R
Evangelical Advocate—R
$-Faith Today
Friends Journal—R
$-Gem—R
$-Generation X—R
Good News Journal
Grand Valley Observer—R
Heartlight—R
$-Home Times—R
$-Inland NW Christian

$-Interim—R
Journal of Church & State
$-Layman
$-Liberty—R
$-Light & Life
$-Living Church
$-Lookout—R
$-Lutheran—R
Maranatha News—R
$-MESSAGE
$-Messenger
Metro Voice—R
$-Montgomery's Journey
Mutuality—R
$-New Freeman—R
$-New Wineskins—R
$-North American Voice—R
$-Our Sunday Visitor
$-Plain Truth—R
$-Prairie Messenger—R
Presbyterian Outlook
Quaker Life—R
$-Relevant
Sacred Journey—R
$-SCP Journal—R
$-Seeds
$-Social Justice—R
$-St. Anthony Messenger
$-Testimony—R
thegoodsteward.com—R
$-Today's Christian—R
Trumpeter—R
$-U.S. Catholic
$-United Church Observer—R
Victory News—R
$-War Cry—R
West Wind Review
$-Wireless Age—R
$-World & I—R

CHILDREN
Barefoot for Kids—R
$-Guideposts for Kids
Skipping Stones

**CHRISTIAN
EDUCATION/LIBRARY**
Catholic Library World

MISSIONS
Missiology
$-New World Outlook
$-One
OpRev Equipper—R
$-PIME World—R
$-World Pulse—R
$-Worldwide Challenge

PASTORS/LEADERS
$-African American Pulpit
$-Building Church Leaders.com
Cell Group—R
$-Emmanuel
$-Evangelicals Today—R
$-Interpreter
$-Ministries Today
$-Pastoral Life—R
Quarterly Review
$-Rev.
Sharing the Practice—R
$-Spiritual Spinach—R
$-Theology Today
$-This Rock
$-Word & World
$-Youthworker

TEEN/YOUNG ADULT
$-Boundless Webzine—R
$-Passageway.org—R
Setmag.com—R
Teen Light—R
$-Teenage Christian—R
TeensForJC.com—R
Transcendmag.com—R
$-Young Christian—R
$-Young Salvationist—R

WOMEN
$-Esprit—R
$-Horizons (women)—R
$-inSpirit—R
$-Journey
$-SpiritLed Woman

WRITERS
$-Areopagus (UK)

WORSHIP

ADULT/GENERAL
AGAIN—R
Alliance Life
$-Angels on Earth
$-Annals of St. Anne
$-Arlington Catholic
Barefoot Path—R
$-BGC World—R
$-Bible Advocate—R
Breakthrough Intercessor—R
$-Bridal Guides—R
$-Cathedral Age
$-Catholic New Times—R
$-CGA World—R
Channels—R
$-Charisma
$-Christian Examiner
$-Christian Leader—R

Christian Motorsports
Christian Online
Christian Ranchman
$-Christian Standard—R
$-Christianity Today—R
$-Christianweek
Church Herald & Holiness—R
$-Columbia
$-Commonweal
$-Cornerstone Christian—R
Creation Care—R
$-Culture Wars—R
$-Cup of Comfort—R
$-Dovetail—R
$-Evangel—R
Evangelical Advocate—R
$-Faith Today
$-Foursquare World Advance—R
$-Interchange
$-Lifeglow—R
$-Light & Life
$-Liguorian
Literary TNT—R
$-Living Church
$-Lutheran—R
Mature Times—R
$-Men of Integrity—R
$-Minnesota Christian—R
$-Montgomery's Journey
$-New Freeman—R
$-New Wineskins—R
$-North American Voice—R
$-Our Sunday Visitor
Perspectives
$-Power for Living—R
$-Prairie Messenger—R
Presbyterian Outlook
$-Presbyterians Today—R
Priscilla Papers—R
Quaker Life—R
$-Relevant
$-Seeds
$-Silver Wings—R
Singles Scoop—R
$-Spiritual Life
Spiritual Voice—R
$-St. Anthony Messenger
$-Stewardship—R
Sword and Trumpet—R
Sword of the Lord—R
$-Testimony—R
thegoodsteward.com—R
Time of Singing—R
$-Today's Christian—R
Trumpeter—R
$-United Church Observer—R

$-War Cry—R
$-Way of St. Francis—R
$-Wesleyan Life—R
$-World & I—R
$-Young Christian—R

CHILDREN
$-BREAD/God's Children—R
$-Passport—R

CHRISTIAN EDUCATION/LIBRARY
$-Children's Ministry
$-Church Educator—R
$-Evangelizing Today's Child—R
$-Group
$-Youth & CE Leadership

MISSIONS
$-Worldwide Challenge

MUSIC
$-Church Pianist
$-Creator—R
Hymn

PASTORS/LEADERS
$-African American Pulpit
$-Barefoot—R
$-Building Church Leaders.com
Cell Group—R
$-Church Growth Network—R
$-Church Worship
$-Clergy Journal—R
$-Emmanuel
$-Enrichment—R
$-Environment & Art
$-Evangelical Baptist—R
$-Evangelicals Today—R
Interpretation
$-Interpreter
$-Leadership—R
$-Let's Worship
$-Lutheran Partners—R
$-Ministries Today
$-Ministry
$-Ministry & Liturgy—R
$-Pastoral Life—R
Pastors.com—R
$-Preaching
Preaching On-Line—R
Pulpit Helps—R
$-Reformed Worship
$-Rev.
$-RevWriter Resource
Sharing the Practice—R
$-Spiritual Spinach—R
Theological Digest—R

$-Theology Today
$-Today's Parish—R
$-Word & World
$-Worship Leader
$-Youthworker

TEEN/YOUNG ADULT
$-Brio—R
$-Brio & Beyond
$-Passageway.org—R
Setmag.com—R
$-Student Leadership—R
Teen Light—R
$-Teenage Christian—R
TeensForJC.com—R
Transcendmag.com—R
$-With—R
$-Young and Alive—R
$-Young Christian—R

WOMEN
$-Esprit—R
$-Godly Business Woman
$-Horizons (women)—R
$-inSpirit—R
Right to the Heart—R
$-Women by Grace—R

WRITING HOW-TO

ADULT/GENERAL
$-Animal Trails—R
Barefoot Path—R
$-Bridal Guides—R
$-CBA Marketplace
Christian Observer
Christian Online
$-Cornerstone Christian—R
Good News Journal
$-Home Times—R
Parents & Teens—R
Penwood Review
Rose & Thorn
$-St. Anthony Messenger
Storyteller—R
$-World & I—R
$-Young Christian—R

CHILDREN
Barefoot for Kids—R
$-Guideposts for Kids

CHRISTIAN EDUCATION/LIBRARY
Christian Librarian—R

PASTORS/LEADERS
$-Evangelicals Today—R
$-Newsletter Newsletter

$-Pastoral Life—R

TEEN/YOUNG ADULT
Setmag.com—R
Teen Light—R
TeensForJC.com—R
Transcendmag.com—R
$-Young Christian—R

WOMEN
$-Esprit—R
$-Godly Business Woman
Just Between Us—R

WRITERS
$-Advanced Chris. Writer—R
$-Areopagus (UK)
Author Network E-zine
Beginnings
$-Brady Magazine—R
$-Byline
$-Christian Communicator—R
$-Cross & Quill—R
$-Exchange—R
$-Fellowscript—R
$-Money the Write Way—R
NW Christian Author—R
Once Upon a Time—R
Romancing the Christian Heart—R
$-Spirit-Led Writer—R
Teachers & Writers
$-Tickled by Thunder
Upper Case
$-WIN-Informer
$-Writing Parent—R
Write to Inspire.com
$-Writer
$-Writer's Apprentice
$-Writer's Digest—R
Writer's Lifeline
Writers Gazette
Writers Manual
$-Writers' Journal
Writes of Passage

YOUNG WRITER MARKETS

Note: These publications have indicated they will accept submissions from children or teens (C or T).

ADULT/GENERAL
African Voices
$-Animal Trails
$-Aujourd'hui Credo (C or T)
Barefoot Path (T)
$-Bridal Guides (C or T)
$-Catholic Peace Voice (T)

$-Celebrate Life (C or T)
Channels (T)
Christian Journal (C or T)
Christian Online (C or T)
Church Herald & Holiness (C or T)
Cochran's Corner (C or T)
$-Creative Nonfiction (T)
$-Drama Ministry (T)
$-Eclectic Homeschool (T)
$-Generation X (C or T)
$-Gospel Today
Hard Row to Hoe (T)
$-History's Women (T)
$-Insight (T)
$-Interchange (C or T)
Jewel Among Jewels
LifeTimes Catholic (T)
$-Light & Life (C or T)
Literary TNT (C or T)
$-Lutheran Journal (C or T)
Maranatha News (C or T)
$-Montgomery's Journey (T)
Parents & Teens (T)
$-Peeks & Valleys (C or T)
$-PIME World (T)
$-Presbyterian Record (T)
Quaker Life (C or T)
$-Relate (C or T)
Spiritual Voice (C or T)
$-Spring Hill Review (T)
Storyteller (C or T)
$-Tickled by Thunder (C or T)
Tributes (T)
Victory News (T)
$-Voice of the Lord (C or T)
Women Today (T)

CHILDREN
$-American Girl (C)
Barefoot for Kids (C)
Cliché Finder
$-Pockets (C)
$-PrayKids! (C)
Skipping Stones (C)

CHRISTIAN EDUCATION/LIBRARY
Journal/Christian Education

PASTORS/LEADERS
$-Barefoot
Cornerstone Youth
$-Joke Writers
$-Let's Worship
Ministry in Motion

TEEN/YOUNG ADULT
$-Campus Life (T)

$-Essential Connection (T)
$-Insight (T)
$-Listen (T)
Setmag.com (T)
Teen Light (T)
TeensForJC.com (T)
Transcendmag.com (T)
$-Young Christian (C or T)

WOMEN
$-Women by Grace

WRITERS
Beginnings
Cochran's Corner (C or T)
$-Merlyn's Pen
$-Money the Write Way
$-Spirit-Led Writer
$-Writers' Journal

YOUTH ISSUES

ADULT/GENERAL
Alliance Life
American Tract Society—R
$-Annals of St. Anne
$-Arlington Catholic
$-Beacon
Breakthrough Intercessor—R
$-Catholic Forester—R
$-Catholic New Times—R
$-Catholic Peace Voice—R
Channels—R
$-Charisma
$-Chicken Soup—R
$-Christian Examiner
$-Christian Home & School
Christian Journal—R
$-Christian Leader—R
Christian Motorsports
Christian News NW—R
Christian Online
$-Christian Parenting—R
Christian Ranchman
$-Christian Renewal—R
$-Christian Social Action—R
$-Christianweek
Church Herald & Holiness—R
$-Columbia
$-Culture Wars—R
$-Dovetail—R
Evangelical Advocate—R
$-Faith & Family
$-Faith Today
Good News Journal
$-Home Times—R
$-Homeschooling Today—R
Jewel Among Jewels

$-Joy & Praise
LifeTimes Catholic
$-Light & Life
$-Liguorian
$-Living Church
$-Lookout—R
$-Lutheran—R
$-Lutheran Digest—R
Maranatha News—R
$-MESSAGE
MESSAGE/Open Bible—R
Metro Voice—R
$-Montgomery's Journey
$-New Freeman—R
Parents & Teens—R
$-Prairie Messenger—R
Presbyterian Outlook
$-Prism—R
Quaker Life—R
$-Seeds
$-Smart Families—R
Spiritual Voice—R
$-St. Anthony Messenger
$-Testimony—R
thegoodsteward.com—R
$-Today's Christian—R
Trumpeter—R
$-U.S. Catholic
Victory News—R
$-World & I—R
$-Young Christian—R

CHILDREN
$-American Girl
$-BREAD/God's Children—R
$-Cadet Quest—R
$-Children's Ministry
$-Club Connection
$-Focus/Clubhouse
$-Focus/Clubhouse Jr.
$-Guideposts for Kids
$-My Friend
$-SHINE brightly—R
Skipping Stones

CHRISTIAN EDUCATION/LIBRARY
$-Church Educator—R
$-Enrichment—R
$-Group
$-Journal/Adventist Educ.—R
$-Leader in C. E. Ministries
$-Momentum
$-Religion Teacher's Journal
$-Resource—R
$-Teachers of Vision—R
$-Youth & CE Leadership

MISSIONS
East-West Church
$-Worldwide Challenge

MUSIC
Quest—R

PASTORS/LEADERS
$-African American Pulpit
$-Catholic Servant
Cell Group—R
$-Christian Camp—R
Cornerstone Youth—R

$-Eucharistic Ministries—R
$-Evangelical Baptist—R
$-Evangelicals Today—R
$-Interpreter
$-Lutheran Partners—R
$-Ministries Today
$-Pastoral Life—R
$-Rev.
Sharing the Practice—R
$-Word & World
Youth Culture
$-Youthworker

TEEN/YOUNG ADULT
$-Breakaway
$-Guideposts Sweet 16—R
Teen Light—R
$-Young Christian—R
YouthWalk

WOMEN
$-Godly Business Woman
Just Between Us—R
P31 Woman—R
Shalom Bayit

ALPHABETICAL LISTINGS OF PERIODICALS AND E-ZINES

Following are the listings of periodicals. They are arranged alphabetically by type of periodical (see table of contents for a list of types). Nonpaying markets are indicated in bold letters within those listings, e.g. **NO PAYMENT**. Paying markets are indicated with a $ in front of the listing.

If a listing is preceded by an asterisk (*), it indicates that publisher did not send updated information and we were unable to contact them by any means. If it is preceded by a number symbol (#) it was updated from current guidelines, their Website, or available sources. If it is preceded by a (+) it is a new listing. It is important that freelance writers request writer's guidelines and a recent sample copy before submitting to any of these publications.

If you do not find the publication you are looking for, look in the General Index. See the introduction of that index for the codes used to identify the current status of each unlisted publication.

For a detailed explanation of how to understand and get the most out of these listings, as well as solid marketing tips, see the "How to Use This Book" section at the front of the book. Unfamiliar terms are explained in the Glossary at the back of the book.

(*) An asterisk before a listing indicates no or unconfirmed information update.
(#) A number symbol before a listing means it was updated from the current writer's guidelines, their Websites, or other sources.
(+) A plus sign means it is a new listing.
($) A dollar sign before a listing indicates a paying market.
($) A dollar sign in parentheses before a listing indicates they sometimes pay.

ADULT/GENERAL MARKETS

$ABILITIES MAGAZINE, 650-340 College St., Toronto ON M5T 3A9 Canada. (416)923-1885, ext. 232. Fax (416)923-9829. E-mail: lbendall@abilities.ca. Website: www.abilities.ca, or www.enablelink.org. Canadian Abilities Foundation; secular. Lisa Bendall, mng. ed. Canada's foremost cross-disabilities lifestyle magazine. Open to freelance. Query; e-query OK. Pays $50-400 for 1st rts. Articles 500-2,000 wds. No simultaneous submissions. Requires disk. Kill fee 50%. Guidelines & theme list on Website. Not in topical listings. (Ads)

AFRICAN VOICES, 270 W. 96th St., New York NY 10025. (212)865-2982. Fax (212)316-3335. E-mail: africanvoices@aol.com. Website: www.africanvoices.com. African Voices Communications, Inc. Maitefa Angaza, mng. ed.; Kim Horne, fiction ed. Publishes original fiction, nonfiction, and poetry by artists of color. Quarterly mag.; 48 pgs.; circ. 20,000. Subscription $12. 75% unsolicited freelance; 25% assigned. Query/clips; e-query OK. **PAYS IN COPIES** for 1st rts. Articles 500-1,500 wds. (25/yr.); fiction 500-1,500 wds. (20/yr.); book reviews 300 wds. Responds in 16 wks. Seasonal 4 mos. ahead. Accepts simultaneous submissions and reprints (tell when/where appeared). Requires accepts submissions by e-mail (copied into message). Uses some sidebars. Guidelines; copy $5/9x12 SAE/$1.42 postage (mark "Media Mail"). (Ads)

Poetry: Accepts 75-80/yr. Free verse, haiku, traditional; to 3 pgs. Submit max. 3 poems.
Fillers: Accepts 10/yr. Cartoons.

AGAIN MAGAZINE, 10090 A Hwy 9, Ben Lomond CA 95005. (831)336-5118. Fax (831)336-8882. E-mail: tzell@conciliarpress.com. Website: www.conciliarpress.com. Antiochian Orthodox Archdiocese of North America/Conciliar Press. Father Thomas Zell, mng. ed. Historic Eastern Orthodox Christianity applied to our modern times. Quarterly mag.; 32 pgs.; circ. 5,000. Subscription $16. 1% unsolicited freelance; 99% assigned. Query; e-query OK. **USUALLY PAYS IN COPIES**. Articles 1,500-2,500 wds. (4/yr.); book reviews 800-1,000 wds. Responds in 6-8 wks. Seasonal 4-6 mos. ahead. Serials 2 parts. Accepts reprints (tell when/where appeared). Prefers requested ms on disk or by e-mail (copied into message). Uses some sidebars. Prefers NKJV. Guidelines (also by e-mail); copy for 9x12 SAE/4 stamps. (No ads)

> **Tips:** "We are Orthodox in orientation, and interested in thoughtful, intelligent articles dealing with church history, Protestant/Orthodox dialog, relations between Protestants and Orthodox in foreign countries, also in modern ethical dilemmas—no fluff."

>**$ALIVE! A Magazine for Christian Senior Adults**, PO Box 46464, Cincinnati OH 45246-0464. (513)825-3681. Christian Seniors Fellowship. David Lang, ed.; submit to June Lang, office ed. Focuses on activities and opportunities for active Christian senior adults, 55 and older; upbeat rather than nostalgic. Bimonthly mag.; 24 pgs.; circ. 3,000. Subscription/membership $18. 60% unsolicited freelance; 10% assigned. Complete ms/cover letter; no e-query. Pays .04-.06/wd. ($18-75) on publication for one-time or reprint rts. Articles 600-1,200 wds. (25-50/yr.); fiction 600-1,200 wds. (12/yr.). Responds in 9 wks. Seasonal 6 mos. ahead. Accepts reprints (tell when/where appeared). No disk. Uses some sidebars. Guidelines; copy for 9x12 SAE/3 stamps. (Ads)

> **Fillers:** Buys 15/yr. Anecdotes, cartoons, quizzes, short humor, and word puzzles, 50-500 wds.; $2-15.

> **Columns/Departments:** Buys 50/yr. Heart Medicine (humor, grandparent/grandchild anecdotes), to 100 wds., $2-25.

> **Tips:** "Most open to fresh material of special appeal to Christian senior adults. Avoid nostalgia. Our market is seniors interested in living in the present, not dwelling on the past. We pay little attention to credits/bios; articles stand on their own merit. Stories of seniors in short-term missions or other Christian activities, or active senior groups involved in service—not just social activities."

$ALIVE NOW! PO Box 340004, Nashville TN 37203-0004. (615)340-7218. Fax (615)340-7267. E-mail: alivenow@upperroom.org. Website: www.alivenow.org. United Methodist/The Upper Room. Melissa Tidwell, ed. Short, theme-based writings in attractive graphic setting for reflection and meditation. Bimonthly mag.; 64 pgs.; circ. 70,000. Subscription $14.95. 25% unsolicited freelance; 75% assigned. Complete ms/cover letter; e-query OK. Pays $50 & up on publication for newspaper, periodical, or electronic rts. Articles 300-500 wds. (25/yr.). Responds 13 wks. before issue date. Seasonal 6-8 mos. ahead. Accepts simultaneous submissions and reprints (tell when/where appeared). Accepts e-mail submissions (copied into message). Uses some sidebars. Prefers NRSV. Guidelines/theme list (also on Website); copy for 6x9 SAE/4 stamps.

> **Poetry:** Avant-garde, free verse, traditional; to 40 lines or one page; $40 & up. Submit max. 5 poems.

> **Fillers:** Prayers.

> **Tips:** "Write for our theme list and make your submission relevant to the topic. Avoid the obvious and heavy-handed preachiness."

ALLIANCE LIFE, PO Box 35000, Colorado Springs CO 80935-3500. (719)599-5999. Fax (719)599-8234. E-mail: alife@cmalliance.org. Website: www.alliancelife.org. The Christian & Missionary Alliance/denominational. Mark Failing, ed. To teach and inspire readers concerning principles of Christian living. Monthly mag.; circ. 21,000. Subscription $13. Open to freelance. Prefers query. **NO PAYMENT.** Articles 900-1,200 wds. Guidelines by e-mail/Website; copy. (Ads)

> **Tips:** "Looking for first-person stories that show God at work and involvement in fulfilling the Great Commission."

> ****2004, 2000 & 1998 EPA Award of Merit—Denominational.

$AMERICA, 106 W. 56th St., New York NY 10019-3893. (212)581-4640. Fax (212)399-3596.

E-mail: articles@americamagazine.org. Website: www.americamagazine.org. Catholic. Thomas J. Reese, S. J., ed-in-chief. For thinking Catholics and those who want to know what Catholics are thinking. Weekly mag. & online version; 32+ pgs.; circ. 46,000. Subscription $48. 100% unsolicited freelance. Complete ms/cover letter; fax/e-query OK. Pays $100-200 on acceptance. Articles 1,500-2,000 wds. Responds in 6 wks. Seasonal 3 mos. ahead. Does not use sidebars. Guidelines (also on Website); copy for 9x12 SAE. (Ads)

Poetry: Buys avant-garde, free verse, light verse, traditional; 20-35 line; $2-3/line.

AMERICAN TRACT SOCIETY, Box 462008, Garland TX 75046. (972)276-9408. Fax (972)272-9642. E-mail: PBatzing@ATSTracts.org. Website: www.ATStracts.org. Peter Batzing, tract ed. Majority of tracts written to win unbelievers. Bimonthly new tract releases; 40 new titles produced annually. 5% unsolicited freelance; 2% assigned. Complete ms/cover letter; e-query OK. **PAYS IN COPIES** on publication for exclusive tract rts. Tracts 600-1,200 wds. Responds in 6-8 wks. Seasonal 1 yr. ahead. Accepts simultaneous submissions and reprints (tell when/where appeared). Accepts requested ms on disk or by e-mail (attached or copied into message). Prefers NIV, KJV. Guidelines (also by e-mail)/free samples for #10 SAE/1 stamp. (No ads)

Special Needs: Youth issues, African American, cartoonists, critical issues.

Tips: "Read our current tracts; submit polished writing; relate to people's needs and experiences. Follow guidelines—almost no one does."

$ANCIENT PATHS, PO Box 7505, Fairfax Station VA 22039. E-mail: ssburris@msn.com. Website: www.literatureclassics.com/ancientpaths. Christian/nondenominational. Skylar Hamilton Burris, ed. For a literate Christian audience, or non-Christians open to and moved by traditional-themed poetry and fiction. Annual mag; 48 pgs.; circ. 150-175. Subscription $5. 100% unsolicited freelance. Complete ms only; no queries. Pays $2 for prose and $2 for artwork on publication for one-time & reprint rts. Not copyrighted. Fiction (or creative essays/true stories) to 2,500 wds. (6/yr.). Responds in 5 wks. No seasonal. Accepts simultaneous submissions and reprints (tell when/where appeared). Accepts e-mail submissions (copied into message for poetry; attached for fiction). No kill fee. No sidebars. Prefers KJV. Guidelines (also by e-mail/Website); copy for 9x12 SAE/3 stamps. (Ads—inserts only)

Poetry: Buys 20-30/yr. Traditional and free verse; 4-60 lines; $1 & 1 copy. Submit max. 5 poems.

Contest: Occasionally sponsors contest; check Website.

Tips: "I receive fewest fiction submissions, so they have a better chance. I need work that communicates profound themes in an interesting, nonpreachy way. I'd like more formal poetry (rhymed) with good (not inconsistent or singsong) meter. It is rare, so I publish more free verse. Master the traditional forms before you experiment. I am always in need of high quality black and white artwork. Read, read, read the great writers."

+ANGEL FACE, PO Box 102, Huffman TX 77336. E-mail: MaryAnkaPress@cs.com. Website: www.maryanka.com. MaryAnka Press/Catholic. Mary Agnes Dalrymple, pub. Religious or secular poetry loosely based on the Rosary, birth, re-birth, joy, light sorrow, epiphany, hope, Jesus, Mary, the seasons of nature and the cycles of life, the search for God in everyday life, etc. Complete ms. **PAYS 1 COPY** for one-time rts. Poetry only. Guidelines on Website.

Poetry: Free-verse poetry to 60 lines. Submit max. 5 poems.

Tips: "Poetry submitted can be secular or religious, Catholic, non-Catholic, ex-Catholic, or non-Christian. I want to see poetry that comes from the life (rather than the head)."

$+ANGELICA, 83 Bellaire Drive, Vicksburg, MS 39180. (601)415-3048. E-mail: lynettewfuller@yahoo.com. Lynette W. Fuller, ed. Art and literature (Christian fiction) on the topics of angels, demons, spiritual warfare, and end times, with references to Christ worked into the story in some way. Quarterly journal. Estab. 2004. 100% freelance. Pays .20/wd. for first story, higher rate after you've been published with them. Short stories 4,000-6,000 words (40/yr.).

Tips: "We prefer compelling, suspense-filled, faith-building short stories with those elements and how those issues play out in the lives of everyday people, Christians, or entire congregations or groups where good wins out over evil. The novels by Frank Peretti are great examples, particularly *This Present Darkness* and *The Visitation.*"

$ANGELS ON EARTH, 16 E. 34th St., New York NY 10016. (212)251-8100. Fax (212)684-1311. E-mail: angelseditors@guideposts.org. Website: www.angelsonearth.com. Guideposts. Colleen Hughes, ed-in-chief; Meg Belviso, depts. ed. for features and fillers. Presents true stories about God's angels and humans who have played angelic roles on earth. Bimonthly mag.; 75 pgs.; circ. 550,000. Subscription $19.95. 90% unsolicited freelance. Complete ms/cover letter; no phone/fax/e-query. Pays $100-400 on publication for all rts. Articles 100-1,500 wds. (100/yr.); all stories must be true. Responds in 13 wks. Seasonal 6 mos. ahead. No disk or e-mail submissions. Guidelines (also by e-mail/Website); copy for 7x10 SAE/4 stamps.

Fillers: Buys many. Anecdotal shorts of similar nature; 50-250 wds.; $50-100.

Columns/Departments: Buys 20-30/yr. Messages (brief, mysterious happenings), $25. Earning Their Wings (good deeds), 150 wds., $50. Only Human? (human or angel?/mystery), 350 wds.; $100.

Tips: "We are not limited to stories about heavenly angels. We also accept stories about human beings doing heavenly duties."

+THE ANGLICAN, 135 Adelaide St. E., Toronto M5C 1L8 Canada. Toll-free (800)668-8932. (416)363-6021, ext. 47. Fax (416)363-7678. E-mail: smann@toronto.anglican.ca. Website: www.toronto.anglican.ca. Anglican Diocese of Toronto. Stuart Mann, ed. Provides timely news, in-depth features, and challenging opinions to Anglicans in this Diocese. Monthly (10X) tabloid; circ. 300. Subscription $8. Open to unsolicited freelance. Not included in topical listings. (Ads)

$ANGLICAN JOURNAL, 80 Hayden St., Toronto ON M4Y 2J6 Canada. (416)924-9192 or 9199. Fax (416)921-4452. E-mail: editor@national.anglican.ca. Website: www.anglicanjournal .com. Anglican Church of Canada. Leanne Larmondin, ed.; Steve Brickenden, ed. asst. (sbrickenden@national.anglican.ca). National newspaper of the Anglican Church of Canada; informs Canadian Anglicans about the church at home and overseas. Newspaper (10x/yr.) and online; 12-16 pgs.; circ. 220,000. Subscription $10 Can., $17 US & foreign. 10% unsolicited freelance. Query only; fax/e-query OK. Pays $50-300 or .23/wd. Can., on acceptance for 1st and electronic rts. Articles 600 wds. (12-15/yr.). Responds in 2 wks. Seasonal 2 mos. ahead. No reprints. Guidelines (also by e-mail). (Ads)

$+ANIMAL TRAILS, 2660 Peterborough St., Herndon VA 20171. Phone/fax (703)715-1129. E-mail: bridalguides@yahoo.com, or weddingandromancewriters@yahoogroups.com. Tellstar Publishing. Shannon Bridget Murphy, ed. Keeping animal memories alive through writing. Quarterly mag. 85% unsolicited freelance. Complete ms/cover letter; e-query OK. Pays .02-.05/wd. on acceptance for 1st, one-time, reprint, and simultaneous rts. Articles to 2,000 wds.; fiction to 2,000 wds. Responds in 2-8 wks. Seasonal 3 mos. ahead. Accepts simultaneous submissions and reprints (tell when/where appeared). Accepts disk or e-mail submissions (attached or copied into message.). No kill fee. Regularly uses sidebars. Prefers KJV. Guidelines by e-mail. (No ads)

Poetry: Buys variable number. Avant-garde, free verse, haiku, light verse, traditional; any length. Pays variable rates. Submit any number.

Fillers: Buys most types, to 1,000 wds.

Tips: "Send a well-written article that is suitable for this publication."

$THE ANNALS OF SAINT ANNE DE BEAUPRE, PO Box 1000, St. Anne de Beaupre QC G0A 3C0 Canada. (418)827-4538. Fax (418)827-4530. E-mail: mag@revuestanne debeaupre.ca. Website: www.ssadb.qc.ca. Catholic/Redemptorist Fathers. Father Roch Achard, C.Ss.R., mng. ed. Promotes Catholic family values. Monthly mag.; 32 pgs.; circ. 45,000. Subscription $12.50 US, $14.50 Can. 80% unsolicited freelance. Complete ms/cover letter; no phone/fax/e-query. Pays .03-.04/wd. on acceptance for 1st N.A. serial rts. only. Articles (350/yr.) & fiction (200/yr.); 500-1,500 wds. Responds in 4-5 wks. Seasonal 6 mos. ahead. No disk or e-mail submission. Does not use sidebars. Prefers NRSV. Guidelines; copy for 9x12 SAE/IRC. (No ads)

   Tips: "Writing must be uplifting and inspirational, clearly written, not filled with long quotations. We tend to stay away from extreme controversy and focus on the family, good family values, devotion, and Christianity." No simultaneous submissions or reprints; rights must be clearly stated. Typed manuscripts only.

$THE APOCALYPSE CHRONICLES, Box 448, Jacksonville OR 97530. Phone/fax (541)899-8888. E-mail: James@ChristianMediaNetwork.com. Websites: www.ChristianMedia Daily.com; www.christianmedianetwork.com; www.christianmediaresearch.com; and www .soundbodycm.com (health articles). Christian Media. James Lloyd, ed./pub. Deals with the apocalypse exclusively. Quarterly & online newsletter; circ. 2,000-3,000. Query; prefers phone query. Payment negotiable for reprint rts. Articles. Responds in 3 wks. Requires KJV. No guidelines; copy for #10 SAE/2 stamps.

   Tips: "It's helpful if you understand your own prophetic position and are aware of its name, i.e., Futurist, Historicist, etc."

$ARKANSAS CATHOLIC, PO Box 7417, Little Rock AR 72217. (501)664-0340. Fax (501)664-6572. E-mail: mhargett@dolr.org. Catholic Diocese of Little Rock. Malea Hargett, ed.; Tara Little, assoc. ed. Statewide newspaper for the local diocese. Weekly tabloid; 16 pgs.; circ. 7,000. Subscription $18. 1% unsolicited freelance; 10% assigned. Query/clips; e-query OK. Pays $2.50/inch on publication for 1st rts. Articles 1,000 wds. Accepts simultaneous submissions & reprints. Accepts requested ms on disk or by e-mail. Uses some sidebars. Prefers Catholic Bible. Guidelines (also by e-mail); copy for 9x12 SAE/2 stamps. (Ads)

   Columns/Departments: Tara Little, ed. Buys 2/yr. Seeds of Faith (education). Complete ms. Pays $15.

   Tips: "All stories and columns must have an Arkansas connection."

$ARLINGTON CATHOLIC HERALD, 200 N. Glebe Rd., Ste. 600, Arlington VA 22203. (703)841-2590. Fax (703)524-2782. E-mail: editorial@catholicherald.com. Website: http://catholicherald.com/index.htm. Catholic Diocese of Arlington. Michael F. Flach, ed. Regional newspaper for the local diocese. Weekly newspaper; 28 pgs.; circ. 53,000. Subscription $14. 10% unsolicited freelance. Query; phone/fax/e-query OK. Pays $50-150 on publication for one-time rts. Articles 500-1,500 wds. Responds in 2 wks. Seasonal 3 mos. ahead. Accepts simultaneous submissions. Prefers accepted ms on disk. Regular sidebars. Guidelines (also on Website); copy for 11x17 SAE. (Ads)

   Columns/Departments: Sports; School News; Local Entertainment; 500 wds.

   Tips: "All submissions must be Catholic-related. Avoid controversial issues within the Church."

$+ATLANTIC CATHOLIC, PO Box 1300, 88 College St., Antigonish NS B2G 2L7 Canada. (902)863-4370. Fax (902)863-1943. E-mail: atlanticcatholic@thecasket.ca. The Casket Printing and Publishing Co. Ken Sims, pub.; Brian Lazzuri, mng. ed. Reports religious news that will inform, educate, and inspire Catholics. Biweekly tabloid; circ. 2,500. Subscription $28. Open to unsolicited freelance. Pays $25/story. Incomplete topical listings. (Ads)

$+AUJOURD'HUI CREDO, 1332 Victoria, Longueuil QC Canada. (450)466-7733. Fax (450)466-2664. E-mail: davidfines@egliseunce.org. Website: www.egliseunce.org. United

Church of Canada. David Fines, dir. The only French Reformed magazine in North America. Monthly mag.; 28 pgs.; circ. 600. Subscription $25 Can. 20% unsolicited freelance. Complete ms; fax/e-query OK. Pays $50 on publication for nonexclusive rts. Not copyrighted. Articles 1,500 wds. (10/yr.); fiction 800 wds. (6/yr.); reviews 100 wds. Responds in 4 wks. Seasonal 2 mos. ahead. Accepts simultaneous submissions & reprints (tell when/where appeared). Requires e-mail submissions (attached or copied into message). No kill fee. Sometimes uses sidebars. Accepts submissions from children or teens. Prefers TOB. Guidelines/theme list by e-mal; free copy. (Ads)

Poetry: Accepts free verse.

Tips: "Most likely to break in by being inclusive and intelligent."

+BAREFOOT PATH, PO Box 3743, Englewood CO 80155. E-mail: jeanne@barefootonholy ground.com. Website: www.barefootpath.com. Jeanne Gowen Dennis, ed. Explores childlike wonder and faith for Christian adults who long for a more intimate relationship with their Father/Creator. Quarterly e-zine. Free online. Estab. 2004. Open to freelance. Complete ms/cover letter; e-query OK. **NO PAYMENT** (will link to Website & include a brief bio) for reprint, simultaneous, electronic, or nonexclusive rts. Articles 300-500 wds. (16/yr.); reviews 25-50 wds. Responds in 4 wks. Seasonal: Submit by August 20 for Thanksgiving or Christmas. Accepts simultaneous submissions & reprints (tell when/where appeared). Requires e-mail submission (copied into message). Uses some sidebars. Accepts submissions from teens. Prefers NIV, NASB, NKJV. Guidelines by e-mail/Website; copy online. (No ads)

Poetry: Accepts several/yr. Free verse, light verse, traditional; 14-20 lines. Submit max. 5 poems.

Fillers: Accepts several/yr. Anecdotes, ideas, kid quotes, prayers, quotes, short humor, and tips; 25-100 wds.

Columns/Departments: Accepts 8+/yr. Barefoot on Tiptoe (activity, exercise, or tip to stimulate childlike wonder or faith), 50-100 wds.; Holy Ground (devotional related to childlike wonder or faith), 100-250 wds., plus scripture verse.

Special Needs: "Writing that will inspire wonder at God's great love for us and a childlike spirit of worship in response."

Tips: "All areas are open to freelancers. To break in, send us quality writing that fits our theme (inspires childlike wonder and faith in readers)."

$B.C. CATHOLIC, 150 Robson St., Vancouver BC V6B 2A7 Canada. (604)683-0281. Fax (604)683-8117. E-mail: bcc@rcav.bc.ca. Website: www.rcav.bc.ca/bcc. Roman Catholic Archdiocese of Vancouver. Paul Schratz, ed. News, education, and inspiration for Canadian Catholics. Weekly (48X) newspaper; 20 pgs.; circ. 20,000. Subscription $32. 20% unsolicited freelance. Query; phone query OK. Pays .15/wd. on publication for 1st rts. Photos $25. Articles 500-1,000 wds. Responds in 6 wks. Seasonal 4 wks. ahead. Accepts simultaneous submissions and reprints. Prefers e-mail submission (Word attached file or copied into message). No guidelines; free copy. (Ads)

Tips: "Items of a Catholic nature are preferred."

$+BC CHRISTIAN NEWS, #200 - 20316—56 Ave., Langley BC V3A 3Y7 Canada. Toll-free (888)899-3777. (604)534-1444. Fax (604)534-2970. E-mail: editor@canadianchristianity .com. Website: www.canadianchristianity.com. Christian Info Society. Flyn Ritchie, ed. A cross-denominational newspaper linking Christians in ministry and purpose. Monthly tabloid; circ. 1,000. Subscription $35 Can.; $50 US. Open to unsolicited freelance. Pays .10/wd. Not in topical listings. (Ads)

$BELIEVER'S BAY, PO Box 6362, Clearwater FL 33758. Toll-free (888)564-3534. E-mail: Publisher@BelieversBay.com, or editor@BelieversBay.com. Website: www.BelieversBay.com.

Ro Lashua, pub./ed-in-chief. To unite the Body of Christ through communication, exhortation, and edification while focusing on ministries in the Body of Christ. Monthly online mag. Mostly freelance. Complete ms by e-mail only; e-query OK. Pays $15 for 1st and electronic rts. (keeps in archives for 3 mos.). Articles or fiction 900-1,000 wds. Guidelines/theme list on Website with topical listings.

Poetry: Occasionally uses some.

Columns/Departments: Columns to 500 wds. Most columns full for now; however, looking for writers who focus on prophecy. Pays $15.

Special Needs: Focus on prayer every month.

Tips: "We will need all submissions to the editor by the first of the month prior to the month of the issue for which it is submitted."

$BGC WORLD, 2002 S. Arlington Heights Rd., Arlington Heights IL 60005-4102. Toll-free (800)323-4215. (847)228-0200. Fax (847)228-5376. E-mail: bputman@baptist general.org. Website: www.bgcworld.org. Baptist General Conference. Bob Putman, ed. Almost exclusively for, about, and by the people and ministries of the Baptist General Conference. Monthly (10X) mag.; 16 pgs.; circ. 40,000. Subscription free. Estab. 2003. 35% unsolicited freelance; 65% assigned. Query; e-query preferred. Pays $30-280 on publication for 1st, reprint, and electronic rts. Articles 800-1,300 wds. (12/yr.). Responds in 6-8 wks. Seasonal 8 mos. ahead. Accepts simultaneous submissions and reprints (tell when/where appeared). Prefers accepted mss by e-mail (attached file). Kill fee 50%. Uses some sidebars. Prefers NIV. Guidelines (also by e-mail); free copy. (Ads)

Columns/Departments: Buys 30/yr. New Life (first-person transformation story), 800 wds.; Profile (third-person story of key leader), 800 wds.; Around the BGC (short news blurb of happenings in churches), 75-200 wds.; Good Ideas (ministries working in BGC churches), 250-400 wds.; $30-115.

Tips: "Report on interesting happenings/ministry in BGC churches close to you for our Around the BGC or Good Ideas columns. Or query on a theme-related article."

$BIBLE ADVOCATE, Box 33677, Denver CO 80233. (303)452-7973. Fax (303)452-0657. E-mail: bibleadvocate@cog7.org. Website: www.cog7.org/BA. Church of God (Seventh-day). Calvin Burrell, ed.; Sherri Langton, assoc. ed. Adult readers; 50% not members of the denomination. Monthly (10X) mag.; 24 pgs.; circ. 13,500. Subscription free. 25-35% unsolicited freelance. Complete ms/cover letter; no phone/fax/e-query. Pays $25-55 on publication for 1st, one-time, reprint, electronic, and simultaneous rts. Articles 1,000-1,500 wds. (10-20/yr.). Responds in 4-8 wks. Seasonal 9 mos. ahead. Accepts simultaneous submissions and reprints (tell when/where appeared). Accepts requested ms on disk or by e-mail (copied into message). Regularly uses sidebars. Prefers NIV, NKJV. Guidelines/theme list (also on Website); copy for 9x12 SAE/3 stamps. (No ads)

Poetry: Buys 6-10/yr. Free verse, traditional; 5-20 lines; $20. Submit max. 5 poems.

Fillers: Buys 5-10/yr. Facts, prose, quotes; 100-400 wds.; $20.

Columns/Departments: Accepts 5/yr. Viewpoint (social or religious issues), 650-675 wds., pays copies.

Special Needs: Articles centering on upcoming themes (ask for theme list).

Tips: "If you write well, all areas are open to freelance, especially personal experiences that tie in with the monthly themes. Articles that run 650-700 words are more likely to get in. Also, fresh writing with keen insight is most readily accepted. Writers may submit sidebars that fit our theme for each issue." This magazine may be undergoing changes in 2005—fewer issues with more pages and a shift in editorial focus. Contact Sherri Langton, associate editor, for details.

**This periodical was #28 on the 2003 Top 50 Christian Publishers list (#36 in 2002).

BOOKS & CULTURE, 465 Gundersen Dr., Carol Stream IL 60188. (630)260-6200. Fax (630)260-0114. E-mail: bceditor@booksandculture.com. Website: www.booksand culture.com. Christianity Today Intl. David Neff, exec. ed.; John Wilson, ed. To edify, sharpen, and nurture the evangelical intellectual community by engaging the world in all its complexity from a distinctly Christian perspective. Bimonthly & online newsletter.; circ. 15,000. Subscription free. Open to freelance. Query. Incomplete topical listings. (Ads)
    **2004 & 2003 EPA Award of Merit—General. 2001 EPA Award of Excellence—General.

$BRAVE HEARTS, 1503 S.W. 42nd St., Topeka KS 66609-1265. Toll-free (800)678-5779, ext. 4345. (785)274-4300. Fax (785)274-4305. Website: www.braveheartsmagazine.com. Ogden Publications/Grit Magazine. Ann Crahan, ed-in-chief; Jean Teller and Traci Smith, mng. eds. Written by ordinary people who have an inspirational message to share. Quarterly magazine; 48 pgs.; circ. 2,000. Subscription $9.95. 100% unsolicited freelance. Complete ms; no phone/fax/e-query. Pays up to $15 on publication for one-time rts. Articles to 900 wds. (100/yr.). Responds in 3-6 mos. Seasonal 6 mos. ahead. Call 800# or e-mail (www.braveheartsmagazine.com/guidelines.htm) for guidelines/theme list (also on Website); copy for $4/6x9 SAE. Incomplete topical listings.
    Poetry: Buys 3-4/yr. Free verse, light verse, traditional, 4-16 lines. Submit max. 5 poems.
    Tips: "All departments open to freelancers."

THE BREAD OF LIFE, 209 MacNab St. N., Box 395, Hamilton ON L8N 3H8 Canada. (905)529-4496. Fax (905)529-5373. E-mail: steeners@cyberus.ca. Website: www.thebreadoflife.ca. Catholic. Fr. Peter Coughlin, ed. Catholic Charismatic; to encourage spiritual growth in areas of renewal in the Catholic Church today. Bimonthly mag.; 32 pgs.; circ. 2,500. Subscription $30. 5% unsolicited freelance. Complete ms/cover letter; fax query OK. **NO PAYMENT**. Articles 1,100-1,300 wds.; biblical fiction; book reviews 250 wds. Responds in 4-6 wks. Seasonal 6 mos. ahead. Accepts reprints (tell when/where appeared). No disk. Does not use sidebars. Prefers NAB, NJB. Guidelines; copy for 9x12 SAE/$1.42 postage (mark "Media Mail"). (Ads)
    Poetry: Accepts little.
    Fillers: Accepts 10-12/yr. Facts, prose, quotes; to 250 wds.
    Tips: "We do appreciate poetry submissions and shorter articles, 750 words. It is best if a writer includes a 2-3 line biography and photo for publication."

THE BREAKTHROUGH INTERCESSOR, PO Box 121, Lincoln VA 20160. (540)338-5522. Fax (540)338-1934. E-mail: breakthrough@intercessors.org. Website: www.intercessors.org. Nondenominational. Andrea Doudera, ed.; Trudi Schwarting, mng. ed. Preparing and equipping people who pray; encouraging in prayer and faith. Quarterly mag.; 44 pgs.; circ. 7,000. Subscription $15. 100% unsolicited freelance. Complete ms/cover letter; fax/e-query OK. **NO PAYMENT**. Articles about 1,000 wds. (50/yr.). Accepts simultaneous submissions and reprints (tell when/where appeared). Accepts requested ms on disk or by e-mail. Regularly uses sidebars. Any Bible version. Guidelines; copy for 6x9 SAE/3 stamps. (No ads)
    Poetry: Accepts very few. Subject must be prayer.
    Special Needs: All articles must deal with prayer.
    Contest: Pays $25 for article with most reader impact.
    Tips: "Break in by submitting true articles/stories about prayer and its miraculous results."
    Manuscripts acknowledged but not returned.

$BRIDAL GUIDES, 2660 Peterborough St., Herndon VA 20171. Phone/fax (703)715-1129. E-mail: bridalguides@yahoo.com, or weddingandromancewriters@yahoogroups.com. Tellstar Publishing. Shannon Bridget Murphy, ed. Theme-based wedding/reception ideas and planning for Christian wedding planners. Quarterly mag. 85% unsolicited freelance. Complete ms/cover letter; e-query OK. Pays .02-.05/wd. on acceptance for 1st, one-time, reprint, and simultaneous rts. Articles to 2,000 wds.; fiction to 2,000 wds. Responds in 2-

8 wks. Seasonal 3 mos. ahead. Accepts simultaneous submissions and reprints (tell when/where appeared). Accepts disk or e-mail submissions (attached or copied into message.). No kill fee. Regularly uses sidebars. Prefers KJV. Guidelines by e-mail. (No ads)

Poetry: Buys variable number. Avant-garde, free verse, haiku, light verse, traditional; any length. Pays variable rates. Submit any number.

Fillers: Buys most types, to 1,000 wds.; .02-.05/wd.

Columns/Departments: Financial Planning (budgeting/planning), 1,000 wds.

Special Needs: All aspects of wedding/reception planning; home-planning articles related to a variety of topics; honeymoon destinations and travel advice. Also romance fiction related to weddings, travel, and home.

$CANADA LUTHERAN, 302-393 Portage Ave., Winnipeg MB R3B 3H6 Canada. (204)984-9170. Fax (204)984-9185. E-mail: editor@elcic.ca, or canaluth@elcic.ca. Website: www.elcic .ca/clweb. Evangelical Lutheran Church in Canada. Ida Reichardt Backman, ed. Denominational. Monthly (8X) mag.; 42 pgs.; circ. 14,000. Subscription $23 US. 40% unsolicited freelance; 60% assigned. Query or complete ms/cover letter; fax/e-query OK. Pays $40-110 (.10/wd.) Can. on publication for one-time rts. Articles 700-1,200 wds. (15/yr.); fiction 850-1,200 wds. (4/yr.). Responds in 5 wks. Seasonal 10 mos. ahead. Accepts simultaneous submissions and reprints. Prefers e-mail submission (copied into message). Uses some sidebars. Prefers NRSV. Guidelines (also by e-mail). (Ads)

Tips: "Canadians/Lutherans receive priority here; others considered but rarely used. Want material that is clear, concise, and fresh. Articles that talk about real life experiences of faith receive our best reader response."

+THE CANADIAN LUTHERAN, 3074 Portage Ave., Winnipeg MB R3K 0Y2 Canada. Toll-free (800)588-4226. (204)895-3433. Fax (204)897-4319. E-mail: communications@lutheran church-canada.ca. Website: www.lutheranchurch-canada.ca. Lutheran Church-Canada. Ian Adnams, ed. Monthly (9X) mag. Subscription $20. Open to unsolicited freelance. Not in topical listings. (Ads)

($)+CANADIAN MENNONITE, 490 Dutton Dr., Unit C5, Waterloo ON N2L 6H7 Canada. Toll-free (800)378-2524. (519)884-3810. Fax (519)884-3331. E-mail: editor@canadian mennonite.org. Website: www.canadianmennonite.org. Canadian Mennonite Publishing Service/Anabaptist Mennonite. Margaret Loewen Reimer, interim ed. Seeks to promote covenantal relationships within the church (Hebrews 10:23-25). Biweekly mag.; circ. 20,000. Subscription $32.50 Can.; $52.50 US. Open to unsolicited freelance. Pays for assignments only. Not in topical listings. (Ads)

$CAPPERS, 1503 S.W. 42nd St., Topeka KS 66609. (785)274-4300. Fax (785)274-4305. E-mail: cappers@cappers.com. Website: www.cappers.com. Ogden Publications. Ann Crahan, ed-in-chief; Andrea Skalland, mng. ed. Timely news-oriented features with positive messages. Biweekly magazine; 40-56 pgs.; circ. 250,000. Subscription $27.98. 40% unsolicited freelance. Complete ms/cover letter by mail only. Pays about $2.50/printed inch for nonfiction on publication, pays $100-400 for fiction on acceptance for one-time rts. Articles to 1,000 wds. (50/yr.); fiction to 2,000 wds., serials to 25,000 wds. (20/yr.). Responds in 2-6 mos. Seasonal 6 mos. ahead. No simultaneous submissions or reprints. Prefers requested ms on CD (Mac). Uses some sidebars. Guidelines (also on Website); copy $4/9x12 SASE/4 stamps. (Ads)

Poetry: Attn: Poetry Editor. Buys 50/yr. Free verse, light verse, traditional; 4-16 lines. Pays $10-15 on acceptance. Submit max. 5 poems.

Fillers: Attn: Fillers Dept. Buys 50/yr. Short humor (humorous or thought-provoking one-liners); 10-50 wds. No payment.

Columns/Departments: Buys 26/yr. Garden Path (gardens/gardening), 500-1,000 wds. Payment varies. This column most open.

Tips: "Our publication is all original material either written by our readers/freelancers or occasionally by our staff. Every department, every article is open. Break in by reading at least 6 months of issues to know our special audience. Most open to nonfiction features and garden stories." Submissions are not acknowledged or status reports given.

$+THE CATALYST, 229 College St., #311, Toronto ON M5T 1R4 Canada. (416)979-2443, ext. 23. Fax (416)979-2458. E-mail: janet@cpj.ca. Website: www.cpj.ca. Citizens for Public Justice. Janet Somerville, ed. pro tem. To act as a catalyst for faith-based political action. Bimonthly newsletter; circ. 3,000. Subscription $15. Open to unsolicited freelance. Pays $50 for 700 wds. Incomplete topical listings. (No ads)

$CATHEDRAL AGE, 3101 Wisconsin Ave. NW, Washington DC 20016. (202)537-5681. Fax (202)364-6600. E-mail: Cathedral_Age@cathedral.org. Website: www.cathedralage.org. Protestant Episcopal Cathedral Foundation. Craig W. Stapert, pub. mngr. News from Washington National Cathedral and stories of interest to friends and supporters of WNC. Quarterly & online mag.; 36 pgs.; circ. 38,000. Subscription $15. 50% assigned freelance. Query; e-query OK. Pays to $500 on publication for all rts. Articles 1,000-1,500 wds. (10/yr.); book reviews 600 wds., ($100). Responds in 6 wks. Seasonal 6 mos. ahead. Requires requested ms on disk or by e-mail (attached file). Kill fee 50%. Uses some sidebars. Prefers NRSV. No guidelines; copy $5/9x12 SAE/5 stamps. (No ads)

Special Needs: Art, architecture, music.

Tips: "We assign all articles, so query with clips first. Always write from the viewpoint of an individual first, then move into a more general discussion of the topic. Human interest angle important."

$THE CATHOLIC ANSWER, 200 Noll Plaza, Huntington IN 46750. Toll-free (800)348-2440. E-mail: tcanswer@osv.com. Website: www.osv.com. Our Sunday Visitor/Catholic. Paul Thigpen, ed. Answers to questions of belief for orthodox Catholics. Bimonthly mag.; 36 pgs.; circ. 50,000. 10% unsolicited freelance. Query/clips. Pays $100-250 on publication for 1st rts. Articles 800-1,200 wds. (25/yr.). Seasonal 6 mos. ahead. Guidelines (also by e-mail); free copy.

$CATHOLIC DIGEST, PO Box 6001, Mystic CT 06355. (860)536-2611. Fax (860)536-5600. E-mail: cdigest@bayard-inc.com. Submissions to: cdsubmissions@bayardpubs.com. Website: www.CatholicDigest.com. Catholic/Bayard Publications. Joop Koopman, ed.; submit to Articles Editor. Readers have a stake in being Catholic and a wide range of interests: religion, family, health, human relationships, good works, nostalgia, and more. Monthly & online mag.; 128 pgs.; circ. 400,000. Subscription $19.95. 15% unsolicited freelance; 20% assigned. Complete ms (for original material)/cover letter, tear sheets for reprints; no e-query. Pays $200-400 ($100 for reprints) on acceptance for one-time rts. Online-only articles receive $100, plus half of any traceable revenue. Articles 1,000-3,500 wds. (60/yr.). Responds in 6-8 wks. Seasonal 5 mos. ahead. Accepts reprints (tell when/where appeared). Accepts requested ms on disk or by e-mail (copied into message). Regularly uses sidebars. Prefers NAB. Guidelines (also on Website:www.catholicdigest.org/stops/info/writers. html); copy for 7x10 SAE/2 stamps. (Ads)

Fillers: Julie Rattey, asst. ed. Buys 200/yr. Anecdotes, cartoons, facts, jokes, quotes; 1 line to 300 wds.; $2/published line on publication.

Columns/Departments: Buys 75/yr. Open Door (personal stories of conversion to Catholicism); 200-500 wds.; $2/published line. See guidelines for full list.

Special Needs: Family and career concerns of Baby Boomers who have a stake in being Catholic.

Contest: See Website for current contest, or send an SASE.

Tips: "We favor the anecdotal approach. Stories must be strongly focused on a definitive topic that is illustrated for the reader with a well-developed series of true-life, interconnected vignettes."

**This periodical was #37 on the 2002 Top 50 Christian Publishers list (#28 in 2001, #44 in 2000, #15 in 1999).

$CATHOLIC FORESTER, Box 3012, Naperville IL 60566-7012. (630)983-3381. Fax (800)811-2140. E-mail: cofpr@aol.com. Website: www.catholicforester.com. Catholic Order of Foresters. Mary Anne File, ed. For mixed audience, primarily parents and grandparents between the ages of 30 and 80+. Quarterly mag.; 40 pgs.; circ. 100,000. Free/ membership. 10% unsolicited freelance. Complete ms/cover letter; no phone/fax/e-query. Pays .30/wd. on acceptance for 1st, or one-time rts. Articles 1,000-1,500 wds. (5/yr.); fiction for all ages 500-1,200 wds. (5/yr.). Responds in 12-16 wks. Seasonal 4-6 mos. ahead. Accepts simultaneous submissions and reprints (tell when/where appeared). Accepts requested ms by e-mail. Kill fee 5%. Uses some sidebars. Prefers Catholic Bible. Guidelines (also on Website); copy for 9x12 SAE/4 stamps. (No ads)

> **Poetry:** Buys 2/yr. Light verse, traditional. Pay varies. Submit max. 5 poems.
> **Fillers:** Keith Halla, fillers ed. Buys 2/yr. Cartoons. Pay varies.
> **Tips:** "Looking for informational, inspirational articles on finances and parenting. Writing should be energetic with good style and rhythm. Most open to general interest and fiction."
> **This periodical was #37 on the 2004 Top 50 Christian Publishers list (#15 in 2003, #24 in 2002, #47 in 2001).

$CATHOLIC INSIGHT, PO Box 625, Adelaide Sta., 31 Adelaide St. E., Toronto ON M5C 2J8 Canada. (416)204-9601. Fax (416)204-1027. E-mail: reach@catholicinsight.com. Website: www.catholicinsight.com. Life Ethics Information Center. Fr. Alphonse de Valk, ed./ pub. News, analysis, and commentary on social, ethical, political, and moral issues from a Catholic perspective. Monthly (10X) mag.; 40-44 pgs.; circ. 3,500. Subscription $32 Can., $38 US. 2% unsolicited freelance; 98% assigned. Query; phone/fax/e-query OK. Pays $200 for 1,500 wds. ($250 for 2,000 wds.) on publication for all rts. Articles 750-1,500 wds. (20-30/yr.); book reviews 750 wds. ($85). Responds in 6-8 wks. Seasonal 2 mos. ahead. Accepts requested ms on disk or by e-mail. Uses some sidebars. Prefers RSV (Catholic). Guidelines (also by e-mail); copy $4 Can./9x12 SAE/.90 Can. postage or IRC. (Ads)

> **Tips:** "We are interested in intelligent, well-researched, well-presented commentary on a political, religious, social, or cultural matter from the viewpoint of the Catholic Church."

$CATHOLIC NEW TIMES, 80 Sackville St., Toronto ON M5A 3E5 Canada. (416)361-0761. Fax (416)361-0796. E-mail: editor@catholicnewtimes.org. Website: www.catholicnewtimes .org. Independent. New Catholic Times, Inc. Ted Schmidt, ed. An independent journal in the Catholic tradition that focuses on faith and social justice. Biweekly newspaper (20X); 20 pgs.; circ. 8,500. Subscription $27.95. 25% unsolicited freelance; 75% assigned. Query; phone/fax/ e-query OK. Pays $75-300 on publication for one-time rts. Articles 500-1,200+ wds. (40/yr.); book reviews 500-800 wds.; music reviews 500 wds.; video reviews 500-700 wds.; pays $50-100. Guidelines (also by e-mail); copy for 9x12 SAE/3 stamps. Not in topical listings. (Ads)

> **Fillers:** Newsbreaks.
> **Columns/Departments:** Buys 40/yr. (assigned). Witness (first-person experience) 1,200 wds.; Frontburner (opinion) 500-600 wds.; Faith & Spirituality (experiences of faith) to 1,200 wds.; Canada (Canadian news/features) 300-1,200+ wds.; World (world news) 300-1,200+ wds.; $100. Query.
> **Tips:** "Call me with an idea and we can chat about it. Our office is in Toronto, but we want to reflect all parts of the country, so writers in all provinces and territories are encouraged to get in touch."

$CATHOLIC NEW YORK, 1011—1st Ave., 17th Fl., New York NY 10022. (212)688-2399. Fax (212)688-2642. E-mail: cny@cny.org. Website: www.cny.org. Catholic. John Woods, ed-in-chief. To inform New York Catholics. Monthly newspaper; 72 pgs.; circ. 135,000. Subscription

$12. 2% unsolicited freelance. Query or complete ms/cover letter. Pays $15-100 on publication for one-time rts. Articles 500-800 wds. Responds in 5 wks. Copy $3.

Columns/Departments: Comment; 325 wds.

$CATHOLIC PARENT, 200 Noll Plaza, Huntington IN 46750. Toll-free (800)348-2440. (219)356-8400. Fax (219)359-9117. E-mail: cparent@osv.com. Website: www.osv.com. Catholic. Woodeene Koenig-Bricker, ed. Practical advice for Catholic parents, with a specifically Catholic slant. Bimonthly mag.; 52 pgs.; circ. 27,000. Subscription $24. 5% unsolicited freelance; 95% assigned. Query/clips or complete ms/cover letter; fax/e-query OK. Pays $100-200 on acceptance for 1st rts. Articles 250-1,000 wds. (50/yr.). Responds in 12 wks. Seasonal 6 mos. ahead. Kill fee. Considers simultaneous submissions. Accepts requested ms on disk. Regularly uses sidebars. Guidelines; copy $3. (Ads)

Fillers: York Young, fillers ed. Parenting tips, 100-200 wds., $25.

Columns/Departments: This Works! (short parenting tips), 200 wds.; $25. Briefly Speaking, 200-500 wds., $50.

Tips: "We need practical, how-to pieces on raising children, building strong marriages, developing a spiritual life, and growing faith-filled families."

**This periodical was #38 on the 2002 Top 50 Christian Publishers list (#39 in 1999).

$CATHOLIC PEACE VOICE, 532 W. 8th, Erie PA 16502-1343. (814)453-4955. Fax (814)452-4784. E-mail: info@paxchristiusa.org. Website: www.paxchristiusa.org. Pax Christi USA. Dave Robinson, ed. For members of Pax Christi USA, the national Catholic Peace Movement. Bimonthly newsmagazine; 16-20 pgs.; circ. 23,000. Subscription $20, free to members. 15-20% unsolicited freelance; 25-30% assigned. Complete ms; phone/fax/e-query OK. Pays $50-75 on publication for all & electronic rts. Articles 500-1,500 wds. (10-15/yr.); reviews 750 wds., $50. Responds in 1-2 wks. Accepts simultaneous submissions and reprints (tell when/where appeared). Accepted ms on disk or by e-mail (attached or copied into message). Uses some sidebars. Accepts submissions from teens. Guidelines (also by e-mail); copy for 9x12 SAE/2 stamps. (Ads)

Poetry: Accepts 1-5/yr. Avant-garde, free verse, haiku, light verse, traditional. Submit max. 2 poems. No payment.

Tips: "Most open to features and news, as well as reviews and resources. E-mailing us and pitching a story is the best way to break into our publication. Emphasis is on nonviolence. No sexist language."

+THE CATHOLIC REGISTER, 1155 Yonge St., #401, Toronto ON M4T 1W2 Canada. (416)934-3410. Fax (416)934-3409. E-mail: editor@catholicregister.org. Website: www.catholic register.org. Michey Conlon, mng. ed. To provide reliable information about the world from a Catholic perspective. Weekly (47X) tabloid; circ. 33,000. Subscription $32.95. Open to unsolicited freelance. Not in topical listings. (Ads)

$CATHOLIC SENTINEL, PO Box 18030, Portland OR 97218. (503)281-1191. Fax (503)460-5496. E-mail: sentinel@ocp.org. Website: www.sentinel.org. Oregon Catholic Press. Bob Pfohman, ed. Weekly newspaper; 16-28 pgs.; circ. 16,000. Subscription $28. 2% unsolicited freelance; 0% assigned. Query/clips. Payment negotiable on publication for one-time rts. Articles 600-1,500 wds. Responds in 4 wks. Seasonal 2 mos. ahead. Accepts requested ms on disk or by e-mail (copied into message). Uses some sidebars. Prefers NAS. Incomplete topical listings. Guidelines; copy for 9x12 SAE/3 stamps. (Ads)

Tips: "We're most open to local church news and feature articles."

$CATHOLIC TELEGRAPH, 100 E. 8th St., Cincinnati OH 45202. (513)421-3131. Fax (513)381-2242. E-mail: tctnews@aol.com. Catholic. Dennis O'Connor, mng. ed. Diocese newspaper for Cincinnati area (all articles must have a Cincinnati or Ohio connection). Weekly newspaper; 24-28 pgs.; circ. 100,000. Limited unsolicited freelance; mostly assigned. Send résumé and writing samples for assignment. Pays varying rates on publication for all rts. Articles. Responds in 2-3 wks. Kill fee. No guidelines; copy $2/#10 SASE.

Fillers: Newsbreaks (local).

Special Needs: Personality features for 'Everyday Evangelists' section. These are feature stories that offer a slice of life of a person who is making a difference as a Roman Catholic Christian in their community. Prefer to have a tie within the Archdiocese of Cincinnati; must be an Ohioan. Complete ms.; 800 wds.; pays $40 (extra for photos of individual interviewed).

Tips: "Most likely to accept an article about a person, event, or ministry with an Ohio connection—Cincinnati-Dayton area."

CATHOLIC WORLD REPORT, Domus Enterprises, Inc., Box 1608, South Lancaster MA 01561. (978)365-7208. Fax (978)365-4307. E-mail: editor@cwnews.com. Website: www.cw news.com. Catholic. A news magazine that not only reports on important events in the Church but helps to shape them. Philip Lawler, ed. Monthly mag. Subscription $19.95. Not in topical listings.

$CBA MARKETPLACE, 9240 Explorer Dr., Colorado Springs CO 80920. Toll-free (800)252-1950. (719)265-9895. Fax (719)272-3510. E-mail: publications@cbaonline.org. Website: www.cbaonline.org. Christian Booksellers Assn. Sue Grise, sr. ed. To provide Christian bookstore owners and managers with professional retail skills, product information, and industry news. Monthly trade journal; 110-260 pgs.; circ. 8,000. Subscription $59.95 (for nonmembers). 0% unsolicited freelance; 30% assigned. Query/clips; fax/e-query OK. Pays .20-.30/wd. on acceptance for all rts. Articles 800-2,000 wds. (30/yr. assigned); book/music/video reviews 150 wds., $30-35. Responds in 8 wks. Seasonal 4-5 mos. ahead. Prefers requested ms on disk. Regularly uses sidebars. Accepts any modern Bible version. Theme list; copy $5/9x12 SAE/$1.42 postage (mark "Media Mail"). (Ads)

Fillers: Buys 12/yr. Cartoons ($100), retail facts, ideas, trends, newsbreaks.

Columns/Departments: Buys 10-20/yr. Industry Watch; Music News; Gift News; Video & Software News; Book News; Kids News; Spanish News; all 100-500 wds. Pays .16-.25/wd. Query.

Special Needs: Trends in retail, consumer buying habits, market profiles. By assignment only.

Tips: "Looking for writers who have been owners/managers/buyers/ sales staff in Christian retail stores. All our articles are by assignment and focus on producing and selling Christian products or conducting retail business. Send cover letter, including related experience and areas of interest, plus samples. We also assign reviews of books, music, videos, Spanish products, kids products, and software. Ask for calendar for product news and market-segment features."

+CBN.COM (CHRISTIAN BROADCASTING NETWORK), 977 Centerville Turnpike, Virginia Beach VA 23464. (757)226-3557. E-mail: craig.vonbuseck@cbn.org. Website: www .CBN.com. Christian Broadcasting Network. Craig von Buseck, programming dir. Online publication. Free online. Open to unsolicited freelance. E-mail submissions (attached as a Word document). Complete ms. **NO PAYMENT.** Devotions 500-700 wds.; Spiritual Life Teaching 700-1,500 wds.; Living Features (Family, Entertainment, Health, Finance) 700-1,500 wds.; Movie/TV/Music Reviews 700-1,000 wds.; Hard News 300-700 wds.; News Features 700-1,500 wds.; News Interviews 1,000-2,000 wds. Accepts reprints (tell when/where appeared). Guidelines; copy online.

$CELEBRATE LIFE, 1179 Courthouse Rd., Stafford VA 22554. (540)659-4171. Fax (540)659-2586. E-mail: clmag@all.org. Website: www.all.org. American Life League. Melissa Solt, asst. ed. A no-exceptions pro-life, pro-family magazine for Christian audience. Bimonthly mag.; 48 pgs.; circ. 70,000. Subscription $12.95 (donation). 40% unsolicited freelance;

40% assigned. Query/clips or complete ms/cover letter; phone/fax/e-query OK. Pays .30/wd. on publication for one-time or reprint rts. Articles 1,000-1,500 wds. (50/yr.). Responds in 2-13 wks. Seasonal 4 mos. ahead. Accepts simultaneous submissions and reprints (tell when/where appeared). Accepts e-mail submissions (attached or copied into message). No kill fee. Uses some sidebars. Accepts submissions from children and teens. Prefers Jerusalem Bible (Catholic). Guidelines/theme list (also by e-mail); copy for 9x12 SAE/4 stamps. (No ads)

Fillers: Buys 5/yr. Newsbreaks (local or special pro-life news); 75-200 wds.; $10.

Special Needs: Personal experience about abortion, post-abortion stress/healing, adoption, activism/young people's involvement, death/dying, euthanasia, eugenics, special needs children, personhood, chastity, and large families.

Tips: "We are no-exceptions pro-life. The importance of that philosophy should be emphasized. Photos are preferred."

$CGA WORLD, PO Box 249, Olyphant PA 18447. (570)586-1091. Fax (570)586-7721. E-mail: cgaemail@aol.com. Website: www.catholicgoldenage.org. Catholic Golden Age. Barbara Pegula, mng. ed. For Catholics 50+. Bimonthly mag.; 8 pgs.; circ. 100,000. Subscription/membership $12. Query. Pays .10/wd. on publication for 1st, one-time, or reprint rts. Articles 600-1,000 wds. & fiction 600-1,000 wds. Responds in 6 wks. Seasonal 6 mos. ahead. Accepts reprints (tell when/where appeared). Accepts requested ms on disk. Guidelines; copy for 9x12 SAE/3 stamps. (Ads)

Fillers: Games, ideas, prayers, word puzzles.

CHANNELS, 3819 Bloor St. W., Toronto ON M9P 1K7 Canada. Phone/fax (519)651-2232. E-mail: cbbrown@rogers.com. Website: www.renewalfellowship.presbyterian.ca. The Renewal Fellowship/Presbyterian (P.C.C.) Calvin Brown, ed. For Presbyterians seeking spiritual renewal and biblical orthodoxy. Quarterly mag.; 20 pgs.; circ. 2,000. Subscription $12. 10% unsolicited freelance; 90% assigned. Query; e-query OK. **PAYS IN COPIES** for one-time rts. Articles 1,000-1,500 wds. (15/yr.); book reviews 300 wds. Responds in 4 wks. Seasonal 4-6 mos. ahead. Accepts reprints (tell when/where appeared). Prefers mss by e-mail (attached file/.RTF). Regularly uses sidebars. Accepts submissions from teens. No guidelines; copy for #10 SAE/3 stamps. (Ads)

Poetry: Accepts 3/yr. Free verse, haiku, light verse, traditional; 3 lines & up. Submit max. 6 poems.

Fillers: Accepts 4/yr. Anecdotes, cartoons, prayers.; 6-100 wds.

$CHARISMA & CHRISTIAN LIFE, Strang Communications, 600 Rinehart Rd., Lake Mary FL 32746. (407)333-0600. Fax (407)333-7133. E-mail: charisma@strang.com. Website: www.charismamag.com. Strang Communications. Lee Grady, exec. ed.; Jimmy Stewart, mng. ed.; Adrienne S. Gaines, book & music review ed. Primarily for the Pentecostal and Charismatic Christian community. Monthly & online mag.; 100+ pgs.; circ. 230,000. Subscription $24.97. 75% assigned freelance. Query only; e-query OK. Pays $100-800 on publication for 1st rts. Articles 1,800-2,500 wds.; book/music reviews, 200 wds., $25-35. Responds in 8-12 wks. Seasonal 4 mos. ahead. Kill fee $50. Prefers accepted ms by e-mail. Regularly uses sidebars. Guidelines; copy $4. (Ads)

Tips: "Most open to news section, reviews, or features. Query (published clips help a lot)." No unsolicited manuscripts.

**#1 Best-selling Magazine in Christian retail stores. 1998 EPA Award of Excellence—General.

+CHATTELS OF THE HEART, 2215 Hall Rd., Hartford WI 53027. (262)673-2775. E-mail: wolfsrosebud@purescreen.net. Patti Wolf, pub. Shows picturesque written work in poetry, devotions, and personal testimony, based on a biblical view and supporting creation. Quarterly booklet; 20-24 pgs. Subscription $18. 90% unsolicited freelance; 10% assigned.

Complete ms/cover letter; e-query OK. **NO PAYMENT** for 1st rts. Not copyrighted. Articles 250-425 wds. Responds in 12 wks. Seasonal 3 mos. ahead. No simultaneous submissions; accepts reprints (tell when/where appeared). Prefers e-mail submissions (copied into message). No sidebars. Accepts submissions from teens. Prefers KJV, NKJV. Guidelines (also by e-mail/Website); copy .90/9x12 SAE. (No ads)

Poetry: Accepts 40/yr. Free verse, haiku, light verse, traditional; 3-20 lines. Submit max. 3 poems.

Contest: God's Creation Poetry Contest. Three poems, 3-20 lines. Entry fee: $5.

Tips: "We also sponsor a yearly conference for writers in the spring (see conference listing)."

$CHICKEN SOUP FOR THE SOUL, PO Box 30880, Santa Barbara CA 93130. (805)563-2935. Fax (805)563-2945. E-mail: webmaster@chickensoupforthesoul.com. Website: www .chickensoup.com. Barbara LoMonaco, story acquisitions (blomonaco@chickensoup forthesoul.com). Inspirational anthologies to open your heart and rekindle your spirit; audience is open to all ages, races, etc. Quarterly trade paperback books; 385 pgs.; circ. 60 million. $12.95/book. 98% unsolicited freelance. Complete ms/cover letter; fax/e-query OK. Pays a fee on publication for reprint, simultaneous, and electronic rts. Articles 1,200 wds. max. Seasonal anytime. Accepts simultaneous submissions and reprints (tell when/where appeared). Accepts e-mail submissions: stories@chickensoupforthesoul.com (attached file/WORD). No kill fee. Guidelines/themes on Website; free sample. (No ads)

Fillers: Anecdotes, cartoons, facts, kid quotes, quotes, short humor; 10-200 wds. Pays.

Special Needs: See Website for a list of upcoming titles.

Contest: See Website for list of current contests.

Tips: "Visit our Website and be familiar with our book series. Send in stories via mail or e-mail, complete with contact information. Submit story typed, double spaced, max. 1,200 words, in a WORD document."

$+CHRISTIAN BIBLE STUDIES.COM, 465 Gundersen Dr., Carol Stream IL 60188-2498. (630)260-6200. Fax (630)260-0114. E-mail: bclstore@christianitytoday.com. Website: www.christianbiblestudies.com. Christianity Today Intl. Lori Quicke, mng. ed. Website with downloadable Bible studies on current issues. Estab. 2003. 100% assigned. Query/clips; e-query OK. Payment varies. Articles 500-2,500 wds.; Bible studies, 1,500-2,500 wds. Prefers full ms by e-mail (attached file). Kill fee 50%. No sidebars. Prefers NIV. Guidelines by e-mail.

THE CHRISTIAN CIVIC LEAGUE OF MAINE RECORD, Box 5459, Augusta ME 04332. (207)622-7634. Fax (207)621-0035. E-mail: e-mail@cclmaine.org. Website: www .cclmaine.org. Natalie Torgeson, ed. Focuses on public policy, political action, some church and public service. Monthly newsletter; 4 pgs.; circ. 4,600. Free. Some freelance. Query; phone/fax/e-query OK. **NO PAYMENT** for one-time rts. Articles 800-1,200 wds. (10-12/yr.). Responds in 4-8 wks. Accepts simultaneous query and reprints. Guidelines by e-mail/Website; free copy. Not in topical listings. (No ads)

CHRISTIAN COMPUTING MAGAZINE, PO Box 319, Belton MO 64012. (816)331-8142. Fax (800)456-1868. E-mail: steve@ccmag.com. Website: www.ccmag.com. Steve Hewitt, ed-in-chief. For Christian/church computer users. Monthly (11X) & online mag.; 2 pgs.; circ. 30,000. Subscription $14.95. 40% unsolicited freelance. Query/clips; fax/e-query OK. **NO PAYMENT** for all rts. Articles 1,000-1,800 wds. (12/yr.). Responds in 4 wks. Seasonal 2 mos. ahead. Accepts reprints. Requires requested ms on disk. Regularly uses sidebars. Guidelines; copy for 9x12 SAE.

Fillers: Accepts 6 cartoons/yr.

Columns/Departments: Accepts 12/yr. Telecommunications (computer), 1,500-1,800 wds.

Special Needs: Articles on Internet, DTP, computing.

$CHRISTIAN COURIER, (Canada), 1 Hiscott St., St. Catherines ON L2R 1C7 Canada. (US address: Box 110, Lewiston NY 14092-0110.) Toll-free (800)969-4838. (905)682-8311. Fax (905)682-8313. E-mail: editor@christiancourier.ca. Website: www.christian courier.ca. Reformed Faith Witness. Harry DerNederlanden, ed. To present Canadian and international news, both religious and secular, from a Reformed Christian perspective. Biweekly tabloid; 24-28 pgs.; circ. 4,000. 20% unsolicited freelance; 80% assigned. Complete ms/cover letter; fax/e-query OK. Pays $75-120 US, up to .10/wd. for assigned ($50-100 for unsolicited); 30 days after publication for one-time, reprint, or simultaneous rts. Not copyrighted. Articles 700-1,500 wds. (40/yr.); fiction to 1,200-2,500 wds. (6/yr.); book discussions 800-1,200 wds. Responds in 1-3 wks. Seasonal 3 mos. ahead. Accepts simultaneous submissions and reprints (tell when/where appeared). Prefers accepted ms by e-mail (attached file). No kill fee. Uses some sidebars. Prefers NIV. No guidelines/theme list/copy. (Ads)

> **Poetry:** Buys 12/yr. Avant-garde, free verse, light verse, traditional; 10-30 lines; $20-30. Submit max. 5 poems.

> **Tips:** "Suggest an aspect of the theme which you believe you could cover well, have insight into, could treat humorously, etc. Show that you think clearly, write clearly, and have something to say that we should want to read. Have a strong biblical world-view and avoid moralism and sentimentality." Responds only if material is accepted.

CHRISTIAN COURIER (WI), 1933 W. Wisconsin Ave., Milwaukee WI 53233. (414)344-7300. Fax (414)345-3544. E-mail: christiancourier@juno.com. ProBuColls Assn. John M. Fisco, Jr., pub.; Rita Bertolas, ed. To propagate the gospel of Jesus Christ in the Midwest. Monthly newspaper; circ. 10,000. 10% freelance. Query; phone/fax/e-query OK. **PAYS IN COPIES**, for one-time rts. Not copyrighted. Articles 300-1,500 wds. (6/yr.). Responds in 4-8 wks. Seasonal 2 mos. ahead. Accepts reprints. Guidelines; free copy. (Ads)

> **Fillers:** Anecdotes, facts, newsbreaks; 10-100 wds.

> **Tips:** "We are always in need of seasonal feature/filler type of articles: Christmas, Easter, 4th of July, etc."

CHRISTIAN DRAMA E-MAGAZINE, 1824 Celestia Dr., Walla Walla WA 99362-3619. (509)522-5242. E-mail: hiddennook@hiddennook.com. Website: http://hiddennook.com. Phillips Music & Drama. Victor R. Phillips, ed./pub. Play scripts and articles related to Christian drama. E-magazine. Distributed free. Open to freelance. Prefers accepted ms by e-mail. **NO PAYMENT FOR NOW.** Articles 300-1,000 wds. Incomplete topical listings.

> **Fillers:** Short articles on what different churches and drama groups are doing and anecdotes of effective results of drama ministries; 300 wds. and up.

> **Special Needs**: Articles on script writing, directing, acting, set design, lighting, costumes, performance reviews, script reviews, and news about Christian drama groups.

> **Tips:** "No monologues or poetry." Features a *Directory of Touring Christian Drama Groups*.

$CHRISTIAN EXAMINER, (formerly Christian Times) PO Box 2606, El Cajon CA 92021. (619)660-5500. Fax (619)660-5505. E-mail: info@christianexaminer.com. Website: www.christianexaminer.com. Keener Communications. Lori Arnold, ed. To report on current events from an evangelical Christian perspective, particularly traditional family values and church trends. Monthly & online newspaper; 24-36 pgs.; circ. 180,000. Subscription $19.95. 0% unsolicited freelance; 5% assigned. Query/clips. Pays .10/wd., on publication for 1st and electronic rts. Articles 600-900 wds. Responds in 4-5 wks. Seasonal 3 mos. ahead. No simultaneous submissions or reprints. Prefers e-mail submissions (copied into message). No kill fee. Uses some sidebars. Guidelines bye-mail; copy $1.50/9x12 SAE. (Ads)

> **Tips:** "We prefer news stories."

> **2004, 2000 & 1999 EPA Award of Merit—Newspaper.

$+THE CHRISTIAN HERALD, PO Box 68526, Branpton ON L6S 6A1 Canada. (905)874-1731. Fax (905)874-1731. E-mail: info@christianherald.ca.. Website: wwwchristianherald.ca. Covenant Communications. Fazal Karim, Jr., ed-in-chief. A Canadian-Christian tabloid with a focus on Christian arts and entertainment. Monthly tabloid; 24 pgs.; circ. 32,000. Subscription free, or $26.75 mailed. 10% unsolicited freelance; 85% assigned. Query; fax/e-query OK. Pays $20-100 or .10/wd. on publication for 1st rts. Articles 500-1,500 wds.; reviews 150-300 wds. (no payment). Responds in 4 wks. Seasonal 3 mos. ahead. Accepts simultaneous submissions & reprints (tell when/where appeared). Prefers e-mail submissions (attached file). No kill fee. Sometimes uses sidebars. Accepts submissions from teens. Prefers KJV, NKJV, NIV, NLT. Guidelines (also by e-mail); copy for 9x12 SAE/$1.60 Canadian postage. (Ads)

Fillers: Accepts 10/yr. Cartoons, facts, games, jokes, prayers, quotes, and word puzzles, 20-100 wds. No payment.

Columns/Departments: Interviews (Christian newsmakers/personalities), 900 wds., $20-50.

Tips: "Most open to articles/columns with specific reference to Canadians, with Canadian quotes, relevance, etc.."

$CHRISTIAN HISTORY & BIOGRAPHY, (formerly Christian History) 465 Gundersen Dr., Carol Stream IL 60188. (630)260-6200. Fax (630)260-0114. E-mail: CHeditor@ christianitytoday.com. Website: www.christianhistory.net. Christianity Today Intl. David Neff, exec. ed.; Chris Armstrong, mng. ed.; submit to Steve Gertz, ed. coordinator. To teach Christian history to educated readers in an engaging manner. Quarterly mag. & newsletter; 52 pgs.; circ. 55,000. Subscription $19.95. 5% unsolicited freelance; 95% assigned. Query/clips; e-query only. Pays .10-.20/wd. on acceptance for 1st rts. Articles 1,000-3,000 wds. (1/yr.). Responds in 2 wks. Accepts reprints (tell when/where appeared). Prefers accepted ms by e-mail (attached or copied into message). Kill fee 50%. Regularly uses sidebars. Prefers NIV. Guidelines/theme list (also by e-mail); copy for 9x12 SASE. (Ads)

Tips: "Let us know your particular areas of specialization and any books or papers you have written in the area of Christian history. The Gallery profiles are usually freelanced. We are purely thematic; only submit queries related to upcoming themes. Most open to non-themed departments: Story Behind; People Worth Knowing; Turning Points."

**2000 & 1998 EPA Award of Merit—General.

$CHRISTIAN HOME & SCHOOL, 3350 East Paris Ave. SE, Grand Rapids MI 49512. (616)957-1070, ext. 239. Fax (616)957-5022. E-mail: RogerS@CSIonline.org, or GBordewyk@ aol.com. Website: www.CSIonline.org. Christian Schools Intl. Gordon L. Bordewyk, exec. ed.; Roger Schmurr, sr. ed. Focuses on parenting and Christian education; for parents who send their children to Christian schools. Bimonthly & online mag.; 32 pgs.; circ. 68,000. Subscription $13.95. 95% unsolicited; 5% assigned. Complete ms or prefers e-query. Pays $175-250 on publication for 1st rts. Articles 1,000-2,000 wds. (30/yr.); Christmas fiction 1,000-2,000 wds. (5/yr.); book reviews $25 (assigned). Responds in 1 wk. Seasonal 5 mos. ahead. Accepts simultaneous query. Accepts requested ms on disk (clean copy they can scan); prefers e-mail submission (attached file). Regularly uses sidebars. Prefers NIV. Guidelines/theme list (also on Website); copy for 9x12 SAE/4 stamps. (Ads)

Fillers: Parenting ideas; 100-250 wds.; $25-40.

Tips: "Most open to feature articles on parenting and education. Looking for articles on teens, and single parenting. Ask to be assigned to do a book review, or send an article on speculation."

**This periodical was #38 on the 2004 Top 50 Christian Publishers list (#33 in 2003, #49 in 2000). 2001 Award of Excellence—Organizational; 1997 EPA Award of Merit—Organizational.

THE CHRISTIAN JOURNAL, 1025 Court St., Medford OR 97501. (541)773-4004. Fax (541)773-9917. E-mail: Info@thechristianjournal.org. Website: www.thechristian journal.org. Chad McComas, ed. Dedicated to sharing encouragement with the Body of Christ in Southern Oregon and Northern California. Bimonthly newspaper; 24-28 pgs.; circ. 20,000. Subscription $15; most copies distributed free. 50% unsolicited freelance; 50% assigned. Complete ms; phone/fax query OK. **NO PAYMENT AT THIS TIME.** Articles and fiction 800-1,000 wds; reviews 300-500 wds.; children's stories 600 wds. Prefer articles on disk or by e-mail (attached file). Accepts submissions from children or teens. Guidelines/ theme list; copy $1.20/9x12 SAE/3 stamps. (Ads)

   Poetry: Accepts 12-20/yr. Free verse, haiku, light verse, traditional; 4-12 lines. Submit max. 2 poems.

   Fillers: Accepts 50/yr. Anecdotes, cartoons, jokes, kid quotes, newsbreaks, prayers, quotes, short humor, or word puzzles; 100-300 wds.

   Columns/Departments: Accepts 6/yr. Youth, 800-1,000 wds; Seniors, 800-1,000 wds.; Children's stories, 600 wds.

   Tips: "Send articles on themes; each issue has a theme. Theme articles get first choice."

$CHRISTIAN LEADER, PO Box 220, Hillsboro KS 67063-0220. (620)947-5543. Fax (620)947-3266. E-mail: editor@usmb.org. Website: www.usmb.org. U.S. Conference of Mennonite Brethren. Submit to The Editor. Denominational. Monthly mag.; 36 pgs.; circ. 9,800. Subscription $16. 15% unsolicited freelance; 85% assigned. Complete ms; e-query OK. Pays .10/wd. on publication for 1st rts. Articles 1,200 wds. (2/yr.). Responds in 8 wks. Seasonal 4 mos. ahead. Accepts simultaneous submissions and reprints (tell when/where appeared). Prefers requested ms on disk or by e-mail (copied into message). Guide-lines/theme list (also by e-mail); no copy. (Ads)

   Tips: "Although we use primarily denominational writers, we are most open to features section. Ask for theme list; query specific topic/article."

CHRISTIAN MEDIA, Box 448, Jacksonville OR 97530. (541)899-8888. E-mail: James@ ChristianMediaNetwork.com. Website: www.ChristianMediaDaily.com, or www.Christian MediaNetwork.com. James Lloyd, ed./pub. Updates on world conditions, politics, econom-ics, in the light of prophecy. Quarterly & online tabloid; 24 pgs.; circ. 25,000. Query; prefers phone query. **NO PAYMENT** for negotiable rts. Articles; book & music reviews, 3 paragraphs. Accepts simultaneous submissions and reprints. Prefers requested ms on disk. Requires KJV. Copy for 9x12 SAE/2 stamps.

   Special Needs: Particularly interested in stories that expose dirty practices in the indus-try—royalty rip-offs, misleading ads, financial misconduct, etc. No flowery pieces on celebrities; wants well-documented articles on abuse in the media.

#CHRISTIAN MOTORSPORTS ILLUSTRATED, PO Box 884, Crowley TX 76036-0884. E-mail: cpo@epix.net. Website: www.christianmotorsports.com. CPO Publishing. Roland Osborne, pub. Covers Christians involved in motorsports. Bimonthly mag.; 64 pgs.; circ. 40,000. Subscription $19.96. 50% unsolicited freelance. Complete ms; no phone/fax/e-query. **NO PAYMENT.** Articles 500-2,000 wds. (30/yr.). Seasonal 4 mos. ahead. Requires requested ms on disk. Regularly uses sidebars. No guidelines; free copy. (Ads)

   Poetry: Accepts 10/yr. Any type. Submit max. 10 poems.

   Fillers: Accepts 100/yr. Anecdotes, cartoons, facts, games, ideas, jokes, newsbreaks, prayers, prose, quizzes, quotes, short humor.

   Columns/Departments: Accepts 10/yr.

   Tips: "Send a story on a Christian involved in motorsports—cars, tractors, motorcycles, airplanes, go-carts, lawnmowers, etc."

$CHRISTIAN NETWORKS JOURNAL, 228 Robert S. Kerr, Ste. 900, Oklahoma City OK 73102. (405)605-3562. E-mail: gordon@cnj.org. Website: http://cnj.org. ChristianNetworks. Rev.

Gordon McClellan, pres. Examines international and timely issues from many perspectives. Quarterly mag. Pays per article. Articles/essays to 1,250 wds. Gives 10% of their sales revenue to missions. Not in topical listings.

CHRISTIAN NEWS NORTHWEST, PO Box 974, Newberg OR 97132. Phone/fax (503)537-9220. E-mail: cnnw@cnnw.com. Website: www.cnnw.com. John Fortmeyer, ed./pub. News of ministry in the evangelical Christian community in western and central Oregon and southwest Washington; distributed primarily through evangelical churches. Monthly newspaper; 28-36 pgs.; circ. 30,000. Subscription $20. 10% unsolicited freelance; 5% assigned. Query; phone/fax/e-query OK. **NO PAYMENT.** Not copyrighted. Articles 300-400 wds. (100/yr.). Responds in 4 wks. Seasonal 3 mos. ahead. Accepts reprints (tell when/where appeared). Accepts e-mail submissions. Regularly uses sidebars. Guidelines (also by e-mail); copy $1.50. (Ads)

> **Tips:** "Most open to ministry-oriented features. Our space is always tight, but stories on lesser-known, Northwest-based ministries are encouraged. Keep it very concise. Since we focus on the Pacific Northwest, it would probably be difficult for anyone outside the region to break into our publication."

THE CHRISTIAN OBSERVER, 9400 Fairview Ave., Ste. 200, Manassas VA 22110. (703)335-2844. Fax (703)368-4817. E-mail: editor@christianobserver.org. Website: www.Christian Observer.org. Christian Observer Foundation; Presbyterian Reformed. Dr. Edwin P. Elliott, ed. To encourage and edify God's people and families; print version of *Presbyterians-Week*. Monthly newspaper; 32 pgs.; circ. 2,000. Subscription $27. 10% unsolicited freelance; 90% assigned. Query; phone/e-query OK. **NO PAYMENT.** Accepts e-mail submissions. (Ads)

CHRISTIAN ONLINE MAGAZINE, PO Box 262, Wolford VA 24658. E-mail: darlene@christian magazine.org. Website: www.ChristianMagazine.org. Darlene Osborne, pub. Endeavors to bring you the best Christian information on the net. Monthly e-zine; circ. 500,000. Subscription free. 90% unsolicited freelance; 10% assigned. E-query. Articles & short stories 500-1,000 wds. Responds in 1 wk. Seasonal 2 mos. Ahead. Prefers accepted ms by e-mail (attached file). **NO PAYMENT.** Seasonal 2 mos. ahead. Regularly uses sidebars. Accepts submissions from children & teens. Prefers KJV. Guidelines on Website. (Ads)

> **Poetry:** Accepts 50/yr. Traditional. Submit max. 2 poems.
> **Fillers:** Accepts 50/yr. Prayers, quizzes, short humor; 500 wds.
> **Columns/Departments:** Variety Column, 700-1,000 wds. Query.
> **Contest:** For contest rules and prizes go to: http://contest.christianmagazine.org.
> **Tips:** Most open to Variety Column, prayers, devotionals.

$CHRISTIAN PARENTING TODAY, 465 Gundersen Dr., Carol Stream IL 60188-2498. (630)260-6200. Fax (630)260-0114. E-mail: cpt@christianparenting.net. Website: www .Christianparenting.net. Christianity Today Intl. Raelynn Eickhoff, ed. coord. To encourage and equip parents to nurture the spiritual and moral development of their children as they walk alongside them in a family journey of faith; practical advice for parents (of kids birth to 14). Bimonthly mag.; 76-96 pgs.; circ. 90,000. Subscription $17.95. 50% unsolicited freelance; 50% assigned. Query only; e-query OK. Pays .15-.25/wd. on acceptance for 1st rts. Articles 450-1,500 wds. (50/yr.); product reviews (games, toys, etc.), 150 wds. Responds in 6-8 wks. Seasonal 6 mos. ahead. Accepts reprints (tell when/where appeared). Accepts requested ms on disk or by e-mail (copied into message). Kill fee 50%. Regularly uses sidebars. Prefers NIV. Guidelines (also on Website); copy $3.95/9x12 SAE. (Ads)

> **Fillers:** Accepts 100/yr. Anecdotes, ideas; 100-400 wds. No payment.
> **Columns/Departments:** Accepts 50/yr. Growing Up, 500 wds.; Ideas That Work (problem-solving ideas), 50 wds.; Life in Our House (funny anecdotes from kids), 50 wds.; Can You Help? (parent-to-parent advice), 50 wds. No payment.

Contest: Sponsors occasional contests.

Tips: "We will now focus solely on the spiritual and moral development of children. While this has always been our distinctive, it will now be our mission."

****#7 Best-selling Magazine in Christian retail stores. This periodical was #14 on the 2004 Top 50 Christian Publishers list (#40 in 2003, #1 in 2002, #4 in 2001, #4 in 2000). 1999 EPA Award of Merit—Most Improved Publication.

$CHRISTIAN PARENTS SECTION—BUSY PARENTS ONLINE, 29 Brook Ave., Hopewell Junction NY 12533. (845)227-2390. E-mail: spirit@busyparentsonline.com. Website: www .busyparentsonline.com. Busy Parents Online. Submit to Section Editor. Quick, useful information for busy parents on the run. Monthly online. Estab. 2003. Pays $10-22 on publication for 1st, one-time, or reprint rts. Articles & juvenile fiction to 1,000 wds.; book reviews 150-250 wds. Guidelines. (Ads) Currently closed to submissions.

CHRISTIAN RADIO WEEKLY: The Information Source for Christian Radio, 5350 N. Academy Blvd., Ste. 200, Colorado Springs CO 80918. (719)536-9000, ext. 123. Fax (719)598-7461. E-mail: veldo@weststarmediagroup.com. Website: www.christianradio weekly.com. Westar Media Group. Jim Veldhuis, mng. ed. For Christian media professionals working in radio and Christian music industry. Weekly mag.; 12 pgs.; circ. 600. Subscription $199/yr. Open to freelance. Query; e-query OK. **NO PAYMENT**. Articles & fiction 800 wds.

THE CHRISTIAN RANCHMAN, 7022-A Lake County Dr., Fort Worth TX 76179. (817)236-0023. Fax (817)236-0024. E-mail: cowboysforchrist@juno.com. Website: www.Cowboys forChrist.net. Interdenominational. Ted Pressley, ed. Monthly tabloid; 20 pgs.; circ. 45,400. No subscription. 85% unsolicited freelance. Complete ms/cover letter. **NO PAYMENT** for all rts. Articles 350-1,000 wds.; book/video reviews (length open). Does not use sidebars.

Poetry: Accepts 40/yr. Free verse. Submit max. 3 poems.

Fillers: Accepts all types.

Tips: "We're most open to true-life Christian stories, Christian testimonies, and Christian or livestock news."

$CHRISTIAN RENEWAL, Box 770, Lewiston NY 14092-0770, or PO Box 777, Jordan Sta., ON L0R 1S0 Canada. (905)562-5719. Fax (905)562-7828. E-mail: JVANDYK@aol.com, or christianrenewal@hotmail.com. Reformed (Conservative). John Van Dyk, mng. ed. Church-related and world news for members of the Reformed community of churches in North America. Biweekly newspaper; 24 pgs.; circ. 4,000. Subscription $36 US/$40 Can. (christianrenewal@hotmail.com). 5% unsolicited freelance; 20% assigned. Query/clips; e-query OK. Pays $25-100 for one-time rts. Articles 500-3,000 wds.; fiction 2,000 wds. (6/yr.); book reviews 50-200 wds. Responds in 9 wks. Seasonal 3 mos. ahead. Accepts simultaneous submissions and reprints. Prefers e-mail submission (copied into message). Uses some sidebars. Prefers NIV, NKJV. No guidelines; copy $2. (Ads: christianrenewal@ hotmail.com)

Tips: "Most open to stories written from a reformed, biblical perspective."

$CHRISTIAN RESEARCH JOURNAL, PO Box 7000, Rancho Santa Margarita, CA 92688-7000. (949)858-6100. Fax (949)858-6111. E-mail: elliot.miller@equip.org. Website: www .equip.org. Christian Research Institute. Elliot Miller, ed-in-chief. Probing today's religious movements, promoting doctrinal discernment and critical thinking, and providing reasons for Christian faith and ethics. Bimonthly journal; 64 pgs.; circ. 22,000. Subscription $30. 5% unsolicited freelance. Query or complete ms/cover letter; fax query OK; e-query and submissions OK. Pays .16/wd. on publication for 1st rts. Articles to 4,200 wds.; book reviews 1,100-2,500 wds. Responds in up to 16 wks. Accepts simultaneous submissions. Kill fee to 50%. Requires requested ms on disk. Guidelines (also by e-mail); copy $6. (Ads)

Columns/Departments: Effective Evangelism, 1,700 wds.; Viewpoint, 875 wds.; News Watch, up to 2,500 wds.

Special Needs: Viewpoint on Christian faith and ethics, 1,700 wds.; news pieces, 800-1,200 wds.

Tips: "Be familiar with the Journal in order to know what we are looking for. We accept freelance articles in all sections (features and departments). E-mail for writer's guidelines." **2003, 1997 EPA Award of Excellence—Organizational. 2000, 1999 EPA Award of Merit—Organizational.

$THE CHRISTIAN RESPONSE, PO Box 125, Staples MN 56479-0125. (218)894-1165. E-mail: hapco2@brainerd.net. Website: www.brainerd.net/~hapco2. HAPCO Industries. Hap Corbett, ed. Exposes anti-Christian bias in America and encourages readers to write letters against such bias. Bimonthly newsletter; 6 pgs. Subscription $13. 10% unsolicited freelance. Complete ms/cover letter; phone/e-query OK. Pays $5-20 on acceptance for one-time rts. Articles 50-500 wds. (4-6/yr.). Responds in 2 wks. Seasonal 6 mos. ahead. Accepts simultaneous submissions and reprints. Does not use sidebars. Guidelines; copy for $1 or 3 stamps. (Ads—classified only)

Fillers: Buys 2-4/yr. Anecdotes, facts, quotes; 150 wds.; $5-20.

Special Needs: Articles on anti-Christian bias; tips on writing effective letters to the editor; pieces on outstanding accomplishments of Christians in the secular media.

Tips: "We are looking for news/articles about anti-Christian bias in the media, and how you, as a writer, responded to such incidents."

$CHRISTIAN RETAILING, 600 Rinehart Rd., Lake Mary FL 32746. (407)333-0600. Fax (407)333-7133. E-mail: butcher@strang.com. Website: www.christianretailing.com. Strang Communications. Andy Butcher, ed. For Christian product industry manufacturers, distributors, retailers. Trade journal published 20X/yr.; circ. 10,000. Subscription $75. 75% assigned. Query/clips; no phone/fax/e-query. Pays .20/wd. on publication. Articles; book reviews. No simultaneous submissions. Accepts requested mss by e-mail (attached file). Kill fee. Uses some sidebars. Prefers NIV. Guidelines on Website. (Ads)

Special Needs: Book reviews should focus on what the book contains and how it might help them in their walk with Christ.

$CHRISTIAN SINGLE, One Lifeway Plaza, Nashville TN 37234. (615)251-2230. Fax (615)251-5008. E-mail: christiansingle@lifeway.com, or christiansingle@bssb.com. Website: www.christiansingle.com. Subscription $20.25. No freelance.

**2003 EPA Award of Merit—General.

CHRISTIAN SINGLE ONLINE, One Lifeway Plaza, Nashville TN 37234-0140. (615)251-2230. Fax (615)251-5008. E-mail: christiansingle@lifeway.com, or christiansingle@bssb.com. Website:www.christiansingle.com.

$CHRISTIAN SOCIAL ACTION, 100 Maryland Ave. NE, Washington DC 20002. (202)488-5632. Fax (202)488-1617. E-mail: editor@umc-gbcs.org. Website: www.umc-gbcs.org. United Methodist. Gretchen Hakola, ed. Information and analysis of critical social issues from a theological, denominational perspective. Bimonthly mag.; 32 pgs.; circ. 42,000. Subscription $15. 10% unsolicited freelance; 15% assigned. Query/clips or complete ms/cover letter; e-query OK. Pays $75-150 on publication for all rts. (negotiable). Articles 1,200 wds. (12/yr.); book reviews 500 wds. ($75). Responds in 4-6 wks. Consider simultaneous submissions and reprints (tell when/where appeared). Requires requested ms on disk or by e-mail. Regularly uses sidebars. Prefers RSV. Guidelines (also by e-mail/Website); copy for 9x12 SAE/2 stamps. (Ads)

Poetry: Benediction poetry; $50-75.

Columns/Departments: Buys 10/yr. Talking (readers write), 1,000 wds.; $50-75.

Special Needs: Lectionary items, responsive readings, prayers, litanies on social justice topics.

Tips: "Send a query letter that states your thesis and how you plan to address it. Stories should help readers understand the justice issues but also provide means for hope and for action by readers (what can they do to bring about justice?). Writers need not be United Methodist, but should do their homework and speak to the United Methodist understanding of issues."

$CHRISTIAN STANDARD, 8121 Hamilton Ave., Cincinnati OH 45231. (513)931-4050. Fax (513)931-0950. E-mail: christianstd@standardpub.com, or standardpub@attmail.com. Website: www.christianstandard.com. Standard Publishing/Christian Churches/Churches of Christ. Mark A. Taylor, ed. Devoted to the restoration of New Testament Christianity, its doctrines, its ordinances, and its fruits. Weekly & online mag.; 16 pgs.; circ. 45,000. Subscription $26.99. 40% unsolicited freelance; 60% assigned. Query; no phone/fax/e-query. Pays $20-160 on publication for one-time, reprint, and electronic rts. Articles 800-1,600 wds. (200/yr.). Responds in 9 wks. Seasonal 8-12 mos. ahead. Accepts reprints (tell when/where appeared). Guidelines & copy on Website. (No ads)
**2004 EPA Award of Merit—Most Improved Publication.

$CHRISTIANITY TODAY, 465 Gundersen Dr., Carol Stream IL 60188-2498. (630)260-6200. Fax (630)260-8428. E-mail: cteditor@christianitytoday.com. Website: www.christianity today.com/ctmag. Christianity Today Inc. David Neff, ed. For evangelical Christian thought leaders who seek to integrate their faith commitment with responsible action. Monthly & online mag.; 65-120 pgs.; circ. 155,000. Subscription $24.95. 80% freelance (mostly assigned). Query only; fax/e-query OK. Pays .20-.30/wd. on publication for 1st rts. Articles 1,000-4,000 wds. (60/yr.); book reviews 800-1,000 wds. (pays per-page rate). Responds in 13 wks. Seasonal 8 mos. ahead. Accepts reprints (tell when/where appeared—payment 25% of regular rate). Kill fee 50%. Does not use sidebars. Prefers NIV. Guidelines; copy for 9x12 SAE/3 stamps. (Ads)
Tips: "Read the magazine."
**#8 Best-selling Magazine in Christian retail stores. This periodical was #50 on the 2000 Top 50 Christian Publishers list (#40 in 1999). 1999 EPA Award of Merit—General. 2004 EPA Award of Merit—Online (for ChristianityToday.Com).

$CHRISTIANWEEK, Box 725, Winnipeg MB R3C 2K3 Canada. Toll-free (800)263-6695. Fax (204)947-5632. E-mail: editor@christianweek.org. Website: www.christianweek.org. Fellowship for Print Witness. Kelly Rempel, mng. ed. Canada's National Christian Newspaper; telling the stories of God and His people in Canada. Biweekly tabloid newspaper (25X/yr.); circ. 5,000. Subscription $34.95. Query; e-query OK. News articles 300-600 wds. Prefers accepted ms by e-mail. Pays $30-100 on publication. Guidelines (also by e-mail/Website). (Ads)
Tips: "Most open to general news, profiles, and features. Writers are encouraged to query first with ideas about people or news events in their own community (Canadian angles, please) or denomination that would be of interest to readers in other denominations or in other areas of the country."
**2004 EPA Award of Excellence—Newspaper.

CHURCH HERALD AND HOLINESS BANNER, 7407 Metcalf (66212), Box 4060, Overland Park KS 66204. (913)432-0331. Fax (913)722-0351. E-mail: HBeditor@juno.com. Website: www.heraldandbanner.com. Church of God (Holiness)/Herald and Banner Press. Mark D. Avery, ed. Offers the conservative holiness movement a positive outlook on their church, doctrine, future ministry, and movement. Monthly mag.; 20 pgs.; circ. 1,600. Subscription $12.50. 25% unsolicited freelance; 50% assigned. Complete ms/cover letter; e-query OK. **NO PAYMENT** for one-time, reprint, or simultaneous rts. Not copyrighted. Articles 750-1,000 wds. (40/yr.). Responds in 4 wks. Seasonal 3 mos. ahead. Accepts simultaneous submissions and reprints (tell when/where appeared). Accepts requested ms on disk or by e-mail (attached or copied into message). Uses some sidebars. Prefers KJV. Accepts submissions from children or teens. Guidelines (also by e-mail); copy for 6x9 SAE/2 stamps. (No ads)

Fillers: Anecdotes, quizzes; 150-400 wds.

Tips: "Most open to short inspirational/devotional articles. Must be concise, well-written, and get one main point across; 200-600 wds."

$CHURCH OF GOD EVANGEL, PO Box 2250, Cleveland TN 37320-2250. (423)476-4512. Fax (423)478-7616. E-mail: wilma_amison@pathwaypress.org. Website: www.pathway press.org. Church of God (Cleveland, TN). Bill George, ed. Denominational. Monthly mag.; 40 pgs.; circ. 49,000. Subscription $15. 10-20% unsolicited freelance; 0% assigned. Complete ms/cover letter; e-query OK. Pays $25-50 on acceptance for 1st, one-time, and simultaneous rts. Articles 300-1,200 wds. (50/yr.). Responds in 6-8 wks. Seasonal 4 mos. ahead. Accepts simultaneous submissions. Uses some sidebars. Prefers KJV, NKJV, NIV. Guidelines (also on Website); free copy. (No ads)

Tips: "We always need short articles (300-500 wds.) with a salvation appeal. Also human interest stories with a spiritual application. Outstanding writing on timely topics will get our attention."

**1999 EPA Award of Merit—Denominational.

$COLUMBIA, PO Box 1670 (06507-0981), 1 Columbus Plaza, New Haven CT 06510-3326. (203)752-4398. Fax (203)752-4109. E-mail: columbia@kofc.org. Website: www.kofc.org. Knights of Columbus (Catholic). Tim S. Hickey, ed. Geared to a general Catholic family audience. Monthly & online mag.; 32 pgs.; circ. 1.6 million. Subscription $6; foreign $8. 25% unsolicited freelance; 75% assigned. Query; fax/e-query OK. Pays $250-600 on acceptance for 1st and electronic rts. Articles 1,500 wds. (12/yr.). Responds in 2 wks. Seasonal 3 mos. ahead. Occasional reprint (tell when/where appeared). Prefers e-mail submission (copied into message). Kill fee. Regularly uses sidebars. Free guidelines (also by e-mail)/copy. (No ads)

Special Needs: Essays on spirituality, personal conversion. Catholic preferred. Query first.

Tips: "We welcome contributions from freelancers in all subject areas. An interesting or different approach to a topic will get the writer at least a second look from an editor. Most open to feature writers who can handle Church issues, social issues from an orthodox Roman Catholic perspective. Must be aggressive, fact-centered writers for these features."

**This periodical was #49 on the 2002 Top 50 Christian Publishers list (#30 in 2001, #18 in 2000).

$COMMON GROUND, Ste. 201, 3091 W. Broadway, Vancouver BC V6K 2G9 Canada. Toll-free (800)365-8897. (604)733-2215. Fax (604)733-4415. E-mail: editor@common ground.ca. Website: www.commonground.ca. Common Ground Publishing. Joseph Roberts, sr. ed. Covers health, environment, spirit, creativity, and wellness. Monthly tabloid; circ. 70,000. 90% unsolicited freelance. Query by e-mail. Pays .10/wd. (Canadian) on publication (although most articles are donated) for one-time or reprint rts. Articles 600-1,500 wds. (to 2,500 wds.), (12/yr.). Responds in 6-13 wks. (returns material only if clearly specified). Seasonal 3 mos. ahead. Accepts simultaneous submissions and reprints. Requires requested ms on disk or by e-mail. Guidelines by e-mail; upcoming needs on Website; copy for $5. Incomplete topical listings. (Ads)

Tips: "Donated articles are given priority over paid articles. Once an article has been published, we will contact you with the final word count, after which you may submit an invoice."

$COMMONWEAL, 475 Riverside Dr., rm. 405, New York NY 10115-0499. (212)662-4200. Fax (212)662-4183. E-mail: editors@commonwealmagazine.org. Website: www.common wealmagazine.org. Commonweal Foundation/Catholic. Patrick Jordan, mng. ed. A review of public affairs, religion, literature, and the arts, for an intellectually engaged readership. Biweekly mag.; 32 pgs.; circ. 20,000. Subscription $47. 20% unsolicited freelance. Query/clips; phone query OK. Pays $50-100 (.03/wd.) on acceptance or publication for all rts. Articles 1,000 or 3,000 wds. (20/yr.). Responds in 4 wks. Seasonal 2 mos. ahead. Prefers requested ms on disk or by e-mail. Kill fee 2%. Uses some sidebars. Guidelines; copy for 9x12 SAE/4 stamps. (Ads)

> **Poetry:** Rosemary Deen, poetry ed. Buys 20/yr. Free verse, traditional; to 75 lines; .50-.75/line (on publication). Submit max. 5 poems. Submit October-May.
>
> **Columns/Departments:** Upfronts (brief, newsy facts and information behind the headlines), 750-1,000 wds.; The Last Word (commentary based on insight from personal experience or reflection), 700 wds.
>
> **Tips:** "Most open to meaningful articles on social, political, religious, and cultural topics; or columns."

($)COMMUNITY SPIRIT, 8835 S. Memorial, Tulsa OK 74133. (918)298-9616. Fax (918)298-9064. E-mail: Tom@communityspiritmagazine.com. Website: www.communityspirit magazine.com. Independent. Tom McCloud, pub. To glorify God by telling stories of individual Christians whose good works testify to God's active presence in Oklahoma. Monthly mag.; circ. 30,000. Subscription free. Accepts freelance. Prefers query. Pays for assignments only. Not in topical listings. No questionnaire returned. (Ads)

$COMPANY: The World of Jesuits and Their Friends, PO Box 60790, Chicago IL 60660. (773)761-9432. Fax (773)761-9443. E-mail: editor@companymagazine.org. Website: www.companymagazine.org. Martin McHugh, ed.; Becky Troha, asst. ed. For people interested in or involved with Jesuit ministries. Quarterly & online mag.; 32 pgs.; circ. 120,000. Free subscription. 40% unsolicited freelance; 60% assigned. Complete ms/cover letter; e-query OK. Pays $250-450 on publication for one-time rts. Articles 1,500 wds. Responds in 6 wks. Seasonal 3 mos. ahead. Accepts simultaneous submissions and reprints (tell when/where appeared). Prefers e-mail submission (attached file). Prefers NRSV, NAB, NJB. Guidelines (also by e-mail); copy for 9x12 SAE/4 stamps. (No ads)

> **Columns/Departments:** Books with a Jesuit connection; Minims and Maxims (short items of interest to Jesuit world), 100-150 wds./photo; Letters to the Editor; Obituaries. No payment (usually).
>
> **Tips:** "We welcome manuscripts as well as outlines of story ideas and indication of willingness to accept freelance assignments (please include résumé and writing samples with the latter two). Articles must be Jesuit-related, and writers usually have some prior association with and/or knowledge of the Jesuits. Looking for feature articles (Jesuit-related), historical, essays, or ministry-related articles."

COMPASS DIRECT, PO Box 27250, Santa Ana CA 92799. (949)862-0314. Fax (949)752-6536. E-mail: info@compassdirect.org. Website: www.compassdirect.org. David Miller, mng. ed. To raise awareness of and encourage prayer for Christians worldwide who are persecuted for their faith. Monthly e-zine; circ. 700. E-mail subscription $25. Open to freelance. Query only. (No ads)

CONNECTING POINT, PO Box 6002, Vero Beach FL 32961. (321)773-2691. Fax (321)773-4921. E-mail: ircgathering@juno.com. Linda G. Howard, ed. For and by the mentally challenged (mentally retarded) community; primarily deals with spiritual and self-advocacy issues. Monthly mag.; 12 pgs.; circ. 1,000. Free. 75% unsolicited freelance. Complete ms; phone/fax/e-query OK. **NO PAYMENT** for 1st rts. Articles (24/yr.) & fiction (12/yr.), 250-300 wds. Responds in 3-6 wks. Seasonal 3 mos. ahead. Accepts simultaneous submissions and reprints. Guidelines (also by e-mail); copy for 9x12 SAE/$1.42 postage (mark "Media Mail").

> **Poetry:** Accepts 4/yr. Any type; 4-30 lines. Submit max. 10 poems.

Fillers: Accepts 12/yr. Cartoons, games, word puzzles; 50-250 wds.

Columns/Departments: Accepts 24/yr. Devotion Page, 250 wds.; Bible Study, 250 wds. Query.

Special Needs: Self-advocacy, integration/normalization, justice system.

Tips: "All manuscripts need to be in primary vocabulary."

$CORNERSTONE CHRISTIAN NEWSPAPER, 1111 Sheri Ln., Carlisle OH 45005. (937)743-2371. Fax (937)743-2329. E-mail: NewsCornerstone@aol.com. Website: www.corner stonenews.com. A Crary Publication. Mark S. Crary, pub./ed.; Vickie Gardner, articles ed. The printed voice for the Tri-State (IN, KY, OH) Christian community. Monthly newspaper; 40 pgs.; circ. 50,000. Subscription $20. 20% unsolicited freelance; 20% assigned. Query; fax/e-query OK. Pays $25-50 on publication for all rts. Articles 1,200 wds. (18/yr.); fiction 1,200 wds.; book/music/video reviews 300 wds. (no payment). Responds in 2 wks. Seasonal 1 mo. ahead. Accepts simultaneous submissions and reprints (tell when/where appeared). Accepts requested ms on disk or by e-mail (copied into message). No kill fee. Some sidebars. Prefers NKJV, NIV. Guidelines (also by e-mail)/theme list; copy for 9x12 SAE/3 stamps. (Ads)

Poetry: Accepts 6-12/yr. Free verse, 50-300 wds. No payment. Submit max. 3 poems.

Fillers: Accepts 24-36/yr. Cartoons, facts, games, ideas, jokes, kid quotes, newsbreaks, party ideas, prayers, short humor, and word puzzles; 50-300 wds. No payment.

Special Needs: Lots of music.

Tips: "We are open and enjoy working with freelancers. The best way a writer can break into our publication is to just get in touch with us and let us see the work they do."

$THE COVENANT COMPANION, 5101 N. Francisco Ave., Chicago IL 60625. (773)784-3000. Fax (773)784-4366. E-mail: communication@covchurch.org. Website: www.covchurch .org. Evangelical Covenant Church. Donald Meyer, ed.; Bob Smietana, features ed. Informs, stimulates thought, and encourages dialog on issues that affect the denomination. Monthly mag.; 40 pgs.; circ. 16,000. Subscription $19.95. 5% unsolicited freelance; 35% assigned. Complete ms/cover letter; fax/e-query OK. Pays $35-100 on publication for one-time or simultaneous rts. Articles 1,200-1,800 wds. (15/yr.). Prefers e-mail submission. Responds in 4 wks. Seasonal 3 mos. ahead. Accepts simultaneous submissions and reprints (tell when/where appeared). Some kill fees. Regularly uses sidebars. Prefers NRSV. Guidelines (also by e-mail/Website); copy for 9x12 SAE/5 stamps or $2.50. (Ads)

CREATION, PO Box 6302, Acacia Ridge QLD 4110 Australia. Phone 07 3273 7650. Fax 07 3273 7672. E-mail: admin@answersingenesis.com. Website: www.answersingenesis.org. Answers in Genesis. Carl Wieland, ed. A family, nature, science magazine focusing on creation/evolution issues. Quarterly mag.; 56 pgs.; circ. 70,000. Subscription $22. 30% unsolicited freelance. Query; phone/fax/e-query OK. **NO PAYMENT** for all rts. Articles to 1,500 wds. (20/yr.). Responds in 2-3 wks. Prefers requested ms on disk or by e-mail (attached file). Regularly uses sidebars. Guidelines (also by e-mail); copy $6.95. (No ads)

Tips: "Get to know the basic content/style of the magazine and emulate."

CREATION CARE, 680 I St. S.W., Washington DC 20024. (202)554-1955. E-mail: jim@ creationcare.org. Website: www.creationcare.org/magazine. Evangelical Environmental Network. Rev. Jim Ball, ed. For Christians who care about reducing pollution and caring for God's creation. Quarterly mag.; 20 pgs.; circ. 5,000. Subscription $25. 90% unsolicited freelance. Query; fax/e-query OK. **NO PAYMENT.** Articles 500-1,200 wds. (20/yr.); book reviews 200 wds. (no payment). Responds in 6-8 wks. Seasonal 4 mos. ahead. Accepts reprints (tell when/where appeared). Prefers accepted ms by e-mail. Regularly uses sidebars. Prefers NRSV, NIV. Guidelines; copy for 10x13 SAE/4 stamps. (Ads)

Tips: "See past issues on our Website."

$CREATION ILLUSTRATED, PO Box 7955, Auburn CA 95604. (530)269-1424. Fax (530)269-

1428. E-mail: creation@foothill.net, or ci@creationillustrated.com. Website: www.creation illustrated.com. Tom Ish, ed./pub. An uplifting, Bible-based Christian nature magazine that glorifies God; for ages 9-99. Quarterly mag.; 68 pgs.; circ. 13,000. Subscription $19.95. 60% unsolicited freelance; 40% assigned. Query or query/clips; fax/e-query OK. Pays $75-125 within 30 days of publication for 1st rts. (holds rts. for 6 mos.). Articles 1,000-2,000 wds. (25/yr.). Responds in 3 wks. Seasonal 6 mos. ahead. Accepts simultaneous submissions and reprints (tell when/where appeared). Prefers e-mail submission (copied into message). Kill fee 25%. Some sidebars. Prefers NKJV. Guidelines/theme list (also on Website); copy $3/9x12 SAE/$1.42 postage (mark "Media Mail"). (Some ads)

Poetry: Buys 8/yr. Light verse, traditional; 10-20 lines; $15. Submit max. 4 poems.

Fillers: Games, 100-200 wds. Pays variable rates.

Tips: "Most open to an experience with nature/creation that brought you closer to God and will inspire the reader to do the same. Include spiritual lessons and supporting scriptures—at least 3 or 4 of each."

$CREATIVE NONFICTION, 5501 Walnut St., Ste. 202, Pittsburgh PA 15232. (412)688-0304. Fax (412)683-9173. E-mail: information@creativenonfiction.org. Website: www.creative nonfiction.org. Lee Gutkind, ed. Semiannual journal; 140 pgs.; circ. 5,000. Subscription $29.95 for 4 issues. 80% unsolicited freelance; 20% assigned. Complete ms/cover letter/SASE for response. Pays $10/published page on publication. Articles (20/yr.). Responds in 3-5 mos. No simultaneous submissions or reprints. No disk or e-mail submissions. Kill fee sometimes. No sidebars. Accepts submissions from teens. Guidelines (also by e-mail/Website); copy for 7x10 SAE/$1.42 postage (mark "Media Mail").

Tips: "All topics have a place with us."

$THE CRESSET: A Review of Arts, Literature & Public Affairs, 1409 Chapel Dr., Valparaiso IN 46383. (219)464-6089. Fax (219)464-5211. E-mail: cresset@valpo.edu. Website: www.valpo.edu/cresset. Valparaiso University/Lutheran. Tom Kennedy, ed. For college educated, professors, pastors, laypeople; serious review essays on religious-cultural affairs. Magazine published 5X/yr.; 60 pgs.; circ. 4,500. Subscription $20. 10% unsolicited freelance; 90% assigned. Query; e-query OK. Pays $100-500 on publication for all rts. Articles 2,000-4,500 wds. (2/yr.); book/music reviews, 1000 wds. ($150). Responds in 15 wks. No simultaneous submissions or reprints. Prefers requested ms by e-mail (attached or copied into message). Regularly uses sidebars. Prefers NRSV. Guidelines on Website; copy $4.

Poetry: John Ruff, poetry ed. Buys 20/yr. Avant-garde, free verse, light verse, traditional; to 40 lines; $15-25. Submit max. 4 poems.

Columns/Departments: Buys 20/yr. Books; Music; Science & Technology; World Views; all 1,000 wds., $100-250. Query.

#CROSSHOME.COM: Your Christian Home on the Net! E-mail: webmaster@cross home.com. Website: www.crosshome.com. Online magazine. Open to unsolicited freelance. Complete ms by e-mail; e-query OK. **NO PAYMENT** for one-time rts. Articles 300-1,000 wds.; devotionals 300-1,000 wds. (prefers 350-650 wds.); book reviews 300-800 wds. Responds in 1-3 wks. (if accepted). Requires accepted ms by e-mail (attached file in Word). Prefers KJV, NKJV, NIV, NASB. Guidelines on Website: www.crosshome.com/guide lines.shtml; copy online. (Ads)

Poetry: Accepts poetry. Free verse, traditional; 30-500 wds.

Columns/Departments: Open to submissions for regular columns, or ideas for new ones. (See guidelines.)

Special Needs: See Website/guidelines for list of channels where your writing might fit.

Tips: "We do archive all writing, but any submission can be deleted by request of the author, by e-mail."

*CROSSWAY MAGAZINE/NEWSLINE NEWSLETTER/AVIATION NEWSPAPER, AAACF c/o

C.B.C. Officeblock Unit 5, Frimley Road, Camberley Surrey GU18 5UJ England. Phone/fax 01276 709474. Airline Aviation & Aerospace Christian Fellowship. C. Cowell, gen. sec. For non-Christians working in aviation. Quarterly publications; 16 pgs. Subscription free. 100% unsolicited freelance. Complete ms/cover letter. **NO PAYMENT.** Not copyrighted. Articles on aviation to 2,000 wds. Accepts simultaneous submissions and reprints. Prefers KJV. Not included in topical listings.

+CRUX, c/o Regent College, 5800 University Blvd., Vancouver BC V6T 2E4 Canada. Toll-free (800)663-8664. (604)224-3245. Fax (604)224-3097. E-mail: crux@regent-college.edu. Website: www.regent-college.edu. Regent College. Donald M. Lewis, ed. Seeks to expound the basic tenets of the Christian faith and to demonstrate that Christian truth is relevant to the whole of life. Quarterly mag.; circ. 1,300. Subscription $14+PST. **PAYS 5 COPIES.** Not in topical listings. (Ads)

    Poetry: Luci Shaw, poetry ed.

$CULTURE WARS, 206 Marquette Ave., South Bend IN 46617-1111. (574)289-9786. Fax (574)289-1461. E-mail: jones@culturewars.com, or letters@culturewars.com. Website: www.culturewars.com. Ultramontagne Associates, Inc. Dr. E. Michael Jones, ed. Issues relating to Catholic families and issues affecting America that affect all people. Monthly (11X) mag.; 48 pgs.; circ. 3,500. Subscription $30. 20% unsolicited freelance. Complete ms/cover letter; fax/e-query OK. Pays $100 & up on publication for all rts. Articles (25/yr.); book reviews $50. Responds in 12-24 wks. Query about reprints. Prefers requested ms on disk. Uses some sidebars. Developing guidelines; copy for 9x12 SAE/5 stamps.

    Poetry: Buys 15/yr. Free verse, light verse, traditional; 10-50 lines; $25. Submit max. 2 poems.

    Fillers: Buys 15/yr. Cartoons, quotes; 25 wds. & up; variable payment.

    Columns/Departments: Buys 25/yr. Commentary, 2,500 wds.; Feature, 5,000 wds.; $100-250.

    Tips: "All fairly open except cartoons. Single-spaced preferred; avoid dot matrix; photocopies must be clear."

$A CUP OF COMFORT BOOK SERIES, 57 Littlefield St., 2nd Floor, Avon MA 02322. Toll-free (800)872-5627. (508)427-7100. Fax (508)427-6790. E-mail: cupofcomfort@adams media.com. Website: www.cupofcomfort.com. Adams Media Corp. Colleen Sell, ed. Each anthology is filled with slice-of-life, positive, inspiring, anecdotal stories, written from the heart, about the extraordinary experiences of ordinary people. Publishes 3-4 anthologies/yr.; 360 pgs. 100% freelance. Query/clips; e-query OK. Pays $100 for each story accepted, plus a $500 Grand Prize for best story in each volume, on publication for worldwide book and archival rts. for 5 yrs. (with exception of books comprised solely of author's original work); on publication. Stories 1,000-2,000 wds. (no fiction or poetry), 150-200/yr.. Responds in 9-12 mos. Accepts simultaneous submissions and reprints (unless published in another anthology). Prefers submissions by disk or e-mail (copied into message). No kill fee. No sidebars. Guidelines (also by e-mail/Website); sample stories posted on Website. (No ads)

    Special Needs: Stories of faith, marriage, love, and personal spirituality. See Website for list of possible future themes and deadlines.

    Tips: "With the exception of designated volumes with themes specific to Christianity (i.e., faith), A Cup of Comfort stories are secular, not religious. We publish creative nonfiction (true) stories and essays." Many of the themes listed in the topical files may refer to inclusion only in one of the upcoming anthologies.

THE DALLAS/FORT WORTH HERITAGE, c/o ROMAR Media Group, PO Box 763127, Dallas TX 75376. Toll-free (888)280-0480. (469)337-3492. Fax (972)293-8566. E-mail: editor@ dfwheritage.com. Website: www.fni.com/heritage. ROMAR Media Group. Contact: Roland

Martin. To help preserve and sustain America's Christian heritage and pass it on to the nation's children. Monthly newspaper; 50-70 pgs.; circ. 45,000. Subscription $25. Open to freelance. E-mail submissions OK. Query. (Ads)

$DECISION/DECISION ONLINE, 1 Billy Graham Pkwy., Charlotte NC 28201-0001. (704)401-2432. Fax (704)401-3009. E-mail: submissions@bgea.org. Website: www.decision mag.org. Billy Graham Evangelistic Assn. Bob Paulson, mng. ed. Evangelism/Christian nurture; all articles must have connection to BGEA or Samaritan's Purse. Monthly & online mag.; 44 pgs.; circ. 1,000,000. Subscription $12. 1% unsolicited freelance; written mostly in-house. Complete ms/cover letter (no queries); no phone/fax/e-query. Pays $55-500 on publication for all, 1st, or electronic rts. Articles 400-1,000 wds. (12-15/yr.). Response time varies. Seasonal 3-5 mos. ahead. Accepts ms by e-mail (attached file). Kill fee. Uses some sidebars. Prefers NIV. Guidelines (also by e-mail/Website); copy for 10x13 SAE/3 stamps. (No ads)

> **Columns/Departments:** Buys 12/yr. Finding Jesus (people who have become Christians through Billy Graham ministries); 400-600 wds.; $85.
>
> **Special Needs:** Personal experience articles telling how a Billy Graham ministry (or Samaritan's Purse) helped you live out your faith.
>
> **Tips:** "Nearly all of our articles have some connection with a ministry of the Billy Graham Evangelistic Assn. or Samaritan's Purse—through the author's participation in the ministry or through the author's being touched by the ministry."
>
> **2003, 2000 EPA Award of Merit—Organizational. 2001 EPA Award of Merit—Most Improved Publication.

DESERT CALL: Christianity for a Vital Culture, Box 219, Crestone CO 81131. (719)256-4778. Fax (719)256-4719. Website: www.spirituallifeinstitute.org. Spiritual Life Institute/Catholic. Submit to The Editor. Practical spirituality and contemplative prayer; interreligious dialog and culture. Quarterly mag.; 32 pgs.; circ. 2,000. Subscription $16. 15% unsolicited freelance; 10% assigned. Complete ms/cover letter; no phone/fax/e-query. **PAYS 3 COPIES** for 1st rts. Articles 1,000-2,500 wds. (4/yr.). Responds in 15 wks. Seasonal 8 mos. ahead. Accepts reprints (tell when/where appeared). No disk or e-mail submissions. Uses some sidebars. No guidelines; copy $2.50/10x13 SAE. (No ads)

> **Poetry:** Accepts 3/yr. Free verse, haiku, traditional; to 25 lines. Submit max. 2 poems.
>
> **Fillers:** Accepts 3/yr. Anecdotes, facts, prayers, prose, quotes; 50-250 wds.
>
> **Special Needs:** Interreligious dialog, arts, and culture.
>
> **Tips:** "Avoid personal reflection/anecdotal pieces. Prefer articles that are informative, well-researched, accessible to a busy, educated readership of interdenominational background. Avoid moralisms and preachy tone."

$DIRECTION, PO Box 436987, Chicago IL 60643. Toll-free (800)860-8642. Fax (708)868-7105. E-mail cywilson@urbanministries.com. Website: www.urbanministries.com. Urban Ministries, Inc. Cheryl Wilson editorial asst. An adult-level Sunday School quarterly publication consisting of a student book and a teacher's guide. Quarterly mag; 64 pgs.; $16.45 (student) and $24.95 (teacher). 0% Unsolicited freelance; 100% assigned. Query or query/clips; phone/fax/e-query OK. Accepts full manuscripts by e-mail. Pays to $150 ($200 for lessons) on acceptance, for all rts. Articles 1,500 wds. Responds in 4 wks. Seasonal 12 mos. ahead. No simultaneous submissions or reprints. Requires accepted ms on disk or by e-mail (attached or copied into message). No kill fee. No sidebars. Prefers KJV. Guidelines by e-mail; copy for SASE. (No ads)

> **Tips:** "Send query with a writing sample, or attend our annual conference on the first weekend in November each year. Manuscripts are evaluated at the conference."

$DISASTER NEWS NETWORK, 9195 C Red Branch Rd., Columbia MD 21045. Toll-free (888)203-9119. (410)884-7350. Fax (410)884-7353. E-mail: info@villagelife.org. Website: www.disasternews.net. Village Life Company. Submit to The Editor. Online; an interactive daily news site on the World Wide Web. Query; phone/fax/e-query (preferred) OK. Pays $85-100 after publication for all rts. Articles 1,000 wds. Requires accepted ms by e-mail. Guidelines on the Website. Not in topical listings.

Tips: "Most open to 'people stories' related to faith-based disaster response and/or mitigation. Also, faith-based response to incidents of public violence. Authors are expected to have an e-mail submission address."

THE DISCERNING POET: Celebrating the Truth, Ethics, and Beauty of the Christian Worldview, W. 4031 Musser Heights Ln., Phillips WI 54555. (715)339-6734. E-mail: bog woman@pctcnet.net. Margaret L. Been, ed. A poetry magazine. Estab. 2003. Quarterly journal; circ. 80. Subscription $14. 75% unsolicited freelance; 25% assigned. Complete ms/cover letter. **PAYS IN COPIES** for 1st, one-time, reprint, or simultaneous rts. Articles 750 wds. (4-8/yr.); book reviews 750 wds. Responds in 2-4 wks. Seasonal 8 mos. ahead. Accepts simultaneous submissions and reprints (tell when/where appeared). Accepts e-mail submissions (copied into message); include all contact information. No sidebars. Prefers KJV. Guidelines (also on Website); copy $4/10x13 SAE.

Poetry: Accepts 120-150/yr. Avant-garde, free verse, haiku, traditional; 3-40 lines. Submit max. 7 poems. Spiritual growth, nature themes, quality of life, and honest expressions of the human condition. 95% of publication is poetry.

Columns/Departments: Accepts 4-8/yr. A Backwards Glance (upbeat memories of past eras), to 750 wds.

Special Needs: Features, essays, and reviews: reviews of classic writers and books, features related to the craft of poetry and the writer's life, and Christian apologetics and "think" pieces. No standard devotionals; no greeting-card verse. Show with figurative language, sensory appeal, and imagery; poems should not be preachy.

Tips: "All areas are open to freelancers. Read centuries of great poetry, and discover what poetry really is. Poems rich in sensory appeal, imagery, figurative language will be considered over marching band rhymes conveying a generic pop sentiment. Remember that poetry is art as well as craft; show—don't preach. Value excellent language and vocabulary."

DISCIPLE'S JOURNAL, 10 Fiorenza Dr., PO Box 100, Wilmington MA 01887-4421. Toll-free (800)696-2344. (978)657-7373. Fax (978)657-5411. E-mail: dddj@disciplesdirectory .com, or info@disciplesdirectory.com. Website: www.disciplesdirectory.com. Kenneth A. Dorothy, ed. To strengthen, edify, inform, and unite the body of Christ. 9X/yr. & online newspaper; 24-32 pgs.; circ. 8,000. Subscription $14.95. 5% unsolicited freelance. Query; fax/e-query OK. **NO PAYMENT** for one-time rts. Articles 400 wds. (24/yr.); book/music/video reviews 200 wds. Responds in 2 wks. Seasonal 2 mos. ahead. Accepts simultaneous submissions and reprints (tell when/where appeared). Prefers requested ms on disk or by e-mail (attached file). Uses some sidebars. Prefers NIV. Guidelines/theme list (also by e-mail); copy for 9x12 SAE/$1.42 postage (mark "Media Mail"). (Ads)

Fillers: Accepts 12/yr. All types; 100-400 wds.

Columns/Departments: Financial; Singles; Men; Women; Business; Parenting; 400 wds.

Tips: "Most open to men's, women's, or singles' issues; missions; or homeschooling. Send sample of articles for review."

$DISCIPLESHIP JOURNAL, Box 35004, Colorado Springs CO 80935. (719)548-9222. Fax (719)598-7128. E-mail: djwriters@navpress.com. Website: www.discipleshipjournal.com. The Navigators. Sue Kline, ed.; Connie Willems, mng. ed. For motivated, maturing Christians desiring to grow spiritually and to help others grow; biblical and practical. Bimonthly mag.; 82+ pgs.; circ. 130,000. Subscription $23.97. 65% unsolicited freelance; 35% assigned. Query/clips; fax/e-query OK. Pays .25/wd.(.05/wd. for reprints) on acceptance for 1st and electronic rts. Articles 1,500-2,500 wds. (60/yr.). Responds in 6-8 wks. Accepts reprints; simultaneous submissions discouraged. Prefers requested ms by e-mail. Kill fee 50%. Regularly uses sidebars. Prefers NIV. Guidelines (also by e-mail/Website); copy for 9x12 SAE/$1.42 postage (mark "Media Mail"). (Ads)

> **Columns/Departments:** Buys 100+/yr. DJ Plus (ministry how-to on missions, evangelism, serving, discipling, teaching, and small groups), to 500 wds., DJ Plus editor: Connie Willems (connie.willems@navpress.com). Query or complete manuscript. Pays .25/wd.
>
> **Special Needs:** Biblical exposition of a passage or topic; maturing in Christian character; applying scripture to current topics; character of God; spiritual disciplines.
>
> **Tips:** "Most open to nontheme articles and DJ Plus. Our articles focus on biblical passages or topics. Articles should derive main principles from a thorough study of Scripture, should illustrate each principle, should show how to put each principle into practice, and should demonstrate with personal illustrations and vulnerability that the author has wrestled with the subject in his or her life."
>
> **#4 Best-selling Magazine in Christian retail stores. This periodical was #3 on the 2004 Top 50 Christian Publishers list (#3 in 2003, #5 in 2002, #2 in 2001, #1 in 2000). 2004 & 2000 EPA Award of Excellence—General; 1998 EPA Award of Merit—General.

$+DISCIPLESWORLD, PO Box 11469, Indianapolis IN 46201-0469. (317)375-8846. Fax (317)375-8849. E-mail: semmons@disciplesworld.com. Website: www.disciplesworld .com. Christian Church (Disciples of Christ). Sherri Wood Emmons, mng. ed. The journal of news, opinion, and mission for this denomination in North America. Monthly mag.; 48 pgs.; circ. 14,000. Subscription $25. 30% unsolicited freelance; 70% assigned. Complete ms/cover letter; e-query OK. Pays .15/wd. on publication for 1st rts. Articles 600-1,200 wds. (30/yr.); fiction 500-1,000 wds. (5/yr.); reviews 600 wds. (no payment). Responds in 6 wks. Seasonal 6 mos. ahead. Accepts simultaneous submissions; no reprints. Requires submissions by disk or e-mail (attached file) No kill fee. Sometimes uses sidebars. Prefers NRSV. Guidelines/theme list on Website; copy for 9x12 SAE/3 stamps. (Ads)

> **Poetry:** Buys 3-4/yr. Free verse, light verse; 12-30 lines. Pays $10-50 . Submit max. 2 poems.
>
> **Fillers:** Buys several/yr. Anecdotes, cartoons, kid quotes, quotes, short humor, 20-200 wds. Pays $10-50.
>
> **Columns/Departments:** Buys 10/yr. Speak Out (opinion on an issue), 600 wds.; Disciples Go (travel to places relevant to Disciples), 600 wds., plus photos; $100. Quotable Quotes, 200 wds, (no pay).
>
> **Tips:** "Looking for humorous short-shorts (200 wds.). Our readers are mostly college-educated, active in their churches, proud of their Disciples heritage, and all over the board politically and theologically. We like things with a Disciples connection."

DISCOVERY: Central Florida's Online Christian Family Newspaper, 1188 Lake View Dr., Altamonte Springs FL 32714. (407)682-9494. Fax (407)682-7005. E-mail: jadams@ wtln.com. Website: www.wtln.com. Radio Stations WTLN & WHIM. John Adams, ed. For the Christian community in Central Florida. Quarterly print and online newspaper. 20% unsolicited freelance. Complete ms/cover letter; fax/e-query OK. **NO PAYMENT**. Not copyrighted. News-driven articles under 500 wds. Seasonal 1+ mo. ahead. Accepts reprints. Regularly uses sidebars. No disk; e-mail submission OK. No guidelines; free copy. (Ads)

> **Fillers:** Accepts several/yr. Cartoons and word puzzles.
>
> **Columns/Departments:** Local/National News, Local Ministries, Broadcaster's Information, Sports, Christian Living, Seasonal-themed features.
>
> **Tips:** "We may submit articles to our other publications in Knoxville and Philadelphia."

+DIVINE ASCENT: A Journal of Orthodox Faith, PO Box 563, Pt. Reyes Station CA 94956. (415)663-1705. Fax (415)663-0359. E-mail: office@monasteryofstjohn.org. Website: www.divineascent.org. Monastery of St. John of Shanghai & San Francisco/Catholic. Fr.

Jonah Paffhausen, Abbot & ed-in-chief. Focuses on contemporary Orthodox spirituality as seen in the lives and writings of saints and holy men and women of our own time. Annual Jour.; 150 pgs. Subscription $25/2 yrs. 20% unsolicited freelance; 65% assigned. Query. **NO PAYMENT** for all rts. Articles (6/yr.); book reviews 500 wds. Responds 4-8 in wks. No reprints. Prefers disk or e-mail submissions (attached file). No sidebars. Prefers RSV. KJV, NKJV. Guidelines by e-mail. (Ads, from Orthodox Christian businesses)

Tips: "Nothing Protestant."

$THE DOOR, 5634 Columbia Ave., Dallas TX 75214. (214)827-2625. Fax (254)752-4915. E-mail (submissions): dooreditor@earthlink.net. Website: www.thedoormagazine.com. Trinity Foundation. Robert Darden, ed. Satire of evangelical church, plus issue-oriented interviews. Bimonthly mag.; 50 pgs.; circ. 14,000. Subscription $29.95. 90% unsolicited freelance; 10% assigned. Complete ms; e-query OK. Pays $60-200 on publication for 1st rts. Articles to 1,500 wds., prefers 750-1,000 wds. (30/yr.). Responds in 8 wks. Accepts simultaneous submissions and reprints (if from noncompeting markets). Kill fee $40-50. Regularly uses sidebars. Guidelines (also by e-mail); copy $7. (Ads)

Tips: "We look for biting satire/humor—*National Lampoon* not *Reader's Digest.* You must understand our satirical slant. Read more than one issue to understand our 'wavelength.' We desperately need genuinely funny articles with a smart, satiric bent. Write funny stuff about religion. Interview interesting people with something to say about faith and/or religion."

$DOVETAIL: A Journal by and for Jewish/Christian Families, 775 Simon Greenwell Ln., Boston KY 40107. (502)549-5499. Fax (549)540-3543. E-mail: di-ifr@bardstown.com. Website: www.dovetailinstitute.org. Dovetail Institute for Interfaith Family Resources. Debi Tenner, ed.; send mss to: 45 Lilac Ave., Hamden CT 06517, or DebiT4RLS@aol.com. Book review ed.: Carol Weiss Rubel, 310 Tulip Cir., Clarks Summit PA 18411-0213, or Carol W44@aol.com. Offers balanced, nonjudgmental articles for interfaith families and the professionals who serve them. Bimonthly mag.; 12-16 pgs.; circ. 1,000. Subscription/membership $59.95. 80% unsolicited freelance; 20% assigned. Query or complete ms; phone/fax/e-query OK. Pays $25 on publication for all rts. Articles 800-1,000 wds. (18-20/yr.); book reviews 500 wds., ($15). Responds in 2-6 wks. Seasonal 4 mos. ahead. Accepts simultaneous submissions and reprints (tell when/where appeared). Prefers requested ms on disk or by e-mail (copied into message). Uses some sidebars. Prefers RSV. Guidelines/theme list (also by e-mail); copy for 9x12 SAE/3 stamps. (Ads)

Poetry: Buys 1-2/yr. Traditional; $15. Submit max. 4 poems.

Columns/Departments: Buys 3-6/yr. Food & Family (Jewish & Christian), 500 wds.; Parent's Page and Reviews; $15. Complete ms.

Special Needs: We are expanding our scope to include other types of interfaith marriages, especially those involving a Muslim partner.

Tips: "Demonstrate real, concrete, practical knowledge of the challenges facing Jewish and Christian partners in a marriage. Do not send pieces of Christian interest only. No proselytizing."

$+DRAGONS, KNIGHTS, AND ANGELS: The Magazine of Christian Fantasy and Science Fiction, 5461 W. 4605 S., West Valley City UT 84120. E-mail: dkamagazine@quixnet.net. Website: www.dkamagazine.net. Rebecca Shelley, ed. Quarterly. Subscription $19.99. Pays $5 for short stories to 4,000 wds. This publication is in transition, so check Website for latest information.

$+DRAMA MINISTRY, 1881 General George Patton Dr., Ste. 203, Franklin TN 37067. (866)859-7622. Fax (615)373-8502. E-mail: service@dramaministry.com. Website: www.dramaministry.com. Belden Street. Kimberlee Stone, ed. Mag. published 8X/yr. & online; page count varies. 50% unsolicited freelance; 50% assigned. Complete ms/cover letter for scripts; query for articles; e-query OK. Pays $100-150 for scripts on publication for one-time rts. Articles 500-700 wds. (10/yr.); scripts 2-10 minutes (80/yr.). Responds in 6-8 wks. Seasonal 6 mos. ahead. Accepts simultaneous submissions & reprints (tell when/where appeared). Requires submissions by e-mail (attached file). No kill fee. No sidebars. Accepts submissions from teens. Any Bible version. Guidelines/theme list on Website. (No ads)

> **Tips:** "If your script is well-written and you have a true understanding of what works within the church drama ministry, then you will break into our publication easily. Please adhere to and read writer's guidelines thoroughly. We do not respond unless we choose to publish your script."

$DREAMS & VISIONS: Spiritual Fiction, 35 Peter St. S., Orillia ON L3V 5A8 Canada. Phone/fax (705)329-1770. E-mail: skysong@bconnex.net. Website: www.bconnex.net/~skysong. Skysong Press. Steve Stanton, ed. An international showcase for short literary fiction written from a Christian perspective. Semiannual journal; 56 pgs.; circ. 200. Subscription $12. 100% unsolicited freelance. Complete ms/cover letter; fax/e-query OK. Pays .01/wd. on publication for 1st rts. and one nonexclusive reprint. Fiction 2,000-6,000 wds. (10/yr.). Responds in 4-6 wks. No seasonal. Accepts simultaneous submissions and reprints (tell when/where appeared). Guidelines (also on Website); copy $4.95 (4 back issues to writers $10).

DREAMSEEKER MAGAZINE, 126 Klingerman Rd., Telford PA 18969. (215)723-9125. E-mail: DSM@CascadiaPublishingHouse.com. Website: www.CascadiaPublishingHouse.com. Cascadia Publishing House. Submit to The Editor. For readers committed to exploring from the heart, with passion, depth, and flair, their own visions and issues of the day. Magazine. Accepts freelance. Not in topical listings. No questionnaire returned.

$+ECLECTIC HOMESCHOOL ONLINE, PO Box 50188, Sparks NV 89435-0188. (775)428-6454. E-mail: eclectic@eho.org. Website: www.eho.org. Eclectic Homeschool Assn. Beverly S. Krueger, sr. ed. Reaches a diverse homeschool audience interested in new ideas, techniques, or resources that will help them creatively tailor their homeschooling to their children's needs. Biweekly online mag.; circ. 50,000. Subscription $19.95. 25% unsolicited freelance; 25% assigned. Complete ms/cover letter; e-query OK. Pays $35-100 on acceptance for 1st, reprint, electronic, and archival rts. Articles. Responds in 6-8 wks. Seasonal 3 mos. ahead. No simultaneous submissions or reprints. Accepts disk or e-mail submissions (copied into message). No kill fee. Some sidebars. Accepts submissions from teens. Prefers NKJV. Guidelines/copy on Website. (Ads)

> **Columns/Departments:** Buys 25/yr. Homeschooling Methods (for arts, language arts, social sciences, critical thinking, computers, etc.); Making Math Marvelous (math how-to or resources); History (how-to or resources); Science (how-to or resources); all 350 wds. $35.
> **Tips:** "We are looking for short (350 word) pieces for all our departments. Articles must be encouraging, practical, and provide useful content for our readers."

$EFCA TODAY, (formerly Beacon) 901 E. 78th St., Minneapolis MN 55420. Toll-free (877)293-5653. (952)853-8438. E-mail: Today@EFCA.org. Website: www.efca.org/today. Evangelical Free Church of America/Journey Communications. Linda Giese, ed. Denominational. Quarterly mag.; 32 pgs.; circ. 28,000. Subscription $10. 5% unsolicited freelance; 95% assigned. Query or complete ms/cover letter; fax/e-query OK. Pays .23/wd. on acceptance for 1st and subsidiary (free use on EFCA Website or church bulletins) rts. Articles 300-1,200 wds. (6/yr.). Responds in 6 wks. Seasonal 6 mos. ahead. Accepts simultaneous submissions; rarely uses reprints (tell when/where appeared). Prefers e-mail (attached file) or hard copy. Kill fee 50%. Regularly uses sidebars. Guidelines (also by e-mail); copy $1/10x13 SAE/$1.42 postage (mark "Media Mail"). (Ads)

> **Columns/Departments:** Buys 6/yr. Home Base (topics affecting women's, men's, and

youth ministries, as well as families); Cover-theme Section (variety of topics applicable to church leadership), 550-1,200 wds., .23/wd.

Special Needs: Stories of EFCA churches in action.

Tips: "Have a unique story about a Free Church in action. The vast majority of articles are geared to sharing the Free Church at work."

**2003 Award of Excellence—Denominational. 2001, 2000 & 1999 EPA Award of Merit— Denominational. This periodical was #44 on the 2004 Top 50 Christian Publishers list.

$+EN CONFIANZA, 8675 Explorer Dr., Colorado Springs CO 80920. (719)548-4660. Fax (719)531-3383. E-mail: abeljl@fotf.org. Website: www.enfoqualafamilia.com. Focus on the Family. Graciela Lelli, ed. To provide family-friendly material to our domestic Spanish constituents and inform the Hispanic community of culturally relevant issues that affect their families. Bimonthly mag.; circ. 30,000. Subscription free. Open to unsolicited freelance. Complete ms/cover letter. Articles. Incomplete topical listings. (No ads)

$EPISCOPAL LIFE, 815—2nd Ave., New York NY 10017. Toll-free (800)334-7626, ext. 6009. (212)716-6009. Fax (212)949-8059. E-mail: jhames@episcopalchurch.org. Website: www.episcopal-life.org. Episcopal Church. Jerrold F. Hames, ed. Denominational. Monthly newspaper; 32 pgs.; circ. 280,000. Subscription $16.95. 0% unsolicited freelance; 10% assigned. Query/clips or complete ms/cover letter; phone query on breaking news only; e-query OK. Pays $50-300 on publication for 1st, one-time, or simultaneous rts. Articles 250-1,200 wds. (12/yr.); assigned book reviews 400 wds. ($35). Responds in 5 wks. Seasonal 4 mos. ahead. Accepts simultaneous submissions and reprints. Accepts e-mail submission. Kill fee 50%. Guidelines (by e-mail); free copy. (Ads)

> **Columns/Departments:** Nan Cobbey, column ed. (ncobbey@dfms.org). Buys 36/yr. Commentary on political/religious topics; 300-600 wds.; $35-75. Query.

> **Tips:** "All articles must have Episcopal Church slant or specifics. We need topical/issues, not devotional stuff. Most open to feature stories about Episcopalians—clergy, lay, churches, involvement in local efforts, movements, ministries."

$EUREKA STREET: A Magazine of Public Affairs, the Arts and Theology, PO Box 553, Richmond VIC 3121, Australia. Phone +613 9427 7311. Fax +613 9428 4450. E-mail: eureka@jespub.jesuit.org.au. Website: www.eurekastreet.com.au/index.html. Jesuit Publications. Marcelle Mogg, ed. Monthly mag. (10X); circ. 13,000. Subscription $70. Accepts freelance. Complete ms by mail or e-mail (attached file). Pays $110 US/1,000 wds. for one-time rts. No reprints. Guidelines online (www.eurekastreet.com.au/ab_write.html). Incomplete topical listings.

$EVANGEL, Box 535002, Indianapolis IN 46253-5002. (317)244-3660. E-mail: evangeleditor@ fmcna.org. Free Methodist/Light and Life Communications. Julie Innes, ed. For young to middle-aged adults; encourages spiritual growth. Weekly take-home paper; 8 pgs.; circ. 16,000. Subscription $9. 100% unsolicited freelance. Complete ms/cover letter; no e-query. Pays .04/wd. ($10 min.) on publication for one-time rts. Articles to 1,200 wds. (100/yr.); fiction to 1,200 wds. (100/yr.). Responds in 6-8 wks. Seasonal 12-15 mos. ahead. Accepts simultaneous submissions and reprints (tell when/where appeared). Accepts requested ms on disk. Some sidebars. Prefers NIV. Guidelines (also by e-mail); copy for #10 SAE/1 stamp. (No ads)

> **Poetry:** Buys 40+/yr. Free verse, light verse, traditional; 3-16 lines; $10. Submit max. 5 poems. Rhyming poetry not usually taken too seriously.

> **Fillers:** Buys 20/yr. Cartoons, word puzzles; to 100 wds; $10.

> **Tips:** "Bring fresh insight to a topic like prayer, faith, etc. Be sure to submit material appropriate for the market and audience. Don't ramble; stick to one thesis or theme. A returned manuscript isn't always because of poor writing. Don't give up—keep writing and submitting."

THE EVANGEL, PO Box 348, Marlow OK 73055. (580)658-5631. Fax (817)277-8098. E-mail: umi@umi.org. Website: www.umi.org, or www.watchman.org. Utah Missions, Inc. Dennis A. Wright, dir. A Christian apologetics ministry that exposes major counterfeit religions with a special emphasis upon Mormonism, and explains their doctrine, history, and current events in the light of biblical Christianity. Monthly mag.; 12 pgs.; circ. 3,500. Subscription $15, 6-month subscription free to new subscribers. Little freelance. Complete ms; phone/fax/e-query OK. **NO PAYMENT.** Articles 1,000-1,500 wds. Copy. (Ads)

THE EVANGELICAL ADVOCATE, Box 30, 1426 Lancaster Pike, Circleville OH 43113. (740)474-8856. Fax (740)477-7766. E-mail: directordoc@cccuhq.org. Website: www.cccuhq.org. Churches of Christ in Christian Union. Ralph Hux, dir. of communications. Provides news, information, and features which emphasize current events and worldview, appealing to the needs of our constituency, emphasizing fundamental evangelical holiness. Monthly mag.; 24-28 pgs.; circ. 4,000. Subscription $12. 15% unsolicited freelance; 15% assigned. Complete ms/cover letter; fax/e-query OK. **NO PAYMENT.** Articles 500-1,000 wds. (15-20/yr.). Seasonal 2-3 mos. ahead. Accepts simultaneous submissions and reprints (tell when/where appeared). Prefers e-mail submissions (attached file). Regularly uses sidebars. Prefers KJV, NIV. Theme list (no guidelines); copy for 9x12 SAE. (No ads)

    Tips: "Best way to break in is to submit material for review."

$FAITH & FAMILY: The Magazine of Catholic Living, 432 Washington Ave., North Haven CT 06473. (203)230-3800. Fax (203)230-3838. E-mail: editor@faithandfamilymag.com. Website: www.faithandfamilymag.com. Catholic/Circle Media, Inc. Tom & April Hoopes, eds.; submit to Robyn Lee, ed. asst. Features writing for Catholics and/or Christian families of all ages. Quarterly magazine; 100 pgs.; circ. 32,000. Subscription $14.95. 10% unsolicited freelance; 90% assigned. Query/clips; e-query OK. Pays .33/wd. on acceptance for 1st rts. Articles 700-3,000 wds. (35/yr.); brief reviews. Responds in 6-8 wks. Seasonal 6-9 mos. ahead. No reprints. Prefers e-mail submission (attached file). Kill fee. Regularly uses sidebars. Accepts illustrations from children. Prefers NAB. Guidelines (also on Website); copy $3/10x13 SAE. (Ads)

    Fillers: Buys 10/yr. Anecdotes, cartoons, prose (brief).

    Columns/Departments: Buys 75/yr. The Home Front (news); The Insider; Flair; The Season; Life Lessons; Faith & Folklore; Celebrations; Entertainment; The Where & How Guide; Spiritual Directions; and Back Porch; 600-1,200 wds. Query.

    Tips: "Most open to well-written feature articles employing good quotations, anecdotes, and transitions about an interesting aspect of family life; departments; news items. To break in, submit ideas for The Home Front." Only wants Catholic theme-related material.

    **This periodical was #5 on the 2004 Top 50 Christian Publishers list.

$FAITH & FRIENDS, 2 Overlea Blvd., Toronto ON M4H 1P4 Canada. (416)422-6226. Fax (416)422-6120. E-mail: faithandfriends@can.salvationarmy.org. Website: www.salvation army.ca. The Salvation Army. Sharon Stinka, ed-in-chief; Geoff Moulton, ed. Monthly mag.; 16 pgs.; circ. 60,000. Subscription $16.50 Can. 90% assigned. Query/clips; e-query OK. Pays up to $200 Can. on publication for one-time rts. Articles 500-1,000 wds. Responds in 2 wks. Seasonal 6 mos. ahead. Accepts simultaneous submissions and reprints (tell when/where appeared). Prefers accepted ms by e-mail (attached file). Uses some sidebars. Prefers NIV. Guidelines (also on Website); free copy. (No ads)

    Fillers: Buys 10/yr. Cartoons, games, jokes, quizzes, quotes, word puzzles, recipes; 50 wds.; $25.

    Columns/Departments: God in My Life (how Christians in the workplace find faith relevant), 600 wds.; Words to Live By (simple Bible studies/discussions of faith), 600 wds.; Faith Builders; Someone Cares.

$FAITH TODAY: Seeking to Inform, Equip and Inspire Christians Across Canada,

M.I.P. Box 3745, Markham ON L3R 0Y4 Canada. (905)479-5885. Fax (905)479-4742. E-mail: ft@efc-canada.com. Website: www.faithtoday.ca. Evangelical Fellowship of Canada. Gail Reid, mng. ed.; Bill Fledderus, sr. ed. A general-interest publication for Christians in Canada; almost exclusively Canadian content. Bimonthly mag.; 56-80 pgs.; circ. 18,000. Subscription $22.05 Can. 20% unsolicited freelance; 80% assigned. Query only; fax/e-query preferred. Pays $100-500 (.15-.30 Can./wd.) within 6 wks. of acceptance for 1st & electronic rts.; reprints .15/wd. Features 800-1,700 wds. (75/yr.); cover stories 2,000 wds.; essays 650-1,200 wds.; profiles 900 wds; reviews 300 wds. Responds in 6 wks. Prefers e-mail submission. Kill fee 30-50%. Regularly uses sidebars. Any Bible version. Guidelines (also by e-mail/Website); copy for 9x12 SAE/$2.05 in Canadian funds. (Ads)

Columns/Departments: Buys 6/yr. Kingdom Matters (short, colorful Canadian news), 250 wds.; Guest Meditation (assigned only), 650 wds.; $50 Can.

Special Needs: "Canadian news. All topics to be approached in a journalistic—not personal viewpoint—style."

Tips: "Most open to short, colorful items, statistics, stories, profiles for Kingdom Matters department. Must be Canadian." All unsolicited manuscripts will not be returned.

$THE FAMILY DIGEST, PO Box 40137, Fort Wayne IN 46804. Catholic. Corine B. Erlandson, manuscript ed.; Kelley Renz, issue ed. Dedicated to the joy and fulfillment of Catholic family life and its relationship to the Catholic parish. Bimonthly booklet; 48 pgs.; circ. 150,000. Distributed through parishes. 90% unsolicited freelance. Complete ms/cover letter; no phone/fax/e-query. Pays $40-60, 4-8 wks. after acceptance, for 1st rts. Articles 700-1,200 wds. (60/yr.). Responds in 4-8 wks. Seasonal 7 mos. ahead. Occasionally buys reprints (tell when/where appeared). No disk. No sidebars. Prefers NAB. Guidelines & copy for 6x9 SAE/2 stamps. (No ads)

Fillers: Buys 15/yr. Anecdotes drawn from experience, cartoons, prayers, 20-100 wds.; $25.

Tips: "Prospective freelance writers should be familiar with the types of articles we accept and publish. We are looking for upbeat articles which affirm the simple ways in which the Catholic faith is expressed in daily life. Articles on family life, parish life, seasonal articles, how-to pieces, inspirational, prayer, spiritual life, and Church traditions will be gladly reviewed for possible acceptance and publication."

FARO DE LUZ, 404 N.W. 14th Ave., Gainesville FL 32601-4215. (352)378-0078. Fax (352)378-0042. E-mail: CCLfarodeluz@cs.com. Website under construction. Pastor Rojas, ed. Monthly newspaper; circ. 9,500. For the whole family; promoting the unity of the family, the church, and the body of Christ in general. Subscription $17. Open to freelance. Complete ms. Not in topical listings. (Ads)

$FELLOWSHIP FOCUS, 3339 N. 109th Plaza, Omaha NE 68164-2908. (402)965-3860. Fax (402)965-3871. E-mail: FellowshipFocus@febcministries.org. Website: www.febcministries.org. Fellowship of Evangelical Bible Churches. Sharon Berg, ed. To inform, educate, and edify members of affiliate churches. Bimonthly mag.; 20 pgs.; circ. 2,100. Subscription $10. 5% freelance. Query or complete ms/cover letter; fax/e-query OK. Pays $15-50 on publication for all rts. Articles (2/yr.) & fiction (1/yr.); 850-1,200 wds. Responds ASAP. Seasonal 3 mos. ahead. Accepts simultaneous submissions and reprints (tell when/where appeared). Accepts requested ms on disk or by e-mail (copied into message). Uses some sidebars. Prefers NIV. Guidelines (also by e-mail); copy for 9x12 SAE/3 stamps. (No ads)

+FELLOWSHIP MAGAZINE, Box 237, Barrie ON L4M 4T3 Canada. Toll-free (800)678-2607. Fax (705)737-1086. E-mail: jhodgins@sympatico.ca, or felmag@csolv.net. Website: www.fellowshipmagazine.org. Fellowship Publications/United Church of Canada. Jane Hodgins, ed. To provide a positive voice for orthodoxy and uphold the historic Christian faith of the denomination. Quarterly mag.; circ. 9,000. Subscription free for donation. Open to unsolicited freelance. Not in topical listings. (Ads)

$FIRST THINGS: A Monthly Journal of Religion and Public Life, 156 Fifth Ave., Ste. 400, New York NY 10010. (212)627-1985. Fax (212)627-2184. E-mail: ft@firstthings.com. Website: www.firstthings.com. Institute on Religion & Public Life. Damon Linker, ed. Shows relation of religion and religious insights to contemporary issues of public life. Monthly (10X) & online mag.; 64-92 pgs.; circ. 32,000. Subscription $34 ($14.97 for students). 60% unsolicited freelance. Complete ms/cover letter; phone/e-query OK. Pays $400-1,000 on publication for all rts. Articles 4,000-6,000 wds.; opinion 1,500 wds. (50-60/yr.); book reviews, 1,500 wds. ($400). Responds in 2-3 wks. Seasonal 4-5 mos. ahead. No simultaneous submissions or reprints. Prefers requested ms by e-mail (attached file). Kill fee. No sidebars. Any Bible version. Guidelines by e-mail or Website; copy for 9x12 SAE/$1.42 postage (mark "Media Mail"). (Ads)

> **Poetry:** Joseph Bottom, poetry ed. (mailed submissions only). Buys 30/yr. Traditional; 4-40 lines; $50.

> **Columns/Departments:** Buys 50-60/yr. Opinion, 1,000-2,000 wds.; $400. Complete ms.

> **Tips:** "Most open to opinion and articles."

$#FLUTTERS OF THE HEART NEWSLETTER, Toll-free (800)854-3143. E-mail: editor@fluttersoftheheart.com. Website: www.fluttersoftheheart.com. Flutters of the Heart Gift Products. Virginia Villasenor, ed. Online newsletter. Personal essays that warm the heart, touch the soul, or just make you smile; must be tied to one of their products. Monthly newsletter. Accepts freelance. Responds in 1 mo. Complete ms only. Pays $40 on publication. Articles 500-700 wds. No reprints. Prefers e-mail submissions (no attachments). No kill fee. Guidelines on Website. Does not acknowledge receipt of manuscripts; will contact if accepted.

$FOCUS ON THE FAMILY MAGAZINE, 8605 Explorer Dr., Colorado Springs CO 80920. (719)548-4588. Fax (719)531-3499. Website: www.family.org. Focus on the Family. Susan Graham Mathis, mng. ed. To help families utilize Christian principles to strengthen their marriages, to improve their child rearing, and to deal with the problems of everyday life. Monthly (10X) mag.; 32 pgs., plus an 8-pg. segment for single parents; circ. 2,200,000. Free to donors. 5% unsolicited freelance; 10% assigned. Query/clips; no phone/fax query. Pays $100-300 on publication for one-time and electronic rts. Articles 400-1,100 wds. Responds in 4-6 wks. Seasonal 6 mos. ahead. Accepts requested ms on disk. Kill fee 25%. Regularly uses sidebars. Prefers NIV. Guidelines (also by e-mail/Website); copy for 9x12 SAE/2 stamps. (No ads)

> **Tips:** "This magazine is 90% generated from within our ministry. It's very hard to break in. Must be a unique look at a subject or very interesting topic not usually seen in our magazine, but still fitting the audience. Interested in unique and practical marriage, parenting, and family articles. All topics indicated must have a connection to parenting or marriage."

$+FOURSQUARE WORLD ADVANCE, 1910 W. Sunset Blvd., Ste. 200, Los Angeles CA 90026-0176. (213)989-4220. Fax (213)989-4590. E-mail: comm@foursquare.org. Website: www.foursquare.org. International Church of the Foursquare Gospel. Bill Shepson, ed. dir. Quarterly mag. with summer bonus issue; circ. 102,000. Subscription free. Open to unsolicited freelance (query first). Query by letter or e-mail. Responds in 2 wks. Seasonal 6 mos. ahead. Accepts simultaneous submissions & reprints. Accepts e-mail submissions (attached file). Regularly uses sidebars. Free guidelines/theme list on Website; free copy. (Ads)

> **2004 EPA Award of Excellence—Most Improved Publication.

#THE FRIEND, 35839 Graystone Dr., Abbotsford BC V3G 1K7 Canada. (604)853-5967. E-mail: dartr@ucfv.bc.ca. University College of the Fraser Valley. Ron Dart, pub. A platform for the humanist Christian tradition. Quarterly mag.; 24 pgs. Not in topical listings.

FRIENDS JOURNAL, 1216 Arch St., 2A, Philadelphia PA 19107-2835. (215)563-5629. Fax

(215)568-1377. E-mail: info@friendsjournal.org. Website: www.friendsjournal.org. Quaker. Robert Dockhorn, sr. ed.. Reflects Quaker life with commentary on social issues, spiritual reflection, Quaker history, and world affairs. Monthly mag.; circ. 8,000. Subscription $29. 70% freelance. Complete ms by e-mail preferred; e-query OK. Articles to 2,500 wds.; news items 50-200 wds.; reports of Quaker events 450 wds. Accepts simultaneous submissions or reprints, if notified. Also accepts disk. Guidelines on Website; free copy. Incomplete topical listings.

Poetry: To 25 lines.

Fillers: Games, short humor, newsbreaks, and word puzzles.

+FUSE MAGAZINE: Where Art & Faith Intersect, PO Box 6513, High Point NC 27262. (336)687-0157. E-mail: Robin@fusemagazine.net. Website: www.fusemagazine.net. Mr. Robin Parrish, ed./pub. Online mag. Open to unsolicited freelance. E-query. **NO PAYMENT FOR NOW**. Fiction 3,000 wds. and up. Guidelines by e-mail; copy online.

Poetry: Accepts poetry. "We prefer poetry about people and what they feel, think, or experience." No length requirements.

Special Needs: Original artwork. See guidelines.

Tips: "No preachy fiction—a thought-provoking moral to the story is enough for us. This publication is unique. Be sure to send for guidelines before submitting."

$GATEWAY S-F MAGAZINE: Stories of Science & Faith, GateWay Publishing House, 1833 S. Westmoreland Ave., Los Angeles CA 90006-4621. Website: www.geocities.com/scifieditor/index.html. John A. M. Darnell, ed. (John.Darnell@walsworth.com); B. Joseph Fekete Jr., ed./pub. (scifieditor@yahoo.com). For science fiction fans who also happen to be Christians, and sci-fi readers who don't mind religious themes. Biannual CD mag. & quarterly e-zine; 144 pgs.; circ. 250. Subscription $27.95 for 4 issues ($7.50 single copy). 100% unsolicited freelance. Complete ms/cover letter; query for longer pieces and serials; e-query/submissions only. Pays $5 on publication for one-time and electronic rts. Not copyrighted. Fiction 500-7,500 wds. (80/yr.). Responds in 2-4 wks. No seasonal material. Accepts reprints (tell when/where appeared). Requires accepted ms by e-mail (attached copy). Guidelines/theme list (also by e-mail/Website: www.geocities.com/scifieditor/guidelines.html); sample CD copy $5. (No ads)

Special Needs: Time-travel stories always welcomed; also stories about the behind-the-scene workings of angels in the sci-fi setting. Also accepts generic sci-fi artwork; payment by agreement with artist.

Tips: "Submit stories that have solid science-based plot lines, easy reading, straightforward writing without 'creative experimentation,' and religious themes. Also read the online guidelines for specific submission requirements. We are a liberal publication, and disdain dogmatism."

$THE GEM, 700 E. Melrose Ave., Box 926, Findlay OH 45839-0926. (419)424-1961. Fax (419)424-3433. E-mail: communications@cggc.org. Website: www.cggc.org. Churches of God, General Conference. Rachel Foreman, ed. Monthly (13X) take-home paper for adults; 8 pgs.; circ. 7,100. Subscription $10. 80% unsolicited freelance; 20% assigned. Complete ms/cover letter; phone/fax/e-query OK. Pays $15 after publication for one-time rts. Articles 300-1,600 wds. (125/yr.); fiction 2,000 wds. (125/yr.); book/music reviews, 750 wds., $10. Responds in 12 wks. Seasonal 3 mos. ahead. Accepts simultaneous submissions and reprints (tell when/where appeared). Accepts requested ms on disk; no e-mail submission. Uses some sidebars. Prefers NIV. Guidelines (also by e-mail)/copy for #10 SAE/2 stamps. (No ads)

Poetry: Buys 100/yr. Any type, 3-40 lines; $5-15. Submit max. 3 poems.

Fillers: Buys 100/yr. All types, except party ideas; 25-100 wds; $5-15.

Special Needs: Missions and true stories. Be sure that fiction has a clearly religious/Christian theme.

Tips: "Most open to real-life experiences where you have clearly been led by God. Make the story interesting and Christian."

**This periodical was #30 on the 2004 Top 50 Christian Publishers list (#35 in 2003, #25 in 2002).

$GEMS OF TRUTH, PO Box 4060, Overland Park KS 66204. (913)432-0331. Fax (913)722-0351. E-mail: sseditor1@juno.com. Church of God (Holiness)/Herald & Banner Press. Arlene McGehee, Sunday school ed. Denominational. Weekly adult take-home paper; 8 pgs.; circ. 14,000. Subscription $2.25. Complete ms/cover letter; phone/fax/e-query OK (prefers mail or e-mail). Pays .005/wd. on publication for 1st rts. Fiction 1,000-2,000 wds. Seasonal 6-8 mos. ahead. Accepts simultaneous submissions and reprints (tell when/where appeared). Prefers KJV. Guidelines/theme list; copy. Not in topical listings. (No ads)

$+GENERATION X NATIONAL JOURNAL, 411 W. Front, Wayland IA 52654. (319)256-4221. E-mail: genxjournal2004@yahoo.com. Website: www.genxnatljournal.com. Kathy Stoops, mng. ed. For those who came of age during the late 80s and early 90s. Quarterly creative jour.; 60 pgs.; circ. 100. Subscription $12. Estab. 2003. 90% unsolicited freelance; 10% assigned. Query; e-query OK. Pays $5-10 on publication for one-time rts. Articles 500-2,000 wds. (100/yr.); fiction 500-2,000 wds. (100/yr.). Responds in 9 wks. Seasonal 6 mos. ahead. Accepts simultaneous submissions & reprints (tell when/where appeared). Requires e-mail submissions (copied into message). No kill fee. No sidebars. Accepts submissions from children & teens. Guidelines/theme list (also by e-mail/Website); copy $3. (Ads)

Poetry: Buys 20-30/yr. Any type; any length; $5. Submit max. 3 poems.

Fillers: Buys 20/yr. Anecdotes, facts, ideas, jokes, prose, quotes, short humor; $5.

Columns/Departments: Buys 100/yr. Ethnic View (personal perspective); Success Story (personal perspective), Political Views (personal or research); all 500-2,000 wds., $5-10.

Contest: Watch Website for future contests.

Tips: "Most of our departments are open to freelancers. We believe in being a place for aspiring and established writers."

$GOD ALLOWS U-TURNS BOOK SERIES, The God Allows U-Turns Project, PO Box 717, Faribault, MN 55021-0717. Fax (507)334-6464. E-mail: editor@godallowsuturns.com. Website: www.godallowsuturns.com. Submit to Editor. For a list of current *God Allows U-Turns* books open to submissions, as well as related opportunities, visit Website. Timelines vary, so send stories any time, as they may fit another volume. You may submit the same story to more than one volume, but you must submit a separate copy to each. When submitting, indicate which volume it is for. Each book in the series will contain up to 100 uplifting, encouraging, and inspirational true short stories written by contributors from all over the world. 100% unsolicited freelance. Includes byline and short bio. Articles 500-1,500 words. Pays $50 on publication, plus 1 copy of book, for one-time, or reprint rts. (no returns). Accepts simultaneous submissions and reprints (tell when/where appeared). Prefers submissions via Website. Accepts e-mail submissions (copied into message). Guidelines and sample story appear on Website, or by sending #10 SAE/1 stamp. (No ads)

Special Needs: True stories. Open to well-written, personal inspirational pieces showing how faith in God can inspire, encourage, and heal. Hope should prevail. Human-interest stories with a spiritual application, affirming ways in which faith is expressed in daily life. These true stories must touch the emotions. Our contributors are a diverse group with no limits on age or denomination. Project topics currently open are Teens; Men; Women; Golden Memories; A Child Shall Lead Them; Medical Miracles; Couples; Military Honor; and Weight Loss. Of particular interest for several special upcoming volumes are true stories on how God allows U-turns via answered prayer. Volumes on the answered prayers of moms, teens, couples, seniors, cancer survivors, military personnel, children, and prisoners are in development. See Website for publication dates and deadlines.

Tips: "Read prior volumes. Keep it real. Ordinary people doing extraordinary things with God's help. Focus on timeless, universal themes like love, forgiveness, salvation, healing, hope, faith, etc. Be able to tell a good story with drama, description, and dialog. Avoid moralisms and preachy tone. The point of the story should be some practical spiritual help the reader receives from what the author learned through his experience. When possible, show how a change of heart, attitude, thought, and/or behavior occurred that clearly describes a U-turn toward God. Using a U-turn lesson/analogy within the story is a plus."
Deadline: Deadlines vary; this is an ongoing book series. Check Website for frequent series updates.

$GOD'S WAY BOOK SERIES, 6528 E. 101st St., Ste. 416, Tulsa OK 74133-6754. WhiteStone Publishing. Mark Gilroy, ed. E-mail: stories@godswaybooks.com. Website: www.godsway books.com. For books created to help readers discover and experience God's love and power in their lives through well-crafted, inspirational, and challenging true life stories; each story enhanced by a compelling quote and Bible verse. True stories 750-2,000 wds. (no fiction). Open to freelance. Complete ms sent electronically. Pays $50/story for non-exclusive book rts., plus a copy of the book. Full guidelines and list of current topics available on Website.

+GOLD COUNTRY FAMILIES, PO Box 723, Meadow Vista CA 95722. (530)878-8353. E-mail: vgbeninga@yahoo.com. Website: www.goldcountryfamilies.com. Sierra Nevada Gold Country. Victoria Beninga, ed. E-magazine. Subscription free. Open to unsolicited freelance. Complete ms. By e-mail (preferred). **NO PAYMENT.** Articles 300-2,000 wds. (can vary). Accepts reprints. No guidelines; copy online.

$GOOD NEWS, PO Box 150, Wilmore KY 40390. (859)858-4661. Fax (859)858-4972. E-mail: steve@goodnewsmag.org. Website: www.goodnewsmag.org. United Methodist/Forum for Scriptural Christianity, Inc. Steve Beard, ed. Focus is evangelical renewal within the denomination. Bimonthly mag.; 44 pgs.; circ. 100,000. Subscription $20. 20% unsolicited freelance. Query first; no phone/fax/e-query. Pays $100-150 on publication for one-time rts. Articles 1,500-1,850 wds. (25/yr.). Responds in 24 wks. Seasonal 4-6 mos. ahead. Accepts simultaneous submissions and reprints (tell when/where appeared). Accepts requested ms on disk. Kill fee. Regularly uses sidebars. Prefers NIV. Guidelines (also on Website); copy $2.75/9x12 SAE. (Ads)
Tips: "Most open to features."

$GOOD NEWS, ETC., PO Box 2660, Vista CA 92085. (760)724-3075. E-mail: rmonroe@good newsetc.com. Website: www.goodnewsetc.com. Good News Publishers, Inc. of California. Rick Monroe, ed. Feature stories and local news of interest to Christians in San Diego County. Monthly tabloid; 24-32 pgs.; circ. 42,000. Subscription $15. 5% unsolicited freelance; 5% assigned. Query; e-query OK. Pays $20 on publication for all, 1st, one-time, or reprint rts. Articles 500-700 wds. (15/yr.). Responds in 2 wks. Seasonal 2 mos. ahead. Accepts simultaneous submissions and reprints (tell when/where appeared). Prefers accepted ms on disk. Regularly uses sidebars. Prefers NIV. Guidelines; copy for 9x12 SAE/4 stamps. (Ads)
Tips: "Most open to local (San Diego), personality-type articles."
**1993 EPA Award of Merit—Newspaper.

#GOOD NEWS JOURNAL, 1901 Hwy. 183 North, Leander TX 78641. Fax (512)259-0892 or (512)260-1800. E-mail:goodnews98@aol.com. Evelyn W. Davison, pub. Christian paper for national circulation by subscription, and Central Texas by free distribution. Monthly newspaper; 24 pgs.; circ. 60,000. Subscription $29.95. 40% unsolicited freelance; 60% assigned. Query; fax/e-query OK. **NO PAYMENT** for one-time rts. Articles 200-600 wds. Accepts reprints. Prefers accepted ms by e-mail. Guidelines (also by e-mail/Website); copy for 9x12 SAE/2 stamps. (Ads)
Poetry: Accepts 4-6/yr. Traditional.

Fillers: Accepts many. All types; 10-50 wds.

Tips: "Most open to short helps, funnies, inspirations, and current issues."

$GOSPEL TODAY MAGAZINE, 286 Highway 314, Ste. C, Fayetteville GA 30214. (770)719-4825. Fax (770)716-2660. E-mail: Gospeltodaymag@aol.com. Website: www.gospel today.com. Horizon Concepts, Inc. Teresa Hairston, pub. Ministry/Christian lifestyle directed toward urban marketplace. Bimonthly (8X) mag.; 64-80 pgs.; circ. 200,000. Subscription $16.97. 5% unsolicited freelance; 90% assigned. Query; e-query OK. Pays $75-250 on publication for all rts. Articles 1,000-3,500 wds. (4/yr.). Responds in 2 wks. Seasonal 3 mos. ahead. Accepts simultaneous submissions and reprints (tell when/where appeared). Prefers accepted ms by e-mail (attached file). Kill fee 15%. Uses some sidebars. Prefers NKJV. Guidelines on Website; copy $3.50. (Ads)

Fillers: Accepts 2-3/yr. Cartoons, word puzzles. No payment.

Columns/Departments: Precious Memories (historic overview of renowned personality), 1,500-2,000 wds.; From the Pulpit (issue-oriented observation from clergy), 2,500-3,000 wds.; Life & Style (travel, health, beauty, fashion tip, etc.), 1,500-2,500 wds.; Broken Chains (deliverance testimony), 1,200 wds. Query. Pays $50-75.

Tips: "Looking for great stories of great people doing great things to inspire others."

GOSPEL TRACT HARVESTER, PO Box 1118, Independence MO 64051. (816)461-6086. Fax (816)461-4305. Gospel Tract Society, Inc. Beth Buttram, ed. For Christians of all ages (few unchurched readers). Monthly mag.; 16 pgs.; circ. 38,000. Subscription free (donations). 20% unsolicited freelance. Query; no phone/fax query. **PAYS UP TO 20 COPIES** for all rts. Not copyrighted. Articles 1,000 wds. (10/yr.). Responds in 4-6 wks. Seasonal 4 mos. ahead. Accepts reprints (tell when/where appeared). Uses some sidebars. Prefers KJV. Guidelines; copy for 9x12 SAE/2 stamps. (No ads)

Fillers: Accepts 8-12/yr. Anecdotes, facts, games, quotes, short humor; 100-500 wds.

Special Needs: Good, fresh, well-written tracts for children and teens.

Tips: "Most open to personal testimonies if well-written and documented. Have a message to share and a sincere desire to share the message of salvation. Be concise. Be correct in grammar and references."

THE GRAND VALLEY OBSERVER, PO Box 112, Howard OH 43028-0112. (740)392-7674. Fax (740)392-7675. E-mail: pjcooper@ecr.net. Website: www.pandocooperstudios.com. Nondenominational/evangelical; Pando-Cooper Studios, Inc. Paul J. Cooper Jr., ed. To build up the Body of Christ with absolute biblical truth. Quarterly newsletter; 8-16 pgs.; circ. 350. Subscription free. 100% unsolicited freelance. Complete ms; e-query OK. **PAYS IN COPIES** for one-time rts. Articles 700-1,800 wds. (18/yr.). Responds in 4 wks. (no response for rejections). Holiday/seasonal 2 mos. ahead. Accepts simultaneous submissions and reprints (tell when/where appeared). Prefers e-mail submissions (copied into message). No sidebars. Prefers NASB, NIV. Guidelines; copy for 6x9 SAE/2 stamps. (No ads)

Poetry: Accepts 8/yr. Free verse, haiku, light verse, traditional; 12-30 lines. Submit max. 4 poems.

Fillers: Accepts 12/yr. Anecdotes, facts; 20-100 wds.

Tips: "Completely open to all freelancers. Be honest. Present the truth of how to walk a Christian life without compromise. Many of our readers are unbelievers or have no church affiliation. We emphasize evangelism 'around-the-back-door,' not the 'in-your-face' method."

$GRIT, 1503 S.W. 42nd St., Topeka KS 66609. (785)274-4300. Fax (785)274-4305. E-mail: grit@grit.com. Website: www.grit.com. Ogden Publications. Ann Crahan, ed-in-chief; Andrea Skalland, mng. ed. Features with positive messages. Monthly tabloid; 64 pgs.; min. circ. 100,000. Subscription $27.98. 90% unsolicited freelance. Complete ms/cover letter by mail only. Pays .15/wd. for nonfiction on publication, see guidelines for fiction pay rates;

for one-time rts. Articles to 2,000 wds. (300/yr.); fiction to 3,500 wds. Responds in 3-6 mos. Seasonal 6 mos. ahead. No simultaneous submissions or reprints. Uses some sidebars. Guidelines; copy $4/9x12 SASE/4 stamps. (Ads)

Poetry: Attn: Poetry Editor. Buys 50/yr. Free verse, light verse, traditional; 4-16 lines. Pays $10-15 on acceptance. Submit max. 5 poems.

Columns/Departments: Buys 100-200/yr. Looking Back (nostalgia with a message), 500 wds.; Cook of the Month (unique people with storyteller recipes), 1,000 wds.; Coping (survivors with a positive message), 1,200 wds.; Gardens/Gardening, 500-1,000 wds.; Little Friends (our children & grandchildren), 100-200 wds.; Best Friends (pets), 200-1,200 wds. Payment varies.

Special Needs: True inspirational stories, miracles, unique family lifestyles, humor, nature. Always needs seasonal stories and photos (Christmas, Thanksgiving, Easter, Mother's Day, Father's Day, Memorial Day, etc.). Avoid first-person or as-told-to techniques in longer pieces. Also accepts historical, mystery, western, adventure, and romance fiction to 3,500 words. Submit to "Fiction Dept."

Tips: "Our publication is all original material either written by our readers/freelancers or occasionally by our staff. Every department, every article is open. Break in by reading at least 6 months of issues to know our special audience." Submissions are not acknowledged or status reports given.

**This periodical was #24 on the 2004 Top 50 Christian Publishers list (#18 in 2003, #13 in 2002).

$GUIDEPOSTS, 16 E. 34th St., 21st Floor, New York NY 10016-4397. (212)251-8100. Website: www.guideposts.com. Interfaith. Mary Ann O'Roark, exec. ed. Personal faith stories showing how faith in God helps each person cope with life in some particular way. Monthly mag.; 52 pgs.; circ. 3 million. Subscription $13.94. 30% unsolicited freelance; 20% assigned. Complete ms/cover letter, by mail only; no electronic submissions. Pays $250-500 on acceptance for all rts. Articles 750-1,500 wds. (40-60/yr.), shorter pieces 250-750 wds ($100-250.). Responds only to mss accepted for publication in 2 mos. Seasonal 6 mos. ahead. Accepts simultaneous submissions and reprints. Uses some sidebars. Free guidelines (also by e-mail/Website)/copy. (Ads)

Columns/Departments: Christopher Davis, column ed. Buys 24/yr. His Mysterious Ways (divine intervention), 250 wds.; What Prayer Can Do, 250 wds.; Angels Among Us, 400 wds.; Divine Touch (tangible evidence of God's help), 400 wds. ("This is our most open area. Write in 3rd person."); $100.

Contest: Writers Workshop Contest held on even years with a late June deadline. Winners attend a week-long seminar in New York (all expenses paid) on how to write for Guideposts. Also Young Writers Contest; $36,000 in college scholarships; best stories to 1,200 wds.; deadline November 29.

Tips: "Be able to tell a good story, with drama, suspense, description, and dialog. The point of the story should be some practical spiritual help that subjects learned through their experience. Use unique spiritual insights, strong and unusual dramatic details." First person only.

**This periodical was #45 on the 2001 Top 50 Christian Publishers list (#31 in 2001, #22 in 1998).

+HANNAH TO HANNAH, PO Box 168, Hanford CA 93232-0168. Phone/fax (775)852-9202. E-mail: newsletter@hannah.org. Website: www.hannah.org. Hannah's Prayer Ministries. Jill Amack, ed. Provides encouragement to couples facing infertility or the loss of a child at any time from conception to early infancy. Monthly newsletter.; 15-20 pgs.; circ. 2,300. Subscription free. 40% unsolicited freelance; 60% assigned. Complete ms; e-query OK. Accepts full mss. by e-mail. **NO PAYMENT** for all rts. Article length open (15/yr.); book reviews

200 wds. Responds in 2 wks. Seasonal 2 mos. ahead. Accepts simultaneous submissions & reprints (tell when/where appeared). Prefers accepted mss. by e-mail (attached file). No sidebars. Prefers NAS/NIV. Guidelines/theme list on Website. (No ads)

Poetry: Accepts 15-20/yr. Free verse, light verse, traditional. Submit max. 10 poems.

Tips: "Articles should be compassionate and practical—all information given should point the reader back to God in difficulties."

HARD ROW TO HOE, PO Box 541-I, Healdsburg CA 95448. (707)433-9786. Secular; Potato Eyes Foundation. Joe E. Armstrong, ed. Focuses on rural literature: poetry, short stories (no blatantly Christian/religious material). Triannual newsletter; 12 pgs.; circ. 200. Subscription $8.00. 90% unsolicited freelance. Complete ms/cover letter; no phone query. **PAYS 2 COPIES** for one-time rts. Rural fiction to 2,000 wds. (3-4/yr.); book reviews 300-400 wds. (no Christian books). Responds in 6-8 wks. No simultaneous submissions or reprints. Sometimes accepts poetry from teens. Guidelines; copy for $3. (no ads)

Poetry: Accepts 20-25/yr. Traditional (rural poems); to 30 lines. Submit max. 6 poems.

Special Needs: Native American.

Tips: "All areas are open—reviews, poetry and fiction; realistic details of rural life—domestic or foreign. Fiction should be rural, environmental, or Native American (for adults)."

HEARTLIGHT INTERNET MAGAZINE, 8332 Mesa Dr., Austin TX 78759. (514)345-6386. Fax (512)345-6634. E-mail: phil@heartlight.org. Website: www.heartlight.org. Westover Hills Church of Christ. Phil Ware & Paul Lee, co-eds. Offers positive Christian resources for living in today's world. Weekly online mag. (see Website above); 20+ pgs.; circ. 70,000+. Subscription free. 20% unsolicited freelance. E-query. **NO PAYMENT** for electronic rts. Articles 300-450 wds. (25-35/yr.); fiction 500-700 wds. (12-15/yr.). Responds in 3 wks. Seasonal 2 mos. ahead. Accepts simultaneous submissions and reprints (tell when/where appeared). Prefers e-mail submission. Regularly uses sidebars. Prefers NIV. Copy available on the Internet.

Fillers: Accepts 12/yr. Anecdotes, cartoons, games, ideas, jokes, newsbreaks, prayers, prose, quotes, short humor, word puzzles; to 350 wds.

Tips: "Most open to feature articles, Just for Men or Just for Women, or Heartlight for Children."

#HEARTWARMERS, Submit to: moderator@heartwarmers.com. Website: www.heartwarmers .com. Lee Simonson, pub.; submit to Laurie Patterson, assoc. pub. Personal, heartwarming experiences. Online mag.; circ. 67,000. Stories to 700 wds. (few to 900 wds.). **NO PAYMENT** for one-time rts., but they will link your story to your Website or e-mail. Requires accepted ms by e-mail (copied into message only). Does not respond to submissions. Guidelines on Website.

Poetry: Short.

Tips: "We like stories with a humorous or surprise twist. Include a 2-3 sentence biography of yourself."

HIGHWAY NEWS AND GOOD NEWS, PO Box 303, Denver PA 17517-0303. (717)859-4870. Fax (717)859-4798. E-mail: tfcio@transportforchrist.org. Website: www.transport forchrist.org. Transport For Christ. Jennifer Landis, ed. For truck drivers and their families; evangelistic, with articles for Christian growth. Monthly mag.; 16 pgs.; circ. 35,000. Subscription $30 or donation. 60% unsolicited freelance. Query or complete ms/cover letter; e-query OK. **PAYS IN COPIES** for rights offered. Articles 600 or 1,500 wds.; fiction to 800 wds. Seasonal 4 mos. ahead. Accepts simultaneous submissions and reprints (tell when/where appeared). Accepts requested ms on disk. Uses some sidebars. Prefers NIV. Guidelines/theme list; free copy for 9x12 SAE. (No ads)

Poetry: Accepts 2/yr.; any type; 3-20 lines. Submit max. 5 poems.

Fillers: Accepts 12/yr. Anecdotes, cartoons, facts, ideas, prayers, prose, short humor, tips; to 100 wds.

Tips: "Looking for items affecting the trucking industry. Need pieces (any length) on health, marriage, and fatherhood. Most open to features and true stories about truckers."

HOLY HOUSE MINISTRIES NEWSLETTER, 9641 Tujunga Canyon Blvd., Tujunga CA 91042. (818)249-3477. Fax (818)249-3432. E-mail: Holy House9@aol.com. Website: http://holy houseministries.tripod.com/. Rev. Kimberlie Zakarian, ed. Bimonthly newsletter. Open to freelance. Prefers accepted ms by e-mail. **PAYS 5 COPIES.** Not included in topical listings. No questionnaire returned.

$HOME TIMES FAMILY NEWSPAPER, 3676 Collins Dr., #16, West Palm Beach FL 33406. (561)439-3509. Fax (561)968-1758. E-mail: hometimes2@aol.com. Website: www.home times.org. Neighbor News, Inc. Dennis Lombard, ed./pub. Conservative, pro-Christian community newspaper. Twice monthly tabloid; 24-28 pgs.; circ. 18,000. Subscription $22. 20% unsolicited freelance; 30% assigned. Complete ms only/cover letter; no phone/fax/ e-query. Pays $5-50 on publication for one-time rts. Articles to 800 wds. (25/yr.); fiction to 800 wds. (6/yr.); book reviews 200 wds. ($5-15). Responds in 2-3 wks. Seasonal 2 mos. ahead. Accepts simultaneous submissions and reprints (tell when/where appeared). Accepts requested ms on disk or by e-mail. No kill fee. Uses some sidebars. Prefers NIV. Guidelines; 3 issues $3. (Ads)

Poetry: Buys several/yr. Light verse, traditional, inspirational; 4-28 lines; $5-10. Submit max. 3 poems.

Fillers: Accepts 30-40/yr. Anecdotes, cartoons, jokes, kid quotes, quotes, short humor; to 100 wds.; pays 3-6 copies.

Columns/Departments: Buys 15/yr. See guidelines for departments, to 600 wds.; $5-15.

Special Needs: Good short stories (creative nonfiction, or fiction). More faith, miracles, and personal experiences.

Tips: "Most open to personal stories or home/family pieces. Very open to new writers, but study guidelines and sample first; we are different. Published by Christians, but not religious. Looking for more positive articles and stories. Open to fiction for all ages."

#HOMECOMING, Contact by e-mail from their Website: www.gaithermusic.com. Click on Magazine. Bill & Gloria Gaither, pubs.; Joy MacKenzie, ed-at-large; Roberta Croteau, ed-in-chief. Estab. 2003. Open to submissions to several columns.

$HOMESCHOOLING TODAY, PO Box 413, Barker TX 77413. (281)492-6050. Fax (832)201-7620. E-mail: editor@homeschooltoday.com. Website: www.homeschoolingtoday.com. Family Reformation LLC. Stacy McDonald, ed-in-chief. Practical articles, encouragement, news, and lessons for homeschoolers. Bimonthly mag.; 96 pgs.; circ. 30,000. Subscription $21.99. 40% unsolicited freelance; 60% assigned. Query; query/clips, or complete ms; e-query OK. Pays .08/wd. on publication for all rts. Articles 600-2,200 wds. (20/yr.); book reviews 800 wds. Responds in 6-8 wks. Accepts reprints (tell when/where appeared). Requires requested ms by e-mail (attached file). Kill fee 25%. Uses some sidebars. Any Bible version. Guidelines (also by e-mail); copy $2/9x12 SAE. (Ads)

Columns/Departments: Buys 20-24/yr. Parents Speak Out, 500-700 wds. (See guidelines for other departments.) Query. Pays .08/wd.

HOPEKEEPERS MAGAZINE, (formerly And He Will Give You Rest) PO Box 502928, San Diego CA 92150. Toll-free (888)751-7378. (858)486-4685. Fax (800)933-1078. E-mail: rest@restministries.org. Website: www.restministries.org. Rest Ministries, Inc. Lisa Copen, ed. For people who live with chronic illness or pain; offers encouragement, support, and hope dealing with everyday issues. Bimonthly mag.; 50 pgs. Subscription $17.97. Estab. 2004. 40% unsolicited freelance; 60% assigned. Query; fax/e-query OK. **PAYS IN COPIES.**

Articles 375-1,500 wds.; book reviews 300 wds. Responds in 6-8 wks. Seasonal 6 mos. ahead. Accepts simultaneous submissions & reprints. Prefers e-mail submissions (attached or copied into message). Regularly uses sidebars. Accepts submissions from teens. Guidelines (also by e-mail/Website); copy $4.

Tips: "Topics should be 'attention grabbers' about specific emotions (Is it okay to be mad at God?), or experiences (parenting with a chronic illness), or helpful (5 things you should know about illness on the job)."

$HORIZONS, 1300 N. Meacham Rd., Schaumburg IL 60173-4888. (847)843-1600. Fax (847)843-3757. E-mail: takehomepapers@garbc.org. Website: www.RegularBaptist Press.org. Regular Baptist. Joan E. Alexander, ed. For adults associated with fundamental Baptist Churches. Weekly take-home paper that supports the adult curriculum by assisting adults in being grounded and growing Christians; 4 pages weekly. Open to freelance. Complete ms/cover letter including personal testimony; no phone/fax/e-query. Pays .05/wd. and up, on acceptance (usually) for 1st rts. Articles 500-1,200 wds. (if over 600 wds., use subheads); fiction 1,000-1,200 wds. Responds in 8-12 wks. Seasonal 1 yr. ahead. No simultaneous submissions; some reprints. Some sidebars. Prefers KJV. Guidelines/theme list by e-mail/Website. Incomplete topical listings. (No ads)

Fillers: Buys 10-15/yr. Word puzzles.

Tips: "We look for personal experience stories (both first person and as-told-to), articles with a story element to them, and well-written fiction that helps readers know more of God's character and ways. Check Website quarterly for updates concerning needs, themes, etc."

$IDEALS MAGAZINE, Ideals Publishing, Inc., 535 Metroplex Dr., Ste. 250, Nashville TN 37211. (615)333-0478. Website: www.idealspublications.com. Guideposts, Inc. Peggy Schaefer, mng. ed. Seasonal, inspirational, nostalgic magazine for mature men and women of traditional values. Bimonthly mag.; 88 pgs.; circ. 180,000. Subscription $15.95. 95% unsolicited freelance. Complete ms/cover letter; no phone/e-query. Pays .10/wd. on publication for one-time rts. Articles 800-900 wds. (20/yr.); fiction. Responds in 6-8 wks. Seasonal 8 mos. ahead. Accepts simultaneous submissions and reprints (tell when/where appeared). No disk. Does not use sidebars. Prefers KJV. Guidelines; copy $4.

Poetry: Buys 100+/yr. Free verse, light verse, traditional; 12-50 lines; $10. Submit max. 15 poems.

Tips: Each issue has a particular theme: Easter, Mother's Day, Country, Friendship, Thanksgiving, and Christmas.

Note: This publication is not currently reviewing unsolicited manuscripts of any kind, including poetry. Also not reviewing unsolicited photographs or art.

$IMAGE, 3307 Third Ave. W., Seattle WA 98119. (206)281-2988. Fax (206)281-2335. E-mail: image@imagejournal.org. Website: www.imagejournal.org. Gregory Wolfe, pub./ed. Publishes the best literary fiction, poetry, nonfiction, and visual arts that engages the Judeo-Christian tradition. Quarterly journal; 128 pgs.; circ. 4,500. Subscription $36. 50% unsolicited freelance; 50% assigned. Complete ms/cover letter; phone/fax/e-query OK. Payment varies on publication for 1st rts. Articles 5,000-8,000 wds. (8/yr.); fiction 5,000-8,000 wds. (4/yr.); book reviews 2,000 wds. Responds in 10 wks. No seasonal. Accepts simultaneous submissions; no reprints. No kill fees. Does not use sidebars. Any Bible version. Guidelines (also on Website); copy $14. (Ads)

Poetry: Buys 30/yr. Good poetry. Payment varies. Submit max. 8 poems.

Tips: "Read the journal to understand what we publish. We're always thrilled to see high quality literary work in the unsolicited freelance pile, but we really can't typify what we're looking for other than good writing that's honest about faith and the life of faith. No genre fiction."

$IMPACT MAGAZINE, 301 Geylang Centre, #03-04 Geylang Rd., Singapore 389 344. Phone 65

6748 1244. Fax 65 748 3744. E-mail: impact@pacific.net.sg. Website: www.impact.com.sg. Impact Christian Comm., Ltd. Andrew Goh, ed.; Loy Chin Fen, copy ed. To help young working adults apply Christian principles to contemporary issues. Bimonthly & online mag.; 56 pgs.; circ. 6,000. Subscription $18. 10% unsolicited freelance. Query or complete ms/cover letter; phone/fax/e-query OK. Ranges from no payment up to $20/pg., for all rts. Articles 1,200-1,500 wds. (12/yr.) & fiction (6/yr.); 1,000-2,000 wds. Seasonal 2 mos. ahead. Accepts reprints. Accepts e-mail submission (attached file). Uses some sidebars. Prefers NIV. Guidelines (also by e-mail); copy for $4/$2 postage (surface mail). (Ads)

Poetry: Accepts 2-3 poems/yr. Free verse, 20-40 lines. Submit max. 3 poems.

Fillers: Accepts 6/yr. Anecdotes, cartoons, jokes, quizzes, short humor, and word puzzles.

Columns/Departments: Closing Thoughts (current social issues), 600-800 wds.; Testimony (personal experience), 1,500-2,000 wds.; Parenting (Asian context), 1,000-1,500 wds.; Faith Seeks Understanding (answers to tough questions of faith/Scripture), 80-1,000 wds.

Tips: "We're most open to fillers."

**1997 EPA Award of Merit—Missionary.

$INDIAN LIFE, PO Box 3765, Redwood Post Office, Winnipeg MB R2W 3R6 Canada. US address: Box 266, Pembina ND 58271-0266. (204)661-9333. Fax (204)661-3982. E-mail: viola.editor@indianlife.org. Website: www.indianlife.org. Indian Life Ministries. Viola Fehr, ed. An evangelistic publication for English-speaking aboriginal people in North America. Bimonthly newspaper; 16 pgs.; circ. 22,000. Subscription $10. 10% unsolicited freelance; 25% assigned. Query (query or complete ms for fiction); e-query OK. Pays .10/wd on publication for 1st rts.; Internet rts. negotiable. Articles 300-1,500 wds. (20/yr.); fiction 300-1,200 wds. (4/yr.); reviews, 500 wds., $40. Responds in 4 wks. Seasonal 4 mos. ahead. Accepts simultaneous submissions and reprints. Accepts requested ms on disk. No kill fee. Uses some sidebars. Prefers New Life Version, NIV. Guidelines (also by e-mail); copy $2.50 (check or money order). (Ads)

Poetry: Buys poetry to 100 wds.; $20-40.

Fillers: Fillers 50-200 wds.; $10-25.

Special Needs: Celebrity pieces must be aboriginal only. Looking for legends.

Tips: "Most open to personality stories, news features, or historical fiction with strong and accurate portrayal of Native American life from the Indian perspective. A writer should have understanding of some Native American history and culture. We suggest reading some Native American authors. Native authors preferred, but some others are published. Aim at a 10th-grade reading level; short paragraphs; avoid multisyllable words and long sentences."

**2003, 2001, 1998 & 1997 EPA Award of Excellence—Newspaper; 2000 EPA Award of Merit—Newspaper.

+INDIANA CHRISTIAN NEWS, 18891 Stockton Dr., Noblesville IN 46060. (317)770-7670. Fax (317)774-8260. E-mail: samgaw@flashpointministry.com. Website: www.indiana christiannews.com. Flashpoint Ministries. Sam Gaw, ed.; Kelly Gaw, assoc. ed. A Christian company dedicated to building up the Church, which is the Body of Christ, unifying churches in our community and giving Christian men, women, and children a voice in our community. Monthly newspaper. Subscription $25. Query on Website. Incomplete topical listings. No questionnaire returned.

$INLAND NORTHWEST CHRISTIAN NEWS, 222 W. Mission, #132, Spokane WA 99201. (509)328-0820. Fax (509)326-4921. E-mail: inldnwchrist@spocom.com. John McKelvey, ed. To inform, motivate, and encourage evangelical Christians in Spokane and the Inland Northwest. Monthly newspaper; 12 pgs.; circ. 8,000. Subscription $17.95. 30% freelance. Query; phone query OK. Pays $1/column-inch on publication for 1st rts. Articles 400 wds. Responds in 9 wks. (Ads)

$INSIDE JOURNAL, PO Box 17429, Washington DC 20041-0429. (703)478-0100, ext. 3553. Fax (703)318-0235. E-mail: Jeff_Peck@pfm.org. Website: www.pfm.org. Prison Fellowship Ministries. Jeff Peck, mng. ed. To proclaim the gospel to non-Christian prisoners within the context of a prison newspaper. Bimonthly (8X) tabloid; 8 pgs.; circ. 395,000. Subscription $10. 5% unsolicited freelance; 10% assigned. Query; phone/fax/e-query OK. Modest payment (depending on situation) on acceptance for one-time rts. Articles to 1,200 wds. (25/yr.). Responds in 4 wks. Seasonal 4 mos. ahead. Accepts requested ms on disk or by e-mail. Regularly uses sidebars. Guidelines (also by e-mail); free copy. (No ads)

> **Columns/Departments:** Buys 15-20/yr. Shortimer (those preparing for release within 6 wks.), 500 wds.; Especially for Women (issues for incarcerated women), 600-800 wds. Variable payment.

> **Tips:** "Always need seasonal material for Christmas, Easter, and Thanksgiving. Also celebrity stories that demonstrate triumph over adversity. Address our prison audience with authenticity. Preachy church talk doesn't work. Be practical. Inspire or equip prisoner to serve his/her sentence or live a new life when released."

> **2003, 2001, 1994 EPA Award of Merit—Newspaper.

+INSIGHT, 40 St. Clair Ave. E., #202, Toronto ON M4T 1M9 Canada. (416)960-3953. Fax (416)960-3570. E-mail: admin@jmsblind.ca. Website: www.jmsblind.ca. John Milton Society for the Blind in Canada. Rebekah Chevalier, ed. To provide Christian inspiration and information to blind and visually impaired Canadians in an accessible format. Bimonthly large-print newspaper; circ. 2,000. Open to unsolicited freelance. Not in topical listings. (No ads)

+INSOUND, 40 St. Clair Ave. E., #202, Toronto ON M4T 1M9 Canada. (416)960-3953. Fax (416)960-3570. E-mail: admin@jmsblind.ca. Website: www.jmsblind.ca. John Milton Society for the Blind in Canada. Graham Down, ed. To provide Christian inspiration and information to blind and visually impaired Canadians in an accessible format. Bimonthly audio cassettes; circ. 200. Open to unsolicited freelance. Not in topical listings. (No ads)

+INSPIRE, Evangel Praise Center, Fresno CA. E-mail: submissions@inspireonline.org. Website: www.inspireonline.org. Terri M., ed.; Robin Ogle, asst. ed. Secular fiction/mystery stories with inspirational or moral undertone, with or without a Christian character. Online mag. Free online. Open to unsolicited freelance. Complete ms by e-mail (attached file). **NO PAYMENT** for one-time rts. Back issues will be archived; notify them if you want your story removed. Fiction 1,000-5,000 wds.; novellas to run as serials up to 15,000 wds. Responds in up to 1 mo. Guidelines/copy on Website.

> **Tips:** "We are not a 'religious-themed' magazine, but are family-friendly with a Christian influence."

+INTERACTIVE E-POETRY, 35 Peter St. S., Orillia ON L3V 5A8 Canada. E-mail: skysong@bconnex.net. Website: www.bconnex.net/~skysong. Skysong Press. Submit to e-mail address. A Christian e-poetry site; all submissions will be posted. Weekly e-zine. Estab. 2004. 100% unsolicited freelance. Complete ms by e-mail only. **NO PAYMENT.**

> **Poetry:** Accepts many; any type.

$INTERCHANGE, 412 Sycamore St., Cincinnati OH 45202-4179. (513)421-0311. Fax (513)421-0315. E-mail: richelle_thompson@episcopal-dso.org. Website: www.episcopal-dso.org. Episcopal Diocese of Southern Ohio. Richelle Thompson, dir. of communications. Regional paper for the Episcopal and Anglican Church in southern Ohio. Monthly tabloid; 16 pgs.; circ. 12,000. Free. 20% unsolicited freelance. Query or complete ms/cover letter. Pays $50-150 on acceptance for all rts. Articles 500-2,000 wds. (8-10/yr.). Responds in 4 wks. Accepts simultaneous submissions. Prefers requested ms on disk, CD. Regularly uses sidebars. Accepts submissions from children or teens. Copy for 9x12 SASE.

Fillers: Cartoons, facts, jokes.

Tips: "Most open to features, especially with a local angle."

$THE INTERIM, 104 Bond St., Toronto ON M5B 1X9 Canada. (416)204-1687. Fax (416)204-1027. E-mail: interim@lifesite.net. Website: www.lifesite.net. The Interim Publishing Co. Paul Tuns, ed. Abortion, euthanasia, pornography, feminism, and religion from a pro-life perspective; Catholic and evangelical Protestant audience. Monthly & online newspaper; 24 pgs.; circ. 30,000. Subscription $25 Can. or US. 60% unsolicited freelance. Query; phone/fax/e-query OK. Pays $50-150 Can., on publication. Articles 400-750 wds.; book, music, video reviews, 500 wds. ($50-75 Can.). Responds in 2 wks. Seasonal 2 mos. ahead. Accepts simultaneous submissions and reprints (tell when/where appeared). Prefers e-mail submission (copied into message). Kill fee. Uses some sidebars. Prefers RSV & others. No guidelines; catalog. (Ads)

Tips: "We are most interested in articles relating to issues of human life and the family."

+INTOUCH, 40 St. Clair Ave. E., #202, Toronto ON M4T 1M9 Canada. (416)960-3953. Fax (416)960-3570. E-mail: admin@jmsblind.ca. Website: www.jmsblind.ca. John Milton Society for the Blind in Canada. Rebekah Chevalier, ed. To provide Christian inspiration and information to blind and visually impaired Canadians in an accessible format. Quarterly Braille mag. Open to unsolicited freelance. Not in topical listings. (No ads)

+ISLAND CATHOLIC NEWS, PO Box 5721, Victoria BC V8R 6S8 Canada. (250)920-0233. Fax (250)920-0262. E-mail: icn@islandnet.com. Website: www.islandnet.com/~icn. Island Catholic News Society. Patrick Jamieson, ed. News and features about spirituality, social justice, health, ethical and poverty issues from a faith perspective. Monthly tabloid; circ. 3,000. Subscription $25. Open to unsolicited freelance. E-submissions OK (copied into message). Incomplete topical listings. (Ads)

JEWEL AMONG JEWELS ADOPTION NEWS, 11444 Lake Stonebridge Ln., Fishers IN 46038. (317)849-5651. Fax (317)915-8636. E-mail: mail@adoptionjewels.org. Website: www.adoptionjewels.org. Jewel Among Jewels Adoption Network, Inc. Sherrie Eldridge, ed. Seeks to bridge the spiritual gap in adoption literature through writing and speaking; presenting adoption from a biblical perspective. Quarterly online newsletter. Subscription free. 90% unsolicited freelance; 10% assigned. Complete ms/cover letter; e-query OK. **NO PAYMENT** for one-time rts. Articles to 600 wds. (40/yr.); book reviews 250 wds. Responds in 2 wks. Seasonal 4 mos. ahead. Requires requested ms on disk or by e-mail (attached file). Uses some sidebars. Prefers NIV. No guidelines; has theme list (contact editor); see online archives. (No ads)

Poetry: Accepts 5-10/yr. Free verse, traditional. Submit max. 2 poems.

Fillers: Accepts very few. Anecdotes, facts, ideas, prayers, quotes, tips; to 150 wds.

Columns/Departments: Accepts 40/yr. Common Threads, Passages of Adoption, The Great Awakening, Trigger Points, Reframing the Loss, The Blessings of Adoption; all 250 wds.

Special Needs: Adoptive parenting, adoption, grief and loss, identity in Christ, bonding and attachment perspectives, 12-step writing about adoption, how to find therapist who understands adoption issues, adoption and mental health professionals.

Tips: "Contact our editor by e-mail with your ideas. We are looking for experience-related adoption articles that include God's teaching or perspective."

JOURNAL OF CHURCH AND STATE, Baylor University, One Bear Pl. #97308, Waco TX 76798-7308. (254)710-1510. Fax (254)710-1571. E-mail: Derek_Davis@Baylor.edu. Website: www.baylor.edu/~church_state. J. M. Dawson Institute of Church-State Studies/Baylor University. Dr. Derek H. Davis, dir. Provides a forum for the critical examination of the interaction of religion and government worldwide. Quarterly jour.; 225 pgs.; circ. 1,700. Subscription $25 (indiv.); $39 (institution). 75% unsolicited freelance; 25% assigned.

Complete ms (3 copies)/cover letter (also by e-mail); phone/fax query OK; no e-query. **NO PAYMENT** for all rights. Articles 25-30 pgs./footnotes (24/yr.). Responds in 9-18 wks. Prefers requested ms on disk, e-mail submission OK. Does not use sidebars. Prefers KJV. Guidelines (also by e-mail); copy $8/$1.42 postage (mark "Media Mail"). (Ads)

Special Needs: Church-state issues.

Tips: "Open to articles only. Send three copies of manuscript and cover letter. Follow writers' guidelines."

$JOY AND PRAISE, PO Box 284, Swarthmore PA 19081-0284. (610)565-5526. Fax (610)565-4553. E-mail: sonya@joyandpraise.org. Website: www.joyandpraise.org. Blessed Communications and Entertainment, Inc. Sonya Crew, pub.; Crystal Morgan, mng. ed. (submissions to: submissions@joyandpraise.org). Youth Ministry Supplement; biblically based articles. Mag.; 60 pgs. Estab. 2003. 40% unsolicited freelance; 60% assigned. Query/clips; e-query OK. Pays $50-250 on acceptance for 1st & electronic rts. Articles; reviews $10-50. Responds in 8 wks. Guidelines on Website. Incomplete topical listings. (Ads).

Fillers: Cartoons, facts, prayers, and word puzzles; $2-25.

Columns/Departments: Pays $50-75.

Tips: "Articles must relay insightful, personal accounts of your Christian experience. Be certain these accounts are original, enlightening, and encouraging to others in their Christian walk." Log onto Website and click on writer's section.

KEYS TO LIVING, 105 Steffens Rd., Danville PA 17821. (570)437-2891. E-mail: owcam@chilitech.net. Connie Mertz, ed./pub. Educates, encourages, and challenges readers through devotional and inspirational writings; also nature articles, focusing primarily on wildlife in eastern U.S. Quarterly newsletter; 12 pgs.; circ. 200. Subscription $10. 20% unsolicited freelance (needs freelance). Complete ms/cover letter; no phone query. **PAYS 2 COPIES** for one-time or reprint rts. Articles 350-500 wds. Responds in 4 wks. Accepts reprints. No disk; e-mail submission OK (copied into message). Prefers NIV. Guidelines/theme list; copy for 7x10 SAE/2 stamps. (No ads)

Poetry: Accepts if geared to family and personal living. Traditional with an obvious message.

Fillers: Facts, jokes, kid quotes, prayers, quotes, short humor; one paragraph.

Columns/Departments: Recipe Roundup (easy, tasty recipes); to 1/2 page.

Special Needs: Nature/Bible activities geared to children.

Tips: "We are a Christ-centered family publication. It's best to request a sample copy. Submissions should focus on our current theme, which is included with Writers' Guidelines. Stay within word count. We are a ministry."

$KIWANIS, 3636 Woodview Trace, Indianapolis IN 46268-3196. (317)875-8755. Fax (317)879-0204. E-mail: magazine@kiwanis.org. Website: www.kiwanis.org. Secular magazine, for business and professional persons and their families. Jack Brockley, mng. ed. Monthly (10X) mag.; circ. 240,000. 10% unsolicited freelance. Query; fax/e-query OK. Pays $400-800 on acceptance for 1st rts. Articles 750-1,000 wds. (40/yr.). Responds in 5 wks. Kill fee 40%. Guidelines (also on Website); copy for 9x12 SAE/5 stamps. Incomplete topical listings.

Tips: "Send us a well-written and researched manuscript that contains a 'human quality' with the use of anecdotes, practical examples, quotations, etc."

$THE LAYMAN, (formerly The Presbyterian Layman) 136 Tremont Dr., PO Box 2210, Lenoir NC 28645. (828)758-8716. Fax (828)758-0920. E-mail: laymanletters@layman.org, or art@abts.net. Website: www.layman.org. Presbyterian Lay Committee. Parker T. Williamson, CEO; Craig M. Kibler, dir. of publications. For members of the Presbyterian Church (USA). Bimonthly newspaper; 24 pgs.; circ. 485,000. No subscriptions. 10% unsolicited freelance. Query. Pays negotiable rates on publication for 1st rts. Articles 800-1,200 wds. (12/yr.). Responds in 2 wks. Seasonal 2 mos. ahead. Prefers requested ms on disk. Regularly uses sidebars. Copy for 9x12 SAE/3 stamps. (No ads)

LEAVES, PO Box 87, Dearborn MI 48121-0087. (313)561-2330. Fax (313)561-9486. E-mail: leaves-mag@juno.com. Website: www.rc.net/detroit/mariannhill/leaves.htm. Catholic/ Mariannhill Mission Society. Jacquelyn M. Lindsey, ed. For all Catholics; it promotes devotion to God and His saints and publishes readers' spiritual experiences, petitions, and thanksgivings. Bimonthly mag.; 24 pgs.; circ. 75,000. Subscription free. 50% unsolicited freelance. Complete ms/cover letter; phone/fax/e-query OK. **NO PAYMENT** for 1st or reprint rts. Not copyrighted. Articles 500 wds. (6-12/yr.). Responds in 4 wks. Seasonal 4 mos. ahead. Accepts reprints. Accepts e-mail submissions (copied into message). Does not use sidebars. Prefers NAB, RSV (Catholic edition). No guidelines or copy. (No ads)

Poetry: Accepts 6-12/yr. Traditional; 8-20 lines. Submit max. 4 poems.

Special Needs: Testimonies of conversion or reversion to Catholicism.

Tips: "Besides being interestingly and attractively written, an article should be confidently and reverently grounded in traditional orthodox Catholic doctrine and spirituality. The purpose of our magazine is to edify our readers."

$LIBERTY, Dept. of Public Affairs and Religious Liberty, 12501 Old Columbia Pike, Silver Springs MD 20904. (301)680-6690. Fax (301)680-6695. E-mail: steeli@nad .adventist.org. Website: www.libertymagazine.org. Seventh-day Adventist. Lincoln Steed, ed. Deals with religious liberty issues for government officials, civic leaders, and laymen. Bimonthly mag.; 32 pgs.; circ. 200,000. Subscription $6.95. 95% unsolicited freelance. Query/clips; phone/fax/e-query OK. Pays $250 & up on acceptance for 1st rts. Articles & essays 1,000-2,500 wds. Responds in 5-13 wks. Requires requested ms on disk or by e-mail. Guidelines; copy.

$LIFEGLOW, Box 6097, Lincoln NE 68506. (402)448-0981. Fax (402)488-7582. Website: www.christianrecord.org. Christian Record Services, Inc. Gaylena Gibson, ed. For sight-impaired adults over 25; interdenominational Christian audience; inspirational/devotional articles. Quarterly mag.; 65-70 pgs. (lg. print); circ. 30,000. Free to sight-impaired. 95% unsolicited freelance. Complete ms; no phone/e-query. Pays .04-.05/wd. on acceptance for one-time rts. Articles & true stories 750-1,400 wds. Responds in 52 wks. Seasonal anytime. Accepts simultaneous submissions and reprints. Accepts requested ms on disk. Does not use sidebars. Guidelines; copy for 7x10 SAE/5 stamps. (No ads) Note: Due to an overabundance of manuscripts, this publication will not be accepting manuscripts until 2009.

#LIFETIMES CATHOLIC eZINE. E-mail: bjubar@parishwebmaster.com. Website: www.Parish Webmaster.com. Catholic. Brandon Jubar, ed. Designed to spread the Good News and minister to people online. Online publication. Open to submissions. Query first. **NO PAYMENT.** Articles 300-600 wds. (300/yr.). Accepts submissions from teens. Guidelines on Website.

Columns: Weekly Reflection; Catholic Catechism; Faith & Spirituality; Family; Self-Improvement; Teen Issues; Teen 2 Teen.

$LIGHT & LIFE, Box 535002, Indianapolis IN 46253-5002. (317)244-3660. Fax (317)248-9055. E-mail: LLMManager@fmcna.org. Website: www.freemethodistchurch.org/Magazine. Free Methodist Church of North America. Doug Newton, ed.; Cynthia Schnereger, mng. ed.; submit to Margie Newton, ms manager. Interactive magazine for maturing Christians; contemporary-issues oriented, thought-provoking; emphasizes spiritual growth, discipline, holiness as a lifestyle. Bimonthly mag.; 32 pgs. (plus pull-outs); circ. 15,000. Subscription $16. 95% unsolicited freelance. Query first; e-query OK. Pays .10-.15/wd. on acceptance for 1st or one-time rts. Articles 500-1,500 wds. (24/yr.). Responds in 8-12 wks. Seasonal 12 mos. ahead. Accepts simultaneous submissions. Prefers e-mail submission (attached file) after acceptance. No kill fee. Uses some sidebars. Prefers NIV. Accepts submissions from children or teens. Guidelines (also on Website); copy $5. (Ads)

Tips: "Best to write a query letter. We are emphasizing contemporary issues articles, well researched. Ask the question, 'What topics are not receiving adequate coverage in the church and Christian periodicals?' Seeking unique angles on everyday topics."

**2001 & 1999 EPA Award of Excellence—Denominational; 2000 & 1998 EPA Award of Merit—Denominational.

$LIGUORIAN, One Liguori Dr., Liguori MO 63057-9999. Toll-free (800)464-2555. (636)464-2500. Fax (800)325-9526 or (636)464-8449. E-mail: liguorianeditor@liguori.org. Website: www.liguorian.org. Catholic/Liguori Publications. William Parker, C.Ss.R., ed-in-chief; Cheryl Plass, mng. ed. To help Catholics of all ages better understand the gospel and Church teachings and to show how these teachings apply to life and the problems confronting them as members of families, the Church, and society. Monthly (10X) mag.; 40 pgs.; circ. 200,000. Subscription $20. 30-40% unsolicited freelance; 60% assigned. Query, query/clips, or complete ms; phone/fax/e-query OK. Pays .12-.15/wd. on acceptance for 1st rts. Articles 1,500-1,800 wds. (30-50/yr.); fiction 2,000 wds. (10/yr.); book reviews 250 wds. No simultaneous submissions or reprints. Responds in 8-12 wks. Seasonal 6-8 mos. ahead. Prefers requested mss by e-mail (attached file). Kill fee 50%. Uses some sidebars. Prefers NRSV. Guidelines (also by e-mail/Website); copy for 9x12 SAE/3 stamps. (Ads)

Fillers: Buys 100/yr. Cartoons, jokes; $50-100.

Tips: "Most open to 1,000 word meditations; 1,800 word fiction; or 1,500 word personal testimonies. Send complete manuscript for fiction. Polish your own manuscript."

**This periodical was #42 on the 2004 Top 50 Christian Publishers list (#39 in 2003).

+LITERARY TNT, (formerly delighters.com) PO Box 6294, Texarkana TX 75505-6294. E-mail: Tonya@literaryTNT.com. Website: www.LiteraryTNT.com. Christian. Tonya Stockton, ed. Weekly e-zine. Estab. 2003. Open to freelance. Complete ms by e-mail. **NO PAYMENT** for 1st or simultaneous rts. Articles 250-1,000 wds. Responds in 2-3 wks. Seasonal 2 mos. ahead. Accepts simultaneous submissions & reprints (tell when/where appeared). Prefers e-mail submissions (copied into message). Some sidebars. Accepts submissions from children or teens. Prefers NIV or Amplified. Guidelines/theme list on Website; copy for #10 SAE/2 stamps. (Ads)

Poetry: Accepts 4-12/yr. Avant-garde, free verse, traditional; 4-30 lines. Submit max. 3 poems.

Fillers: Accepts 12/yr. Prayers, quizzes, short humor, 25-100 wds.

Columns/Departments: Accepts 50/yr. Your Voice (opinion), 250-1,000 wds.; Worship Matters (teaching & testimonials), to 500 wds.; Light Waves (prayers), to 200 wds.; Light Therapy (warfare, testimonials, deliverance), to 1,000 wds.

Tips: "Most open to the Your Voice and Light Waves columns."

$LIVE, 1445 N. Boonville Ave., Springfield MO 65802-1894. (417)862-2781. Fax (417)862-6059. E-mail: rl-live@gph.org. Website: www.radiantlife.org. Assemblies of God/Gospel Publishing House. Paul W. Smith, adult ed. Inspiration and encouragement for adults. Weekly take-home paper; 8 pgs.; circ. 70,000. Subscription $13. 100% unsolicited freelance. Complete ms/cover letter; no phone/fax query. Pays .10/wd. (.07/wd. for reprints) on acceptance for 1st, one-time, simultaneous, or reprint rts. Articles 500-1,200 wds. (80-90/yr.); fiction 800-1,200 wds. (20/yr.). Responds in 4-6 wks. Seasonal 12-18 mos. ahead. Accepts simultaneous submissions and reprints (tell when/where appeared). Accepts e-mail submissions (copied into message). Few sidebars. Prefers NIV, KJV. Guidelines (also by e-mail/ Website); copy for #10 SAE/1 stamp. (No ads)

Poetry: Buys 15/yr. Any type; 12-20 lines; $60 ($35 for reprints) when scheduled. Submit max. 3 poems.

Fillers: Buys 6-8/yr. Anecdotes, prose; 200-700 wds.; .10/wd. (.07/wd. for reprints).

Tips: "All areas open to freelance—human interest, inspirational, and difficulties over-come with God's help. Fiction must be especially good with biblical application. Follow our guidelines. Most open to well-written personal experience with biblical application. Send no more than two articles in the same envelope and send an SASE. We always need holiday articles, other than Christmas."

**This periodical was #6 on the 2004 Top 50 Christian Publishers list (#5 in 2003, #4 in 2002, #12 in 2001, #13 in 2000).

$LIVING, 1251 Virginia Ave., Harrisonburg VA 22802. Toll-free (888)833-3333. (540)433-5351. Fax (540)434-0247. E-mail: Tgether@aol.com. Website: www.churchoutreach.com. Shalom Foundation, Inc. Melodie Davis, ed. A positive, practical, and uplifting publication for the whole family; mass distribution. Quarterly tabloid; 32 pgs.; circ. 50,000. Subscription free. 95% unsolicited freelance. Query or complete ms/cover letter; e-query OK. Pays $35-50 on publication for one-time rts. Articles 500-1,000 wds. (40-50/yr.); fiction (4/yr.). Responds in 12-16 wks. Seasonal 4 mos. ahead. Accepts simultaneous submissions and reprints (tell when/where appeared). Accepts requested ms on disk or by e-mail (copied into message; include e-mail address in message). Uses some sidebars. Prefers NIV. Guidelines/theme list (also by e-mail); copy for 9x12 SAE/4 stamps. (Ads)

Fillers: Buys 4-8/yr. Anecdotes, short humor; 100-200 wds.; $20-25.

Tips: "We are directed toward the general public, many of whom have no Christian inter-ests, and we're trying to publish high-quality writing on family issues/concerns from a Christian perspective. That means religious language must be low key. Too much of what we receive is directed toward a Christian reader. We get far more than we can use, so some-thing really has to stand out. Please carefully consider before sending. Need more articles of interest to men. Our articles need to have a family slant, or fit the descriptor, 'encour-agement for families.'" When submitting by e-mail, put title of magazine and title of your piece in subject line. Also include your e-mail address in body of message.

$THE LIVING CHURCH, PO Box 514036, Milwaukee WI 53203-3436. (414)276-5420, ext. 11. Fax (414)276-7483. E-mail: tlc@livingchurch.org. Website: www.livingchurch.org. Episcopal/The Living Church Foundation, Inc. John Schuessler, mng. ed. Independent news coverage of the Episcopal Church for clergy and lay leaders. Weekly mag.; 24+ pgs.; circ. 9,000. Subscription $39.50. Open to freelance. Query; phone/fax/e-query OK. Pays $25-100 (for solicited articles, nothing for unsolicited) for one-time rts. Articles 1,000 wds. (10/yr.). Responds in 2-4 wks. Seasonal 2 mos. ahead. Prefers requested ms on disk or by e-mail (attached or copied into message). Uses some sidebars. Guidelines (by e-mail); free copy. (Ads)

Columns/Departments: Accepts 5/yr. Benediction (devotional/inspirational), 200 wds. Complete ms. No payment.

Tips: "Most open to features, as long as they have something to do with the Episcopal Church."

$LIVING LIGHT NEWS, #200, 5306—89th St., Edmonton AB T6E 5P9 Canada. (780)468-6397. Fax (780)468-6872. E-mail: shine@livinglightnews.org. Website: www.livinglight news.org. Living Light Ministries. Jeff Caporale, ed. To motivate and encourage Christians; witnessing tool to the lost. Bimonthly (7X) tabloid; 36 pgs.; circ. 30,000. Subscription $19.95 US. 40% unsolicited freelance; 60% assigned. Query; fax/e-query OK. Pays $20-125 (.05-.10/wd. Can. or .08/wd. US) on publication for all, 1st, one-time, simultaneous, or reprint rts. Articles 350-700 wds. (75/yr.); fiction 500-1,200 wds. (3/yr. for Christmas only). Responds in 4 wks. Seasonal 3-4 mos. ahead. Accepts simultaneous submissions and reprints (tell when/where appeared). Accepts requested ms on disk or by e-mail (attached file in rich text format or copied into message). Regularly uses sidebars. Prefers NIV. Guidelines (also by e-mail/Website); copy for 9x12 SAE/$2.50 Can. postage or IRCs (no US postage). (Ads)

Columns/Departments: Buys 20/yr., 450-600 wds., $10-30. Parenting; relationships. Query.

Special Needs: Celebrity interviews/testimonials of well-known personalities; humorous fiction and interesting nonfiction stories related to Christmas (Christmas fiction only). Fun or informative articles (250-700 wds.) for Christian education supplement.

Tips: "Most open to a timely article about someone who is well known in North America, in sports or entertainment, and has a strong Christian walk."

**2002, 2001, 1999, 1998 EPA Award of Merit—Newspaper; 1996 & 2000 EPA Award of Excellence—Newspaper. This publication was #25 on the 2004 Top 50 Christian Publishers list (#14 in 2003, #10 in 2002).

+LOOKING UP MAGAZINE, PO Box 24, Southington OH 44470. E-mail: LookingUpMag@aol.com or LookingUpMag@yahoo.com. Website: www.lookingupmagazine.com. Jeannie Schmucker, ed-in-chief. Monthly mag. **PAYS ONE COPY**. Articles and devotions to 700 wds.; poetry. Guidelines/theme list on Website. Not included in topical listings.

$THE LOOKOUT, 8121 Hamilton Ave., Cincinnati OH 45231-9981. (513)931-4050. Fax (513)931-0950. E-mail: lookout@standardpub.com. Website: www.lookoutmag.com. Standard Publishing. Shawn McMullen, ed. For adults in Sunday school who are interested in learning more about applying the gospel to their lives. Weekly take-home paper & online version; 16 pgs.; circ. 100,000. Subscription $24.99, plus $5 postage. 40% unsolicited freelance; 45% assigned. Query for theme articles; complete ms for others; e-query OK. Pays .09-.12/wd. on acceptance for 1st reprint rts. Articles 500-1,600 wds. or 400-700 wds. (200/yr.). Responds in 10 wks. Seasonal 6 mos. ahead. Accepts simultaneous submissions and reprints rarely (tell when/where appeared). No disks or e-mail submissions. Kill fee 50%. Regularly uses sidebars. Prefers NIV. Guidelines/theme list (also by e-mail/Website); copy for #10 SAE/$1.06 postage. (No ads)

Columns/Departments: Buys 24/yr. The Outlook (personal opinion); Salt & Light (innovative ways to reach out into the community); Faith Around the World; all 500-800 wds.; .09/wd. Query.

Contest: Sponsors article writing contests for teens and senior adults. See Nonfiction Contest section for details.

Tips: "Most open to feature articles. Get a copy of our theme list and query about a theme-related article at least six months in advance. Request sample copies of our magazine to familiarize yourself with our publishing needs. Send samples of published material."

**This periodical was #2 on the 2004 Top 50 Christian Publishers list (#24 in 2003, #11 in 2002, #49 in 2001, #39 in 2000). 1999 & 1998 EPA Award of Excellence—Sunday School Take-Home.

$THE LUTHERAN, 8765 W. Higgins Rd., Chicago IL 60631-4183. (773)380-2540. Fax (773)380-2751. E-mail: lutheran@elca.org. Website: www.thelutheran.org. Evangelical Lutheran Church in America. David L. Miller, ed. Addresses broad constituency of the church. Monthly & online mag.; 68 pgs.; circ. 500,000. Subscription (see Website). 15% unsolicited freelance. Query/clips; fax/e-query OK. Pays $400-700 (assigned), $100-500 (unsolicited) on acceptance for 1st rts. Articles 400-1,500 wds. (40/yr.). Responds in 6 wks. Seasonal 4 mos. ahead. Accepts reprints. Accepts requested ms on disk or by e-mail. Kill fee 50%. Guidelines/theme list (also on Website); free copy.

Fillers: Julie Sevig, fillers ed. Buys 50/yr. Cartoons, jokes, short humor. Uses only true anecdotes from ELCA congregations; 25-100 wds.; $10.

Tips: "Most open to feature articles."

**This periodical was #29 on the 2004 Top 50 Christian Publishers list (#29 in 2003, #27 in 2002, #20 in 2001, #7 in 2000).

$THE LUTHERAN DIGEST, Box 4250, Hopkins MN 55343. (952)933-2820. Fax (952)933-5708. E-mail: tldi@lutherandigest.com. Website: www.lutherandigest.com. Lutheran. David L. Tank, ed. Blend of secular and light theological material used to win nonbelievers to the Lutheran faith. Quarterly & online mag.; 64 pgs.; circ. 105,000. Subscription $14. 100% unsolicited freelance. Query/clips or complete ms/cover letter; no phone/fax query. Pays $25-50 on acceptance for one-time rts. Articles to 1,000 wds. (25-30/yr.). Responds in 4-9 wks. Seasonal 6-9 mos. ahead. Accepts reprints (70% is reprints). No disk. Uses some sidebars. Guidelines (also on Website); copy $3.50/6x9 SAE/3 stamps. (Ads)

> **Poetry:** Accepts 45-50/yr. Light verse, traditional; any length; no payment. Submit max. 3 poems.
>
> **Fillers:** Anecdotes, cartoons, facts, jokes, short humor; to 100 wds.; no payment.
>
> **Tips:** "We need more nature articles. Compose well-written, short pieces that would be of interest to middle-age and senior Christians—and also acceptable to Lutheran church pastors. (The word *hope* is frequently associated with our publication.) So much of the material we receive is poorly written and we spend too much time trying to clean it up. Research your market first. To catch our attention, the topic has to be catchy or stand out from the usual and must be well-written."

$THE LUTHERAN JOURNAL, 7010—6th St. N., PO Box 28158, Oakdale MN 55128. (651)702-0086. Fax (651)702-0074. E-mail: christianad2@msn.com. Submit to The Editor. Family magazine for, by, and about Lutherans, and God at work in the Lutheran world. Semiannual mag.; 24-32 pgs.; circ. 100,000. Subscription $6. 60% unsolicited freelance; 40% assigned. Complete ms/cover letter; fax query OK. Pays $5-50 on publication for 1st rts. Articles 750-1,500 wds. (20/yr.). Response time varies. Seasonal 4-5 mos. ahead. Accepts reprints. Uses some sidebars. Prefers NIV, NAS, KJV. Accepts requested ms on disk. Accepts submissions from children or teens. Guidelines; copy for 9x12 SAE/3 stamps. (Ads)

> **Poetry:** Buys 10/yr. Light verse, traditional; 50-150 wds.; $5-30. Submit max. 3 poems.
>
> **Fillers:** Buys 5-10/yr. Anecdotes, facts, games, prayers, quizzes, quotes; 50-300 wds.; $5-30.
>
> **Columns/Departments:** Buys 40/yr. Apron Strings (short recipes); About Books (reviews), 50-150 wds.; $5-25.
>
> **Tips:** "Most open to Lutheran lifestyles or Lutherans in action."

MARANATHA NEWS, PO Box 328, Jupiter FL 33468. (561)744-9336. Fax (561)744-8897. E-mail: maranews@aol.com. Assemblies of God. Waldir DeOliveira, ed. Quarterly tabloid; 16 pgs.; circ. 4,000. Subscription free. Open to freelance. Complete ms; e-query OK. **NO PAYMENT** for 1st rts. Not copyrighted. Articles (2/yr.). Responds in 2 wks. Seasonal 2 mos. ahead. Accepts reprints (tell when/where appeared). No kill fee. Uses some sidebars. Accepts submissions from children or teens. No guidelines; copy for 7x10 SAE. (Ads)

> **Fillers:** Anecdotes, cartoons, jokes, newsbreaks, short humor, and word puzzles.

$MARIAN HELPER, Marian Helpers Center, Eden Hill, Stockbridge MA 01263. (413)298-3691. Fax (413)298-3583. E-mail: came@marian.org. Website: www.marian.org. Catholic/Marians of the Immaculate Conception. Dave Came, exec. ed.; Steve LaChance, review ed. Quarterly & online mag.; circ. 500,000. Rarely uses unsolicited; 25% assigned freelance. Query/clips or complete ms/cover letter. Pays $250 for 1,000-1,200 wds. (2-page feature), for 1st rts. Articles 500-900 wds. Responds in 6 wks. Seasonal 6 mos. ahead. Kill fee 30%. Guidelines/copy for #10 SAE. (No ads)

> **Tips:** "Write about God's mercy touching people's everyday lives, or about devotion to the Blessed Virgin Mary in a practical, inspirational, or fresh way."

MARKETPLACE, 12900 Preston Rd., Ste. 1215, Dallas TX 75230-1328. Toll-free (800)775-7657. (972)385-7657. Fax (972)385-7307. E-mail: art.stricklin@marketplaceministries

.com. Website: www.marketplaceministries.com. Marketplace Ministries. Art Stricklin, ed. Focus is on working in the corporate workplace. Triannual mag.; 12 pgs.; circ. 16,000. Subscription free. 10% assigned. Query or complete ms; e-query OK. **NO PAYMENT** for all rts. Articles. Prefers e-mail submission. No copy. Incomplete topical listings. (No ads)

> **Tips:** "We are attempting to cut back on freelance and use only assigned stories."

$MARRIAGE PARTNERSHIP, 465 Gundersen Dr., Carol Stream IL 60188. (630)260-6200. Fax (630)260-0114. E-mail: mp@marriagepartnership.com. Website: www.marriage partnership.com, or www.christianitytoday.com/marriage. Christianity Today Intl. Ginger Kolbaba, mng. ed. To promote and strengthen Christian marriages. Quarterly mag.; 74 pgs.; circ. 53,000. Subscription $19.95. 5% unsolicited freelance; 95% assigned. Query only; fax/e-query OK. Pays .15-.25/wd. on acceptance for 1st rts. Articles 500-2,000 wds. Responds in 8-10 wks. Seasonal 9 mos. ahead. Accepts reprints (tell when/where appeared). Prefers accepted ms by e-mail (copied into message). Kill fee 50%. Regularly uses sidebars. Prefers NIV. Guidelines (also on Website); copy $5/9x12 SAE. (Ads)

> **Columns/Departments:** Buys 4/year/department. Work It Out (working out a marriage problem); Back from the Brink (real-life story of a marriage in recovery), 1,800 wds.; Starting Out (views from the early years, married 5 years or less), 900 wds.; That Thing We Do (unique hobby you share as a couple), 400 wds. Query with ideas. Pays $150.

> **Tips:** "Know the magazine. Read a few issues to get the correct tone and feel. Most open to the departments listed above. Be fresh, creative, and have a thorough, well-crafted query."
> **2000 EPA Award of Merit—General.

($)+MARS HILL REVIEW, PO Box 10506, Bainbridge Island WA 98110-0506. Toll-free (800)990-MARS. Fax (877-349-7880). E-mail from Website. Website: www.marshill review.com. Sarah Koops Vanderveen, ed. Revealing Christ in the various texts of our contemporary culture. Triannual literary jour.; 200 pgs. Subscription $36. Open to unsolicited freelance. For longer submissions query first. Pays for solicited submissions only; **NO PAYMENT** for unsolicited. Essays/studies up to 3,000-5,000 wds.; fiction up to 3,000-5,000 wds. Responds in 10-12 wks. Requires disk. Guidelines on Website.

> **Poetry:** Marlene Muller, poetry ed.

> **Special Needs:** Deadlines for issues are: Spring/Winter, October 1; Summer, February 1; and Fall, June 1.

$MATURE LIVING, One Lifeway Plaza, MSN 175, Nashville TN 37234-0175. (615)251-2485. Website: www.lifeway.com. LifeWay Christian Resources/Southern Baptist. David T. Seay, ed-in-chief. Christian leisure reading for senior adults (50+) characterized by human interest and Christian warmth. Monthly mag.; circ. 320,000. Subscription $19.95. 75-90% unsolicited freelance; 10% assigned. Complete ms/cover letter; no phone/fax/e-query. Pays $75-105 on publication for all rts. Articles 600-1,100 wds. (100/yr.); senior adult fiction 800-1,200 wds. (12/yr.). Responds in 13 wks. Seasonal 1 yr. ahead. No simultaneous submissions or reprints. No kill fee. Uses some sidebars. Prefers KJV, HCSB. Guidelines (also by e-mail); copy for 9x12 SAE/4 stamps. (Ads)

> **Poetry:** Buys 24/yr. Haiku and light verse; 12-16 lines; $15-25. Submit max. 3 poems.

> **Fillers:** Buys 120/yr. Anecdotes, cartoons, facts, games, short humor, word puzzles; to 50 wds.; $15.

> **Columns/Departments:** Buys 250/yr. Cracker Barrel (brief humor), 25-30 wds., $15; Grandparent's Brag Board, 50-100 wds. Columns pay $15-40. See guidelines for full list.

> **Tips:** "Most open to gardening, crafts, travel, hidden-word puzzles, poetry, or devotionals."
> **This periodical was #47 on the 2004 Top 50 Christian Publishers list (#46 in 2003, #44 in 2001, #43 in 1999).

MATURE TIMES, 374 Sheppard Ave. E., Toronto ON M2N 3B6 Canada. (416)222-3341, ext. 142. Fax (416)222-3344. E-mail: timothy@peoplesministries.org. The Peoples Church/Toronto

Canada. Dr. T. Starr, mng. ed. For readers aged 55 and older. Quarterly mag.; 24 pgs. Subscription free/donation. 15% unsolicited freelance; 85% assigned. Complete ms/cover letter. **NO PAYMENT.** Articles 500 wds. (20/yr.); fiction 350-500 wds.; book/video reviews 150 wds. Responds in 2 wks. Seasonal 3 mos. ahead. Accepts simultaneous submissions and reprints (tell when/where appeared). Accepts requested ms on disk. Regular sidebars. Prefers NIV. Guidelines/theme list; copy for 9x12 SAE/$1.20 Can. postage. (Ads)

Poetry: Accepts 1-2/yr.

Fillers: Accepts 1-5/yr.; 50 wds. Anecdotes, cartoons, facts, games, quizzes, short humor; 25-40 wds.

Columns/Departments: Accepts 20/yr. Complete ms.

$MATURE YEARS, Box 801, Nashville TN 37202. (615)749-6292. Fax (615)749-6512. E-mail: matureyears@umpublishing.org. United Methodist. Marvin W. Cropsey, ed. Inspiration, information, and leisure reading for persons of retirement age. Quarterly mag.; 112 pgs.; circ. 70,000. Subscription $19. 60% unsolicited freelance; 40% assigned. Complete ms/cover letter; fax/e-query OK. Pays .05/wd. on acceptance for one-time rts. Articles 900-2,000 wds. (60/yr.); fiction 1,200-2,000 wds. (4/yr.). Responds in 9 wks. Seasonal 14 mos. ahead. Accepts reprints. Prefers accepted ms by e-mail (copied into message). Regularly uses sidebars. Prefers NRSV, NIV. Guidelines (also by e-mail); copy $5. (No ads)

Poetry: Buys 24/yr. Free verse, haiku, light verse, traditional; 4-16 lines; pays $.50-1.00/line. Submit max. 6 poems.

Fillers: Buys 20/yr. Anecdotes (to 300 wds.), cartoons, jokes, prayers, word puzzles (religious only); to 30 wds.; $5-25.

Columns/Departments: Buys 20/yr. Health Hints, 900-1,200 wds.; Modern Revelations (inspirational), 900-1,100 wds.; Fragments of Life (true-life inspirational), 250-600 wds.; Going Places (travel), 1,000-1,500 wds.; Money Matters, 1,200-1,800 wds.

Special Needs: Articles on crafts and pets. Fiction on older adult situations. All areas open except Bible studies.

**This periodical was #35 on the 2004 Top 50 Christian Publishers list (#43 in 2003, #33 in 2002, #34 in 2001, #33 in 2000).

$MEN OF INTEGRITY, 465 Gundersen Dr., Carol Stream IL 60188. (630)260-6200. Fax (630)260-0114. E-mail: mail@menofintegrity.net. Website: www.MenofIntegrity.net. Christianity Today, Inc. Harry Genet, mng. ed. Uses narrative to apply biblical truth to specific gritty issues men face. Bimonthly pocket-sized mag.; 64 pgs.; circ. 85,000. Subscription $19.95. 10% unsolicited freelance. Complete ms. Pays $50 on acceptance for one-time and electronic rts. Articles 225 wds. (15/yr.). Responds in 4 wks. Accepts simultaneous submissions and reprints (tell when/where appeared). Accepts requested ms on disk or by e-mail (attached file or copied into message). Does not use sidebars. Prefers NLT. Guidelines/theme list (also by e-mail); copy $4/#10 SAE. (No ads)

+MEN OF THE CROSS, 920 Sweetgum Creek, Plano TX 75023. E-mail: info@menofthecross.com. Website: www.menofthecross.com. Greg Paskal, ed./pub.(greg@gregpaskal.com). Encouraging men in their walk with the Lord; strong emphasis on discipleship and relationship. Online community. Open to unsolicited freelance. Complete ms. by e-mail; e-query OK. **NO PAYMENT.** Articles 500-2,000 wds. Accepts reprints.

Tips: "Appropriate topic could be first-hand account of how God worked in the author's life. View online forums for specific topics."

$MENNONITE BRETHREN HERALD, 3169 Riverton Ave., Winnipeg MB R2L 2E5 Canada. (204)654-5760. Fax (204)654-1865. E-mail: mbherald@mbconf.ca. Website: www.mbherald.com. Canadian Conference of Mennonite Brethren Churches. Susan Brandt, acting ed.; Dora Dueck, assoc. ed. Denominational; for information, communication, and spiritual enrichment. Biweekly mag.; 32 pgs.; circ. 17,000. Subscription $30. 75% unsolicited freelance; 25% assigned. Query or complete ms/cover letter; phone/e-query OK. Pays $30-40 (.07/wd.) on publication for 1st or one-time rts. Not copyrighted. Articles 250-1,500 wds. (40/yr.); fiction 1,000-2,000 wds. (10/yr.). Responds in 26 wks. Seasonal 5 mos. ahead. Accepts reprints (tell when/where appeared). Prefers requested ms on disk or by e-mail. Regularly uses sidebars. Prefers NIV. Guidelines/theme list; copy for 9x12 SAE/$1 Canadian postage. (Ads)

Poetry: Buys 6-12/yr. Avant-garde, free verse, traditional; to 25 lines; pays to $10.

Tips: "Most open to feature articles on relevant topics, but not with an American bias."

*MENNONITE FAMILY HISTORY**, 219 Mill Rd., Morgantown PA 19543-9516. Lois Ann Mast, ed. Not in topical listings. No questionnaire returned. (No ads)

($)MENNONITE HISTORIAN, 600 Shaftesbury Blvd., Winnipeg MB R3P 0M4 Canada. (204)888-6781. Fax (204)831-5675. E-mail: aredekopp@mennonitechurch.ca. Website: www.mennonitechurch.ca. Mennonite Church Canada. Alf Redekopp, ed. dir. Gathers and shares historical material related to Mennonites; focus on North America, but also beyond. Quarterly newsletter; 8 pgs.; circ. 2,600. Subscription $11. 40% unsolicited freelance; 20% assigned. Complete ms/cover letter; phone/e-query OK. **NO PAYMENT EXCEPT BY SPECIAL ARRANGEMENT** for 1st rts. Articles 250-1,000 wds. (6/yr.). Responds in 3 wks. Seasonal 3 mos. ahead. Accepts simultaneous submissions and reprints (tell when/where appeared). Prefers e-mail submission (attached file). Does not use sidebars. Guidelines (also by e-mail); copy $1/9x12 SAE. (Ads)

Tips: "Must be Mennonite related (i.e., related to the life and history of the denomination, its people, organizations, and activities). Most open to lead articles. Write us with your ideas. Also genealogical articles."

$MESSAGE, Review and Herald Pub. Assn., 55 W. Oak Ridge Dr., Hagerstown MD 21740. (301)393-4099. Fax (301)393-4103. E-mail: message@RHPA.org, or ronsmith@rhpa.org. Website: www.Messagemagazine.org. Review & Herald/Seventh-day Adventist. Ron Smith, ed. African Americans and all people seeking practical Christian guidance on current events and a better lifestyle. Bimonthly mag.; 48 pgs.; circ. 80,000. Subscription $12.95. Most articles assigned. Query or complete ms/cover letter; fax/e-query OK. Pays $50-300 ($50-75 for fiction) on acceptance for 1st rts. Articles 700-1,200 wds. (50/yr.); parables; fiction (6/yr.) for children (ages 5-8), 500 wds. Responds in 6-10 wks. Seasonal 6 mos. ahead. Prefers requested ms on disk, no e-mail submission. Regularly uses sidebars. Prefers NIV. Guidelines (also by e-mail/Website); copy for 9x12 SAE/2 stamps. (No ads)

Columns/Departments: Buys 12/yr. Healthspan (health issues), 700 wds.; MESSAGE Jr. (biblical stories or stories with clear-cut moral for ages 5-8), 500 wds.; $75-150.

Tips: "As with any publication, writers should have a working knowledge of *Message*. They should have some knowledge of our style and our readers."

**This periodical was #47 on the 1999 Top 50 Christian Publishers list. Also 1995 EPA Award of Merit—Missionary.

MESSAGE OF THE OPEN BIBLE, 2020 Bell Ave., Des Moines IA 50315-1096. (515)288-6761. Fax (515)288-2510. E-mail: message@openbible.org. Website: www.openbible.org. Open Bible Standard Churches. Andrea Johnson, ed. To inspire, inform, and educate the Open Bible family. Bimonthly mag.; 16 pgs.; circ. 3,000. Subscription $9.95. 3% unsolicited freelance; 3% assigned. Query or complete ms/cover letter; e-query OK. **PAYS 5 COPIES**. Not copyrighted. Articles 750 wds. (2/yr.). Responds in 4 wks. Seasonal 4 mos. ahead. Accepts simultaneous submissions and reprints (tell when/where appeared). Accepts requested ms on disk or by e-mail. Regularly uses sidebars. Prefers NIV. Guidelines/theme list (also by e-mail); copy for 9x12 SAE/2 stamps. (No ads)

Fillers: Accepts 6/yr. Cartoons, facts, quotes, short humor; 50 wds.

Tips: "A writer can best break in by giving us material for an upcoming theme, or something inspiring, specifically as it would relate to an Open Bible lay person."
**1995 EPA Award of Merit—Denominational.

\$*MESSENGER, Box 18068, Covington KY 41018-0068. Fax (859)283-6226. Catholic. Diane Reder, news ed. Diocese paper of Covington KY. Weekly (45X) newspaper; 24 pgs.; circ. 16,000. Subscription \$18. 40% unsolicited freelance. Query/clips. Pays \$1.25/column inch on publication for 1st rts. Articles 500-800 wds. Responds in 1 wk. Seasonal 1 mo. ahead. Accepts simultaneous submissions. Guidelines; free copy. (Ads)

\$THE MESSENGER OF SAINT ANTHONY, Via Orto Botanico 11, 35123 Padova, Italy (US address: Anthonian Assn., 101 Saint Anthony Dr., Mt. Saint Francis IN 47146). (812)923-6356 or 049 8229924. Fax (812)923-3200 or 049 8225651. E-mail: m.conte@mess-s-antonio.it (editor); messenger@mess-s-antonio.it (ed. sec.), or info@saintanthonyofpadua.net. Website: www.saintanthonyofpadua.net. Catholic/Provincia Padovana F.M.C. Fr. Mario Conte OFM, ed.; Karen Brookes, ed. sec. For middle-aged and older Catholics in English-speaking world; articles that address current issues. Monthly & online mag.; 50 pgs.; circ. 35,000. Subscription \$25 US. 10% unsolicited freelance; 90% assigned. Query (complete ms for fiction); phone/fax/e-query OK. Pays \$40/pg. (600 wds./pg.) for one-time rts. Articles 600-2,400 wds. (40/yr.); fiction 900-1,200 wds. (11/yr.). Responds in 8-10 wks. Seasonal 3 mos. ahead. Prefers e-mail submission (attached file or copied into message). Regularly uses sidebars. Prefers NEB (Oxford Study Edition). Guidelines (also by e-mail); free copy. (No ads)

  Columns/Departments: Buys 50-60/yr. Documentary (issues), 600-2,000 wds.; Spirituality, 600-2,000 wds.; Church Life, 600-2,000 wds.; Saint Anthony (devotional), 600-1,400 wds.; Living Today (family life), 600-1,400 wds.; \$55-200. Complete ms.

  Special Needs: Short story of a moral or religious nature; St. Anthony.

  Tips: "Most open to short stories; Saint Anthony, and devotional articles on parishes named after Saint Anthony, local feasts/shrines in Saint Anthony's honour."

\$MESSENGER OF THE SACRED HEART, 661 Greenwood Ave., Toronto ON M4J 4B3 Canada. (416)466-1195. Catholic/Apostleship of Prayer. Rev. F. J. Power, S.J., ed. Help for daily living on a spiritual level. Monthly mag.; 32 pgs.; circ. 13,000. Subscription \$14. 20% freelance. Complete ms; no phone query. Pays .06/wd. on acceptance for 1st rts. Articles 800-1,500 wds. (30/yr.); fiction 800-1,500 wds. (12/yr.). Responds in 5 wks. Seasonal 5 mos. ahead. No disk. Does not use sidebars. Guidelines; copy \$1/9x12 SAE. (No ads)

  Tips: "Most open to inspirational stories and articles."

\$+MESSIAH MAGAZINE, PO Box 620099, Littleton CO 80162-0099. Fax (303933-0997. Website: www.ffoz.org. First Fruits of Zion. Hope Egan, ed. Dedicated to the study, exploration, and celebration of our righteous and sinless Torah—observant King—Yeshua of Nazareth. Mag. published 5X/yr.; 34 pgs.; circ. 10,000. Subscription for donation. Open to freelance. Query; fax query OK. Pays on acceptance for all rts. Articles (15-20/yr.). Responds in 3 wks. Seasonal 6 mos. ahead. Accepts simultaneous submissions; no reprints. Requires e-mail submissions (attached file). No sidebars. Prefers NASB. Copy for \$4/9x12 SAE/5 stamps. Incomplete topical listings. (No ads)

  Tips: "F.F.O.Z. is a nonprofit ministry devoted to strengthening the love and appreciation of the Body of the Messiah for the land, people, and scriptures of Israel. Since our focus is unique, please be very familiar with our magazine before submitting your query. Our Torah Testimony column is always open, as are some of the others. Looking for something on Hebrew roots."

\$MESSIANIC SCI-FI ONLINE. E-mail: msf-submit@heartofisrael.org. Website: www.heartofisrael.org/msf. Pia Cruz, Stephanie Lutz, Joe Applegate, eds. Quarterly e-zine. 100% freelance.

Heavily Bible-based science fiction that glorifies God. Welcomes new writers. Authors paid per download through offsite service. All legal issues/rights/finances are between that service and the author. Publishes (a) author's testimony (b) introduction (like a book jacket cover) and (c) "Teaser": first 200 words of ms. Will maintain archives so new visitors/readers can buy older stories from authors and will allow (and may help) authors create their own individual Website to promote their work to increase sales of their story. Pays 1/8 cent/wd., for original stories only, for one-time rts. Articles to 2,000 words (also accepts serials). Responds within 1-3 mos. No simultaneous submissions. Requires submissions by e-mail (copied into message). See Website for guidelines, topics, and deadlines, and suggested biblical Scripture references (for inspiration) for 2005.

Tips: "For classic topics (e.g., apocalyptic fiction), we seek a very fresh approach in an area that has been done to death! Primary motivation for writing: glorify God with your talent."

THE MESSIANIC TIMES, PO Box 2190, Niagara Falls NY 14302. (905)685-4072. Fax (905)685-7371. E-mail: editor@messianictimes.com. Website: www.messianictimes.com. Rosalind Golden, ed. To unify the Messianic Jewish community around the world, to serve as an evangelistic tool to the Jewish community, and to educate Christians about the Jewish roots of their faith. Bimonthly newspaper; circ. 35,000. Subscription free. Accepts freelance. Not in topical listings. No questionnaire returned. (Ads)

METHODIST HISTORY, PO Box 127, Madison NJ 07940. (973)408-3189. Fax (973)408-3909. E-mail: cyrigoyen@gcah.org. Website: www.gcah.org. United Methodist. Charles Yrigoyen Jr., ed. History of the United Methodism and Methodist/Wesleyan churches. Quarterly jour.; 64 pgs.; circ. 800. Subscription $20. 100% unsolicited freelance. Query; phone/fax/e-query OK. **PAYS IN COPIES** for all rts. Historical articles to 5,000 wds. (15/yr.); book reviews 500 wds. Responds in 8 wks. Requires requested ms on disk. Does not use sidebars. Guidelines (also on Website); no copy. (Ads)

Special Needs: United Methodist church history.

METRO VOICE, 305 S.W. Market, Ste. 4, Lee's Summit MO 64063. (816)524-4522. Fax (816)282-0010. E-mail: editor@metrovoicenews.com. Website: www.metrovoicenews .com. Nondenominational. Dwight & Anita Widaman, pubs. To promote Christian business, ministries, and organizations and provide thought-provoking commentary for edification of the body of Christ. Monthly newspaper; circ. 35,000. Subscription $14. 50% unsolicited freelance. Complete ms/cover letter; short phone query OK. **PAYS IN COPIES** or limited amount for well-researched pieces, for one-time or reprint rts. Not copyrighted. Articles to 1,200 wds. (100/yr.). Responds in 6 wks. Seasonal 6 mos. ahead. Accepts reprints. Guidelines; copy for 9x12 SAE/$1 postage.

Fillers: Accepts 12/yr. Anecdotes, cartoons, ideas, newsbreaks, quotes, short humor; to 500 wds.

Tips: "We look for up-to-date information. Willing to work with new writers who want to learn. Interested in investigative features and current events."

MIDNIGHT CALL MAGAZINE, PO Box 280008, Columbia SC 29228. Toll-free (800)845-2420. (803)755-0733. Fax (803)755-6002. E-mail: info@midnightcall.com. Website: www.mid nightcall.com. Arno Froese, ed. The world's only international voice of prophecy regarding end-time events.

MID-SOUTH CHRISTIAN BANNER, PO Box 40086, Memphis TN 38174-0086. (662)280-1304. Fax (662)280-1301. E-mail: abholmes@bellsouth.net; publisher@christian banner.com. Website: www.christianbanner.com. Independent. Mary Ann Marchbanks, pub.; Warren Smith, ed. Holding forth truth and traditional Judeo-Christian values as found in God's Word, and seeking to increase awareness and activism among its readers related to moral, ethical, political, and biblical issues that affect the Christian community. Monthly newspaper. Subscription $24 (free to churches). Open to freelance articles, press releases, and news of interest to readers. Guidelines on Website. Not in topical listings. No questionnaire returned. (Ads)

$MINNESOTA CHRISTIAN CHRONICLE, 7317 Cahill Rd., #201, Minneapolis MN 55439. Toll-free (800)257-4972. (952)562-1234, ext. 213. Fax (952)941-3010. E-mail: editor@ mcchronicle.com. Website: www.mcchronicle.com. World Newspaper Publishing. Bryan Malley, ed. Local news and features of interest to the Christian community. Biweekly & online newspaper; 28 pgs.; circ. 20,000. Subscription $19.95 (some free distribution). 5% unsolicited freelance; 5% assigned. Query; e-query OK. Accepts e-mail submissions (attached or copied into message). Pays $20-200 one month after publication for one-time rts. Articles 500-2,000 wds. (36/yr.). Responds in 5 wks. Seasonal 2 mos. ahead. Accepts simultaneous query and reprints (tell when/where appeared). Regularly uses sidebars. Guidelines (also by e-mail); copy $2. (Ads)

> **Tips:** "We most often use freelancers in our local news and feature article sections. Stories with a strong Minnesota hook will be accepted. Unique ministries, events, and/or people interest our readers the most. We also encourage participation in communities." Loves e-queries.
>
> **1996 EPA Award of Merit—Newspaper; 1995 EPA Award of Excellence—Newspaper.

$THE MIRACULOUS MEDAL, 475 E. Chelten Ave., Philadelphia PA 19144-5785. (215)848-1010. Fax (215)848-1014. Website: www.cammonline.org. Catholic. Rev. James O. Kiernan, C.M., ed. Fiction and poetry for Catholic adults, mostly women. Quarterly mag.; 36 pgs.; circ. 340,000. Subscription free to members. 25% unsolicited freelance. Query by mail only. Pays .02/wd. and up, on acceptance, for 1st rts. Religious fiction 1,000-2,400 wds.; some 1,000-1,200 wds. (6/yr.). Responds in 26 wks. Seasonal anytime. Accepts simultaneous submissions. Guidelines (also by e-mail); copy for 6x9 SAE/2 stamps. (No ads)

> **Poetry:** Buys 6/yr. Free verse, traditional; to 20 lines; .50 & up/line. Send any number. "Must have religious theme, preferably about the Blessed Virgin Mary."
>
> **Tips:** "Most open to good short stories, 1,500-2,500 wds., or poetry, with light religious theme."

$MONTGOMERY'S JOURNEY, 555 Farmington Rd,, Montgomery AL 36109-4609. (334)213-7940. Fax (334)213-7990. E-mail: Journey@watsonmedia.com. Website: www.watsonmedia.com. True Life Publishing, LLC. DeAnne Watson, pub. For protestant Christians and Christian families. Monthly mag.; 40-48 pgs.; circ. 7,000. Subscription $20. Open to freelance. Query or complete ms/cover letter; fax/e-query OK. Pays $25 on publication for one-time or reprint rts. Articles 1,800-2,000 wds. Seasonal 3 mos. ahead. Accepts requested ms on disk or by e-mail (attached file). No kill fee. Regularly uses sidebars. Accepts submissions from teens. No guidelines or copy. (Ads)

> **Tips:** "Mainly open to feature stories."

+MOSAIC (Canadian Baptist), 7185 Millcreek Dr., Mississauga ON L5N 5R4 Canada. (905)821-3533. Fax (905)826-3441. E-mail: mosaic@cbmin.org. Website: www.cbmin.org. Canadian Baptist. Jennifer Lau, ed. A community forum of local and global voices united by a shared mission—to serve as a catalyst to stimulate and encourage passionate discipleship. Quarterly mag.; circ. 20,000. Open to unsolicited freelance. Incomplete topical listings. (No ads)

+MOSAIC (Free Methodist), 4315 Village Centre Ct., Mississauga ON L4Z 1S2 Canada. (905)848-2600. Fax (905)848-2603. E-mail: howdenl@fmc-canada.org. Website: www.fmc-canada.org. Free Methodist Church in Canada. Lisa Howden, ed. To equip and inform Free Methodists so the entire church may be built up in Jesus Christ. Bimonthly mag.; circ. 2,100. Subscription $10. Open to unsolicited freelance. Not in topical listings. (Ads)

MOVIEGUIDE, 2510-G Los Posas Rd. #502, Camarillo CA 93010. (805)383-2000. Fax (805)383-4089. E-mail: office@movieguide.org. Website: www.movieguide.org. Good News Communications/Christian Film & TV Commission. Dr. Theodore Baehr, pub. Family guide to media entertainment from a biblical perspective. Biweekly mag.; 23+ pgs.; circ. 3,000. Subscription $40. 40% unsolicited freelance. Query/clips. **NO PAYMENT** for all rts. Articles 1,200 wds. (100/yr.); book/music/video/movie reviews, 1,200 wds. Responds in 6 wks. Seasonal 6 mos. ahead. Accepts requested ms on disk. Regularly uses sidebars. Guidelines/theme list; copy for SAE/4 stamps. (Ads)

    Fillers: Accepts 1,000/yr.; all types; 20-50 wds.

    Columns/Departments: MovieGuide; TravelGuide; VideoGuide; CDGuide, etc.; 1,200 wds.

($)MUTUALITY, 122 W. Franklin Ave., Ste. 218, Minneapolis MN 55404-2451. (612)872-6898. Fax (612)872-6891. E-mail: mutuality@cbeinternational.org. Website: www.cbeinter national.org. Christians for Biblical Equality. Jaime Hunt, ed. Seeks to provide inspiration, encouragement, and information about equality within the Christian church around the world. Quarterly mag.; 32 pgs.; circ. 2,200. Subscription $30/free to members & donors. 80% assigned freelance. Query/clips; fax/e-query OK. **PAYS A GIFT CERTIFICATE TO THEIR BOOKSTORE** on publication for 1st or electronic rts. Articles 500-2,500 wds. (12/yr.); book reviews 600 wds. Responds in 6 wks. Accepts reprints (tell when/where appeared). Accepts requested ms on disk or by e-mail (attached file). Regularly uses sidebars. Prefers NRSV, NIV, TNIV. Guidelines (also on Website); copy for 9x12 SAE/3 stamps. (Ads)

$NATIONAL CATHOLIC REPORTER, 115 E. Armour Blvd., Kansas City MO 64111. (816)531-0538. Fax (816)968-2280. E-mail: ncr_editor@natcath.org. Catholic. Thomas Fox, pub; Tom Roberts, ed-in-chief. Independent. Weekly (44X) & online newspaper; 44-48 pgs.; circ. 120,000. Query/clips. Pays .20/wd. on publication, or varying rates by agreement. Articles & short stories, varying lengths. Responds in up to 6 wks. Accepts simultaneous submissions. Guidelines (also by e-mail/Website); copy on Website.

    Columns/Departments: Query with ideas for columns.

NETWORK, PO Box 131165, Birmingham AL 35213-6165. (205)328-7112. E-mail: network newspaper@earthlink.net. Website: www.networknewspaper.org. Interdenominational. Dolores Milazzo Hicks, ed./pub. (dolores@networknewspaper.org). To encourage and nurture dialog, understanding, and unity in Christian communities. Monthly tabloid; 12-16 pgs.; circ. 10,000. Subscription $25. 50% unsolicited freelance. Phone/fax/e-query OK. **NO PAYMENT**. Not copyrighted. Articles to 500 wds. Accepts simultaneous submissions. Articles and news.

    Tips: "Most open to feature stories that express the unity of the Body of Christ and articles that encourage and uplift our readers. We also cover state, local, national, and international news."

$THE NEW FREEMAN, One Bayard Dr., Saint John NB E2L 3L5 Canada. (506)653-6806. Fax (506)653-6818. E-mail: tnf@nbnet.nb.ca. Roman Catholic Diocese of St. John. Submit to The Editor. Weekly tabloid; 12 pgs.; circ. 7,300. Subscription $18.69 Can., $30 US. 70% unsolicited freelance; 30% assigned. Query/clips; phone/fax/e-query OK. Pays variable rates on publication. Not copyrighted. Articles about 200 wds. Seasonal 2 mos. ahead. Accepts simultaneous submissions and reprints (tell when/where appeared). Accepts requested ms on disk or by e-mail (attached/.txt format or copied into message). Kill fee. Uses some sidebars. No guidelines/copy. (Ads)

    Tips: "We are very open to all sorts of freelance possibilities."

NEW FRONTIER, 180 E. Ocean Blvd., 4th Fl., Long Beach CA 90802. (562)491-8343. Fax (562)491-8791. E-mail: safrontier@aol.com, or newfrontier@usw.salvationarmy.org. Website: www.salvationarmy.usawest.org/newfrontier. Salvation Army—Western Territory.

Robert L. Docter, ed. To share the good news of the gospel and the work of The Salvation Army in the western territory with salvationists and friends. Biweekly newspaper; circ. 25,500. Subscription $10. Open to freelance. Prefers query. Not in topical listings. (Ads) **2000 & 1997 EPA Award of Merit—Newspaper.

A NEW HEART, Box 4004, San Clemente CA 92674-4004. (949)496-7655. Fax (949)496-8465. E-mail: HCFUSA@juno.com. Website: www.HCFUSA.com. Aubrey Beauchamp, ed. For Christian healthcare givers; information regarding medical/Christian issues. Quarterly mag.; 16 pgs.; circ. 5,000. Subscription $25. 20% unsolicited freelance; 10% assigned. Complete ms/cover letter; phone/fax/e-query OK. **PAYS 2 COPIES** for one-time rts. Not copyrighted. Articles 600-1,800 wds. (20-25/yr.). Responds in 2-3 wks. Accepts simultaneous submissions and reprints. Accepts e-mail submission. Does not use sidebars. Guidelines (also by fax); copy for 9x12 SAE/3 stamps. (Ads)

> **Poetry:** Accepts 1-2/yr. Submit max. 1-3 poems.
>
> **Fillers:** Accepts 3-4/yr. Anecdotes, cartoons, facts, jokes, short humor; 100-120 wds.
>
> **Columns/Departments:** Accepts 20-25/yr. Chaplain's Corner, 200-250 wds.; Physician's Corner, 200-250 wds.
>
> **Tips:** "Most open to real-life situations which may benefit and encourage healthcare givers and patients. True stories with medical and evangelical emphasis."

$NEW MAN, 600 Rinehart Rd., Lake Mary FL 32746-4872. (407)333-0600. Fax (407)333-7133. E-mail: newman@strang.com. Website: www.newmanmagazine.com. Strang Communications Co. Robert Andresik, ed. America's #1 Christian men's magazine. Bimonthly mag.; 72 pgs.; circ. 125,000. Subscription $19.95. 5% unsolicited freelance; 95% assigned. Prefers query/clips (complete ms OK); e-query OK. Pays .15/wd. and up on publication for all rts. (negotiable). Articles 2,000 wds.; book/music/video reviews, 300 wds. ($70). Responds in 9 wks. Seasonal 4 mos. ahead. Accepts reprints (tell when/where appeared). Accepts e-mail submissions (attached or copied into message). Kill fee. Uses some sidebars. Guidelines (also on Website); copy $4. Incomplete topical listings. (Ads)

> **Fillers:** Short clips of interest to men, 50-250 wds.
>
> **Special Needs:** "Every man" stories: ordinary people who have extraordinary testimonies; men who overcome difficult circumstances; men who do things the rest of us only dream about; men with unusual jobs.
>
> **Tips:** "Send in clips of where you have been published before."
>
> **2001 EPA Award of Merit—General.

$+NEW WINESKINS, PO Box 41028, Nashville TN 37204-1028. (615)292-2940. Fax (615)292-2931. E-mail: gtaylor@woodmont.org, or wineskinsmagazine@msn.com. Website: www.wineskins.org. The ZOE Group, Inc. Greg Taylor, mng. ed. Combines biblical and cultural scholarly focus with popular-level articles and art for a powerful journal/magazine hybrid. Bimonthly mag. & e-zine; 40-60 pgs.; circ. 5,000. Subscription $19.95 (online). 40% unsolicited freelance; 60% assigned. Query; phone query OK; e-query preferred. Pays $50-100 for online, and $50-250 for print, 2-3 mos. after publication for one-time and electronic rts. Articles 800-2,500 wds. (100/yr.); fiction 1,000-2,500 wds. (10/yr.); book reviews 800-1,200 wds. ($50-100). Responds in 8-10 wks. Seasonal 6 mos. ahead. Accepts simultaneous submissions & reprints (tell when/where appeared). Prefers e-mail submissions (attached or copied into message). No kill fee. Sometimes uses sidebars. Accept submissions from children or teens. Prefers NIV or NRSV. Guidelines by e-mail/Website; copy on Website. (Ads)

> **Poetry:** Buys 4-5/yr. Avant-garde, free verse, light verse; 100-2,000 wds. Pays $50. Submit max. 1 poem.
>
> **Tips:** "Best way to break in is by reviewing books, specifically ones we request. Also by writing well-shaped and well-researched pieces that are more than just opinions." Note: This publication is transitioning to online, but still publishes a print edition twice a year.

$THE NORTH AMERICAN VOICE OF FATIMA, 1023 Swann Rd., Youngstown NY 14174-0167. (716)754-7489. Fax (716)754-9130. E-mail: Voice@fatimashrine.com. Website: www .fatimashrine.com. Barnabite Fathers, Inc./Catholic. Rev. Peter M. Calabrese, CRSP, ed. A magazine of Catholic spirituality dedicated to Our Lady of Fatima, to share the joy and challenge of the gospel and to foster devotion to Our Lady. Quarterly mag.; 28 pgs.; circ. 1,200. Subscription $4.50. 90% unsolicited freelance; 10% assigned. Complete ms/cover letter; phone/fax/e-query OK. Pays .05/wd. on publication for 1st, one-time, reprint, and electronic rts. Articles 500-1,500 wds. (32/yr.); book reviews to 500 wds. Responds in 12 wks.; unsolicited mss are not returned. Seasonal 2 mos. ahead. Accepts simultaneous submissions and reprints (tell when/where appeared). Accepts requested ms on disk or by e-mail (attached or copied into message). Some kill fees. Uses some sidebars. Prefers RSV, NRSV, NAB. Guidelines (also by e-mail); free copy. (No ads)

> **Poetry:** Buys 16-20/yr. Free verse, traditional; 4 lines and up; $10-25. Publishes a page of poetry in each issue.
>
> **Fillers:** Buys 3/yr. Anecdotes, cartoons, facts, ideas, kid quotes, prayers, quizzes, quotes, short humor, and word puzzles, 15-200 wds.; $1-10.
>
> **Columns/Departments:** Pro-Life (stories that promote respect for life—conception to death), 800-1,500 wds.; .05/wd. Complete ms.
>
> **Tips:** "All areas are open. Mary, Sacraments, biblical reflections, discipleship, and ecumenical articles as well as practical applications of spirituality are desired."

$+NOSTALGIA MAGAZINE, 1703 N. Normandie St., Spokane WA 99205. (509)323-2086. Fax (509)323-2096. E-mail: mcarter@NostalgiaMagazine.us. Website: www.nostalgia magazine.us. King's Publishing Group, Inc. Mark Carter, ed. Stories and photos from 1970 and previous—both memories and history. Monthly mag.; 48 pgs.; circ. 6,000+. Subscription $24.95. 90% unsolicited freelance; 10% assigned. Complete ms/cover letter. Pays negotiable rate or copies/subscription on publication for one-time, reprint, simultaneous, electronic, or nonexclusive rts. Articles 400+ wds. (120/yr.). Responds in 4 wks. Seasonal 4 mos. ahead. Accepts simultaneous submissions & reprints (tell when/where appeared). Prefers e-mail submissions (copied into message). No kill fee. Regularly uses sidebars. Guidelines (also by e-mail); query for themes/topics; copy $1.50/9x12 SAE. (Ads)

> **Poetry:** Accepts 6/yr. Free verse, light verse, traditional; variable length. Pays in copies. Submit max. 1 poem. Send photo with poem.
>
> **Fillers:** Accepts 100+/yr. Anecdotes, facts, games, quizzes, historic photos. Pays copies/ subscription
>
> **Columns/Departments:** Buys 60/yr. Old Recipes; Hitch-Hiking; Games We Used to Play; Historic Household Hints; Old Movie Reviews; all 400 wds.
>
> **Tips:** "Looking for quality photo essays—pre-1970s only. Send interesting pre-1970s photos with episodic captions. Also personal experiences with interesting photos; write about how you used to do things, supported by photos. No genealogies."

$NOW WHAT?, Box 33677, Denver CO 80233. (303)452-7973. Fax (303)452-0657. E-mail: bibleadvocate@cog7.org. Website: http://nowwhat.cog7.org. Church of God (Seventh-day). Calvin Burrell, ed.; Sherri Langton, assoc. ed. Articles on salvation, Jesus, social issues, life problems that are seeker sensitive. Monthly online mag.; available only online. 100% unsolicited freelance. Complete ms/cover letter; no query. Pays $25-55 on publication for first, one-time, electronic, simultaneous, and reprint rts. Articles 1,000-1,500 wds. (20/yr.). Responds in 4-8 wks. Accepts simultaneous submissions and reprints (tell when/where appeared). Accepts requested ms on disk or by e-mail (copied into message). Regularly uses sidebars. Prefers NIV. Guidelines (also on Website); copy of online article for #10 SAE/1 stamp. (No ads)

> **Fillers:** Buys 5-10/yr. Anecdotes, facts, prose, quotes; 50-100 wds.; $20.

Special Needs: "Personal experiences must still show a person's struggle that either brought him/her to Christ or deepened faith in God. The entire *Now What?* site is built around a personal experience each month."

Tips: "The whole e-zine is open to freelance. Think how you can explain your faith, or how you overcame a problem, to a non-Christian. It's a real plus for writers submitting a personal experience to also submit an objective article related to their story. Or they can contact Sherri Langton for upcoming personal experiences that need related articles."

($)NRB MAGAZINE, 9510 Technology Dr., Manassas VA 20110-4167. (703)330-7000. Fax (703)330-6996. E-mail: cpryor@nrb.org. Website: www.nrb.org. National Religious Broadcasters. Christine L. Pryor, ed.; V. Fraedrich, asst. ed. Topics relate to Christian radio, television, satellite, church media, Internet and all forms of communication; promoting access and excellence in Christian communications. Monthly (9X) & online mag.; 52 pgs.; circ. 10,000. Subscription $24; Canadians add $6 US; foreign add $24 US. 70% unsolicited freelance. Complete ms/cover letter; fax/e-query OK. **PAYS 6 COPIES** ($100-200 for assigned) on publication for 1st or reprint rts. Articles 1,000-2,000 wds. (30/yr.). Responds in 6 wks. Seasonal 6 mos. ahead. Accepts simultaneous submissions and reprints (tell when/where appeared). Prefers accepted ms by e-mail. Regularly uses sidebars. Prefers NAS. Guidelines/theme list (also by e-mail); free copy. (Ads)

Columns/Departments: Valerie Fraedrich, asst. ed. Accepts 9/yr. Trade Talk (summary paragraphs of news items/events in Christian broadcasting), 50 wds.; Opinion (social issues), 750 wds. Columns coordinated in-house, 500 wds.

Special Needs: Electronic media; education. All articles must relate in some way to broadcasting: radio, TV, programs on radio/TV, or Internet.

Tips: "Most open to feature articles relevant to Christian communicators. Become acquainted with broadcasters in your area and note their struggles, concerns, and victories. Find out what they would like to know, research the topic, then write about it." Contact assistant editor for guidelines, reprint permission, classified ads, additional copies, etc. **1999 EPA Award of Merit—Most Improved Publication.

$OBLATES, 9480 N. De Mazenod Dr., Belleville IL 62223-1160. Toll-free (888)330-6264. (618)398-4848. Fax (618)398-8788. E-mail: mami@oblatesusa.org. Website: www .oblatesusa.org. Catholic/Missionary Assn. of Missionary Oblates of Mary Immaculate. Mary Mohrman, mss ed. To inspire, comfort, uplift, and motivate a Catholic/Christian audience. Bimonthly mag.; 24 pgs.; circ. 500,000. Free to members. 15% unsolicited freelance. Complete ms only/cover letter; no phone/fax/e-query. Pays $150 on acceptance for 1st rts. Articles 500-600 wds. Responds in 9 wks. Seasonal 6 mos. ahead. Considers simultaneous submissions. No disk. Does not use sidebars. Prefers NAB. Guidelines; copy for 6x9 SAE/2 stamps. (No ads)

Poetry: Free verse, traditional; 8-12 lines; $50. Submit max. 2 poems.

Tips: "Need personal, inspirational articles with a strong spiritual theme firmly grounded to a particular incident, and poetry." No Christmas material.

$ON MISSION, 4200 North Point Pkwy., Alpharetta GA 30022-4176. (770)410-6284. Fax (770)410-6105. E-mail: onmission@namb.net, or cpipes@namb.net. Website: www .onmission.com. North American Mission Board, Southern Baptist. Submit to The Managing Editor. Helping readers share Christ in the real world. Bimonthly & online mag.; 56 pgs.; circ. 90,000. Subscription $14.95. 1-5% unsolicited freelance; 50-60% assigned. Query/clips for assignments; no phone/fax/e-query. Pays .25-.50/wd. on acceptance for all, 1st, one-time, reprint, or electronic rts. Articles 250-1,200 wds., most 750-1,000 wds. (6/yr.). Responds in 6-12 wks. Seasonal 8 mos. ahead. Accepts e-mail submission (attached and copied into message). Kill fee. Regularly uses sidebars. Prefers NIV. Guidelines on Website. (Ads)

Special Needs: Needs 700-1,000 word, principle-based articles with practical applications for how to live a lifestyle of personal evangelism, how to have a successful mission experience, or how to plant a church.

Tips: "Write a solid, 750-word, how-to article geared to 20- to 40-year-old men and women who want fresh ideas and insight into sharing Christ in the real world in which they live, work, and play. Send a résumé, along with your best writing samples. We are an on-assignment magazine, but occasionally a well-written manuscript gets published."

**2000 EPA Award of Merit—Missionary; 1999 EPA Award of Excellence—Missionary; many EPA Higher Goals Awards, 1999-2002.

$OUR SUNDAY VISITOR, 200 Noll Plaza, Huntington IN 46750. (260)356-8400. Fax (260)359-9117. E-mail: oursunvis@osv.com. Website: www.osv.com. Catholic. Gerald Korson, ed. Vital news analysis, perspective, spirituality for today's Catholic. Weekly newspaper; 24 pgs.; circ. 68,000. 10% unsolicited freelance; 90% assigned. Query or complete ms; fax/e-query OK. Pays $100-300 on acceptance for 1st & electronic rts. Articles to 1,100 wds. (25/yr.). Responds in 6 wks. Seasonal 2 mos. ahead. No simultaneous submissions; rarely accepts reprints (tell when/where appeared). Kill fee. Regularly uses sidebars. Prefers RSV. Guidelines (also by e-mail/Website); copy for 10x13 SASE. (Ads)

Columns/Departments: Faith; Family; Trends; and Profile. See guidelines for details.

Tips: "Our mission is to examine the news, culture, and trends of the day from a faithful and sound Catholic perspective—to see the world through the eyes of faith.

$OVER THE BACK FENCE, 14 S. Paint St., Ste. 69, PO Box 756, Chillicothe OH 45601. (740)772-2165. Fax (740)773-7626. E-mail: backfenc@bright.net. Website: www.panther publishing.com. Panther Publishing, Inc. Sarah Williamson, mng. ed. Positive news about Southern Ohio. Quarterly mag.; 64 pgs.; circ. 15,000. Subscription $9.97. 60% unsolicited freelance. Query/clips; fax/e-query OK. Pays .10-.20/wd. on publication for one-time rts. Articles 750-1,000 wds. (9-12/yr.); fiction 300-850 wds. (4/yr.). Responds in 13 wks. Seasonal 1 yr. ahead. Accepts simultaneous submissions and reprints (tell when/where appeared). Requires requested ms on disk or by e-mail (copied into message). Regularly uses sidebars. Guidelines (also on Website); copy $4/9x12 SAE, or on Website. (Ads)

Poetry: Buys 4/yr. Free verse, light verse, traditional; 1 pg.; $25 min. Submit max. 5 poems.

Columns/Departments: Buys 10-20/yr. Profiles From the Past (interesting history that never made the headlines), 800-1,000 wds.; Heartstrings (touching essays), 800 wds.; Shorts (humorous essays), 800 wds. Complete ms. Pays $80-120.

Special Needs: Think upbeat and positive. Articles on nature, history, travel, nostalgia, and family.

Tips: "We need material for our columns most often—Humor, Profiles from the Past, and Heartstrings. It is best for writers to send things with appeal for Midwest readers and be generally positive. We do not publish articles that criticize or create a negative feeling about a geographical area or people."

$PARABOLA: Myth, Tradition, and the Search for Meaning, 656 Broadway, New York NY 10012. (212)505-9037. Fax (212)979-7325. E-mail: editors@parabola.org, or parabola@ panix.com. Website: www.parabola.org. The Society for the Study of Myth and Tradition. Natalie Baan, mng. ed. Devoted to the exploration of the search for meaning as expressed in the myths, symbols, rituals, and art of the world's religious traditions. Quarterly jour.; 144 pgs.; circ. 40,000. Subscription $24. 60% unsolicited freelance; 40% assigned. Query; fax/e-query OK. Pays $150-400 on publication for 1st, one-time, or reprint rts. Articles 1,000-3,000 wds. (40/yr.); book/video reviews 500-700 wds., $75. Responds in 12 wks. Accepts simultaneous submissions and reprints (tell when/where appeared). Accepts e-mail submissions after query (attached file or copied into message). Kill fee varies. Uses some sidebars. Prefers KJV. Guidelines/theme list (also by e-mail/Website); copy $7.50. (Ads)

Columns/Departments: Buys 40/yr. Reviews (books, audios, videos, software), to 700 wds.; Epicycles (retellings of traditional stories), to 1,500 wds.; $75-150.

Tips: "All submissions must relate to themes. We look for well-researched, well-written, and authentic material that strikes a balance between the personal and the objective. No journalistic or self-improvement articles, evangelism, or profiles of specific persons or organizations. No witnessing, no pieces solely focused on Christianity as the only religious truth. We are a multifaith journal and seek reflections on the truths that underlie all forms of religious and spiritual search. Visit our hints page at www.parabola.org/hints.html, for suggestions."

$PARENTLIFE, One Lifeway Plaza, Nashville TN 37234-0172. (615)251-2021. Fax (615)277-8142. E-mail: parentlife@lifeway.com. Website: www.lifeway.com. LifeWay Christian Resources. William Summey, ed-in-chief. A child-centered magazine for parents of children 12 and under. Monthly mag.; 52 pgs.; circ. 100,000. Subscription $22.05. 5% unsolicited freelance; 95% assigned. Query; e-query OK. Pays on publication for nonexclusive rts. Articles 1,000 wds. Responds in 8 wks. Seasonal 1 yr. ahead. Accepts simultaneous submissions; no reprints. Accepts e-mail submissions (attached file). No kill fee. Regularly uses sidebars. Accepts submissions from children. Prefers Holman CSB. Guidelines (also by e-mail); copy for 10x13 SASE. (No ads)

Columns/Departments: Buys 60/yr. The Funny Life (funny family stories), 100 wds.; $20. Complete ms.

Tips: "Most open to a feature article with cutting edge approach to current issues affecting parents/children."

#PARENTS & TEENS. E-mail: submissions@parentsandteens.com. Website: www.parentsandteens.com. Lyn Gregory, ed./pub. (lyngregory@ntlworld.com). To help parents connect with their teens. Biweekly e-zine; 20 pgs.; circ. 10,000. Subscription free. 10% unsolicited freelance. E-mail submissions only. Accepts full ms by e-mail. **PAYS IN COPIES AND LINK TO YOUR WEBSITE/BIO OR EBOOKS** for 1st, one-time, reprint, or electronic rts. Articles 400-1,200 wds. (12/yr.); reviews 500 wds. ($5). Responds in 1-2 wks. Seasonal 3 mos. ahead. Accepts simultaneous submissions and reprints (tell when/where appeared). Prefers e-mail submission (copied into message). Does not use sidebars. Accepts submissions from teens. Guidelines on Website; copy on site archive. (Ads)

Special Needs: Parenting teens and frugal living. Also articles from dads of teens.

Tips: "Query by e-mail."

$PEEKS & VALLEYS: A New England Fiction Journal, PO Box 708, Newport NH 03773-0708. (603)863-5896. Fax (603)863-8198. E-mail: hotdog@nhvt.net. Website: www.peeksandvalleys.com. Davis Publications. Cindy Davis, ed. Literary magazine of short stories. Quarterly mag. 100% freelance. Complete ms; fax/e-query OK. Pays $5 & up on acceptance for one-time or reprint rts. Not copyrighted. Fiction to 3,000 wds. (30/yr.). Responds in 4-9 wks. Seasonal 6 mos. ahead. Accepts simultaneous submissions and reprints. Accepts submissions from children & teens. Guidelines; copy $4.

Poetry: Buys 5/yr. Light verse, traditional; to 30 lines. Submit max. 2 poems.

Special Needs: Short story submissions by children.

Tips: "No talking animals, sex, or obscenity."

THE PEGASUS REVIEW, PO Box 88, Henderson MD 21640-0088. (410)482-6736. E-mail: bounds1@comcast.net. Art Bounds, ed. Theme-oriented poetry, short fiction, and essays; not necessarily religious; in calligraphy format. Bimonthly mag.; 10-12 pgs.; circ. 125. Subscription $12. 100% unsolicited freelance. Query or complete ms/cover letter; e-query OK. **PAYS 2 COPIES** for one-time rts. Fiction 2.5 pgs. is ideal, single-spaced (6-10/yr.); also one-page essays. Responds in 4-5 wks. Seasonal 2 mos. ahead. Accepts simultaneous submissions and reprints (tell when/where appeared). No disk or e-mail submissions.

Does not use sidebars. Prefers KJV. Accepts submissions from teens. Guidelines/theme list (also by e-mail); copy $2.50. (No ads)

Poetry: Accepts 100/yr. Any type; 4-25 lines (shorter the better—pay attention to line length). Theme oriented. Submit max. 3 poems.

Fillers: Accepts 10-20/yr. Cartoons, prose, essays; 100-150 wds.

Special Needs: 2005 themes: Jan/Feb—Adventure; Mar/Apr—History/Custom/Tradition; May/Jun—Imagination; Jul/Aug—Parents; Sep/Oct—Teaching/Knowledge; and Nov/Dec—Music.

Tips: "Above all, persevere."

PENTECOSTAL MESSENGER, PO Box 850, Joplin MO 64802. Toll-free (800)444-4674. (417)624-7050. Fax (417)624-7102, or (800)982-5687. E-mail: johnm@pcg.org. Website: www.pcg.org. Denominational/Pentecostal Church of God. John Mallinak, ed. Monthly (11X) mag.; circ. 6,000. Subscription $12. Accepts freelance. Prefers query. Complete ms. Articles and reviews. Copy $1.50. Not in topical listings. No questionnaire returned. (Ads)

THE PENWOOD REVIEW, PO Box 862, Los Alamitos CA 90720-0862. E-mail: penwoodreview@charter.net. Website: http://webpages.charter.net/penwoodreview/penwood.htm. Lori Cameron, ed. Poetry, plus thought-provoking essays on poetry, literature, and the role of spirituality and religion in the literary arts. Biannual jour.; 40+ pgs.; circ. 50-100. Subscription $12. 99% unsolicited freelance; 1% assigned. Complete ms (February 25 & August 25 deadlines); no e-query. **NO PAYMENT** ($2 off subscription & 1 free copy), for one-time and electronic rts. Articles 2 pgs. Responds in 9-12 wks. Accepts requested ms on disk or by e-mail (copied into message). Guidelines (also by e-mail/Website); copy $6.

Poetry: Accepts 100-120/yr. Avant-garde, free verse, traditional; to 2 pgs. Submit max. 5 poems.

Special Needs: Faith and the literary arts; religion and literature. Needs essays (up to 2-pages, single spaced).

Tips: "We publish poetry almost exclusively and are looking for well-crafted, disciplined poetry, not doggerel or greeting-card-style poetry. Poets should study poetry, read it extensively, and send us their best, most original work. Visit our Website or buy a copy for an idea of what we publish."

PERSPECTIVES: A Journal of Reformed Thought, PO Box 1196, Holland MI 49422-1196. (616)526-6528. Fax (616)526-8508. E-mail: perspectives_@hotmail.com. Reformed Church Press. Dr. Leanne Van Dyk, Dr. David Timmer, and Dr. Roy Anker, eds. To express the Reformed faith theologically; to engage issues that Reformed Christians meet in personal, ecclesiastical, and societal life. Monthly (10X) mag.; 24 pgs.; circ. 3,000. Subscription $30. 70% unsolicited freelance; 30% assigned. Complete ms/cover letter or query; fax/e-query OK. **PAYS 5 COPIES** for all rts. (usually). Articles (10/yr.) and fiction (3/yr.), 2,000-2,500 wds.; book & movie reviews 500-1,500 wds. Responds in 4-6 wks. Seasonal 4 mos. ahead. Prefers requested ms on disk. Sidebars rare. Prefers NRSV. Guidelines by e-mail; copy for 9x12 SAE/$1.42 postage (mark "Media Mail"). (Ads)

Poetry: Francis Fike, poetry ed. Free verse, traditional. Accepts 5-7/yr. Submit max. 2 poems.

Columns/Departments: Accepts 20-24/yr. As We See It (editorial/ opinion) 750-1,500 wds.; Inside Out (biblical exegesis) 750 wds. Complete ms.

Tips: "I would say that a reading of past issues and a desire to join in a contemporary conversation on the Christian faith would help you break in here."

$PHYSICIAN, 8605 Explorer Dr., Colorado Springs CO 80920. (719)531-3400. Fax (719)531-3499. E-mail: physician@family.org. Website: www.family.org/physmag. Focus on the Family. Scott DeNicola, ed. To encourage physicians in their faith, family, and medical practice. Bimonthly mag.; 24 pgs.; circ. 93,900. Free to medical profession/donors. 20% unsolicited freelance. Query or complete ms/cover letter; fax/e-query OK. Pays $100-500 on acceptance for 1st rts. Articles 900-2,400 wds. (20-30/yr.). Responds in 9 wks. Accepts reprints. Kill fee. Regularly uses sidebars. Prefers NIV. Copy for SASE. (No ads)

Fillers: Cartoons; $50.

**2001, 2000 & 1997 EPA Award of Merit—Christian Ministries; 2004 &1996 EPA Award of Excellence—Christian Ministries.

$THE PLAIN TRUTH, 300 W. Green St., Pasadena CA 91129. (626)304-6181. Fax (626)304-8172. E-mail: phyllis.duke@ptm.org. Website: www.ptm.org. Plain Truth Ministries. Greg Albrecht, ed.; submit to Phyllis Duke, asst. ed. Proclaims Christianity without the religion, emphasizing the central, main and plain, core teachings of historic Christianity. Bimonthly mag.; 32 pgs.; circ. 80,000. Subscription $12.95. 20% unsolicited freelance; 80% assigned. Query/clips or complete ms/cover letter; fax/e-query OK. Pays .25/wd.(.15/wd. for reprints) on publication for 1st, one-time, reprint, or world (all languages) rts. Articles 750-2,500 wds., prefers 800-1,200 wds. (48-50/yr.); fiction. Responds in 4-6 wks. Seasonal 6 mos. ahead. Accepts simultaneous submissions and reprints (tell when/where appeared). Requires requested ms on disk or by e-mail (attached or copied into message). Kill fee $50. Regularly uses sidebars. Prefers NIV. Guidelines (also by e-mail/Website); copy for 9x12 SAE/5 stamps. (Ads)

Columns/Departments: Buys 18/yr. Family (family issues), 1,500 wds.; Commentary (hot topic editorials), 550-650 wds.

Tips: "Most open to articles. Best to send tear sheets of previously published articles and submit detailed query for standard articles."

**This periodical was #39 on the 2004 Top 50 Christian Publishers list (#26 in 2003, #12 in 2002, #22 in 2001, #30 in 2000).

THE PLOWMAN, Box 414, Whitby ON L1N 5S4 Canada. (905)668-7803. The Plowman Ministries/Christian. Tony Scavetta, ed./pub. Poetry and prose of social commentary; any topics. Semiannual newsletter; 20 pgs.; circ. 5,000. Subscription $10 US. 100% unsolicited freelance. Query; phone query OK. **NO PAYMENT**. Articles (10/yr.) & fiction (50/yr.), 1,000 wds. Responds in 2-4 wks. Accepts simultaneous submissions and reprints. No disk. Does not use sidebars. Free guidelines/copy for 9x12 SAE. (Ads)

Poetry: Accepts 100/yr. All types; to 38 lines (55 characters across max.). Submit max. 4 poems.

Fillers: Accepts 25/yr. Cartoons, prayers, short humor; 25-30 wds.

Special Needs: Also publishes chapbooks; 20% royalties.

Contest: Sponsors monthly poetry contests; $2/poem entry fee.

Tips: "All sections open, especially poetry and short stories. Send in submissions."

$#PORTLAND MAGAZINE: The University of Portland Quarterly, 5000 N. Willamette Blvd., Portland OR 97203. Catholic. Brian Doyle, ed. University of Portland news, issues, and concerns; spirituality issues (especially Catholic). Quarterly mag.; circ. 28,000. 70% unsolicited freelance. Query/clips or complete ms. Pays $100-500 on publication for 1st rts. Articles 1,000-3,000 wds. (6/yr.). Responds in 5 wks. Seasonal 8 mos. ahead. Free guidelines/copy. Incomplete topical listings.

$POSITIVE THINKING: Finding Joy & Fulfillment Every Day, 66 E. Main St., Pauling NY 12564. (845)855-5000. Fax (845)855-1036. E-mail: azaengle@guideposts.org. Website: www.guideposts.org. Guideposts. Patricia Planeta, ed. Spiritually oriented, based on positive thinking and faith. Monthly (10X) mag.; 36 pgs.; circ. 600,000. Subscription $10. 30% unsolicited freelance. Complete ms/cover letter; phone/fax/e-query OK. Pays $75/pg. on publication for 1st or one-time rts. Articles 500-2,500 wds. (8/yr.). Responds in 3-4 wks. Seasonal 6 mos. ahead. Accepts reprints. Accepts submissions by e-mail. No sidebars. Guidelines; copy for #10 SAE/1 stamp.

Special Needs: Contemporary heroes; overcoming (addiction, etc.) through faith. (1) Life-changing experiences that bring about faith in Jesus Christ. (2) Ways to improve prayer and spiritual life. (3) How positive thinking and faith provide answers to life's problems.

Tips: "Most open to true stories of finding faith through difficult circumstances. Avoid preachiness. How-tos (if applicable), stories (nonfiction only) that touch the heart and soul. Have a deep, living knowledge of Christianity. Our audience is 65-70% female, average age is 55."

$POWER FOR LIVING, 4050 Lee Vance View, Colorado Springs CO 809118. Toll-free (800)708-5550. (719)536-0100. Fax (719)535-2928. Website: www.cookministries.org. Cook Communications/Scripture Press Publications. Don Alban Jr., ed. To expressly demonstrate the relevance of specific biblical teachings to everyday life via reader-captivating profiles of exceptional Christians. Weekly take-home paper; 8 pgs.; circ. 250,000. Subscription $12. 15% unsolicited freelance; 85% assigned. Complete ms; no phone/fax/e-query. Pays up to .175/wd. (reprints up to .10/wd.) on acceptance for 1st rts. Profiles 700-1,500 wds. (20/yr.). Responds in 10 wks. Seasonal 1 yr. ahead. Accepts simultaneous submissions and reprints (tell when/where appeared). Accepts requested ms on disk. Kill fee. Requires KJV. Guidelines/copy for #10 SAE/1 stamp. (No ads)

Special Needs: Third-person profiles of truly out-of-the-ordinary Christians who express their faith uniquely. We use very little of anything else.

Tips: "Most open to vignettes, 450-1,500 wds., of prominent Christians with solid testimonies or profiles from church history. Focus on the unusual. Signed releases required."

$PRAIRIE MESSENGER: Catholic Journal, PO Box 190, Muenster SK S0K 2Y0 Canada. (306)682-1772. Fax (306)682-5285. E-mail: pm.editor@stpeters.sk.ca. Website: www.stpeters.sk.ca/prairie_messenger. Catholic/ Benedictine Monks of St. Peter's Abbey. Peter Novecosky, OSB, ed.; Maureen Weber, assoc. ed. For Catholics in Saskatchewan and Manitoba, and Christians in other faith communities. Weekly tabloid (46X); 20 pgs.; circ. 7,300. Subscription $27.50 Can. 10% unsolicited freelance; 90% assigned. Complete ms/cover letter; phone/fax/e-query OK. Pays $40-60 ($2/column inch for news items) on publication for 1st, one-time, simultaneous, and reprint rts. Not copyrighted. Articles 800-900 or 2,500 wds. (15/yr.). Responds in 9 wks. Seasonal 3 mos. ahead. Accepts simultaneous submissions and reprints. Regularly uses sidebars. Guidelines (also by e-mail/Website); copy for 9x12 SAE/$1 Can./$1.29 US. (Ads)

Poetry: Accepts 30/yr. Avant-garde, free verse, haiku, light verse; 4-30 lines. Pays $15 ($11 US)

Columns/Departments: Accepts 5/yr. Pays $50.

Special Needs: Ecumenism; social justice; native concerns.

Tips: "Comment/feature section is most open; send good reflection column of about 800 words; topic of concern or interest to Prairie readership. It's difficult to break into our publication."

**This periodical was selected #1 for general excellence by the Canadian Church Press (10 times during the last 16 years).

THE PRAYER CLOSET, 595 Stratton Rd., Decatur, MS 39327. (601)635-2180. Fax (601)635-4025. E-mail: prayer@prayerclosetministries.org. Website: www.prayerclosetministries.org. Dr. Kevin Meador, ed. Challenges and equips believers in the area of prayer, fasting, spiritual warfare, journaling, and healing. Monthly newsletter; circ. 3,000. Free subscription. **PAYS IN COPIES.** Prefers NKJV. Guidelines.

Tips: "We are looking for sound, biblically based articles concerning the above-listed topics."

PRAYERWORKS, PO Box 301363, Portland OR 97294. (503)761-2072. E-mail: VannM1@aol.com. Website: www.prayerworks.org. V. Ann Mandeville, ed. For prayer warriors in retirement centers; focuses on prayer. Weekly newspaper and online (soon); 4 pgs.; circ. 1,000. Subscription free. 100% unsolicited freelance. Complete ms. **PAYS IN COPIES/SUBSCRIPTION** for one-time rts. Not copyrighted. Articles (30-40/yr.) & fiction (30/yr.); 300-500 wds. Responds in 3 wks. Seasonal 2 mos. ahead. Accepts simultaneous submissions and reprints. Does not use sidebars. Guidelines; copy for #10 SAE/1 stamp. (No ads)

> **Poetry:** Accepts 20-30/yr. Free verse, haiku, light verse, traditional. Submit max. 10 poems.
>
> **Fillers:** Accepts up to 50/yr. Facts, jokes, prayers, quotes, short humor; to 50 wds.
>
> **Tips:** "Write tight and well. Half our audience is over 70, but 30% is young families. Subject matter isn't important as long as it is scriptural and designed to help people pray. Have a strong, catchy takeaway."

$PRECEPTS FOR LIVING UMI, Annual Sunday School Commentary, PO Box 436987, Chicago IL 60643. Toll-free (800)860-8642. Fax (708)868-6759. Website: www.urban ministries.com. Urban Ministries, Inc. K. Hall, mng. ed. *Precepts for Living* is a verse-by-verse Sunday School commentary geared toward an African American adult audience. Word studies are presented in the original Greek and Hebrew languages to further illuminate understanding of the text. KJV Scriptures. 500 pgs. $16.95 complete with an enhanced CD-ROM Bible study tool for interactive learning. The CD-ROM contains electronic versions of the New Living Translation Bible, Strong's Concordance, Strong's Greek and Hebrew Dictionary, and other helpful resources including a video tutorial feature. Strict adherence to guidelines. Query/clips; fax/e-query OK., Pays $200 per Bible Study lesson and $250 per verse-by-verse commentary which includes Greek and Hebrew word studies, 120 days after acceptance, for all rts. Requires accepted ms on disk.

THE PRESBYTERIAN OUTLOOK, Box 85623, Richmond VA 23285-5623. Toll-free (800)446-6008. (804)359-8442. Fax (804)353-6369. E-mail: editor@pres-outlook.com. Website: www.pres-outlook.com. Presbyterian Church (USA)/Independent. O. Benjamin Sparks, ed. For ministers, members, and staff of the denomination. Weekly (43X) mag.; 16-40 pgs.; circ. 12,734. Subscription $39.95. 5% unsolicited freelance; 95% assigned. Query; phone/fax/e-query OK. **NO PAYMENT** for all rts. Not copyrighted. Articles to 1,000 wds.; book reviews 1 pg. Responds in 1-2 wks. Seasonal 2 mos. ahead. Requires requested ms on disk; accepts e-mail submissions. Uses some sidebars. Prefers NRSV. Guidelines (also by e-mail); free copy. (Ads)

> **Tips:** "Correspond (mail or e-mail) with editor regarding current needs; most open to features. Most material is commissioned; anything submitted should be of interest to Presbyterian church leaders."

$PRESBYTERIAN RECORD, 50 Wynford Dr., Toronto ON M3C 1J7 Canada. (416)444-1111. Fax (416)441-2825. E-mail: pcrecord@presbyterian.ca. Website: www.presbyterian.ca/record. Presbyterian Church in Canada. David Harris, ed. Denominational. Monthly (11X) mag.; 52 pgs.; circ. 44,400. Subscription $18 Can.; $25 US & foreign. 5% unsolicited freelance; 95% assigned. Query (preferred/with 150 wds.) or complete ms/cover letter; fax/e-query OK. Pays .15 Can./published word on publication for one-time & electronic rts. Articles 700-1,000 wds.; book/music reviews to 400 wds. Responds in 6 wks. Seasonal 3 mos. ahead. Accepts simultaneous submissions and reprints. Accepts e-mail submission (attached or copied into message). Kill fee 50%. Regularly uses sidebars. Prefers NRSV. Accepts submissions from teens. Copy for 9x12 SAE/$2.50 Canadian postage or IRCs from US writers. (Ads)

> **Poetry:** Thomas Dickey, poetry ed. Buys 11/yr. Free verse, haiku, light verse, traditional; 10-30 lines preferred; $35. Send any number.
>
> **Fillers:** Cartoons.
>
> **Tips:** "Nonpietistic reflections of faith in life. It helps if submissions have some connection to Canada and/or the Presbyterian Church. Query."

$PRESBYTERIANS TODAY, 100 Witherspoon St., Louisville KY 40202-1396. Toll-free (888)728-7228, ext. 5637. (502)569-5637. Fax (502)569-8632. E-mail: today@ pcusa.org. Website: www.pcusa.org/today. Presbyterian Church (U.S.A.). Catherine Cottingham, mng. ed.; submit to Eva Stimson, ed. Denominational; not as conservative or evangelical as some. Monthly (10X) mag.; 48 pgs.; circ. 58,000. Subscription $19.95. 65% unsolicited freelance. Query or complete ms/cover letter; phone/fax/e-query OK. Pays $75-300 on acceptance for 1st rts. Articles 800-2,000 wds. (prefers 1,000-1,500). (20/yr.). Also uses short features 250-600 wds. Responds in 5 wks. Seasonal 3 mos. ahead. Few reprints. Accepts requested ms on disk or by e-mail. Kill fee 50%. Prefers NRSV. Guidelines (also by e-mail/Website: www.pcusa.org/today/guidelines/guidelines.htm); free copy. (Ads)

> **Fillers:** Cartoons, $25; and short humor to 150 wds., no payment.
>
> **Tips:** "Most open to feature articles about Presbyterians—individuals, churches with special outreach, creative programs, or mission work. Do not often use inspirational or testimony-type articles."
>
> **This periodical was #32 on the 2004 Top 50 Christian Publishers list (#27 in 2003, #21 in 2000).

$PRIORITY! 440 W. Nyack Rd., West Nyack NY 10994. (845)620-7450. Fax (845)620-7753. E-mail: priority@salvationarmy.org, or linda_johnson@use.salvationarmy.org. Website: www.prioritypeople.org. The Salvation Army. Linda D. Johnson, ed.; Robert Mitchell, assoc. ed. Quarterly mag.; 48 pgs.; circ. 30,000. Subscription $6.95. 20% assigned. Query/clips; e-query OK. Pays .25/wd. or $150 & up on acceptance for all rts. Articles 750-1,500 wds. (5-10/yr.). All articles assigned. Seasonal 4 mos. ahead. Prefers accepted ms by e-mail (in Word or copied into message). Kill fee 25%. Regularly uses sidebars. Prefers NIV. No guidelines; copy $1/9x12 SAE. (Ads from nonprofits only)

> **Columns/Departments:** Buys 20/yr. Prayer Power (stories about answered prayer, or harnessing prayer power), 400-500 wds.; Who's News (calling attention to specific accomplishments or missions), 400-500 wds; $100-200. Query.
>
> **Special Needs:** All articles must have a connection to The Salvation Army. Looking especially for freelancers with Salvation Army connections. Christmas recollections.
>
> **Tips:** "Most open to features on people. The more a writer knows about The Salvation Army, the better. We are interested in finding a group of freelancers we can assign to specific features."

PRISCILLA PAPERS, 122 W. Franklin Ave., Ste. 218, Minneapolis MN 55404-2451. (612)872-6898. Fax (612)872-6891. E-mail: cbe@cbeinternational.org. Website: www.cbeinternational.org. Christians for Biblical Equality. William D. Spencer, ed. Addresses biblical interpretation and its relationship to gender, race/ethnicity, economic class, and age issues in the society, the Christian community, and the family. Quarterly journal; 32 pgs.; circ. 2,000. Subscription $30. 85% unsolicited freelance; 15% assigned. Query or complete ms/cover letter; fax/e-query OK. **PAYS 3 COPIES, PLUS A FREE BOOK** for 1st & electronic rts. Articles 600-5,000 wds.; book review 600 wds (free book). Responds in 4 wks. Seasonal 3 mos. ahead. Accepts simultaneous submissions and reprints (tell when/where appeared). Prefers accepted ms on disk or by e-mail (attached file). No kill fee. Uses some sidebars. Prefers NIV, TNIV, NRSV. Guidelines (also by e-mail/Website); copy for 9x12 SAE/$1.06 postage. (Ads)

> **Poetry:** Accepts 1/yr. Avant-garde, free verse, traditional; pays a free book.
>
> **Tips:** "All sections are open to freelancers. Any article presenting a solid exegetical and hermeneutical approach to biblical equality will be considered for publication."

$PRISM: America's Alternative Evangelical Voice, 10 E. Lancaster Ave., Wynnewood PA 19096-3495. (610)645-9390. Fax (610)649-8090. E-mail: prism@esa-online.org, or kristyn@esa-online.org. Website: www.esa-online.org. Evangelicals for Social Action.

Kristyn Komarnicki, ed. America's alternative Evangelical voice; for Christians who are interested in the social and political dimensions of the gospel. Bimonthly mag.; 44 pgs.; circ. 9,000. Subscription $25. 25% unsolicited freelance. Query/clips; fax/e-query OK. Pays to $200 ($100 for fiction) 6 wks. after publication for 1st or reprint rts. Articles 500-2,800 wds. (10-12/yr.); fiction, 700-1,600 wds. (1/yr.); book/video reviews, 500 wds., $0-100. Responds in 2-9 wks. Seasonal 6 mos. ahead. Accepts reprints (tell when/where appeared). Prefers requested ms on disk. Regularly uses sidebars. Prefers NRSV. Guidelines; copy $3. (Ads)

> **Tips:** "Looking for analysis on religious right; social justice fiction. Understand progressive evangelicals and E.S.A. Read Tony Campolo, Ron Sider, and Richard Foster. Most open to features."
>
> **1997 EPA Award of Merit—Organizational.

$PSYCHOLOGY FOR LIVING, 250 W. Colorado Blvd., Ste. 200, Arcadia CA 91007. (626)821-8400. Fax (626)821-8409. E-mail: rwi@ncfliving.org. Website: www.ncfliving.org. Narramore Christian Foundation. Dick Innes, ed. Addresses issues of everyday life from a Christian and psychological viewpoint. Quarterly mag.; 8 pgs. (one issue 24 pgs.); circ. 7,000. Subscription for $20 donation. Open to freelance. Complete ms/cover letter; fax OK, e-query preferred. Pays $75-200, plus a subscription, on publication for 1st, one-time, or reprint rts. Articles 1,000-1,700 wds. Responds in 2-4 wks. Seasonal 4 mos. ahead. Accepts reprints (tell when/where appeared). Prefers accepted ms by e-mail (attached file). Uses some sidebars. Prefers NIV. Guidelines (also by e-mail); free copy. (No ads)

> **Tips:** "Tell a story or illustration that tells how a psychological/emotional problem was dealt with in a biblical and psychologically sound manner. Not preachy."

$PURPOSE, 616 Walnut Ave., Scottdale PA 15683-1999. (724)887-8500. Fax (724)887-3111. E-mail: Horsch@mph.org. Website: www.mph.org. Mennonite Publishing Network. James E. Horsch, ed. Denominational, for older youth and adults. Weekly take-home paper; 8 pgs.; circ. 9,000. Subscription $20.95. 95% unsolicited freelance; 5% assigned. Complete ms (only)/cover letter; e-query OK. Pays .05/wd. on acceptance for one-time rts. Articles & fiction, to 750 wds. (50/yr.). Responds in 13 wks. Seasonal 6 mos. ahead. Accepts simultaneous submissions and reprints (tell when/where appeared). Regularly uses sidebars. Guidelines (also by e-mail); copy $2/6x9 SAE/2 stamps. (No ads)

> **Poetry:** Buys 130/yr. Free verse, light verse, traditional; 3-12 lines; up to $2/line ($7.50-20). Submit max. 10 poems.
>
> **Fillers:** Buys 80/yr. Anecdotes, cartoons, short humor; 300-600 wds.; .04/wd. max.
>
> **Tips:** "All areas are open. Articles must carry a strong story line. First person is preferred. Don't exceed maximum word length, send no more than 3 works at a time, and e-mail submissions preferred."
>
> **This periodical was #28 on the 2004 Top 50 Christian Publishers list (#48 in 2003, #40 in 2002, #9 in 2001, #10 in 2000, #44 in 1999).

QUAKER LIFE, 101 Quaker Hill Dr., Richmond IN 47374. (765)962-7573. Fax (765)962-1293. E-mail: quakerlife@fum.org. Website: www.fum.org/ql. Friends United Meeting. Trish Edwards-Konic, ed. For Christian Quakers, focusing on news around the world, peace and justice, simplicity, and inspiration. Monthly (10X) mag.; 36 pgs.; circ. 7,000. Subscription $24. 50% unsolicited freelance; 50% assigned. Query; fax/e-query OK. Accepts full ms by e-mail. **PAYS 3 COPIES** on publication for 1st rts. Articles to 1,500 wds. (40/yr.); book reviews 300 wds.; music/video reviews, 200 wds. Responds in 4 wks. Seasonal 4 mos. ahead. Accepts some reprints (tell when/where appeared). Accepts e-mail submissions (attached in WORD or copied into message). No kill fee. Uses some sidebars. Prefers RSV. Accepts submissions from children or teens. Guidelines/theme list (also by e-mail); copy for 9x12 SAE. (Ads)

Poetry: Accepts 4/yr.

Columns/Departments: Turning Point (first-person spiritual experiences); Ideas That Work (ideas from churches); Peace Notes (peace and justice news and ideas); each 750 wds. Query or complete ms.

Special Needs: Leadership, church growth, personnel.

Tips: "Write on current issues or a personal spiritual experience from a Christian perspective. Be more practical than academic. For general readers who are Christian Quakers."

$QUEEN OF ALL HEARTS, 26 S. Saxon Ave., Bay Shore NY 11706-8993. (631)665-0726. Fax (631)665-4349. E-mail: montfort@optonline.net. Website: www.montfortmissionaries .com. Catholic/Montfort Missionaries. Rev. Roger M. Charest, SMM, mng. ed. Focus is Mary, the Mother of Jesus. Bimonthly mag.; 48 pgs.; circ. 2,000. Subscription $22. 80% unsolicited freelance. Not copyrighted. Query or complete ms/cover letter; phone/fax query OK. Pays $40-60 on publication for one-time rts. Not copyrighted. Articles 1,000-2,000 wds. (40/yr.) and fiction 1,500-2,000 wds. (6/yr.); book reviews 100 wds. Responds in 1 mo. Seasonal 4 mos. ahead. No simultaneous submissions or reprints. No disk. Uses some sidebars. Prefers NRSV. Guidelines (also by e-mail); copy for $3.50/9x12 SAE. (No ads)

Poetry: Joseph Tusiani, poetry ed. Buys 12/yr. Free verse; to 25 lines; Marian themes only. Pays 2-year subscription and 6 copies. Submit max. 2 poems.

+RADIX MAGAZINE, PO Box 4307, Berkeley CA 94704. (510)548-5329. E-mail: Radix Mag@aol.com. Website: www.RadixMagazine.com. Sharon Gallagher, ed.; Luci Shaw, poetry ed. Features in-depth articles for thoughtful Christians who are interested in engaging the culture. Quarterly mag.; 32 pgs. Subscription $15. 10% unsolicited freelance. E-queries only. **PAYS IN COPIES** for 1st rts. Meditations, 300-500 wds.; book reviews 700 wds. Responds in 2 wks. to e-mail only. No seasonal. No simultaneous submissions; accepts reprints (tell when/where appeared). Uses some sidebars. Prefers NRSV. Guidelines by e-mail. (Ads - few)

Poetry: Accepts 8/yr. Avant-garde, free verse, haiku; 4-30 lines. Submit max. 4 poems.

Tips: "Most open to poetry, book reviews, meditations. Familiarity with the magazine is key."

+THE REFORMED QUARTERLY, 1231 Reformation Dr., Oviedo FL 32765. (407)366-9425. Fax (407)366-9425. E-mail: lperez@rts.edu. Website: www.rts.edu. Reformed Theological Seminary. Lyn Perez, ed. To provide theological and biblical articles and other information helpful to the church. Quarterly mag.; circ. 40,000. Subscription free. Open to unsolicited freelance. Prefers query. Articles/reviews. Not in topical listings. (No ads)

RE:GENERATION QUARTERLY, 1770 Massachusetts Ave. #220, Cambridge MA 02140. (617)491-2055. Fax (617)249-0270. E-mail: editor@regenerator.com. Website: www .veritas.org. The Veritas Forum. Andy Crouch, ed. To equip the emerging generation to transform their world by providing commentary, critique, and celebration of communities and contemporary culture; college-educated Christians mostly in their 20s and 30s. Quarterly mag. Open to unsolicited freelance. Complete ms or query by e-mail only, unless OK'd by editor. Personal but theologically informed reflections (1,000-2,500 wds.); analytical essays (2,000-3,000 wds); opinion pieces (600-900 wds.); reports on important trends (1,000-3,000 wds.); humor/satire (about 800 wds.); book and culture reviews (300-1,000 wds.). Responds in 6-8 wks. Seasonal 4 mos. ahead. No simultaneous submissions or reprints. Guidelines/themes on Website.

Poetry: Actively seeking poetry.

Columns/Departments: Short Takes, 200-799 wds.

Tips: "No footnotes; integrate your sources into the text."

REGENT BUSINESS REVIEW, 1000 Regent University Dr., Virginia Beach VA 23464. (757)226-4427. Fax (757)226-4369. E-mail: michzig@regent.edu. Website: www.regent.edu/review.

Regent University School of Business. Michael A Zigarelli, ed. For Christian leaders and managers who take their faith seriously and who give genuine thought to how to live out that faith in the workplace and everywhere else. Bimonthly e-zine; 30 pgs.; circ. 10,000. Free online. 25% unsolicited freelance; 75% assigned. Query/clips by e-mail only. **NO PAYMENT** for electronic rts. Articles 1,500-3,000 wds. (10/yr.); case studies 500-700 wds.; book reviews 400 wds. Responds in 2 wks. Seasonal 6 mos. ahead. No simultaneous submissions; accepts reprints. Requires accepted mss by e-mail (attached file). Regularly uses sidebars. Prefers NIV. Guidelines on Website. (Ads)

> **Columns/Departments:** Toolkit (tips and resources), 1,500 wds.; Case Studies, 1,500 wds.; Best Practices (stories/interviews), 1,500 wds.; Legal Advice, 1,000 wds.; Inspired Ideas (exegesis), 1,500 wds.

> **Tips:** "Anyone can offer an idea for Christian leadership. We're looking to publish only those ideas that have a proven track record for success."

$RELATE MAGAZINE, 64096 Mangano Rd., Lot 157, Pearl River LA 70452-5348. (985)781-0628. Fax (707)922-1027. E-mail: editor@relatemagazine.org. Website: www.Relate Magazine.org. The online magazine for disabled Christians and those who care for them. David Hudson, sr. ed. Monthly online mag.; circ. 1,000. Free online. 100% unsolicited freelance. Query or complete ms/cover letter; e-query OK. Pays $40/article (as budget is met by donations) for one-time rts. Articles to 800 wds. (24-30/yr.). Responds in 4-6 wks. Seasonal 2 mos. ahead. Accepts simultaneous submissions and reprints (tell when/where appeared). Requires accepted ms by e-mail (copied into message). No kill fee. Does not use sidebars. Accepts submissions from children or teens. Guidelines on Website. (No ads)

> **Tips:** "Currently accepting two articles per issue from disabled Christians or caregivers. May increase in the future. Focus on personal/spiritual/inspirational pieces, not social/political issues. Paste entire ms into e-mail (plain text) and include a 1-paragraph bio (plus e-mail or Website) with submissions."

$+RELEVANT & RELEVANTMAGAZINE.COM, Toll-free (866)512-1108. (407)3433-7152. Website: www.RelevantMediaGroup.com. Cara Davis, ed. dir. (cara@relevantmedia group.com); Erika Larson, asst. ed. (erika@relevantmediagroup.com); submit to Won Kim (won@relevantmediagroup.com). Targets culture-savvy twentysomethings who are looking for purpose, depth, and spiritual truth. Bimonthly & online mag.; 100 pgs. Send a one-paragraph query; prefers e-mail; no phone/fax query. Pays .10/wd. within 45 days of publication for 1st rts. and all electronic rts. for 6 mos.; nonexclusive rts. thereafter. Features 1,000 wds.; reviews 400-600 wds. Prefers submissions as Word attachments. Guidelines on Website; copy $2.98. No questionnaire returned.

+RHUBARB, 606-100 Arthur St., Winnipeg MB R3B 1H3 Canada. E-mail: rhubarb@mts.net. Website: www.mennolit.com. Mennonite Literary Society. Submit to The Editor. Designed to provide an outlet for the (loosely defined) Mennonite voice, reflecting the changing face of the Mennonite community, promoting dialog, and encouraging the Anabaptist tradition of reformation and protest. Quarterly mag. Open to unsolicited freelance. Query for nonfiction; e-query OK. **NO REFERENCE TO PAYMENT.** Articles and fiction to 2,500 wds. Guidelines/ theme list on Website.

> **Poetry:** Accepts poetry to 30 lines.

> **Special Needs:** Black & white art work; commentary, issues analysis.

+ROCK & SLING: A Journal of Literature, Art and Faith, 2119 S. Monroe Street, Spokane, WA 99203. Fax (509)276-2971. E-mail: editor@rockandsling.org. Website: www.rockandsling.org. Kris Christensen, Susan Cowger, Laurie Klein, eds. Semiannual jour. Subscription $18 US/$22 Intl. 70% unsolicited freelance; 30% assigned. Complete ms/cover letter; no phone/fax/e-query. **PAYS 2 COPIES** for 1st NA serial rights. Nonfiction & fiction, 5,000 wds. (longer pieces accepted if exceptional). Responds in 2 mos.

Accepts simultaneous submissions (if notified). Any Bible version. Guidelines (also on Website); copy $10.

Poetry: Accepts poetry; 60 lines max. Longer poems accepted if exceptional. Submit max. 5 poems. "Formal verse is discouraged unless experimental."

Art: Rock & Sling publishes b & w artwork. Submit slides, not originals. See guidelines.

Tips: "No devotions or testimonies. We publish writing with broad or explicit associations to Christian faith or its history, including fiction, nonfiction (including creative nonfiction and memoir), poetry, translations, interviews, critical reviews of books, music, and film, and scholarly articles by qualified authors. Rock & Sling wants complexity of thought and emotion but not esotericism to the point of inaccessibility. We also publish art and photography. Submissions accepted year round."

#THE ROSE & THORN: A Literary E-zine. E-mail: BAQuinn@aol.com. Website: www.the roseandthornezine.com. Secular. B. A. Quinn, ed. Showcases short fiction, poetry, essays, and anything of a literary nature; no children's or juvenile stories. Quarterly online literary mag. Open to freelance. Complete ms. **NO PAYMENT** but will provide a link to your Website. One-time nonexclusive rts. Articles, fiction, reviews; all to 2,000 wds. Requires accepted ms by e-mail (copied into message). Guidelines on Website.

Poetry: Now accepting poetry. Submit max. 3 poems; prefers shorter poems. E-mail to: poetryeditor@hotmail.com.

Special Needs: Fiction, vignettes, and flash fiction; creative essays, perspective, humor, reviews, and interviews. Author interviews and writing how-to articles.

Tips: "We have eclectic tastes, so go ahead and give us a shot."

$+SABBATH MOMENTS SERIES, PO Box 836, Hillsboro OH 45133. (937)393-4974. E-mail: busha@lifewisebooks.com. Website: www.lifewisebooks.com. LifeWise Books. A series of books of devotionals on a variety of themes, yet to be decided. Open to suggestions. Needs 100 or more selections for each book. Pays $25 and 2 copies of the book. Devotionals/inspirational commentaries 400-500 wds. Accepts mailed or e-mailed submissions.

SACRED JOURNEY: The Journal of Fellowship in Prayer, 291 Witherspoon St., Princeton NJ 08542. (609)924-6863. Fax (609)924-6910. E-mail: editorial@sacredjourney.org. Website: www.sacredjourney.org. Fellowship in Prayer, Inc. Louise Hutner, ed. Multifaith spirituality. Bimonthly journal & e-zine; 48 pgs.; circ. 4,500. Subscription $18. 70% unsolicited freelance; 30% assigned. Complete ms/cover letter; phone/fax/e-query OK. **PAYS 5 COPIES & SUBSCRIPTION** for one-time & electronic rts. Articles to 1,500 wds. (30/yr.); reviews 500 wds. Responds in 8 wks. Seasonal 4 mos. ahead. Accepts simultaneous submissions and reprints (tell when/where appeared). Requires requested ms on disk or by e-mail. No sidebars. Guidelines (also by e-mail/Website); copy $1.70/6x9 SAE. (No ads)

Poetry: Accepts 6-8/yr. Free verse, haiku, light verse, traditional; 10-35 lines. Submit max. 3 poems.

Columns/Departments: Accepts 30/yr. A Transforming Experience (personal experience of spiritual significance); Pilgrimage (journey taken for spiritual growth or service); Spirituality and the Family; Spirituality and Aging; to 1,500 wds.

Special Needs: Meditation and service to others.

Tips: "Write well about your own spiritual experience and we'll consider it. Most open to a transforming experience feature."

+SALT OF THE EARTH: Your Online Resource for Social Justice, 205 W. Monroe St., Chicago IL 60606. (312)236-7782. Fax (312)236-8201. E-mail: clarkek@claretian pubs.org. Website: http://salt.claretianpubs.org. The Claretians/Catholic. Kevin Clarke, mng. ed. Monthly online mag.

$SCIENCE & SPIRIT MAGAZINE, 5 Radnor Corporate Ctr. Ste. 100, Wayne PA 19087-4534.

(617)769-2904. Fax (617)745-3932. E-mail: editorial@science-spirit.org. Website: www.science-spirit.org. Science & Spirit Resources, Inc./Heldref Publications. Karl Giberson, ed. Well-researched and reported articles on the intersection of science and religion in health, environment, human relationships, technology, and ethics. Bimonthly mag; circ. 10,000. Subscription $23.95. 20% freelance. Query by mail first. Pays $700 for feature articles on publication for all rts. No reprints. Feature articles 1,500-1,800 wds. Responds in 6 mos. Guidelines: copy $4.95.

Columns/Departments: Interlude (social/science environmental topic), 1,200 wds.; Critical Mass (news briefs covering all areas of science—physics, gender, space, psychology, etc.); pays $200-300. See Website for samples of departments.

Tips: "Common mistakes include shallow reporting, lack of in-depth writing, lack of diversity in religious perspectives. We're looking for well-researched articles that include interviews with scientists, theologians, and everyday people. The best articles include citations for recent research and current books. Thoughtful leads, transitions, and conclusions based on the writer's research and insight are a must."

$SCP JOURNAL & NEWSLETTER, (Spiritual Counterfeits Project), PO Box 4308, Berkeley CA 94704-4308. (510)540-0300. Fax (510)540-1107. E-mail: scp@scp-inc.org. Website: www.scp-inc.org. Tal Brooke, ed. Christian apologetics for the college educated. Quarterly journal (55 pgs.) & newsletter; circ. 15,000. Subscription $25. 100% assigned. Query only/clips; phone query encouraged; e-query from Website. Pays $20-35/typeset pg. on publication for negotiable rts. Articles 2,500-3,500 wds. (5/yr.); book reviews 1,500 wds. Responds in 13 wks. Accepts simultaneous query and reprints. Requires requested ms on disk or by e-mail (attached file). Some sidebars. Guidelines (also by e-mail); copy $8.75. (No ads)

Tips: "Must be an extremely good writer who is aware of the issues. Most of our writers come from the top 20 universities. No unsolicited manuscripts. May not respond to queries."

SEEDS OF HOPE, 602 James Ave., Waco TX 76706-1476. (254)755-7745. Fax (254)753-1909. E-mail: SeedsHope@aol.com. Website: www.seedspublishers.org. Seeds of Hope Publishers. Katie Cook, ed. Committed to the healing of hunger and poverty in our world. Quarterly worship packet; 20 pgs. of camera-ready resources. Subscription $120. Individual packet $50. Back issues less expensive. Also quarterly newsletter, *Hunger News & Hope,* published through denominational offices of national churches. E-query OK. **NO PAYMENT.**

$SEEK, 8121 Hamilton Ave., Cincinnati OH 45231. (513)521-1789. Fax (513)931-0950. E-mail: seek@standardpub.com. Website: www.Standardpub.com. Standard Publishing. Dawn Medill, ed. Light, inspirational, take-home reading for young and middle-aged adults. Weekly take-home paper; 8 pgs.; circ. 29,000. Subscriptions $14.69 (sold only in sets of 5). 75% unsolicited freelance; 25% assigned. Complete ms; no phone/fax/e-query. Pays .07/wd. on acceptance for 1st rts., .05/wd. for reprints. Articles 400-1,200 wds. (150-200/yr.); fiction 400-1,200 wds. Responds in 18 wks. Seasonal 1 yr. ahead. Accepts reprints (tell when/where appeared). Prefers submissions by e-mail (attached file). Kill fee. Uses some sidebars. Guidelines/theme list (also on Website); copy for 6x9 SAE/2 stamps. (No ads)

Fillers: Buys 50/yr. Ideas, jokes, short humor; $15.

Tips: "We now work with a theme list. Only articles tied to these themes will be considered for publication. Check Website for theme list and revised guidelines."

**This periodical was #20 on the 2004 Top 50 Christian Publishers list (#49 in 2003, #29 in 2002, #45 in 2001, #47 in 2000).

$SENIOR LIVING NEWSPAPERS, 318 E. Pershing St., Springfield MO 65806. (417)862-0852. Fax (417)862-9079. E-mail: elefantwalk@msn.com. Website: www.seniorlivingnews papers.com. Metropolitan Radio Group, Inc. Joyce Yonker O'Neal, mng. ed. Positive, upbeat magazine for people 55+; includes religious articles. Monthly newspaper; circ. 40,000. 25-50% unsolicited freelance. Complete ms/cover letter; e-query OK. Pays $20-35 for assigned, $5-35 for unsolicited, 30 days after publication for 1st, reprint, and electronic rts. Articles 600-700 wds. (65/yr.). Responds in 2-5 wks. Seasonal 4 mos. ahead. Guidelines; copy for 9x12 SAE/5 stamps.

$THE SHANTYMAN, 1885 Clements Rd. Unit 226, Pickering ON L1W 3V4 Canada. Toll-free (877)4-SHANTY. (905)686-2030. Fax (905)427-0334. E-mail: shanty@pathcom.com. Website: www.shantymen.org. Shantymen's Christian Assn. Phil Hood, mng. ed. Distributed by their missionaries in remote areas of Canada and northern US as an evangelism tool. Quarterly mini-tabloid; 16 pgs.; circ. 17,000. 90% unsolicited freelance. Complete ms/cover letter; no phone/fax query. Pays $20-50 Can., on publication for one-time or reprint rts. Articles 800-1,600 wds. (30/yr.). Responds in 4-6 wks. Seasonal 6 mos. ahead. Accepts reprints (tell when/where appeared). No disk; e-mail attachment preferred. Uses some sidebars. Prefers NAS. Guidelines; copy for #10 SAE/2 stamps or IRCs.

   Columns/Departments: Accepts 6/yr. Way of Salvation (fresh look at gospel message), 300-400 wds.

   Tips: "We always have a need for salvation testimonies, first person (preferred) or as-told-to. We always have too many inspirational stories."

SHARING: A Journal of Christian Healing, 6807 Forest Haven St., San Antonio TX 78240-3343. Toll-free (888)824-5387. (210)681-5146. Fax (210)681-5146. E-mail: Marjorie_George@dwtx.org. Website: www.orderofstluke.org. Order of St. Luke the Physician. Marjorie George, ed. For Christians interested in spiritual and physical healing. Monthly (11X) jour.; 32 pgs.; circ. 9,000. Subscription $16. 100% unsolicited freelance. Complete ms/cover letter. **NO PAYMENT** for one-time or reprint rts. Articles 750-900 wds. (50/yr.). Responds in 3 wks. Seasonal 2 mos. ahead. Accepts simultaneous submissions and reprints (tell when/where appeared). Prefers requested ms on disk. Some sidebars. Prefers RSV. Guidelines; copy for 8x10 SAE/2 stamps.

   Poetry: Accepts 10-12/yr. Free verse, traditional; 6-14 lines.

   Tips: "The entire magazine is open. We're looking for crisp, clear, well-written articles on the theology of healing and personal witness of healing. We do not return mss or poems, nor do we reply to inquiries regarding manuscript status."

$SIGNS OF THE TIMES, Box 5398, Nampa ID 83653-5398. (208)465-2579. Fax (208)465-2531. E-mail: signs@pacificpress.com or mmoore@pacificpress.com. Website: www.signs times.com. Seventh-day Adventist. Marvin Moore, ed. Biblical principles relevant to all of life; for general public. Monthly mag. & partial online version; 32 pgs.; circ. 200,000. Subscription $18.95. 40% unsolicited freelance; 60% assigned. Complete ms/cover letter. Pays $100-300 (.10-.20/wd.) on acceptance for all, 1st, reprint rts. Articles 500-1,500 wds. (75/yr.). Responds in 4-9 wks. Seasonal 1 yr. ahead. Accepts simultaneous submissions and reprints (tell when/where appeared). Prefers requested ms by e-mail (copied into message). Kill fee 50%. Uses some sidebars. Guidelines (also by e-mail/Website); copy for 9x12 SAE/3 stamps. (No ads)

   Tips: "Most open to gospel, Christian lifestyle, or Amazing Grace column (conversion, answers to prayer, victory over temptation, or God's leading)."

$SILVER WINGS, (formerly Silver Wings Mayflower Pulpit), PO Box 2340, Clovis CA 93613-2340. (559)347-0194. E-mail: cloviswings@aol.com. Poetry on Wings/Baptist—Evangelical. Jackson Wilcox, ed. Christian understanding and uplift through poetry, plus a sermon. Bimonthly mag.; 16 pgs.; circ. 275. Subscription free with donation. 100% unsolicited freelance. Query; phone query OK. Pays .01/wd for articles for 1st rts.; book reviews 200 wds. Not copyrighted. Poetry only. Responds in 3 wks. Seasonal 6 mos. ahead. Sometimes accepts simultaneous submissions and reprints (tell when/where appeared). No disk or e-mail submissions. No kill fee or sidebars. Prefers KJV. Accepts submissions from teens. Guidelines/theme list; copy for 6x9 SAE/2 stamps. (No ads)

Poetry: Accepts 170/yr. Free verse, haiku, light verse, traditional; 3-20 lines. Submit max. 3 poems. No payment.

Fillers: Original sayings. No payment.

Contest: Annual poetry contest on a theme(December 31 deadline); send SASE for details. Winners published in March. $200 in prizes. $3 entry fee. Theme for 2005: All things New.

Tips: "We like poems with clear Christian message, observation, or description. Poetry should be easy to read and understand. Short poems get best attention."

$SINGLE AGAIN.COM WEBZINE & MAGAZINE, 1237 Crescendo Dr., Roseville CA 95678-5165. (916)773-7337. E-mail: editor@singleagain.com. Website: www.singleagain.com. Rev. Paul Scholl, pub.; Donalee Hill, ed. Caters to people trying to put their lives back together after divorce, separation, or death of a significant other. Online and print mag. Open to freelance. Complete ms by mail or e-mail (preferred). **NO PAYMENT** for online material; payment for print version to be determined; for nonexclusive continuous rts. for electronic and print publishing. Articles 500 wds. and up. Responds in 2 wks. by e-mail and 6 wks. by mail. Guidelines on Website. Incomplete topical listings. No questionnaire returned.

Tips: "Write from your heart first. Don't worry about your article being perfect. We will help you with any final editing."

SINGLES SCOOP, 374 Sheppard Ave. E., Toronto ON M2N 3B6 Canada. (416)222-3341, ext. 142. Fax (416)222-3344. E-mail: timothy@peoplesministries.org. The Peoples Church/ Toronto Canada. Dr. T. Starr, mng. ed. For singles, ages 35-65. Quarterly mag.; 24 pgs. Subscription free/donation. 15% unsolicited freelance; 85% assigned. Complete ms/cover letter. **NO PAYMENT.** Articles 500 wds. (20/yr.); fiction 350-500 wds.; book/video reviews 150 wds. Responds in 2 wks. Seasonal 3 mos. ahead. Accepts simultaneous submissions and reprints (tell when/where appeared). Accepts requested ms on disk. Regularly uses sidebars. Prefers NIV. Guidelines/theme list; copy for 9x12 SAE/$1.20 Can. postage. (Ads)

Poetry: Accepts 1-2/yr.

Fillers: Accepts 1-5/yr.; 50 wds. Anecdotes, cartoons, facts, games, quizzes, short humor; 25-40 wds.

Columns/Departments: Accepts 20/yr. Complete ms. No payment.

$SMART FAMILIES, PO Box 1125, Murrieta CA 92564-1125. (858)513-7150. Fax (909)461-3526. E-mail: plewis@smartfamilies.com. Website: www.smartfamilies.com. Smart Families, Inc. Paul Lewis, ed./pub. Christian parenting, with strong crossover to secular families. Quarterly & online newsletter; 16 pgs.; circ. 140,000. 20% unsolicited freelance. Complete ms preferred; fax/e-query OK. Pays $50-250 on publication for 1st rts. Articles 200-1,000 wds. Responds in 1-3 wks. Seasonal 4 mos. ahead. Accepts simultaneous submissions and reprints. Prefers requested ms on disk; accepts e-mail submission (attached file). Uses some sidebars. Prefers NIV. No guidelines or copy. (No ads)

Fillers: Games, ideas, quotes.

Tips: "We are not a typical 'magazine' and have tight length requirements. Because of crossover audience, we do not regularly print Scripture references or use traditional God-word language."

$SOCIAL JUSTICE REVIEW, 3835 Westminster Pl., St. Louis MO 63108-3472. (314)371-1653. E-mail: centbur@juno.com. Website: www.socialjusticereview.org. Catholic Central Union of America. Rev. John H. Miller, C.S.C., ed. For those interested in the social teaching of the Catholic Church. Bimonthly jour.; 32 pgs.; circ. 4,950. Subscription $20. 90%

unsolicited freelance. Query or complete ms/cover letter. Pays .02/wd. on publication for one-time rts. Not copyrighted. Articles to 3,000 wds. (80/yr.); book reviews 500 wds. (no pay). Responds in 1 wk. Seasonal 3 mos. ahead. Accepts reprints (tell when/where appeared). Does not use sidebars. Guidelines; copy for 9x12 SAE/3 stamps. (No ads)

Columns/Departments: Virtue; Economic Justice; variable length. Query.

Tips: "Fidelity to papal teaching and clarity and simplicity of style; thoughtful and thought-provoking writing."

$SOJOURNERS/SOJO NET, 2401—15th St. NW, Washington DC 20009. (202)328-8842. Fax (202)328-8757. E-mail: sojourners@sojo.net. Website: www.sojo.net. Submit to Manuscript Editor; Jim Rice, online mng. ed. For those who seek to turn their lives toward the biblical vision of justice and peace. Monthly & online mag.; 54 pgs.; circ. 20,000. Subscription $40. 5% unsolicited freelance; 25% assigned. Complete ms/cover letter; e-query OK. Pays $50-400 on publication for all rts. Articles 600-3,000 wds. (10/yr.); reviews, 650 wds., $50-100. Responds in 8 wks. Seasonal 6 mos. ahead. No simultaneous submissions or reprints. Kill fee. Prefers NRSV. Regularly uses sidebars. Guidelines (also by e-mail/Website); copy for 9x12 SAE. (Ads)

Poetry: Rose Marie Berger, poetry ed. Buys 6-10/yr. Free verse, haiku; $25. Submit max. 3 poems.

Fillers: Accepts 6 cartoons/yr.; also other unsolicited artwork and photographs.

Tips: "Most open to features, Culture Watch reviews, and short pieces on individuals and groups working successfully in their communities to empower the poor, create jobs, and promote peace and reconciliation."

**1996 EPA Award of Merit—General; 2000 & 1999 ACP Award: Best in Class.

$+SOUND BODY, Box 448, Jacksonville OR 97530. Phone/fax (541)899-8888. E-mail: James@ChristianMediaNetwork.com. Websites: www.SoundBodycm.com. Christian Media. James Lloyd, ed./pub. A health newsletter with an alternative slant. Quarterly & online newsletter. Query; prefers phone query. Payment negotiable for reprint rts. Articles. Responds in 3 wks. Requires KJV. No guidelines; copy for #10 SAE/2 stamps.

***SOUTHERN RENAISSANCE**, PO Box 1199, Boutte LA 70039. E-mail: Boris3128@aol.com. Catholic. Allen Lottinger, ed. Articles & columns to 1,200 wds. Include your e-mail address. Looking mainly for Catholic writers.

SOUTHWEST KANSAS FAITH AND FAMILY, PO Box 1454, Dodge City KS 67801. (620)225-4677. Fax (620)225-4625. E-mail: stan@swkfaithandfamily.org. Website: www.swkfaith andfamily.org. Independent. Stan Wilson, pub. Dedicated to sharing the Word of God and news and information that honors Christian beliefs, family traditions, and values that are the cornerstone of our nation. Monthly newspaper; circ. 5,000. Subscription $15. Accepts freelance. Prefers e-query. Complete ms. Incomplete topical listings. (Ads)

$SPECIAL LIVING, PO Box 1000, Bloomington IL 61702. E-mail: gareeb@aol.com. Website: www.specialiving.com. Betty Garee, pub./ed. For and about physically disabled adults, mobility impaired individuals. Quarterly mag.; 88 pgs.; circ. 12,000. Subscription $12. 90% unsolicited freelance; 5% assigned. Query; phone/fax/e-query OK. Pays .10/wd. on publication for 1st rts. Articles 300-800 wds. (50/yr.). Responds in 3 wks. Seasonal 6 mos. ahead. Accepts simultaneous submissions and reprints (tell when/where appeared). Prefers requested ms on disk. No kill fee. Uses some sidebars. No guidelines; copy $2. (Ads)

Fillers: Buys 20/yr. Cartoons, tips.

Tips: "Query with a specific idea. Have good photos to accompany your article."

$SPIRITUAL LIFE, 2131 Lincoln Rd. NE, Washington DC 20002-1199. Toll-free (888)616-1713. (202)832-8489. Fax (202)832-8967. E-mail: editorSL@aol.com. Website:

www.Spiritual-Life.org. Catholic. Edward O'Donnell, O.C.D., ed. Essays on Christian spirituality with a pastoral application to everyday life. Quarterly jour.; 64 pgs.; circ. 11,000. Subscription $18. 90% unsolicited freelance. Complete ms/cover letter; phone/fax/e-query OK. Pays $50-250 ($50/pg.) on acceptance for 1st rts. Articles/essays 5,000-8,000 wds. (20/yr.); book reviews 1,500 wds. ($15). Responds in 8-10 wks. Seasonal 9 mos. ahead. Accepts simultaneous submissions. Requires requested ms on disk. Does not use sidebars. Prefers NAB. Guidelines; copy for 7x10 SAE/5 stamps.

> **Tips:** "No stories of personal healing, conversion, miracles, etc."

SPIRITUAL VOICE NEWS, PO Box 45, Kennett Square PA 19348. (610)347-6766. Fax (610)347-6765. E-mail: Linda@Kennett.net. Website: www.spiritualvoyages.cc. Regional news. Linda T. Eckman, ed./pub. For backslid Christians or the unsaved; available free at convenience stores, restaurants, etc. Quarterly newspaper; 16 pgs.; circ. 10,000. Subscription free. 100% unsolicited freelance. Complete ms/cover letter; phone/fax/e-query OK. **PAYS IN COPIES** for one-time, reprint, or simultaneous rts. Not copyrighted. Articles (500 wds.); all genres of fiction; book/music/movie reviews. Responds in 2 wks. Seasonal 1 mo. ahead. Accepts simultaneous submissions and reprints. Accepts e-mail submissions (attached file). Uses some sidebars. Accepts submissions from children or teens. Guidelines/theme list (also by e-mail); copy for 6x9 SAE/3 stamps. (Ads)

> **Poetry:** Accepts 30/yr. Any type. Send any number. No payment. Needs more.
>
> **Fillers:** Accepts many. Any type. No payment. Needs more.
>
> **Special Needs:** Column writers.
>
> **Tips:** "This paper is very open to new writers."

$SPIRITUALITY & HEALTH, 74 Trinity Pl., 13th Floor, New York NY 10001-2088. (212)602-0705. Fax (212)602-0726. E-mail: editor@spiritualityhealth.com. Website: www.spirituality health.com. Nondenominational. Betsy Robinson, mng. ed.; Stephen Kiesling, ed. For spiritual seekers who may or may not be affiliated with organized religion; cultural creatives; open skeptics. Bimonthly mag. (back issues online); 76 pgs.; circ. 70,000. Subscription $24.95. 60% unsolicited freelance. Query by e-mail preferred; no phone query; fax query OK. Pays flat fee on acceptance for 1st rts. Articles 300-1,500 wds. Responds in 12-16 wks. No simultaneous submissions or reprints. Requires submissions by e-mail (attached file; copied into message OK). Kill fee 50%. Regularly uses sidebars. Guidelines (also by e-mail/ Website); copy online. (Ads)

> **Tips:** "We currently need queries from writers who are familiar with the magazine and who have read our guidelines thoroughly. No new age."

+SPIRITUALITY FOR TODAY, PO Box 7466, Greenwich CT 06836. (203)316-9394. Fax (203)316-9396. E-mail: Clemons10@aol.com. Website: www.spirituality.org. Clemons Productions, Inc. Dorothy Riera, asst. ed. Adults spiritual renewal with articles that challenge reflection. Monthly mag.; 13-15 pgs.; circ. 425,000. Subscription free. Open to freelance. E-query OK. **NO PAYMENT** Articles 1.5 pgs. Incomplete topical listings.

$SPORTS SPECTRUM, 105 Corporate Blvd. Ste. 2, Indian Trail NC 28105. (704)821-2971. Fax (704)821-2669. E-mail: dbranon@rbc.org. Website: www.sportsspectrum.com. Sports Spectrum Publishing. Dave Branon, mng. ed. A high-quality national sports magazine that features Christian athletes. Bimonthly daily devotional mag.; 56 pgs.; circ. 30,000. Subscription $27.52. 0% unsolicited freelance; 80% assigned. Query/clips; e-query OK. Pays .21/wd. on acceptance for all rts. Not copyrighted. Articles 1,200-2,000 wds. (40/yr.). Responds in 3-4 wks. Requires accepted ms by e-mail. Kill fee 30-50%. Regularly uses sidebars. Prefers NIV. Guidelines (also by e-mail); copy for 9x12 SAE. (Ads)

> **Columns/Departments:** Buys 15/yr. Legends (past/retired Christian athletes), 800 wds.; Champions (lesser-known athletes), 300 wds. Pays .21/wd. Query.

Tips: "The best thing a writer can do is to be aware of the special niche *Sports Spectrum* has developed in sports ministry. Then find athletes who fit that niche and who haven't been covered in the magazine."

**2004, 2003, 1998 EPA Award of Merit—General.

$SPRING HILL REVIEW, PO Box 621, Brush Prairie WA 98606. (360)892-1178. E-mail: Springhillreview@aol.com. Carolyn Schultz-Rathbun, pub.; Lucy S.R. Austen, ed. A general market publication that examines and challenges Pacific Northwest U.S. culture, seeking to encourage its audience to re-view contemporary culture through the lens of biblical truth. Monthly journal; 16 pgs.; circ. 6,200. Subscription $20. 80% unsolicited freelance; 20% assigned. Complete ms/cover letter; e-query preferred. Pays $10-15 on publication for 1st, reprint, or simultaneous rts. Articles 500-800 wds. (20/yr.); fiction to 2,000 wds. (10/yr.); reviews 500-700 wds. Responds in 4-6 wks. Seasonal 2 mos. ahead. Accepts simultaneous submissions and reprints (tell when/where appeared). Prefers accepted ms on disk or by e-mail (attached file); accepts disk in MS Word only. No kill fee. Uses some sidebars. Accepts submissions from teens. Guidelines (also by e-mail); copy $2. (Ads)

Poetry: Buys 30/yr. Avant-garde, free verse, haiku, traditional; to 35 lines; $5-10. Submit max. 6 poems.

Fillers: Buys 12/yr. Cartoons (single-frame, B & W cartoons; would consider a regular monthly multiframe cartoon), games, word puzzles, poetry, and essays; 500 wds./20 lines; $5-10.

Columns/Departments: Buys 50/yr. Book of the Hour (new book reviews); The Reel Deal (movie reviews); The Play's the Thing (Northwest Theater reviews); Northwest Book Nook (books with a NW connection); Video Corner (old and new video reviews); The Poetry Corner; all 600-800 wds.; $10-15.

Special Needs: Occasionally uses an in-depth examination of multiple books/CDs/movies on the same theme or by the same author/artist/director, up to 1,000 wds. Needs seasonal material. Information and opinion pieces on politics, arts, history, social and spiritual issues, especially those with a N.W. U.S. angle.

Tips: "We are always looking for good reviews of books (especially Northwest authors), movies, CDs, and videos. And we never have enough good fiction. No overtly evangelistic material, please, and no material written for a specifically Christian audience. Write to connect with a secular, post-modern audience, but don't check your faith at the door. Our tone and approach are quite different from those of most Christian publications. We receive a large number of submissions written for a Christian audience, but we can't use them because our audience is primarily non-Christian. You can write a wonderful story or article dealing with spiritual issues from a Christian perspective, but if your reader stops reading after the first paragraph, you haven't communicated. Read a sample copy before submitting." Deadline is the 15th of each month.

**This periodical was #30 on the 2003 Top 50 Christian Publishers list (#48 in 2002).

SR: A JOURNAL FOR LUTHERAN REFORMATION. E-mail: jglange@allwest.net. Website: http://members.aol.com/SemperRef. Semper Reformada. Rev. Jonathan G. Lange, ed. Publishes reformation theses only. Query from Website. Open to original articles and reprints of essays from old theological journals. No mention of payment. Submissions must be sent to full editorial board from the Website. Guidelines on Website.

$ST. ANTHONY MESSENGER, 28 W. Liberty St., Cincinnati OH 45210-1298. (513)241-5615. Fax (513)241-0399. E-mail: StAnthony@AmericanCatholic.org. Website: www.American Catholic.org. Pat McCloskey, O.F.M., ed. For Catholic adults & families. Monthly & online mag.; 60 pgs.; circ. 310,000. Subscription $25. 40% unsolicited freelance. Query; fax/e-query OK. Pays .15/wd. on acceptance for 1st, reprint (right to reprint), and electronic rts. Articles 1,500-3,000 wds., prefers 2,000-2,500 (45-50/yr.); fiction 1,500-2,500 wds. (12/yr.); book reviews 500 wds., $40. Responds in 8 wks. Seasonal 6+ mos. ahead. Kill fee. Uses some sidebars. Prefers NAB. Guidelines (also on Website); copy for 9x12 SAE. (Ads)

Poetry: Christopher Heffron, poetry ed. Buys 20/yr. Free verse, haiku, traditional; 3-25 lines; $2/line ($20 min.) Submit max. 2 poems.

Fillers: Cartoons.

Tips: "Most open to articles, fiction, profiles, interviews of Catholic personalities, personal experiences, and prayer. Writing must be professional; use Catholic terminology and vocabulary. Writing must be faithful to Catholic belief and teaching, life, and experience. Our online writers' guidelines indicate the seven categories of articles. Texts of articles reflecting each category are linked to the online writers' guidelines for nonfiction articles."

****This periodical was #40 on the 2004 Top 50 Christian Publishers list (#45 in 2003, #36 in 2001, #35 in 2000, #45 in 1999).

$ST. JOSEPH'S MESSENGER AND ADVOCATE OF THE BLIND, PO Box 288, Jersey City NJ 07303-0288. (201)798-4141. Catholic/Sisters of St. Joseph of Peace. Sister Mary Kuiken, CSJP, ed. For older Catholics interested in supporting ministry to the aged, young, blind, and needy. Triannual mag.; 16 pgs.; circ. 14,000. Subscription $5. 30% unsolicited freelance. Complete ms. Pays $30-40 on acceptance for 1st rts. Articles 800-1,000 wds. (24/yr.); fiction 800-1,000 wds. (30/yr.). Responds in 5 wks. Seasonal 3 mos. ahead. Accepts simultaneous submissions and reprints (tell when/where appeared). Does not use sidebars. Guidelines; copy for 9x12 SAE/2 stamps. (No ads)

Poetry: Buys 25/yr. Light verse, traditional; 4-16 lines; $5-20 on publication. Submit max. 4 poems.

Fillers: Buys 20/yr. Ideas, 50-100 wds.; $5-10.

Tips: "Most open to contemporary fiction. No Christmas issue."

+ST. LINUS REVIEW, 5239 S. Sandusky, Tulsa OK 74135. (918)906-7059. E-mail: editor@stlinusreview.com. Website: www.stlinusreview.com. Catholic. William Ferguson, ed./pub. Poetry and short prose by and for orthodox Catholics. Semiannual mag.; circ. 50. Subscription $12. Estab. 2003. 90% unsolicited freelance; 10% assigned. Complete ms.; e-query OK. **PAYS 1 COPY** for 1st rts. Fiction 2,500 wds. (8/yr.). Responds when selections are made. Seasonal poetry only . No simultaneous submissions or reprints. Accepts e-mail submissions (MS Word attachment). No sidebars. Accepts submissions from teens. Prefers RSV for Catholics. Guidelines on Website; copy for $6/9x12 SAE. (Ads)

Poetry: Accepts 30-50/yr. All types; prefers rhyming. Pays 1 copy. Submit max. 5 poems.

Contest: Offers small cash prize for "Best of Review."

Tips: "Send us poetry or fiction."

$STANDARD, 6401 The Paseo, Kansas City MO 64131. (816)333-7000. Fax (816)333-4439. E-mail: evlead@nazarene.org. Website: www.nazarene.org. Nazarene. Dr. Everett Leadingham, ed. Examples of Christianity in everyday life for adults, college-age through retirement. Weekly take-home paper; 8 pgs.; circ. 150,000. Subscription $11.95. 100% unsolicited freelance. Complete ms. Pays .035/wd.(.02/wd. for reprints) on acceptance for one-time rts. Articles (20/yr.) or fiction (200/yr.) 700-1,500 wds. Responds in 12 wks. Seasonal 6-9 mos. ahead. Accepts simultaneous submissions and reprints (tell when/where appeared). No disk; accepts e-mail submissions (copied into message). Kill fee. Does not use sidebars. Prefers NIV. Guidelines (also by e-mail); copy for #10 SAE/2 stamps. (No ads)

Poetry: Buys 50/yr. Free verse, haiku, traditional; to 50 lines; .25/line. Submit max. 5 poems.

Fillers: Buys 50/yr. Word puzzles; $20.

Tips: "Fiction or true-experience stories must demonstrate Christianity in action. Show us, don't tell us. Action in stories must conform to Wesleyan-Arminian theology and practices." Themes follow the Christian year, not celebrating national holidays.
**This periodical was #38 on the 2003 Top 50 Christian Publishers list (#30 in 2002, #23 in 2001, #22 in 2000, #18 in 1999).

STAR OF ZION, PO Box 26770, Charlotte NC 28221-6770. (704)599-4630. Fax (704)688-2546. E-mail: editor@starofzion.org. Website: www.starofzion.org. African Methodist Episcopal Zion Church. Mike Lisby, ed. Religious denominational newspaper for A.M.E. Zion church members, pastors, and national officers. Bimonthly newspaper; 16 pgs.; circ. 9,200. Subscription $38. 10% unsolicited freelance; 75% assigned. Query/clips; fax/e-query OK. **NO PAYMENT; SUBSCRIPTION FOR ESTABLISHED COLUMNS** for 1st rts. Articles to 750 wds.; book reviews 500-750 wds. Responds in 4 wks. Seasonal 2 mos. ahead. Accepts simultaneous submissions. Prefers e-mail submissions (attached file or copied into message). No kill fee. Uses some sidebars. Copy of 9x12 SAE/$1.42 postage (mark "Media Mail"). (Ads)

   Poetry: Accepts 12-24/yr. African American themes; traditional. Submit max. 12 poems.

   Fillers: Accepts 24/yr. Anecdotes, cartoons, games, jokes, prayers, and word puzzles; 25-175 wds.

   Columns/Departments: Accepts 24/yr. Motivational Message (sermon text), 500-1,000 wds.; 5-Minute Sermon (brief lesson), 500-750 wds.; From the Pulpit (pastor recollections and anecdotes). Query.

   Contest: Annual essay contest: What Zion Means to Me.

   Tips: "Most open to columns, Black history articles, religious poems, humor, church (AME Zion) histories, and pastor biographies."

STEPS: A Magazine of Hope and Healing for Christians in Recovery, PO Box 215, Brea CA 92822-0215. (714)529-6227. Fax (714)529-1120. E-mail: barbaram@christian recovery.com. Website: www.nacronline.com. National Assn. for Christian Recovery. Barbara Milligan, assoc. ed. Serves a broad audience of individuals, families, couples, church leaders, pastors, support-group leaders, and mental-health professionals. Quarterly mag. Subscription with $30 membership. Open to freelance. E-query only (see guidelines first on Website); no complete mss. **PAYS ONE YEAR HONORARY MEMBERSHIP/SUBSCRIPTION.** Articles to 1,000 wds. Uses some sidebars.

   Special Needs: Healing, restoration, reconciliation, depression, substance abuse, co-dependency, domestic violence, loss, sexual abuse, spiritual abuse, eating disorders, shame, bitterness, guilt, distorted images of self, distorted images of God, distorted images of others, sexual addiction, broken relationships, anger/rage, grief, family dysfunction, victimization, woundedness, fear, workaholism, the Twelve Steps, self-disclosure, support groups, boundaries, forgiveness, trust, God's grace, God's love, God's help.

   Tips: "Be sure to visit our Website and read sample articles from back issues. Emphasize in your article a specific way that the love and grace of God made a difference in your life or in the life of the person you are writing about."

$STEWARDSHIP, PO Box 1561, New Canaan CT 06840. (203)966-6470. Fax (203)966-4654. E-mail: guy@parishpublishing.org. Website: www.parishpublishing.org. Parish Publishing, LLC. Guy Brossy, principal. Inspires parishioners to give to their church—abilities, time, and monies. Monthly newsletter; 4 pgs.; circ. 1 million. 50% unsolicited freelance; 50% assigned. Fax/e-query with cover letter. Pays $50 on acceptance for all & reprint rts. Articles 160, 200, or 250 wds. (50/yr.) Responds in 2 wks. Seasonal 3 mos. ahead. Accepts simultaneous submissions and reprints. Accepts e-mail submissions (attached or copied into message). Regularly uses sidebars. Free guidelines/copy. (No ads)

Tips: "Write articles that zero in on stewardship—general, time, talent, or treasure—as it relates to the local church."

THE STORYTELLER, 2441 Washington Rd., Maynard AR 72444. (870)647-2137. Fax (870)647-2137. Fax (870)847-2454. E-mail: storyteller1@cox-internet.com. Website: http://freewebz.com/fossilcreek. Fossil Creek Publishing. Regina Cook Williams, ed./pub.; Ruthan Riney, review ed. Family audience; geared to (but not limited to) new writers. Quarterly mag.; 72 pgs.; circ. 525. Subscription $20. 100% unsolicited freelance. Complete ms/cover letter; phone/e-query OK. **NO PAYMENT** for 1st rts. Articles 1,500 wds. (60/yr.); fiction 1,500 wds. (100-125/yr.). Responds in 3-4 wks. Seasonal 3 mos. ahead. Accepts simultaneous submissions and reprints (tell when/where appeared). No disk or e-mail submissions. Does not use sidebars. Accepts submissions from children or teens. Guidelines (also on Website); copy $6/#10 SAE/5 stamps. (Ads)

Poetry: Accepts 100/yr. Free verse, haiku, light verse, traditional; 3-40 lines. Submit max. 3 poems.

Fillers: Accepts 10-20/yr. Cartoons, quotes, tips; 25-50 wds. Writing-related only.

Special Needs: Original artwork. Funny or serious stories about growing up as a pastor's child or being a pastor's wife.

Contest: Offers 1 or 2 paying contests per year, along with People's Choice Awards, and Pushcart Prize nominations. Go to: www.expage.com/Fossilcreekpub, for announcements of all forthcoming contests for the year.

Tips: "All sections of the magazine are open to freelancers. To break in, write a good story, of course, but send as clean a copy as possible, learn how to set up the manuscript, and include a cover letter. We like to know who wrote the story. Show us you are a serious writer."

STUDIO: A Journal of Christians Writing, 727 Peel St., Albury NSW 2640 Australia. Phone/fax +61 2 6021 1135. E-mail: pgrover@bigpond.com. Submit to Studio Editor. Quarterly journal; 36 pgs.; circ. 300. Subscription $60 AUD. 90% unsolicited freelance; 10% assigned. Query. **PAYS IN COPIES** for one-time rts. Articles 3,000 wds. (15/yr.); fiction 3,000 wds. (50/yr.); book reviews 300 wds. Responds in 3 wks. Accepts simultaneous submissions and reprints (tell when/where appeared). No disks or e-mail submissions. Does not use sidebars. Guidelines (send IRC); copy for $10 AUD. Incomplete topical listings. (Ads)

Poetry: Accepts 200/yr. Any type; 4-100 lines. Submit max. 3 poems.

Contest: See copy of journal for details.

$STUDIO CLASSROOM, 130 S. First Ave., Arcadia CA 91006. (626)462-0880. Fax (626)462-0008. E-mail: ruth@imt.net. Website: www.studioclassroom.com. Overseas Radio & Television (a Christian ministry). Ruth Seamans Devlin, exec. ed. Used to teach English to the Chinese in Taiwan. Print and online version. 50% unsolicited freelance. Query or complete ms; fax/e-query OK. Pays .25/wd. on acceptance. Articles 600-800 wds. (Ads)

Special Needs: Stories with good moral point; can be personal anecdote or fiction.

Tips: "Most readers are not Christians, so articles shouldn't be religious (except material for the Christmas and Easter issues). Our magazine content is similar to *Reader's Digest*."

THE SWORD AND TRUMPET, PO Box 575, Harrisonburg VA 22803-0575. Phone/fax (540)867-9419. Mennonite. Paul Emerson, ed. Primarily for conservative Bible believers. Monthly mag.; 37 pgs.; circ. 3,300. Subscription $12. **NO PAYMENT.** Articles. Prefers KJV. (No ads)

SWORD OF THE LORD NEWSPAPER, PO Box 1099, Murfreesboro TN 37133. (615)893-6700. Fax (615)895-7447. E-mail through Website. Website: www.swordofthelord.com. Independent Baptists and other fundamentalists. Dr. Terry Frala, editorial dept. supervisor.

Revival and soul-winning. Biweekly newspaper; 24 pgs.; circ. 70,000. Subscription $15. Open to freelance. Query; phone/fax/e-query OK. **NO PAYMENT**. Articles 500-1,000 wds.; fiction for preteens and teenagers. Responds in 13 wks. Seasonal 3 mos. ahead. Accepts simultaneous submissions and reprints (tell when/where appeared). Accepts disk or e-mail submissions (attached file). No kill fee. Does not use sidebars. Prefers KJV. Guidelines (also by e-mail); no copy. (Ads)

Poetry: Accepts variable number. Free verse, light verse, traditional; any length.

Fillers: Accepts variable number. Facts, newsbreaks, prose.

Columns/Departments: Accepts variable number. Kid's Korner (children's stories); Teen Talk (teen issues); both 500-700 wds.

Tips: "Most open to Bible study, Christian growth, and soul-winning materials. Breaking in would require material from a fundamentalist perspective."

$TESTIMONY, (title is all lowercase), 2450 Milltower Ct., Mississauga ON L5N 5Z6 Canada. (905)542-7400. Fax (905)542-7313. E-mail: testimony@paoc.org. Website: www.paoc .org. The Pentecostal Assemblies of Canada. Submit to The Editor. Focus is inspirational and Christian living; Pentecostal holiness slant. Monthly & online mag.; 24 pgs.; circ. 20,000. Subscription $24 US/$19.05 Can. (includes GST). 10% unsolicited freelance; 90% assigned. Query; fax/e-query OK. Pays $20-75 on publication for 1st or reprint rts. Articles 800-1,000 wds. Responds in 6-8 wks. Seasonal 4 mos. ahead. Accepts reprints (tell when/where appeared). Prefers e-mail submission (copied into message). Regularly uses sidebars. Prefers NIV. Guidelines/theme list (also by e-mail/Website); copy $2/9x12 SAE. (Ads)

Special Needs: See Website.

Tips: "View our theme list on our Website and query us about a potential article regarding one of our themes. Our readership is 98% Canadian. We prefer Canadian writers or at least writers who understand that Canadians are not Americans in long underwear."

THEGOODSTEWARD.COM, 2514 Plantation Dr., Ste. B, Matthews NC 28105. (828)396-7966. Fax (828)396-9490. E-mail: editor@thegoodsteward.com. Website: www.thegoodsteward .com. Wall Watchers. Michael Barrick, ed. (michaelb@thegoodsteward.com). To increase the level of giving to Christian ministries and provide a central source of information on those ministries. Weekly e-zine. 2% unsolicited freelance; 10% assigned. Query; e-query OK. **USUALLY NO PAYMENT**, except for providing a link to your e-mail or Website on publication. Articles 500-750 wds.; book reviews 500-750 wds. Responds in 2 wks. Seasonal 2 mos. ahead. Accepts simultaneous submissions and reprints. Requires e-mail submissions (attached file). Does not use sidebars. Guidelines on Website. (No ads)

Special Needs: Looking for information/articles that match well with the site's themes— biblical stewardship, life stewardship, environmental stewardship, and responsible giving. Books reviewed must have been published within last 90 days.

Tips: "Subject areas include: Biblical Principles (general precepts of biblical stewardship); Life Stewardship (physical health, fitness and well being, spiritual gifts, talents, use of time, and relationships); Financial Matters (saving, budgeting, investing, tax strategy, insurance, and estate planning); Giving Wisely (tithing and responsible giving); and Environment (ecology, recycling, environmental management, and conservation)." Is working on design/content changes; check Website for updated guidelines.

$+TIDEWATER PARENT, 1300 Diamond Springs Rd., Ste. 102, Virginia Beach VA 23455. (757)222-3100. Fax (757)363-1767. E-mail: jodonnel@pilotonline.com. Portfolio Publishing. Jennifer O'Donnell, ed. For parents of children 0-11 years; help for facing the everyday challenges of parenting. Monthly tabloid; circ. 40,000. 85% unsolicited freelance. Complete ms. or query; fax/e-query OK. Pays $35-200 on publication for 1st rts. Articles 500-3,000 wds. (60/yr.); reviews 600-800 wds. ($35-50). Responds in 1-4 mos. Seasonal

3 mos. ahead. Accepts simultaneous submissions & reprints. Kill fee 10%. Free guidelines & copy. (Ads)

Tips: "Write in an informal, familiar tone." A secular publication that accepts religious articles.

TIME FOR RHYME, PO Box 1055, Battleford SK S0M 0E0 Canada. (306)445-5172. Family Books. Richard W. Unger, ed. Poetry only; not strictly Christian (but editor is). Quarterly mag.; 32 pgs.; circ. about 100. Subscription $12 US/Can.; $17 foreign. 80% unsolicited freelance; 0% assigned. Complete ms/cover letter; phone query OK. **PAYS IN COPIES** for 1st rts. Responds as soon as possible. Seasonal 1 yr. ahead. Accepts reprints (tell when/where appeared). Prefers KJV. Guidelines; copy $3.25 US/Can.; $5.50 foreign. (Classified ads)

Poetry: Accepts 70/yr.; light verse or traditional; 2-32 lines. Rhyming only; light or serious. Submit max. 5 poems.

Tips: "Write poetry honest to the heart. Truly see, smell, etc., the experience first—focus. Then write. Don't hold readers at arm's length; let them experience it with you (show, don't tell)." US authors can send a $1 US bill to cover return postage—no US stamps.

TIME OF SINGING: A Magazine of Christian Poetry, PO Box 149, Conneaut Lake PA 16316. (814)382-8667. E-mail: timesing@zoominternet.net. Website: www.timeofsinging.bizland .com. Lora Zill, ed. We try to appeal to all poets and lovers of poetry. Quarterly booklet; 44 pgs.; circ. 250. Subscription $17. 95% unsolicited freelance; 5% assigned. Complete ms; e-query OK. **PAYS IN COPIES** for 1st, one-time, or reprint rts. Poetry only (some book reviews by assignment). Responds in 12 wks. Seasonal 6 mos. ahead. Accepts simultaneous submissions and reprints (tell when/where appeared). Accepts e-mail submission (attached file). Guidelines (also by e-mail/Website); copy $4 ea. or 2/$6.

Poetry: Accepts 150-200/yr. Free verse, haiku, light verse, traditional; 3-60 lines. Submit max. 5 poems. Always need form poems (sonnets, villanelles, triolets, etc.) with Christian themes. Fresh verse. "Cover letter not needed—-your work speaks for itself."

Contest: Sponsors 1-2 annual poetry contests on specific themes or forms ($2 entry fee/poem) with cash prizes (send SASE for rules).

Tips: "Study poetry, read widely—both Christian and non-Christian. Work at the craft. Be open to suggestions and critique. If I have taken time to comment on your work, it is close to publication. If you don't agree, submit elsewhere. I appreciate poets who take chances, who write outside the box. *Time of Singing* is a literary poetry magazine, so I'm not looking for greeting card verse or sermons that rhyme."

TJ: The In-depth Journal of Creation, PO Box 6302, Acacia Ridge D. C., QLD 4110 Australia. Phone 07 3273 7650. Fax 07 3273 7672. E-mail: admin@answersingenesis.com. Website: www.answersingenesis.org. Answers in Genesis. Pierre Jerlstrom, chief editorial coord. An international journal devoted to the presentation and discussion of the technical aspects of the sciences as they relate to biblical creation and Noah's flood. Triannual & online journal; 128 pgs.; circ. 5,000. Subscription $37. 90% unsolicited freelance; 10% assigned. Complete ms/cover letter; phone/fax/e-query OK. **NO PAYMENT** for all rts. Articles to 5,000 wds.; include an abstract of 200 wds. Responds in 2-3 wks. Prefers requested ms on disk or by e-mail (attached file). Guidelines on Website (www.answersingenesis.org/ Home/Area/Magazines/TJ/Tjguidelines.asp). Not included in topical listings. (No ads)

$TODAY'S CHRISTIAN, (formerly Christian Reader) 465 Gundersen Dr., Carol Stream IL 60188-2498. (630)260-6200. Fax (630)260-0114. E-mail: tceditor@christianity today.com. Website: www.todays-christian.com. Christianity Today Intl. Ed Gilbreath, mng. ed. A Christian *Reader's Digest* that uses both reprints and original material. Bimonthly & online mag.; 64 pgs.; circ. 125,000. Subscription $17.95. 35% unsolicited freelance; 20%

assigned. Complete ms/cover letter; phone/fax/e-query OK. Pays .10/wd. on acceptance for 1st, reprint & electronic rts. Articles 500-1,500 wds. (50/yr.). Responds in 6-8 wks. Seasonal 9 mos. ahead. Accepts reprints ($50-100, tell when/where appeared). Accepts e-mail submissions (copied into message). Kill fee. Sidebars, 150-300 wds. Prefers NIV. Guidelines/theme list (also on Website); copy for 6x9 SAE/4 stamps. (Ads)

> **Columns/Departments:** Cynthia Thomas, columns ed. Buys 150/yr. Lite Fare (adult church humor); Kids of the Kingdom (kids say and do funny things); all to 250 wds.; $35.
> **This periodical was #16 on the 2004 Top 50 Christian Publishers list (#6 in 2003, #14 in 2002, #7 in 2001, #14 in 2000). 2001 & 2000 EPA Award of Merit—General.

$TODAY'S PENTECOSTAL EVANGEL, 1445 N. Boonville, Springfield MO 65802-1894. (417)862-2781. Fax (417)862-0416. E-mail: pe@ag.org. Website: www.pe.ag.org. Assemblies of God. Hal Donaldson, ed-in-chief; Ken Horn, mng. ed.; submit to Ashli O'Connell, asst. ed. Denominational; Pentecostal. Weekly & online mag.; 32-48 pgs.; circ. 264,000. Subscription $24.99. 5% unsolicited freelance; 95% assigned. Query or complete ms/cover letter; fax/e-query OK. Pays .08/wd. (.04/wd. for reprints) on acceptance for 1st and electronic rts. Articles 500-1,200 wds.; testimonies 200-300 wds. Responds in 6-8 wks. Seasonal 6-8 mos. ahead. Kill fee 100%. Prefers e-mail submission (attached file). Regularly uses sidebars. Prefers NIV, KJV. Guidelines (also on Website); no copy. (Ads)

> **Fillers:** Practical, how-to pieces on family life, devotions, evangelism, seasonal, current issues, Christian living; 50-200 wds.; $20.
> **Tips:** "Most of the material published from unsolicited submissions centers on the personal experience of the writer. Bible exposition and most teaching articles, as well as controversial issues, are assigned to tested writers. Send samples of previous things published and indicate you are open for assignments. Special themes done mostly by assignment, but holiday themes are used if submitted well in advance (preferably 6 months). Our news editor is open to news leads and gives small stories on assignment occasionally. Best opportunity for first-time feature writer is an article about a compelling personal experience written in a down-to-earth manner. Avoid a melodramatic or preachy tone."
> **2003, 2001 EPA Award of Merit—Denominational.

$TOGETHER, 1251 Virginia Ave., Harrisonburg VA 22802. Toll-free (888)833-3333. (540)433-5351. Fax (540)434-0247. E-mail: Tgether@aol.com. Website: www.churchout reach.com. Shalom Foundation, Inc. Melodie Davis, ed. An outreach magazine distributed by churches to attract the general public to Christian faith and life. Quarterly tabloid; 8 pgs.; circ. 150,000. Free. 95% unsolicited freelance. Complete ms/cover letter; e-query OK. Pays $30-60 after publication for one-time rts. Articles 500-1,200 wds. (16/yr.). Responds in 12-16 wks. Seasonal 4 mos. ahead. Accepts simultaneous submissions and reprints. Accepts requested ms on disk or by e-mail (copied into message). Uses some sidebars. Prefers NIV. Guidelines/theme list (also by e-mail/Website); copy for 9x12 SAE/4 stamps. (No ads)

> **Tips:** "Deal with contemporary themes with fresh style. We need a variety of salvation testimonies from all racial/ethnic groups, with excellent photos available (don't submit photos until requested)." When submitting by e-mail, put title of magazine and title of your piece in subject line. Also include your e-mail address in body of message.

TRIBUTES, 5008 Rolling Meadows Dr., Durham NC 27703. (919)596-7663. E-mail: wisler@mindspring.com. Website: www.geocities.com/griefhope/index.html. Daniel's House Publications. Alice Wisler, ed. To reach those who have had a child or sibling die, and for those who care and want to help the bereaved. Monthly online mag; circ. 500+. Free (send blank e-mail to wisler@mindspring.com). 95% unsolicited freelance; 5% assigned. Complete ms. by e-mail only. **NO PAYMENT**, but gives generous bio and Website links. Articles 800-900 wds.; reviews 600-700 wds. Responds in 1 wk. Seasonal 2 mos.

ahead. Accepts reprints. Accepts mss by e-mail (copied into message). Accepts submissions from teens. Guidelines by e-mail. (Ads)

Poetry: Accepts 35/yr. Free verse, haiku, light verse, traditional; to 60 lines. Submit max. 2 poems.

Fillers: Accepts 15/yr. Anecdotes and prayers to 100 wds.

Tips: *"Tributes* is geared to helping those in grief, specifically bereaved parents and bereaved siblings. Make sure articles and poetry are within the range of this theme."

#THE TRUMPETER, 6790 Miller Dr., Ste. 200, Miami FL 33155. (305)668-6462. Website: www.thetrumpeter.com. Swanko Communications. Martiele Swanko, ed-in-chief. Unites all South Florida Christian denominations, ethnic groups, and cultures. Bimonthly & online mag.; 80+ pgs.; circ. 20,000. Subscription $19.95. 90% unsolicited freelance. Query; fax/e-query OK. **NO PAYMENT** for one-time rts. Features & sports, 900-1,000 wds.; articles 500-1,200 wds.; book/music/video reviews, 100 wds. Responds in 4 wks. Accepts reprints (tell when/where appeared). Requires requested ms on disk or by e-mail. Regularly uses sidebars. Prefers KJV. Guidelines/theme list (also by e-mail/Website). (Ads)

Fillers: Cartoons.

Columns/Departments: Accepts 100/yr. Around Town (local talk), 100-125 wds.; Arts & Entertainment, 400 wds.; Legal, 450 wds.; Political/Viewpoint, 100-125 wds.

Tips: "Call us for a special feature assignment. Be a good writer. Know how to effectively write a paragraph by the rules and use active verbs instead of adjectives."

$THE UNITED CHURCH OBSERVER, 478 Huron St., Toronto ON M5R 2R3 Canada. (416)960-8500. Fax (416)960-8477. E-mail: mduncan@ucobserver.org. Website: www.ucobserver.org. United Church of Canada. Muriel Duncan, ed. To voice hope for individual Christians, for the United Church, for God's World. Monthly mag: circ. 81,000. Subscription $20. Uses a limited amount of material from non-United Church freelancers. (Ads)

$+UP: The Magazine of Hope & Encouragement, 1987 Dwight Ln., Dresser WI 54009. (715)294-4580. E-mail: jeff@upmagazine.us. Website: www.upmagazine.us. Julie Holmquist, pub. Regional stories about how God is working in lives and through ministries. Bimonthly mag.; 36 pgs.; circ. 10,000. Subscription $18. Estab. 2003. 0% unsolicited freelance; 10% assigned. Query/clips; e-query OK. Pays $40, copies & subscription, on publication for all rts. Articles 1,500-2,000 wds. (4/yr.) Responds in 2 wks. No simultaneous submissions or reprints. Accepts submissions by e-mail (attached file). Regularly uses sidebars. No guidelines; copy for $1.50/9x12 SAE. (Ads)

$UPSCALE MAGAZINE: Exposure to the World's Finest, 600 Bronner Brothers Way SW, Atlanta GA 30310. (404)758-7467. Fax (404)755-9892. E-mail: features@upscale mag.com. Website: www.upscalemagazine.com. Upscale Communications, Inc. Sheila Bronner, ed-in-chief.; Tiffany Anderson, online ed. To inspire, inform, and entertain African Americans. Monthly mag.; circ. 242,000. Subscription $12. 75-80% unsolicited freelance. Query; fax/e-query OK. Pays $100 & up for all rts. Articles (135/yr.); novel excerpts. Seasonal 6 mos. ahead. Accepts simultaneous submissions. Kill fee 25%. Guidelines; copy $2.

Columns/Departments: Buys 6-10/yr. Positively You (personal inspiration/perspective); Viewpoint (social/political perspective). Query. Pays $75. These columns most open to freelance.

Tips: "We are open to queries for exciting and informative nonfiction." Uses inspirational and religious articles.

$U.S. CATHOLIC, 205 W. Monroe St., Chicago IL 60606. (312)236-7782. Fax (312)236-8207. E-mail: editors@uscatholic.org. Website: www.uscatholic.org. The Claretians. Meinrad Schrer Emunds, editorial dir.; Heidi Schlumpf, mng. ed. Rev. Mark J. Brummel, ed. Devoted to starting and continuing a dialog with Catholics of diverse lifestyles and opinions about the way they live their faith. Monthly & online mag.; 52 pgs.; circ. 40,000. Subscription $22. 95% unsolicited freelance. Complete ms/cover letter; phone/fax/e-query OK. Pays $250-600 (fiction $300-400) on acceptance for all rts. Articles 2,500-4,000 wds.; fiction 2,500-3,500 wds. Responds in 5 wks. Seasonal 6 mos. ahead. Accepts requested ms on disk or by e-mail. Regularly uses sidebars. Guidelines; copy for 10x13 SASE. (Ads: Dianne Wade, 312-236-7782, ext. 474)

Poetry: Submit poetry (and fiction) to: literaryeditor@uscatholic.org. All types but light verse, to 50 lines; $75.

Columns/Departments: (See guidelines first.) Sounding Board, 1,100-1,300 wds., $250; Practicing Catholic, 750 wds., $150.

Tips: "All articles (except for fiction or poetry) should have an explicit religious dimension that enables readers to see the interaction between their faith and the issue at hand. Fiction should be well written, creative, with solid character development."

**This periodical was #33 on the 2004 Top 50 Christian Publishers list.

+**VALPARAISO POETRY REVIEW**, Dept. of English, Valparaiso University, Valparaiso IN 46383. E-mail: VPR@Valpo.edu. Website: www.valpo.edu. Academic. Edward Byrne, ed. Presents new, emerging, and well-known voices in contemporary poetry. Online literary journal. Reads unsolicited submissions year round. Complete ms/cover letter; e-submissions OK (copied into message). **NO PAYMENT** for one-time rts. Essays, book reviews, author interviews. Accepts simultaneous submissions & reprints (tell when/where appeared). Guidelines on Website; copy online.

Poetry: Accepts unpublished and previously published poems. Submit max. 5 poems, once per month.

Tips: "Unsolicited book reviews are welcome. Small press publishers and poets are encouraged to send books for review to address above."

$**VIBRANT LIFE**, 55 W. Oak Ridge Dr., Hagerstown MD 21740-7390. (301)393-4019. Fax (301)393-4055. E-mail: chmills@rhpa.org. Website: www.vibrantlife.com. Seventh-day Adventist/Review & Herald. Charles Mills, ed. Total health publication (physical, mental, and spiritual); plus articles on family and marriage improvement; ages 30-50. Bimonthly mag.; 32 pgs.; circ. 28,000. Subscription $19.95. 50% unsolicited freelance; 30% assigned. Query/clips; fax/e-query OK. Pays $75-300 on acceptance for 1st, one-time, reprint, or electronic rts. Articles 600-1,500 wds. (35-40/yr.). Responds in 9 wks. Seasonal 9 mos. ahead. Accepts simultaneous submissions and reprints (tell when/where appeared). Accepts e-mail submissions (attached file). Kill fee 25-50%. Regularly uses sidebars. Prefers NIV. Guidelines (also by e-mail/Website); copy $1/9x12 SAE. (Ads)

Fillers: Buys 6-8/yr. Facts, quizzes; 50-500 wds.; $25-100.

Columns/Departments: Buys 12-18/yr. Fit People (people whose lives are changed for the better when applying timeless health principles/before and after photos), 500-650 wds.; Times of Your Life (family-oriented, everyday tips), 500-600 wds.; $75-200. Query.

Tips: "Articles need to be very helpful, practical, and well documented. Don't be preachy. Sidebars are a real plus."

**This periodical was #7 on the 2004 Top 50 Christian Publishers List (#4 in 2003, #22 in 2002, #26 in 2001, #16 in 2000).

VICTORY NEWS, 2723 Steamboat Circle, Arlington TX 76006. (817)548-1124. E-mail: luotto@comcast.net. Website: wwwfranklinpublishing.net. Franklin Publishing Company. Dr. Ludwig Otto, pub. Positive news about the Christian experience. Quarterly jour.; 200 pgs.; circ. 1,000. Subscription $185. 100% unsolicited freelance. Complete ms.; phone/ e-query OK. **NO PAYMENT** for nonexclusive rts. Articles (100/yr.) & fiction (75/yr.) to 7,000 wds.; reviews to 1,000 wds. Responds in 3 wks. Seasonal 1 mo. ahead. Accepts simultaneous submissions and reprints. Requires requested ms on disk or by e-mail (attached file). No sidebars. Accepts submissions from teens. Any Bible version. Guidelines/theme list on Website; no copy. (Ads)

Poetry: Accepts 100/yr.; all types. Submit max. 10 poems.

Fillers: Accepts 25/yr.; all types.

Columns/Departments: Accepts 20/yr.

Special Needs: Communications; public relations; marketing, management; fund-raising; grant development; TV, newspaper, and radio projects; music; building or construction; government relations; public and private education; and special event planning.

Tips: "Articles and stories may advocate any Christian position for all issues concerning our mission."

$THE VISION, 8855 Dunn Rd., Hazelwood MO 63042-2299. (314)837-7300. Fax (314)837-4503. E-mail: WAP@upci.org. Website: www.upci.org. United Pentecostal Church. Richard M. Davis, ed.; submit to Lisa Henson, ed. designer. Denominational. Weekly take-home paper; 4 pgs.; circ. 10,000. Subscription $1.39/quarter. 95% unsolicited freelance. Complete ms/cover letter; no e-query. Pays $18-25 on publication for 1st rts. Articles 1,200-1,600 wds. (to 120/yr.); fiction 1,200-1,600 wds. (to 120/yr.). Seasonal 9 months ahead. Accepts simultaneous submissions and reprints. Guidelines (also by e-mail); free copy. (No ads)

Poetry: Buys 30/yr.; $3-12.

Tips: "Most open to fiction short stories, real-life experiences, and short poems. Stay within word count. Be sure manuscript has a pertinent, spiritual application."

$VOICE OF THE LORD, 3675 S. Westshore Blvd. PMB 156, Tampa FL 33639-8235. (412)232-6801. E-mail: SwordofTruthmin@hotmail.com. Website: www.SwordofTruth.org. International Charismatic Bible Ministries (ICBM)/Sword of Truth Ministries. Rev. Jay Baldwin, gen. overseer. Healing, spiritual warfare, and prayer from a Charismatic/Pentecostal perspective. Quarterly mag.; up to 40 pgs.; circ. 1,850-2,150. Free subscription. 25-35% unsolicited freelance; 65-75% assigned. Query only; e-query OK. Pays negotiable rates on publication for 1st North American & international rts., and all electronic rts. Articles 150-700 wds. Responds in 6-8 wks. No simultaneous submissions or reprints. No disk or e-mail submissions. Uses some sidebars. Prefers KJV. Accepts submissions from children or teens. Guidelines; copy for #10 SAE/3 stamps.

Special Needs: Charismatic deliverance.

Tips: "Issues are topic oriented—the same each year. Most open to fiction or monthly topic. Must be Pentecostal/Charismatic in doctrine, and writer will have to agree to adhere to our Statement of Beliefs (charismatic) before publication will be done. Articles dealing with first person and/or reports of physical healing have a much better chance of publication if confirmed documentation from a physician is included. Be truthful—we check."

WALK THIS WAY: Extreme Discipleship Web-zine, Prolongacion de Paraiso #153-A, Colonia Rincon de San Juan, Tepic, Nayarit 63138 Mexico. (311)214-6200. E-mail: editor@walk-this-way.com. Website: www.walk-this-way.com. Walk This Way Ministries. Submit to: R. Cody Smith, ed., at submissionseditor@walk-this-way.com. Monthly e-zine; 20 pgs. Subscription free. 50% unsolicited freelance; 50% assigned. Complete ms/cover letter; e-query OK. **NO PAYMENT** for 1st, one-time, reprint, simultaneous, or electronic rts. Articles 800-1,600 wds. (25/yr.); fiction 800-1,600 wds. (2/yr.); book reviews 300-500 wds. Responds in 4 wks. Seasonal 3 mos. ahead. Accepts simultaneous submissions and reprints (tell when/where appeared). Requires submissions by e-mail (attached or copied into message). No sidebars. Prefers NIV. Guidelines on Website; copy online. (No ads)

Special Needs: New Testament Reformation; house church.

$WAR CRY, 615 Slaters Ln., Alexandria VA 22313. (703)684-5500. Fax (703)684-5539. E-mail: War_cry@USN.salvationarmy.org. Website: www.salvationarmyusa.org. The Salvation Army. Lt. Col. Marlene Chase, ed-in-chief; Jeff McDonald, mng. ed. Pluralistic readership reaching all socioeconomic strata and including distribution in institutions. Biweekly & online mag.; 24 pgs.; circ. 500,000. Subscription $7.50. 10% unsolicited freelance. Complete ms/brief cover letter; no phone/fax query; e-query OK. Pays .15-.20/wd.(.12/wd. for reprints) on acceptance for 1st or reprint rts. Articles (40/yr.) & fiction (5-10/yr.) 800-1,500 wds. Responds in 4-6 wks. Seasonal 1 yr. ahead. Accepts simultaneous submissions and reprints (tell when/where appeared). Prefers accepted ms by e-mail. Regularly uses sidebars. Prefers NIV. Guidelines/theme list (also on Website); copy free or online. (No ads)

> **Poetry:** Buys 10-20/yr. Free verse, traditional; to 16 lines. Inspirational only. Pays $25 and up. Submit max. 5 poems.
>
> **Fillers:** Buys 10-20/yr. Anecdotes (inspirational), 200-500 wds.; .15-.20/wd.
>
> **Tips:** "We are soliciting more short fiction, inspirational articles, and poetry; interviews with Christian athletes, evangelical leaders, and celebrities; and theme-focused articles. Always looking for theologically sound coverage of essential Christian doctrine and how it applies to daily living. Also short, contemporary articles (400 wds.) with an evangelical message."
>
> **This periodical was #21 on the 2004 Top 50 Christian Publishers list (#23 in 2003, #43 in 2002, #17 in 2001, #17 in 2000).

+THE WAR CRY (Canada), 2 Overlea Blvd., Toronto ON M4H 1P4 Canada. (416)422-6114. Fax (416)422-6120. E-mail: warcry@can.salvationarmy.org, or Kenneth_Smith@can .salvationarmy.org. Website: www.salvationarmy.ca/magazines/thewarcry. The Salvation Army/Canada. Kenneth Smith, ed. To provide news and information about the people, programs, and potential of The Salvation Army at work. Monthly mag.; 24 pgs.; circ. 25,000. Subscription $26.50. Open to unsolicited freelance. Complete ms/with cover letter; e-submissions OK (attached or copied into message). **PAYS 3 COPIES.** Feature articles; news 100-150 wds.; departments 650-750 wds. Accepts reprints (tell when/where appeared). Guidelines on Website. Incomplete topical listings. (Ads)

$THE WAY OF ST. FRANCIS, 1112—26th St., Sacramento CA 95816-5610. (916)443-5717, ext. 16. Fax (916)443-2019. E-mail: ofmcaway@att.net. Website: www.sbfranciscans.org. Franciscan Friars of California/Catholic. David Elliott, mng. ed. For those interested in the message of St. Francis of Assisi as lived out by contemporary people. Bimonthly mag.; 48 pgs.; circ. 5,000. Subscription $12. 10% unsolicited freelance; 65% assigned. Complete ms/cover letter; no phone/fax query; e-query OK. Pays $25-100 (or copy & subscription) on publication for 1st rts. Articles 500-1,500 wds. (4-6/yr.). Responds in 8 wks. (manuscripts are not returned). Seasonal 6 mos. ahead. Accepts simultaneous submissions and reprints (tell when/where appeared). Prefers requested ms on disk or by e-mail (attached file). Regularly uses sidebars. Any Bible version. Guidelines/theme list (also by e-mail); copy for 6x9 SAE/$1.42 postage (mark "Media Mail"). (No ads)

> **Fillers:** Anecdotes, cartoons, facts, prayers, prose; to 100 wds.; $25-50.
>
> **Columns/Departments:** Buys 12/yr. First Person (opinion/issue), to 900 wds.; Portrait (interview or personality), to 1,200 wds.; Inspirations (spiritual), to 1,200 wds.; $25-50.
>
> **Tips:** "Make direct connection to St. Francis, St. Clare, or a recognizable aspect of their life and vision."

$WEAVINGS, 1908 Grand Ave., PO Box 340004, Nashville TN 37203-0004. (615)340-7200. E-mail: weavings@upperroom.org. Website: www.upperroom.org. The UpperRoom. Submit to The Editor. For clergy, lay leaders, and all thoughtful seekers who want to deepen their understanding of, and response to, how God's life and human lives are being woven together. Bimonthly mag. Open to freelance. Complete ms. Pays .12/wd. & up on acceptance. Articles 1,250-2,500 wds.; sermons & meditations 500-2,500 wds.; stories (short vignettes or longer narratives) to 2,500 wds.; book reviews 750 wds. Responds within 13 wks. Accepts reprints. Accepts requested ms on disk or by e-mail. Guidelines (also on Website: www.upperroom.org/weavings/guidelines.asp)/theme list; copy for 7.5 x 10.5 SAE/5 stamps. Incomplete topical listings. No questionnaire returned.

Poetry: Pays $75 & up.

Tips: "All contributions should reflect simplicity, authenticity, and inclusiveness."

$WESLEYAN LIFE, (formerly Wesleyan Advocate) Box 50434, Indianapolis IN 46250-0434. (317)774-7909. Fax (317)774-7913. E-mail: communications@wesleyan.org. Website: www.wesleyan.org. The Wesleyan Church Corp. Dr. Norman G. Wilson, gen. ed.; Jerry Brecheisen, mng. ed. Denominational. Quarterly mag.; 34 pgs.; circ. 50,000. Subscription controlled. 25% unsolicited freelance; 25% assigned. Complete ms/cover letter. Pays $50-80 for unsolicited on publication for 1st or simultaneous rts. Articles 400-500 wds. (50/yr.). Responds in 2 wks. Seasonal 6 mos. ahead. Accepts simultaneous submissions and reprints (tell when/where appeared). Guidelines (also by e-mail/Website); copy $2. (Ads—limited)

Tips: "Most open to ministry pieces, personal testimonies, and general articles. No poetry."

WEST WIND REVIEW, 1250 Siskiyou Blvd., Ashland OR 97520. (541)552-6518. E-mail: West Wind@students.sou.edu. Website: www.sou.edu/English/westwind. Southern Oregon University. Student editor changes each year. Strives to bring well-written, insightful stories and poems to the public. Annual jour; 100-200 pgs.; circ. 250-500. 100% unsolicited freelance. Complete ms/cover letter & bio; no phone/e-mail query. **PAYS 1 COPY OF ANTHOLOGY** for 1st rts. Not copyrighted. Fiction (8-15/yr.). Accepts mss from May 15 through November 20. Responds in 5-10 wks. No simultaneous submissions or reprints. Does not use sidebars. No e-mail submissions. Guidelines; copy $3. (No ads)

Poetry: Any type; any length. Submit max. 5 poems. Pays one copy of the anthology.

Special Needs: Poetry or short stories that reflect moving, human interest—in a tasteful manner. Fiction should be thoughtful, literary, and contemporary.

Tips: "We accept all submissions for consideration, and observe no borders in order to encourage original creativity. We accept all forms of poetry, prose, short story, and black & white photos. No erotica, sci-fi/fantasy, or racial bias."

WHITE WING MESSENGER, PO Box 2910, Cleveland TN 37320-2910. (423)559-5128. Fax (423)559-5444. Website: www.cogop.org. Church of God of Prophecy. Virginia Chatham, mng. ed. Official voice of the denomination. Monthly mag.; 36 pgs.; circ. 7,000. Subscription $12. Open to freelance. Query; phone/fax/e-query OK. **NO PAYMENT.** Articles 500-1,000 wds. Responds in 3-4 wks. Not in topical listings. (No ads)

WINSOME WIT, 12971 Fieldstone Rd., Milaca MN 56353. (320)983-5910. E-mail: jbeuoy@winsomewit.com. Website: www.winsomewit.com. Nondenominational. Jay Beuoy, ed. We write to persuade the unbeliever through the use of satire, from a Christian worldview. Online e-zine. 75% unsolicited freelance. Complete ms; e-query OK. **NO PAYMENT FOR NOW** for one-time and electronic rts. Not copyrighted. Articles & short stories 500-2,000 wds.; reviews 500-700 wds. Responds in 1 wk. No seasonal. Accepts simultaneous submissions and reprints (tell when/where appeared). Prefers accepted ms by e-mail (attached as word.doc or copied into message). Guidelines & copy on Website. (Ads)

Poetry: Open to poetry if it fits their style; any type; to 100 lines. Submit max. 10 poems.

Fillers: Short humor.

Special Needs: "Writers with a good sense of humor. We want satire, but keep it friendly."

Contest: Details on Website.

Tips: "Check our Website. We encourage you to submit if you can write from a Christian perspective; use satire, parody, and the like; and be creative. We do not lampoon the church. Please don't send religious satire; we satirize secular culture."

$WIRELESS AGE: The Information Source for Christian Media, 5350 N. Academy Blvd., Ste. 200, Colorado Springs CO 80918. (719)536-9000. Fax (719)598-7461. E-mail: wireless age@westarmediagroup.com. Website: www.westarmediagroup.com. Westar Media Group, Inc. Dave Koch, pub./ed. For Christian media professionals working in the industry—especially those in radio. Quarterly mag.; 48 pgs.; circ. 4,100. 15% unsolicited freelance; 85% assigned. Query; fax/e-query OK. Pays variable rates for 1st rts. Articles 300-2,500 wds.; book reviews 150-250 wds. Responds in 2 wks. Accepts simultaneous submissions and reprints (tell when/where appeared). Prefers accepted ms by e-mail (attached or copied into message). Regularly uses sidebars. Prefers NIV. Guidelines (also by e-mail); copy for 10x13 SAE/$1.42 postage (mark "Media Mail"). (Ads)

   Fillers: Buys 3/yr. Cartoons, prose, 50-300 wds.; pay varies.

   Columns/Departments: Buys 48-55/yr. TV/Film (Christian TV/film issues/concerns); Radio (Christian broadcasting issues/concerns); Internet (using the Internet effectively); Programming/Production (radio program and production development); Music (profiles, reviews, news); Publishing (publishing concerns/issues); Technology (reviews, technology issues); Ministry (highlights, development of); plus others; all 800 wds., payment varies.

   Special Needs: Technology pieces: affecting the way Christians communicate the gospel.

$THE WORLD & I: The Magazine for Lifelong Learners, 3600 New York Ave. NE, Washington DC 20002-1947. (202)635-4000. Fax (202)269-9353. E-mail: editor@world andimag.com, or research@worldandi.com. Washington Times Corp. Morton A. Kaplan, ed./pub.; Michael Marshall, exec. ed.; submit to Gary Rowe, editorial office mngr. Scholarly and encyclopedic. Monthly & online journal.; 350 pgs.; print circ. 30,000. Subscription rates on Website. 5-8% unsolicited freelance; 85% assigned. Query/clips; e-query OK. Pays $400-800 on publication for all rts. Articles 2,500 wds. (1,200/yr.); book reviews 2,000-2,500 wds. ($400-500). Responds in 6-10 wks. Seasonal 5 mos. ahead. Accepts reprints. Prefers requested ms on disk. Kill fee 20%. Uses some sidebars. Guidelines (also by e-mail); copy $7.95/9x12 SAE/$1.42 postage (mark "Media Mail"). (Ads)

   Poetry: Buys few. Haiku (Asian translation); $30-75. Submit max. 5 poems.

   Columns/Departments: Buys 60/yr., plus 12 photo essays. Seven different columns, various lengths. See sample copy.

   Tips: "Life and Culture areas most open to freelancers. Offer a great/original idea (with established background as a writer), and writing samples. We especially appreciate scholarly contributions."

   **This periodical was #49 on the 2004 Top 50 Christian Publishers list (#31 in 2003).

+XAVIER REVIEW, 1 Drexel Dr., Box 110C, Xavier University of Louisiana, New Orleans LA 70125. (504)520-7549. E-mail: rcollins@xula.edu. Richard Collins, ed. Publishes nondogmatic, thought-provoking, and sometimes humorous and even irreverent work on religious subject matters. Semiannual literary jour; 75 pgs.; circ. 300. Subscription $10 (individuals), $15(institutions). 90% unsolicited freelance; 10% assigned. Complete ms/cover letter; e-query OK. **PAYS IN COPIES** for 1st rts. Articles 250-5,000 wds. (3/yr.); fiction 250-5,000 wds.(6/yr.); book reviews 250-750 wds. Responds in 4 wks. Accepts simultaneous submissions; no reprints. Prefers accepted mss by e-mail (attached). No kill fee. No sidebars. Guidelines by e-mail; copy for $2/7x10 SAE/3 stamps. (No ads)

   Poetry: Accepts 25/yr. Avant-garde; 4-100 lines. Submit max. 5 poems.

CHILDREN'S MARKETS

$ADVENTURES, 6401 The Paseo, Kansas City MO 64131-1213. (816)333-7000, ext. 2247. Fax (816)333-4439. E-mail: dfillmore@nazarene.org. Website: www.wordaction.com. Donna Fillmore, ed.; submit to Andrea Callison, ed. asst. For 6- to 8-yr.-olds (1st & 2nd graders);

emphasis on principles, character building. Weekly take-home paper; 4 pgs.; circ. 40,000. Subscription $11.96 ($2.99/child/quarter). Estab. 2003. 45% unsolicited freelance. Query; e-query OK. Pays $15-25 on publication for all rts. Biblical or contemporary fiction 100 wds. Responds in 4-6 wks. Accepts simultaneous submissions; no reprints. Accepts requested ms by e-mail (attached file). Prefers NIV. Guidelines/theme list (also by e-mail); copy for #10 SAE/1 stamps. (No ads)

Poetry: Buys free verse, light verse, traditional; 4-8 lines; .25/line, with $2 min. Submit any number.

Fillers: Buys cartoons, facts, games, party ideas, quotes, tips, word puzzles. Pays $15 for cartoons; $25 for 4-panel strip.

Special Needs: Rebus stories; interesting facts/trivia; trivia puzzles; recipes and crafts; activities. Also needs material for Parent Connections: activities for parent/child; upbeat advice for parents or caretakers.

Tips: "We accept a limited amount of material."

$#AMERICAN GIRL, 8400 Fairway Pl., Middleton WI 53562. (608)836-4848. Fax (608)831-7089. E-mail: im_agmag_editor@pleasantco.com. Website: www.americangirl.com. Pleasant Company Publications. Kristi Thom, ed.; Barbara E. Stretchberry, mng. ed. Secular; for girls ages 8-12 to recognize and celebrate girls' achievements yesterday and today, inspire their creativity, and nurture their hopes and dreams. Bimonthly & online mag.; 50 pgs.; circ. 650,000. Subscription $19.95. 5% unsolicited freelance; 10% assigned. Query (complete ms for fiction); no e-query. Pays $1/wd. on acceptance for all rts. Articles 150-1,000 wds. (10/yr.); fiction to 2,500 wds. (1/yr.). Responds in 13 wks. Seasonal 6 mos. ahead. Accepts simultaneous submissions. Kill fee 50%. Uses some sidebars. Guidelines (also on Website); copy $3.95 (check)/9x12 SAE/$1.42 postage (mark "Media Mail"). (No ads)

Poetry: All poetry is by children.

Fillers: Cartoons, puzzles, word games; $50.

Columns/Departments: Buys 10/yr. Girls Express (short profiles on girls), to 150 wds. (query); Giggle Gang (visual puzzles, mazes, word games, math puzzles, seasonal games/puzzles), send complete ms. Pays $50-200.

Contest: Contests vary from issue to issue.

Tips: "Girls Express offers the most opportunities for freelancers. We're looking for short profiles of girls who are doing great and interesting things. A key: a girl must be the 'star' and the story written from her point of view. Be sure to include the ages of the girls you are pitching to us. Write for 8- to 12-year-olds—not teenagers."

+BAREFOOT FOR KIDS, PO Box 3743, Englewood CO 80155. E-mail: jeanne@barefooton holyground.com. Website: www.barefootforkids.com. Jeanne Gowen Dennis, ed. Encourages children, ages 6-12, to live their lives fully in a loving relationship with God. Quarterly e-zine/interactive Website for kids. Free online. Estab. 2004. Open to freelance. Complete ms/cover letter; e-query OK. **NO PAYMENT**(will link to Website & include a brief bio) for all rts. (from children only), reprint, simultaneous, electronic, or nonexclusive rts. Articles 300-500 wds. (16/yr.); fiction. Responds in 4 wks. Seasonal: Submit by August 20 for Thanksgiving or Christmas. Accepts simultaneous submissions & reprints (tell when/where appeared). Requires e-mail submission (copied into message). Encourages submissions from children. Prefers NIV. No guidelines; copy online. (No ads)

Poetry: Accepts several/yr. Free verse, haiku, light verse, traditional; 4-12 lines. Submit max. 5 poems.

Fillers: Accepts several/yr. Cartoons, facts, games, ideas, jokes, kid quotes, party ideas, prayers, quizzes, quotes, short humor, tips; 25-100 wds.

Tips: "Most open to fun, quality writing that engages children and encourages them to have an active life and faith. Guide them gently toward greater intimacy with God and away from worldliness."

$BEGINNER'S FRIEND, PO Box 4060, Overland Park KS 66204. (913)432-0331. Fax (913)722-0351. E-mail: sseditor1@juno.com. Church of God (Holiness)/Herald and Banner Press. Arlene McGehee, Sunday school ed. Denominational; for young children. Weekly take-home paper; 4 pgs.; circ. 2,700. Subscription $1.50. Complete ms/cover letter; phone/fax/e-query OK (prefers mail or e-mail). Pays .005/wd. on publication for 1st rts. Fiction 500-800 wds. Seasonal 6-8 mos. ahead. Accepts simultaneous submissions and reprints (tell when/where appeared). Prefers KJV. Guidelines/theme list; copy. Not in topical listings.

$BREAD FOR GOD'S CHILDREN, Box 1017, Arcadia FL 34265-1017. (863)494-6214. Fax (863)993-0154. E-mail: BREAD@sunline.net. Website: www.breadministries.org. Bread Ministries, Inc. Judith M. Gibbs, ed. A family magazine for serious Christians who are concerned about their children or grandchildren. Bimonthly mag.; 32 pgs.; circ. 10,000. Subscription free. 20-25% unsolicited freelance. Complete ms; no e-query. Pays $20-30 ($30-50 for fiction) on publication for 1st or one-time rts. Not copyrighted. Articles 600-800 wds. (6/yr.); fiction & true stories 600-900 wds. for 4-10 yrs., 900-1,500 wds. for teens aged 14 and up (15/yr.). Responds in 8-12 wks. (may hold longer). Uses some simultaneous submissions and reprints (tell when/where appeared). Some sidebars. Prefers KJV. Guidelines (also by e-mail); 3 magazine copies for 9x12 SAE/5 stamps; 1 copy 3 stamps. (No ads)

> **Columns/Departments:** Buys 5-8/yr. Let's Chat (discussion issues facing children), 500-800 wds.; Teen Page (teen issues), 600-900 wds.; and Idea Page (object lessons or crafts for children), 300-800 wds.; $10-30.
>
> **Tips:** "We need good stories for the younger children—ages 4-10 years. Most open to fiction or real-life stories of overcoming through faith in Jesus Christ and/or guidance from godly principles. No tag endings or adult solutions coming from children. Create realistic characters and situations. No 'sudden inspiration' solutions. Open to any areas of family life related from a godly perspective."

$CADET QUEST, PO Box 7259, Grand Rapids MI 49510. (616)241-5616. E-mail: submissions@CalvinistCadets.org. Website: www.CalvinistCadets.org. Calvinist Cadet Corps. G. Richard Broene, ed. To show boys ages 9-14 how God is at work in their lives and in the world around them. Mag. published 7X/yr.; 24 pgs.; circ. 9,500. Subscription $13.30. 35% unsolicited freelance. Complete ms/cover letter. Pays .04-.06/wd. on acceptance for 1st, one-time, or reprint rts. Articles 500-1,000 wds. (7/yr.); fiction 900-1,500 wds. (14/yr.). Responds in 4 wks. Accepts simultaneous submissions and reprints (tell when/where appeared). Accepts ms by e-mail (copied into message). Uses some sidebars. Prefers NIV. Guidelines, theme list (also on Website); copy for 9x12 SAE/4 stamps. (Ads—limited)

> **Fillers:** Buys several/yr. Quizzes, tips, word puzzles; 20-200 wds.; $5 & up.
>
> **Tips:** "Most open to fiction or fillers tied to themes; request new theme list in January of each year (best to submit between January and April each year). Also looking for simple projects/crafts, and puzzles (word, logic)."

$CELEBRATE, 6401 The Paseo, Kansas City MO 64131. (816)333-7000, ext. 2358. Fax (816)333-4439. E-mail: mhammer@nazarene.org. Website: www.wordaction.com. Word-Action Publishing Co., Church of the Nazarene. Melissa Hammer, ed.; Andrea Callison, ed. asst. Weekly activity/story paper connects Sunday school learning to life for preschoolers (3 & 4), kindergartners (5 & 6), and their families. Weekly take-home paper; 4 pgs.; circ. 40,000. Subscription $10. 50% unsolicited freelance. Query or complete ms/cover letter; e-query OK. Pays $15 or .25/line on acceptance for multiple-use rts. Responds in 4-6 wks.

No seasonal. Accepts simultaneous submissions; no reprints. Accepts e-mail submissions (attached file). Prefers NIV. Guidelines (also by e-mail)/theme list/copy for #10 SAE/1 stamp. (No ads)

Special Needs: Activities, recipes, poems, piggyback songs, and crafts for 3- to 6-year-olds.

Tips: "We accept a limited amount of material."

$CHILDREN'S MAGIC WINDOW, PO Box 390, Perham MN 56573. (701)306-2859. E-mail: johncmwm@yahoo.com. Website: www.magicwindowmagazine.com. ProMark Publishing. Joan Foster, ed-in-chief. Encourages reading for fun and leisure for children ages 6-12 years. Bimonthly digest mag.; 96 pgs.; circ. 18,000. Subscription $19.95. 60% unsolicited freelance; 40% assigned. Complete ms/cover letter; no phone/fax/e-query. Pays $40-400 on publication for all, one-time, or reprint rts. Articles (16/yr.) & fiction (16/yr.) to 1,000 wds. Responds in 10 wks. No seasonal. Very rarely accepts simultaneous submissions and rarely accepts reprints (tell when/where appeared). No submission on disk or by e-mail. Kill fee 10%. Some sidebars. Guidelines; copy $5/6x9 SAE.

Poetry: Buys 10/yr. Free verse; to 20 lines; $10-40. Submit max. 2 poems.

Fillers: Buys 100/yr. Anecdotes, cartoons, facts, games, ideas, jokes, kid quotes, short humor, tips, word puzzles; to 150 wds.; no set payment.

Columns/Departments: Fun Facts (100/yr.), 70 wds.; crafts (8/yr.), 2-page spread; and Puzzles (16/yr.), 1 or 2 page spread. "We avoid sex, drugs, alcohol, violence, or social issues—all else is acceptable."

Tips: "We want fiction that would interest teens, but should be on an 8- to 12-year-old reading level. No particular area the most open to submissions. If we like your submission, we'll buy it. If we don't like it—we won't."

$CLUB CONNECTION, 1445 N. Boonville Ave., Springfield MO 65802-1894. (417)862-2781. Fax (417)862-0503. E-mail: clubconnection@ag.org. Website: www.clubconnection .ag.org, or www.ag.org/missionettes. Gospel Publishing House. Submit to The Editor. For girls, ages 6-12 (with leader edition for Missionettes leaders). Quarterly mag.; 32 pgs.; circ. 14,700. Subscription $6.50 (leader's $7.50). 30-40% freelance. Complete ms/cover letter. Pays $10-50 on publication for 1st or one-time rts. Articles 300 wds. or 750 wds. (4-6/yr.). Responds in 10 wks. Seasonal 10-12 mos. ahead. Accepts requested ms on disk. Regular sidebars. Prefers NIV. Guidelines/theme list (also on Website); copy for 9x12 SAE/3 stamps.

Fillers: Buys 6-8/yr. Anecdotes, cartoons, facts, games, ideas, jokes, newsbreaks, party ideas, quizzes, short humor, word puzzles; 20-50 or 100 wds.; $5-20.

Columns/Departments: Buys 4-6/yr.; $10-50.

Special Needs: Send for theme list each year.

$COURAGE, 1300 N. Meacham Rd., Schaumburg IL 60173-4888. (847)843-1600. Fax (847)843-3757. E-mail: takehomepapers@garbc.org. Website: www.garbc.org/rbp. Regular Baptist Press. Joan Alexander, ed. For children, 9-11, in Sunday school. Weekly take-home paper; 4 pgs. Subscription $2.49/quarter. Complete ms/cover letter including personal testimony; no phone/fax/e-query. Pays .05/wd. and up, on acceptance for first and reprint rts. (needs multiple reprint rights so they can reprint 2-3 times until next revision). Lead stories 800-1,200 wds. (40/yr.). Fiction and true stories (40-50/yr.); some serials. Responds in 8-12 wks. Seasonal 1 yr. ahead. No simultaneous submissions; occasionally accepts reprints (tell when/where appeared). No mss by e-mail. Uses some sidebars. Accepts submissions from children. Requires KJV. Guidelines/theme list (also by e-mail/Website); copy for 9x12 SAE/3 stamps. (No ads)

Fillers: Accepts 15-25/yr. Puzzles and projects. "Not word puzzles; we're looking for logic puzzles, visual puzzles, and other innovative approaches to solving problems." Pays for fillers.

Columns/Departments: Now done on assignment.

Special Needs: Looking for well-written stories that show the truth about God (related to the weekly Sunday school lesson) as it comes to bear in the lives of children today. Need stories for boys, or that have both boy and girl characters.

Tips: "Writer can best break into our market by being well acquainted with our audience and writing well in a way that supports the RBP mission. Check Website quarterly for updates concerning needs, themes, etc.: www.RegularBapristPress.org."

$DISCOVERIES, 6401 The Paseo, Kansas City MO 64131. (816)333-7000. Fax (816)333-4439. E-mail: vfolsom@nazarene.org. Website: www.nazarene.org. Nazarene/Word Action Publishing. Virginia Folsom, ed.; submit to Julie J. Smith, ed. asst. (jjsmith@nazarene.org). For 8- to 10-yr.-olds, emphasizing Christian values and holy living; follows theme of Sunday school curriculum. Weekly take-home paper; 4 pgs.; circ. 30,000. 80% unsolicited freelance; 20% assigned. This publication has announced that it will be accepting no more freelance submissions until 2007.

    **This periodical was #41 on the 2004 Top 50 Christian Publishers list (#44 in 2003).

$+FACES, 30 Grove St., Ste. C, Peterborough NH 03458. (603)924-7209. E-mail: faces mag@yahoo.com. Website: www.cobblestonepub.com. Cobblestone Publishing/secular. Submit to The Editor. Introduces young readers (ages 8-14) to different world cultures, religion, geography, government, and art. 9X/yr. mag.; circ. 11,000. Subscription $29.95. 80% freelance. Query only; e-query OK. Pays .20-.25/wd. on publication for all rts. Articles 600-800 wds.; fiction to 800 wds. (retold folktales, legends, plays; related to theme). Responds in 4 wks. to 4 mos. Prefers disk or hard copy. Kill fee. Guidelines/themes on Website.

    Fillers: Activities, 100-600 wds.; .20-.25/wd.

$FOCUS ON THE FAMILY CLUBHOUSE, 8605 Explorer Dr., Colorado Springs CO 80920. (719)531-3400. Website: www.clubhousemagazine.com. Focus on the Family. Jesse Florea, ed.; Suzanne Hadley, assoc. ed. For children 8-12 years who desire to know more about God and the Bible. Monthly & online mag.; 24 pgs.; circ. 101,100. Subscription $15. 15% unsolicited freelance; 25% assigned. Complete ms/cover letter; no phone/fax/e-query. Pays .15-.25/wd. for articles, up to $200 for fiction on acceptance for 1st, one-time, electronic rts. Articles to 800 wds. (5/yr.); fiction 500-1,800 wds. (30/yr.). Responds in 8 wks. Seasonal 6 mos. ahead. Accepts simultaneous submissions; no reprints. No disk or e-mail submissions. Kill fee. Uses some sidebars. Prefers NIV. Accepts submissions from children. Guidelines; copy (call 1-800-232-6459). (No ads)

    Fillers: Buys 6-8/yr. Quizzes, word puzzles, recipes; 200-800 wds.; .15-.25/wd.

    Tips: "Most open to fiction, biblical fiction, and how-to pieces with a theme. Avoid stories dealing with boy-girl relationships, poetry, and contemporary, middle-class family settings (current authors meet this need). Biggest need is for biblical fiction stories (less than 1,000 wds.) that stay true to the Bible, but bring text to life; also historical or other cultures; or how-to with a theme (doing stuff for dad, making neighborhood beautiful, Christmas crafts, etc.). Send mss with list of credentials. Read past issues."

    **2004, 1997 & 1994 EPA Award of Merit—Youth.

$FOCUS ON THE FAMILY CLUBHOUSE JR., 8605 Explorer Dr., Colorado Springs CO 80920. (719)531-3400. Website: www.clubhousemagazine.org. Focus on the Family. Annette Bourland, ed.; Suzanne Hadley, assoc. ed. For 4-8 year olds growing in a Christian family. Monthly & online mag.; 16-24 pgs.; circ. 78,000. Subscription $15. 25% unsolicited freelance; 50% assigned. Complete ms/cover letter; no phone/fax/e-query. Pays $25-200 ($50-100 for fiction) on acceptance for 1st, one-time, electronic rts. Articles 100-500 wds.

(1-2/yr.); fiction 250-1,000 wds. (10/yr.); Bible stories 250-800 wds.; one-page rebus stories to 200 wds. Responds in 4-6 wks. Seasonal 5-6 mos. ahead. Kill fee 25%. Uses some sidebars. Guidelines; copy (call 1-800-232-6459). (No ads)

Poetry: Buys 8-12/yr. Traditional; 10-25 lines (to 250 wds.); $50-100.

Fillers: Buys 18-12/yr. Recipes/crafts; 100-500 wds.; $50-100.

Special Needs: Bible stories, rebus, fiction, and crafts.

Tips: "Most open to short, nonpreachy fiction, beginning reader stories, and read-to-me. Be knowledgeable of our style and try it out on kids first."

**2004 & 1996 EPA Award of Excellence—Youth.

$GOD'S WORLD NEWS, PO Box 2330, Asheville NC 28802. (828)253-8063. Fax (828)253-1556. E-mail: nbomer@gwpub.com. God's World Publications. Norman W. Bomer, sr. ed. No longer accepting freelance.

$GUIDE, 55 W. Oak Ridge Dr., Hagerstown MD 21740. (301)393-4037. Fax (301)393-4055. E-mail: Guide@rhpa.org. Website: www.guidemagazine.org. Seventh-day Adventist/Review and Herald Publishing. Randy Fishell, ed.; Rachel Whitaker, asst. ed. A Christian journal for 10- to 14-yr.-olds, presenting true stories relevant to their needs. Weekly mag.; 32 pgs.; circ. 30,000. Subscription $45.95/yr. 65% unsolicited freelance. Complete ms/cover letter; fax/e-query OK. Pays .06-.12/wd. on acceptance for 1st, one-time, reprint, or electronic rts. Not copyrighted. True stories 500-1,200 wds. (200/yr.). Responds in 4-6 wks. Seasonal 6 mos. ahead. Accepts reprints (tell when/where appeared; pays 50% of standard rate). Prefers requested ms on CD or by e-mail (attached file). Prefers NIV. Guidelines (also by e-mail); copy for 6x9 SAE/2 stamps.

Fillers: Buys 100/yr. Games, quizzes, word puzzles on a spiritual theme; 20-50 wds.; $20-50. Accepting very few games, only the most unusual concepts.

Special Needs: "Most open to true action/adventure and Christian humor. Kids want that. Put it together with dialog and a spiritual slant, and you're on the 'write' track for our readers. School life."

Tips: "We use only true stories, including school situations, humorous circumstances, adventure, short historical and biographical stories, and almost any situation relevant to 10- to 14-year-olds. Stories must have a spiritual point or implication."

**This periodical was #34 on the 2004 Top 50 Christian Publishers list (#19 in 2003, #8 in 2002, #11 in 2001, #12 in 2000, #14 in 1999).

$GUIDEPOSTS FOR KIDS ON THE WEB, 1050 Broadway, Ste. 6, Chesterton IN 46304. (219)929-4429. Fax (219)926-3839. E-mail: rtolin@guideposts.org. Website: www.gp4k.com. Guideposts, Inc. Mary Lou Carney, ed.; submit to Rosanne Tolin, mng. ed. For kids 6-11 yrs. (emphasis at upper level). Online mag. only. Free online. 40% unsolicited freelance; 60% assigned. Query/clips (complete ms for fiction); no phone/fax/e-query. Pays $50-350 ($100-350 for fiction) on acceptance for all electronic rts. and nonexclusive print rts. Articles 300-1,200 wds. (24/yr.); fiction to 900 wds. (6/yr.). Responds in 4-6 wks. Seasonal 6 mos. ahead. No disk or e-mail submissions. Kill fee. Regularly uses sidebars. Prefers NIV. Guidelines (also on Website); copy online. (No ads)

Poetry: Buys 4-6/yr. Any type; 3-20 lines; $15-50. Submit max. 5 poems.

Fillers: Buys 15-20/yr. Anecdotes, cartoons, facts, games, ideas, jokes, party ideas, prose, quizzes, short humor, word puzzles; to 300 wds.; $20-75.

Columns/Departments: Buys 20/yr. Cool Kids (amazing kids doing great things to help their communities, or excelling in a sport, etc.), 300-600 wds.; Tips from the Top (Christian celebrities/sports figures), 500-700 wds.; $100-200.

Contest: Has giveaways, art and writing contests in Home School Zone (section of the e-zine).

Tips: "Keep online links in mind that might be of interest on your topic. Polaroid snapshots are helpful as well. Cool Kids column is a good place to break in. Also stories on school and sports; craft and recipe ideas; animals; and celebrity profiles."

**This periodical was #32 on the 2001 Top 50 Christian Publishers list (#32 in 2000, #31 in 1999).

$HIGH ADVENTURE, 1445 N. Boonville Ave., Springfield MO 65802-1894. (417)862-2781, ext. 4177. Fax (417)831-8230. E-mail: RoyalRangers@ag.org. Website: www.rangers .ag.org. Assemblies of God. Jerry Parks, ed-in-chief. For the Royal Rangers (boys), from kindergarten through high school; emphasis toward elementary through high school. Quarterly mag.; 16 pgs.; circ. 86,000. 25% unsolicited freelance; 60% assigned. Complete ms/cover letter; e-query OK. Pays .06/wd. on publication for 1st, one-time, simultaneous, or reprint rts. Articles 500-900 wds. (30/yr.); fiction 500-900 wds. (15/yr.). Responds in 4-5 wks. Seasonal 7 mos. ahead. Accepts simultaneous submissions and reprints (tell when/where appeared). Regularly uses sidebars. Prefers NIV. Guidelines (also by e-mail); copy for 9x12 SAE/3 stamps. (No ads)

   Fillers: Buys 30/yr. Cartoons, jokes, short humor; 50 wds., $25-30; quizzes, word puzzles, $12-15.

   **This periodical was #46 on the 2002 Top 50 Christian Publishers list.

$JUNIOR COMPANION, PO Box 4060, Overland Park KS 66204. (913)432-0331. Fax (913)722-0351. E-mail: sseditor1@juno.com. Church of God (holiness)/Herald and Banner Press. Arlene McGehee, Sunday school ed. Denominational; for 4th-6th graders. Weekly take-home paper; 4 pgs.; circ. 3,500. Subscription $1.50. Complete ms/cover letter; phone/fax/e-query OK (prefers mail or e-mail). Pays .005/wd. on publication for 1st rts. Fiction 500-1,200 wds. Seasonal 6-8 mos. ahead. Accepts simultaneous submissions and reprints (tell when/where appeared). Prefers KJV. Guidelines/theme list; copy. Not in topical listings.

$JUNIORWAY, PO Box 436987, Chicago IL 60643. Toll-free (800)860-8642. Fax (708)868-6759. Website: www.urbanministries.com. Urban Ministries, Inc. Submit to The Editor. Sunday school take-home paper for 4th-6th graders. Open to freelance. Query/clips; fax/e-query OK. Pays $150, 120 days after acceptance, for all rts. Articles. Responds in 4 wks. Seasonal 6 mos. ahead. Accepts simultaneous submissions. Requires accepted ms on disk. Prefers NIV. Guidelines; copy for #10 SASE. (No ads)

   Tips: "Send query with a writing sample, or attend our annual conference on the first weekend in November each year. Manuscripts are evaluated at the conference."

$KEYS FOR KIDS, Box 1, Grand Rapids MI 49501. (616)451-2009. E-mail: kfk@cbhministries .org. Website: www.cbhministries.org. CBH Ministries. Hazel Marett, ed.; Geri Walcott, ed. A daily devotional booklet for children (8-14) or for family devotions. Bimonthly booklet and online version; 80 pgs.; circ. 100,000. Subscription free. 100% unsolicited freelance. Complete ms. Pays $20-25 on acceptance for 1st, reprint, or simultaneous rts. Not copyrighted. Devotionals (includes short fiction story) 375-425 wds. (60-70/yr.). Responds in 2-4 wks. Seasonal 4-5 mos. ahead. Accepts simultaneous submissions and reprints. Prefers NKJV. Guidelines (also by e-mail); copy for 6x9 SAE. (No ads)

   Tips: "We want children's devotions. If you are rejected, go back to the sample and study it some more."

$LIVE WIRE, 8121 Hamilton Ave., Cincinnati OH 45231. (513)931-4050. Fax (513)931-0950. E-mail: cgirton@standardpub.com. Website: www.StandardPub.com. No freelance.

$MY FRIEND: A Catholic Magazine for Kids, 50 Saint Pauls Ave., Boston MA 02130-3491. (617)522-8911. Fax (617)541-9805. E-mail: mgdateno@paulinemedia.com. Website: www.myfriendmagazine.org. Pauline Books & Media. Sr. Maria Grace Dateno, ed. Christian formation, inspiration, and entertainment for Catholic children, ages 7-12. Monthly (10X)

& online mag.; 32 pgs.; circ. 9,000. Subscription $21.95. 30% unsolicited freelance; 30% assigned. Complete ms/cover letter; e-query OK for nonfiction. Pays $70-150 for articles and fiction on acceptance for 1st, electronic, and worldwide rts. Articles 200-1,000 wds. (5/yr.); fiction 500-1,200 wds. (25/yr.). Responds in 8 wks. Seasonal 11 mos. ahead. Kill fee. Uses some sidebars. Prefers CEV. No submissions from children or teens. Guidelines/theme list (also on Website); copy $2/9x12 SAE/5 stamps. (No ads)

Poetry: Buys 5-6/yr. Light verse, traditional; theme-related or seasonal; $20-50. Submit any number.

Fillers: Buys 5-6/yr. Math puzzles. Pays $5-20.

Special Needs: Needs more nonfiction and fiction for Christmas issue. Also profiles of kids making a difference in the world. Theme-related fiction.

Tips: "We publish freelance fiction in every issue. We are looking for engaging stories with realistic dialog, good character development, and current lingo. Watch out for being too predictable or too preachy. Please check out our guidelines, theme list, and a sample copy. Go to Website and click on 'For Contributors'."

$NATURE FRIEND, 2673 Township Rd. 421, Sugarcreek OH 44681-9486. (330)852-1900. Fax (330)852-3285 or (800)852-4482. Carlisle Press. Marvin Wengerd, ed. For children (ages 6-14); about God's wonderful world of nature and wildlife. Monthly mag.; 24 pgs.; circ. 13,000. Subscription $22. 10% unsolicited freelance; 40% assigned. Complete ms/cover letter; no phone/fax query. Pays .05/wd. on publication for 1st or one-time rts. Articles 250-750 wds. (50/yr.); or fiction 500-750 wds. (40/yr.). Responds in 12-13 wks. Seasonal 4 mos. ahead. Accepts simultaneous submissions; no reprints. No disk. Uses some sidebars. Requires KJV. Guidelines $4; copy $2.50/9x12 SAE/3 stamps. (No ads)

Fillers: Buys 12/yr. Quizzes, word puzzles; 100-500 wds.; $10-25.

Tips: "Don't bother submitting to us unless you have seen our guidelines and a sample copy. We are very conservative in our approach. Everything must be nature-related. Write on a children's level—stories, facts, puzzles about animals, and nature subjects. No evolution."

$ON THE LINE, 616 Walnut Ave., Scottdale PA 15683-1999. (724)887-8500. Fax (724)887-3111. E-mail: otl@mph.org. Website: www.mph.org/otl. Mennonite Publishing House/Herald Press. Mary Clemens Meyer, ed. Reinforces Christian values in 9- to 14-yr.-olds. Monthly mag.; 24 pgs.; circ. 5,000. Subscription $27.95. 90% unsolicited freelance; 10% assigned. Complete ms; fax/e-query OK. Pays .03-.05/wd. on acceptance for one-time or reprint rts. Articles 300-500 wds. (25-30/yr.); fiction 1,000-1,800 wds. (45-50/yr.). Responds in 4 wks. Seasonal 6 mos. ahead. Accepts simultaneous submissions and reprints (tell when/where appeared). No e-mail submission. Regularly uses sidebars. Prefers NIV, NRSV. Guidelines (also by e-mail or Website); copy for 7x10 SAE/2 stamps. (No ads)

Poetry: Buys 10-15/yr. Free verse, haiku, light verse, traditional; 3-24 lines; $10-25.

Fillers: Buys 25-30/yr. Cartoons, facts, games, jokes, party ideas, quizzes, word puzzles; to 350 wds.; $10-25.

Tips: "Watch kids 9-14. Listen to them talk. Write stories that sound natural—not moralizing, preachy, with adults quoting Scripture. We look for stories of ordinary kids solving everyday problems; humor helps. Our readers like puzzles, especially theme crosswords and word-finds. Most sections of our magazine rely on freelancers for material; especially need fiction, puzzles, how-tos, and recipes for each issue."

**This periodical was #27 on the 2004 Top 50 Christian Publishers list. (#36 in 2003, #28 in 2002, #19 in 2001, #29 in 2000, #28 in 1999)

$OUR LITTLE FRIEND, Box 5353, Nampa ID 83653-5353. (208)465-2580. Fax (208)465-2531. E-mail: ailsox@pacificpress.com. Website: www.pacificpress.com. Seventh-day Adventist. Aileen Andres Sox, ed. To teach children Christian belief, values, and practice;

God loving us and our loving Him makes a difference in every facet of life, from how we think and act to how we feel. Weekly take-home paper for 0 to 5-yr.-olds; 8 pgs. 25% unsolicited freelance (or reprints); 50% assigned. Complete ms by e-mail. Pays $25-40 on acceptance for one-time or reprint rts. True stories 450-550 wds. (52/yr.); no articles. Responds in 26 wks. Seasonal 7 mos. ahead. Accepts simultaneous submissions and reprints; no serials. Prefers e-mail submissions (attached file). Guidelines (also on Website); copy for 9x12 SAE/2 stamps. (No ads)

$PARTNERS, Christian Light Publications, Inc., Box 1212, Harrisonburg VA 22803-1212. (540)434-0768. Fax (540)433-8896. Mennonite. Etta Martin, ed. Helping 9- to 14-yr.-olds to build strong Christian character. Weekly take-home paper; 4 pgs.; circ. 6,389. Subscription $9.20. 99% unsolicited freelance; 1% assigned. Complete ms; e-query OK. Pays up to .03-.05/wd. on acceptance for 1st, multiuse, or reprint rts. Articles 200-1,000 wds. (50/yr.); fiction & true stories 1,000-1,600 wds. (70/yr.); serial stories up to 1,600 wds./installment; short-short stories to 400 wds. Responds in 6 wks. Seasonal 6 mos. ahead. Accepts reprints (tell when/where appeared); serials 2-4 parts. Prefers e-mail submissions (attached or copied into message). No kill fee. Does not use sidebars. Requires KJV. Guidelines/theme list (also by e-mail); copy for 9x12 SAE/3 stamps. (No ads)

Poetry: Buys 100/yr. Traditional, story poems; 4-24 lines; .50-.70/line. Submit max. 6 poems.

Fillers: Buys 100/yr. Prose, quizzes, quotes, word puzzles (Bible related); 200-800 wds.; .03-.05/wd. Must be theme-related.

Columns/Departments: Character Corner; Cultures & Customs; Historical Highlights; Maker's Masterpiece; Missionary Mail; Torches of Truth; or Nature Nook; all 200-800 or 1,000 wds.

Tips: "Most open to character-building articles and stories that teach a spiritual lesson. Many new writers will submit their manuscript without asking for or reading our guidelines. That is folly and a waste of everyone's time. Someone who has experienced a genuine spiritual 'rebirth' has a much better chance of receiving an acceptance. Write in a lively way (showing, not telling) and on a child's level of understanding (ages 9-14). We do not require that you be Mennonite, but we do send a questionnaire for you to fill out if you desire to write for us."

**This periodical was #12 on the 2004 Top 50 Christian Publishers list (#21 in 2003, #21 in 2002, #25 in 2001, #34 in 2000).

$PASSPORT, 6401 The Paseo, Kansas City MO 64131. (816)333-7000, ext. 2243. Fax (816)333-4439. E-mail: efreeburg@nazarene.org, or khendrixson@nazarene.org. Church of the Nazarene. Emily J. Freeburg, ed.; submit to Katherine Hendrixson, ed. asst. For preteens, 10- to 12-year-olds; supports the Sunday school lesson and provides an exciting way to learn about God and life. Weekly take-home paper; 4 pgs.; circ. 18,000. 30% unsolicited freelance. NO FREELANCE UNTIL 2007.

$POCKETS, PO Box 340004, Nashville TN 37203-0004. (615)340-7333. Fax (615)340-7267. E-mail: pockets@upperroom.org. Website: www.pockets.org. United Methodist. Submit to Lynn W. Gilliam, ed. Devotional magazine for children (6-11 yrs.). Monthly (11X) mag.; 48 pgs.; circ. 93,000. Subscription $19.95. 75% unsolicited freelance. Complete ms/brief cover letter. Pays .14/wd. on acceptance for 1st rts. Articles 400-800 wds. (20/yr.) & fiction 500-1,500 wds. (40/yr.). Responds in 4 wks. Seasonal 1 yr. ahead. Accepts reprints (tell when/where appeared). No mss by e-mail. Uses some sidebars. Prefers NRSV. Accepts submissions from children through age 12. Guidelines/theme list (also by e-mail/Website); copy for 9x12 SAE/4 stamps. (No ads)

Poetry: Buys 25/yr. Free verse, haiku, light verse, traditional; 4-24 lines; $2/line. Submit max. 7 poems.

Fillers: Buys 44/yr. Games, ideas, jokes, prayers, riddles, word puzzles; $25.

Columns/Departments: Buys 40/yr. Kids Cook; Pocketsful of Love (ways to show love), 200-300 wds.; Peacemakers at Work (children involved in environmental, community, and peace/justice issues; include action photos and name of photographer), to 600 wds.; Pocketsful of Prayer, 400-600 wds.; Someone You'd Like to Know (preferably a child whose lifestyle demonstrates a strong faith perspective).

Special Needs: Two-page stories for ages 5-7, 600 words max. Need role model stories, retold Biblical stories, Someone You'd Like to Know, and Peacemakers at Work.

Contest: Fiction-writing contest; submit between 3/1 & 8/15 every yr. Prize $1,000 and publication in Pockets. Length 1,000-1,500 wds. Must be unpublished and not historical fiction. Previous winners not eligible. Send to Pockets Fiction Contest at above address, and include an SASE for return of manuscript and response.

Tips: "Well-written fiction that fits our themes is always needed. Make stories relevant to the lives of today's children and show faith as a natural part of everyday life. All areas open to freelance. Nonfiction probably easiest to sell for columns (we get fewer submissions for those). Read, read, read and study—be attentive to guidelines, themes, and study past issues."

**This periodical was #4 on the 2004 Top 50 Christian Publishers list (#1 in 2003, #9 in 2002, #5 in 2001, #27 in 2000).

$PRAYKIDS! PO Box 35004, Colorado Springs CO 80935. (719)531-3555. Fax (719)598-7128. E-mail: sandie.higley@navpress.com. Website: www.praykids.com. Pray! Magazine/NavPress. Sandie Higley, asst. ed. Focus is on prayer for 8- to 12-year-olds. Bimonthly take-home paper; 8 pgs. Complete ms/cover letter; e-query OK. Pays .10/wd. on acceptance for 1st rts. Articles 250-500 wds. (6/yr.). Responds in 6-8 wks. Accepts reprints (tell when/where appeared). Prefers e-mail submissions (copied into message). Kill fee 50%. Uses some sidebars. Prefers NIV. Accepts submissions from children. Guidelines (also by e-mail); copy for #10 SAE/2 stamps. (No ads)

Special Needs: Bible stories on prayer.

Tips: "We want articles from kids (8-12 years) writing about how God answered prayer that affected their community or made a global impact. Also Bible stories on prayer (fiction based on biblical fact)."

$PRESCHOOL PLAYHOUSE, PO Box 436987, Chicago IL 60643. (708)868-7100. Fax (708)868-6759. Website: www.urbanministries.com. Urban Ministries, Inc. K. Steward, ed. Sunday school magazine with activities for 2- to 5-year-olds with accompanying teacher's manual. Quarterly magazine for teachers; take-home paper for students; 96 pgs. Subscription $4.85 (teacher) and $2.85 (student). 80% assigned. Query/clips; fax/e-query OK. Pays $150, 120 days after acceptance, for all rts. Articles 6,000 characters for teacher, 2,900 characters for student (4/yr.). Responds in 4 wks. Seasonal 6 mos. ahead. Accepts simultaneous submissions. Requires accepted ms on disk. Prefers NIV. Guidelines; copy $2.25/#10 SASE. (No ads)

Tips: "Send query with a writing sample."

$PRIMARY PAL (IL), 1300 N. Meacham Rd., Schaumburg IL 60173-4888. (847)843-1600. Fax (847)843-3757. E-mail: takehomepapers@garbc.org. Website: www.garbc.org/rbp. Regular Baptist Press. Joan Alexander, ed. For ages 6-8; fundamental, conservative. Weekly take-home paper. Complete ms/cover letter including personal testimony; no e-query. Pays .04/wd. and up, on acceptance for all rts. Lead stories 450-525 wds. Requires KJV. Currently in a reprint cycle. (No ads)

Fillers: Buys 40+/yr. Word Puzzles; one page (include copy of solution). Payment. "We need items with a bit of visual puzzling. Writers also need to set the puzzle in a 'frame,' writing something to help child anticipate the challenge in solving the puzzle and receiving a take-away in finding the solution."

Tips: "We also use crafts and service projects. In fiction, we want mainstream stories of daily life for children of this age. May have elements of suspense, adventure, or humor— but pointed toward an understanding of God's character and ways as they apply today. Check Website quarterly for updates concerning needs, themes, etc."

$PRIMARY PAL (KS), PO Box 4060, Overland Park KS 66204. (913)432-0331. Fax (913)722-0351. E-mail: sseditor1@juno.com. Church of God (holiness)/Herald and Banner Press. Arlene McGehee, Sunday school ed. Denominational; for 1st-3rd graders. Weekly take-home paper; 4 pgs.; circ. 2,900. Subscription $1.50. Complete ms/cover letter; phone/fax/e-query OK (prefers mail or e-mail). Pays .005/wd. on publication for 1st rts. Fiction 500-1,000 wds. Seasonal 6-8 mos. ahead. Accepts simultaneous submissions and reprints (tell when/where appeared). Prefers KJV. Guidelines/theme list; copy. Not in topical listings.

$PRIMARY STREET, 1551 Regency Ct., Calumet City IL 60409. (708)868-7100. Fax (708)868-7105. E-mail: Jhull@urbanmisnistries.com. Website: www.urbanministries.com. Urban Ministries, Inc. Dr. Judith Hull, sr. ed. Sunday school curriculum for African American children, ages 6 to 8. Quarterly lesson folder for students and teacher's guide; 96 pgs. for teacher, 4 pages weekly for students. 100% assigned. Query/clips; phone/e-query OK. Pays $150/lesson on acceptance for all rts. Requires submissions on disk or by e-mail (attached file). No sidebars. Prefers NIV. Guidelines by e-mail; copy for 9x12 SAE/3 stamps.

Tips: "Writer may submit a résumé, testimony, and writing sample to be considered for an assignment."

$PRIMARY TREASURE, Box 5353, Nampa ID 83653-5353. (208)465-2500. Fax (208)465-2531. E-mail: ailsox@pacificpress.com. Website: www.pacificpress.com. Seventh-day Adventist. Aileen Andres Sox, ed. To teach children Christian belief, values, and practice. God's loving us and our loving him makes a difference in every facet of life, from how we think and act to how we feel. Weekly take-home paper for 6- to 9-yr.-olds (1st-4th grades); 16 pgs. 50% freelance (assigned), 25% reprints or unsolicited. Complete ms by e-mail preferred. Pays $25-50 on acceptance for one-time or reprint rts. True stories 900-1,000 wds. (52/yr.); articles used rarely (query). Responds in 13 wks. Seasonal 7 mos. ahead. Accepts simultaneous submissions and reprints; serials to 10 parts (query). E-mail submission preferred (attached file). Guidelines (also on Website); copy for 9x12 SAE/2 stamps. (No ads)

Tips: "We need true adventure stories with a spiritual slant; positive, lively stories about children facing modern problems and making good choices. We always need strong stories about boys and stories featuring dads. We need a spiritual element that frequently is missing from submissions."

$PROMISE, 2621 Dryden Rd., Moraine OH 45439. (937)293-1415. Fax (937)293-1310. E-mail: service@pflaum.com. Website: www.pflaum.com. Catholic. Joan Mitchell CSJ, ed. For kindergarten and grade 1; encourages them to participate in parish worship. Weekly (32X) take-home paper. Not in topical listings.

$SEEDS, 2621 Dryden Rd., Moraine OH 45439. (937)293-1415. Fax (937)293-1310. E-mail: service@pflaum.com. Website: www.pflaum.com. Catholic. Joan Mitchell CSJ, ed. Prepares children to learn about God; for preschoolers. Weekly (32X) take-home paper; 4 pgs. Not in topical listings.

$SHINE BRIGHTLY, Box 7259, Grand Rapids MI 49510. (616)241-5616, ext. 3024. Fax (616)241-5558. E-mail: sara@gemsgc.org, or servicecenter@gemsgc.org. Website: www.gemsgc.org. GEMS Girls Clubs. Sara Lynne Hilton, mng. ed. To show girls ages 9-14 that God is at work in their lives and in the world around them. Monthly (9X) mag.; 24

pgs.; circ. 13,000. Subscription $12.50. 80% unsolicited freelance; 20% assigned. Complete ms; no e-query. Pays .03-.05/wd. on publication for 1st or reprint rts. Articles 100-400 wds. (10/yr.); fiction 400-900 wds. (30/yr.). Responds in 4-6 wks. Seasonal 10 mos. ahead. Accepts simultaneous submissions and reprints. Accepts requested ms on disk. Regularly uses sidebars. Prefers NIV. Guidelines/theme list (also by e-mail/Website); copy $1/9x12 SAE/3 stamps. (No ads)

Fillers: Buys 10/yr. Cartoons, games, party ideas, prayers, quizzes, short humor, word puzzles; 50-200 wds.; $5-10.

Special Needs: Craft ideas that can be used to help others. Articles on how words can help build others up or tear people down.

Tips: "Be realistic—we get a lot of fluffy stories with Pollyanna endings. We are looking for real-life-type stories that girls relate to. We mostly publish short stories but are open to short reflective articles. Know what girls face today and how they cope in their daily lives. We need angles from home life and friendships, peer pressure, and the normal growing-up challenges girls deal with."

SKIPPING STONES: A Multicultural Magazine, PO Box 3939, Eugene OR 97403. Phone/fax (541)342-4956. E-mail: editor@skippingstones.org. Website: www.skippingstones.org. Interfaith/multicultural. Arun N. Toké, exec. ed.; Mary Drew, asst. ed. A multicultural awareness and nature appreciation magazine for young people 7-17, worldwide. Bimonthly (5X) mag.; 36 pgs.; circ. 2,500. Subscription $25. 85% unsolicited freelance; 15% assigned. Query or complete ms/cover letter; no phone query; e-query/submissions OK. **PAYS IN COPIES** for 1st, electronic, and nonexclusive reprint rts. Articles (15-25/yr.) 500-750 wds.; fiction for teens, 750-1,000 wds. Responds in 9-13 wks. Seasonal 2-4 mos. ahead. Accepts simultaneous submissions. Accepts requested ms on disk. Regularly uses sidebars. Guidelines/theme list (also by e-mail/Website); copy $5/4 stamps. (No ads)

Poetry: Only from kids under 18. Accepts 100/yr. Any type; 3-30 lines. Submit max. 4-5 poems.

Fillers: Accepts 10-20/yr. Anecdotes, cartoons, games, quizzes, short humor, word puzzles; to 250 wds.

Columns/Departments: Accepts 10/yr. Noteworthy News (multicultural/nature/international/social, appropriate for youth), 200 wds.

Special Needs: Stories and articles on your community and country, peace, nonviolent communication, compassion, kindness, spirituality, tolerance, and giving.

Contest: Annual Book Awards for published books and authors (deadline January 20); Annual Youth Honor Awards for students 7-17. Send SASE for guidelines. June 20 deadline.

Tips: "Most of the magazine is open to freelance. We're seeking submissions by minority, multicultural, international, and/or youth writers. Do not be judgmental or preachy; be open or receptive to diverse opinions."

$SPARKLE, Box 7259, Grand Rapids MI 49510. (616)241-5616. Fax (616)241-5558. E-mail: sara@gemsgc.org, or servicecenter@gemsgc.org. Website: www.gemsgc.org. GEMS Girls Clubs (nondenominational). Christina Malone, mng. ed. To show girls, grades 1-3, that God is at work in their lives and the world around them. Triannual mag. Subscription $5. 80% unsolicited freelance; 20% assigned. Complete ms; no e-query. Pays .03/wd. on publication for 1st, reprint, or simultaneous rts. Articles 200-400 wds. (10/yr.); fiction 400-1,000 wds. (30/yr.). Responds in 6 wks. Seasonal 10 mos. ahead. Accepts simultaneous submissions and reprints. Accepts requested ms on disk. Regularly uses sidebars. Prefers NIV. Guidelines/theme list (also by e-mail/Website); copy $1/9x12 SAE/3 stamps. Not included in topical listings. (No ads)

Fillers: Buys 10/yr. Games, party ideas, prayers, quizzes, short humor; 50-200 wds.; $5-15.

$STORY FRIENDS, 616 Walnut St., Scottdale PA 15683. (724)887-8500. Fax (724)887-3111. E-mail: rstutz@mph.org. Website: www.mph.org. Faith and Life Press/Mennonite Publishing House. Rose Mary Stutzman, ed. For children 4-9 yrs.; reinforces Christian values in a nonmoralistic manner. Monthly mag.; 20 pgs.; circ. 6,000. Subscription $18. 70% freelance. Complete ms/cover letter; no e-query. Pays .03-.05/wd. on acceptance for 1st or one-time rts. Articles (5-10/yr.) & fiction (30/yr.), 300-800 wds. Responds in 8 wks. Seasonal 6 mos. ahead. Accepts simultaneous submissions and reprints (tell when/where appeared). Prefers NIV. Guidelines; copy for 9x12 SAE/2 stamps.

> **Poetry:** Buys 12/yr. Traditional; 8-20 lines; $10. Submit max. 3 poems.
>
> **Fillers:** Buys 2-3/yr. Cartoons, word puzzles.
>
> **Ethnic:** Targets all ethnic groups involved in the Mennonite church.
>
> **Tips:** "Send stories that show rather than tell. Realistic fiction (no fantasy). Send good literary quality with a touch of humor that will appeal to children. Cover letter should give your experience with children."

$STORY MATES, Christian Light Publications, Inc., Box 1212, Harrisonburg VA 22803-1212. (540)434-0768. Fax (540)433-8896. E-mail: StoryMates@clp.org. Mennonite. Crystal Shank, ed. For 4- to 8-yr.-olds. Weekly take-home paper; 4 pgs.; circ. 6,200. Subscription $9.80. 90% unsolicited freelance. Complete ms. Pays up to .04/wd. on acceptance for 1st rts. (.05/wd. for 1st rts., plus reprint rts.). Realistic or true stories to 800-900 wds. (50-75/yr.); picture stories 120-150 wds. Responds in 6 wks. Seasonal 6 mos. ahead. Accepts simultaneous submissions and reprints (tell when/where appeared). No disk. Requires KJV. Guidelines/theme list (also by e-mail); copy for 9x12 SAE/3 stamps. Will send questionnaire to fill out. (No ads)

> **Poetry:** Buys 25/yr. Traditional, any length. Few story poems. Pays up to .50/line.
>
> **Fillers:** Quizzes, word puzzles, craft ideas. "Need fillers that correlate with theme list; Bible related." Pays about $7.
>
> **Tips:** "Carefully read our guidelines and understand our conservative Mennonite applications of Bible principles." Very conservative.
>
> **This periodical was #50 on the 1999 Top 50 Christian Publishers list.

$WINNER MAGAZINE, 55 W. Oak Ridge Dr., Hagerstown MD 21740. (301)393-4010. Fax (301)393-3294. E-mail: winner@healthconnection.org. Website: www.winnermagazine.org. The Health Connection. Anita Jacobs, ed. For elementary school children, grades 4-6. Monthly (during school year) mag.; 16 pgs.; circ. 15,000. Subscription $18.25. 30% unsolicited freelance; 70% assigned. Query by e-mail. Pays $40-80 on acceptance for 1st rts. Articles 600-650 wds. (25-30/yr.); fiction 600-650 wds. Responds in 4-13 wks. Seasonal 9 mos. ahead. Accepts simultaneous submissions and reprints (tell when/where appeared). Prefers e-mail submission (attached file). Uses some sidebars. Guidelines; copy $2/9x12 SAE/2 stamps.

> **Tips:** "*Winner* is a positive lifestyle magazine. Most open to self-help stories, factuals on tobacco, alcohol, and other drugs—in story format (include sources), with a catchy ending. Each article needs at least three questions relating to the story and a puzzle/activity."

YOUNG GENTLEMAN'S MONTHLY, PO Box 23, West Charleston VT 05872-0023. Stepping Out of the Darkness. Sharon White, ed. For Christian boys, ages 7-11. Monthly (8X). Subscription $12, includes club membership. Open to freelance. Complete ms. **NO PAYMENT.** Articles 200-600 wds.; fiction 200-800 wds. No guidelines; copy $2/SASE. Incomplete topical listings. (Ads)

> **Fillers:** Accepts 8/yr. Historical fillers, 200 wds. (What did boys learn and do 200-300 years ago?)
>
> **Columns/Departments:** Diligence; Work Ideas; Manners; Sabbath Keeping; How to Care for and Protect the Family; 200-600 wds.

Special Needs: Short stories need to be old-fashioned—moral, character building. No contemporary problems or situations. Articles should be devout Christian/Messianic Jewish based.

Tips: "Please request a sample issue before submitting. We're always willing to work with new writers. Be sensitive to the growing need of leading our children away from modernism and back to the old paths of moralism, courage, and men being men."

CHRISTIAN EDUCATION/LIBRARY MARKETS

$CARAVAN: A Resource for Adult Catechesis, 2500 Don Reid Dr., Ottawa ON K1H 2J2 Canada. (613)241-9461, ext. 109. Fax (613)241-9048. E-mail: jchafe@cccb.ca. Website: www.cccb.ca. Canadian Conference of Catholic Bishops. Joanne Chafe, ed. A resource for adult religious educators. Quarterly mag.; 16 pgs.; circ. 1,000. Subscription $27.82 Can.; $27 US. 10% unsolicited freelance; 90% assigned. Complete ms/cover letter. Pays variable rate on acceptance or publication. Copyrighted; rights released on request. Articles 600-1,500 wds. (30-40/yr.). Responds in 4-6 wks. Seasonal 3 mos. ahead. Accepts simultaneous submissions. Regularly uses sidebars. Guidelines/copy. (No ads)

    Columns/Departments: Adult religious education: New Initiatives, New Releases, Creative Program Ideas.

    Special Needs: Workshop models.

    Tips: "Send suggested annotated outline of material. Request guidelines and sample copy."

$CATECHIST, 2621 Dryden Rd., 3rd Floor, Dayton OH 45439. (937)293-1415. Fax (937)293-1410. E-mail: kdotterweich@peterli.com. Website: www.catechist.com. Catholic; Peter Li Education Group. Kass Dotterweich, ed. For Catholic school teachers and parish volunteer catechists. Mag. published 7X/yr.; 52 pgs.; circ. 52,000. 30% unsolicited freelance; 70% assigned. Query (preferred) or complete ms. Pays $25-150 on publication. Articles 1,200-1,500 wds. Responds in 9-18 wks. Guidelines (also on Website); copy $3.

    Tips: "Most open to short features and how-to lesson plans and crafts."

CATHOLIC LIBRARY WORLD, 100 North St., Ste. 224, Pittsfield MA 01201-5109. (413)443-2252. Fax (413)442-2252. E-mail: cla@cathla.org. Website: www.cathla.org. Catholic Library Assn. Sr. Mary E. Gallagher, gen. ed. For libraries at all levels—preschool to post-secondary to academic, parish, public, and private. Quarterly jour.; 80 pgs.; circ. 1,000. Subscription $60/$70 foreign. 90% unsolicited freelance; 10% assigned. Query or complete ms; phone/fax/e-query OK. **PAYS 1 COPY.** Articles; book/video reviews, 300-500 wds. Accepts requested ms on disk. Uses some sidebars. No guidelines; copy for 9x12 SAE. (Ads)

    Special Needs: Topics of interest to academic libraries, high school and children's libraries, parish and community libraries, archives, and library education. Reviewers cover areas such as theology, spirituality, pastoral, professional, juvenile books and material, and media.

    Tips: "Review section considers taking on new reviewers who are experts in field of librarianship, theology, and professional studies. No payment except a free copy of the book or materials reviewed. Query us by mail or e-mail."

$CHILDREN'S MINISTRY MAGAZINE, 1515 Cascade Ave., Loveland CO 80539. Toll-free (800)447-1070. Fax (970)292-4360. E-mail: cyount@cmmag.com. Website: www .cmmag.com. Group Publishing/nondenominational. Christine Yount, ed.; submit to Jennifer Hooks, assoc. ed. (jhooks@cmmag.com). The leading resource for adults who work with children (ages 0-12) in the church. Bimonthly mag.; 140 pgs.; circ. 90,000. Subscription $24.95. 80% unsolicited freelance; 20% assigned. Complete ms/cover letter; e-query OK. Pays $25-400 on acceptance for all & electronic rts. Articles 50-1,800 wds.

(250-300/yr.). Responds in 8-10 wks. Seasonal 6-9 mos. ahead. No simultaneous submissions or reprints. Accepts requested ms by e-mail (attached or copied into message). Kill fee 100%. Regularly uses sidebars. Accepts submissions from children and teens. Prefers NIV. Guidelines (also by e-mail/Website); copy $2/9x12 SAE/.80 postage. (Ads)

Fillers: Buys 25-50/yr. Cartoons, kid quotes; 25-50 wds.; $25-60.

Columns/Departments: Buys 200+/yr. Age-level insights (age-appropriate ideas); Family Ministry (family ideas); Reaching Out (outreach ideas); 150-250 wds. Teacher Telegram (ideas for teachers); For Parents Only (parenting ideas); 150-300 wds.; $40-150. Complete ms.

Special Needs: Seasonal ideas, outreach ideas, volunteer management, and family ministry.

Tips: "All areas open to freelancers. We're looking for stand-out ideas. Big need for cartoons depicting kids and faith. Break in with ideas unless you are a published writer. We seek features from 'experts'—through practice or theory."

**This periodical was #13 on the 2004 Top 50 Christian Publishers list.

+CHRISTIAN EARLY EDUCATION, PO Box 35097, Colorado Springs CO 80935. (719)528-6906. Fax (719)531-0631. E-mail: earlyeducation@acsi.org. Website: www.acsi.org. Assn. of Christian Schools Intl. D'Arcy Maher, sr. ed. Equips individuals serving children ages birth to five from a biblical perspective. Quarterly mag.; 40 pgs.; circ. 5,500. Subscription $14. 10% unsolicited freelance; 90% assigned. Query; phone/fax/e-query OK. **PAYS IN COPIES**. Not copyrighted. Articles 600-1,800 wds. (12-15/yr.). Responds in 4 wks. Seasonal 10 mos. ahead. Accepts reprints (tell when/where appeared). Prefers e-mail submissions (attached file). No sidebars. Prefers NIV. Guidelines/theme list (also by e-mail); copy $1.50/9x12 SAE. (Ads)

Columns/Departments: Accepts up to 10/yr. Staff Training (training for teachers of young children, to use in staff meeting), 400 wds.; Parents Place (material suitable for parents of young children), 400 wds. Complete ms.

$CHRISTIAN EDUCATORS JOURNAL, 73 Highland Ave., St. Catherines ON L2R 4H9 Canada. Phone/fax (905)684-3991. E-mail: bert.witvoet@sympatico.ca. Christian Educators Journal Assn. Bert Witvoet, mng. ed. For educators in Christian day schools at the elementary, secondary, and college levels. Quarterly jour.; 36 pgs.; circ. 4,200. Subscription $7.50 (c/o James Rauwerda, 2045 Boston St. SE, Grand Rapids MI 49506, 616-243-2112). 50% unsolicited freelance; 50% assigned. Query; phone/e-query OK. Pays $30 on publication for one-time rts. Articles 750-1,500 wds. (20/yr.); fiction 750-1,500 wds. Responds in 5 wks. Seasonal 4 mos. ahead. Accepts simultaneous submissions and reprints. Guidelines/theme list; copy $1.50 or 9x12 SAE/4 stamps. (Limited ads)

Poetry: Buys 6/yr. On teaching day school; 4-30 lines; $10. Submit max. 5 poems.

Tips: "No articles on Sunday school, only Christian day school. Most open to theme topics and features."

THE CHRISTIAN LIBRARIAN, Ryan Library, PLNU 3600 Lomaland Dr., San Diego CA 92106. (619)849-2208. Fax (619)849-7024. E-mail: apowell@ptloma.edu. Website: www.acl.org. Assn. of Christian Librarians. Anne-Elizabeth Powell, ed-in-chief. Geared toward academic librarians of the Christian faith. Quarterly (3X) jour.; 40 pgs.; circ. 800. Subscription $30. 50% unsolicited freelance; 50% assigned. E-mail; fax/e-query OK. **NO PAYMENT** for one-time rts. Not copyrighted. Articles 1,000-3,000 words; research articles to 5,000 wds. (6/yr.); reviews 150-300 wds. Responds in 5 wks. Accepts simultaneous submissions and reprints (tell when/where appeared). Prefers accepted ms by e-mail (attached file). Uses some sidebars. Guidelines (also by e-mail/Website); copy $5. (No ads)

Fillers: Anecdotes, ideas, short humor; 25-300 wds.

Special Needs: Articles dealing with the intersection of faith and professional duties in libraries. Interviews with library leaders, profiles of Christian academic libraries, international librarianship.

Tips: "Reviews are a good way to gain publication. Write a tight, well-researched article about a current 'hot topic' in librarianship as it is defined in a Christian setting; or ethics of librarianship. Articles on 'how we did it right' are good entry publications."

CHRISTIAN LIBRARY JOURNAL, 331 Valley Mall Pkwy., Ste. 416, East Wenatchee WA 98802-4829. (509)662-7455. Fax (509)884-9504. E-mail: nlhesch@ChristianLibraryJ.org. Website: www.christianlibraryj.org. Christian Library Services. Nancy Hesch, ed./pub. Provides reviews of library materials and articles about books, authors, and libraries for the Christian librarian. Irregular online mag. (about 4/yr.); 70+ pgs.; circ. 20,000. Subscription $20. 10% unsolicited freelance; 90% assigned. Query by e-mail only. Publisher overseas; correspond by e-mail only. **PAYS A SUBSCRIPTION** for 1st or reprint rts. Articles 1,000-1,500 wds. (20/yr.); book/video reviews, 200-300 wds. (see the Website if you want to be a reviewer), book or other item plus subscription in payment. Responds in 10-12 wks. Accepts reprints (tell when/where appeared). Prefers accepted ms by e-mail (attached file or copied into message). Copy online.

Special Needs: Library how-tos, Websites, author profiles, and annotated bibliographies.

Tips: "Most open to articles, book reviews, especially written by librarians and teachers."

+CHRISTIAN SCHOOL EDUCATION, PO Box 35097, Colorado Springs CO 80935-3509. (719-528-6906. Fax (719)531-0631. E-mail: cse@acsi.org. Website: www.acsi.org. Association of Christian Schools, Intl. Steven C. Babbitt, ed. To provide accurate information as well as provoke thought and reflection about the ministry of Christian school education worldwide. 5X/yr. mag.; circ. 70,000. Subscription $20. Open to unsolicited freelance. Query preferred. Articles/reviews. Incomplete topical listings. (Ads)

CHURCH & SYNAGOGUE LIBRARIES, PO Box 19357, Portland OR 97280-0357. (503)244-6919. Fax (503)977-3734. E-mail: csla@worldaccessnet.com. Website: www.worldaccess net.com/~csla. Church and Synagogue Library Assn. Judith Janzen, exec. dir. To help librarians run congregational libraries. Bimonthly; 24 pgs.; circ. 3,000. Subscription $25, $35 Can., $45 foreign. Query; no e-query. **NO PAYMENT.** Requires accepted ms on disk. Articles. Book & video reviews 1-2 paragraphs. Guidelines; copy available. (Ads)

Fillers: Ideas.

$CHURCH EDUCATOR, 165 Plaza Dr., Prescott AZ 86303. Toll-free (800)221-0910. (928)771-8601. Fax (928)771-8621. E-mail: edmin2@aol.com. Website: www.education alministries.com. Educational Ministries, Inc. Robert G. Davidson, ed. For mainline Protestant Christian educators. Monthly jour.; 32 pgs.; circ. 3,000. Subscription $28, Can. $34, foreign $36. 95% unsolicited freelance. Complete ms/cover letter; phone/fax/e-query OK. Pays .03/wd., 60 days after publication, for 1st or one-time rts. Articles 500-1,750 wds. (200/yr.); fiction 500-1,500 wds. (10/yr.). Responds in 1-13 wks. Seasonal 7 mos. ahead. Accepts simultaneous submissions and reprints (tell when/where appeared). Regularly uses sidebars. Guidelines/theme list; copy for 9x12 SAE/4 stamps.

Fillers: Bible games and Bible puzzles.

Tips: "Talk to the educators at your church. What would they find useful? Most open to seasonal articles dealing with the liturgical year. Write up church programs with specific how-tos of putting the program together."

**This periodical was #17 on the 2004 Top 50 Christian Publishers list (#16 in 2003, #38 in 2002, #39 in 2001).

$CHURCH LIBRARIES, 9731 N. Fox Glen Dr., #6F, Niles IL 60714-4222. (847)296-3964. Fax (847)296-0754. E-mail: lin@ECLAlibraries.org. Website: www.ECLAlibraries.org. Evangelical Church Library Assn. Lin Johnson, managing ed. To assist church librarians in setting up, maintaining, and promoting church libraries and media centers. Quarterly mag.; 40 pgs.; circ. 600. Subscription $30. 25% unsolicited freelance. Complete ms or queries by e-mail only. Pays .04/wd. on acceptance for 1st or reprint rts. Articles 500-1,000 wds. (24-30/yr.); book/music/video/cassette reviews by assignment, 75-150 wds., free product. Responds in 4-6 wks. Seasonal 6 mos. ahead. Accepts reprints (tell when/where appeared). Requires e-mail submission. Regularly uses sidebars. Prefers NIV. Guidelines (also by e-mail/Website); copy for 9x12 SAE/$1.42 postage (mark "Media Mail"). (Ads)

> **Tips:** "Talk to church librarians or get involved in library or reading programs. Most open to articles and promotional ideas; profiles of church libraries; roundups on best books in a category (query on topic first). Need for reviewers fluctuates; if interested e-mail for availability."

**This periodical was #48 on the 2002 Top 50 Christian Publishers list (#45 in 2000).

$EVANGELIZING TODAY'S CHILD, PO Box 348, Warrenton MO 63383-0348. (636)456-4321. Fax (636)456-9935. E-mail: ETCeditor@cefonline.com. Website: www.etczine.com. Child Evangelism Fellowship. Elsie C. Lippy, ed. To equip Christians to lead the world's children (ages 4-11) to Christ and disciple them in the Word of God. Bimonthly mag.; 64 pgs.; circ. 14,500. Subscription $24. 25% unsolicited freelance; 75% assigned. Complete ms; no phone/fax query; e-query OK. Pays .12-.14/wd. (.08/wd. for fiction) within 60 days of acceptance for one-time rts. Articles 1,000-1,200 wds. (24/yr.); fiction 800-850 wds. (12/yr.). Responds in 4-6 wks. Seasonal 1 yr. ahead. Accepts few reprints (tell when/where appeared). Disk or e-mail submission OK. Kill fee 30%. Regularly uses sidebars. Prefers NIV. Guidelines (also by e-mail/Website); copy $3/9x12 SAE. (Ads)

> **Resource Center:** Buys 40-60/yr. Complete ms, 200-300 wds.; $35 for teaching tips, bulletin board ideas, object lessons, missions incentives, seasonal ideas, crafts with spiritual focus.

> **Special Needs:** Bible-related ideas for the Resource Center, i.e., seasonal, missions. We would like to receive more reproducible activity pages on Christian growth that the child can do with the family, articles on teaching methods, and testimonies of adults saved as children; 200-300 wds. ($35)

> **Tips:** "Fictional read-aloud stories and Resource Center are good areas to break into. A writer should be actively working with children in order to gain fresh anecdotes and insight to share with the readers. Fiction should be written at the third- to fourth-grade level. Feature contemporary settings with scriptural solutions to problems faced by children."

**This periodical was #45 on the 2004 Top 50 Christian Publishers list.

$GROUP MAGAZINE, Box 481, Loveland CO 80538. (970)669-3836. Fax (970)679-4392. E-mail: rlawrence@grouppublishing.com, or kdieterich@grouppublishing.com. Website: www.grouppublishing.com, or www.groupmag.com. Rick Lawrence, ed.; Kathleen Dieterich, asst. ed. For leaders of Christian youth groups; to supply ideas, practical help, inspiration, and training for youth leaders. Bimonthly mag.; 85 pgs.; circ. 55,000. Subscription $29.95. 55% unsolicited freelance; 45% assigned. Query; e-query OK. Pays $40-300 on acceptance for all rts. Articles 500-2,000 wds. (150/yr.). Responds in 8 wks. Seasonal 5 mos. ahead. No simultaneous submissions or reprints. Accepts e-mail submissions (copied into message). No kill fee. Uses some sidebars. Any Bible version. Guidelines (also on Website); copy $2/9x12 SAE/4 stamps. (Ads)

> **Fillers:** Buys 5-10/yr. Cartoons, games, ideas; $40.

> **Columns/Departments:** Buys 30-40/yr. Try This One (youth group activities), to 300 wds.; Hands-on Help (tips for leaders), to 175 wds.; Good News About Kids (positive news about teens), 150 wds.; $40. Complete ms.

> **Special Needs:** Articles geared toward working with teens; programming ideas; youth ministry issues.

Tips: "We're always looking for effective youth ministry ideas—especially those tested by youth leaders in the field. Most open to Hands-On-Help column (use real-life examples, personal experiences, practical tips, scripture, and self-quizzes or checklists)."

$IDEAS UNLIMITED FOR EFFECTIVE CHILDREN'S MINISTRY, PO Box 12624, Roanoke VA 24027. (540)342-7511. E-mail: ccmbbr@juno.com. Website: www.Creative ChristianMinistries.com. Betty Robertson, ed. For anyone ministering to children. Quarterly e-newsletter; circ. 4,200. 25% unsolicited freelance; 75% assigned. Query; no phone/fax query; e-query OK. Pays $5-10 on acceptance for 1st, one-time, or simultaneous rts. Not copyrighted. Articles 100-600 wds. Responds in 3 wks. Seasonal 6 mos. ahead. Accepts simultaneous submissions and reprints. Guidelines by e-mail.

$#THE JOURNAL OF ADVENTIST EDUCATION, 12501 Old Columbia Pike, Silver Springs MD 20904-6600. (301)680-5075. Fax (301)622-9627. E-mail: 74617.1231@compu serve.com. General Conference of Seventh-day Adventists. Beverly J. Rumble, ed.; Enrique Becerra, assoc. ed. For Seventh-day teachers teaching in the church's school system, kindergarten to university. Bimonthly (5X) jour.; 48 pgs.; circ. 7,500. Subscription $17.25 (add $1 outside US). Percentage of freelance varies. Query or complete ms; phone/fax/ e-query OK. Pays $25-300 on publication for 1st North American and translation rts. Articles 1,000-1,500 wds. (2-20/yr.). Responds in 6-18 wks. Seasonal 6 mos. ahead. Accepts reprints (tell when/where appeared). Accepts requested ms on disk. Kill fee to 25%. Regularly uses sidebars. Guidelines (also by e-mail); copy for 10x12 SAE/5 stamps.

Fillers: Cartoons only, no pay.

Special Needs: "All articles in the context of parochial schools (*not* Sunday school tips); professional enrichment and teaching tips for Christian teachers. Need feature articles."

JOURNAL OF CHRISTIAN EDUCATION, PO Box 602, Epping NSW 1710 Australia. Phone/fax 61 2 9868 6644. E-mail: ahukins@bigpond.com, submit to: editor@acfe.org.au. Website: http://jce.acfe.org.au. Australian Christian Forum on Education, Inc. Dr. Allan G. Harkness, ed. To consider the implications of the Christian faith for the entire field of education. Tri-annual jour.; 64 pgs.; circ. 500. Subscription $40 AUS, $35 US for individuals; $50 AUS, $45 US for institutions. 40% unsolicited freelance; 60% assigned. Complete ms/cover letter; phone/fax/e-query OK. **NO PAYMENT** for one-time rts. Articles 3,000-5,000 wds. (6/yr.); book reviews 400-600 wds. Responds in 4 wks. Seasonal 6 mos. ahead. Accepts requested ms on disk or by e-mail (attached file). Does not use sidebars. Accepts submissions from children & teens. Free guidelines (also on Website) & copy. (No ads)

Tips: "Send for a sample copy, study guidelines, and submit manuscript. Most open to articles or book reviews. Open to any educational issue from a Christian perspective."

JOURNAL OF CHRISTIANITY AND FOREIGN LANGUAGES, Dept. of Germanic and Asian Languages, Calvin College, 3201 Burton St. SE, Grand Rapids MI 49546. (616)957-8609. Fax (616)526-8583. E-mail: dsmith@calvin.edu. Website: www.spu.edu/orgs/NACFLA. North American Christian Foreign Language Assn. Dr. David Smith, ed. Scholarly articles dealing with the relationship between Christian belief and the teaching of foreign languages and literatures; mainly for college faculty. Annual jour.; 100 pgs.; circ. 100. Subscription $16 (indiv.), $27 (library). Open to freelance. Complete ms/cover letter; phone/fax/ e-query OK. **PAYS IN COPIES/OFFPRINTS.** Articles 2,000-4,000 wds. (6/yr.); book/video reviews, 750 wds. Responds in 12-16 wks. Rarely accepts reprints (tell when/where appeared). Requires requested ms on disk or by e-mail (attached file). Does not use sidebars. Guidelines (also on Website); no copy. (Ads)

Columns/Departments: Accepts 1-3/yr. Forum (position papers, pedagogical suggestions), 1,000-1,500 wds.

Tips: "Most open to Forum column; see www.spu.edu/orgs/nacfla/ for guidelines. Also see Website for abstracts and samples."

JOURNAL OF EDUCATION & CHRISTIAN BELIEF, Dept. of Germanic Languages, Calvin College, 3201 Burton St. SE, Grand Rapids MI 49546. (616)957-8609. Fax (616)526-8583. E-mail: jecb@stapleford-centre.org. Website: www.stapleford-centre.org. Association of Christian Teachers. Editors: Dr. David Smith (use above address) & Dr. John Shortt, 1 Kiteleys Green, Leighton Buzzard, Beds LU7 3LD, United Kingdom. Phone +44 0 1525 379709. Semiannual jour.; 80 pgs.; circ. 400. Subscription 20-80 pounds. 80% unsolicited freelance; 20% assigned. Complete ms/cover letter; e-query OK. **NO PAYMENT** for 1st rts. Articles 5,000 wds. (12/yr.). Responds in 4-8 wks. Accepts reprints (tell when/where appeared). Prefers requested ms on disk or by e-mail (attached file). Does not use sidebars. Guidelines by e-mail; no copy. (No ads)

JOURNAL OF RESEARCH ON CHRISTIAN EDUCATION, Andrews University, Information Services Bldg., Ste. 211, Berrien Springs MI 49104. (269)471-6080. Fax (269)471-6224. E-mail: jrce@andrews.edu. Website: www.andrews.edu/jrce. Andrews University. Paul Brantley, ed.; Jane Thayer, book rev. ed. Research related to Christian schooling (all levels) within the Protestant tradition. Semiannual jour.; 150+ pgs.; circ. 400. Subscription $15.100% unsolicited freelance. Complete ms/cover letter; phone/fax/e-query OK. **NO PAYMENT**. Articles 13-26, double-spaced pgs. (12-18/yr.); book reviews, 2-5 pgs. Responds in 1 wk.; decision within 6 mos. (goes through review board). No simultaneous submissions. Requires requested ms on disk. Does not use sidebars. Guidelines (also by e-mail). (No ads)

> **Tips:** "This is a research journal. All manuscripts should conform to standards of scholarly inquiry. Manuscripts are submitted to a panel of 3 experts for their review. Publication decision is based on recommendation of reviewers. Authors should submit manuscripts written in scholarly style and focused on Christian schooling. Submit 5 copies along with a 100-word abstract and 30-word bio-sketch indicating institutional affiliation."

$KIDS' MINISTRY IDEAS, 55 W. Oak Ridge Dr., Hagerstown MD 21740. (301)393-4082. Fax (301)393-3209. E-mail: KidsMin@rhpa.org. Seventh-day Adventist. Ginger Church, ed. For adults leading children (birth-8th grade) to Christ. Quarterly mag.; 32 pgs.; circ. 1,700. Guidelines on request. Note: This publication is in transitions and current needs are undetermined at this time.

$LEADER IN CHRISTIAN EDUCATION MINISTRIES, PO Box 801, Nashville TN 37202-0801. (615)749-6791. Fax (615)749-6512. E-mail: jshoup@umpublishing.org. Website: www.cokesbury.com. United Methodist Publishing House. Joan M. Shoup, assoc. ed. Estab. 2003. Focuses on issues of concern to leaders in the field of Christian education. Quarterly mag.; 40 pgs.; circ. 3,500. Subscription $19. 5% unsolicited freelance; 95% assigned. Query; fax/e-query OK. Pays $50-150 on acceptance for all rts. Articles 650-5,000 wds. (5/yr.). Responds in 8-10 wks. Seasonal 1 yr. ahead. No simultaneous submissions or reprints. Prefers disk or e-mail submission (attached file). No kill fee. Regularly uses sidebars. Prefers NRSV (never The Living Bible). Guidelines/theme list (also by e-mail); copy for #10 SAE. (No ads)

> **Columns/Departments:** Features on Christian education, 600-5,000 wds.; $50-100.
>
> **Tips:** "We occasionally accept articles in our features section or for the Holiday column. Most of our articles are assigned, however. We rarely accept freelance submissions." Online version is available through the Teaching & Learning Portal.

$MOMENTUM, 1077—30th St. NW, Ste. 100, Washington DC 20007-3852. (202)337-6232. Fax (202)333-6706. E-mail: momentum@ncea.org. Website: www.ncea.org. National Catholic Educational Assn. Brian Gray, ed. Features outstanding programs, issues, and research in education. Quarterly jour.; 88 pgs.; circ. 25,000. Subscription $20 (free to members). 40% unsolicited freelance; 25% assigned. Query or complete ms; phone/

e-query OK. Pays $35-100 on publication for 1st rts. Articles 500-1,500 wds. (25-30/yr.); book reviews 400 wds. ($50). No simultaneous submissions. Accepts full mss by e-mail. Regularly uses sidebars. Guidelines (also by e-mail/Website); copy $5/9x12 SAE/$1.42 postage (mark "Media Mail"). (Ads)

   Columns/Departments: From the Field (success ideas that can be used by other Catholic schools); DRE Directions (guidance for directors of religious education programs); both 700 wds.

   Special Needs: Religious education; teaching methods.

   Tips: "We recommend that writers call or send e-mail before submitting. Conversation often leads to additional ideas. Articles should have applicability to Catholic elementary and high schools. Especially need brief articles about successful youth religious education programs in Catholic parishes. Also, how are weekend religious education programs absorbing students in areas where Catholic schools are closing."

$PRESCHOOL PLAYHOUSE, PO Box 436987, Chicago IL 60643. Toll-free (800)860-8642. (708)868-7100. Fax (708)868-7105. Website: www.urbanministries.com. Urban Ministries, Inc. K. Steward, ed. Sunday school magazine with activities for 2- to 5-year-olds with accompanying teacher's manual. Quarterly magazine for teachers; take-home paper for students; 96 pgs. Subscription $4.85 (teacher) and $2.85 (student). 80% assigned. Query/clips; fax/e-query OK. Pays $150, 120 days after acceptance, for all rts. Articles 6,000 characters for teacher, 2,900 characters for student (4/yr.). Responds in 4 wks. Seasonal 6 mos. ahead. Accepts simultaneous submissions. Requires requested ms on disk. Prefers NIV. Guidelines; copy $2.25/#10 SASE. (No ads)

   Tips: "Send a query with writing samples."

$RELIGION TEACHER'S JOURNAL, Box 180, Mystic CT 06355. (860)536-2611. Fax (860)572-0788. E-mail: aberger@twentythirdpublications.com. Website: www.twenty thirdpublications.com. Catholic Publishers/Bayard. Alison Berger, ed. For volunteer religion teachers who need practical, hands-on information as well as spiritual and theological background for teaching religion to kindergarten through high school. 7X yearly mag.; 40 pgs.; circ. 32,000. Subscription $21.95. 40% unsolicited freelance; 60% assigned. Complete ms/cover letter; fax/e-query OK. Pays $50-125 on acceptance for 1st rts. Articles to 1,300 wds. (40/yr.); plays. Responds in 2-4 wks. Seasonal 6 mos. ahead. Accepts simultaneous submissions and rarely accepts reprints (tell when/where appeared). Prefers requested ms on disk or by e-mail (attached file). No kill fee. Regularly uses sidebars. Prefers NRSV (Catholic edition). Guidelines/theme list (also by e-mail); copy for 9x12 SAE/3 first class stamps. (Ads)

   Fillers: Buys 20-30/yr. Anecdotes (about teaching), games, ideas, quizzes, crafts, successful class activities (especially seasonal); 50-300 wds.; $20-50.

   Special Needs: Partnering with families; teaching the sacraments; prayer and prayer services; celebrating the seasons; spiritual formation for religion teachers/catechists; successful faith formation programs.

   Tips: "Most open to articles on teaching skills; successful activity ideas/lessons; involving parents in religious education, especially in sacrament preparation; celebrating Advent and Lent; spiritual formation. Looking for clear, concise articles written from experience, for catechists and religion teachers (K-12). Articles should help readers move from theory/doctrine to concrete application." Unsolicited manuscripts not returned without an SASE.

   **This periodical was #43 on the 2004 Top 50 Christian Publishers list (#22 in 2003, #47 in 2002).

$RESOURCE, 6401 The Paseo, Kansas City MO 64131. (816)333-7000, ext. 2343. Fax (816)363-7092. E-mail: ssmith@nazarene.org. Website: www.nazarene.org. Church of the

Nazarene. David Graves, ed.; submit to Shirley Smith, ed. asst. To provide information, training, and inspiration to those who are involved in ministering within the Christian Life and Sunday school departments of the local church. Quarterly mag.; 32 pgs.; circ. 25,000. Subscription $6.25. 95% unsolicited freelance; 5% assigned. Complete ms; phone/fax/ e-query OK. Pays .05/wd. on publication for all, one-time, reprint, or simultaneous rts. Articles 1,000-2,000 wds. (150/yr.). Seasonal 9-12 mos. ahead. Accepts simultaneous submissions and reprints. Accepts requested ms on disk or by e-mail (attached or copied into message). Uses some sidebars. Prefers NIV, NRSV. Guidelines/theme list (also by e-mail); copy for 9x12 SAE/2 stamps. (No ads)

   Tips: "Focus on issues, skills, concerns central to a particular age group; how-tos, examples, illustrations; skill development; roles of teachers/leaders; organizational tips."

   **This periodical was #41 on the 2002 Top 50 Christian Publishers list (#46 in 2000).

$TEACHERS INTERACTION, 3558 S. Jefferson Ave., St. Louis MO 63118-3968. (314)268-1083. Fax (314)268-1329. E-mail: tom.nummela@cph.org. Concordia Publishing House/Lutheran Church-Missouri Synod. Tom Nummela, ed. Supports volunteer Sunday school teachers and those who serve with teaching ideas, resources, and articles about education and theology. Quarterly mag.; 32 pgs.; circ. 11,000. Subscription $16.60. 20% unsolicited freelance. Query; fax/e-query OK. Pays $55-110 on acceptance for all rts. One-page articles, 450 wds., feature articles 1,200 wds. (4/yr.). Responds in 4-8 wks. Seasonal 1 yr. ahead. Prefers requested ms on disk or by e-mail. Uses some sidebars. Prefers NIV or ESV. Guidelines/theme list (also by e-mail); copy $4.99. (No ads)

   Songs: Buys occasionally. First rts.; $50.

   Fillers: Buys 48/yr. Teacher tips/ideas, 50-150 wds.; $20-40 on publication.

   Columns/Departments: Departments for early childhood teachers, lower elementary grade teachers, middle school teachers, The Adaptive Teacher, Parents as Teachers, Law and Gospel, Outreach/Evangelism, and support staff (pastors, directors of CE, and superintendents); 450 wds., $55.

   Special Needs: Practical, how-to articles that will help the volunteer church worker.

   Tips: "Most freelance material is used in our 'Teacher's Toolbox' section; practical teaching ideas for the Sunday school classroom. We also need feature articles in four areas— inspiration, theology, practical application, and information—in the area of volunteer Christian education. Theology must be compatible with Lutheranism."

$TEACHERS OF VISION MAGAZINE, Box 41300, Pasadena CA 91114. (626)798-1124. Fax (626)798-2346. E-mail: judy@ceai.org. Website: www.ceai.org. Christian Educators Assn., Intl. Judy Turpen, contributing ed.; F. L. Turpen, editorial dir.; Denise Trippett, mng. ed. To encourage, equip, and empower Christian educators serving in public and private schools. Biannual mag.; circ. 10,000. Subscription $20. 50-60% unsolicited freelance; 40-50% assigned. Query; phone/fax/e-query OK. Pays $40 ($30 for reprints) on publication for 1st or reprint rts. Articles 1,000-2,500 wds. (12-15/yr.); mini-features 400-750 wds., $25; very few book reviews 50 wds., (pays copies). Responds in 4-6 wks. Seasonal 4 mos. ahead. Accepts simultaneous submissions and reprints (tell when/where appeared). Accepts requested ms on disk or by e-mail (attached or copied into message). Regularly uses sidebars. Any Bible version. Guidelines/theme list (also by e-mail/Website); copy for 9x12 SAE/5 stamps. (Ads)

   Poetry: Accepts 2-3/yr. Free verse, haiku, light verse, traditional; 4-16 lines; no payment. Submit max. 3 poems.

   Fillers: Accepts 6/yr. Cartoons, facts; 20-100 wds.; no payment. Educational only.

   Special Needs: Legal and other issues in public education. Interviews; classroom resource reviews; living out your faith in your work.

Tips: "Know public education; write from a positive perspective as our readers are involved in public education by calling and choice. Most open to tips for teachers for living out their faith in the classroom in legally appropriate ways. All topics covered must be public-education related."

$TODAY'S CATHOLIC TEACHER, 2621 Dryden Rd., Dayton OH 45439. (937)293-1415. Fax (937)293-1310. E-mail: mnoschang@peterli.com. Website: www.catholicteacher.com. Catholic; Peter Li Education Group. Mary C. Noschang, ed. Directed to personal and professional concerns of teachers and administrators in K-12 Catholic schools. Monthly mag. (6X during school yr.); 60 pgs.; circ. 45,000. Subscription $14.95. 30% unsolicited freelance; 30% assigned. Query; phone/fax/e-query OK. Pays $100-250 on publication for 1st rts. Articles 600-800, 1,000-1,200, or 1,200-1,500 wds. (40-50/yr.). Responds in 18 wks. Seasonal 3 mos. ahead. Accepts simultaneous submissions and reprints (tell when/where appeared). Prefers requested ms by e-mail (attached file). Regularly uses sidebars. Guidelines/theme list (also on Website); copy $3/9x12 SAE. (Ads)

> **Special Needs:** Activity pages teachers can copy and pass out to students to work on. Try to provide classroom-ready material teachers can use to supplement curriculum.

> **Tips:** "Looking for material teachers in grades 3-9 can use to supplement curriculum material. Most open to articles or lesson plans."

$YOUTH AND CHRISTIAN EDUCATION LEADERSHIP, 1080 Montgomery Ave., Cleveland TN 37311. (423)478-7597. Fax (423)478-7616. E-mail: wanda_griffith@pathwaypress.org. Website: www.pathwaypress.org. Church of God/Pathway Press. Wanda Griffith, ed. To inform, equip, and inspire Christian education teachers and leaders. Quarterly mag.; 32 pgs.; circ. 13,000. Subscription $8. 10% unsolicited freelance; 90% assigned. Query; phone/fax/e-query OK. Pays $25-50 on publication for 1st rts. Articles 500-1,200 wds. (4/yr.). Responds in 4 wks. Seasonal 6 mos. ahead. Accepts requested ms on disk or by e-mail (attached file). No kill fee. Uses some sidebars. Accepts submissions from teens. Prefers NIV. Guidelines by e-mail/Website; copy for 9x12 SAE/4 stamps. (No ads)

> **Fillers:** Cartoons, ideas, word puzzles.

> **Special Needs:** Most open to how-to articles relating to Christian education. Local church ministry stories; articles on youth ministry, children's ministry, Christian education, and Sunday school.

> **2004 EPA Award of Excellence—Denominational.

DAILY DEVOTIONAL MARKETS

Due to the nature of the daily devotional market, the following market listings give a limited amount of information. Because most of these markets assign all material, they do not wish to be listed in the usual way.

If you are interested in writing daily devotionals, send to the following markets for guidelines and sample copies, write up sample devotionals to fit each one's particular format, and send to the editor with a request for an assignment. **DO NOT** submit any other type of material to these markets unless indicated.

+ANCHOR DEVOTIONAL, PO Box 5100, Costa Mesa CA 92628. Toll-free (800)65HAVEN. Fax (714)918-4299. E-mail: staff@havenministries.com. Website: www.havenministries.com. Haven Ministries. Joyce Gibson, ed. Quarterly devotional mag. Devotions 200 wds. Assigns one month of devotions on a theme (author picks theme). Query first for theme.

+CLOSER WALK, PO Box 562, Mt. Morris IL 61054-8197. (770)458-9300. Fax (770)454-9313. Website: www.walkthru.org. Walk Thru the Bible. Read through the New Testament in a year. Monthly mag. Requires NKJV.

DAILY DEVOTIONS FOR THE DEAF, 21199 Greenview Rd., Council Bluffs IA 51503-4190. (712)322-5493. Fax (712)322-7792. E-mail: DeafMissions@deafmissions.com. Website: www.deafmissions.com. Jo Krueger, ed. Quarterly. Circ. 26,000. Prefers to see completed devotionals; 225 wds. **NO PAYMENT**. E-mail submissions OK.

$DAILY MEDITATION, PO Box 2710, San Antonio TX 78299. (210)735-5247. Emilia Devno, ed. Inspirational religious articles. Semiannual booklet; circ. 775. Subscription $16. Complete ms; no e-query. Pays .015-.02/wd. on acceptance for 1st rts. Articles 300-1,650 wds. Responds in 3-8 wks.

　　Poetry: Buys poetry; 4-12 lines; .14/line.

　　Fillers: Buys fillers, to 350 wds.

THE DAILY WALK, 4201 N. Peachtree Rd., Atlanta GA 30341. (770)458-9300. Fax (770)454-9313. E-mail: pkirk@walkthru.org. Website: www.walkthru.org. Walk Thru the Bible Ministries, Inc. Paula A. Kirk, ed. To encourage people to read and study God's word on a daily basis; read the entire Bible in one year. Monthly mag.; circ. 50,000. Subscription $18. Open to freelance. Query or complete ms. (Ads)

$DEVOTIONS, 8121 Hamilton Ave., Cincinnati OH 45231. (513)931-4050. Fax (513)931-0904. E-mail: gwilde1@cfl.rr.com. Website: www.standardpub.com. Gary Allen, ed. Assigned by work-for-hire contract to previously published writers only. Query by e-mail only. Pays $20/devotion. Send list of credits rather than a sample.

FAMILY WALK, PO Box 562, Mt. Morris IL 61054-8197. (770)458-9300. Fax (770)454-9313. Website: www.walkthru.org. Walk Thru the Bible. Topical devotional guide for families with children 6 years and older. Explores a different issue each week (rather than daily Bible readings). Monthly mag. Subscription $18. Requires NIV.

FORWARD DAY BY DAY, 412 Sycamore St., Cincinnati OH 45202-4195. Toll-free (800)543-1813. (513)721-6659. Fax (513)721-0729. E-mail: esgleason@forwarddaybyday.com. Website: www.forwardmovement.org. Edward S. Gleason, ed. Also online version. Send complete devotions, or send samples and request an assignment. Also likes author to complete an entire month's worth of devotions. E-mail submissions OK. Length: 2 paragraphs. **NO PAYMENT**. (No ads)

FRUIT OF THE VINE, Barclay Press, 211 N. Meridian St., #101, Newberg OR 97132. (503)538-9775. Fax (503)554-8597. E-mail: info@barclaypress.com. E-mail submissions accepted at: phampton@barclaypress.com. Website: www.barclaypress.com. Editorial team: Susan Fawver, Sherry Macy, Paula Hampton. Send samples and request assignment. Prefers 250-290 wds. **PAYS FREE SUBSCRIPTION & 6 COPIES.** Guidelines.

*THE HOME ALTAR, Box 1209, Minneapolis MN 55440-1209. Cynthia Biddlecomb, ed. Sample writing and inquiries are welcome.

INDEED, PO Box 562, Mt. Morris IL 61054-8197. (770)458-9300. Fax (770)454-9313. Website: www.walkthru.org. Walk Thru the Bible. Chris Tiegreen, ed. Bimonthly mag. By assignment only.

　　**2004 EPA Award of Excellence—Devotional.

PENNED FROM THE HEART, 51 Greenfield Rd., New Wilmington PA 16142. Toll-free (800)358-0777. Fax (724)946-8700. Florence W. Biros, pub. Annual devotional book. Poetry and homily to 250 wds. Deadline is the end of August annually. **PAYS ONE FREE COPY** of the book.

$THE QUIET HOUR, 4050 Lee Vance View, Colorado Springs CO 80919. (719)536-0100. Fax (407)359-2850. E-mail: gwilde1@cfl.rr.com. Website: www.cookministries.com. Cook Communications Ministries. Gary Wilde, ed. 100% unsolicited freelance. Pays $15-35/devotional on acceptance. Send list of credits only, rather than a sample. Accepts e-mailed sample devotional. Responds in 3 mos.

QUIET WALK, 4201 N. Peachtree Rd., Atlanta GA 30341. (770)458-9300. Fax (770)454-9313. E-mail: pubsinfo@walkthru.org. Website: www.walkthru.org. Walk Thru the Bible. Emphasis on personal worship and prayer. Monthly mag. Requires NKJV.

$REJOICE! 600 Shaftesbury Blvd., Winnipeg MB R3P 0M4 Canada. (204)888-6781. Fax (204)831-5675. E-mail: ByronRB@mph.org. Mennonite/Faith & Life Resources. Byron Rempel-Burkholder, ed. Devotional ministry to individuals and families. Quarterly. Pays $125 for 7-day assigned meditations, 280 wds. Prefers that you send a couple of sample devotions and inquire about assignment procedures. Don't apply for assignment unless you are familiar with the publication and Anabaptist theology.

$THE SECRET PLACE, Box 851, Valley Forge PA 19482-0851. (610)768-2000. Fax (610)768-2441. E-mail: thesecretplace@abc-usa.org. Website: www.judsonpress.com. Kathleen Hayes, sr. ed. Prefers to see completed devotionals, 200 wds. (use unfamiliar Scripture passages). 64 pgs. Circ. 150,000. 100% freelance. Pays $15 for 1st rts. Accepts poetry and buys photos (B & W). Accepts e-mail submissions. Guidelines.

+SOUL JOURNEY, 3000 Kraft Ave. SE, Grand Rapids MI 49512. (616)974-2663. E-mail: articles@soul-journey.org. Website: www.soul-journey.org. RBC Ministries. Tom Felton, ed. Devotionals for today's young adult. Quarterly mag. Subscription $5. Open to unsolicited freelance. Complete ms. as a Word attachment. **PAYS 10 COPIES.** Articles/devotions 325-350 wds. Guidelines on Website.

   Special Needs: Art and photographs. See guidelines.

   Tips: "Submit one article at a time, once a month."

$THESE DAYS, 100 Witherspoon St., Louisville KY 40202-1396. (502)569-5052. Fax (502)569-8308. E-mail: vpatton@presbypub.com. Website: www.ppcpub.com. Presbyterian Publishing Corp. Vince Patton, ed. Subscription $6.95. Query/samples. 95% unsolicited freelance. Pays $14.25/devotion for 1st and nonexclusive reprint rts. (makes work-for-hire assignments); 200 wds. (including key verse and short prayer). Uses poetry (2-6/yr.), pays $15. Wants short, contemporary poetry on church holidays and seasons of the year—overtly religious (15 lines, 33-character/line maximum). Query for their two feature segments (short articles): "These Moments" and "These Times."

$THE UPPER ROOM, PO Box 340004, Nashville TN 37203-0004. (615)340-7252. Fax (615)340-7267. E-mail: TheUpperRoomMagazine@upperroom.org. Website: www.upperroom.org. Mary Lou Redding, mng. ed. 95% unsolicited freelance. Pays $25/devotional on publication. 72 pgs. Note: This publication wants freelance submissions and does not make assignments. Phone/fax/e-query OK. Send devotionals up to 250 wds. Buys explicitly religious art, in various media, for use on covers only (transparencies/slides requested); buys one-time, worldwide publishing rts. Accepts e-mail submissions (copied into message). Guidelines (also on Website); copy for 5x7 SAE/2 stamps.(No ads)

   Tips: "We do not return submissions. Accepted submissions will be notified in 6-9 wks. Follow guidelines. Need meditations from men." Always include postal address with e-mail submissions.

$THE WORD IN SEASON, PO Box 1209, Minneapolis MN 55440-1209. Fax (612)330-3215. E-mail: rochelle@liferhymecoaching.com. Website: www.augsburgfortress.org. Augsburg Fortress. Rev. Rochelle Y. Melander, ed./mngr. 96 pgs. Devotions to 200 wds. Pays $18/devotion; $50 for prayers. Accepts e-mail submissions (copied into message) after reading guidelines. Guidelines for #10 SAE/2 stamps; copy for 9x12 SAE/4 stamps.

   Tips: "We prefer that you write for guidelines. We will send instructions for preparing sample devotions. We accept new writers based on the sample devotions we request and make assignments after acceptance. Do not send samples or request guidelines by e-mail."

$WORDS OF LIFE: Daily Reflections for Your Spirit, St. Paul University, 223 Main St., Ottawa ON K1S 1C4 Canada. (613)782-3036. Fax (613)782-3004. E-mail: words-of-life@ustpaul.ca. Caryl Green, ed. Send samples and request an assignment. Prefers 135 wds. Pays $45 Can. Buys photos.

MISSIONS MARKETS

$#AMERICAN BAPTISTS IN MISSION, PO Box 851, Valley Forge PA 19482-0851. (610)768-2000. Fax (610)768-2320. E-mail: richard.schramm@abc-usa.org. Website: www.abc-usa .org. Richard W. Schramm, ed. Denominational. Bimonthly mag.; 24-32 pgs.; circ. 39,000. Subscription free. 10% unsolicited freelance; 90% assigned. Query; fax/e-query OK. Pays negotiable rates on publication. Articles 750-1,000 wds. (few/yr.). Prefers e-mail submission (attached file). Uses some sidebars. Prefers NRSV. Guidelines (also by e-mail); copy. Not in topical listings but will accept any article of substantial interest to American Baptists. (Ads)

+CATHOLIC MISSIONS IN CANADA, 1155 Yonge St., #201, Toronto ON M4T 1W2 Canada. (416)934-3424. Fax (416)934-3425. E-mail: patria@cmic.info. Website: www.cmic.info. Catholic Missions in Canada. Patria C. Rivera, ed. To share the faith journeys of their missionaries as they share the love of Jesus in needy Catholic missions across Canada. Quarterly digest-sized mag.; circ. 37,000. Subscription free to donors. Open to unsolicited freelance. Not in topical listings. (No ads)

EAST-WEST CHURCH & MINISTRY REPORT, The Global Ctr./Beeson Divinity School, Samford University, Birmingham AL 35229-2268. (205)726-2170. Fax (205)726-2271. E-mail: ewcmreport@samford.edu. Website: www.samford.edu/groups/global. The Global Center/Samford University. Dr. Mark Elliott, ed. Encourages Western Christian ministry in Central and Eastern Europe and the former Soviet Union that is effective, culturally sensitive, and cooperative. Quarterly newsletter; 16 pgs.; circ. 400. Subscription $44.95. 25% unsolicited freelance; 75% assigned. Complete ms/cover letter; phone/fax/e-query OK. **NO PAYMENT** for all rts. Articles 1,500 wds. (4/yr.); book reviews, 100 wds. Responds in 4 wks. Prefers requested ms on disk or by e-mail. Regularly uses sidebars. Any Bible version. Guidelines (also by e-mail/Website); copy $11.95. (No ads)

> **Tips:** "All submissions must relate to Central and Eastern Europe or the former Soviet Union."

> ****2001, 1999, 1998, 1997 EPA Award of Merit—Newsletter.**

$EVANGELICAL MISSIONS QUARTERLY, PO Box 794, Wheaton IL 60189. (630)752-7158. Fax (630)752-7155. E-mail: emqjournal@aol.com, or emis@wheaton.edu. Website: www.BillyGrahamCenter.org/emis. Evangelism and Missions Information Service (EMIS). Gary Corwin, ed.; Minnette Northcutt, mng. ed. For missionaries and others interested in missions trends, strategies, issues, problems, and resources. Quarterly journal; 136 pgs.; circ. 7,000. Subscription $24.95. 65% unsolicited; 35% assigned. Query; fax/e-query OK. Pays $100 on publication for all rts. Articles 2,500 wds. (30/yr.); book reviews 400 wds. (query—$25). Responds in 4 wks. Accepts few reprints (tell when/where appeared). Prefers requested ms on disk or by e-mail (copied into message). Uses some sidebars. Prefers NIV. Free guidelines (also by e-mail)/copy. (Ads)

> **Columns/Departments:** Buys 4/yr. In the Workshop (tips to increase missionary effectiveness), 1,500-2,000 wds.; $100.

> **Tips:** "We consider all submissions. It is best to check our Website for examples and guidelines. Present an article idea and why you are qualified to write it. All articles must target evangelical, cross-cultural missionaries. 'In the Workshop' is most open to freelancers. Most authors have a credible connection to and experience in missions."

+GLAD TIDINGS, 50 Wynford Dr., Toronto ON M3C 1J7 Canada. Toll-free (800)619-7301.(416)441-1111. Fax (416)441-2825. E-mail: hwilson@presbyterian.ca. Website: wwwpresbyterian.ca. Women's Missionary Society/Presbyterian. Holly Wilson, ed. To challenge concerned Christians to reflect on their faith through art; encourage readers to become informed, educated, inspired, and motivated to action; and provide a forum for a broad spectrum of opinion and information. Bimonthly mag.; circ. 5,500. Subscription $10. Open to unsolicited freelance. Not in topical listings. (Ads)

I.E., PO Box 628200, Orlando FL 32862-8200. (407)852-3600. Fax (407)852-3601 E-mail: editors.pub@wycliffe.org. Website: www.wycliffe.org. Wycliffe Bible Translators. Susan Van Wynen, ed. To inform friends and supporters of Wycliffe about the ministry of Bible translation and to inspire them to greater involvement. Triannual mag.; 16 pgs.; circ. 260,000. Subscription free. 5% assigned. Query; e-query preferred. **PAYS IN COPIES**.

   Tips: "We rarely accept anything from outside writers. If you would like to write for us, send us an e-mail detailing your writing experience and the types of pieces you'd be available to write. We will contact you when we have possible assignments."

INTERNATIONAL JOURNAL OF FRONTIER MISSIONS, 1539 E. Howard St., Pasadena CA 91104. (626)398-2108. Fax (626)398-2185. E-mail: ijfm@wciu.edu. Website: www.ijfm.org. Rory Clark, mng. ed. Dedicated to frontiers in missions. Quarterly jour.; 48 pgs.; circ. 600. Subscription $15. 75% unsolicited freelance. Complete ms/cover letter; phone/fax/e-query OK. **NO PAYMENT** for one-time rts. Articles 2,000-8,500 wds. Seasonal 3 mos. ahead. Accepts simultaneous submissions and reprints. Accepts e-mail submission. No sidebars. Guidelines/theme list (also by e-mail/Website); copy $2/10x13 SAE. (Ads)

   Special Needs: Contextualization, church in missions, training for missions, mission trends and paradigms, de-westernization of the gospel and missions from the Western world, biblical world-view development, mission theology, Animism, Islam, Buddhism, Hinduism, nonliterate peoples, tent making, mission member care, reaching nomadic peoples, mission history, new religious movements and missions, science and missions, etc.

   Tips: "Writers on specific issues we cover are always welcome. Although the circulation is small, the print run is 3,000 and used for promotional purposes. Highly recommended for mission schools, libraries, and mission executives."

$LEADERS FOR TODAY, Box 13, Atlanta GA 30370. (770)449-8869. Fax (770)449-8457. E-mail: hiatlanta@haggai-institute.com. Website: www.haggai-institute.com. Haggai Institute. Scott Schreffler, ed. (scotts@haggai-institute.com). Primarily for donors to ministry; focus is alumni success stories. Quarterly mag.; 16 pgs.; circ. 7,500. Subscription free. 100% assigned to date. Query; fax query OK. Pays .10-.25/wd. on acceptance for all rts. Articles 1,000-2,000 wds. Responds in 2-3 wks. Requires requested ms on disk or by e-mail (attached file). Kill fee 100%. Regularly uses sidebars. Prefers NIV. Guidelines/theme list; copy for 9x12 SAE/4 stamps. (No ads)

   Tips: "If traveling to a developing country, check well in advance regarding the possibility of doing an alumni story. All articles are preassigned; query first."

   **1999 EPA Award of Merit—Missionary; 1998 EPA Award of Excellence—Missionary.

MISSIOLOGY: An International Review, 204 N. Lexington Ave., Wilmore KY 40390. (859)858-2216. Fax (859)858-2375. E-mail: Terry_Muck@asburyseminary.edu. Website: www.asmweb.org. American Society of Missiology/Asbury Theological Seminary. Terry C. Muck, ed.; Robert Danielson, book ed. An academic journal for mission studies. Quarterly jour.; 128 pgs.; circ. 2,000. Subscription $24. 75% unsolicited freelance; 25% assigned. Complete ms/cover letter. **PAYS 20 COPIES** for 1st rts. Articles 3,000 wds. (20/yr.); book reviews, 300-400 wds. Responds in 8 wks. No seasonal. No simultaneous submissions or reprints. Prefers requested ms by e-mail (attached file). Uses some sidebars. Any Bible version. Guidelines (also by e-mail); no copy. (Ads)

Tips: "We accept many unsolicited manuscripts and book reviews. The best way to be published is to submit a manuscript that conforms to our style and to communicate with the editorial office. Most open to essays."

MISSION FRONTIERS, 1605 Elizabeth St., Pasadena CA 91104. (626)797-1111. Fax (626) 398-2263. E-mail: mission.frontiers@uscwm.org. Website: www.missionfrontiers .org. U.S. Center for World Mission. Darrell Dorr, mng. ed. To stimulate a movement to establish indigenous churches where still needed around the world. Bimonthly & online mag.; 40 pgs.; circ. 75,000. Subscription $18. No unsolicited freelance; 100% assigned. Query. **NO PAYMENT.** Articles. Rarely responds. Accepts requested ms on disk or by e-mail (copied into message). Regularly uses sidebars. No guidelines; free copy. Not in topical listings. (Ads)

Fillers: Cartoons.

Tips: "Be a published missionary or former missionary. Be on the cutting edge of strategic breakthrough or methods of reaching an unreached ethnic group." Looking for true-life, short sidebars of Muslims accepting Jesus, or impact of prayer in missions.

**1999 EPA Award of Merit—Most Improved Publication.

$NEW WORLD OUTLOOK, 475 Riverside Dr., rm. 1476, New York NY 10115-1476. (212)870-3765. Fax (212)870-3940. E-mail: nwo@gbgm-umc.org. Website: http:// gbgm-umc.org/nwo. United Methodist. Alma Graham, ed. Denominational missions. Bimonthly mag.; 48 pgs.; circ. 22,000. Subscription $15. 20% unsolicited freelance. Query; fax/e-query OK. Pays $50-300 on publication for all and electronic rts. Articles 500-2,000 wds. (24/yr.); book reviews 200-500 wds. (assigned). No guaranteed response time. Seasonal 4 mos. ahead. Kill fee 50% or $100. Prefers e-mail submission (Word Perfect 6.1 or 8.1 in attached file). Regularly uses sidebars. Prefers NRSV. Guidelines; copy $3. (Ads)

Tips: "Ask for a list of United Methodist mission workers and projects in your area. Investigate them, propose a story, and consult with the editors before writing. Most open to articles and/or color photos of US or foreign mission sites visited as a stringer, after consultation with the editor."

$ONE (formerly CNEWA World), 1011 First Ave., New York NY 10022-4195. Toll-free (877)228-8239. (212)826-1480. Fax (212)826-8979. E-mail: mjl@cnewa.org. Website: www.cnewa.org. Catholic Near East Welfare Assn. Michael La Civita, exec. ed. Interest in cultural, religious, and human rights development in Middle East, NE Africa, India, and Eastern Europe. Bimonthly mag.; 32 pgs.; circ. 100,000. Subscription $12. 20% unsolicited freelance; 30% assigned. Query/clips; fax query OK. Pays .20/edited wd.($200) on publication for all rts. Articles 1,500-2,000 wds. (15/yr.). Responds in 9 wks. Accepts requested ms on disk. Kill fee $200. Prefers NAS. Guidelines (also by e-mail); copy for 7x10 SAE/2 stamps.

Tips: "We strive to educate our readers about the culture, faith, history, issues, and people who form the Eastern Christian churches. Anything on people in Palestine/Israel, Eastern Europe, or India. Material should not be academic. Include detailed photographs with story or article."

OPREV EQUIPPER, (formerly Operation Reveille Shofar), PO Box 26396, Colorado Springs CO 80936-6396. (719)572-5908. Fax (775)248-8147. E-mail: bside@oprev.org. Website: www.oprev.org. Mission To Unreached Peoples. Bruce T. Sidebotham, dir. Provides information to equip U.S. military Christians for cross-cultural ministry. Bimonthly & online newsletter; 8 pgs.; circ. 1,500. Subscription free. 40% unsolicited freelance; 60% assigned. Query; phone/e-query OK. **PAYS IN COPIES** for one-time rts. Not copyrighted. Articles 250-1,000 wds. (4/yr.). Responds in 4 wks. Seasonal 4 mos. ahead. Accepts simultaneous submissions and reprints (tell when/where appeared). Accepts requested ms on disk. No kill fee. Regularly uses sidebars. Prefers NIV. No guidelines; copy 50 cents/9x12 SAE/4 stamps. (No ads)

Fillers: Accepts 4/yr. Newsbreaks, to 150 wds.

Columns/Departments: Accepts 4/yr. Agency Profile (describes a mission agency's history and work), 200-300 wds.; Area Profile (describes spiritual landscape of a military theater of operations), 300-750 wds., Resource Review (describes a cross-cultural ministry tool), 100-200 wds. Query.

Special Needs: Ministry in Afghanistan and Iraq. World news and analysis; cross-cultural communication; area profiles and people profiles on military theaters of operation.

Tips: "We need insights and case studies on US service personnel being used in cross-cultural Christian ministry."

$PFI WORLD REPORT, Box 17434, Washington DC 20041. (703)481-0000. Fax (703)481-0003. E-mail: info@pfi.org, or chris@pfi.org. Website: www.pfi.org. Prison Fellowship, Intl. Christopher P. Nicholson, ed. Targets issues and needs of prisoners, ex-prisoners, justice officials, victims, families, PFI staff, and volunteers in 75 countries. Bimonthly newsletter; 4-8 pgs.; circ. 4,750. Subscription free. 10% unsolicited freelance. Query; fax/e-query OK. Pays $100-350 on acceptance for all rts. Articles 500-750 wds. (4/yr.). Responds in 2 wks. Seasonal 4 mos. ahead. Accepts simultaneous submissions and reprints (tell when/where appeared). Accepts requested ms on disk. Kill fee. Regularly uses sidebars. Guidelines (also on Website); copy for #10 SAE/1 stamp. (No ads)

Special Needs: Prison issues, justice issues, anything that relates to international prison ministry.

Tips: "Looking for personal profiles of people active in prison ministry (preferably PFI officials); ex-prisoner success stories; how-to articles about various aspects of prison ministry. Avoid American slant."

$PIME WORLD, 17330 Quincy St., Detroit MI 48221-2765. (313)342-4066. Fax (313)342-6816. E-mail: pimeworld@pimeusa.org. Website: www.pimeusa.org. Pontifical Inst. for Foreign Missions/Catholic. Cari Hartman, publications mngr. For those interested in and supportive of foreign missions. Published 5X/yr., plus newsletter supplement; 24 pgs.; circ. 16,000. Subscription $15. 10% unsolicited freelance. Complete ms; e-query OK. Pays $15-25 on publication for one-time rts. Photos $10. Articles 500-1,000 wds. Responds in 2 wks. Seasonal 4 mos. ahead. Accepts reprints (tell when/where appeared). Prefers e-mail submission (attached file). Uses some sidebars. Prefers NAB. Accepts submissions from teens. Guidelines/theme list; copy for 6x9 SAE/2 stamps. (No ads)

Tips: "Features are open to freelancers. Needs missionary profiles; articles on PIME missionaries; interfaith dialog/experiences; and missions in Africa, especially Ivory Coast, Guinea Bissau, and Cameroon. Also issues like hunger, human rights, women's rights, peace, and justice as they are dealt with in developing countries by missionaries and locals alike."

THE RAILROAD EVANGELIST, PO Box 5026, Vancouver WA 98668-5026. (360)699-7208. E-mail: rrjoe@comcast.net. Railroad Evangelistic Assn. Joe Spooner, ed. For railroad and transportation employees and their families. Quarterly (3X) mag.; 16 pgs.; circ. 2,500. Subscription $8. 100% unsolicited freelance. Complete ms/no cover letter; phone query OK. **NO PAYMENT.** Articles 100-700 wds. (10-15/yr.); railroad-related fiction only, for children or teens. Seasonal 4 months ahead. Accepts simultaneous submissions and reprints. Accepts e-mail submissions. Does not use sidebars. Guidelines (also by e-mail); copy for 9x12 SAE/2 stamps. (No ads)

Poetry: Accepts 4-8/yr. Traditional, any length. Send any number.

Fillers: Accepts many. Anecdotes, cartoons, quotes; to 100 wds.

Tips: "We need 400- to 700-word railroad-related salvation testimonies; or railroad-related human-interest stories; or model railroads. Since we publish only three times a year, we are focusing on railroad-related articles only. Just write and tell us or send us what you have. We'll let you know if we can use it or not."

WESLEYAN WORLD, 13300 Olio Rd., Noblesville IN 46060. (317)774-7943. Fax (317)774-7958. E-mail: djbray42@msn.com. Website: www.globalpartnersnet.net. The Wesleyan Church. Joy Bray, ed. For members and those who attend a Wesleyan church and are world-missions minded. Quarterly mag.; 34 pgs.; circ. 38,700. Subscription free or $15 (suggested donation). 10% unsolicited freelance; 90% assigned. Complete ms/cover letter. **NO PAYMENT**. Articles 500-700 wds. Accepts simultaneous submissions and reprints (tell when/where appeared). Regularly uses sidebars. (Ads—denominational only)

> **Special Needs:** Leadership in missions; children's ministries; biblical teaching on spiritual warfare.

WOMEN OF THE HARVEST, PO Box 151297, Lakewood CO 80215-9297. (303)985-2148. Fax (303)989-4239. E-mail: snelson@womenoftheharvest.com. Website: www.womenof theharvest.com. Women of the Harvest Ministries Intl., Inc. Stephanie Nelson, ed.; Blair Sellke, submissions ed. To support and encourage women serving in cross-cultural missions. Bimonthly mag.; 16 pgs.; circ. 2,500. Subscription $24. 90% unsolicited freelance; 10% assigned. Complete ms; e-query OK. **NO PAYMENT** for one-time rts. Articles 350-650 wds. Seasonal 3 mos. ahead. Prefers requested ms on disk or by e-mail. Guidelines (also by e-mail); copy for SASE. (No ads)

> **Poetry:** Free verse, traditional, haiku; variable length. Submit max. 5 poems.
>
> **Fillers:** Anecdotes, short humor; 100 wds.
>
> **Tips:** "This is a magazine designed especially for women serving cross-culturally. We need articles, humor, and anecdotes related to this topic. Best way to break in is by having a cross-cultural missions experience or to be heading to the mission field."
>
> **2004 EPA Award of Merit—Christian Ministries.

$WORLD PULSE, PO Box 794, Wheaton IL 60189. (630)752-7158. Fax (630)752-7155. E-mail: pulsenews@aol.com. Website: www.worldpulseonline.com. Evangelism & Missions Information Service (EMIS). Dawn Herzog Jewell, ed. Articles and news items from around the world, related to missions and Christians. Print & online newsletter (20X/yr.); 8 pgs.; circ. 2,600. Subscription $29.95 (print); $14.95 (online). 20% unsolicited; 80% assigned. Complete ms; fax/e-query OK. Pays $50-100 on publication for 1st rts. Articles 750-1,000 wds. Accepts reprints (tell when/where appeared). Prefers requested ms on disk or by e-mail (copied into message). Kill fee 60%. Accepts sidebars. Prefers NIV. Free guidelines (also by e-mail)/copy. (No ads)

> **Tips:** "Most open to cover stories, articles, interviews/profiles. Query via e-mail. Send specific ideas on what missions and national churches are actually doing and tell why you are qualified to write it."

$WORLDWIDE CHALLENGE, 100 Lake Hart Dr., #1600, Orlando FL 32832-0100. (407)826-2390. Fax (407)826-2374. E-mail: Worldwide.Challenge@ccci.org. Website: www.wwc magazine.org. Campus Crusade for Christ. Mark Winz, mng. ed. For financial supporters of Campus Crusade. Bimonthly mag.; 48 pgs.; circ. 95,000. Subscription $13.95. 5% unsolicited freelance. Query only/clips; no e-query. Pays .10/wd. plus a flat fee of $100-200 (depending on research) on acceptance for 1st rts. (all rts. for assigned articles). Articles 800-1,600 wds. (6/yr.). Responds in 6-8 wks. Seasonal 6-8 mos. ahead. Accepts simultaneous submissions. Kill fee 50%. Regularly uses sidebars. Prefers NAS. Guidelines; copy for 9x12 SAE/5 stamps. (Ads)

> **Columns/Departments:** Erik Segalini, columns ed. Buys 6/yr. Insight (personal experience/commentary); 400-800 wds.; query or complete ms.

Tips: "Give the human face behind a topic or story. Show how the topic relates to evangelism and/or discipleship. Wants articles about Campus Crusade staff. Most open to column." ******2004, 2003, 2002, 2001 EPA Award of Merit—Organizational; 2000 EPA Award of Excellence—Organizational.

MUSIC MARKETS

\$CCM MAGAZINE, 104 Woodmont Blvd., Ste. 300, Nashville TN 37205-2245. (615)312-4246. Fax (615)386-3380. E-mail: CCMWebEditors@ccmcom.com. Website: www.ccm magazine.com. Salem Communications, Inc. Christa Farris, Web ed.; April Hefner, mng. ed. Encourages spiritual growth through contemporary music; provides news and information about the Christian music market. Monthly & online mag.; 80 pgs.; circ. 70,000. Subscription \$19.95. 75% unsolicited freelance. Query/clips; phone/fax query OK. Pays .20/wd. for short pieces, or \$100/published pg. for features, on publication for all rts. Articles 500-2,500 wds.; music reviews 250-350 wds. Responds slowly. Seasonal 3 mos. ahead. Kill fee 50%. Prefers requested ms on disk or by e-mail (copied into message). Regularly uses sidebars. Guidelines; copy for 9x12 SAE/\$4. (Ads)

> ******#2 Best-selling Magazine in Christian retail stores. 1995 EPA Award of Merit—Youth.

CHRISTIAN MUSIC WEEKLY, 7057 Bluffwood Ct., Brownsburg IN 46112-8650. (317)892-5031. Fax (317)892-5034. E-mail through Website. Website: www.ChristianMusic Weekly.com. Joyful Sounds. Rob Green, ed. Trade paper for Worship, Inspirational, Adult Contemporary, and Southern Gospel Music radio formats. Weekly trade paper; 12 pgs.; circ. 300-1,200. Subscription \$104 (paper) or \$52 (PDF via e-mail). 25% unsolicited freelance; 75% assigned. Query by e-mail only. **PAYS IN COPIES** (will publish photo of writer and tiny bio). Articles 600-2,000 wds.; music reviews, 100-300 wds. Responds in 2 wks. Seasonal 2 mos. ahead. Accepts reprints. Requires requested ms on disk (DOS-ASCII), prefers e-mail submission. Guidelines by e-mail; copy for 9x12 SAE/2 stamps. (Ads)

> **Fillers:** Cartoons, short humor (particularly radio or music related).
>
> **Columns/Departments:** Insider (artist interview); Programming 101 (radio technique); retail, inspirational, especially for musicians and radio people; 600-2,000 wds.
>
> **Special Needs:** Songwriting and performance.
>
> **Tips:** "Most open to artist interviews. Must be familiar with appropriate music formats."

\$*CHURCH PIANIST/SAB CHOIR/THE CHOIR HERALD, Box 268, Alcoa TN 37701. Now a division of The Lorenz Corp. Hugh S. Livingston Jr., ed. Each of these music magazines has one page devoted to articles that deal with problems/solutions of choirs and accompanists. Bimonthly mag.; 36-52 pgs.; circ. 25,000. 45% unsolicited freelance. Complete ms/cover letter. Pay \$15-150 on publication for all rts. Articles 250-1,250 wds. (10-20/yr.). Seasonal 1 yr. ahead. Responds in 3-6 wks. Guidelines; copy for 9x12 SAE/3 stamps.

> **Poetry:** Buys 25/yr. Free verse, light verse, traditional, or poetry suitable for song lyrics; \$10. Submit max. 5 poems.
>
> **Fillers:** Buys 5-10/yr. Anecdotes, cartoons.
>
> **Special Needs:** Choir experiences; pianist/organist articles.
>
> **Tips:** "Best approach is from direct experience in music with the small church."

\$CREATOR MAGAZINE, PO Box 480, Healdsburg CA 95448. Toll-free (800)777-6713. (707)837-9071. E-mail: creator@creatormagazine.com. Website: www.creatormagazine .com. Rod Ellis, ed. For interdenominational music ministry; promoting quality, diverse music programs in the church. Bimonthly mag.; 48-56 pgs.; circ. 6,000. Subscription \$32.95. 35% unsolicited freelance. Query or complete ms/cover letter; fax/e-query OK. Pays \$30-75 for assigned, \$30-60 for unsolicited, on publication for 1st, one-time, or reprint rts. Articles 1,000-10,000 wds. (20/yr.); book reviews ($20). Responds in 4-12 wks. Seasonal 4 mos. ahead. Accepts simultaneous submissions and reprints (tell when/where appeared). Prefers requested ms on disk. Regularly uses sidebars. Prefers NRSV. Guidelines/theme list; copy for 9x12 SAE/5 stamps. (Ads)

Fillers: Buys 20/yr. Anecdotes, cartoons, ideas, jokes, party ideas, short humor; 10-75 wds.; $5-25.

Special Needs: Articles on worship; staff relationships.

THE HYMN: A Journal of Congregational Song, School of Theology, Boston University, 745 Commonwealth Ave., Boston MA 02215-1401. Toll-free (800)THEHYMN. Fax (617)353-7322. E-mail: hymneditor@aol.com. Website: www.bu.edu/sth/hymn, or www.hymn society.org. Hymn Society in the US & Canada. Beverly A. Howard, ed. (5423 Via Alberca, Riverside CA 92507-6477). For church musicians, hymnologists, scholars; articles related to the congregational song. Quarterly jour.; 60 pgs.; circ. 3,000. Subscription $65. 85% unsolicited freelance; 15% assigned. Query; phone/e-query OK. **NO PAYMENT** for all rts. Articles any length (12/yr.); book and music reviews any length. Responds in 4 wks. Seasonal 4 mos. ahead. Prefers requested ms on disk, no e-mail submission. Regularly uses sidebars. Any Bible version. Guidelines (also on Website); free copy. (Ads)

Special Needs: Articles on history of hymns or practical ways to teach or use hymns. Controversial issues as related to hymns and songs. Contact editor.

Contest: Hymn text and tune contests for special occasions or themes.

Note: Also see "Resources: Songwriting" in the Resources section at the front of this book.

*QUEST, PO Box 14804, Columbus OH 43214. Rick Welke, ed. Geared to 16- to 30-year-olds and radio personnel. Monthly newsletter. Query. **PAYS A SUBSCRIPTION.** Articles 100-500 wds. (4/yr.); fiction, 150-750 wds. (4/yr.); book/music reviews, 30-75 wds. Seasonal 3 mos. ahead. Accepts simultaneous submissions and reprints. Theme list; copy for #10 SAE/2 stamps.

Poetry: Accepts 12/yr. Any type, 4-24 lines. Submit max. 4 poems.

Fillers: Accepts 36/yr. Cartoons, facts, jokes, quizzes, quotes, short humor, word puzzles.

Columns/Departments: Artist Action (any specific artist information).

Special Needs: Organizational pieces; new music releases/photos; artist's concert schedules; radio station playlists.

Tips: "Submit between the 10th and 20th of each month for best review."

$THE SENIOR MUSICIAN, One Lifeway Plaza., Nashville TN 37234-0170. (615)251-2913. Fax (615)251-2614. E-mail: jere.adams@lifeway.com. Website: www.lifeway.com. Southern Baptist. Jere V. Adams, ed. Easy choir music for senior adult choirs to use in worship, ministry, and recreation; for music directors, pastors, organists, pianists, and choir coordinators. Quarterly mag.; 32 pgs.; circ. 32,000. 90% unsolicited freelance; 10% assigned. Complete ms. Pays .07/wd. on publication for 1st rts. Articles 500-900 wds. (6-7/yr.). Responds in 2-4 wks. Seasonal 1 yr. ahead. Some simultaneous submissions; reprints. Guidelines; free copy. (No ads for now)

Poetry: Buys 2-3/yr. Traditional.

Fillers: Buys 3-4/yr. Cartoons, ideas, party ideas, musical quizzes, short humor.

Special Needs: Leisure reading, music training, fellowship suggestions, and choir projects for personal growth.

Tips: "All topics must relate to senior adult musicians and senior choirs—anything else will be returned. Our publication includes 8 pages of literary and 24 pages of music."

TRADITION MAGAZINE, PO Box 492, Anita IA 50020. Phone/fax (712)762-4363. E-mail: bobeverhart@yahoo.com. Website: www.oldtimemusic.bigstep.com. National Traditional Country Music Assn., Inc. Bob Everhart, pres./ed. Bimonthly mag.; 56 pgs.; circ. 3,500. Subscription $25. 30% unsolicited freelance; 70% assigned. Query. **PAYS IN COPIES** for one-time rts. Articles 1,000-2,000 wds. (4/yr.). Responds in 6-8 wks. Uses some sidebars. Prefers KJV. Guidelines; copy for 9x12 SAE/2 stamps. (Ads)

Fillers: Cartoons.

Columns/Departments: Accepts 4-6/yr. Query.

Tips: "Most articles need to deal with traditional or old-time music."

PASTOR/LEADERSHIP MARKETS

$THE AFRICAN AMERICAN PULPIT, PO Box 15347, Pittsburgh PA 15237. Toll-free (800)509-8227. Phone/fax (412)364-1688. E-mail: Info@theafricanamericanpulpit.com. Website: www.TheAfricanAmericanPulpit.com. Hope for Life Intl., Inc. Victoria McGoey, project mngr.; Martha Simmons, pub. The only journal focused exclusively on the art of black preaching. Quarterly journal; 96 pgs.; circ. 3,000. Subscription $35 ($48 to libraries). 50% unsolicited freelance; 50% assigned. Complete ms/cover letter; phone/e-query OK. Pays $50 (flat fee) on publication for 1st rts. Articles 1,500 wds., sermons 2,500 wds. Responds in 13-26 wks. Seasonal 6-9 mos. ahead. Requires requested ms on disk or by e-mail. Does not use sidebars. Any Bible version. Guidelines (also by e-mail/Website); copy. (Ads)

Special Needs: Any type of sermon by African American preachers, and related articles or essays.

Contest: Sponsors contest occasionally; advertised in the magazine.

Tips: "The entire journal is open to freelancers. We strongly encourage freelancers to submit to us (as many pieces as you can), and freelancers can call anytime with questions. We are always looking for how-to articles, sermon helps, homiletic method essays, seminarian pieces, and practical pieces."

ANGELOS, PO Box 757800, Memphis TN 38175-7800. (901)757-7977. Fax (901)757-1372. E-mail: OMI@olford.org. Website: www.olford.org. Olford Ministries Intl. Mark N. Boorman, dir. of communications. Quarterly mag.; 4-8 pgs.; circ. 9,500. Subscription $10 (voluntary). 5% unsolicited freelance; 95% assigned. Query; phone/e-query OK. **NO PAYMENT** for one-time rts. Articles (1-3/yr.) 500 wds. Responds in 2-3 wks. Seasonal 3-4 mos. ahead. Might accept reprints (tell when/where appeared). Prefers requested ms on disk or by e-mail (attached file). Prefers NKJV. Guidelines by e-mail; copy for 9x12 SAE/4 stamps. (No ads)

Fillers: Accepts 4-6/yr. Prayers, 100-200 wds.

Tips: "Need articles on prayer. Call and ask if we need article complementary to theme of upcoming issue. Understand our ministry's purpose and objectives."

$BAREFOOT, PO Box 419527, Kansas City MO 64141. (816)931-1900. Fax (816)412-8312. E-mail: bfeditor@barefootministries.com. Website: www.barefootministries.com. Bo Cassell, ed. Dedicated to resourcing and equipping youth workers and youth. Weekly e-zine. Subscription free online. 10% unsolicited freelance; 90% assigned. E-query preferred; fax query OK. Pays $50-100 on publication for all rts. Articles for youth workers 1,000 wds. (15-20/yr.); articles for youth 500 wds. (15-20/yr.); fiction 500-1,000 wds.; reviews 500 wds. ($25). Responds in 8 wks. Seasonal 6 mos. ahead. Accepts reprints (tell when/where appeared). Accepts e-mail submissions (attached or copied into message). Some kill fees. Does not use sidebars. Prefers NIV. Accepts submissions from teens. Guidelines by e-mail; copy online. (No ads)

Fillers: Buys 20-40/yr. Anecdotes, cartoons, games, ideas, party ideas, short humor, and tips, 100-200 wds.; $20-40.

Special Needs: Youthworker and youth issues.

Tips: "We are most open to freelancers in the areas of product, music, and entertainment reviews. Also for fillers and any materials written for teens. Where youth ministry articles and curricular pieces are concerned, we usually assign those to established youth ministry professionals."

$BUILDING CHURCH LEADERS.COM, 465 Gundersen Dr., Carol Stream IL 60188-2498. (630)260-6200. Fax (630)260-0114. E-mail: bclstore@christianitytoday.com. Website: www.buildingchurchleaders.com. Christianity Today Intl. Lori Quicke, mng. ed. Website with downloadable resources. Estab. 2003. 100% assigned. Query/clips; e-query OK. Articles 500-2,500 wds.; 8-14 pg. training guides for church leaders. Prefers full ms by e-mail (attached file). Kill fee 50%. No sidebars. Prefers NIV. Guidelines by e-mail.

$CATECHUMENATE: A Journal of Christian Initiation, 1800 N. Hermitage Ave., Chicago IL 60622-1101. Toll-free (800)933-1800. (773)486-8970. Fax (800)933-7094. E-mail: editors@ltp.org. Website: www.LTP.org. Catholic. Victoria M. Tufano, ed. For clergy and laity who work with those who are planning to become Catholic. Bimonthly jour.; 48 pgs.; circ. 5,600. Subscription $20. Complete ms/cover letter; phone/fax/e-query OK. Pays $100-250 on publication for all rts. Articles 1,500-3,000 wds. (10/yr.). Responds in 2-6 wks. Accepts simultaneous submissions. Prefers requested ms on disk. Kill fee. Does not use sidebars. Guidelines; copy for 6x9 SAE/4 stamps.

> **Poetry:** Buys 6/yr. Free verse, traditional; 5-20 lines; $75. Submit max. 5 poems. One-time rts.

> **Columns/Departments:** Buys 12/yr. Sunday Word (Scripture reflection on Sunday readings, aimed at catechumen); 450 wds.; $200-250. Query for assignment.

> **Special Needs:** Christian initiation; reconciliation.

> **Tips:** "It helps if the writer has experience working with Christian initiation. Approach is that this is something we are all learning together through experience and scholarship."

$THE CATHOLIC SERVANT, PO Box 24142, Minneapolis MN 55424. (612)729-7321. Fax (612)724-8695. E-mail: jcsondag@mninter.net. Catholic. John Sondag, ed./pub. For Catholic evangelization, catechesis, and apologetics. Monthly mag.; 12 pgs.; circ. 33,000. Query/clips; fax query OK. Pays $50-60 on publication. Articles 750-1,000 wds. (12/yr.). Responds in 4 wks. Seasonal 3 mos. ahead. Prefers requested ms on disk; no e-mail submissions. Uses some sidebars. (Ads)

> **Fillers:** Cartoons & short humor.

> **Columns/Departments:** Opinion column, 500-750 wds.

> **Tips:** "We buy features or column only."

CELL GROUP JOURNAL, 10055 Regal Row, Ste. 180, Houston TX 77040. Toll-free (800)735-5865. (713)896-7478. Fax (713)896-1874. E-mail: randall@touchusa.org. Website: www.touchusa.org. Touch Outreach Ministries. Randall Neighbour, ed. dir. For Cell Church pastors, leaders, and consultants working to impact the world for Christ through the church. E-newsletter; 32 pgs.; circ. 12,000. Subscription $14. 70-80% unsolicited freelance. Query/clips; fax/e-query OK. **PAYS 10 COPIES.** Articles 1,000-1,500 wds. (20-30/yr.). Responds in 2 wks. Seasonal 3 mos. ahead. Accepts simultaneous submissions and reprints (tell when/where appeared). Prefers requested ms on disk. Uses some sidebars. Prefers NIV. Guidelines/theme list; copy $3.50/9x12 SAE/3 stamps. (Ads)

> **Columns/Departments:** Accepts 20-25/yr. Youth, Children's Ministry, Transitioning (to Cell Church), Global Input, Pastor's Pilgrimage (pastor's testimonial about Cell Church), ToolKit (500-wd. testimonies about cell life, tips from cell leaders/interns, icebreakers), and Heart to Heart (heartfelt testimony about cell life); all 1,000-1,500 wds.

> **Special Needs:** Global issues; practical tips and ideas relevant to Cell Church concept. Needs youth Cell Church writers.

$CHRISTIAN CAMP & CONFERENCE JOURNAL, PO Box 62189, Colorado Springs CO 80962-2189. (719)260-9400. Fax (719)260-6398. E-mail: editor@cciusa.org. Website: www.christiancamping.org. Christian Camping Intl./USA. Alison Hayhoe, ed.; Justin Boles, mng. ed. To inform, inspire, and motivate all who serve in Christian camps and conferences. Bimonthly & online mag.; 40 pgs.; circ. 8,750. Subscription $26.95. 15% unsolicited freelance; 85% assigned. Query; e-query OK. Pays .16/wd. on publication for 1st and electronic rts. Articles 1,500-2,000 wds. (12/yr.); features 1,000-1,200 wds. (30/yr.); sidebars 500 wds. (15-20/yr.) Responds in 4 wks. Seasonal 6 mos. ahead. Accepts simultaneous submissions and reprints (tell when/where appeared). Prefers e-mail submission (attached file) with fax backup. Kill fee. Regularly uses sidebars. Prefers NIV. Guidelines (also by e-mail); copy $4.95/10x13 SAE/$1.60 postage. (Ads)

Special Needs: Outdoor setting; purpose and objectives; administration and organization; personnel development; camper/guest needs; programming; health and safety; food service; site/facilities maintenance; business/operations; marketing and PR; relevant spiritual issues; and fund raising.

Tips: "Most open to nonfiction; get guidelines, then query first. Don't send general camping-related articles. We print stories specifically related to Christian camp and conference facilities; changed lives or innovative programs; how a Christian camp or conference experience affected a present-day leader. Review several issues so you know what we're looking for."
**2004 EPA Award of Merit—Christian Ministries.

$#THE CHRISTIAN CENTURY, 104 S. Michigan Ave., Ste. 700, Chicago IL 60603. (312)263-7510. Fax (312)263-7540. E-mail: main@christiancentury.org. Website: www.christian century.org. Christian Century Foundation. Submit to: Attention Manuscripts. For ministers, educators, and church leaders interested in events and theological issues of concern to the ecumenical church. Biweekly mag.; 48 pgs.; circ. 30,000. Subscription $49. 20% unsolicited freelance; 80% assigned. Query (complete ms for fiction); phone/fax query OK. Pays $75-200 ($75-150 for unsolicited) on publication for all or one-time rts. Articles 1,500-3,000 wds. (150/yr.); fiction 1,000-3,000 wds. (3/yr.); book reviews, 800-1,500 wds.; music or video reviews 1,000 wds.; pays $0-75. Responds in 1-9 wks. Seasonal 4 mos. ahead. No simultaneous submissions. Accepts reprints (tell when/where appeared). No kill fee. Regularly uses sidebars. Prefers NRSV. Guidelines/theme list (also by e-mail); copy $5. (Ads)

Poetry: Buys 50/yr. Any type (religious but not sentimental); to 20 lines; $50. Submit max. 10 poems.

Special Needs: Film, popular culture commentary; news topics and analysis.

Tips: "Keep in mind our audience of sophisticated readers, eager for analysis and critical perspective that goes beyond the obvious. We are open to all topics if written with appropriate style for our readers."

$CHRISTIAN CREATIVE ARTS ASSN., PO Box 1128, Franklin TN 37065. (877)CH-DRAMA. E-mail: info@ccaaonline.org. Website: www.ccaaonline.org. Christy Haines, exec. dir. Conservative, evangelical dramas for stage, street, and sanctuary. Open to freelance. Scripts must adhere to guidelines for submissions; e-mail for guidelines first. Looking for any-length scripts for drama, puppetry, clowning, mime, interpretive movement, and comedy.

+CHRISTIAN EDUCATION JOURNAL (CA), 13800 Biola Ave., LaMirada CA 90639. (562)903-6000, ext. 5528. Fax (562)906-4502. E-mail: editor.cej@biola.edu. Website: www.biola.edu.cej. Talbot School of Theology, Biola University. Kevin E. Lawson, ed. Academic journal on the practice of Christian education; for students, professors, and thoughtful ministry leaders in Christian education. Semiannual jour.; 200-250 pgs.; circ. 750. Subscription $25. Open to freelance. Query; e-query OK. Accepts full mss by e-mail. **NO PAYMENT** for 1st rts. Articles 3,000-6,000 wds. (20/yr.); book reviews 2-5 pgs. Responds in 4-6 wks. No seasonal. Might accept simultaneous submissions & reprints (tell when/where appeared). Requires e-mail submissions (attached file in Word format). No sidebars. Any Bible version. Guidelines on Website; no copy. (Ads)

Tips: "Focus on foundations and/or research with implications for the conception and practice of Christian education."

CHRISTIAN MANAGEMENT REPORT, PO Box 4090, San Clemente CA 92674. (949)487-0900. Fax (949)487-0927. E-mail: DeWayne@CMAonline.org. Website: www.CMA online.org. Christian Management Assn. DeWayne Herbrandson, exec. ed. Management resources and leadership training for Christian nonprofit organizations and growing churches. Bimonthly jour.; 48 pgs.; circ. 3,500+. Subscription $39.95. 100% assigned. Complete ms; e-query encouraged. **PAYS 10 COPIES** for all, 1st, one-time, reprint, or electronic rts. Articles 770-1,500 wds./bio; book reviews 100-200 wds. Responds in 4 wks. Seasonal 6 mos. ahead. No simultaneous submissions; limited reprints. CMA members first choice. Prefers accepted ms by e-mail (attached file). No kill fee. Regularly uses sidebars. Prefers NIV, NLT. Guidelines (also by e-mail); free copy. (Ads)

Fillers: Cartoons.

Columns/Departments: Accepts 6/yr. Living with Integrity (leadership integrity issues), 750-1,500 wds.; Ministry Profile (management issues with various ministries), 1,500 wds.; Coaching as Ministry (how to mentor and coach one's staff), 750-1,500 wds.

Special Needs: Evangelical Calendar of Events, Ministry Profiles/Case Studies; hot ministry news, and trends.

Tips: "All areas open. Submit a synopsis of article idea dealing with leadership and management issues relevant to megachurches or parachurch organizations. Send by e-mail (attached file)."

$CHURCH ADMINISTRATION, One Lifeway Plaza, Nashville TN 37234. (615)251-2297. Fax (615)251-3866. Website: www.lifeway.com. Southern Baptist. Chris Johnson, ed. Practical pastoral ministry/church administration ideas for pastors and staff. Quarterly mag.; 50 pgs.; circ. 12,000. 15% unsolicited freelance. Query. Pays .065/wd. on acceptance for all rts. Articles 1,600-2,000 wds. (60/yr.). Responds in 8 wks. Guidelines/copy for #10 SAE/2 stamps.

Columns/Departments: Buys 60/yr. Weekday Dialogue; Minister's Mate; Secretary's File; all 2,000 wds.

Tips: "Manuscripts must be typed and have return postage."

$CHURCH GROWTH NETWORK, PO Box 892589, Temecula CA 92589-2589. Phone/fax (909)506-3086. E-mail: cgnet@earthlink.net. Website: www.mcintoshcgn.com. Dr. Gary L. McIntosh, ed. For pastors and church leaders interested in church growth. Monthly newsletter; 2 pgs.; circ. 8,000. Subscription $16. 10% unsolicited freelance; 90% assigned. Query; fax/e-query OK. Pays $25 for one-time rts. Not copyrighted. Articles 1,000-2,000 wds. (2/yr.). Responds in 4 wks. Accepts simultaneous submissions and reprints. Accepts requested ms on disk. Does not use sidebars. Guidelines; copy for #10 SAE/1 stamp. (No ads)

Tips: "Write articles that are short (1,200 words), crisp, clear, with very practical ideas that church leaders can put to use immediately. All articles must have a pro church-growth slant, be very practical, have how-to material, and be very tightly written with bullets, etc."

$CHURCH WORSHIP, 165 Plaza Dr., Prescott AZ 86303. (928)771-8601. Fax (928)771-8621. E-mail: edmin2@aol.com. Website: www.educationalministries.com. Educational Ministries. Robert Davidson, ed. Supplementary resources for church worship leaders. Monthly jour.; 24 pgs.; circ. 1,500. Subscription $24. 100% unsolicited freelance. Complete ms/cover letter; phone/fax/e-query OK. Pays .03/wd., 60 days after publication, for 1st rts. Articles 500-1,500 wds.; fiction 100-1,500 wds. Responds in 3-18 wks. Seasonal 6 mos. ahead. Guidelines/ theme list; copy for 9x12 SAE/4 stamps. (No ads)

Special Needs: Complete worship services; seasonal sermons.

Tips: "Most open to creative worship services using music, drama, or art."

$THE CLERGY JOURNAL, 6160 Carmen Ave. E., Inver Grove Heights MN 55076-4422. (651)451-9945. Fax (651)457-4617. E-mail: fig@logosstaff.com. Website: www.join hands.com. Logos Productions, Inc. Sharilyn Figueroa, mng. ed. Directed mainly to clergy—a practical guide to church leadership and personal growth. Monthly (10X) mag.; 56 pgs.; circ. 8,000. Subscription $36.95. 5% unsolicited freelance; 95% assigned. Complete ms/cover letter. Pays $100-150 on publication for 1st rts. Articles 1,000-1,500 wds. Responds in 2-3 wks. Seasonal 6 mos. ahead. Accepts reprints (tell when/where appeared). Prefers requested ms on disk or by e-mail (attached file). Uses some sidebars. Prefers NRSV. Guidelines/theme list (also by e-mail); copy for 9x12 SAE/4 stamps. (Ads)

> **Fillers:** Cartoons, $25.
>
> **Columns/Departments:** Ministry Issues; Preaching & Worship; Personal Issues.
>
> **Special Needs:** Humorous fiction for pastors, and sermons for children.
>
> **Tips:** "Our greatest need is sermon writers who can write on assigned texts. Instructions sent on request. Our readers are mainline Protestant. We are interested in meeting the personal and professional needs of clergy in areas like worship planning, church and personal finances, and self-care—spiritual, physical, and emotional."

$CORNERSTONE YOUTH RESOURCES, 55 W. Oak Ridge Dr., Hagerstown MD 21740. (301)393-4019. Fax (817)926-5845. E-mail: plhumphrey@earthlink.net. Seventh-day Adventist. Patricia Humphrey, ed. For Christian youth leaders; a practical resource filled with ideas for creative youth ministry and programming. Quarterly mag.; 48 pgs.; circ. 2,200. 5% unsolicited freelance; 95% assigned. Query/clips; fax query OK; best to e-mail as editor lives in Texas. Pays $25-350 on acceptance for 1st rts. Articles 700-900 wds. (16/yr.). Responds in 8-12 wks. Seasonal 12 mos. ahead. Accepts reprints (tell when/where appeared). Accepts e-mail submissions (attached file). No kill fee. Regularly uses sidebars. Prefers KJV, NKJV, NIV. Accepts submissions from teens. Guidelines (also by e-mail); copy for 9x12 SAE/$1.42 postage (mark "Media Mail"). (Ads)

> **Columns/Departments:** Outreach Ideas (service activity ideas for teens), 800-1,000 wds.; Super Social Suggestions (social activities and games for teen groups), 800-1,000 wds.; Program Ideas (creative youth programming ideas), variable lengths.
>
> **Special Needs:** Articles dealing with understanding and teaching youth. Innovative concepts in youth ministry.
>
> **Tips:** "Areas most open to freelancers are the Super Social and Outreach Ideas. We are always looking for creative activity ideas that teen leaders can do with youth, ages 14-18. The activities should be fun to do and well-written with clear, easy-to-follow instructions. Ideas that are tested and have worked well with your own youth group are preferred."

CROSS CURRENTS, 475 Riverside Dr., Ste. 1945, New York NY 10015. (212)870-2544. Fax (212)870-2539. E-mail: chashenderson@mindspring.com. Website: www.crosscurrents .org. Association for Religion and Intellectual Life. Carey Monserrate, mng. ed. For thoughtful activists for social justice and church reform. Quarterly mag.; 144 pgs.; circ. 5,000. Subscription $30. 25% unsolicited freelance; 75% assigned. Mostly written by academics. Complete ms/cover letter; e-query OK. **PAYS IN COPIES** for all rts. Articles 3,000-5,000 wds.; fiction 3,000 wds.; book reviews 1,000 wds. Responds in 6-8 wks. Seasonal 6 mos. ahead. No simultaneous submissions or reprints. Prefers requested ms on disk or by e-mail (attached file). No kill fee. Does not use sidebars. Guidelines (also on Website); no copy. (Ads)

> **Poetry:** Beverly Coyle, poetry ed. Accepts 12/yr. Any type or length; no payment. Submit max. 5 poems.
>
> **Tips:** "Looking for focused, well-researched articles; creative fiction and poetry. Send two, double-spaced copies; SASE; use *Chicago Manual of Style* and nonsexist language."

$DIOCESAN DIALOGUE, 16565 S. State St., South Holland IL 60473. (708)331-5485. Fax (708)331-5484. E-mail: acp@acpress.org. Website: www.americancatholicpress.org. A Mexican Catholic Press. Fr. Michael Gilligan, editorial dir. Targets Latin-Rite dioceses in the US that sponsor a mass broadcast on TV or radio. Annual newsletter; 8 pgs.; circ. 750. Free. 20% unsolicited freelance. Complete ms/cover letter; no phone/fax/e-query. Pays on publication for all rts. Responds in 10 wks. Accepts simultaneous submissions and reprints. Uses some sidebars. Prefers NAB (Confraternity). No guidelines; copy $3/9x12 SAE/2 stamps. (No ads)

> **Fillers:** Cartoons, 2/yr.

> **Tips:** "Writers should be familiar with TV production of the Mass and/or the needs of senior citizens, especially shut-ins."

$EMMANUEL, 5384 Wilson Mills Rd., Cleveland OH 44143. (440)449-2103. Fax (440)449-3862. E-mail: Emmanuelpublishing@sbcglobal.net. Website: www.blessedsacrament.com. Catholic. Submit to The Editor; books for review to Dr. Patrick Riley. Eucharistic spirituality for priests and others in church ministry. Bimonthly mag.; 96 pgs.; circ. 3,000. Subscription $26; $31 foreign. 30% unsolicited freelance. Query or complete ms/cover letter; e-query OK. Pays $75-150 for articles, $50 for meditations, on publication for all rts. Articles 2,000-2,750 wds.; meditations 1,000-1,250 wds.; book reviews 500-750 wds. Responds in 2 wks. Seasonal 4 mos. ahead. Accepts manuscripts on disk or as e-mail attachments. Guidelines (also by e-mail)/theme list. (Ads)

> **Poetry:** Buys 15/yr. Free verse, light verse, traditional; 8 lines & up; $35. Submit max. 3 poems.

> **Tips:** "Most open to articles, meditations, poetry oriented toward Eucharistic spirituality, prayer, and ministry."

$ENRICHMENT: A Journal for Pentecostal Ministry, 1445 N. Boonville Ave., Springfield MO 65802. (417)862-2781, ext. 4096. Fax (417)862-0416. E-mail: enrichmentjournal @ag.org. Website: www.enrichmentjournal.ag.org. Assemblies of God. Gary R. Allen, exec. ed.; Rick Knoth, mng. ed. (rknoth@ag.org). Directed to part- or full-time ministers and church leaders. Quarterly jour.; 128-144 pgs.; circ. 33,000. Subscription $24, $42/2 yrs.; foreign add $10. 5-10% unsolicited freelance. Complete ms/cover letter. Pays .10/wd. ($75-175) on acceptance for one-time rts. Articles 1,200-1,500 wds. (25/yr.); book reviews, 250 wds. ($25). Responds in 8-12 wks. Seasonal 1 yr. ahead. Accepts simultaneous submissions and reprints (tell when/where appeared). Requires requested ms on disk or by e-mail (copied into message). Kill fee 50%. Regularly uses sidebars. Prefers NIV. Guidelines/theme list; copy for $3/10x13 SAE. (Ads)

> **Fillers:** Cartoon; $50-75.

> **Columns/Departments:** Buys many/yr. For Women in Ministry (leadership ideas), Associate Ministers (related issues), Managing Your Ministry (how-to), Financial Concepts (church stewardship issues), Family Life (minister's family), When Pews Are Few (ministry in smaller congregation); Worship in the Church; Leader's Edge; Preaching That Connects; all 1,200-1,500 wds.; $125-150.

> **Tips:** "Most open to sermon outlines, how-to articles (fillers), sermon illustrations, practical ideas on ministry-related topics."

> **2000 & 1997 EPA Award of Excellence—Denominational; 1999 EPA Award of Merit—Denominational; 1997 EPA Most Improved Publication.

$#ENVIRONMENT & ART LETTER, 1800 N. Hermitage Ave., Chicago IL 60622-1101. Toll-free (800)933-1800. (773)486-8970, ext. 267. Fax (773)486-7094. E-mail: mbrennan@ LTP.org. Website: www.LTP.org. Catholic. Margaret Brennan, ed. For artists, architects, building professionals, pastors, parish committees interested in church architecture, art, and decoration. Monthly newsletter; 12 pgs.; circ. 2,500. Subscription $20. 80% unsolicited freelance. Query/clips; phone/fax query OK. Pays $25/ms page on publication for all rts. Responds in 18 wks. Seasonal 2 mos. ahead. Accepts simultaneous submissions. Theme list; copy for 9x12 SAE/3 stamps.

Tips: "Need a thorough knowledge of the liturgical documents pertaining to architecture and art, especially environment and art for Catholic worship."

$EUCHARISTIC MINISTRIES: A Resource for Parish Life, 115 E. Armour Blvd., Box 419493, Kansas City MO 64111. (816)531-0538. Fax (816)968-2291. E-mail: nwagner@ natcath.org. Website: www.ncrpub.com. National Catholic Reporter Publishing Co. Nick Wagner, ed. For Eucharistic ministers. Monthly newsletter; 8 pgs.; circ. 50,000. 20% unsolicited freelance; 80% assigned. Complete ms/cover letter; phone/fax/e-query OK. Pays $50-125 on publication for one-time rts. Articles 500-1,250 wds. (12/yr.). Responds in 1-2 wks. Seasonal 6 mos. ahead. Accepts reprints (tell when/where appeared). Prefers accepted ms by e-mail (attached or copied into message). Does not use sidebars. Guidelines (also by e-mail); copy for 10x13 SAE/2 stamps. (Ads—e-mail for specifications).

Fillers: Buys 10-12/yr. Anecdotes, cartoons, short humor.

Columns/Departments: Buys 12/yr. Living My Ministry (reflections on minister's experiences, anecdotes, inspirational personal experiences), 500 wds., $50. Complete ms.

Tips: "Feature articles need to be eucharistically, theologically, and/or ministerially based; practical, inspirational, or motivational. They need to be simple and direct enough for the average person to read easily—no heavy theology, pious inspiration, or excess verbiage. General focus—rather than personal accounts—a must."

$THE EVANGELICAL BAPTIST, 679 Southgate Dr., Guelph ON N1G 4S2 Canada. (519)821-4830. Fax (519)821-9829. E-mail: eb@fellowship.ca. Website: www.fellowship.ca. Fellowship of Evangelical Baptist Churches in Canada. Ginette Cotnoir, mng. ed., (18 Louvigny, Lorraine QC J6Z 1T7 Canada). To enhance the life and ministry of pastors and leaders in local churches. Bimonthly (5X) mag.; 32 pgs.; circ. 3,000. Subscription $12. 5-10% unsolicited freelance; 20% assigned. Complete ms/cover letter; e-query preferred. Pays $25-75 on publication for one-time rts. Articles 800-2,400 wds. Responds in 6-8 wks. Accepts simultaneous submissions and reprints. Guidelines (also by e-mail); copy for 9x12 SAE/.90 Canadian postage. (Ads)

Columns/Departments: Buys 5/yr. Joy in the Journey (inspiration in everyday life), 600-800 wds.; Point of View (respectful and well-argued opinion pieces about a subject relevant to believers or the church), 800-900 wds; $30-50. Complete ms.

Special Needs: Church Life department looking for practical church ministry ideas; how to enhance Sunday school, small groups, worship, youth ministry, women's ministries, etc.; 600-800 wds.

Tips: "This magazine is for church leaders—pastors, elders, deacons, and anyone involved in a church ministry. Most articles are assigned. Most open to columns. Preference given to writers from Fellowship Baptist Churches in Canada."

$*EVANGELICALS TODAY, 62 Molave St., Project 3, Quezon City 1102, Philippines. (632)433-1546 to 1549. Fax (632)913-1675. Philippine Council of Evangelical Churches. Bishop Efraim M. Tendero, exec. ed. To equip pastors, Christian leaders/workers and the rest of Christ's Body in the various areas of Christian life and ministry by providing inspiring and enriching articles and relevant news reports. Bimonthly mag.; 36 pgs.; circ. 3,000. Subscription $6.25 (local) or $50 (foreign). 5% unsolicited freelance; 95% assigned. Complete ms by e-mail. Pays $12.50/article on publication. Articles 1,000-1,500 wds. Responds in 2 wks. Seasonal 2 mos. ahead. Accepts simultaneous submissions and reprints (tell when/where appeared). Prefers requested ms on disk or by e-mail (attached file or copied into message). Prefers NIV. No guidelines. (Ads)

$THE FIVE STONES, 155 Brown St., Providence RI 02906. Phone/fax (401)861-9405. E-mail:

pappas@tabcom.org. Website: www.tabcom.org. American Baptist. Anthony G. Pappas, ed. Primarily to small church pastors and laity, denominational staff, and seminaries; to equip for service. Quarterly jour.; 16 pgs.; circ. 1,000. Subscription $8-12. 100% unsolicited freelance. Complete ms/cover letter. Pays $5 on publication for one-time rights. Not copyrighted. Articles (20/yr.) & fiction (4/yr.), 500-2,000 wds.; book reviews 500 wds. ($5). Responds in 10-12 wks. Seasonal 10 mos. ahead. Accepts simultaneous submissions and reprints. Prefers requested ms on disk or by e-mail. Uses some sidebars. Any Bible version. Guidelines/theme list; copy for 9x12 SAE/4 stamps. (Ads)

> **Tips:** "Always looking for everything related to small church life (nature and dynamics of small churches); fresh programming. Good place for unpublished to break in. Use first person. Best to call and talk."

$HORIZONS, 2 Overlea Blvd., Toronto ON M4H 1P4 Canada. (416)422-6226. Fax (416)422-6120. E-mail: horizons@can.salvationarmy.org. Website: www.horizons.salvationarmy.ca. The Salvation Army. Geoff Moulton, sr. ed. For officers and lay leaders of The Salvation Army; focusing on leadership, discipleship, theology, social issues, and Christian ministry. Bimonthly mag.; 24 pgs.; circ. 4,600. Subscription $14 Can. 100% assigned. Query/clips; fax/e-query OK. Pay negotiated for 1st rts. Articles 1,500 wds. (30/yr.); reviews 250 wds. Responds in 2 wks. Accepts simultaneous submissions and reprints (tell when/where appeared). Prefers e-mail submission (attached file). Uses some sidebars. Prefers NIV. Guidelines (also on Website); free copy. Incomplete topical listings. (No ads)

> **Fillers:** Cartoons.

> **Columns/Departments:** Accepts 20/yr. Future Frontiers (what's new in church ministry), 850 wds.; Practical Ministry (practical helps), 850 wds.; Strategic Advance (church leadership/growth issues), 1,500 wds.; Reaching Out (evangelism), 1,500 wds.; Bookmarks (reviews), 250-300 wds.; Creed & Deed (theology), 850 wds. No payment.

+INTERPRETATION, 3401 Brook Rd., Richmond VA 23227. Toll-free (877)522-7799. Website: www.interpretation.org. James A. Brashler, ed.; Jenna A. Bowen, mng. ed. Enhances lifelong theological education and recharges ministers in their work with individuals, study groups, and congregations. Quarterly & online mag. Subscription $23. Incomplete topical listings. No questionnaire returned.

$INTERPRETER MAGAZINE, PO Box 320, Nashville TN 37202-0320. (615)742-5107. Fax (615)742-5460. E-mail: tsimmons@umcom.org. Website: www.InterpreterMagazine.org. United Methodist Church. Kathy Noble, ed. For lay leaders and pastors of the United Methodist Church. Published 8X/yr.; 44 pgs.; circ. 275,000. Subscription $12. 10% unsolicited freelance; 30% assigned. Query/clips; e-query OK (form online). Pays $150-500 on acceptance for 1st and reprint rts. Articles 500-800 wds. (10/yr.); book/music/video reviews, $100. Responds in 8 wks. Seasonal 6 mos. ahead. No simultaneous submissions or reprints. Prefers requested ms on disk or by e-mail (attached file). No kill fee. Regularly uses sidebars. Prefers NRSV. Guidelines/theme list (also by e-mail); copy for 9x12 SAE/4 stamps. (Ads)

> **Fillers:** Buys several/yr. Facts, ideas, short humor; 50-75 wds.

> **Columns/Departments:** Buys 10/yr. One of Us; It Worked for Us; Youth (how parents/church can reach and serve); Worship (new ideas/special days); Evangelism (new ideas for); Singles (how to reach/issues facing); Relationships (strengthening); all to 200 wds., $50-100.

> **Tips:** "All articles must have a specific and prominent United Methodist connection."

> **This periodical was #31 on the 2004 Top 50 Christian Publishers list (#42 in 2003, #32 in 2002).

$JOKE WRITERS GUILD NEWSLETTER, PO Box 605, Times Plaza Sta., Brooklyn NY 11217. E-mail: makinsonrobert@hotmail.com. Website: www.angelfire.com//biz7/rbmakinson/

index.html. Robert Makinson, ed./pub. Short jokes to be done orally by comedians, pastors, and public speakers. Quarterly newsletter; 3 pgs. Subscription $24 for guild members; $5 single issue. 10% unsolicited freelance; 10% assigned. Query; e-query OK. Pays $2-4/joke on acceptance for all rts. Short jokes 1-3 lines. Responds in 2-4 wks. Seasonal 6 mos. ahead. No simultaneous submissions or reprints. No submissions by disk or e-mail. Guidelines; copy $5.(No ads)

   Fillers: Jokes: one-, two-, and three-liners for public speakers. Buying nothing else at this time.

THE JOURNAL OF PASTORAL CARE & COUNSELING, 1068 Harbor Dr. SW, Calabash NC 28467. Phone/fax (910)579-5084. E-mail: OrloS@aol.com. Website: www.jpcp.org. Dr. Orlo Strunk Jr., mng. ed. For chaplains/pastors/professionals involved with pastoral care and counseling in other than a church setting. Quarterly jour.; 116 pgs.; circ. 10,000. Subscription $32. 95% unsolicited freelance; 5% assigned. Query; phone/fax/e-query OK. **PAYS 10 COPIES** for 1st rts. Articles 5,000 wds. or 20 pgs. (30/yr.); book reviews 5 pgs. Responds in 8 wks. Accepts requested ms on disk. No sidebars. Guidelines (also on Website); no copy. (Ads)

   Poetry: Accepts 16/yr. Free verse; 5-16 lines. Submit max. 3 poems.

   Special Needs: "We publish brief (500-600 wds.) 'Personal Reflections'—but they need to deal with clinical experiences that have led the writer to reflect on the religious and/or theological meaning generated."

   Tips: "Most open to poems and personal reflections. Readers are highly trained clinically, holding professional degrees in religion/theology. Writers need to be professionals on topics covered."

JOURNAL OF THE AMERICAN SOCIETY FOR CHURCH GROWTH, c/o Dr. Gary L. McIntosh, ed., Talbot School of Theology, 13800 Biola Ave., LaMirada CA 90639. (562)944-0351. Fax (562)906-4502. E-mail: gary.mcintosh@biola.edu. Website: www.ascg.org. American Society for Church Growth. Dr. Gary L. McIntosh, ed. Targets professors, pastors, denominational executives, and seminary students interested in church growth and evangelism. Quarterly jour. (3X—fall, winter, spring); 100 pgs.; circ. 400. Subscription $24. 66% unsolicited freelance; 33% assigned. Complete ms/cover letter; phone/fax/e-query OK. **PAYS IN COPIES** for one-time rts. Not copyrighted. Articles 15 pgs. or 4,000-5,000 wds. (10/yr.); book reviews 750-2,000 wds. Responds in 8-12 wks. Accepts simultaneous submissions and reprints (tell when/where appeared). Prefers requested ms on disk or by e-mail. Does not use sidebars. Any Bible version. Guidelines (also in journal)/theme list; copy $10. (Ads)

   Tips: "Provide well-researched and tightly written articles related to some aspect of church growth. Articles should be academic in nature, rather than popular in style. We're open to new writers at this time."

LEADERS IN ACTION, PO Box 150, Wheaton IL 60189. (630)871-1424. Fax (630)871-1797. E-mail: bslinger@csbministries.org. Website: www.csbministries.org. CSB Ministries. B.J. Slinger, ed. To motivate and train leaders—men who lead in Christian Service Brigade and women who lead in Girls Alive. Triannual mag.; circ. 6,500. Subscription $6. Open to freelance. Prefers query. Not in topical listings. (No ads) Note: This publication is currently on hold; query for current status.

$LEADERSHIP, 465 Gundersen Dr., Carol Stream IL 60188. (630)260-6200. Fax (630)260-0114. E-mail: LJEditor@LeadershipJournal.net. Website: www.leadershipjournal.net. Christianity Today Intl. Marshall Shelley, ed.; Eric Reed, mng. ed. Practical help for pastors/church leaders. Quarterly & online jour.; 130 pgs.; circ. 65,000. Subscription $24.95. 20% unsolicited freelance; 80% assigned. Query or complete ms; fax/e-query OK. Pays $75-375 (.15/wd) on acceptance for 1st rts., right to reprint, and electronic rts. Articles

500-3,000 wds. (50/yr.). Responds in 3-5 wks. Seasonal 6 mos. ahead. Accepts reprints (tell when/where appeared). Accepts requested ms on disk or by e-mail (copied into message). Kill fee 50%. Regularly uses sidebars. Prefers NIV, NLT. Guidelines/theme list (also on Website); copy $3. (Ads)

Fillers: Buys 80/yr. Cartoons, short humor; to 150 wds.; $25-50.

Columns/Departments: Buys 80/yr. Ideas That Work, 150 wds.; To Illustrate (sermon illustrations), 150 wds.; $25-50. Complete ms.

Tips: "*Leadership* is a practical journal for pastors. We look for articles that provide practical help for problems church leaders face, not essays expounding on a topic, editorials arguing a position, or homilies explaining biblical principles. We want 'how-to' articles based on first-person accounts of real-life experiences in ministry."

**2004, 2003, 2001 EPA Award of Merit—Christian Ministries; 2000 & 1999 EPA Award of Excellence—Christian Ministries; 1998 EPA Award of Merit—General. This periodical was #8 on the 2004 Top 50 Christian Publishers list (#12 in 2003, #16 in 2002, #14 in 2001, #19 in 2000).

$LET'S WORSHIP, One Lifeway Plaza, MSN 175, Nashville TN 37234-0170. (615)251-2769. Fax (615)251-2795. E-mail: mtullos@lifeway.com. Website: www.lifeway.com. Southern Baptist/LifeWay Christian Resources. Matt Tullos, ed-in-chief. Resources for pastors and worship leaders; countering the norm with contagious ideas. Quarterly mag.; 96 pgs.; circ. 5,500. Subscription $14.95. 10% unsolicited freelance; 90% assigned. Complete ms by e-mail only. Pays .105/wd. on acceptance for all, 1st, or one-time rts. Articles 1,500 wds. (50/yr.); book reviews 300 wds. ($50). Responds in 10 wks. Seasonal 10 mos. ahead. Accepts simultaneous submissions. Requires ms by e-mail (attached file or copied into message). Regularly uses sidebars. Prefers HCSB. No guidelines/copy. (No ads)

Columns/Departments: Wednesday Words (4-week Bible study with listening sheets); Bible study, 625 wds.; listening sheet, 200 wds.; Drama (original scripts), 900 wds.

Special Needs: Offer testimonials: How we do drama, start a drama ministry, use mime, transition worship, etc. in our church. Offer original scripts for short drama or reader's theater.

Tips: "Most open to short dramas, dramatic readings, dramatic monologues/dialogs."

LUTHERAN FORUM, PO Box 327, Delhi NY 13753-0327. (607)746-7511. E-mail: dkralpb@aol.com. Website: www.alpb.org. American Lutheran Publicity Bureau. Ronald Bagnall, ed. For church leadership—clerical and laity. Quarterly jour.; 64 pgs.; circ. 3,200. Subscription $24.95. 80% unsolicited freelance. Complete ms/cover letter. **NO PAYMENT.** Articles 1,000-3,000 wds. Responds in 26-32 wks. Accepts simultaneous submissions and reprints. Requires requested ms on disk. Guidelines; copy for 9x12 SAE/$1.42 postage (mark "Media Mail"). (Ads)

$LUTHERAN PARTNERS, 8765 W. Higgins Rd., Chicago IL 60631-4195. Toll-free (800)638-3522, ext. 2884. (773)380-2884. Fax (773)380-2829. E-mail: lpartmag@elca.org or LUTHERAN_PARTNERS@ecunet.org. Website: www.elca.org/lp. Evangelical Lutheran Church in America. William A. Decker, ed. To encourage and challenge rostered leaders in the ELCA, including pastors and lay ministers. Bimonthly mag.; 40+ pgs.; circ. 20,000. Subscription $12.50 (free to leaders), $18.75 outside North America. 10-15% unsolicited freelance; 85-90% assigned. Query; phone/fax/e-query OK. Pays $120-170 on publication for one-time rts. Articles 500-1,500 wds. (12-15/yr.). Responds in 16 wks. Seasonal 9 mos. ahead. Accepts simultaneous submissions and reprints (tell when/where appeared). Kill fee (rare). Prefers requested ms on disk or by e-mail (attached file). Regularly uses sidebars. Prefers NRSV. Guidelines/theme list (also by e-mail/Website); copy $2/9x12 SAE/5 stamps. (Ads)

Poetry: Buys 6-10/yr. Free verse, traditional; $50-75. Keep concise. Submit max. 6 poems.

Fillers: Buys 4-5/yr. Cartoons; ideas for parish ministry (called Jottings); to 500 wds.; $25.
Special Needs: Book reviews. Query the editor. Uses books predominately from mainline denominational and some evangelical publishers. Payment is copy of book. Youth and family issues, rural and urban ministry issues, men's issues. More articles from women and ethnic authors (especially if ordained or are in official lay ministry leadership roles).
Tips: "Query us with solid ideas. First, we are a leadership publication. Our audience includes pastors and lay church staff. Your articles must answer concerns that leadership has, especially ordained leadership. Secondly, understand Lutheran Church theology and ELCA congregational life. Pertinent topics include: youth leadership and discipleship; faith and science; Lutheran identity among other denominations or religions; and use of the Bible in a biblically illiterate church and society."

$MINISTRIES TODAY, 600 Rinehart Rd., Lake Mary FL 32746. (407)333-0600. Fax (407)333-7100. E-mail: ministries@strang.com. Website: www.ministriestoday.com. Strang Communications. Rob Andrescik, ed.; Adrienne Gaines, review ed. Helps for pastors and church leaders, primarily in Pentecostal/charismatic churches. Bimonthly mag.; 90 pgs.; circ. 30,000. Subscription $24.95. 60-80% freelance. Query; fax/e-query preferred. Pays $50 or $500-800 on publication for all rts. Articles 1,800-2,500 wds. (25/yr.); book/music/video reviews, 300 wds., $25. Responds in 4 wks. Prefers accepted ms by e-mail. Kill fee. Regularly uses sidebars. Prefers NIV. Guidelines; copy $6/9x12 SAE. (Ads)
   Columns/Departments: Buys 36/yr.
   Tips: "Most open to columns. Write for guidelines and study the magazine."

$MINISTRY & LITURGY, 160 E. Virginia St., #290, San Jose CA 95112. (408)286-8505. Fax (408)287-8748. E-mail: mleditor@rpinet.com. Website: www.rpinet.com/ml. Resource Publications, Inc. Donna M. Cole, ed. dir. To help liturgists and ministers make the imaginative connection between liturgy and life. Monthly (10X) mag.; 50 pgs.; circ. 20,000. Subscription $50. Query only; fax/e-query OK. Pays a stipend on publication for 1st rts. Articles 1,500 wds. (30/yr.). Responds in 4 wks. Seasonal 6 mos. ahead. Accepts reprints (tell when/where appeared). Requires requested ms on disk. Regularly uses sidebars. Guidelines/theme list; copy $4/11x14 SAE/2 stamps. (Ads)
   Contest: Visual Arts Awards.

MINISTRY IN MOTION E-ZINE, 451 Hawthorne Ln., Benicia CA 94510. (707)751-3703. E-mail: contribute@ministryinmotion.net. Website: www.ministryinmotion.net. Nondenominational. Teena Stewart, ed. Dedicated to helping individuals uncover and use their gifts and abilities for ministry, and to providing ministry resources and tips for volunteers and church leaders. Biweekly e-zine; circulation 200+. Subscription free. 50% unsolicited freelance; 50% assigned. Complete ms/cover letter; e-query OK. **NO PAYMENT** (for now—may start by 2005) for 1st, reprint, electronic, nonexclusive rts., but provides a blurb on the author or the author's Website, ministry, or book. Not copyrighted. Articles 500-1,000 wds. (20/yr.); book reviews 250 wds. Responds in 1-2 wks. Seasonal 3 mos. ahead. Accepts simultaneous submissions and reprints (tell when/where appeared). Prefers submissions by e-mail (copied into message). No sidebars. Prefers NIV or MSG (no KJV). Guidelines and theme list by e-mail/Website; copy online. (Ads)
   Fillers: Accepts anecdotes and tips, to 2 paragraphs.
   Columns/Departments: Evangelism/outreach (from a church perspective), 500-1,000 wds.; Christian Living, Small Groups, Lay Counseling, Single's Ministry, Worship Arts Ministry, Teaching, Small Groups, Men's Ministry, Discipleship, etc.; 800-1,000 wds. We are looking for columnists. If you have one you think will fit, query us.
   Special Needs: Practical how-tos and interviews with people in successful ministry. We want to hear about what churches are doing as they minister. Let us see how you do what you do.

Tips: "Share leadership tips and insights. We are open to anything related to leadership. The more practical and how-to, the better. No theology or heavily scholastic articles; we are for the everyday church worker."

$MINISTRY MAGAZINE: International Journal for Pastors, 12501 Old Columbia Pike, Silver Spring MD 20904. (301)680-6510. Fax (301)680-6502. E-mail: norcottj@gc.adventist.org. Website: www.ministrymagazine.org. Seventh-day Adventist. Willmore D. Eva, ed.; Julia W. Norcott, asst. ed. For pastors. Monthly jour.; 32 pgs.; circ. 20,000. Subscription $29.95. 90% unsolicited freelance. Query; fax/e-query OK. Pays $50-300 on acceptance for all rts. Articles 1,000-1,500 wds.; book reviews 100-150 wds. ($25). Responds within 13 wks. Prefers requested ms on disk. Uses some sidebars. Guidelines (also on Website)/theme list; copy for 9x12 SAE/5 stamps. (Ads)

+MINISTRY MATTERS, 80 Hayden St., Toronto ON M4Y 3G2 Canada. (905)833-6200. Fax (905)833-2116. E-mail: ministry.matters@national.anglican.ca, or cmccormick@canadads.com. Website: www.national.anglican.ca/mm. Anglican Church of Canada. Vianney (Sam) Carriere, ed. To produce articles, resources, and information to inspire you and support your ministry. Mag. published 3X/yr. Open to unsolicited freelance. Not in topical listings. (Ads)

NET RESULTS, 5001 Ave. N, Lubbock TX 79412. (806)726-8094. Fax (806)762-8873. E-mail: netresults@netresults.org. Website: www.netresults.org. Net Results, Inc. Karen Medlin, mng. ed. Offers Christian church leaders practical, ministry vitalization ideas and methods. Monthly (10X) & online mag.; 32 pgs.; circ. 12,000. Subscription $29.95. 20% unsolicited freelance; 80% assigned. Query; fax/e-query OK. Accepts full ms through e-mail. **PAYS IN COPIES/SUBSCRIPTION** on publication for one-time rts. Articles 1,000-2,000 wds. (20/yr.). Response time varies. Seasonal 6 mos. ahead. No simultaneous submissions and reprints. Requires accepted ms by e-mail (attached file). No kill fee. Regularly uses sidebars. Prefers NRSV. Copy for 9x12 SAE. (Limited ads)

Tips: "We prefer practical, how-to articles on ideas that have worked in a local church setting."

$THE NEWSLETTER NEWSLETTER, PO Box 36269, Canton OH 44735. Toll-free (800)992-2144. E-mail: jburns@comresources.com. Website: www.newsletternewsletter.com. Communication Resources. John Burns, ed. To help church secretaries and church newsletter editors prepare their newsletter. Monthly & online newsletter; 14 pgs. Subscription $44.95. 0% unsolicited freelance; 70% assigned. Complete ms; e-query OK. Pays $50-150 on acceptance for all rts. Articles 800-1,000 wds. (12/yr.). Responds in 4 wks. Seasonal 8 mos. ahead. Accepts simultaneous submissions. Requires requested ms on disk; accepts e-mail submissions. Kill fee. Regular sidebars. Guidelines (also by e-mail); copy for 9x12 SAE/3 stamps.

Tips: "Most open to how-to articles on various aspects of newsletter production—writing, graphics, layout and design, postal, printing, etc."

OUTREACH MAGAZINE, 2560 Progress St., Vista CA 92083. (760)940-0600. Fax (760)597-2314. E-mail: lwarren@outreachmagazine.com. Website: www.outreachmagazine.org. Lindy Warren, mng. ed. Creative outreach ideas for churches. Bimonthly mag. Subscription $29.95. Not in topical listings. No questionnaire returned.

$PARISH LITURGY, 16565 S. State St., South Holland IL 60473. (708)331-5485. Fax (708)331-5484. E-mail: acp@acpress.org. Website: www.americancatholicpress.org. Catholic. Father Michael Gilligan, ed. dir. A planning tool for Sunday and holy day liturgy. Quarterly mag.; 40 pgs.; circ. 1,200. Subscription $24. 5% unsolicited freelance. Query; no phone/e-query. Pays variable rates for all rts. Articles 400 wds. Responds in 4 wks. Seasonal 4 mos. ahead. Accepts simultaneous submissions and reprints (tell when/where appeared). Uses some sidebars. Prefers NAB. No guidelines; copy available. (No ads)

Tips: "We only use articles on the liturgy—period."

$PASTORAL LIFE, PO Box 595, Canfield OH 44406-0595. (330)533-5503. Fax (330)533-1076. E-mail: plmagazine@hotmail.com. Website: www.albahouse.org. Catholic/Society of St. Paul. Fr. Arthur J. Palisada, assoc. ed. Focuses on the current problems, needs, issues, and all important activities related to all phases of pastoral work and life. Monthly mag.; 64 pgs.; circ. 2,000. Subscription $20. 66% unsolicited freelance; 34% assigned. Query; phone/fax/e-query OK. Pays .04/wd. on publication for 1st or one-time rts. Articles 1,600-2,000 wds., 3,500 wds. max. (30/yr.); book/music/video reviews 500 wds. (no payment). Responds in 5 wks. Seasonal 3-4 mos. ahead. Accepts reprints (tell when/where appeared). Prefers accepted ms by e-mail (attached file or copied into message). No kill fee. Does not use sidebars. Prefers NAB. Guidelines/theme list (also by e-mail); copy for 6x9 SAE/4 stamps. (No ads)

> **Fillers:** Buys 12/yr. Anecdotes, facts, ideas, prayers, prose, quotes, and short humor; to 50 wds; no payment.

> **Special Needs:** Enculturation and minority issues; church and media issues; articles and reflections.

> **Tips:** "Research your work, check our guidelines, and be of use to pastors. We feature pastoral homilies for Sundays and Holy days. Articles should be eminently pastoral in approach and content."

> **This periodical was #47 on the 2003 Top 50 Christian Publishers list (#17 in 2002, #35 in 2001).

PASTORS.COM, 20 Empire Dr., Lake Forest CA 92630-2244. Toll-free (866)829-0300. (929)829-0300. Fax (949)829-0400. E-mail: editor@pastors.com. Website: www.pastors.com. Jon Walker ed. dir. To mentor pastors worldwide. Weekly e-zine; circ. 80,000. Free e-mail newsletter. 30% unsolicited freelance; 30% assigned. Query; fax/e-query OK. **NO PAYMENT** for one-time, reprint, simultaneous, and electronic rts. Articles 500-1,000 wds. (250/yr.); fiction 500-1,000 wds. (25/yr.). Responds in 6-8 wks. Seasonal 4 mos. ahead. Accepts simultaneous submissions and reprints (tell when/where appeared). Prefers accepted ms by e-mail (attached file). Uses some sidebars. Guidelines by e-mail; copy by e-mail. (No ads)

> **Special Needs:** Time management, conflict resolution, facilitating change, communication and preaching, stewardship, worship, lay ministry, temptation, spiritual vitality, family matters, finances, creative ideas for ministry, vision, power, and authority.

> **Tips:** "We're very open to freelance contributions. Although we are unable to pay, this is a worldwide ministry to pastors."

PLUGGED IN, 8605 Explorer Dr., Colorado Springs CO 80920. Toll-free (800)232-6459. (719)531-3400. Fax (719)531-3347. E-mail: waliszrs@fotf.org, or pluggedin@family.org. Website: www.pluggedinmag.com. Focus on the Family. Bob Smithouser, print ed.; Steven Isaac, online ed. Helping parents and youth leaders guide teens through the world of popular youth culture. Monthly & online newsletter; 12 pgs.; circ. 50,000. Subscription $20. Freelance OK. Query. **NO PAYMENT**. No guidelines. Not in topical listings. (No ads)

> **2003 & 1998 EPA Award of Excellence—Newsletter; 2004, 2001, 2000 & 1999 EPA Award of Merit—Newsletter.

$PRAY! PO Box 35004, Colorado Springs CO 80935-3504. (719)531-3555. Fax (719)598-7128. E-mail: pray.mag@navpress.com. Website: www.praymag.com. The Navigators. Jonathan L. Graf, ed.; submit to Sandie Higley, asst. ed. (sandie.higley@navpress.com). A magazine entirely about prayer, geared toward intercessors and prayer mobilizers (pastors and leaders who encourage prayer). Bimonthly mag.; 40-48 pgs.; circ. 39,000. Subscription $19.97. 75% unsolicited freelance; 25% assigned. Complete ms/cover letter (no query); fax/e-query OK. Pays .10/wd. (.05/wd. for reprints) on acceptance for 1st, reprint, and electronic rts. Articles 800-1,500 wds., or 500 wds. or less. (30/yr.). Responds in 12-16 wks. Accepts simultaneous submissions and reprints (tell when/where appeared). Prefers e-mail submission (copied into message). Kill fee 50%. Regularly uses sidebars. Prefers NIV. Guidelines (also by e-mail/Website); copy for 9x12 SAE/$1.42 postage (mark "Media Mail"). (Ads)

Fillers: Ideas on prayer; 75-500 wds.; $20.

Special Needs: Starting an 8-page section just for pastors, so needs articles for pastors, written by pastors. Also needs nontheme feature articles on various aspects of prayer.

Tips: "We most frequently purchase short material for our Ideas section. If you submit a general article it better be unique. Most of our theme articles are assigned."

**#9 Best-selling Magazine in Christian retail stores. This periodical was #36 on the 2004 Top 50 Christian Publishers list (#37 in 2003, #34 in 2002, #18 in 2001, #28 in 2000).

$PREACHING, PO Box 681868, Franklin TN 37068-1868. (615)599-9889. Fax (615)599-8985. E-mail: editor@preaching.com. Website: www.preaching.com. American Ministry Resources LLC. Dr. Michael Duduit, ed. Professional magazine for evangelical preachers; focus is on preaching and worship leadership. Bimonthly mag.; 80 pgs.; circ. 9,000. Subscription $39.95. 70% unsolicited freelance; 20% assigned. Query; fax/e-query OK. Pays $35-50 on publication for one-time & electronic rts. Articles 1,200-1,500 wds. (25-35/yr.). Responds in 4-8 wks. Seasonal 1 yr. ahead. No simultaneous submissions or reprints. Accepts requested ms by e-mail (attached file). Uses some sidebars. Guidelines on Website; copy $5. (Ads)

Fillers: Buys 10-15/yr. Cartoons only; $25.

Tips: "Need how-to articles about specific areas of preaching and worship leadership. We only accept articles from pastors or seminary/college faculty."

PREACHING ON-LINE, 133 Holiday Ct., Ste. 111, Franklin TN 37067. (615)599-9889. Fax (615)599-8985. E-mail: mail@preaching.com. Website: www.preaching.com. American Ministry Resources. Dr. Michael Duduit, ed. An online professional resource for pastors. Monthly online e-zine; circ. 1,500. Subscription $39.95. 30% unsolicited freelance; 70% assigned. Query; fax/e-query OK. **PAYS A SUBSCRIPTION** for one-time and electronic rts. Responds in 4-8 wks. Seasonal 10-12 mos. ahead. Reprints from books only. Prefers requested ms on disk or by e-mail (attached file). Uses some sidebars. Guidelines on Website; copy online. (Ads)

$PREACHINGTODAY.COM, 465 Gundersen Dr., Carol Stream IL 60188-2498. (630)260-6200. Fax (630)260-8428. E-mail: editor@preachingtoday.com. Website: www.preaching today.com. Christianity Today Intl. Open to fresh sermon illustrations from various sources for preachers (no recycled illustrations from other illustration sources). E-mail submissions only. Guidelines on Website. Sermon illustrations only.

$THE PRIEST, 200 Noll Plaza, Huntington IN 46750-4304. (260)356-8400. Fax (260)359-0029. E-mail: tpriest@osv.com. Website: www.osv.com. Catholic/Our Sunday Visitor, Inc. Msgr. Owen F. Campion, ed. For Catholic priests, deacons, and seminarians; to help in all aspects of ministry. Monthly jour.; 48 pgs.; circ. 6,500. Subscription $39.95. 25% unsolicited freelance. Query (preferred) or complete ms/cover letter; phone/fax/e-query OK. Pays $175-250 on acceptance for 1st rts. Articles 1,500-5,000 wds. (45/yr.); some 2-parts. Responds in 3-5 wks. Seasonal 6 mos. ahead. Uses some sidebars. Prefers disk or e-mail submissions (attached file). Prefers NAB. Free guidelines; copy for 9x12 SASE. (Ads)

Fillers: Murray Hubley, fillers ed. Cartoons; $35.

Columns/Departments: Buys 36/yr. Viewpoint, to 1,000 wds.; $75.

Tips: "Write to the point, with interest. Most open to nuts-and-bolts issues for priests, or features. Keep the audience in mind; need articles or topics important to priests and parish life. Include Social Security number."

**This periodical was #41 on the 2001 Top 50 Christian Publishers list (#43 in 2000, #49 in 1999).

$PROCLAIM, PO Box 1561, New Canaan CT 06840. (203)966-6470. Fax (203)966-4654. E-mail: meg@parishpublishing.org. Website: www.parishpublishing.org. Parish Publishing, LLC. Guy Brossy, principal. The leading inspirational preaching resource for church leaders. Weekly newsletter; 4 pgs. Subscription $59.95. 20% unsolicited freelance; 80% assigned. Query/clips. Pays to $100 on publication or acceptance for reprint rts. Articles or fiction. Responds in 2 wks. Seasonal 3 mos. ahead. Prefers accepted mss by e-mail (attached file). (No ads)

> **Tips:** "*Proclaim* follows the Catholic Lectionary and the Revised Common Lectionary (RCL). Writers are usually priests and ministers, or in seminary."

PULPIT HELPS, 6815 Shallowford Rd., Chattanooga TN 37421. Toll-free (800)251-7206. (423)894-6060. Fax (423)510-8074. E-mail: publisher@pulpithelps.com. Website: www.pulpithelps.com. AMG International. Bob Dasal, ed-in-chief. To help evangelical preachers and serious students of the Bible. Monthly & online tabloid; 36 pgs.; circ. 75,000. Subscription $22.99. 25% unsolicited freelance; 75% assigned. Query; e-query OK. **NO PAYMENT**. Articles 700-900 wds. (60-80/yr.); book reviews 400 wds. Responds in 4 wks. Seasonal 4 mos. ahead. Accepts simultaneous submissions and reprints (tell when/where appeared). Accepts e-mail submission (attached or copied into message). Uses some sidebars. Prefers KJV. Guidelines/theme list (also by e-mail); copy for 9x12 SAE/2 stamps. (Ads)

> **Poetry:** Accepts 10-12/yr. Traditional; short. Submit max. 3 poems.
>
> **Fillers:** Ted Kyle, fillers ed. Accepts 10-20/yr. Anecdotes, cartoons, prose, quotes, short humor, word puzzles; 300-500 wds.
>
> **Columns/Departments:** Ted Kyle, mng. ed. Family Helps, 100-1,000 wds.; Illustrations (for sermons), 50-100 wds.; Sermon Starters (brief).
>
> **Tips:** "Most open to Illustrations and Sermon Starters—short, pointed anecdotes/articles preachers can use as illustrations. Follow submission guidelines."

QUARTERLY REVIEW: A Journal of Theological Resources for Ministry, 1001—19th Ave. S., PO Box 340007, Nashville TN 37203-0007. (615)340-7334. Fax (615)340-7048. E-mail: hpieterse@gbhem.org. Website: www.quarterlyreview.org. United Methodist. Dr. Hendrik R. Pieterse, ed. A theological approach to subjects of interest to clergy—Scripture study, ethics, and practice of ministry in Wesleyan tradition. Quarterly jour.; 112 pgs.; circ. 1,100. Subscription $24. 20% unsolicited; 80% assigned. Complete ms/cover letter; phone/fax/e-query OK. **PAYS IN COPIES** for 1st rts. Articles to 5,000 wds. (20/yr.); book reviews to 1,000 wds. Responds in 6-8 wks. Seasonal 8 mos. ahead. Prefers requested ms on disk, no e-mail submission. No sidebars. Prefers NRSV. Guidelines/theme list (also by e-mail); copy for 9x12 SAE/$1.42 postage (mark "Media Mail"). (No ads)

> **Tips:** "A section called 'Outside the Theme' is reserved for articles of high quality unrelated to the theme of the issue. I often consider unsolicited manuscripts for this section. We look for writers who have strong academic/theological training and whose work addresses concerns and interests of those in ministry. Awareness of current scholarly literature, a well-developed argument, and clear expository prose are essential."

$REFORMED WORSHIP, 2850 Kalamazoo SE, Grand Rapids MI 49560-0001. Toll-free (800)777-7270. Fax (616)224-0834. E-mail: info@reformedworship.org. Website: www.reformedworship.org. Christian Reformed Church in North America. Dr. Emily R. Brink, ed. To provide liturgical and musical resources for pastors, church musicians, and other worship leaders. Quarterly mag.; 48 pgs.; circ. 5,000. Subscription $25.95. 10% unsolicited freelance; 70% assigned. Query or complete ms/cover letter; e-query OK. Pays .05/wd. on publication for all rts. (negotiable). Articles 2,000 wds.; book reviews 250 wds.

Responds in 4 wks. Seasonal 6 mos. ahead. Rarely accepts reprints (tell when/where appeared). Prefers e-mail submission (copied into message). Regularly uses sidebars. Prefers NRSV. Guidelines/theme list (also by e-mail); copy for 9x12 SAE/$1.42 postage (mark "Media Mail"). (No ads)

Columns/Departments: Songs for the Season (music and background notes, usually 3 songs), 2,000 wds.; Worship Technology (intersection of worship and technology), 900 wds. Query.

Tips: "You need to understand the Reformed tradition of worship."

**2004 EPA Award of Merit—General.

$REV. MAGAZINE, PO Box 481, Loveland CO 80539-0481. (970)669-3836. Fax (970)292-4373. E-mail: info@grouppublishing.com. Website: www.onlinerev.com. Group Publishing, Inc. Kristi Rector, ed.; Cary Dunlap, Web ed. For pastors; partnering with pastors. Bimonthly & online mag.; 104 pgs.; circ. 30,000. Subscription $24.86. 40% unsolicited freelance; 60% assigned. Complete ms/cover letter; e-query OK. Pays $300-500 on acceptance for all rts. Articles 1,500-2,000 wds. Responds in 6-8 wks. Seasonal 6-8 mos. ahead. Prefers requested ms on disk or by e-mail (attached file). Regularly uses sidebars. Guidelines (also on Website); copy $2/9x12 SAE/5 stamps. (Ads)

Fillers: Buys 5-10/yr. Cartoons, ideas, sermon illustrations; $30-50.

Columns/Departments: Ministry (preaching, worship, discipleship, outreach, family); Life (personal growth, health beat, home front); Leadership (church business, team work, leadership); Insight (today's trends, current culture, in the know); all 150-300 wds; $35-50.

Tips: "We are most open to short (250 word) practical articles for our departments. Write articles that deal with personal and professional topics for pastors."

$REVIEW FOR RELIGIOUS, 3601 Lindell Blvd., Rm. 428, St. Louis MO 63108-3393. (314)977-7363. Fax (314)977-7362. E-mail: review@slu.edu. Website: www.reviewforreligious.org. Catholic/Jesuits of Missouri Province. Rev. David L. Fleming, S.J., ed. A forum for shared reflection on the lives and experience of all who find that the church's rich heritages of spirituality support their personal and apostolic Christian lives. Quarterly mag.; 112 pgs.; circ. 7,000. Subscription $24. 100% unsolicited freelance. Complete ms/cover letter; no phone/fax/e-query. Pays $6/pg. on publication for 1st rts. Articles 1,500-5,000 wds. (50/yr.). Responds in 9 wks. Seasonal 8 mos. ahead. Accepts requested ms on disk. Does not use sidebars. Prefers RSV, NAB. Guidelines (also by e-mail); copy for 10x13 SAE/5 stamps. (No ads)

Poetry: Buys 10/yr. Light verse, traditional; 3-12 lines; $6. Submit max. 4 poems.

Tips: "Be familiar with at least three past issues. Submit an article based on our guidelines."

$THE REVWRITER RESOURCE, PO Box 81, Perkasie PA 18944. (215)453-5066. Fax (215)453-8128. E-mail: editor@revwriter.com. Website: www.revwriter.com. Nondenominational. Rev. Susan M. Lang, ed. An electronic newsletter for busy lay and clergy congregational leaders. Monthly e-zine.; circ. 200. Subscription free. 50% unsolicited freelance; 50% assigned. Query; e-query preferred. Pays $20 on publication for 1st electronic rts. and one-year archival rts. Articles 800-1,000 wds.; questions or exercises for group use 250-500 wds. No simultaneous submissions or reprints. Guidelines on Website; copy online. Incomplete topical listings. (No ads)

Fillers: Buys 10/yr. Ideas; Ministry Resources List to accompany article; 250-400 wds. These are usually written by the feature-article writer.

Tips: "Articles should be practical how-tos for busy church leaders—materials they can use in their ministry settings. Be sure to read archived issues for previous formats and ministry resources already covered. Looking for a new approach to stewardship. Most open to devotion writing in Lent and Advent, and the monthly articles and discussion questions. Send me an e-query detailing the article you'd like to write and include your expertise in this area. The material must be practical and applicable to life as a busy congregational leader. They want information they can use."

$SABBATH SCHOOL LEADERSHIP, 55 W. Oak Ridge Dr., Hagerstown MD 21740. (301)393-4094. E-mail: fcrumbly@rhpa.org. Website: www.Sabbathschool.com. Seventh-day Adventist/Review & Herald. Faith Crumbly, ed. Nurtures, educates, and supports adult Bible study and program leaders by providing training in leadership and interpersonal skills plus programs. Monthly mag.; 32 pgs.; circ. 9,000. Subscription $30.95 (add $6 for addresses outside US, Canada, and Bermuda). 10% unsolicited freelance; 90% assigned. Complete ms. Pays $25-100 on acceptance for 1st rts. Articles 600-1,200 wds. (120-150/yr.). Responds in 1-2 wks. Seasonal 6-8 mos. ahead. Accepts reprints (tell when/where appeared). Prefers accepted ms by e-mail (attached file). Uses some sidebars. Guidelines/theme list; copy. (For ads, contact: Margie Tooley at margie.tooley@rhpa.org.)

Fillers: Cartoons; $70-100.

Columns/Departments: Buys 5/yr. Leadership Tips (interpersonal skills, organization, mentoring, training), 600-800 wds. Query. Pays $70-100.

$SERMON NOTES, 1420 Osborne St., Ste. 10, PO Box 68, Humboldt TN 38343. (731)784-3400. Fax (731)784-7469. E-mail: stevemay@sermonnotes.com. Website: www.sermonnotes.com. Christianity Today. Stephen May, ed. Sermon helps for ministers. Quarterly & online mag.; 96 pgs.; circ. 5,000. Subscription $39. 25% unsolicited freelance. Complete ms/cover letter; fax/e-query OK. Pays $35-50 for articles and sermons ($5 for illustrations) on publication for one-time rts. Sermons & articles (8/yr.) 1,500 wds.; illustrations 80-100 wds.; book reviews 500 wds., $20. Responds in 5 wks. Seasonal 4 mos. ahead. Accepts reprints (tell when/ where appeared). Prefers requested ms on disk. Regularly uses sidebars. Prefers NIV. Guidelines/theme list; copy $2/6x9 SAE. (Ads)

Fillers: Buys 12/yr. Cartoons, short humor, or church newsletter ideas; $15.

Columns/Departments: Buys 6/yr. Q&A (interview with Christian leader), 1,000-1,500 wds.; Pastor's Library (book or product review), 500 wds.; $35-50.

Tips: "We are always interested in sermons. Right now we have an even greater interest in articles about church growth, preaching, or about a particular minister who is pastoring a growing church of any size." Also publishes on diskette.

SEWANEE THEOLOGICAL REVIEW, University of the South, 335 Tennessee Ave., Sewanee TN 37383-0001. (931)598-1475. E-mail: STR@sewanee.edu. Website: www.sewanee.edu/theology/str/strhome. Anglican/Episcopal. Jim D. Jones, mng. ed. For Anglican/Episcopal clergy and interested laity. Quarterly jour.; 120 pgs. Subscription $21. Open to freelance. Complete ms/cover letter; no e-query. **NO PAYMENT** for all rts. Articles (24/yr.). Responds in 9-26 wks. Seasonal 24 mos. ahead. No simultaneous submissions or reprints. Prefers requested ms on disk or by e-mail (attached file). Prefers NRSV. No guidelines; copy $7. Incomplete topical listings.

Special Needs: Anglican and Episcopal theology, religion, history, doctrine, ethics, homiletics, liturgies, hermeneutics, biography, prayer, practice.

SHARING THE PRACTICE, 100 S. Chestnut St., Kent OH 44240-3402. (330)678-0187. E-mail: dunmovin720@aol.com. Website: www.apclergy.org. Academy of Parish Clergy/Ecumenical/Interfaith. Dr. Donald W. Shilling, ed-in-chief. Growth toward excellence through sharing the practice of parish ministry. Quarterly international jour.; 40 pgs.; circ. 250 (includes 80 seminary libraries and publishers). Subscription $25/yr. (send to: APC, 2249 Florinda St., Sarasota FL 34231-1414). 100% unsolicited freelance. Complete ms/cover letter; e-query OK. **PAYS IN COPIES** for 1st, reprint, simultaneous, or electronic rts. Articles 500-2,500 wds. (25/yr.); reviews 200 wds. Responds in 2 wks. Seasonal 6 mos. ahead.

Accepts simultaneous submissions and reprints (tell when/where appeared). Prefers e-mail submissions (copied into message). Uses some sidebars. Prefers NRSV. Guidelines/theme list (also by e-mail); free copy. (No ads)

Poetry: Accepts 12/yr. Any type; 25-35 lines. Submit max. 2 poems.

Fillers: Accepts 6/yr. Anecdotes, cartoons, jokes, short humor; 50-100 wds.

Contest: Book of the Year Award ($100+), Top Ten Books of the Year list, Parish Pastor of the Year Award ($200+). Inquire by e-mail to: DIELPADRE@aol.com.

Tips: "We desire articles and poetry by practicing clergy of all kinds who wish to share their practice of ministry."

$SMALL GROUP DYNAMICS, PO Box 621, Zionville IN 46077. (317)769-0945. E-mail: office@smallgroups.com. Website: http://smallgroups.com. Small Group Network. Dan Lentz, owner. How-to for small groups. Online e-zine/newsletter. Query; e-query OK. Pays $40-60 for all rts. Articles 500-1,000 wds. Seasonal 2-3 mos. ahead. Prefers requested ms by e-mail (attached file). Accepts reprints. Prefers NIV. Guidelines/theme list: http://small groups.com/themes.htm.

Fillers: Small group cartoons.

Special Needs: Brief testimonies of how God has worked in your group; humor in groups; icebreaker ideas, etc.

Tips: "Follow our themes. We use mostly practical, how-to oriented articles."

$SPIRITUAL SPINACH, PO Box 3102, Margate NJ 08402. Toll-free (800)827-9401. (609)822-9401. Fax (609)822-1638. E-mail: sermons@voicings.com. Website: www .voicings.com. Voicings Publications. James Colaianni Jr., pub. Sermon illustration resource for professional clergy. Monthly newsletter, 12 pgs. Subscription $37.50. 5% unsolicited freelance; 0% assigned. Complete ms; e-query OK. Pays .10/wd. on publication for any rts. Illustrations/anecdotes 50-250 wds. Responds in 6 wks. Seasonal 4 mos. ahead. Accepts reprints. Prefers requested ms on disk or by e-mail. Guidelines/topical index (also by e-mail); copy for 9x12 SAE. (Ads)

Poetry: Light verse, traditional; 50-250 lines; .10/wd. Submit max. 3 poems.

Fillers: Various; sermon illustrations; 50-250 wds.; .10/wd.

Tips: "All sections open."

STRATEGIC ADULT MINISTRIES ONLINE JOURNAL, 4050 Lee Vance View, Colorado Springs CO 80918. (719)536-0100, ext. 3438. Fax (719)536-3202. E-mail: samresources@cook ministries.org. Website: www.samresources.com. Cook Communications Ministries. Susan Tjaden, mng. ed. For pastors and lay leaders involved in ministry with single or young adults. Online jour. 10% unsolicited freelance. Query; fax/e-query OK. **USUALLY NO PAYMENT** for 1st rts. Articles 200-2,500 wds. (2/yr.); book reviews 50-300 wds. ($15-75). Responds in 4 wks. Seasonal 1 yr. ahead. Accepts simultaneous submissions and reprints (tell when/where appeared). Prefers e-mail submission (copied into message). Prefers NIV. Theme list; copy online.

Fillers: Buys 0-5/yr. Facts, newsbreaks, quotes; 25-200 wds.; $10-50.

Tips: "Write to the pastor or leader, not to the singles or young adults themselves. Interview young adults or the leaders who work with them. Want very practical, how-to or 600-word essay on a controversial topic of interest to young adult leaders." This publication is making the transition from a print to an online publication.

STRATEGIES FOR TODAY'S LEADER, 1230 US Hwy. 6, Corunna IN 46730. Accepts freelance. Not in topical listings. No questionnaire returned.

$SUNDAY SERMONS, PO Box 3102, Margate NJ 08402. Toll-free (800)827-9401. (609)822-9401. Fax (609)822-1638. E-mail: sermons@voicings.com. Website: www.voicings.com. Voicings Publications. James Colaianni Jr., pub. Full-text sermon resource serving professional clergy since 1970. Bimonthly booklet; 60 pgs. Subscription $77. 5% unsolicited freelance; 0% assigned. Complete ms; e-query OK. Pays .10/wd. on publication for any rts. Complete sermon manuscripts 1,200-1,500 wds.; illustrations/anecdotes 50-250 wds. Responds in 6 wks. Seasonal 4 mos. ahead. Accepts reprints. Prefers requested ms on disk or by e-mail. Guidelines/topical index (also by e-mail); copy for 9x12 SAE. Not in topical listings.

Fillers: Various; sermon illustrations; 50-250 wds.; .10/wd.

Tips: "Submit complete sermon, 1,200-1,500 words."

#TECHNOLOGIES FOR WORSHIP, 3891 Holborn Rd., Queensville ON L0G 1R0 Canada. (905)473-9822. Fax (905)473-9928. E-mail: krc@tfwm.com, or info@tfwm.com. Website: www.tfwm.com. ITC Inc. Kevin Rogers Cobus, ed. Bimonthly & online mag.; 92+ pgs.; circ. 35,000. Subscription $29.95 US. 100% unsolicited freelance. Query; phone/fax/e-query OK. **NO PAYMENT** for one-time rts. Articles 700-1,200 wds. Responds in 2 wks. Seasonal 2 mos. ahead. Accepts simultaneous submissions and reprints (tell when/where appeared). Prefers accepted ms by e-mail (attached or copied into message). Uses some sidebars. Free guidelines/theme list (also on Website)/copy. (Ads)

Special Needs: Website streaming resources for churches and ministries; technologies: audio, video, music, computers, broadcast, lighting, and drama; 750-2,500 wds.

Tips: "Call/fax/e-mail the editor to discuss idea for article or column. The publication is open to technical, educational articles that can benefit the church, providing hints, tips, guidelines, examples, studies, tutorials, etc. on new technology and new uses for it in the church."

+THEOLOGICAL DIGEST & OUTLOOK, 415 Linwell Rd., St. Catherines ON L2M 2P3 Canada. (905)935-5369. Fax (905)935-7134. E-mail: p-d@magara.com. Website: www.church alivecanada.org. United Church of Canada. Paul Miller, ed. For clergy and informed laity; evangelical/orthodox slant within denomination. Semiannual mag.; 32 pgs.; circ. 400. Subscription $15 CAN, $19 US. 100% unsolicited freelance. Complete ms; phone/fax/e-query OK. **NO PAYMENT.** Articles 1,500-5,000 wds. (6-8/yr.). Responds in 2 wks. Accepts reprints (tell when/where appeared). Prefers disk or e-mail submissions. No sidebars. Any Bible version. No guidelines. (No ads)

$THEOLOGY TODAY, PO Box 821, Princeton NJ 08542-0803. (609)497-7714. Fax (609)497-7870. E-mail: theology.today@ptsem.edu. Website: http://theologytoday.ptsem.edu. Patrick D. Miller (patrick.miller@ptsem.edu) & Ellen T. Charry (ellen.charry@ptsem.edu), eds. Explores key issues, current thoughts and trends in the fields of religion and theology. Quarterly jour.; 144-160 pgs.; circ. 14,000. Subscription $29. 50% unsolicited freelance; 50% assigned. Complete ms/cover letter and disk; phone query OK. Pays to $250 on publication for all rts. Articles 13-17 manuscript pgs. Responds in several wks. Seasonal 1 yr. ahead. Regularly uses sidebars. Guidelines (also by e-mail/Website); free copy. (Display ads)

Poetry: Buys 12/yr. Free verse, traditional; $50. Submit max. 5 poems.

Tips: "We rarely accept unsolicited material, but do look for new talent. The best route to acceptance is strong familiarity with the journal and types of articles we publish. We expect inclusive language."

$THIS ROCK, 2020 Gillespie Way, El Cajon CA 92020. (619)387-7200. Fax (619)387-0042. E-mail: editor@catholic.com. Website: www.catholic.com. Catholic Answers. Tim Ryland, ed. Deals with doctrine, evangelization, and apologetics. Monthly (10X) mag.; 48 pgs.; circ. 20,745. Subscription $39.95. 60% unsolicited freelance. Query or complete ms/cover letter; e-query OK. Pays .10/wd. on acceptance for 1st or one-time rts. Articles 1,500-2,500 wds. (25/yr.); book reviews 800 wds. Responds in 4-6 wks. Prefers RSV (Catholic version). No simultaneous submissions or reprints. Prefers e-mail submissions (attached file). Kill fee. Uses some sidebars. Guidelines (also by e-mail); copy for 9x12 SAE/$1.42 postage (mark "Media Mail"). (No ads)

$TODAY'S CHRISTIAN PREACHER, PO Box 100, Morgantown PA 19543. (610)856-6830. Fax (610)856-6831. E-mail: publications@rightideas.us. Right Ideas, Inc. Jerry Thacker, ed. To provide material on current topics to help preachers in their personal lives. Quarterly mag.; 20 pgs.; circ. 25,000. Subscription free. 20% unsolicited freelance; 80% assigned. Complete ms/cover letter; fax/e-query OK. Pays $150 on publication for one-time or simultaneous rts. Articles 800-1,000 wds. (16/yr., 2-3 freelance). Responds in 6-8 wks. Seasonal 1 yr. ahead. Accepts simultaneous submissions and reprints (tell when/where appeared). Prefers requested ms by e-mail. Requires KJV. Guidelines (also by e-mail); copy for 9x12 SAE/3 stamps. (No ads)

> **Tips:** "Most open to very practical articles on everyday life—not sermons or how to run a church."

$TODAY'S PARISH, Box 180, Mystic CT 06355. (860)536-2611. Fax (860)536-5674. Catholic. Daniel Connors, ed. Practical ideas and issues relating to parish life, management, and ministry. Mag. published 7X/yr.; 40 pgs.; circ. 14,800. Subscription $24.95. Very little unsolicited freelance. Query or complete ms. Pays $75-100 on publication for 1st rts. Articles 800-1,800 wds. (15/yr.). Responds 13 wks. Seasonal 6 mos. ahead. Guidelines; copy for 9x12 SASE.

$WCA NEWS, PO Box 3188, Barrington IL 60011-5046. (847)765-0070. Fax (847)765-5046. E-mail: BraoudaP@willowcreek.org. Website: www.willowcreek.com. Willow Creek Assn. Paul Braoudakis, mng. ed. For church leaders who are willing to take risks for the sake of the gospel. Quarterly & online newsletter; 28 pgs.; circ. 10,000. Subscription $39. 10% unsolicited; 25-30% assigned. Query/clips or complete ms; phone/fax/e-query OK. Pays .20/wd. on publication for all rts. Articles 500-1,000 wds.; book/music reviews 500 wds., video reviews 300 wds. Responds in 2 wks. Seasonal 2 mos. ahead. Accepts simultaneous submissions and reprints (tell when/where appeared). Requires requested ms on disk or by e-mail (attached file). Some sidebars. Prefers NIV. Free copy. (No ads)

> **Fillers:** Buys cartoons, ideas, short humor; 50-75 wds.; $10.

> **Columns/Departments:** News From the Frontlines (creative ministries within the church), 50-100 wds.; Strategic Trends (trends from growing churches), 200-250 wds.; $10-25. Complete ms.

> **Tips:** "Submit articles that will help other churches do what they do better. Any articles that pertain to doing a seeker-sensitive type of ministry will be considered. Also leadership issues in the church, outreach ideas, and effective evangelism."

$WORD & WORLD: Theology for Christian Ministry, 2481 Como Ave., St. Paul MN 55108. (651)641-3482. Fax (651)641-3354. Website: www.luthersem.edu/word&world. E.L.C.A./Luther Theological Seminary. Frederick J. Gaiser, ed. Addresses ecclesiastical and secular issues from a theological perspective and addresses pastors and church leaders with the best fruits of theological research. Quarterly jour.; 104 pgs.; circ. 2,500. Subscription $24. 10% unsolicited freelance. Complete ms/cover letter; phone query OK. Pays $50 on publication for all rts. Articles 3,500 wds. Responds in 2-8 wks. Guidelines/theme list; copy $7.

> **Tips:** "Most open to general articles. We look for serious theology addressed clearly and interestingly to people in the practice of ministry. Creativity and usefulness in ministry are highly valued."

$WORSHIP LEADER, 26311 Junipero Serra, Ste. 130, San Juan Capistrano CA 92675. (949)240-9339. Fax (949)240-0038. E-mail: editor@wlmag.com. Website: www.worship leader.com. Worship Leader Partnership. Julie Reid, exec. ed. A resource for current trends, theological insights, and planning programs for all those involved in church worship. Bimonthly mag.; 64-72 pgs.; circ. 45,000. Subscription $19.95. 20% unsolicited freelance; 80% assigned. Complete ms. by fax/e-mail OK. Pays $200-800 for assigned, $200-

500 for unsolicited, on publication for all or 1st rts. Articles 1,200-2,000 wds. (15-30/yr.); reviews 300 wds. Responds in 6-13 wks. Seasonal 6 mos. ahead. Accepts e-mail submissions (attached file—MS Word). Kill fee 50%. Uses some sidebars. Prefers NIV. Guidelines/theme list (also by e-mail); copy $5. (Ads)

Tips: "Read our magazine. Become familiar with our themes. Submit a detailed and well-thought-out idea that fits our vision."

**2003 EPA Award of Merit—Christian Ministries.

$YOUR CHURCH, 465 Gundersen Dr., Carol Stream IL 60188. (630)260-6200. Fax (630)260-0114. E-mail: YCEditor@yourchuch.net. Website: www.yourchurch.net. Christianity Today Intl. Harold Smith, exec. ed.; submit to Mike Schreiter, mng. ed. We give pastors and church leaders practical information to help them in managing the business side of the church. Bimonthly trade journal; 80+ pgs.; circ. 150,000. Subscription free to church administrators. 10% unsolicited freelance; 90% assigned. Query; phone/fax/e-query OK. Query for electronic submissions. Pays .15/wd. on acceptance for 1st and electronic rts. Articles 1,000-2,000 wds. (60/yr.). Responds in 2-4 wks. Seasonal 6 mos. ahead. Accepts reprints (tell when/where appeared). Prefers e-mail submission (attached file). Accepts full manuscripts by e-mail. Kill fee 50%. Uses some sidebars. Prefers NIV. Guidelines/theme list; copy for $1 postage. (Ads: 630-260-6202)

Fillers: Cartoons, $125.

Columns/Departments: Leadership Notes (tips on leadership from high-profile writer—often an article or book excerpt, but also original material).

Special Needs: Church management articles; audio/visual equipment; books/curriculum resources; music equipment; church products; furnishings; office equipment; computers/software; transportation (bus, van); video projectors; church architecture/construction.

Tips: "Write and ask to be considered for an assignment; tell of your background, experience, strengths, and writing history. Most assigned articles include a list of companies that must be interviewed. Unsolicited manuscripts should be informative, how-to articles without referring to any companies. Direct information to nontechnical readership (pastors and church administrators)."

**This periodical was #46 on the 2004 Top 50 Christian Publishers list (#50 in 2003, #44 in 2002, #46 in 2001, #48 in 2000).

YOUTHCULTURE@TODAY, PO Box 414, Elizabethtown PA 17022-0414. (717)361-8429. Fax (717)361-8964. E-mail: cpyu@cpyu.org, or media@cpyu.org. Website: www.cpyu.org. Center for Parent/Youth Understanding. Walt Mueller, pres. To equip parents, teens, and youth workers with analysis and commentary on youth culture and cross-generational ministry. Quarterly & online mag.; 24 pgs.; circ. 10,000. Subscription $15 donation. 100% assigned. (No ads)

**2003, 2000 EPA Award of Merit—Newsletter.

$YOUTHWORKER: The Contemporary Journal for Youth Ministry, 104 Woodmont Blvd., Ste. 300, Nashville TN 37205. (615)312-4250. Fax (615)385-4112. E-mail: Will@Youth-Specialties.com. Website: www.Youthworker.com. Salem Communications. Will Penner, ed. For youth workers/church and parachurch. Bimonthly & online jour.; 72 pgs.; circ. 20,000. Subscription $39.95. 80% unsolicited freelance. Query or complete ms (only if already written); e-query preferred. Pays $200-300 on acceptance for all rts. Articles 1,500-3,000 wds. (30/yr.); length may vary. Responds in 8 wks. Seasonal 10 mos. ahead. No reprints. Kill fee $50. Guidelines/theme list (also on Website); copy $3/10x13 SAE. (Ads)

Columns/Departments: Buys 10/yr. International Youth Ministry, and Technology in Youth Ministry.

Tips: "Read *Youthworker*; imbibe its tone (professional, though not academic; conversational,

though not chatty). Query me with specific, focused ideas that conform to our editorial style. It helps if the writer is a youth minister, but it's not required. Check *Youthworker* Website for additional info, upcoming themes, etc."
**This periodical was #38 on the 1999 Top 50 Christian Publishers list. 2003 Award of Merit—Most Improved Publication & 2003 Award of Excellence—Christian Ministries; 2000, 1999, 1998 EPA Award of Merit—Christian Ministries.

TEEN/YOUNG ADULT MARKETS

$BOUNDLESS WEBZINE, 8605 Explorer Dr., Colorado Springs CO 80920. (714)548-5928. Fax (719)548-5860. E-mail: roeberdb@fotf.org, or editor@boundless.org. Website: www.boundless.org. Focus on the Family. Blake Roeber, ed. For college students exploring love, faith, and cultural issues in the context of a Christian world-view. Online Web mag. 20,000 visitors/wk. 15% unsolicited freelance; 85% assigned. E-query. Pays .35-.40/wd. on publication for one-time rts. Articles 700-1,200 wds. (5/yr.); reviews 700-1,200 wds. Responds in 3 wks. Seasonal 1-2 mos. ahead. Accepts simultaneous submissions and reprints (tell when/where appeared). Requires e-mail submission (attached and copied into message). Prefers NIV. Guidelines (by e-mail/Website); copy online. (No ads)
   Columns/Departments: Pages (book reviews/excerpt); @Play (entertainment/culture); Beyond Buddies (relationships); Campus Culture (college life/issues); Head and Heart (spirituality); Finding Your Place (career/future planning); Isms & Ologies (world-view); The Podium (speeches); all 1,000-2,000 wds., 20-.40/wd.
   Tips: "Develop an understanding of Web journalism and a voice that will compel college students."
   **2004 EPA Award of Merit—Online. This periodical was #22 on the 2004 Top 50 Christian Publishers list (#32 in 2003, #23 in 2002, #27 in 2001, #23 in 2000).

$BREAKAWAY, 8605 Explorer Dr., Colorado Springs CO 80921. (719)531-3400. Fax (719)531-3499. E-mail: breakaway@family.org. Website: www.breakawaymag.com. Focus on the Family. Michael Ross, ed. The 15-year-old unchurched teen (boy) in the public school is our target; boys 12-17 yrs. Monthly mag.; 32 pgs.; circ. 95,000. Subscription $18. 10% unsolicited freelance; 75% assigned. Complete ms/cover letter only; no phone/fax/e-query. Pays .12-.15/wd. on acceptance for 1st, one-time, or electronic rts. Articles 400-1,000 wds. (2-3/yr.); fiction to 2,000 wds. (2-3/yr.). Responds in 8-10 wks. Seasonal 6 mos. ahead. No simultaneous submissions or reprints. Kill fee 25%. Uses some sidebars. Accepts submissions from teens. Prefers NIV. Guidelines & copy (call 1-800-232-6459). (No ads)
   Columns/Departments: Buys 5-6/yr. Truth Encounter (devotional); 700-900 wds.
   Tips: "Most open to nontypical, historical, and biblical fiction. Need strong lead. Brevity and levity a must. Have a teen guy or two read it. Make sure the language is up to date, but not overly hip." Needs drama-in-life stories involving boys.
   **2004, 2003, 1999 EPA Award of Merit—Youth. This periodical was #7 on the 2003 Top 50 Christian Publishers list (#2 in 2002, #10 in 2001,#8 in 2000, #7 in 1999).

$BRIO, 8605 Explorer Dr., Colorado Springs CO 80920. (719)531-3400. Fax (719)531-3499. E-mail: brio@mm.fotf.org. Website: www.briomag.com. Focus on the Family. Susie Shellenberger, ed.; submit to Mrs. Marty Kasza, assoc. ed. For teen girls, 12-15 yrs. Monthly mag.; 38-48 pgs.; circ. 206,000. Subscription $18. 25-50% unsolicited freelance; 50-75% assigned. Complete ms/cover letter; e-query OK. Pays .08-.15/wd. on acceptance for 1st rts. Articles 800-1,000 wds. (10/yr.); fiction 1,200-2,000 wds. (10/yr.). Accepts requested ms by e-mail or disk. Responds in 2-4 wks. Seasonal 8 mos. ahead. Rare kill fee $100. Uses some sidebars. Guidelines (also by e-mail); copy $1.50. (No ads)

Special Needs: All topics of interest to female teens are welcome: boys, makeup, dating, weight, ordinary girls who have extraordinary experiences, female adjustments to puberty, etc. Also teen-related female fiction.

Tips: "Study at least 3 issues of *Brio* before submitting. We're looking for a certain fresh, hip-hop, conversational style. Most open to fiction, articles, and quizzes."

**#5 Best-selling Magazine in Christian retail stores. Also 2001 & 1995 EPA Award of Merit—Youth. This periodical was #50 on the 2004 Top 50 Christian Publishers list.

$BRIO AND BEYOND, 8605 Explorer Dr., Colorado Springs CO 80920. (719)531-3400. Fax (719)531-3499. E-mail: brio@macmail.fotf.org. Focus on the Family. Susie Shellenberger, ed. Brings a Christian perspective to tough issues faced specifically by high school upper-classmen and college students (16-19 yrs.). Monthly mag.; 40-48 pgs.; circ. 55,000. Sub-scription $18. Much the same material as *Brio,* plus 10 segmented pages with more mature subject matter for older teens. 10% unsolicited freelance. Complete ms/cover letter; fax/e-query OK. Articles 800-1,000 wds. (10/yr.); fiction to 2,000 wds. Pays .08-.15/wd. on acceptance for 1st & electronic rts. Accepts requested ms by e-mail. Responds in 4-6 wks. Seasonal 8 mos. ahead. Rarely pays kill fee. Guidelines (also by e-mail); copy $1.50. (No ads)

Tips: "Most open to nonfiction currently—we are overloaded with fiction."

$CAMPUS LIFE, 465 Gundersen Dr., Carol Stream IL 60188. (630)260-6200. Fax (630)260-0114. E-mail: clmag@campuslife.net. Website: www.campuslife.net. Christianity Today Inc. Christopher Lutes, ed. Seeks to help teenagers navigate adolescence with their Christian faith intact. Bimonthly (plus 4 special Christian college issues) mag.; 68-94 pgs.; circ. 100,000. Subscription $19.95. 20% assigned. Query; fax/e-query OK. Pays .15-.20/wd. on acceptance for 1st rts. Articles 1,200-2,000 wds. (5-10/yr.); fiction 1,000-2,000 wds. (1-5/yr.). Responds in 6 wks. Seasonal 6 mos. ahead. Accepts reprints (tell when/where appeared). Accepts requested ms by e-mail (attached file). Kill fee 50%. Uses some side-bars. Accepts queries from teens. Guidelines (also on Website); copy $3/9x12 SAE. (Ads)

Poetry: Buys 1-5/yr. Free verse; 5-20 lines; $25-50. Submit max. 2 poems. Rarely purchase.

Tips: "Most open to as-told-to stories. Interview students and get their stories."

**This periodical was #42 on the 2001 Top 50 Christian Publishers list (#41 in 2000, #30 in 1999). 2003, 2002, 2001, 2000 EPA Award of Merit—Youth; 1999, 1998 EPA Award of Excellence—Youth.

$THE CONQUEROR, 8855 Dunn Rd., Hazelwood MO 63042. (314)837-7300. Fax (314)837-4503. E-mail: youth@pentecostalyouth.org. Website: www.pentecostalyouth.org. United Pentecostal Church, Intl. Travis Miller, ed. (tmiller@upci.org). For teenagers in the denomination. Bimonthly mag.; 16 pgs.; circ. 6,000. Subscription $10.97. 75% unsolicited freelance; 25% assigned. Complete ms; e-query OK. Pays $20-50 on publication for vari-ous rts. Articles & fiction (many/yr.) 600-1,250 wds. Responds in 10 wks. Seasonal 4 mos. ahead. Accepts simultaneous submissions and reprints. Prefers KJV. Guidelines (also by e-mail); copy for 11x14 SAE/2 stamps. (No ads)

Fillers: Various.

Tips: "Articles should be written with the idea of conservative morals, standards, and ethics in mind." Cutting down on their backlog of submissions.

$DEVO'ZINE, PO Box 340004, Nashville TN 37203-0004. (615)340-7247. Fax (615)340-1783. E-mail: devozine@upperroom.org, or smiller@upperroom.org. Website: www.devozine.org. Upper Room Ministries. Sandy Miller, ed. Devotional; to help teens (12-18) develop and maintain their connection with God and other Christians. Bimonthly mag.; 64 pgs.; circ. 104,000. Subscription $20. 85% unsolicited freelance; 15% assigned. Query; phone/fax/e-query OK. Pays $25 for meditations, $100 for feature articles (assigned) on acceptance for these one-time rts.: newspaper, periodical, electronic, and software-driven rts., and the right to use in future anthologies. Meditations 150-250 wds. (350/yr.), articles 350-500 wds.; book/music/video reviews, 350-500 wds., $100. Responds in 16 wks. Seasonal 6-8 mos. ahead. Accepts reprints (tell when/where appeared). Accepts requested ms by e-mail. Regular sidebars. Prefers NRSV, NIV, CEV. Guidelines/theme list (also by e-mail/Website); copy/7x10 SASE. (No ads)

> **Poetry:** Buys 25-30/yr. Free verse, light verse, haiku, traditional; to 150 wds. or 10-20 lines; $25. Submit max. 1 poem/theme, 9 themes/issue.
>
> **Tips:** "E-mail with ideas for weekend features related to specific themes."
>
> **This periodical was #1 on the 2004 Top 50 Christian Publishers list (#2 in 2003, #3 in 2002, #3 in 2001, #3 in 2000).

$ESSENTIAL CONNECTION, One Lifeway Plaza, Nashville TN 37234-0174. (615)251-2008. Fax (615)277-8271. E-mail: ec@lifeway.com. LifeWay Christian Resources of the Southern Baptist Convention. Bob Bunn, ed-in-chief. Christian leisure reading and devotional guide for 7th-12th graders. Monthly mag.; 60 pgs.; circ. 120,000. Subscription $1.32/issue. 10% unsolicited freelance; 90% assigned. Query; e-query OK. Pays $80-120 on acceptance for all rts. Articles 800-1,200 wds. (12/yr.); fiction 1,200 wds. (12/yr.). Responds in 10 wks. Seasonal 9 mos. ahead. No simultaneous submissions or reprints. Prefers e-mail submission (attached file or copied into message). No kill fee. Uses some sidebars. Prefers NIV. Guidelines (also by e-mail); free copy. (No ads)

> **Poetry:** Accepts 36/yr. All types. From teens only.
>
> **Special Needs:** Always in search of Christian humor; sports profiles. Most open to fiction (send complete ms).

GO! 4200 North Point Pkwy, Alpharetta GA 30022. (770)410-6251 or 6000. Fax (770)410-6006. E-mail: go@namb.net. Website: www.gomag.com. North American Mission Board/Southern Baptist Convention. Brent Moxley, ed. To encourage Christian teens to make an impact on their world for Christ. Bimonthly mag.; circ. 85,000. Subscription $14.95. Open to freelance. Prefers query. Not included in topical listings. (Ads)

> **2003, 2001 EPA Award of Excellence; 2000 EPA Award of Merit—Youth.

$GUIDEPOSTS SWEET 16, (formerly Guideposts for Teens) 1050 Broadway, Ste. 6, Chesterton, IN 46304. (219)929-4429. Fax (219)926-3839. E-mail: sweet16writers@guide posts.org. Guideposts, Inc. Mary Lou Carney, ed-in-chief; Betsy Kohn, mng. ed.; Allison Payne, assoc. ed. For teen girls 11-17; features true, first-person stories about real teens. Our watchwords are "wholesome," "current," "fun," and "inspiring." Bimonthly mag.; 48 pages.; circ. 150,000. Subscription $19.95. 50% unsolicited freelance; 50% assigned. Query/clips; fax/e-query OK. Pays $300-500 for true stories, $100-300 for shorter pieces on acceptance for all rts. Articles 500-1,500 wds. Responds in 4 wks. Seasonal 6 mos. ahead. Accepts simultaneous submissions and reprints (tell when/where appeared). Accepts disk or e-mail submission (copied into message). Kill fee 25%. Some sidebars. Guidelines (also by e-mail); copy $4.50.

> **Columns/Departments:** Allison Payne, assoc. ed. Buys 40/yr. Query. Positive Thinker (single-page feature on teen girl who has overcome something remarkable and kept a positive outlook), 300 wds; My Own Thing (profile of teen girl who has followed her passion to do something extraordinary, often something that helps others), 300 wds; Too Good to Be True (profile of teen guy who is cute, wholesome, and doing something very, very cool), 250 wds; DIY (trendy crafts, DIY fashion/beauty, bedroom accessories, anything a teen girl would find cool, fun, easy to create); Fashion/Beauty/Self-Help (fun, trendy, seasonal pieces about a single topic in beauty or fashion); 500-1,000 wds; Quizzes (teen issues, approached with humor), 500-900 wds. Pays $175-400.
>
> **Special Needs:** Need 1st-person (ghostwritten) true stories of teen girls (5/issue); see

guidelines. Also need Mysterious Moments ("strange-but-true" stories of miracles, unexplained coincidences, by teen girl or boy narrators), 250 words.

Tips: "We'll publish the occasional action/adventure true story, but our ongoing focus will be on relationships and real-life teen issues: friendship, romance, peer pressure, etc. We need 'light' true stories about finding a date and learning to drive, as well as 'catch-in-the-throat' stories. Language and subject matter must be current, uplifting, and teen-friendly. No preaching or lecturing, please! NOTE: We do not publish fiction or poetry."

**This periodical was #11 on the 2003 Top 50 Christian Publishers list.

$INSIGHT, 55 W. Oak Ridge Dr., Hagerstown MD 21740-7301. (301)393-4038. Fax (301)393-3292. E-mail: insight@rhpa.org. Website: www.insightmagazine.org. Review and Herald/Seventh-day Adventist. Lori Peckham, ed. A magazine of positive Christian living for Seventh-day Adventist high school and college students. Weekly take-home mag.; 16 pgs.; circ. 16,600. Subscription $45.95. 60% unsolicited freelance. Complete ms/cover letter; e-query OK. Pays $10-125 on acceptance for one-time rts. Not copyrighted. Articles 500-1,500 wds. (100/yr.). Responds in 4 wks. Seasonal 6 mos. ahead. Accepts reprints (tell when/where appeared). Prefers e-mail submission (attached file). Kill fee. Regularly uses sidebars. Prefers NIV. Accepts submissions from teens. Guidelines (also by e-mail/Website); copy $2/9x12 SAE/2 stamps. (No ads)

Poetry: Buys to 36/yr. All types; to 1 pg.; $10. By high school and college students only.

Columns/Departments: Buys 50/yr. On the Edge (drama in real life), 800-1,500 wds., $50-100; It Happened To Me (personal experience in first person), 600-900 wds., $50-75; Big Deal (big topics, such as prayer, premarital sex, knowing God's will, etc.) with sidebar, 1,200-1,700 wds., $75 + $25 for sidebar; So I Said (first-person opinion), 300-500 wds., $25-100.

Contest: Sponsors a nonfiction and poetry contest; includes a category for students under 21. Prizes to $250. June deadline (may vary). Send SASE for rules.

Tips: "We are desperately in need of true, dramatic stories involving Christian young people. Also need stories by male authors, particularly some humor. Also profiles of Seventh-day Adventist teenagers who are making a notable difference."

**This periodical was #19 on the 2004 Top 50 Christian Publishers list (#20 in 2003, #26 in 2002, #24 in 2001, #41 in 1999). 1998 EPA Award of Merit—Youth.

$INTEEN, PO Box 436987, Chicago IL 60643. Toll-free (800)860-8642. (708)868-7100, ext. 239. Fax (708)868-7107. E-mail: kawashington@urbanministries.com. Website: www.urban ministries.com. Urban Ministries, Inc. Katara Washington, ed. Teen curriculum for ages 15-17 (student and teacher manuals). Quarterly booklet; 32 pgs.; circ. 20,000. Subscription $11.25. 1% unsolicited freelance; 99% assigned. Query/clips; phone query OK; no e-query. Pays $75-150 on acceptance for all rts. Articles & fiction 1,200 wds. Responds in 4 wks. Seasonal 9 mos. ahead. Accepts some reprints (tell when/where appeared). Accepts requested ms on disk or by e-mail (copied into message). Prefers NIV. Free guidelines/theme list/copy for 10x13 SAE. (No ads)

Poetry: Buys 4/yr. Free verse; variable length; $25-60.

Tips: "Write in with sample writings and be willing and ready to complete an assignment. We prefer to make assignments. Most open to Bible study guides applicable and interesting for teens. Writers who can accurately explain scriptures to teens are always welcome."

$J.A.M.: JESUS AND ME, PO Box 436987, Chicago IL 60643. (708)868-7100, ext. 290. Fax (708)868-6759. E-mail: ctaylor@urbanministries.com. Website: www.urbanministries .com. Urban Ministries, Inc. C. Taylor, ed. Magazine for 12- to 14-year-olds. Open to freelance. Query/clips; fax/ e-query OK. Pays up to $150, 120 days after acceptance, for all rts. Articles 200-400 wds. Responds in 4 wks. Seasonal 6 mos. ahead. Accepts simultaneous submissions. Requires accepted ms on disk. Prefers NIV. Guidelines; copy for #10 SASE. (No ads)

Tips: "Send query with a writing sample, or attend our annual conference on the first weekend in November each year. Manuscripts are evaluated at the conference."

$LISTEN, 55 W. Oak Ridge Dr., Hagerstown MD 21740. (301)393-4019. Fax (301)393-3294. E-mail: editor@listenmagazine.org. Website: www.listmagazine.org. The Health Connection. Celeste Perrino Walker, ed. Positive lifestyle magazine for teens/young adults; emphasizes values in a secular tone. Monthly mag. (September-May); 32 pgs.; circ. 50,000. Subscription $26.95. 50% unsolicited freelance; 50% assigned. Query or complete ms; phone/fax/e-query OK. Pays .06-.10/wd.($50-150) on acceptance for 1st or reprint rts. Articles 1,000-1,200 wds. (30-50/yr.); fiction 1,000-1,200 wds. (15/yr.). Responds in 2 wks.-3 mos. Seasonal 1 yr. ahead. Accepts simultaneous submissions and reprints (tell when/where appeared). Accepts requested ms on disk or by e-mail (attached file). Regularly uses sidebars. Guidelines/theme list (also by e-mail/Website); copy $2/9x12 SAE/2 stamps. (No ads)

    Poetry: From high school students only. Pays a *Listen* T-shirt.

    Special Needs: Anti-drug, tobacco, alcohol; positive role models. In fiction: true-to-life stories dealing with everyday problems.

    Tips: "Need good activity articles. Address a specific lifestyle topic (i.e., alcohol, tobacco, marijuana, etc.). Make it believable and interesting to teen readers. We like an upbeat article with a catchy ending."

    **This periodical was #11 on the 2004 Top 50 Christian Publishers List (#9 in 2003).

$LIVING MY FAITH, 1300 N. Meacham Rd., Schaumburg IL 60173-4888. (847)843-1600. Fax (847)843-3757. E-mail: livingmyfaith@garbc.org. Website: www.rbpstudentministries.org. Regular Baptist Press. Mel Walker, dir. of student ministries. For junior high youth (12-14); conservative/fundamental. Weekly devotional booklet; 12 pgs. Complete ms; no e-query. Pays .04/wd. and up, on acceptance. Lead stories 450-550 wds; articles 300-800 wds.; true and fiction stories to 1,000 wds. Requires KJV. Check Website for guidelines before submitting at: www.rbpstudentministries.org/contribute.

    Tips: "Check Website quarterly for updates concerning needs, themes, etc."

$PASSAGEWAY.ORG, 1 Billy Graham Pkwy, Charlotte NC 28201. (704)401-2432. E-mail: ed@passageway.org. Website: www.passageway.org. Billy Graham Evangelistic Assn. Steve Knight, sr. ed. Online publication for teens, 15-17 yrs. Biweekly e-zine. 10% unsolicited freelance; 90% assigned. Complete ms/cover letter; no phone query/e-query OK. Pays $100-250 on publication, for all, electronic, or reprint rts. Articles 500-1,000 wds. (52/yr.); no fiction. Responds in 6-8 wks. Seasonal 2 mos. ahead. Accepts simultaneous submissions and reprints (tell when/where appeared). Prefers e-mail submission (attached or copied into message). Some kill fees 50%. Uses some sidebars. Prefers NIV. Guidelines on Website (www.passageway.org/guidelines); copy online. (No ads)

    Columns/Departments: Grow and Pop Culture sections.

    Tips: "Most open to a well-written article for the Grow section; it is the best way to break in. Also open to unique Pop Culture features that are relevant to teens. This is a youth Website, and writing that does not work for youth or the Web will not be considered."

    **2004 EPA Award of Merit—Online.

$REAL FAITH IN LIFE, 1300 N. Meacham Rd., Schaumburg IL 60173-4888. (847)843-1600. Fax (847)843-3757. E-mail: realfaith@garbc.org. Website: www.rbpstudentministries.org. Regular Baptist Press. Mel Walker, dir. of student ministries. For senior high youth (15-18); conservative/fundamental. Quarterly devotional planner; 96 pgs. Complete ms; no e-query. Pays .04/wd. and up, on acceptance for first (preferred) or one-time rts. Articles 400-1,200 wds. (if more than 600 words, include subheads). Using mostly assignment writers who are using the RBP student ministries materials or are familiar with churches who do. Some reprints. Guidelines (also on Website: www.rbpstudentministries.org/contribute); copy.

Tips: "Check Website quarterly for updates concerning needs, themes, etc."

SETMAG.COM, 2855 Lawrenceville-Suwanee Rd., Ste. 760-355, Suwanee GA 30024. Phone/fax (770)831-8622. E-mail: uvaldes@aol.com. Website: www.setmag.com. PLGK Communications, Inc. Quentin Plair, pres./CEO. Helping teens get set for life. Monthly e-zine. 70% unsolicited freelance; 30% assigned. Complete ms/cover letter; no phone/fax/e-query. Accepts requested ms on disk or by e-mail (attached file). **NO PAYMENT** for one-time rts. Not copyrighted. Articles 100-5,000 wds. (15/yr.) & fiction 100-5,000 wds. (12/yr.); reviews 200 wds. ($10). Responds in 12 weeks. Seasonal 4 months ahead. Accepts simultaneous submissions and reprints (tell when/where appeared). No kill fee. Uses some sidebars. Accepts submissions from teens. Guidelines (also on Website). (Ads)

Poetry: Accepts many; any type; 1-200 lines.

Fillers: Accepts many; cartoons, facts, games, jokes, party ideas, prayers, prose, quizzes, short humor, tips, word puzzles; 10-750 wds.

Columns/Departments: Accepts 36/yr. School tips (teen tips for scholarly excellence); Scoop (current info); Music (music reviews/stories); Speak Out (opinion articles by teens); all 100-500 wds.

Tips: "Provide information teens need to lay a foundation for a successful life. Looking for great stories."

$SHARING THE VICTORY, 8701 Leeds Rd., Kansas City MO 64129-1680. Toll-free (800)289-0909. (816)921-0909. Fax (816)921-8755. E-mail: stv@fca.org. Website: www.Fca.org. Fellowship of Christian Athletes (Protestant and Catholic). Jill Ewert, ed. Equipping and encouraging athletes and coaches to take their faith seriously, in and out of competition. Monthly (9X—double issues in Jan., Jun. & Aug.) mag.; 40 pgs.; circ. 70,000. Subscription $18. 10% unsolicited freelance; 40% assigned. Query only/clips; e-query OK. Pays $150-400 on publication for one-time rts. Articles 500-1,500 wds. (20/yr.). Responds in 10-15 wks. Seasonal 6 mos. ahead. Accepts reprints, pays 50% (tell when/where appeared). Accepts requested ms on disk or by e-mail (attached or copied into message). Kill fee .05%. Uses some sidebars. Prefers NIV. Guidelines (also by e-mail/Website); copy $1/9x12 SAE. (Ads)

Special Needs: Articles on FCA camp experiences. All articles must have an athletic angle. Need stories featuring Christian female professional athletes with a FCA connection.

Tips: "FCA angle important; pro and college athletes and coaches giving solid Christian testimony; we run stories according to athletic season. Need articles on Christian pro athletes—all sports. It is suggested that writer actually look at the magazine for general style and presentation."

**1996 EPA Award of Merit—Organizational.

$STUDENT LEADERSHIP JOURNAL, Box 7895, Madison WI 53707-7895. (608)274-9001x425. Fax (608)274-7882. E-mail: slj@ivcf.org. Website: www.ivcf.org/slj. InterVarsity Christian Fellowship. Jeff Yourison, ed. Undergraduate college student Christian leaders, single, ages 18-26. Triannual & online jour.; 32 pgs.; circ. 9,500. Subscription $12. 2% unsolicited; 20% assigned. Query/clips; no e-query. Pays $35-125 on acceptance for 1st or one-time rts. Articles to 2,000 wds. (3/yr.). Responds in 16 wks. Seasonal 8 mos. ahead. Accepts reprints. No e-mail submission. Regularly uses sidebars. Guidelines/theme list; copy $4/9x12 SAE/4 stamps. (No ads)

Poetry: Buys 4-6/yr. Avant-garde, free verse; to 15 lines; $25-50. Submit max. 5 poems.

Columns/Departments: Buys 6-10/yr. Collegiate Trends, 20-100 wds.; Student Leadership Network, 500-800 wds.; Chapter Strategy (how-to planning strategy for campus groups), 500-800 wds.; $10-75. Query.

Special Needs: Campus issues/trends/ministry/spiritual growth/leadership; Kingdom values; multiethnic reconciliation.

Tips: "Most open to main features targeted to college-age students. Be upbeat, interesting, and fresh. Writers who were involved in campus fellowship as students have the 'write' perspective and experience."

**1997 & 1995 EPA Award of Merit—Christian Ministry.

TEEN LIGHT: The Teen 2 Teen Christian Magazine, 6118 Bend of River, Dunn NC 28334. (910)980-1126. Fax (910)980-1126. E-mail: publisher@teenlight.org. Website: www.teenlight.org. Writers' Ministries, Inc. Annette Dammer, pub.; submit to Rebekah Hamrick. Totally teen authored; uses professional Christian writers to mentor their teen journalists so they may reach the world for Christ. Bimonthly & online mag.; circ. 5,000. Subscription $11.95. 20% unsolicited freelance; 80% assigned. Complete ms/cover letter; e-query OK. **PAYS IN COPIES & FREE CLASSES** for nonexclusive rts. Articles 500-1,000 wds. (25/yr.); short fiction (12/yr.). Responds in 2 wks. Seasonal 4-6 mos. ahead. Accepts simultaneous submissions and reprints (tell when/where appeared). Prefers accepted mss by e-mail (copied into message). Uses some sidebars. Prefers NIV. Accepts submissions from children and teens. Guidelines (also by e-mail/Website); copy for 9x12 SAE/3 stamps. (Ads)

> **Poetry:** Accepts 26/yr. All types; pays in copies. Submit max. 5 poems.
>
> **Fillers:** Accepts 26/yr. Anecdotes, cartoons, facts, games, jokes, party ideas, prayers, prose, quizzes, quotes, short humor, tips, and word puzzles; pays in copies.
>
> **Special Needs:** Fashion, art, photo journalism; true-life teen triumphs and testimonies.
>
> **Contest:** We sponsor contests sporadically. See e-zine.
>
> **Tips:** "Write from your heart and your life. Be honest, open, and fallible. Most of all, our writers must be 22 years old or younger. Even our publisher doesn't write for us. By teens, for teens—that is our appointed mission."

$TEENAGE CHRISTIAN, PO Box 92, Hohenwald TN 38462. Toll-free (800)637-2613. E-mail: teenagechristian@bellsouth.net. Website: www.teenagechristian.net. Church of Christ/Christian Publishing Inc. Ben Forrest, ed. Spiritual answers to tough questions for Christian teens (13-19 yrs.). Quarterly mag.; 32 pgs.; circ. 10,500. Subscription $14.95. 50% unsolicited freelance. Prefers submissions through e-mail or Website. Pays $35 on publication for one-time and reprint rts. Articles 600-1,200 wds. (20/yr.); fiction 600-1,500 wds. (9/yr.). Responds in 2-3 mos. Accepts requested ms on disk. Seasonal 6 mos. ahead. Accepts simultaneous submissions and reprints (tell when/where appeared). Rarely uses sidebars. Prefers NIV. Copy $2.50/9x12 SAE. (Ads)

> **Poetry:** Buys 3-4/yr. Free verse; 10-25 lines; $15-25. Submit max. 5 poems.
>
> **Fillers:** Buys 5-10/yr. Cartoons, quizzes, prayers, word puzzles; 150-350 wds.; $15-25.
>
> **Tips:** "Most open to practical nonfiction. Fiction should be excellent, realistic, and up to date."

TEENS FOR JC.COM, 2855 Lawrenceville-Suwanee Rd., Ste. 760-355, Suwanee GA 30024. Phone/fax (770)831-8622. E-mail: uvaldes@aol.com. Website: www.teensforjc.com. PLGK Communications, Inc. Quentin Plair, pres./CEO. Salutes the fun and exhilaration of being a Christian teen. Monthly e-zine. 90% unsolicited freelance; 10% assigned. Complete ms/cover letter; no phone/fax/e-query. Accepts requested ms on disk or by e-mail (attached file). **NO PAYMENT** for one-time rts. Not copyrighted. Articles 100-5,000 wds. (15/yr.) & fiction 100-5,000 wds. (12/yr.); reviews 200 wds. Responds in 12 weeks. Seasonal 4 months ahead. Accepts simultaneous submissions and reprints (tell when/where appeared). No kill fee. Uses some sidebars. Accepts submissions from teens. Guidelines (also on Website). (Ads)

> **Poetry:** Accepts many; any type; 1-200 lines.
>
> **Fillers:** Accepts many; cartoons, facts, games, jokes, party ideas, prayers, prose, quizzes, short humor, tips, word puzzles; 10-750 wds.

Columns/Departments: Accepts 36/yr. School tips (teen tips for scholarly excellence); Scoop (current info); Music (music reviews/stories); Speak Out (opinion articles by teens); all 100-500 wds.

Tips: "Provide information teens need to lay a foundation for a successful life. Looking for great stories."

TRANSCENDMAG.COM, 2855 Lawrenceville-Suwanee Rd., Ste. 760-355, Suwanee GA 30024. Phone/fax (770)831-8622. E-mail: uvaldes@aol.com. Website: www.transcendmag.com. PLGK Communications, Inc. Travis Lucas, mng. ed.; submit to Quentin Plair, pres. Salutes the fun and exhilaration of being an African American teen. Monthly e-zine. 100% assigned. Complete ms/cover letter (for fiction query/clips); no phone/fax/e-query. **NO PAYMENT** for one-time rts. Not copyrighted. Articles 100-5,000 wds. (15/yr.); fiction 100-5,000 wds. (12/yr.); reviews 200 wds. Responds in 12 weeks. Seasonal 4 mos. ahead. Accepts simultaneous submissions and reprints (tell when/where appeared). Prefers requested ms on disk or by e-mail (attached file). No kill fee. Uses some sidebars. Accepts submissions from children or teens. Guidelines (also on Website); copy on Website. (Ads)

Poetry: Accepts many; 1-200 lines. Submit any number.

Fillers: Accepts many; cartoons, facts, games, jokes, party ideas, prayers, prose, quizzes, short humor, tips, word puzzles; 10-750 wds.

Columns/Departments: Accepts 36/yr. School Tips (tips for scholarly excellence); Speak Out (opinion articles by teens); Scoop (current info); Music (music reviews/stories); all 100-500 wds.

Tips: "Looking for great stories. Provide information teens need to lay a foundation for a successful life. Great publication for freelancers."

$WITH: The Magazine for Radical Christian Youth, Box 347, Newton KS 67114-0347. (316)283-5100. Fax (316)283-0454. E-mail: carold@mennoniteusa.org. Website: www.withonline.org. Faith & Life Press/Mennonite, Brethren & Mennonite Brethren. Carol Duerksen, ed. For high-school teens (15-18 yrs.), Christian and non-Christian. Bimonthly mag.; 32 pgs.; circ. 4,000. Subscription $23.50. 20% unsolicited freelance; 80% assigned. Query (on first-person and how-to articles); complete ms on others/cover letter; no phone/fax/e-query. Pays .06/wd. (.03/wd. for reprints) on acceptance for 1st, one-time, simultaneous, or reprint rts. Articles 500-1,800 wds. (15/yr.); fiction 1,000-2,000 wds. (15/yr.); music reviews 500 wds., .05/wd. (query for assignment). Responds in 4 wks. Seasonal 6 mos. ahead. Accepts simultaneous submissions and reprints (tell when/where appeared). No disk. Kill fee 25-50%. Regularly uses sidebars. Prefers NRSV. Guidelines/theme list (also by e-mail); copy for 9x12 SAE/4 stamps. Separate guidelines for 1st-person and how-to articles sent only when requested. (No ads)

Fillers: Buys 20 cartoons/yr.; $35-40.

Tips: "We need good Christmas stories; true, powerful stories or fiction that reads as well as truth. Send for theme list and write for the theme. Write a story from a teen's perspective that grabs the reader and leaves the reader thinking and going away with a new insight. Humor—both cartoons and short articles—are hard to find. Our readers expect high-quality humor."

**This periodical was #35 on the 2002 Top 50 Christian Publishers list. 2000 EPA Award of Excellence—Youth; 1999 & 1998 EPA Award of Merit—Youth.

$YOUNG ADULT TODAY, PO Box 436987, Chicago IL 60643. Toll-free (800)860-8642. (708)868-7100, ext. 239. Fax (708)868-7107. E-mail: kawashington@urbanministries .com. Website: www.urbanministries.com. Urban Ministries, Inc. Katara Washington, ed. Young adult curriculum for ages 18-24 (student and teacher manuals). Quarterly booklet; 80 pgs.; circ. 10,000. Subscription $14.75. 99% assigned. Query/clips; phone query OK; no e-query. Pays $75-150 on acceptance for all rts. Articles (24/yr.) & fiction (12/yr.);

under 1,000 wds. Responds in 4 wks. Seasonal 9 mos. ahead. Accepts some reprints (tell when/where appeared). Accepts requested ms on disk or by e-mail (copied into message). Prefers KJV. Free guidelines/theme list/copy for 10x13 SAE. (No ads)

Poetry: Buys 4/yr. Free verse; variable length; $25-60.

Tips: "We assign articles based on the Uniform Lesson Series for Sunday schools. Writers should send samples of their writing to be considered for an assignment. We very rarely publish unassigned submissions. Assignments are made to writers who demonstrate knowledge of the audience and the publication as well as biblical text and life application."

$YOUNG AND ALIVE, Box 6097, Lincoln NE 68506. (402)488-0981. E-mail: info@christian record.org. Website: www.christianrecord.org. Christian Record Services, Inc. Gaylena Gibson, ed. For sight-impaired young adults, 16-25 yrs.; for interdenominational Christian audience. Quarterly mag.; 65-70 pgs.; circ. 25,000. Free to sight-impaired. 90% unsolicited freelance. Pays .03-.05/wd. on acceptance for one-time rts. Articles & true stories 800-1,400 wds. (40/yr.). Responds in 52 wks. Seasonal anytime. Accepts simultaneous submissions and reprints (tell when/where appeared, no tear sheets). Accepts requested ms on disk. Does not use sidebars. Guidelines; copy for 7x10 SAE/5 stamps. (No ads) Note: due to an overabundance of manuscripts, this publication will not be accepting submissions until 2009.

$YOUNG CHRISTIAN, 2660 Petersborough St., Herndon VA 20171. Phone/fax (703)715-1129. E-mail: youngchristianmagazine@yahoo.com. Website: http://groups.yahoo.com/group/youngchristianmagazine. Tellstar Publishing. Shannon Bridget Murphy, ed. Christian writing with the Lord's message for children and teens. Quarterly mag. 85% unsolicited freelance. Complete ms/cover letter; e-query OK. Pays .02-.05/wd. on acceptance for 1st or one-time rts. Articles 500-2,000 wds.; fiction 500-2,000 wds.; book/tape reviews. Responds in 2-8 wks. Seasonal 3-6 mos. ahead. Accepts simultaneous submissions and reprints (tell when/where appeared). Accepts disk; prefers e-mail submissions (attached or copied into message). No kill fee. Regularly uses sidebars. Prefers KJV. Guidelines by e-mail. (No ads)

Poetry: Buys variable number. Avant-garde, free verse, haiku, light verse, traditional; any length; variable rates. Submit any number.

Fillers: Buys anecdotes, cartoons, facts, ideas, kid quotes, party ideas, prayers, prose, quizzes, quotes, short humor, tips, and word puzzles, to 1,000 wds.

Tips: "Freelancers have the best chance of breaking in if they send a manuscript that is well-written and suitable for our audience."

$YOUNG SALVATIONIST, PO Box 269, Alexandria VA 22313-0269. (703)684-5500. Fax (703)684-5539. E-mail: ys@usn.salvationarmy.org. Website: http://publications.salvation armyusa.org. The Salvation Army. Laura Ezzell, mng. ed. For teens & young adults in the Salvation Army. Monthly (10X) & online mag.; 20 pgs.; circ. 48,000. Subscription $4. 80% unsolicited freelance; 20% assigned. Complete ms preferred; e-query OK. Pays .15/wd.(.10/wd. for reprints) on acceptance for 1st, one-time, or reprint rts. Articles (60/yr.) & fiction (10/yr.), 600-1,200 wds.; short evangelistic pieces, 350-600 wds. Responds in 9 wks. Seasonal 6 mos. ahead. Accepts reprints (tell when/where appeared). Accepts requested ms on disk or by e-mail. Uses some sidebars. Prefers NIV. Guidelines/theme list (also on Website); copy for 9x12 SAE/3 stamps. (No ads)

Contest: Sponsors a contest for fiction, nonfiction, poetry, original art, and photography. Send SASE for details.

Tips: "Our greatest need is for nonfiction pieces that are relevant to the readers and offer clear application to daily life. We are most interested in topical pieces on contemporary issues that affect a teen's daily life, and pieces that work with the day-to-day challenges of faith. Although we use fiction and poetry, they are a small percentage of the total content of each issue."

**This periodical was #9 on the 2004 Top 50 Christian Publishers list (#10 in 2003, #6 in 2002, #6 in 2001, #5 in 2000).

$YOUTH COMPASS, PO Box 4060, Overland Park KS 66204. (913)432-0331. Fax (913)722-0351. E-mail: sseditor1@juno.com. Church of God (holiness)/Herald and Banner Press. Arlene McGehee, Sunday school ed. Denominational; for teens. Weekly take-home paper; 4 pgs.; circ. 4,800. Subscription $1.50. Complete ms/cover letter; phone/fax/e-query OK (prefers mail or e-mail). Pays .005/wd. on publication for 1st rts. Fiction 800-1,500 wds. Seasonal 6-8 mos. ahead. Accepts simultaneous submissions and reprints (tell when/where appeared). Prefers KJV. Guidelines/theme list; copy. Not in topical listings.

YOUTHWALK (GA), 4201 N. Peachtree Rd., Atlanta GA 30341. (770)451-9300. Fax (770)454-9313. E-mail: twalker@walkthru.org. Website: www.youthwalk.org. Walk Thru the Bible Ministries. Tim Walker, ed.; Laurin Makohon, asst. ed. To encourage teens to have a real faith by reading their Bible daily and to have a real relationship with a real God who cares about every aspect of their lives. Monthly mag.; circ. 55,000. Subscription $18. Open to freelance. Query or complete ms. Requires NIV. (No ads)

>   **Tips:** "We accept freelance for feature articles and profiles only; no devotionals."

>   **2001 Award of Merit—Youth.

WOMEN'S MARKETS

ANNA'S JOURNAL, PO Box 341, Ellijay GA 30540. Phone/fax (706)276-2309. E-mail: annas@ellijay.com. Website: www.annasjournal.com. Catherine Ward-Long, ed. Spiritual support for childless couples who for the most part have decided to stay that way. Print publication being converted to an e-zine. 80% unsolicited freelance; 20% assigned. Complete ms/cover letter; fax/e-query OK. 1st, simultaneous, or reprint rts. Not copyrighted. Articles 500-2,000 wds. (8-12/yr.); fiction 1,000-2,000 wds. (1-3/yr.). Seasonal 3 months ahead. Accepts simultaneous submissions and reprints (tell when/where appeared). No disk; e-mail OK (copied into message). Does not use sidebars. Prefers KJV. No guidelines or copy. (No ads) Note from publisher: "Thank you for your patience and support of *Anna's Journal.*"

>   **Poetry:** Accepts 4-10/yr. Any type. Submit max. 3 poems.

>   **Fillers:** Accepts 3-4/yr. Anecdotes, facts, newsbreaks, prose, prayers, quizzes, quotes, letters; 50-250 wds.

>   **Special Needs:** Articles from married, childless men; articles discussing the meaning of childless, childfree, and childless by choice.

>   **Tips:** "Looking for innovative ways to improve the child-free lifestyle and self-esteem. It helps if writer is childless."

$AT THE CENTER, PO Box 100, Morgantown PA 19543. Toll-free (800)588-7744. (610)856-6830. Fax (610)856-6831. E-mail: publications@rightideas.us, or elaine@rightideas.us. Website: www.atcmag.com. Marketing Partners, Inc. Jerry Thacker, ed.; submit to Elaine Williams, asst. ed. Designed to help staff, volunteers, and board members of Crisis Pregnancy Centers/Pregnancy Care Centers with relevant information and encouragement. Quarterly (3X) & online mag.; 24 pgs.; circ. 30,000. Subscription free. 20% unsolicited freelance; 80% assigned. Complete ms; phone/fax query OK; e-query preferred. Pays $150 on publication for 1st, reprint, or simultaneous rts. Articles 800-1,000 wds. (15/yr.). Responds in 8-10 wks. Seasonal 6-8 mos. ahead. Accepts simultaneous submissions and reprints. Accepts e-mail submissions (attached or copied into message). No kill fee. Uses some sidebars. Prefers KJV, ESV, or NASB. Guidelines/idea list (also by e-mail); copy for 9x12 SAE/3 stamps. (Ads; marjori@rightideas.us)

Special Needs: Articles that give ideas for other centers in the areas of recruiting and retaining volunteers, ways to reach abortion-minded clients, and creative fund-raising ideas.

Tips: "Looking for practical articles of help and encouragement for those involved in the work of CPC/PCC ministry. If someone has been involved in crisis pregnancy work, their insight into many areas of the ministry can be helpful to staff and board."

**This periodical was #49 on the 2000 Top 50 Christian Publishers list. 2000 Award of Excellence—Organizational; 2001 & 1997 EPA Award of Merit—Organizational.

THE CHRISTIAN WOMAN'S PAGE, PO Box 84, Comstock MN 56525. E-mail: writer@christian womanspage.org. Website: www.christianwomanspage.org. Nondenominational. Encouraging women of all ages, in all walks of life, with topics you would find in a print magazine, while being easily accessible 24/7 online. Janel Messenger, ed./pub.; Elizabeth Fabiani, asst. ed. Quarterly e-zine. 80% unsolicited freelance. Complete ms/cover letter; e-query OK. **NO PAYMENT** for one-time, reprint, simultaneous, or electronic rts. Articles 300-1,800 wds.; fiction to 1,800 wds. Responds in 2-3 wks. Accepts simultaneous submissions and reprints (tell when/where appeared). Requires e-mail submission (copied into message). Prefers NIV, NKJV. Guidelines/theme list by e-mail/Website; copy online. (No ads)

Tips: "We accept freelance for all departments. We are also open to submissions containing 4-6 articles written with a theme that could be used as a column (submit articles together). Follow guidelines on Website. Be passionate about your subject matter. Our mission is to encourage women to live with passion and love for Jesus Christ. Write with passion, love, and honesty."

CHRISTIAN WOMEN TODAY, Box 300, Vancouver BC V6C 2X3 Canada. (604)514-2000. Fax (604)514-2124. E-mail: editor@christianwomentoday.com. Website: www.christian womentoday.com. French Website: www.chretiennes.com. Campus Crusade for Christ, Canada. Karen Schenk, pub.; Stacy Wiebe, ed. For Christian women, 20-60 yrs. Monthly online mag.; 2 million hits/mo. 30% unsolicited freelance. Query first; e-query preferred. **NO PAYMENT**. Lifestyle articles 200-500 wds.; features 500-1,000 wds.; life stories 500 wds. Seasonal 4 mos. ahead. Accepts simultaneous submissions and reprints (tell when/where appeared). Prefers e-mail submission (attached file). Guidelines/theme list on Website (www.christianwomentoday.com/volunteer/submissions.html). (Ads)

Tips: "The writer needs to have a global perspective, have a heart to build women in their faith, and help develop them to win others to Christ. Text should be written for online viewing with subheads and bullets in the body of the article."

CHURCHWOMAN, 475 Riverside Dr., Ste. 1626, New York NY 10115. Toll-free (800)298-5551. (212)870-2347. Fax (212)870-2338. E-mail: cwu@churchwomen.org. Website: www.churchwomen.org. Church Women United. Annie Llamoso-Songco, ed. Shares stories of women acting on their faith and engaging in the work for peace and justice around the world. Quarterly mag.; 28 pgs.; circ. 3,000. Subscription $10. 1% unsolicited freelance. Query. **PAYS IN COPIES**. Articles to 3 pgs. Prefers accepted ms by e-mail (copied into message). Guidelines; copy $1.

+CROWNED WITH SILVER, PO Box 10, Masonville CO 80541. E-mail: crownedwithsilver@ yahoo.com. Website: www.crownedwithsilver.com. Submit to The Editor. Return to biblical femininity; Christian homemaking encouragement regarding home schooling, etiquette, marriage, womanhood, and nostalgic wisdom from the past. Quarterly mag. Subscription $14. Incomplete topical listings. No questionnaire returned.

$ESPRIT, Evangelical Lutheran Women, 302-393 Portage Ave., Winnipeg MB R3B 3H6 Canada.

(204)984-9160. Fax (204)984-9162. E-mail: esprit@elcic.ca. Website: www.elw.ca. Evangelical Lutheran Church in Canada. Gayle Moore-Morrans, ed. For Christian women. Quarterly mag.; 56 pgs.; circ. 5,800. Subscription $17 Can., $26 US. 50% unsolicited freelance; 50% assigned. Complete ms/cover letter; phone/fax/e-query OK. Pays $16.50/pg. Can. on publication for 1st or one-time rts. Articles (34/yr.) and fiction (4/yr.) 325-1,400 wds.; book reviews 150 wds., $16.50 Can. Responds in 2-4 wks. Seasonal 4 mos. ahead. Accepts simultaneous submissions and reprints (tell when/where appeared). Prefers accepted mss by e-mail (copied into message). Uses some sidebars. Prefers NRSV. Guidelines/theme list (also on Website); copy for #10 SAE/.90 Can. postage or $1 US. (Limited ads)

Poetry: Buys 4-8/yr. Light verse, traditional; 8-100 lines; $10-20. Submit max. 3 poems.

Columns/Departments: Buys 4/yr., 325 wds.

Tips: "Articles must be in accordance with Lutheran theology. Preference is given to Canadian Lutheran women writers. Use inclusive language (no male pronoun references to God), focus on women and spiritual/faith issues. Check our theme calendar; almost all articles and poems are theme related."

**This periodical was #18 on the 2004 Top 50 Christian Publishers list (#34 in 2003, #19 in 2002).

$*EXTREME JOY. E-mail: JeanAnn@simplejoy.org. Website: www.simplejoy.org. Jean Ann Duckworth, pub.; submit to The Editor. To increase productive energy and enhance joy. Monthly online mag. Open to freelance. Query first; e-query OK (extremequery@simple joy.org). Pays $25 honorarium for feature articles, $10 for other articles, on publication for one-time rts. Features 1,500-2,000 wds.; articles 500-1,000 wds. Seasonal 4 mos. ahead. Prefers e-mail (attached file in Word format). Guidelines by e-mail (extremeguide lines@simplejoy.org). Incomplete topical listings.

Columns/Departments: Volunteerism (ideas for serving others and the community), 500-1,000 wds.; The WOW Factor (life experiences that caused you to say WOW to life), 500 wds.; Extreme Women (tell us about a woman who lives a life of extreme joy), 500-1,000 wds.; The Great Outdoors (how do you increase your energy outdoors), 500-1,000 wds.

FOOTPRINTS, PO Box 1962, Cleveland DC, Qld 4163, Australia. E-mail: footprints australia@hotmail.com. Website: www.footprints.vze.com. Janet Camilleri, ed. To encourage women of all ages, stages, and walks of life to grow and develop spiritually, emotionally, mentally, physically, and relationally. Quarterly mag. Subscription $10 AUS; $20 AUS for outside Australia. E-query OK. **NO PAYMENT.** Articles 600 wds.; fiction to 1,000 wds.; book reviews to 500 wds. Guidelines on Website. Not in topical listings.

Poetry: Usually runs one/issue.

Fillers: Kid quotes, quizzes, puzzles, quotes, crossword puzzles, recipes (use Australian ingredients and the metric system).

Columns/Departments: My Favourite Scripture, to 600 wds.; God Answered My Prayer, to 600 wds.; and Evangelistic pieces.

Tips: "Preference given to contributions by subscribers. We especially want testimonies of how God has been at work in your life."

$THE GODLY BUSINESS WOMAN, PO Box 181004, Casselberry FL 32718-1004. Toll-free (800)560-1090. (407)696-2805. Fax (407)695-8033. E-mail: info@godlybusiness woman.com, or tracey@godlybusinesswoman.com. Website: www.godlybusinesswoman .com. Kathleen B. Jackson, pub; Tracey Davison, mng. ed. Our goal is to educate, inspire, and encourage women to be all they can be through Jesus Christ; to be a resource that will shed light on God's view of the responsibilities we have been given. Mag.; 48 pgs.; circ. 25,000. Subscription $15.99. 30% unsolicited freelance; 70% assigned. Query; prefers e-queries. Pays $20. Articles 750-1,500 wds. Regularly uses sidebars. Guidelines. (Ads)

Columns/Departments: Women on the Move; Missions Hall of Fame; Mind; 250-650 wds. Query. No payment.

Tips: "Our goal is to encourage educated decision making and harmony in women's lives whether they are in or out of the workplace."

THE HANDMAIDEN, PO Box 76, Ben Lomond CA 95005. (831)336-5118. Fax (831)336-8882. E-mail: czell@conciliarpress.com, or vhnieuwsma@prodigy.com. Website: www .conciliarpress.com. Antiochian Orthodox Archdiocese of North America. Virginia Nieuwsma & Carla Zell, co-eds. For women serving God within the Eastern Orthodox tradition. Quarterly jour.; 64 pgs.; circ. 3,000. Subscription $16.50. 5% unsolicited freelance; 95% assigned. Query; e-query OK. **PAYS IN COPIES/SUBSCRIPTION.** Articles 1,000-2,000 wds. (8/yr.). Responds in 6-8 wks. Seasonal 6 mos. ahead. Accepts reprints (tell when/where appeared). Prefers hard copy or e-mail submissions (copied into message). Uses some sidebars. Prefers NKJV. Guidelines (also by e-mail)/theme list; copy for 7x10 SAE/4 stamps. (No ads)

Poetry: Donna Farley, poetry ed. Accepts 4-8/yr. Free verse, light verse, traditional. Submit max. 3 poems.

Columns/Departments: Heroines of the Faith (lives of women saints within Orthodox tradition), 1,000-2,000 wds.

Tips: "Most open to theme features, sidebars, and poetry."

*HEARTS AT HOME, 900 W. College Ave., Normal IL 61761. (309)888-6667. Fax (309)888-4525. E-mail: hearts@hearts-at-home.org. Website: www.hearts-at-home.org. Connected to annual conferences by the same name (held in Bloomington IL, Lansing MI, and Minneapolis MN). Marilyn Snook, co-ed; Rachel Kitson, ed. for columns, poetry, and fillers. To encourage and educate mothers at home. Monthly mag.; 16 pgs.; circ. 2,000. Subscription $15. 30-40% unsolicited freelance; 60-70% assigned. Complete ms by mail or e-mail; e-query OK. **PAYS 5 COPIES** for one-time rts. Articles 350-900 wds. (40-50/yr.); devotionals to 750 wds.; book reviews 500 wds. Responds in 2 wks. Seasonal 3 mos. ahead. Accepts reprints (tell when/where appeared). Prefers e-mail submissions (attached Word file, to: heart-to-heart@hearts-at-home.org). No kill fee. Some sidebars. Any Bible version. Guidelines/theme list (also by e-mail/Website); copy $2/6x9 SAE/2 stamps. (No ads)

Poetry: Accepts 5-8/yr. Light verse, traditional; 10-25 lines (to 250 wds.). Submit max. 3 poems.

Fillers: Accepts 100/yr. Anecdotes, cartoons, facts, ideas, party ideas, short humor; 25-100 wds.

Columns/Departments: Accepts 15-20/yr., Motherhood; Parenting; Marriage; Personal Growth; Spiritual Growth; Family Management; to 900 wds.

Special Needs: Articles that challenge mothers in their growth as a parent; uplift spouses in relationship with each other and children; encourage spiritual growth; educate mothers on networking, finding time for themselves, or overcoming personal challenges; tips on saving time and money; and using personal experiences to better parent kids. Looking for more articles by, for, and about moms at home with older children (preteen and older).

Tips: "Submit a well-written, balanced, positive article which will encourage, educate, and/or entertain our audience. Personal stories of the triumphs and trials of being an at-home mom are preferred. This publication is designed to be by moms and for moms. Please include a short biography to go with your article."

$HISTORY'S WOMEN, 22 Williams St., Batavia NY 14020. (585)343-2810. Fax (585)343-3245. E-mail: patti@historyswomen.com. Website: www.historyswomen.com. PC Publications. Patti Chadwick, ed. Online magazine highlighting the extraordinary achievements of women throughout history. Biweekly e-zine; 20 pgs.; circ. 17,000. Subscription free. 20% unsolicited freelance. E-query/e-submissions only. **PAYS IN COPIES & FREE E-BOOKS**

(occasionally pays $10, if budget permits) for 1st, one-time, reprint, or electronic rts. Articles 500-1,000 wds. (20/yr.). Responds in 1-2 wks. Seasonal 3 mos. ahead. Accepts simultaneous submissions and reprints (tell when/where appeared). Prefers e-mail submission (copied into message). Does not use sidebars. Accepts submissions from teens. Guidelines on Website; copy on site archive. (Ads)

Columns/Departments: Buys 10-20/yr. Women to Admire, in these columns: Women of Faith; First Women (pioneers in their field); Social Reformers; Amazing Moms; Women Who Ruled (women rulers); Early America; all 500-1,000 wds., $10. Query or complete ms.

$HORIZONS, 100 Witherspoon St., Louisville KY 40202-1396. (502)569-5688. Fax (502)569-8085. E-mail: sdunne@ctr.pcusa.org. Website: www.pcusa.org/horizons. Presbyterian Church (USA). Presbyterian Women. Sharon Dunne, assoc. ed. Justice issues and spiritual life for Presbyterian women. Bimonthly mag. & annual Bible study; 40 pgs.; circ. 25,500. Subscription $18. 10% unsolicited freelance; 90% assigned. Query; fax/e-query OK. Pays $50-125/printed pg. on acceptance for 1st rts. Articles 600-1,800 wds. (10/yr.) & fiction 1,200-1,800 wds. (5/yr.); book reviews 100 wds. ($25). Seasonal 6 mos. ahead. Accepts simultaneous submissions and reprints (tell when/where appeared). Accepts requested ms on disk or by e-mail (attached file or copied into message). Kill fee. Regularly uses sidebars. Prefers NRSV. Guidelines/theme list (also by e-mail/Website); copy $4. (No ads)

Poetry: Buys 5/yr. All types; $50-100. Submit max. 5 poems.

Fillers: Cartoons, church-related graphics; $50.

Tips: "Most open to devotionals, mission stories, justice and peace issues. Writer should be familiar with constituency of Presbyterian women and life in the Presbyterian Church (USA)."

**This periodical was #10 on the 2004 Top 50 Christian Publishers list (#8 in 2003, #15 in 2002).

$INSPIRIT MAGAZINE, 5101 N. Francisco Ave., Chicago IL 60625. (773)907-3332. Fax (773)784-1128. E-mail: cwm@covchurch.org. Website: www.covchurch.org./cov/cwm. Dept. of Covenant Women's Ministries. Suzannah V. Worl, mngr. To inform and inspire women across the Covenant denomination. Quarterly mag.; 50 pgs.; circ. 2,500. Subscription $10. 95% unsolicited freelance; 5% assigned. Complete ms/cover letter; phone/fax/e-query OK. Pays $20-35 on publication. Articles about 800 wds. (36/yr.); fiction 500-800 wds. (4/yr.). Seasonal 2.5 mos. ahead. Accepts simultaneous submissions & reprints (tell when/where appeared). Accepts e-mail submissions (attached file). Uses some sidebars. Prefers TNIV or NIV. Guidelines/theme list (also by e-mail); copy for 6x9 SAE & $1. (Ads)

Poetry: Buys 2-3/yr. Free verse, light verse, traditional; 25-50 lines; $25. Submit max. 3 poems.

Tips: "Looking for articles on racial reconciliation. Follow our themes and guidelines. We are very strict about article length."

$JOURNEY: A Woman's Guide to Intimacy with God, One Lifeway Plaza, Nashville TN 37234-0175. (615)251-5659. Fax (615)277-8272. E-mail: journey@lifeway.com. Website: www.lifeway.com. Lifeway Christian Resources. Pamela Nixon, lead ed.; Tammy Drolsum, ed. Devotional magazine for women 30-50 years old. Monthly mag.; 44 pgs.; circ. 215,000. 15% unsolicited freelance; 85% staff or assigned. Subscription $20.75. Query/clips or complete ms/cover letter; no phone/fax/e-query or e-submissions. Pays $50-100 on acceptance for all rts. Articles 350-1,000 wds. (10-12/yr.). Responds in 8 wks. Seasonal 6-7 mos. ahead. Regularly uses sidebars. Prefers HCSB. Accepts requested ms on disk. Guidelines; copy for 6x9 SAE/2 stamps.

Special Needs: Strong feature articles, 750-1,000 words (including sidebars) on topics of interest to women 30-50 years old ranging from practical applications of faith to spiritual growth, as well as profiles of Christian women in leadership positions.

Tips: "Most open to feature articles that are well-written with a thorough understanding of our magazine and target audience. Strong sample devotionals written in *Journey* style may be considered for assignment of a devotional."

JUST BETWEEN US, 777 S. Barker Rd., Brookfield WI 53045. Toll-free (800)260-3342. (262)786-6478. Fax (262)796-5752. E-mail: jbu@elmbrook.org. Website: www.just betweenus.org. Elmbrook Church, Inc. Shelly Esser, ed. Ideas, encouragement, and resources for wives of evangelical ministers and women in leadership. Quarterly mag.; 32 pgs.; circ. 7,000. Subscription $14.95. 85% unsolicited freelance; 15% assigned. Query; phone/fax/e-query OK. **NO PAYMENT** for one-time rts. Articles 250-500 wds. or 1,200-1,500 wds. (50/yr.). Responds in 8 wks. Accepts simultaneous submissions and reprints. Regularly uses sidebars. Prefers NIV. Guidelines/theme list (also by e-mail/Website); copy $4/9x12 SAE. (Ads)

Fillers: Accepts 15/yr. Anecdotes, cartoons, ideas, prayers, quotes, short humor; 50-250 wds.

Columns/Departments: Accepts 12/yr. Hospitality; Keeping Your Kids Christian; Women's Ministry (program ideas); all 700-900 wds.

Tips: "Most open to feature articles addressing the unique needs of women in leadership (Bible-study leaders, women's ministry directors, pastor's wives, missionary wives, etc.). Some of these needs would include relationship with God, staff, leadership skills, ministry how-tos, balancing ministry and family, and marriage. The best way to break in is to contact the editor directly. Follow themes."

KEEPING HEARTS & HOME, W9109 Holmes Junction Rd., Beecher WI 54156. E-mail: articles@keepinghearts.org. Website: www.keepinghearts.org. Jocelyn Zichterman, ed/pub.; Sarah Burton, asst. ed. Uplifting and heart-warming; to encourage and inspire women in every stage of life. Quarterly mag.; 30 pgs. Subscription $14. Estab. 2003. Open to freelance. Complete ms by e-mail. **NO PAYMENT.** Articles 1,000-1,200 wds. Prefers e-mail submissions. Guidelines on Website. Incomplete topical listings. (Ads)

Fillers: Accepts games, household tips, party plans, prayers, short humor.

Columns/Departments: Has several columns.

Tips: "We prefer testimony-type articles—not necessarily instructional."

LIFE TOOLS FOR WOMEN, 40 Macewan Park Rise, NW, Calgary AB T3K 3Z9 Canada. (403)295-1932. Fax (403)291-2515. E-mail: editor@lifetoolsforwomen.com. Website: www.lifetoolsforwomen.com. Judy Rushfeldt, ed. Equipping women to reach their potential. Monthly online mag. Monthly page views: 26,000. Articles 500-1,200 wds. **NO PAYMENT**. Provides a byline and up to 50-word bio, including e-mail and Website link. Prefers e-query and e-submission (attached file). Guidelines on Website.

$THE LINK & VISITOR, 1—315 Lonsdale Rd., Toronto ON M4V 1X3 Canada. (416)544-8550. E-mail: linkvis@baptistwomen.com. Website: www.baptistwomen.com. Baptist Women of Ontario and Quebec. Esther Barnes, ed. A positive, practical Baptist magazine for Canadian women who want to reach others for Christ. Bimonthly mag.; 24 pgs.; circ. 4,000. Subscription $16 Can., $16 US. 15% unsolicited freelance; 85% assigned. Complete ms; e-query OK. Pays .06-.10/wd., .05-.10/wd. Can., on publication for one-time or simultaneous rts.; some work-for-hire. Articles 750-1,500 wds. (30/yr.). Responds in 16 wks. Seasonal 3 mos. ahead. Accepts simultaneous submissions and reprints (tell when/where appeared). Requires e-mail submission (copied into message). No kill fee. Uses some sidebars. Prefers NIV (inclusive language), NRSV, NLT. Guidelines/theme list on Website; copy for 9x12 SAE/.90 Canadian postage. (Ads—limited/Canadian)

Poetry: Buys 3/yr. Free verse; 12-32 lines; $10-20. Submit max. 3 poems.

Tips: "Feature writers who know our magazine and our readers will know what topics and types of stories we are looking for. Canadian writers only, please."

LUTHERAN WOMAN'S QUARTERLY, 3121 Chelsea Ct., South Bend IN 46614-2207. Phone/fax (574)291-8297. E-mail: donnajs@michiana.org, or lwml@lwml.org. Website: www.lwml .org. Lutheran Women's Missionary League. Donna Streufert, ed-in-chief. For women of the Lutheran Church—Missouri Synod. Quarterly mag.; 44 pgs.; circ. 200,000. Subscription $4.50. 25% unsolicited freelance; 75% assigned. Complete ms/cover letter. **NO PAYMENT.** Not copyrighted. Articles 750-1,200 wds. (4/yr.); fiction 750-1,200 wds. (4/yr.). Responds in 2 wks. Seasonal 5 mos. ahead. Regularly uses sidebars. Prefers NIV. Guidelines/theme list (also by e-mail); no copy.

> **Tips:** "Most open to articles. Must reflect the Missouri Synod teachings. Most of our writers are from the denomination. We set themes two years ahead. Contact us for themes and guidelines."

+MAKING WAVES, 394 Bloor St. W., #201, Toronto ON M5S 1X4 Canada. (416)929-5184. Fax (416)929-4064. E-mail: barfoot@wicc.org. Website: www.wicc.org. Women's Inter-Church Council of Canada. Karen Hincke, pub. A Christian feminist journal committed to addressing issues related to women, justice, and theology from ecumenical faith perspective. Bimonthly mag.; circ. 4,000. Subscription $16. Open to unsolicited freelance. Incomplete topical listings. (Ads)

> **Tips:** "We are connected to a wider network of women and men working to free church and society from racism, ageism and sexism, and from the teachings and practices that discriminate against women."

$MELODY OF THE HEART E-ZINE: Reconciling Hearts; Offering Hope, 8409 S. Elder Glenwood St., Broken Arrow OK 74011. (918)451-4017. Cell (918)695-4528; Website: http://epistleworks.com/HeartMelody E-mail: editor1@epistleworks.com (do not e-mail directly, use submission form at site). No fax or postal submissions. Published by Epistle-Works Creations—JoAnn Reno Wray, owner, ed./pub. For women, 30-60+ yrs. Vivid writing with scriptural accuracy to bring a practical and joyful approach to life. Quarterly e-zine; 130,000 hits a month. Open to freelance. Query ONLY (using only the online form provided on Website). Pays $15-20 for articles, $20-25 for fiction, $5-8 for poetry on publication for 1st or reprint electronic rts. Contracts issued for work used (archived for one issue only; market elsewhere after 1 month display). Articles 500-900 wds.; short fiction 600-900 wds. Poetry to 24 lines only. Tries to respond but normally can't unless they'd like to use the material. Seasonal 6 mos. prior. Guidelines/theme list/submission form on Website. PDF guidelines available online to download.

> **Poetry:** Music of the Poet Department—poems on theme of targeted issue. Buys 12+/yr.; 4-24 lines. Submit max. 2 poems; theme related. Wait for response before submitting more. Complete ms. Pays $6-8.50. First or one-time electronic rts. Submit max. 2 poems. "Avoid common overused rhymes; try forms other than iambic pentameter; use words to paint vivid images and scenes to help readers see scriptural truths. More poetry received than anything. More poetry is rejected than any other type of writing due to telegraphed end rhymes and overused, tired ideas."
>
> **Fillers:** Short humor, news, kids sayings, anecdotes, husband/wife shorts, animal antics, interesting facts, health info, household tips, devotions. Buys 15-30 fillers/year. Send complete ms. via online form. Under 200 wds.; prefers under 150. Pays $3-10.
>
> **Columns/Departments:** Life Steps (illustrates the work of God in your life in some way), 500-900 wds.; How Do I? (how-to), 500-750 wds.; Just Do It! (what you do that ministers God's love to others), 500-900 wds.; It's the Little Things (lessons learned or insights gained from the seemingly insignificant), 500-750 wds.; Teen Quest (teen interest), 500-750 wds.; Crafting Love (instructions for craft projects), 900 wds.; Cooking with Taste (recipes), 900 wds. Book Reviews (new and about to be released books), 350-800 wds. Query only via online form. Pays $15-25 for articles or fiction; $6.00-8.50 for poems (submit poems

whole with cover note). Regular columns written by staff columnists. Open to new column proposals from writers. If accepted, they become staff columnists. Must include 2 sample columns and commit to 4/year. Use online form. Pays $30 per column.

Tips: "We hope to increase from a quarterly to six times a year in 2005 and that will mean more opportunities for freelancers. 2004 was a spotty year in getting new issues up due to personal and health problems, but the number of readers more than doubled. God has a plan! Biggest lack in quality submissions is in Fiction Fountain (short fiction), Cook's Corner (recipes and their stories) and Crafting Love (crafts). Being previously unpublished is no hindrance to being published here. However, over 65% of submissions miss the mark due to failure to study guidelines and read content of the e-zine. Follow guidelines to the best of your ability. If you have questions, then e-mail only send them by e-mail using the form on the Connections Page. (http://epistleworks.com/HeartMelody/INFO/connections.html) Always include a short bio with your query or submission. Target your submission or query to a specific issue's theme and to a specific department in the e-zine. Have patience waiting on responses. I know what freelancing is like since I've done it for over 35 years. I'm the whole kazoo here with minimal help. Wait until we have an editor/writer relationship to submit without using the submission form."

$MOMSENSE, 2370 S. Trenton Way, Denver CO 80231. (303)733-5353. Fax (303)733-5770. E-mail: MOMsense@mops.org. Website: www.mops.org. MOPS Intl., Inc. (Mothers of Preschoolers). Elizabeth Jusino, ed. Nurtures mothers of preschoolers from a Christian perspective with articles that both inform and inspire on issues relating to womanhood and motherhood. Bimonthly mag.; 24 pgs.; circ. 100,000. 20% unsolicited freelance; 30% assigned. Query; fax/e-query OK. Pays .15/wd. on publication for 1st rts. Articles 600-1,000 wds. (15/yr.). Responds in 6-8 wks. Seasonal 6 mos. ahead. Accepts simultaneous submissions and reprints (tell when/where appeared). Prefers requested ms by e-mail (attached file or copied into message). Kill fee 10%. Uses some sidebars. Prefers NIV. Guidelines/theme list (also by e-mail); copy for 9x12 SAE. (No ads)

   Contest: Sponsors several contests per year for writing and photography. Check Website for details on current contests.

   Tips: "Most open to theme-specific features. Writers are more seriously considered if they are a mother with some connection to MOPS (but not required). Looking for original content ideas that appeal to Christian and non-Christian readers."

   **2001 EPA Award of Merit—Most Improved Publication.

+PRAISE MAGAZINE (PRA!SE), PO Box 11492, Baltimore MD 21239. E-mail: submissions@praisemagazine.com. Website: www.praisemagazine.com. Geared toward African American women. Submit to The Editor. Bimonthly mag. Open to freelance. Complete ms; e-query OK. **NO PAYMENT** for one-time rts. (Articles may be held for use in future issues.) Articles 500-1,500 wds.; book reviews (fiction & nonfiction). Accepts e-mail submissions (copied into message). Guidelines by e-mail; themes on Website.

   Poetry: Accepts poetry.

   Special Needs: Skin, hair, fashion design/trends/tips, health advice, home decorating, recipes. Movie & music reviews.

   Tips: "Relax. Be warm and personal. Think about what information the readers can take away with them. How can this help create balance in their life?"

P31 WOMAN, 616-G Matthews-Mint Hill Rd., Matthews NC 28105. (704)849-2270. Fax (704)849-7267. E-mail: editor@proverbs31.org. Website: www.proverbs31.org. Proverbs 31 Ministries. Glynnis Whitwer, ed. Seeks to offer a godly woman's perspective on life. Monthly mag.; 16 pgs.; circ. 7,000. Subscription for donation. 50% unsolicited freelance; 50% assigned. Complete ms; e-query OK. **PAYS IN COPIES** for one-time rts. Not copyrighted. Articles 200-1,000 wds. (40/yr.). Responds in 4-6 wks. Seasonal 3 mos. ahead.

Accepts simultaneous submissions and reprints (tell when/where appeared). Prefers accepted ms by e-mail (attached file or copied into message). Uses some sidebars. Prefers NIV. Guidelines/theme list (also on Website); copy on Website. (No ads)

> **Fillers:** Accepts 12/yr. Ideas, party ideas, prose; to 100 wds.
>
> **Tips:** "Looking for articles that encourage women and offer practical advice as well."

REFLECTIONS, 5351 N.W. 11th St., Lauderhill FL 33313-6406. (954)587-0129. E-mail: thesilentwoman2@aol.com. Ellen Waldron, pub. Good news and inspiration for all ages. Quarterly newsletter; 20+ pgs. Subscription $15. 90% unsolicited freelance; 10% assigned. Complete ms/cover letter. **PAYS 4 COPIES.** Not copyrighted. Articles 400 wds. (6/yr.); fiction 1,000 wds. (6/yr.). Responds in 6-8 wks. Seasonal 2 mos. ahead. Accepts e-mail submissions. Uses some sidebars. Guidelines/theme list; copy for $2/10x13 SAE/$1.42 postage (mark "Media Mail"). (Ads)

> **Poetry:** Accepts 10/yr. Free verse, haiku, light verse, traditional; 5-30 lines. Submit max. 5 poems. Poetry to reach those who have suffered abuse and found the Lord.
>
> **Columns/Departments:** Accepts 6/yr. Pen Pals Corner (write service families in armed forces); Helpful Hints (ideas to help others), 400 wds.; Joy, Joy, Joy (good news), 400 wds.; Chicklette Gazette (children ages 4-12), 200 wds.; Teen Corner (sharing ideas for 13- to 19-year-olds), 400 wds.; On the Road (travel).
>
> **Tips:** "Have an interest in writing; write from the heart. No foul language or anything offensive. Writers must send a notarized release before we can print their work (under 18 years, parent must sign). Fiction is for children or teens."

RIGHT TO THE HEART OF WOMEN E-ZINE, 2217 Lake Park Dr., Longmont CO 80503. (303)772-2035. Fax (303)678-0260. E-mail: Rebekah@rebekahmontgomery.com. Website: www.righttotheheartofwomen.com. Rebekah Montgomery, ed. Encouragement and helps for women in ministry. Bimonthly online e-zine; 20 pgs.; circ. 4,000. Subscription free. 10% unsolicited freelance; 90% assigned. Query; e-query OK. **NO PAYMENT** for nonexclusive rts. Articles 100-300 wds. (20/yr.); book reviews 100 wds. Responds in 2 wks. Seasonal 4 mos. ahead. Accepts simultaneous submissions and reprints (tell when/where appeared). Requires accepted mss by e-mail (copied into message). No sidebars. No guidelines; copy on Website. (Ads)

> **Fillers:** Accepts 12/yr. Anecdotes, ideas, party ideas, prayers, quotes; 50-200 wds.
>
> **Columns/Departments:** Accepts 10/yr. Women Bible Teachers; Profiles of Women in Ministry; Women's Ministry Tips; Author's and Speaker's Tips; 100 wds. Query.
>
> **Special Needs:** Book reviews must be in first person, by the author. Looking for women's ministry event ideas.
>
> **Tips:** "For free subscription, subscribe at Website above; also view e-zine. We want to hear from those involved in women's ministry or leadership. Also accepts manuscripts from AWSAs (see www.awsawomen.com). Query with your ideas."

+SHALOM BAYIT: Peace in the Home, PO Box 23, West Charleston VT 05872. E-mail: puritanstore@aol.com. Website: www.thepuritanlight.com. The Puritan Light Ministry. Sharon White, ed. For homeschooling mothers, from a Puritan/Jewish perspective. Quarterly mag.; 32 pgs. Subscription free. 20% unsolicited freelance; 10% assigned. Complete ms/cover letter; e-query OK (no attachments). **PAYS 2 COPIES.** Articles 400-1,500 wds. (8/yr.). Responds in 2 wks. Seasonal 2 mos. ahead. No simultaneous submissions or reprints. Accepts e-mail submissions (copied into message). No sidebars. Accepts submissions from children or teens. No guidelines; free copy. (No ads)

> **Columns/Departments:** Memories of Grandmother (nostalgic stories of grandmother), 500 wds.; Dear Daughter (letter to a future keeper at home), 800 wds.; Etiquette (share how ladies behaved long ago), 400 wds. Complete ms.
>
> **Tips:** "This is our new magazine (formerly published Stepping Out of the Darkness). The

editor owns and operates a country store in rural Vermont. We focus on home business, homeschooling, tender mothering, peaceful marriage, and old-fashioned living. Ask for a free subscription; read a few issues; then start writing."

SHARE, 10 W. 71st St., New York NY 10023-4201. (212)877-3041. Fax (212)724-5923. E-mail: CDofANatl@aol.com. Website: www.catholicdaughters.org. Catholic Daughters of the Americas. Margaret O'Brien, exec. dir.; submit to Peggy Eastman, ed. For Catholic women. Quarterly mag.; circ. 100,000. Free with membership. Most articles come from membership, but is open. **NO PAYMENT.** Buys color photos and covers. Guidelines/copy. Not in topical listings. (Ads)

   Tips: "We use very little freelance material unless it is written by Catholic Daughters."

$#SIMPLE JOY. E-mail: JeanAnn@simplejoy.org. Website: www.simplejoy.org. Jean Ann Duckworth, pub.; submit to The Editor. For women (target age 30-55) interested in a simpler way of life. Monthly online mag. Open to freelance. Query first; e-query OK (queries@simplejoy.org). Pays $25 honorarium on publication for articles 1,500-2,000 wds.; $10 for under 1,000 wds.; within 60 days of publication; for one-time rts. Seasonal 4 mos. ahead. Prefers e-mail (attached file in Word format). Guidelines by e-mail (guidelines@simplejoy.org). For list of upcoming needs, send an e-mail to: topics@simplejoy.org. Incomplete topical listings.

   Columns/Departments: Simple Home, 1,500-2,000 wds.; Simple Celebrations, 1,000-1,500 wds.; Simple Traditions, 1,000-1,500 wds.; Joy for Couples, 1,5000-2,000 wds.; Joy with Children, 1,500-2,000 wds.; Simple Garden, 1,000-1,500 wds.; Simple Cooking, 1,000-1,500 wds.

   Special Needs: Creating a simpler life, guilt- and stress-free parenting, organization, turning house into home, comfort, relaxation, journaling, spirituality, strengthening relationships, and home cooking.

   Tips: "Keep in mind our Three Rules of Simple Joy as you write your articles. (See Website.)"

$SPIRITLED WOMAN, 600 Rinehart Rd., Lake Mary FL 32746. (407)333-0600. Fax (407)333-7133. E-mail: spiritledwoman@strang.com. Website: www.spiritledwoman.com. Strang Communications. Brenda J. Davis, ed. To call women, ages 20-60, into intimate fellowship with God so He can empower them to fulfill His purpose for their lives. Bimonthly mag.; 100 pgs.; circ. 100,000. Subscription $17.95. 1% unsolicited freelance; 99% assigned. Query (limit to 500 wds.); e-query OK. Pays to $300 ($50 for humor, $75 for testimonies) on publication for 1st and all electronic rts. Articles 1,200-2,000 wds. Responds in 18-26 wks. No simultaneous submissions. Guidelines (also by e-mail); copy. (Ads)

   Columns/Departments: Testimonies; Final Fun (funny stories or embarrassing moments, to 200 wds.); cartoons; $25-50.

   Tips: "Mainly we want high impact feature articles that depict a practical and spiritual application of scriptural teachings. Need brief testimonies of 300 words or less; profiles of women in ministry. Articles need to deal with the heart issues that hold a woman back. Also humor and book excerpts."

+TAPESTRY, 2816 Calder Ave., Saskatoon SK S7J 1W1 Canada. (306)343-7396. Fax (306)683-7296. E-mail: hollinger@sasktel.net. Lutheran Women's Missionary League of Canada. Marion Hollinger, ed-in-chief. To enable readers to know and reflect their Saviour and to understand how the LWML can help them do so. Quarterly mag.; circ. 3,700. Subscription $7. Open to unsolicited freelance. Not in topical listings. (Ads)

TAPESTRY: A Woman's Guide to Intimacy with God, 4201 N. Peachtree Rd., Atlanta GA 30341. (770)458-9300. Fax (770)454-9313. E-mail: pubsinfo@walkthru.org. Website: www.walkthru.org. Walk Thru the Bible. Monthly mag. Requires NIV.

$TODAY'S CHRISTIAN WOMAN, 465 Gundersen Dr., Carol Stream IL 60188-2498. (630)260-6200. Fax (630)260-0114. E-mail: TCWedit@christianitytoday.com. Website: www.Todays ChristianWoman.com. Christianity Today Intl. Jane Johnson Struck, ed.; submit to Holly Robaina, asst. ed. To help Christian women (20-49 yrs.) grow in their relationship to God by providing practical, biblical perspectives on marriage, sex, parenting, work, health, friendship, single life, and self. Bimonthly mag.; 80-150 pgs.; circ. 250,000. Subscription $17.95. 25% unsolicited freelance; 75% assigned. Query only; fax/e-query OK. Pays .20/wd. on publication (on acceptance for assignments) for 1st rts. Articles 1,000-1,800 wds. (6-12/yr.); no fiction. Responds in 8 wks. Seasonal 6 mos. ahead. Accepts reprints (tell when/where appeared); no simultaneous submissions. Accepts e-mail submission (copied into message). Regularly uses sidebars. Prefers NIV. Guidelines; copy $5. (Ads)

> **Columns/Departments:** Camerin Courtney, ed. of My Story. Buys 6/yr. My Story (dramatic story of overcoming a difficult situation), 1,500 wds., $300. Faith@Work (how you shared faith in the marketplace), 300 wds., $25. Reader's Picks (personal book or CD review), 200 wds. Small Talk (funny things kids say), 100 wds.
>
> **Special Needs:** Articles slanted for mature Christians that deal with spiritual life topics; short humor pieces.
>
> **Tips:** "Break in by submitting to our reader-solicited questions or My Story. Make sure your writing has a fresh approach to a relational topic and that it has a personal tone and anecdotal approach. Please query first."
>
> **#3 Best-selling Magazine in Christian retail stores. Also 2000 & 1996 EPA Award of Merit—General.

TRUEWOMAN, PO Box 8732, Columbia SC 29202. Fax (775)908-9660. E-mail: webmaster@ faithwebbin.net. Website: www.faithwebbin.net/truewoman. Mrs. Tyora Moody, owner. For Christian women. Online mag. Complete ms by e-mail submission. **NO PAYMENT.** Guidelines on Website.

> **Fillers:** Beauty, health, and household tips.
>
> **Special Needs:** Arts and crafts, mentoring, mothering, any articles of interest to women.
>
> **Tips:** "If you are the writer, please send information about yourself as well (a short bio and contact e-mail submission address for readers). If you are not the writer, please include proper credits."

$WELCOME HOME, 9493-C Silver King Ct., Fairfax VA 22031. Toll-free (800)783-4MOM. (703)352-1072. Fax (703)352-1076. E-mail: fahn@familyandhome.org. Website: www.familyandhome.org. Mothers at Home, Inc. Laura M. Jones, ed-in-chief; submit to Manuscript Coordinator. For women who have chosen to stay at home with their children. Monthly jour.; 30 pgs.; circ. 10,000. Subscription $22. 100% unsolicited freelance. Complete ms/cover letter; no e-query. Pays gift certificate for first-time submissions, $20-30 for subsequent submissions, for one-time rts. Articles to 2,400 wds., most 500-1,500 wds. (60/yr.). Acknowledges receipt in 2-4 wks., decision in 3-6 mos. Seasonal 1 yr. ahead. No e-mail submission. Uses some sidebars. Guidelines (request specific guidelines for departments interested in; also on Website); copy for 7x10 SAE/3 stamps. (No ads)

> **Poetry:** Winnie Peterson Cross, poetry ed. Accepts 48/yr. Free verse, haiku, light verse, traditional. Responds in up to 1 yr.
>
> **Columns/Departments:** Accepts 36/yr. From a Mother (surprising/sudden insights); Resource Roundup (books/resources); New Dimensions (personal growth/development); Heartwarming (cooking/recipes); Health & Safety (mother's/child's health, family safety); Time to Care (volunteer work); all 700-1,000 wds.
>
> **Tips:** "This is a publication for all mothers at home, and not for those with any particular religious background. Articles which focus on a religious theme will not be accepted."

$WOMAN'S TOUCH, 1445 N. Boonville Ave., Springfield MO 65802-1894. (417)862-2781. Fax (417)862-0503. E-mail: womanstouch@ag.org. Website: www.ag.org/womanstouch. Assemblies of God Women's Ministries Dept. Darla J. Knoth, mng. ed. Inspirational magazine for women. Bimonthly mag.; 36 pgs.; circ. 12,200. Subscription $9.95. 20% unsolicited freelance; 80% assigned. Query only; fax/e-query OK. Pays $20-35 (.03/wd) on publication for one-time and electronic rts. Articles 500-800 wds. (20/yr.). Responds in 13 wks. Seasonal 10 mos. ahead. Accepts simultaneous submissions and reprints (tell when/where appeared). Accepts e-mail submission. Kill fee. Regularly uses sidebars. Prefers NIV. Guidelines/theme list (also by e-mail); copy for 9x12 SAE/3 stamps. (No ads)

> **Columns/Departments:** Buys 30/yr. Body Wise (health/fitness), 300 wds.; The Single Woman (never married, widowed, divorced), 400 wds.; Family Matters (single or married moms); I Still Do! (marriage), 400 wds.; $10-40.
>
> **Tips:** "Request guidelines and theme list for guidance on types of articles needed."
>
> **2003 EPA Award of Excellence—Most Improved Publication.

$WOMEN ALIVE! PO Box 480052, Kansas City MO 64148. Phone/fax (913)402-1369. E-mail: ahinthorn@kc.rr.com. Website: www.womenalivemagazine.org. Aletha Hinthorn, ed. To encourage women to live holy lives by applying Scripture to their daily lives. Bimonthly mag.; 20 pgs.; circ. 5,000-6,000. Subscription $13.95. 50% unsolicited freelance; 0% assigned. Complete ms/no cover letter; no phone/fax query. Pays $25-50 on publication for 1st or reprint rts. Articles 300-1,800 wds. (7/yr.). Responds in 4-6 wks. Seasonal 4 mos. ahead. Accepts reprints. Uses some sidebars. No disk. Prefers KJV, NIV. Guidelines/theme list (also by e-mail); copy for 9x12 SAE/4 stamps. (No ads)

> **Fillers:** Buys 0-1/yr. Cartoons, jokes, short humor.
>
> **Tips:** "We look for articles that draw women into a deeper spiritual life—articles on surrender, prayer, Bible study—yet written with personal illustrations."

$WOMEN BY GRACE, PO Box 691, Gaylord MI 49734. E-mail: kelly@womenbygrace.com. Website: www.womenbygrace.com. Gaylord Community Church. Kelly McCausey, ed. Monthly e-zine; circ. 300+. Subscription free. 25% unsolicited freelance. Complete ms; e-query OK. Pays $5-10 on acceptance for online permanent archive rts. Articles 500-900 wds. (50/yr.); fiction 500-900 wds. (10/yr.). Responds in 1 wk. Seasonal 2 mos. ahead. Accepts simultaneous submissions and reprints. Prefers submissions by e-mail (copied into message). No kill fee. Uses some sidebars. Prefers NIV. Guidelines (also by e-mail); copy online only. (No ads)

> **Fillers:** Buys 25/yr. Anecdotes, jokes, short humor; 50-250 wds.; $5.
>
> **Columns/Departments:** Buys 20/yr. Building a Home By Grace (home, recipes, crafts); Divorce By Grace (devotions for the divorced); $5-10.
>
> **Tips:** "All areas open to freelance. Do not use religious language."

+WOMEN OF THE CROSS, 920 Sweetgum Creek, Plano TX 75023. E-mail: info@womenof thecross.com. Website: www.menofthecross.com. Greg Paskal, ed./pub.(greg@gregpaskal .com). Encouraging women in their walk with the Lord; strong emphasis on discipleship and relationship. Online community. Open to unsolicited freelance. Complete ms. by e-mail; e-query OK. **NO PAYMENT.** Articles 500-2,000 wds. Accepts reprints.

> **Tips:** "Appropriate topics could be first-hand accounts of how God worked in the author's life. View online forum for specific topics."

WOMEN TODAY MAGAZINE, Box 300 Sta. A, Vancouver BC V6C 2X3, Canada. (604)514-2000 (no phone calls). Fax (604)514-2124. E-mail: editor@womentodaymagazine.com. Website: www.womentodaymagazine.com. Campus Crusade for Christ, Canada. Karen Schenk, pub.; Claire Colvin, ed. For the professional, pre-seeking woman, 20-60 years; provides quality information that leads into a discussion of spiritual things and a presentation of the gospel. Monthly online e-zine; 1.8 million hits/mo.; 60,000 unique visitors/mo. 90% unsolicited freelance; up to 10% assigned. Query; fax/e-query OK. Accepts full ms by e-mail. **NO PAYMENT** for one-time or reprint rts. Articles 300-1,000 wds. (12-24/yr.). Responds in 8-12 wks. Seasonal 2 mos. ahead. Accepts simultaneous submissions and reprints (tell when/where appeared). Prefers e-mail submission (attached or copied into message). Does not use sidebars. Accepts submissions from teens. Guidelines (also by e-mail/Website). (Ads)

Columns/Departments: Columns tend toward how-to; 600-1,000 wds. Beauty & Fashion; Health & Fitness; Food & Cooking; Advice.

Tips: "Beauty/fashion, relationships, and self-esteem are big draws on our site, and we can always use more great content. To break in, make your article approachable to an unchurched audience, avoid Christian jargon, and speak the truth plainly."

$*WOMEN'S FAITH & SPIRIT, 125 Park Ave., New York NY 10017. Meredith Corp. Pamela Guthrie O'Brien, ed. Explores what faith means to the reader and how it affects daily life and the way women view the world. Monthly mag.; 112 pgs.; circ. 350,000. No information on openness to freelance. Not included in topical listings. No questionnaire returned.

WOMEN'S MINISTRY MAGAZINE, 1730 E. Republic Rd., Ste. A-220, Springfield MO 65804. (417)888-2067. Fax (417)888-2095. E-mail: publisher@womensministry.net. Website: www.womensministry.net. Jennifer and Philip Rothschild, pubs. Where more than 9,000 women's ministry leaders find news, events, and tips for women's ministry in the local church. Online newsletter. Subscription free. Open to freelance. Guidelines by e-mail.

Special Needs: Punchy, practical tips and ideas related to leading effective women's ministry.

WRITERS' MARKETS

$ADVANCED CHRISTIAN WRITER, 9731 N. Fox Glen Dr., #6F, Niles IL 60714-4222. (847)296-3964. Fax (847)296-0754. E-mail: lin@wordprocommunications.com. Website: www.ACWriters.com. American Christian Writers/Reg Forder, Box 110390, Nashville TN 37222. Toll-free (800)21-WRITE. E-mail: ACWriters@aol.com. Lin Johnson, mng. ed. A professional newsletter for published writers. Bimonthly newsletter; 8 pgs.; circ. 500. Subscription $19. 60% unsolicited freelance; 0% assigned. Query, correspondence, and mss by e-mail only. Pays $20 on publication for 1st or reprint rts. Articles 500-1,000 wds. (18/yr.). Responds in 4-6 wks. Seasonal 6 mos. ahead. Accepts reprints (tell when/where appeared). Regularly uses sidebars. Requires e-mail submission. Prefers NIV. Guidelines (also by e-mail); copy for #10 SAE/1 stamp. (Ads)

Special Needs: Behind the scenes look at a publishing house (how it started, how editorial operates, current needs, submission procedures).

Tips: "We accept articles only from professional, well-published writers and from editors. We need manuscripts about all aspects of being a published freelance writer and how to increase sales and professionalism; on the advanced level; looking for depth beyond the basics."

$AREOPAGUS MAGAZINE (UK), 101 Maytree Close, Winchester SO22 4JF, United Kingdom. Fax 0870 1346384. E-mail for UK: areopagus@churchnet.org.uk. E-mail for US: Areopag USA@aol.com. Website: www.churchnet.org.uk/areopagus/index.html. Areopagus Publications. Julian Barritt, ed. For amateur and semiprofessional Christian writers, producing both secular and Christian writing. Quarterly mag.; 32 pgs.; circ. 150. Subscription $17 (now on sale in US). 80% unsolicited freelance; 20% assigned. Complete ms/cover letter (if subscriber); e-query OK. Pays 3-7 pounds (or equivalent in dollars) on publication for 1st and electronic rts. Articles 1,800 wds. (40/yr.); fiction 1,800 wds. (15/yr.); book reviews 300 wds. Responds in 2 wks. Seasonal 4 mos. ahead. Accepts e-mail submissions (attached or copied into message). Does not use sidebars. Any Bible version. Guidelines; copy (also on Website) for 9x12 SAE/equivalent of 31 pence for postage. (Ads)

Poetry: Buys 40/yr. Any type; to 60 lines. Pays 3 pounds. Submit max. 5 poems.

Fillers: Accepts 12/yr. Facts, ideas, newsbreaks, prayers, prose, short humor, to 200 wds. No payment.

Contest: Sponsors a quarterly, subscribers-only, writing competition (fiction, nonfiction, or poetry theme) with prizes of 25 pounds.

Tips: "Send an idea with short sample in the first instance. Items are selected by merit from subscribers only. If not accepted, a recommendation for re-submission is given if there is potential." Purchases from subscribers only.

#AUTHOR-ME.COM. E-mail: ccfictioneditor@aol.com. Website: www.Author-Me.com. Independent. Rena Williams, mng. ed. Endeavors to encourage and nurture new writers in their craft. Accepts freelance. Complete ms. **NO PAYMENT.** No submissions from writers under age 14. Edit manuscripts before submitting. Requires e-mail submissions (attached or copied into message). Guidelines on Website.

Poetry: Submit max. 4 poems.

THE AUTHOR NETWORK E-ZINE, 35A Lower Park Rd., Brightlingsea, Essex CO7 OJX, England. Phone/fax 44 01206 303607. E-mail: submissions@author-network.com. Website: www.author-network.com/submissions.html. Karen Scott, pub. (karen@author-network .com). A distinctive and cutting-edge resource site for writers seeking material that challenges, questions, and pushes out the boundaries. Online mag. Open to freelance. Query or complete ms by e-mail (attached or copied into message). **NO PAYMENT,** but lists bio and links for author, for one-time rts. (stays on Website indefinitely). Articles 1,500-2,000 wds. Responds in wks. Guidelines on Website. Incomplete topical listings.

Special Needs: Also does novellas and novels as e-books under Puff Adder Books. Guidelines on Website: www.puff-adder.com/submissions.html. "We are looking for well-written, original novels with strong characterization, lifelike dialog, evocative setting, and compelling themes. We strongly advise studying material on site before submitting."

Tips: "We are looking for well-written material to add to the site, but only interested in articles, essays, columns, etc., on writing-related issues."

BEGINNINGS: A Magazine for Novice Writers, PO Box 92, Shirley NY 11967. (631)205-5542. Fax (631)924-3019. E-mail: jenine@optonline.net. Website: www.scbeginnings .com. Caters only to the aspiring writer. Jenine Boisits, ed-in-chief. Triannual mag.; 48 pgs.; circ. 1,500. Subscription $14. 95% unsolicited freelance; 5% assigned. Charges a reading fee of $10 if you send more than one ms or 5 poems at a time. Complete ms/cover letter or query (for nonfiction); query/clips or complete ms (for fiction); e-query OK. **PAYS IN COPIES** for one-time rts. Articles (2-4/yr.) & short stories (30/yr.) to 3,000 wds. Responds in 16 wks. Accepts simultaneous submissions; no reprints. Prefers requested ms by e-mail (copied into message), or on disk. Uses some sidebars. Guidelines (also by e-mail/Website—www.scbeginnings.com/guidelines.htm); copy $4/10x13 SAE/5 stamps.

Poetry: Freada Dillon, poetry ed. Reasonable length. Submit only by mail. Submit max. 5 poems.

Fillers: Buys cartoons; $5.

Special Needs: Short stories, poetry, or artwork written by children. Written work: ages 5-12. Or same material from young adults: 13-19 yrs. Artwork must be on plain, unruled white paper.

Contest: Sponsors poetry and short story contests, 4 contests for each season. See Website for current contests and details.

$#BOOK: The Magazine for the Reading Life, 417 Overhill Rd., South Orange NJ 07079-1213. Toll-free (800)317-2665. (212)659-7070. Fax (212)736-4455. E-mail: alanger@

bookmagazine.com. Website: www.bookmagazine.com. West Egg Communications, LLC; secular. Jerome V. Kramer, ed.; submit to Adam Langer. Focuses on books and reading. Bimonthly mag.; circ. 900,000. 80% unsolicited freelance. Query/clips for nonfiction; complete ms for fiction; fax/e-query OK. Pays $.50-1.50/wd. for nonfiction, $300-5,000 for fiction, 30 days after publication for 1st and electronic rts.; makes work-for-hire assignments. Articles 1,000-4,000 wds.; fiction 1,000-10,000 wds. Seasonal 4 mos. ahead. Kill fee. Copy online. Incomplete topical listings. No questionnaire returned.

Columns/Departments: Buys 36/yr. Shop Watch (bookstore profiles); Locations (literary travel); Group Dynamics (book-group tips, stories); Web Catches (related to books online); all to 1,500 wds.

$BRADY MAGAZINE, 165 Old Muskoka Rd., Ste. 306, Gravenurst ON P1P 1N3 Canada. E-mail: info@bradymagazine.com. Website: www.bradymagazine.com. Independent. Krissy Brady, ed. Where writers meet writers; writing related material only. Bimonthly mag. Open to freelance. Complete ms by e-mail only (submissions@bradymagazine.com, or submissions form on Website); no attached files. Pays $15 Canadian on publication. Articles 1,000-2,500 wds. Accepts simultaneous submissions and reprints (tell when/where appeared). Guidelines on Website. (Ads)

Fillers: Tips 50-200 wds.; pays $5.

Special Needs: Writing success stories, 200-500 wds.; pays $10.

$BYLINE, Box 5240, Edmond OK 73083-5240. Phone/fax (405)348-5591. E-mail: Mpreston@ bylinemag.com. Website: www.BylineMag.com. Secular. Marcia Preston, ed.; Carolyn Wall, fiction ed. Offers practical tips, motivation, and encouragement to freelance writers and poets. Monthly (11X) mag.; 32 pgs.; circ. 3,000+. Subscription $22. 80% unsolicited freelance. Query or complete ms; no phone/fax query; e-query OK. Pays $75 for features; $100 for fiction; less for shorts, on acceptance for 1st rts. Articles 1,500-1,800 wds. (75/yr.); personal essays 700 wds.; fiction 2,000-4,000 wds. (11/yr.). Responds in 6 wks. Seasonal 6 mos. ahead. Accepts simultaneous submissions. No e-mail submissions. Encourages sidebars. Guidelines on Website; copy $4. (Ads)

Poetry: Sandra Soli, poetry ed. Buys 50-100/yr. Any type; to 30 lines; $10. Writing themes only. Submit max. 3 poems.

Fillers: Anecdotes, prose, short humor for humor page; 50-400 wds.; $15-25. Must pertain to writing.

Columns/Departments: Buys 50-60/yr. End Piece (personal essay on writing theme), 700 wds., $35; First Sale accounts, 300 wds., $20; Only When I Laugh (writing humor), short, $15-25. Complete ms.

Contests: Sponsors many year round; details included in magazine, on Website, or send SASE for flier.

Special Needs: Accepts articles only about writing and selling; likes mainstream fiction.

Tips: "All areas except our regular columns are open to freelancers. We get much more fiction than nonfiction. Always looking for instructive, well-written articles."

**This periodical was #48 on the 2004 Top 50 Christian Publishers list.

$CANADIAN WRITER'S JOURNAL, White Mountain Publications, Box 1178, New Liskeard ON P0J 1P0 Canada. Canada-wide toll-free (800)258-5451. (705)647-5424. Fax (705)647-8366. E-mail: cwj@cwj.ca. For submissions: submissions@cwj.ca. Website: www.cwj.ca. Deborah Ranchuk, ed./pub. How-to articles for writers. Bimonthly mag.; 64 pgs.; circ. 350. Subscription $37.45. 85% unsolicited freelance; 15% assigned. Complete ms/cover letter or query; e-query OK. Pays $7.50 Can./published pg. on publication (2-9 mos. after acceptance) for one-time rts. Articles 400-2,000 wds. (150/yr.); fiction to 1,200 wds (see contest below); book/music/video reviews 250-500 wds., $7.50. Responds in 12 wks. Seasonal 3 mos. ahead. Accepts simultaneous submissions and reprints (tell when/where appeared). Prefers e-mail submission (copied into message only). Some sidebars. Prefers KJV. Accepts submissions from teens. Guidelines (also by e-mail/Website); copy $8. (Ads)

Poetry: Buys 40-60/yr. All types; to 40 lines; $2-5. Submit max. 10 poems.

Fillers: Buys 15-20/yr. Anecdotes, cartoons, ideas, quotes; 20-200 wds.; $3-5.

Contest: Sponsors semiannual short fiction contest (March 31 and September 30 deadlines); to 1,200 wds. Entry fee $5. Prizes $100, $50, $25. All fiction needs are filled by this contest. E-mail: cwc-calendar@cwj.ca.

Tips: "Send clear, complete, concise how-to-write articles with a sense of humor and usefulness. Read the guidelines and follow them, please."

$THE CHRISTIAN COMMUNICATOR, 9731 N. Fox Glen Dr., #6F, Niles, IL 60714-4222. (847)296-3964. Fax (847)296-0754. E-mail: lin@wordprocommunications.com. Website: www.ACWriters.com. American Christian Writers/Reg Forder, Box 110390, Nashville TN 37222. Toll-free (800)21-WRITE (for samples, advertising or subscriptions), fax (615)834-0450; ACWriters@aol.com. Lin Johnson, mng. ed. For Christian writers/speakers who want to improve their writing craft and speaking ability, stay informed about writing markets, and be encouraged in their ministries. Monthly (11X) mag.; 20 pgs.; circ. 3,000. Subscription $25. 70% unsolicited freelance. Complete ms/queries by e-mail only. Pays $5-10 on publication for 1st or reprint rts. Articles 600-1,000 wds. (80/yr.). Responds in 4-6 wks. Seasonal 6 mos. ahead. Accepts reprints (tell when/where appeared). Requires e-mail submission. Guidelines by e-mail; copy for 9x12 SAE/3 stamps to Nashville address. (Ads)

Poetry: Buys 11/yr. Poems on writing or speaking; $5. Send to Gretchen Sousa, gretloriat@earthlink.net.

Columns/Departments: Buys 80/yr. A Funny Thing Happened on the Way to Becoming a Communicator (humor), 75-300 wds.; Interviews (published authors or editors), 650-1,000 wds.; Speaker's Corner (techniques for speakers), 600-1,000 wds.

Tips: "I need editor profiles and articles for speaker's column."

$CHRISTIAN WRITER, PO Box 22416, Denver CO 80222-0416. (303)758-6556. Fax (303)758-9272. E-mail: Suwriter@aol.com. Su Wright, ed. Focuses on Christians who are writing for both the Christian and general market. This publication currently suspended.

#CHRISTIANWRITERS.COM. Website: www.christianwriters.com. A free online writers' resource community to provide a supportive, family atmosphere where writers may easily access the tools and resources to create, market, and publish their work. Accepts articles, short fiction, poetry, and devotionals. Submit through Website. Guidelines on Website.

COCHRAN'S CORNER, 1003 Tyler Ct., Waldorf MD 20602-2964. (361)645-2476. John Treasure, ed. asst. To encourage a greater interest in writing for art's sake and provide a publication where aspiring and young writers can be published; a family magazine. Quarterly mag.; 25 pgs. Circ. 100. Subscription $20. 95% unsolicited freelance. Complete ms/cover letter; no phone query. **PAYS 1 COPY** for one-time & reprint rts. Articles 1,000 wds. (5/yr.); fiction 1,000 wds. (50/yr.); book reviews 100 wds. Responds in 5 wks. Seasonal 3 mos. ahead. Accepts simultaneous submissions and reprints. No disk. Does not use sidebars. Accepts submissions from children & teens. Guidelines; copy $6/9x12 SAE/3 stamps. (Ads)

Poetry: Billy Keene, poetry ed. Accepts 30/yr. All types; 3-20 lines. Submit max. 5 poems.

Fillers: Accepts 25/yr. Anecdotes, cartoons, games, prayers; to 150 wds.

Columns/Departments: Accepts 5/yr. Gardening (how to grow something, for adults, but simple enough a child could do it), 1,000 wds.

Contest: Annual contest; see magazine or ask to be put on mailing list for contest updates.

Tips: "All sections are open to freelancers. A well-crafted story without violence, pornography, or blue language has the best chance with us."

$CROSS & QUILL, 1624 Jefferson Davis Rd., Clinton SC 29325-6401. (864)697-6035. E-mail: cwfi@cwfi-online.org. Website: www.cwfi-online.org. Christian Writers Fellowship Intl. Sandy Brooks, ed./pub. For Christian writers, editors, agents, conference directors. Bimonthly newsletter; 16 pgs.; circ. 1,000+. Subscription $20; CWFI membership $40. 75% unsolicited freelance; 25% assigned. Complete ms; query for electronic submissions. Pays honorarium for feature articles on publication for 1st or reprint rts. Articles 800-1,000 wds. (24/yr.); book reviews 100 wds. (pays copies). Responds in 2 mos. Seasonal 6 mos. ahead. Accepts reprints (tell when/where appeared). Regularly uses sidebars. Accepts e-mail submission to: CQArticles@cwfi-online.org. Guidelines; copy $2/9x12 SAE/2 stamps. (Ads)

> **Poetry:** Accepts 12/yr. Any type; to 12 lines. Submit max. 3 poems. Must pertain to writing/publishing.
>
> **Fillers:** Accepts 12/yr. Anecdotes, cartoons, prayers; 25-100 wds. Pays in copies.
>
> **Columns/Departments:** Accepts 36/yr. Writing Rainbows! (devotional), 500-600 wds.; Writers Helping Writers (how-to), 200-800 wds.; Editor's Roundtable (interview with editor), 200-800 wds.; Tots, Teens & In-Betweens (juvenile market), 200-800 wds.; Business-Wise (business side of writing), 200-800 wds.; Connecting Points (how-to on critique group), 200-800 wds.
>
> **Special Needs:** Good "meaty" informational articles on children's writing; writing for teens; how-tos on organizing and operating writers' groups; program ideas for groups; and how to organize and run a writer's workshop, conference, or seminar.
>
> **Tips:** "Most open to informational articles that explain how to improve writing skills, how to keep records, how to organize and run a writers' group. Keep in mind our audience is primarily writers and others associated with Christian publishing."

$EXCHANGE, 1275 Markham Rd., #305, Toronto ON M1H 3A2 Canada. (416)439-4320. Fax (416)439-5089. E-mail: audrey@dorschedit.ca. Website: www.dorschedit.ca. Audrey Dorsch, ed. A forum for Christian writers to share information and ideas. Quarterly newsletter; 8 pgs.; circ. 300. Subscription $19.26 Can., $15 US. 65% unsolicited freelance; 30% assigned. Complete ms/cover letter; fax/e-query OK. Pays .12 Can. & .08 US on publication for one-time rts. Not copyrighted. Articles 400-600 wds. (20/yr.). Responds in 4-6 wks. Accepts reprints (tell when/where appeared). Accepts requested ms on disk, prefers e-mail submission (attached file). Does not use sidebars. Prefers NIV. Guidelines (also by e-mail)/copy for #10 SAE/2 Canadian stamps. (Ads—classified)

> **Special Needs:** Material geared to experienced, professional writers.
>
> **Tips:** "Take a very deliberate approach to the 'how' of good writing. I get too much for the novice writer. If you submit something an experienced writer will learn from, you face much less competition."

$FELLOWSCRIPT, 333 Hunter's Run, Edmonton AB T6R 2N9 Canada. (780)988-5622. Fax (780)430-0139. E-mail: submissions@inscribe.org. Website: www.inscribe.org. Inscribe Christian Writers' Fellowship. Elsie Montgomery & Janet Sketchley, eds. To provide encouragement, instruction, news, and helpful information to Christians who write. Quarterly newsletter; 32-44 pgs.; circ. 175-250. Subscription $40 (includes membership, if desired). 55% unsolicited freelance; 45% assigned. Complete ms/cover letter; no e-query. Accepts full mss by e-mail. Pays .015-.025/wd. Can. on publication for 1st, one-time rts. Articles 400-1,200 wds. (30-50/yr.); book reviews, 400 wds. Responds in 1-4 wks. Seasonal 6 mos. ahead. Accepts simultaneous submissions & reprints (nothing from Internet; tell when/where appeared/pays .015/wd. Can.). Prefers requested ms by e-mail (copied into message). No kill fee. Uses some sidebars. Prefers NIV. Guidelines (also by e-mail/Website); copy $3.50 Can., $3.50 US, plus $1.60 in Canadian stamps or IRCs. (Ads if writing related)

Fillers: Accepts 5-10/yr. Anecdotes, short humor, tips; 100-200 wds. Pays one tear sheet.

Columns/Departments: Accepts 20-25/yr. Opportunities (market news, publishing opportunities, contests, etc.), 25-100 wds., no payment.

Special Needs: Articles of practical help to writers, from beginners to advanced.

Contest: Fall contest in conjunction with Inscribe's Fall Conference. Details on Website, or write and ask to be on mailing list. Spring contest for members only.

Tips: "Most open to short, specific instructional or inspirational articles about writing and the writing life."

$#FICTION FIX NEWSLETTER: The Nuts and Bolts of Crafting Better Fiction. Articles@ coffeehouseforwriters.com. Website: www.coffeehouseforwriters.com/news.html. Carol Lindsay, ed. For writers and aspiring writers of short stories and novels. Monthly; circ. 5,000. To subscribe, send blank e-mail to: FictionFix-subscribe@topica.com. E-query only. Responds in 2-3 wks. Pays to $20 ($30-50 for assigned) within 10 days of publication for 1st electronic rts. How-to articles 300-500 wds. Prefers submission by e-mail (copied into message/see guidelines for specifics). Guidelines on Website.

Columns/Departments: This Writer's Opinion (reviews of writing books), 300-500 wds.; The Writing Life (personal writing stories). No payment.

HEAVEN, 207 Willow Wind Dr., Artemas PA 17211. (814)458-3102. E-mail: willowwind@ hereintown.net. Kay Weems, ed. Published every even year. $7/copy. 100% unsolicited freelance. Phone/e-query OK. **NO PAYMENT.** Short stories to 2,500 wds. Responds before typing begins. Accepts simultaneous submissions and reprints.

Poetry: All types of poetry on heaven, to 36 lines (or slightly longer). Submit max. 10 poems. Helpful hints: Subject could be "finding the right road to heaven," "suppose through a mistake you go to the wrong place," "would you have a memory of earth?" "can you still see earth or visit?" or "are animals there?" Use your imagination. This is an endless subject.

Tips: "In addition to this collection, I also publish 2-3 different themes throughout the year, along with my regular publications."

$MERLYN'S PEN: Fiction, Essays, and Poems by America's Teens, Box 910, East Greenwich RI 02818. Toll-free (800)247-2027. (401)885-5192. Fax (401)885-5199. E-mail: merlyn@merlynspen.org. Website: www.merlynspen.com. Secular. Jim Stahl, ed. Magazine; circ. 5,000. Subscription $29.95. Query; no e-query. Pays $20-200 on publication for all rts. Articles 500-5,000 wds.; fiction to 8,500 wds. Responds in 10-12 wks.

Poetry: Free verse, metric verse; $20-50.

$MONEY THE WRITE WAY, PO Box 3405, Auburn CA 95604. (916)205-4763. E-mail: carmel@moneythewriteway.com. Website: www.moneythewriteway.com. Write Spirit Publishing. Carmel Mooney, pub. Educates, inspires, and supports Christian writers, travel writers, authors, and e-publishing enthusiasts in making money as a writer of integrity. Monthly e-zine; 8-15 pgs.; circ. 4,000. Subscription free. 80% unsolicited freelance; 10% assigned. Query; e-query OK. **PAYS IN COPIES**, free advertising for writer, and occasionally up to $10; for one-time rts. Articles 300-800 wds. (36/yr.); book reviews 300-500 wds. Responds in 2-4 wks. Seasonal 2 mos. ahead. Accepts simultaneous submissions and reprints (tell when/where appeared). Accepts mss by e-mail (attached file). No sidebars. Prefers NIV. Guidelines; copy for #10 SAE or by e-mail. (Ads)

Fillers: Accepts 6-12/yr. Anecdotes, facts, ideas, quotes, tips; 50-100 wds. No payment (usually), or up to $5.

Columns/Departments: Accepts 36+/yr. Marketing for Writers—Marketing with Integrity, 300-800 wds.; monthly guest article (how-to or personal experience essay), 300-800 wds.; Boast Post (short pieces on personal writing accomplishments), 50-100 wds.

Special Needs: Christian writing: tips, resources, how-to, reviewing, travel writing, success stories. and marketing. Propose a column for us.

Contest: Occasionally sponsors writing contests.

Tips: "Most open to Boast Post (column), or how-to-write/marketing/breaking-in articles. Send a concise, focused query that is an example of writer's tone and expertise."

$MY LEGACY, 207 Willow Wind Dr., Artemas PA 17211. (814)458-3102. E-mail: willowwind@hereintown.net. Kay Weems, ed. For young adults and up. Quarterly booklet; 70-80 pgs.; circ. 200+. Subscription $16. 100% unsolicited freelance. Pays $5 for editor's favorite stories. No articles; fiction to 2,500 wds. Responds in 16-20 wks. Accepts simultaneous submissions and reprints. Guidelines; copy $4.50/6x9 SAE/4 stamps.

NORTHWEST CHRISTIAN AUTHOR, 1111 Pierce Ave. N.E., Renton WA 98056. (425)228-4835. E-mail: NovelConcept2@aol.com. Northwest Christian Writers Assn. Marcy Fomin, ed. To encourage Christian authors to share the gospel through the written word and to promote excellence in writing. Bimonthly newsletter; 8 pgs.; circ. 120. Subscription $10. 100% unsolicited freelance. Complete ms/cover letter; e-query OK. **PAYS 3 COPIES** for 1st, one-time, reprint, or simultaneous rts. Not copyrighted. Articles 500-800 wds. (18/yr.). Responds in 8 wks. Accepts simultaneous submissions and reprints (tell when/where appeared). Prefers e-mail submission (attached file). Regularly uses sidebars. No guidelines; copy for 6x9 SAE/2 stamps. (No ads)

Special Needs: How-tos on nonfiction and fiction writing. Focus on genre techniques.

Tips: "Most open to articles on writing techniques, particularly for specific genres. We've had too many how-to-submit articles. Stay within word count. E-queries should have 'NW Christian Author' in subject line. Include 1-2 sentence author bio with article."

OMNIFIC, 207 Willow Wind Dr., Artemas PA 17211. (814)458-3102. E-mail: willowwind@hereintown.net. Kay Weems, ed. Family-type publication for writers/adults. Semiannual booklet; approx. 100 pgs.; circ. 300+. Subscription $10 ($5/issue). 100% unsolicited freelance. **NO PAYMENT.** Accepts simultaneous submissions and reprints. No articles; poetry only. Guidelines; copy for 6x9 SAE/4 stamps & $5 (payable to Weems Concepts).

Poetry: Any type; to 36 lines. Submit max. 4-8 poems.

ONCE UPON A TIME, 553 Winston Ct., St. Paul MN 55118. (651)457-6223. E-mail: audrey ouat@comcast.net. Website: http://onceuponatimemag.com. Audrey B. Baird, ed./pub. Highly specialized magazine for children's writers and illustrators, offering help, instruction, encouragement in an over-the-fence-type friendly way. Quarterly mag.; 32 pgs.; circ. 1,000. Subscription $26. 50% unsolicited freelance. Complete ms/cover letter; no phone/fax/e-query. **PAYS IN COPIES** for one-time rts. Articles 100-900 wds. (80-100/yr.). Responds in 6 wks. Seasonal anytime. Accepts simultaneous submissions and reprints (tell when/where appeared—must be 1 yr. from last publication). Uses some sidebars. Guidelines (also on Website); copy $5. (Ads)

Poetry: Accepts 80-100/yr. Free verse, haiku, light verse, traditional; to 24 lines. Writing/illustrating related. Submit max. 6 poems. "About rhyming poetry: pay attention to rhythm—it's not enough to rhyme—rhyming poetry must have rhythm (and near rhyme is not enough). I'm willing to help and to edit and to suggest, but do your part first with revision until the piece is as good as you can get it."

Fillers: Accepts 20-30/yr. Anecdotes, cartoons, ideas, short humor, tips (all writing/illustrating related); to 100 wds.

Special Needs: How-to articles on writing & illustrating (by those qualified to write them) up to 800 wds.; short pieces on writing & illustrating, 100-400 wds.

Tips: "Send a good, tight article on the writing life—any aspect—that is either educational, informative, entertaining, humorous, or inspiring. We like a friendly, upbeat tone. Humor is always looked for. We get too many articles on rejection. I am open to them if you state what you learned from them or how you persevered in spite of them. Articles on good advice you've received that resulted in publication for you are always good. We like success stories and particularly look for how-to pieces. Perseverance is a strong theme for us. Read the writing books. Read the market guides. Attend conferences. Learn how to write before you attempt it."

ROMANCING THE CHRISTIAN HEART. Website: www.romancingchristianheart.com. E-zine for fiction writers of romance and women's fiction; how-to. One-time rts. Prefers initial contact through "Contact Us" form on Website. **NO PAYMENT**. Articles 300 wds. & up; fiction to 3,000 wds. Guidelines on Website.

> **Poetry:** Accepts poetry; any type; to 50 lines.
>
> **Fillers:** Anecdotes, prose, quotes, tips; min. 50 wds.

$#SHADES OF ROMANCE MAGAZINE. E-mail: sormag@mail.com. Website: www.sormag .com. LaShaunda Hoffman, ed. A guide for readers and writers of multicultural romance and fiction. Bimonthly magazine. E-query only. Pays $20 for articles, $25 for fiction within 30 days of publication (through PayPal). Articles 500-800 wds.; short stories 500-1,500 wds.; devotions 200-500 wds. Responds in 2-4 wks. Accepts reprints (pays $10). Guidelines/themes online.

> **Poetry:** Buys romantic poetry to 1 pg.; $5.
>
> **Fillers:** Buys fillers; $10. Tips on freelancing time management, writing exercises, and romance. Humorous anecdotes.
>
> **Columns/Departments:** The Writer's Path (articles on writing multicultural romance and fiction); Shades of Motivation (inspiring thoughts on writing); The Marketing Path (how to market); The Publishing Path (business of writing and promoting).

$SPIRIT-LED WRITER. E-mail: spiritwriter@att.net. Website: www.SpiritLedWriter.com. Lisa A. Crayton, pub./ed. Internet magazine for Christian beginning, intermediate, and advanced writers. Monthly e-zine. Query by e-mail (put "Query: [subject]" in subject line). Pays $10-20 on publication for one-time, reprint, and electronic rts. Articles to 1,200 wds. (70+/yr.); reviews to 500 wds. Responds in 8 wks. Accepts reprints. Submit accepted mss by e-mail (no attachments). Regularly uses sidebars. Accepts submissions from teens. Guidelines by e-mail/Website; copy online. (Ads)

> **Columns/Departments:** Buys several/yr. Musing Dept. (writing-related personal reflections), 700-900 wds.; God's Glory Dept. (writing success stories), 500-700 wds.; Business (articles on the business of writing), to 1,200 wds.; Children's Column (how-to on writing for youth), to 1,200 wds.; $10-20.
>
> **Special Needs:** Writing-related devotionals; conference coverage (700-900 wds.); and book reviews of writing books, 250-500 wds. ($5-10, depending on whether they supply the book). Also articles on writing for youth, or on advanced writing topics.
>
> **Tips:** "Easiest to break in with a success story (God's glory), musing article, or devotional. We seek how-to and feature articles with a writing theme. We are not a general, Christian-living publication. We reject many manuscripts because they are general, not writing-related. Make it relevant to writing and writers."

TEACHERS & WRITERS, 5 Union Square W., New York NY 10003-3306. (212)691-6590. Fax (212)675-0171. E-mail: info@twc.org. Website: www.twc.org. Christopher Edgar, pub. dir. (cedgar@twc.org) & Christina Davis, ed. (cdavis@twc.org). On teaching creative and imaginative writing for children. Mag. published 5X/yr. & online mag.; circ. 3,000. Query; phone/fax/e-query OK. **PAYS IN COPIES**. Articles 3,000-6,000 wds. Guidelines by e-mail; copy $2.50.

$TICKLED BY THUNDER, 14076—86A Ave., Surrey BC V3W 0V9 Canada. (604)591-6095.

E-mail: info@tickledbythunder.com. Website: www.tickledbythunder.com. Larry Lindner, ed. For writers wanting to better themselves. Quarterly chapbook (3-4X); 24 pgs.; circ. 1,000. Subscription $12 (or $10 US). 90% unsolicited freelance; 10% assigned. Complete ms/cover letter; e-query OK from subscribers only. Pays $2-5 (in Canadian or US stamps) on publication for one-time rts. Articles 1,500 wds. (5/yr.); fiction 2,000 wds. (20/yr.); book/music/video reviews 1,000 wds. Responds in 16 wks. Seasonal 6 mos. ahead. Accepts simultaneous submissions. Prefers requested ms on disk, no e-mail submission. Uses some sidebars. Accepts submissions from children or teens. Guidelines (also by e-mail/ Website); copy $2.50/6x9 SAE. (Ads)

Poetry: Accepts 20-40/yr. Any type; to 40 lines. Submit max. 5-7 poems.

Contest: For fiction (February 15 annual deadline) and poetry (February 15, May 15, August 15, and October 15 annual deadlines). Article contests for subscribers only (February 15, May 15, August 15, and October 15 deadlines). Send SASE for guidelines.

Tips: "Write a 300-word article describing how you feel about your successes/failures as a writer. Be specific, and focus—don't be at all general or vague, tell what works for you. Be original, say something classic in a new way. Use imagery. I also like fiction that surprises me."

$THE UPPER CASE, PO Box 2505, Cranberry PA 16066. Fax (724)776-7228. E-mail: gracie@pathway.net. Website: www.StDavidsWriters.com. St. Davids Christian Writers' Assn. Nancy E. James, ed. Quarterly (3X) newsletter. Subscription $10 to nonmembers. Open to freelance. Complete ms. or query. Pays $10/half page for one-time rts. Articles 300-900 wds.; short, short stories 150-300 wds.; devotionals 150-200 wds.; book reviews 200-300 wds. Guidelines in newsletter/on Website; copy for 9x12 SAE/3 stamps. (No ads)

Poetry: Any form; to 20 lines.

Fillers: Short fillers and cartoons.

Special Needs: Articles on writing, book reviews, devotions, interviews with published writers (query first for interviews).

$WIN-INFORMER, PO Box 11337, Bainbridge Island WA 98110. (206)842-9103. Fax (206)842-0536. E-mail: writersinfonetwork@juno.com. Website: www.christianwriters info.net. Writers Information Network. Elaine Wright Colvin, ed. CBA industry news and trends to keep professional writers, editors, agents, and speakers in touch with the changing marketplace. Bimonthly (6X) mag.; 24-32 pgs. Subscription $40 ($50 Canada/foreign). 30% unsolicited; 20% assigned. Complete ms submitted in body of e-mail only. Pays $10-50 (or subscription) on publication for 1st rts. Articles 100-800 wds. (30/yr.); book reviews, 100-300 wds. Accepts e-mail submissions only. Uses some sidebars. Guidelines (also by e-mail/Website); copy $8/9x12 SAE/$1.42 postage (mark "Media Mail"). (No ads, but likes to announce news of members' successes)

Poetry: Any type; writing related.

Fillers: Anecdotes, facts, ideas, newsbreaks, quizzes, quotes, prayers, short humor; 50-300 wds.; $10-20.

Columns/Departments: Columns are continuously changing to meet the needs of an evolving industry. Check a recent copy for current column needs.

Special Needs: "Hot news of our growing, changing market whenever and wherever you hear it: at a writers conference, in a magazine news announcement, from your editor or agent, at your writers group—pass it on. If you make it into a round-up article of what many industry insiders are saying, we'll even pay you. Our readers want to be kept on the cutting-edge of what is happening in the CBA industry."

Tips: "If it works for you, we want to hear about it. If it is a hot tip, we want you to share it. We are in a tough economy and a tight book-publishing industry, and no one has time to learn it all and live through his mistakes and challenges by himself. We want tried and proven ideas on what's working for you and other professional writers and speakers. Give us great hints on book promotion, preparing for radio and TV appearances, promoting book signings, and other speaking engagements. 'Without good direction, people lose their way; the more wise counsel you follow, the better your chances' (Prov. 11:14, MSG)."

WRITE TO INSPIRE.COM. E-mail: editor@writetoinspire.com?subject=Submission. Website: www.writetoinspire.com. Online publication. Provides good how-to information for Christian writers. **NO PAYMENT**. Articles 500-700 wds., written in an online style. Send submissions in body of e-mail (no attachments). Guidelines on Website.

*****THE WRITE TOUCH**, 1714 Soland Dr. N.E., Albuquerque NM 87110-4930. Tim Anderson, ed. For writers trying to get published. Monthly newsletter; 12 pgs.; circ. 40. Subscription $15/yr. 100% unsolicited freelance. Complete ms/cover letter. **PAYS 3 COPIES**, for one-time rts. Essays on various subjects (120/yr.) & fiction for all ages (120/yr.), 100-500 wds. Responds in 2-4 wks. Seasonal 2 mos. ahead. Discourages simultaneous submissions and reprints. Accepts requested ms on disk. Guidelines; copy $1.

> **Poetry:** Any type; 4-30 lines. Submit max. 3 poems.
>
> **Fillers:** Anecdotes, facts, ideas, prose, short humor; 15-50 wds.

$THE WRITER, 21027 Crossroads Cir., Waukesha WI 53189. (262)796-8776. Fax (262)798-6468. E-mail: editor@writermag.com. Website: www.writermag.com. Secular. Elfrieda Abbe, ed.; Jeff Reich, mng. ed. How-to for writers; lists religious markets periodically. Monthly mag.; 68 pgs.; circ. 38,000. Subscription $29 (single issue $4.95). 80% unsolicited freelance. Query; no phone/fax query (prefers hard copy, but will accept e-query at query@writermag.com). Pays $75-600 for feature articles; book reviews ($50—varies); on acceptance for 1st rts. Features 2,000-3,000 wds. (60/yr.). Responds in 4 wks. Uses some sidebars. Guidelines (also on Website), copy $4.95. (Ads)

> **Fillers:** Prose; cartoons $50; photos related to writing.
>
> **Columns/Departments:** Buys 24+/yr. Bottom Line (shorter pieces on the business of writing); Off the Cuff (personal essays about writing, avoid writer's block stories); Net//working (articles about Internet resources for writers and how to use the Internet effectively); Poet to Poet (a poet writes on writing poetry—should show a technique); Syntax (on language; please, no articles on basic grammar or punctuation); Ethics (ethical questions pertaining to writing and how they can be resolved). All 800-1,200 wds. Pays $150-500 for columns; $50-75 for reviews. Query 4 months ahead.
>
> **Special Needs:** How-to on the craft of writing only.
>
> **Contests:** Occasionally sponsors a contest.
>
> **Tips:** "Material must be practical, targeted to beginning writers, and include plenty of how-to, advice, and tips on techniques. Be specific. Query for features six months ahead."

$WRITER'S APPRENTICE, 607 N. Cleveland St., Merrill WI 54452. Phone/fax (715)536-3167. E-mail: tina@writersapprentice.com. Website: www.writersapprentice.com. Prairie River Publishing. Tina Miller, ed./pub. For aspiring, beginning, and intermediate writers. Monthly mag. Estab. 2004. Subscription free. Accepts freelance. Prefers e-mail query or complete ms. Articles 300-900 wds. ($15-50), essays 300-600 wds. ($10-25). First rts.; no reprints. Pays on publication. Responds in 6-9 mos. Guidelines on Website. (Ads)

> **Tips:** "Your best chance of breaking in is with a very niche-specific, fair, and objective article that presents both sides of an issue relevant to aspiring, beginning, or intermediate writers, and include at least two quotes from experts or others with actual experience on each side of the issue."

$WRITER'S CHRONICLE: The Magazine for Serious Writers, Associated Writing Programs, George Mason University, MSN 1E3, Fairfax VA 22030. (703)993-4301. Fax (703)993-4302. E-mail: awpchron@gmu.edu. Website: www.awpwriter.org. D. W. Fenza, ed-in-chief. Bimonthly mag. Subscription $20. Pays $8/100 wds. on publication for 1st rts. No kill fee. Guidelines on Website.

Special Needs: Author interviews, essays, trends, and literary controversies. No poetry or fiction.

$WRITER'S DIGEST, 4700 E. Galbraith Rd., Cincinnati OH 45236. (513)531-2690, ext. 1483. E-mail: wdsubmissions@fwpubs.com. Website: www.writersdigest.com. Secular/F & W Publications. Submit to Submissions Editor. To inform, instruct, or inspire the freelancer. Monthly mag.; 76 pgs.; circ. 150,000. Subscription $27. 20% unsolicited; 60% assigned. Strongly prefers e-query (responds in 2 wks.). Pays .25-.40/wd. on acceptance for 1st and electronic (sometimes) rts. Articles 1,000-2,000 wds. (60/yr.). Responds to mail query in 3 mos. Seasonal 8 mos. ahead. Requires requested ms on disk or by e-mail (attached file or copied into message). Kill fee 25%. Regularly uses sidebars. Guidelines/editorial calendar on Website; copy $7 (attn: Debbie Paolello). (Ads)

Contests: Sponsors annual contest for articles, short stories, poetry, and scripts. Also The National Self-Publishing Book Awards. Send SASE for rules.

Tips: "We're looking for fiction technique pieces by published authors."

WRITERS GAZETTE, 7231—120th St., Ste. 105, Delta BC V4C 6P5 Canada. E-mail: editor@ writersgazette.com. Website: www.writersgazette.com (click on "Submit to Us."). Krista Barrett, ed-in-chief. Looking for submissions on the craft of writing and book/product reviews. One-time rts.

$WRITERS' JOURNAL, PO Box 394, Perham MN 56573-0394. (218)346-7921. Fax (218)346-7924. E-mail: writersjournal@lakesplus.com. Website: www.writersjournal.com. Val-Tech Media/Secular. Leon Ogroske, ed. Advice, tools, and markets for writers, communicators, and poets. Bimonthly mag.; 68 pgs.; circ. 24,000. Subscription $19.97. 60% unsolicited freelance; 10% assigned. Complete ms/cover letter; e-query OK. Pays $10-30, plus subscription, on publication for one-time rts. Articles 1,800 wds. (60/yr.). Responds in 24 wks. Accepts simultaneous submissions; no reprints. Accepts requested ms by e-mail (copied into message). No kill fee. Uses some sidebars. Guidelines (also by e-mail); copy $5/#10 SAE. (Ads)

Poetry: Esther M. Leiper, poetry ed. Buys 30/yr. All types; to 10 lines; $5/poem. Submit max. 4 poems.

Fillers: Any type, 10-200 wds. Pays $1-10.

Contest: Runs several contests each year. Prizes up to $300. Categories are short story, horror/ghost, romance, travel writing, and fiction; 3 poetry; 2 photo. Send an SASE requesting guidelines.

Tips: "We are looking for a well-written article on freelance income; articles on how to write better and how to sell what authors write. Also looking for articles on obscure income markets for writers. General story construction and grammar tips."

WRITER'S LIFELINE, Box 1641, Cornwall ON K6H 5V6 Canada. (613)932-2135. Fax (613)932-7735. E-mail: stefgill@hotmail.com. Stephen Gill, mng. ed. For professional freelancers and beginning writers. Bimonthly mag.; 16-35 pgs.; circ. 1,500. Needs articles of interest to writers, news items of national and international interest, letters to the editor, poetry, interviews. Needs book reviewers; **PAYS IN BOOK REVIEWED & COPIES**.

WRITERS MANUAL, 7231—120th St., Ste. 105, Delta BC V4C 6P5 Canada. E-mail: writers manual@yahoo.com. Website: www.writersmanual.com (click on "Get Interviewed!"). Krista Barrett, ed-in-chief. Looking for author and/or freelance interviews. One-time rts.

WRITES OF PASSAGE, Heart of America Christian Writers' Network. Jeanette Littleton, ed.

E-mail: JeanetteDL@aol.com. Website: www.hacwn.org. Monthly newsletter; 4 pgs. Distributed to writer's group only. Open to short how-to articles from freelancers. E-query. **NO PAYMENT.** Articles 400 wds.

$*THE WRITING PARENT: For Parents Striving to Become Professional Writers. This publication has been sold and is currently on hiatus.

MARKET ANALYSIS

PERIODICALS IN ORDER BY CIRCULATION

ADULT/GENERAL

Guideposts 3,000,000
Focus on the Family 2,200,000
Columbia 1,600,000
Decision 1,200,000
Positive Thinking 600,000
Angels on Earth 550,000
Christian Online 500,000 (online)
The Lutheran 500,000
Marion Helpers 500,000
Oblates 500,000
War Cry 500,000
Spirituality for Today 425,000
Catholic Digest 400,000
Miraculous Medal 340,000
Mature Living 320,000
St. Anthony Messenger 310,000
Anglican Journal 272,000
Today's Pentecostal Evangel 264,000
Power for Living 250,000
Upscale Magazine 242,000
Kiwanis 240,000
Charisma 230,000
Gospel Today 200,000
Liberty 200,000
Liguorian 200,000
Signs of the Times 200,000
Ideals 180,000
Christianity Today 155,000
Family Digest 150,000
Standard 150,000
Tomorrow's Christian Graduate
    150,000
Smart Families 140,000
Discipleship Journal 130,000
New Man 125,000
Today's Christian 125,000
Company 120,000
Live 115,000
Lutheran Digest 105,000
Presbyterian Survey 105,000
Foursquare World Advance 102,000
Catholic Forester 100,000
CGA World 100,000
Good News (KY) 100,000
Lookout 100,000
Lutheran Journal 100,000
ParentLife 100,000
United Church Observer 100,000

Physician 93,900
On Mission 90,000
Men of Integrity 85,000
Message 80,000
Plain Truth 80,000
Christian Parenting Today 78,000
Leaves 75,000
alive now! 70,000
Celebrate Life 70,000
Common Ground 70,000
Creation 70,000
Heartlight Internet 70,000
Mature Years 70,000
Spirituality & Health 70,000
Sword of the Lord 70,000
Christian Home & School 68,000
Our Sunday Visitor 68,000
Heartwarmers 67,000
Presbyterians Today 62,000
Christian Standard 60,000
Christian History 55,000
Marriage Partnership 53,000
Bridal Guides 50,000
Catholic Answer 50,000
Daily Walk 50,000
Faith & Friends 50,000
Wesleyan Life 50,000
Church of God Evangel 49,000
Christian Social Action 48,000
Annals of St. Anne 45,000
Presbyterian Record 44,400
America 41,000
BGC World 40,000
Christian Motorsports 40,000
Parabola 40,000
Reformed Quarterly 40,000
Senior Living 40,000
U.S. Catholic 40,000
Cathedral Age 38,000
Gospel Tract 38,000
Highway News 35,000
Messenger of St. Anthony 35,000
Messianic Times 35,000
Faith & Family 32,000
First Things 32,000
Christian Computing 30,000
Christian News Northwest 30,000
Community Spirit 30,000
en confianza 30,000
Homeschooling Today 30,000

Interim 30,000
Lifeglow 30,000
Priority! 30,000
Sports Spectrum 30,000
World & I 30,000
Seek 29,000
EFCA Today 28,000
Portland Magazine 28,000
Vibrant Life 28,000
Catholic Parent 27,000
Canadian Lutheran 26,000
War Cry (Canada) 25,000
Catholic Peace Voice 23,000
Christian Research Journal 22,000
Alliance Life 21,000
African Voices 20,000
Canadian Mennonite 20,000
Commonweal 20,000
Mosaic (Canadian Baptist) 20,000
Sojourners 20,000
Testimony 20,000
Trumpeter 20,000
Faith Today 18,000
Mennonite Brethren Herald 17,000
Covenant Companion 16,000
The Door 16,000
Evangel 16,000
Marketplace 16,000
Books & Culture 15,000
Light & Life 15,000
Over the Back Fence/SW 15,000
SCP Journal 15,000
Canada Lutheran 14,000
DisciplesWorld 14,000
Gems of Truth 14,000
St. Joseph's Messenger 14,000
Bible Advocate 13,500
Creation Illustrated 13,000
Messenger/Sacred Heart 13,000
Presbyterian Outlook 12,734
Special Living 12,000
Spiritual Life 11,000
Christian Retailing 10,000
Disciple's Journal 10,000
Messiah Magazine 10,000
NRB Magazine 10,000
Parents & Teens 10,000
Regent Business Review 10,000
Spiritual Voice News 10,000
Vision 10,000

Christian Leader 9,800
Breakthrough Intercessor 9,300
Fellowship Magazine 9,000
Living Church 9,000
Prism 9,000
Purpose 9,000
Sharing 9,000
Catholic New Times 8,500
CBA Marketplace 8,000
The Gem 7,100
MN Christian Chronicle 7,000
Montgomery's Journey 7,000
Psychology for Living 7,000
Quaker Life 7,000
Review for Religious 7,000
White Wing Messenger 7,000
Nostalgia Magazine 6,000+
Impact 6,000
Pentecostal Messenger 6,000
Spring Hill Review 5,400
AGAIN 5,000
Creation Care 5,000
Creative Nonfiction 5,000
New Heart 5,000
New Wineskins 5,000
Plowman 5,000
TJ 5,000
Way of St. Francis 5,000
Social Justice Review 4,950
Christian Civic League (ME) 4,600
Cresset 4,500
Resource 4,500
Sacred Journey 4,500
Wireless Age 4,100
Christian Courier (CAN) 4,000
Christian Renewal 4,000
Evangelical Advocate 4,000
Image 4,000
Maranatha News 4,000
Catholic Insight 3,700
Cross Currents 3,500
Culture Wars 3,500
Evangel 3,500
Sword and Trumpet 3,300
Alive! 3,000
Catalyst 3,000
Evangelical Baptist 3,000
Message/Open Bible 3,000
MovieGuide 3,000
Perspectives 3,000
Prayer Closet 3,000
Mennonite Historian 2,600
Bread of Life 2,500
Railroad Evangelist 2,500
Hannah to Hannah 2,300
Mutuality 2,200
Fellowship Focus 2,100

Mosaic (Free Methodist) 2,100
Apocalypse Chronicles 2,000-3,000
Brave Hearts 2,000
Channels 2,000
Desert Call 2,000
Priscilla Papers 2,000
Queen of All Hearts 2,000
Voice of the Lord 1,850-2,150
Jour./Church & State 1,700
Church Herald/Holiness Banner 1,600
Connecting Point 1,500
Crux 1,300
North American Voice 1,200
BC Christian News 1,000
Dovetail 1,000
Relate 1,000
Victory News 1,000
Methodist History 800
Compass Direct 700
Eternal Ink 675
Aujourd'hui Credo 600
Christian Radio Weekly 600
The Storyteller 525
Tributes 500+
Grand Valley Observer 350
Studio 300
Xavier Review 300
Silver Wings 275
West Wind Review 250-500
Gateway S-F 250
Time of Singing 250
Dreams & Visions 200
Hard Row to Hoe 200
Insound 200
Keys to Living 200
Ancient Paths 150-175
Pegasus Review 125
Time for Rhyme 100
Discerning Poet 80
Penwood Review 50-100
St. Linus Review 50

CHILDREN

American Girl 650,000
Guideposts for Kids Online 200,000+
FOF Clubhouse 101,100
Keys for Kids 100,000
Pockets 93,000
High Adventure 86,000
FOF Clubhouse Jr. 78,000
Our Little Friend 45,000-50,000
Adventure 40,000
Celebrate 40,000
Courage 40,000
Primary Treasure 35,000
GUIDE 30,000
Children's Magic Window 18,000

Passport 18,000
The Winner 15,000
Club Connection 14,700
Nature Friend 13,000
SHINE brightly 13,000
BREAD for God's Children 10,000
Cadet Quest 9,500
My Friend 9,000
Partners 6,389
Story Mates 6,200
Story Friends 6,000
On the Line 5,000
Junior Companion 3,500
Primary Pal (KS) 2,900
Beginner's Friend 2,700
Skipping Stones 2,500

CHRISTIAN EDUCATION/LIBRARY

Christian School Education 70,000
Children's Ministry 60,000
Group 55,000
Catechist 52,000
Today's Catholic Teacher 45,000
Religion Teacher's Journal 32,000
Momentum 25,000
Resource 25,000
Christian Library Journal 20,000
Evangelizing Today's Child 14,500
Youth & CE Leadership 13,000
Teachers Interaction 11,000
Teachers of Vision 10,000
Jour./Adventist Ed. 7,500
Christian Early Education 5,500
Christian Educator's Journal 4,200
Ideas Unlimited 4,200
Church Educator 4,000
Leader/Chr. Ed. Ministries 3,500
Church & Synagogue Libraries 3,000
Kids' Ministry Ideas 1,700
Caravan 1,000
Catholic Library World 1,000
Christian Librarian 800
Christian Education Journal (CA) 750
Church Libraries 600
Jour./Christian Education 500
Jour./Ed. & Christian Belief 400
Jour./Research on C. E. 400
Jour./Christianity/Foreign Languages 100

MISSIONS

I.E. 260,000
CNEWA World 100,000
Worldwide Challenge 95,000
Mission Frontiers 80,000
American Baptists in Mission 39,000

Wesleyan World 38,700
Catholic Missions in Canada 37,000
New World Outlook 22,000
PIME World 16,000
Leaders for Today 7,500
Evangelical Missions 7,000
Glad Tidings 5,500
PFI World Report 4,750
World Pulse 2,600
Women of the Harvest 2,500
Cornerstone Youth Resource 2,200
Missiology 2,000
OpRev Equipper 1,500
Intl. Jour./Frontier 600
East-West Church 400

MUSIC

CCM Magazine 70,000
Church Pianist 35,000
Senior Musician 32,000
Creator 6,000
Tradition 3,500
The Hymn 3,000
Christian Music Weekly 300-1,200

NEWSPAPERS

Layman 485,000
Inside Journal 395,000
Episcopal Life 280,000
Anglican Journal 220,000
Christian Examiner 180,000
Together 150,000
Catholic New York 135,000
National Catholic Reporter 120,000
Catholic Telegraph 100,000
Grit 100,000
Living 90,000
Pulpit Helps 75,000
Common Ground 70,000
Sword of the Lord 70,000
Our Sunday Visitor 68,000
Good News Journal 60,000
Arlington Catholic Herald 53,000
Cornerstone Christian 50,000
Living 50,000
Christian Ranchman 45,400
Dallas/Ft. Worth Heritage 45,000
Good News, Etc. 42,000
Senior Living 40,000
Tidewater Parent 40,000
Messianic Times 35,000
Metro Voice 35,000
Catholic Register 33,000
Christian Herald 32,000
Christian News NW 30,000
Interim 30,000
Living Light News 30,000

New Frontier 25,500
Christian Media 25,000
Life Gate 23,000
Indian Life 22,000
B.C. Catholic 20,000
Christian Journal 20,000
Minnesota Chr. Chronicle 20,000
Home Times 18,000
Shantyman 17,000
Catholic Sentinel 16,000
Messenger 16,000
Christian Voice 15,000
Interchange 12,000
Christian Courier (WI) 10,000
Network 10,000
Spiritual Voice News 10,000
Faro de Luz 9,500
Star of Zion 9,200
Catholic New Times 8,500
Disciple's Journal 8,000
Inland NW Christian 8,000
New Freeman 7,300
Prairie Messenger 7,300
Arkansas Catholic 7,000
Christianweek 5,000
SW KS Faith & Family 5,000
Christian Courier (Canada) 4,000
Christian Renewal 4,000
Maranatha News 4,000
Island Catholic News 3,000
Atlantic Catholic 2,500
Christian Observer 2,000
Insight (for the blind) 2,000
B.C. Christian News 1,000
Hunted News 1,000
Prayerworks 1,000
Anglican 300

PASTORS/LEADERS

Interpreter 275,000
Your Church 150,000
Growing Churches 85,000
Pastors.com 80,000
Pulpit Helps 75,000
Leadership 65,000
Eucharistic Ministries 50,000
Plugged In 50,000
Worship Leader 43,000
Pray! 39,000
Technologies/Worship 35,000
Catholic Servant 33,000
Enrichment 33,000
Christian Century 30,000
Ministries Today 30,000
Rev. 30,000
Today's Christian Preacher 25,000
This Rock 20,745

Lutheran Partners 20,000
Ministry 20,000
Ministry & Liturgy 20,000
Youthworker 20,000
Today's Parish 14,800
Theology Today 14,000
Cell Group 12,000
Church Administration 12,000
Net Results 12,000
Jour./Pastoral Care 10,000
Watchman Expositor 10,000
WCA News 10,000
YouthCulture 10,000
Angelos 9,500
Student Leadership Journal 9,500
Preaching 9,000
Sabbath School Leadership 9,000
Christian Camp & Conference 8,750
Church Growth Network 8,000
Clergy Journal 8,000
The Priest 8,000
Review for Religious 7,000
Christian Ministry 6,500
Leaders in Action 6,500
Jour./Christian Camping 6,000
Catechumenate 5,600
Let's Worship 5,600
Cross Currents 5,000
Reformed Worship 5,000
Ministry Matters 4,500
Christian Management Report 3,500+
Lutheran Forum 3,200
African American Pulpit 3,000
Emmanuel 3,000
Evangelicals Today 3,000
Sermon Notes 3,000
Single Adult Min. Jour. 3,000
Environment & Art 2,500
Word & World 2,500
Pastoral Life 2,000
Reaching Children at Risk 2,000
Preaching On-Line 1,500
Church Worship 1,200
Parish Liturgy 1,200
Quarterly Review 1,100
Five Stones 1,000
Hunted News 1,000
Jour./Amer. Soc./Chur. Growth 400
Theological Digest 400
Ministry in Motion 200+
RevWriter Resource 200

TEEN/YOUNG ADULT

Brio 206,000
Essential Connection 120,000
Devo'Zine 104,000

Campus Life 100,000
Breakaway 95,000
Sharing the Victory 70,000
Brio & Beyond 55,000
YouthWalk/GA 55,000
Listen 50,000
Young Salvationist 48,000
Young & Alive 25,000
Inteen 20,000
Real Faith in Life 18,000
Insight 16,600
Living My Faith 16,000
Teenage Christian 10,500
Young Adult Today 10,000
Student Leadership 8,500
The Conqueror 6,000
Beautiful Christian Teen 5,000
Teen Light 5,000
Youth Compass 4,800
With 4,000

WOMEN

Today's Christian Woman 250,000
Journey 215,000
Lutheran Woman's Quarterly
    200,000

MOMSense 100,000
Share 100,000
SpiritLed Woman 100,000
At the Center 30,000
Horizons 25,500
Godly Business Women 25,000
History's Women 17,000
Women of Spirit 15,000
Woman's Touch 12,200
Welcome Home 10,000
Women's Ministry 8,000
Just Between Us 7,000
P31 Woman 7,000
Esprit 5,800
Women Alive! 5,000-6,000
Link & Visitor 4,000
Making Waves 4,000
Right to the Heart 4,000
Tapestry 3,700
ChurchWoman 3,000
Handmaiden 3,000
inSpirit 2,500
Hearts at Home 2,000
Women of God's Word 1,700
Melody of the Heart 500+
Women by Grace 300+

WRITERS

Writer's Digest 150,000
The Writer 38,000
Writers' Journal 24,000
Fiction Fix Newsletter 5,000
Money the Write Way 4,000
Byline 3,000+
Christian Communicator 3,000
Teachers & Writers 3,000
Beginnings 1,500
Writer's Lifeline 1,500
Cross & Quill 1,000+
New Writing 1,000
Once Upon a Time 1,000
Tickled by Thunder 1,000
Advanced Christian Writer 500
Canadian Writer's Journal 385
Omnific 300+
Exchange 300
Gotta Write Network 300
My Legacy 200+
FellowScript 175-250
Areopagus (UK) 150
Northwest Christian Author 120
Cochran's Corner 100
The Write Touch 40

PERIODICAL TOPICS IN ORDER OF POPULARITY

NOTE: Following is a list of topics in order by popularity. To find the list of publishers interested in each of these topics, go to the Topical Listings for periodicals and find the topic you are interested in. The numbers indicate how many periodical editors said they were interested in seeing something of that type or on that topic. (*—new topic this year)

1. Christian Living 261
2. Photographs 259
3. Family Life 248
4. Prayer 220
5. Inspirational 218
6. Current/Social Issues 210
7. Personal Experience 204
8. Holiday/Seasonal 194
9. Spirituality 191
10. Poetry 191
11. Book Reviews 191
12. Faith 188
13. Interviews/Profiles 187
14. Evangelism/Witnessing 187
15. Humor 184
16. Relationships 183
17. Women's Issues 171
18. Marriage 171
19. Devotionals/Meditations 168
20. Discipleship 164

21. Christian Education 162
22. Parenting 159
23. Church Outreach 154
24. Worship 146
25. Personal Growth 146
26. Controversial Issues 143
27. True Stories 142
28. Fillers: Cartoons 141
29. Short Story: Adult/Religious
    138
30. Ethnic/Cultural Pieces 136
31. Church Life 134
32. Leadership 133
33. Online Publications 133
34. Missions 132
35. Theological 127
36. Ethics 125
37. How-to 123
38. World Issues 119
39. Essays 118

40. Youth Issues 117
41. Health 116
42. Death/Dying 113
43. Men's Issues 112
44. Historical 112
45. Church Growth 109
46. Bible Studies 106
47. Social Justice 104
48. Stewardship 102
49. Singles Issues 102
50. Religious Freedom 101
51. Divorce 99
52. Opinion Pieces 98
53. Short Story: Contemporary 97
54. Fillers: Anecdotes 96
55. Money Management 95
56. Canadian/Foreign Markets 93
57. Salvation Testimonies 93
58. Think Pieces 92
59. Celebrity Pieces 92

60. Fillers: Short Humor 92
61. Church History 91
62. Short Story: Humorous 91
63. Church Traditions 88
64. Time Management 88
65. Environmental Issues 86
66. Spiritual Gifts 85
67. Christian Business 84
68. Spiritual Life 83
69. Church Management 82
70. Doctrinal 81
71. Spiritual Warfare 79
72. Healing 76
73. Music Reviews 75
74. Encouragement 75
75. Fillers: Facts 75
76. Book Excerpts 73
77. Short Story: Biblical 72
78. Senior Adult Issues 71
79. Young Writer Markets 70
80. How-to Activities (juv.) 70
81. Short Story: Juvenile 70
82. Fillers: Ideas 69
83. Short Story: Parables 69
84. Miracles 68
85. Nature 67
86. Fillers: Word Puzzles 66
87. Racism 64
88. Sports/Recreation 63
89. Short Story: Adventure 63
90. News Features 63
91. Fillers: Prayers 62
92. Short Story: Historical 61

93. Inner Life 61
94. Economics 61
95. Liturgical 60
96. Food/Recipes 60
97. Fillers: Quotes 60
98. Writing How-to 59
99. Newspapers/Tabloids 59
100. Short Story: Teen/Young Adult 58
101. Religious Tolerance 58
102. Travel 57
103. Workplace Issues 56
104. Fillers: Quizzes 56
105. Fillers: Prose 56
106. Political 56
107. Homeschooling 55
108. Fillers: Jokes 52
109. Video Reviews 50
110. Self-help 50
111. Fillers: Games 50
112. Short Story: Mystery/Suspense 49
113. Creation Science 49
114. Short Story: Literary 47
115. Prophecy 46
116. Crafts 44
117. Sociology 44
118. Fillers: Newsbreaks 43
119. Short Story: Fantasy 42
120. Science 42
121. Short Story: Allegory 41
122. Cults/Occult 40
123. Psychology 39

124. Exegesis 37
125. Sermons 36
126. Short Story: Romance 35
127. Spiritual Renewal 34*
128. Homiletics 33
129. Short Story: Ethnic 33
130. Short Story: Science Fiction 32
131. Photo Essays 32
132. Website Reviews 32
133. Apologetics 30
134. Fillers: Party Ideas 30
135. Take-home Papers 29
136. Short Story: Mystery/Romance 27
137. Short Story: Frontier 26
138. Fillers: Tips 25
139. Short Story: Historical/Romance 24
140. Short Story: Plays 20
141. Short Story: Frontier/Romance 20
142. Fillers: Kid Quotes 20
143. Peace Issues 18*
144. Short Story: Skits 17
145. Short Story: Speculative 16
146. Nostalgia 16*
147. Puppet Plays 10
148. Movie Reviews 9*
149. Short Story: Westerns 4
150. Spiritual Life 1
151. Pastor's Helps 1
152. Politics 1

COMMENTS

If you are a short story writer, the biggest market is for adult fiction (138 markets, 13 more than last year). Children's is still in second place with 70 (12 more than last year), followed by teen with 58 (6 more than last year). It's nice to see increases in each of these areas. The most popular genres (in order) are Contemporary, Humorous, Biblical, Parables, Adventure, Historical, Mystery/Suspense, and Literary. This represents several changes in order from last year—although the topics are the same. The least popular are still the genre romances. It is interesting to note that Fantasy and Science Fiction are continuing to move up the list.

This year poetry dropped to 191 markets, down from 197 last year, 200 the year before, and 210 the year before that. The total number of poems expected to be bought or accepted by those markets has gone from 4,935 three years ago to about 4,342 two years ago, 4,677 last year, and is up this year to 5,190. Taking into consideration that there are fewer publications represented, that's a healthy increase. Since we have lost poetry book markets the last two years, the number of publishers doing books of poetry is up slightly to 37. I still recommend that the serious poet pursue the periodical markets and establish a good reputation as a poet before ever attempting to sell a book of poetry.

This year the same topics are in the top 10 again, although Current/Social Issues and Spirituality have both moved up slightly.

SUMMARY OF INFORMATION ON CHRISTIAN PERIODICAL PUBLISHERS FOUND IN THE ALPHABETICAL LISTINGS

NOTE: The following numbers are based on the maximum total estimate for each periodical. For example, if they gave a range of 4-6, the average was based on the higher number, 6. These figures were all calculated from those periodicals that reported information in each category.

WANTS QUERY OR COMPLETE MANUSCRIPT

Of the 623 periodicals that indicated a preference, 47% ask for or will accept a complete manuscript, and 37% want or will accept a query. Only 3% require a query. Thirteen percent of all reporting will accept either. Although the number of periodicals varies from year to year, these percentages stay pretty much the same. However, there was a 5% increase this year for complete manuscripts and a 5% drop for queries.

ACCEPTS PHONE QUERY

This year, 129 periodical publishers are accepting phone queries—nine more than last year. Many seem now to prefer fax or e-mail to phone queries. It is suggested that you reserve phone queries for timely material that won't wait for the regular mailed query. If you phone in a query, be sure you have your idea well thought out and can present it succinctly and articulately.

ACCEPTS FAX QUERY

Most publishers have faxes, but many are asking for their fax number to be dropped from their listing—mostly because they prefer an e-mail query or are trying to avoid having complete manuscripts come by fax. Last year, 30% of all the periodical publishers accepted fax queries. This year, 217 publishers (28%) will accept them. Since a fax query will not have an SASE, it is suggested that you make fax queries only if you have your own fax machine to accept their response.

ACCEPTS E-MAIL QUERY

As expected, the number of publishers with e-mail addresses continues to grow. Last year 392 publishers were open to receiving messages or submissions by e-mail. This year it is up to 419. Because most publishers now have both e-mail and Websites, we are no longer tracking the actual numbers who have them.

SUBMISSIONS ON DISK

Of the 241 periodicals that responded to the question about whether or not they accepted, preferred, or required accepted submissions on disk, 96 (40%) said they accepted disks, 70 (29%) preferred disks, only 40 (16%) required disks, and 35 (15%) do not want disks.

SUBMISSIONS BY E-MAIL

This area is beginning to show some significant changes in editors' perceptions of e-mail submissions. When asked if they would accept submissions by e-mail, 184 said yes. Of those, 38% wanted them copied into the message, 40% wanted them sent as an attached file, and the last 22% would accept them either way. These percentages are almost the same as last year. Generally speaking, those who prefer it copied into the message fear viruses, while those who prefer an attached copy don't like losing the coding when you copy it into the message.

PAYS ON ACCEPTANCE OR PUBLICATION

Of the 381 publishers that indicated, 40% of the publishers pay on acceptance (down 4% from last year), while 60% pay on publication (up 4%). Not encouraging.

PERCENTAGE OF FREELANCE

Many of the publishers responded to the question about how much freelance material they use. We now make the question more definitive by asking them to specify the percentage unsolicited and the percentage assigned, and each year a greater number of them give us both figures. Based on the figures we have, for the average publisher, 45.6% of the material purchased is unsolicited freelance and 50.2% is assigned.

CIRCULATION

In dividing the list of periodicals into three groups, according to size of circulation, the list comes out as follows: Publications with a circulation of 100,000 or more (up to 3,000,000), 13.4%; publications with a circulation between 50,000 and 100,000, 10.4%; the remaining 76.2%, a circulation of 50,000 or less. These percentages are slightly lower for the higher two categories and slightly higher for the lowest category compared to last year. If we break that last group into three more groups by circulation, we come out with 10% of those from 33,000-50,000; 16% from 17,000-32,000; and the remaining 74% with less than 17,000. That means that 56% of all the periodicals that reported their circulation are at a circulation of 17,000 or less—nearly 2 percentage points higher than last year. Circulations are dropping overall.

RESPONSE TIME

According to the 378 publishers who indicated response time, the average response time moved up to about 8 weeks, one week longer than reported two years ago. Those who are writing and submitting regularly will have no problem confirming that most publishers are taking longer to respond to submissions.

REPRINTS

Nearly 50% of the periodicals included in the market guide accept reprints; that's down almost 5% from last year. Although until the last few years it was not necessary to tell a publisher where a piece had been published previously, that has changed. Most Christian publishers are now wanting a tear sheet of the original publication and a cover letter telling when and where it appeared originally. Be sure to check the individual listings to see if a publisher wants to know when and where a piece has appeared previously. Most are also paying less for reprints than for original material.

PREFERRED BIBLE VERSION

Although we are not running the percentages anymore, it is obvious that the most preferred Bible version is the New International Version, the preference of more than half the publishers. Other preferred versions are the King James Version, the New Revised Standard Version, the New American Bible, New American Standard, Revised Standard Version, and New King James. The NIV seems a good choice for those who didn't indicate a preference, although the more conservative groups seem to favor the KJV.

GREETING CARD/GIFT/SPECIALTY MARKETS

PLEASE NOTE: This listing contains both Christian/religious card publishers and secular publishers who have religious lines or produce some religious or inspirational cards. Keep in mind that the secular companies may produce other lines of cards that are not consistent with your beliefs, and that for a secular company, inspirational cards usually do not include religious imagery.

(*) Indicates that publisher did not return questionnaire
(#) Indicates that listing was updated from guidelines or other sources
(+) Indicates new listing
($) Indicates a paying market

NOTE: See the end of this listing for specialty product lists.

CARD PUBLISHERS

$AFRICAN AMERICAN EXPRESSIONS, 3127 Fite Circle, Ste. I, Sacramento CA 95827. (916)424-5000. Fax (916)424-5053. E-mail: gperkins@black-gifts.com. Website: www.black-gifts.com. Greg Perkins, pres. Christian card publishers and specialty products. Open to freelance; buys 5-10 ideas/yr. Prefers outright submissions. Pays $35 on acceptance. No royalty. Responds in 2 wks. Uses rhymed, unrhymed, traditional, and light verse. Produces invitations and conventional, humorous, informal, inspirational, juvenile, novelty, and religious cards. Needs anniversary, birthday, Christmas, friendship, get well, graduation, keep in touch, love, miss you, Mother's Day, new baby, relatives (all occasions), sympathy, valentines, wedding, and pastor appreciation. Holiday/seasonal 9 mos. ahead. Open to ideas for new card lines, calendars/journals, novelty/gift items, magnets, and stationery. No guidelines; free catalog.

$+ALEGRIA COLLECTION, PO Box 835008, Miami FL 33283-5008. (305)271-6183. Fax (786)551-7985. E-mail: ventas@alegriacollection.com. Website: www.alegriacollection.com. Spanish greeting cards.

AMERICAN GREETINGS, 1 American Rd., Cleveland OH 44144-2398. (216)252-7300. Website: www.americangreetings.com. Kathleen McKay, ed. No unsolicited material.

$ARTFUL GREETINGS, PO Box 52428, Durham NC 27717. (919)598-7599. Fax (919)598-8909. Website: www.artfulgreetings.com. Black art greeting cards and gifts.

$+BLESS HIS NAME GREETINGS, 7316 River Pointe Dr., #18, Maumelle AR 72113. (501)612-2935. Website: www.blesshisnamegreetings.com. L. Marie Trotter, pub. A Christian/religious card publisher. Open to freelance. Prefers outright purchases. Pays $35-50 on publication for all rts. No royalties. Responds in 3-4 wks. Uses rhymed, unrhymed, traditional; variable lengths. Produces inspirational and religious cards. Needs anniversary, birthday, Christmas, congratulations, Easter, Father's Day, friendship, get well, graduation, keep in touch, love, miss you, Mother's Day, new baby, relative (all occasion), sympathy, Thanksgiving, thank you, valentines, and wedding. Holiday seasonal 3 mos. ahead. Open to ideas for new card lines. Submit max. 5 ideas. Open to ideas for bookmarks, calendars/journals, gift books, greeting books, prints, stationery, and T-shirts. Guidelines; catalog for 9x12 SAE/$1.50 postage.

$BLUE MOUNTAIN ARTS, INC., PO Box 1007, Boulder CO 80306-1007. (303)449-0536. Fax (303)447-0939. E-mail: editorial@spsstudios.com. Website: www.sps.com. Submit to Editorial Department. General card publisher that does a few inspirational cards. Open to freelance; buys 50-100 ideas/yr. Prefers outright submissions. Pays $300 for all rts. for use on a greeting card, or $50 for one-time use in a book, on publication. No royalties. Responds in 12-16 wks. Uses unrhymed or traditional poetry; short or long, but no one-liners. Produces inspirational and sensitivity. Needs anniversary, birthday, Christmas, congratulations, Easter, Father's Day, friendship, get well, graduation, keep in touch, love, miss you, Mother's Day, new baby, please write, relatives, sympathy, thank you, valentines, wedding, reaching for dreams. Holiday/seasonal 3 mos. ahead. Open to ideas for new card lines. Send any number of ideas (1 per pg.). Open to ideas for calendars and gift books. Guidelines; no catalog.

Contest: Sponsors a poetry card contest online. Details on Website.

Tips: "We are interested in reviewing poetry and writings for greeting cards, and expanding our field of freelance poetry writers."

BOB SIEMON DESIGNS INC., 3501 W. Segerstrom Ave., Santa Ana CA 92704-6497. (714)549-0678. Fax (714)979-2627. Website: www.bobsiemon.com. No freelance.

$CELEBRATION GREETINGS, (a div. of Leanin' Tree), Box 9500, Boulder CO 80301. (303)530-1442. Website: www.celebrationgreetings.com. Nancy Trumble Fox, VP Product. Christian/religious card publisher and specialty products. No freelance for now.

$CHRISTIAN INSPIRATIONS, 30 E. 33rd St., New York NY 10016. (212)685-0751. Fax (212)889-6868. Suzanne Kruck, VP. Christian card publisher. No unsolicited submissions; request permission in writing to send submissions. Pays on acceptance; no royalty. Responds in 4-6 wks. All types of verse, 4-6 lines. All kinds of cards and greetings, except Halloween and St. Patrick's. Seasonal 12 months ahead. Not open to new card lines or specialty products. No guidelines; catalog.

$+CREATIVE CHRISTIAN GIFTS. Toll-free (866)325-8565. (407)788-1151. E-mail: sales@creativechristiangifts.com. Website: www.creativechristiangifts.com. Greeting cards & note cards.

CURRENT, INC., PO Box 2559, Colorado Springs CO 80901. (719)594-4100. Fax (719)534-6259. Mar Porter, freelance coordinator. No freelance.

$DAYSPRING CARDS, INC., Box 1010, 20984 Oak Ridge Rd., Siloam Springs AR 72761. (479)549-6303. Fax (479)524-8959. E-mail: info@dayspring.com (type "write" in message or subject line). Website: www.dayspring.com. Christian/religious card publisher. Please read guidelines before submitting. Prefers outright submission. Pays $60/idea on acceptance for all rts. No royalty. Responds in 4-8 wks. Uses unrhymed, traditional, light verse, conversational, contemporary; various lengths. Looking for inspirational cards for all occasions, including anniversary, birthday, relative birthday, congratulations, encouragement, friendship, get well, new baby, sympathy, thank you, wedding. Also needs seasonal cards for friends and family members for Christmas, Valentine, Easter, Mother's Day, Father's Day, Thanksgiving, graduation, and Clergy Appreciation Day. Include scripture verse with each submission. Send 10 ideas or less. Guidelines by phone or e-mail; no catalog.

Tips: Prefers submissions on 8 x 11 inch sheets, not 3x5 cards (one idea per sheet).

$DESIGNER GREETINGS, PO Box 140729, Staten Island NY 10314. (718)981-7700. E-mail: info@designergreetings.com. Website: www.designergreetings.com. Fern Gimbelman, art dir. 50% freelance. Holiday/seasonal 6 mos. ahead. Responds in 2 mos. Pays on acceptance for greeting card rts. Guidelines on Website. Uses rhymed or unrhymed verse. Produces announcements, conventional, humorous, informal, inspirational, invitations, juvenile, sensitivity, soft line, studio. Up to 50% freelance.

*GIBSON GREETINGS, PO Box 371804, Cincinnati OH 45222-1804. E-mail: wcallah@gibsongreetings.com. Website: www.gibsongreetings.com. No freelance.

$#THE HERITAGE COLLECTION, 2 Forest Ln., Monroe NJ 08831-3256. Submit to Creative Director. General card publisher with a religious line. 20% freelance; buys 50-60 ideas/yr. Outright submission. Pays $35 on publication for domestic rts. No royalties. Responds in

4 wks. Prefers unrhymed; to 3 paragraphs. Produces announcements, inspirational, religious, and sensitivity. Needs anniversary, birthday, congratulations, friendship, get well, keep in touch, love, miss you, new baby, sympathy, thank you, and wedding. Also open to ideas for mugs. Guidelines/needs list; free catalog.

$INSPIRATIONART & SCRIPTURE, INC., PO Box 5550, Cedar Rapids IA 52406-5550. Toll-free (800)728-5550. (319)365-4350. Fax (319)861-2103. E-mail: Charles@inspiration art.com. Website: www.inspirationart.com. Publishes Christian posters. Charles Edwards, creative dir. Open to freelance. Buys 20-30 ideas/yr. Prefers e-mail contact. Pays $150-250, 30 days after publication, for right to publish as a poster. Royalties 5% of net. Responds in 4 wks. Seasonal 6 mos. ahead. Open to new ideas for posters, bookmarks, or puzzles. Submit up to 3 ideas. Guidelines (also on Website); catalog on Website.

$INSPIRATIONS UNLIMITED, PO Box 5097, Crestline CA 92325. (909)338-6758. Fax (909)338-2907. E-mail: Inspirations@aol.com. Website: www.InspirationsUnlimited.org. General card publisher that does a few inspirational/religious cards. Open to freelance. Buys 50 ideas/yr. Prefers outright submission. Pays $25 on acceptance. No royalties. Responds in 4 wks. Prefers unrhymed verse (something that tugs at the heart). Produces conventional, informal, inspirational, religious, sensitivity. All types. Holiday/seasonal 1 yr. ahead. Open to ideas for new card lines, plaques, stationery, note cards, and gift tags. Send up to 10 ideas. No guidelines or catalog.

$LAURA LEIDEN CALLIGRAPHY, INC., PO Box 141, Watkinsville GA 30677. (706)769-6989. Fax (706)769-0628. E-mail: llc@lauraleiden.com. Website: www.lauraleiden calligraphy.com. Submit to: Freelance submissions. General card publisher with one or more inspirational lines, and producer of specialty products. Open to freelance. Buys 10-20 ideas/yr. Outright submission. Responds in 12 wks. Buys all rts. on acceptance. No royalties. Prefers rhymed verse; sentimental/nostalgic; 4 stanzas, 4 lines ea. stanza. Produces conventional, inspirational. Needs Christmas, friendship, get well, relative (all occasion), sympathy. Prefers 4-10 ideas/submission. Holiday/seasonal 8 mos. ahead. Not open to ideas for new card lines or specialty items. Also produces plaques. Send SASE for guidelines first; no catalog.

$*LAWSON FALLE PUBLISHING, 1245 Franklin Blvd./290 Pinebush Rd., Cambridge ON N1R 5X9 Canada. Toll-free (800)265-8673. Fax (800)565-2755. E-mail: Rick@lawson-falle .com. Website: www.lawsonfalle.com. Rick Tocquigny, exec. VP. General card publisher with an inspirational line. Open to freelance; buys 20 ideas/yr. Prefer outright submission or e-mail contact. Buys rights to publish in CBA. Pays variable amounts. Royalties 3-5% of wholesale on publication. Responds in 3 wks. Prefers rhymed, unrhymed, traditional, and light verse, under 40 wds. Produces announcements, conventional, humorous, informal, inspirational, invitations, juvenile, novelty. Needs all types except Halloween; especially humorous birthday cards. Seasonal 18 mos. ahead. Not open to new card lines. Send 10 ideas. Open to ideas for calendars/journals, gift/novelty items, greeting books, and stationery. No guidelines or catalog.

    Tips: "We need good but clean humor."

$*LIFE GREETINGS, Box 468, Little Compton RI 02837. Website: www.LifeGreetings.com. (401)635-8535. Fax (401)635-4918. Kathy Brennan, ed. Christian/religious card publisher. 100% freelance. Outright purchases. Pays $10 on acceptance for all rts. No royalties. Responds in 2 wks. Uses rhymed, unrhymed, traditional; 6-8 lines. Produces announcements, conventional, humorous, inspirational, juvenile, religious, sensitivity. Needs congratulations, friendship, get well, new baby, sympathy, thank you, and wedding. Also clergy reassignment, ordination, anniversary of ordination, and pro-life Christmas. Holiday/seasonal 6 mos. ahead. Open to new card lines. Prefers 12 ideas/submission. Guidelines; no catalog.

$+NORTHERN CARDS, Creative Department, 5694 Ambler Dr., Mississauga ON L4W 2K9

Canada. E-mail: artists@northerncards.com. Website: www.northerncards.com/docs/ artists.shtml. Open to writers and artists. Greeting cards.

$*NOVO CARD PUBLISHERS, INC., 3630 W. Pratt Ave., Lincolnwood IL 60712. (847)763-0077. Fax (847)763-0020. E-mail: art@novocard.net. Website: www.novocard.net. Submit to Art Production. General card publisher that does a few inspirational and religious cards. Open to freelance; buys 10 ideas/yr. Prefers outright submissions. Pays $2/line on acceptance for all rts. No royalties. Responds in 5 wks. Uses traditional and light verse; 5-20 lines (nothing too brief). Produces baby announcements, conventional, humorous, inspirational, invitations, juvenile, religious, studio. Needs anniversary, birthday, Christmas, congratulations, Easter, Father's Day, friendship, get well, miss you, Mother's Day, new baby, relatives (all occasions), sympathy, Thanksgiving, thank you, valentines, wedding. Seasonal 6-8 mos. ahead. Open to ideas for new card lines. Submit enough ideas to show style. Guidelines/needs list; no catalog.

Tips: "We don't want anything too brief or too lengthy. We like verse that holds everyone's hearts, especially the male gender."

$+PRINTESSDI, PMB 520, 2058 N. Mills Ave., Claremont CA 91711. (909)437-0808. Fax (435)514-5425. E-mail: cards@printessdi.com. Website: www.printessdi.com. Diane Cooley, design ed. A general card publisher with one or more inspirational lines. Open to freelance. Buys 10-20 ideas/yr. Prefers outright submissions (read guidelines first). Buys all rts. Pays on acceptance in merchandise or $5-25. No royalties. Responds in 3-4 wks. Uses unrhymed, traditional, light verse; brief and to the point. Produces conventional, humorous, informal, inspirational, novelty. Needs anniversary, birthday, Christmas, congratulations, Easter, friendship, get well, love, Mother's Day, new baby, sympathy, thank you, valentines, wedding—with relationship-building messages. Holiday/seasonal 9 mos. ahead. Open to new card lines. Prefers 3-10 ideas/submission tied together by theme and/or style. Guidelines/needs list (also by e-mail/Website); no catalog.

Tips: "Need artwork: fresh, simple images (any media) with plain or no background. We do not use 'all over' card designs. Think 'clean, simple, classy.'"

$*P. S. GREETINGS, 5730 N. Tripp Ave., Chicago IL 60646-6723. Toll-free (800)621-8823. (773)267-6150. Fax (773)267-6055. E-mail: artdirector@psgreetings.com. Website: www.psgreetings.com. Jennifer Dodson, art dir. 100% freelance; 200-300 ideas/yr. Holiday/seasonal 6 mos. ahead. Responds in 1 mo. Pays flat fee on acceptance; no royalty. Rhymed or unrhymed verse. Produces conventional, humorous, inspirational, invitations, juvenile, sensitivity, soft line, and studio. Send 10 ideas. Submit on disk or by e-mail (copied into message). Guidelines/market list for #10 SASE (also on Website).

$*RED FARM STUDIO, 1135 Roosevelt Ave., Pawtucket RI 02861-0347. (401)728-9300. Fax (401)728-0350. Submit to Production Coordinator. General card publisher with a religious line. 100% freelance; buys 100 ideas/yr. Outright submission. Pays variable rates (about $4/line) within 1 mo. of acceptance for exclusive rts. No royalties. Responds in 2 mos. Use traditional and light verse; 1-4 lines. Produces announcements, invitations, religious. Needs anniversary, birthday, Christmas, friendship, get well, new baby, sympathy, wedding. Holiday 6 months ahead. Not open to ideas for new card lines. Submit any number of ideas. Guidelines/needs list for SASE.

$+RIVER M, 29742—400th St., Le Sueur MN 56058. Toll-free (866)474-8376. Inspirational display cards.

$SUZY'S ZOO, PO Box 85490, San Diego CA 92186-5490. (619)282-9401. Fax (619)285-5730. E-mail: jbush@suzyszoo.com. Website: www.suzyszoo.com. Judi Bush, acq. ed. Secular card publisher that does some inspirational cards. Responds in 4 mos. Pays on acceptance for all rts. Prefers unrhymed verse. Needs announcements, conventional, humorous, informal, inspirational, invitations. Holiday 18 mos. ahead. Submit 15 ideas. Guidelines/market list for #10 SAE/1 stamp.

Tips: "Most of our cards are purchased by women to give to their friends and family. We look for fresh, happy, witty verse that reflects the culture of today's family and makes people smile."

$#TON COMMUNICATIONS, 2295 Towne Lake Pkwy, #116-127, Woodstock GA 30189-5520. Toll-free (800)2000LBS. Christian humor cards. Willing to look at ideas from freelancers.

$WARNER PRESS INC., 1200 E. 5th St., PO Box 2499, Anderson IN 46018-9988. (765)644-7721. Fax (765)640-8005. E-mail: krhodes@warnerpress.org. Website: www.warnerpress.com. Karen Rhodes, sr. ed. Produces greeting cards. 30% freelance; buys 15-25 ideas/yr. Pays on acceptance. No royalties. Responds in 10-12 wks. Uses unrhymed prose, traditional & free verse for cards. Devotionals for bulletins—reflective, 110-150 wds. Accepts 10 ideas/submission. Prefers e-mail submissions; be sure name and address are on each page. Guidelines on Website; no catalog.

Tips: "Send greeting card submissions August-September and January-February. Those received at other times will be returned or held for possible use later, IF requested by the sender." Manuscripts/requests sent by regular mail without an SASE will not be returned.

ADDITIONAL CARD PUBLISHERS

NOTE: Following is a list of card publishers who did not respond to our questionnaire. You may want to contact them on your own to see if they are open to freelance submissions.

*ALFRED MAINZER, INC., 27-08—40th Ave., Long Island City NY 11101. Toll-free (800)22-cards. (718)392-4200. Fax (718)392-2681.

*APPALACHIAN BIBLE CO. INC., 506 Princeton Rd., Johnson City TN 37601.

*BERG CHRISTIAN ENTERPRISES, 4525 S.E. 63rd Ave., Portland OR 97206.

*BLACK FAMILY GREETING CARDS, 20 Cortlandt Ave., New Rochelle NY 10801. Bill Harte, pres.

*BLACKSMITH CARDS & PRINTS, 37535 Festival Dr., Palm Desert CA 92211. Bob Smith, pres.

*CAROL WILSON FINE ARTS, PO Box 17394, Portland OR 97217. Gary Spector, ed.

*CD GREETING CARDS, PO Box 5084, Brentwood TN 37024-5084.

*CRT CUSTOM PRODUCTS, INC., 7532 Hickory Hills Ct., Whites Creek TN 37189.

*DESIGNS FOR BETTER LIVING, 1716 N. Vista St., Los Angeles CA 90046.

*EXPRESSIONS OF FAITH, PO Box 35777, Colorado Springs CO 80935-3577.

*FREDERICK SINGER & SONS, INC., 2–15 Borden Ave., Long Island City NY 11101.

*GOOD NEWS IN SIGHT, 2610 Mirror Lake Dr., Fayetteville NC 28303-5212.

*GRACE PUBLICATIONS, 2125 Martindale S.W., Grand Rapids MI 49509.

#GREENLEAF, INC., 951 S. Pine St. #250, Spartanburg SC 29302-3370. Greenleaf Foundation, Inc.

*HERMITAGE ART CO., INC., 5151 N. Ravenswood Ave., Chicago IL 60640.

*HIGHER HORIZONS, PO Box 78399, Los Angeles CA 90016-0399.

*JOAN BAKER DESIGNS, 1130 Via Callejon, San Clemente, CA 92673.

*JODY HOUGHTON DESIGNS, INC., 2253 Lois Ln., West Linn OR 97068.

*KRISTIN ELLIOTT, INC., 6 Opportunity Way, Newburyport MA 01950.

*LORENZ CO., 1208 Cimmaron Dr., Waco TX 76712-8174.

*LUCY & ME GALLERY, 13232 Riviera PL. NE, Seattle WA 98125-4645. Diane Roger, card ed.

*MCBETH CORP, PO Box 400, Chambersburg PA 17201.

*MORE THAN A CARD, 5010 Baltimore Ave., Bethesda MD 20816.

*OAKSPRINGS IMPRESSIONS, PO Box 572, Woodacre CA 94973-0572.

*RANDALL WILCOX PUBLISHING, 826 Orange Ave., #544, Coronado CA 92118.

*SOUL-SEARCHER GREETING CARDS, 1336 N. 6th St., Mankato MN 56001-4216.

#THESE THREE, INC., 314 Washington Rd., #1001, South Hills PA 15216-1638. Jean P. Bridgers, card ed.

GAME MARKETS

NOTE: Some of the following markets for games, gift items, and videos have not indicated their interest in receiving freelance submissions. Contact these markets on your own for information on submission procedures before sending them anything.

$BIBLE GAMES CO., 14389 Cassell Rd., PO Box 237, Fredericktown OH 43019. (740)694-8042. Fax (740)694-8072. E-mail: info@biblegamescompany.com. Website: www.bible gamescompany.com. JoAnn Vozar, operations mngr. Produces Bible games. 10% freelance. Buys 1-2 ideas/yr. Query. Pays on publication for all rts. (negotiable). Royalties 8%. Responds in 6-8 wks. Open to new ideas. One game per submission. Guidelines & catalog online.
  Tips: "Send developed and tested game play; target market and audience. Must be totally nonsectarian and fully biblical—no fictionalized scenarios." Board games, CD-ROMs, computer games, and video games.

$*J. D. BRODIE, INC., PO Box 384, Bensalem PA 19020. Board games.

$+CACTUS GAME DESIGN, INC., 751 Tusquittee St., Hayesville NC 28904. (828)389-1536. Fax (828)389-1534. E-mail: cactusrob@brmemc.net. Website: www.cactusgamedesign.com. Rob Anderson, pres. Produces card games, board games, and computer games. Open to freelance submissions. Buys 2-4 ideas/yr. Query by e-mail. Pays variable amounts on acceptance for game rts. Pays 5-15% royalty for complete games only. Responds in 4 wks. Open to new ideas for games. Guidelines; catalog for .60 postage.

$GOODE GAMES INTERNATIONAL, 211 Stirrup Cir., Nicholasville KY 40356. Toll-free (800)257-7767. (859)881-4513. Fax (859)881-0765. Website: www.goodegames.com. Contact: Mike Goode.

$*GOOD STEWARD GAME CO., 6412 Sunnyfield Way, Sacramento CA 95823-5781. William Parker, ed.

$+PRISMATECH PUBLISHING, 4025 Pleasantdale Rd., Ste. 220, Atlanta GA 30340. Toll-free (888)316-3206. (770)242-1898. E-mail: WFWilliams@prismatech-inc.com. Website: www.prismatech-inc.com. Board games.

$*TALICOR, 14175 Telephone Ave., Ste. A, Chino CA 91710. (909)517-0076. Fax (909)517-1962. E-mail: webmaster@Talicor.com. Website: www.Talicor.com. Lew Herndon, pres. Produces board games and puzzles. 100% freelance; buys 10 ideas/yr. Outright submissions. Pays variable rates on publication for all rts. Royalty 4-6%. Responds in 4 wks. Seasonal 6 mos. ahead. Open to new ideas for puzzles or toys. Submit 1-4 ideas. No guidelines; catalog for 9x12 SAE/$1.42 postage (mark "Media Mail").

$*WISDOM TREE, PO Box 8682, Tucson AZ 85738-8682. (520)825-5702. Fax (520)825-5710. E-mail: wisdom@christianlink.com. Website: www.christianlink.com/media/wisdom. Brenda Huff, owner. Produces Bible-based computer games. 30% freelance (Beta versions). Query. Negotiable rights. Pays variable rates on publication. Variable royalties. Responds in 1-6 wks. Seasonal 8 mos. ahead. Open to review beta versions of computer games, computer software, or video games. No guidelines; catalog on request.
  Special Needs: "Storybook/puzzle game engine."

GIFT/SPECIALTY ITEM MARKETS

$ACTIVE DISCIPLE, PO Box 2045, Redmond WA 98073-2045. (425)260-6936. Fax (425)861-5777. E-mail: steveo@activedisciple.com. Website: www.activedisciple.com. Apparel.

$+ANCHOR WALLACE PUBLISHERS, 1000 Hwy 4 S., PO Box 7000, Sleepy Eye MN 56085-0007. Toll-free (800)582-2352. E-mail: contactus@anchorwallace.com. Website: www.anchor wallace.com. Calendars and bulletins.

$ARGUS COMMUNICATIONS, 200 E. Bethany Dr., Allen TX 75002-3804. Toll-free (800)328-5540. (972)396-6500. Fax (972)396-6789. Website: www.argus.com. Beth Davis, ed. Produces posters and other message-based products. 90% freelance. Query. Outright purchase. Pays $50-75 on acceptance for all rts. Responds in 6-8 wks. Open to ideas for banners, magnets, postcards, and posters. Guidelines (also on Website); no catalog.

Special Needs: "We need messages for teens and adults that are positive, inspirational, and motivational. We're looking for direct messages that have an impact and relevance to today's issues."

$ARTBEATS, 129 Glover Ave., Norwalk CT 06850-1311. (203)847-2000. Fax (203)846-2105. E-mail: Richard@nygs.com. Website: www.NYGS.com. New York Graphic society. Richard Fleischmann, pub. Produces prints and posters. Open to freelancers; purchases 100 ideas/yr. Outright submissions. Pays on publication. Royalties 10%. Responds in 3 wks. Does conventional, inspirational, juvenile, religious, and sensitivity prints and posters. Open to new ideas. Guidelines; no catalog.

$BE ONE CHRISTIAN SPORTSWEAR, 3208 Merrywood Dr., Sacramento CA 95825. (916)483-7630. Christian clothing.

$BROADMAN & HOLMAN GIFTS, a division of Broadman & Holman, 127 Ninth Ave. N., Nashville TN 37234. (615)251-3638. Website: www.broadmanholman.com.

$#CARPENTREE, INC., Carpentree Design, 2724 N. Sheridan, Tulsa OK 74115. (918)582-3600. Fax (918)587-4329. E-mail: design@carpentree.com. Website: www.carpentree.com. Submit to Design Dept. Produces framed art and verse. Buys several ideas/yr. Prefers outright submission. Rights purchased are negotiable. Pays on publication; negotiable royalty. Responds in 12-15 wks. Uses rhymed, unrhymed, and traditional verse for framed art; 4-16 lines. Open to ideas for new specialty items. Submit max 3-10 ideas. Open to ideas for framed art, tabletop items, and gift/novelty items. Guidelines; catalog $5/10x13 SAE.

$CATHEDRAL ART METAL CO., 25 Manton Ave., Providence RI 02909-3349. Toll-free (800)493-GIFT. (401)273-7200, ext. 227. Fax (401)273-6262 or (800)472-6435. E-mail: camco@cathedralart.com, or information@cathedralart.com. Website: www.cathedralart.com. Fritzi Frey, art dir. Producer of specialty products. Open to freelance; buys 2 ideas/yr. Outright submissions; e-query OK. Pays $50 on acceptance for all rights. Royalties 3-5%. Responds in 1-4 wks. Uses rhymed, unrhymed, traditional, light verse; 2-8 lines (for plaques). Produces plaques and pins with inspirational messages for special occasions: baby, communion, confirmation, graduation, wedding, and anniversary. Holiday/seasonal 6 mos. ahead. Open to ideas for bookmarks, figurines, plaques, jewelry/pins, wind chimes, frames. Guidelines; catalog for 9x12 SAE/$3.85 postage.

$+CHRISTIAN ART GIFTS, 1025 N. Lombard Rd., PO Box 1443, Lombard IL 60148. Toll-free (800)521-7807. (630)599-0240. Fax (630)599-0245. Friendship cards, greeting books, bookmarks, mugs.

$CONTEMPORARY CHRISTIAN ART POSTERS, 140 E. 52nd St., New York NY 10022. Toll-free (888)999-4188. (212)486-7700. Fax (212)486-7077.

$+DEPENDING ON THE SON CHRISTIAN PATCHWORKS, 639 S. Everett Ave., Columbus OH 43213-2778. Toll-free (866)204-6011. E-mail: vistor@dependingontheson.com. Website: www.jcpatch.com. Iron-on patches.

$DESTINY IMAGE GIFTS, PO Box 310, Shippensburg PA 17257. (717)532-3040. Fax (717)532-9291. E-mail: dlm@destinyimage.com. Website: www.destinyimage.com. Don Milam, ed. mngr. Gift books.

$DEXSA, The Giving Company, PO Box 109, Hudson WI 54016. Toll-free (800)933-3972. (715)386-8701. Fax (888)559-1603. Website: www.dexsa.com.

$DICKSONS, INC., 709 B Ave. East, PO Box 368, Seymour IN 47274. (812)522-1308. Fax (812)522-1319. E-mail: rdeppen@dicksonsgifts.com. Website: www.dicksonsgifts.com. Rita

Deppen, prod. dev. Produces gift items. Open to freelance (1-2%). Submit cover letter/ sample (no originals). Outright purchase; all rts. preferred. Pays $50 on acceptance. Variable royalties. Responds in 4-6 wks. Uses rhymed verse. Needs Christmas, Father's Day, friendship, graduation, love, Mother's Day, thank you, and wedding. Holiday/seasonal 1 yr. ahead. Send any number of ideas. Uses religious/inspirational verses for bookmarks, Quik Notes, plaques, etc. Open to ideas for banners, board games, bookmarks, calendars/journals, comic books, gift/novelty items, magnets, mugs, plaques, stationery, T-shirts, and toys. Guidelines; no copy.

Tips: "Return postage required for return of submitted material." Recently acquired Cross Gifts.

$*FAMILYLIFE, PO Box 23840, Little Rock AR 72221-3840. Toll-free (800)358-6329. Website: www.familylife.com. Mark Whitlock, acq. ed. Producer of specialty products. Open to freelance. Prefers a query/SASE; e-query OK. Buys all rts. Payment negotiable. Pays 1/4 on acceptance and 3/4 on publication. Royalty 2-18% of gross. Responds within 24 mos. Holiday/seasonal 24 mos. ahead. Open to ideas for specialty items. Does activity/coloring books, audiotapes, bookmarks, calendars/journals, gift books, gift/novelty items, magnets, videos, and interactive multipiece resources. Guidelines; catalog for 9x12 SAE/4 stamps.

Tips: "We do content product. Please do not send us trinkets or cheap specialties. Study our resources and read our guidelines on our Website."

$*GREGG GIFT COMPANY, 17762 Mitchell Ave., Irvine CA 92614. Toll-free (800)447-3440. (949)955-5900. Fax (949)955-1198. E-mail: sales@gregggiftcompany.com. Website: www .gregggiftcompany.com. Makes a variety of gift items. Open to freelance art. Prefers e-mail submissions.

$HERITAGE PUZZLE, INC., 340 Witt St., Winston-Salem NC 27103. Toll-free (888)348-3717. Website: www.heritagepuzzle.com. Religious jigsaw puzzles.

$INSPIRIO GIFTS/ZONDERVAN PUBLISHING HOUSE, 5300 Patterson S.E., Grand Rapids MI 49530-0002. Toll-free (800)727-1309. Website: www.inspiriogifts.com. Gift company offering Bible and book covers, gift books, devotionals, boutique products, and home decor lines.

$JAMES LAWRENCE COMPANY, 1501 Livingstone Rd., PO Box 188, Hudson WI 54016. (715)386-3082. Fax (715)386-3699. Website: www.jameslawrencecompany.com. Chuck Hetland, product development. Produces wall decor. Open to freelance. Buys 12-20 ideas/yr. Prefers outright submissions. Prefers exclusive rts. Pays $50-100/verse on acceptance. No royalties. Responds in 3 wks. Inspirational verse no shorter than 4 lines and no longer than 5 stanzas of 4 lines ea. Holiday 9-12 mos. ahead. Open to new ideas for mugs, plaques, pictures. Send any number of ideas. Guidelines; no catalog.

$KNOW HIM, 6200 S. Troy Cir., #240, Englewood CO 80111. Toll-free (888)256-6944. (303)662-9512. Fax (303)662-9942. E-mail: Doug.Mckenna@knowhim.com. Website: www.knowhimcom. Contact: Doug McKenna. Christian apparel.

$+LIVING EPISTLES, 3401 Greensboro Ave., Tuscaloosa AL 35401. Toll-free (800)294-8637. Website: www.livingepistles.com. Apparel.

$MULTNOMAH GIFTS, A Division of Multnomah Publishers, Inc., PO Box 1720, Sisters OR 97759. (541)549-1144. Fax (541)549-8048. E-mail: lstilwell@multnomahgifts.com. Website: www.multnomahbooks.com. Lisa Stilwell, dev. ed. Produces 4-color gift books. Not open to freelance submissions. Guidelines; no catalog.

$*PEELE ENTERPRISES SHIRT PRINTS, 3401 Hwy. 25N, Hodges SC 29653. Shirts.

$+POWERMARK: Comics Worth Reading, 380 E. Hwy. CC, Ste. B104, Nixa MO 65714. Toll-free (877)769-2669. Fax (417)724-0119. E-mail: webmaster@powermarkcomics.com. Website: www.powermarkcomics.com. Contact: Steve Benintendi. Christian comic books.

$*PRINTS OF PEACE, PO Box 717, Camino CA 95709. (530)644-7044.

$*RED LETTER 9, 2910 Kerry Forest Pkwy, D4, Tallahassee FL 32309. (866)804-4833. Fax (866)804-4832. Apparel and gift items.

$#REVELATIONS, 21241 N 23rd Ave., Ste. 1, Phoenix AZ 85027-2537. Toll-free (800)886-5420. (623)582-0802. Fax (623)582-4004. E-mail: info@revgifts.com. Website: www.giftware company.com. Variety of gift products.

$*SCANDECOR, 430 Pike Rd., Southampton PA 18966. (215)355-2410. Fax (215)364-8737. Dan Griffin, VP of operations. A general poster publisher that does a few inspirational posters for children, teens, and adults. 40% freelance; buys 50 ideas/yr. Makes outright purchase, for worldwide, exclusive rts. Pays $100 on publication, depends on size of poster. No royalties. Responds in 9 wks. Uses rhymed, unrhymed, and light verse; one line up to 20 lines. Produces humorous, inspirational, juvenile, novelty, and soft line. No holiday posters. Submit several ideas. Open to ideas for calendars, posters, and novelty products/copy. Guidelines; no catalog.

$+SOLID LIGHT CO., PO Box 330, Lewis Center OH 43035-0330. Toll-free (800)726-9606. Fax (740)548-1223. E-mail: info@solidlightco.com. Website: www.solidlightco.com. Apparel.

$+SONTEEZ CHRISTIAN T-SHIRTS, PO Box 44106, Phoenix AZ 85064. Toll-free (800)874-4485. E-mail: info@sonteez.com. Website: www.sonteez.com. T-shirts.

$*SWANSON INC., 1200 Park Ave., Murfreesboro TN 37129. (615)896-4114. Fax (866)431-1313. E-mail: adam@swansoninc.com. Website: www.swansoninc.com. Adam Swanson, marketing. Produces specialty products. Just opening up to freelancers. Query. Pays on publication. No royalties. Responds in 8-10 wks. Uses rhymed, unrhymed, traditional, and light verse; short. Inspirational/Christian. Open to new ideas. Send any number. Open to ideas for coloring books, gift/novelty items, magnets, mugs, postcards, puzzles, T-shirts. No guidelines or catalog.

$+WARFARE STORE, PO Box 681, Ocoee FL 34761. Toll-free (888)769-9931. Fax (208)972-1164. E-mail: info@warfarestore.com. Website: www.warfarestore.com. Submit by e-mail to: submit@warfarestore.com. Produces and distributes specialty products and cards. Open to freelance. Buys 3-4 ideas/yr. Prefers outright submissions. Pays on publication. Royalties 5-8%. Responds in 8-10 wks. Produces conventional cards; keep in touch, wedding, and humor. Open to ideas for new card lines or specialty items. Prefers more than one idea per submission. Guidelines; no catalog.

　　Special Needs: Apparel for teen audience (skater, goth, punk, rave, etc.).

　　Tips: "Visit our Website to see if your idea fits our audience. We resell products as well as manufacture our own products. Please send us your 'out of the box' ideas."

$WARNER PRESS INC., 1200 E. 5th St., PO Box 2499, Anderson IN 46018-9988. (765)644-7721. Fax (765)640-8005. E-mail: krhodes@warnerpress.org. Website: www.warner press.com. Karen Rhodes, product mktg. ed. Producer of church resources (greeting cards, bulletins, coloring books, puzzle books). 30% freelance; buys 30-50 ideas/yr. Query for guidelines. Pays $30-35 on acceptance (for bulletins); material for bulletins cannot be sold elsewhere for bulletin use, but may be sold in any other medium. No royalties. Responds in 6-8 wks. Uses rhymed, unrhymed, traditional verse, and devotionals for bulletins; 16-24 lines. Accepts 10 ideas/submission. Also open to ideas for coloring books, church resource items. Guidelines for bulletins; no catalog.

　　Tips: "Most of our present purchases are for church bulletins. Send bulletin submissions August-October only. Those received at other times will be returned or held for possible use later, IF requested by the sender. Manuscripts/requests without an SASE will not be returned."

SOFTWARE DEVELOPERS

AMG PUBLISHERS, 6815 Shallowford Rd. (37421), PO Box 22000, Chattanooga TN 37422. Toll-free (800)266-4977. (423)894-6060, ext. 275. Fax (800)265-6690 or (423)894-

9511. E-mail: danp@amginternational.org. Website: www.amgpublishers.org. AMG International. Dan Penwell, dir. of prod. dev./acq. Bible software.

BAKER BOOKS, Box 6287, Grand Rapids MI 49516-6287. (616)676-9185. Fax (616)676-9573. Website: www.BakerBooks.com. Baker Publishing Group.

BIBLESOFT, 22014—7th Ave. S., Seattle WA 98198-6235. (206)824-0547. Fax (206)824-1828. Website: www.biblesoft.com.

BROADMAN & HOLMAN SOFTWARE, 127 Ninth Ave. N., Nashville TN 37234. (615)251-3638. Website: www.broadmanholman.com.

DISCOVERY HOUSE, PO Box 3566, Grand Rapids MI 49501. Toll-free (800)653-8333. Website: www.dhp.org. Does Bible study software.

ELLIS ENTERPRISES, INC., 5100 N. Brookline #465, Oklahoma City OK 73112. (405)749-6878. E-mail: mail@ellisenterprises.com. Website: www.ellisenterprises.com. Contact person: John Ellis. Produces the Micro Bible, Ultra Bible, Mega Bible, and Maxima Bible. Check out additional products on their Website.

+LARIDIAN, 1733 Lake Terrace Rd. SE, Cedar Rapids IA 52403. (319)378-4940. Fax (413)208-8477. E-mail: craigr@laridian.com. Website: www.laridian.com. Craig Rairdin, pres. Send ideas by e-mail. Bible software for hand-held and palmtop computers.

LOGOS RESEARCH SYSTEMS, 1313 Commercial St., Bellingham WA 98225-4372. Phone/fax (360)527-1700. E-mail: info@logos.com. Website: www.logos.com. Contact: Dan Pritchett (DAN@logos.com). Publishes the Logos Bible Software Series X—Scholar's Library, Pastor's Library, and Bible Study Library. Over 3,800 titles from more than 100 publishers now compatible with the system.

*NAVPRESS SOFTWARE, 16002 Pool Canyon Rd., Austin TX 78734.

*SILAS PUBLISHING, 1154 Westchester Dr., Lilburn GA 30047. E-mail: scott@silasinteractive.com. Website: www.silasinteractive.com. Christian self-help books and software.

ZONDERVAN NEW MEDIA, 5300 Patterson St. S.E., Grand Rapids MI 49530. Toll-free (800)226-1122. (616)698-6900. Fax (616)698-3483. Website: www.zondervan.com. Contact: T.J. Rathbun. Software.

VIDEO/CD MARKETS

AMG PUBLISHERS, 6815 Shallowford Rd. (37421), PO Box 22000, Chattanooga TN 37422. Toll-free (800)266-4977. (423)894-6060, ext. 275. Fax (800)265-6690 or (423)894-9511. E-mail: danp@amginternational.org. Website: www.amgpublishers.org. AMG International. Dan Penwell, dir. of prod. dev./acq. Bible CD-ROMs.

+BIG IDEA PRODUCTIONS, INC., 206 Yorktown Shopping Center, Lombard IL 60148-5526. (630)652-6000. Query; no unsolicited ideas. Movies, videos, music, books, and games.

+CANDLELIGHT MEDIA GROUP, 566 Watson Branch Rd., Franklin TN 37064. Toll-free (800)747-2696. E-mail: info@candlelightmedia.com. Website: www.candlelightmedia.com. Videos, DVDs.

CHRISTIAN DUPLICATIONS INTL., INC., 1710 Lee Reed Rd., Orlando FL 32810. Toll-free (800)327-9332. Fax (407)299-6004. Website: www.CDIMediaSolutions.com. Videos.

CLOUD TEN PICTURES, PO Box 1440, Niagara Falls NY 14302. Or, One St. Paul St., Ste. 401, The Penthouse, St. Catherines ON L2R 7L2 Canada. (905)684-5561. Fax (905)684-7946. E-mail: movies@cloudtenpictures.com. Website: www.cloudtenpictures.com. Mario Falvo, corp. controller. Film production, theatrical release, video distribution and marketing. Cloud Ten Pictures (maker of the Left Behind movies) is committed to maintaining its position as the industry leader in the production, distribution, and acquisition of quality faith-based family entertainment. For all media inquiries, contact Jessica Parker, Publicist. (905)684-5561, ext. 47, or e-mail: jessicap@cloudtenpictures.com.

+CROWN VIDEO, PO Box 1108, Edmonton AB T5J 2M1 Canada. Toll-free (800)661-9467. (780)471-1417. Fax (780)474-0418. E-mail: info@crownvideo.com. Website: www.crown video.com. Precision Media Group. Videos, DVDs.

DALLAS CHRISTIAN VIDEO, PO Box 450474, Garland TX 75045-0474. Toll-free (800)350-9458. Fax (972)644-5926. E-mail: DCV6681@aol.com. Website: www.DallasChristian Video.com. Contact: Bob Hill.

#EXEGESES BIBLES CD-ROM—The Only Literal Translations and Transliterations—Ever. PO Box 1031, Chiloquin OR 97624-1031. Toll-free phone/fax (800)9BIBLE9. E-mail: exege ses@exegesesbibles.org. Website: www.exegesesbibles.org.

+GOODTIMES ENTERTAINMENT, 16 E. 40th St., New York NY 10016. Toll-free (800)285-6920. (212)951-3000. Fax (212)951-9319. E-mail: information@goodtimes.com. Website: www.goodtimesentertainmsnt.com. Videos.

+GOSPEL COMMUNICATIONS, PO Box 455, Muskegon MI 49443-0455. Toll-free (800)467-7353. (231)774-3361. Fax (231)777-1847. Website: www.ChristianMediaSource.com. Videos, DVDs, books, Bibles, and music.

*PROPHECY PUBLICATIONS, PO Box 7000, Oklahoma City OK 73153. Toll-free (800)475-1111. Fax (405)636-1054. Religious education videos; fiction videos.

*RANDOLF PRODUCTIONS, INC., 18005 Sky Park Cir., Ste. K, Irvine CA 92614-6514. Toll-free (800)266-7741. (949)794-9109. Fax (949)794-9117. E-mail: randy@randolf productions.com. Website: www.randolfproductions.com. Distributor of music and video from Campus Crusade for Christ. Contact: Randy Ray. Videos, CD-ROMs, and DVD.

*RUSS DOUGHTEN FILMS, INC., 5907 Meredith Dr., Des Moines IA 50322. Toll-free (800)247-3456. (515)278-4737. Fax (515)334-0460. E-mail: trachford@rdfilms.com. Website: www.rdfilms.com. Submit to Production Dept. Produces feature-length Christian movies, DVDs. Open to ideas. Guidelines; free catalog.

*SILAS PUBLISHING, 1154 Westchester Dr., Lilburn GA 30047. E-mail: info@silasinteractive .com. Website: www.silasinteractive.com. Dr. Scott Philip Stewart, ed. Interactive multi-media; book/CD sets.

*SOLDIERS OF LIGHT PRODUCTIONS, 18701 Victory Blvd., Reseda CA 91335-6459.

ST. ANTHONY MESSENGER PRESS. See book listing.

TOMMY NELSON VIDEOS, PO Box 141000, Nashville TN 37214. (615)902-3305. Fax (615)902-3325. E-mail: breeves@tommynelson.com. Website: www.tommynelson.com. Contact: Bill Reeves, entertainment dir. Video producer.

+TYNDALE FAMILY VIDEO, 351 Executive Dr., Carol Stream IL 60188. (630)668-8300. Website: www.tyndale.com. Videos.

VISION VIDEO/GATEWAY FILMS, PO Box 540, Worcester PA 19490-0540. (610)584-3500. Fax (610)584-6643. E-mail: info@VisionVideo.com. Website: www.VisionVideo.com.

*VISUAL ENTERTAINMENT, INC., 1235 Bay St., Ste. 300, Toronto ON M5R 3K4 Canada. Toll-free (888)387-2200. E-mail: info@visualbible.com. Website: www.visualbible.com. Videos and CD-ROMs.

+WACKY WORLD STUDIOS, 148 E. Douglas Rd., Oldsmar FL 34677. (813)818-8277. Fax (813)818-8396. E-mail: info@wackyworld.tv. Website: www.wackyworld.tv. Full service custom art and design studio. Videos, DVDs.

+WORLD WIDE PICTURES, INC., PO Box 668029, Charlotte NC 28266-8029. Toll-free (800)745-4318. E-mail: info@wwp.org. Website: www.wwp.org. Billy Graham Assn. DVDs.

ZONDERVAN NEW MEDIA, 5300 Patterson St. S.E., Grand Rapids MI 49530. Toll-free (800)226-1122. (616)698-6900. Fax (616)698-3483. Website: www.zondervan.com. contact: T. J. Rathbun. Videos.

SPECIALTY PRODUCTS TOPICAL LISTINGS

NOTE: Most of the following publishers are greeting card/specialty market publishers, but some will be found in the book publisher listings.

ACTIVITY/COLORING BOOKS

Chariot Books
FamilyLife
Rainbow Publishers
Shining Star
Swanson
Warfare Store
Warner Press

AUDIOTAPES

AMG Publishers
Bible Games Co.
Eldridge Pub.
Fair Havens
FamilyLife
Liguori
McRuffy Press
Success Publishers
Tyndale House
W Publishing Group
Warfare Store
World Publishing
Zondervan New Media

BANNERS

Argus Communications

BOARD GAMES/GAMES

Bethel Publishing
Bible Games Co.
Big Idea, Inc.
Brodie, Inc., J. D.
Cactus Game Company
Chariot Books
Dicksons
Good Steward Game Co.
Goode Games
Joshua Morris Publishing
Lightwave Publishing
Master Books
Prismatech Publishing
Review and Herald
Shining Star
Standard Publishing
Talicor
Tyndale House
Warfare Store

BOOKMARKS

Bless His Name
Cathedral Art
Christian Art Gifts
Dexsa
Dicksons
FamilyLife
InspirationArt

BULLETINS

Anchor Wallace Publishers
Warner Press

CALENDARS/DAILY JOURNALS

Abingdon Press
African American Expressions
American Tract Society
Anchor Wallace Publishers
Argus Communications
Barbour Publishing
Bless His Name
Blue Mountain Arts
Dicksons
FamilyLife
Group Publishing
Lawson Falle
Neibauer Press
Read 'N Run Books
Scandecor
Tyndale House
Women of the Promise

CD-ROMs

AMG Publishers
Bible Games Co.
Cactus Game Company
Chariot Books
Doubleday
Fair Havens
Georgetown Univ. Press
Group Publishing
NavPress
Our Sunday Visitor
Talicor
Twenty-Third Publications
World Publishing

CHARTS

Rose Publishing

COMIC BOOKS

Dicksons
Kaleidoscope Press
Nelson Books
Powermark

COMPUTER GAMES

Bible Games Co.
Big Idea, Inc.
Brown-ROA
Cactus Game Company
Chariot Books
Editores Betania-Caribe
NavPress
Robbie Dean Press
Talicor
Wisdom Tree
Wood Lake Books

COMPUTER SOFTWARE

AMG Publishers
Baker
BibleSoft
Concordia
Gospel Light
Laridian
Logos Research Systems
NavPress
Resource Publications
Talicor
Wisdom Tree
Zondervan New Media

DVDs*

Big Idea, Inc.
Candlelight Media
Crown Video
Gospel Communications
Wacky World Studios
World Wide Pictures

GIFT BOOKS

Bless His Name
Blue Mountain Arts
Destiny Image
FamilyLife
Inspirio Gifts
Review and Herald

GIFT/NOVELTY ITEMS

Abingdon Press
African American Expressions
Carpentree
Cathedral Art
Chariot Books
Christian Art Gifts
Depending on the Son
Dexsa
Dicksons
FamilyLife
Lawson Falle
New Boundary Designs
River M
Scandecor
Swanson
Zondervan New Media

GREETING BOOKS

Bless His Name
Blue Mountain Arts
Christian Art Gifts
Lawson Falle
New Boundary Designs

MAGNETS

African American Expressions
Argus Communications
Dexsa
Dicksons
FamilyLife
New Boundary Designs
Swanson

MUGS

Christian Art Gifts
Dicksons
Heritage Collection
James Lawrence
Swanson
Warfare Store

NOTECARDS*

Creative Christian Gifts

PLAQUES

Cathedral Art
Dexsa
Dicksons

Inspirations Unlimited
James Lawrence
Laura Leiden
New Boundary Designs

POSTCARDS

Abingdon Press
Argus Communications
New Boundary Designs
Read 'N Run Books
Swanson
Warner Press
Zondervan New Media

POSTERS

Argus Communications
ArtBeats
Bless His Name (prints)
InspirationArt
Life Cycle Books
Read 'N Run Books
Scandecor
Warfare Store

PUZZLES

Bible Games Co.
InspirationArt
Swanson
Talicor
Warfare Store

STATIONERY

African American Expressions
Bless His Name
Dicksons
Inspirations Unlimited
Lawson Falle

SUNDAY BULLETINS

Warner Press

T-SHIRTS/APPAREL

Active Disciple
Be One Christian
Bless His Name
Dicksons
Know Him
Living Epistles
Peele Enterprises
Red Letter 9

Solid Light Co.
SonTeez
Swanson

TOYS

Dicksons
Standard Publishing
Talicor
Warfare Store

VIDEOS/VIDEO GAMES

Abingdon Press
Augsburg
Bible Games Co.
Big Idea Productions
Big Idea, Inc.
Brentwood
Broadman & Holman
Brown-ROA
Candlelight Media
Chariot Books
Christian Duplications
Crown Video
Destiny Image
Editorial Unilit
Fair Havens
FamilyLife
Focus on the Family
GoodTimes Entertainment
Gospel Communications
Gospel Light
Group Publishing
Howard Publishing
Liguori
Master Books
Moody Press
Paraclete Press
Pauline Books
Prophecy Publications
Russ Doughten Films
Talicor
Tommy Nelson
Tyndale House
Vermont Story Works
Victor Books
W Publishing Group
Wacky World Studios
Warfare Store
Wisdom Tree

CHRISTIAN WRITERS' CONFERENCES AND WORKSHOPS

(*) Indicates information was not verified or updated by the conference director
(+) Indicates a new listing

Note: Visit the following Websites for information on these and other conferences available across the country: www.freelancewriting.com/conferences, or www.screenwriter.com/insider/Writers Calendar.html. Link to the following conference sites at: www.stuartmarket.com.

ALABAMA

SOUTHERN CHRISTIAN WRITERS CONFERENCE. Tuscaloosa/First Baptist Church; June 2005. Contact: Joanne Sloan, SCWC, PO Box 1106, Northport AL 35473. (205)333-8603. Fax (205)339-4528. E-mail: SCWCworkshop@aol.com. Website www.magazinewriting .com/scwc. Attendance: 220.

ARIZONA

AMERICAN CHRISTIAN WRITERS PHOENIX CONFERENCE. October 28-29, 2005. Contact: Reg A. Forder, Box 110390, Nashville TN 37222. 1-800-21-WRITE. Website: www.ACWriters .com. Attendance: 40-75.

CATHOLIC WRITERS RETREATS. Redemptorist Renewal Center at Picture Rocks/near Tucson; February 11-15, 2005. Contact: Thomas M. Santa, CSSR, 7101 W. Picture Rocks Rd., Tucson AZ 85743. (520)744-3400. Fax (520)744-8021. E-mail: tmscssr@cs.com. Website: www.desertrenewal.org. Speakers: Working professionals and select editors from Catholic publishers. Attendance: 50. Awards an annual $500 scholarship to attend this conference. Applicants must send a 250-word statement, explaining why they should receive the scholarship, by e-mail only to: CBPA3@aol.com. Also Sessions One and Two for Beginning Writers on January 25-30, 2005 and February 11-15, 2005.

+THE PUBLISHING GAME WORKSHOP. Phoenix; March 21, 2005. Contact: Alyza Harris, Peanut Butter and Jelly Press, PO Box 590239, Newton MA 02459. Phone/fax (617)630-0945. E-mail: workshop@PublishingGame.com. Website: www.PublishingGame.com (registration form on Website). Speaker: Fern Reiss. Attendance: limited to 18.

*SOUTH-EASTERN ARIZONA CHRISTIAN WRITERS WORKSHOP. Benson; November 5, 2005 (always the 1st Saturday of November). Contact: Floyd Pierce, 6565 Jeffords Trail, Willcox AZ 85643. (520)384-3064.

ARKANSAS

+ANNUAL ARKANSAS WRITERS CONFERENCE. Little Rock; June 3-4, 2005 (always 1st Friday & Saturday of June). Contact: Barbara Mulkey, 9317 Claremore, Little Rock AR 72227. (501)312-1747. E-mail: blm@aristotle.net. Attendance: 200. Sponsors 32 contests; one $6 entry free covers all contests.

OZARK CREATIVE WRITERS CONFERENCE. Eureka Springs; October 6-8, 2005 (always 2nd weekend Thursday-Saturday of October). Contact: Clarissa Willis, 2603 W. Walnut, Johnson City TN 37604. (423)929-1049. E-mail: ozarkcreativewriters@earthlink.net. Website: www.ozarkcreativewriters.org. Editors and agents in attendance. Sponsors 25-30 contests each year. Attendance: 200.

SILOAM SPRINGS WRITERS' CONFERENCE. Siloam Springs; September 17, 2005. Contact: Margaret Weathers, 716 W. University, Siloam Springs AR 72761-2658. (479)524-6598. Website: http://sswc.flash57.com. Attendance: 30.

CALIFORNIA

ACT ONE: WRITING FOR HOLLYWOOD. Hollywood; July 2005. Contact: Barbara R. Nicolosi, 1763 N. Gower St., Hollywood CA 90028. (323)462-1348. Fax (323)462-2550. E-mail: Actone@fpch.org. Website: www.ActOneprogram.com. Speakers include: Dean Batali, Ralph Winter. These are month-long intensive training session for screenwriters. No editors or agents in attendance. Limited to 30 students (by application).

ALL DAY FICTION. Tehachapi; April 2006 (not being held in 2005). Contact: Lauraine Snelling (instructor), 19872 Highline Rd., Tehachapi CA 93561. (661)823-0669. Fax (661)823-9427. E-mail: TLSnelling@yahoo.com. Website: www.LauraineSnelling.net. Attendance: Limited to 15.

AMERICAN CHRISTIAN WRITERS ANAHEIM CONFERENCE. October 21-22, 2005. Contact: Reg A. Forder, Box 110390, Nashville TN 37222. 1-800-21-WRITE. Website: www .ACWriters.com. Attendance: 40-75.

AMERICAN CHRISTIAN WRITERS SACRAMENTO CONFERENCE. October 15, 2005. Contact: Reg A. Forder, Box 110390, Nashville TN 37222. 1-800-21-WRITE. Website: www .ACWriters.com. Attendance: 40-75.

+BIOLA MEDIA CONFERENCE. La Mirada; May 2005. Contact: Craig Detweiler, Biola University, 13800 Biola Ave., La Mirada CA 90639. Toll-free (866)334-2266. Website: www.biola.edu/media.

CASTRO VALLEY CHRISTIAN WRITERS SEMINAR. Castro Valley; February 18-19, 2005. Contact: Pastor Jon Drury, 19300 Redwood Rd., Castro Valley CA 94546-3465. (510)886-6300. Fax (510)581-5022. E-mail: jdrury@redwoodchapel.org. Website: www.christian writer.org. Speaker: Sally E. Stuart. One or two editors in attendance. Attendance: 160-220.

CHRISTIAN WRITERS FELLOWSHIP OF ORANGE COUNTY WRITERS DAYS. Location to be announced; February or March 2005, and possibly fall 2005. Contact: Beverly Bush Smith or Bonnie Compton Hanson, PO Box 538, Lake Forest CA 92609. (949)458-8981. Fax (949)458-1807. E-mail: bonnieh1@worldnet.att.net, or b2smith@pacbell.net. Attendance: 100.

FICTION INTENSIVE, for fiction writers who want to go deeper. Tehachapi; no session planned for 2005. Contact: Lauraine Snelling (instructor), 19872 Highline Rd., Tehachapi CA 93561. (661)823-0669. Fax (661)823-9427. E-mail: TLSnelling@yahoo.com. Website: www.LauraineSnelling.net. Attendance: Limited to 10.

+HANDS-ON WRITER'S WEEKEND. Lake Elsinore; March & October 2005. Contact: Beverly Caruso, 18550 Timberline Dr., Lake Elsinore CA 92532-7325. (909)245-4082. Fax (909)245-9068. E-mail: admin@across2u.com. Website: www.cross2u.com/rancho.html. This is a small (no more than 10) interactive workshop/instruction & personal time with Beverly Caruso. No editors or agents in attendance.

*LODI ALL-DAY WRITERS SEMINAR. Stockton; July 2005. General writing conference; not just Christian writers. Contact: Dee Porter, PO Box 1863, 103 Koni Ct. (95240), Lodi CA 95241. Phone/fax (209)334-0603. E-mail: crcomm@lodinet.com. Write and ask to be put on mailing list.

MARKETING SEMINAR. Tehachapi; September 2006 (tentative); not being held in 2005. Contact: Lauraine Snelling (instructor), 19872 Highline Rd., Tehachapi CA 93561. (661)823-0669. Fax (661)823-9427. E-mail: TLSnelling@aol.com. Website: www.Lauraine Snelling.net. Attendance: Limited to 10.

MOUNT HERMON CHRISTIAN WRITERS CONFERENCE. Mount Hermon (near Santa Cruz); March 18-22, 2005; mid-April 2006. Offers an advanced track and a professional forum. Also offers a teen track. Contact: David R. Talbott, Box 413, Mount Hermon CA 95041-0413. (831)335-4466. Fax (831)335-9413. E-mail: rachelw@mhcamps.org. Website: www.mounthermon.org/writers. Keynote speaker (2005): Liz Curtis Higgs. Many editors and agents in attendance. Attendance: 450.

+THE PUBLISHING GAME WORKSHOP. Los Angeles; check Website for date. Contact: Alyza Harris, Peanut Butter and Jelly Press, PO Box 590239, Newton MA 02459. Phone/fax (617)630-0945. E-mail: workshop@PublishingGame.com. Website: www.Publishing Game.com (registration form on Website). Speaker: Fern Reiss. Attendance: limited to 18.

+THE PUBLISHING GAME WORKSHOP. San Francisco; check Website for date. Contact: Alyza Harris, Peanut Butter and Jelly Press, PO Box 590239, Newton MA 02459. Phone/fax (617)630-0945. E-mail: workshop@PublishingGame.com. Website: www.Publishing Game.com (registration form on Website). Speaker: Fern Reiss. Attendance: limited to 18.

SAN DIEGO CHRISTIAN WRITERS GUILD FALL CONFERENCE. San Diego; September 16-17, 2005. Contact: Robert Gillespie, PO Box 270403, San Diego CA 92198. (619)221-8183 or (858)673-3921. Fax (619)255-1131 or (858)673-3921. E-mail: info@sandiegocwg .org. Website: www.sandiegocwg.org. Editors and agents in attendance. Attendance: 100.

*SAN DIEGO STATE UNIVERSITY WRITERS CONFERENCE. San Diego/Doubletree Hotel Mission Valley; January 2005. To advanced writers offers a read and critique by editors and agents. Contact: Diane Dunaway, 8465 Jane St., San Diego CA 92129. (619)594-2517. Fax (619)594-8577. E-mail: ddunaway@aol.com. Website: www.writersconferences.com. Attendance: 500.

SANTA BARBARA CHRISTIAN WRITERS CONFERENCE. Westmont College; October 1, 2005; October 7, 2006. Contact: Rev. Opal Mae Dailey, PO Box 42429, Santa Barbara CA 93140. Phone/fax (805)682-0316. E-mail: opalmae@bigplanet.com. Attendance: 50.

SCBWI WRITERS & ILLUSTRATORS CONFERENCE IN CHILDREN'S LITERATURE. Los Angeles; early August 2005. Society of Children's Book Writers & Illustrators. Contact: Lin Oliver, 8271 Beverly Blvd., Los Angeles CA 90048. (323)782-1010. Fax (323)782-1892. E-mail: scbwi@scbwi.org. Website: www.scbwi.org. Includes a track for professionals. Editors and agents in attendance. Attendance: 900.

WRITERS SYMPOSIUM BY THE SEA. San Diego/Point Loma Nazarene University; late February 2005. Contact: Dean Nelson, Professor, Journalism Dept. PLNU, 3900 Lomaland Dr., San Diego CA 92106. (619)849-2592. Fax (619)849-2566. E-mail: deannelson@ ptloma.edu. Website: www.ptloma.edu. Sometimes has editors and agents in attendance. Attendance: 300. Past speakers include Anne Lamont, George Plimpton, Ray Bradbury, Amy Tan, Rick Reilly, Roy Blount Jr., Kathleen Norris, Barbara Bradley Hagerty, Frederica Mathewes-Green, Lauren Winner, and Joseph Wambaugh.

COLORADO

AD LIB CHRISTIAN ARTS RETREAT. St. Malo Retreat and Conference Center/Allenspark; September 2005. Contact: Judith Deem Dupree, PO Box 365, Pine Valley CA 91962-0365. Phone/fax (619)473-8683, or (303)823-9938. E-mail: adlib@ixpres.com, or joanne kirwin@yahoo.com. Website: www.adlibchristianarts.org. Retreat and forum for literary, visual, and performing arts. Designed as a forum and format for renewal. Solitude, fellowship, issues and ideas, critiquing. Notable speakers. No "working" editors or agents. Attendance: 35-40.

AMERICAN CHRISTIAN WRITERS COLORADO SPRINGS CONFERENCE. September 9-10, 2005. Contact: Reg A. Forder, Box 110390, Nashville TN 37222. 1-800-21-WRITE. Website: www.ACWriters.com. Attendance: 40-75.

CBA INTERNATIONAL CONVENTION. (Held in a different location each year.) July 9-14, 2005, Denver CO. Contact: CBA, Box 62000, Colorado Springs CO 80962-2000. Toll-free (800)252-1950. (719)265-9895. Website: www.cbaonline.org. Entrance badges available through book publishers or Christian bookstores. Attendance: 14,000.

COLORADO CHRISTIAN WRITERS CONFERENCE. Estes Park; May 11-14, 2005 at the YMCA of the Rockies. Director: Marlene Bagnull, LittD, 316 Blanchard Rd., Drexel Hill, PA 19026-3507. Phone/fax (610)626-6833. E-mail: mbagnull@aol.com. Website: www .writehisanswer.com/Colorado. Conferees choose six hour-long workshops from 42 offered or a Fiction Clinic (by application) plus one 6-1/2 continuing session from seven offered. One-on-one appointments, paid critiques, editors panels, and general sessions focused on the conference theme: Holding Out the Word of Life (from Phil. 2:16). Thursday evening concert by Marty Goetz. Teens Write Saturday afternoon plus teens are welcome to attend the entire conference half-price. Contest (registered conferees only) awards four $75 discounts off May 17-20, 2006, conference. Faculty of 40-45 authors, editors, and agents. Attendance: 250.

COLORADO WRITERS FELLOWSHIP SEMINARS. Denver; no seminars scheduled for 2005. Contact: Su Wright, CWF Executive Director, PO Box 22416, Denver CO 80222-0416. (303)758-6556. Fax (303)758-9272. E-mail: ColWritersFellow@aol.com. Sponsors a writing contest in conjunction with their seminar; none for 2005.

GLEN EYRIE WRITER'S CONFERENCE. Colorado Springs; February 24-27, 2005. Contact: Craig Dunham, 3820 N. 30th, Colorado Springs CO 80904. Toll-free (800)944-GLEN. (719)272-7749. E-mail: craig_dunham@navigators.org. Website: www.gleneyrie group.org. Some editors/agents in attendance. Attendance: 100.

JERRY B. JENKINS CHRISTIAN WRITERS GUILD WRITING FOR THE SOUL CONFERENCE. Colorado Springs; February 17-20, 2005. Hosted by Left Behind author Jerry B. Jenkins. Held at historic Broadmoor Hotel. Speakers include: Rick Warren and Sammy Tippit. Offers multiple general sessions with national keynote speakers and in-depth workshops on 6 tracks; plus appointments with publisher's reps. Contact: Wayne Atcheson, PO Box 88196, Black Forest CO 80908. (866)495-5177, ext. 37. Fax (719)495-5181. E-mail: ContactUs@christianwritersguild.com. Website: www.christianwritersguild.com. Editors and agents in attendance. Attendance: 300-350. See contest listings for Operation First Book Contests.

*SOUTHWEST CHRISTIAN WRITERS ASSOCIATION SEMINAR. Hesperus; September 2005. Contact: Gayle Davis, pres., SCWA, PO Box 544, Bayfield CO 81122-0544. (505)325-3717. E-mail: scwa@frontier.net. Website: www.swchristianwriter.org. No editors or agents in attendance. Attendance: 40.

CONNECTICUT

WESLEYAN WRITERS CONFERENCE. Wesleyan University/Middletown; 3rd week of June 2005. Contact: Anne Greene, 279 Court St., Middletown CT 06457. (860)685-3604. Fax (860)685-2441. E-mail: agreene@wesleyan.edu. Website: www.wesleyan.edu/writers. Includes an advanced track. Editors and agents in attendance. Offers fellowship and scholarship awards. Attendance: 100.

DISTRICT OF COLUMBIA

ACT ONE: WRITING FOR HOLLYWOOD. Washington DC; May 1-31, 2005. Contact: Barbara R. Nicolosi, 1763 N. Gower St., Hollywood CA 90028. (323)462-1348. Fax (323)462-2550. E-mail: Actone@fpch.org. Website: www.ActOneprogram.com. Speakers: Dana

Gioia, Ron Maxwell, Linda Seger. Limited to 30 students. These are month-long intensive training session for screenwriters.

THE PUBLISHING GAME WORKSHOP. Washington DC; check Website for date. Contact: Alyza Harris, Peanut Butter and Jelly Press, PO Box 590239, Newton MA 02459. Phone/fax (617)630-0945. E-mail: workshop@PublishingGame.com. Website: www.Publishing Game.com (registration form on Website). Speaker: Fern Reiss. Attendance: limited to 18.

FLORIDA

+AMERICAN CHRISTIAN WRITERS ORLANDO CONFERENCE. November 19, 2005. Contact: Reg A. Forder, Box 110390, Nashville TN 37222. 1-800-21-WRITE. Website: www.ACWriters.com. Attendance: 40-75.

CLASS REUNION. Orlando; July 2005 (limited to first 80 CLASS graduates). Marketing conference for writers. Includes appointments with editors. Contact: Marita Littauer, PO Box 66810, Albuquerque, NM 87193-6810. (505)899-4283. Fax (505)899-9282. E-mail: info@classervices.com. Website: www.classervices.com.

FLORIDA CHRISTIAN WRITERS CONFERENCE. Bradenton; March 3-6, 2005. Contact: Billie Wilson, 2344 Armour Ct., Titusville FL 32780. (321)269-5831. Fax (321)264-0037. E-mail: billiewilson@cfl.rr.com. Website: www.flwriters.org. Offers advanced track; Eva Marie Everson leading this track for 2005. Speakers include Heather Gemmen. Editors and agents in attendance. Offers awards in 10 categories. Attendance: 225.

THE PUBLISHING GAME WORKSHOP. Boca Raton; check Website for date. Contact: Alyza Harris, Peanut Butter and Jelly Press, PO Box 590239, Newton MA 02459. Phone/fax (617)630-0945. E-mail: workshop@PublishingGame.com. Website: www.Publishing Game.com (registration form on Website). Speaker: Fern Reiss. Attendance: limited to 18.

+WORD WEAVERS CHRISTIAN WRITERS RETREAT. Vero Beach; January 21-23, 2005. Contact: Eva Marie Everson, 122 Fairway Ten Dr., Casselberry FL 32707-4823. (407)695-9366. E-mail: PenNHand@aol.com. Speaker: Vernon Rainwater.

WRITING STRATEGIES FOR THE CHRISTIAN MARKET. Not offered in seminar; only as independent studies, with manual and assignments. Contact instructor: Rosemary J. Upton, 2712 S. Peninsula Dr., Daytona Beach FL 32118-5706. Phone/fax (386)322-1111. E-mail: rupton@cfl.rr.com. E-mail name and address to request a brochure on Writing Strategies for the Christian Market course.

GEORGIA

AMERICAN CHRISTIAN WRITERS ATLANTA CONFERENCE. March 18-19, 2005. Contact: Reg Forder, Box 110390, Nashville TN 37222. 1-800-21-WRITE. Website: www.ACWriters .com. Attendance: 40-75.

*SOUTHEASTERN WRITERS CONFERENCE. Epworth-by-the-Sea, St. Simons Island; June 2005. Contact: Holly McClure, Dir., 210 Harrington Rd., St. Simons Island GA 31522 (holly.mcc@mindspring.com). E-mail: info@southeasternwriters.com. Website: www .southeasternwriters.com. Attendance: limited to 100. Awards cash prizes to attendees in every genre, and free manuscript critiques.

HAWAII

MAUI WRITERS RETREAT AND CONFERENCE. Retreat, August 26-31, 2005; Conference, Labor Day weekend, September 1-5, 2005. Maui Writers Foundation, PO Box 1118, Kihei HI 96753. Toll-free (888)974-8373, or (808)879-0061. Fax (808)879-6233. E-mail:

writers@mauiwriters.com. Website: www.mauiwriters.com. Download forms or sign up from Website. Secular. Editors and agents in attendance.

ILLINOIS

#ASSOCIATED CHURCH PRESS 2005 ANNUAL CONVENTION. Chicago; April 24-27, 2005. Contact: Mary Lynn Hendrickson, The Associated Church Press, 1410 Vernon St., Stoughton WI 53589-2248. (608)877-0011. Fax (608)877-0062. E-mail: theacp@earthlink.net. Website: www.theacp.org.

EVANGELICAL PRESS ASSOCIATION CONVENTION. Chicago; April 24-27, 2005. (held in different location each year.) Contact: Doug Trouten, dir., PO Box 28129, Crystal MN 55428. (763)535-4793. Fax (763)535-4794. E-mail: mailto:director@epassoc.org. Website: www.epassoc.org. Attendance: 300-400. Annual convention for editors of evangelical periodicals; freelance communicators welcome.

KARITOS CHRISTIAN ARTS CONFERENCE. Chicago area; July 2005. Contact: Bob Hay, 1116 State St., PMB 21, Lemont IL 60439. (847)749-1284 or (630)243-8375. E-mail: bob@karitos.com. Website: www.karitos.com. Offers beginner and advanced track. Karitos is a festival conducting classes and showcases in all areas of the arts, including writing. Attendance: 500-600.

THE PUBLISHING GAME WORKSHOP. Chicago; check Website for date. Contact: Alyza Harris, Peanut Butter and Jelly Press, PO Box 590239, Newton MA 02459. Phone/fax (617)630-0945. E-mail: workshop@PublishingGame.com. Website: www.Publishing Game.com (registration form on Website). Speaker: Fern Reiss. Attendance: limited to 18.

WRITE-TO-PUBLISH CONFERENCE. Wheaton (Chicago area); June 8-11, 2005. Contact: Lin Johnson, 9731 N. Fox Glen Dr., #6F, Niles IL 60714-4222. (847)299-4755. Fax (847)296-0754. E-mail: lin@WriteToPublish.com. Website: www.WriteToPublish.com. Offers advanced track (prerequisite 2 published books). Majority of faculty are editors; also has agents. Attendance: 250.

INDIANA

AMERICAN CHRISTIAN WRITERS FORT WAYNE CONFERENCE. Holiday Inn; April 29-30, 2005. Contact: Reg A. Forder, Box 110390, Nashville TN 37222. 1-800-21-WRITE. Website: www.ACWriters.com. Attendance: 40-75.

AMERICAN CHRISTIAN WRITERS INDIANAPOLIS CONFERENCE. August 5-6, 2005. Contact: Reg A. Forder, Box 110390, Nashville TN 37222. 1-800-21-WRITE. Website: www.ACWriters.com. Attendance: 40-75.

BETHEL COLLEGE CHRISTIAN WRITERS' WORKSHOP. Bethel College/Mishawaka; planning a conference with American Christian Writers (date undecided). Contact: Kim Peterson, 1001 W. McKinley Ave., Mishawaka IN 46545-5509. (574)257-3375. E-mail: petersk@ bethelcollege.edu. Offers a track for advanced writers. May sponsor a contest. Attendance: 75-90.

EARLHAM SCHOOL OF RELIGION ANNUAL COLLOQUIUM: THE MINISTRY OF WRITING. Richmond; October 14-15, 2005 (always 3rd weekend). Editors in attendance. Contact: '05 Writing Colloquium, Director, Earlham School of Religion, 228 College Ave., Richmond IN 47374. Toll-free (800)432-1377. (765)983-1423. Fax (765)983-1688. E-mail: esr@earlham.edu. Website: www.esr.earlham.edu/events.html. Attendance: 150.

MIDWEST WRITERS WORKSHOP. Muncie/Ball State University Alumni Center; July 28-30, 2005 (always the last Thursday, Friday, and Saturday of July). Contact: Dept. of Journalism, Ball State University, Muncie IN 47306-0484. Director: Jama Kehoe Bigger. (765)282-

1055. Fax (765)285-7997. E-mail: info@midwestwriters.org. Website: www.midwest
writers.org. Fiction instructor: Best-selling author Jeffery Deaver. Editors and sometimes
agents in attendance. Attendance: 125.

IOWA

IOWA SUMMER WRITING FESTIVAL. University of Iowa/Iowa City; June & July 2005. This is
a secular writer's conference that comes highly recommended for good, solid instruction.
Contact: Iowa Summer Writing Festival, 100 Oakdale Campus, Ste. W310, University of
Iowa, Iowa City IA 52242. (319)335-4160. Fax (319)335-4039. E-mail: iswfestival@
uiowa.edu. Website: www.uiowa.edu/~iswfest. For two months, June and July, you can sign
up for either one-week workshops or weekend workshops on a wide variety of topics.
Write for a catalog of offerings (available in February).

KANSAS

CALLED TO WRITE. Girard; April 2005. Contact: Carol Russell, Walkertown 894—165th St.,
Fort Scott KS 66701. (620)547-2472. E-mail: rlrussell@ckt.net. Sponsors a contest for
attendees only. Attendance: 40.

HEART OF AMERICA CHRISTIAN WRITERS' NETWORK TWICE YEARLY CONFERENCES.
Overland Park; April and late October. Contact: Mark and Jeanette Littleton, 3706 N.E.
Shady Lane Dr., Gladstone MO 64119. Phone/fax (816)459-8016. E-mail: MarkLitt@
aol.com. Offers classes for new and advanced writers. Has editors and sometimes agents in
attendance. Major conference in late October of each year, mentoring conference in April.

*LITERARY ARTS FESTIVAL. The Milton Center/Wichita; February 2005. Cosponsored with
Newman University English Department. Contact: Dr. Bryan Dietrich, Newman University,
3100 McCormick, Wichita KS 67213-2097. (316)942-4291. Fax (316)942-4483. Website:
www.newmanu.edu/miltoncenter. Offers advanced track. Sometimes has editors in attendance; usually not agents. Sponsors a contest.

KENTUCKY

+AMERICAN CHRISTIAN WRITERS LOUISVILLE CONFERENCE. July 30, 2005. Contact:
Reg A. Forder, Box 110390, Nashville TN 37222. 1-800-21-WRITE. Website: www.AC
Writers.com. Attendance: 40-75.

ANNUAL KENTUCKY CHRISTIAN WRITERS' CONFERENCE. Memorial United Methodist
Church, Elizabethtown; June 2005. Contact: Crystal Murray, 1440 Shingo Ave., Louisville KY
40215-1132. (502)361-7078. E-mail: crystalamurray@insightbb.com. Speaker: Dr. Dennis Hensley. Editors in attendance. Attendance: 60-100.

*WRITERS WORKSHOP AT LOUISVILLE PRESBYTERIAN SEMINARY. Louisville; March
2005. Contact: Kathryn Mates, Coord. of Academic Support, Louisville Presbyterian Seminary, 1044 Alta Vista Rd., Louisville KY 40205. Toll-free (800)264-1839, ext. 384. Fax
(502)895-1096. Attendance: 40.

MAINE

*ANNUAL CHRISTIAN WRITERS' CONFERENCE. China Lake Conference Center; August
2005. Contact: Vicki Reynolds Schad, 180 S. Stanley Hill, Vassalboro ME 04989-3505.
(207)923-3956. E-mail: jvschad@psouth.net. Sponsors Dorothy Templeton Writer's Contest
(for paying conferees) and publishes an anthology of writing by conferees. Attendance: 60.

+MAINE CHRISTIAN WRITERS CONFERENCE. China ME; August 2005. Contact: Beth Rogers, 720 Essex St., Bangor ME 04401. (207)942-1616. E-mail: BethR58@aol.com. Sponsors contest open to conference attendees.

STATE OF MAINE WRITERS' CONFERENCE. Ocean Park; August 23-27, 2005. Contact: Jeff Belyea/Jim Brosnan, 16 Foley Ave., Saco ME 04072. (207)284-4119. E-mail: jeff@mind goal.com. Speaker: Michael White. Attendance: 30. Sponsors several contests. Editors in attendance.

MARYLAND

MID-ATLANTIC CHRISTIAN WRITERS CONFERENCE. Hagerstown or Gaithersburg; no conference scheduled for 2005. Editors and agents in attendance. Contact: Rajendra Pillai, Turning Point, PO Box 255, Clarksburg MD 20871-0255. (301)972-6351. E-mail: info@reachingtheworld.com. Website: www.reachingtheworld.com. Attendance: 200-250. Also offers one-day workshops for beginning and intermediate Christian writers in several locations at various times throughout the year.

SANDY COVE CHRISTIAN WRITERS CONFERENCE. Sandy Cove/North East; October 2-5, 2005. Offers Advanced and Teen Tracks. Contact: Jim Watkins, Writers' Conference Director, Sandy Cove Ministries, 60 Sandy Cove Rd., North East MD 21901. Toll-free (800)234-2683. E-mail: info@sandycove.com. Website: www.jameswatkins.com/sandycove.htm. Editors and agents in attendance. Attendance: 150.

WISE PEN CHRISTIAN WRITERS GUILD SEMINAR. Bel Air; October 2005. Contact: Anne Perry, 1258 Collier Ln., Belcamp MD 21017. (410)297-6656. E-mail: bunniesarefree@ aol.com. Speaker: Marlene Bagnull. Attendance: 50

MASSACHUSETTS

CAPE COD ANNUAL SUMMER WRITERS' CONFERENCE AND YOUNG WRITERS' WORKSHOP (ages 12-16). Craigville Conference Center; August 2005. Contact: Jacqueline M. Loring, dir., Box 408, Osterville MA 02665. (508)420-0200. Fax (508)420-0212. E-mail: ccwc@capecod.net. Website: www.capecodwriterscenter.com. Editors and agents in attendance. Attendance: 150.

+THE PUBLISHING GAME WORKSHOP. Boston; check Website for date. Contact: Alyza Harris, Peanut Butter and Jelly Press, PO Box 590239, Newton MA 02459. Phone/fax (617)630-0945. E-mail: workshop@PublishingGame.com. Website: www.Publishing Game.com (registration form on Website). Speaker: Fern Reiss. Attendance: limited to 18.

MICHIGAN

"ADVANCED SPEAK UP WITH CONFIDENCE" SEMINAR. Hillsdale; June 2005. Contact: Carol Kent, 1614 Edison Shores Pl., Port Huron MI 48060. (810)982-0898. Fax (810)987-4163. E-mail: Speakupinc@aol.com. Website: www.SpeakUpSpeakerServices.com. Speakers: Carol Kent and Jennie Afman Dimkoff. Speaking seminar. Offers advanced training. Also offers a seminar on writing for speakers who write. Attendance: 100. Also offers several Basic Speak Up Seminars.

AMERICAN CHRISTIAN WRITERS GRAND RAPIDS CONFERENCE. June 24-25, 2005. Contact: Reg Forder, Box 110390, Nashville TN 37222. 1-800-21-WRITE. Website: www .ACWriters.com. Attendance: 40-75.

MARANATHA CHRISTIAN WRITERS SEMINAR. Maranatha Bible & Missionary Conference/

Muskegon; August 2005. Contact: Maranatha, 4759 Lake Harbor Rd., Muskegon MI 49441-5299. (231)798-2161. E-mail: info@maranatha-bmc.org. Website: www.maranatha-bmc.org. Attendance: 50.

MINNESOTA

AMERICAN CHRISTIAN WRITERS MINNEAPOLIS CONFERENCE. August 12-13, 2005. Contact: Reg Forder, Box 110390, Nashville TN 37222. 1-800-21-WRITE. Website: www .ACWriters.com. Attendance: 40-75.

MINNESOTA CHRISTIAN WRITERS SPRING & FALL SEMINARS. Minneapolis; spring seminar, April 8-9, 2005; fall seminar, October 2005. Contact: Barbara Majchrzak, 18469 Jaeger Path, Lakeville MN 55044. (952)892-0438. E-mail: barbara.majchrzak@charter.net. Website: www.mnchristianwriters.org. No editors or agents in attendance. Attendance: 50.

THE WRITING ACADEMY SEMINAR. Mount Olivet Retreat Center outside Minneapolis; July 21-25, 2005. Sponsors year-round correspondence writing program and annual seminar in various locations. Contact: Mar Korman, 1128 Mule Lake Dr. N.E., Outing MN 56662. (218)792-5144. E-mail: pattyk@wams.org. Website: www.wams.org. Attendance: 30-40. Sponsors a contest open to nonattendees (rules are posted on Website).

WRITING SEMINARS NORTH HENNEPIN COMMUNITY COLLEGE. Brooklyn Park/Minneapolis; new classes every quarter. Instructor: Louise B. Wyly. Topics include Fiction I, II, III; children and teen writing, personal experiences; Beginning & Advanced; The Artist's Way; and memoirs. Now offers a Creative Writing Certificate. Attendance: 24 (2 classes each quarter). Contact: Louise Wyly, 7411—85th Ave. N., Brooklyn Park MN 55445. (763)533-6207. E-mail: Lsnowbunny@aol.com. Website: www.nh.cc.mn.us (click on Training and Development); watch NHCC Bulletin for details, or call (612)424-0880 to inquire.

MISSOURI

+AMERICAN CHRISTIAN WRITERS SPRINGFIELD CONFERENCE. Springfield MO; August 20, 2005. Contact: Reg A. Forder, Box 110390, Nashville TN 37222. 1-800-21-WRITE. Website: www.ACWriters.com. Attendance: 40-75.

NEBRASKA

MY THOUGHTS EXACTLY WRITERS RETREAT. St. Benedict Retreat Center/Schuyler; October/November 2005. Contact: Cheryl Paden, PO Box 1073, Fremont NE 68026-1073. (402)727-6508. Geared toward the beginning writer. Attendance: 12.

NEW HAMPSHIRE

WRITERS WORKSHOPS BY MARY EMMA ALLEN. Taught as requested by writer's groups, conferences, schools, and libraries. Topics include: Workshops for Young Writers (for schools and home parenting groups); Workshops for Teachers and Home-parenting Parents; Writing for Children Workshop; Travel Writing Workshop; Writing for Regional Markets; Poetry Writing Workshop; Writing Family History Workshop; Self-Publishing Workshop; Writer & the Internet Workshop; Writing for the Weekly Newspaper Workshop; Writing Columns for Newspaper, Magazine, and Online Publications; and Writing for Publication Workshop. Contact: Mary Emma Allen (instructor), 55 Binks Hill Rd., Plymouth NH 03264. Fax (603)536-4851. E-mail: me.allen@juno.com. Website: http://homepage.fcgnetworks.net/jetent/mea.

NEW MEXICO

THE GLEN WORKSHOP. St. John's College/Santa Fe; August 2005. Includes fiction, poetry, nonfiction, memoir, on-site landscape painting, figure drawing, collage and mixed media, and several master classes. Contact: Gregory Wolfe, Image, 3307 Third Ave. W., Seattle WA 98119. (206)281-2988. Fax (206)281-2335. E-mail: glenworkshop@imagejournal.org. Website: www.imagejournal.org/glen_home.asp. No editors/agents in attendance. Attendance: 200.

GLORIETA CHRISTIAN WRITERS' CONFERENCE. Glorieta (18 mile N. of Santa Fe); October 26-30, 2005. Offers 7 continuing classes (including beginning, advanced, fiction, nonfiction, magazines, children, and at least one specialty topic); 80+ workshops, paid critiques, and much more. Editors and agents in attendance. Contact: CLASServices, PO Box 66810, Albuquerque, NM 87193-6810. Toll-free (800)433-6633. (505)899-4283. Fax (505)899-9282. E-mail: info@classervices.com. Website: www.glorietaCWC.com. Attendance: 250.

SOUTHWEST CHRISTIAN WRITERS ASSN. SEMINAR. Farmington; April 16, 2005. Contact: Connie Peters, 240 S. Ash, Cortez CO 81321. (970)564-9449. E-mail: CoFun77@yahoo .com. Website: www.swchristianwriter.org. No editors/agents in attendance. Attendance: 20-25.

SOUTHWEST WRITERS MINI CONFERENCES. Albuquerque; February, May, August, and November 2005. Contact: Southwest Writers, 3721 Morris St. NE, Ste. A, Albuquerque NM 87111-3611. (505)265-9485. Fax (505)265-9483. E-mail: contactus@southwest writers.org. Website: www.southwestwriters.org. Send SASE/2 stamps for brochure. Secular. Sponsors the Southwest Writers Contest (send SASE for details and entry form).

NEW YORK

AMERICAN CHRISTIAN WRITERS BUFFALO CONFERENCE. June 10-11, 2005. Contact: Reg Forder, Box 110390, Nashville TN 37222. 1-800-21-WRITE. Website: www.ACWriters.com. Attendance: 40-75.

+THE PUBLISHING GAME WORKSHOP. Manhattan; check Website for date. Contact: Alyza Harris, Peanut Butter and Jelly Press, PO Box 590239, Newton MA 02459. Phone/fax (617)630-0945. E-mail: workshop@PublishingGame.com. Website: www.Publishing Game.com (registration form on Website). Speaker: Fern Reiss. Attendance: limited to 18.

THE PUBLISHING GAME WORKSHOP. New York City; May 29 & June 6, 2005. Contact: Alyza Harris, Peanut Butter and Jelly Press, PO Box 590239, Newton MA 02459. Phone/fax (617)630-0945. E-mail: workshop@PublishingGame.com. Website: www.Publishing Game.com (registration form on Website). Speaker: Fern Reiss. Attendance: limited to 18.

20TH ANNUAL INTERNATIONAL CONFERENCE ON HUMOR, HOPE AND HEALING. Saratoga Springs; April 2005. Secular. Contact: The HUMOR Project, Inc., 480 Broadway, Ste. 210, Saratoga Springs NY 12866. (518)587-8770. Fax (800)600-4242. E-mail: joel@humorproject.com.

NORTH CAROLINA

AMERICAN CHRISTIAN WRITERS CHARLOTTE CONFERENCE. Marriott Hotel; April 1-2, 2005. Contact: Reg A. Forder, Box 110390, Nashville TN 37222. 1-800-21-WRITE. Website: www.ACWriters.com. Attendance: 40-75.

BLUE RIDGE MOUNTAIN CHRISTIAN WRITERS CONFERENCE. Lifeway Ridgecrest Conference Center; April 17-21, 2005. Contact: Ron Pratt, Lifeway Christian Resources, One Lifeway Plaza, Nashville TN 37234-0106. (615)241-2065. Fax (615)277-8232. E-mail: ron. pratt@lifeway.com, or Yvonne Lehman, PO Box 188, Black Mountain NC 28770. Website:

www.lifeway.com/conferencecenter. Editors and agents in attendance. Sponsors a contest. Attendance: 200.

JERRY B. JENKINS CHRISTIAN WRITERS GUILD WRITING FOR THE SOUL CONFERENCE. Ashville/The Cove; no August conference offered in 2005. Hosted by Left Behind author Jerry B. Jenkins. Held at the Billy Graham Training Center. Offers morning and evening general sessions with national keynote speakers, 6 continuing classes, and 6 workshop tracks, plus appointments with publisher's reps and agents. Contact: Wayne Atcheson, PO Box 88196, Black Forest CO 80908. (866)495-5177, ext. 37. Fax (719)495-5181. E-mail: ContactUs@christianwritersguild.com. Website: www.christianwritersguild.com. Editors and agents in attendance. Attendance: 200-250.

WRITE IT! SPEAK IT! LIVE IT!: Helping Writers Speak and Speakers Write their God-Given Word of Power! Durham; October 9, 2005; held annually, usually in late winter or early fall. Contact: Gail M. Hayes, PO Box 71017, Durham NC 27722-1017. Phone/fax (919)286-4200. E-mail: gmhayes@daughtersoftheking.org. Website: www.daughter softheking.org. Speakers: Dr. Gail Hayes and others. Attendance: 50+.

OHIO

AMERICAN CHRISTIAN WRITERS CLEVELAND CONFERENCE. April 15-16, 2005. Contact: Reg A. Forder, Box 110390, Nashville TN 37222. 1-800-21-WRITE. Website: www.ACWriters .com. Attendance: 40-75.

AMERICAN CHRISTIAN WRITERS COLUMBUS CONFERENCE. June 3-4, 2005. Hosted by Columbus Christian Writers Assn./Pat Zell, (937)593-9207. Contact: Reg Forder, Box 110390, Nashville TN 37222. 1-800-21-WRITE. Website: www.ACWriters.com. Attendance: 40-75.

DAYTON CHRISTIAN WRITERS GUILD, INC. Contact: Tina V. Toles, PO Box 251, Englewood OH 45322-2227. Phone/fax (937)836-6600. E-mail: Poet11@earthlink.net. Website: www.geocities.com/dtolessr. Sponsoring a seminar in August 2005.

NORTHWEST OHIO CHRISTIAN WRITERS SEMINAR. Toledo; September 2005. Contact: Judy Gyde, 3072 Muirfield, Toledo OH 43614-3766. (419)382-7582. E-mail: begyde@ glasscity.net. No editors or agents in attendance. Attendance: 50.

OKLAHOMA

AMERICAN CHRISTIAN WRITERS OKLAHOMA CITY CONFERENCE. La Quinta Hotel; February 25-26, 2005. Contact: Reg Forder, Box 110390, Nashville TN 37222. 1-800-21-WRITE. Website: www.ACWriters.com. Attendance: 40-75.

WRITING WORKSHOPS. Various locations and dates. Contact: Kathryn Fanning, PO Box 18472, Oklahoma City OK 73154-0472. (405)524-9619. E-mail: oklahomawriter@earth link.net. Attendance varies: 25-200.

OREGON

DRAMA IMPROVEMENT CONFERENCE. Portland; no conference planned for 2005; unknown for 2006. Contact: Judy Straalsund, PO Box 19844, Portland OR 97280-0844. (503)245-6919. E-mail: ttc.pdx@att.net. Website: www.tapestrytheatre.org (click on Drama Conferences). Geared to all Christian dramatists, and features workshops, performances, networking, forums, and a book table. Playwrights are encouraged to attend. No editors or agents in attendance. Attendance: 100. Note: If interested in having drama workshop leaders for your event, contact Judy Straalsund at ttc.pdx@att.net or (503)245-6919; or Andy Rice at dramatic.impact@att.net, (360)694-2525, ext. 16.

HEART TALK '05. A workshop for women beginning to write for publication. Portland/Western Seminary; March 12, 2005. Beverly Hislop, dir. Contact: Women's Center for Ministry, Western Seminary, 5511 S.E. Hawthorne Blvd., Portland OR 97215. Toll-free (800)547-4546, ext. 1931. (503)517-1931. Fax (503)517-1889. E-mail: kstein@westernseminary .edu (Kenine Stein), or wcm@westernseminary.edu. Website: www.westernseminary .edu. Attendance: 100-120. This conference alternates with a writing conference one year and a speaking conference the next. The 2005 conference is on writing for publication. Check Website for details.

OREGON CHRISTIAN WRITERS COACHING CONFERENCE. Canby Grove Christian Conference Center/Portland area; July 31-August 4, 2005. Contact: Sandy Cathcart, 341 Flounce Rock Rd., Prospect OR 97536. (541)560-2367. E-mail: Summconf@oregonchristian writers.com. Website: www.OregonChristianWriters.com. Includes about 7 hours of training under a specific coach/topic. Offers advanced track. Editors and agents in attendance. Attendance: 250.

PENNSYLVANIA

GREATER PHILADELPHIA CHRISTIAN WRITERS' CONFERENCE. Philadelphia Biblical University, Langhorne; August 18-20, 2005. Founder and director: Marlene Bagnull, LittD, 316 Blanchard Rd., Drexel Hill, PA 19026-3507. Phone/fax (610)626-6833. E-mail: mbag null@aol.com. Website: www.writehisanswer.com/Philadelphia. Conferees choose six hour-long workshops from 42 offered or a Fiction Clinic (by application) plus one 6-1/2 continuing session from seven offered. One-on-one appointments, paid critiques, editors panels, and general sessions focused on the conference theme: Holding Out the Word of Life (from Phil. 2:16). Contest (registered conferees only) awards four $75 discounts off 2006 conference. Especially encourages African American writers. Faculty of 40-50 authors, editors, and agents. Attendance: 225.

MERCER ANNUAL ONE-DAY WRITERS' WORKSHOP (sponsored by St. David's Writers' Conference); April 2005. Contact: Gloria C. Peterman. (724)253-2635. E-mail: gloworm@ certainty.net. Website: www.stdavidswriters.com. Attendance: 135.

MONTROSE CHRISTIAN WRITERS CONFERENCE. Montrose; July 24-29, 2005; July (end of) 2006. Contact: Patti Souder, c/o Montrose Bible Conference, 5 Locust St., Montrose PA 18801-1112. Toll-free (800)598-5030. (570)278-1001. Fax (570)278-3061. E-mail: mbc@montrosebible.org. Website: www.montrosebible.org. Features wide range of classes for beginning and advanced writers in many different areas. Attendance: 120.

+THE PUBLISHING GAME WORKSHOP. Philadelphia; check Website for date. Contact: Alyza Harris, Peanut Butter and Jelly Press, PO Box 590239, Newton MA 02459. Phone/fax (617)630-0945. E-mail: workshop@PublishingGame.com. Website: www.Publishing Game.com (registration form on Website). Speaker: Fern Reiss. Attendance: limited to 18.

+REVWRITER WRITERS CONFERENCE. Sellersville PA; October 8, 2005. Contact: RevWriter, Sue Lang, PO Box 81, Perkasie PA 18944. (215)453-5066. Fax (215)453-8128. E-mail: conference@revwriter.com. Website: www.revwriter.com, or www.suelang.com. Editors in attendance. Focuses on supporting those writing for the local congregation and for the larger Christian market. Attendance: 50+.

ST. DAVIDS CHRISTIAN WRITERS' CONFERENCE. Geneva College/Beaver Falls, near Pittsburgh; June 2005. Offers writer's retreat and a special pastor's day. Contest in 10 categories for attendees only. Lora Zill, director. Contact: Audrey Stallsmith, registrar, 87 Pines Rd. E., Hadley PA 16130-1019. (724)253-2738. Fax (724)946-3689. E-mail: audstall@ nauticom.net. Website: www.stdavidswriters.com. Attendance: 70.

+WEST BRANCH CHRISTIAN WRITERS MINI-CONFERENCE. Williamsport. Contact: Eileen Berger, 866 Penn Dr., Hughesville PA 17737. (570)584-2280. E-mail: emberger@ sunlink.net. Sponsors an annual one-day mini-conference each fall, usually in October.

TENNESSEE

AMERICAN CHRISTIAN WRITERS MENTORING RETREAT EAST. Nashville; May 20-21, 2005. Contact: Reg Forder, Box 110390, Nashville TN 37222. 1-800-21-WRITE. Website: www.ACWriters.com. Attendance: 40-75.
CBA ADVANCE. (Held in a different location each year.) January 31-February 4, 2005; January 23-27, 2006. Contact: CBA, Box 62000, Colorado Springs CO 80962-2000. Toll-free (800)252-1950. (719)265-9895. Website: www.cbaonline.org. Entrance badges available through book publishers or Christian bookstores.
CLASS CAREER COACHING CONFERENCE. January 31-February 3, 2005 in Nashville, TN (limited to first 80 CLASS graduates). Marketing conference for writers, includes training and appointments with editors. CLASS, PO Box 66810, Albuquerque, NM 87193-6810. Toll-free (800)433-6633. (505)899-4283. Fax (505)899-9282. E-mail info@classervices .com. Website www.classervices.com.

TEXAS

AMERICAN CHRISTIAN WRITERS DALLAS CONFERENCE. Best Western North; February 18-19, 2005. Contact: Reg Forder, Box 110390, Nashville TN 37222. 1-800-21-WRITE. Website: www.ACWriters.com. Attendance: 40-75.
AMERICAN CHRISTIAN WRITERS HOUSTON CONFERENCE. Hobby Marriott; February 12, 2005. Contact: Reg A. Forder, Box 110390, Nashville TN 37222. 1-800-21-WRITE. Website: www.www.ACWriters.com. Attendance: 40-75.
ART & SOUL INTL. FESTIVAL OF RELIGIOUS FAITH AND LITERARY ART AT BAYLOR UNIVERSITY. Baylor University, Waco; April 7-9, 2005 (held biennially in odd years). Contact: Robert Darden or Joy Jordan-Lake, Institute for Faith & Learning, One Bear Pl. #97270, Waco TX 76798-7270. Toll-free (800)BAYLOR-U. (254)710-4805. E-mail: IFL@baylor.edu. Website: www.baylor.edu/Rel_Lit. Speakers include: Kaye Gibbons, Madison Smart Bell, Phyllis Tickle, and Jeremy Begbie. Editors and agents in attendance.
AUSTIN CHRISTIAN WRITERS' SEMINAR. February 2005. Contact: Lin Harris, 129 Fox Hollow Cove, Cedar Creek TX 78612-4844. (512)601-2216. Fax (240)208-3201. E-mail: linharris@austin.rr.com. Attendance: 100.
+EAST TEXAS CHRISTIAN WRITERS CONFERENCE. Marshall; June 2005. Contact: Dr. Jerry Hopkins, East Texas Baptist University, 1209 N. Grove St., Marshall TX 75670. (903)923-2269. Website: www.etbu.edu/CWC2005/default.htm.
INSPIRATIONAL WRITERS ALIVE!/AMARILLO SEMINAR. April (first weekend) 2005. Contact: Helen Luecke, 2921 S. Dallas, Amarillo TX 79103-6713. (806)376-9671. E-mail: hcoluecke@arn.net. Attendance: 50. Sponsors a contest.
***NORTH TEXAS CHRISTIAN WRITERS' CONFERENCE.** Dallas; October 2005. Contact: James H. Pence, PO Box 8942, Greenville TX 75404-8942. (903)450-4944. E-mail: info@green villechristianwriters.com. Website: www.greenvillechristianwriters.com. Attendance: 50.
+THE PUBLISHING GAME WORKSHOP. Dallas; check Website for date. Contact: Alyza Harris, Peanut Butter and Jelly Press, PO Box 590239, Newton MA 02459. Phone/fax (617)630-0945. E-mail: workshop@PublishingGame.com. Website: www.PublishingGame.com (registration form on Website). Speaker: Fern Reiss. Attendance: limited to 18.

TEXAS CHRISTIAN WRITERS CONFERENCE. Houston; August 6, 2005; August 5, 2006. Contact: Martha Rogers, 6038 Greenmont, Houston TX 77092-2332. (713)686-7209. E-mail: marthalrogers@sbcglobal.net. Speaker 2005: Cecil Murphey. Editors in attendance; agents when available. Sponsors a contest. Attendance: 65.

WOMAN THOU ART LOOSED CONFERENCE. Houston (location may vary). Contact: Jeanie Colston, conf. coord., T. D. Jakes Ministries/The Potter's House, 3635 Dan Morton Dr., Dallas TX 75236. (214)333-6441. E-mail: jcolston@TDJakes.org. Offers workshop at conference on book writing/publishing. Attendance: 8,500.

YWAM HANDS-ON SCHOOL OF WRITING AND WRITERS TRAINING WORKSHOPS. Lindale; March 30-June 23, 2005. Contact: Carol Scott, PO Box 1380, Lindale TX 75771-1380. (903)882-9663. Fax (903)882-1161. E-mail: writingschooltx@yahoo.com. Website: www.ywamwoodcrest.com. Send SASE for list of workshops. Speakers include: Janice Rogers, Janet Benge, Patricia Rushford, Elaine Wright Colvin, and Mona Gansberg Hodgson. Attendance: 10-20.

VIRGINIA

+AMERICAN CHRISTIAN WRITERS OGDEN CONFERENCE. Ogden, UT; September 17, 2005. Contact: Reg A. Forder, Box 110390, Nashville TN 37222. 1-800-21-WRITE. Website: www.ACWriters.com. Attendance: 40-75.

AMERICAN CHRISTIAN WRITERS RICHMOND CONFERENCE. Wyndam Airport Hotel; April 8-9, 2005. Contact: Reg A. Forder, Box 110390, Nashville TN 37222. 1-800-21-WRITE. Website: www.ACWriters.com. Attendance: 45-70.

RICHMOND CHRISTIANS WHO WRITE SEMINAR. Richmond; October 2005. Contact: Rev. Thomas C. Lacy, 12114 Walnut Hill Dr., Rockville VA 23146-1854. (804)749-4050. Fax (804)749-4939. E-mail: RichmondCWW@aol.com. Website: http://rchristianswhowrite .tripod.com.

WASHINGTON

AMERICAN CHRISTIAN WRITERS SEATTLE CONFERENCE. September 24, 2005. Contact: Reg Forder, Box 110390, Nashville TN 37222. 1-800-21-WRITE. Website: www.ACWriters .com. Attendance: 40-75.

IMAGE FESTIVAL OF LITERATURE AND THE ARTS. No conference for 2005; next one fall 2006. Contact: Gregory Wolfe, Image, 3307 Third Ave. W., Seattle WA 98119. (206)281-2988. Fax (206)281-2335. E-mail: conference@imagejournal.org. Website: www.image journal.org.

THE PUBLISHING GAME WORKSHOP. Seattle; check Website for date. Contact: Alyza Harris, Peanut Butter and Jelly Press, PO Box 590239, Newton MA 02459. Phone/fax (617)630-0945. E-mail: workshop@PublishingGame.com. Website: www.PublishingGame.com (registration form on Website). Speaker: Fern Reiss. Attendance: limited to 18.

SEATTLE PACIFIC CHRISTIAN WRITERS WEEKEND. Seattle; June 3-4, 2005. Contact: Judy Bodmer, 11108 N.E. 141st Pl., Kirkland WA 98034. (425)488-2900. E-mail: jbodmer@ msn.com. Speaker: novelist Stephen Bly.

WRITE ON THE BEACH. Ocean Shores; January 28-30, 2005. Contact: Don Clark, Write on the Beach, PO Box 2284, Ocean Shores WA 98569. Toll-free (800)76-BEACH. (360)289-2451. Website: www.wotbeach.com. Speakers include: Yasmine Cealenorn. Editors and agents in attendance. Sponsors a contest. Secular. Attendance: 100.

WRITERS HELPING WRITERS. Spokane; March 17-19, 2005, March 16-18, 2006. This is not a conference, but a booth offering manuscript evaluation and help to writers during the annual Christian Workers Conference, plus one workshop. Contact: Darrel Bursch, 510 E. Francis Ave., Spokane WA 99207-1038. (509)487-0149. Attendance: 20-35.

WRITER'S WEEKEND AT THE BEACH. Ocean Park; February 25-27, 2005. Contact: Birdie Etchison/Pat Rushford, PO Box 877, Ocean Park WA 98640-0877. (360)665-6576. E-mail: etchison@pacifier.com. Website: www.patriciarushford.com. (Registration form on Website.) Offers an advanced track. Sponsors a limerick contest. Editors and sometimes agents in attendance. Attendance: 50-60.

WASHINGTON, DC

CATHOLIC PRESS ASSOCIATION ANNUAL CONVENTION. Washington DC; late May or early June 2005. Contact: Owen McGovern, exec. dir., 3555 Veterans Memorial Hwy., Unit O, Ronkonkoma NY 11779-7636. (631)471-4730. Fax (631)471-4804. E-mail: CathJourn@aol.com. Website: www.catholicpress.org. For media professionals. Annual book awards. Attendance: 400.

WISCONSIN

+CHRISTIANS IN THEATRE ARTS (CITA) NATIONAL NETWORKING CONFERENCE. Milwaukee; June 15-18, 2005. Contact: Dr. Dale Savidge, dir., PO Box 26471, Greenville SC 29616. (864)679-1898. Fax (864)679-1899. E-mail: admin@cita.org. Website: www.conference.cita.org. Sponsors a play contest (rules on Website). Editors in attendance; no agents. Attendance: 400-500.

GREEN LAKE CHRISTIAN WRITER'S CONFERENCE. Green Lake; July 30-August 5, 2005. Contact: Russann Hadding, Green Lake Conference Center, W2511 State Hwy. 23, Green Lake WI 54941-9300. Toll-free (800)558-8898. (920)294-7364. Fax (920)294-3848. E-mail for information: RussannHadding@glcc.org. Website: www.glcc.org. Sometimes has editors or agents. Attendance: 100. Also provides Christian Writer's Weeks when you can stay at the conference center for writing time; January, March, November (may vary).

+OBADIAH PRESS CHRISTIAN WRITER'S CONFERENCE. Merrill; April 8-9, 2005. Contact: Tina L. Miller, 607 N. Cleveland St., Merrill WI 54452. (715)536-3167. E-mail: tina@obadiahpress.com. Website: www.obadiahpress.com. Speakers: Lin Johnson, Billie Williams, Tina L. Miller, and Alyice Edrich. No editors or agents in attendance.

+WISCONSIN'S CHRISTIAN PAW CONFERENCE. Neosho; April 9, 2005. Contact: Patti Wolf, 2215 Hall Rd., Hartford WI 53027. (262)673-2775. E-mail: wolfrosebud@purescreen.net. Website: www.4safeinternet.net/~chattelstheheart. Sponsored by *Chattels of the Heart,* a quarterly inspirational magazine. Register on Website.

CANADA/FOREIGN

AMERICAN CHRISTIAN WRITERS CARIBBEAN CRUISE. November 27-December 4, 2005. Contact: Reg A. Forder, Box 110390, Nashville TN 37222. 1-800-21-WRITE. Website: www.ACWriters.com. Attendance: 15-30.

ASSOCIATION OF CHRISTIAN WRITERS. London + network of area groups in England. Contact: Jenny Kyriacou, Administrator, All Saints Vicarage, 43 All Saints Close, Edmonton, London, N9 9AT, United Kingdom. Phone/fax 020 8884 4348. E-mail: admin@christian writers.org.uk. Membership (900) open. Sponsors a biennial writers' weekend for members only. Next one first weekend in July 2006 in Hertfordshire.

CARIBBEAN CHRISTIAN WRITER'S CONFERENCES. Various Caribbean locations; none scheduled for 2005. Contact: Patricia Varlack, PO Box 645, St. Maarten, Netherlands

Antilles. Phone/fax 5995 475393. E-mail: pvarlack@sintmaarten.net. Website: www.greater things.an. Attendance: 20.

*COMIX35 CHRISTIAN COMICS TRAINING. Various international locations; no dates set yet for 2004. Contact: Nathan Butler, PO Box 27470, Albuquerque NM 87125-7470. (505)232-3500. Fax (775)307-8202. E-mail: comix35@comix35.org. Website: www .comix35.org. Often has editors in attendance; no agents.

INSCRIBE CHRISTIAN WRITERS' FELLOWSHIP FALL CONFERENCE. Edmonton AB Canada; September 2005. Contact: Marcia Laycock, 5007 42 A Street, Ponoka AB T4J 1M3 Canada. (403)783-3044. Fax (403)783-6500. E-mail: info@inscribe.org. Website: www.inscribe.org. Some editors in attendance, no agents. Sponsors a fall contest open to nonmembers; details on Website. Attendance: 115.

*LITT-WORLD CONFERENCE. Various locations worldwide; November 2006 (held every two years on even years). Contact: John D. Maust, director, 130 N. Bloomingdale Rd., Ste. 101, Bloomingdale IL 60108-1035. (630)893-1977. Fax (630)893-1141. E-mail: MaiLitt World@cs.com. Website: www.littworld.org. Editors in attendance. Attendance: 140.

WRITE! CANADA. Guelph, Ontario; June 16-18, 2005. Contact: Nancy J. Lindquist, Box 487, Markham ON L3P 3R1 Canada. (905)294-6482. Fax (905)471-6912. E-mail: conference@ thewordguild.com. Website: www.thewordguild.com. Hosted by The Word Guild, an association of Canadian writers and editors who are Christian. Editors and agents in attendance. Contests for attendees. Attendance: 240. Also sponsors one-day conferences in various Canadian cities.

+WRITING SERVICES INSTITUTE (WSI)/MARSHA L. DRAKE. #109 4351 Rumble St., Burnaby BC V5J 2A2, Canada. Phone/fax (604)321-3555. E-mail: write@shaw.ca. Offers several correspondence and online courses: Write for Fun and Profit; Write for Success; Write Fiction from Plot to Print; Write with Power; Write for You; Magazine Article Writing; Write Yes!; Write Now; Young Author's Tutorial; Write Write—with Computers; and Write On! Write or e-mail for details and information on correspondence courses. Also writes company histories, biographies, résumés, and offers online tutorial. Charges negotiable fees for consultation, editing, and critique. See www.vsb-adult-ed.com for further information on courses and author biography.

CONFERENCES THAT CHANGE LOCATIONS

AMERICAN CHRISTIAN ROMANCE WRITERS CONFERENCE/WRITE FROM THE HEART. September 15-18, 2005 in Nashville; September 2006. Speaker 2005: Karen Ball. Contact: Tammy Alexander, PO Box 101066, Palm Bay FL 32910-1066. E-mail: alexander tammy@yahoo.com. Website: www.acrw.net. Editors and agents in attendance. Sponsors a contest (details on Website).

AMERICAN CHRISTIAN WRITERS CONFERENCES. Various dates and locations (see individual states where held). Also sponsors an annual Caribbean cruise, November 27-December 4, 2005. Contact: Reg A. Forder, Box 110390, Nashville TN 37222. 1-800-21-WRITE. Website: www.ACWriters.com.

ASSOCIATED CHURCH PRESS 2005 ANNUAL CONVENTION. Chicago; March/April 2005. Contact: Mary Glenn Hendrickson, The Associated Church Press, PO Box 30379, Chicago IL 60630-0379. (608)877-0011. Website: www.associatedchurchpress.org.

BEFORE ACT ONE WEEKEND SEMINARS. See Website for dates and locations. Contact: Kitty Bucholtz, 1760 N. Gower St., Hollywood CA 90028. (323)462-1348. Fax (323)462-2550. E-mail: Actone@fpch.org. Website: www.ActOneprogram.com. Speakers: Barbara Nicolosi, James Scott Bell, Ken Wales. Open to anyone who is interested in learning more about the craft of screenwriting.

CATHOLIC PRESS ASSOCIATION ANNUAL CONVENTION. Washington DC; late May or early June 2005. Contact: Owen McGovern, exec. dir., 3555 Veterans Memorial Hwy., Unit O, Ronkonkoma NY 11779-7636. (631)471-4730. Fax (631)471-4804. E-mail: CathJourn@ aol.com. Website: www.catholicpress.org. For media professionals. Annual book awards. Attendance: 400.

CBA CONVENTION. Held in a different location each year. July 9-14, 2005, Denver CO. Contact: CBA, Box 62000, Colorado Springs CO 80962-2000. Toll-free (800)252-1950. (719)265-9895. Website: www.cbaonline.org. Entrance badges available through book publishers or Christian bookstores. Attendance: 14,000. Future dates: July 8-13, 2006, Denver CO; July 7-12, 2007, Atlanta GA; July 12-17, 2008, Orlando FL; July 11-16, 2009, Denver CO.

CHILDREN'S AUTHORS' BOOTCAMPS. Held in several locations each year; various dates. Secular. Contact: Bootcamp c/o Linda Arms White, PO Box 231, Allenspark CO 80510. Phone/fax (303)747-1014. E-mail: CABootcamp@aol.com. Website: www.WeMake Writers.com. Upcoming dates and details on Website.

CHRISTIAN LEADERS AND SPEAKERS SEMINARS (The CLASSeminar). Sponsors 6 seminars across the country each year. Check Website for CLASSeminar dates and locations. For anyone who wants to improve their communication skills for either the spoken or written word, for professional or personal reasons. Speakers: Florence Littauer and Marita Littauer. Contact: CLASS, PO Box 66810, Albuquerque, NM 87193-6810. Toll-free (800) 433-6633. (505) 899-4283. Fax (505) 899-9282. E-mail: info@classervices.com. Website: www.classervices.com. Attendance: 70-120.

CHRISTIAN WRITER'S WORKSHOPS. Various cities nationwide; various dates (see Website for dates and locations). A fast-paced, one-day workshop for beginning writers. Contact: Rajendra Pillai, Turning Point, PO Box 255, Clarksburg MD 20871-0255. (301)972-6351. E-mail: tpworkshops@yahoo.com. Website: www.ChristianWritersWorkshop.com. Attendance: 25-50.

EVANGELICAL PRESS ASSOCIATION CONVENTION. Chicago IL; May 2005. (held in different location each year.) Contact: Doug Trouten, dir., PO Box 28129, Crystal MN 55428. (763)535-4793. Fax (763)535-4794. E-mail: director@epassoc.org. Website: www.epassoc .org. Attendance: 300-400. Annual convention for editors of evangelical periodicals; freelance communicators welcome.

JERRY B. JENKINS CHRISTIAN WRITERS GUILD, PO Box 88196, Black Forest CO 80908. Toll-free (866)495-5177. Fax (719)495-5181. E-mail: contactus@christianwriters guild.com. Website: www.christianwritersguild.com. Contact: Wayne Atcheson. Owned by Jerry B. Jenkins, author of the Left Behind series. Students enrolled in correspondence courses are personally mentored by seasoned professional writers or editors. The Guild also offers annual memberships, a critique service, associated benefits (advocacy, supplemental insurance, etc.), conferences, and contests. Call for a Free Starter Kit.

*ORTHODOX AUTHOR'S ASSN. ANNUAL CONVENTION. National organization. Contact: Donna Jones, 1563 Three Sisters Way, Kodiak AK 99615. (907)486-2529. E-mail: seraphima@ak.net. Membership (70) open. May hold a conference in 2005. This group is currently reorganizing, but not defunct.

THE PUBLISHING GAME WORKSHOP. Various cities throughout the year (see individual states or check Website for dates and locations). Contact: Alyza Harris, Peanut Butter and Jelly Press, PO Box 590239, Newton MA 02459. Phone/fax (617)630-0945. E-mail: work shop@PublishingGame.com. Website: www.PublishingGame.com (dates, locations, and registration forms on Website). Speaker: Fern Reiss. Most workshops held at the Four Seasons Hotel. Attendance: limited to 18.

SPAN's SMALL PUBLISHERS MARKETING CONFERENCE. Philadelphia Renaissance Marriott;

October 22-24, 2005. Sponsored by the Small Publishers Assn. of North America. A marketing-specific, information-packed conference for authors, self-publishers, and independent presses. Contact: Scott Flora, PO Box 1306, Buena Vista CO 81211-1306. (719)395-4790. Fax (719)395-8374. E-mail: scott@SPANnet.org. Website: www.SPAN net.org/2005. No editors or agents in attendance. Attendance: 100.

WINSUN COMMUNICATIONS WRITING SEMINARS/MARK LITTLETON. Various dates and locations. Available for your conference at your location. Contact: Mark Littleton, WINSUN Communications, 3706 N.E. Shady Lane Dr., Gladstone MO 64119. Phone/fax: (816)459-8016. E-mail: Mark Litt@aol.com.

"WRITE HIS ANSWER" SEMINARS & RETREATS. Various locations around U.S.; dates throughout the year; a choice of focus on periodicals or books (includes self-publishing or mastering the craft). Contact: Marlene Bagnull, LittD, 316 Blanchard Rd., Drexel Hill PA 19026-3507. Phone/fax (610)626-6833. E-mail: mbagnull@aol.com. Website: www.write hisanswer.com. Attendance: 20-50. One and two-day seminars by the author of *Write His Answer: A Bible Study for Christian Writers.*

AREA CHRISTIAN WRITERS' CLUBS, FELLOWSHIP GROUPS, AND CRITIQUE GROUPS

(*) An asterisk before a listing means the information was not verified or updated by the group leader.
(+) A plus sign before a listing indicates a new listing.

ALABAMA

CHRISTIAN FREELANCERS. Tuscaloosa. Contact: Joanne Sloan, 4195 Waldort Dr., Northport AL 35473. (205)333-8603. Fax (205)339-4528. E-mail: cjosloan@aol.com. Membership (25) open.

*OAKWOOD COLLEGE LITERARY GUILD. Huntsville. Contact: Dr. Cicely Daly, 3903 Nelson Dr. N.W., Huntsville AL 35810-3919. (256)852-8656. Fax (256)726-7020. E-mail: cdaly@oakwood.edu. Website: www.oakwood.edu/english (click on Literary Guild). Membership (15-18) open. ACW Chapter. Sponsors writers' event, November 2005, at Oakwood College.

ALASKA

*PUSHKIN LITERARY SOCIETY CHAPTER OF THE ORTHODOX AUTHORS' ASSN. Kodiak. Contact: Mamas Poussen, St. Innocent's Academy, PO Box 1517, Kodiak AK 99615. (907)486-4376. Fax (907)486-1758. Also publishes the *Pushkin Gazette*.

ARIZONA

FOUNTAIN HILLS CHRISTIAN WRITERS GROUP. Contact: Jewell Johnson, 14223 N. Westminster Pl., Fountain Hills AZ 85268. (480)836-8968. E-mail: TykeJ@juno.com. Membership (15) open. ACW Chapter.

*PHOENIX CHRISTIAN WRITERS' FELLOWSHIP. Contact: Victor J. Kelly Sr., 2135 W. Cactus Wren Dr., Phoenix AZ 85021-7724. (602)864-1390. E-mail: vjk@ntwrld.com. Membership (20+) open.

TEMPE CHRISTIAN WRITERS' CLUB. Contact: Heather Bilodeau, 5353 S. El Camino Dr., Tempe AZ 85283-1822. (602)499-7417. Membership (20) open.

ARKANSAS

ACW FAMILYLIFE CHAPTER. Little Rock. Contact: Marla Rogers, 5800 Ranch Rd., Little Rock AR 72212. Toll-free (800)358-6329. E-mail: mrogers@familylife.com. Membership (29) open. ACW Chapter. Sponsors a contest for members only.

+ARK-LA-TEX PEN-SHELL ACW CHAPTER. Texarkana. Contact: Rosalind Morris, 1400 E. 35th St., Apt. 61, Texarkana AR 71854. (870)772-4983.

#NORTHWEST ARKANSAS CREATIVE WRITERS GUILD. Rogers. Contact: Karin S. Croft, 729 N. Wharton Rd., Lowell AR 72745-9366. (479)936-7945. Membership (6+) open.

OZARK MOUNTAIN CHRISTIAN WRITERS GUILD. Osage. Contact: Judith Gillis, PO Box 770, Alpena AR 72611. (870)553-2512. Fax (870)553-2519. Membership (4) open.

ROGERS AREA CHRISTIAN WRITERS GUILD. Rogers. Contact: Karin Croft, 729 N. Wharton Rd., Lowell AR 72745-9366. (479)936-7945. Membership (6) open.

SILOAM SPRINGS WRITERS. Contact: Margaret Weathers, 716 W. University, Siloam Springs AR 72761-2658. (479)524-6598. Website: http://sswc.flash57.com. Membership (20) open. Sponsoring a contest open to nonmembers and a seminar. September 17, 2005.

CALIFORNIA

AMERICAN CHRISTIAN WRITERS OF VENTURA COUNTY. Camarillo. Contact: Pat Loomis, 5750 Terra Bella Ln., Camarillo CA 93012. (805)551-4217. Fax (805)384-0360. E-mail: ploomis@adelphia.net. Membership (10) open.

BAY AREA WRITERS CRITIQUE GROUP. Castro Valley. Contact: Launa Herrmann, 21555 Eden Canyon Rd., Castro Valley CA 94552-9721. (510)889-7564. E-mail: Wordroom@ aol.com. Membership (6) open to experienced writers only.

CASTRO VALLEY CHRISTIAN WRITERS GROUP. Contact: Pastor Jon Drury, 19300 Redwood Rd., Castro Valley CA 94546-3465. (510)886-6300. Fax (510)581-5022. E-mail: jdrury@ redwoodchapel.org. Website: www.christianwriter.org. Membership (10) open. Sponsoring a Christian Writers Seminar, February 18-19, 2005. Keynote speaker: Sally Stuart.

CHINO VALLEY CHRISTIAN WRITERS CRITIQUE GROUP. Chino Hills. Contact: Nancy I. Sanders, 6361 Prescott Ct., Chino CA 91710-7105. (909)590-0226. E-mail: JNDB Sand@ juno.com. Membership (10-15) open.

CHRISTIAN WRITERS' GROUP INTERNATIONAL. Fountain Valley. Contact: Penelope Alexander, PO Box 1122, Huntington Beach CA 92647-1122. (714)434-8308. Membership (1) open.

DIABLO VALLEY CHRISTIAN WRITERS GROUP. Danville. Marcy Weydemuller, leader. Contact: Sue Massie, 2674 Derby Dr., San Ramon CA 94583. (925)828-8667. Fax (925)556-1590. E-mail: redfox@ix.netcom.com. Membership (10-14) open.

GARDENA VALLEY BAPTIST CHURCH ACW WRITERS GROUP. Gardena. Contact Susan J. Shelley or Stan Terasaki, 1630 W. 158th St., Gardena CA 90247. (310)323-5683. Fax (310)768-2783. E-mail: gvbc@gvbc.net (put ACW Writers Group in subject line). Website: www.gvbc.net. Has a free monthly print newsletter: *Writer's Workshop.* Membership (7) open.

HIGH DESERT CHRISTIAN WRITERS GUILD. Lancaster. Contact: Don Patterson, 43543—51st St. W., Quartz Hill CA 93536. (661)722-5695. E-mail: don@theology.edu. Membership (25) open.

*****LODI WRITERS ASSOCIATION.** (General membership, not just Christian.) Contact: Dee Porter, PO Box 1863, Lodi CA 95241. Phone/fax (209)334-0603. E-mail: crcomm@ lodinet.com. Membership (70) open. Sponsors one-day workshop, usually in July.

*****MARIPOSA CHRISTIAN WRITERS.** Contact: Steve Radanovich, 4194 Sebastopol Rd., Mariposa CA 95338-9775. Phone/fax (209)742-5463 or (209)966-3047. E-mail: oz333@ sierratel.com. Membership (8) open. ACW Chapter.

NOVEL IDEA, CHRISTIAN WRITERS SWARM. Norwalk. Contact: Derrell B. Thomas, 11239 1/2 Ferina St., Norwalk CA 90650-5507, (562)863-3132. E-mail: luv2writ@yahoo.com. Membership (6) open.

ORANGE COUNTY CHRISTIAN WRITERS FELLOWSHIP. Various groups meeting throughout the county. Contact: Bonnie Compton Hanson (bonnieh1@worldnet.att.net.) and Beverly Bush Smith (b2smith@pacbell.net), PO Box 538, Lake Forest CA 92609. (949)458-8981. Membership (200+) open. Annual $20 membership includes a bimonthly newsletter, information on local critique groups, and reduced registration fees for annual Spring Writer's Day, which includes keynote speakers, workshops, and consultations. Officers: John DeSimone (jdesimone@socal.rr.com); Peggy Matthews Rose (proseunltd@cox.net); and Jeanne Pallos (jlpallos@cox.net). Membership inquiries to Jeanne Pallos by e-mail or phone (949-249-3728). Questions or information for newsletter, mail to: OC CWF, PO Box 982, Lake Forest CA 92609. See Website for details: www.occwf.org.

SACRAMENTO CHRISTIAN WRITERS. Citrus Heights. Contact: Beth Miller Self, 2012 Rushing River Ct., Elverta CA 95626-9756. (916)992-8709. E-mail: cwbself@msn.com. Membership (32) open. Sponsors a contest open to members only. Sponsors a seminar every 5 years; May 2005 will be their 25th anniversary seminar; in Sacramento.

SAN DIEGO COUNTY CHRISTIAN WRITERS' GUILD. Contact: Jennie & Robert Gillespie, PO Box 270403, San Diego CA 92198. (619)221-8183. Fax (619)255-1131. E-mail: info@sandiegocwg.org. Website: www.sandiegocwg.org. Membership (150) open. To join their Internet newsgroup, e-mail your name and address to: info@sandiegocwg.com. Sponsors critique groups, fall seminar (September 2005) and spring awards banquet.

SANTA CLARA VALLEY CHRISTIAN WRITER'S GROUP. Los Gatos. Contact: Richard M. Hinz, 550 S. 4th St. Apt. E, San Jose CA 95112. (408)297-3336. E-mail: Rickhinz@yahoo.com. Membership (10) open.

S.C.U.M. San Leandro. Contact: John B. Olson, 1261 Estrudillo Ave., San Leandro CA 94577. (510)357-4441. E-mail: john@litany.com. Membership (15) open, by invitation.

SONRISE CHRISTIAN WRITERS. East of Sacramento. Contact: Marlys Norris, 8524 Oak Harbour Ct., Fair Oaks CA 95628. (916)961-0575. Membership (18-20) open.

SOUTH VALLEY CHRISTIAN WRITERS. Hanford. Contact: Mary Kirk, 247 E. Cortner St., Hanford CA 93230-1845. (559)582-8442. E-mail: mkirk@sti.net. Membership (7) open. ACW Chapter.

SOUTHERN CALIFORNIA WRITERS ASSN. Fountain Valley. Contact: Roy King, 15772 Heatherdale Rd., Victorville CA 92394-1317. (760)955-9027. Fax (760)851-3689. E-mail: 3kings@urs2.net. Website: www.ocwriter.com. Membership (120) open. Secular group/ many Christians.

+TEMECULA CHRISTIAN WRITERS CRITIQUE GROUP. Contact: Rebecca Farnbach, 41403 Bitter Creek Ct., Temecula CA 92591-1545. (909)699-5148. Fax (909)699-4208. E-mail: sunbrook@hotmail.com. Website: www.sandiegocwg.org. Membership (10) open.

VALLEY BIBLE CHRISTIAN WRITERS GROUP. Hercules. Contact: Sandy Ormeo, 1477 Willow Ave., Hercules CA 94547. (510)779-3171. Fax (510)799-3174. E-mail: Sandywrites@ yahoo.com. Membership (10-15) open.

THE WRITE BUNCH. Stockton. Contact: Shirley Cook, 3123 Sheridan, Stockton CA 95219. (209)477-8375. E-mail: shirleyc@softcom.net. Membership (7-8) not currently open.

COLORADO

CHRISTIAN WRITERS GROUP. Colorado Springs area. Contact: Julie Schroeder, PO Box 202, Simla CO 80835-0202. E-mail: WriteHeart@aol.com. Membership open in this new group.

CONNECTICUT

+SOUTHERN NEW ENGLAND ACW CHAPTER. Putnam area. Contact: Blanche Gosselin, 218 Woodstock Ave., #24, Putnam CT 06260. (860)963-7801.

DELAWARE

DELMARVA CHRISTIAN WRITERS' FELLOWSHIP. Georgetown. Contact: Candy Abbott, PO Box 777, Georgetown DE 19947-0777. (302)856-6649. Fax (302)856-7742. E-mail: candy.abbott@verizon.net. Website: www.delmarvawriters.com. Membership (36) open.

FLORIDA

BRANDON CHRISTIAN WRITERS. Contact: Ruth C. Ellinger, 1405 S. Lithia Pinecrest Rd., Brandon FL 33511-6719. (813)685-7387. E-mail: WrightandRuth@cs.com. Membership (8) open.

BROWARD COUNTY ACW CHAPTER. Coral Springs. Contact: Lynne Cooper Sitton, 105 N.W. 104th Ter., Coral Springs FL 33071-7364. (954)341-2627. E-mail: LynneCSitton@cs.com. Membership (5-15) open.

CHRISTIAN WRITERS GROUP. Contact: Roy Proctor, 1715 Dalby Ct., Middleburg FL 32068. E-mail: royp2000@bellsouth.net. Membership (5) open.

MIAMI AMERICAN CHRISTIAN WRITERS CHAPTER. Contact: Karen Whiting, 10936 S.W. 156th Pl., Miami FL 33196-3547. (305)388-8656. Fax (305)388-2488. E-mail: whiting@gate.net. Membership (8) open.

MID-FLORIDA CHRISTIAN WRITERS. Clermont. Contact: Joy Shelton, 1040 Glensprings Ave., Winter Garden FL 34787. (407)654-9076. Fax (407)654-9079. E-mail: JoySprinkles@aol.com. Membership (13) open.

SUNCOAST CHRISTIAN WRITERS. Clearwater. Contact: Elaine Creasman, 13014—106th Ave. N., Largo FL 33774. Phone/fax (727)595-8963. E-mail: emcreasman@aol.com. Membership (10) open.

WORD WEAVERS. Casselberry. Contact: Eva Marie Everson, 122 Fairway Ten Dr., Casselberry FL 32707-4823. Phone/fax (407)695-9366. E-mail: penNhand@aol.com. Membership (40+) open. Yearly contest for members. Planning a conference for January 2005 in Vero Beach, Florida.

WRITING STRATEGIES CRITIQUESHOP. Daytona Beach. Meets monthly (10X). Sponsors workshops the 2nd Friday of each month for working authors who have completed one course of Writing Strategies (see conference listing). Send SASE for brochure. Contact: Rosemary J. Upton. Phone/fax (386)322-1111. E-mail: rupton@cfl.rr.com. Website: www.ruptonbooks.com. Membership (10) open.

GEORGIA

AMERICAN CHRISTIAN WRITERS IN ATLANTA. Contact: Kay Shostak, 2242 Blenheim Ct., Marietta GA 30066. (770)591-9057. E-mail: kshostak@comcast.net. Membership (20) open.

CHRISTIAN AUTHORS GUILD (formerly Cherokee Christian Writers Group). Woodstock. Contact: Dick Byrum or Diana Baker. E-mail: info@christianauthorsguild.com. Website: www.christianauthorsguild.org. Membership (40) open.

*GEORGIA WRITERS, INC./CHRISTIAN WRITERS POD. Contact: Lloyd Blackwell, 3049 Scott Rd. N.E., Marietta GA 30066. (770)421-1203. E-mail: lloydblackwell@worldnet.att.net. Membership open.

LAMBLIGHTERS CRITIQUE GROUP. Roswell area. Contact: Cisi Morrow-Smith, 248 Quail Run, Roswell GA 30076-3182. (770)518-6101. Membership (4-6) open.

+NORTHEAST GEORGIA WRITERS. Gainesville. Contact: Elouise Whitten, 660 Crestview Ter., Gainesville GA 30501-3110. (770)532-3007. Membership (32) open. Sponsors contest open to members.

SOUTHEASTERN WRITERS ASSN. Contact: Amy Munnell, PO Box 20161, St. Simons Island GA 31522. E-mail: purple@southeasternwriters.com. Website: www.southeasternwriters.com. Sponsors an annual conference; June 2005. Membership open.

*W.R.I.T.E. Covington. Contact: Colleen Jackson, 215 High Point Dr., Covington GA 30016. (770)787-2951. E-mail: cjac401992@aol.com. Membership (5) open.

IDAHO

CHRISTIAN WRITERS OF IDAHO. Boise. Contact: Diana L. James, 393 W. Willowbrook Dr., Meridian ID 83642-1689. (208)288-0983. Membership (35+) open. ACW Chapter. Cosponsors an ACW Conference in Boise in September.
*INTERNATIONAL NETWORK OF CHRISTIANS 'N THE ARTS. Coeur d'Alene. Contact: Sheri Stone, Box 1754, Post Falls ID 83877. (208)667-9730. Fax (208)667-7317. Membership open. Sponsors various contests.

INDIANA

+ACW INDIANAPOLIS. Contact: Diana Sturm, 4108 Londonderry Dr., Indianapolis IN 46221. (317)821-1244. ACW Chapter.
BLOOMINGTON AREA CHRISTIAN WRITERS. Bloomington/Ellettsville. Contact: Kathi Adams, 9576 W. St. Rd. 48, Bloomington IN 47404-9737. (812)876-8265. E-mail: katadams55@aol.com. Membership (15-20) open.
FORT WAYNE CHRISTIAN WRITERS CLUB. Fort Wayne. Contact: Linda R. Wade, 739 W. Fourth St., Fort Wayne IN 46808-2613. (260)422-2772. E-mail: linda_wade@juno.com. Membership (20) open.
OPEN DOOR CHRISTIAN WRITERS. Westport. Contact: Janet Teitsort, PO Box 129, Westport IN 47283-0129. Phone/fax (812)591-2210. E-mail: JTWrites4Him@insightbb.com. Membership (12) open.
*STEUBEN CHRISTIAN WRITERS GROUP (ACW CHAPTER). Angola. Contact: Tatiana Claudy, 6160 S. 800 W., Pleasant Lake IN 46779-9763. (260)475-5908. E-mail: akclaudy@netscape.net. Membership (10) open.

IOWA

CEDAR RAPIDS CHRISTIAN WRITER'S GROUP. Contact: Susan Fletcher, 513 Knollwood Dr. S.E., Cedar Rapids IA 52403. (319)365-9844. Membership (5) open.
*RIVER CITY WRITERS. Council Bluffs. Contact: Dee Barrett, 16 Susan Ln., Council Bluffs IA 51503. (712)322-7692. Fax (712)329-9615. Membership (30) open.

KANSAS

CHRISTIAN WRITERS FELLOWSHIP. Girard. Contact: Carol Russell, 894—165th St., Fort Scott KS 66701. (620)547-2472. E-mail: rlrussell@ckt.net. Membership (29) open. Sponsors a contest and a seminar, April 2005.
CREATIVE WRITERS FELLOWSHIP. North Newton, Hesston, and Moundridge. Contact: Esther Groves, sec., 500 W. Bluestem, Apt. H4, North Newton KS 67117-8004. (316)283-7224. E-mail: estherbg@southwind.net. Membership (20) open.
HEART OF AMERICA CHRISTIAN WRITERS' NETWORK. Overland Park KS. Contact: Mark and Jeanette Littleton, 3706 N.E. Shady Lane Dr., Gladstone MO 64119. Phone/fax (816)459-8016. E-mail: MarkLitt@aol.com. Membership (120) open. Sponsors monthly meetings, a contest (open to nonmembers), and two conferences: a major one in late October and a mentoring conference in April.

KENTUCKY

JACKSON CHRISTIAN WRITERS' CLUB. Near Campton. Contact: Donna J. Woodring, Box 10, Vancleve KY 41385-0010. (606)666-5000. E-mail: donnaw@kmbc.edu. Membership (6) open (if advanced).

LOUISVILLE CHRISTIAN WRITERS. Contact: Lana Jackson, pres., 8516 Missionary Ct., Louisville KY 40291. (502)968-3602. E-mail: LanaHJackson@aol.com. Membership (25) open. ACW Chapter.

LOUISIANA

SOUTHERN CHRISTIAN WRITERS GUILD. Slidell. Contact: Grace Booth or Marlaine Peachey, 146 Pebble Beach Dr., Slidell LA 70458-5742. E-mail: ruwriting@datastar.net, or marlaine@juno.com. Membership (35) open.

MAINE

MAINE FELLOWSHIP OF CHRISTIAN WRITERS. China ME. Contact: Beth Rogers, 720 Essex St., Bangor ME 04401. (207)942-1616. E-mail: BethR58@aol.com. Membership (20) open. Sponsors contest open to conference attendees. Conference, August 2005.

MARYLAND

ANNAPOLIS FELLOWSHIP OF CHRISTIAN WRITERS. Annapolis. Contact: Jeri Sweany, 3107 Ervin Ct., Annapolis MD 21403-4620. (410)267-0924. Membership (10-15) open.

HARFORD COUNTY WRITERS GROUP. Bel Air. Contact: Danny L. Imwold, 1304 Mazeland Dr., Bel Air MD 21015. (410)734-7760. Fax (410)734-7599. E-mail: dimoi@bellatlantic .net. Or contact: Joyce Seabolt, (410)941-1120. E-mail: joyceseabolt@hotmail.com. Membership (15) open.

+MARYLAND CHRISTIAN WRITERS GROUP/ACW. Bowie, Forestville, and via teleconference. Contact: Sharon Ricks, 9900-E Greenbelt Rd. #190, Lanham MD 20706-2264. (301)919-0211. E-mail: marylandcwg@aol.com. Website: http://home.regent.edu/ sharric/sharric. Membership (10) open.

*SOUTHERN MARYLAND WRITER'S GROUP. White Plains. Contact: Angela Dion, PO Box 2131, LaPlata MD 20646-2131. E-mail: SMWGroup@aol.com. Website: http://members .truepath.com/SMWG. Membership (15) open. Sponsors a contest open to nonmembers.

THIRD SATURDAY CHRISTIAN WRITERS GROUP. Columbia area. Contact: Claire DeBakey. (410)715-4863. E-mail: c.debakey@att.net. Membership (8) open.

WISE PEN CHRISTIAN WRITERS GUILD. Belcamp. Contact: Anne Perry, 1258 Collier Ln., Belcamp MD 21017-1349. (410)297-6656. E-mail: bunniesarefree@aol.com. Nonfiction group. Membership (7) open. Sponsors a seminar in October in Bel Air MD.

MASSACHUSETTS

CENTRAL MASSACHUSETTS CHRISTIAN WRITERS FELLOWSHIP. Sturbridge. Contact: Barbara Shaffer, 168 Warren Rd., Brimfield MA 01010. (413)245-9620. Membership (10) open.

WESTERN MASSACHUSETTS CHRISTIAN WRITERS FELLOWSHIP. Springfield. Contact: Barbara A. Robidoux, 127 Gelinas Dr., Chicopee MA 01020-4813. (413)592-4386. Fax

(413)594-8375. E-mail: ebwordpro@aol.com. Website: www.scribesnscribblers.com. Membership (55) open.

MICHIGAN

THE CALLED AND READY WRITERS. Detroit. Contact: Mary Edwards, 20700 Civic Center Dr. Ste. 170, Southfield MI 48076. (248)663-2363. Fax (313)861-7578. E-mail: mwwginc@ aol.com. Website: www.thecalledandreadywriters.org. Membership (60) open.

CAPSTONE COMPOSERS. Bancroft. Contact: Rebecca L. Durling, 6986 Cole Rd., Bancroft MI 48414. (989)634-9237. Fax (989)634-5984. E-mail: durfar@michonline.net. Membership (8) open.

CHRISTIAN WRITERS GROUP. Vassar. Contact: Arlene Knickerbocker, 810-793-0316. E-mail: writer@thewritespot.org. Membership (6+) open.

*CREATIVE CHRISTIAN WRITERS. Grandville. Contact: Flavia Crowner, 211 S. Maple St., Fennville MI 49408. (289)561-5296. E-mail: flacro@datawise.net. Membership (10) open. ACW Chapter.

DETROIT ACW CHAPTER. Southfield. Contact: Pamela Perry, 21442 Hamilton Ave., Farmington Hills MI 48336-5840. (248)426-2300. Fax (248)471-2422. E-mail: info@ministry marketingsolutions.com. Website: www.ministrymarketingsolutions.com. Membership (100) open. Sponsors a summer seminar in Detroit and book signing parties.

SOUTHEASTERN MICHIGAN ACW CHAPTER. Ypsilanti. Contact: Debbie Mitchell, 1191 Stamford Rd, Yypsilanti MI 48198. (734)483-5444. Fax (734)769-5134. E-mail: allthings@ ameritech.net. Membership (10) open.

MINNESOTA

MINNESOTA CHRISTIAN WRITERS GUILD. Edina. Contact: Sharon Knudson, pres., 1596 Beechwood Ave., St. Paul MN 55116-2408. (651)695-0609. Fax: same/call first. E-mail: sharonknudson@hotmail.com. Website: www.mnchristianwriters.org. Sponsors a spring contest for members only and annual spring (April 8-9, 2005) and fall (October) seminars. Monthly meetings (Sept.-May); monthly newsletter. Sponsors critique circles throughout Minnesota. Membership (125) open.

MISSISSIPPI

+BYHALIA CHRISTIAN WRITERS/ACW CHAPTER. Byhalia. Contact: Marylane Wade Koch, 2573 W. Church St., Byhalia MS 38611-9576. (662)838-2451. E-mail: rwkoch@att.net. Membership open.

*NORTH MISSISSIPPI CHRISTIAN WRITERS. Byhalia. Contact: Earl Adams, PO Box 76, Byhalia MS 38611-0067. (901)3811289. E-mail: erladms@connect.com. ACW Chapter. Membership (10) open.

MISSOURI

*CHRISTIAN WRITERS WORKSHOP OF ST. LOUIS. Day group contact: Ruth Houser, 3148 Arnold-Tenbrook Rd., Arnold MO 63010-4732. (636)464-1187. E-mail: HouserRA@juno .com. Also contact: Ruth McDaniel (636)464-1187. Membership (15-20) open. ACW Chapter.

*GREATER ST. LOUIS CHRISTIAN WRITERS. This group is no longer meeting, but contact person for writers in the area is Lila Shelburne, 707 Gran Lin Dr., St. Charles MO 63303-6025. (636)441-2131. Fax (636)922-2459. E-mail: lila@anet-stl.com.

MONTANA

WRITERS IN THE BIG SKY. Helena. Contact: Lenore Puhek, 1215 Hudson, Helena MT 59601-1848. (406)443-2552. Membership (9) currently closed. There is a waiting list.

NEBRASKA

CENTRAL NEBRASKA FELLOWSHIP OF CHRISTIAN WRITERS, ARTISTS, AND MUSICIANS. Kearney. Contact: Carolyn Scheidies, 415 E. 15th, Kearney N.E. 68847-6959. (308)234-3849. E-mail: crscheidies@hotmail.com (put C-WAM on subject line). Membership (15) open.

MY THOUGHTS EXACTLY WRITERS GROUP. Fremont. Contact: Cheryl A. Paden, PO Box 1073, Fremont NE 68025. (402)727-6508. Membership (6) open. Periodically sponsors a writers' retreat; October/November 2005.

WORDSOWER'S CHRISTIAN WRITER'S GROUP. Omaha. Contact: Kelly Haack, 5712 S. 91st St., Omaha NE 68127. (402)593-7936. E-mail: haackkj@cox.net. Membership (10) open. ACW Chapter.

NEW HAMPSHIRE

WORDSMITHS' CHRISTIAN WRITERS' FELLOWSHIP. Nashua. Contact: Susan Peel, 165 Village Circle Way #3, Manchester NH 03102-7112. (603)669-0264. E-mail: speel@icwriters.com. Website: www.icwriters.com/Wordsmiths/index.htm. Membership (40) open.

NEW JERSEY

CENTRAL JERSEY CHRISTIAN WRITERS' FELLOWSHIP. Zarephath. Contact: Catherine J. Barrier, 13 Oliver St., Somerset NJ 08873-2142. (732)545-5168. Fax (732)545-0640. E-mail: JCMajesty@juno.com. Membership (15) open.

NEW JERSEY SOCIETY OF CHRISTIAN WRITERS. Three chapters: Vineland, Voorhees, and Delanco. Liz Fabiani, dir. Contact: Lillian Baker, membership dir., 1370 S. Main Rd., PMB #7, Vineland NJ 08360. (856)690-0186. Fax (856)327-0291. E-mail: Newriter57@aol.com. Website: www.njscw.com. Membership in all (49) open.

NORTH JERSEY CHRISTIAN WRITER'S GROUP. Ringwood. Contact: Louise Bergmann DuMont, PO Box 36, Ringwood NJ 07456. (973)962-9267. E-mail: word.worker@verizon.net. Website: www.louisedumont.com. Membership (26) open. E-mail for information.

NEW MEXICO

SOUTHWEST CHRISTIAN WRITERS ASSOCIATION. Farmington. Contact: Connie Peters, pres., SCWA, 240 S. Ash, Cortez CO 81321. (970)564-9449. E-mail: CoFun77@yahoo.com. Website: www.swchristianwriter.org. Membership (12) open. Sponsors annual one-day seminar the third Saturday in April (April 16, 2005) in Farmington NM.

SOUTHWEST WRITERS. Albuquerque. Contact: Robert Spiegel, pres., SWW, 3721 Morris St. N.E., Ste. A, Albuquerque NM 87111-3611. (505)265-9485. Fax (505)265-9483. E-mail: contactus@southwestwriters.com. Website: www.southwestwriters.com. Membership (800) open. Sponsors a contest (open to nonmembers) and a series of mini-conferences in Albuquerque, in February, May, August, and November 2005. Secular.

NEW YORK

BROOKLYN WRITER'S CLUB. Contact: Ann Dellarocco, PO Box 184, Bath Beach Station, Brooklyn NY 11214-0184. (718)680-4084. Membership (10-20) open.

NEW YORK CHRISTIAN WRITERS GROUP. New York City. Contact: Marilyn Driscoll, 350—First Ave., New York NY 10010-4911, (212)529-6087. E-mail: madrisc@rcn.com. Membership (12) open.

THE SCRIBBLERS. Riverhead. Contact: Bill Batcher, pres., c/o First Congregational Church, 103 First St., Riverhead NY 11901. E-mail: bbatcher@optonline.net. Membership (12) open. ACW Chapter #3049.

SOUTHERN TIER CHRISTIAN WRITERS' FELLOWSHIP. Binghamton (Johnson City). Contact: Kenneth Cetton, 20 Pine St., Port Crane NY 13833-1512. (607)648-7249. E-mail: KC1933@juno.com. Membership (5) open.

NORTH CAROLINA

COVENANT WRITERS. Lincolnton. Contact: Robert Redding, 3392 Hwy. 274, Cherryville NC 28021. (704)445-4962. E-mail: minwriter@yahoo.com. Call for location of meeting. Membership (10) open.

SEVEN SERIOUS SCRIBES. Cary. Contact: Katherine W. Parrish, 103 Chimney Rise Dr., Cary NC 27511-7214. (919)467-1924. E-mail: servantsong@aol.com. Critique group. Membership (7) not currently open, but encourages others to start similar groups in the area. ACW chapter.

OHIO

+ACWRITERS NORTHEAST OHIO CHAPTER. Contact: Christopher Flucker, 15716 Broadway Ave., Maple Heights OH 44137. (216)851-7214. ACW Chapter.

ASHLAND AREA CHRISTIAN WRITERS GUILD. Contact: April Boyer, 1552 County Rd. 995, Ashland OH 44805. (419)281-1766. E-mail: oboy@bright.net. Website: http://april boyer.com (includes pertinent information). Membership (15) open. Meets twice a month. Holds a variety of events, activities, and speakers.

+BLACK SWAMP WRITERS GUILD. Contact: Sister Jacinta Neargardner, CPPS, 1745 S. Agner St., Ottawa OH 45875. (419)523-3598. ACW Chapter.

***CHRISTIAN WRITERS GUILD.** Youngstown area. Contact: Susan K. Virgalitte, 240 Sawmill Run Dr., Canfield OH 44406. Phone/fax (330)533-5833. Membership (30) open.

COLUMBUS CHRISTIAN WRITERS ASSN. Contact: Barbara Taylor Sanders, 9220 Shawnee Trl., Powell OH 43065. (614)764-9220. E-mail: BTSanders@columbus.rr.com. Website: www.ccwaohio.com. Membership (25) open. Cosponsoring a writers' workshop with the American Christian Writers, May 2005.

DAYTON CHRISTIAN SCRIBES. Kettering. Contact: Lois Pecce (secretary), Box 41613, Dayton OH 45441-0613. (937)433-6470. E-mail: epecce@compuserve.com. Membership (36) open.

DAYTON CHRISTIAN WRITERS GUILD, INC. Contact: Tina V. Toles, PO Box 251, Englewood OH 45322-2227. Phone/fax (937)836-6600. E-mail: Poet11@earthlink.net. Website: www .dougtoles.com/dtolessr. Membership (40) open. Sponsoring a seminar in August 2005.

GREATER CINCINNATI CHRISTIAN WRITERS' FELLOWSHIP. Contact: Wayne Holmes, 5499 Yellowstone Dr., Fairfield OH 45014-3868. Phone/fax (513)858-6609. E-mail: wwriter@ fuse.net. Website: http://gccwf.com. Membership (20) open.

+GREATER OHIO ACW CHAPTER. Contact: Kandy Williams, 3241 Oak Bend Blvd., Canal Winchester OH 43110. (614)834-1682.
NORTHWEST OHIO CHRISTIAN WRITERS. Toledo. Contact: Judy Gyde, 3072 Muirfield Ave., Toledo OH 43614-3766. (419)382-7582. E-mail: begyde@glasscity.net. Membership (45) open. Sponsors a Saturday seminar in September.

OKLAHOMA

FELLOWSHIP OF CHRISTIAN WRITERS (FCW). Tulsa. Membership 80+; 3 satellite groups w/ total memberships 40+; at-large membership 75+. Ready Writer Online, FCW's Website at http://fcwreadywriter.com. Ten-member board headed by Sue R. Dodd, chairman (suerd@fcwreadywriter.com). JoAnn R. Wray, Web master, e-mail newsletter director (epistle1@fcwreadywriter.com). Linda Cravens, secretary/treasurer (lcravens@fcwready writer.com). James Tate, poetry director/greeter (jetate@fcwreadywriter.com). Trudy Graham, print newsletter editor/publicist (gfgram@fcwreadywriter.com). Satellite groups: Granbury TX, Dena Dyer, director (denad@fcwreadywriter.com); Vinita OK, Lavon Lewis, director (lavonl@fcwreadywriter.com). Suwanee GA, LeAnne Benfield, director (leannb@fcwreadywriter.com). Local groups meet monthly or more often. FCW-Tulsa meets 2nd Tuesday monthly at Kirk of the Hills Presbyterian, Tulsa OK. Meetings feature hands-on workshops and dynamic outside speakers. 2004 included Lin Carlson of Dayspring Greeting Cards; Rene Gutteridge, Christian fiction author; and Cecil Murphey, author of over 90 books. FCW also has a Free List Serve at Yahoo Groups—http://groups .yahoo.com/group/FCW—or send an email to FCW-subscribe@yahoogroups.com. List is moderated. Must apply online at Yahoo groups and fill out questionnaire. 600+ members. Has daily interaction, markets, encouragement, tips, definitions, prayer, contests, and more. Online critique groups for fiction, nonfiction, children's, and poetry for list members. May also be paired with an accountability partner, if you wish. See Website for details on joining. Free e-mail newsletter: (over 750 subscribers), Ready Writer Light, with different content than the print newsletter which goes to paid members only. Subscribe at the Website through provided form. Paid local memberships: yearly fee $35 offers many benefits including our 10-page monthly print newsletter, membership card, resources, bookmarks, magnets, eligibility to members' only contests with cash prizes, product discounts, critique groups, special speakers, and workshops, free listing at the Members Online bookstore, and much more. Tapes of speakers and workshops available for sale online. At-large memberships for those not near a local group $25/year. See Website for more details and form. Special rates for teens and for more than one person per household. Contact: JoAnn R. Wray, 8409 S. Elder, Broken Arrow, OK 74011; Phone (918)451-4017; cell (918)695-4528; e-mail: epistle1@fcwreadywriter.com. Brochure on request.
WORDWRIGHTS OKLAHOMA CITY CHRISTIAN WRITERS. Contact: Milton Smith, 6457 Sterling Dr., Oklahoma City OK 73132. (405)721-5026. E-mail: jerri-milton@juno.com. Membership (20) open. Cosponsors an annual writers' conference with American Christian Writers, spring 2005, in Oklahoma City; send an SASE for information. Sponsors 2 or 3 contests through the year for members only.

OREGON

GOD'S WORDSMITHS—ADVANCED. King City. Contact: Crystal Ortmann, 11625 S.W. King George Dr., King City OR 97224-2624. (503)372-0529. Fax (503)372-0529. E-mail: cjortmann@earthlink.net. Membership (4) open.

GOD'S WORDSMITHS—BEGINNERS. King City. Contact: Crystal Ortmann, 11625 SW King George Dr., King City OR 97224-2624. Phone/fax (503)372-0529. E-mail: cjortmann@ earthlink.net. Membership (5) open.

OREGON CHRISTIAN WRITERS. Contact: Jennifer Anne Messing. 6214 S.E. Sherman St., Portland OR 97215. (503)775-6039. E-mail: president@oregonchristianwriters.org. Website: www.oregonchristianwriters.org. Meets for 4 all-day Saturday conferences annually: February in Salem, May in Eugene, September in Medford area, and October in Portland. Newsletter published one month before each one-day conference. Annual 4-day Coaching Conference July 31-August 4, 2005 & 2006 in Canby Grove. Occasionally sponsors a contest. Membership (300+) open.

PORTLAND CHRISTIAN WRITERS GROUP. Contact: Stan Baldwin, (503)659-2974. Serious group; must write regularly. Waiting list available.

SALEM I CHRISTIAN WRITERS GROUP. Contact: Marcia Mitchell, 4144 Sunnyview Rd. N.E., #115, Salem OR 97305-1893. (503)588-0372. Membership (10) not currently open.

WORDSMITHS. Gresham/sometimes E. Portland or Vancouver WA. Contact: Susan Thogerson Maas, 27526 S.E. Carl St., Gresham OR 97080-8215. (503)663-7834. E-mail: susan .maas@verizon.net. Membership (6) open. Christian and secular writers.

WRITER'S DOZEN CRITIQUE GROUP. Eugene. Contact: Geni White, 1455 Larkspur Ave., Eugene OR 97401. (541)465-2268. E-mail: geniwhite@comcast.net. Membership (8) possibly open.

PENNSYLVANIA

BLOCK BUSTERS. Bedford. Contact: Julie Leppert, (814)839-4786. E-mail: kllepp@yellow bananas.com. Membership (new) open.

THE FIRST WORD. Sewickley/Bellevue. Contact: Shirley S. Stevens, 326 B Glaser Ave., Pittsburgh PA 15202-2910.(412)761-2618. E-mail: poetcat@earthlink.net. Membership (12) open. Affiliated with the St. Davids Conference.

GREATER PHILADELPHIA CHRISTIAN WRITERS' FELLOWSHIP. Newtown Square. Contact: Marlene Bagnull, 316 Blanchard Rd., Drexel Hill, PA 19026. Phone/fax (610)626-6833. E-mail: Mbagnull@aol.com. Website: www.writehisanswer.com. Membership (20) open. Meets one Thursday morning a month, October-June. Sponsors annual writers' conference (August 11-13, 2005) and contest (open to registered conferees only).

INDIAN VALLEY CHRISTIAN WRITERS FELLOWSHIP. Telford. Contact: Cheryl Wallace, 952 Route 113, Sellersville PA 18960. (215)453-0415. E-mail: daphni@voicenet.com. Membership (25-30) open. ACW Chapter. Sponsors a seminar every other year; next one tentatively 3/05.

INDIANA CHRISTIAN WRITERS FELLOWSHIP. Indiana PA. Contact: Jan Woodard, 270 Sunset Dr., Indiana PA 15701. (724)465-5886. E-mail: jwoodard@wpia.net. Membership (9) open. Annual fall and winter writers' retreats.

INSPIRATIONAL WRITERS FELLOWSHIP. Brookville. Contact: Jan R. Sady, 2026 Langville Rd., Mayport PA 16240. (814)856-2560. E-mail: janfran@alltel.net. Membership (10) open. Sponsors a contest in February.

JOHNSTOWN CHRISTIAN WRITERS' GROUP. Contact: Betty Rosian, 108 Deerfield Ln., Johnstown PA 15905-5703. (814)255-4351. E-mail: BLRosian@charter.net. Membership (15) open.

LANCASTER AREA CHRISTIAN WRITERS FELLOWSHIP. Contact: A. Martha Stahl, 1001 E. Oregon Rd., Lititz PA 17543. (717)509-5829. E-mail: omstahl@juno.com. Membership open.

WEST BRANCH CHRISTIAN WRITERS. Williamsport. Contact: Eileen Berger, 866 Penn Dr., Hughesville PA 17737. (570)584-2280. E-mail: emberger@sunlink.net. Membership (20) open. Sponsors an annual one-day mini-conference each fall, usually in October.

SOUTH CAROLINA

CHRISTIAN WRITERS' GROUP. Columbia area. Contact: Kim Andrysczyk, 201 Sutton Way, Irmo SC 29063. E-mail: kimbocraig@juno.com. Meets monthly. Membership open.

GREENVILLE CHRISTIAN WRITERS GROUP. Contact: Nancy Parker, 3 Ben St., Greenville SC 29601. (864)232-1705. E-mail: Nancy@jjparker.com. Membership (14) open.

STEVENS CREEK WRITERS GROUP. Augusta. Contact: Gene Jennings, pres., 1203 Crestview Dr., North Augusta SC 29841. (706)863-7002. Fax (706)869-8777. E-mail: gene pjennings@aol.com. Membership (12) open. ACW Chapter.

+WRITING 4 HIM. Spartanburg. Contact: Linda Gilden, Christian Supply Store, 1600 Reidville Rd., Spartanburg SC 29301. (864)595-2626. E-mail: Rosewriter@aol.com. Membership open.

TENNESSEE

+CHATTANOOGA ACW CHAPTER. Contact: Keith Troop, 3207 Mount View Dr., Chattanooga TN 37411. (423)629-6990.

*WEST TENNESSEE WORD WEAVERS. Henderson. Contact: Sue Hite, pres., PO Box 12, Henderson TN 38340. (731)989-0265. E-mail: fright@earthlink.net. Membership (16) open. ACW Chapter.

TEXAS

AUSTIN CHRISTIAN WRITERS' GUILD. Contact: Lin Harris, 129 Fox Hollow Cv., Cedar Creek TX 78612-4844. (512)601-2216. Fax (240)208-3201. E-mail: linharris@austin.rr.com. Website: http://pw1.netcom.com/~linjer/acwg.html. Membership (60) open. Meetings, workshops, and conferences announced on Website. February conference.

CHRISTIAN WRITERS GROUP OF GREATER SAN ANTONIO. Universal City/San Antonio area. Contact: Brenda Blanchard, 2827 Olive Ave., Schertz TX 78154-3719. (210)945-4163. Fax (210)945-6613. E-mail: ZBGP1@aol.com. Has 4-8 speakers/yr. Sponsors a contest. Membership (25) open.

+CONGRESS OF CHRISTIAN WRITERS. Dallas. Contact: Eyo Umoh, PO Box 550654, Dallas TX 75355-0654. (214)341-8338. ACW Chapter.

DALLAS CHRISTIAN WRITERS GUILD. Plano. Contact: Jan Winebrenner, 2709 Winding Hollow, Plano TX 75093. (972)867-1119. E-mail: janwrite@earthlink.net. Website: www .dallaschristianwriters.com. Membership (50) open.

FCW TEXAS SATELLITE GROUP. Granbury/Dallas-Ft. Worth area. Small group for support, encouragement, and fellowship. Has some guest speakers and holds an annual conference. Dues $25/year. Contact: Dena Dyer, 505 Heather Dr., Granbury TX 76048. (817)573-4469. E-mail: thedyers@hcnews.com. Membership (5-10) open.

*HARLINGEN CHRISTIAN WRITERS GROUP. Meets rarely. Contact: Herschel Whittington, 2910 Treasure Hills Blvd., Harlingen TX 78550. (956)423-8048. E-mail: thyrzawhit@ aol.com. Membership (5) open.

INSPIRATIONAL WRITERS ALIVE! Groups meet in Houston, Pasadena, Jacksonville, Amarillo, and Humble. Contact: Martha Rogers, 6038 Greenmont, Houston TX 77092-2332. (713)686-7209. E-mail: marthalrogers@sbcglogal.net. Membership (130 statewide) open. Sponsors summer seminar, August 6, 2005, monthly newsletter, and annual contest (November 1-April 1) open to nonmembers.

INSPIRATIONAL WRITERS ALIVE!/AMARILLO CHAPTER. Contact: Helen Luecke, 2921 S.

Dallas, Amarillo TX 79103. (806)376-9671. E-mail: hcoluecke@arn.net. Sponsors a seminar, first weekend in April 2005.

*INSPIRATIONAL WRITERS ALIVE!/EAST TEXAS CHAPTER. Jacksonville. Contact: Maxine Holder, director & founding member, Rt. 4, Box 81-H, Rusk TX 75785-9410. (903)795-3986. E-mail: mholder787@aol.com. President of chapter: Judith Robinson, 15777 Meadow Cr., Bullard TX 75757. (903)825-2416. Membership (16) open. Connects with chapters in Houston and Amarillo for spring (Amarillo) and summer (Houston) conferences. When possible, East Texas chapter holds a fall, one-day seminar in Tyler. New: A new chapter has formed in Marshall, at East Texas Baptist University. Contact: Jerry Hopkins, Asst. Professor/History. E-mail: jhopkins@etbu.edu.

*INSPIRATIONAL WRITERS ALIVE!/FIRST BAPTIST HOUSTON CHAPTER. Contact: Carl Grjalba. (281)531-9034. E-mail: csgrjalba@yahoo.com.

*INSPIRATIONAL WRITERS ALIVE!/HUMBLE CHAPTER. Contact: Dalphna Barnes, 20319 Belleau Wood Dr., Humble TX 77338. (281)852-3521.

*INSPIRATIONAL WRITERS ALIVE!/PASADENA CHAPTER. Contact: Pat Vance. (713)477-4986.

+NORTH DALLAS CHAPTER OF ACW. Dallas. Contact: Earma Brown, PO Box 11046, Carrollton TX 75011. (469)892-1574. Website: www.acwchapter.com.

READY WRITERS. Lewisville. Contact: Frank Ball, PO Box 820802, Fort Worth TX 76182-0802. (817)741-0558. E-mail: journalist@1scom.net. Membership (5) open. ACW Chapter.

ROCKWALL CHRISTIAN WRITERS' GROUP. Contact: Leslie Wilson, 535 Cullins Rd., Rockwall TX 75032-6017. (972)772-3442. Fax (972)771-6656. E-mail: les5points@aol.com. Membership (15) open. Tentative plans for a conference.

SCRIBES FOR CHRIST/MANOR AREA. Contact: Azzie Spiers, 8315 Burleson Manor Rd., Manor TX 78653-5108. (512)272-8209. E-mail: auntlitty1@aol.com. ACW Chapter.

SEED SOWERS. Arlington. Contact: Frank Ball, PO Box 820802, Fort Worth TX 76182-0802. (817)741-0558. E-mail: journalist@1scom.net. Membership (8) open. ACW Chapter.

SUPER SCRIBES. Keller. Contact: Frank Ball, PO Box 820802, Fort Worth TX 76182-0802. (817)741-0558. E-mail: journalist@1scom.net. Membership (6) open. ACW Chapter.

UTAH

*UTAH CHRISTIAN WRITERS FELLOWSHIP. Salt Lake City area. Contact: Kimberly Malkogainnis, 117 W. Park St., Bingham Canyon UT 84006-1134. Phone/fax (801)568-7761. E-mail: kimmalkos@hotmail.com. Membership (20+) open.

VIRGINIA

CAPITAL CHRISTIAN WRITERS. Fairfax. Leader: Betsy Dill, PO Box 873, Centreville VA 20122-0873. Phone/fax (703)803-9447. E-mail: ccwriters@juno.com. Website: www.ccwriters.org. Meets the second Monday of each month except August and December. Speakers one month, critiquing the next. Sponsors a contest for members only. Membership (75-100) open.

CHRISTIAN WRITER'S CIRCLE. Fredericksburg. Contact: Sarah Sumpolec, dir., 6210 Forest Grove Dr., Fredericksburg VA 22407. E-mail: Sarah@sarahannesumpolec.com. Membership (15) open.

NEW COVENANT WRITER'S GROUP. Newport News. Contact: Mary Tatem, 451 Summer Dr., Newport News VA 23606-2515. Phone/fax (757)930-1700. E-mail: rwtatem@juno.com. Membership (6) open.

+PENINSULA CHRISTIAN WRITERS. Contact: Yvonne Ortega, PO Box 955, Yorktown VA 23692. (757)564-3262. E-mail: yvonne@whro.net. ACW Chapter.

RICHMOND CHRISTIANS WHO WRITE. Contact: Rev. Thomas C. Lacy, 12114 Walnut Hill Dr., Rockville VA 23146-1854. (804)749-4050. Fax (804)749-4939. E-mail: Richmond CWW@aol.com. Website: http://Rchristianswhowrite.tripod.com. Membership (40) open. Sponsors a seminar, October 2005. ACW Chapter.

+TIDEWATER CHRISTIAN WRITERS FORUM. Contact: Peter D. Mallett, 1270 Pall Mall St., #A, Norfolk VA 23513. (757)889-9917. E-mail: F18Pete@aol.com. ACW Chapter.

WASHINGTON

ADVENTIST WRITERS ASSOCIATION OF WESTERN WASHINGTON. Auburn. Contact: Marian Forschler, PO Box 58785, Renton WA 98058-1785. (425)235-1435. Fax (425)204-2070. E-mail: msf1944@cs.com. Membership (40) open. Newsletter $10/yr. Sponsors annual writers' conference in late June.

CHRISTIAN WRITERS FELLOWSHIP OF MOSES LAKE. Contact: Judith Gonzales, 1108 W. Rose Ave., Moses Lake WA 98837-2062. (509)765-4829. Fax: (509)766-4284. E-mail: gonzalesjm92@genext.net. Membership (6-10) open.

MEMOIR WRITERS. Federal Way. Contact: Bernice Large, 1013 S. 325th St., Federal Way WA 98003-5933. (253)946-2782. Membership (12-13) open.

NORTHWEST CHRISTIAN WRITERS ASSN. Bellevue WA. Contact: Carla Williams, PO Box 428, Enumclaw WA 98022. (360)802-2547. Fax (360)802-2551. E-mail: president@ nwchristianwriters.org. Website: www.nwchristianwriters.org. Membership (100) open. Sponsoring an Alaskan Cruise (leaving from Seattle) in August 2005.

*SPOKANE CHRISTIAN WRITERS. Contact: Niki Anderson, PO Box 30222, Spokane WA 99223-3003. Bus. phone/fax (509)448-2277. E-mail: Nander1405@aol.com. Or Christine Tangvald, 6016 E. Willow Springs Rd., Spokane WA 99223-9235. (509)448-0593. Membership (10) open. No dues.

SPOKANE NOVELISTS. Contact: Joan Mochel, 12229 N. Ruby Rd., Spokane WA 99218-1924.(509)466-2938. E-mail: MOCHEL@aol.com. Membership (18) open. Secular group with mostly Christian members.

WALLA WALLA CHRISTIAN WRITERS. Contact: Dolores Walker, 904 Ankeny, Walla Walla WA 99362-3705. (509)529-2974. E-mail: Klinker@bmi.net. Membership (10) open.

WALLA WALLA VALLEY CHRISTIAN SCRIBES. College Place. Contact: Helen Heavirland, PO Box 146, College Place WA 99324-0146. Phone/fax (541)938-3838. E-mail: hlh@bmi.net. Membership (15) open.

WENATCHEE CHRISTIAN WRITERS' FELLOWSHIP. Contact: David Peckham, PO Box 236, Chelan WA 98816. (509)682-5591. E-mail: david@onhisshoulders.com. Membership (25) open.

WISCONSIN

WORD AND PEN CHRISTIAN WRITERS CLUB. Menasha. Contact: Chris Stratton, 107 E. McArthur St., Appleton WI 54911-2109. (920)739-0752. E-mail: wordandpen@my christiansite.com. Website: http://mychristiansite.com/ministries/wordandpen. Membership (10) open. ACW Chapter.

WORDSMITHS (W.R.W.A.). Marinette/Menominee. Wisconsin Regional Writers Assn. (secular group that includes Christians). Contact: Mildred Utke, 2709 Northland Cir. Dr., Marinette WI 54143-4277. (715)735-0127. Membership (6) open.

CANADA

*FRASER VALLEY CHRISTIAN WRITERS GROUP. Abbotsford BC. Contact: Helmut Fandrich, 2461 Sunnyside Pl., Abbotsford BC V2T 4C4 Canada. Phone/fax (604)850-0666. E-mail: helmut@coneharvesters.com. Membership (20) open.

INSCRIBE CHRISTIAN WRITERS' FELLOWSHIP. Calgary & Edmonton (various locations across Canada). Contact: Marcia Laycock, 5007—42 A St., Ponoka AB T4J 1M3 Canada. (403)783-3044. E-mail: info@inscribe.org. Website: www.inscribe.org. Membership (250) open. Sponsors a newsletter and 2 contests, details on Website (one open to non-members). Also sponsors annual conferences in April and September.

LIFELINES CHRISTIAN WRITERS' GROUP. Richmond, British Columbia. Contact: Dauna Biggs, Unit 9—4711 Blair Dr., Richmond BC V6X 4E6 Canada. Phone/fax (604)244-2993. E-mail: buzz4@telus.net. Membership (6) open.

MANITOBA CHRISTIAN WRITERS ASSN. Winnipeg. Contact: Maria Rogalski, 409 Lynbrook Dr., Winnipeg MB R3R 0T2 Canada. (204)832-2846. E-mail: hansm@mts.net. Membership (25-30) open. May sponsor a conference in March 2005 in Winnipeg.

+PLC ONTARIO WRITES! Sudsbury area. Contact: Emily Betty, 374 Bressie St., Unit 3, Sudsbury ON P3C Canada. (705)673-0544. ACW Chapter.

THE WORD GUILD, an association of Canadian writers and editors who are Christian. Exec. Director: N. J. Lindquist, Box 487, Markham ON L3P 3R1 Canada. (905)294-6482. Fax (905)471-6912. E-mail: info@thewordguild.com. Website: www.thewordguild.com. Sponsors the Write! Canada Conference (formerly God Uses Ink), plus additional one-day conferences in various locations, and several contests open to nonmembers. Membership (200+) open.

FOREIGN

*ASSOCIATION OF CHRISTIAN WRITERS. London + network of area groups in England. Contact: Jenny Kyriacou, Administrator, All Saints Vicarage, 43 All Saints Close, Edmonton, London, N9 9AT, United Kingdom. Phone/fax 020 8884 4348. E-mail: admin@christian writers.org.uk. Membership (900) open. Sponsors a biennial writers' weekend for members only. Next one first weekend in July 2006 in Hertfordshire.

*CARIBBEAN CHRISTIAN WRITER'S GROUPS. St. Maarten, Netherlands Antilles; biweekly meetings; call Patricia Varlack: 599-5-95730. Curaçao, Netherlands Antilles; monthly meetings on western side of island; call Ingrid Jacobus Quarton at 599-9-868-3890. Curaçao, Netherlands Antilles; monthly meetings on eastern side of the island; call Lisette Quarton at 599-9-736-6107.

CONGRESS OF CHRISTIAN WRITERS. Nigeria. Contact: Dr. Austin J. Caleb, Embassy of Grace, PO Box 380, Etinan, Akwa Ibom State, Nigeria. Phone (GMS) (234) 802 321 9810. E-mail: austinjcaleb@hotmail.com. Membership (26) open. Conferences: Port Harcourt, Nigeria, November 2005; Lagos, Nigeria, November 2005. ACW Chapter.

NATIONAL/INTERNATIONAL GROUPS (no state location)

AMERICAN CHRISTIAN ROMANCE WRITERS. Rachel Hauck, pres.; PO Box 101066, Palm Bay FL 32910-1066. Website: www.acrw.net. E-mail loop, online courses, critique groups, and newsletter for members. Send membership inquiries to address above. Membership (470) open. Sponsors a contest open to nonmembers. Sponsoring a seminar in Nashville, September 15-18, 2005, speaker: Karen Ball; and in Houston, September 2006.

AMERICAN CHRISTIAN WRITERS SEMINARS. Sponsors conferences in various locations around the country (see individual states for dates and places). Call or write to be placed on mailing list for any conference. Events are Friday and Saturday unless otherwise noted. Brochures usually mailed three months prior to event. Contact: Reg Forder, Box 110390, Nashville TN 37222. 1-800-21-WRITE. Website: www.ACWriters.com.

CHRISTIAN WRITERS FELLOWSHIP INTL. (CWFI). Contact: Sandy Brooks, 1624 Jefferson Davis Rd., Clinton SC 29325-6401. (864)697-6035. E-mail: cwfi@cwfi-online.org. Website: www.cwfi-online.org. To contact Sandy Brooks personally: sandybrooks@cwfi-online.org. No meetings, but offers market consultations, critique service, writers books, and conference workshop tapes. Connects writers living in the same area, and helps start writers' groups. Membership (1,000+) open.

FAITH, HOPE & LOVE is the inspirational chapter of Romance Writers of America. Dues for the chapter are $24/yr., but you must also be a member of RWA to join (dues $75/yr.). Chapter offers these services: online list service for members, a Web page, 20-pg. bimonthly newsletter, annual contest, monthly online guest chats with multipublished authors and industry professionals, connects critique partners by mail or e-mail, and latest romance-market information. To join, contact RWA National Office, 16000 Stuebner Airline Rd., Ste. 140, Spring TX 77379. (832)717-5200. Fax (832)717-5201. Website: www.rwanational.org. Or go to FHL Website: www.faithhopelove-rwa.org. Inspirational Readers Choice Contest by subgenre categories for published works; deadline April 1, 2005; cash prizes. Send SASE for guidelines. Membership (150+) open.

NATIONAL ASSN. OF WOMEN WRITERS. Secular. Box 183812, Arlington TX 76096. Phone/fax toll-free (866)821-5829. E-mail: naww@onebox.com. Website: www.naww.org.

*ORTHODOX AUTHOR'S ASSN. National organization. Contact: Donna Jones, 1563 Three Sisters Way, Kodiak AK 99615. (907)486-2529. E-mail: seraphima@ak.net. Membership (70) open. May hold a conference in 2005. This group is currently reorganizing, but not defunct.

PEN-SOULS (prayer and support group, not a critique group). Conducted entirely by e-mail. Contact: Janet Ann Collins, PO Box 3083, Alameda CA 94501-3415. (510)522-7681. E-mail: onwords@alamedanet.net. Membership (14) open.

THE PRESBYTERIAN WRITERS GUILD. No regular meetings. National writers' organization with a quarterly newsletter. Dues $15/year. Contact: Nancy Regensburger, 3111 Greenridge Dr., Lancaster PA 17601-1369. Membership (220) open. Sponsors contests for members each year. Sponsors annual conference.

*WORDS OF WORSHIP ONLINE CRITIQUE GROUP. For fiction writers only. Members are placed in a group with 2-5 writers of similar interests. This is a Yahoo group and there is no charge for joining. Leader: Meredith Efken. Sign up on their Website at: http://groups.yahoo.com/group/wordsofworship. Membership (20) open.

THE WRITING ACADEMY. Contact: Inez Schneider, 4010 Singleton Rd., Rockford IL 61114. (815)877-9675. E-mail: Inezmarie@aol.com. Website: www.wams.org. Membership (75) open. Sponsors year-round correspondence writing program and annual seminar in August (held in various locations); currently in Minneapolis.

Note: If your group is not listed here, please send information to Sally Stuart, 1647 S.W. Pheasant Dr., Aloha OR 97006. June 20 is the deadline for next year's edition.

EDITORIAL SERVICES

The following listing is included because so many writers contact me looking for experienced/qualified editors who can critique or evaluate their manuscripts. These people from all over the country offer this kind of service. I cannot personally guarantee the work of any of those listed, so you may want to ask for references or samples of their work.

The following abbreviations indicate what kinds of work they are qualified to do:

GE—general editing/
   manuscript evaluation
LC—line editing or
   copyediting

GH—ghostwriting
CA—coauthoring
B—brochures

NL—newsletters
SP—special projects
BCE—book contract evaluation

The following abbreviations indicate the types of material they evaluate:

A—articles
SS—short stories
P—poetry
F—fillers
N—novels
NB—nonfiction books

BP—book proposals
JN—juvenile novels
PB—picture books
QL—query letter
BS—Bible studies

GB—gift books
TM—technical material
E—essays
D—devotionals
S—scripts

Always send a copy they can write on and an SASE for return of your material.

(*) Indicates that editorial service did not return questionnaire
(#) Indicates updated from Website, brochure or other sources
(+) Indicates new listing

ARIZONA

CARLA'S MANUSCRIPT SERVICE/CARLA BRUCE, 10229 W. Andover Ave., Sun City AZ 85351-4509. Phone/fax (623)876-4648. E-mail: CarlaBrc@aol.com. Call/e-mail/write. GE/LC/GH/typesetting. Does A/SS/P/F/NB/BS/GB/TM/E/D. Charges by the page or gives project estimate after evaluation. Does ghostwriting for pastors and teachers; professional typesetting. Twenty-two years ghostwriting/editing; 10 years typesetting.

PROFESSIONAL PROOFREADING/JODI DECKER, 5642 W. Carol Ave., Glendale AZ 85302. (623)939-1199. E-mail: jodidecker@msn.com. Call/e-mail/write. GE/LC. Does N/NB/BP/QL/JN/E. Charges by the page. Has MEd in education; BA in communication; college writing teacher, editor of 5 books; award-winning freelance writer. References available.

CALIFORNIA

CHRISTIAN COMMUNICATOR MANUSCRIPT CRITIQUE SERVICE/SUSAN TITUS OSBORN, 3133 Puente St., Fullerton CA 92835-1952. (714)990-1532. Toll-free (877)428-7992. (714)990-1532. Fax (714)990-0310. E-mail: Susanosb@aol.com. Website: www.christiancommunicator.com. Call/e-mail/write. For book, send material with $115 deposit. Staff of 14 editors. GE/LC/GH/CA/SP/BCE. Does A/SS/P/F/N/NB/BP/JN/PB/QL/

BS/GB/TM/E/D/S. $72 for short pieces/picture books. Three chapter-book proposal $115. Additional editing $25/hr. Twenty-six years experience.

DARLENE HOFFA, 512 Juniper St., Brea CA 92821. (714)990-5980. E-mail: jack.darlene .hoffa@adelphia.net. E-mail contact. GE. Does A/F/NB/BP/D. Eighteen years experience; author of 11 books. Charges $20/hr. or $1.50/ms pg.

KAREN O'CONNOR COMMUNICATIONS/KAREN O'CONNOR, 2050 Pacific Beach Dr., #205, San Diego CA 92109-6269. (858)483-3184. Fax (858)483-0427. E-mail: karen@karen oconnor.com. Website: www.karenoconnor.com. E-mail. GE/LC/SP/BCE. Does A/F/NB/BP/ QL/PB/BS/GB/E/D. One-hour free consultation; $75/hr or flat fee depending on project. Has 25+ years of teaching writing for universities and other accredited institutions.

LAURA JENSEN WALKER, PO Box 601325, Sacramento CA 95860. (916)489-9269. E-mail: Ljenwalk@aol.com. Website: www.laurajensenwalker.com. Write/e-mail/call (before 9 p.m. PT); send $50 deposit. GE/B. Does A/NB/BP/QL (nonfiction only). Charges $50/hr. Freelance editor; writing workshop instructor; former copywriter at a secular publishing house; former reporter, newspaper columnist, and copyeditor for a newspaper wire service; BA in journalism; author of 7 books and hundreds of articles.

LAURAINE SNELLING/KMB COMMUNICATIONS, INC., 19872 Highline Rd., Tehachapi CA 93561-7796. (661)823-0669. Fax (661)823-9427. E-mail: TLsnelling@yahoo.com. Website: www.LauraineSnelling.net. Call/write/e-mail. GE. Does N/BP/QL/JN. Charges $50/hr. with $100 deposit, or by the project after discussion with client. Author of 45 books (YA and adult fiction, 2 nonfiction).

LIGHTHOUSE EDITING/DR. LON ACKELSON, 13326 Community Rd., #11, Poway CA 92064-4754. (858)748-9258. Fax (858)748-7431. E-mail: Isaiah68LA@aol.com. Website: www.lighthouseedit.com. E-mail/write. GE/LC/GH/CA/B/NL/BCE. Does A/SS/N/NB/BP/ QL/BS/E/D. Charges $30 for article/short story critique; $50 for 3-chapter book proposal. Send SASE for full list of fees. Editor since 1981; senior editor 1984-2002.

*PATRICIA M. BELCHER TRANSCRIPTION SERVICE, 21909 Tranquil Ln., Anderson CA 96007-8331. Transcribes tapes and the spoken word into the computer.

SHIRL'S EDITING SERVICE/SHIRL THOMAS, 9379 Tanager Ave., Fountain Valley CA 92708-6557. (714)968-5726. E-mail: Shirlth@aol.com. Call/e-mail/write, and send material with $60 deposit. GE/LC/GH/CA/Rewriting. Does A/SS/P/F/N/NB/BP/QL/BS/GB/TM/E/D/greeting cards/synopses. Consultation/evaluation, $60/hr.; evaluation/critique, $60/hr.; copyediting $55/hr.; content editing/rewriting, $65/hr. Teaches two 6-week classes, three times a year, "Stepping Stones to Getting Published," and "Writing for the Greeting Card Market."

VICKI HESTERMAN, PhD/WRITING, EDITING, PHOTOGRAPHY, PO Box 6788, San Diego CA 92166. E-mail: vhvh@earthlink.net. E-mail/write; will follow with phone call. GE/LC/CA/SP. Does A/NB/BP/QL/BS/GB/E/D/photo books, memoirs. Quotes/rates based on project. Edits/develops nonfiction material, including editorials; works with book and article writers and publishers as coauthor, line editor, or in editorial development.

COLORADO

ALPHA TRANSCRIPTION/CHERYL A. JONES/MIKE COLCHIN, 1832 S. Lee St., Unit G, Lakewood CO 80232-6255. (303)978-9596. E-mail: alphatranscription@juno.com. E-mail/write. Typing for authors, preferably from cassette tapes, but will consider legible longhand material. Rate determined after discussion with client. Has worked with Dr. Larry Crabb, David Wilkerson, and other authors since 1996.

+ARIEL COMMUNICATIONS & DESIGN, INC./DEBBIE BARKER, 18445 Shady Knoll Ct., Peyton CO 80831. (719)749-0166. Fax (719)749-0188. E-mail: dbarker@cnonline.net. Editing and proofreading. No poetry. Call for rates and turn-around times.

MARKETING CONSULTANT/CECILE COOPER HIGGINS, 11126 W. 69th Pl., Arvada CO 80004. (303)456-1511. E-mail: cecilehiggins@yahoo.com. A marketing consultant for the publishing world. Regularly leads workshops and gives talks on self-publishing marketing. Consults on an individual basis with people seeking marketing advice on self-publishing.

OMEGA EDITING/MICHAEL P. COLCHIN, 1832 S. Lee St., Unit G, Lakewood CO 80232-6255. (303)978-0880. E-mail: omegaediting@juno.com. E-mail. GE/LC/GH/CA/B/NL/SP. Does A/SS/NB/BP/QL/BS/TM/D. Charges $45/hr. and up, or by the project after discussion with client. Works in partnership with authors and publishers as ghostwriter, coauthor, editor, or in editorial development. Published book and article author, 10 years experience as freelance editor.

+SCRIBBLE COMMUNICATIONS/BRAD LEWIS, Colorado Springs CO. Phone/fax (719)260-8651. E-mail: scribblecom@adelphia.net. Website: www.scribblecom.com. E-mail contact. GE/GH/CA/SP/developmental/substantive editing. Does A/NB/BP/BS/Website content. Edited 60 books; former senior book and magazine editor; 5+ years as a freelancer. Charges $40/hr. for developmental editing, or will negotiate a project rate.

STANFORD CREATIVE SERVICES/ERIC STANFORD, 7645 N. Union Blvd. PMB 235, Colorado Springs CO 80920. (719)599-7808. Fax (719)590-7555. E-mail: eric@stanford creative.com. Website: www.stanfordcreative.com. E-mail. GE/LC/GH/CA/B/NL/SP. Does A/SS/F/N/NB/BP/QL/BS/TM/D/book doctoring. Charges $20/hr. and up. Former senior editor; independent since 1998.

A WAY WITH WORDS/RENEE GRAY-WILBURN, 1820 Smoke Ridge Dr., Colorado Springs CO 80919-3458. (719)265-6626. Fax (719)266-8040. E-mail: waywords@earthlink.net. Call/e-mail. LC/CA/B/NL/SP. Does A/SS/F/N/NB/JN/PB/BS/GB/TM/E/D. Line editing/copyediting: $20/hr. Project prices negotiable. Has had a writing company for over 10 years. Works with authors, Christian publishers, ministries, and small businesses.

+THE WELL-WRITTEN WORD/NICKIE DUMKE, 1877 Polk Ave., Louisville CO 80027-1117. Phone/fax (303)666-8253. E-mail: dumke@earthlink.net. Website: www.food-allergy.org. Call or e-mail. GE/LC/GH/CA/NL/SP/health and medical editing and writing. Does A/SS/F/N/NB/JN/PB/BS/TM/E/D/cookbooks. Fifteen years experience in writing, editing, and publishing; author of 4 books and several booklets. Charges $25/hr.; flat rate for project after evaluating material.

FLORIDA

LESLIE SANTAMARIA, 1024 Walnut Creek Cove, Winter Springs FL 32708-4735. E-mail: san tamaria@mpinet.net. E-mail inquiry or send material by surface mail (1-chapter book proposal, article up to 2,500 words, or poems to 5 pages) with $50 for an initial review. GE/LC. Does A/SS/N/NB/BP/QL/JN/BS/TM/E/D. Charges $30 per 2,500 words for initial review; by the page or project for additional editing. Published author, book reviewer, and experienced book editor. Will give an overall critique, edit content, and copyedit. Articles/stories to 1,500 wds. $65. Book Proposals $100. Children's picture book $65. Juvenile fiction $80. E-query about other services.

LIGHTPOST COMMUNICATIONS/SEAN FOWLDS, 305 Pinecrest Rd., Mount Dora FL 32757-5929. (352)383-2485. Fax (775)249-5732. E-mail: sfowlds@earthlink.net. Website: www.home.earthlink.net/~sfowlds. E-mail. GE/LC/B/NL/SP. Does A/SS/P/F/NB/BP/QL/PB/BS/GB/TM/E/D/S. Offers speaking, writing, and editing services. Negotiated sliding scale starting at $25/hr. Former editor of a national publication.

+REACH OUT EXPRESSIONS, INC./CAROL C. TONGUE, PO Box 1861, Mt. Dora FL 32756. (352)669-6789. E-mail: reachoutpress@earthlink.net.

*WILDE CREATIVE SERVICES/GARY A. WILDE, 183 Lawn St., Oviedo FL 32765-8089.

(407)977-3869. GE/GH/CA/SP. A publishing support company providing book doctoring, editorial project management, collaborative writing, and copywriting services. Negotiated flat fee based on $50/hr. Former staff editor for major publisher.

GEORGIA

BONNIE C. HARVEY, PhD, 5579B Chamblee Dunwoody Rd., Ste. 357, Atlanta GA 30338. (404)299-6149. Fax (404)297-6651. E-mail: BoncaH@aol.com. Call/e-mail. GE/LC/ GH/CA/SP/theology. Does A/SS/P/N/NB/QL/JN/BS/GB/E/D/S/theological and academic articles. Charges $20/hr. for reading/critiquing; $20/hr. for proofreading; $25/hr. for editing, $45-75/hr. for rewriting. Has PhD in English; 13 years teaching college-level English; 24 years experience as editor; has ghostwritten books and authored 22 books. Also does some agenting.

+JANICE CHRISTIAN, PO Box 60, Tate GA 30177. (770)735-3200. Cell (615)414-7855. E-mail: janice.christian@lifeway.com. Write with deposit of 50%. GE/LC/B/NL/SP/typesetting & design. Does A/SS/P/N/NB/JN/PB/BS/TM/E/D/S/catalogs, ads, typesetting galleys, music masters, scientific, mathematics, course textbooks (school or Sunday school). Thirty-five year in typesetting and design business with copyediting; graphics director for three quarterly journals. Charges by the hour, page, or project (after evaluation).

+JILL COX'S WRITE MIND, 1986 Morning Walk, Acworth GA 30102. Phone/fax (770)917-1539. E-mail: jcoxwritemind@aol.com. E-mail/write. GE/LC/SP/BCE/media-related résumés and book proposals. Does A/N/NB/BP/QL/BS/GB/E/D/S. Thirteen years in television; 3 years as a professor; currently a magazine editor. Charges $15-25/hr or $5-9/pg., depending on service provided.

LAMBLIGHTERS LITERARY SERVICE/CISI MORROW-SMITH, 248 Quail Run, Roswell GA 30076-3182. (770)518-6101. Call/write/send with $25-35 deposit. GE/LC/GH/CA/ SP/BCE/tutors writing (child or adult). Does A/SS/P/F/N/NB/BP/QL/JN/PB/TM/E/D/S. Phone consultation $25 (initial hour free). Charges $35-75/hr., $30 min.; long-term projects negotiable. Has BA in journalism/creative writing; 28 years experience.

POSITIVE DIFFERENCE COMMUNICATIONS/ROSS WEST, 100 Martha Dr., Rome GA 30165-4138. (706)232-9325. Fax (706)235-2716. E-mail: drrwest@aol.com. Website: www.positivedifference.com. Call/write/e-mail. GE/LC/GH. Does A/NB/BS. Charges by the page or provides a project cost estimate. Published professional; author of two books and several articles; more than 20 years editing experience.

IDAHO

*MAX JAMES, 393 W. Willowbrook Dr., Meridian ID 83642. (208)288-0983. E-mail: Max Diana@aol.com.

ILLINOIS

ALICE 'N INK/ALICE PEPPLER, 6007 N. Sheridan Rd., Apt. 6D, Chicago IL 60660-3061. (773)878-5943. Fax (773)878-6264. E-mail: apeppler@aol.com. Website: www.apeppler .com. Call/e-mail/write. GE/LC. Does A/SS/P/F/N/NB/BP/QL/JN/PB/BS/GB/E/D. Three-chapter book proposal, including market analysis $103; additional editing $30/hr. Publishing experience of 25 years. Quality work; quick turnaround.

+AMACK EDITING SERVICES/JILL S. AMACK, 808 Corday Dr., #202, Naperville IL 60540. (630)848-1948. E-mail: amackediting@earthlink.net. Website: www.pensite.org (listed under Membership). E-mail. GE/LC. Does A/N/NB/BP/QL/PB/BS/GB/TM/D/back-cover copy.

Full-time copy editor; freelance editing for over 6 years; newsletter editor; graduate of Denver Publishing Institute. Charges $25/hr. or flat rate.

+INNOVATIVE MEDIA SOLUTIONS/BILL SPILMAN, 529 N. Cherry St., Galesburg IL 61401. (309)342-3211. Fax (309)342-3212. E-mail: Bill@innovativemediasolutions.com. Provides PR and editorial services.

THE WRITER'S EDGE, PO Box 1266, Wheaton IL 60189. E-mail: info@writersedge service.com. Website: www.WritersEdgeService.com. No phone calls. A manuscript screening service for 75 cooperating Christian publishers. Charges $79 to evaluate a book proposal and if publishable, they will send a synopsis of it to 75 publishers who might be interested. If not publishable they will tell how to improve it. If interested, send an SASE for guidelines and a Book Information Form; request a form via e-mail or copy from Website. The Writer's Edge now handles previously published books that are out of print and available for reprint. Requires a different form, but cost is the same. Reviews novels, nonfiction books, juvenile novels, Bible studies, devotionals, biography, and theology. See Website for details.

INDIANA

APRIL STIER, 7768 N. 100 E., Ossian IN 46777-9360. (260)622-4756. E-mail: april_lynn03 @hotmail.com. E-mail/Write. GE/LC/CA. Does A/SS/F/N/NB/BP/QL/BS/GB/E/D. Charges $2-3/pg.; fillers $10; queries $15; devotionals $10-15. Send SASE for rate sheet. BA in English, AA in writing, BA in biblical literature; published writer.

DENEHEN, INC./DR. DENNIS E. HENSLEY, 6824 Kanata Ct., Fort Wayne IN 46815-6388. (260)744-8647. Fax (260)485-9891. E-mail: dnhensley@H51mail.com. E-mail; send ms. With full payment. GE/LC. Does A/SS/P/F/N/NB/JN/BS/GB/E/D/comedy/academic articles/editorials/Op-Ed pieces/columns/speeches/interviews. Rate sheet for SASE. Author of 43 books; PhD in English; college English professor.

EPIPHANY LANE PRODUCTIONS/STEPHEN R. CLARK, PO Box 551, Fishers IN 46038-0551. (317)435-9673. E-mail: stephen@stephenrclark.com. Website: www.StephenRClark.com. E-mail. LC/GH/CA/SP/Websites/speechwriting/consulting. Does A/NB/BS/TM/E/D. Charges $95/hour (negotiable). Projects negotiable. Ghostwriting $5,000 and up. Details on Website. Writer/editor for 20+ years.

+XARIS COM/JAMES WATKINS, PO Box 117, Laotto IN 46763-0117. (260)897-2575. E-mail: jim@jameswatkins.com. Website: www.jameswatkins.com. E-mail; send $50 deposit. GE. Does A/NB/BP/D. Award-winning author & editor; 20+ years experience. Charge $50 for 2,000 words of critique, editing, market suggestions.

KENTUCKY

BETTY L. WHITWORTH, 15763 Leitchfield Rd., Leitchfield KY 42754. (270)257-2461. E-mail: Blwhit@bbtel.com. Call/e-mail/write. GE/CA/SP. Does A/SS/N/NB/BP/QL/JN/BS/E/D. Typing, $2 pg.; proofreading/moderate corrections $1.00-1.50/pg.; negotiable fees on projects. Retired language arts teacher, newspaper columnist, and feature writer; helped 7 writers get books published. Clergy get 10% discount.

MARILYN A. ANDERSON, 127 Sycamore Dr., Louisville KY 40223-2956. (502)244-0751. Fax (502)452-9260. E-mail: shelle12@aol.com. Call/e-mail. GE/LC. Does A/F/NB/BS/TM/E/D. Charges $15-20/hr. for proofreading; $25/hr. for extensive editing; or negotiable by the job or project. Holds an MA and BA in English; former high school English teacher; freelance consultant since 1993. References available.

MARYLAND

+OPINE PUBLISHING INTERACTIVE SERVICE FOR FIRST BOOK AUTHORS. This service gives writers a direct, interactive publisher's contact. Gain a unique view of key elements most likely to influence a publisher. Obtain publisher's view of frequently overlooked items, a unique query packet, personal guidance and critique of documents, plus thorough critique of three manuscript chapters. Contact: publisher@opinebooks.com. Participation does not insure consideration for publication by Opine.

*OWEN-SMITH & ASSOCIATES, INC./RHONDA OWEN-SMITH, 2916 Old Court Rd., Pikesville MD 21208. (410)659-2247. Fax (410)659-9758. E-mail: mapreos@aol.com. Does GH/CA/B/NL/SP/BP / Biographies / Market Analysis / Marketing and PR Plans / Potential Publisher Identification / Press Kits / Interview Scheduling / Book Signings. Will consider other requests. Charges a flat fee or hourly rate based upon the project.

MASSACHUSETTS

LESLIE H. STOBBE, 229 Brickett Hill Circle, Haverhill MA 01830-1587. (978)374-5289. Fax (978)945-0517. E-mail: lstobbe@gis.net. E-mail. GE/GH/CA/NL/SP/BCE. Does NB/BP/BS/D. Considers writing assignments of all kinds, including promotional and fundraising, coauthoring with pastors and professionals, biographies, research-based Bible studies, adult curriculum, small group Bible studies, major rewriting of manuscripts, specialized editing. Fifty years as writer/editor/agent. Able to meet client needs despite tight deadlines. Charges $50-75/hr.; rate sheet on request.

WORD PRO/BARBARA A. ROBIDOUX, 127 Gelinas Dr., Chicopee MA 01020-4813. (413)592-4386. Fax (413)594-8375. E-mail: Ebwordpro@aol.com. Call/e-mail. GE/LC/GH/CA. Does A/SS/F/N/NB/BP/QL/BS/GB/TM/E/D. Charges $25/hr.; $115 for book proposal/3 chapters. BA in English; 18 years as freelancer; book reviewer; on staff of TCC Manuscript Critique Service.

MICHIGAN

CALLED AND READY WRITERS CONSULTATION SERVICE/MARY EDWARDS, 20700 Civic Center Dr.. Ste. 170, Southfield MI 48076. (248)663-2363. Fax (313)861-7578. E-mail: mwwginc@aol.com. Website: www.thecalledandreadywriters.org. E-mail. GE/LC/CA/B/NL/SP. Does A/SS/F/N/NB/QL/BS/GB/E/D. Charges $45/hr. Twenty plus years editing books and writing; copyeditor for secular newspaper.

WALLIS EDITORIAL SERVICES/DIANA WALLIS, 547 Cherry St. S.E., #6C, Grand Rapids MI 49503-4755. Phone/fax (616)459-8836. E-mail: WallisEdit@sirus.com. Call/e-mail. GE/LC/GH/CA/B/NL/SP / research / fact and reference checking / rewriting / proofreading / markup for typesetting / coding for electronic publications. Does A/SS/F/N/NB/BS/TM/E/D/advertising and promotional material, Website content, technical material for nontechnical readers. Charges $25/hr. Will negotiate on larger projects (20+ hours). Deposit of 50% required for first-time clients. Commercial advertising and technical writing experience; published book author and editor.

MINNESOTA

NORTH COUNTRY TRANSCRIPTION: Writing, Editing and Secretarial Services/CONNIE PETTERSEN, (Psalm 96:13). (218)927-6176. E-mail: sonshinegirl56431@yahoo.com.

Call or e-mail. Manuscript typing; edit for punctuation/spelling/grammar, etc. Published freelance writer (fiction & nonfiction); 27 years secretarial/transcription experience. IBM compatible computer, satellite Internet, Windows XP, Corel 8, and Microsoft Office 2000; voice file digital transcription or standard and microcassette transcribers. Fees: Negotiable (about $12/hr., $1.50/double-spaced page or .10-.11/65-character line), plus postage. Free estimates.

MISSOURI

BLUE MOUNTAIN EDITORIAL SERVICE/BARBARA WARREN, Rte. 3 Box 3200, Exeter MO 65647. (417)835-3235. E-mail: barbarawarren@mo-net.com. E-mail. GE/LC. Does N/BP/QL/JN. Fees negotiable. Seventeen years experience.

PRO WORD WRITING & EDITORIAL SERVICES/MARY R. RUTH, PO Box 155, Labadie MO 63055-0155. (636)742-3663. E-mail: prowordusa@juno.com. Call/e-mail. GE/LC/SP/manuscript or script typing, scan hard copy to disk, proofreading, indexing. Does A/SS/N/NB/BP/JN/BS/TM/E/D/S/biographies/textbooks. Call to discuss your project. Reasonable rates/professional results. MC/Visa available.

MONTANA

NOVELEDIT/JIM COTTON, 652 Treece Gulch Rd., Stevensville MT 59870. (406)777-5191. E-mail: noveledit2003@yahoo.com. Website: www.noveledit.com. Call/e-mail/write; send 1/2 of estimated fee. GE/LC. Does N only; specializes in tutorial critique for novels. Also online editing using MS Word 2000. Charges $3/pg. for critique; electronic rates available. Has 25 years experience in journalism and magazine editing; novel critiquing since 1995.

NEW HAMPSHIRE

AMDG ENTERPRISES/SALLY WILKINS, Box 273, Amherst NH 03031-0393. (603)673-9331. E-mail: SEDWilkins@aol.com. Write. GE/LC. Does A/F/JN/ PB/BS/TM. Rate sheet for SASE.

NEW JERSEY

DAYSTAR WRITING CONSULTANTS/DR. MARY ANN DIORIO, Box 405, Millville NJ 08332-0405. (856)327-1231. Fax (856)327-0291. E-mail: daystar405@aol.com. Website: www.daystarministries.com/writcons.htm. E-mail. GE/LC. Does A/SS/P/copy for ads and PR material/résumés/business letters; also translations in French, Italian, and Spanish. Rates on request. Freelance writer, 25 yrs.; editor, 11 yrs.; former college instructor; PhD in literature/language.

D'EDRA Y. ARMSTRONG. New Jersey. E-mail: MLHUB21@aol.com or thesoulssolace @aol.com. E-mail. LC/GH/CA/B/NL/SP. Does SS/N/NB/QL/E/D. Charges $20/hr.; technical $40/hr. Over 15 years copywriting/editing experience.

WRITER'S RELIEF, INC./RONNIE L. SMITH, 245 Teaneck Rd., #3, Ridgefield Park NJ 07660-2003. (201)641-3003. Fax (201)641-1253. E-mail: Ronnie@wrelief.com. Website: www.wrelief.com. E-mail. GE/LC. Does SS/P/N/NB/BP/QL/JN/PB/E. An author's submission service, handling your manuscript submissions for an hourly rate of $45-60 (plus postage and copying), or a flat fee after completing review. Prepares manuscripts, proofreads, writes query and cover letters, tracks submissions, keeps records, etc.

NEW YORK

ELIZABETH CRISPIN, Box 134 Schulyer Rd., Oswegatchie NY 13670-3126. (315)848-7401. Fax (315)848-9860. E-mail: JMYPoet@aol.com. Write/call/e-mail, or send with $25 deposit and SASE. GE/LC/GH/CA/B/SP. Does A/SS/P/BP/JN/PB/BS/GB/E/D. Charges $25 basic charge; others on contractual basis. Published book and magazine author.

+I AM THE VINE PUBLISHING SERVICES/SUSAN RESCIGNO, PO Box 497, Crompond NY 10517. (914)844-5217. E-mail: susan311@att.net. Website: www.iamthevine.net. Call/e-mail. GE/LC/NL. Does A/SS/N/NB/JN. Fifteen years experience in publishing industry. Hourly or page rates available for copyediting or proofreading.

LAST WORD OFFICE WORKS/MARY A. LACLAIR, PO Box 435, Vernon NY 13476-0435. (315)829-3356. Fax (315)829-3356 (auto switch). E-mail: mlaclair1@juno.com. Write; send material with $25 deposit. GE/LC. Does A/SS/N/JN/BS/D. Estimates for projects, about $2-5/pg. or $10-20/hr. (depending on amount of editing needed). Published writer; Op-Ed guest column in NY and FL newspapers, weekly columnist in VA newspaper, published articles in 5 different national magazines.

*WRITING-RELATED SERVICES/LAURA S. MCCORMICK, PO Box 300, Scottsville NY 14546-0300. Toll-free phone/fax (866)733-3769. Phone/fax (585)889-5256. E-mail: Laura SueMordoff@juno.com, or LSMcCormick@juno.com. GE/LC/B/NL/SP. Does A/NB/TM/E/presentation and training materials. Fees negotiable; min. consulting fee $30/hr., plus travel expenses for over 50 miles from Rochester NY.

NORTH CAROLINA

ANNA W. FISHEL, 3416 Hunting Creek Dr., Pfafftown NC 27040. (336)924-5880. E-mail: awfishel@triad.rr.com. Call/write/e-mail. GE/CA/SP. Does A/SS/P/N/NB/JN/E/D. Charges by the hour. Estimates offered. Professional editor for over 17 years; editor with major Christian publishing house for over 10 years; published author.

*PREP PUBLISHING/PATTY SLEEM, 1110 1/2 Hay St., Fayetteville NC 28305. (910)483-6611. Fax (910)483-2439. E-mail: preppub@aol.com. Website: www.prep-pub.com. Write. GE/LC/SP. Does N/NB. Project price based on written query and initial free telephone consultation. BA in English, MBA from Harvard, author of more than 25 books.

OKLAHOMA

CHRISTY PHILLIPPE, 5736 S. Quincy Pl., Tulsa OK 74105. (918)749-0098. E-mail: christy 6871@aol.com. E-mail. GE/LC/GH/SP/research/indexing. Does A/SS/NB/BP/QL/BS/GB/D. Critiques: $3/pg.; line editing: $15-17/hr.; other projects negotiable. Deposit usually required. Ten year's experience in Christian publishing; former editor; ghostwritten books on bestseller list; former college English instructor.

EPISTLEWORKS CREATIONS/JOANN RENO WRAY, 812 W. Glenwood St., Broken Arrow OK 74011-6419. (918)451-4017. E-mail: epistle1@epistleworks.com. Website: http://epistle works.com. Call/write/e-mail (prefers). GE/LC/GH/CA/B/NL/SP/research. Does A/SS/P/F/N/NB/BP/D. Charges start at $25/hr. Accepts checks, money orders, or payment by PayPal. See site for details on services. Most editing requires min. $25 deposit. Binding estimates given. Designs and creates Websites. Offers e-mail classes on writing. Available as speaker/teacher. Experienced artist, writer, and editor since 1974.

*KNUTH EDITORIAL SERVICES/DEBORAH L. KNUTH, 7642 E. 49th St., Apt. A, Tulsa OK 74145. (918)384-0787. E-mail: austriabound@yahoo.com. E-mail or send with $50 deposit. GE/LC/GH/CA/B/NL/SP/BCE. Does A/SS/F/N/NB/BP/QL/JN/PB/BS/GB/TM/E/D/S.

Charges $20/hr. Specializes in historical fiction. Has a BA in English/creative writing, is a graduate of the Writer's Digest Writing School, and has 6 years editing experience.

WINGS UNLIMITED/CRISTINE BOLLEY, PO Box 691532, Tulsa OK 74169-1532. (918)250-9239. Fax (918)250-9597. E-mail: WingsUnlimited@aol.com. Website: www.wingsunlimited.com. E-mail. GE/GH/CA/SP. Does NB/D. Charges by the page; negotiated in advance. Former editorial acquisition editor with 25 yrs. experience in book development of best-selling titles and author/coauthor/ghostwriter of 30+ titles. Also available to teach workshops at writer's conferences.

+THE WRITE WORD/IRENE MARTIN, PO Box 300332, Midwest City OK 73140-5641. E-mail: write1word@aol.com. Write/e-mail (detailing project). GE/LC. Does A/SS/F/N/BP/QL/JN. Charges $3/pg., min. $15 for 5 pgs. Workshops and editorial consulting done on a project-by-project basis. Has MA in English Creative Writing; published novelist; instructor/editor for Writer's Digest School; former college writing instructor.

OREGON

***ANNA LLOYD STONE**, PO Box 2251, Lake Oswego OR 97035. (503)638-3705. Fax (503)638-6131. E-mail: mizanna@att.net. E-mail. LC/SP. Does A/SS/P/F/N/NB/BP/QL/JN/PB/BS/GB/TM/E/D/S/advertising/copywriting. Charges $35/hr. for copyediting; $50/hr. for copywriting. Send ms/SASE or can edit by e-mail. BA in humanities/writing, 3 years copywriting experience.

BALDWIN WRITERS SERVICES/STANLEY C. BALDWIN, 12900 S.E. Nixon, Portland OR 97222. (503)659-2974. E-mail: scbaldwin@juno.com. Evaluation of your organizational publication; Writers Workshops; manuscript critiquing by mail, contract evaluation. Send an SASE for rate sheet.

BONNIE LEON, PO Box 774, Glide OR 97443. (541)496-3787. E-mail: leon@rosenet.net. Call/write/e-mail. GE/LC/GH/NL/SP. Does A/SS/F/N/BP/QL/D. Charges $25/hr. ($50 min.); larger projects negotiated. Author of 10 books; editorial services, writing instructor, speaker.

BOOKHOUSE COMMUNICATIONS/TRICIA LAWRENCE, Box 24687, Federal Way WA 98093-1687. Phone/fax (253)661-0371. E-mail: sensibility@proaxis.com. Website: www.realbrilliant.com. Call. GE/LC/GH/CA/B/NL/SP. Does A/SS/N/NB/BP/QL/JN/PB/GB. Nine years as a published author and freelance editor. Charges $5/pg. and up, or $250 for a book proposal evaluation. Call or e-mail for details.

EDITING INTERNATIONAL, LLC./ELIZABETH LYON, 2123 Marlow Ln., Eugene OR 97401-6431. 541-344-9118. E-mail: info@4-edit.com. Website: www.4-edit.com. Call/e-mail/write. GE/LC/SP. Does A/SS/N/NB/BP/QL/JN/TM/E/screenplays. Charges $75/hr. for consulting and editing short manuscripts; $7/pg. For longer manuscripts; $1,200 for book proposal. Staff of editors with many published clients, and many publishing credits of their own.

+EDITING INTERNATIONAL, LLC/CAROL CRAIG, 2622 Willona Dr., Eugene OR 97408. (541)342-7300. E-mail: carollcraig@cs.com. Website: www.4-edit.com. Call/e-mail. GE/LC/GH/CA/B/NL/SP/BCE. Does A/SS/N/NB/BP/QL/JN/PB/BS/GB/TM/E/D/S. Offers multiple services with varying prices. See Website for full price list.

I'LL READ IT! EDITORIAL SERVICES/DONNA FLEISHER, 3404 S.W. Anchor Ave., #3, Lincoln City OR 97367. (541)994-2630. E-mail: donna@illreadit.com. Website: www.illreadit.com. Call/e-mail/write. GE/LC. Does SS/N/JN. Charges $300 flat fee for entire manuscript, which includes a complete edit and free future consultations.

MARCIA A. MITCHELL, 4144 Sunnyview Rd. N.E. #115, Salem OR 97305-1893. (503)588-0372. E-mail: b2nytr@msn.com. E-mail/write; send $25 deposit with ms. GE/LC/GH/CA/NL.

Does A/SS/F/N/NB/JN/D. Charges $25/hr for long projects; $25 for up to 5,000 wds.; $50 for 5,000-10,000 wds. Published writer.

*NANCY SUE BRANNEN, 183—63 S.W. 135th Ter., Tualatin OR 97062. (503)625-5807. E-mail: branfam@eschelon.com. LC.

PICKY, PICKY INK/SUE MIHOLER, 1075 Willow Lake Road N., Salem OR 97303-5790. (503)393-3356. E-mail: miholer@viser.net. E-mail. GE/LC. Does A/F/N/NB/BS/D. Manuscript preparation available. $20 an hour or negotiable by job. Freelance writer and copyeditor for several publishers for 6 years. "Helping you write it right," whether it's a postcard or a doctoral dissertation.

PRINT PREVIEW, INC./PAT JOHNSON, 10214 S.W. 36th Ct., Portland OR 97219-6100. (503)244-4460. Fax (503)244-4153. E-mail: pjdj01@aol.com. Call/e-mail/write. LC/NL/SP. Does A/SS/F/N/NB/BP/QL/JN/PB/BS/TM/D/S/typing. Charges $18/hr.; $35 min. Editing, proofreading experience.

SALLY STUART, 1647 S.W. Pheasant Dr., Aloha OR 97006. (503)642-9844. Fax (503)848-3658. E-mail: stuartcwmg@aol.com. Website: www.stuartmarket.com. Call/write/e-mail. GE/BCE/agent contracts. Does A/SS/N/NB/BP/GB/JN/E. Charges $35/hr. for critique; $40/hr. for consultations. Contact for availability. For books, send a copy of your book proposal: cover letter, chapter-by-chapter synopsis, and the first three chapters. Comprehensive publishing contract evaluation $75-125. Author of 31 books and over 37 years experience as a writer, teacher, marketing expert.

PENNSYLVANIA

IMPACT COMMUNICATIONS/DEBRA PETROSKY, 604 Chestnut St., 1st Floor, Irwin PA 15642-3536. Phone/fax (724)863-5906. E-mail: Editing4U@aol.com. Call. GE/LC. Does N/NB/TM. Charges $20/hr.; per page rates available. Satisfied self-publishers endorse our typesetting services. Very reasonable rates.

*SPREAD THE WORD/MAURCIA DELEAN HOUCK, 106 Danny Rd., Sanatoga PA 19464-7215. (610)970-6931. E-mail: mhouck@voicenet.com. E-mail/write. GE/LC. Does A/SS/F/NB/BP/QL/BS. Charges $1.75/pg. (double-spaced), or as quoted. Discount for over 200 pgs. Author of 2 books and over 1,500 articles and former newspaper editor.

*STRONG TOWER PUBLISHING/HEIDI NIGRO, PO Box 11412, Lancaster PA 17605. E-mail: strongtowerpub@earthlink.net. Website: www.strongtowerpublishing.com. GE/LC. Does A/SS/P/F/N/NB/QL/JN/PB/BS/GB/TM/E/D. Manuscript evaluation, $59-109; proofing, $2 per 250-word-page; copyediting, $3/pg. Provides free 5-page sample edit.

VAL CINDRIC EDITING & WRITING SERVICES, 662 N. Main St., Greensburg PA 15601-1695. (724)838-9011. Fax (724)838-9336. E-mail: pcindric@earthlink.net. Call/e-mail. GE/LC/GH/CA. Does A/SS/F/N/NB/BP/QL/JN/PB/BS/GB/TM. Fee based on complexity and subject matter of the material (call for rate); generally $1-2/pg. Reduced rate for nonprofits. Over twenty years experience in professional editing and coauthoring for Christian publishers, authors, pastors, and mission organizations.

WORDS FOR ALL REASONS/ELIZABETH ROSIAN, 108 Deerfield Ln., Johnstown PA 15905-5703. (814)255-4351. E-mail: words@charter.net. Write/e-mail (preferred). GE/LC/GH/CA/BCE. Does A/SS/P/F/N/NB/BP/QL/JN/PB/BS/GB/TM/E/D/S. Over 30 years experience in publishing/editing. Charges $1-1.50/pg.; send SASE for rate sheet.

WRITE HIS ANSWER MINISTRIES/MARLENE BAGNULL, LittD, 316 Blanchard Rd., Drexel Hill PA 19026-3507. Phone/fax: (610)626-6833. E-mail: mbagnull@aol.com. Website: www.writehisanswer.com. Call/write. GE/LC/typesetting. Does A/SS/N/NB/BP/JN/BS/D. Charges $30/hr.; estimates given. Call or write for information on At-Home Writing Workshops, a correspondence study program. Author of 5 books; compiler/editor of 3 books; over 1,000 sales to Christian periodicals.

TENNESSEE

+AT HOME WITH WORDS/SHARLA TAYLOR & MARYLANE WADE KOCH, PO Box 1513, Collierville TN 38027-1513. (901)853-6007. Fax (901)853-2071. E-mail: athomewith words@msn.com. Website: www.athomewithwords.com. E-mail or send material with $50 deposit. GE/LC/GH/CA/NL/SP. Does A/SS/F/N/NB/BP/QL/JN/BS/GB/TM (health-related)/ E/D/speech writing. Marylane edits graduate thesis papers and doctoral dissertations; contact her at rwkoch@worldnet.att.net. Charges $36/$50/$76 per hour, depending on work done (see Website for details).

CHRISTIAN WRITERS INSTITUTE MANUSCRIPT CRITIQUE SERVICE, PO Box 110390, Nashville TN 37222. Toll-free (800)21-WRITE. E-mail: ACWriters@aol.com. Website: www.ACWriters.com. Call/write. GE/LC/GH/CA/SP/BCE. Does A/SS/P/F/N/NB/BP/JN/PB/BS/ TM/E/D/S. Send SASE for rate sheet and submission slip.

DENNIS L. PETERSON EDITING & WRITING SERVICES, 7909 Tressa Cir., Powell TN 37849-3534. Phone/fax (865)947-0496. E-mail: DLPEdit@aol.com. Website: http://go .to/editing. Write/e-mail. LC/proofreading/workshops/seminars. Does A/SS/N/NB/BP/QL/ JN/BS/TM/E/D. Proofreading $15-20/hr.; copyediting $18-25/hr.; writing/rewriting $20-30/hr.; send SASE for rate card. Published writer since 1981; former sr. tech editor with Lockheed Martin; 13 years teaching experience; edited more than 90 books for Christian publishers.

EDIT PLUS/CHARLES STROHMER, PO Box 4325, Sevierville TN 37876. (865)453-7120. Fax (865)428-0029. E-mail: wiselife@esper.com. Call/e-mail. GE/LC/CA/NL/SP. Does A/NB/BP/QL/BS/TM/E/D. Twenty years of experience as author and editor for major Christian publishers. Call/e-mail to discuss project and rates. Rates vary according to the type of work, e.g., ms. Evaluation, line editing, rewriting, or book proposal.

THE YEOMAN'S SERVICE/VIRGINIA S. YOUMANS, 3227 Ella West Cir., Lynnville TN 38472-5228. (931)527-0101. E-mail: sergevirge@bellsouth.net. Website: www.bellsouthpwp .net/s/v/svyoumans. E-mail (preferred), write, or see Website; send ms/full payment. GE. Does N/NB/JN/BS/D. Charges $20/hour. BS in English, plus over 20 years experience as an editor.

TEXAS

+CARL F. PHILLIPS, 415 W. Hwy 100, Apt. 10, Port Isabel TX 78578. Phone/fax (956)943-2372. E-mail: CarlPhil10@aol.com. Contact by e-mail. GE/LC/GH/CA/B/NL/SP. Does A/SS/N/NB/BS/E/D. Has written a weekly column for 10 years. Hourly rate or page rate, depending on the project and time involved.

DALE SHOCKLEY, 25510 Foxbriar, Spring TX 77373. (281)350-2902. E-mail: dale@ daleshockley.com. Website: www.dayleshockley.com. E-mail or write. GE/LC/GH/CA/B/ NL/SP. Does A/SS/NB/GB/TM/E/D. Proofreading $45/hr.; critique $55/hr.; editing $65/hr. Details on Website (or by e-mail). Writing instructor, author, freelancer.

PWC EDITING/PAUL W. CONANT, 527 Bayshore Pl., Dallas TX 75217-7755. (972)913-9123. Fax (972)557-7558. E-mail: editor@pwc-editing.com. Website: www.pwc-editing.com. E-mail. LC/B/NL/SP/magazine editing. Does A/SS/N/NB/BS/TM/E/D/S/dissertations/text-books/Web pages. Writer, editor; proofreader for book publishers and magazines. Proofreading $15-25/hr.; word processing $15-18/hr.; and copyediting $20-25/hr. Projects by the hour; rush charges may also apply.

SYLVIA BRISKEY, Dallas TX. (214)521-7507. Call. GE/LC. Does P/JN/PB/BS/GB/children's stories/secular articles. Poetry, charges $5.60 plus $1/line; fiction $30 to 2,000 wds., $2.50/page thereafter. Writing teacher; writes children's books and poetry.

WORDS IN PROGRESS/CARRIE M. WOOD, 310 Lakewood Dr., Buda TX 78610-2575. (512)295-2592. E-mail: pclwood@netzero.net. Website: www.carriewood.com. E-mail or send synopsis and first three chapters with $30 deposit. GE. Does A/SS/N/NB/BP/QL/JN/PB/ BS/GB/D/S/ audio dramas. Charges $30/hr. (negotiable), discount for ACW and CWFI members. Introductory offer for new clients: $30 flat fee for 3 chapters. Quick turnaround. Project estimates after evaluation of services needed. Four years editing experience. References available.

UTAH

RIVERWRITERS.COM/KATHLEEN DAMP WRIGHT, (801)572-5227. Fax (801)572-5227. E-mail: kathleen@riverwriters.com. Website: www.riverwriters.com. E-mail. GE/LC. Does SS/N/synopsis. Also a writing coach. Charges by the hour; e-mail for current rate. Requires half payment up front. BA in journalism, 20+ years editing/writing experience.

VIRGINIA

+EDITOR FOR YOU/MELANIE RIGNEY, 4201 Wilson Blvd. #110328, Arlington VA 22203-1859. (571)235-1743. E-mail: info@editorforyou.com. Website: www.editorforyou.com, or www.melanierigney.com. Contact by e-mail. GE/LC/SP. Does N/NB/BP/E/memoirs. Charges $2.50/250 word ms. page; $200 for ms. evaluation & 5-page report; variable rates for content editing. Editor of Writer's Digest Magazine for 5 years; book editor/manager of Writer's Digest Books for 3 years; 25+ years of editing experience.

SCRIVEN COMMUNICATIONS/KATHIE NEE SCRIVEN, 1902 Stevens Rd., #1406, Woodbridge VA 22191-2748. Phone/fax (703)492-6442. Call/write. GE/LC/B/N/SP. Does A/SS/P/ F/N/NB/BP/QL/JN/PB/BS/GB/TM/E/D/S/ tracts / pamphlets / résumés / job application letters / biographical sketches / grant proposals. Charges $18-20/hr (negotiable); 1/2 deposit up front. Discount for ministries. Brochure available for SASE. Has a BS in mass communication/journalism; 17 years experience in print media; has edited 26+ books. Specializes in spiritual growth books for adults.

*SOLUTIONS UNLIMITED/SHARLENE WADE, PO Box 1, Fisherville VA 22939. E-mail: solutions@rockbridge.net.

WASHINGTON

BRISTOL EDITING SERVICES/SANDRA E. HAVEN, PO Box 1000, Carlsborg WA 98324-1000. (360)582-9478. E-mail: mailto:services@bristolservicesintl.com. Website: www.bristol servicesintl.com. E-mail contact. GE/SP. Does A/SS/N/NB/BP/QL/JN/E. Critique (comprehensive edit) is .01/wd. Offers a "Write as We Go" service for writers working on book-length manuscripts. Fees and services fully explained on Website, or send SASE for services and rate sheet. Editor of *Writers' Intl. Forum,* 1990-1999 (award-winning publication); contributing editor to *1995 Novel & Short Story Writer's Market;* profiled as a leading editor for young writers in latest *Market Guide for Young Writers;* 14 years experience in general editing.

DUE NORTH PUBLISHING/SCOTT R. ANDERSON, 7372 Guide Meridian, Lynden WA 98264. (360)354-0234. Fax (360)354-0834. E-mail: northbooks@earthlink.net. Website under construction. Write only; no e-mail contact. GE/LC/GH/CA/B/NL/SP. Does A/NB/BP/E.

Charges $25/hr. for copy and content editing or by the project (estimate given). Offers wide range of editorial and prepress (design/layout) services, including layout and design for brochures. Send SASE for current rates.

KALEIDOSCOPE PRESS/PENNY LENT, 2507—94th Ave. E., Edgewood WA 98371-2203. (253)848-1116. Fax (253)848-5610. E-mail: penny.lent@integrity.com. Call/e-mail/write. GE/LC/CA/B/NL/SP/BCE. Does A/SS/P/F/N/NB/BP/QL/JN/PB/BS/GB/TM/E/D/S. Also market analysis. All editing contracted by negotiated agreement. Discount given on larger projects. Has edited two dozen books for 4 different publishers; newsletters for 5 organizations; and teaches editing at 2 local colleges.

+LOGOS WORD DESIGNS, INC./LINDA L. NATHAN, PO Box 735, Maple Falls WA 98266-0735. (360)599-3429. Fax (360)392-0216. E-mail: linda@logosword.com. Website: www.logosword.com. Call/e-mail. GE/LC/GH/CA/B/NL/SP/résumés, consultations, writing assistance, manuscript submission services. Does A/SS/F/N/NB/BP/QL/JN/PB/BS/TM/ E/D/S/academic, legal, apologetics, conservative political. Over 30 years experience in wide variety of areas, including publicity, postdoctoral; BA Psychology; some MA work. Charges $25-35/hr.; e-mail for rate sheet.

MARION DUCKWORTH, 15917 N.E. 41st St., Vancouver WA 98682-7473. (360)896-8599. E-mail: mjduck@comcast.net. Call/e-mail/write. GE. Does A/SS/F/N/NB/BP/QL/BS/D. Charges $25/hr. for critique or consultation. Negotiates on longer projects. Author (for 26 years) of 18 books and 300 articles.

+MONICA COGLAS, PO Box 331, Mountlake Terrace WA 98043-0331. (425)337-7710. E-mail: info@monicacoglas.com. Website: www.monicacoglas.com. E-mail / write / $20 deposit. GE/LC/B. Does A/SS/N/NB/BP/QL/JN/PB/BS/GB/E/D. National award-winning author, business editor, newsletter editor, critique service, contest judge, and legal secretary. Charges $25/hr. or $5/pg. (4-page min.). Payment agreement must be signed in advance.

MOODY LITERARY AGENCY/VIRGINIA A. MOODY, 17402—114th Pl. N.E., Granite Falls WA 98252-9667. (360)691-2616. E-mail: vamoody638@hotmail.com. Call/e-mail/write. LC/GH/CA/NL/SP/BCE. Does A/SS/N/NB/BP/QL/JN/PB/BS/GB/D/S. Charges $3.50/pg. or as agreed. Initially, send three pages and $9 for evaluation. Has edited spiritual romance and Bible study books.

NANCY SWANSON, 10234—38th Ave. S.W., Seattle WA 98146-1118. (206)932-2161. E-mail: sannanvan@yahoo.com. Call, write or e-mail. GE/LC/GH/CA/NL/SP. Does A/SS/P/F/N/NB/ JN/BS/TM/E/D/S. Charges $1/pg. or as agreed by project. Former English teacher; 30+ years experience editing.

WEST VIRGINIA

THE WRITE HELP/ROSEMARY MENTZ-SUTTON, PO Box 1296, Scott Depot WV 25560. Phone/fax (304)757-0183. E-mail: writespirit64@msn.com. Write/SASE. GE/LC/market-ready mss / résumé creation / query & cover letters / edit & type school papers. Does A/SS/P/NB/BP/QL/BS/E/D. Published writer with 15 years freelance editing. Charges $1.25-3.00/pg.; $115 for book proposal. Free evaluation and information for SASE.

WISCONSIN

+BRIAR PEN EDITORIAL SERVICES/SALLIE BACHAR, N1261 Briarwood Ln., Merrill WI 54452. (715)536-2450. E-mail: briarpen@msn.com. Call/e-mail/write. GE/LC. Does A/SS/F/E/D. Proofreading $15/hr.; copyediting $20/hr.; rewriting $30/hr. Associate editor of a national Christian magazine, published author, columnist, and news correspondent.

MARGARET HOUK, West 2355 Valleywood Ln., Appleton WI 54915-8712. (920)687-0559. Fax

(920)687-0259. E-mail: marghouk@juno.com. Call / write. GE/LC. Does A/F/NB/BP/ QL/E/D (all for teens or adults). Charges *Writer's Market* suggested rates. Author of 5 books and 700 articles; has taught writing and manuscript marking for many years.

+**STONE COTTAGE LITERARY SERVICES/JONATHAN RICE**, 404 Meadow View Lane, DeForest WI 53532. E-mail: jrice@ivcf.org.

CANADIAN/FOREIGN

BERYL HENNE, 52 Moira St. W., Belleville ON K8P 1S3 Canada. (613)961-1791. Fax (613)961-1792. E-mail: b.henne@sympatico.ca. Write or e-mail. GE/LC/B/NL/SP. Does A/SS/NB/ BS/TM/E/D. Charges $25/hr., will negotiate on larger projects. Has 5 years book and magazine editing, plus 18 years freelancing. Has worked with many self-publishing authors.

CHRISTIAN WRITERS' WEBSITE. Website: www.christianwriter.co.uk. An online resource for Christian writers primarily in the UK and Europe. E-mail: Abidemi@christianwriter.co.uk.

+**DORSCH EDITORIAL/AUDREY DORSCH.** Toronto, Ontario. (416)439-4320. Fax (416)439-5089. E-mail: Audrey@dorschedit.ca. Website: www.dorschedit.ca. Editorial services: substantive editing, copyediting, indexing, proofreading, layout.

KEVIN MILLER, 35842 Graystone Dr., Abbotsford BC V3G 1K7 Canada. (604)853-4920. E-mail: author@kevinwrites.com. Website: www.kevinwrites.com. E-mail. GE/LC/GH/CA/ B/NL/SP/BCE. Does A/SS/P/N/NB/BP/QL/JN/PB/BS/GB/E/D/S. Charges per word, per page, or per project. Send e-mail for free estimate and free samples. Has written, cowritten, or contributed to more than 24 books, fiction and nonfiction; helped dozens of writers prepare their work for publication.

VINEMARC LITERARY SERVICES/MARCIA LEE LAYCOCK, 5007—42A St., Ponoka AB T4J 1M3 Canada. (403)783-3044. Fax (403)783-6500. E-mail: Marcia@vinemarc.com. Website: www.vinemarc.com. GE. Does SS/P/F/N/NB/JN/PB/D; others by arrangement. Speaks at conferences and teaches writing workshops and online courses through Inscribe Christian Writers' Fellowship.

+**WENDY SARGEANT**, PO Box 4163, Manuka Act 2603 Australia. Phone/fax +611-07-3822-3054. (Call Australia first). E-mail:WendySargeant@bigpond.com. Website: www.editors qld.com/freelance/Wendy_Sargeant.htm. Editing, newsletters, proofreading, research, writing. Special interests: Annual/business reports, children's books, educational books (primary, secondary, tertiary and above), fiction, history, legal, technical material (business humour). Manuscript assessor and instructional designer with The Writing School. Award-winning author published in major newspapers and magazines. Editing educational manuals. Project officer and instructional designer for Global Education Project, United Nationals Assoc. Information specialist for Australian National University.

+**WRITING SERVICES INSTITUTE (WSI)/MARSHA L. DRAKE**, #109 4351 Rumble St., Burnaby BC V5J 2A2, Canada. Phone/fax (604)321-3555. E-mail: writeone@shaw.ca. Call/e-mail/write. GE/LC/GH/CA/B; also book reviews, biographies, résumés, or company history. Does A/SS/F/N/NB/BP/QL/D. Offers correspondence course: Write for Fun and Profit. Charges negotiable fees. Write for details and information on correspondence course.

CHRISTIAN LITERARY AGENTS

The references in these listings to "published authors" refer to those who have had one or more books published by royalty publishers, or who have been published regularly in periodicals. If a listing indicates that the agent is "recognized in the industry," it means they have worked with the Christian publishers long enough to be recognized (by the editors) as credible agents.

Note: Visit this Website to find information on agents or agents other writers have found less than desirable: www.agentresearch.com, or contact Professor Jim Fisher, Criminal Justice Dept., Edinboro University of Pennsylvania, Edinboro PA 16444, (814)732-2409, e-mail: Jfisher@ edinboro.edu. Another such site, www.sfwa.org/beware/agents.html, is sponsored by the Science Fiction and Fantasy Writers of America. At the site for the Association of Authors' Representatives, www.aar-online.org, you will find a list of agents who don't charge fees, except for office expenses. You may also send for their list of approved agents (send $7 with a #10 SAE/1 stamp) to: PO Box 237201, Ansonia Station, New York NY 10003. I also suggest that you check out any potential agents at their local Better Business Bureau or local attorney general's office. For a database of over 500 agencies, go to: www.literaryagent.com; additional agent sites: http://fictionaddiction.net/agents.html; www.anotherealm.com/prededitors; http://mailer.fsu .edu/~tjp4773/agent.html, and www.sfwa.org/prededitors/peala.htm.

As the information is available, listings will indicate which agents belong to the Association of Authors' Representatives, Inc. (address above). Those members have subscribed to a set code of ethics. However, lack of such a designation does not indicate the agent is unethical; most Christian agents are not members. If they do happen to be members, it should give an extra measure of confidence. For a full list of member agents, go to: www.publishersweekly.com/aar.

(*) Indicates that agent did not return questionnaire
(#) Indicates that listing was updated from Website, brochure, or other sources
(+) Indicates new listing

AGENT RESEARCH & EVALUATION, INC., 25 Barrow St., New York, New York 10014. (212)924-9942. Fax (212)924-1864. E-mail: info@agentresearch.com. Website: www .agentresearch.com. This is not an agency but a service that tracks the public record of literary agents and helps authors use the data to obtain effective literary representation. Charges fees for this service. Offers a free "agent verification" service at the site. (Answers the question of whether or not the agent has created a public record of sales.) Also offers a newsletter, *Talking Agents,* that is $35/yr. US, slightly higher elsewhere. See Jerry Jenkins' comments on this service on their Website, in the Story So Far section.

ALAN YOUNGREN, LITERARY AGENT, 1243 Hawthorne, Downers Grove IL 60515. Fax (530)905-5978. E-mail: Ayoungren@worldnet.att.net. Estab. 1998. Recognized in the industry. Represents 15 clients. Open to unpublished authors and new clients. Handles adult fiction and nonfiction, crossover books.
   Contact: Letter, fax, or e-mail (no phone calls).
   Commission: 15%; 20% foreign.
   Fees: No reading fees.

+ALISON J. PICARD, LITERARY AGENT, PO Box 2000, Cotuit MA 02635. Phone/fax (508)477-7192 (contact before faxing). E-mail: ajpicard@aol.com. Agent: Alison Picard. Estab. 1985. Represents 48 clients. Open to unpublished authors and new clients. Secular agent; handles adult religious/inspirational novels & nonfiction.

Contact: Query with SASE. Responds in 1-6 wks.
Commission: 15%; foreign 20%.
ALIVE COMMUNICATIONS, 7680 Goddard St., Ste. 200, Colorado Springs CO 80920. (719)260-7080. Fax (719)260-8223. E-mail: submissions@alivecom.com. Website: www.alivecom.com. Agents: Rick Christian, president; Jerry "Chip" MacGregor, Lee Hough, and Andrea Christian. Well known in the industry. Estab. 1989. Represents 200+ clients. New clients on referral. Handles adult and teen novels and nonfiction, gift books, children's books, crossover and general market books. Deals in both Christian (70%) and general market (30%). Member Author's Guild.
Contact: E-mail to: submissions@alivecom.com.
Commission: 15%
Fees: Only extraordinary costs with client's preapproval; no review/reading fee.
ALLRED AND ALLRED LITERARY AGENTS, 7834 Alabama Ave., Canoga Park CA 91304-4905. Fax (818)346-4313. Agents: Robert Allred & Kim Allred. Estab. 1991. Not yet recognized in industry. Represents 5 clients. Open to unpublished authors and new clients. Handles religious/inspirational fiction and nonfiction for all ages, screenplays, TV/movie scripts, and secular/crossover books.
Contact: Query. Responds in 3 wks. to 2 mos.
Commission: 10%; foreign 10%.
Fees: None.
Tips: "Be professional. If a project has a certain doctrinal slant that makes it of interest to a limited audience, let us know that."
AMBASSADOR AGENCY, PO Box 50358, Nashville TN 37205. (615)370-4700. Fax (615)661-4344. E-mail: Wes@AmbassadorAgency.com. Website: www.AmbassadorAgency.com. Agent: Wes Yoder. Estab. 1973. Recognized in the industry. Represents 15 clients. Open to unpublished authors and new clients. Handles adult novels and nonfiction, crossover books. Also has a Speakers Bureau.
Contact: E-mail.
+AUTHORS & ARTISTS GROUP, INC., 41 E. 11th St., 11th Floor, New York NY 10003. (212)944-6484. Agent: Al Lowman. Estab. 1984. Represents 50 clients. Open to unpublished authors and new clients. Considers simultaneous queries. Responds in 3 wks. Secular agent; handles adult religious/inspirational nonfiction.
Contact: Query by fax (1 pg.).
Commission: 15%; foreign 20%.
Fees: Office expenses; not to exceed $1,000 without author's permission.
BIGSCORE PRODUCTIONS, INC., PO Box 4575, Lancaster PA 17604. (717)293-0247. Fax (717)293-1945. E-mail: bigscore@bigscoreproductions.com. Website: www.bigscore productions.com. Agents: David A. Robie, Sharon Hanby Robie. Recognized in industry. Estab. 1995. Represents 40-50 clients. Open to unpublished and new clients. Handles all types of fiction and nonfiction, gift books, secular, crossover books, self-help, health, history, business, teen/children, and general nonfiction.
Contact: Query by e-mail only. No longer accepts queries or proposals by mail.
Commission: 15%, foreign and film 20%.
Fees: Photocopying, overnight, etc. No reading fees.
Tips: "Very open to taking on new clients. Bigscore deals extensively with the general market, as well as the Christian market. Submit a well-prepared proposal that will take minimal fine tuning for presentation to publishers. Fiction: Your work must be extremely well written. Nonfiction: You must be highly marketable and media savvy. The more established in speaking or your profession, the better."
BK NELSON LITERARY AGENCY, 1565 Paseo Vida, Palm Springs CA 92264. (760)778-8800.

Fax (760)778-0034. E-mail: bknelson4@cs.com. Website: www.bknelson.com. Agent: John W. Benson. Recognized in the industry. Estab. 1980. Represents 8 clients. Open to unpublished authors and new clients. Handles adult fiction and nonfiction, teen fiction and nonfiction, children's fiction and nonfiction, TV/movie scripts, screenplays, gift books, secular books. Also open to history, women's issues, health care, and books of forms (legal, health, movie producers/directors/etc.).

Contact: Query by letter first, or by e-mail (include mailing address).

Commission: 20%, foreign 25%.

Fees: $395 reading fee for complete mss or $4/pg. for proposals with sample chapters. Nonrefundable. SASE required. Takes two weeks to read.

Comments: "Our success with first-book authors is outstanding. Work with us. Listen and follow agency guidelines to insure a good presentation. We'll do the business part; you write the bestsellers."

BOOKENDS, LLC, 136 Long Hill Rd., Gillette NJ 07933. E-mail: jsach@bookends-inc.com, or jfaust@bookends-inc.com. Website: www.bookendsinc.com. Agents: Jacky Sach, Jessica Faust, and Kim Lionetti. Member of AAR. Open to new clients. Handles adult nonfiction, including spirituality, and fiction.

Contact: Accepting mailed queries.

Commission: 15%

Fees: No reading or evaluation fees.

Tips: "Spirituality titles should be sent to Jacky Sach."

BOOKS & SUCH/JANET KOBOBEL GRANT, 4788 Carissa Ave., Santa Rosa CA 95405 (707)538-4184. E-mail: janet@janetgrant.com. Website: www.janetgrant.com. Agent: Janet Kobobel Grant. Recognized in industry. Estab. 1997. Represents 40 clients. Open to new or unpublished authors (with recommendation only). Handles fiction and nonfiction for all ages, picture books, gift books.

Contact: Letter or e-mail (no attachments).

Commission: 15%.

Fees: Photocopying and phone calls.

Tips: "Especially looking for women's nonfiction. Also fiction that depicts everyday life and everyday faith struggles. Always interested in a strong nonfiction manuscript."

*THE BOSTON LITERARY GROUP, 156 Mount Auburn St., Cambridge MA 02138-4875. (617)547-0800. Fax (617)876-8474. E-mail: agent@bostonliterary.com. Agent: Elizabeth Mack. Estab. 1994. Represents 30 clients. Open to unpublished authors and new clients. Handles nonfiction books, including religious/inspirational.

Contact: Query. Responds in 6 wks.

Commission: 15%; foreign 10%.

Fees: Office expenses. Makes referrals to editing services.

BROWNE & MILLER LITERARY ASSOCIATES, 410 S. Michigan Ave., Ste. 460, Chicago IL 60605. (312)922-3063. Fax (312)922-1905. E-mail: mail@browneandmiller.com. Website: www.browneandmiller.com. Agent: Danielle Egan-Miller. Recognized in the industry. Estab. 1971. Represents 15 clients. Open to unpublished authors and new clients if talented and professional. Handles teen and adult fiction, adult nonfiction, gift books, crossover and secular books. Member AAR.

Contact: Query letter/SASE only; no fax/e-query.

Commission: 15%, foreign 20%.

Fees: No fees.

#CAMBRIDGE LITERARY ASSOCIATES, 253 Low St., Newburyport MA 01950-3510. (978)499-0374. Fax (978)499-9774. Website: www.cambridgeliterary.com. Agent: Michael R. Valentino. Represents 20 clients. Open to unpublished authors and new clients.

Open to adult and teen fiction and nonfiction, screenplays, TV/movie scripts, and secular/crossover books. Member AAR.

Contact: Query letter.

Commission: 15%; 20% foreign.

Fees: None.

Tips: "Christian fiction has become increasingly popular, especially works dealing with contemporary issues. Touch the readers where they live."

CASTIGLIA LITERARY AGENCY, 1155 Camino del Mar, Ste. 510, Del Mar CA 92014. (858)755-8761. Fax (858)755-7063. Agents: Julie Castiglia and Sally Van Haitsma. Estab. 1993. Recognized in the industry. Represents 50 clients. Open to unpublished authors (with credentials) and selected new clients. Handles adult religious/inspirational nonfiction and secular crossover books. Member AAR.

Contact: Letter/SASE.

Commission: 15%; 25% foreign.

Fees: For excessive postage and copying.

Tips: "I do not look at unsolicited manuscripts."

CHERYL MOELLER MANAGEMENT, 2069 Old Willow Rd., Northfield IL 60093. (847)446-7892. E-mail: cherylmoeller@hotmail.com. Agent: Cheryl Moeller. Estab. 1992. Recognized in the industry. Represents 10 clients. Open to unpublished authors and new clients. Handles novels for all ages, picture books, adult and teen nonfiction.

Contact: By phone, letter, or e-mail.

Commission: 15%; foreign 20%.

Fees: Charges for office supply expenses.

*CIRCLE OF CONFUSION, 666 Fifth Ave., Ste. 303, New York NY 10103. (212)969-0653. Fax (718)997-052. E-mail: circleltd@aol.com. Agents: Rajeev K. Agarwal, Lawrence Mattis, Annmarie Negretti, and John Sherman. Estab. 1990. Represents 25 clients. Open to unpublished authors and new clients. Handles adult religious/inspirational nonfiction and scripts.

Contact: Query with SASE. Responds in 1-2 months.

Commission: 10%; foreign 10%.

#CLAUSEN, MAYS & TAHAN, LLC, PO Box 1015, New York NY 10276-1015. (212)239-4343. Fax (212)239-5248. E-mail: marytahan@aol.com. Agents: Stedman Mays, Mary M. Tahan. Estab. 1976. Open to some unpublished authors and new clients. Handles adult religious fiction and nonfiction; secular/crossover books.

Contact: Query or proposal. Responds in 1 month.

Commission: 15%; foreign 20%.

Fees: Charges office expenses.

+CRAWFORD LITERARY AGENCY, 94 Evands Rd., Barnstead NH 03218. (603)269-5851. Fax (603)269-2533. Winter address: 3920 Bayside Rd., Fort Meyers Beach FL 33931. E-mail:crawfordlit@att.net. Agents: Susan Crawford, Lorne Crawford, and Scott Neister. Estab. 1988. Represents 45 clients. Open to unpublished authors and new clients. Secular agent; handles adult religious/inspirational nonfiction.

Contact: Query with SASE.

Commission: 15%; foreign 20%.

Fees: None.

CS INTERNATIONAL, (formerly CVK International) 43 W. 39th St., New York NY 10018. (212)921-1610. E-mail: csliterary@aol.com. Website under construction. Agent: Cynthia Neeseman. Handles adult fiction and nonfiction; screenplays; and seeks foreign sales for translations of books published in the US.

Contact: Query.

+CURTIS BROWN, LTD., 10 Astor Pl., New York NY 10003-6935. (212)473-5400. West coast office: 1750 Montgomery St., San Francisco CA 94111. (415)954-8566. Agent: Perry Knowlton, chairman. Member AAR. Secular agent; handles adult religious/inspirational novels & nonfiction.

  Contact: Query with SASE; no fax/e-query.

DAMARIS ROWLAND AGENCY, 5 Peter Cooper Rd., #13H, New York NY 10010. (212)475-8942. Fax (212)358-9411. Agent: Damaris Rowland. Estab. 1994. Represents 40 clients. Open to unpublished authors and new clients. Handles religious/inspirational nonfiction. Very selective.

  Contact: Query letter.

  Commission: 15%; foreign 20%.

  Fees: Some office expenses.

DEE MURA ENTERPRISES, INC., 269 W. Shore Dr., Massapequa NY 11758-8225. (516)795-1616. Fax (516)795-8797. E-mail: samurai5@ix.netcom.com. Agents: Dee Mura, Karen Roberts, Frank Nakamura. Estab. 1987. Open to unpublished authors and new clients. Secular agency; handles religious/inspirational scripts.

  Contact: Query with SASE; e-query OK. Responds in 2 weeks.

  Commission: 15%; foreign 20%.

  Fees: Charges for photocopying, long distance phone calls and faxes, and postage.

DEFIORE & CO., 72 Spring St., Ste. 304, New York NY 10012. (212)925-7744. Fax (212)925-9803. E-mail: info@defioreandco.com. Website: www.defioreandco.com. Agent: Brian Defiore. Estab. 1999. Represents 35 clients. Open to new and unpublished authors. Secular agent; handles religious/inspirational nonfiction. Member of AAR.

  Contact: Query with SASE.

  Commission: 15%; foreign 20%.

  Fees: Charges office expenses after book has sold.

DYSTEL & GODERICH LITERARY MANAGEMENT, INC., 1 Union Square W., Ste. 904, New York NY 10003. (212)627-9100. Fax (212)627-9313. E-mail: Miriam@dystel.com. Website: www.dystel.com. Agents: Jane Dystel, Miriam Goderich, Stacey Glick, Michael Bourret, Jessica Papin, and Jim McCarthy. Estab. 1994. Recognized in the industry. Represents 5-10 religious book clients. Open to unpublished authors and new clients. Handles fiction and nonfiction for adults, gift books, secular/crossover books. Member AAR.

  Contact: Query letter.

  Commission: 15%; foreign 19%.

  Fees: Photocopying is author's responsibility.

*ELLEN LEVINE LITERARY AGENCY, 15 E. 26th St., Ste. 1801, New York NY 10010. (212)889-0620. Fax (212)725-4501. Agent: Ellen Levine. Represents 200 clients. Handles inspirational/religious nonfiction. Member of AAR.

  Contact: Query. Responds in 2-6 wks.

  Commission: 15%; foreign 20%.

  Fees: Charges various office expenses.

+EPIC LITERARY AGENCY, 7107 S. Yale Ave., #327, Tulsa OK 74136. (918)267-3248. Fax (918)267-3244. E-mail: KevinD@EpicLiterary.com. Agent: Kevin D. Decker. Estab. 1996. Represents up to 12 clients. Not currently open to unpublished authors; possibly open to new clients. Handles adult & children's novels & nonfiction, picture books, screenplays, TV/movie scripts, gift books, crossover books.

  Contact: Letter or e-mail.

  Commission: 15%; foreign 20%.

  Fees: Charges only for special travel or out-of-ordinary expenses.

  Tips: "Please query first; we do not accept unsolicited manuscripts."

FARRIS LITERARY AGENCY, INC., PO Box 570069, Dallas TX 75357-0069. (972)203-8804. Fax (972)226-1799. E-mail: farris1@airmail.net, or agent@farrisliterary.com. Website: www.farrisliterary.com. Agents: Mike Farris and Susan Morgan Farris. Open to unpublished authors and new clients. Handles Christian adult and teen fiction, spiritual or inspirational nonfiction, screenplays, secular/crossover books.

Contact: Mail or e-mail query (no attachments).
Commission: 15%; foreign 20%.
Fees: Expense for copies and postage only.
Tips: Please keep your query to one page and allow 2 weeks for a response to queries and 4-6 weeks for response to submissions.

THE FOGELMAN LITERARY AGENCY, 7515 Greenville Ave., Ste. 712, Dallas TX 75231, (214)361-9956. Fax (214)361-9553. And 599 Lexington Ave., Ste. 2300, New York NY 10022. (212)836-4803. E-mail: foglit@aol.com. Website: www.fogelman.com. Agent: Evan M. Fogelman. Estab. 1990. Recognized in the industry. Represents 100 clients. Open to few unpublished authors and new clients. Handles adult novels and nonfiction, women's fiction and nonfiction, gift books, secular/crossover books. Member AAR.

Contact: Query by e-mail, phone, or letter; no unsolicited manuscripts.
Commission: 15%; foreign 10%.
Fees: None.

GAIL ROSS LITERARY AGENCY, 1666 Connecticut Ave. N.W., #500, Washington DC 20009. (202)328-3282. Fax (202)328-9162. E-mail: jennifer@gailross.com. Website: www.gail ross.com. Contact: Jennifer Manguera. Estab. 1988. Represents 200 clients. Open to unpublished authors and new clients. Secular agent; handles adult religious/inspirational nonfiction, history, health, and business books.

Contact: Query letter/SASE; no e-query.
Commission: 15%; foreign 25%.
Fees: Office expenses.

GENESIS CREATIVE GROUP, 28126 Peacock Ridge, Ste. 104, Rancho Palos Verdes CA 90275. (310)541-9232. Fax (310)541-9532. E-mail: KenRUnger@aol.com. Agent: Ken Unger. Estab. 1998; developing recognition in industry. Represents 10 clients. Open to new clients. Handles completed screenplays only; no books.

Contact: Send one-page query with personal information, project description, and target market, by mail or e-mail only. NO phone calls; NO unsolicited manuscripts.
Commission: 15%; may vary by type of project.
Fees: Office fees for long distance calls and postage only.
Tips: "We formed this company to represent material to film and television community. We want material that presents values based on Judeo-Christian tradition."

GROSVENOR LITERARY AGENCY, 5510 Grosvenor Ln., Bethesda MD 20814. Phone/fax (301)564-6231. E-mail: dcgrosveno@aol.com. Agent: Deborah Grosvenor. Estab. 1995. Represents 30 clients. Open to few unpublished authors and new clients. Secular agent; handles adult religious/inspirational nonfiction.

Contact: Letter. Responds in 1-2 mos.
Commission: 15%; foreign 20%.
Fees: None.

HARTLINE LITERARY AGENCY, 123 Queenston Dr., Pittsburgh PA 15235. (412)829-2483. Fax (412)829-2450. E-mail: joyce@hartlineliterary.com. Website: www.hartlineliterary .com. Agents: Joyce A. Hart, adult novels (romance, mystery/suspense, women's fiction) and nonfiction; Janet Benrey, adult fiction (romance, mystery/suspense, women's) and nonfiction, Janet@hartlineliterary.com; Tamela Hancock Murray, children's and young adult fiction, adult fiction (romance, mystery/suspense, women's) and nonfiction, tamela@hartlineliterary.com; Andrea Boeshaar, women's fiction and romance, andrea@hartlineliterary.com. Recognized in industry. Estab. 1992. Represents 150 clients. Open to published authors (or selected unpublished). Handles novels and nonfiction for all ages, gift books, secular/crossover books. No science fiction or poetry.

    Contact: Phone, letter, fax, or e-mail.

    Commission: 15%; foreign negotiable.

    Fees: Office expenses; no reading fee.

    Tips: "Be sure to include your biography and publishing history with your proposal. Please ask for our literary guidelines if you have questions about preparing proposals. Working together we can make sure your manuscript gets the exposure and attention it deserves."

+HORNFISCHER LITERARY MANAGEMENT, PO Box 50067, Austin TX 78763-0067. E-mail: jim@hornfischerliterarymanagement.com. Website: www.hornfischerliterarymanagement.com. Agent: James D. Hornfischer. Estab. 2001. Represents 45 clients. Open to unpublished authors and new clients. Considers simultaneous submissions. Responds in 1 mo. Secular agent; handles adult religious/inspirational nonfiction.

    Contact: Proposal package/2 chapters.

    Commission: 15%; foreign 20%.

*JAN DENNIS LITERARY AGENCY, 19350 Glen Hollow Circle, Monument CO 80132. (719)481-0118. E-mail: jpdennislit@msn.com. Agent: Jan Dennis.

JEFF HERMAN AGENCY, PO Box 1522, Stockbridge MA 01262. (413)298-0077. Fax (413)298-8188. E-mail: Jeff@jeffherman.com. Website: www.jeffherman.com. Agents: Jeff Herman and Deborah Herman. Estab. 1987. Recognized in the industry. Represents 20+ clients with religious books. Open to unpublished authors and new clients. Handles adult nonfiction (spirituality), gift books, and secular/crossover.

    Contact: Query by mail.

    Commission: 15%; foreign 10%.

    Fees: No reading or management fees; just copying and shipping.

    Tips: "I love a good book from the heart. Have faith that you will accomplish what has been appointed to you."

+JELLINEK & MURRAY LITERARY AGENCY, 2024 Mauna Pl., Honolulu HI 96822. (808)521-4057. Fax (808)521-4058. E-mail: jellinek@lava.net. Agent: Roger Jellinek. Estab. 1995. Represents 5 clients. New to this market. Open to unpublished authors and new clients. Handles adult religious/inspirational novels & nonfiction for teens and adults, nonfiction for children, crossover books, and secular books.

    Contact: Prefers e-mail.

    Commission: 15%, foreign 20%.

    Fees: Charges for copying, mailing, and travel.

*JOY HARRIS LITERARY AGENCY, 156 Fifth Ave., Ste. 617, New York NY 10010. (212)924-6269. Fax (212)924-6609. E-mail: gen.office@jhlitagent.com. Agent: Joy Harris. Represents 100 clients. Handles religious/inspirational fiction. Member of AAR.

    Contact: Proposal/outline. Responds in 2 mos.

    Commission: 15%; foreign 20%.

    Fees: Charges some office expenses.

JOY OF WRITING LITERARY AGENCY, PO Box 836, Hillsboro OH 45133-0836. (937)393-4974. E-mail: joyofwriting45@yahoo.com. Agent: Mary Busha. Estab. 2002. Represents 16 clients. Open to unpublished authors and new clients. Handles fiction and nonfiction for adults, and crossover books.

    Contact: Letter or e-mail query; regular mail for proposals and sample chapters.

    Commission: 15-18%; foreign 20%.

    Fees: Charges for office expenses. Writer encouraged to call for details.

KATHI J. PATON LITERARY AGENCY, 19 W. 55th St., New York NY 10019-4907. (212)265-6586. (908)647-2117. E-mail: KJPLitBiz@aol.com. Agent: Kathi Paton. Estab. 1987. Handles adult religious/inspirational nonfiction.
> **Contact:** Proposal/1 chapter.
> **Commission:** 15%; foreign 20%.
> **Fees:** For photocopying.

KELVIN C. BULGER AND ASSOCIATES, 1525 E. 53rd St., Ste. 534, Chicago IL 60615. (312)692-1002. Fax (773)256-1505. Agent: Kelvin C. Bulger. Estab. 1992. Represents 25 clients. Open to unpublished authors and new clients. Handles religious/inspirational screenplays and TV/movie scripts. Currently handles 75% movie scripts and 25% TV scripts.
> **Contact:** Query with SASE. Responds in 3-9 wks.
> **Commission:** 10%; foreign 10%.
> **Fees:** None mentioned.

KEN SHERMAN & ASSOCIATES, 9507 Santa Monica Blvd., Beverly Hills CA 90210. (310)273-3840. Fax (310)271-2875. Agent: Ken Sherman. Estab. 1989. Represents 50 clients. Open to unpublished authors and new clients. Handles adult religious/inspirational novels, nonfiction, and scripts.
> **Contact:** By referral only. Responds in 1 mo.
> **Commission:** 15%; foreign 15%; dramatic rts. 15%.
> **Fees:** Charges office expenses and other negotiable expenses.

THE KNIGHT AGENCY, Madison GA. (706)752-0096. Fax (706)752-1158. E-mail: knight agent@aol.com. Website: www.knightagency.net. Agents: Deidre Knight and Pamela Harty. Recognized in industry. Estab. 1996. Represents 65 clients (15 Christian). Open to unpublished and new clients (very selective). Handles adult, teen, and children's fiction and nonfiction, secular/crossover books. Member AAR.
> **Contact:** E-mail only (no attachments); no phone or fax.
> **Commission:** 15%; 20-25% on foreign and film rights (includes subagent commission).
> **Fees:** None.
> **Tips:** "We're always looking for strong nonfiction, particularly with crossover appeal to the ABA. In children's or young adult, we're only considering authors who have published previously. In fiction, we're no longer accepting mystery or action-adventure submissions."

LAWRENCE JORDAN AGENCY, 345 W. 121st St., New York NY 10027. (212)662-7871. Fax (212)662-8138. E-mail: LJLAgency@aol.com. Agent: Lawrence Jordan. Estab. 1978. Represents 50 clients. Open to unpublished authors and new clients. Recognized in the industry. Responds in 3-6 wks. Handles teen and adult novels, adult nonfiction (including religious/inspirational), gift books, short stories, crossover, and secular books.
> **Contact:** Letter or e-mail only.
> **Commission:** 15%; foreign 20%.
> **Fees:** Office expenses only.
> **Tips:** "Actively seeking spiritual and religious books."

LESLIE H. STOBBE, 300 Doubleday Rd., Tryon NC 28782. (828)859-5964. Fax (978)945-0517. E-mail: lstobbe@alltel.net. Well recognized in the industry. Estab. 1993. Represents 72 clients. Open to unpublished authors and new clients. Handles adult fiction and nonfiction.
> **Contact:** By e-mail or letter.
> **Commission:** 15%
> **Fees:** Only when engaged as a consultant/mentor.
> **Tips:** "I will not accept clients whose theological positions in their book differ significantly from mine."

+LEVINE GREENBERG LITERARY AGENCY, INC., 307 7th Ave., Ste. 1906, New York NY 10001. (212)337-0934. Fax (212)337-0948. Website: www.jameslevine.com. Agent:

James Levine. Estab. 1989. Represents 250 clients. Open to unpublished authors and new clients. Secular agent; handles adult religious/inspirational nonfiction. Member AAR.
   Contact: See guidelines on Website; prefers e-query.
   Commission: 15%; foreign 20%.
   Fees: Office expenses.
   Tips: "Our specialties include spirituality and religion."
+**LINDSEY'S LITERARY SERVICES**, 7502 Greenville Ave., Ste. 500, Dallas TX 75231. (214)890-9262. Fax (214)890-9265. E-mail: bonedges001@aol.com. Agents: Bonnie James and Emily Armenta. Estab. 2002. Represents 10 clients. Open to unpublished authors and new clients. Considers simultaneous submissions. Responds in 6 wks. to 3 mos. Secular agency; handles adult religious/inspirational novels.
   Contact: Query with SASE.
   Commission: 15%; foreign 20%.
THE LITERARY GROUP INTL, 270 Lafayette St., #1505, New York NY 10012. (212)274-1616. Fax (212)274-9876. E-mail: Fweimann@theliterarygroup.com. Website: www.theliterary group.com. Agent: Frank Weimann. Recognized in the industry. Estab. 1986. Represents 300 clients (120 for religious books). Open to new and unpublished authors. Handles adult fiction and nonfiction, history, secular, crossover, gift books, how-to, health, spiritual guidance.
   Contact: Letter.
   Commission: 15%; foreign 20%.
   Fees: No fees.
   Tips: "Looking for fresh, original spiritual fiction and nonfiction. We offer a written contract which may be canceled after 30 days."
LITERARY MANAGEMENT GROUP, INC., 4238 Morriswood Dr., Nashville TN 37204-4440, Phone/fax (615)832-7231, E-mail: BRB@brucebarbour.com. Website: www.literary managementgroup.com. Agent: Bruce R. Barbour. Estab. 1995. Recognized in the industry. Represents 50+ clients. No unpublished authors. Open to new clients. Handles adult and teen fiction and nonfiction, crossover, and secular books from published authors only.
   Contact: E-mail.
   Commission: 15%; foreign 20%.
   Fees: No fees or expenses.
   Tips: Check Website for editorial guidelines and submission format.
+**LITWEST GROUP, LLC**, E-mail: kboyle1@mindspring.com. Website: www.litwest.com. Agents: Katie Boyle or Nancy Ellis. Represents 160 clients. Open to unpublished authors and new clients. Considers simultaneous submissions. Responds in 1 mo. or more. Secular agency; handles adult religious/inspirational novels & nonfiction.
   Contact: Query with SASE.
   Commission: 15%; foreign 20%.
****LUKEMAN LITERARY MANAGEMENT, INC.**, 101 N. 7th St., Brooklyn NY 11211. E-mail: Agency@lukeman.com. Website: www.lukeman.com. Agent: Noah Lukeman. Estab. 1996. Recognized in the industry. Represents 10 clients. Rarely open to unpublished authors or new clients (most are already publishing). Handles adult religious/inspirational novels and nonfiction.
   Contact: Not accepting submissions at this time. Check Website for availability.
   Commission: 15%; foreign 20%.
   Fees: None.
+**MANUSCRIPT PLACEMENT SERVICE**, PO Box 428, Newburg PA 17240. 717)423-6621. Fax (717)423-6944. E-mail: keith@manuscriptplacementservice.com, or MPS@innernet.net. Agent: Keith Carroll . Estab. 2000. Represents 55 clients. Open to unpublished authors and

new clients. Handles adult and teen religious/inspirational novels & nonfiction, picture books, gift books, and crossover books.

Contact: E-mail, letter, or phone.

Commission: 10%.

Fees: Charges $75 as an introductory consultation fee, which includes a 30-90 minute consultation phone call, following an initial examination of a prospective author's material.

*MARCH MEDIA, INC., 1114 Oman Dr., Brentwood TN 37027. (615)377-1146. Fax (615)373-1705. E-mail: marchmed@bellsouth.net. Agents: Etta Wilson & Cathey Clark. Estab. 1989. Recognized in the industry. Represents 27 clients. Handles teen/YA and children's novels and nonfiction, picture books, and gift books for adults.

Contact: Letter only.

Commission: 15%.

Fees: Only if agreed on in contract. Offers consultation services on a fee basis for authors regarding contract negotiation.

Tips: "I prefer humor, tight plotting, and strong Christian values."

MARK GILROY COMMUNICATIONS, INC., 6528 E. 101st St., Ste. 416, Tulsa OK 74133. (918)298-4526. Fax (918)298-0041. E-mail: mark@markgilroy.com. Website: www .markgilroy.com. Agent: Mark K. Gilroy. Recognized in the industry. Represents 10 clients. Open to a limited number of new or unpublished clients. Handles adult nonfiction, gift books, crossover books, and secular books.

+MCHUGH LITERARY AGENCY, 1033 Lyon Rd., Moscow ID 83843. (208)882-0107. Fax (847-628-0146. E-mail: elisabetmch@turbonet.com. Agent: Elisabet McHugh. Estab. 1995. Represents 2 clients. Recognized in the industry. Open to unpublished authors and new clients. Secular agent; handles adult and teen religious/inspirational nonfiction, crossover, and secular books.

Contact: E-mail.

Commission: 15%; foreign 20%.

Fees: None, but clients provide copies of manuscripts.

Comments: Be professional!

MEREDITH BERNSTEIN LITERARY AGENCY, 2112 Broadway, Ste. 503A, New York NY 10023. (212)799-1007. Fax (212)799-1145. Agents: Meredith Bernstein and Elizabeth Cavanaugh. Estab. 1981. Represents 75 clients. Open to unpublished authors and new clients. Handles nonfiction on spirituality. Member AAR.

Contact: Query with SASE.

Commission: 15%; foreign 20%.

Fees: Charges $75/yr. disbursement fee.

Tips: "We obtain most of our new clients through conferences and referrals from others."

+MICHAEL SNELL LITERARY AGENCY, PO Box 1206, Truro MA 02666-1206. (508)349-3718. Agent: Michael Snell. Estab. 1978. Represents 200 clients. Open to unpublished authors and new clients. Secular agent: handles adult religious/inspirational nonfiction.

Contact: Query with SASE. No simultaneous submissions. Responds in 1-2 wks.

Commission: 15%; foreign 15%.

NATASHA KERN LITERARY AGENCY INC., PO Box 2908, Portland OR 97208-2908. (503)297-6190. Fax (503)297-8241. Website: www.natashakern.com. Agent: Natasha Kern. Recognized in the industry. Estab. 1987. Represents 12 religious clients. Open to unpublished authors and new clients. Secular agent; handles adult religious/inspirational fiction and nonfiction, crossover, and secular books.

Contact: Accepts queries by letter only; 3 pg. synopsis & 3 sample pgs.; SASE.

Commission: 15%; 20% foreign (includes foreign-agent commission).

Fees: No reading fee.

Tips: "We represent a wide range of inspirational fiction and nonfiction; adult only."

ORACLE ASSOCIATES: A Literary Agency, PO Box 87170, Tucson AZ 85754. (520)743-8465. Fax (520)743-1842. E-mail: priscpalmer@aol.com. Agent: Priscilla M. Palmer. Recognized in the industry. Estab. 2001. Represents 6 clients. Open to unpublished authors and new clients. Handles religious/inspirational novels and nonfiction for all ages, picture books, and secular/crossover books.

Contact: Query letter with 1-page synopsis, or e-mail.

Commission: 15%.

Fees: One-time fee of $100 for unpublished authors. No reading/editing fees.

Tips: "No Eastern religions, occult, New Age, science fiction or romance fiction. Do your homework. Know your category and its requirements."

+PAUL S. LEVINE LITERARY AGENCY, 1054 Superba Ave., Venice CA 90291-3940 (310)450-6711. Fax (310)450-0181. E-mail: pslevine@ix.netcom.com. Website: www.netcom.com/~pslevine/lawliterary.html. Agent: Paul S. Levine. Estab. 1996. Represents 100 clients. Open to unpublished authors and new clients. Considers simultaneous submissions. Responds in one day to 2 mos. Secular agent; handles adult religious/inspirational novels, nonfiction, and scripts.

Contact: Query with SASE.

Commission: 15%; foreign 20%.

Fees: Actual office expenses; no up-front payment.

PELHAM LITERARY AGENCY, 2451 Royal St. James Dr., El Cajon CA 92019-4408. (619)447-4468. E-mail: jmeals@pelhamliterary.com. Website: www.pelhamliterary.com. Agent: Jim Meals. Not yet known in the Christian industry. Estab. 1993. Open to unpublished authors and new clients. Handles adult and teen novels, adult nonfiction, secular/crossover books.

Contact: Brief query letter preferred; e-query OK. Provides a list of published clients and titles.

Commission: 15%; foreign 20%.

Fees: Charges for postage and copying only.

Tips: "We are actively seeking writers for the Christian fiction market although also open to Christian nonfiction. We specialize in genre fiction and enjoy working with new writers."

PEMA BROWNE LTD., 11 Tena Pl., Valley Cottage NY 10989-2215. (845)268-0029. E-mail: ppbltd@earthlink.net. Website: www.pemabrowneltd.com. Agents: Perry Browne & Pema Browne. Recognized in industry. Estab. 1966. Represents 20 clients (1 religious). Open to unpublished authors; no new clients at this time. Handles novels for adults and teens, nonfiction for all ages; picture books/novelty books, gift books, crossover books. Only accepts mss not previously sent to publishers.

Contact: Letter query with credentials; no phone, fax or e-mail. Must include SASE.

Commission: 15%; 20% foreign.

Fees: None.

Tips: "Check at the library in reference section, in *Books in Print,* for books similar to yours. Have good literary skills, neat presentation. Know what has been published and research the genre that interests you."

A PICTURE OF YOU AGENCY, 1176 Elizabeth Dr., Hamilton OH 45013. Phone/fax (513)863-1108. E-mail: apoy1@aol.com. Agent: Lenny Minelli. Estab. 1995. Branching out into Christian market. Represents 15 clients. Open to unpublished authors and new clients. Handles only screenplays, TV/movie scripts.

Contact: Query with proposal.

Commission: 10%; 15% foreign.

Fees: Charges $125/yr.

Tips: "Make sure your material is the best it can be before seeking an agent. Always enclose an SASE."

+QUICKSILVER BOOKS ONLINE. E-mail: QBOnline@artsnet.net. Website: www.quicksilver books.com. Agent: Bob Silverstein. Estab. 1987. Represents 50 clients. Open to unpublished authors and new clients. Secular agent; handles adult religious/inspirational nonfiction.
> **Contact:** Query by e-mail. Considers simultaneous submissions. Responds in 2-5 wks.
> **Commission:** 15%; foreign 20%.
> **Fees:** No fees.

RICIA MAINHARDT AGENCY, 612 Argyle Rd. #L5, Brooklyn NY 11230. (718)434-1893. Fax (718)434-2157. E-mail: ricia@ricia.com. Website: www.ricia.com. Handles adult and young adult fiction, nonfiction, picture books and early readers.
> **Contact:** For fiction send a 3-5 page synopsis with first 20-30 pages (ending at a chapter break); for nonfiction a chapter-by-chapters synopsis and 2 chapters; for children's send complete ms. Call for e-mail submissions instructions.
> **Fees:** No reading fees.

+RITA ROSENKRANZ LITERARY AGENCY, 440 West End Ave., Ste. 15D, New York NY 10024-5358. (212)873-6333. Agent: Rita Rosenkranz. Estab. 1990. Represents 30 clients. Open to unpublished authors and new clients. Secular agent; handles adult religious/inspirational nonfiction. Member AAR.
> **Contact:** Proposal package; no fax/e-query.
> **Commission:** 15%; foreign 20%.

+RLR ASSOCIATES, LTD., Literary Dept., 7 W. 51st St., New York NY 10019. (212)541-8641. Fax (212)541-6052. Website: www.rlrassociates.net/literary. Agents: Jennifer Unter, Ezra Fitz. Represents 50 clients. Open to unpublished authors and new clients. Secular agency; handles adult religious/inspirational nonfiction.
> **Contact:** Query with SASE. Considers simultaneous submissions. Responds in 5 wks.
> **Commission:** 15%; foreign 20%.

SAMUEL FRENCH, INC., 45 W. 25th St., New York NY 10010-2751. (212)206-8990. Fax (212)206-1429.E-mail: samuelfrench@earthlink.net. Website: www.samuelfrench.com. Editor: Lawrence Harbison. Estab. 1830. Handles rights to some religious/inspirational stage plays.
> **Contact:** Query or send complete manuscript.
> **Commission:** Varies.
> **Fees:** None.

SANFORD J. GREENBURGER ASSOCIATES, INC., 55 Fifth Ave., New York NY 10003. (212)206-5600. Fax (212)463-8718. Website: www.greenburger.com. Agents: Heide Lange, Faith Hamlin, Theresa Park, Elyse Cheney, Dan Mandel, Julie Barer. Estab. 1945. Represents 500 clients. Open to unpublished authors and new clients. Secular agent; handles adult religious/inspirational nonfiction. Member of AAR.
> **Contact:** Query with SASE. Responds in 3-9 weeks.
> **Commission:** 15%; foreign 20%.
> **Fees:** Charges for photocopying and foreign submissions.

*SARA A. FORTENBERRY LITERARY AGENCY, 1001 Halcyon Ave., Nashville TN 37204. (615)385-9074. Recognized in the industry. Estab. 1995. Represents 40 clients. Open to unpublished authors or new clients only by referral. Handles adult nonfiction and novels, picture books, gift books, and secular crossover books.
> **Contact:** Unpublished authors query by mail; published authors by phone or mail. Query letters should be accompanied by referral, book proposal, and SASE.
> **Commission:** 15%; foreign 10%, plus subagent commission.

Fees: Standard expenses directly related to specific projects (copies, messenger, overnight shipping, and postage).

Tips: "For my purposes, a published author is one who has had a book published by a commercial (royalty) publisher."

SCHIAVONE LITERARY AGENCY, INC., 236 Trails End, West Palm Beach FL 33413-2135. Phone/fax (561)966-9294. E-mail: profschia@aol.com. Website: www.publishersmarket place.com/members/profschia. Agent: James Schiavone, EdD. Recognized in the industry. Estab. 1997. Represents 6 clients. Open to unpublished and new clients. Handles adult, teen and children's fiction and nonfiction; picture books; celebrity biography; secular/crossover books.

   Contact: Query letter/SASE; one-page e-mail query (no attachments).

   Commission: 15%, foreign 20%.

   Fees: No reading fees; authors pay postage only.

   Tips: Works primarily with published authors; will consider first-time authors with excellent material. Actively seeking books on spirituality, major religions, and alternative health. Very selective on first novels.

*SE LITERARY PROPERTIES, PO Box 25, Portland CT 06480. E-mail: stephen@excellent novels.com. Website: www.seliterary.homestead.com. Agent: Stephen Everett.

   Contact: Mail or e-mail (no attachments).

   Commission: 15%.

   Fees: Office expenses only.

*SEDGEBAND LITERARY ASSOCIATES, 7312 Martha Ln., Fort Worth TX 76112-5336. (817)496-3652. Fax (425)952-9518. E-mail: queries@sedgeband.com. Website: www .sedgeband.com. Agents: Ginger Norton and David Duperre. Estab. 1997. Recognized in the industry. Represents 10 clients with religious books. Open to unpublished authors and new clients. Handles religious fiction and nonfiction, gift books, secular/crossover books. Manuscripts must be at least 70,000 wds., and complete.

   Contact: E-mail (no attachments) or letter; fax if necessary; complete ms only on request.

   Commission: 15%; foreign 20%.

   Fees: Office expenses only.

   Tips: "Write your query with as much care as you wrote your manuscript. Watch spelling and grammar. Never be rude or egotistical; impress the agent with your style and ability."

+SERENDIPITY LITERARY AGENCY, LLC, 732 Fulton St., Ste. 3, Brooklyn NY 11238. Phone/fax (718)230-7689. E-mail: rbrooks@serendipitylit.com. Website: www.serendipity lit.com. Agent: Regina Brooks. Estab. 2000. Represents 30 clients. Open to unpublished authors and new clients. Secular agent; handles adult religious/inspirational nonfiction.

   Contact: Outline/1 chapter. No simultaneous submissions. Responds in 2-3 mos.

   Commission: 15%; foreign 20%.

   Fees: $200 for office expenses.

THE SEYMOUR AGENCY, 475 Miner St. Rd., Canton NY 13617. (315)386-1831. Fax (315)386-1037. E-mail: mseymour@slic.com. Website: www.theseymouragency.com. Agent: Mary Sue Seymour. Estab. 1992. Recognized in the industry. Represents 25 religious clients. Open to unpublished authors and new clients. Handles romance novels, and nonfiction for all ages, gift books, secular/crossover books.

   Contact: Query letter or e-mail with first 50 pages of mss; no fax query. For nonfiction, send proposal with chapter one.

   Commission: 15% for unpublished authors; 12% for published authors; foreign 20%.

   Fees: None.

   Tips: Mary Sue is a New York State certified (but retired) teacher. Former Sunday school teacher and superintendent.

*SHAPIRO-LICHTMAN, 8827 Beverly Blvd., Los Angeles CA 90048. (310)859-8877. Fax (310)859-7153. E-mail: ppatrick@shapiro-lichtman.com. Agent: Peggy Patrick. Estab. 1965. Well-known agency in Hollywood; just started religious division. Open to unpublished authors and new clients. Handles religious/inspirational novels for all ages, screenplays, TV/movie scripts, crossover books, and secular books and screenplays.

    Contact: Query by letter, fax, or e-mail; no calls.

    Commission: 10%.

    Fees: None.

    Tips: "We are primarily an agency that represents books in the film and television market, but are just opening up to the Christian book market. We are a full-service agency that represents writers, directors, producers. We also specialize in animation, kids and family programming."

THE SHEPARD AGENCY, 73 Kingswood Dr., Bethel CT 06801. (203)790-4230. Fax (203)798-2924. E-mail: shepardagcy@mindspring.com. Website: http://home.mindspring.com/~shepardagcy. Agent: Jean Shepard. Recognized in the industry. Estab. 1987. Represents 12 clients. Open to unpublished authors; no new clients at this time. Handles fiction and nonfiction for all ages; no picture books; especially business, reference, professional, self-help, cooking, and crafts. Books only.

    Contact: By e-mail.

    Commission: 15%; foreign variable.

    Fees: None except long-distance calls and copying.

SHEREE BYKOFSKY ASSOCIATES, INC., 16 W. 36th St., 13th Floor, New York NY 10018. E-mail: ShereeBee@aol.com. Website: www.shereebee.com. Agent: Sheree Bykofsky. Estab. 1984. Agent is a former editor and an author. Represents a limited number of clients. Open to unpublished authors and new clients. Handles adult religious/inspirational nonfiction. Member AAR.

    Contact: Query with SASE.

    Commission: 15%; foreign 15%.

    Fees: Charges for postage, photocopying, and fax.

    Tips: "I get new clients through the recommendations of others. No poetry, children's material, or screenplays."

*SOUTHEAST LITERARY AGENCY, PO Box 910, Sharpes FL 32959. (321)632-5019. Agent: Debbie Fine. Recognized in the industry. Estab. 1996. Open to new clients and unpublished authors. Handles fiction and nonfiction for all ages, few picture books, gift books, short story collections, secular/crossover books, some poetry books.

    Contact: Query letter with overview, postage for return, and SASE for correspondence. Disposable complete manuscript with synopsis preferred.

    Commission: 10%, foreign 20%.

    Fees: For out-of-pocket expenses for postage, packaging, long-distance calls and copying. Charges a $150-175 up-front fee.

    Tips: Include return postage and packaging if you want submissions returned, and keep calls to a minimum.

SPENCERHILL ASSOCIATES, LTD./KAREN SOLEM, 24 Park Row, PO Box 374, Chatham NY 12037. (518)392-9293. Fax (518)392-9554. E-mail: ksolem@klsbooks.com. Agent: Karen Solem. Recognized in the industry. Estab. 2001 (previously with Writers House). Represents 20 clients. Open to unpublished authors and new clients. Handles adult novels and nonfiction, secular, and crossover books.

    Contact: A brief e-mail query is OK. If sending a proposal with chapters, send by mail.

    Commission: 15%; foreign 20%.

    Fees: Photocopying and Express Mail charges only.

STEPHEN PEVNER, INC., 382 Lafayette St., 8th Floor, New York NY 10003. (212)674-8403. Fax (212)529-3692. E-mail: spevner@aol.com. Agent: Stephen Pevner. Estab. 1991. Represents under 50 clients. Open to unpublished authors and new clients. Responds in 2-5 wks. Secular agent; handles religious/inspirational nonfiction.
    Contact: Query/outline/proposal.
    Commission: 15%; foreign 20%.
    Fees: Commission only.
+THE STEVE LAUBE AGENCY, 5501 N. 7th Ave., #502, Phoenix AZ 85013. (602)336-8910. E-mail: steve@stevelaube.com. Website: www.stevelaube.com. Agent: Steve Laube. Estab. 2004. Open to new and unpublished authors. Handles adult fiction and nonfiction, history, secular, crossover, gift books, how-to, health, spiritual guidance.
    Contact: Letter.
    Commission: 15%; foreign 20%.
    Fees: No fees.
    Tips: "Looking for fresh, original spiritual fiction and nonfiction."
STONE MANNERS AGENCY, 8436 W. Third St., Ste. 740, Los Angeles CA 90048. (323)655-1313. Fax (323)655-7676. Agent: Michael Sheehy. Handles religious/inspirational scripts and well as all others.
    Contact: Queries only.
SUITE A MANAGEMENT TALENT AGENCY, 120 El Camino Dr., Ste. 202, Beverly Hills CA 90212. (310)278-0801. Fax (310)278-0807. E-mail: suite-A@juno.com. Agent: Lloyd D. Robinson. Recognized in the industry. Estab. 2001. Several clients. Open to new and unpublished clients (if published in other media). Specializes in screenplays and novels for adaptation to TV movies.
    Commission: 10%
    Comments: Representation limited to adaptation of novels and true-life stories for film and television development. Work must have been published for consideration.
SUSAN HERNER RIGHTS AGENCY, PO Box 57, Pound Ridge, NY 10576. (914)234-2864. Fax (914)234-2866. E-mail: sherneragency@optonline.net. Agent: Susan Herner. Estab. 1987. Represents 100 clients. Very open to unpublished authors and new clients. Handles adult religious/inspirational nonfiction.
    Contact: Proposal/2-3 sample chapters. Responds in one month.
    Commission: 15%; foreign 20%.
    Fees: Charges only for extraordinary copying costs.
    Tips: "Particularly interested in revisionist biblical history, women's religious/spiritual experience, and comparative religious thought rather than traditional religious viewpoints."
*SUSAN SCHULMAN, A LITERARY AGENCY, 454 W. 44th St., New York NY 10036. (212)713-1622. Fax (212)581-8830. E-mail: schulman@aol.com. Website: www.susanschulman agency.com. Religious/spiritual nonfiction. Member AAR.
    Contact: Query/SASE.
    Commission: 15%; foreign 20% (shared 50/50 with foreign coagent).
    Fees: No fees.
    Tips: "We are interested in sophisticated religious and spiritual material, especially nonfiction or historically based or appropriate for a well-educated audience."
+3 SEAS LITERARY AGENCY, PO Box 8571, Madison WI 53708. (608)221-4306. E-mail: threeseaslit@aol.com. Website: www.threeseaslit.com. Agent: Michelle Grajkowski. Estab. 2000. Represents 40 clients. Open to unpublished authors and new clients. Secular agent; handles adult religious/inspirational novels & nonfiction.
    Contact: Query with proposal/first 3 chapters. Considers simultaneous submissions. Responds in 2-3 mos.

Commission: 15%; foreign 20%.

TOAD HALL, INC., RR 2 Box 2090, Laceyville PA 1863. (570)869-2942. Fax (570)869-1031. E-mail: toadhallco@aol.com. Website: www.laceyville.com/toad-hall. Agent: Sharon Jarvis. Not yet known in the industry. Estab. 1983. Represents 1 religious client. Open to unpublished authors and new clients. Handles adult religious/inspirational nonfiction; fiction only from published authors.

> **Contact:** Hard-copy query only. Do not send any text unless requested.
>
> **Commission:** 15%; foreign 10%.
>
> **Fees:** Office expenses (photocopying, bank fees, special postage). $50 fee to read the first 50 pages plus synopsis/table of contents and provide a detailed written analysis.
>
> **Tips:** "All queries should include (1) the category, (2) the word count, (3) brief summary, (4) bio, (5) SASE." Has their own small press, plus a partnership with an independent e-book company for authors considering self-publishing or a co-op arrangement.

THE VINES AGENCY, INC., 648 Broadway, Ste. 901, New York NY 10012. (212)777-5522. Fax (212)777-5978. E-mail: jv@vinesagency.com. Website: www.vinesagency.com. Agents: James C. Vines, Paul Surdi, Ali Ryan, and Gary Neuwirth. Estab. 1995. Represents 52 clients. Open to unpublished authors and new clients. Secular agency; handles adult religious/inspirational nonfiction.

> **Contact:** Send outlines/3 sample chapters/SASE; fax/e-mail query OK.
>
> **Commission:** 15%; foreign 25%.
>
> **Fees:** For foreign postage, photocopying, and messenger service.
>
> **Tips:** "We get most of our clients through query letters, conferences, recommendations from others."

WILLIAMS AGENCY, 909 Knox Rd., Kosciusko MS 39090. (662)290-0617. Fax (270)517-7167. E-mail: submissions@williamsliteraryagency.com (no attachments). Website: www.williamsliteraryagency.com. Agents: Sheri Homan Williams (book rts.); Maxx Williams (film & TV rts.). Estab. 1997. Recognized in the industry. Represents 25 clients. Not open to unpublished authors; open to new clients (1-page query first). Handles adult and teen fiction and nonfiction, TV/movie scripts, gift books, crossover books, and secular books (secular books must be family-friendly). Foreign commission 20%.

> **Contact:** Query by mail or e-mail; 1-page letter with synopsis only. No complete mss unless requested (unsolicited returned or discarded). No phone calls. Adhere to guidelines on Website. Allow up to 3 months for reply.
>
> **Commission:** 15%; 25% foreign.
>
> **Fees:** No reading or signing fees.
>
> **Tips:** "No unsolicited manuscripts. SASE for reply. No calls. Always follow guidelines as posted on our Website. Multiple e-mails or calls inquiring as to the status of your manuscript does not increase your chances; in fact, it hurts them."

WINSUN LITERARY AGENCY, 3706 N.E. Shady Ln. Dr., Gladstone MO 64119. Phone/fax (816)459-8016. E-mail: MarkLitt@aol.com. Agents: Mark and Jeanette Littleton. Recognized in the industry. Represents 20 clients. Somewhat open to unpublished authors and open to new clients. Handles fiction and nonfiction for all ages, picture books, gift books.

> **Contact:** E-mail.
>
> **Commission:** 15%; foreign 20%.
>
> **Fees:** Postage and copying for new clients only.
>
> **Tips:** "Send only your absolutely best work, i.e., work that has been rewritten to perfection, put through critique groups, and so on."

WOLGEMUTH & ASSOCIATES, INC., 8600 Crestgate Circle, Orlando FL 32819. (407)909-9445. Fax (407)909-9446. E-mail: rwolgemuth@cfl.rr.com. Agent: Robert D. Wolgemuth.

Well recognized in the industry. Estab. 1992. Represents 18 clients. No new clients or unpublished authors. Handles mostly adult nonfiction, most other types of books handled only for current clients.

Contact: By letter.

Commission: 15%.

Fees: None.

Tips: "We work with authors who are either best-selling authors or potentially best-selling authors. Consequently, we want to represent clients with broad-market appeal."

+#WOMACK PUBLISHING AGENCY, PO Box 1367, Somerton AZ 85350. (928)246-8847. E-mail: WomacjAgency@aol.com. Agent: David A. Womack.

+WORDSERVE LITERARY GROUP, 2235 Ashwood Pl., Highlands Ranch CO 80129. (303)471-6675. Fax (303)471-1297. E-mail: greg@wordserveliterary.com. Website: www.wordserveliterary.com. Agent: Greg Johnson. Estab. 2003. Represents 20+ clients. Recognized in the industry. Open to unpublished authors (fiction primarily) and new clients. Handles novels & nonfiction for all ages, gift books, crossover books, and secular books.

Contact: Short e-mail initially; then letter with samples by mail, with SASE.

Commission: 15%; foreign 10-15%.

Fees: None.

Tips: "Nonfiction: First impressions count. Make sure your proposal answers all the questions on competition, outline, audience, felt need, etc. Fiction: Make sure your novel is completed before you submit a proposal (synopsis, plus 5 chapters)."

*THE WRITER'S EDGE. See listing under Editorial Services—Illinois.

WRITERS HOUSE, 21 W. 26th St., New York NY 10010. (212)685-2400. Fax (212)685-6550. Estab. 1974. Represents 440 clients. Handles religious/inspirational fiction. Secular agency; handles adult religious/inspirational fiction. Member of AAR.

Contact: Query by mail. Responds in 1 mo.

Commission: 15%; foreign 20%.

Fees: No fees.

+WYLIE-MERRICK LITERARY AGENCY, 1138 S. Webster St., Kokomo IN 46902-6357. (765)459-8258, or (765)457-3783. E-mail: smartin@wylie-merrick.com, or rbrown@wylie-merrick.com. Website: www.wylie-merrick.com. Agents: S. A. Martin and Robert Brown. Estab. 1999. Represents clients. Secular agent; handles juvenile and adult religious/inspirational novels.

Contact: Query with SASE/first 10 pages. Considers simultaneous submissions. Responds in 1-3 mos.

Commission: 15%; foreign 20%.

Fees: Office expenses.

YATES & YATES, LLP, 1100 W. Town and Country Rd., Ste. 1300, Orange CA 92868-4654. (714)480-4000. Fax (714)480-4001. E-mail: email@yates-yates.com. Website: www.yates-yates.com. Estab. 1989. Recognized in the industry. Represents 50+ clients. Not currently open to unpublished authors or new clients. Handles novels and nonfiction for all ages, gift books, secular/crossover, and business books.

Contact: Letter or fax.

Commission: Negotiable

Fees: Negotiable.

Tips: "The law firm of Yates & Yates, LLP, in addition to providing traditional literary agenting services, also serves the legal needs of its author clients, having extensive experience in intellectual property law (including copyright and trademark), entertainment law, tax law, estate planning, and business law."

ADDITIONAL AGENTS

NOTE: The following agents did not return a questionnaire, but most have been identified as secular agents who handle religious/inspirational manuscripts. Be sure to send queries first if you wish to submit to them. Always check out an agent thoroughly before committing to work with him or her. Ask for references and a list of books represented, check with the Better Business Bureau, and ask your writing friends.

*AVATAR LITERARY AGENCY, 3389 Sheridan St., Ste. 308, Hollywood FL 33021. Agent: Karen Weiss.

*CRAIG NELSON CO. INC., 115 W. 18th St., 5th Floor, New York NY 10011. Agent: Craig Nelson. Member of AAR.

*DENISE MARCIL LITERARY AGENCY, 685 West End Ave., New York NY 10025. Agent: Denise Marcil. Member of AAR.

*JACQUELINE SIMENAUER LITERARY AGENCY, PO Box AG, Mantoloking NJ 08738-0390.

*JAMES LEVINE COMMUNICATIONS INC., 307 Seventh Ave., Ste. 1906, New York NY 10001. Agent: Arielle Eckstut.

*LIZA DAWSON ASSOCIATES, 240 W. 35th St., Ste. 500, New York NY 10001. Agent: Liza Dawson.

*THE MIDWEST LITERARY AND ENTERTAINMENT MANAGEMENT GROUP, 2545 Hilliard-Rome Rd., Ste. 320, Hilliard OH 43026. Website: www.hwei.com. Agent: Vivian Hall. Handles religious fiction, and can negotiate film, music, and TV production rights.
    Commission: 15%; foreign 20%.
    Fees: Charges $450 on acceptance of new client. No reading fee.

*NEW BRAND AGENCY GROUP. E-mail: office manager@literaryagent.net. Handles inspirational, spirituality/religious fiction and nonfiction. Member AAR.

*SHERRY JACKSON LITERARY AGENCY, 2448 E. 81st St., Ste. 154, Tulsa OK 74137. Agent: Sherry Jackson.

*STEPHANIE VON HIRSCHBERG LITERARY AGENCY, 1385 Baptist Church Rd., Yorktown Heights NY 10598. (914)243-9250.

*WILLIAM MORRIS LITERARY AGENCY, 2100 West End Ave., #1000, Nashville TN 37203. (615)963-3000. Member AAR.

CONTESTS

Note: Below is a listing of all the contests mentioned throughout this guide, plus additional contests that will be of interest. Some are sponsored by book publishers or magazines, some by conferences or writers' groups included in this guide. The contests are arranged by genre or type of material they are looking for such as poetry, fiction, nonfiction, etc. Send an SASE to each one you are interested in to obtain a copy of their complete contest rules and guidelines, or copy from their Website. A listing here does not guarantee the legitimacy of a contest. For guidelines on evaluating contests and to determine if a contest is legitimate or just a scam, go to: www.sfwa.org/beware/contests.html. Also note that because many contests had not set deadlines and final details for the next year's contests when this guide was written, details as given may change, so always get a copy of their current guidelines before entering.

CHILDREN/YOUNG ADULT CONTESTS, WRITING FOR

CHILDREN'S STORY WRITING CONTESTS. Various contests on Website: http://achieve-the-dream.net.

DELACORTE PRESS CONTEST FOR FIRST YOUNG ADULT NOVEL. Random House, 1745 Broadway, 9th Fl., New York NY 10019. For writers who have not previously published a young adult novel (for ages 12-18). No fee. Submit between October 1 and December 31 (may vary). Prize is $1,500, plus a $7,500 advance against royalties. Details: www.random house.com/kids/games/delacorte.html.

DEVOTED TO YOU BOOKS, PO Box 300, Sartell MN 56377. Toll-free (800)704-7250. E-mail: info@devotedtoyoubooks.com. Website: www.devotedtoyoubooks.com. Nondenominational. Tracy Ryks, pub. Seeks to teach children that God is present in their lives today; children's picture books for ages 1-8. Publishes 2 titles/yr. Sponsors a contest.

HIGHLIGHTS FOR CHILDREN, 803 Church St., Honesdale PA 18431. *Highlights for Children* Fiction Contest. Offers 3 prizes of $1,000 each for stories up to 800 words for children. Stories for beginning readers to 500 words. Send SASE for guidelines and current topic. No crime, violence, or derogatory humor. No entry fee or form required. Entries must be postmarked between January 1 and February 28.

MARGUERITE DE ANGELI PRIZE. Sponsored by Delacorte Press/Random House, Inc. Open to U.S. and Canadian authors who have not previously published a book for middle-grade readers. Submissions must be contemporary or historical fiction for ages 7-10 (80-144 manuscript pages) that examines the diversity of the American experience. Deadline: April 1-June 30th. Winner receives a $1,500 cash prize and book contract with a $3,500 advance against royalties. For rules, send SASE to: Marguerite de Angeli Contest, Bantam Doubleday Dell BFYR, 1745 Broadway, New York NY 10019. (212)782-9000. Website: www.random house.com/kids/games/marguerite.html.

MILKWEED PRIZE FOR CHILDREN'S FICTION, Milkweed Editions, Open Book Bldg., Ste. 300, 1011 Washington Ave. S., Minneapolis MN 55415-1246. Toll-free (800)520-6455. (612)332-3192. Fax (612)215-2550. E-mail: webmaster@milkweed.org. Website: www.milkweed.org/2_1_2.html. Children's novels for ages 8-13 years. Ongoing competition. Prize: $10,000 advance against royalties with publication of the book. Follow guidelines for their children's books on Website (no picture books, poetry, or short story collections).

+NEW WORLDS FIRST NOVEL AWARD, Hyperion Books for Children, PO Box 6000, Manhasset NY 11030-6000. For children's fiction, ages 8-12 yrs. Guidelines on Website: http://disney.go.com/disneybooks/hyperionbooks/rules.html. Prize is $1,500, plus book contract with $7,500 advance. April 30 deadline.

POCKETS, PO Box 340004, Nashville TN 37203-0004. (615)340-7333. Fax (615)340-7267. E-mail: pockets@upperroom.org. Website: www.pockets.org. United Methodist. Janet Knight, ed.; submit to Lynn W. Gilliam, ed. Devotional magazine for children (6-11 yrs.). Fiction-writing contest; submit between 3/1 and 8/15 every yr. Prize $1,000 and publication in Pockets. Length 1,000-1,600 wds. Must be unpublished and not historical fiction. Previous winners not eligible. Send to Pockets Fiction Contest at above address, designating "Fiction Contest" on outside of envelope. Send an SASE for return and response.

SKIPPING STONES: A Multicultural Magazine, PO Box 3939, Eugene OR 97403. Phone/fax (541)342-4956. E-mail: editor@skippingstones.org. Website: www.skippingstones.org. Not specifically Christian. Arun N. Toké, ed.; Mary Drew, asst. ed. A multicultural awareness and nature appreciation magazine for young people 8-17, worldwide. Annual Book Awards for published books and authors (deadline January 20); Annual Youth Honor Awards for students 7-17. Send SASE for guidelines. June 20 deadline.

FICTION CONTESTS

+AMERICAN CHRISTIAN ROMANCE WRITERS CONTEST. Rachel Hauck, pres.; PO Box 101066, Palm Bay FL 32910-1066. Website: www.acrw.net. E-mail loop, online courses, critique groups, and newsletter for members. Sponsors a contest open to nonmembers. Sponsoring a seminar in Nashville, September 15-18, 2005, speaker: Karen Ball; and in Houston, September 2006.

ANCIENT PATHS, PO Box 7505, Fairfax Station VA 22039. E-mail: ssburris@msn.com. Website: www.literatureclassics.com/ancientpaths. Christian/nondenominational. Skylar Hamilton Burris, ed. For a literate Christian audience, or non-Christians open to and moved by traditional-themed literature. Occasionally sponsors contest; check Website.

BLACKBERRY HILL CREATIVE ARTS AWARDS/SHORT STORY WRITING CONTEST, PO Box 368, Suttons Bay MI 49682. E-mail: KMCreativearts@aol.com. Website: www.black berryhillcreativeartsawards.com. Kristine Morris, dir. May 30 deadline. Prizes of $1,500, $500, $300. Check Website for contest details.

+BOULEVARD SHORT FICTION CONTEST FOR EMERGING WRITERS, PMB 325, 6614 Clayton Rd., Richmond Heights MO 63117. (314)862-2643. Website: www.boulevard magazine.com/contest.htm. Prize of $1,500, plus publication in Boulevard Magazine. For writers who have not had a book published with a nationally distributed publisher. Story to 8,000 wds. Entry fee $15. December 15 deadline.

BULWER-LYTTON FICTION CONTEST. For the worst opening line to a novel. Deadline: April 15. Website: www.bulwer-lytton.com. Rules on Website.

CANADIAN WRITER'S JOURNAL, White Mountain Publications, Box 1178, New Liskeard ON P0J 1P0 Canada. (705)647-5424. Canada-wide toll-free (800)258-5451. Fax (705)647-5424. E-mail: cwj@cwj.ca. Website: www.cwj.ca. Deborah Ranchuk, ed./pub. Sponsors semiannual short fiction contest (March 31 and September 30 deadlines); to 1,200 wds. Entry fee $5. Prizes $100, $50, $25. All fiction needs are filled by this contest. E-mail: cwc-calendar@cwj.ca.

+CHIAROSCURO SHORT STORY CONTEST. Website: www.thechiaroscuro.com. Up to 4,000 wds. No entry fee. Prize is publication and payment. Deadline June 15.

THE CHRISTY AWARDS. Donna Kehoe, Administrator, 1571 Glastonbury Rd., Ann Arbor MI 48103. Phone/fax (734)663-7931. E-mail: CA2000DK@aol.com. Website: www.christy awards.com/home.htm. Awards in 9 fiction genres for excellence in Christian fiction: allegory, contemporary/general, futuristic, historical (international and North American), romance, suspense/mystery, western, plus first novel. For submission guidelines and other information, see Website: www.christyawards.com. Awards are presented at an Annual

Christy Awards Banquet held Friday prior to the annual CBA international convention in June or July.

C. S. LEWIS CONTESTS. Check Website for current contests: www.cslewisclassics.com.

+DARK OAK MYSTERY CONTEST, 2743 S. Veterans Pkwy., #135, Springfield IL 62704-6402. Website: www.oaktreebooks.com. Mystery novels. July 31 deadline. Entry fee $35. 1st prize: book contract and promotional package; 2nd prize: complete ms critique and analysis; 3rd prize: $100 worth of Oak Tree books.

+THE FLANNERY O'CONNOR AWARD FOR SHORT FICTION. For submission guidelines, go to Website: www.ugapress.uga.edu/pressinfo/subguide_flan.html. Cash award of $1,000, plus publication under royalty book contract. Submission fee: $20. Submit between April 1 and May 31 (postmark).

GLIMMER TRAIN PRESS FICTION OPEN. Secular. Must be postmarked by June 30. Entry fee: $15. Prizes: $2,000 and publication, $1,000, and $600. Open to all writers, all themes, any length. Submit original, unpublished stories. Send SASE for results. Glimmer Train Press, 1211 N.W. Glisan St., #207, Portland OR 97209. (503)221-0836. Fax (503)221-0837. Website: www.glimmertrain.com.

GLIMMER TRAIN PRESS SHORT STORY AWARD FOR NEW WRITERS. Secular. Must be postmarked between February 1 and March 31. Also sponsors a fall contest with deadline between August 1 and September 30. Open to any writer who hasn't been published in a national magazine with a circulation over 5,000; unpublished stories 1,200-7,500 wds.; no children's stories; prizes $1,200, $500, and $300; staple pages together with name, address, and phone on first page, no SASE (will not be returned); $12 entry fee/story. Send to: Short-Story Award, Glimmer Train Press, 1211 N.W. Glisan St., #207, Portland OR 97209. (503)221-0836. Fax (503)221-0837. E-mail: info@glimmertrain.com. Website: www.glimmertrain.com. Results announced on July 1.

GLORY BOUND BOOKS/ONCE UPON A TWISTED TALE, PO Box 278, Cass City MI 48726. (989)635-7520. E-mail: info@gloryboundenterprises.com. Website: www.thegloryboundbookcompany.com. Leah Berry, pub. Annual contest for previously unpublished Christian authors for this series. Winner(s) will first be published on the Web and then in a paperback volume of "Tales," receiving 25% of the profit from all sales. Simultaneous submissions acceptable. Preview the current stories for "Once Upon a Twisted Tale" on the Website in the Collect-A-Book category to understand what they are looking for. Submit a 12-chapter manuscript of similar length to those on the site by December 31. Entry fee $20. Guidelines on Website.

HIDDEN TALENTS ANNUAL SHORT STORY CONTEST. Sponsored by Tall Tales Press (a small Canadian publisher), 20 Tuscany Valley Park N.W., Calgary BC T3L 2B6 Canada. (403)874-4293. E-mail: talltalespress@shaw.ca. May 31 deadline. Prizes of $25-500. Entry fee $10 US or Canadian. Details on Website: www.talltalespress.com/pages/882188/index.htm.

IOWA SHORT FICTION AWARD and **JOHN SIMMONS SHORT FICTION AWARD** are open to any writer who has not published a volume of prose fiction. Award-winning manuscripts will be published by the University of Iowa Press under their standard contract. The manuscript must be a collection of short stories of at least 150 pages. Submit between August 1 and September 30. No submission fee. Also sponsors a poetry contest. (319)335-2000. E-mail: uipress@uiowa.edu. Details: www.uiowa.edu/uiowapress/prize-rules.htm. Submit to: Iowa Short Fiction Award, Iowa Writers Workshop, 102 Dey House, Iowa City IA 52242-1000.

JAMES JONES FIRST NOVEL FELLOWSHIP for an American author with a first novel in progress. Offers a $6,000 fellowship/award. Deadline is March 1. Winners notified by September 1. Entry fee $20. Details: www.wilkes.edu/humanities/jones.asp. E-mail:

english@wilkes.edu. James Jones First Novel Fellowship, c/o Dept. of English, Wilkes University, Wilkes-Barre PA 18766.

+KATHERINE ANNE PORTER PRIZE IN SHORT FICTION. Submission guidelines at Website: www.unt.edu/untpress/series/kaporter.htm. Prize is $1,000 plus book publication. August 29 deadline. Entries can be a combination of short-shorts, short stories and novellas; 100-200 pgs.; 27,500-50,000 wds. Entry fee: $20.

+THE LONG FICTION CONTEST. Website: http://members.aol.com/wecspress/page4.htm. Stories 8,000-14,000 wds. December 15 postmark.

LORIAN HEMINGWAY SHORT STORY COMPETITION, PO Box 993, Key West FL 33041. E-mail: info@shortstorycompetition.com, or Calico2419@aol.com. Website: www.short storycompetition.com. First prize $1,000; 2nd and 3rd $500 apiece. Up to 3,000 wds. Details on Website.

+THE MARY MCCARTHY PRIZE IN SHORT FICTION, PO Box 4456, Louisville KY 40204. Website: www.sarabandebooks.org. Prize: $2,000 and publication of a collection of short stories, novellas, or a short novel. Postmark between January 1 and February 15. Entry fee: $20.

MEMPHIS MAGAZINE FICTION CONTEST with $1,000 grand prize, plus two $500 honorable mentions. August 1 deadline. Entrants must live within 150 miles of Memphis. Reading fee $10. Stories 3,000-5,000 wds. Details on Website: www.memphismagazine.com/fiction contestrules.asp. Fiction Contest, c/o *Memphis Magazine,* PO Box 1738, Memphis TN 38101.

MID-LIST PRESS SERIES AWARD FOR SHORT FICTION, 4324—12th Ave. S., Minneapolis MN 55407-3218. (612)822-3733. Fax (612)823-8387. E-mail: guide@midlist.org. Website: www.midlist.org. Annual contest of short fiction for previously unpublished writers. Send #10 SASE for guidelines and entry form; also on Website..

MID-LIST PRESS SERIES AWARD FOR THE NOVEL, 4324—12th Ave. S., Minneapolis MN 55407-3218. (612)822-3733. Fax (612)823-8387. E-mail: guide@midlist.org. Website: www.midlist.org. Annual contest of novels for previously unpublished writers. Mss 50,000 words and up. Send #10 SASE for guidelines and entry form; also on Website.

+NELLIGAN PRIZE FOR SHORT FICTION. Website: www.coloradoreview.com. Best short story. First prize $1,000, plus publication in the fall issue of *Colorado Review.* Entry fee $10. Deadline April 5 (may vary).

OPERATION FIRST BOOK/FICTION. Sponsored by Jerry B. Jenkins Christian Writers Guild, PO Box 88196, Black Forest CO 80908. For unpublished authors who are students or annual member of the Christian Writers Guild. One prize of publication by Tyndale House Publishers, plus $10,000 advance against royalties. Length 50,000-100,000 wds. Entry deadline October 19, 2005. Winner announced February 2006. For rules, go to: www .ChristianWritersGuild.com/contest.

+PARACLETE FICTION AWARD. Website: www.paracletepress.com/fictionaward, or http://calvin.edu/academic/engl/festival.htm. For a new or emerging writer unpublished by a major house. Christian themes. Winner receives $2,000 advance against royalties and publication by Paraclete Press. Deadline February 1.

+SARA ANN FREED MEMORIAL AWARD. For a first mystery novel. Website: www.twbook mark.com. Offers a $10,000 advance on a publishing deal. No entry fee. Deadline July 1.

+TAMARAK AWARD. Website: www.minnesotamonthly.com/edit/edit_tamarack.htm. Short fiction to 4,000 words. $10,000 prize. Winning story to be published in the fall issue of *Minnesota Monthly.* For residents of Minnesota, North Dakota, South Dakota, Iowa, Wisconsin, and Michigan only. Spring deadline.

TOBIAS WOLFF AWARD FOR FICTION. Short story or novel excerpt to 9,000 wds. Entries must be postmarked between December 1 and March 4 (may vary). Entry fee $15/story or chapter. First prize of $1,000. Unpublished works only. Send manuscripts to: The Tobias Wolff Award for Fiction, Mail Stop 9053, Western Washington University, Bellingham WA 98225. (360)650-4863. E-mail: bhreview@cc.wwu.edu. Website: www.wwu.edu/~bhreview.

WORD SMITTEN ANNUAL TEN TEN FICTION COMPETITION. For literary fiction (no genre fiction); exactly 1,010 wds. Award provides a grant of $1010. July deadline. Details on Website: www.wordsmitten.com/fiction.html.

NONFICTION CONTESTS

THE AFRICAN AMERICAN PULPIT, PO Box 15347, Pittsburgh PA 15237. Toll-free (800)509-8227. Phone/fax (412)364-1688. E-mail: Info@theafricanamericanpulpit.com. Website: www.TheAfricanAmericanPulpit.com. Hope for Life Intl., Inc. Victoria McGoey, project mngr.; Martha Simmons, pub. The only journal focused exclusively on the art of black preaching. Sponsors contest occasionally; advertised in the magazine.

THE AMY FOUNDATION sponsors the Amy Writing Awards, which is a call to present spiritual truth reinforced with biblical references in secular, nonreligious publications. First prize is $10,000 with a total of $34,000 given annually. The Amy Writing Awards is designed to recognize creative, skillful writing that presents in a sensitive, thought-provoking manner a biblical position on issues affecting the world today. To be eligible, submitted articles must be published in a secular, nonreligious publication, and must be reinforced with at least one passage of Scripture. For details on The Amy Writing Awards and a copy of last year's winning entries, contact: The Amy Foundation, PO Box 16091, Lansing MI 48901-6091. (517)323-6233. E-mail: amyfoundtn@aol.com. Website: www.amyfound.org.

AMY PASTOR AWARDS, PO Box 16091, Lansing MI 48901. Toll-free (877)727-4260. E-mail: amyfoundtn@aol.com. Website: www.amyfound.org. $10,000 first prize, plus 14 additional prizes from $200-$5,000, for 10 sermon outlines. Only open to pastors or associate pastors actually serving an organized congregation. Details on Website. Deadline is June 30.

ANNIE DILLARD AWARD IN CREATIVE NONFICTION. Contact: Brenda Miller. Essays on any subject to 9,000 wds. Entries must be postmarked between December 1 and March 15. Entry fee $15. First prize: $1,000. Unpublished works only, to 8,000 wds. Send manuscripts to contest at: Bellingham Review, Mail Stop 9053, Western Washington University, Bellingham WA 98225. (360)650-4863. E-mail: bhreview@cc.wwu.edu. Website: www.wwu.edu/~bhreview.

THE BROSE PRIZE, The Brose Foundation, Lake Forest College, 555 N. Sheridan, Lake Forest IL 60045. (847)735-5175. Fax (847)735-6192. E-mail: rmiller@lfc.edu. Professor Ron Miller, contact person. Offered only every 10 years for unpublished work; next contest 2010. September 1 deadline in contest year. Prizes from $4,000-$15,000; entries become the property of the college. Open to a book or treatise on the relationship between any discipline or topic and the Christian religion. Send SASE for guidelines.

+ERMA BOMBECK WRITING COMPETITION. Website: www.wcpl.lib.oh.us/adults/erma .html. No entry fee. Offers cash prizes. Personal essay, 450 wds. Submit between January 6 and February 20 (may vary).

GUIDEPOSTS CONTEST, 16 E. 34th St., New York NY 10016. (212)251-8100. Website: www.guideposts.org. Interfaith. Submit to The Editor. Writers Workshop Contest held on even years with a late June deadline. True, first-person stories (yours or someone else's), 1,500 words. Needs one spiritual message, with scenes, drama, and characters. Winners attend a week-long seminar (all expenses paid) on how to write for *Guideposts*. Also Young Writers Contest (see separate listing).

GUIDEPOSTS YOUNG WRITERS CONTEST, 16 E. 34th St., New York NY 10016. (212)251-

8100. Website: www.gp4teens.com. Interfaith. Submit to Kathryn Stattery. Offered annually for high school juniors and seniors. Write about an experience that affected you and deeply changed your life. True stories only. Contest and deadline announced in the October issue each year. Usually late November. Prizes: 1st $10,000; 2nd $8,000; 3rd $6,000; 4th $4,000; 5th $3,000; 6th-10th $1,000; 11th-20th $250 gift certificate for college supplies.

+LAMAR YORK PRIZE FOR NONFICTION, The Chatahoochee Review, Georgia Perimeter College, 2101 Womack Rd., Dunwoody GA 30338-4497. (770)551-3091. Website: www.gpc.edu/~gpccr/lamaryork.html. Reading fee $10. Prize $1,000. Unpublished essays to 5,000 wds. January 15 deadline.

*__THE LOOKOUT SENIOR ADULT WRITING CONTEST__, 8121 Hamilton Ave., Cincinnati OH 45231. For ages 70 and older. Articles only, 500-800 wds. Deadline April 15. Three winners of $100 each, plus publication and a free book; Honorable Mention $20, plus a free book; every entrant gets a $10 gift certificate for a Standard Publishing product.

*__THE LOOKOUT TEEN WRITING CONTEST__, 8121 Hamilton Ave., Cincinnati OH 45231. For ages 13-18. Articles only, 500-800 wds. Deadline August 31. Three winners of $100 each, plus publication and a free book; Honorable Mention $20, plus a free book; every entrant gets a $10 gift certificate for a Standard Publishing product.

MID-LIST PRESS SERIES AWARD FOR CREATIVE NONFICTION, 4324—12th Ave S., Minneapolis MN 55407-3218. (612)822-3733. Fax (612)823-8387. E-mail: guide@midlist.org. Website: www.midlist.org. Annual contest of creative nonfiction for previously unpublished writers. Mss 50,000 wds. & up. Submit entire manuscript between April 1 and July 1. Prize is $1,000 advance against royalties, plus publication. Entry fee: $20.

MONEY THE WRITE WAY, PO Box 3405, Auburn CA 95604. (916)205-4763. E-mail: carmel@moneythewriteway.com. Website: www.moneythewriteway.com. Write Spirit Publishing. Carmel Mooney, pub. Educates, inspires, and supports Christian writers, travel writers, authors, and e-publishing enthusiasts in making money as a writer of integrity. Occasionally sponsors writing contests.

+THE NUEBY AWARD. Sponsored by WordWright.biz, Inc. and the Writer's League of Texas. Website: www.wordwright.biz/neubyaward.shtml. For authors of nonfiction books, previously unpublished by royalty houses. First place, royalty contract; 2nd place, $250; 3rd place, $150.

+OPERATION FIRST BOOK/NONFICTION. Sponsored by Jerry B. Jenkins Christian Writers Guild, PO Box 88196, Black Forest CO 80908. For unpublished authors who are students or annual member of the Christian Writers Guild. One prize of publication by Tyndale House Publishers, plus $10,000 advance against royalties. Length 50,000-100,000 wds. Entry deadline October 19, 2005. Winner announced February 2006. For rules, go to: www.ChristianWritersGuild.com/contest.

+THE POWER OF PURPOSE AWARDS, A Worldwide Essay Competition. Website: www.powerofpurpose.org. Essays to 3,500 wds. No entry fee. Nineteen prizes totaling $500,000. Deadline. May 31.

+TRINITY PRIZE/CONTINUUM INTERNATIONAL PUBLISHERS, Tower Bldg., 11 York Rd., London SE1 7NX England. U.S. submissions: Henry Carrigan Jr., North American Publisher, T & T Clark Intl., 4775 Linglestown Rd, Harrisburg PA 17112. (0207)922 0880. Fax (0207)922 0881. E-mail: info@continuumbooks.com, or hcarriga@morehousegroup.com. Website: www.continuumbooks.com. R. J. Baird-Smith, pub. dir. Sponsors the Trinity Prize. See Website. March 1 deadline each year. $10,000 prize.

WINSOME WIT, 12971 Fieldstone Rd., Milaca MN 56353. (320)983-5910. E-mail: jbeuoy@winsomewit.com. Website: www.winsomewit.com. Nondenominational. Jay Beuoy, ed. We write to persuade the unbeliever through the use of satire, from a Christian worldview. Online e-zine. Contest details on Website.

PLAY/SCRIPTWRITING/SCREENWRITING CONTESTS

+THE AMERICAN ACCOLADES SCREENWRITING COMPETITION. Website: http://american accolades.com/contest_rules.htm.

BAKER'S PLAYS, PO Box 699222, Quincy MA 02269. (617)745-0805. Fax (617)745-9891. E-mail: 411@bakersplays.com. Website: www.bakersplays.com. John B. Welch, chief ed.; Re Herman, assoc. ed. High School Play Writing Contest. Deadline: January 30. No entry fee. Prizes: $500 (with publication), $250, $100. Plays about the high-school experience or appropriate for high-school productions. Requires a signature from a sponsoring drama or English teacher. May not be held every year.

+CHESTERFIELD FILM COMPANY WRITER'S FILM PROJECT. Website: www.chesterfield-co.com. Any genre. Awards up to five winners $20,000 stipends for a one-year fellowship based in Los Angeles to learn more about the craft of screenwriting.

CITA PLAYWRITING CONTEST, PO Box 26471, Greenville SC 29616. E-mail: information@cita.org. Website: www.CITA.org. (click on "Playwriting"). To encourage Christian playwrights, the writing of new plays and musicals that are informed by a biblical world-view in influencing our culture and furthering the Kingdom of God. Entries may be a full-length play, approximately 60+ pages, or a one-act play to 60 pages. Deadline for entries: March 1 (may vary).

CITA THEATRICAL SKETCH WRITING CONTEST, Lin Sexton, 501 Coronado Way, Modesto CA 95350. E-mail: information@cita.org. Dramatic or comedy sketch not to exceed 8 minutes in length. Deadline for entries: March 1 annually. Writers must be members of CITA (go to www.CITA.org for info on membership). Contest categories are Comedy and Drama. Download entry form and rules on Website.

FADE IN ON LINE. Annual screenplay and fiction competition. May 29 deadline. Over $10,000 in prizes. Website: www.fadeinonline.com.

+THE FIREHOUSE THEATRE PROJECT. Website: www.firehousetheatre.org/contest.htm. Annual Festival of New American Plays. First prize is $1,000 with staged reading and possible full production, and second prize is $500 and a stage reading. Deadline September 30 (may vary).

INTERNATIONAL SCREENPLAY COMPETITION. Presented by the American Screenwriters Association and Writer's Digest. More than $10,000 in prizes, including a trip to the "2005 Selling to Hollywood International Screenwriters Conference." Deadline: December 15 (may vary). Go to Website guidelines and an entry form: www.writersdigest.com/contests.

+MOONDANCE INTERNATIONAL FILM FESTIVAL. Website: www.moondancefestival.com. International contest to promote and encourage women screenwriters and filmmakers. Screenplays, animation, stage plays, and short stories are all eligible for review. Judges encourage nonviolence as a solution to conflict, and place high emphasis on character-driven, intelligent, and nonstereotypical roles for females.

+NICHOLL FELLOWSHIPS IN SCREENWRITING. Website: www.oscars.org/nicholl/index.html. An international contest held annually is open to any writer who has not optioned or sold a treatment, teleplay, or screenplay for more than $5,000. Up to five $25,000 fellowships are offered each year to promising authors.

OPEN DOOR SCREENPLAY COMPETITION. Website: www.scriptmag.com/contests/index.htm.

SCREENPLAY FESTIVAL. Annual festival where you can submit your screenplay. $1,000 grand prize in each category. Website: www.screenplayfestival.com.

+WALT DISNEY STUDIOS FELLOWSHIP PROGRAM. Website: www.members.tripod.com/disfel. Spring competition. Awards a residency program in Los Angeles for 8 lucky winners, with round-trip airfare and one month's accommodations.

POETRY CONTESTS

+ALLEN GINSBERG POETRY AWARDS. Website: www.pccc.edu/poetry/Prize/Allen2005.html. $1,000 first prize. Entry fee $15.

ANHINGA PRIZE FOR POETRY, PO Box 10595, Tallahassee FL 32302. (850)521-9920. Fax: (850)442-6363. E-mail: info@anhinga.org. A $2,000 prize for original poetry book in English. Winning manuscript published by Anhinga Press. For poets trying to publish a first or second book of poetry. Self-published books and chapbooks do not make you ineligible. Submissions must be 48-80 pages, excluding front matter (do not staple or bind manuscript). Number pages and include $20 reading fee. Submissions must be received between February 15 and May 1 each year. For details, go to: www.anhinga.org/contest .html.

ANNUAL ALDRICH POETRY COMPETITION, 258 Main St., Ridgefield CT 06877. (203)438-4519. Fax (203)438-0198. E-mail: general@aldrichart.org. Website: www.aldrichart.org. Send up to 15 poems, which may include work previously published in journals or self-published chapbooks. Prize: Honorarium and publication. Entry fee: $15. Deadline: September 30.

ANNUAL CAVE CANEM POETRY PRIZE. Supports the work of African American poets with excellent manuscripts who have not found a publisher for their first book. May 15 deadline. Winner receives $500, publication of their book by a national press, and 50 copies of the book. Details on Website: www.cavecanempoets.org/pages/prize.html#guidelines.

ANNUAL KENYON REVIEW PRIZE FOR POETRY, c/o Zoo Press, PO Box 22990, Lincoln NE 68542. E-mail: editors@zoopress.org. Website: http://zoopress.org. For previously unpublished book of poems in English, 48-100 pages, by an author who has not yet published a full-length book of verse. First prize $3,500 advance against royalties, publication by Zoo Press. Entry fee: $25. Deadline in mid-March (see Website to verify date). Mail or e-mail for rules.

ATLANTA REVIEW INTERNATIONAL POETRY COMPETITION, PO Box 8248, Atlanta GA 31106. E-mail: contest@atlantareview.com. Website: www.atlantareview.com. Dan Veach, ed. Prize of $1,000 and publication in the *Atlanta Review* given for an unpublished poem; five prizes of $100 each. Twenty International Publication Awards appear in over 120 countries in *Atlanta Review*. May 10 (postmark) deadline. Submit poems of any length with a $5 entry fee for the first poem, and $3 each for any additional poems. Discount on subscriptions and contest issue to all entrants. Send SASE, e-mail, or visit Website for details.

BARBARA MANDIGO KELLY PEACE POETRY AWARDS, An Annual Series of Awards to Encourage Poets to Explore and Illuminate Positive Visions of Peace and the Human Spirit. Deadline, July 1. Prizes: $1,000 for Adult; $200 for Youth 13-18 years; and $200 for Youth ages 12 and under. Adult entry fee: $15 for up to 3 poems (no youth fee). Details on Website: www.wagingpeace.org/new/programs/awardscontests/bmk/index.htm.

BLACKBERRY HILL CREATIVE ARTS AWARDS/POETRY CONTEST, PO Box 368, Suttons Bay MI 49682. E-mail: KMCreativearts@aol.com. Website: www.blackberryhillcreativearts awards.com. Kristine Morris, dir. June 30 deadline. Check Website for contest details.

BLUE MOUNTAIN ARTS, INC., PO Box 1007, Boulder CO 80306-1007. (303)449-0536. Fax (303)447-0939. E-mail: editorial@spsstudios.com. Website: www.sps.com. Submit to Editorial Department. General card publisher that does a few inspirational cards. Sponsors a poetry card contest online. Prizes for this biannual contest range from $50-300. June 30 deadline (may vary). Details on Website.

BOLLINGEN PRIZE FOR POETRY 2006. Awarded every two years to an American poet for the best book published in the previous two years, or for a lifetime achievement in poetry;

includes a $50,000 cash prize. For details visit Yale University Press Website: www
.yale.edu/yup.

BOSTON REVIEW ANNUAL POETRY CONTEST. Deadline is June 1. First prize is $1,000, plus
publication. Submit up to 5 unpublished poems; $15 entry fee (includes a subscription to
Boston Review). Submit manuscripts in duplicate with cover note. Send manuscript and
fee to: Poetry Contest, *Boston Review*, E53-407 MIT, Cambridge MA 02139. Website:
www.bostonreview.net

CAMPBELL CORNER POETRY PRIZE. Once a year, on October 15, a prize of $2,500 for best
entry is awarded by an outside panel of distinguished poets and writers. No entry fee. Winner and two finalists invited to give a reading at Sarah Lawrence College, plus publication.
Submit 1-3 poems. See Website for theme: http://pages.slc.edu/~eraymond/corner. Twelve
pages max. Send three sets in hard copy and one disk in ASCII text format only. Submit to:
Poetry Contest Director, c/o Office of Graduate Studies, Sarah Lawrence College, 1 Mead
Way, Bronxville NY 10708-5999. Deadline: March 15.

+CHATTELS OF THE HEART CONTEST, 2215 Hall Rd., Hartford WI 53027. (262)673-2775.
E-mail: wolfsrosebud@purescreen.ney. Patti Wolf, pub. Shows picturesque written work in
poetry, devotions, and personal testimony, based on a biblical view and supporting creation. Quarterly booklet; 20-24 pgs. Subscription $18. **NO PAYMENT** for 1st rts. Articles
250-425 wds. Responds in 12 wks. Seasonal 3 mos. ahead. No simultaneous submissions;
accepts reprints (tell when/where appeared). Prefers e-mail submissions (copied into
message). No sidebars. Accepts submissions from teens. Prefers KJV, NKJV. Guidelines
(also by e-mail/Website); copy .90/9x12 SAE. Contest: God's Creation Poetry Contest; 3
poems; $5 entry fee; publication in summer issue.

+CHERRY GROVE POETRY PRIZE. Website: www.cherry-grove.com. Deadline: June 15. Submit full-length ms. of poetry (48 pg. min.). Reading fee: $20. Cash prize of $1,000, plus
25 copies of the book.

+CHRISTIAN ONLINE CONTESTS, PO Box 262, Wolford VA 24658. E-mail: darlene@
christianmagazine.org. Website: www.ChristianMagazine.org. Darlene Osborne, pub.
Endeavors to bring you the best Christian information on the net. Monthly e-zine; circ.
500,000. Guidelines on Website. (Ads) Sponsors a monthly contest. No cash prizes. For
details go to http://contest.christianmagazine.org. Poetry contest; categories may vary from
month to month.

+CHRISTIAN POETRY CONTEST. Website: www.visionpage.info/id41.html. Submit up to 5
poems. First prize $1,750. Open April 9 to August 9.

DREAM HORSE PRESS ORPHIC PRIZE FOR POETRY, PO Box 640746, San Jose CA 95164.
Send 48-80 pages of poetry (paginated), plus two title pages (one with title, name, address,
phone number, and e-mail address, and one with title only), table of contents, acknowl-
edgment page, bio, and SASE. Entry fee: $20. Deadline May 1 (may vary). Prize: $500 and
100 copies of the book. Previously published OK, if not in book form. Manuscripts will be
recycled. See Website for details: www.dreamhorsepress.com. Electronic submissions OK, with
electronic fee payment. Dream Horse Press, PO Box 640746, San Jose CA 95164-0746.

+EMILY DICKINSON AWARDS IN POETRY. Website: www.popularpicks.com/Dickinson.htm.
Entry fee $12. Three prizes: $1,200, $750, and $500. Submit 3 poems, up to six pages.
Deadline: August 31. Not held every year. Check Website for current status.

49TH PARALLEL POETRY CONTEST. Contact: Brenda Miller. Poems in any style or on any
subject. Entries must be postmarked between December 1, and March 15. Entry fee $15.
First prize of $1,000. Unpublished works only. Send manuscripts to: 49th Parallel Poetry
Award, Mail Stop 9053, Western Washington University, Bellingham WA 98225. (360)650-
4863. E-mail: bhreview@cc.wwu.edu. Website: www.wwu.edu/~bhreview.

GRIFFIN POETRY PRIZE. Contact: Ruth Smith, mngr., The Griffin Trust for Excellence in

Poetry, 6610 Edwards Blvd., Mississauga ON L5T 2V6 Canada. (905)565-5993. E-mail: info@griffinpoetryprize.com. Website: www.griffinpoetryprize.com. Makes two $40,000 awards (one to a Canadian and one to a poet from anywhere in the world) for a collection of poetry published in English during the preceding year. Details on Website.

HEART SONGS, PO Box 3192, Williamsport PA 17701. (570)974-6225. E-mail: webmaster@ christianpoetry.org. Cross Way Publications. Jerry Hoffman, ed. For Christians desiring to focus on the attributes of our God through Jesus Christ; poetry only. Sponsors a semi-annual poetry contest. January through June 30; prizes $15, $30, $50. Details on Website at: www.christianpoetry.org/poetry_contest.html.

HOLLIS SUMMERS POETRY PRIZE COMPETITION, Ohio University Press, Scott Quadrangle, Athens OH 45701. Details on Website: www.ohiou.edu/oupress/poetryprize.htm. For unpublished collection of original poems, 60-95 pages. Entry fee $15. Deadline October 31. Prize: $500, plus publication.

HONICKMAN FIRST BOOK PRIZE IN POETRY is sponsored by The American Poetry Review. Open to any U.S. citizen who has not published a book of poetry. Prize is $3,000 and publication. Entry fee $20. Deadline October 31. Details: www.aprweb.org.

*****HOWARD NEMEROV SONNET AWARD**, The Formalist, 320 Hunter Dr., Evansville IN 47711. Entry fee: $3/sonnet. Original, unpublished sonnets. Winning entries will be published in *The Formalist.* June 15 deadline. Prize: $1,000. Put name, address, and phone number on back of entry. Send SASE for complete list of rules or for contest results.

KATE TUFTS DISCOVERY AWARD is presented annually for a first or very early work by a poet of genuine promise. Award is $10,000. Work submitted must be a book published between September 15, 2004, and September 15, 2005. Deadline is September 15. Details on Website: www.cgu.edu/tufts.

+KATHRYN A. MORTON PRIZE IN POETRY, PO Box 4456, Louisville KY 40204. Website: www.sarabandebooks.org. Prize: $2,000, plus publication of a book of poetry. Submit a minimum of 48 pages of poetry. Entry fee: $20.

THE MAY SWENSON POETRY AWARD, Utah State University Press, 7800 Old Main Hill, Logan UT 84322-7800. Annual. Prize: $1,000 award, publication the following spring, and royalties. Reading fee $25. Details on Website: www.usu.edu/usupress/poetcomp.htm.

MID-LIST PRESS SERIES AWARD FOR POETRY, 4324—12th Ave S., Minneapolis MN 55407-3218. (612)822-3733. Fax (612)823-8387. E-mail: guide@midlist.org. Website: www.midlist.org. Annual contest of poetry for previously unpublished writers. Manuscript must be at least 60 pages. Send #10 SASE for guidelines and entry form.

*****THE MILTON CENTER AWARD FOR EXCELLENCE IN WRITING-POETRY.** Award is given for a single poem in English that elevates the human spirit. Three prizes: $1,000, $500, $250. Entry fee $15 (payable to the Milton Center). Submissions must be postmarked between April 1 and November 15 (may vary). For guidelines, contact: Program Director, The Milton Center, Newman University, 3100 McCormick Ave., Wichita KS 67213-2097. (316)942-4291x326. Fax (316)942-4483. E-mail: miltonc@newmanu.edu. Or download from: www.newmanu.edu/MiltonCenter/contest.html.

MURIEL CRAFT BAILEY MEMORIAL POETRY AWARD. Awarded annually. July 1 deadline. Prizes of $100 to $1,000. Finalists published in the Comstock Review. Unpublished poems under 40 lines. Details on Website: www.comstockreview.org.

*****PENUMBRA'S ANNUAL POETRY & HAIKU CONTEST**, PO Box 15995, Tallahassee FL 32317-5995. Poems to 50 lines or 3-line haiku. Original, unpublished, and any theme. Reading fee required. Cash prizes. Deadline: June 30. Send SASE for guidelines.

*****THE PLOWMAN**, Box 414, Whitby ON L1N 5S4 Canada. (905)668-7803. The Plowman Ministries/Christian. Tony Scavetta, ed./pub. Poetry and prose of social commentary; any topics. Sponsors monthly poetry contests; $2/poem entry fee.

POETRY OF TODAY PUBLISHING, 2075 Stanford Village Dr., Antioch TN 37013-4450. (615)337-2725. Fax (347)823-9608. E-mail: editor@poetryoftoday.com. Website: www.poetryoftoday.com. Christian Business. Patrice M. Brooks, pub. Sponsors a monthly poetry contest.

POETRY SOCIETY OF VIRGINIA POETRY CONTEST, PO Box 35160, Richmond VA 23235. Website: www.poetrysocietyofvirginia.org. Categories for adults and students. Prizes from $10-100. Entry fee per poem for nonmembers: $3.

*READ 'N RUN BOOKS, PO Box 294, Rhododendron OR 97049. (503)622-4798. Fax (503)658-6233. Crumb Elbow Publishing. Michael P. Jones, pub. Poetry contest. Send SASE for information.

+ROSE VELARDI ANNUAL POETRY SHOWCASE. Website: www.purple-rose.com. January 31 deadline. Three prizes: $150, $200, and $50, plus publication and a subscription to *Promise Magazine.*

SARA HENDERSON HAY PRIZE, The Pittsburgh Quarterly, 36 Haberman Ave., Pittsburgh PA 15211-2144. Enter up to 3 poems of no more than 100 lines each. Prize is $500. Entry fee $10. Unpublished poems only. Details: www.city-net.com/~tpq.

*SHORT STORIES BIMONTHLY, 5713 Larchmont Dr., Erie PA 16509. Phone/ fax (814)866-2543. E-mail: 75562.670@compuserve.com. Website: www.thepoetryforum.com. Poetry Forum. Gunvor Skogsholm, ed. Poetry and prose that takes an honest look at the human condition. Chapbook contest, $12 entry fee. Prize: publication and 20 copies. Send SASE for information. December 15 deadline (may vary).

SILVER WINGS CONTEST, PO Box 2340, Clovis CA 93613-2340. (559)347-0194. E-mail: cloviswings@aol.com. Poetry on Wings/Baptist Evangelical. Jackson Wilcox, ed. Christian understanding and uplift through poetry, plus a sermon. Contest: Annual poetry contest on a theme(December 31 deadline); send SASE for details. Winners published in March. $200 in prizes. $3 entry fee.

SLIPSTREAM ANNUAL POETRY CHAPBOOK COMPETITION, Box 2071, Niagara Falls NY 14301. Website: www.slipstreampress.org/contest.html. Prize: $1,000, plus 50 copies of chapbook. December 1 deadline annually. Send up to 40 pages of poetry. Reading fee: $15.

STORY LINE PRESS' ANNUAL NICHOLAS ROERICH POETRY PRIZE. Roerich Competition, Three Oaks Farm, PO Box 1240, Ashland OR 97520-0055. E-mail: contest@storyline press.com. Website: www.storylinepress.com/projects/roerich.htm. Manuscripts of original poetry must be in English, and at least 48 pages in length. Poems may have previously appeared in magazines (including online), anthologies, or chapbooks, or in printed press runs of less than 500 copies. Prize: $1,000. Entry fee: $20. Deadline: October 31.

THOMAS MERTON POETRY OF THE SACRED CONTEST. Poetry that expresses, directly or indirectly, a sense of the holy or that, by mode of expression, evokes the sacred. The tone may be religious, prophetic, or contemplative. Deadline: December 31. First prize: $500; three Honorable Mentions, $50 each. Submit 1 poem. No entry fee. No poems returned. Submit poems to: The Thomas Merton Prize, The Thomas Merton Foundation, 2117 Payne St., Louisville KY 40206-2011, or e-mail to: hgraffy@mertonfoundation.org. For additional information, call (502)899-1991 or visit Website: www.mertonfoundation.org.

*TIME OF SINGING: A Magazine of Christian Poetry, PO Box 149, Conneaut Lake PA 16316. (814)382-8667. E-mail: timesing@toolcity.net. Website: www.timeofsinging .bizland.com. Lora Zill, ed. Sponsors 1-2 annual poetry contests on specific themes or forms ($2 entry fee/poem) with cash prizes (send SASE for rules).

UTMOST CHRISTIAN POETRY CONTEST, New Leaf Works, 121 Morin Maze, Edmonton AB T6K 1V1 Canada. E-mail: nathan@snowfaux.com. Website: www.utmostchristian writers.com/poetry-contest/poetrycontest.htm. Nathan Harms. Prizes of $25-750. Deadline is February 15 (may vary). Contest details on Website.

+WAR POETRY CONTEST. Website: www.winningwriters.com/annualcontest.htm. Sponsored by Winning Writers. Submit 1-3 unpublished poems on the theme of war, up to 500 lines total. $1,000 first prize; $2,250 in total prizes. Submit between March 1 and May 31. Entry fee $10.

+WORDS WORDS WORDS ANNUAL POETRY CONTEST, PO Box 61542, Fennell RPO, Hamilton ON L8T 5A1 Canada. E-mail: contest@wordswordswords.8k.com. Website: www.wordswordswords.4t/contests.html. Entry fee: $3, plus .50 for each additional poem (make check payable to Marylin Houle). First prize $250 Can. No specific theme. September 1 deadline.

YALE UNIVERSITY PRESS, 302 Temple St. (06511), PO Box 209040, New Haven CT 06520. (203)432-0960. Fax (203)432-0948. E-mail: robert.flynn@yale.edu. Website: www.yale.edu/yup. Robert Flynn, ed./religion. Yale Series of Younger Poets competition. Open to poets under 40 who have not had a book of poetry published. Submit manuscripts of 48-64 pages in February only. Entry fee $15. Send SASE for guidelines (also on Website).

MULTIPLE-GENRE CONTESTS

+ALEXANDRA WRITERS' CENTRE SOCIETY FREEFALL FICTION & POETRY CONTEST. Website: www.alexandrawriters.org/ctest.html. October 1 deadline. Fiction to 3,000 wds.; 5 poems. Prizes of $200 & $100 in both categories. Entry fee: $10.

AMERICAN LITERARY REVIEW CONTEST, PO Box 311307, University of North Texas, Denton TX 76203. Category is different each year. Winner receives $1,000 and publication in fall issue of the magazine. Reading fee $10. Check Website for current category and details: www.engl.unt.edu/alr/contest.htm.

ANNUAL DANA AWARDS. Categories include novel, short fiction, poetry, and portfolio (3 mss). Reading fees $10-20. Prizes up to $3,000 and $1,000. Details on Website: www.danaawards.com/guidelines.htm. E-mail: danaawards@pipeline.com (questions only).

ANTHOLOGY PROSE & POETRY CONTESTS, PO Box 4411, Mesa AZ 85211. Winners will be published in future editions of *Anthology Magazine*. First prize $150, additional prizes include subscriptions and T-shirts. Entry fee $5. Details on Website: www.anthology.org/Contests.html.

AUTHOR LINK CONTESTS. Website: www.authorlink.com. Sponsors a variety of contests each year; check Website for current listings. Scroll down to "Authorlink News/Info" and click on "Contests."

+BAKELESS LITERARY PUBLICATION PRIZES. Website: www.bakelessprize.org. Book series competition for new authors of literary works of poetry, fiction, and nonfiction. Processing fee: $10. Submit between October 1 and November 15.

BEGINNINGS: A Magazine for Novice Writers, PO Box 92, Shirley NY 11967. (631)205-5542. E-mail: jenineb@optonline.net. Website: www.scbeginnings.com. Partnered with Coffeehouse for Writers. Jenine Boisits, ed-in-chief. Sponsors poetry and short story contests, 4 contests for each season. See Website for current contests and details.

+BRIAR CLIFF REVIEW POETRY AND FICTION COMPETITION. Website: www.briarcliff.edu/bcreview/contest.htm. $500 first place, plus publication. Short stories to 6,000 wds. Entry fee: $15 per story or 3 poems. Deadline: November 1.

BRISTOL SERVICES WRITING COMPETITIONS, PO Box 1000, Carlsborg WA 98324-1000. E-mail: services@bristolservicesintl.com. Website: www.bristolservicesintl.com. Recent contests for short stories and stories for children. Check Website for current contests.

BYLINE, Box 5240, Edmond OK 73083-5240. Phone/fax (405)348-5591. E-mail: Mpreston@bylinemag.com. Website: www.BylineMag.com. Secular. Marcia Preston, ed.; Carolyn Wall, fiction ed. Sponsors many contests year-round; details included in magazine, on Website, or send SASE for flier.

$CATHOLIC DIGEST, PO Box 6001, Mystic CT 06355. (860)536-2611. Fax (860)536-5600. E-mail: cdigest@bayardpubs.com. Submissions to: cdsubmissions@bayardpubs.com. Website: www.CatholicDigest.com. Catholic/Bayard Publications. Joop Koopman, ed.; submit to Articles Editor. Readers have a stake in being Catholic and a wide range of interests: religion, family, health, human relationships, good works, nostalgia, and more. See Website for current contest, or send an SASE.

CHICKEN SOUP BOOKS. Website: www.chickensoup.com. See Website for list of current contests.

COCHRAN'S CORNER, 1003 Tyler Ct., Waldorf MD 20602-2964. (361)644-2476. John Treasure, ed. asst. Sponsors an annual contest; see magazine or ask to be put on mailing list for contest info.

+COLUMBIA FICTION/POETRY/NONFICTION CONTEST. Website: www.columbia.edu/cu/arts/journal. Length: 20 double-spaced pages or up to 5 poems. Prize: $500, plus publication. Deadline: March 31.

ESSENCE PUBLISHING CO., INC., 20 Hanna Ct., Belleville ON K8P 5J2 Canada. (613)962-2360. Toll-free (800)238-6376. Fax (613)962-3055. E-mail: publishing@essence group.com. Website: www.essencegroup.com. Essence Communications Group. Cathy Jol, submissions ed. Sponsors The Essence Treasury Writing Competition.

+GENERATION X NATIONAL JOURNAL CONTESTS, 411 W. Front, Wayland IA 52654. (319)256-4221. E-mail: genxjournal2004@yahoo.com. Website: www.genxnatljournal .com. Kathy Stoops, mng. ed. For those who came of age during the late 80s and yearly 90s. Quarterly creative jour.; 60 pgs.; circ. 100. Guidelines/theme list (also by e-mail/Website); copy $3. (Ads)

    Contests: Watch Website for future contests.

GUIDEPOSTS FOR KIDS ON THE WEB, 1050 Broadway, Ste. 6, Chesterton IN 46304. (219)929-4429. Fax (219)926-3839. E-mail: gp4k@guideposts.org. Website: www.gp4k.com. Guideposts, Inc. Mary Lou Carney, ed.; submit to Rosanne Tolin, mng. ed. For kids 7-12 yrs. (emphasis at upper level). Online mag. only. Has giveaways, art and writing contests for kids in Home School Zone (section of the e-zine).

*THE HYMN: A Journal of Congregational Song, School of Theology, Boston University, 745 Commonwealth Ave., Boston MA 02215-1401. Toll-free (800)THE-HYMN. Fax (617)353-7322. E-mail: hymneditor@aol.com. Website: www.bu.edu/sth/hymn, or www.hymn society.org. Hymn Society in the US & Canada. Beverly A. Howard, ed. (5423 Via Alberca, Riverside CA 92507-6477). For church musicians, hymnologists, scholars; articles related to the congregational song. Quarterly journal; 60 pgs.; circ. 3,000. Subscription $55. 85% unsolicited freelance; 15% assigned. Query; Hymn text and tune contests for special occasions or themes.

INSIGHT, 55 W. Oak Ridge Dr., Hagerstown MD 21740-7301. (301)393-4038. Fax (301)393-4055. E-mail: insight@rhpa.org. Website: www.insightmagazine.org. Review and Herald/Seventh-day Adventist. Lori Peckham, ed. A magazine of positive Christian living for Seventh-day Adventist high school and college students. Sponsors a nonfiction and poetry contest; includes a category for students under 22. Prizes to $250. June deadline (may vary). Send SASE for rules.

INTERNATIONAL LIBRARY OF PHOTOGRAPHY FREE PHOTO CONTEST, 3600 Crondall Ln., Ste. 101, Owings Mills MD 21117. Website: www.picture.com. Ongoing contest. $10,000 first prize; $60,000 in prizes to amateur photographers. Send one photo in one of these categories: Action, Children, Humor, Nature, People, Animals/Pets, Portraiture, Sports, Travel, or Other. Color or black & white, up to 8x10. Photos will not be returned, but photographer retains all rights to the photo.

"IN THE BEGINNING WAS THE WORD…" LITERARY ARTS CONTEST. Sponsored by the

Lake Oswego, Oregon, United Church of Christ. Categories include short fiction, creative nonfiction, or poetry; previously unpublished; to 4,000 words. One submission per person. Deadline: September 1 each year. Prizes of $500, $250, and $100 for first three places. Also sponsors a Young Writers' Contest for those 18 years and younger (write or call for details). Send SASE for official entry form to: Lake Oswego United Church of Christ, 1111 S.W. Country Club Rd., Lake Oswego OR 97034, (503)635-4348, or e-mail: loucc@pacifier.com.

+**JOHN T. LUPTON NEW VOICES IN LITERATURE AWARDS.** Website: www.booksfor lifefoundation.com/php/luptonawards.php#guidelines. Professional query letters and proposals to submit to agents or publishers. Prizes are $10,000 for each category. Entry fee: $25. Deadline May 5 (may vary).

MINISTRY & LITURGY, 160 E. Virginia St., #290, San Jose CA 95112. (408)286-8505. Fax (408)287-8748. E-mail: mleditor@rpinet.com. Website: www.rpinet.com/ml, or www .rpinet.com/vaaentry.pdf. Resource Publications, Inc. Nick Wagner, ed. dir. To help liturgists and ministers make the imaginative connection between liturgy and life. Visual Arts Awards.

+**MISSISSIPPI REVIEW PRIZE.** Website: www.mississippireview.com/contest.html. Fiction & Poetry. $1,000 prize in each category. April 2 to October 1 (may vary). Entry fee: $15 per entry.

MOMSENSE, 2370 S. Teenton Way, Denver CO 80231. (303)733-5353. Fax (303)733-5770. E-mail: info@mops.org. Website: www.mops.org. MOPS Intl., Inc. (Mothers of Preschoolers). Elizabeth Jusino, mng. ed. Nurtures mothers of preschoolers from a Christian perspective with articles that both inform and inspire on issues relating to womanhood and motherhood. Sponsors several contests per year for writing and photography. Check Website for details on current contests.

+**MONA SCHREIBER PRIZE FOR HUMOROUS FICTION AND NONFICTION.** Website: http://home.pcmagic.net/brashcyber/mona.htm. Humorous fiction and nonfiction to 750 wds. Prizes: $500, $250, and $100. Entry fee: $5.

+**NEW MILLENNIUM AWARDS.** Website: www.newmillenniumwritings.com/awards.html. Fiction, poetry and nonfiction; $1,000 award for each. Fiction and nonfiction to 6,000 wds.; 3 poems to 5 pgs. Total. Entry fee: $17.

*__SHARING THE PRACTICE__, 100 S. Chestnut St., Kent OH 44240-3402. (330)678-0187. E-mail: dunmovin720@aol.com. Website: www.apclergy.org. Academy of Parish Clergy/ Ecumenical/Interfaith. Dr. Darryl Zoller, ed-in-chief. (journal@apclergy.org); Dr. Forrest V. Fitzhugh, book rev. ed. (bond007@texas.net). Growth toward excellence through sharing the practice of parish ministry. Book of the Year Award ($100+), Top Ten Books of the Year list, Parish Pastor of the Year award ($200+). Inquire by e-mail to: DIELPADRE@ aol.com.

SOUL-MAKING LITERARY COMPETITION. November 30 deadline. Prose and poetry. Submit up to 3 poems, one per page. First prize $100; $5 entry fee. For complete guidelines, send SASE to: Soul-Making Literary Competition, Webhallow House, 1544 Sweetwood Dr., Colma CA 94015-2029; or e-mail: PenNobHill@aol.com. Website: www.SoulMakingContest.us.

SOWING SEEDS ANNUAL WRITING CONTEST. Soliciting entries in four categories: Devotions (600-750 wds.); Sermons (to 2,000 wds.); Prayer; and Poetry. Winner in each category gets $100, plus publication on their Web page. Winners will also be submitted to other publications. Entries must be postmarked by June 30, 2005. Entry fee is $20 for first submission, $15 each additional. For details and sample entries, go to their Website at www.sowingseedsoffaith.com/writing.htm. Send submissions to: Sowing Seeds Ministry, 47 Greenwell Ct., Lynchburg VA 24502.

THE STORYTELLER, 2441 Washington Rd., Maynard AR 72444. (870)647-2137. Fax (870)647-2454. Fax (870)647-2454. E-mail: storyteller1@cox-internet.com. Contest

Website: www.expage.com/fossilcreekpub. Fossil Creek Publishing. Regina Cook Williams, ed./pub.; Ruthan Riney, review ed. Family audience; geared to (but not limited to) new writers. Offers 1 or 2 paying contests per year, along with People's Choice Awards, and Pushcart Prize nominations.

*STUDIO: A Journal of Christians Writing, 727 Peel St., Albury NSW 2640 Australia. Phone/fax +61 2 6021 1135. E-mail: pgrover@bigpond.com. Submit to Studio Editor. See copy of journal for contest details.

TEEN LIGHT: The Teen 2 Teen Christian Magazine, 6118 Bend of River, Dunn NC 28334. (910)980-1126. E-mail: publisher@teenlight.org. Website: www.teenlight.org. Writers' Ministries, Inc. Annette Dammer, pub.; submit to Rebekah Hamrick. Totally teen authored; uses professional Christian writers to mentor their teen journalists so they may reach the world for Christ. We sponsor contests for teens sporadically. See e-zine.

TICKLED BY THUNDER, 14076 86A Ave., Surrey BC V3W 0V9 Canada. (604)591-6095. E-mail: info@tickledbythunder.com. Website: www.tickledbythunder.com. Larry Lindner, ed. Contest for fiction (February 15 annual deadline) and poetry (February 15, May 15, August 15, and October 15 annual deadlines). Article contests for subscribers only (February 15, May 15, August 15, and October 15 deadlines). Prizes range from $5-150 & up. Send SASE for guidelines.

*VIRGINIA PINES PRESS, 7092 Jewell-North, Kinsman OH 44428. (330)876-3504. Fax (209)882-5803. E-mail: virginiapines@nlc.net. Website: http://virginiapines.com. Helen C. Caplan, pub. Publishes fiction with a Christian viewpoint and creative nonfiction that helps document 21st-century America. Sponsors several cover design contests each year. See Website for details of current contest.

THE WHITBREAD BOOK AWARDS. Go to: www.whitbread-bookawards.co.uk. The site lists a number of writing contests in the UK.

WOMEN'S EMPOWERMENT AWARDS WRITING COMPETITION, E.F.S. Enterprises, Inc., 2844 Eighth Ave., Ste. 6E, New York NY 10039. (212)283-8899. E-mail: info @efs-enterprises.com. Website: www.efs-enterprises.com. Rita Baxter, contest director. Deadline: Preliminary October 1; Final November 30. Entry fee $20. Prizes: Online publishing contract for 1st and 2nd place winners. For fiction, plays, and essays. See Website for entry form and additional information.

THE WRITER, 21027 Crossroads Cir., Waukesha WI 53189. (262)796-8776. Fax (262)798-6468. E-mail: editor@writermag.com. Website: www.writermag.com. Secular. Elfreida Abbe, ed. How-to for writers; lists religious markets periodically. Occasionally sponsors a contest. Check Website.

WRITER'S DIGEST, 4700 E. Galbraith Rd., Cincinnati OH 45207. (513)531-2690, ext. 1483. Fax (513)531-1843. E-mail: wdsubmissions@fwpubs.com. Website: www.writers digest.com. Secular/F & W Publications. Jane Friedman, mng. ed. To inform, instruct, or inspire the freelancer. Sponsors annual contest for articles, short stories, poetry, children's fiction and scripts (categories vary); May deadline (varies). More than $25,000 in prizes. Also The National Self-Publishing Book Awards with $6,000+ in prizes, including $1,500 grand prize. Send SASE for rules, or visit Website: www.writersdigest.com/novalearn.asp. Plus National Zine Publishing Awards. Official rules and entry forms are available online at: www.writersdigest.com/catalog/contest_frame.html. And International Screenplay Competition; $5,000, plus trip to a screenwriting conference; deadline October 31.

WRITER'S JOURNAL, PO Box 394, Perham MN 56573-0394. (218)346-7921. Fax (218)346-7924. E-mail: writersjournal@lakesplus.com. Website: www.writersjournal.com. Val-Tech Media/Secular. Leon Ogroske, ed. Runs several contests each year. Prizes up to $300. Categories are short story, horror/ghost, romance, travel writing, and fiction; 3 poetry; 2 photo. Send an SASE requesting guidelines.

WRITERS' UNION OF CANADA AWARDS & COMPETITIONS, 96 Richmond St. E., Ste. 200, Toronto ON M5C 1P1 Canada. (416)703-8982. Fax (416)504-7656. E-mail: info@writers union.ca. Website: www.writersunion.ca/compete.htm. Various competitions. See Website for details.

$THE WRITING PARENT: For Parents Striving to Become Professional Writers, 127 Bishop Rd. N.W., Cartersville GA 30121-7324. E-mail: agklocke@bellsouth.net, or editor@thewritingparent.com, or shelley@thewritingparent.com. Website: www.thewritingparent.com. The Write Side Up, Inc.; secular. Angela Giles Klocke, pub. For writers who are also parents (not a parenting-in-general market). Current contests listed on Website.
   Contest: Current contests listed on Website.

YOUNG SALVATIONIST, PO Box 269, Alexandria VA 22313-0269. (703)684-5500. Fax (703)684-5539. E-mail: ys@usn.salvationarmy.org. Website: http://publications.salvation armyusa.org. The Salvation Army. Laura Ezzell, mng. ed. For teens & young adults in the Salvation Army. Sponsors a contest for fiction, nonfiction, poetry, original art, and photography. Send SASE for details.

SPONSORED BY WRITERS' CONFERENCES/GROUPS

(This list includes only those contests that are open to nonmembers of the groups or nonattendees at the conferences.)

AMERICAN CHRISTIAN ROMANCE WRITERS NOBLE THEME CONTEST. Novel contests for those who have not had a novel-length fiction book published in the last 5 years (up to 40,000 wds.) Complete guidelines for contest on Website: www.acrw.net/conference/contest.shtml.

+ARKANSAS WRITERS CONTEST. Conference in Little Rock, AR; June 3-4, 2005 (always 1st Friday & Saturday of June). Contact: Barbara Mulkey, 9317 Claremore, Little Rock AR 72227. (501)312-1747. E-mail: blm@aristotle.net. Attendance: 200. Sponsors 32 contests; one $6 entry free covers all contests.

+BETHEL CHRISTIAN WRITERS' CONTEST. Bethel College. Contact: Kim Peterson, 1001 W. McKinley Ave., Mishawaka IN 46545-5509. (574)257-3375. E-mail: petersk@bethel college.edu. May sponsor a contest.

BLUE RIDGE MOUNTAIN CHRISTIAN WRITERS CONFERENCE. Lifeway Ridgecrest Conference Center; April 17-21, 2005. Contact: Ron Pratt, LifeWay Christian Resources, One Lifeway Plaza, Nashville TN 37234-0106. (615)241-2065. Fax (615)277-8232. E-mail: ron.pratt@lifeway.com, or Yvonne Lehman, PO Box 188, Black Mountain NC 28770. Website: www.lifeway.com/conferencecenter. Sponsors a contest.

+CHRISTIAN WRITERS GROUP OF GREATER SAN ANTONIO AREA CONTEST. Contact: Brenda Blanchard, 2827 Olive Ave., Schertz TX 78154-3719. (210)945-4163. Fax (210)945-6613. E-mail: ZBGP1@aol.com. Has 4-8 speakers/yr. Sponsors a contest.

EVANGELICAL PRESS ASSOCIATION, PO Box 28129, Crystal MN 55428. (763)535-4793. Fax (763)535-4794. E-mail: mailto:director@epassoc.org. Website: www.epassoc.org. Sponsors annual contest for member publications. New "Best Freelance Article" category open to articles in EPA publications authored by freelancers who are members of EPA.

FAITH, HOPE & LOVE is the inspirational chapter of Romance Writers of America. Dues for the chapter are $24/yr., but you must also be a member of RWA to join (dues $75/yr.). Chapter offers these services: online list service for members, a Web page, 20-pg. bimonthly newsletter, annual contest, monthly online guest chats with multipublished authors and industry professionals, connects critique partners by mail or e-mail, and latest romance-market information. To join, contact RWA National Office, 16000 Stuebner

Airline Rd., Ste. 140, Spring TX 77379. (832)717-5200. Fax (832)717-5201. Website: www.rwanational.org. Or go to FHL Website: www.faithhopelove-rwa.org. Inspirational Readers Choice Contest by subgenre categories for published works; deadline April 1, 2005; cash prizes. Send SASE for guidelines. Membership (150+) open.

FELLOWSCRIPT CONTEST. Marcia Laycock, 5007—42A St., Ponoka AB T4J 1M3 Canada. (403)783-3044. E-mail: info@inscribe.org. Website: www.inscribe.org. Inscribe Christian Writers' Fellowship. Fall contest in conjunction with Inscribe's Fall Conference. Details on Website, or write and ask to be on mailing list. Sponsors two conferences each year, one open and one for members only.

FELLOWSHIP OF CHRISTIAN POETS ANNUAL CONTESTS, PO Box 93345, Lakeland FL 33804. E-mail: john@christianpoets.com. Website: www.christianpoets.com. Sponsors 6 contests a year. Check Website for current contests and details.

HEART OF AMERICA CHRISTIAN WRITERS' NETWORK. Overland Park KS. Contact: Mark and Jeanette Littleton, 3706 N.E. Shady Lane Dr., Gladstone MO 64119. Phone/fax (816)459-8016. E-mail: MarkLitt@aol.com. Sponsors a contest (open to nonmembers).

*INSCRIBE CHRISTIAN WRITERS' FELLOWSHIP. Calgary & Edmonton (various locations across Canada). Contact: Marcia Laycock, 5007—42 A Street, Ponoka AB T4J 1M3 Canada. (403)783-3044. Fax (403)783-6500. E-mail: info@inscribe.org. Website: www.inscribe .org. Sponsors a fall contest open to nonmembers; details on Website.

INSPIRATIONAL WRITERS ALIVE! Groups meet in Houston, Pasadena, Jacksonville, Amarillo, and Humble TX. Contact: Martha Rogers, 6038 Greenmont, Houston TX 77092-2332. (713)686-7209. E-mail: marthalrogers@sbcglobal.net. Sponsors annual contest November 1-April 1 (may vary). Seven categories. Entry fees $10 for short pieces; $15 for book proposals. Prizes are $25 first prize, $15 second prize, and $10 third prize. Include 10x13 SAE for return. E-mail for official rules and entry form.

+INSPIRATIONAL WRITERS ALIVE! AMARILLO CONTEST. Contact: Helen Luecke, 2921 S. Dallas, Amarillo TX 79103. (806)376-9671. E-mail: hcoluecke@arn.net. Sponsors a seminar, first weekend in April 2005. Sponsors a contest; one category opened to nonmembers.

+INSPIRATIONAL WRITERS FELLOWSHIP CONTEST. Contact: Jan R. Sady, 2026 Langville Rd., Mayport PA 16240. (814)856-2560. E-mail: janfran@alltel.net. Sponsors a contest in February (February 14 deadline).

*INTERNATIONAL BLACK WRITERS. Chicago area. Contact: Mabel Terrell, PO Box 437134, Chicago IL 60654. (773)468-5754. Membership (2,000) open. Sponsors a contest open to nonmembers.

*LITERARY ARTS FESTIVAL. The Milton Center/Wichita KS. February 2005. Cosponsored with Newman University English Department. Contact: Dr. Bryan Dietrich, Newman University, 3100 McCormick, Wichita KS 67213-2097. (316)942-4291. Fax (316)942-4483. E-mail: miltonc@newmanu.edu. Website: www.newmanu.edu/miltoncenter. Sponsors a contest.

OZARK CREATIVE WRITERS CONFERENCE. Contact: Clarissa Willis, 2603 W. Walnut, Johnson City TN 37604. (423)929-1049. E-mail: ozarkcreativewriters@earthlink.net. Website: www.ozarkcreativewriters.org. Sponsors 25-30 contests each year.

SILOAM SPRINGS WRITERS. Contact: Margaret Weathers, 716 W. University, Siloam Springs AR 72761-2658. (479)524-6598. Website: http://sswc.flash57.com. Sponsoring a contest open to nonmembers. Prose and poetry. Awards from $5 to $25. July 1 deadline. Send SASE for rules.

SOUTHWEST WRITERS ANNUAL CONTEST. Contact: Southwest Writers, 3721 Morris St. N.E., Ste. A,, Albuquerque NM 87111-3611. (505)265-9485. Fax (505)265-9483. E-mail: contactus@southwestwriters.com. Website: www.southwestwriters.com. Sponsors the Southwest Writers Contest (send SASE for details and entry form). Prizes: $150, $100, $75.

STATE OF MAINE WRITERS' CONFERENCE. Contact: Jeff Belyea/Jim Brosnan, 16 Foley Ave., Saco ME 04072. (207)284-4119. E-mail: jeff@mindgoal.com. Sponsors several contests.

+THE WORD GUILD, an association of Canadian writers and editors who are Christians. Exec. Director: N. J. Lindquist, Box 487, Markham ON L3P 3R1 Canada. (905)294-6482. Fax (905)471-6912. E-mail: info@thewordguild.com. Website: www.thewordguild.com. Sponsors the Write! Canada Conference (formerly God Uses Ink), plus additional one-day conferences in various locations, and several contests open to nonmembers.

+WRITE ON THE BEACH WRITING CONTEST. Don Clark, Write on the Beach, PO Box 2284, Ocean Shores WA 98569. Toll-free (800)76-BEACH. (360)289-2451. Website: www .wotbeach.com. Sponsors a contest. Check Website for guidelines. Secular.

+WRITERS WEEKEND AT THE BEACH LIMERICK CONTEST. Contact: Birdie Etchison/Pat Rushford, PO Box 877, Ocean Park WA 98640-0877. (360)665-6576. E-mail: etchison@ pacifier.com. Website: www.patriciarushford.com. Sponsors a limerick contest.

THE WRITING ACADEMY SEMINAR. Sponsors year-round correspondence writing program and annual seminar in various locations. Contact: Mar Korman, 1128 Mule Lake Dr. N.E., Outing MN 56662. (218)792-5144. E-mail: pattyk@wams.org. Website: www.wams.org. Sponsors a contest open to nonattendees (rules are posted on Website).

RESOURCES FOR CONTESTS

BYLINE MAGAZINE CONTEST LISTINGS. www.bylinemag.com.

CONTESTS LINK PAGE. www.wordsmithshoppe.com.

FREELANCE WRITING: WEBSITE FOR TODAY'S WORKING WRITER. www.freelance writing.com/contests.html.

KIMN SWENSON GOLLNICK'S WEBSITE. Contest listings. Website: www.KIMN.net.

WRITER'S DIGEST WEBSITE FOR CONTESTS. www.writersdigest.com. Search: Contests.

DENOMINATIONAL LISTING OF BOOK PUBLISHERS AND PERIODICALS

An attempt has been made to divide publishers into appropriate denominational groups. However, due to the extensive number of denominations included, and sometimes incomplete denominational information, some publishers inadvertently may have been included in the wrong list. Additions and corrections are welcome.

ANTIOCHIAN ORTHODOX

Book Publishers:
Conciliar Press
Periodicals:
Again
The Handmaiden

ASSEMBLIES OF GOD

Book Publishers:
Gospel Publishing House
Logion Press
Periodicals:
Club Connection
Discovery Trails
Enrichment
High Adventure
Live
Maranatha News
Testimony (Canada)
Today's Pentecostal Evangel
Woman's Touch

BAPTIST, FREE WILL

Periodicals:
CoLaborer
Heartbeat

BAPTIST, SOUTHERN

Book Publishers:
Baylor Univ. Press
Broadman & Holman
New Hope Publishers
Southern Baptist Press
Periodicals:
Church Administration
Crusader
Glory Songs
HomeLife
Journey
Let's Worship
Light
Living with Teenagers
Mature Living
Music Makers
Music Time
On Mission

ParentLife
Senior Musician
Stand Firm

BAPTIST (other)

Book Publishers:
Baptist Publishing House
R.H. Boyd (Missionary)
Judson Press (American)
Mercer Univ. Press (Baptist)
Periodicals:
African American Pulpit (American)
American Baptist in Missions
BGC World
CoLaborer (Free Will)
Courage (Regular)
Friends Journal
Heartbeat (Free Will)
Link & Visitor
Living My Faith (Regular)
Primary Pal (Regular)
Real Faith in Life (Regular)
Secret Place (American)
Sword of the Lord (Independent)
Writer's Forum

CATHOLIC

Book Publishers:
ACTA Publications
Alba House
American Catholic Press
Canticle Books
Catholic Book Publishing
Catholic Univ. of America Press
Cistercian Publications
Cross Cultural Publications
Dimension Books
HarperSanFrancisco (Cath. bks.)
ICS Publications
Libros Liguori
Liguori Publications
Liturgical Press
Loyola Press
Thomas More
Novalis
Oregon Catholic Press

OSL Publications
Our Sunday Visitor
Pauline Books
Paulist Press
Pflaum Publishing
Regnery Publishing
St. Anthony Messenger
Small Helm Press
Tau-Publishing
Twenty-Third Publications
Periodicals:
America
Angel Face
Annals of St. Anne
Arkansas Catholic
Arlington Catholic Herald
Atlantic Catholic
Bread of Life
Canticle
Caravan
Catechist
Catechumenate
Catholic Answer
Catholic Courier
Catholic Digest
Catholic Faith & Family
Catholic Forester
Catholic Insight
Catholic Library World
Catholic Missions in Canada
Catholic New Times
Catholic New York
Catholic Parent
Catholic Peace Voice
Catholic Register
Catholic Rural Life
Catholic Sentinel
Catholic Servant
Catholic Telegraph
Celebration
CGA World
CNEWA WORLD
Columbia
Commonweal
Culture Wars
Desert Call

Diocesan Dialogue
Divine Ascent
Emmanuel
Environment & Art
Eucharistic Ministries
Faith & Family
Family Digest
Good News for Children
Immaculate Heart Messenger
Interim
Island Catholic News
Leaves
Liguorian
Marian Helper
Messenger (KY)
Messenger/Sacred Heart
Messenger/St. Anthony
Miraculous Medal
Montana Catholic
My Friend
National Catholic Reporter
New Covenant
New Freeman
N.A. Voice of Fatima
Notre Dame
Oblates
Oblate World
Our Sunday Visitor
Parish Liturgy
Pastoral Life
Portland Magazine
Prairie Messenger
Priest
Queen of All Hearts
Religion Teacher's Journal
Review for Religious
St. Anthony Messenger
St. Joseph's Messenger
St. Linus Review
St. Willibrord Journal
Seeds
Share
Social Justice Review
Southern Renaissance
Spiritual Life
Sursum Corda!
This Rock
Today's Catholic Teacher
Today's Parish
U.S. Catholic
Visions
Way of St. Francis

CHRISTIAN CHURCH/ CHURCH OF CHRIST

Book Publishers:
ACU Press

Chalice Press (Disciples of Christ)
College Press (Church of Christ)
Periodicals:
Christian Standard
DisciplesWorld (Disciples of Christ)
Encounter
Kidz Chat
Lookout
Teenage Christian (Church of Christ)

CHURCH OF GOD (Anderson, IN)

Book Publisher:
Warner Press
Periodical:
Pathways to God

CHURCH OF GOD (Cleveland, TN)

Book Publishers:
Editorial Evangelica
Pathway Press
Periodicals:
Church of God EVANGEL
Save Our World
Youth and CE Leadership

CHURCH OF GOD (holiness)

Periodicals:
Beginner's Friend
Church Herald and Holiness Banner
Gems of Truth
Junior Companion
Primary Pal (KS)
Youth Compass

CHURCH OF GOD (other)

Periodicals:
Bible Advocate (Seventh-day)
Church Advocate
Gem
Now What? (Seventh-day)
Spirit (Pentecostal Church of God)
2 Soar (Church of God in Christ)
White Wing Messenger (Church of God of Prophecy)

CHURCH OF THE NAZARENE

Book Publishers:
Beacon Hill Press
Lillenas (music)
Periodicals:
Adventures
Celebrate

Children's Church Exch.
Discoveries
Holiness Today
Passport
Preacher's Magazine
Resource
Standard
Team NYI

EPISCOPAL/ANGLICAN

Book Publishers:
Alban Institute
Forward Movement
Morehouse Publishing
Periodicals:
Cathedral Age
Episcopal Life
Interchange
Living Church
Sewanee Theological Review

LUTHERAN

Book Publishers:
Concordia
Langmarc Publishing
Northwestern Publishing
Openbook Publishers
Periodicals:
Canada Lutheran (ELCC)
Canadian Lutheran
Cresset
Esprit (ELCC)
Forward in Christ
Lutheran (ELCA)
Lutheran Digest
Lutheran Educ. (MO Synod)
Lutheran Forum
Lutheran Journal
Lutheran Parent
Lutheran Parent's Wellspring
Lutheran Partners (ELCA)
Lutheran Witness (MO Synod)
Lutheran Woman's Quarterly (MO Synod)
Lutheran Woman Today (ELCA)
Northwestern Lutheran
Teachers Inter. (MO Synod)
Word & World (ELCA)

MENNONITE

Book Publishers:
Green Pastures Press
Kindred Productions
Periodicals:
Canadian Mennonite
Christian Leader
Companions

Mennonite Brethren Herald
Mennonite Historian
Mennonite Weekly Review
On the Line
Partners
Purpose
Story Friends
Story Mates
With

METHODIST, FREE

Book Publisher:
Light and Life Communications
Periodicals:
Evangel
Light and Life
World Mission People

METHODIST, UNITED

Book Publishers:
Abingdon Press
Cokesbury
Dimensions for Living
United Methodist Publishing House
Upper Room Books
Periodicals:
alive now!
Christian Social Action
Good News
Interpreter
Leader/Christian Education Ministries
Mature Years
Methodist History
Michigan Christian Advocate
New World Outlook
Pockets
Quarterly Review
Upper Room

MISSIONARY CHURCH

Periodical:
Emphasis/Faith & Living

PENTECOSTAL, UNITED

Periodicals:
Conqueror
Vision (adult)

PRESBYTERIAN

Book Publishers:
Canon Press
P & R Publishing
Westminster John Knox
Periodicals:
Channels (PCC)
Glad Tidings
Horizons (USA)
PCA Messenger
Presbyterian Layman (USA)
Presbyterian Outlook (USA)
Presbyterian Record
Presbyterians Today
Reflections (EPC)

QUAKER/FRIENDS

Book Publishers:
Barclay Press
Friends United Press
Periodicals:
Fruit of the Vine
Quaker Life

REFORMED CHURCHES

Periodicals:
Perspectives
Reformed Worship
Vision (MI)

SEVENTH-DAY ADVENTIST

Book Publishers:
Pacific Press
Review and Herald
Periodicals:
Cornerstone Youth Resources
GUIDE Magazine
Insight (MD)
Journal/Adventist Ed
Kids' Ministry Ideas
Liberty
Message
Ministry
Our Little Friend
Primary Treasure
Sabbath School Leadership

Signs of the Times
Vibrant Life
Young and Alive

WESLEYAN CHURCH

Book Publisher:
Wesleyan Publishing House
Periodicals:
Friend
Wesleyan Life
Wesleyan World

MISCELLANEOUS DENOMINATIONS

Armenian Holy Apostolic
Pourastan
Christian & Missionary Alliance
Christian Publications
Covenant Church
inSpirit
Evangelical Covenant Church
Cornerstone
Covenant Companion
Evangelical Free Church
EFCA Today
Evangelical Beacon
Pursuit
Fellowship of Evangelical Bible Churches
Fellowship Focus
Foursquare Gospel Church
Foursquare World Advance
Greek Orthodox
Holy Cross Orthodox Press
Open Bible Standard Churches
MESSAGE of the Open Bible
United Church of Canada
Aujourd'hui Credo
Fellowship Magazine
Theological Digest & Outlook
United Church Observer
United Church Publishing House
United Church of Christ
Pilgrim Press
United Church Press

LIST OF BOOK PUBLISHERS AND PERIODICALS
BY CORPORATE GROUP

Following is a listing of book publishers first and then periodicals that belong to the same group or family of publications.

CCM COMMUNICATIONS

CCM
Worship Leader
Youthworker
The CCM Update

CHRISTIANITY TODAY, INTL.

Books & Culture
Campus Life
Christian Bible Studies.com
Christian History
Christianity Today
Christianity Today.com
Christian Parenting Today
Leadership Journal
Marriage Partnership
Men of Integrity
PreachingToday.com
Sermon Notes
Today's Christian
Today's Christian Woman
Your Church

CHRISTIAN MEDIA

Christian Media (books)
The Apocalypse Chronicles
Christian Media

COOK COMMUNICATIONS MINISTRIES

Chariot Books
Chariot Victor Books
Honor Books
Lion Publishing (books)
RiverOak Publishing
Counselor
I.D.
Power for Living
Primary Days
Quiet Hour
Real Time
The Rock
Strategic Adult Ministries Online

FOCUS ON THE FAMILY

Focus on the Family (books)

Boundless Webzine
Breakaway
Brio
Brio and Beyond
Citizen
Clubhouse
Clubhouse Jr.
Focus on the Family Physician
Plugged-In

BILLY GRAHAM EVANG. ASSN.

Decision
Passageway.org

GROUP PUBLICATIONS, INC.

Group Publishing, Inc. (books)
Group's Faithweaver Bible Curriculum
Children's Ministry
Group Magazine

GUIDEPOSTS

Guideposts Books
Angels on Earth
Clarity
Guideposts
Guideposts for Kids on the Web
Guideposts Sweet 16
Ideals Magazine
Ideals Publications
Positive Thinking

HARPERCOLLINS

HarperSanFrancisco
ZonderKidz
Zondervan

THE NAVIGATORS

NavPress
Pray!
PrayKids!

THOMAS NELSON PUBLISHERS

J. Countryman
Thomas Nelson Publishers (books)

Tommy Nelson (books)
W Publishing Group (books)

PLGK COMMUNICATIONS

Setmag.com
TeensforJC.com
Transcendmag.com

THE SALVATION ARMY

Faith & Friends
Horizons
War Cry
Young Salvationist

STANDARD PUBLISHING

Standard Publishing (books)
Christian Standard
Encounter
Kidz Chat
The Lookout
Seek

STRANG COMMUNICATIONS

Charisma House (books)
Creation House Press (co-publishing)
Charisma & Christian Life
Christian Retailing
Ministries Today
New Man
Vida Cristiana

THE UPPER ROOM

Upper Room Books
alive now!
Devo'Zine
The Upper Room
Weavings

URBAN MINISTRIES

Direction
InTeen
J.A.M.: Jesus and Me
Juniorway
Precepts for Living
Preschool Playhouse
Primary Street
Young Adult Today

GLOSSARY OF TERMS

NOTE: This is not intended to be an exhaustive glossary of terms. It includes primarily those terms you will find within the context of this market guide.

Advance. Amount of money a publisher pays to an author up front, against future royalties. The amount varies greatly from publisher to publisher, and is often paid in two or three installments (on signing contract, on delivery of manuscript, and on publication).

All rights. An outright sale of your material. Author has no further control over it.

Anecdote. A short, poignant, real-life story, usually used to illustrate a single thought.

Assignment. When an editor asks a writer to write a specific piece for an agreed-upon price.

Avant-garde. Experimental; ahead of the times.

Backlist. A publisher's previously published books that are still in print a year after publication.

Bar code. Identification code and price on the back of a book read by a scanner at checkout counters.

Bible versions. CEV—Contemporary English Version; ESV—English Standard Version; GNB—Good News Bible; HCSB—Holman Christian Standard Bible; ICB—International Children's Bible; KJV—King James Version; MSG—The Message; NAB—New American Bible; NAS—New American Standard; NEB—New English Bible; NIV—New International Version; NIrV—New International Reader's Version; NJB—New Jerusalem Bible; NKJV—New King James Version; NLT—New Living Translation; NRSV—New Revised Standard Version; RSV—Revised Standard Version; TNIV—Today's New International Version.

Bimonthly. Every two months.

Biweekly. Every two weeks.

Bluelines. Printer's proofs used to catch errors before a book is printed.

Book proposal. Submission of a book idea to an editor; usually includes a cover letter, thesis statement, chapter-by-chapter synopsis, market survey, and 1-3 sample chapters.

Byline. Author's name printed just below the title of a story, article, etc.

Camera-ready copy. The text and artwork for a book that are ready for the press.

Chapbook. A small book or pamphlet containing poetry, religious readings, etc.

Circulation. The number of copies sold or distributed of each issue of a publication.

Clips. See "Published Clips."

Column. A regularly appearing feature, section, or department in a periodical using the same heading; written by the same person or a different freelancer each time.

Contributor's copy. Copy of an issue of a periodical sent to the author whose work appears in it.

Copyright. Legal protection of an author's work.

Cover letter. A letter that accompanies some manuscript submissions. Usually needed only if you have to tell the editor something specific or to give your credentials for writing a piece of a technical nature. Also used to remind the editor that a manuscript was requested or expected.

Critique. An evaluation of a piece of writing.

Devotional. A short piece that shares a personal spiritual discovery, inspires to worship, challenges to commitment or action, or encourages.

Editorial guidelines. See "Writer's guidelines."

Electronic submission. The submission of a proposal or article to an editor by electronic means, such as by e-mail or on disk.

Endorsements. Flattering comments about a book; usually carried on the back cover or in promotional material.

EPA/Evangelical Press Assn. A professional trade organization for periodical publishers and associate members.

E-proposals. Proposals sent via e-mail.

E-queries. Queries sent via e-mail.

Eschatology. The branch of theology that is concerned with the last things, such as death, judgment, heaven, and hell.

Essay. A short composition usually expressing the author's opinion on a specific subject.

Evangelical. A person who believes that one receives God's forgiveness for sins through Jesus Christ, and believes the Bible is an authoritative guide for daily living.

Exegesis. Interpretation of the Scripture.

Feature article. In-depth coverage of a subject, usually focusing on a person, an event, a process, an organization, a movement, a trend or issue; written to explain, encourage, help, analyze, challenge, motivate, warn, or entertain as well as to inform.

Filler. A short item used to "fill" out the page of a periodical. It could be a timeless news item, joke, anecdote, light verse or short humor, puzzle, game, etc.

First rights. Editor buys the right to publish your piece for the first time.

Foreign rights. Selling or giving permission to translate or reprint published material in a foreign country.

Foreword. Opening remarks in a book introducing the book and its author.

Freelance. As in 50% freelance: means that 50% of the material printed in the publication is supplied by freelance writers.

Freelancer or freelance writer. A writer who is not on salary but sells his material to a number of different publishers.

Free verse. Poetry that flows without any set pattern.

Galley proof. A typeset copy of a book manuscript used to detect and correct errors before the final print run.

Genre. Refers to type or classification, as in fiction or poetry. Such types as westerns, romances, mysteries, etc., are referred to as genre fiction.

Glossy. A black-and-white photo with a shiny, rather than matte, finish.

Go-ahead. When a publisher tells you to go ahead and write up or send your article idea.

Haiku. A Japanese lyric poem of a fixed 17-syllable form.

Hard copy. A typed manuscript, as opposed to one on disk or in an e-mail.

Holiday/seasonal. A story, article, filler, etc., that has to do with a specific holiday or season. This material must reach the publisher the stated number of months prior to the holiday/season.

Homiletics. The art of preaching.

Honorarium. If a publisher indicates they pay an honorarium, it means they pay a small flat fee, as opposed to a set amount per word.

Humor. The amusing or comical aspects of life that add warmth and color to an article or story.

Interdenominational. Distributed to a number of different denominations.

International Postal Reply Coupon. See "IRC."

Interview article. An article based on an interview with a person of interest to a specific readership.

IRC or IPRC. International Postal Reply Coupon: can be purchased at your local post office and should be enclosed with a manuscript sent to a foreign publisher.

ISBN number. International Standard Book Number; an identification code needed for every book.

Journal. A periodical presenting news in a particular area.

Kill fee. A fee paid for a completed article done on assignment that is subsequently not published. Amount is usually 25-50% of original payment.

Libel. To defame someone by an opinion or a misquote and put his or her reputation in jeopardy.

Light verse. Simple, lighthearted poetry.

Little/Literary. Small circulation publications whose focus is providing a forum for the literary writer, rather than on making money. Often do not pay, or pay in copies.

Mainstream fiction. Other than genre fiction, such as romance, mystery or science fiction. Stories of people and their conflicts handled on a deeper level.

Mass market. Books intended for a wide, general market, rather than a specialized market. These books are produced in a smaller format, usually with smaller type, and are sold at a lower price. The expectation is that their sales will be higher.

Ms. Abbreviation for manuscript.

Mss. Abbreviation for more than one manuscript.

Multiple submissions. Submitting more than one piece at a time to the same publisher, usually reserved for poetry, greeting cards, or fillers, not articles. Also see "Simultaneous submissions."

NASR. Abbreviation for North American serial rights.

Newsbreak. A newsworthy event or item sent to a publisher who might be interested in publishing it because it would be of interest to his particular readership.

Nondenominational. Not associated with a particular denomination.

Not copyrighted. Publication of your piece in such a publication will put it into public domain and it is not then protected. Ask that the publisher carry your copyright notice on your piece when it is printed.

On acceptance. Periodical or publisher pays a writer at the time manuscript is accepted for publication.

On assignment. Writing something at the specific request of an editor.

One-time rights. Selling the right to publish a story one time to any number of publications (usually refers to publishing for a nonoverlapping readership).

On publication. Publisher pays a writer when his/her manuscript is published.

On speculation/On spec. Writing something for an editor with the agreement that he will buy it only if he likes it.

Overrun. The extra copies of a book printed during the initial print run.

Over the transom. Unsolicited articles that arrive at a publisher's office.

Payment on acceptance. See "On acceptance."

Payment on publication. See "On publication."

Pen name/Pseudonym. Using a name other than your legal name on an article or book in order to protect your identity or the identity of people included, or when the author wishes to remain anonymous. Put the pen name in the byline under the title, and your real name in the upper, left-hand corner.

Permissions. Asking permission to use the text or art from a copyrighted source.

Personal experience story. A story based on a real-life experience.

Personality profile. A feature article that highlights a specific person's life or accomplishments.

Photocopied submission. Sending an editor a photocopy of your manuscript, rather than an original. Some editors prefer an original.

Piracy. To take the writings of others just as they were written and put your name on them as the author.

Plagiarism. To steal and use the ideas or writings of another as your own, rewriting them to make them sound like your own.

Press kit. A compilation of promotional materials on a particular book or author, usually organized in a folder, used to publicize a book.

Public domain. Work that has never been copyrighted, or on which the copyright has expired. Subtract 75 from the current year, and anything copyrighted prior to that is in public domain.

Published clips. Copies of actual articles you have had published, from newspapers or magazines.

Quarterly. Every three months.

Query letter. A letter sent to an editor telling about an article you propose to write and asking if he or she is interested in seeing it.

Reporting time. The number of weeks or months it takes an editor to get back to you about a query or manuscript you have sent in.

Reprint rights. Selling the right to reprint an article that has already been published elsewhere. You must have sold only first or one-time rights originally, and wait until it has been published the first time.

Review copies. Books given to book reviewers or buyers for chains.

Royalty. The percentage an author is paid by a publisher on the sale of each copy of a book.

SAE. Self-addressed envelope (without stamps).

SAN. Standard Account Number, used to identify libraries, book dealers, or schools.

SASE. Self-addressed, stamped envelope. Should always be sent with a manuscript or query letter.

SASP. Self-addressed, stamped postcard. May be sent with a manuscript submission to be returned by publisher indicating it arrived safely.

Satire. Ridicule that aims at reform.

Second serial rights. See "Reprint rights."

Semiannual. Issued twice a year.

Serial. Refers to publication in a periodical (such as first serial rights).

Sidebar. A short feature that accompanies an article and either elaborates on the human interest side of the story or gives additional information on the topic. It is often set apart by appearing within a box or border.

Simultaneous rights. Selling the rights to the same piece to several publishers simultaneously. Be sure everyone is aware that you are doing so.

Simultaneous submissions. Sending the same manuscript to more than one publisher at the same time. Usually done with nonoverlapping markets (such as denominational or newspapers) or when you are writing on a timely subject. Be sure to state in a cover letter that it is a simultaneous submission and why.

Slanting. Writing an article so that it meets the needs of a particular market.

Slush pile. The stack of unsolicited manuscripts that have arrived at a publisher's office.

Speculation. See "On speculation."

Staff-written material. Material written by the members of a magazine staff.

Subsidiary rights. All those rights, other than book rights, included in a book contract such as paperback, book club, movie, etc.

Subsidy publisher. A book publisher who charges the author to publish his book, as opposed to a royalty publisher who pays the author.

Synopsis. A brief summary of work from one paragraph to several pages long.

Tabloid. A newspaper-format publication about half the size of a regular newspaper.

Take-home paper. A periodical sent home from Sunday school each week (usually) with Sunday school students, children through adults.

Think piece. A magazine article that has an intellectual, philosophical, or provocative approach to a subject.

Third World. Reference to underdeveloped countries of Asia and Africa.

Trade magazine. A magazine whose audience is in a particular trade or business.

Traditional verse. One or more verses with an established pattern that is repeated throughout the poem.

Transparencies. Positive color slides, not color prints.

Unsolicited manuscript. A manuscript an editor didn't specifically ask to see.

Vanity publisher. See "Subsidy publisher."

Vignette. A short, descriptive literary sketch or a brief scene or incident.

Vitae/Vita. An outline of one's personal history and experience.

Work-for-hire. Signing a contract with a publisher stating that a particular piece of writing you are doing for him is "work-for-hire." In the agreement you give the publisher full ownership and control of the material.

Writers' guidelines. An information sheet provided by a publisher that gives specific guidelines for writing for the publication. Always send an SASE with your request for guidelines.

GENERAL INDEX

This index includes periodicals, books, and greeting cards/specialty markets, as well as some of the various organizations/resources and specialty lists or areas you may need to find quickly. Conferences, groups, and editorial services are listed alphabetically by state; agents are listed alphabetically by the name of the agency. Check the table of contents for the location of supplementary listings.

Note: Due to the many changes in the market, and to help you determine the current status of any publisher you might be looking for, all markets will be listed in this index. If they are not viable markets, their current status will be indicated here, rather than in separate listings as they were in earlier years. The following codes will be used: (ABD) asked to be deleted, (BA) bad address or phone number, (ED) editorial decision, (NF) no freelance, (NR) no recent response, (OB) out of business. These changes will be noted in this listing for five years before being dropped altogether.

MORE TOOLS FROM THE WRITERS' RESOURCE LIBRARY

WriterSpeaker.com: Internet Research and Marketing for Writers and Speakers
by Carmen Leal

"If a writer and speaker could only have one book on the Internet, this is it."
—MARY WESTHEIMER,
CEO of BookZone.com

"*WriterSpeaker.com* is *the* resource for writers and speakers."
—MARITA LITTAUER,
president of CLASServices, Inc.

*How to Write What You Love...
and Make a Living at It*
by Dennis E. Hensley, Ph.D.

"Hensley's enthusiasm, energy, and encyclopedia of ideas are captured here in print. If you've always wanted to do something with your writing, here's how to get going!"
—LIZ CURTIS HIGGS,
author of *Bad Girls of the Bible*

Effective Magazine Writing: Let Your Words Reach the World
by Roger C. Palms

"With uncommon common sense, Roger Palms will help you turn the ordinary experiences of ordinary people into outstanding articles that have potential to change readers' lives."
—DAVID NEFF,
editor, *Christianity Today*

SHAW BOOKS
www.shawbooks.com

Available in bookstores everywhere.

To learn more about Shaw Books and view our catalog of products, log on to our Web site:
www.shawbooks.com

SHAW BOOKS

an imprint of WATERBROOK PRESS